D0570820

INTERMEDIATE ACCOUNTING

FIFTH CANADIAN EDITION

VOLUME TWO

INTERMEDIATE ACCOUNTING

FIFTH CANADIAN EDITION
VOLUME TWO

Donald E. Kieso PhD, CPA
KPMG Peat Marwick Professor of Accounting
Northern Illinois University
DeKalb, Illinois

Jerry J. Weygandt PhD, CPA
Arthur Anderson Alumni Professor of Accounting
University of Wisconsin
Madison, Wisconsin

Canadian Edition prepared by

V. Bruce Irvine PhD, CMA, FCMA
University of Saskatchewan
Saskatoon, Saskatchewan

W. Harold Silvester PhD, CPA, CA
University of Saskatchewan (Emeritus)
Saskatoon, Saskatchewan

Nicola M. Young MBA, FCA
St. Mary's University
Halifax, Nova Scotia

JOHN WILEY & SONS CANADA, LTD.
Toronto • New York • Chichester • Weinheim • Brisbane • Singapore

Copyright © 1998, 1994, 1991, 1990, 1989, 1986, 1982 by John Wiley & Sons Canada Ltd
Copyright © 1998, 1995, 1992, 1989, 1983, 1980, 1977, 1975 by John Wiley & Sons Inc. All rights reserved. No part of this work covered by the copyrights herein may be reproduced or used in any form or by any means—graphic, electronic, or mechanical—without the prior written permission of the publisher.

Any request for photocopying, recording , taping or information storage and retrieval systems of any part of this book shall be directed in writing to CANCOPY (Canadian Reprography Collective), 6 Adelaide Street East, Toronto, Ontario, M5C 1H6.

Care has been taken to trace ownership of copyright material contained in this text. The publishers will gladly receive any information that will enable them to rectify any reference or credit line in subsequent editions.

Canadian Cataloguing in Publication Data

Kieso, Donald E.
    Intermediate accounting

5th Canadian ed./prepared by V. Bruce Irvine,
W. Harold Silvester, Nicola M. Young.
Includes bibliographical references and indexes.
ISBN 0-471-64183-9 (v. 1)
ISBN 0-471-64184-7 (v. 2)

1. Accounting. I. Irvine, V. Bruce.
II. Silvester, W. Harold. III. Weygandt
Jerry J. IV. Young, Nicola M. V. Title.

HF5635.I573 1997   657'.044   C97–931411–9

Production Credits

Acquisitions Editor: John Horne

Publishing Services Director: Karen Bryan

Developmental Editor: Karen Staudinger

Assistant Editor: Michael Schellenberg

Copy Editor: Leah Johnson

Proofreader: Claudia Kutchukian

Graphic Designer: Christine Rae, RGD

Cover Photo Credits: I. Barrett / First Light

Typesetting & Film: Compeer Typographic Services

Printing and Binding: Tri-Graphic Printing Limited

Printed and bound in Canada
10 9 8 7 6 5 4 3

Dedicated To

Marilyn	_Viola_	_John_
Lee-Ann	_Susan_	_Hilary_
Cameron	_Dianne_	_Tim_
Sandra	_Daniel_	_Megan_

ABOUT THE AUTHORS

CANADIAN EDITION

V. Bruce Irvine PhD, CMA, FCMA, is a professor of Accounting at the University of Saskatchewan. He received his PhD in accounting from the University of Minnesota. Among his publications are articles and reviews in such journals as *CMA: The Management Accounting Magazine, CA Magazine, Managerial Planning, and The Accounting Review.* Designated "Professor of the Year" several times, Dr. Irvine has extensive teaching experience in financial and managerial accounting and has been instrumental in establishing innovative pedagogical techniques and instructional materials at the University of Saskatchewan. He has had considerable involvement with practising accountants through serving on various local, provincial, national, and international committees and boards of the Society of Management Accountants. At the international level, Dr. Irvine has been a Canadian delegate to the board of the International Accounting Standards Committee and a technical advisor to the International Federation of Accountants. Additionally, Dr. Irvine has served in various executive committee positions of the Canadian Academic Accounting Association.

W. Harold Silvester PhD, CPA, CA, received his doctorate from the University of Missouri, Columbia, and is Professor Emeritus of Accounting at the University of Saskatchewan. In his teaching capacity, he played a key role in introducing pedagogical improvements at the University of Saskatchewan and in developing instructional materials for the Accounting program there. He was named "Professor of the Year" in recognition of his substantial contributions to the College of Commerce. An important contribution has been the development of materials to integrate computers with accounting instruction. Articles by Professor Silvester have appeared in *CA Magazine* and other academic and professional journals.

Nicola M. Young, MBA, FCA, is an associate professor of accounting in the Frank H. Sobey Faculty of Commerce at Saint Mary's University in Halifax, Nova Scotia where her teaching responsibilities vary from the non-accounting major introductory course to final year advanced financial courses to the survey course in the Executive MBA program. She is the recipient of the Commerce Professor of the Year and the university-wide alumni teaching medal, and contributes to the academic and administrative life of the university through membership on the Senate and Board of Governors. Professor Young has been involved with the Atlantic School of Chartered Accountancy for many years on a variety of levels from program and course development and design to teaching, and authored a report on examination and evaluation objectives and processes for this organization. In addition to contributions to the accounting profession at the provincial level, Professor Young has served on various national boards of the CICA dealing with licensure, education and standard setting.

U.S. EDITION

Donald E. Kieso PhD, CPA, received his bachelors degree from Aurora University and his doctorate in accounting from the University of Illinois. He has served as chairman of the Department of Accountancy at Northern Illinois University. He has done postdoctorate work as a Visiting Scholar at the University of California at Berkeley and is a recipient of NIU's Teaching Excellence Award and four Golden Apple Teaching Awards (1986, 1990, 1992, and 1994). He has served as a member of the Board of Directors of the CPA Society, the Board of Governors of the American Accounting Association's Administrators of Accounting Programs Group, the AACSB's Accounting Accreditation and Visitation Committees, the State of Illinois Comptroller's Commission, as Secretary-Treasurer of the Federation of Schools of Accountancy, and as Secretary-Treasurer of the American Accounting Association. From 1989 to 1993 he served as a charter member of the national Accounting Education Change Commission. In 1988 he received the Outstanding Accounting Educator Award from the Illinois CPA Society, and in 1992 he received the FSA's Joseph A. Silvoso Award of Merit and the NIU Foundation's Humanitarian Award for Service to Higher Education.

Jerry J. Weygandt, PhD, CPA, is Arthur Andersen Alumni Professor of Accounting of the University of Wisconsin-Madison and has also served as President of the American Accounting Association. He holds a PhD in accounting from the University of Illinois. Articles by Professor Weygandt have appeared in the *Accounting Review, Journal of Accounting Research, The Journal of Accountancy,* and other professional journals. These articles have examined such financial reporting issues as accounting for price-level adjustments, pensions, convertible securities, stock option contracts, and interim reports. He has served on numerous committees of the American Accounting Association and as a member of the editorial board of the Accounting Review. In addition, he has been involved with the American Institute of Certified Public Accountants and has been a member of the Accounting Standards Executive Committee (AcSEC) of that organization. Professor Weygandt has received the Chancellor's Award for Excellence in Teaching; he also has served as Secretary-Treasurer of the American Accounting Association. In 1991 he received the Wisconsin Institute of CPA's Outstanding Educator's Award.

PREFACE

Accounting is an exciting, dynamic field of study; its body of knowledge, theories, and practices, as well as the methodologies for teaching these concepts, are constantly evolving. In the writing of this fifth Canadian edition of *Intermediate Accounting*, we have thoroughly revised and updated the text to include the latest developments in the financial accounting profession.

Continuing to keep pace with the complexities of the modern business enterprise and professional accounting pronouncements, we have added new topics, deleted obsolete material, clarified existing coverage, added illustrations, and updated material where necessary. To provide the instructor with greater flexibility in choosing topics to cover or omit, we have continued the use of judiciously selected appendices. The appendices are concerned primarily with complex subjects, less commonly used methods, or specialized topics.

Benefitting from the comments and recommendations of the many adopters of our previous editions, we have made significant revisions. Explanations have been expanded where necessary, complicated discussions and illustrations have been simplified; realism has been integrated to heighten interest and relevance; and new topics and coverage have been added to maintain currency.

Accountants must act as well as think; therefore, we believe it is important for students to understand the how as well as the why. The study of concepts develops an understanding of the procedures, and the performance of procedures enriches the understanding of the concepts. Keeping this in mind, we have maintained the balance in our coverage so the conceptual discussion and procedural presentation are mutually reinforcing.

We believe that individuals learn to account for financial events and phenomena best if they fully understand the nature of the business transactions and comprehend the behavioural and economic consequences of the events for which firms account and report. The ability to critically evaluate accounting alternatives and their consequences is important. Throughout this edition, we have provided coverage to help students develop a real understanding of how accounting can be used to make effective financial decisions.

NEW FEATURES

Based on extensive reviews and interactions with other intermediate accounting instructors and students, we have developed a number of new pedagogical features designed both to help students learn more effectively and to answer the changing needs of the course.

Using Your Judgement: We have created a new section of end-of-chapter assignments that go beyond routine problem solving and calculations. "Using Your Judgement" sections, appearing at the end of every chapter, help students develop analytical and critical thinking skills in an accounting environment, and include:

> *Financial Reporting Problems,* often involving analysis and interpretation of Moore Corporation's financial statements (Appendix 5A).

> *Ethics Cases* that sensitize students to ethical considerations, situations, and dilemmas encountered by practising accountants.

Summary of Learning Objectives: Completely rewritten end-of-chapter summaries reinforce important ideas from each chapter and link them to the learning objectives introduced at the beginning and integrated throughout.

Key Terms: Key terms used in each chapter are listed in the margin next to the Summary of Learning Objectives. The numbers after each term refer to the page on which the term appears (in bold, blue type for easy reference) with its definition.

Topical Boxes: Many chapters now feature short vignettes that relate to material covered in the chapter and either contrast international practices or discuss an ethical consideration or emerging issue pertaining to this material. Boxes were contributed by Kevin Berry, Lucie Laliberté, Arline Savage, Peter Secord and Irene Wiecek.

ENHANCED FEATURES

Real-World Emphasis: To help make material relevant and readily understandable to students, numerous real-world examples, most of them new, have been used throughout the text. Excerpts from the annual reports of over 50 Canadian corporations have been reprinted exactly as they originally appeared.

Ethics: Ethics in the accounting environment is introduced as a topic in chapter 1 and is included in every chapter in at least one Ethics Case in the "Using Your Judgement" section. These cases help students learn to identify when ethical issues are involved and how to approach ethical decision making.

Currency and Accuracy: Accounting continually changes as its environment changes, making an up-to-date book a necessity. As with past editions we have striven to make this edition the most up-to-date and accurate text available. This is exemplified by our coverage of the *Exposure Drafts* on Cash Flows Statements and Employees' Future Benefits and the new *Handbook* Section 3465 concerning Corporate Income Tax.

Readability: Adopters of previous editions have praised the readability of our text. In this edition, we have carefully reviewed each line of the text to further improve clarity and directness of language, to take out unnecessary detail, and to simplify complex presentations. Our streamlining efforts have both improved user-friendliness and allowed us to add needed new material while still maintaining the overall length of the text.

Design: The design of any text is an integral part of its pedagogical framework. The design of the fifth edition was conceived with this in mind. It presents the material in an open and eye-catching manner and facilitates use of all of the elements of the text.

CHANGES IN CHAPTER ORDER

In response to suggestions, Chapter 18 on Investments: Temporary and Long-Term in the fourth edition has been moved to Chapter 10 to include it with the other chapters covering assets topics. Section 1 on Temporary Investments and Section 2 on Long-Term Investments can be taught as stand-alone material for instructors who prefer a different placement in their courses.

CONTENT CHANGES

The list below outlines major revisions and improvements of the fifth edition by chapter.

Volume 1

Chapter 1	Material included regarding business reporting as considered by the Jenkins Committee.
	Section on Environmental Factors that Influence Financial Accounting restructured.
	Ethics section is given more significance and is moved to an earlier position in the chapter.
Chapter 2	Material on new Exposure Draft on Going Concern added.
	Examples illustrating trade-offs among qualitative characteristics expanded.
	Definitions for "investment by owners" and "distributions to owners" added.
Chapter 3	Appendix 3A, section on End of Period Procedures for Inventory and Related Accounts and exhibits for Prepaid Expenses and Unearned Revenues all completely rewritten.
Chapter 4	Discussion of intraperiod tax allocation simplified.
	Illustration of a foreign income statement added.

Chapter 5   Statement of Cash Flows introduced.
                 Illustration of a foreign balance sheet added.

Chapter 6   Material on the Percentage-of-Completion Method rewritten.
                 Complex entries regarding Continuing Fees, Bargain Purchases and
                 Options deleted from Appendix 6B.

Chapter 7   Coverage of notes receivable reorganized and simplified.
                 Appendix 7A deleted.

Chapter 8   Inventory Errors section expanded; examines impact of errors on ratios.
                 Management incentives in choosing inventory methods are covered.
                 Appendix 8B deleted.

Chapter 9   Ethics box added.

Chapter 10   Cash Surrender Value and Accounting for Funds given appendix status.
                 References to *Handbook* Section 3860 and section on consolidations added.

Chapter 11   Definitions from *Handbook* Section 3060 and coverage of GST added.

Chapter 12   Compound Interest Method discussed.
                 Basic issues and accounting for Future Removal and Site Restoration
                 Costs added.
                 Sum-of-Years-Digits Method deleted.

Chapter 13   Explanation of terminology of *Handbook* Section 3060 updated.
                 New section on Impairment of Intangibles added.

Volume 2

Chapter 14   Discussion of GST added.

Chapter 15   Updated to reflect *Handbook* Section 3860, including an expanded section
                 on Financial Instrument Complexities.
                 Reporting Long-Term Debt, the illustration covering the reacquisition of
                 debt and Notes Payable have all been expanded.

Chapter 16   Updated to reflect *Handbook* Section 3860.
                 Sections on Instalment Receipts and Shares Issued Financed by Company
                 Loans added.

Chapter 17   Exhibit on Contributed Surplus expanded.
                 Discussion on Dividends reorganized.
                 Disclosure Requirements moved to the end of the chapter.

Chapter 18   Discussion of Dilutive Securities revised to reflect *Handbook* Section 3860.

Chapter 19   Chapter completely revised to conform to new *Handbook* Section 3465.

Chapter 20   Chapter revised to reflect June 1997 *Exposure Draft* on Employees' Future Benefits.

Chapter 21   Examples of actual lease disclosures increased.
New appendix added featuring relevant flowcharts from the *Handbook*.

Chapter 22   Revised to incorporate current proposals.

Chapter 23   Chapter revised to reflect *Exposure Draft* on Cash Flow Statements.
Both Worksheet and T Account Methods now in an appendix as chapter emphasizes Balance Sheet Approach.

Chapter 24   New introduction of the Ratio Analysis section added.
Summary of Ratios chart substantially revised.
Emphasis on Cash Flow Ratios increases.

Chapter 25   New illustrations of segment reporting added.
Coverage of auditor's report upgraded.

EXERCISES, PROBLEMS, AND CASES

At the end of each chapter we have provided a comprehensive set of review and homework material consisting of exercises, problems, and cases. For this edition many of the exercises and problems have been revised, and a new section, "Using Your Judgement," has been added. Typically, an exercise covers a specific topic and requires less time and effort to solve than a problem or case. The problems are designed to develop a professional level of achievement and are more challenging and time consuming to solve than the exercises. The cases generally require an essay as opposed to quantitative solutions; they are intended to confront the student with situations calling for conceptual analysis and the exercise of judgement in identifying problems and evaluating alternatives. The "Using Your Judgement" assignments are designed to develop students' critical thinking and analytical skills.

In the fourth edition, all exercises, problems, and cases included a short description of the topic tested. These descriptions have been retained in the exercises, but removed from the problems and cases in the fifth edition so that students are required to determine what the key issues are themselves.

Probably no more than one-fourth of the total exercise, problem, and case material must be used to adequately cover the subject matter; consequently, problem assignment may be varied from year to year.

ACKNOWLEDGEMENTS

We thank the many users of our fourth edition who contributed to this revision through their comments and instructive criticism. Special thanks are extended to the reviewers of and contributors to our fifth edition manuscript.

Primary Text Reviewers

Judy Cumby
  Memorial University of Newfoundland

Pauline Downer
  Memorial University of Newfoundland

Margaret Forbes
  Lakehead University

Leo Gallant
  St Francis-Xavier University

Louise Hayes
  York University

Ron Hill
  Southern Alberta Institute of Technology

James Hughes
  British Columbia Institute of Technology

Wayne Irvine
  Mount Royal College

Larry Knechtel
  Grant MacEwan Community College

Robin Hemmingsen
  Centennial College

Michael Lee
  Humber College

Bruce McConomy
  Carleton University

David McPeak, CGA

Patrick O'Neill
  Algonquin College

Morina Rennie
  University of Regina

Tom Shoniker
  Ryerson Polytechnic University

Barbara Trenholm
  University of New Brunswick

Marilyn Willie
  Northern Alberta Institute of Technology

Betty Wong
  Athabasca University

Walter Woronchak
  Sheridan College

Preliminary Reviewers of the Fourth Edition

Judy Cumby
  Memorial University of Newfoundland

Sandra Felton
  Brock University

Bruce Hazelton
  Sheridan College

James Hughes
  British Columbia Institute of Technology

Wayne Irvine
  Mount Royal College

Michael Lee
  Humber College

Valorie Leonard
  Laurentian University

Terry Litovitz
  University of Toronto

Bruce McConomy
  Carleton University

Alistair Murdoch
  University of Manitoba

Peter Nissen
  Northern Alberta Institute of Technology

Patrick O'Neill
  Algonquin College

Wendy Roscoe
  Concordia University

Michael Welker
  Queen's University

Betty Wong
  Athabasca University

Focus Groups

Before the commencement of our writing the fifth edition, John Wiley & Sons Canada, Ltd held focus groups with both instructors and students of Intermediate Accounting from the following schools: Sheridan College, Mohawk College, Humber College, McMaster University, University of Toronto, Sir Sandford Fleming College and Brock University. These discussions lead to some of the pedagogical enhancements in this edition and we thank everyone who participated for their input.

Appreciation is also extended to our colleagues at the University of Saskatchewan and Saint Mary's University who worked on and examined portions of this work and who made valuable suggestions. These include David Bateman, John Brennan, Gary Entwistle, Len Gerspacher, Daryl Lindsay, Jack Vicq, and Mardell Volls.

We are most grateful to the staff at John Wiley & Sons Canada, Ltd: Diane Wood, John Horne, Karen Staudinger, Karen Bryan, Carolyn Wells, Michael Schellenberg and all of the sales representatives. As well, we would like to acknowledge the editorial contributions of Leah Johnson and Claudia Kutchukian.

Sincere appreciation is also extended to the following who provided the authors with excellent word-processing services and suggestions: Jill Mierke, Valerie Fink, Bernie Rodier, Evadne Merz, Eilene Sabat, and Lyla Sheppard. We also thank Jim Wightman and Dan L'Abbé for providing excellent research and proofreading assistance.

We appreciate the cooperation of the Canadian Institute of Chartered Accountants in permitting us to quote from their materials. We thank the Moore Corporation Limited for permitting us to use its 1995 Annual Report for our specimen financial statements. We also wish to acknowledge the cooperation of many Canadian companies from whose financial statements we have drawn excerpts.

If this book helps teachers instill in their students an appreciation of the challenges, worth, and limitations of accounting, if it encourages students to evaluate critically and understand financial accounting theory and practice, and if it prepares students for advanced study, professional examinations, and the successful and ethical pursuit of their careers in accounting or business, then we will have attained out objective.

Suggestions and comments from users of this book will be appreciated. We have striven to produce an error-free text. However, should anything have slipped through the variety of checks undertaken, we would like to know so corrections can be made to subsequent printings.

V. Bruce Irvine	W. Harold Silvester	Nicola M. Young
Saskatoon, Saskatchewan	*Olds, Alberta*	*Halifax, Nova Scotia*

July 1997

BRIEF TABLE OF CONTENTS

TABLE OF CONTENTS

LIABILITIES: RECOGNITION, MEASUREMENT, AND DISCLOSURE

part

3

chapter

14

CURRENT LIABILITIES AND CONTINGENCIES

Current Liabilities and Contingencies

Learning Objectives

After studying this chapter, you should be able to:

1. Define current liabilities and describe how they are valued.

2. Identify the nature and types of current liabilities.

3. Explain financial statement classification issues related to short-term debt that is expected to be refinanced.

4. Identify types of employee-related liabilities.

5. Indicate how current liabilities are disclosed.

6. Identify the criteria used to account for and disclose loss contingencies.

7. Explain the accounting for different types of contingent liabilities.

The credit quality of many corporations has substantially declined. For many Canadian corporations, liabilities have increased in relation to shareholders' equity. The proportion of interest payments to pretax income has also increased. Increased liabilities have resulted from Canadian corporations that, like the federal government, went on an unprecedented debt binge. Companies borrowed money to expand in a booming economy. They also borrowed heavily to fend off takeovers by other companies. Currently many companies are paying off or refinancing much of that debt. As a result, both investors and the accounting profession now have to pay more attention to liabilities.

SECTION 1: CURRENT LIABILITIES

WHAT IS A LIABILITY?

"What is a liability?" is not an easy question to answer. The acquisition of goods or services on credit terms gives rise to liabilities. But it seems clear that liabilities include more than debts that arise from borrowings. Less similar are liabilities that result from taxes, withholdings from employees' wages and salaries, dividend declarations, pension plans and employee benefits, and product warranties.

To illustrate the complexity of this issue, one might ask whether preferred shares represent a liability or an ownership claim. The first reaction is to say that preferred shares are in fact an ownership claim and should be reported as part of shareholders' equity. In fact, preferred shares often have many elements of debt as well.[1] The issuer (and in some

---

[1] It should be noted that this illustration is not just a theoretical exercise. In practice, there are a number of preferred share issues that have all the characteristics of a debt instrument, except that they are called—and legally classified as—preferred shares. In some cases, Revenue Canada has even permitted the dividend payments to be treated as interest expense for tax purposes. This issue is discussed further in Chapter 15.

cases the holder) often has the right to call the shares within a specific period of time—making it similar to a repayment of principal. The dividend is in many cases almost guaranteed (cumulative provision), which makes it look like interest. And preferred shares are but one of many financial instruments that are difficult to classify.[2]

To help resolve some of these controversies, the Accounting Standards Committee defined **liabilities** in Section 1000 of the *CICA Handbook* as "**obligations of an enterprise arising from past transactions or events, the settlement of which may result in the transfer of assets, provision of services or other yielding of economic benefits in the future.**"[3] In other words, a liability has three essential characteristics.

1. It is an obligation to others that entails settlement by future transfer or use of cash, financial assets, goods, or services on a determinable date or upon the occurrence of some specified event;

2. The entity has little or no opportunity to avoid the obligation; and

3. The transaction or other event that obligates the enterprise must have already occurred.[4]

Because liabilities involve future disbursements of assets or services, one of the most important features is the date on which they are payable. Currently maturing obligations represent a demand on the current assets of the enterprise—a demand that must be satisfied promptly and in the ordinary course of business if operations are to be continued. Liabilities with a more distant due date do not, as a rule, represent a claim on the enterprise's current resources and are in a slightly different category. This feature gives rise to the basic division of liabilities into (1) current liabilities; and (2) long-term debt.

The distinction between current liabilities and long-term debt is important because it provides information about the liquidity of the company. Liquidity regarding a liability is the time that is expected to elapse before the liability has to be paid. In other words, a liability soon to be paid is a current liability. A liquid company—one that has more liquid assets than current liabilities—is less likely to fail. A liquid company is better able to withstand a financial downturn. Also, it has a better chance to take advantage of investment opportunities that develop.

WHAT IS A CURRENT LIABILITY?

OBJECTIVE 1
Define current liabilities and describe how they are valued.

Current assets are cash or other assets that can reasonably be expected to be converted into cash, sold, or consumed in operations within a single operating cycle or within a year if more than one cycle is completed each year.

Current liabilities "**should include amounts payable within one year from the date of the balance sheet or within the normal operating cycle, where this is longer than a year.**"[5] This definition has gained wide acceptance because it recognizes operating cycles of varying lengths in different industries and takes into consideration the important relationship between current assets and current liabilities. The AcSB affirmed this concept of

---

[2] As examples of the diversity within preferred shares, companies now issue (1) mandatorily redeemable preferred shares (redeemable at a specified price and time); (2) Dutch auction preferred shares (holders have the right to change the rate at defined intervals through a bidding process); and (3) increasing rate (exploding rate) preferred shares (holder receives an increasing dividend rate each period with the user having the right to call the shares at a certain date in the future). In all three cases, the issuer either has to redeem the shares per the contract or has to have strong economic reasons for calling the shares. These securities are more like debt than equity. The CICA issued *Handbook* Section 3860, "Financial Instruments," in September, 1995, which addresses the problem of distinguishing debt and equity instruments.

[3] *CICA Handbook*, Section 1000, par. .28.

[4] *CICA Handbook*, Section 1000, par. .33.

[5] *CICA Handbook*, Section 1510, par. .03.

"**maturity within one year or the operating cycle whichever is longer**" in its definition of current liabilities.[6]

The **operating cycle** is the period of time that elapses between the acquisition of the goods and services involved in the manufacturing process and the final cash realization that results from product sales and subsequent collections. Industries that manufacture products requiring an aging process and certain capital-intensive industries have an operating cycle of considerably more than one year; on the other hand, most retail and service establishments have several operating cycles within one year.

There are many different types of current liabilities. The following ones are covered in this chapter in this order.

OBJECTIVE 2
Identify the nature and types of current liabilities.

1. Accounts payable.

2. Notes payable.

3. Current maturities of long-term debt.

4. Short-term obligations expected to be refinanced.

5. Dividends payable.

6. Returnable deposits.

7. Unearned revenues.

8. Goods and Services Tax.

9. Sales taxes payable.

10. Property taxes payable.

11. Income taxes payable.

12. Employee-related liabilities.

ACCOUNTS PAYABLE

Accounts payable, or **trade accounts payable**, are balances owed to others for goods, supplies, and services purchased on open account. Accounts payable arise because of the time lag between the receipt of services or acquisition of title to assets, and the payment for them. This period of extended credit is usually found in the terms of the sale (e.g., 2/10, n/30 or 1/10, E.O.M.) and is commonly 30 to 60 days.

Most accounting systems are designed to record liabilities for purchase of goods when the goods are received or, practically, when the invoices are received. Frequently there is some delay in recording the goods and the related liability on the books. If title has passed to the purchaser before the goods are received, the transaction should be recorded at the time of title passage. Attention must be paid to transactions occurring near the end of one accounting period and at the beginning of the next to ascertain that the record of goods received (the inventory) is in agreement with the liability (accounts payable) and that both are recorded in the proper period.

Measuring the amount of an account payable poses no particular difficulty because the invoice received from the creditor specifies the due date and the exact outlay in money that is necessary to settle the account. The only calculation that may be necessary concerns the amount of cash discount. See Chapter 8 for examples of entries that relate to accounts payable and purchase discounts.

NOTES PAYABLE

Notes payable are written promises to pay a certain sum of money on a specified future date and may arise from sales, financing, or other transactions. In some industries, notes

---

[6] *CICA Handbook*, Section 1510, par. 03.

(often referred to as **trade notes payable**) are required as part of the sales/purchase transaction in lieu of the normal extension of open account credit. Notes payable to banks or loan companies generally arise from cash loans. Notes may be classified as short-term or long-term, depending upon the payment due date. Notes may also be interest-bearing or zero-interest-bearing.

Interest-Bearing Note.   Assume that Castle Mountain Bank agrees to lend $100,000 on March 1, 1998 to Landscape Ltd. provided Landscape Ltd. signs a $100,000, 12%, four-month note. The entry to record the cash received by Landscape Ltd. on March 1 is:

March 1

Cash	100,000	
Notes Payable		100,000
(To record issuance of 12%, four-month note to Castle Mountain Bank)		

If Landscape Ltd. prepares financial statements semiannually, an adjusting entry is required to recognize interest expense and interest payable of $4,000 ($100,000 × 12% × 4/12) at June 30. The adjusting entry is:

June 30

Interest Expense	4,000	
Interest Payable		4,000
(To accrue interest for four months on Castle Mountain Bank note)		

If Landscape prepared financial statements monthly, the adjusting entry at the end of each month would have been $1,000 ($100,000 × 12% × 1/12).

At maturity (July 1) Landscape Ltd. must pay the face value of the note ($100,000) plus interest ($100,000 × 12% × 4/12).

The entry to record payment of the note and accrued interest is as follows.

July 1

Notes Payable	100,000	
Interest Payable	4,000	
Cash		104,000
(To record payment of Castle Mountain Bank interest-bearing note and accrued interest at maturity)		

Zero-Interest-Bearing Note.   A zero-interest-bearing note may be issued instead of an interest-bearing note. A zero-interest-bearing note does not explicitly state an interest rate on its face. Interest is still charged, however, because the borrower is required at maturity to pay back an amount greater than the cash received at the issuance date. In other words, the borrower receives in cash the present value of the note. The present value equals the face value of the note at maturity minus the interest or discount charged by the lender for the term of the note. In essence, the bank takes its fee "up front" rather than on the date the note matures.

To illustrate, we will assume that Landscape Ltd. issues a $104,000, four-month, zero-interest-bearing note to the Castle Mountain Bank. The present value of the note is $100,000.[7] The entry to record this transaction for Landscape Ltd. is as follows.

March 1

Cash	100,000	
Discount on Notes Payable	4,000	
Notes Payable		104,000
(To record issuance of four-month, zero-interest-bearing note to Castle Mountain Bank)		

---

[7] The bank discount rate used in this example to find the present value is 11.538%.

The Notes Payable account is credited for the face value of the note, which is $4,000 more than the actual cash received. The difference between the cash received and the face value of the note is debited to Discount on Notes Payable. **Discount on Notes Payable is a contra account to Notes Payable and therefore is subtracted from Notes Payable on the balance sheet.** The balance sheet presentation on March 1 is as follows.

Current liabilities		
Notes payable	$104,000	
Less: Discount on notes payable	**4,000**	$100,000

The amount of the discount, $4,000 in this case, represents the cost of borrowing $100,000 for four months. Accordingly, the discount is charged to interest expense over the life of the note. That is, the Discount on Notes Payable balance **represents interest expense chargeable to future periods**. Thus, it would be incorrect to debit Interest Expense for $4,000 at the time the loan is obtained. Additional accounting issues related to notes payable are discussed in Chapter 15.

CURRENT MATURITIES OF LONG-TERM DEBT

The portion of bonds, mortgage notes, and other long-term indebtedness that matures within the next fiscal year—**current maturities of long-term debt**—is reported as a current liability. When only a part of a long-term debt is to be paid within the next 12 months, as in the case of serial bonds that are to be retired through a series of annual instalments, **the maturing portion of long-term debt is reported as a current liability**, the balance as a long-term debt.

Long-term debts maturing currently should not be included as current liabilities if they are to be:

1. retired by assets accumulated for this purpose that properly have not been shown as current assets;

2. refinanced, or retired from the proceeds of a new debt issue (see next topic); or

3. converted into share capital.

In these situations, the use of current assets or the creation of other current liabilities does not occur. Therefore, classification as a current liability is inappropriate. The plan for liquidation of such a debt should be disclosed either parenthetically or by a note to the financial statements.

However, a liability that is **due on demand** (callable by the creditor) or will be due on demand within a year (or operating cycle, if longer) should be classified as a current liability. Liabilities often become callable by the creditor when there is a violation of the debt agreement. For example, most debt agreements specify a level of equity to debt that must be maintained, or specify that working capital be of a minimum amount. If an agreement is violated, classification of the debt as current is required because it is a reasonable expectation that existing working capital will be used to satisfy the debt. Only if it can be shown that it is **probable** that the violation will be cured (satisfied) within the grace period usually given in these agreements can the debt be classified as noncurrent.

SHORT-TERM OBLIGATIONS EXPECTED TO BE REFINANCED

Short-term obligations are those debts that are scheduled to mature within one year after the date of an enterprise's balance sheet or within an enterprise's operating cycle, whichever is longer. Some **short-term obligations** are **expected to be refinanced** on a

OBJECTIVE 3
Explain financial statement classification issues related to short-term debt that is expected to be refinanced.

long-term basis and, therefore, are not expected to require the use of working capital during the next year (or operating cycle).[8]

At one time, the accounting profession generally supported the exclusion of short-term obligations from current liabilities if they are "expected to be refinanced." Because the profession provided no specific guidelines, however, the determination of whether a short-term obligation was "expected to be refinanced" was usually based solely on management's **intent** to refinance on a long-term basis. A company could obtain a five-year bank loan but, because the bank preferred it, handle the actual financing with 90-day notes, which it kept turning over (renewing). It was then unclear whether the loan was a long-term debt or a current liability.

Refinancing Criteria. As a result of these classification problems, the accounting profession requires the exclusion of short-term obligations from current liabilities "to the extent that contractual arrangements have been made for settlement from other than current assets."[9] Professional judgement must be used to determine whether the particular contractual arrangement is adequate to permit classification of the short-term obligation as noncurrent. The following conditions in the agreement help substantiate its adequacy.

1. The agreement should be noncancellable as to all parties.

2. It should extend beyond the normal operating cycle of the company or one year, whichever is longer.

3. At the balance sheet date and the date of issuance of the financial statements, the company must not be in violation of the agreement.

4. The lender or investor should be financially capable of honouring the agreement.

The amount of short-term debt that may be excluded from current liabilities:

1. Should not exceed the amount available for refinancing under the agreement.

2. Should be adjusted for any limitations or restrictions in the agreement that indicate that the full amount obtainable will not be available to retire the short-term obligations.

3. Should not exceed a reasonable estimate of the **minimum** amount expected to be available, if the amount available for refinancing will fluctuate (that is, the most conservative estimate should be used).

If any of these three amounts **cannot be reasonably estimated, the entire amount of the short-term debt should be included in current liabilities**.

As an illustration of a fluctuating amount (item 3 above), consider the following.

Yorkton Furniture Limited enters into an agreement with the Royal Bank to borrow up to 80% of the amount of its trade receivables. During the next fiscal year, the receivables are expected to range between a low of $900,000 in the first quarter and a high of $1,700,000 in the third quarter. The minimum amount expected to be available to refinance the short-term obligations that mature during the first quarter of the next year is $720,000 (80% of the expected low for receivables during the first quarter). Consequently, no more than $720,000 of short-term obligations may be excluded from current liabilities at the balance sheet date.

---

[8] *Refinancing a short-term obligation on a long-term basis* means either replacing it with a long-term obligation or with equity securities, or renewing, extending, or replacing it with short-term obligations for an uninterrupted period extending beyond one year (or operating cycle, if longer) from the date of the enterprise's balance sheet.

[9] *CICA Handbook*, Section 1510, par. .06.

An additional question relates to whether a short-term obligation should be excluded from current liabilities if it is paid off after the balance sheet date and subsequently replaced by long-term debt before the balance sheet is issued. To illustrate, Marquardt Company pays off short-term debt of $40,000 on January 17, 1998 and issues long-term debt of $100,000 on February 3, 1998. Marquardt's financial statements dated December 31, 1997 are to be issued March 1, 1998. Because repayment of the short-term obligation **before** funds were obtained through long-term financing required the use of **existing** current assets, the short-term obligation should be included in current liabilities at the balance sheet date (see graphical presentation below).

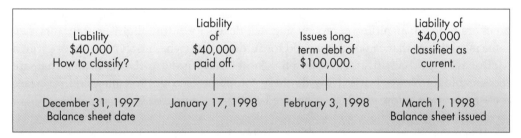

Disclosure. If a short-term obligation is excluded from current liabilities because of refinancing, the note to the financial statements should include:

1. A general description of the financing agreement.
2. The terms of any new obligation incurred or to be incurred.
3. The terms of any equity security issued or to be issued.

When refinancing on a long-term basis is expected to be accomplished through the issuance of equity securities, it is not appropriate to include the short-term obligation in owners' equity. At the date of the balance sheet, the obligation is a liability and not owners' equity.

DIVIDENDS PAYABLE

A **cash dividend payable** is an amount owed by a corporation to its shareholders as a result of an authorization by the board of directors. At the date of declaration, the corporation assumes a liability that places shareholders in the position of creditors in the amount of dividends declared. Because cash dividends are normally paid within one year of declaration (generally within three months), they are classified as current liabilities.

Accumulated but undeclared dividends on cumulative preferred shares are not a recognized liability because **preferred dividends in arrears** are not an obligation until formal action is taken by the board of directors to authorize the distribution of earnings. Nevertheless, the amount of cumulative dividends unpaid should be disclosed as a note or it may be shown parenthetically in the share capital section.

Dividends payable in the form of additional shares are not recognized as a liability. Such **stock dividends** (as discussed in Chapter 17) do not require future outlays of assets or services and they are revocable by the board of directors at any time prior to issuance. Even so, such undistributed stock dividends are generally reported in the shareholders' equity section because they represent retained earnings in the process of transfer to contributed surplus.

RETURNABLE DEPOSITS

Current liabilities of a company may include **returnable cash deposits** received from customers and employees. Deposits may be received from customers to guarantee performance of a contract or service, or as guarantees to cover payment of expected future obligations. For example, telephone companies often require a deposit upon installation of a phone. Deposits may also be received from customers as guarantees for possible damage to property left with the customer. Some companies require that their employees make deposits for the return of keys or other company property. The classification of these items as current or noncurrent liabilities is dependent on the time between the date of the deposit and the termination of the relationship that requires the deposit.

UNEARNED REVENUES

A magazine publisher such as Golf Digest may receive a customer's cheque when magazines are ordered; an airline company may sell tickets for future flights; restaurants may issue meal tickets that can be exchanged for future meals (who hasn't received or given a McDonald's gift certificate?), and retail stores may issue gift certificates that are redeemable for merchandise. How do these companies account for **unearned revenues** that are received before goods are delivered or services rendered?

1. When the advance is received, Cash is debited, and a current liability account identifying the source or the unearned revenue is credited.

2. When the revenue is earned, the unearned revenue account is debited, and an earned revenue account is credited.

To illustrate, assume that the Raiders Hockey Club sells 10,000 season hockey tickets at $50 each for its five-game home schedule. The entry for the sales of season tickets is:

August 6

Cash	500,000	
Unearned Ticket Revenue		500,000
(To record sale of 10,000 season tickets)		

As each game is completed, the following entry is made:

October 7

Unearned Ticket Revenue	100,000	
Ticket Revenue		100,000
(To record ticket revenues earned)		

Unearned Ticket Revenue is, therefore, unearned revenue and is reported as a current liability in the balance sheet. As revenue is earned, a transfer from unearned revenue to earned revenue occurs. Unearned revenue is material for some companies: In the airline industry, tickets sold for future flights represent almost 50% of total current liabilities.

Exhibit 14-1 shows specific unearned and earned revenue accounts used in selected types of businesses.

EXHIBIT 14-1

Type of Business	Account Title	
	Unearned Revenue	Earned Revenue
Airline	Unearned Passenger Ticket Revenue	Passenger Revenue
Magazine Publisher	Unearned Subscription Revenue	Subscription Revenue
Hotel	Unearned Rental Revenue	Rental Revenue
Auto Dealer	Unearned Warranty Revenue	Warranty Revenue

The balance sheet should report obligations for any commitments that are redeemable in goods and services; the income statement should report revenues earned during the period.

SALES TAXES PAYABLE

Sales taxes on transfers of tangible personal property and on certain services must be collected from customers and remitted to the tax authority. The Sales Taxes Payable account should reflect the liability for sales taxes due the government. The entry below is the proper one for a sale of $3,000 when a 4% sales tax is in effect.

Cash or Accounts Receivable	3,120	
Sales		3,000
Sales Taxes Payable		120

When the sales tax collections credited to the liability account are not equal to the liability computed by the governmental formula, an adjustment of the liability account may be made by recognizing revenue or a loss on sales tax collections.

In many companies, however, the sales tax and the amount of the sale are not segregated at the time of sale; both are credited in total in the Sales account. In that case, to reflect correctly the actual amount of sales and the liability for sales taxes, the Sales account must be debited for the amount of the sales taxes due the government on these sales and the Sales Taxes Payable account credited for the same amount. As an illustration, assume that the Sales account balance is $150,000 and includes sales taxes of 4%. Because the amount recorded in the Sales account is equal to sales plus 4% of sales, or 1.04 times the sales total, the sales are $150,000 divided by 1.04, or $144,230.77. The sales tax liability is $5,769.23 ($144,230.77 × 0.04; or $150,000 − $144,230.77), and the following entry would be made to record the amount due the taxing unit.

Sales	5,769.23	
Sales Taxes Payable		5,769.23

GOODS AND SERVICES TAX

Most businesses in Canada are subject to a Goods and Services Tax (GST). The GST is a tax on the value added by each taxable entity. The amount payable is determined by deducting the amount of GST paid to suppliers on goods and services purchased from the amount of GST collected on sales to customers.

Accounting for GST involves setting up a liability account to be credited with GST charged on sales. This account is debited for the amount of GST paid to suppliers. Normally, the amount collected on sales exceeds the amount paid on purchases and the account will have a credit balance until a remittance is made. Since GST is paid on purchases of fixed assets, it is possible that the GST Payable account will have a debit balance. In these instances, a claim for reimbursement is made to Revenue Canada.

Purchases of taxable goods and services are recorded by debiting the GST Payable account for the amount of GST and debiting the appropriate account(s) for the purchase price. Since the amount of GST paid is a recoverable amount, the cost of items acquired should not normally include this tax. As an example, Kindersley Limited purchases merchandise for $150,000 plus GST of 7% ($10,500). The entry to record this transaction would be as follows.

Merchandise Purchases	$150,000	
GST Payable	10,500	
Accounts Payable		160,500

When these goods are sold for $210,000 plus GST of 7% ($14,700) the entry would be:

Accounts Receivable	$224,700	
Sales		210,000
GST Payable		14,700

The GST Payable account shows the amount of tax charged to customers on sales as credits and the amount of tax paid to suppliers as debits. The balance represents the net amount that must be remitted periodically to the Receiver General for Canada. If the amount of tax paid to suppliers exceeds the amount of tax collected from customers, the account will have a debit balance. In this case, a claim for a refund is filed. A credit balance in the GST Payable account would be reported as a current liability and a debit balance would be shown as a current asset.

PROPERTY TAXES PAYABLE

Local governments generally depend on property taxes as their primary source of revenue. Such taxes are based on the assessed value of real and personal property and become a lien against property at a date determined by law. This lien is a liability of the property owner and is a cost of the services of such property. The accounting questions that arise from property taxes are:

1. When should the property owner record the liability?
2. To which income period should the cost be charged?

The accounting profession, in considering the various periods to which property taxes might be charged and how the liability should be reported, contends that generally, the most acceptable basis of providing for property taxes is monthly accrual on the taxpayer's books during the fiscal period of the taxing authority for which the taxes are levied. Charging the taxes to the period subsequent to the levy relates the expense to the period in which the taxes are used by the governmental unit to provide benefits to the property owner.

Assume that Seaboard Limited, which closes its books each year on December 31, receives its property tax bill in May each year. The fiscal year for the city in which Seaboard Limited is located begins on January 1 and ends on the following December 31. Property taxes of $36,000 are levied against Seaboard Company for the 1998 calendar year. However, notice of taxes is sent out in May, and taxes are payable in equal instalments on July 1 and September 1. Prior to receipt of the tax notice, the company estimated the 1998 taxes at $33,600.

Entries to record the liability, monthly tax charges, and tax payments for the 1998 property taxes are shown below.

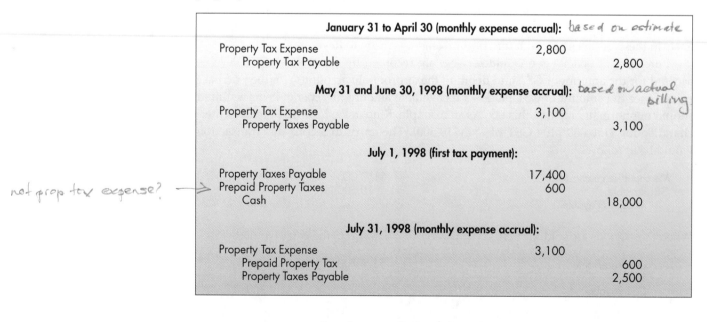

January 31 to April 30 (monthly expense accrual): *based on estimate*		
Property Tax Expense	2,800	
Property Tax Payable		2,800
May 31 and June 30, 1998 (monthly expense accrual): *based on actual billing*		
Property Tax Expense	3,100	
Property Taxes Payable		3,100
July 1, 1998 (first tax payment):		
Property Taxes Payable	17,400	
Prepaid Property Taxes	600	
Cash		18,000
July 31, 1998 (monthly expense accrual):		
Property Tax Expense	3,100	
Prepaid Property Tax		600
Property Taxes Payable		2,500

[handwritten margin note: not prop tax expense?]

August 31, 1998		
Property Tax Expense	3,100	
Property Tax Payable		3,100
September 1, 1998 (second tax payment):		
Property Taxes Payable	5,600	
Prepaid Property Tax	12,400	
Cash		18,000
Sept. 30, Oct. 31, Nov. 30, and Dec. 31, 1998 (monthly expense accrual):		
Property Tax Expense	3,100	
Prepaid Property Taxes		3,100

Prepaid property taxes of $600 on July 1 represent a prepayment and $12,400 on September 1 represent a four-month prepayment. At December 31, both the prepaid property tax and property taxes payable will have zero balances.

Some accountants advocate accruing property taxes by charges to expense during the fiscal year ending on the lien date, rather than during the fiscal year beginning on the lien date (the fiscal year of the taxing authority). In such instances the property tax for the coming fiscal year must be estimated and charged monthly to Property Tax Expense and must be credited to Property Tax Payable. Under this method, the entire amount of the tax accrued by the lien date and the expense is therefore charged to the fiscal period preceding payment of the tax. Justification for this method exists when the assessment date precedes the lien date by a year or more, as is the case in some taxing units. In such instances, since the amount is estimated and accrued by the property owner before receipt of the tax bill, it is proper to categorize property taxes as an estimated current liability rather than as determinable current liability.

Recognizing that special circumstances may suggest the use of alternative accrual periods, it is important that the period chosen be consistent from year to year. The selection of any of the alternative periods mentioned is a matter of individual judgement.

INCOME TAXES PAYABLE

Any federal or provincial income tax varies in proportion to the amount of annual income. Some accountants consider the amount of income tax on annual income as an estimate because the computation of income (and the tax thereon) is subject to Revenue Canada review and approval. The meaning and application of numerous tax rules, especially new ones, are debatable and often dependent on a court's interpretation. Using the best information and advice available, a business must prepare an income tax return and compute the income tax payable resulting from the operations of the current period. The taxes payable on the income of a corporation, as computed per the tax return, should be classified as a current liability.

Unlike a corporation, the proprietorship and the partnership are not taxable entities. Because the individual proprietor and the members of a partnership are subject to personal income taxes on their share of the business's taxable income, income tax liabilities do not appear on the financial statements of proprietorships and partnerships.

Most corporations make periodic tax payments based on estimates of their current year's income tax. As the estimated total tax liability changes, the periodic contributions also change. If in a later year an additional tax is assessed on the income of an earlier year, Income Taxes Payable should be credited. The related debit should be charged to current operations.

Differences between taxable income under the tax laws and accounting income under generally accepted accounting principles have become greater in recent years.

Because of these differences, the amount of income tax payable to the government in any given year, based on taxable income, may differ substantially from the amount of income tax that relates to the income before taxes, as reported on the financial statements. Chapter 19 is devoted solely to the problems of accounting for income tax matters and presents an extensive discussion on this complex and controversial problem.

EMPLOYEE-RELATED LIABILITIES

OBJECTIVE 4
Identify types of employee-related liabilities.

Amounts owed to employees for salaries or wages at the end of an accounting period are reported as a current liability. In addition, the following items related to employee compensation are often reported as current liabilities.

1. Payroll deductions.
2. Compensated absences.
3. Post-retirement benefits.
4. Bonuses.

Payroll Deductions.   The most common types of payroll deductions are taxes and miscellaneous items such as insurance premiums, employee savings, and union dues. To the extent that the deductions have not been remitted to the proper authority at the end of the accounting period, they should be recognized as current liabilities.

Canada (Quebec) Pension Plan (CPP/QPP).   The Canada and Quebec pension plans are funded through the imposition of taxes on both the employer and the employee. All employers are required to collect the employee's share of this tax. They deduct it from the employee's gross pay and remit it to the government along with the employer's share. Both the employer and the employee are taxed at the same rate, currently 2.8% (1996) based on the employee's gross pay up to a $35,400 annual limit. The amount of unremitted employee and employer CPP contributions should be reported by the employer as a current liability.

Employment Insurance.   Another payroll tax levied by the federal government provides a system of employment insurance. This tax is levied on both employees and employers. Employees must pay a premium of 2.95% (1996) of insurable earnings while the employer is required to contribute 1.4 times the amount of employee premiums. Insurable earnings are gross wages above a prescribed minimum and below a maximum amount. Both the premium rates and insurable earnings are adjusted frequently.

Income Tax Withholding.   Federal income tax laws require employees to withhold from the pay of each employee an amount approximating the applicable income tax due on those wages. The amount of income tax withheld is computed by the employer according to a government-prescribed formula or a government-provided income tax deduction table and is dependent on the length of the pay period and each employee's wages, marital status, and claimed dependants.

Illustration.   Assume a weekly payroll of $10,000 entirely subject to CPP (2.8%), employment insurance (2.95%), income tax withholdings of $1,320, and union dues of $88.

The entry to record the wages and salaries paid and the employee payroll deductions would be:

Wages and Salaries Expense	10,000	
Employee Income Tax Deductions Payable		1,320
CPP Contributions Payable		280
EI Premiums Payable		295
Cash		8,027
Union Dues Payable		88

The entry to record the employer payroll taxes would be:

Payroll Tax Expense	693	
CPP Contributions Payable		280
EI Premiums Payable		413

The employer is required to remit to the Receiver General for Canada the employees' CPP(QPP) contributions and EI taxes along with the employer's share of these payroll taxes. All unremitted employer CPP(QPP) contributions and EI premiums should be recorded as payroll tax expense and payroll taxes payable. In a manufacturing enterprise, all of the payroll costs (wages, payroll taxes, and fringe benefits) are allocated to appropriate cost accounts such as Direct Labour, Indirect Labour, Sales Salaries, Administrative Salaries, and the like. This abbreviated and somewhat simplified discussion of payroll costs and deductions is not indicative of the volume of records and clerical work that may be involved in maintaining a sound and accurate payroll system.

Compensated absences. **Compensated absences** are absences from employment—such as vacation, illness, and holidays—for which employees will be paid. Employers are required under provincial statutes to give each employee an annual vacation of a stipulated number of days or compensation in lieu of the vacation. As a result, employers have an obligation for vacation pay that accrues to the employees. Usually this obligation is satisfied by paying employees their regular salary for the period that they are absent from work while taking an annual vacation.

Vested rights exist when an employer has an obligation to make payment to an employee even if his or her employment is terminated; thus, vested rights are not contingent on an employee's future service. **Accumulated rights** are those that can be carried forward to future periods if not used in the period in which earned. For example, assume that you have earned four days of vacation pay as of December 31, the end of your employer's fiscal year. In a province where vacation pay is prescribed by statute, your employer will have to pay you for these four days even if you terminate employment. In this situation, your four days of vacation pay are considered vested and should be accrued. Now assume that your vacation days are not vested, but that you can carry the four days over into later periods. Although the rights are not vested, they are accumulated rights for which the employer should provide an accrual, allowing for estimated forfeitures due to turnover.

Entitlement to **sick pay** varies considerably among employers. In some companies, employees are allowed to accumulate unused sick pay and take compensated time off from work even though they are not ill. In other companies, employees receive sick pay only if they are absent because of illness. In the first case sick pay benefits vest, while in the second case the benefits do not vest and may or may not accumulate. When benefits vest, accrual of the estimated liability is recommended. However, if the sick pay benefits are paid only when employees are absent from work due to illness, then *Handbook* Section 3290 should be applied. Under this section, accruals are required only if the probability of occurrence is high and the amount can be reasonably estimated.[10] Thus, if the actual amount of sick pay payable in future periods as a consequence of services rendered in the current period can be reasonably estimated, accruals should be recorded. Otherwise, a note to the financial statements would be sufficient.

The authors believe that the expense and related liability for compensated absences should be recognized in the year in which they are earned by employees.[11] For example, if new employees receive rights to two weeks' paid vacation at the beginning of their sec-

---

[10] *CICA Handbook*, Section 3290, par. .12.

[11] Canadian accounting standards permit both accrual and pay-as-you-go accounting for compensated absences with a note disclosing the method used.

ond year of employment, the vacation pay is considered to be earned during the first year of employment.

After it is determined in what period the employee earned the right to the vacation, an issue arises as to what rate should be used to accrue the compensated absence cost—the current rate or an estimated future rate. It is likely that companies will use the current rate rather than the future rate, which is less certain and raises issues concerning the discounting of the future amount.

To illustrate, assume that Amutron Limited began operations on January 1, 1997. The company employed 10 individuals who were paid $480 per week. Vacation weeks earned by all employees in 1997 were 20 weeks, but none was used during this period. In 1998, the vacation weeks were used when the current rate of pay was $540 per week for each employee. The entry at December 31, 1997 to accrue the accumulated vacation pay was as follows.

Wages Expense	9,600	
Vacation Wages Payable		9,600*

*($480 × 20)

At December 31, 1997 the company would report on its balance sheet a liability of $9,600. In 1998, the vacation pay related to 1997 would be recorded as follows.

Vacation Wages Payable	9,600	
Wages Expense	1,200	
Cash		10,800*

*($540 × 20)

In 1998 the vacation weeks were used; therefore, the liability was extinguished. Note that the difference between the amount of cash paid and the reduction in the liability account was recorded as an adjustment to Wages Expense in the period when paid. This difference arose because the liability account was accrued at the rates of pay in effect during the period when compensated time was earned. The cash paid, however, was based on the rates in effect during the period compensated time was used. If the future rates of pay were used to compute the accrual in 1997, then the cash paid in 1998 would be equal to the liability.

Post-retirement Benefits.   The accounting and reporting standards for post-retirement benefit payments are complex. These standards relate to two different types of **post-retirement benefits**: (1) pensions; and (2) post-retirement health care and life insurance benefits.[12]

Bonus Agreements.   For various reasons, many companies give a **bonus** to certain or all officers and employees in addition to their regular salary or wage. Frequently, the bonus amount is dependent on the company's yearly profit. From the standpoint of the enterprise, **bonus payments to employees** may be considered additional wages and should be included as a deduction in determining the net income for the year.

To illustrate the entries for an employee bonus, assume a company whose income for the year 1997 is $100,000 will pay out bonuses of $10,714.29 in January, 1998. An adjusting entry dated December 31, 1997, is made to record the bonus as follows.

Employees' Bonus Expense	10,714.29	
Accrued Profit-Sharing Bonus Payable		10,714.29

---

[12] These issues are discussed extensively in Chapter 20.

In January 1998, when the bonus is paid, the journal entry will be:

Accrued Profit-Sharing Bonus Payable	10,714.29	
Cash		10,714.29

The expense account should appear in the income statement as an operating expense. The liability, Accrued Profit-Sharing Bonus Payable, is usually payable within a short period of time and should be included as a current liability in the balance sheet.

Similar to bonus arrangements are contractual agreements covering rents or royalty payments that are conditional on the amount of revenues earned or the quantity of product produced or extracted. Conditional expenses based on revenues or units produced are usually less difficult to compute than bonus arrangements. For example, if a lease calls for a fixed rent payment of $500 per month and 1% of all sales over $300,000 per year, the annual rent obligation will amount to $6,000 plus $0.01 of each dollar of revenue over $300,000. Or, a royalty agreement may accrue to the patent owner $1.00 for every tonne of product resulting from the patented process, or accrue to the owner of the mineral rights $0.50 on every barrel of oil extracted. As each additional unit of product is produced or extracted, an additional obligation, usually a current liability, is created.

DISCLOSURE OF CURRENT LIABILITIES IN THE FINANCIAL STATEMENTS

Theoretically, liabilities should be measured by the present value of the future outlay of cash required to liquidate them. But, in practice, current liabilities are usually recorded in accounting records and reported in financial statements at their full maturity value. Because of the short time periods involved, frequently less than one year, the difference between the present value of a current liability and its maturity value is not usually large. The slight overstatement of liabilities that results from carrying current liabilities at maturity value is accepted as immaterial.

OBJECTIVE 5
Indicate how current liabilites are disclosed.

The current liability accounts are commonly presented as the first classification in the Liabilities and Shareholders' Equity section of the balance sheet. In some instances, current liabilities are presented as a group immediately below current assets, with the total of the current liabilities deducted from the total current assets to obtain "working capital" or "current assets in excess of current liabilities."

Within the Current Liability section, the accounts may be listed in order of maturity, in descending order of amount, or in order of liquidation preference. The authors' review of published financial statements in 1991–1994 disclosed that a significant majority of the companies examined listed "notes payable" first (sometimes called "commercial paper," or "bank loans," or "short-term debt"), regardless of relative amount, followed most often with "accounts payable," and ended the current liability section with "current portion of long-term debt."

Detailed and supplemental information concerning current liabilities should be sufficient to meet the requirement of full disclosure. Secured liabilities should be identified clearly, and the related assets pledged as collateral indicated. If the due date of any liability can be extended, the details should be disclosed. Current liabilities should not be offset against assets that are to be applied to their liquidation. Current maturities of long-term debt should be classified as current liabilities.

A major exception exists when a currently maturing obligation is to be paid from assets classified as long-term. For example, if payments to retire a bond payable are made from a bond sinking fund classified as a long-term asset, the bonds payable should be reported in the Long-Term Liability section. Presentation of this debt in the Current Liability section would distort the working capital position of the enterprise.

Existing commitments that will result in obligations in succeeding periods that are material in amount may require disclosure. For example, commitments to purchase goods or services, as well as for construction, purchase, or lease of equipment or properties, may require disclosure in notes accompanying the balance sheet.

Presented below is an example of a published financial statement that is a representative presentation of the current liabilities with appropriate notes as found in the reports of large corporations.

EXHIBIT 14-2　POTASH CORPORATION OF SASKATCHEWAN INC.

(DOLLARS IN THOUSANDS)— DECEMBER 31

	1996	1995
Liabilities		
Current Liabilities		
Bank indebtedness (Note 8)	$ 6,330	$ –
Accounts payable and accrued charges (Note 9)	180,008	199,222
Current portion of long-term debt (Note 10)	1,520	164,971
Current obligations under capital leases (Note 11)	300	870
	188,158	365,063

8. Bank Indebtedness

Bank indebtedness consists of cheques issued in excess of funds on deposit.

The Company has available lines of credit for short-term financing in the amount of $95,000 at December 31, 1996 (1995 – $91,600). The lines of credit are unsecured.

9. Accounts Payable and Accrued Charges

	1996	1995
Trade accounts	$ 151,723	$ 155,891
Accrued interest	6,853	2,993
Accrued payroll	9,015	14,968
Income taxes	395	13,351
Dividends	12,022	12,019
	$ 180,008	$ 199,222

SECTION 2: CONTINGENCIES

A **contingency** is defined in *Handbook* Section 3290 "as an existing condition or situation involving uncertainty as to possible gain **(gain contingency)** or loss **(loss contingency)** to an enterprise that will ultimately be resolved when one or more future events occur or fail to occur."[13] As discussed in Chapter 5, gain contingencies are not recorded and are disclosed in the notes only when it is likely that a gain contingency will be realized. As a result, it is unusual to find information about contingent gains in the financial statements and the accompanying notes. A liability incurred as a result of a "loss contingency" is by definition a contingent liability. **Contingent liabilities** are obligations that are dependent upon the occurrence or nonoccurrence of one or more future events to confirm either the amount payable, the payee, the date payable, or its existence. That is, one or more of these factors depend upon a contingency.

---

[13] *CICA Handbook*, Section 3290, par. .02.

ACCOUNTING FOR LOSS CONTINGENCIES

OBJECTIVE 6
Identify the criteria used to account for and disclose loss contingencies.

When a loss contingency exists, the likelihood that the future event or events will confirm the incurrence of a liability can range from highly probable (likely) to only slightly probable (unlikely). The *CICA Handbook* uses the terms **likely** and **unlikely** to identify two areas within that range and assigns the following meaning.

Likely. The chance of occurrence (or nonoccurrence) of the future event is high.

Unlikely. The chance of the occurrence (or nonoccurrence) of the future event is slight.

An estimated loss from a loss contingency should be accrued by a charge to income and a liability recorded only if both of the following conditions are met.

1. Information available prior to the issuance of the financial statements indicates that it is likely that a future event will confirm that an asset had been impaired or a liability incurred as of the date of the financial statements.

2. The amount of the loss can be reasonably estimated.

Neither the exact payee nor the exact date payable need be known to record a liability. **What must be known is whether it is likely that a liability has been incurred.**

The second criterion indicates that an amount for the liability must be reasonably determined; otherwise, it should not be accrued as a liability. Evidence to determine a reasonable estimate of the liability may be based on the company's own experience, experience of other companies in the industry, engineering or research studies, legal advice, or educated guesses by personnel in the best position to know.

The following excerpt from the 1996 annual report of The Oshawa Group Limited is an example of disclosure of a loss contingency.

EXHIBIT 14-3 THE OSHAWA GROUP LIMITED

9. Contingency

The Company's designation of certain income for income tax purposes is under review by taxation authorities, which could give rise to additional taxes and interest of $8.6. Should income tax assessments be issued, appropriate appeal procedures would be implemented. Recognition of prior years' income tax adjustments would be recorded as a prior period adjustment in the year ending January 25, 1997.

Use of the terms likely and unlikely as guidelines for classifying contingencies involves judgement and subjectivity. The items below are examples of loss contingencies and the general accounting treatment accorded them.

Accounting Treatment of Loss Contingencies			
	Usually Accrued	Not Accrued	May Be Accrued*
Loss Related to			
1. Collectibility of receivables	X		
2. Obligations related to product warranties and product defects	X		

Accounting Treatment of Loss Contingencies *(Continued)*	Usually Accrued	Not Accrued	May Be Accrued*
3. Premiums offered to customers	X		
4. Risk of loss or damage of enterprise property by fire, explosion, or other hazards		X	
5. General or unspecified business risks		X	
6. Risk of loss from catastrophes assumed by property and casualty insurance companies including reinsurance companies		X	
7. Threat of expropriation of assets			X
8. Pending or threatened litigation			X
9. Actual or possible claims and assessments**			X
10. Guarantees of indebtedness of others			X
11. Obligations of commercial banks under "standby letters of credit"			X
12. Agreements to repurchase receivables (or the related property) that have been sold			X

*Should be accrued when both criteria are met (likely and reasonably estimable).
**Estimated amounts of losses incurred prior to the balance sheet data but settled subsequently should be accrued as of the balance sheet date.

The accounting concepts and procedures relating to contingent items are relatively new and unsettled. Practising accountants express concern over the diversity that now exists in the interpretation of "likely" and "unlikely." Current practice relies heavily on the exact language used in responses received from lawyers (such language is necessarily biased and protective rather than predictive). As a result, accruals and disclosures of contingencies vary considerably in practice. Some of the more common loss contingencies discussed in this chapter are:[14]

1. Litigation, claims, and assessments.

2. Guarantee and warranty costs.

3. Premiums, coupons, and air miles.

4. Environmental liabilities.

5. Self-insurance risks.

LITIGATION, CLAIMS, AND ASSESSMENTS

OBJECTIVE 7
Explain the accounting for different types of contingent liabilities.

The following factors, among others, must be considered in determining whether a liability should be recorded with respect to pending or threatened **litigation** and actual or possible **claims** and **assessments**.

1. The **time period** in which the underlying cause for action occurred.

2. The **probability** of an unfavourable outcome.

3. The ability to make a **reasonable estimate** of the amount of loss.

To report a loss and a liability in the financial statements, the event giving rise to the litigation must have occurred on or before the date of the financial statements. It does not matter that the company did not become aware of the existence or possibility of the lawsuit or claims until after the date of the financial statements but before they are issued. To evaluate the probability of an unfavourable outcome, consider the nature of the litigation,

---

[14] *Financial Reporting in Canada—1995* reports that of the 325 companies surveyed, loss contingencies of the following nature and number were reported: litigation, 117; guarantees of indebtedness of others, 37; environmental matters, 29; possible tax reassessments, 18; and other, 34.

the progress of the case, the opinion of legal counsel, the experience of your company and others in similar cases, and any management response to the lawsuit.

The outcome of pending litigation, however, can seldom be predicted with any assurance. Even if the evidence available at the balance sheet date does not favour the defendant, it is hardly reasonable to expect the company to publish in its financial statements a dollar estimate of the probable negative outcome. Such specific disclosures could weaken the company's position in the dispute and encourage the plaintiff to intensify its efforts. A typical example of the wording of such a disclosure is the following note to the financial statements of Abitibi-Price relating to its pending litigation.

EXHIBIT 14-4 · ABITIBI-PRICE CORPORATION

21. CONTINGENT LIABILITY

In a lawsuit commenced in 1995 in the state of Alabama, but not served on the Company until after the year end, the Company and its wholly-owned U.S. subsidiary, Abitibi-Price Corporation, were named as defendants in a conditionally certified nationwide class action suit. This claim asserts that hardboard siding manufactured by Abitibi-Price Corporation in its Building Products business, sold in 1992, was defective. While the lawsuit appears to seek substantial damages in a trial by jury, the amount of damages claimed has not been specified. However, as the claims have only recently been served, the Company has not yet filed its statement of defence or position with respect to the class action status. The Company denies the allegations and will vigorously defend itself against the claim. No amount has been accrued in these financial statements for this claim.

The Company is subject to a number of other claims in respect of which either an adequate provision has been made or for which no material liability is expected.

With respect to **unfiled suits** and **unasserted claims and assessments**, a company must determine (1) the degree of **probability** that a suit may be filed or a claim or assessment may be asserted; and (2) the **probability** of an unfavourable outcome. For example, assume that Nawtee Company is being investigated by the federal government for possible violations of anti-combines legislation, and that enforcement proceedings have been instituted. Such proceedings may be followed by private claims. In this case, Nawtee Company must determine the probability of the claims being asserted **and** the probability of damages being awarded. If both are likely, the loss is reasonably estimable, and the cause for action is dated on or before the date of the financial statements, the liability should be accrued.

GUARANTEE AND WARRANTY COSTS

A **warranty (product guarantee)** is a promise made by a seller to a buyer to make good on a deficiency of quantity, quality, or performance in a product. It is commonly used by manufacturers as a sales promotion technique. Automakers, for instance, recently "hyped" their sales by extending their new-car warranty to seven years or 115,000 km. For a specified period of time following the date of sale to the consumer, the manufacturer may promise to bear all or part of the cost of replacing defective parts, to perform any necessary repairs or servicing without charge, to refund the purchase price, or even to "double your money back."

Warranties and guarantees entail future costs that are sometimes called "after costs" or "post-sale costs," and are frequently significant. Although the future cost is indefinite as to amount, due date, and even customer, a liability does exist and should be recognized in the accounts if it can be reasonably estimated. The amount of the liability is an estimate of all the costs that will be incurred after sale and delivery and that are incident to the correction of defects or deficiencies required under the warranty provisions. Warranty costs are a good example of a loss contingency. There are two basic methods of accounting for warranty costs: (1) the cash basis method; and (2) the accrual method.

Cash Basis.   Under the **cash basis method,** warranty costs are charged to expense as they are incurred. In other words, **warranty costs are charged to the period in which the seller or manufacturer complies with the warranty**. No liability is recorded for future costs arising from warranties, nor is the period in which the sale is recorded necessarily charged with the costs of making good on outstanding warranties. Use of this method, the only one recognized for income tax purposes, is frequently justified for accounting on the basis of expediency when warranty costs are immaterial or when the warranty period is relatively short. The cash basis method is required when a warranty liability is not accrued in the year of sale either because:

1. It is not likely that a liability has been incurred; or

2. The amount of the liability cannot be reasonably estimated.

Accrual Basis.   If it is likely that customers will make claims under warranties relating to goods or services that have been sold, and a reasonable estimate of the costs involved can be made, the accrual method must be used. Under the **accrual method,** warranty costs are charged to operating expense **in the year of sale**. It is the generally accepted method and should be used whenever the warranty is an integral and inseparable part of the sale and is viewed as a loss contingency. We refer to this approach as the **expense warranty method**.

Illustration of Expense Warranty Method.   To illustrate the expense warranty method, assume that the Denson Machinery Company begins production on a new machine in July 1998 and sells 100 units at $5,000 each by its year end, December 31, 1998. Each machine is under warranty for one year and the company has estimated, from past experience with a similar machine, that the warranty cost will probably average $200 per unit. Further, as a result of parts replacements and services rendered in compliance with machinery warranties, the company incurs $4,000 in warranty costs in 1998 and $16,000 in 1999.

Sale of 100 machines at $5,000 each, July through December 1998		
Cash or Accounts Receivable	500,000	
Sales		500,000
Recognition of warranty expense, July through December 1998		
Warranty Expense	4,000	
Cash, Inventory, or Accrued Payroll		4,000
(Warranty costs incurred)		
Warranty Expense	16,000	
Estimated Liability Under Warranties		16,000
(To accrue estimated warranty costs)		

The 12/31/98 balance sheet would report Estimated Liability Under Warranties as a current liability of $16,000, and the income statement for 1998 would report Warranty Expense of $20,000.

Recognition of warranty costs incurred in 1999 (on 1998 machinery sales)

Estimated Liability Under Warranties	16,000	
Cash, Inventory, or Accrued Payroll		16,000
(Warranty costs incurred)		

If the cash basis method was applied to the facts in the Denson Machinery Company example, $4,000 would be recorded as warranty expense in 1998 and $16,000 as warranty expense in 1999, with all of the sale price being recorded as revenue in 1998. In many instances, application of the cash basis method does not match the warranty costs relating to the products sold during a given period with the revenues derived from such products. Where ongoing warranty policies exist year after year, the differences between the cash and the expense warranty basis probably would not be so great.

Sales Warranty Method. A warranty is sometimes **sold separately from the product**. For example, when you purchase a television set or VCR, you will be entitled to the manufacturer's warranty. You will likely be offered an extended warranty on the product at an additional cost.[15]

In this case, the seller should recognize separately the sale of the television or VCR with the manufacturer's warranty, and the sale of the extended warranty. This approach is referred to as the **sales warranty method**. **Revenue on the sale of the extended warranty is deferred** and is generally recognized on a straight-line basis over the life of the contract. Revenue is deferred because the seller of the warranty has an obligation to perform services over the life of the contract. Only costs that vary with and are directly related to the sale of the contracts (mainly commissions) should be deferred and amortized. Costs such as employees' salaries, advertising, and general and administrative expenses that would have been incurred even if no contract was sold should be expensed as incurred.

To illustrate, assume that you just purchased a new automobile from Sundre Auto for $20,000. In addition to the regular warranty on the auto (all repairs will be paid by the manufacturer for the first 60,000 km or three years, whichever comes first), you purchase at a cost of $600 an extended warranty that protects you for an additional three years or 60,000 km. The entry to record the sale of the automobile (with regular warranty) and the sale of the extended warranty on January 2, 1998 on Sundre Auto's books is as follows.

Cash	20,600	
Sales		20,000
Unearned Warranty Revenue		600

The entry to recognize revenue at the end of the fourth year (using straight-line amortization) would be as follows.

Unearned Warranty Revenue	200	
Warranty Revenue		200

Because the extended warranty contract does not start until after the regular warranty expires, revenue is not recognized until the fourth year. If the costs of performing services under the extended warranty contract are incurred on other than a straight-line basis (as historical evidence might indicate), revenue should be recognized over the contract period in proportion to the costs expected to be incurred in performing services under the contract.

---

[15] A contract is separately priced *if the customer has the option to purchase* the services provided under the contract for an expressly stated amount separate from the price of the product. An extended warranty or product maintenance contract usually meets these conditions.

PREMIUMS, COUPONS, REBATES, AND AIR MILES

Numerous companies offer premiums on either a limited or a continuing basis to customers in return for box tops, certificates, coupons, labels, or wrappers. The **premium** may be silverware, dishes, a small appliance, toys, or other goods. Also, **printed coupons** that can be redeemed for a cash discount on items purchased are extremely popular. A more recent marketing innovation gaining popularity is the **cash rebate**, which the buyer can obtain by returning the store receipt, a rebate coupon, and Universal Product Code (UPC label) or "bar code" to the manufacturer. Free air miles are another rapidly developing method of promoting sales. These premiums, coupon offers, air miles, and rebates are made to stimulate sales, and their **costs should be charged to expense in the period of the sale** that benefits from the premium plan. At the end of the accounting period many of these premium offers may be outstanding and, when presented in subsequent periods, must be redeemed. **The number of outstanding premium offers that will be presented for redemption must be estimated in order to reflect the existing current liability and to match costs with revenues.**[16] The cost of premium offers should be charged to Premium Expense, and the outstanding obligations should be credited to an account titled Estimated Premium Claims Outstanding.

Premium offers are not included in the CICA's list of loss contingencies. The authors believe that **premium offers result in an existing condition that involves uncertainty as to a possible loss to an enterprise that is likely to occur and can be reasonably estimated in amount and, therefore, are a loss contingency** within the guidelines of *Handbook* Section 3290.

The following example illustrates the accounting treatment accorded a premium offer. The Fluffy Cakemix Company offers its customers a large, nonbreakable mixing bowl in exchange for 25 cents and 10 boxtops. The mixing bowl costs the Fluffy Cakemix Company 75 cents, and the company estimates that 60% of the boxtops will be redeemed. The premium offer begins in June, 1998 and results in the following transactions and entries during 1998.

1. To record purchase of 20,000 mixing bowls at 75 cents each:

Inventory of Premium Mixing Bowls	15,000	
Cash		15,000

2. To record sales of 300,000 boxes of cake mix at 80 cents each:

Cash	240,000	
Sales		240,000

3. To record redemption of 60,000 boxtops, receipt of 25 cents per 10 boxtops, and delivery of the mixing bowls:

Cash [60,000 ÷ 10] × $0.25]	1,500	
Premium Expense	3,000	
Inventory of Premium Mixing Bowls		4,500
(Computation: [60,000 ÷ 10] × $0.75 = $4,500)		

4. To record estimated liability for outstanding premium offers:

Premium Expense	6,000	
Estimated Premium Claims Outstanding		6,000

Computation:

Total boxes sold in 1998	300,000
Total estimated boxtop redemptions (60%)	180,000
Boxtops redeemed in 1998	60,000
Estimated future redemptions	120,000
Cost of estimated claims outstanding (120,000 ÷ 10) × ($0.75 − $0.25)	$6,000

---

[16] In 1987 more than 13 billion coupons with a total value of $6.24 billion were distributed. However, only about 5% were redeemed.

The December 31, 1998 balance sheet of Fluffy Cakemix Company will report an Inventory of Premium Mixing Bowls of $10,500 as a current asset and Estimated Premium Claims Outstanding of $6,000 as a current liability. The 1998 income statement will report a $9,000 Premium Expense among the selling expenses.

ENVIRONMENTAL LIABILITIES

Estimates to clean up existing toxic waste sites in Canada run into billions of dollars. In addition, the cost of cleaning up our air and preventing future deterioration of the environment is estimated to cost even more. These costs will increase when one considers the trend to more stringent environmental laws and their enactments.

Effective December 1, 1990 firms are required to accrue future removal and site restoration costs if the amounts are reasonably determinable.[17] When the amounts are not reasonably determinable, a contingent liability may exist. Rio Algom Limited reported a liability of $108 million ($28 million current and $80 million long term) to provide for expected costs to restore mine sites. The accompanying note explaining this procedure is reproduced below.

EXHIBIT 14-5   RIO ALGOM LIMITED

SITE RESTORATION AND RELATED OBLIGATIONS
Estimated reclamation and site restoration costs to be incurred following closure are accrued over the life of the mine using the units of production method.

In determining expected costs, recoveries to be made at the time of shutdown are estimated and taken into account. The process of cost estimation is a continuous one, subject to changing regulations, regulatory approvals, technology and other external factors which will be recognized when applicable.

Any current expenditures relating to environmental costs at operating mines are charged to earnings in the period they are incurred.

SELF-INSURANCE RISKS

Uninsured risks may arise in a number of ways, including **noninsurance** of certain risks or **coinsurance** or **deductible clauses** in an insurance contract. But **the absence of insurance** (frequently referred to as **self-insurance**) **does not mean that a liability has been incurred at the date of the financial statements**. For example, fires, explosions, and other similar events that may cause damage to a company's own property are random in occurrence and unrelated to the activities of the company prior to their occurrence. The conditions for accrual stated in *CICA Handbook*, Section 3290, are not satisfied prior to the occurrence of the event because until that time there is no diminution in the value of the property. And, unlike an insurance company, which has contractual obligations to reimburse policyholders for losses, a company can have no such obligations to itself and, hence, **no liability either before or after the occurrence of damage**.[18]

Exposure to **risks of loss resulting from uninsured past injury to others**, however, is an existing condition involving uncertainty about the amount and the timing of losses that may develop, in which case a contingency exists. A company with a fleet of vehicles would have to accrue uninsured losses resulting from injury to others or damage to the property of others that took place prior to the date of the financial statements (if the experience of the company or other information enables it to make a reasonable estimate of the liability).

---

[17] *CICA Handbook*, Section 3060, par. .39.

[18] CICA *Handbook*, Section 3290.

However, it should not establish a liability for **expected future injury** to others or damage to the property of others even if the amount of losses is reasonably estimable.

DISCLOSURE OF LOSS CONTINGENCIES

A loss contingency and a liability are recorded if the loss is both likely and estimable. But if the loss is **either likely or estimable but not both** then the following disclosure in the notes is required.

1. The nature of the contingency.

2. An estimate of the possible loss or a statement that an estimate cannot be made.

3. How the resulting settlement will be accounted for.[19]

Presented below is a disclosure note (taken from the financial statements of Donohue Inc.) that shows that although actual losses have not been charged to operations, a liability for which no estimate is possible may exist.

EXHIBIT 14-6   DONOHUE INC.

16. LITIGATION

(a) Normick Perron Inc. instituted an action in nullity against Donohue Inc. and Donohue Normick Inc. to cancel the issue of 1,400,000 common shares of Donohue Normick Inc. to Donohue Inc. in connection with the financing of $20,000,000 for construction cost overruns of the Amos newsprint mill. The issue of these shares increased Donohue's ownership in this subsidiary from 51% to 58.1%.

Donohue Inc. and Donohue Normick Inc. are contesting this action and maintain that the common shares, which are the subject of the litigation, were issued by Donohue Normick Inc. to Donohue Inc. in accordance with the agreements entered into by Donohue Inc., Normick Perron Inc., Donohue Normick Inc. and the lenders of the first mortgage bonds of Donohue Normick Inc. As a result of an interlocutory injunction and a court order, these shares are under judicial sequestration.

In the event of an unfavourable judgment, retained earnings would be reduced by an estimated $7,300,000.

(b) Normick Perron Inc. instituted an action for a declaratory judgment requesting that the Court gives its interpretation of the Newsprint sales contract dated June 30, 1980 and entered into by Donohue Inc., Normick Perron Inc. and Donohue Normick Inc. regarding the calculation of the selling price of newsprint, the sales made to a certain category of customers and the reimbursement of certain sales expenses for the years 1982 through 1989 inclusively.

Donohue Inc. and Donohue Normick Inc. maintain that the sales of newsprint were calculated in accordance with the terms and conditions of the Newsprint sales contract and intend to justify their position in defence of this action.

In the event of an unfavourable judgment, retained earnings would be reduced by an estimated $3,100,000.

The Company believes that its legal position is sound in each of the litigations mentioned above. In the event of unfavourable judgments, the financial statements would be adjusted retroactively.

Contingencies involving an unasserted claim or assessment need not be disclosed when no claimant has come forward unless (1) it is considered likely that a claim will be asserted; and (2) it is likely that the outcome will be unfavourable.

Certain other contingent liabilities that should be disclosed even though the possibility of loss is remote are as follows.

1. Guarantees of indebtedness of others.

2. Obligations of commercial banks under "stand-by letters of credit."

---

[19] *CICA Handbook*, Section 3290, par. .15.

3. Guarantees to repurchase receivables (or any related property) that have been sold or assigned.

Disclosure should include the nature and amount of the guarantee and, if estimable, the amount that could be recovered from outside parties. Trimin Enterprises Inc. disclosed its guarantees of indebtedness of others in the following note.

EXHIBIT 14-7 TRIMIN ENTERPRISES INC.

15. Contingencies

The Company has provided a guarantee with respect to bank indebtedness of Wabi Iron & Steel Corp. ("Wabi") for an amount not to exceed $1,600,000. The indebtedness is collateralized by substantially all of Wabi's assets. Wabi purchased a substantial portion of Norcast's New Liskeard division assets effective December 31, 1992.

Summary of Learning Objectives

1. **Define current liabilities and describe how they are valued.** Current liabilities are obligations whose liquidation is reasonably expected to require the use of current assets or the creation of other current liabilities. Theoretically, liabilities should be measured by the present value of the future outlay of cash required to liquidate them. In practice, current liabilities are usually recorded in accounting records and reported in financial statements at their full maturity value.

2. **Identify the nature and types of current liabilities.** There are several types of liabilities: (1) accounts payable; (2) notes payable; (3) current maturities of long-term debt; (4) short-term obligations expected to be refinanced; (5) dividends payable; (6) returnable deposits; (7) unearned revenue; (8) taxes payable; and (9) employee-related liabilities.

3. **Explain financial statement classification issues related to short-term debt that is expected to be refinanced.** An enterprise is required to exclude a short-term obligation from current liabilities if both of the following conditions are met: (1) it has made contractual arrangements to refinance the obligation on a long-term basis; and (2) it demonstrates an ability to consummate the refinancing.

4. **Identify types of employee-related liabilities.** The employee-related liabilities are: (1) payroll deductions; (2) compensated absences; (3) post-retirement benefits, which consist of pensions and post-retirement health care and life insurance benefits; and (4) bonuses.

5. **Indicate how current liabilities are disclosed.** The current liability accounts are commonly presented as the first classification in the Liabilities and Shareholders' Equity section of the balance sheet. Within the Current Liability section the accounts may be listed in order of maturity, in descending order of amount, or in order of liquidation preference. Detail and supplemental information concerning current liabilities should be sufficient to meet the requirements of full disclosure.

6. **Identify the criteria used to account for and disclose loss contingencies.** An estimated loss from a loss contingency should be accrued by a charge to expense. A liability should be recorded only if both of the following conditions are met: (1) information available prior to the issuance of the financial statements indicates that it is likely that a liability has been incurred at the date of the financial statements; and (2) the amount of the loss can be reasonably estimated. If the loss is either likely or estimable, but not both, and if there is at least a reasonable possibility that a liability may have been incurred, disclosure should be made in the notes of the nature of the contingency and an estimate should be made of the possible loss.

7. **Explain the accounting for different types of loss contingencies.** (1) The following factors must be considered in determining whether a liability should be recorded with respect to pending or threatened litigation, and actual or possible claims and assessments: (a) the time period in which the underlying cause for action occurred; (b) the probability of an unfavourable outcome; and (c) the ability to make a reasonable estimate of the amount of loss. (2) If it is likely that customers will make claims under warranties relating to goods or services that have been sold and a reasonable estimate of the costs involved can be made, the accrual method should be used. Warranty costs under the accrual basis are charged to operating expense in the year of sale. (3) Premiums, coupon offers, rebates, and air miles are made to stimulate sales, and their costs should be charged to expense in the period of the sale that benefits from the premium plan.

EXERCISES

E14-1 **(Balance Sheet Classification of Various Liabilities)** How would each of the following items be reported on the balance sheet?

1. Accrued vacation pay.
2. Estimated taxes payable.
3. Service warranties on appliance sales.
4. Bank overdraft.
5. Employee payroll deductions unremitted.
6. Unpaid bonus to officers.
7. Deposit received from customer to guarantee performance of a contract.
8. Gift certificates sold to customers but not yet redeemed.
9. Premium offers outstanding.
10. Discounts on notes payable.
11. Personal injury claim pending.
12. Current maturities of long-term debts to be paid from current assets.
13. Cash dividends declared but unpaid.
14. Dividends in arrears on preferred shares.
15. Loans from officers.

E14-2 **(Accounts and Notes Payable)** The following are selected 1998 transactions of Alpha Romero Limited:

Sept. 1   Purchased inventory from Corto Company on account for $50,000. Romero records purchases gross and uses a periodic inventory system.
Oct. 1   Issued a $50,000, 12-month, 10% note to Corto in payment of account.
Oct. 1   Borrowed $50,000 from the Guilia Bank by signing a 12-month, noninterest-bearing $55,000 note (discounted by bank).

Instructions

(a) Prepare journal entries for the preceding transactions.
(b) Prepare adjusting entries at December 31.
(c) Compute the total net liability to be reported on the December 31 balance sheet for:
   1. the interest-bearing note;
   2. the noninterest-bearing note.

(Refinancing of Short-Term Debt) On December 31, 1998 Sharri Fano Company had $1,200,000 of short-term debt **E14-3** in the form of notes payable due February 2, 1999. On January 21, 1999 the company issued 25,000 of its common shares for $39 per share, receiving $975,000 proceeds after brokerage fees and other costs of issuance. On February 1, 1999 the proceeds from the share issue, supplemented by an additional $225,000 cash, were used to liquidate the $1,200,000 debt. The December 31, 1998 balance sheet was issued on February 23, 1999.

Instructions
Show how the $1,200,000 of short-term debt should be presented on the December 31, 1998 balance sheet, including note disclosure.

(Refinancing of Short-Term Debt) On December 31, 1998 Austin Healy Company has $7,000,000 of short-term **E14-4** debt in the form of notes payable to the Scotia Bank due periodically in 1999. On January 18, 1999 Healy enters into a refinancing agreement with the Scotia Bank that will permit it to borrow up to 60% of the gross amount of its accounts receivable. Receivables are expected to range between a low of $5,000,000 in May to a high of $6,000,000 in October during the year 1999. The interest cost of the maturing short-term debt is 15%, and the new agreement calls for a fluctuating interest at 1% above the prime rate on notes due in 2006. Healy's December 31, 1998 balance sheet is issued on February 15, 1999.

Instructions
Prepare a partial balance sheet for Healy at December 31, 1998 showing how its $7,000,000 of short-term debt should be presented, including note disclosures.

(Compensated Absences) Mercer Company began operations on January 2, 1997. It employs nine individuals who **E14-5** work eight-hour days and are paid hourly. Each employee earns 10 paid vacation days and 6 paid sick days annually. Vacation days may be taken after January 15 of the year following the year in which they are earned. Sick days may be taken as soon as they are earned; unused sick days accumulate. Additional information is as follows:

Actual Hourly Wage Rate		Vacation Days Used by Each Employee		Sick Days Used by Each Employee	
1997	1998	1997	1998	1997	1998
$6.00	$7.00	0	9	4	5

Mercer Company has chosen to accrue the cost of compensated absences at rates of pay in effect during the period when earned and to accrue sick pay when earned.

Instructions
(a) Prepare journal entries to record transactions related to compensated absences during 1997 and 1998.
(b) Compute the amounts of any liability for compensated absences that should be reported on the balance sheet at December 31, 1997 and 1998.

(Compensated Absences) Assume the facts in the preceding exercise, except that Mercer Company has chosen not **E14-6** to accrue paid sick leave until used, and has chosen to accrue vacation time at expected future rates of pay without discounting. The company uses the following projected rates to accrue vacation time:

Year in Which Vacation Time Was Earned	Projected Future Pay Rates Used to Accrue Vacation Pay
1997	$6.90
1998	7.60

Instructions
(a) Prepare journal entries to record transactions related to compensated absences during 1997 and 1998.
(b) Compute the amounts of any liability for compensated absences that should be reported on the balance sheet at December 31, 1997 and 1998.

(Adjusting Entry for Sales Tax) During the month of June, Shier's Boutique had cash sales of $234,000 and credit **E14-7** sales of $137,000, both of which include the 6% sales tax that must be remitted to the province by July 15.

Instructions
Prepare the adjusting entry that should be recorded to fairly present the June 30 financial statements.

E14-8   (Payroll Tax Entries) The payroll of the Bentley Company for September 1998 is as follows:

Total payroll $480,000, of which $120,000 represents amounts paid in excess of the maximum pensionable (CPP) and insurable (EI) earnings of certain employees. Income taxes in the amount of $90,000 are withheld, as are $9,000 in union dues. Also, assume that the current CPP contribution rate is 2.8% for employees and 2.8% for employers, and the rate for employee employment insurance deduction is 2.95% and the employer's share is 4.13%.

Instructions

Prepare the necessary journal entries if the wages and salaries paid and the employer payroll taxes are recorded separately.

E14-9   (Payroll Tax Entries) Triumph Company's payroll for August, 1998 is summarized below.

Payroll	Wages Due	Amount Subject to Payroll Taxes	
		CPP	Employment Insurance
Factory	$120,000	$120,000	$40,000
Sales	44,000	32,000	4,000
Administrative	36,000	36,000	4,000
Total	$200,000	$188,000	$48,000

At this point in the year some employees have already received wages in excess of those to which payroll taxes apply. Assume that the employment insurance rate for employees is 2.95% and is 4.13% for employers. The CPP rate is 2.8% for both employee and employer. Income tax withheld amounts to $14,000 for factory, $6,000 for sales, and $7,000 for administrative.

Instructions

(a) Prepare a schedule that shows the employer's total cost of wages for August by function. (Round all computations to nearest dollar.)

(b) Prepare the journal entries to record the factory, sales, and administrative payrolls, including the employer's payroll taxes.

E14-10   (Warranties) Doppler Company sold 200 photocopiers in 1998 for $4,000 apiece, together with a one-year warranty. Maintenance on each machine during the warranty period averages $320.

Instructions

(a) Prepare entries to record the sale of the machines and the related warranty costs, assuming that the accrua method is used. Actual warranty costs incurred in 1998 were $51,200.

(b) On the basis of the data above, prepare the appropriate entries assuming that the cash basis method was used.

E14-11   (Warranties) Stavely Equipment Company sold 500 Rollomatics during 1998 at $6,000 each. During 1998, Stavely spent $30,000 servicing the two-year warranties that accompany the Rollomatic. All applicable transactions were on a cash basis.

Instructions

(a) Prepare 1998 entries for Stavely using the expense warranty treatment. Assume that Stavely estimates the total cost of servicing the warranties to be $120,000 for two years.

(b) Prepare 1998 entries for Stavely assuming that the warranties are not an integral part of the sale. Assume that of the sales total, $160,000 relates to sales of warranty contracts. Stavely estimates the total cost of servicing the warranties will be $120,000 for two years. Estimate revenues earned on the basis of costs incurred and estimated costs.

E14-12   (Liability for Returnable Containers) Vauxhall Company sells its products in expensive, reusable containers. The customer is charged a deposit for each container delivered and receives a refund for each container returned within two years after the year of delivery. Vauxhall accounts for containers not returned within the time limit as being sold at the deposit amount. Information for 1998 is as follows:

Containers held by customers at December 31, 1997, from deliveries in:	1996	$170,000	
	1997	480,000	$650,000
Containers delivered in 1998			870,000
Containers returned in 1998 from deliveries in:	1996	$100,000	
	1997	280,000	
	1998	314,000	694,000

Instructions
(a) Prepare all journal entries required for Vauxhall Company during 1998 for the returnable containers.
(b) Compute the total amount Vauxhall should report as a liability for returnable containers at December 31, 1998.
(c) Should the liability computed in (b) above be reported as current or long-term?   (AICPA adapted)

(Premium Entries) Tucker Company includes one coupon in each box of soap powder that it packs, and 10 coupons **E14-13** are redeemable for a premium (a kitchen utensil). In 1998, Tucker Company purchased 8,800 premiums at 88 cents each and sold 110,000 boxes of soap powder at $3.30 per box; 44,000 coupons were presented for redemption in 1998. It is estimated that 60% of the coupons will eventually be presented for redemption.

Instructions
Prepare all the entries that would be made relative to sales of soap powder and to the premium plan in 1998.

(Contingencies) Presented below are three independent situations. Answer the question at the end of each situation. **E14-14**
1. During 1998, Peugeot Inc. became involved in a tax dispute with Revenue Canada. Peugeot's attorneys have indicated that they believe it is probable that Peugeot will lose this dispute. They also believe that Peugeot will have to pay Revenue Canada between $800,000 and $1,400,000. After the 1998 financial statements are issued, the case is settled with Revenue Canada for $1,100,000. What amount, if any, should be reported as a liability for this contingency as of December 31, 1998?
2. On October 1, 1998 Schumtz Chemical was identified as a potentially responsible party by the provincial Environmental Protection Agency. Schumtz's management, along with its counsel, have concluded that it is probable that Schumtz will be responsible for damages, and a reasonable estimate of these damages is $5,000,000. Schumtz's insurance policy of $9,000,000 has a deductible clause of $600,000. How should Schumtz Chemical report this information in its financial statements at December 31, 1998?
3. Bugatti Inc. had a manufacturing plant in Kuwait, that was destroyed in the Gulf War. It is not certain who will compensate Bugatti for this destruction, but Bugatti has been assured by governmental officials that it will receive a definite amount for this plant. The amount of the compensation will be less than the fair value of the plant, but more than its book value. How should the contingency be reported in the financial statements of Bugatti Inc.?

(Premiums) Presented below are three independent situations. Answer the question at the end of each situation. **E14-15**
1. Invicta Stamp Company records stamp service revenue and provides for the costs of redemption in the year stamps are sold to licensees. Invicta's past experience indicates that only 80% of the stamps sold to licensees will be redeemed. Invicta's liability for stamp redemption was $13,000,000 at December 31, 1997. Additional information for 1998 is as follows:

Stamp service revenue from stamps sold to licensees	$9,500,000
Cost of redemption (stamps sold prior to 1/1/98)	6,000,000

If all the stamps sold in 1998 were presented for redemption in 1999, the redemption cost would be $5,000,000. What amount should Invicta report as a liability for stamp redemptions at December 31, 1998?

2. In packages of its products, Daimler Inc. includes coupons that may be presented at retail stores to obtain discounts on other Daimler products. Retailers are reimbursed for the face amount of coupons redeemed plus 10% of that amount for handling costs. Daimler honours requests for coupon redemption by retailers up to three months after the consumer expiration date. Daimler estimates that 60% of all coupons issued will ultimately be redeemed. Information relating to coupons issued by Daimler during 1998 is as follows:

Consumer expiration date	12/31/98
Total face amount of coupons issued	$800,000
Total payments to retailers as of 12/31/98	290,000

What amount should Daimler report as a liability for unredeemed coupons at December 31, 1998?
                                                                                        (AICPA adapted)

3. Cord Company sold 700,000 boxes of pie mix under a new sales promotion program. Each box contains one coupon that, submitted with $5.00, entitles the customer to a baking pan. Cord pays $6.00 per pan and $0.50 for handling and shipping. Cord estimates that 70% of the coupons will be redeemed, even though only 250,000 coupons had been processed during 1998. What amount should Cord report as a liability for unredeemed coupons at December 31, 1998?

E14-16 **(Financial Statement Impact of Liability Transactions)** Presented below is a list of possible transactions:

1. Purchased inventory for $75,000 on account (assume perpetual system is used).
2. Issued an $80,000 note payable in payment on account (see item 1 above).
3. Recorded accrued interest on the note from item 2 above.
4. Borrowed $100,000 from the bank by signing a six-month, $110,000 noninterest-bearing note.
5. Recognized four months' interest expense on the note from item 4 above.
6. Recorded cash sales of $74,500, which includes 6% sales tax.
7. Recorded wage expense of $35,000. The cash paid was $25,000; the difference was due to various amounts withheld.
8. Recorded employer's payroll taxes.
9. Accrued accumulated vacation pay.
10. Recorded accrued property taxes payable.
11. Recorded bonuses due to employees.
12. Recorded a contingent loss on a lawsuit that the company will likely lose.
13. Accrued warranty expense (assume expense warranty treatment).
14. Paid warranty costs that were accrued in item 13 above.
15. Recorded sales of product and related warranties (assume sales warranty treatment).
16. Paid warranty costs under contracts from item 15 above.
17. Recognized warranty revenue (see item 15 above).
18. Recorded estimated liability for premium claims outstanding.

Instructions

Set up a table using the format below and analyse the effect of the 18 transactions on the financial statement categories indicated.

#	Assets	Liabilities	Owners' Equity	Net Income
1				

Use the following code:
I: Increase D: Decrease NE: No net effect

PROBLEMS

P14-1 Described below are certain transactions of Shao Yu Ltd.

1. On February 2, the corporation purchased goods from Richard Siu for $50,000 subject to cash discount terms of 2/10, n/30. Purchases and accounts payable were recorded by the corporation at net amounts after cash discounts. The invoice was paid on February 26.
2. On April 1, the corporation bought a truck for $30,000 from General Motors Company, paying $4,000 in cash and signing a one-year, 12% note for the balance of the purchase price.
3. On May 1, the corporation borrowed $80,000 from the Royal Bank by signing a $90,200 note due one year from May 1.
4. On August 1, the board of directors declared a $200,000 cash dividend that was payable on September 10 to shareholders of record on August 31.

Instructions

(a) Make all the journal entries necessary to record the preceding transactions using appropriate dates.
(b) Shao Yu Ltd.'s year end is December 31. Assuming that no adjusting entries relative to the transactions above have been recorded at year end, prepare any adjusting journal entries concerning interest that are necessary to present fair financial statements at December 31. Assume straight-line amortization of discounts.

Listed below are selected transactions of Bono Department Store for the current year ending December 31.

P14-2

1. On December 5, the store received $1,000 from the Bob Sadlemyer Players as a deposit to be returned after certain furniture to be used in stage production was returned on January 15.

2. During December, sales totalled $819,000, which included the 5% sales tax that must be remitted to the province by the fifteenth day of the following month.

3. On December 10, the store purchased three delivery trucks for $66,000 in cash. The trucks were purchased in a province that applied no sales tax, but the store was located in and must register the trucks in a province that applies an education and health tax of 5% to nonsalable goods bought outside of the province.

4. The store followed the practice of recording its property tax liability on the ~~lien~~ date/and amortizing the tax over the subsequent 12 months. Property taxes of $84,000 became a lien on May 1 and were paid in two equal instalments on July 1 and October 1.

bill is rec'd

Instructions

Prepare all the journal entries necessary to record the transactions noted above as they occurred and any adjusting journal entries relative to the transactions that would be required to present fair financial statements at December 31. Date each entry.

Liverpool Company pays its office employee payroll weekly. Below is a partial list of employees and their payroll data for August. Because August is their vacation period, vacation pay is also listed.

P14-3

Employee	Earnings to July 31	Weekly Pay	Vacation Pay To Be Received in August
Ringo Starr	$4,200	$180	—
George Harrison	3,500	150	$300
Yoko Ono	2,700	110	220
Paul McCartney	6,400	250	—
John Lennon	8,000	290	580

Assume that the federal income tax collected is 10% of wages. Union dues collected are 3% of wages. Vacations are taken the second and third week of August by Harrison, Ono, and Lennon. The employment insurance rate is 2.95% for employees and 1.4 times the employee rate for employers, both on a $6,000 monthly maximum. The CPP rate is 2.8% for employee and employer on an annual maximum of $33,000 per employee.

Instructions

Make the journal entries necessary for each of the four August payrolls. The entries for the payroll and for the company's liability are made separately. Also make the entry to record the monthly payment of accrued payroll liabilities.

Following is a payroll sheet for Hasselback Export Company for the month of September 1998. The employment insurance rate is 2.95%, and the maximum monthly amount per employee is $96.85. The employer's obligation for employment insurance is 1.4 times the amount of employee deductions. Assume a 10% income tax rate for all employees, and a 2.8% CPP premium charged on both employee and employer on a maximum of $33,400 annual earnings per employee.

P14-4

Name	Earnings to Aug. 31	September Earnings	Income Tax Withholding	CPP	Employment Insurance
A. Stahl	$ 5,800	$ 700			
W. Heck	5,300	500			
K. Loree	7,600	800			
K. Kruger	13,600	1,700			
E. Bannerman	120,000	15,000			
E. Lindsay	130,000	16,000			

Instructions

(a) Complete the payroll sheet and make the necessary entry to record the payment of the payroll.

(b) Make the entry to record the payroll tax expenses of Hasselback Export Company.

(c) Make the entry to pay the payroll liabilities created. Assume that the company pays all payroll liabilities at the end of each month.

P14-5 Earl Adams Ltd. sells portable computers under a two-year warranty contract that requires the corporation to replace defective parts and to provide the necessary repair labour. During 1998 the corporation sells for cash 300 computers at a unit price of $2,500. On the basis of past experience, the two-year warranty costs are estimated to be $110 for parts and $130 for labour per unit. (For simplicity, assume that all sales occurred on December 31, 1998.)

Instructions

(a) Record any necessary journal entries in 1998, applying the cash basis method.

(b) Record any necessary journal entries in 1998, applying the expense warranty accrual method.

(c) What liability relative to these transactions would appear on the December 31, 1998 balance sheet, and how would it be classified if the cash basis method is applied?

(d) What liability relative to these transactions would appear on the December 31, 1998 balance sheet, and how would it be classified if the expense warranty accrual method is applied?

In 1999 the actual warranty costs to Earl Adams Ltd. were $15,300 for parts and $17,800 for labour.

(e) Record any necessary journal entries in 1999, applying the cash basis method.

(f) Record any necessary journal entries in 1999, applying the expense warranty accrual method.

P14-6 Mind Benders Inc. sells televisions at an average price of $700 each and offers to each customer a three-year warranty contract for $75 that requires the company to perform periodic services and to replace defective parts. During 1998, the company sold 300 televisions and 250 warranty contracts for cash. It estimates the three-year warranty costs as $20 for parts and $40 for labour and accounts for warranties on the sales warranty accrual method. Assume sales occur on December 31, 1998, profit is recognized on the warranties, and straight-line recognition of revenues occurs.

Instructions

(a) Record any necessary journal entries in 1998.

(b) What amounts relative to these transactions would appear on the December 31, 1998, balance sheet, and how would they be classified?

In 1999, Mind Benders Inc. incurred actual costs relative to 1998 television warranty sales of $2,000 for parts and $3,000 for labour.

(c) Record any necessary journal entries in 1999 relative to 1998 television warranties.

(d) What amounts relative to the 1998 television warranties would appear on the December 31, 1999 balance sheet, and how would they be classified?

P14-7 Gordon Dixon Company sells a machine for $7,400 under a 12-month warranty agreement that requires the company to replace all defective parts and to provide the repair labour at no cost to the customers. With sales being made evenly throughout the year, the company sells 650 machines in 1998 (warranty expense is incurred half in 1998 and half in 1999). As a result of product testing, the company estimates that the warranty cost is $240 per machine ($110 parts and $130 labour).

Instructions

Assuming that actual warranty costs are incurred exactly as estimated, what journal entries would be made relative to these facts:

(a) Under application of the expense warranty accrual method for:
1. Sale of machinery in 1998?
2. Warranty costs incurred in 1998?
3. Warranty expense charged against 1998 revenues?
4. Warranty costs incurred in 1999?

(b) Under application of the cash basis method for:
1. Sale of machinery in 1998?
2. Warranty costs incurred in 1998?
3. Warranty expense charged against 1998 revenues?
4. Warranty costs incurred in 1999?

(c) What amount, if any, is disclosed in the balance sheet as a liability for future warranty cost as of December 31, 1998 under each method?

(d) Which method best reflects the income in 1998 and 1999 of Gordon Dixon Company? Why?

To stimulate the sales of its Captain Kanga Roo breakfast cereal, the Greenjeans Company places one coupon in each **P14-8** box. Five coupons are redeemable for a premium consisting of a children's hand puppet. In 1998, the company purchases 40,000 puppets at $1.50 each and sells 400,000 boxes of Captain Kanga Roo at $3.75 a box. From its experience with other similar premium offers, the company estimates that 40% of the coupons issued will be mailed back for redemption. During 1998, 95,000 coupons are presented for redemption.

Instructions

Prepare the journal entries that should be recorded in 1998 relative to the premium plan.

Yummy Candy Company offers a CD single as a premium for every five chocolate bar wrappers presented by cus- **P14-9** tomers together with $1.00. The chocolate bars are sold by the company to distributors for $0.30 each. The purchase price of each CD to the company is $0.90; in addition it costs $0.25 to mail each CD. The results of the premium plan for the years 1997 and 1998 are as follows (all purchases and sales are for cash):

	1997	1998
CDs purchased	250,000	330,000
Chocolate bars sold	2,895,400	2,743,600
Wrappers redeemed	1,200,000	1,500,000
1997 wrappers expected to be redeemed in 1998	290,000	
1998 wrappers expected to be redeemed in 1999		350,000

Instructions

(a) Prepare the journal entries that should be made in 1997 and 1998 to record the transactions related to the premium plan of the Yummy Candy Company.

(b) Indicate the account names, amounts, and classifications of the items related to the premium plan that would appear on the balance sheet and the income statement at the end of 1997 and 1998.

On November 24, 1998, 26 passengers on Flutterbye Airlines Flight No. 901 were injured upon landing when the **P14-10** plane skidded off the runway. Personal injury suits for damages totalling $4,000,000 were filed on January 11, 1999 against the airline by 18 injured passengers. The airline carried no insurance. Legal counsel studied each suit and advised Flutterbye that it could reasonably expect to pay 60% of the damages claimed. The financial statements for the year ended December 31, 1998 were issued February 17, 1999.

Instructions

(a) Prepare any disclosures and journal entries required by the airline in preparation of the December 31, 1998 financial statements.

(b) Ignoring the November 24, 1998 accident, what liability due to the risk of loss from lack of insurance coverage should Flutterbye Airlines record or disclose? During the past decade the company has experienced at least one accident per year and incurred average damages of $2,500,000. Discuss fully.

Ruby Sommerfeld Ltd., in preparation of its December 31, 1998 financial statements, is attempting to determine the **P14-11** proper accounting treatment for each of the following situations:

1. As a result of uninsured accidents during the year, personal injury suits for $60,000 and $350,000 have been filed against the company. It is the judgement of Sommerfeld's legal counsel that an unfavourable outcome is unlikely in the $60,000 case but that an unfavourable verdict approximating $200,000 will probably result in the $350,000 case.

2. Ruby Sommerfeld Ltd. owns a subsidiary in a foreign country that has a book value of $5,690,000 and an estimated fair value of $8,700,000. The foreign government has communicated to Sommerfeld its intention to expropriate the assets and business of all foreign investors. On the basis of settlements other firms have received from this same country, Sommerfeld expects to receive 40% of the fair value of its properties as final settlement.

3. Sommerfeld's chemical product division consisting of five plants is uninsurable because of the special risk of injury to employees and losses due to fire and explosion. The year 1998 is considered one of the safest (luckiest) in the division's history because there is no loss due to injury or casualty. Having suffered an average of three casualties a year during the rest of the past decade (ranging from $60,000 to $700,000), management is certain that next year the company will probably not be so fortunate.

Instructions

(a) Prepare the journal entries that should be recorded as of December 31, 1998 to recognize each of the situations above.

(b) Indicate what should be reported relative to each situation in the financial statements and accompanying notes. Explain why.

P14-12   Charlie Parker's Music Emporium carries a wide variety of musical instruments, sound reproduction equipment, recorded music, and sheet music. Parker uses two sales promotion techniques—warranties and premiums—to attract customers.

Musical instruments and sound equipment are sold with a one-year warranty for replacement of parts and labour. The estimated warranty cost, based on past experience, is 1% of sales.

The premium is offered on the recorded and sheet music. Customers receive a coupon for each dollar spent on recorded music or sheet music. Customers may exchange 200 coupons and $20 for a cassette player. Parker pays $32 for each cassette player and estimates that 60% of the coupons given to customers will be redeemed.

Parker's total sales for 1998 are $7,200,000—$5,400,000 from musical instruments and sound reproduction equipment and $1,800,000 from recorded music and sheet music. Replacement parts and labour for warranty work total $82,000 during 1998. A total of 6,500 cassette players used in the premium program are purchased during the year and there are 1,200,000 coupons redeemed in 1998.

The accrual method is used by Parker's to account for the warranty and premium costs for financial reporting purposes. The balances in the accounts related to warranties and premiums on January 1, 1998 are as shown below.

Inventory of Premium Cassette Players	$37,600
Estimated Premium Claims Outstanding	38,400
Estimated Liability from Warranties	68,000

Instructions

Charlie Parker's Music Emporium is preparing its financial statements for the year ended December 31, 1998. Determine the amounts that will be shown on the 1998 financial statements for the following:

1. Warranty Expense.
2. Estimated Liability from Warranties.
3. Premium Expense.
4. Inventory of Premium Cassette Players.
5. Estimated Premium Claims Outstanding.

(CMA adapted)

P14-13   Jann MacDonald Inc. must make computations and adjusting entries for the following independent situations at December 31, 1998:

1. Its line of amplifiers carries a three-year warranty against defects. On the basis of past experience the estimated warranty costs related to dollar sales are: first year after sale—2% of sales; second year after sale—3% of sales; and third year after sale—4% of sales. Sales and actual warranty expenditures for the first three years of business are:

	Sales	Warranty Expenditures
1996	$ 800,000	$ 5,800
1997	1,100,000	17,000
1998	1,200,000	61,200

Instructions

Compute the amount that Jann MacDonald Inc. should report as a liability in its December 31, 1998 balance sheet. Assume that all sales are made evenly throughout each year, with warranty expenses also evenly spaced relative to the rates above.

2. With some of its products, Jann MacDonald Inc. includes coupons that are redeemable in merchandise. The coupons have no expiration date and, in the company's experience, 40% of them are redeemed. The liability for unredeemed coupons at December 31, 1997 is $9,000. During 1998, coupons worth $23,000 are issued, and merchandise worth $8,000 is distributed in exchange for coupons redeemed.

Instructions

Compute the amount of the liability that should appear on the December 31, 1998 balance sheet.   (AICPA adapted)

CASES

Presented below is the current liability section of Maytag Limited.

	($000)	
	1998	1997
Current Liabilities		
Notes payable	$ 68,713	$ 7,700
Accounts payable	179,496	101,379
Compensation to employees	60,312	31,649
Accrued liabilities	158,198	77,621
Income taxes payable	5,486	21,491
Current maturities of long-term debt	16,592	6,649
Total current liabilities	$488,797	$246,489

Instructions

Answer the following questions.

(a) What are the essential characteristics that make an item a liability?

(b) How does one distinguish between a current liability and a long-term liability?

(c) What are accrued liabilities? Give three examples of accrued liabilities that Maytag might have.

(d) What is the theoretically correct way to value liabilities? How are current liabilities usually valued?

(e) Why are notes payable reported first in the current liability section?

(f) What might be the items that comprise Maytag's liability for "Compensation to employees?"

A. Torbert Limited includes the following items in their liabilities at December 31, 1998:

1. Notes payable, $20,000,000, due June 30, 1999.

2. Deposits from customers on equipment ordered by them from Korbert, $5,000,000.

3. Salaries payable, $3,000,000 due January 14, 1999.

Instructions

Indicate in what circumstances, if any, each of the three liabilities above would be excluded from current liabilities.

The following items are listed as liabilities on the balance sheet of Bing Crosby Corporation on December 31, 1998:

Accounts payable	$ 280,000
Notes payable	500,000
Bonds payable	1,500,000

The accounts payable represent obligations to suppliers that were due in January, 1999. The notes payable mature on various dates during 1999. The bonds payable mature on July 1, 1999.

These liabilities must be reported on the balance sheet in accordance with generally accepted accounting principles governing the classification of liabilities as current and noncurrent.

Instructions

(a) What is the general rule for determining whether a liability is classified as current or noncurrent?

(b) Under what conditions may any of Crosby Corporation's liabilities be classified as noncurrent? Explain your answer. (CMA adapted)

Spinney Corporation reflects in the Current Liability section of its balance sheet at December 31, 1998 (its year end) short-term obligations of $15,000,000, which includes the current portion of 12% long-term debt in the amount of $10,000,000 (matures in March, 1999). Management has stated its intention to refinance the 12% debt whereby no portion of it will mature during 1999. The date of issuance of the financial statements is March 25, 1999.

Instructions

(a) Is management's intent enough to support long-term classification of the obligation in this situation?

(b) Assume that Spinney Corporation issues $12,000,000 of 10-year debentures to the public in January, 1999 and that management intends to use the proceeds to liquidate the $10,000,000 debt maturing in March, 1999. Furthermore, assume that the debt maturing in March, 1999 is paid from these proceeds prior to the issuance of the financial statements. Will this have any impact on the balance sheet classification at December 31, 1998? Explain your answer.

(c) Assume that Spinney Corporation issues common shares to the public in January and that management intends to entirely liquidate the $10,000,000 debt maturing in March, 1999 with the proceeds of this equity securities issue. In light of these events, should the $10,000,000 debt maturing in March, 1999 be included in current liabilities at December 31, 1998?

(d) Assume that Spinney Corporation entered into a financing agreement on February 15, 1999 with a commercial bank that permits Spinney Corporation to borrow at any time through 2000 up to $15,000,000 at the bank's prime rate of interest. Borrowings under the financing agreement mature three years after the date of the loan. The agreement is not cancellable except for violation of a provision with which compliance is objectively determinable. No violation of any provision exists at the date of issuance of the financial statements. Assume further that $10,000,000 representing the current portion of long-term debt does not mature until August, 1999. In addition, management intends to refinance the $10,000,000 obligation under the terms of the financial agreement with the bank, which is expected to be financially capable of honouring the agreement. Given these facts, should the $10,000,000 be classified as current on the balance sheet at December 31, 1998?

C14-5 Ken Dewar Ltd. issued $9,000,000 of short-term commercial paper during the year 1997 to finance construction of a plant. At December 31, 1997, the corporation's year end, Dewar intends to refinance the commercial paper by issuing long-term debt. However, because the corporation temporarily has excess cash, in January, 1998 it liquidates $3,000,000 of the commercial paper as the paper matures. In February, 1998, Dewar completes an $18,000,000 long-term debt offering. Later, during the month of February, it issues its December 31, 1997 financial statements. The proceeds of the long-term debt offering are to be used to replenish $3,000,000 in working capital, to pay $6,000,000 of commercial paper as it matures in March, 1998, and to pay $9,000,000 of construction costs expected to be incurred later that year to complete the plant.

Instructions

(a) How should the $9,000,000 of commercial paper be classified on the balance sheets of December 31, 1997, January 31, 1998, and February 28, 1998? Give support for your answer and also consider the cash element.

(b) What would your answer be if, instead of a completed financing at the date of issuance of the financial statements, a financing agreement existed at that date?

C14-6 Wop May Company is a manufacturer of toys. During the present year, the following situations arise:

1. A safety hazard related to one of its toy products is discovered. It is considered probable that liabilities have been incurred. On the basis of past experience, a reasonable estimate of the amount of loss can be made.

2. One of its small warehouses is located on the bank of a river and can no longer be insured against flood losses. No flood losses have occurred after the date that the insurance becomes unavailable.

3. This year, May begins promoting a new toy by including a coupon, redeemable for a movie ticket, in each toy's carton. The movie ticket, which costs May $3, is purchased in advance and then mailed to the customer when the coupon is received by May. May estimates, based on past experience, that 60% of the coupons will be redeemed. Forty percent of the coupons are actually redeemed this year, and the remaining 20% of the coupons are expected to be redeemed next year.

Instructions

(a) How should May report the safety hazard? Why?

(b) How should May report the uninsurable flood risk? Why?

(c) How should May account for the toy promotion campaign in this year?   (AICPA adapted)

C14-7 (a) What is the meaning of the term "contingency" as used in accounting?

(b) Contrast accounting for a "gain contingency" that is never accrued in the accounting records and accounting for a "loss contingency."

(c) How should the following situations be recognized in the calendar year-end financial statements of Barney Phillips Chemical Company? Explain.

1. Pending in a provincial court is a suit against Phillips Chemical. The suit, which asks for token damages, alleges that Phillips has infringed on a 15-year-old patent. Briefs will be heard on March 31.

2. The TUF Union, sole bargaining agent of Phillips' production employees, has threatened a strike unless the company agrees to a proposed profit-sharing plan. Negotiations begin on March 1.

3. A recently completed (during the calendar year in question) government contract is subject to renegotiation. Although Phillips suspects that a refund of approximately $175,000 may be required by the government, the company does not wish, for obvious reasons, to publicize this fact.

4. Phillips has a $200,000, 9% note receivable due next May 1 from Lebed Company, its largest customer. Phillips discounted the note on December 20, with recourse, at the bank to raise needed cash. Lebed Company has never defaulted on a debt and possesses a high credit rating. (Treated as a sale on December 20.)

On February 1, 1998 one of the huge storage tanks of Strum Manufacturing Company exploded. Windows in houses and other buildings within a 2 km radius of the explosion were severely damaged, and a number of people were injured. As of February 15, 1998 (when the December 31, 1997 financial statements were completed and sent to the publisher for printing and public distribution), no suits had been filed or claims asserted against the company as a consequence of the explosion. The company fully anticipates that suits will be filed and claims asserted for injuries and damages. Because the casualty was uninsured and the company considered at fault, Strum Manufacturing will have to cover the damages from its own resources.

C14-8

Instructions

Discuss fully the accounting treatment and disclosures that should be accorded the casualty and related contingent losses in the financial statements dated December 31, 1997.

Presented below is a note disclosure for Shumway Limited:

C14-9

> **Litigation and Environmental:** The Company has been notified, or is a named or a potentially responsible party, in a number of governmental (federal, provincial, and local) and private actions associated with environmental matters, such as those relating to hazardous wastes, including certain Canadian sites. These actions seek clean-up costs, penalties, and/or damages for personal injury or to property or natural resources.
>
> In 1997, the Company recorded a pretax charge of $51,229,000, included in the "Other Expense (Income)— Net" caption of the Company's Consolidated Statements of Income as an additional provision for environmental matters. These expenditures are expected to take place over the next several years and are indicative of the Company's commitment to improve and maintain the environment in which it operates. At December 31, 1997 environmental accruals amounted to $63,931,000, of which $56,535,000 were considered noncurrent and included in the "Deferred Credits and Other Liabilities" caption of the Company's Consolidated Balance Sheets.
>
> While it is impossible at this time to determine with certainty the ultimate outcome of environmental matters, it is management's opinion, based in part on the advice of independent counsel (after taking into account accruals and insurance coverage applicable to such actions) that when the costs are finally determined, they will not have a materially adverse effect on the financial position of the Company.

Instructions

Answer the following questions.

(a) What conditions must exist before a loss contingency can be recorded in the accounts?

(b) Suppose that Shumway Limited could not reasonably estimate the amount of the loss, although it could establish with a high degree of probability the minimum and maximum loss possible. How should this information be reported in the financial statements?

(c) If the amount of the loss was uncertain, how would the loss contingency be reported in the financial statements?

The following three independent sets of facts relate to (1) the possible accrual or (2) the possible disclosure by other means of a loss contingency.

C14-10

Situation I. Subsequent to the date of a set of financial statements, but prior to the issuance of the financial statements, a company enters into a contract that will likely result in a significant loss to the company. The amount of the loss can be reasonably estimated.

Situation II. A company offers a one-year warranty for the product that it manufactures. A history of warranty claims has been compiled and the probable amount of claims related to sales for a given period can be determined.

Situation III. A company has adopted a policy of recording self-insurance for any possible losses resulting from injury to others by the company's vehicles. The premium for an insurance policy for the same risk from an independent insurance company would have an annual cost of $3,000. During the period covered by the financial statements, there were no accidents involving the company's vehicles that resulted in injury to others.

Instructions

Discuss the accrual or type of disclosure necessary (if any) and the reason(s) why such disclosure is appropriate for each of the three independent sets of facts above.

Complete your response to each situation before proceeding to the next situation.   (AICPA adapted)

C14-11   The following two independent situations involve loss contingencies.

Part I. Ya Ha Tinda Company sells two types of merchandise, Type A and Type B. Each carries a one-year warranty.

1. Type A merchandise—Product warranty costs, based on past experience, will normally be 1% of sales.

2. Type B merchandise—Product warranty costs cannot be reasonably estimated because this is a new product line. However, the chief engineer believes that product warranty costs are likely to be incurred.

Instructions

How should Ya Ha Tinda report the estimated product warranty costs for each of the two types of merchandise above? Discuss the rationale for your answer. Do not discuss deferred income tax implications, or disclosures that should be made in Ya Ha Tinda's financial statements or notes.

Part II. Morgan Limited is being sued for $3,000,000 for an injury caused to a child as a result of alleged negligence while the child was visiting a Morgan plant in March, 1998. The suit was filed in July, 1998. Morgan's lawyer states that it is probable that Morgan will lose the suit and be found liable for a judgement costing anywhere from $300,000 to $1,500,000. However, the lawyer states that the most probable judgement is $600,000.

Instructions

How should Morgan Limited report the suit in its 1998 financial statements? Discuss the rationale for your answer. Include in your answer disclosures, if any, that should be made in Morgan's financial statements or notes.

(AICPA adapted)

C14-12   Presented below is the Current Liability section and related note of the Hamilton Company.

	1998	1997
	(Dollars in thousands)	
Current liabilities:		
Current portion of long-term debt	$ 15,000	$ 10,000
Short-term debt	2,668	405
Accounts payable	29,495	42,427
Accrued warranty	16,843	16,741
Accrued marketing programs	17,512	16,585
Other accrued liabilities	35,653	33,290
Accrued and deferred income taxes	6,206	7,348
Total current liabilities	$123,377	$126,796

Notes to Consolidated Financial Statements

1(in Part): Summary of Significant Accounting Policies and Related Data
Accrued Warranty— The company provides an accrual for future warranty costs based upon the relationship of prior years' sales to actual warranty costs.

Instructions
Answer the following questions.

(a) What is the difference between the cash basis and the accrual basis of accounting for warranty costs?

(b) Under what circumstance, if any, would it be appropriate for Hamilton Company to recognize deferred revenue on warranty contracts?

(c) If Hamilton Company recognized deferred revenue on warranty contracts, how would it recognize this revenue in subsequent periods?

USING YOUR JUDGEMENT

FINANCIAL REPORTING PROBLEM

Refer to the financial statements and other documents of Moore Corporation Limited presented in Appendix 5A and answer the following questions.

1. What are Moore's current portions of long-term debt at December 31, 1995 and 1994? What are the amounts of the remaining scheduled maturities of long-term debt for the years 1997 to 2000?

2. How are contingencies reported in Moore's financial statements? What is management's rationale for its reporting practice for these contingencies?

3. Is Moore likely to experience a bank overdraft? Explain.

ETHICS CASE I

Mail Order Company has a bonus arrangement that grants the financial vice-president and other executives a $15,000 bonus if net income exceeds the previous year's by $1,000,000. Noting that the current financial statements report an increase of $950,000 in net income, Vice-President Glenn Close asks Christopher Walkin, the controller, to reduce the estimate of warranty expense by $60,000. The present estimate of warranty expense is $500,000 and is known by both Close and Walkin to be a fairly "soft" amount.

Instructions

(a) Should Walkin lower his estimate?

(b) What ethical issue is at stake? Is anyone harmed?

(c) Is Close acting unethically?

ETHICS CASE 2

Old Manitoba Company, the owner of Camptown Mall, charges Old Folks Home Store a rental fee of $600 per month plus 5% of yearly profits over $500,000. Stephen Foster, the owner of the store, directs his accountant, Osue Sanna, to increase the estimate of bad debt expense, warranty costs, and depreciation on the computerized inventory system in order to keep profits at $475,000.

Instructions

(a) Should Sanna follow her boss's directive?

(b) Who is harmed if her estimates are increased?

(c) Is Foster's directive unethical?

ETHICS CASE 3

On January 2, 1998, Workman Steel Company received notice from the provincial government's Environmental Protection Agency that the Prior Lake Toxic Disposal Site needs to be cleaned up and that Workman Steel will be assessed 1/25 of the $25,000,000 cost. The clean-up will begin in 2001 and will take an estimated five years. Workman Steel has been using this disposal site for several decades. The vice-president and the controller discuss the proper recording of the environmental liability. Vice-President Renea Rhodes advocates recording the entire liability in 1998. Controller Jared Wagner suggests footnote disclosure at most and prefers nondisclosure until clean-up begins in 2001.

Instructions

(a) What is the appropriate manner of reporting?

(b) Is there an ethical issue involved in this discussion?

(c) Who is harmed by nondisclosure?

chapter 15

LONG-TERM LIABILITIES

Learning Objectives

After studying this chapter, you should be able to:

1. Explain the nature of long-term liabilities.

2. Identify various types and characteristics of bonds.

3. Explain how proceeds from the issuance of bonds are determined and why a discount or premium can result.

4. Account for bonds payable and related interest expense for bonds issued at par, or at a discount or premium, on an interest date or between interest dates, using the straight-line and effective interest methods of amortization.

5. Identify the balance sheet presentation of bond discount and bond premium accounts.

6. Account for the costs of issuing bonds.

7. Account for the reacquisition of debt prior to maturity.

8. Differentiate between legal and in-substance defeasance and recognize the accounting issues involved.

9. Account for long-term notes payable.

10. Differentiate between a financial liability and an equity instrument.

11. Determine the appropriate balance sheet classification of, and reporting for, financial instruments according to their economic substance.

12. Explain the basic accounting and reporting issues related to derivatives and off-balance-sheet financing arrangements.

13. Describe the disclosure requirements for long-term debt and financial liabilities.

14. Account for the settlement of troubled debt at less than its carrying amount (Appendix 15A).

15. Account for the modification of the terms of troubled debt (Appendix 15A).

16. Account for serial bonds (Appendix 15B).

"Let us all be happy and live within our means, even if we have to borrow the money to do it . . ."[1] appeared to be a motto of the 1980s. Companies and consumers took on increasing levels of debt to finance expansion, take over companies, satisfy consumption needs, and obtain advantages of favourable financial leverage.[2]

With the recession of the early 1990s, however, many companies with significant amounts of debt found it increasingly difficult to meet their high interest and principal payments. Companies needed cash flows. They responded by selling off assets, restruc-

---

[1] A comment by Artemus Ward in *Investment Vision*, September/October, 1990.

[2] Favourable financial leverage means a company earns a greater return from the use of borrowed funds than the interest cost to them. This concept is examined in Chapter 24.

turing, cutting dividends, laying off workers, and selling new equity. As interest rates declined and the economy and earnings improved, much of the debt was refinanced at lower rates and debt, in general, was brought down to more reasonable levels.

Long-term financing is a key responsibility of management. Borrowing carries a lower cost of capital for the firm than does equity financing (through issuing shares and internal financing through earnings), and the financial leverage it brings can be very beneficial to shareholders. These advantages have to be weighed against the disadvantages in the form of increased risk—of higher fixed costs associated with interest payments and commitments for debt repayment. Financial analysts commonly look to the ratio of debt to equity in assessing a company's financial risk.

Over the past 10 to 15 years, the financial services industry has made available to corporations an incredible variety of new and innovative financing vehicles tailored, in many cases, to the specific needs of individual companies. Accounting standards have not kept pace with the proliferation of types of financial instruments available. The Accounting Standards Board of the CICA issued and reissued exposure drafts on financial instruments in the early and mid-1990s, but the complexity of the project resulted in the recognition and measurement issues being sent back to the Board for further study. *CICA Handbook* Section 3860 on Financial Instruments—Disclosure and Presentation was released effective for December 31, 1996.

The objectives of this chapter are to consider the nature of long-term debt and to examine the accounting issues related to its recognition, measurement, and disclosure. Bonds and long-term notes payable are the basic instruments used to demonstrate the underlying concepts. The reporting issues and disclosure requirements for financial instruments whose underlying economic substance differs from their legal form are explained, and the complex issues associated with off-balance-sheet financing are introduced. Troubled debt restructuring and accounting for serial bonds are considered in Appendix 15A and 15B, respectively. Leases, another important source of long-term financing, are covered in Chapter 21.

NATURE OF LONG-TERM LIABILITIES

OBJECTIVE 1
Explain the nature of long-term liabilities.

A **long-term liability** is an *obligation of an entity arising from past transactions or events for which settlement will not take place within the next year or operating cycle of the business, if longer.*

Incurring long-term debt is often accompanied by considerable formality. For example, by-laws of corporations often require approval by the board of directors and shareholders before bonds can be issued or other long-term debt arrangements can be contracted.

Generally, long-term debt is issued subject to various **covenants** or **restrictions** for the protection of the lenders. The covenants and other terms of the agreement between the borrower and the lender are stated in the **bond indenture** or **note agreement**. Items often mentioned in the indenture or agreement include the amounts authorized to be issued, interest rate, due date or dates, property pledged as security, sinking fund requirements, working capital and dividend restrictions, and limitations concerning the assumption of additional debt. When these stipulations are important for a complete understanding of the financial position and the results of operations, they should be described in the body or notes of the financial statements. In many cases, the loan instrument or contract is held by a trustee, usually a financial institution, which acts as an independent third party to protect the interests of both lender and borrower.

A **debt instrument** *usually has a maturity date* when the face value (principal amount) must be repaid to the lender, *confers no voting rights*, and *bears interest that* *must be paid on a regular basis* (usually annually or semiannually). An **equity instrument**, in contrast, generally *does not have a maturity date, may or may not have voting rights,* and *the entitlement to a return in the form of dividends is at the discretion and direction of the issuing corporation's board of directors.* Situations where the legal form of instrument differs from its underlying characteristics are covered later in this chapter.

BONDS PAYABLE

A **bond** arises from a contract known as an indenture and represents a promise to pay (1) a sum of money at a designated maturity date and (2) periodic interest at a specified (fixed or variable) rate on the maturity amount or face value. Individual bonds are evidenced by a certificate and typically have a face value of $1,000. Bond interest payments are usually made semiannually, although the interest rate is generally expressed as an annual rate.

An entire bond issue may be sold to an investment banker. In such arrangements, investment bankers may either underwrite the entire issue by guaranteeing a certain sum to the corporation, thus taking the risk of selling the bonds for whatever price they can get (firm underwriting), or they may sell the bond issue for a commission to be deducted from the proceeds of the sale (best efforts underwriting). Alternatively, the issuing company may choose to sell the bonds directly to a large institution, financial or otherwise, without the aid of an underwriter (private placement).

TYPES AND CHARACTERISTICS OF BONDS

Various terms are used to describe bonds. Following are some of the more common characteristics that a bond may have, either singly or in combination.

Bonds may be **secured** (e.g., mortgage bonds that have a claim on real estate, and collateral trust bonds that have securities of other corporations as security) or **unsecured** (e.g., debenture bonds). A **junk bond** is unsecured and also very risky, and therefore pays a high rate of interest. These bonds are often used to finance leveraged buyouts.

Bond issues that mature on a single date are called **term bonds**, and issues that mature in instalments are called **serial bonds**. The accounting for serial bonds is illustrated in Appendix 15B. If bonds are exchangeable into other securities of the corporation, such as preferred or common shares, they are called **convertible bonds**. Accounting for bond conversion is discussed later in this chapter and in Chapter 18. If the *issuer* has the right to call in and retire the bonds prior to maturity, they are **callable** or **redeemable bonds**. Where the *holder* has the option to sell the bonds back to the company, typically restricted to specified time periods and prices, the bonds are termed **retractable**. Stelco Inc. has retraction rights in some of its long-term debt instruments. **Extendable bonds** allow the holder, at his or her option, to extend the date of maturity under specified terms and conditions.

Registered bonds are issued in the name of the owner and require surrender of the certificate and issuance of a new certificate to complete a sale. **Bearer bonds**, on the other hand, are not recorded in the name of the owner and may be transferred from one owner to another by mere delivery. Coupons attached to such bonds are submitted by the holder to receive interest payments. **Income bonds** pay no interest unless the issuing company is profitable, whereas **revenue bonds** pay interest from specified revenue sources.

Commodity-backed bonds (also called **asset-linked bonds**) or loans are redeemable in measures of a commodity, such as barrels of oil, bushels of wheat, or ounces of rare metal. For example, in the 1980s Sunshine Mining, a silver mining producer, sold two issues of bonds redeemable with either $1,000 in cash or 50 ounces of silver (or the cash

OBJECTIVE 2
Identify various types and characteristics of bonds.

equivalent), whichever was greater at maturity. Goldcorp Inc. reported two gold loans on recent financial statements. The accounting problem for these bonds is one of appropriate liability measurement, especially as prices for commodities tend to fluctuate significantly over time.

Deep-discount bonds or **zero-interest bonds** pay very low or no stated interest. When no periodic interest is paid, the buyer's total interest payoff is at maturity, the amount of interest being the difference between the maturity amount and the price for which the bonds were sold. A unique version of a zero-interest bond (with overtones of a commodity-backed bond) was proposed by Caesar's World Inc., a Las Vegas/Lake Tahoe gambling casino operator. Caesar's World was to issue 5,000 of $15,000 face value bonds that would entitle each bondholder to spend two weeks a year at its Lake Tahoe resort in lieu of interest on the bond.[3] In Canada, **stripped bonds** or **zero-coupon bonds** are created by detaching (or stripping) the interest coupons from a coupon bond and selling the stripped bond as a contract in itself.[4] For example, Nova Scotia Power Inc.'s bonds that mature on January 10, 2009 are sold by brokers as stripped bonds. Marketing names such as "Cats," "Cougars," and "Tigers" have been used in Canada to describe some deep-discount bonds.

In summary, bonds have many different features and vary in level of risk and return. The main purpose of bonds is to borrow from the general public or from institutional investors for the long term when the amount of capital needed is too large for one lender to supply. By issuing bonds in $1,000 or $10,000 denominations, a large amount of long-term indebtedness can be divided into many small investing units, thus enabling more than one lender to participate in the loan.

VALUATION OF BONDS PAYABLE

The issuance and marketing of bonds is not an overnight happening—it takes time, often weeks or months. Approval must be obtained, audits and issuance of a prospectus may be required, certificates must be printed, and underwriters must be arranged. Frequently, the terms in a bond indenture are established well in advance of the sale of bonds. Between the time the terms are set and the bonds are sold, the market conditions and the financial position of the issuing corporation may change significantly. Such changes affect the marketability of the bonds and thus their selling price.

OBJECTIVE 3
Explain how proceeds from the issuance of bonds are determined and why a discount or premium can result.

As explained in Chapter 10, the selling price of a bond issue is set by such familiar economic phenomena as supply and demand of buyers and sellers, relative risk, market conditions, and the state of the economy. *The investment community values a bond at the present value of its future cash flows, usually consisting of a lump sum at maturity and an annuity of interest payments.* The interest rate used to compute the present value of these cash flows is the rate that provides an acceptable return on the investment commensurate with the issuer's risk characteristics, that is, the **market**, **yield**, or **effective rate**.

The interest rate written in the terms of the bond indenture and ordinarily appearing on the bond certificate is known as the **stated**, **coupon**, or **nominal rate**. This rate, set by the issuer of the bonds, is expressed as a percentage of the **face value**, also called the **par value**, **principal amount**, or **maturity value** of the bonds. If the effective rate used to discount the cash flows in determining the value of the bonds differs from the stated rate,

---

[3] "Caesar's World May Try Bond Issue Paying in Vacations," *The Wall Street Journal* (January 22, 1982), p. 32.

[4] The stripped coupons are sold to investors separately from the bond. Investors interested in a steady flow of income may buy the coupons, while those interested in accumulating capital (such as in a Registered Retirement Savings Plan) would buy the stripped bond.

the value of the bonds computed by the market will differ from the face value of the bonds.[5]

When investors can earn a higher return in the market from other investments of equal risk, a company's bonds will sell, but at an amount less than their face value. That is, the bonds will sell at a **discount**. The present value of the cash flows promised by the bond indenture, discounted at the higher market rate, results in a bond value that is less than face value. As the issuing company will have to pay back more at maturity than it received, this additional cost is amortized over the period to maturity as increased interest expense. Interest expense, therefore, is the total of the cash interest paid or payable and the amount of discount amortized.

When a bond promises to pay interest at a higher rate than other bonds of equivalent risk (i.e., higher than the market rate), investors will bid up the price of the bond above its par or face value and it will sell at a **premium**. Its price will be bid up to an amount equal to the present value of the cash flows discounted at the lower market rate of return. As the issuing company receives more cash for the bonds than it has to repay at maturity, this benefit, the premium, must be taken into income over the periods that benefit from the bond financing, that is, from the date of issue to the maturity date. Thus, as the premium is amortized, the effect is to reduce the amount of interest expense reported. Interest expense, therefore, is the cash interest paid or payable, reduced by the amount of premium amortized.

When the rate required by the investment community is the same as the nominal rate the bond pays, the bond will sell at its face value: the present value of the promised cash flows, discounted at the market rate (also the nominal rate). Interest expense recognized by the issuer in this case is equal to the cash interest paid or payable.

To illustrate the computation of the present value of a bond issue, assume that Servicemaster Corp. issues $100,000 in bonds due in five years with 9% interest payable annually at year end when the market rate for such bonds is 11%. The actual principal and interest cash flows are discounted at an 11% rate as follows:

EXHIBIT 15-1

Present value of the amount of the principal:	
$a(p_{\overline{5}\rceil 11\%}) = \$100,000 \,(.59345)$ (Table A-2)	$59,345
Present value of the annuity of interest payments:	
$R(P_{\overline{5}\rceil 11\%}) = \$9,000 \,(3.69590)$ (Table A-4)	33,263
Present value (selling price) of the bonds	**$92,608**
Discount on bonds: $100,000 − $92,608	$7,392

Because these bonds pay interest at a rate less than the going market rate, we would expect investors to pay less than face value for them. By paying $92,608 (that is, at a discount of $7,392) at the date of issue, investors will earn an effective rate or yield of 11% over the five-year term of the bonds.[6] Although investors cannot change the cash flows to be received, *they can change the return they earn by changing the amount paid for the bond.*

As shown in Exhibit 15-2, if investors required only an 8% return, they would bid up the price of the 9% bond to $103,992, the present value of the future cash flows discounted at the 8% market rate. It would then sell at a premium of $3,992.

---

[5] Companies attempt to align the stated rate as closely as possible with the market or effective rate. Nevertheless, because the stated rate is set prior to the sale of the bonds, it often differs, but is usually small in amount. For deep-discount or zero-interest bonds, however, the difference is substantial.

[6] Bond prices are typically stated as a percentage of par or face value. For example, the Servicemaster bonds sold at 92.6 (92.6% of par). If $102,000 has been received, the bonds would have sold at 102.

EXHIBIT 15-2

Present value of the amount of the principal:	
$a(p_{\overline{5}|8\%}) = \$100,000\ (.68058)$ (Table A-2)	$ 68,058
Present value of the annuity of interest payments:	
$R(P_{\overline{5}|8\%}) = \$9,000\ (3.99271)$ (Table A-4)	35,934
Present value (selling price) of the bonds	**$103,992**
Premium on bonds: $103,992 − $100,000	$3,992

The key variables in bond pricing, aside from the cash flows themselves, are the number of interest periods to maturity (n) and the market or yield rate of return (i). For example, if the 9% Servicemaster bonds paid interest quarterly (four times per year), and were sold to yield 8%, the value of the bonds would be as shown below.

EXHIBIT 15-3

Present value of the amount of the principal:	
$a(p_{\overline{20}|2\%}) = \$100,000\ (.67297)$ (Table A-2)	$ 67,297
Present value of the annuity of interest payments:	
$R(P_{\overline{20}|2\%}) = \$2,250\ (16.35143)$ (Table A-4)	36,791
Present value (selling price) of the bonds	**$104,088**
Premium on bonds: $104,088 − $100,000	$4,088

Three changes were necessary to the calculations in the previous illustration. First, the interest cash flows are now $2,250 ($100,000 × .09 × 1/4); the market rate of interest (i) must correspond to the interest period, that is, the rate per quarter year; and the number of interest periods (n) must be consistent with (i). Note that the revised interest rate and number of periods are used in discounting *both the principal and the interest* flows.

ACCOUNTING FOR BONDS PAYABLE: STRAIGHT-LINE METHOD

OBJECTIVE 4
Account for bonds payable and related interest expense for bonds issued at par, or at a discount or premium, on an interest date or between interest dates, using the straight-line effective interest methods of amortization.

Similar to accounting for investments in bonds as described in Chapter 10, accounting for bonds payable by the issuer requires decisions about measurements at the date of issue, at interest dates and year ends, and at maturity or extinguishment. These aspects are examined in the following paragraphs, which consider the various circumstances that may exist for a bond issue.

Bonds Issued at Par on an Interest Date. When bonds are issued on an interest payment date at face value, the accounting entry simply records the cash proceeds and the face value of the bonds. To illustrate, if 10-year 10% bonds with a par value of $800,000, dated January 1, 1998, with interest payable semiannually on January 1 and July 1, are sold on January 1, 1998 at par, the entry on the books of the issuing corporation is:

Cash	800,000	
Bonds Payable		800,000

The entry to record the first semiannual interest payment of $40,000 ($800,000 × .10 × 6/12) on July 1, is:

Bond Interest Expense	40,000	
Cash		40,000

If the year end is December 31, then six months' accrued interest is recorded on that date as follows:

Bond Interest Expense	40,000	
Bond Interest Payable		40,000

Bonds Issued at a Discount or Premium on an Interest Date. If the $800,000 of bonds illustrated above were sold on January 1, 1998 at 97, the issuance would be recorded as follows:

Cash ($800,000 × .97)	776,000	
Discount on Bonds Payable	24,000	
Bonds Payable		800,000

Unlike accounting for an investment in bonds, bonds payable are usually recorded at their face or maturity value and the discount (or premium) on bonds is set up in a separate contra or adjunct account. The bond in this case sold at less than face value because the interest to be paid by the issuer is less than the market rate; therefore *the resulting discount should be amortized and charged to interest expense over the period the bonds are outstanding*. The discount (or premium) may be amortized using either the straight-line method or the effective interest method.[7]

Under the **straight-line method**, the amount amortized each year is a constant amount. For example, using the above bond discount of $24,000, the amount amortized to interest expense each year for 10 years is $2,400 ($24,000 × 1/10) and, *if amortization is recorded annually*, the December 31 adjustment for the discount would be:

Bond Interest Expense	2,400	
Discount on Bonds Payable		2,400

At the end of the first year, 1998, as a result of the amortization entry, the unamortized balance in the Discount on Bonds Payable account is $21,600 ($24,000 − $2,400). Interest expense for the year is $82,400: $40,000 on both July 1 and December 31, as shown previously, plus the $2,400 debit to interest expense resulting from the discount amortization.

If the bonds were dated and sold on November 1, 1998 with interest dates of November 1 and May 1, and the fiscal year of the corporation ended on December 31, the discount amortized for 1998 would be only 2/12 of 1/10 of $24,000, or $400. Amortization of this amount and recognition of the accrued interest payable of $13,333 ($800,000 × .10 × 2/12) would result in interest expense of $13,733 for 1998, which is recorded on December 31 as follows:

Bond Interest Expense	13,733	
Bond Interest Payable		13,333
Discount on Bonds Payable		400

If no reversing entries are made, the entry on May 1, 1999 for the first interest payment, *assuming the amortization of the discount is recorded on the interest date*, is:

Bond Interest Expense [($800,000 × .10 × 4/12) + $800]	27,467	
Bond Interest Payable (see December 31 entry)	13,333	
Cash		40,000
Discount on Bonds Payable ($24,000 × 1/10 × 4/12)		800

---

[7] Although the effective interest method is preferred, the less complex straight-line method is used initially to emphasize the concepts. The straight-line method is acceptable if the results are not materially different from those produced by the effective interest method, examined shortly.

Premium on bonds payable is accounted for in a manner similar to that described for discount on bonds payable. If the 10-year bonds dated January 1, 1998 with a par value of $800,000 are sold on January 1 at 103, then the cash proceeds are $824,000 ($800,000 × 1.03).

The entry to record this is:

Cash	824,000	
Bonds Payable		800,000
Premium on Bonds Payable		24,000

Given interest dates of July 1 and January 1, a company year end of December 31, and amortization of the premium recorded on interest dates, the following entries would be made:

July 1, 1998

Bond Interest Expense [($800,000 × .10 × 6/12) − $1,200)	38,800	
Premium on Bonds Payable ($24,000 × 1/10 × 6/12)	1,200	
Cash		40,000

December 31, 1998

Bond Interest Expense	38,800	
Premium on Bonds Payable	1,200	
Bond Interest Payable		40,000

As is evident from these examples, ***bond interest expense is increased by amortization of a discount and decreased by amortization of a premium.***

Bonds Issued at Par Between Interest Dates.   Bond interest payments are usually made semi-annually on dates specified in the bond indenture. When bonds are issued on other than an interest payment date, buyers of the bonds pay the seller the interest accrued from the last interest payment date to the date of issue. The purchasers of the bonds, in effect, pay the bond issuer in advance for that portion of the full six-month interest payment to which they are not entitled, not having held the bonds during this period. The purchasers will receive the full six-month interest payment on the semiannual interest payment date.

To illustrate, if 10-year, 10% bonds of a par value of $800,000, dated January 1, 1998, with interest payable semiannually on January 1 and July 1, are issued at ***par plus accrued interest on March 1, 1998,*** the entry on the books of the issuing corporation is:

Cash	813,333	
Bonds Payable		800,000
Bond Interest Expense ($800,000 × .10 × 2/12)		13,333

The purchaser advances two months' interest because on July 1, 1998, four months after the date of purchase, six months' interest will be received from the issuing company. The company makes the following entry on July 1, 1998:

Bond Interest Expense	40,000	
Cash		40,000

The expense account now contains a debit balance of $26,667, representing the appropriate amount of four months' interest expense at 10% on $800,000.[8]

Bonds Issued at a Discount or Premium Between Interest Dates.   The above illustration was simplified by having the January 1, 1998 bonds issued on March 1, 1998 ***at par.*** If, how-

---

[8] Instead of crediting Bond Interest Expense on March 1, Bond Interest Payable could have been credited for the $13,333. In this case, the July 1 debit to Bond Interest Expense would be for $26,667 and the Bond Interest Payable account would be debited for $13,333. The entry to record the first interest payment susequent to issue has to appropriately link to the method chosen to account for the accrued interest when the bonds were issued. The authors base all subsequent examples on the assumption that the accrued interest is credited on issue to Bond Interest Expense.

ever, these bonds were issued at 102, the entry on March 1 on the books of the issuing corporation would be:[9]

Cash [($800,000 × 1.02) + $13,333]	829,333	
Bonds Payable		800,000
Premium on Bonds Payable ($800,000 × .02)		16,000
Bond Interest Expense ($800,000 × .10 × 2/12)		13,333

Since these bonds mature on January 1, 2008, the period over which the premium should be amortized is 118 months, 10 years less two months. Therefore, the entry on July 1, 1998 for the interest payment and straight-line premium amortization is:

Bond Interest Expense	39,458	
Premium on Bonds Payable	542	
Cash		40,000

The premium amortization ($16,000 × 4/118 = $542) is deducted from the cash interest amount to derive the debit to interest expense. Considering both the March 1 and July 1 entries, the net amount charged to interest expense for the four months is $26,125 (the July 1 debit for $39,458 less the March 1 credit for $13,333). Note that this is also equivalent to four months' cash interest of $26,667 ($800,000 × .10 × 4/12) less four months' premium amortization of $542.

ACCOUNTING FOR BONDS PAYABLE: EFFECTIVE INTEREST METHOD

The straight-line method for amortizing a premium or discount as illustrated above results in a *constant amount* being charged to interest expense for each full year during the life of the bonds. Charging an equal amount to interest expense each year is not conceptually correct. The relationship of the constant interest expense to the changing **carrying value** or **book value** (face value less discount or plus the premium) of the bonds results in an apparent change in the *rate* of interest each year.

The **effective interest method** overcomes this problem. Under the effective interest method:

1. Bond interest expense is computed first by multiplying the carrying value of the bonds at the beginning of the period by the effective interest rate.

2. The bond interest to be paid (or payable) is computed by multiplying the face value of the bonds by the stated or nominal rate of interest.

3. The bond discount or premium amortization is then determined by comparing the bond interest expense to the interest to be paid.

The computation of the amortization is depicted as follows:

ILLUSTRATION 15-1

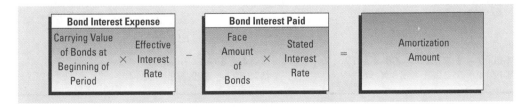

The effective interest method produces a periodic interest expense equal to a *constant percentage of the carrying value of the bonds*. Since the percentage is the effective rate of interest incurred by the borrower at the time of issuance, the effective interest method results in a better matching of expenses with revenues than the straight-line method.

[9] Prices given are for the bond only, unless stipulated otherwise.

Both the effective interest and straight-line methods result in the same total amount of interest expense over the term of the bonds, and the annual amounts of interest expense are generally quite similar. However, *when the annual amounts are materially different, the effective interest method is preferred.*[10]

Bonds Issued at a Discount. To illustrate amortization of a discount using the effective interest method, assume that Evermaster Corp. issued $100,000 of 8% bonds on January 1, 1998, due on January 1, 2003, with interest payable each July 1 and January 1. Because the investors required an effective interest rate of 10%, they paid $92,278 for the $100,000 of bonds, creating a $7,722 discount. The $7,722 discount is calculated as follows:

EXHIBIT 15-4

Maturity value of bonds payable		$100,000
Present value of $100,000 ($n = 10$, $i = 5$)		
$100,000 × .61391 (Table A-2)	$61,391	
Present value of $4,000 interest ($n = 10$, $i = 5$)		
$4,000 × 7.72173 (Table A-4)	30,887	
Proceeds from sale of bonds		92,278
Discount on bonds payable		$ 7,722

The five-year (10-period) amortization schedule appears below. *Note that when using the effective interest method, the carrying value at each interest payment date also equals the present value of the* **remaining** *cash flows discounted at the effective or yield rate.*

EXHIBIT 15-5

SCHEDULE OF BOND DISCOUNT AMORTIZATION

Effective Interest Method: Semiannual Interest Payments
Five-Year, 8% Bonds Sold to Yield 10%

Date	Credit Cash	Debit Interest Expense	Credit Bond Discount	Carrying Value of Bonds
1/1/98				$ 92,278
7/1/98	$ 4,000[a]	$ 4,614[b]	$ 614[c]	92,892[d]
1/1/99	4,000	4,645	645	93,537
7/1/99	4,000	4,677	677	94,214
1/1/00	4,000	4,711	711	94,925
7/1/00	4,000	4,746	746	95,671
1/1/01	4,000	4,783	783	96,454
7/1/01	4,000	4,823	823	97,277
1/1/02	4,000	4,864	864	98,141
7/1/02	4,000	4,907	907	99,048
1/1/03	4,000	4,952	952	100,000
	$40,000	$47,722	$7,722	

[a]$4,000 = $100,000 × .08 × 6/12   [c]$614 = $4,614 − $4,000
[b]$4,614 = $92,278 × .10 × 6/12   [d]$92,892 = $92,278 + $614

The entries to record the issuance of Evermaster Corp.'s bonds, the first interest payment and the accrual of interest at year end are as follows.

---

[10] At the time of writing, there was no Canadain standard requiring the use of the effective interest method when discounts or premiums are large. The CICA *Re-exposure Draft* on "Financial Instruments" (Toronto: CICA, April, 1994) which was subsequently withdrawn, contained a proposed recommendation (par. .170) that the effective interest method be used, as is required in the United States.

January 1, 1998

Cash	92,278	
Discount on Bonds Payable	7,722	
Bonds Payable		100,000

July 1, 1998

Bond Interest Expense	4,614	
Cash		4,000
Discount on Bonds Payable		614

December 31, 1998

Bond Interest Expense	4,645	
Bond Interest Payable		4,000
Discount on Bonds Payable		645

Bonds Issued at a Premium. If investors were willing to accept an effective interest rate of 6% on the 8% bond issue described above, they would have paid $108,530, or a premium of $8,530, based on present value computations. The applicable five-year amortization schedule appears below.

EXHIBIT 15-6

SCHEDULE OF BOND PREMIUM AMORTIZATION

Effective Interest Method: Semiannual Interest Payments
Five-Year, 8% Bonds Sold to Yield 6%

Date	Credit Cash	Debit Interest Expense	Debit Bond Premium	Carrying Value of Bonds
1/1/98				$108,530
7/1/98	$ 4,000[a]	$ 3,256[b]	$ 744[c]	107,786[d]
1/1/99	4,000	3,234	766	107,020
7/1/99	4,000	3,211	789	106,231
1/1/00	4,000	3,187	813	105,418
7/1/00	4,000	3,162	838	104,580
1/1/01	4,000	3,137	863	103,717
7/1/01	4,000	3,112	888	102,829
1/1/02	4,000	3,085	915	101,914
7/1/02	4,000	3,057	943	100,971
1/1/03	4,000	3,029	971	100,000
	$40,000	$31,470	$8,530	

[a]$4,000 = $100,000 × 0.08 × 6/12   [c]$744 = $4,000 − $3,256
[b]$3,256 = $108,530 × 0.06 × 6/12   [d]$107,786 = $108,530 − $744

The entries to record the issuance of the Evermaster bonds at a premium and the first interest payment and amortization of the premium are:

January 1, 1998

Cash	108,530	
Premium on Bonds Payable		8,530
Bonds Payable		100,000

July 1, 1998

Bond Interest Expense	3,256	
Premium on Bonds Payable	744	
Cash		4,000

Bonds Issued Between Interest Dates. When using the effective interest method for bonds issued at a premium or discount between interest dates, the question is how to measure the premium or discount amortization from the issue date to the first interest payment date. The answer is that *the amount amortized equals the difference between the amount received for the bonds (excluding accrued interest) and the present value of the bonds at the first interest date following their issuance.* In the following periods, the amount to be amortized is based on an amortization schedule that starts with the carrying value of the bonds after the first interest payment.

To illustrate, refer to the Schedule of Bond Premium Amortization in Exhibit 15-6. Rather than assuming the bonds were sold on January 1, 1998 for $108,530 as in that example, assume the bonds were sold for $108,282[11] on March 1, 1998. The buyers also pay for two months' accrued interest of $1,333 ($100,000 × .04 × 2/6). The following entry is made on March 1:

Cash ($108,282 + $1,333)	109,615	
Bonds Payable		100,000
Premium on Bonds Payable		8,282
Interest Expense		1,333

On July 1, 1998, the first interest payment date after issuance of the bonds, the following entry is made:

Interest Expense	3,504	
Premium on Bonds Payable	496	
Cash		4,000

The debit to the Premium account is the difference between the $108,282 received for the bonds and their present value of $107,786 on July 1 after the interest payment (see carrying value of these bonds for 7/1/98 in the amortization schedule). *Amounts in entries* to recognize the premium amortization, interest expense, and cash paid or payable *after the first interest payment are the same as those applicable to the situation of the bonds being issued on an interest date.*

Interest Dates Do Not Coincide with Year End. In our previous examples, the interest periods corresponded with the company's fiscal year. However, what happens if Evermaster, having issued its 8% bonds on January 1, 1998, wishes to prepare financial statements at the end of February 1998? In this case, the premium is prorated to arrive at the appropriate interest expense, as shown below.

EXHIBIT 15-7

COMPUTATION OF INTEREST EXPENSE

Interest accrual ($4,000 × 2/6)	$1,333
Premium amortization ($744 × 2/6)	(248)
Interest expense (Jan.–Feb.) ($3,256 × 2/6)	**$1,085**

---

[11] To determine the price received for bonds sold at other than an interest date: (1) determine the present value of the bonds on the interest dates immediately before and after the issuance using the effective rate of interest at date of issuance; and (2) interpolate the price based on the time of issuance between the dates. For Evermaster Corp.:
  (1) Present value, January 1, 1998 = $108,530
      Present value, July 1, 1998   = $107,786
  (2) Since the bonds were issued two months into the six-month period, interpolation results in a March 1, 1998 value of:
      $108,530 − 2/6(108,530 − $107,786) = $108,282.

The journal entry to record this accrual is as follows:

Interest Expense	1,085	
Premium on Bonds Payable	248	
Interest Payable		1,333

If the company prepared interim financial statements six months later on August 31, 1998, the same procedure is followed; that is, the premium amortized would be determined as follows.

EXHIBIT 15-8

Premium amortized (March–June) ($744 × 4/6)	$496
Premium amortized (July–August) ($766 × 2/6)	255
Premium amortized (March–August, 1998)	$751

The computation is much simpler if the straight-line method is employed. For example, in the Evermaster situation the total premium of $8,530 is allocated evenly over the period from the date of issue to maturity. Thus, premium amortization per month is $142 ($8,530 × 1/60).

BALANCE SHEET PRESENTATION OF UNAMORTIZED BOND DISCOUNT OR PREMIUM

OBJECTIVE 5
Identify the balance sheet presentation of bond discount and bond premium accounts.

Discount on Bonds Payable is not an asset because it does not provide any future economic benefit. The enterprise has the use of the borrowed funds, but for that use it must pay interest. A bond discount means that the company received less than the face or maturity value of the bond and therefore is faced with an actual (effective) interest rate higher than the stated (nominal) rate. Conceptually, Discount on Bonds Payable is a liability valuation account, that is, a reduction of the face or maturity amount of the related liability. As such it is reported as a **contra account** to the maturity value of the related bonds payable.

Premium on Bonds Payable is not itself a liability—it has no existence apart from the related debt. A lower interest cost results because the proceeds of borrowing exceed the face or maturity amount of the debt. Conceptually, Premium on Bonds Payable is a liability valuation account; that is, an addition to the face or maturity amount of the related liability. It is reported as an **adjunct account** to the maturity value of the related bonds payable.

In practice, the unamortized portion of a Discount on Bonds Payable is frequently shown on the balance sheet under Deferred Charges (a separate category under assets or as an item under the heading "Other Assets"). Correspondingly, an unamortized Premium on Bonds Payable is frequently shown as a deferred credit item under liabilities. Separating the maturity value and the related discount or premium into different parts of the balance sheet tends to obscure the *effective liability* of the bonds. The conceptually correct approach as identified above overcomes this criticism. Section 3070 (par. .02) of the *CICA Handbook* on Deferred Charges states that "major items among the deferred charges should be shown separately, e.g., debt discount and expenses . . ." While the *Handbook* recognizes the acceptability of showing bond discounts as deferred charges, the authors prefer the practice of reporting discounts and premiums as liability valuation accounts, as illustrated in Exhibit 15-9.

EXHIBIT 15-9

Long-term debt		
10% Bonds Payable, at face value	$100,000	
Less: Unamortized discount	(2,370)	$ 97,630
11% Bonds Payable, at face value	$400,000	
Add: Unamortized premium	7,900	407,900
Total long-term debt		$505,530

When a corporation has numerous bond issues outstanding, each with its own related discount or premium, the total unamortized discount or premium may be shown net at the bottom of a schedule of listed bond issuances.

COSTS OF ISSUING BONDS

OBJECTIVE 6
Account for the costs of issuing bonds.

The issuance of bonds involves engraving and printing costs, legal and accounting fees, commissions, promotion expenses, and other similar charges. One practice is to *merge these items with the discount or premium on bonds*, increasing the balance of the discount or decreasing the balance of the premium account. The debt issue costs, therefore, increase the effective interest rate and interest expense when they are accounted for as part of the amortization of the discount or premium.

Alternatively, it is acceptable to debit debt issue costs to a *deferred charge* account, such as Unamortized Bond Issue Costs, and amortize them over the life of the debt. This account appears in the asset section of the balance sheet under the category Deferred Charges or Other Assets. The acceptability of this approach is implied in Section 3070 of the *CICA Handbook*, which indicates that "debt expenses" are an example of deferred charges. This procedure is called for in *APB Opinion No. 21* governing U.S. financial reporting. In Canada, the choice of balance sheet presentation remains, although the tendency is to treat such costs as deferred charges.

To illustrate the accounting for costs of issuing bonds as a deferred charge, assume that Microchip Inc. sold $20,000,000 of 10-year bonds for $20,795,000 on January 1, 1998 (also the date of the bonds). Costs of issuing the bonds were $245,000. The entries at January 1, 1998 and December 31, 1998 for issuance of the bonds and amortization of the bond issue costs are as follows.

January 1, 1998

Cash	20,550,000	
Unamortized Bond Issue Costs	245,000	
Premium on Bonds Payable		795,000
Bonds Payable		20,000,000

December 31, 1998

Bond Issue Expense ($245,000 × 1/10)	24,500	
Unamortized Bond Issue Costs		24,500
(To amortize one year of bond issue costs, straight-line method)		

While the bond issue costs could be amortized using the effective interest method, the straight-line method is generally used in practice because it is easier and the results are not materially different.

EXTINGUISHMENT OF DEBT

How is the payment (often referred to as the extinguishment) of debt recorded? If the bonds (or any other form of debt security) are held to maturity, the answer is relatively straightforward—no gain or loss is computed because the amount of cash required to retire the debt will be equal to its carrying amount. Any premium or discount and issue costs will have been fully amortized at the date the bonds mature. As a result, the carrying amount will be equal to the maturity (face) value of the bonds at that time.

The problems, however, become more complex when the debt is extinguished *prior to maturity*. Two types of early extinguishment include the reacquisition of debt, and legal and in-substance (economic) defeasance.

REACQUISITION OF DEBT

Reacquisition of debt can occur either by payment to the creditor or by purchase in the open market. A reacquisition could be for all or any portion of the bonds outstanding.

The amount paid on extinguishment or redemption before maturity, including any call premium and expense of reacquisition, is called the **reacquisition price**. The **net carrying amount** of the bonds is the face value adjusted for the unamortized premium or discount and issue costs at the reacquisition date. *At the time of reacquisition, the premium or discount and any issue costs applicable to the bonds must be amortized up to the reacquisition date.* The difference between the net carrying amount and the reacquisition price is the gain or loss on redemption.

To illustrate, assume that on January 1, 1994 General Bell Corp. issued at a price of 97 (at a discount of $24,000), 12% (payable annually) bonds of a par value of $800,000 due in 20 years. Bond issue costs of $16,000 were incurred. On June 1, 1999 the entire issue is redeemed at 101 and cancelled.

On June 1, 1999, the company first must recognize interest expense and the interest payable to the bondholders that has accrued since January 1, and amortize the discount and bond issue costs up to the reacquisition date (assume straight-line amortization for both).

OBJECTIVE 7
Accounting for the reacquisition of debt prior to maturity.

June 1, 1999

Bond Issue Expense ($16,000 × 5/240)	333	
Interest Expense ($40,000 + $500)	40,500	
Unamortized Bond Issue Costs ($16,000 × 5/240)		333
Discount on Bonds Payable ($24,000 × 5/240)		500
Interest Payable ($800,000 × .12 × 5/12)		40,000

The up-to-date balances at June 1, 1999, therefore, are as follows:

ILLUSTRATION 15-2

	Discount on Bonds Payable		Unamortized Bond Issue Costs	
Jan. 1/94	$24,000		$16,000	
Amortization				
–Jan. 1/94 to Dec. 31/98	$6,000	($24,000 × 60/240)	$4,000	($16,000 × 60/240)
			$ 333	
–Jan. 1/99 to June 1/99	$ 500			
			$11,667	
Balance, June 1/99	$17,500			

Bonds Payable	
	$800,000 Jan. 1/94

June 1/99 net carrying amount: $800,000 − $17,500 − $11,667 = $770,833

The entry to record the redemption and cancellation of the bonds does three things: (1) records the amount of cash paid for the bonds and accrued interest; (2) takes the book value of all accounts associated with the bonds redeemed off the books; and (3) recognizes the gain or loss at an amount equal to the difference between the reacquisition price and the net carrying amount:

June 1, 1999

Bonds Payable	800,000	
Interest Payable (see entry on page 731)	40,000	
Loss on Redemption of Bonds ($808,000 − $770,833)	37,167	
Discount on Bonds Payable		17,500
Unamortized Bond Issue Costs		11,667
Cash [($800,000 × 1.01) + $40,000]		848,000

Had only one-quarter of the bonds been reacquired, the *accounts* in the above journal entries would be the same but the *amounts* would be one-quarter of those shown. The subsequent accounting for the remaining bonds would be done in the normal manner. Gains and losses on the redemption of bonds do not meet the definition of extraordinary items and are therefore reported in income before extraordinary items.

In some cases, bonds may be reacquired by the issuing corporation or its agent or trustee but not formally cancelled. These are known as **treasury bonds** of the issuing corporation. If the above bonds had been required to be held in treasury instead of cancelled, the entry to record the transaction is the same as shown except the debit to Bonds Payable would be to an account entitled Treasury Bonds. The treasury bonds would then be shown on the balance sheet at their face value as a deduction from the bonds payable issued to arrive at a net figure representing bonds payable outstanding. When they are subsequently sold or cancelled, the Treasury Bonds account is credited.

It is sometimes advantageous for a corporation to acquire its entire bond issue outstanding and replace it with a new bond issue bearing a lower rate of interest. The replacement of an existing issue with a new one is called **refunding**. If refunding takes place prior to the maturity date of a bond issue, a difference between the issue price of the new bonds and the net carrying amount of the refunded issue is likely to result. When this occurs, there are three alternative approaches to accounting for the amount of the difference:

1. Treat it as a gain or loss on bond refunding in the current year's income statement.
2. Amortize it over the remaining life of the bonds that have been refunded.
3. Amortize it over the life of the new bonds issued.

To date, the choice is left to judgement as the *CICA Handbook* contains no recommendations regarding a preferred method. U.S. GAAP requires the first alternative, based on the opinion that differing reasons for early redemption or differing means by which the bonds are redeemed should have no bearing on how the loss or gain is accounted for.

LEGAL AND IN-SUBSTANCE DEFEASANCE

OBJECTIVE 8
Differentiate between legal and in-substance defeasance and recognize the accounting issues involved.

The reacquisition of debt as explained above results in removing the liability from the books and recording a gain or loss on redemption. Companies have developed other methods of removing debt from the balance sheet. Usually, they set aside sufficient assets (cash and investments) to meet the cash interest and maturity requirements associated with a particular long-term liability, then remove both the assets and the liability from the books, recording a gain (usually) for the difference.

What motivation is there for extinguishing debt in this manner? First, the company may not be able to buy back the publicly held debt in large enough quantities, or it may be too costly if a high call premium is required to be paid. Second, the company may want to reduce its debt-to-equity ratio to meet the requirements of other borrowing contracts, to secure more favourable terms on issuance of new debt, or to reduce reported interest expense in the income statement. Third, management may be motivated by the reporting of a gain on the income statement when the cost of the securities set aside is less than the carrying value of the company's debt. This is possible when interest rates rise and the cost of an investment with cash flows matching those of the debt is less than the recorded book value of the debt.

The issue of whether or not the investments, debt, and related interest expense should be removed from the financial statements is controversial. The arguments regarding various accounting treatments focus on whether the terms of the arrangement result in legal defeasance or in-substance defeasance.

Legal Defeasance. **Legal defeasance** means the debtor is released from all legal liability as a result of the arrangement. This occurs when (1) the party (such as a trustee) receiving the cash or securities agrees to assume the debtor's obligations; and (2) the creditors agree that the trustee will be responsible for paying the principal and interest. In such situations the company is fully discharged from its contractual obligations and the creditor does not retain any right of recourse against the company. Consequently, a legal defeasance is accounted for in a manner similar to that illustrated for reacquisition of debt, except that the carrying value of the securities provided to the trustee would be removed from the company's assets.

To illustrate, assume that PanCan Inc. deposited government securities with a cost of $252 million in an irrevocable trust to solely satisfy the scheduled interest and principal requirements on a long-term debt carried at $269 million, and that the arrangement satisfies the requirements of a legal defeasance. As such, PanCan would make the following entry:

Long-term Debt Payable	269,000,000	
Investment in Securities		252,000,000
Gain from Legal Defeasance		17,000,000

In-Substance Defeasance. When a company deposits cash and securities in an irrevocable trust that is to be used to pay the principal and interest obligation on a debt of the company, *but the creditor is not a party to the arrangement and may not even know it exists*, a legal defeasance does not occur. It is argued, however, that the end result is, in substance, economically the same as a legal defeasance. Hence, such an arrangement is called **an in-substance defeasance.** The fact that the creditor has not released the company from its obligation to pay the principal and interest may not be considered a material risk because the assets placed in trust are sufficient to cover known payments contracted for in the future. Consequently, many conclude that an in-substance defeasance should be accounted for like a legal defeasance (i.e., as a debt extinguishment), with appropriate disclosure of a contingent, but remote, liability.

Air Canada has applied this accounting treatment to its in-substance defeasances, as is indicated by the following excerpt.

EXHIBIT 15-10   AIR CANADA

FROM THE NOTES TO THE DECEMBER 31, 1995
FINANCIAL STATEMENTS
(MILLIONS OF DOLLARS)

5. Long-Term Debt

b) In 1990 and 1989, the Corporation concluded agreements with a substantial U.S. financial institution whereby, upon payment by the Corporation, the financial institution assumed liability for scheduled payments relating to certain long-term obligations in amounts of $98 in 1990 and $107 in 1989 and interest thereon. These obligations (which amount to $85 and $93 respectively at December 31, 1995) are considered extinguished for financial reporting purposes and have been removed from the Corporation's statement of financial position. Until the assumed liabilities have been fully discharged by the financial institution, the Corporation remains contingently liable for such obligations in the remote event that the counter party fails to perform.

While *CICA Handbook* Section 3860, Financial Instruments, makes recommendations on when netting of assets and liabilities is appropriate, the removal of both from the balance sheet as required in accounting for an in-substance defeasance has not yet been resolved. Air Canada's accounting treatment follows *Statement No. 76* issued by the FASB in the U.S.[12]

Statement No. 76 is controversial and has been subjected to much criticism. Dissenters believe that gain or loss recognition should not be extended to situations where the debtor is not legally released from being the primary obligor of the debt obligation. They contend that "the setting aside of assets in trust does not, in and of itself, constitute either the disposition of assets with potential gain or loss recognition or the satisfaction of a liability with potential gain or loss recognition."[13] In other words, committing specific assets to a single purpose might ensure that the debt is serviced in a timely fashion, but that event alone just matches up cash flows; it does not satisfy, eliminate, or extinguish the obligation. For a debt to be satisfied, the risk associated with the obligation must be transferred and the creditor must be satisfied. This is not the case in an in-substance defeasance. Therefore, the assets deposited in trust and the debt obligation they are pledged to service should be reported separately as an asset and liability respectively.

The Accounting Standards Board is studying in-substance defeasance as part of its project on the recognition and measurement of financial instruments.

LONG-TERM NOTES PAYABLE

OBJECTIVE 9
Account for long-term notes payable.

The difference between current notes payable and **long-term notes payable** is the maturity date. As discussed in Chapter 14, short-term notes payable are expected to be paid within a year or the operating cycle, whichever is longer. Long-term notes are similar in substance to bonds in that both have fixed maturity dates and carry either a stated or implicit interest rate. However, notes do not trade as readily as bonds in the organized public securities markets. Noncorporate and smaller corporate enterprises issue notes as their long-term instruments, while larger corporations issue both long-term notes and bonds.

Accounting for notes and bonds is quite similar. *Like a bond, a note is valued at the present value of its future interest and principal cash flows with any discount or premium being amortized over the life of the note.* The computation of the present value of an interest-bearing note, the recording of its issuance, the amortization of any discount or premium, and the accrual of interest are as shown for bonds in this chapter.

As expected, accounting for long-term notes payable parallels accounting for long-term notes receivable as presented in Chapter 7.

---

[12] "Extinguishment of Debt," *Statement of Financial Accounting Standards No. 76* (Stamford, Conn.: FASB, 1983).
[13] *Ibid.*, p. 5.

Notes Issued at Face Value

In Chapter 7, the discounting and recognition of a $10,000, three-year note issued at face value by Scandinavian Imports to Bigelow Corp. was illustrated. In this transaction, the stated rate and the effective rate were both 10%. The time diagram and present value computation on page 337 of Chapter 7 for Bigelow Corp. is the same for the issuer of the note, Scandinavian Imports, in recognizing a note payable. Because the present value of the note and its face value are the same, $10,000, no premium or discount is recognized. The issuance of the note is recorded by Scandinavian Imports as follows:

Cash	10,000	
Notes Payable		10,000

Scandinavian Imports recognizes the interest incurred each year as follows:

Interest Expense	1,000	
Cash		1,000

Notes Not Issued at Face Value

Zero Interest-Bearing Note.[14] If a noninterest-bearing (zero-coupon) note is issued solely for cash, its present value is equal to the cash proceeds received by the issuer of the note. The **implicit interest rate** is the rate that equates the cash received with the maturity value to be paid in the future. *The difference between the face amount and the present value (cash received) is recorded as a discount and is amortized to interest expense over the life of the note.*

    An example of such a transaction was Beneficial Corporation's offering of $150 million of zero-coupon notes having an eight-year life. With a face value of $1,000 each, these notes sold for $327—a deep discount of $673 each. The present value of each note is the cash proceeds of $327. The effective interest rate can be calculated by determining the discount rate that equates the amount currently paid by the investor with the amount to be received in the future.[15] Thus, Beneficial amortized the discount over the eight-year life of the notes using the effective interest rate of 15%.

    To illustrate the entries and the amortization schedule, assume that your company issued the three-year, $10,000 zero interest note to Jeremiah Company as illustrated on page 338 in Chapter 7. With cash proceeds of $7,721.80 at the date of issue, the implicit rate that equates the proceeds with the $10,000 to be paid at maturity is 9%. (The present value of $1 for 3 periods at 9% is $0.77218.)

    The entry to record the issue of the note is as follows:

Cash	7,721.80	
Discount on Notes Payable ($10,000.00 − $7,721.80)	2,278.20	
Notes Payable		10,000.00

The discount is amortized and interest expense is recognized annually using either the straight-line method or the effective interest method as is illustrated in the amortization schedule in Exhibit 15-11.

---

[14] Although the term "note" is used, the basic principles and methodology are equally applicable to other long-term debt instruments, such as bonds.

[15] Derived using the present value of an amount of 1 in Table A-2 of the Appendix:

$327 = $1,000p$_{\overline{8}|i}$

$P_{\overline{8}|i} = $327/$1,000 = .327$

$.327 = 15%$ column interest rate at the 8-year row.

EXHIBIT 15-11

SCHEDULE OF NOTE DISCOUNT AMORTIZATION
EFFECTIVE INTEREST METHOD
0% NOTE, DISCOUNTED AT 9%

	Cash Paid	Interest Expense	Discount Amortized	Carrying Amount of Note
Date of issue				$ 7,721.80
End of year 1	$ —	$ 694.96[a]	$ 694.96[b]	8,416.76[c]
End of year 2	—	757.51	757.51	9,174.27
End of year 3	—	825.73[d]	825.73	10,000.00
	$ —	$2,278.20	$2,278.20	

[a]$694.96 = $7,721.80 × .09   [c]$8,416.76 = $7,721.80 + $694.96
[b]$694.96 = $694.96 − 0   [d]5-cent rounding adjustment

Interest expense at the end of the first year using the effective interest method is recorded as follows:

Interest Expense ($7,721.80 × .09)	694.96	
Discount on Notes Payable		694.96

The total amount of the discount, $2,278.20 in this case, represents the interest expense to be reported on the note over the three years.

Interest-Bearing Note. The zero interest-bearing note above is an example of an extreme difference between the stated rate and the effective rate. In many cases, the difference between these rates is not so great. Take, for example, the illustration from Chapter 7, in which Marie Co. issued a $10,000, three-year note bearing interest at 10% to Morgan Corp. for cash at a time when the market rate of interest for a note of similar risk is 12%. The time diagram depicting the cash flows and the computation of the present value of this note are shown on page 339 in Chapter 7. From Marie Co.'s perspective, the accounting for the issuance of the note, the amortization of the discount, and the recognition of interest expense is exactly the same as for a 10% bond issued when the market rate is 12%.

NOTES ISSUED FOR A COMBINATION OF CASH AND OTHER RIGHTS

Sometimes when a note is issued, additional rights or privileges are given to the recipient of the note. For example, a corporation may issue at face value a noninterest-bearing note payable over five years with no stated interest in exchange for cash and an agreement to sell merchandise to the lender at less than the prevailing prices. In this circumstance, *the difference between the present value of the payable and the amount of cash received should be recorded by the issuer of the note (borrower/supplier) as both a discount (debit) on the note and as unearned revenue (credit) on the future sales.* The discount is amortized as a charge to interest expense over the life of the note. The unearned revenue, equal in amount to the discount, reflects a partial prepayment for sales transactions that will occur over the next five years. This unearned revenue is recognized as revenue when sales are made to the lender over the next five years.

To illustrate, assume that a company receives $100,000 cash in exchange for a five-year, noninterest-bearing note with a face or maturity value of $100,000. The appropriate rate of interest is determined to be 10%. The conditions of the note provide that the recipient of the note, the lender/customer, can purchase $500,000 of merchandise from the issuer of the note, the borrower/supplier, at something less than regular selling prices over the next five years. To record the loan, the issuer records a discount of $37,908, the difference between the $100,000 face amount of the note and its present value of $62,092 ($100,000 × .62092, the present value of an amount of $1 received in five years using 10%). As the supplier of the merchandise, the issuer also records a credit to unearned revenue of $37,908. The issuer's journal entry is:

Cash	100,000	
Discount on Notes Payable	37,908	
Notes Payable		100,000
Unearned Revenue		37,908

The Discount on Notes Payable is subsequently amortized to interest expense using the effective interest or straight-line method. The Unearned Revenue is recognized as revenue from the sale of merchandise and is prorated on the basis that each period's sales to the lender-customer bear to the total sales to that customer for the term of the note. In this situation, the amortization of the discount and the recognition of the unearned revenue are different amounts.

NOTES ISSUED FOR PROPERTY, GOODS, OR SERVICES

Another type of situation involves the issuance of a note for noncash consideration, such as property, goods, or services. When this occurs in a bargained transaction entered into at arm's length, the stated interest rate is presumed to be fair unless:

1. no interest rate is stated, or

2. the stated interest rate is unreasonable, or

3. the face amount of the note is materially different from the current cash sales price for the same or similar items acquired or from the current market value of the debt instrument.

In these circumstances, the present value of the debt instrument is measured as the fair value of the property, goods, or services or by an amount that reasonably approximates the market value of the note. *The implicit interest element, other than that evidenced by any stated rate of interest, is the difference between the face amount of the note and the fair value of the property, goods, or services received.*

For example, assume that Scenic Development Corp. sold land having a fair market value of $200,000 to Health Spa Inc. in exchange for Health Spa's five-year, $293,860 non-interest-bearing note. The $200,000 fair value of the land represents the present value of the $293,860 note discounted at 8% for five years. If the transaction is recorded on the sale date at the face amount of the note, $293,860, by both parties, Health Spa's Land account and Scenic's Sales would both be overstated by $93,860. In addition, interest revenue to Scenic and interest expense to Health Spa would be understated by $93,860 over the corresponding five-year period.

The difference between the fair market value of the land and the face amount of the note represents interest. Therefore, the transaction should be recorded at the exchange date as follows.

EXHIBIT 15-12

Health Spa Inc. Books			Scenic Development Corp. Books		
Land	200,000		Notes Receivable	293,860	
Discount on Notes Payable	93,860		Discount on Notes Receivable		93,860
Notes Payable		293,860	Sales		200,000

not required

During the five-year life of the note, Health Spa amortizes annually a portion of the discount of $93,860 as a charge to interest expense. Scenic Development records interest revenue totalling $93,860 over the five-year period also by amortizing the discount. The effective interest method is appropriate, although the straight-line method may be used if the results obtained are not materially different.

IMPUTING AN INTEREST RATE

In each of the previous illustrations, the effective interest rate was evident or determinable by other factors involved in the exchange, such as the fair market value of what was either given or received. If the fair value of the property, goods, or services is not determinable and if the debt instrument has no ready market, the problem of determining the present value of the debt instrument is more difficult. To estimate the present value of a debt instrument under such circumstances, an appropriate interest rate must be determined that may differ from the stated interest rate. This process of interest rate approximation is called **imputation**, and the resulting interest rate is called an **imputed interest rate**. The imputed interest rate is used to establish the present value of the debt instrument and the cost of what was acquired. Once this information is determined, accounting for the debt follows the methods previously illustrated.

For example, assume that on December 31, 1998, Wunderlich Company issues a promissory note to Brown Interiors Company for architectural services. The note has a face value of $550,000, has a due date of December 31, 2003, and bears a stated interest rate of 2%, payable at the end of each year. The fair value of the architectural services is not readily determinable, nor is the note readily marketable. On the basis of the credit rating of Wunderlich Company, the absence of collateral, the prime interest rate at that date, and the prevailing interest on Wunderlich's other outstanding debt, an 8% interest rate is determined to be appropriate in the circumstances.

The present value of the note and the imputed value of the architectural services can then be determined as follows.

EXHIBIT 15-13

Face value of the note		$550,000
Present value of $550,000 due in 5 years at 8%: $550,000 × .68058	$374,319	
Present value of $11,000 annuity of interest payments for 5 years at 8%: $11,000 × 3.99271	43,920	
Present value of the note and fair value of architectural services		418,239
Discount on notes payable		$131,761

The issuance of the note is recorded as follows:

Building (or Construction in Process)	418,239	
Discount on Notes Payable	131,761	
Notes Payable		550,000

The Discount on Notes Payable is amortized to interest expense in the usual way.

The choice of an imputed rate requires the exercise of judgement. Determination of this rate is made at the time the debt instrument is issued, and any subsequent changes in prevailing interest rates are ignored.

MORTGAGE NOTES PAYABLE

The most common form of long-term note payable is a mortgage note payable. A **mortgage note payable** is a promissory note secured by a document called a mortgage that pledges title to property as security for the loan. Mortgage notes payable tend to be used more frequently by proprietorships and partnerships than by corporations, as corporations usually find that note and bond issues offer advantages in obtaining large loans.

The borrower usually receives cash in the face amount of the mortgage note. In that case, the face amount of the note is the amount of the liability and no premium or discount is involved.

Mortgages may be payable in full at maturity but commonly are paid in blended instalments of principal and interest over the life of the loan. While the mortgage contract may have a term of one to five years or longer, at which time the interest rate and other terms of the arrangement are renegotiated with the financial institution, the amount of the instalment is usually determined with reference to a longer amortization period, typically 20 or 25 years. The principal portion of current instalments due along with interest accrued to the balance sheet date are reported as current liabilities, with the remaining principal shown as a long-term liability.

FINANCIAL INSTRUMENT COMPLEXITIES

SUBSTANCE OVER FORM

A primary quality of accounting information identified in the conceptual framework (see Chapter 2) is *reliability*. A component of reliability is *representational faithfulness*, which means that a transaction or event affecting an entity is presented in the financial statements in a manner that is in agreement with the underlying economic nature of the transaction or event. This concept is reinforced in *CICA Handbook* Section 3860, Financial Instruments, which states that the "substance of a financial instrument, rather than its legal form, governs its classification on the issuer's balance sheet."[16] Consequently, the appropriate classification depends on the instrument's form being consistent with the definition of a financial liability or an equity instrument. These terms are defined as follows:

> A **financial liability** is any liability that is a contractual obligation:
> i) to deliver cash or another financial asset to another party; or
> ii) to exchange financial instruments with another party under conditions that are potentially unfavourable.
> An **equity instrument** is any contract that evidences a residual interest in the assets of an entity after deducting all of its liabilities.
> . . . "contract" and "contractual" refer to an agreement between two or more parties that has clear economic consequences that the parties have little, if any, discretion to avoid, usually because the agreement is enforceable at law. Contracts, and thus financial instruments, may take a variety of forms and need not be in writing.[17]

The key issue on which the classification hinges is whether there is a contractual requirement by one party (the issuer) to deliver cash or other financial assets to the other party. If there is a contractual requirement to do so, the instrument is a financial liability; if not, it is an equity instrument. Because classification is not always straightforward, the *Handbook* provides additional guidance. Restrictions on the ability of the issuer to deliver

OBJECTIVE 10
Differentiate between a financial liability and an equity instrument.

OBJECTIVE 11
Determine the appropriate balance sheet classification of, and reporting for, financial instruments according to their economic substance.

---

[16] Section 3860, par. .19.

[17] *Ibid.*, par. .05 and .06.

under the contract, such as the need to obtain approval from a regulatory body, does not change the nature of the issuer's obligation; and the right of shareholders to dividends does not qualify as a contractual obligation of the entity to make such distributions.[18]

Section 3860 also emphasizes that financial liabilities require settlement through the delivery of cash or other financial assets. Contracts that provide for settlement through delivery of a commodity that is not a financial asset (such as oil) *are not financial liabilities*, while those to be settled in cash but give the issuer the option of settling through delivery of a commodity or those where the cash settlement is indexed to a commodity price *are financial liabilities*.[19]

Further, the classification decision is made when the instrument is first given accounting recognition, and this classification continues until the item is removed from the balance sheet. Where the delivery of cash or financial assets in the future is contingent upon a future event or condition, the issuer must base the classification on its best estimate of the likely outcome, with a change in that likelihood over time requiring note disclosure rather than a change in classification.[20]

EQUITY WITH DEBT CHARACTERISTICS

Term-Preferred Shares. Term-preferred shares provide an example of a financial instrument that has the legal form of equity, but which carries provisions that may lead to the conclusion that its economic substance is that of a liability. Preferred shares are considered to be a residual interest (shareholders' equity item) in the assets of a corporation. Various rights, privileges, and restrictions can accompany a particular issue of preferred shares. While traditional preferred shares are sold to provide a perpetual source of financing until the corporation liquidates, some preferred shares are issued for a limited period of time. Forms of such limitation on their life occur when the company can buy them back from holders (**redeemable preferreds**), when the holder can require the company to buy them back (**retractable preferreds**), and when the company is required to retire all or a specified proportion of the shares on some future date. Because such shares are limited in the term of their lives, they are referred to as **term-preferred shares**.

Those term-preferred shares that provide for mandatory redemption or give the holder the right to require redemption in effect carry a contractual provision for the issuer of the securities to deliver cash to the holder, and thus they meet the definition of a financial liability. In the absence of a direct contractual obligation, the *Handbook* suggests that if the "issuer has little, if any, discretion to avoid redeeming the instrument" or if the "share gives the holder an option to require redemption upon the occurrence of a future event that is highly likely to occur," the share should be classified as debt.[21] Professional judgement must be brought to bear in assessing the likelihood of future events and circumstances.

Along with the instrument being reported as part of current or long-term liabilities depending on when redemption is likely, dividends on these shares are reported in the income statement either with interest on other liabilities or as a separate item (separate disclosure is suggested but not required), and gains or losses on their redemption or refinancing are reported in the income statement as well.[22] Although measurement issues related to financial instruments have been referred to the Accounting Standards Board for study and resolution, the CICA's Emerging Issues Committee reached a consensus that a

---

[18] *Ibid.*, par. .20 and .21.

[19] *Ibid.*, par. A13 to A17.

[20] *Presentation of a Financial Instrument When a Future Event or Circumstance May Affect the Issuer's Obligations, EIC-70*, (Toronto: CICA, April 8, 1996).

[21] *CICA Handbook*, Section 3860, par. .22.

[22] *Ibid.*, par. .31 to 33.

company should account for any premium or discount on redeemable preferred shares classified as a financial liability "in the same manner as it accounts for an issue premium or discount on a bond or debenture."[23] The general principle is that such instruments should be treated as debt in all respects.

The following excerpts from the financial statements of Empire Company Limited illustrate the reporting of redeemable preferred shares, some as debt and some as equity.

EXHIBIT 15-14   EMPIRE COMPANY LIMITED

YEAR ENDED APRIL 30, 1995

($ in thousands)

Balance Sheet	1995	1994
Current liabilities:		
Payable for preferred shares redeemed	$ —	$ 45,814
Long-term debt (Note 4)	648,024	633,622
Shareholders' equity		
Capital stock (Note 5)	277,865	282,639
Note 4. Long-term Debt		
Term-preferred shares at rate fluctuating with the prime rate, due 1997	46,932	48,000
Note 5. Capital Stock		
Senior preferred 5 $\frac{1}{2}$% series	875	875
Senior preferred 8% series	3,748	4,223

DEBT WITH EQUITY CHARACTERISTICS

There are liabilities with some or all of the following characteristics of equity: there is no maturity date, the return of principal is unlikely or is far into the future, no regular return is paid on the principal, and the entitlement to assets is subordinate to all other debt. The question arises as to whether such liabilities should be classified as equity rather than debt.

Perpetual Debt. Air Canada is an example of a company that has issued subordinated **perpetual debt**. The principal is not secured, is payable only when the corporation is liquidated, and is paid only after all other debt has been paid. Interest is at a specified rate but is subordinated to all other corporate debt. These characteristics are similar to traditional preferred shares in terms of being a residual interest in the assets of the corporation. Also, because the interest is subordinated to the payment of interest on other financial liabilities and is not guaranteed, it may be thought of as a stated dividend on preferred shares. Should this instrument be classified as equity?

As stated above, the critical feature in differentiating between debt and equity is whether an obligation exists for the issuer to deliver cash or other financial assets to the holder of the security. *CICA Handbook* Section 3860, par. A19 indicates that where the issuer has contracted to make periodic interest payments on perpetual debt, the instrument meets the definition of a financial liability.

---

[23] *Recognition and Measurement of Financial Instruments Presented as Liabilities or Equity under CICA 3860, EIC-69,* (Toronto: CICA, April 8, 1996).

Shareholder Loans. It is not uncommon for closely held companies to have accounts due to major shareholders or other related parties. The loans are often noninterest-bearing and their repayment is subordinated to other debt. It is not easy to classify such instruments because the ultimate test is the likelihood of the payment of cash or other financial assets to the holder. The decision will differ with the circumstances, as the judgement is made about the economic substance of the item.

If debt instruments are classified as part of contributed capital in the shareholders' equity section of the balance sheet, any distributions made to holders of such instruments are reported as if they were dividends, by a direct reduction of equity rather than through the income statement. Similarly, gains and losses on the subsequent settlement of these items are not reported through the income statement, but are reported as direct changes in equity, exactly the same as if they were common or preferred shares (see Chapter 16).

COMPOUND FINANCIAL INSTRUMENTS

Convertible Bonds. Accounting for financial instruments that are comprised of both a liability and an equity element is also based on the principle of substance over form. The most common example is that of a **convertible bond**, a debt security that allows the holder to exchange the bond for or to convert the bond into preferred or common shares of the issuing corporation. The conversion rights specify when the bond may be exchanged and the exercise price, that is, the number of shares into which it may be converted.

A convertible bond is viewed as being a compound financial instrument. Because the issuing company has a contractual obligation to make periodic interest payments and/or a principal repayment at maturity, one element of the financial instrument is a financial liability. The embedded call option giving the holder the right to convert the liability into shares of the issuer is an equity instrument. The compound features of this single instrument are so similar in nature to a bond issued with detachable stock warrants that it is recommended that each component be accounted for and reported separately.[24] Accounting for convertible debt and bonds issued with detachable warrants are covered in Chapter 18, which deals with these and other dilutive securities.

DERIVATIVE FINANCIAL INSTRUMENTS

CICA Handbook Section 3860 covers *primary* financial instruments, such as receivables, payables and equity securities, and *derivative* instruments, such as financial options, futures and forwards, interest rate swaps and currency swaps. **Derivative financial instruments** or **derivatives** are so named because their value is derived from the value of some underlying instrument, such as stocks, bonds, or commodities, or is tied to a basic indicator such as interest rates, foreign exchange rates, or Toronto Stock Exchange averages.

OBJECTIVE 12
Explain the basic accounting and reporting issues related to derivatives and off-balance-sheet financing arrangements.

Standard setters are particularly interested in derivatives because they create rights and obligations that transfer financial risks associated with a primary instrument, and they raise questions about off-balance-sheet financing, unjustifiable deferrals of losses, premature recognition of gains, and inadequate disclosure of information about risks, fair values, and other attributes of these instruments.

Many of the accounting problems associated with derivatives stem from the limitations of the conventional transactions-based historical cost model where recognition of the effects of changes in market prices or rates are postponed until disposition or settlement. The underlying objective of accounting for mitigating exposure to risk (sometimes called hedge accounting) is to recognize the effects of changes in market prices or rates on

---

[24] *CICA Handbook* (Toronto: CICA), Section 3860, par. .24 to .26.

two or more opposing positions that share an exposure to a market factor and that management has expressly designated as linked, in income at the same time.[25] The problems referred to above exist in large part because our conventional model does not recognize changes in fair value until realized.

There have been sensational reports in the press about losses suffered by organizations such as the Barings Bank (U.S.$1.4 billion), Metaligesellschaft (U.S.$1.3 billion), Proctor & Gamble (U.S.$102 million), and California's Orange County (U.S.$1.7 billion) due to their trading of derivatives. Although these losses are substantial, derivatives do not introduce risks that are fundamentally different from the risks already present in the financial markets, and thousands of companies use them as a powerful tool in managing risks. The challenge for the accounting profession is to develop appropriate standards so that relevant information is reported to investors, creditors, and others.

At the time of writing, the Accounting Standards Board is grappling with recognition and measurement issues associated with financial instruments. *CICA Handbook* Section 3860 deals only with reporting and disclosure requirements for both recognized and unrecognized (derivative) financial instruments.

OFF-BALANCE-SHEET FINANCING

Off-balance-sheet financing is an attempt to borrow monies in such a way that the obligations are not recorded or reported in the balance sheet.[26] It is an issue of extreme importance to accountants as well as general management. As one writer sarcastically noted, "The basic drives of humans are few: to get enough food, to find shelter, and to keep debt off the balance sheet."

There are several reasons for companies to arrange off-balance-sheet financing. First, many believe that removing debt enhances the quality of the balance sheet and permits credit to be obtained more readily or at a lower cost. Second, loan covenants often impose a limitation on the amount of debt a company may have. As a result, off-balance-sheet financing is used because these commitments might not be considered. Third, it is argued by some that off-balance-sheet financing offsets understatements on the asset side of the balance sheet. For example, companies that write off all research and development costs and depreciate assets on an accelerated basis will often have carrying amounts for deferred development costs and plant and equipment that are much lower than their current values. If assets were reported at current values, less pressure would exist for off-balance-sheet financing arrangements.

Whether these arguments have merit is debatable, and many users of financial statements indicate that they factor off-balance-sheet financing into their analyses and decisions.

Some off-balance-sheet financing techniques have been discussed earlier. In Chapter 7, for example, transfers of receivables to third parties with recourse may be reported either as a sale of the receivable or as a borrowing, depending on the facts. When deemed to be a sale, no liability is recorded on the balance sheet. In this chapter, in-substance defeasance is viewed as an off-balance-sheet financing transaction when the debt is not reported on the balance sheet even though it is not legally retired.

---

[25] Jane B. Adams and Corliss J. Montesi, Principal Authors, *Major Issues Related to Hedge Accounting*, Special Report of a working group of the Boards and staff of the Standards Setting bodies of Australia, Canada, the United Kingdom, and the United States, and the International Accounting Standards Committee (FASB, 1995), p. iv.

[26] James L. Goodfellow, "Now You See Them, Now You Don't," *CA Magazine*, December, 1988, pp. 16-23 provides an interesting insight into the motivation for off-balance-sheet financing and the accounting problems related to reporting substance over form.

Two additional off-balance-sheet approaches, interest rate swaps and project financing arrangements, are considered below. In subsequent chapters, off-balance-sheet financing transactions associated with leasing and pensions are examined.

Interest Rate Swaps. Comments similar to the following continue to appear in the financial press:

> With today's volatile interest rates, you can be certain of one thing. Nothing is certain. However, you have one option that could considerably lessen the risks involved.
>
> Hedging flourishes as rates fluctuate.
>
> If you're confused about the timing of economic recovery and how that affects the nation's credit markets, you might want to hedge your bet. Whether interest rates are headed up or down, diversify now, and you can ride out the storm safely.

As these comments indicate, interest rates are volatile and companies often want protection against the effects of their fluctuations. As a result, many companies use sophisticated types of financial instruments, such as interest rate futures, forward rate agreements, and interest rate swaps, to hedge their bets.

A corporation in the early 1980s went to its investment banker and presented the following problem: It wanted to borrow at a fixed rate for protection, but either such borrowing was too expensive or no suitable market existed. The investment banker found a borrower who had a fixed-rate loan but wanted a floating rate. The match was made, the two companies swapped interest payments, and the **interest rate swap** was born.

Many companies find interest rate swaps a convenient way to manage interest rate exposure. A company with a substantial amount of variable rate debt may wish to swap into fixed-rate debt to limit its exposure to rising interest rates. A company with a low credit rating often cannot borrow in the fixed-rate market but can swap into it.

Swap participants report only their original borrowings on their balance sheets. As a result, swaps as well as many other types of financial instruments give rise to off-balance-sheet financing because the right to receive interest payments and the obligation to make interest payments by the swap agreement are not reported on the balance sheet. These swap agreement rights and obligations are related to performance in the future, not past completed economic transactions, and as such are a form of unexecuted contract.

Nova Corporation's financial statements for its year ended December 31, 1995 included the following note about its interest rate swaps.

EXHIBIT 15-15   NOVA CORPORATION

22. Financial Instruments

(b) Interest rate risk management

NOVA uses interest rate swaps to manage the fixed and floating interest rate mix of the total debt portfolio. By entering into interest rate swap agreements, NOVA agrees to exchange with counterparties the difference between fixed rate and floating rate interest amounts calculated by reference to banker's acceptance rates and London Inter Bank Offered Rates and to an agreed notional amount. The notional amounts do not represent the amount exchanged by the counterparties, and therefore are not a measure of market or credit exposure.

EXHIBIT 15-15 NOVA CORPORATION (Continued)

December 31

(millions of dollars, except for rates)	**1995**	1994	1993
Floating to fixed rate swaps			
Notional amount	**$ 205**	$ 316	$ 298
Average receive rate	**6.28%**	5.89%	4.02%
Average pay rate	**8.95%**	9.12%	9.45%
Weighted average years to maturity	**4.9**	3.9	4.9
Fixed to floating rate swaps			
Notional amount	**$ 131**	$ 131	$ –
Average receive rate	**9.02%**	9.02%	–%
Average pay rate	**6.16%**	6.20%	–%
Weighted average years to maturity	**4.3**	5.3	–
Estimated fair value of all swaps[1]	**$ (10)**	$ (5)	$ (30)
Carrying value of all swaps	**$ –**	$ –	$ –

(1) Asset (liability). The fair values of these instruments are estimated based on quoted market prices of comparable contracts, adjusted for maturity differences.

Project Financing Arrangements. **Project financing arrangements** arise when, for example, (1) two or more entities form another entity to construct an operating plant that will be used by both parties; (2) the new entity borrows funds to construct the project and repays the debt from proceeds received from project operations; and (3) payment of the debt is guaranteed by the companies that formed the new entity. The advantage of such an arrangement is that *the companies that formed the new entity do not have to report the liability on their books*. To illustrate, assume that PanCanadian Petroleum and Imperial Oil each put up $1 million to form a separate company to build a chemical plant that will be used by both companies. The newly formed company borrows $48 million to construct the plant. This arrangement is illustrated below.

ILLUSTRATION 15-3

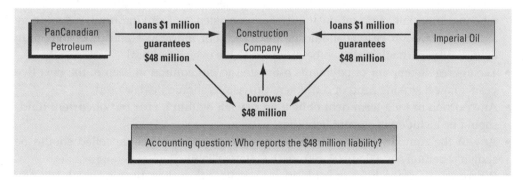

Through this arrangement, neither PanCanadian nor Imperial reports the debt on its balance sheet. The contingent obligation by both parties, however, meets the definition of a financial liability (even though it may not qualify for recognition in the financial statements) and so both PanCanadian Petroleum and Imperial Oil must disclose information about the maximum amount of their exposure to credit risk, that is, should Construction Company fail to pay. Their only disclosure is that they guarantee debt repayment if the project's proceeds are inadequate to pay off the loan.[27]

[27] *CICA Handbook* (Toronto: CICA), Section 3860, par. .67 and .74, and Section 3290. It should also be noted that, by the nature of particular agreements, such arrangements may become joint ventures, in which case the provisions of Section 3055 would apply.

In some cases, these project financing arrangements become more formalized through the use of a variety of contracts. In a simple **take-or-pay contract**, a purchaser of goods signs an agreement with a seller to pay specified amounts periodically in return for an option to receive products. The purchaser must make specified minimum payments even if delivery of the contracted products is not taken. Often these take-or-pay contracts are associated with project financing arrangements. For example, in the illustration above, PanCanadian and Imperial might sign an agreement that they will purchase products from the new plant and that they will make certain minimum payments even if they do not take delivery of the goods.

Through-put agreements are similar in concept to take-or-pay contracts, except that a service instead of a product is provided by the asset under construction. Assume that PanCanadian and Imperial become involved in a project financing arrangement to build a pipeline to transport their various products. An agreement is signed that requires each to pay specified amounts in return for transportation of the product. In addition, these companies are required to make cash payments even if they do not provide the minimum quantities to be transported.

In practice, inconsistent methods have been used to account for and disclose the unconditional obligation in a take-or-pay or through-put contract involved in a project financing arrangement. In general, many companies have attempted to develop these types of contracts to "get the debt off the balance sheet." The general provisions in Section 3280 of the *Handbook* regarding disclosure of significant contractual obligations would apply.

REPORTING LONG-TERM DEBT AND FINANCIAL LIABILITIES

OBJECTIVE 13
Describe the disclosure requirements for long-term debt and financial liabilities.

The presentation and disclosure requirements for long-term debt and financial liabilities are found in Sections 3210 and 3860 of the *CICA Handbook*. Section 3210 requires the following disclosures for long-term debt.

- For bonds, debentures, and similar securities, the title of the issue, interest rate, maturity date, amount outstanding, and existence of sinking fund, redemption, and conversion provisions should be disclosed. For mortgages and other long-term debt, similar particulars should be provided to the extent practical.
- The aggregate amount of payments estimated to be required in each of the next five years to meet sinking fund or retirement provisions should be disclosed.
- Any portion of long-term debt obligation payable within a year out of current funds should be included in current liabilities.
- Any of the company's own securities purchased and not yet cancelled should be shown separately as a deduction from the relative liability.
- Where long-term debt is payable in a currency other than that in which the balance sheet is stated, the currency in which the long-term debt is payable should be indicated.
- If any of the liabilities are secured, they should be stated separately and the fact that they are secured should be indicated.
- The details of any defaults of the company in principal, interest, sinking fund, or redemption provisions with respect to any outstanding obligation should be disclosed.
- The income statement should distinguish interest on indebtedness initially incurred for a term of more than one year (including the amortization of debt discount or premium and issue expenses).

Companies that have numerous types of long-term debt usually report only the total amount in the balance sheet and support this with comments and schedules in the accompanying notes. The illustration drawn from financial statements of Unican Security Systems Ltd. shown below provides an example of such reporting. Also refer to note 7 on long-term liabilities in the financial statements of Moore Corporation Limited presented in Appendix 5A.

EXHIBIT 15-16	UNICAN SECURITY SYSTEMS LTD.

YEAR ENDED JUNE 30, 1995

6. Long-Term Debt

Long-term debt comprises the following:

	1995	1994
Loan bearing interest at Libor plus 1.4% due April 1996 (U.S. $900,000)	$ 1,235	$ 2,267
Note bearing interest at Libor plus 1.4% due April 1996 (U.S. $483,000)	663	1,693
Debenture bearing interest at bank prime rate, due January 1998	4,798	6,657
13.14% mortgage, due June 2001 (Lira 1,050,000)	884	1,009
Industrial Development Revenue Bond bearing interest at 86.946% of bank prime rate	–	581
7.25% notes due June 2000 (U.S. $7,149,000)	9,812	–
7.5% notes due February 2004 (U.S. $1,860,000)	2,553	2,774
7.25% notes due July 2000 (U.S. $4,952,000)	6,797	7,714
Unsecured non-interest bearing loan, due December 2000	1,285	1,285
Other, non-interest bearing and not subject to specified terms of repayment	958	1,015
	28,985	24,995
Current maturity	7,061	5,649
	$ 21,924	$ 19,346

The aggregate amount of capital to be repaid in each of the next five years is as follows:

1996	$	7,061
1997		5,123
1998		4,996
1999		3,992
2000		4,294

As security for any bank indebtedness and substantially all of its long-term debt, the Company has pledged all of its assets. The terms of certain loan agreements require, amongst other things, the maintenance of minimum working capital, debt to equity and interest coverage ratios and restrictions on capital expenditures and borrowings.

Increasingly, companies are adding a separate note for disclosures related to financial instruments. The reporting requirements for financial instruments in Section 3860 are divided into *presentation* and *disclosure* standards. The presentation recommendations deal with the substance over form issue and require that:

1. A financial instrument, or its component parts, be classified as a liability or as equity in accordance with the substance of the contractual arrangement on initial recognition and the definitions of a financial liability and an equity instrument.

2. The component parts of a financial instrument that contains both a liability and an equity element be classified separately.

3. Interest, dividends, losses, and gains relating to a financial instrument, or a component part, that is classified as a financial liability be reported in the income statement as expense or income, while distributions to holders of a financial instrument that is classified as an equity instrument be reported directly in equity.

4. A financial asset and a financial liability be offset and the net amount reported in the balance sheet when an entity (a) has a legally enforceable right to set off the recognized amounts; and (2) intends either to settle on a net basis or to realize the asset and settle the liability simultaneously.

The disclosure standards were designed to provide information useful to users in gaining a better understanding of the significance of recognized and unrecognized financial instruments to an entity's financial position, performance, and cash flows. While many of the specifics are beyond the scope of this book, the minimum required disclosures include the following.

1. The nature and extent of such instruments, including significant terms and conditions that may affect the amount, timing, and certainty of future cash flows.

2. The entity's exposure to interest rate risk, including information about contractual repricing or maturity dates and effective interest rates.

3. The entity's exposure to credit risk, including the amount that best represents the maximum exposure at the balance sheet date, without taking any collateral into account, and information about significant concentrations of credit risk.

4. The fair value of financial assets and liabilities.

5. For financial instruments accounted for as hedges of anticipated transactions, a description of the transaction and hedging instruments involved and information on any deferred gains or losses.

Suggested additional disclosures for financial instruments with off-balance-sheet risk include:

1. The principal or face amount; for many derivative instruments called the **notional amount**, that is, the amount on which future payments are based.

2. Terms and conditions such as the maturity or expiry date, early settlement or conversion options, and collateral pledged.

3. The amount and timing of scheduled cash receipts or payments of principal; the rate or amount and timing of interest and dividends.

4. Conditions, if contravened, that would change any other terms.

In addition, company management is encouraged to provide either as part of or accompanying the financial statements a discussion of their policies for controlling risks associated with financial instruments, the extent to which financial instruments are used, and the associated risks and business purposes served.

NOVA Corporation includes a separate note on financial instruments in its financial statements as illustrated in Exhibit 15-17.

EXHIBIT 15-17   NOVA CORPORATION

YEAR ENDED DECEMBER 31, 1995

22. Financial Instruments

FINANCIAL INSTRUMENT FAIR VALUES

Financial instrument fair values represent a reasonable approximation of amounts NOVA would have received or paid to counterparties on December 31 to unwind the positions prior to maturity. At December 31, 1995, NOVA had no plans to unwind these positions prior to maturity. Carrying amounts represent the receivable or payable recorded in the Consolidated Balance Sheet. The carrying amounts reported in the balance sheet for cash, accounts receivable and payable, and current bank loans approximate their fair value. NOVA does not have a significant exposure to any individual customer or counterparty. Fair values and carrying amounts for derivative instruments are disclosed below in their respective sections.

	Carrying Amount			Estimated Fair Value[1]		
December 31 (millions of dollars)	**1995**	1994	1993	**1995**	1994	1993
Long-term debt[2]						
Regulated businesses	**$ 3,722**	$ 3,412	$ 3,017	**$ 4,140**	$ 3,499	$ 3,286
Non-regulated businesses	**$ 654**	$ 494	$ 560	**$ 666**	$ 494	$ 588

(1) The fair value of long-term debt is based on quoted market prices, where available. If market prices are not available, fair values are estimated using discounted cash flow analyses, based on NOVA's current incremental borrowing rates for similar borrowing arrangements.

(2) Includes debt instalments due within one year.

DERIVATIVES AND OTHER HEDGING INSTRUMENTS

NOVA sells petrochemical products at prices based on U.S. dollars, purchases energy commodities, invests in foreign operations and issues short- and long-term debt, including amounts in foreign currencies. These activities result in exposures to fluctuations in foreign currency exchange rates, energy prices and interest rates.

NOVA manages its exposures by entering into contractual arrangements (derivatives) which reduce (hedge) the exposure by creating an offsetting position. The estimated fair values only represent the value of the hedge component of these transactions and do not consider the value of the contracted and anticipated transactions that are being hedged. NOVA does not provide or require security on its derivative positions. NOVA also has a joint venture interest in a natural gas marketing company, Novagas Clearinghouse Limited Partnership (NCL), which enters into fixed-price forward contracts in connection with its natural gas activities (see Note 22(e)).

Note 22 continues at length with additional information about

(a) foreign exchange risk management
(b) interest rate risk management (see interest rate swap example, Exhibit 15-15)
(c) commodity price risk management
(d) credit risk management
(e) price risk management activities of NCL

The variety and complexity of long-term debt arrangements have grown considerably, with the consequence that many accounting recognition and measurement problems have emerged. Resolving such issues will not be easy, as our understanding of long-term financing and the components of a conceptual framework to guide accounting are sufficiently imprecise that arguments can always be made for accounting for a financial instrument in a particular manner or, perhaps, not accounting for it at all. As financial markets and institutions continue to develop innovative and unique financial instruments, Section 3860 disclosures and those related to management's policies and controls over such instruments become increasingly important.

INTERNATIONAL PERSPECTIVE

Reporting of Long Term Debt: PetroFina S.A. (Belgium)

The variables which are useful to readers of the financial statements are diverse, as many different items can affect the pattern of future cash flows and so affect the solvency and profitability of the firm. For example, the complex nature of the financial structure of modern corporations necessitates innovative disclosure of many details underlying the balance of long term debt, often shown as only one line on the balance sheet. Long term debt potentially has different characteristics, and frequently staggered maturities. The introduction of multiple currencies to the mix adds further complexity. Changes during the year are also of interest.

The consolidated balance sheet of **PetroFina S.A.** of Belgium includes the amount of 48,855 million Belgian francs as long term debt for 1996 (1995, 43,948). These amounts are cross referenced to footnote XIII, presented below as an illustrative summary of how these variables might be presented to provide all relevant details to the users of the financial statements, in a manner which is both effective and efficient.

XIII LONG TERM DEBT

| | 1995 | | 1996 | |
| | Less than 5 years | More than 5 years | Less than 5 years | More than 5 years |
1ᵉ Analysis by category				
– Bonds and notes	16,397	15,380	20,795	14,022
– Capital lease obligations	495	291	418	236
– Banks and financial institutions	7,246	3,452	1,979	10,588
– Other debt	7	680	19	798
TOTAL	24,145	19,803	23,211	25,644

2ᵉ Analysis by maturity	1995 (million BEF)	1996 (million BEF)
– 1997	1,136	—
– 1998	6,851	1,999
– 1999	3,234	2,235
– 2000	12,924	13,601
– 2001	2,449	5,376
– 2002	3,583	8,689
– 2003	6,069	7,349
– Later	7,702	9,606
	43,948	48,855

3ᵉ Analysis by currency	1995 (%)	1996 (%)
– Belgian francs	26	23
– US dollars	67	75
– Pounds sterling	1	1
– French francs	1	1
– Other currencies	5	0
This analysis includes the effect of swap transactions	100	100

4ᵉ Analysis by nature		1995 (million BEF)		1996 (million BEF)
a) Bonds and notes		31,777		34,817
b) Capital lease obligations		786		654
c) Banks and financial institutions		10,698		12,567
– fixed rates	5,668		2,945	
– variable rates	5,030		9,622	
d) Other loans		687		817
		43,948		48,855

5ᵉ Changes in the year	1995 (million BEF)	1996 (million BEF)
At beginning of year	50,384	43,948
New loans	2,424	13,877
Transfers to short term debt	−5,825	−1,200
Anticipated repayments	−895	−10,712
Exchange adjustments	−2,004	2,942
Changes in the scope of consolidation	−136	
At end of year	43,948	48,855

Contributed by: Peter Secord, St. Marys University

Summary of Learning Objectives

1. **Explain the nature of long-term liabilities.** Long-term liabilities are existing obligations that will require the use of company resources or services usually later than one year from the balance sheet date. Liabilities or debt generally have a maturity date, confer no voting or management rights, have a priority right to company assets in the event of dissolution, and bear interest representing the cost of borrowed funds.

2. **Identify various types and characteristics of bonds.** Bonds can be described in a variety of ways: according to whether or not they are secured and the type of security; when the maturities fall due (term and serial bonds); if they are exchangeable for cash, shares, or other assets (convertible, commodity-backed, and asset-linked bonds); if there are other conditions relating to their redemption (callable, redeemable, retractable, and extendable bonds); whether the payment of interest is restricted (income and revenue bonds); how ownership is evidenced (registered and bearer bonds); and whether the return to the holder is solely the difference between the purchase price and the maturity value (deep-discount or zero-coupon bonds).

3. **Explain how proceeds from the issuance of bonds are determined and why a discount or premium can result.** Bonds are priced at the present value of the future cash flows promised by the bond indenture, discounted at the market rate of interest on the date of sale. Because the interest and principal cash flows

KEY TERMS

adjunct account, 729

asset-linked bond, 719

bearer bond, 719

bond, 719

bond indenture, 718

book value, 725

callable bond, 719

carrying value, 725

commodity-backed bond, 719

contra account, 729

convertible bond, 719

coupon rate, 720

covenants, 718

debt instrument, 718

deep-discount bond, 720

derivative financial instrument, 742

derivative, 742

discount, 721

are fixed by the indenture, investors ensure they will earn the going market rate of return by adjusting the price they pay for the bond. For bonds promising cash interest payments at a higher rate than the market offers, the price is bid up and the bond will sell at more than its par value, that is, at a premium. For bonds offering cash interest payments at a lower than market rate, investors will pay less than par value, and the bonds will sell at a discount.

4. **Account for bonds payable and related interest expense for bonds issued at par, or at a discount or premium, on an interest date or between interest dates, using the straight-line and effective interest methods of amortization.** The primary accounting issue related to bonds is ensuring that the proper amount of interest expense is recognized. Because interest is a cost of borrowing money and is a function of the passage of time, interest expense must be related to the time over which the debt is outstanding. If the proceeds of a bond issue exceed the amount to be repaid at maturity (at a premium) because they pay a higher than market rate of interest, the excess is taken into income as a reduction of interest expense over the life of the indebtedness. If the proceeds of a bond issue are less than the amount to be repaid at maturity (at a discount) because they pay a lower than market rate of return, the deficiency is charged to income as increased interest expense over the life of the bond. There are two patterns by which the excess (premium) or deficiency (discount) can be taken into income between the issue date and the maturity date: constant or equal *amounts* each period (the straight-line method), or at a constant *rate* on the debt's carrying or book value each period (the effective interest method). The effective interest method is the preferred approach, but the simpler straight-line method is permitted where the results are not materially different.

5. **Identify the balance sheet presentation of bond discount and bond premium accounts.** Bond discounts and premiums are commonly reported in financial statements as deferred charges and deferred credits, respectively, although the preferred presentation is to subtract the discount or add the premium to the face value of the liability account affected. Because discounts and premiums do not meet the *Handbook* definitions of assets and liabilities, the liability valuation approach is preferred.

6. **Account for the costs of issuing bonds.** Accounting for the costs of issuing bonds is an application of the matching principle in that the cost is recognized over the periods benefitting from the bond financing. One approach is to recognize the issue costs as a deferred charge, allocating them over the period from the date of issue to the maturity date on a straight-line basis. Another approach is to add the issue costs to the discount (or subtract them from the premium) and calculate a revised effective interest rate taking both into account. The higher revised effective rate is used to amortize the increased discount or reduced premium balance to interest expense using the effective interest method.

7. **Account for the reacquisition of debt prior to maturity.** Accounting for the reacquisition of debt prior to maturity requires (1) recognition of interest payable and interest expense to the date of reacquisition, including the amortization of bond discount or premium and any bond issue costs; (2) removal of the up-to-date book value of the bonds from the books; (3) recording of the consideration paid to reacquire the bonds; and (4) recognition of a gain or loss on retirement equal to the difference between the carrying value of the bonds and their reacquisition price.

8. **Differentiate between legal and in-substance defeasance and recognize the accounting issues involved.** Legal defeasance occurs when the debtor is legally discharged from its contractual obligations to a creditor. This could occur by transferring the obligation to a third party with the concurrence of the creditor. In-substance defeasance occurs when a debtor has set aside sufficient assets to cover the cash flows required to service the debt obligation, but without the transfer of the risk associated with that debt. The main accounting issue concerns the fact that the obligation has not been satisfied, even though it appears that arrangements have been made to meet the cash flow requirements of a particular debt.

9. **Account for long-term notes payable.** Notes payable, as well as bonds payable, are valued at the present value of their future cash flows discounted at the market rate of return when the instrument is issued. To the extent that the proceeds on issuance differ from the face or maturity value, the issuer must account for the difference according to its nature. Any premium or discount must be amortized to interest expense similar to the accounting for a bond.

10. **Differentiate between a financial liability and an equity instrument.** Financial liabilities are obligations to deliver cash or other financial assets to another party (or to exchange financial instruments under conditions that are potentially unfavourable), whereas equity instruments represent residual interests in the assets of an entity after deducting its liabilities.

11. **Determine the appropriate balance sheet classification of and reporting for financial instruments according to their economic substance.** The decision as to whether an item is a liability or an item of equity rests on the nature of the contractual obligation, the form of consideration to be given, and the likelihood of the transfer of cash or other financial assets. These criteria help in deciding the economic substance of the instrument. Regardless of the legal form, an item that is in substance a liability is reported as an item of debt, the return paid to the holder of the instrument is charged to the income statement, and any gains or losses on retirement are recognized in income. If the item is equity in substance, it is reported in shareholders' equity, any return to the holder of the instrument is charged directly to a shareholders' equity account, and any gain or loss on retirement or redemption is excluded from the determination of income.

12. **Explain the basic accounting and reporting issues related to derivatives and off-balance-sheet financing arrangements.** The use of derivatives and other off-balance-sheet financing arrangements by companies is of interest to readers of financial statements because they tend to create rights and obligations that transfer financial risks resulting in unrecognized obligations, deferral of losses, and premature recognition of gains. Much of the motivation appears to be an interest in minimizing the amount of debt reported, but increasingly, the problem revolves around the inability of the historic cost model to report the economic substance of hedging activities. To reduce the problems associated with such instruments, and as a stop-gap measure, standard setters have significantly increased the disclosure requirements relative to these financial instruments.

13. **Describe the disclosure requirements for long-term debt and financial liabilities.** The objectives of the disclosure requirements for long-term debt and financial liabilities are to provide information to enable financial statement readers to determine the amount, the timing, and the certainty of future cash outflows of the firm related to its obligations and to provide information useful in gaining a better understanding of the significance of recognized and unrecognized financial instruments to the entity's financial performance, position, and future cash flows.

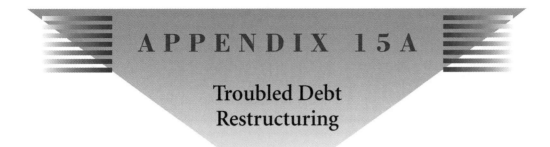

APPENDIX 15A

Troubled Debt Restructuring

Depressed economic conditions and mismanagement are just some of the causes of financial hardship for various companies, provinces, and countries. Such hardship is typically reflected in serious cash flow problems, which in turn results in some debtors encountering difficulty in meeting their obligations to pay interest and/or principal amounts. Well-publicized Canadian examples include Campeau Corp. and companies in the Reichmann's Olympia & York Developments Ltd. group or the Edper Bronfman real estate empire; however, thousands of companies each year run into similar financial difficulties.

While bankruptcy and corporate liquidation may be the eventual result of such problems, organizations may be able to recover by negotiating with debt holders regarding their debt obligations. Successful negotiations result in a troubled debt restructuring.

Troubled debt restructuring occurs when "the creditor for economic or legal reasons related to the debtor's financial difficulties grants a concession to the debtor that it would not otherwise consider."[28] A financial institution such as a bank recognizes that granting some concessions by restructuring the debt in a troubled loan situation is more likely to maximize recovery than forcing the debtor into bankruptcy.

Troubled debt restructuring involves one of two basic types of transactions:

1. Settlement of debt at less than its carrying amount.

2. Continuation of debt with a modification of terms.

Whether the troubled debt restructuring is a settlement or a continuation of the debt with a modification of terms, concessions granted to the debtor (borrower) by the creditor (lender) generally result in a *gain to the debtor* and a *loss to the creditor*.[29] Such a gain or loss, if material, is separately disclosed in the income statement with note disclosure of the nature of the restructuring. It would not be identified as an extraordinary item under Canadian GAAP because it results from decisions or determinations of management or owners.

SETTLEMENT OF DEBT AT LESS THAN ITS CARRYING AMOUNT

A transfer of noncash assets (real estate, receivables, or other assets) or the issuance of the debtor's shares can be used to settle a debt obligation in a troubled debt restructuring. In these situations, *the noncash assets or equity interest given should be accounted for at their fair market value*. The debtor determines the excess of the carrying amount of the payable over the fair value of the assets or equity transferred and recognizes a gain equal

OBJECTIVE 14
Account for the settlement of troubled debt at less than its carrying amount.

---

[28] "Accounting by Debtors and Creditors for Troubled Debt Restructurings," *Statement of Financial Accounting Standards No. 15* (Stamford, Conn.: FASB, 1977), par. 1.

[29] While the restructuring may result in the recognition of no gains or losses by either party, it is the nature of a troubled debt situation that the creditor cannot have a gain and the debtor cannot have a loss from restructuring.

to the excess. Likewise, the creditor determines the excess of the receivable over the fair value of those same assets or equity interests transferred, recognizing a charge to the income statement. In addition, the debtor recognizes a gain or loss on disposition of assets to the extent that the fair value of those assets differs from their carrying or book value.

To illustrate a transfer of assets, assume that City Bank has loaned $20 million to Mortgage Company. Mortgage Company in turn has invested these monies in residential apartment buildings, but because of low occupancy rates it cannot meet its loan obligations. City Bank agrees to accept from Mortgage Company real estate with a fair market value of $16 million in full settlement of the $20 million loan obligation. The real estate has a recorded value of $21 million on the books of Mortgage Company. The entry to record this transaction on the books of City Bank (creditor) is as follows.

Real Estate	16,000,000	
Loss on Restructured Debt	4,000,000	
Note Receivable from Mortgage Company		20,000,000

The real estate is recorded at the lower of the recorded investment in the loan foreclosed and the estimated net proceeds from the sale of the assets (if they are held for sale) or the fair market value of the assets (if held to produce income). If the loss had previously been provided for through an allowance account, the debit could be to the allowance account instead of the loss.

The entry to record this transaction on the books of Mortgage Company (debtor) is as follows.

Note Payable to City Bank	20,000,000	
Loss on Disposition of Real Estate	5,000,000	
Real Estate		21,000,000
Gain on Restructuring of Debt		4,000,000

Mortgage Company has a loss on the disposition of real estate in the amount of $5 million, the difference between the $21 million book value and the $16 million fair market value. In addition, it has a gain on restructuring of debt of $4 million, the difference between the $20 million carrying amount of the note payable and the $16 million fair market value of the real estate accepted as full payment.

CONTINUATION OF DEBT WITH MODIFICATION OF TERMS

OBJECTIVE 15
Account for the modification of the terms of troubled debt.

In some cases, a debtor will have serious short-run cash flow problems that lead the debtor to request one or a combination of the following modifications.

1. Reduction of the stated interest rate.

2. Extension of the maturity date of the face amount of the debt.

3. Reduction of the face amount of the debt.

4. Reduction or deferral of any accrued interest.

In Canada, there appears to be general acceptance that proper accounting entails a reduction in the carrying value of the financial liability and the recognition of a gain equal to the change in the recorded value of the debt. However, there has not been agreement on how to measure the carrying value of the restructured liability.

Two approaches can be taken. In the first, the existing liability is eliminated and a new liability assumed. Consistent with this approach, the new liability is measured at the present value of the revised future cash flows discounted at the currently prevailing market rate of interest. The gain is, therefore, the difference between the current present value of the revised debt taken on and the carrying value of the restructured debt removed from the accounts. This treatment is similar to a refunding or refinancing of a bond payable as identified in this chapter.

Underlying the second approach is the assumption that all that has happened is a change in the terms of the existing debt. In this case, the restructured liability is remeasured at the present value of the revised future cash flows discounted at the rate of interest inherent in the financial liability when initially recognized. The gain is equal to the change in the liability balance.[30] In either case, the gain is generally classified separately in the income statement and the nature of the restructuring is disclosed.

To illustrate these approaches, assume that on December 31, 1998, Canadian Bank enters into a debt restructuring agreement with Resorts Development Ltd. The bank restructures a $10,000,000 note issued at par by:

1. Reducing the principal obligation from $10,000,000 to $9,000,000.

2. Forgiving $500,000 of accrued interest due December 31, 1998, which has been recorded by Resorts.

3. Extending the maturity date from December 31, 1998 to December 31, 2004.

4. Reducing the interest rate from 12% to 8%, with interest payments being due each December 31. The current prevailing market rate of interest is 9%. As the original note was issued at par, the effective rate when the liability was initially recognized was 12%.

The amounts related to the note and accrued interest on Resorts Development's records at December 31, 1998 and the determination of the present value of the restructured note under both approaches are shown below.

EXHIBIT 15A-1

		Approach 1 (new liability)	Approach 2 (old liability remeasured)
Note payable, December 31, 1998			
Principal balance	$10,000,000		
Accrued interest	500,000		
Carrying value of note to be restructured	$10,500,000		
Revised interest payments			
9,000,000 × .08	$720,000		
Present value of new liability:			
Principal, discounted at $n = 6, i = 9$			
$9,000,000 × .59627		$5,366,430	
Interest, discounted at $n = 6, i = 9$			
$720,000 × 4.48592		3,229,862	
		$8,596,292	
Discount on note payable:			
$9,000,000 − $8,596,292		$ 403,708	

---

[30] At the time of writing, there was no Canadian recommendation on this issue. The original *Exposure Draft* on financial instruments (1991) supported the first approach, while the *Re-Exposure Draft* (1994) supported the second. This is one of the measurement issues now under study by the Accounting Standards Board. In the United States, *FASB Statement No. 15* requires a substantially different treatment. Unless the carrying amount at the time of restructure exceeds the *undiscounted* total future cash flows, the debtor will not change the carrying amount of the payable. But when the carrying amount of the debt at the time of restructure is greater than the *undiscounted* total future cash flows, the debtor will adjust the carrying amount, recognizing a gain. No interest is recognized as part of the future payments. This treatment is based on the argument that a troubled debt restructuring by modification of terms is a continuation of the existing debt arrangement.

EXHIBIT 15A-1	(Continued)	

Present value of restructured liability:
  Principal, discounted at $n = 6$, $i = 12$
    $9,000,000 × .50663 $4,559,670

  Interest, discounted at $n = 6$, $i = 12$
    $720,000 × 4.11141   2,960,215
                                                          7,519,885

Discount on note payable: $1,480,115
  $9,000,000 − $7,519,885

The journal entries below illustrate the accounting for the restructuring by Resorts Development under both approaches. Resorts Development Ltd. would account for the remeasured liability in the normal manner.

EXHIBIT 15A-2				

Approach 1 (new liability)			Approach 2 (old liability remeasured)	
Note Payable (12%)	10,000,000		Note Payable	1,000,000[b]
Interest Payable	500,000		Interest Payable	500,000
Discount on			Discount on	
Note Payable (8%)	403,708		Note Payable	1,480,115
Note Payable (8%)		9,000,000	Gain on Restructuring	
Gain on Restructuring			of Debt	2,980,115[c]
of Debt		1,903,708[a]		

[a]$10,500,000 − $8,596,292   [b]$10,000,000 − $9,000,000   [c]$10,500,000 − $7,519,885

Balance Sheet Presentation of Liability
Following Restructuring

Long-term liabilities			Long-term liabilities	
Note payable, 8%	$9,000,000		Note payable, 8%	$9,000,000
Less discount on note	403,708		Less discount on note	1,480,115
	$8,596,292			$7,519,885

Summary of Learning Objectives for Appendix 15A

KEY TERMS

troubled debt restructuring, 755

14. **Account for the settlement of troubled debt at less than its carrying amount.** When troubled debt is settled for less than its carrying amount, a gain should be recognized by the debtor equal to the difference between the book value of the debt and the fair value of the consideration given.

15. **Account for the modification of the terms of troubled debt.** When the terms of troubled debt are modified, the debt is revalued to the discounted present value of the revised future cash flows, and a gain equal to the change in the liability balance is recognized. Under the assumption that the existing debt is settled and a new liability incurred, the currently prevailing market rate of interest should be the discount rate used; under the assumption that the exisiting debt is being carried forward with different terms, the yield rate of interest inherent in the original debt should be the discount rate used. Canadian GAAP permits either approach at the present time.

APPENDIX 15B

Serial Bonds:
Amortization and Redemption
Before Maturity

A serial bond issue may be sold as though each series is a separate bond issue. Alternatively, it may be sold as a package. Whether sold separately or as a package, only one account for the total premium or discount is usually used in the general ledger for that serial issue. The total premium or discount to be amortized, whether computed for each series separately or for the entire issue, is entered as one amount in the Premium or Discount on Bonds Payable account. *The straight-line, bonds outstanding, or effective interest methods may be used to amortize the premium or discount.* These methods and accounting for the redemption of serial bonds before maturity under them are illustrated in this Appendix.

AMORTIZATION OF A PREMIUM OR DISCOUNT ON SERIAL BONDS

A serial bond issue in the amount of $1,000,000, dated January 1, 1998, bearing 8% interest payable at December 31 each year, is sold by Yorkville Inc. to yield 9% per annum; the bonds mature in the amount of $200,000 on January 1 of each year beginning in 1999. The bond price and discount are computed as follows.

OBJECTIVE 16
Account for serial bonds.

EXHIBIT 15B-1

			Selling Price	Discount
Bonds due 1/1/99 (one year away):				
Principal: $200,000 × 0.91743 (Table A-2)		$183,486		
Interest: $16,000 × 0.91743 (Table A-4)		14,679		
			$198,165	$ 1,835*
Bonds due 1/1/00 (two years away)	Computation		196,482	3,518
Bonds due 1/1/01 (three years away)	similar to		194,937	5,063
Bonds due 1/1/02 (four years away)	those for		193,522	6,478
Bonds due 1/1/03 (five years away)	1/1/99 bonds		192,220	7,780
Total price for all series			$975,326	
Total discount on all series				$24,674

*$1,835 = $200,000 − $198,165

STRAIGHT-LINE METHOD

The **straight-line method** of amortization may be used if the results are not materially different from those of the effective interest method. The total discount for the Yorkville issue would be apportioned for each series over the five years as shown in Exhibit 15B-2.

EXHIBIT 15B-2

AMORTIZATION SCHEDULE: STRAIGHT-LINE METHOD

Series Due Jan. 1	Total Discount		Term		Periodic Amortization	Apportioned to				
						1998	1999	2000	2001	2002
1999	$ 1,835	÷	1 year	=	1,835	$1,835				
2000	3,518	÷	2 years	=	1,759	1,759	$1,759			
2001	5,063	÷	3 years	=	1,688	1,688	1,688	$1,687		
2002	6,478	÷	4 years	=	1,619	1,619	1,619	1,620	$1,620	
2003	7,780	÷	5 years	=	1,556	1,556	1,556	1,556	1,556	$1,556
	$24,674					$8,457	$6,622	$4,863	$3,176	$1,556

BONDS OUTSTANDING METHOD

When the entire issue of serial bonds is sold to underwriters at a stated price, the discount or premium is frequently amortized by the **bonds outstanding method,** since the discount or premium on each series is not definitely determinable. *The bonds outstanding method is an application of the straight-line method to serial bonds and assumes that the discount applicable to each bond of the issue is the same dollar amount per bond per year.*

The total discount for the Yorkville issue would be apportioned over the five years as shown below.

EXHIBIT 15B-3

AMORTIZATION SCHEDULE: BONDS OUTSTANDING METHOD

Year Ending Dec. 31	Bonds Outstanding During the Year	Proportion of Bonds Outstanding During the Year to Total of Bonds Outstanding Column	×	Total Discount to Be Amortized	=	Discount to Be Amortized During Each Year
1998	$1,000,000	10/30		$24,674		$ 8,224
1999	800,000	8/30		24,674		6,580
2000	600,000	6/30		24,674		4,935
2001	400,000	4/30		24,674		3,290
2002	200,000	2/30		24,674		1,645
	$3,000,000	30/30				$24,674

The purpose of the column for Bonds Outstanding During the Year is to convert all the bonds into terms of bonds outstanding for each year, for a total of $3,000,000 for five years. Accordingly, during 1998 the premium to be amortized is $1,000,000/$3,000,000 × $24,674, or $8,224. Similarly, during 2001 the premium to be amortized is $400,000/ $3,000,000 × $24,674, or $3,290.

An amortization schedule should be prepared for serial bonds in the same manner as the amortization schedule for single-maturity bonds, except that the maturity value of each series must be deducted from the total carrying amount of the bonds as each series comes due. The schedule in Exhibit 15B-4 illustrates the amortization of the discount and the reduction in carrying amount for the serial bond issue described above using the bonds outstanding method.

EXHIBIT 15B-4

SCHEDULE OF BOND DISCOUNT AMORTIZATION: SERIAL BONDS
BONDS OUTSTANDING METHOD

Date	Credit Cash	**Credit Bond Discount**	Debit Interest Expense	Debit Bonds Payable	Carrying Value of Bonds
1/1/98					$975,326
12/31/98	$ 80,000ᵃ	$ 8,224ᵇ	$ 88,224ᶜ	—	983,550ᵈ
1/1/99	200,000	—	—	$ 200,000	783,550
12/31/99	64,000	6,580	70,580	—	790,130
1/1/00	200,000	—	—	200,000	590,130
12/31/00	48,000	4,935	52,935	—	595,065
1/1/01	200,000	—	—	200,000	395,065
12/31/01	32,000	3,290	35,290	—	398,355
1/1/02	200,000	—	—	200,000	198,355
12/31/02	16,000	1,645	17,645	—	200,000
1/1/03	200,000	—	—	200,000	—
	$1,240,000	$24,674	$264,674	$1,000,000	

ᵃ$80,000 = $1,000,000 × .08
ᵇ$8,224 = $1,000,000/$3,000,000 × $24,674
ᶜ$88,224 = $80,000 + $8,224
ᵈ$983,550 = $975,326 + $8,224

Note: Interest expense is a function of the stated interest rate plus a pro rata share of discount amortization or less a pro rata share of premium amortization.

A schedule with similar debit and credit columns could be prepared using the data from the straight-line amortization schedule. The credit to Bond Discount on December 31, 1998 is $8,457 using the straight-line data.

Effective Interest Method

Application of the **effective interest method** to serial bonds is similar to that illustrated in the chapter for single-maturity bonds. Interest expense for the period is computed by multiplying the effective interest rate times the carrying amount of bonds outstanding during the period. The amount of amortization of bond discount or premium is the difference between the effective interest expense for the period and the actual interest payments. Under this method, the interest expense is at a constant rate relative to the carrying amount of the bonds outstanding. Exhibit 15B-5 illustrates the amortization of discount and the reduction in carrying amount for the Yorkville serial bond issue using the effective interest method.

The journal entries that would be recorded for the payment of the interest, amortization of the discount, and retirement of each series of bonds can be determined from the column headings in the amortization schedule.

REDEMPTION OF SERIAL BONDS BEFORE MATURITY

If bonds of a certain series are redeemed before the maturity date, it is necessary to compute the amount of unamortized discount or premium applicable to those bonds and to remove it from the Discount or Premium on Bonds Payable account.

EXHIBIT 15B-5

SCHEDULE OF BOND DISCOUNT AMORTIZATION: SERIAL BONDS
EFFECTIVE INTEREST METHOD

8% Bonds Sold to Yield 9%

Date	Credit Cash	Credit Bond Discount	Debit Interest Expense	Debit Bonds Payable	Carrying Value of Bonds
1/1/98					$975,326
12/31/98	$ 80,000[a]	$ 7,779[b]	$ 87,779[c]	—	983,105[d]
1/1/99	200,000	—	—	$ 200,000	783,105
12/31/99	64,000	6,479	70,479	—	789,584
1/1/00	200,000	—	—	200,000	589,584
12/31/00	48,000	5,063	53,063	—	594,647
1/1/01	200,000	—	—	200,000	394,647
12/31/01	32,000	3,518	35,518	—	398,165
1/1/02	200,000	—	—	200,000	198,165
12/31/02	16,000	1,835	17,835	—	200,000
1/1/03	200,000	—	—	200,000	—
	$1,240,000	$24,674	$264,674	$1,000,000	

[a]$80,000 = $1,000,000 × .08
[b]$7,779 = $87,779 − $80,000
[c]$87,779 = $975,326 × .09
[d]$983,105 = $975,326 + $7,779

Note: Interest expense is a function of the effective interest rate times the book carrying amount outstanding during the period.

STRAIGHT-LINE METHOD

Assume that on January 1, 2000, $200,000 of the Yorkville serial bonds due January 1, 2003 are redeemed for $201,000. The unamortized discount on the $200,000 of bonds due on January 1, 2003 is $4,668 ($1,556 + $1,556 + $1,556; the discount apportioned to 2000, 2001, and 2002, respectively) as determined from the straight-line amortization schedule in Exhibit 15B-2. The loss on early redemption of these bonds is computed as follows.

EXHIBIT 15B-6

Purchase price of bonds redeemed	$201,000
Carrying value of 1/1/03 series bonds:	
($200,000 − $7,780 + $1,556 + $1,556) or	
($200,000 − $4,668)	195,332
Loss on bond redemption	**$ 5,668**

BONDS OUTSTANDING METHOD

Using the same data, the computation of the applicable unamortized discount under the bonds outstanding method is as follows.

EXHIBIT 15B-7

$$\frac{3 \text{ (number of years before maturity)} \times \$200,000 \text{ (par of bonds)} \times \$24,674 \text{ (total discount)}}{\$3,000,000 \text{ (total of bonds outstanding column)}} = \$4,935$$

Expressed a little differently, the discount to be amortized each year for each $200,000 of bonds is $200,000/$3,000,000 × $24,674, or $1,645. Therefore, if $200,000 of bonds are retired three years before maturity, the discount to be eliminated is 3 × $1,645, or $4,935. Under the bonds outstanding method of amortization, the loss on early retirement of these bonds is computed as follows.

EXHIBIT 15B-8

Purchase price of bonds redeemed	$201,000
Carrying value of 1/1/03 series bonds:	
($200,000 − $4,935)	195,065
Loss on bond redemption	**$ 5,935**

EFFECTIVE INTEREST METHOD

Under the effective interest method, the carrying value of all the serial bonds outstanding at the time of an early retirement must be reduced by the present value of the bonds being retired. Reference to the effective interest amortization schedule shows that the carrying value of all the Yorkville bonds still outstanding at January 1, 2000 is $589,584. The present value of the bonds being retired is computed as follows (three years at 9%).

EXHIBIT 15B-9

Purchase value of principal ($200,000 × .77218)	$154,436
Present value of interest payments ($16,000 × 2.53130)	40,501
Carrying value of bonds to be retired	$194,937

The entry to record the early redemption using the effective interest method is as follows on January 1, 2000.

Bonds Payable	200,000	
Loss on Redemption of Bonds	6,063	
Discount on Bonds Payable ($200,000 − $194,937)		5,063
Cash		201,000

The gain or loss on redemption is the difference between the carrying value of the bonds ($194,937) and the cost to retire the bonds ($201,000); in this example, the loss is $6,063.

Summary of Learning Objective for Appendix 15B

16. Account for serial bonds. Amortization of bond discount or premium for serial bonds is more complex than for single maturity bonds, but both the straight-line and effective interest methods can be adapted to serial maturities. As with single maturity bonds, the gain or loss on the redemption of serial bonds before maturity is determined by comparing the carrying amount of the bond with the consideration given up.

KEY TERMS

bonds outstanding method, 758

effective interest method, 759

straight-line method, 757

Note: All *asterisked* Exercises, Problems, or Cases relate to material contained in the appendices to this chapter.

EXERCISES

E15-1   **(Classification of Liabilities)** Presented below are various accounts and related information for a December 31, 1998 year end:

1. Unamortized premium on bonds payable, of which $1,500 will be amortized during the next year.
2. Bank loans payable due March 10, 1999. (The company expects it will refinance these loans with long-term notes in March, 1999.)
3. Serial bonds payable, $500,000, of which $100,000 are due each July 31.
4. Dividends payable in common shares of the company on January 20, 1999.
5. Noninterest bearing, subordinated loan payable to controlling shareholder, no maturity date.
6. Notes payable due January 15, 2000.
7. Term preferred shares, 6%, redeemable on July 15, 1999.
8. Bonds payable of $900,000 maturing June 30, 1999.
9. Overdraft of $500 in a bank account. (No other accounts are carried in this bank.)
10. Deposits made by customers who have ordered goods.

Instructions

Indicate whether each of the items above should be classified on December 31, 1998 as a current liability, a long-term liability, or under some other classification. Consider each one independently from all others; that is, do not assume that all of them relate to one particular business. If the classification of any of the items is doubtful, explain why.

E15-2   **(Entries for Bond Transactions)** Maria Corp. issued $500,000 of 10%, 20-year bonds on January 1, 1998 at 102. Interest is payable semiannually on July 1 and January 1. Maria Corp. uses the straight-line method of amortization for bond premium or discount.

Instructions

(a) Prepare the journal entries to record:
   1. The issuance of the bonds.
   2. The accrual of interest and the premium amortization on June 30, 1998.
   3. The accrual of interest and the premium amortization on December 31, 1998.
(b) If the effective interest method of amortization for bond premium or discount was used, what would be the (1) interest expense reported on June 30, 1998; and (2) premium amortization for the six month period from July 1 to December 31, 1998? Assume an effective interest rate of 9.75%.

E15-3   **(Entries and Questions for Bond Transactions)** On June 30, 1998, Potter Corp. issued $3,000,000 face value of 13%, 20-year bonds at $3,225,690, a yield of 12%. Potter uses the effective interest method to amortize bond premium or discount. The bonds pay semiannual interest on June 30 and December 31.

Instructions

(a) Prepare the journal entries to record the following transactions.
   1. The issuance of the bonds on June 30, 1998.
   2. The payment of interest and the amortization of the premium on December 31, 1998.
   3. The payment of interest and the amortization of the premium on June 30, 1999.
   4. The payment of interest and the amortization of the premium on December 31, 1999.
(b) Show the presentation for the liability for bonds payable on the December 31, 1999 balance sheet.
(c) Provide answers to the following questions.
   1. What amount of interest expense is reported for 1999?
   2. Will the bond interest expense reported in 1999 be the same as, greater than, or less than the amount that would be reported if the straight-line method of amortization were used?
   3. Determine the total cost of borrowing over the life of the bond.
   4. Will the total bond interest expense be greater than, the same as, or less than the total interest expense if the straight-line method of amortization were used?

(Determining Amounts in Account Balances) Presented below are three independent situations:

1. Renata Corporation incurred the following cost in connection with the issuance of bonds:

   (a) printing and engraving costs, $12,000;

   (b) legal fees, $37,000; and

   (c) commissions paid to underwriter, $60,000.

   What amount should be reported as unamortized bond issue costs, and where should this amount be reported on the balance sheet?

2. Scotto Ltd. sold $2,000,000 of 10%, 10-year bonds at 103 plus accured interest on March 1, 1998. The bonds were dated January 1, 1998 and pay interest on July 1 and January 1. If Scotto uses the straight-line method to amortize bond premium or discount, determine the amount of interest expense to be reported on July 1, 1998 and December 31, 1998.

3. Sutherland Inc. issued $480,000 of 9%, 10-year bonds on June 30, 1998 for $450,000. This price provided a yield of 10% on the bonds. Interest is payable semiannually on December 31 and June 30. If Sutherland uses the effective interest method, determine the amount of interest expense to record if financial statements are issued on October 31, 1998 and October 31, 1999.

E15-4

(Bond Issuance and Interest with Issuance at Other Than an Interest Date) Carrie Inc. issued $500,000 par value 8% bonds on March 1, 1998 for proceeds of $462,414 plus accrued interest. The bonds were dated January 1, 1998, from which date they had a five-year life. Interest is payable semiannually on June 30 and December 31. The effective interest rate on the issue date was 10%.

E15-5

Instructions
Give the necessary journal entries to record the issuance of these bonds and interest costs to be recorded on June 30 and December 31, 1998 assuming the discount is amortized on (a) the straight-line basis; and (b) the effective interest basis. (Hint: To help determine the discount amortization from March 1 through June 30 under the effective interest method, calculate the present value of the bond obligations at June 30 using the effective interest rate.)

(Entry for Retirement of Bond; Bond Issue Costs) On January 2, 1993, Tosca Corporation issued $1,500,000 of 10% bonds at 96 due December 31, 2002. Legal and other costs of $24,000 were incurred in connection with the issue. Interest on the bonds is payable annually each December 31. The $24,000 issue costs are being deferred and amortized on a straight-line basis over the 10-year term of the bonds. The discount on the bonds is also being amortized on a straight-basis over the 10 years (straight-line is not materially different in effect from the effective interest method).

The bonds are callable at 101, and on April 2, 1998, Tosca called $900,000 face amount of the bonds and retired them.

E15-6

Instructions
Ignoring income taxes, compute the amount of loss, if any, to be recognized by Tosca as a result of retiring the $900,000 of bonds in 1998, and prepare the journal entry to record the retirement.   (AICPA adapted)

(Entries for Retirement and Issuance of Bonds) Winter Inc. had outstanding $6,000,000 of 11% bonds (interest payable July 31 and January 31) due in 10 years. On July 1, it issued $9,000,000 of 10% 15-year bonds (interest payable July 1 and January 1) at 97. A portion of the proceeds were used to call the 11% bonds at 102 on July 31. Unamortized bond discount and issue cost applicable to the 11% bonds were $90,000 and $30,000, respectively.

E15-7

Instructions
Prepare the journal entries necessary to record the refunding of the bonds.

(Entries for Retirement and Issuance of Bonds) On June 30, 1989, Aida Inc. issued 12% bonds with a par value of $700,000 due in 20 years. They were issued at 98 and were callable at 104 at any date after June 30, 1997. Because of lower interest rates and a significant change in the company's credit rating, it was decided to call the entire issue on June 30, 1998 and to issue new bonds. New 10% bonds with a face value of $800,000 were sold at 102; they mature in 20 years. The company uses straight-line amortization. Interest payment dates are December 31 and June 30.

E15-8

Instructions
(a) Prepare journal entries to record the retirement of the old issue and the sale of the new issue on June 30, 1998.

(b) Prepare the entry required on December 31, 1998 to record the payment of the first six months' interest and the amortization of the premium on the bonds.

· E15-9   **(Entries for a Zero-Interest Bond)** Clipper Corporation needed funding to finance the construction of a project with high up-front costs and a payback that was substantial, but eight years in the future. The company therefore issued $5,000,000 zero-interest bonds on September 1, 1998 at a price to yield investors an 8% return. The bonds mature on September 1, 2006, and Clipper Corporation has a December 31 year end.

Instructions

(a) Calculate the price at which the bonds sold.

(b) Prepare journal entries required on September 1, 1998, December 31, 1998, and December 31, 1999.

(c) Prepare the journal entry required on September 1, 2006 to record the repayment of the bond at maturity.

E15-10   **(Entries for Noninterest-Bearing Debt)** On July 1, 1998, Rigoletto Inc. makes the two following acquisitions:

1. Purchases land having a fair market value of $200,000 by issuing a five-year noninterest-bearing promissory note in the face amount of $337,012.

2. Purchases equipment by issuing a 6%, eight-year promissory note having a maturity value of $180,000 with interest payable annually each July 1.

The company has to pay 11% interest for funds from its bank.

Instructions

(a) Provide the journal entries that should be recorded by Rigoletto Inc. for the two purchases on July 1, 1998.

(b) Record the interest at December 31, 1998, the company's year end, and at the end of the first year (July 1, 1999) on both notes using the effective interest method.

E15-11   **(Noninterest-Bearing Debt: With Rights)** Presented below are two independent situations:

1. On January 1, 1998, Tristan Furniture Company borrowed $4,000,000 (face value) from Isolde Ltd., a major customer, through a noninterest-bearing note due in four years. Because the note was noninterest-bearing, Tristan agreed to sell furniture to this customer at lower than market price. A 10% rate of interest is normally charged on this type of loan. Prepare the journal entry to record this transaction, and determine the amount of interest expense to report for 1998.

2. On January 1, 1998, Parsifal Inc. purchased land that had an assessed value of $325,000 at the time of purchase. A $500,000 noninterest-bearing note due January 1, 2001 was given in exchange. There was no established exchange price for the land, nor a ready market value for the note. The interest rate charged on notes of this type is 12%. Determine the amount at which the land should be recorded on January 1, 1998 and the interest expense to be reported in 1998.

E15-12   **(Long-Term Debt Disclosure)** To secure a long-term supply, Lalo Corp. entered into a take-or-pay contract with an aluminum recycling plant on January 1, 1997. Lalo is obligated to purchase 40% of the output of the plant each period while the debt incurred to finance the plant remains outstanding. The annual cost of the aluminum to Lalo will be the sum of 40% of the raw material costs, operating expenses, depreciation, interest on the debt used to finance the plant, and return on the owner's investment. The minimum amount payable to the plant under the contract, whether or not Lalo is able to take delivery, is $6 million annually through December 31, 2016. Lalo's total purchases under the agreement were $7 million in 1997 and $7.5 million in 1998. Funds to construct the plant were borrowed at an effective interest rate of 9%. Lalo's incremental borrowing rate was 10% at January 1, 1997 and is 11% at December 31, 1998. Lalo intends to disclose the contract in the notes to its financial statements at December 31, 1998.

Instructions

Assuming that the contract is an "unconditional purchase obligation," prepare the note disclosure for the contract at December 31, 1998.

E15-13   **(Equity with Debt Features)** Morrison Corp., needing funds to finance the acquisition of new equipment, issued 3,000 term preferred shares on July 31, 1998 for $300,000. The preferred shares carry a 10% dividend rate payable each July 31 and are redeemable on July 31, 2003.

Instructions

Assume the preferred shares meet the definition of a financial liability.

(a) Prepare journal entries to record the issue of the shares on July 31, 1998, any adjusting entries needed on December 31, 1998 (Morrison's year end), and on July 31, 1999.

(b) Indicate how all accounts associated with this issue will be reported on Morrison's December 31, 1998 financial statements.

(Mortgage Note Payable) On May 1, 1998 Mirror Corporation entered into a mortgage note payable with the Bank of Nova Commerce whereby it borrowed $130,000 against the purchase of a property that cost $200,000. The remainder of the financing was provided by cash on deposit in the company's bank account.

    The mortgage note payable had a five-year term, carried an interest rate of 10%, and required blended semiannual payments of $7,576.16 every six months beginning November 1, 1998, based on a 20-year amortization period. The municipal assessor's office indicated a value for the land of $50,000 and a value for the building of $125,000.

E15-14

Instructions
(a) Illustrate how the bank calculated the semiannual payment of $7,576.16.
(b) Prepare journal entries to record:
    1. The purchase of the property on May 1, 1998.
    2. The payment of the first mortgage payment on November 1, 1998.
    3. The adjustment for accrued interest on December 31, 1998.
    4. The payment of the second mortgage payment on May 1, 1999.

(Note with Unreasonable Stated Rate) Caster Products Limited purchased an automobile for its sales manager from Stone Motors on May 30, 1998. Stone Motors had been advertising that it would provide 2% financing on the purchase of its vehicles and, since his bank was currently charging 10%, Joe Caster, the president of Caster Products, thought this was too good an opportunity to pass up. The purchase price of the new automobile was $20,000 and Caster Products Limited gave a $5,000 cash down payment and signed a note payable to Stone Motors for the remainder that called for equal annual payments over five years, beginning on May 30, 1999.

E15-15

Instructions
(a) Calculate the amount of the annual payment on the note payable.
(b) Calculate the present value of the note on May 30, 1998 and the GAAP cost of the automobile at acquisition.
(c) Prepare journal entries required on May 30, 1998, December 31, 1998 (Caster's year end), and May 30, 1999.

(Debtor/Creditor Entries for Settlement and for Continuation of Troubled Debt)

*E15-16

Part I
Toshiba Co. Ltd. owes $180,000 plus $19,800 of accrued interest to Zimmer Inc. The debt is a 10-year, 11% note. Because Toshiba is in financial trouble, Zimmer agrees to accept some property and cancel the entire debt. The property had a cost of $75,000 to Toshiba but its fair market value is now $120,000.

Instructions
(a) Prepare the journal entry on Toshiba's books for the debt restructure.
(b) Prepare the journal entry on Zimmer's books for the debt restructure.

Part II
Eaton Corp. owes $200,000 plus $24,000 of accrued interest to First Trust Co. Inc. The debt is a 10-year, 12% note due December 31, 1998. Because Eaton Corp. is in financial trouble, First Trust agrees on December 31, 1998 to forgive the accrued interest, extend the maturity date to December 31, 2000, and reduce the interest rate to 5%, with the interest to be paid annually on December 31. The market rate of interest when the funds were originally borrowed was 12% and is now 10%.

Instructions
(a) Prepare the journal entry on Eaton's books on December 31, 1998 regarding the debt restructure, assuming the old debt is considered eliminated and a new liability is taken on.
(b) Prepare the journal entry on Eaton's books on December 31, 1998 assuming the restructuring is considered a change in terms of the existing liability.

(Restructure of Note Under Different Circumstances) Downunder Corporation is having financial difficulty and therefore has asked Second Canadian Bank to restructure its $3 million note outstanding. The present note has three years remaining and pays a current rate of interest of 10%. The currently prevailing market rate for a loan of this nature is 12%. The note was issued at its face value.

*E15-17

Instructions
Presented below are four independent situations. Prepare the journal entry that Downunder would make for each of these restructurings.
(a) Second Canadian Bank agrees to take an equity interest in Downunder by accepting common shares valued at $2,500,000 in exchange for relinquishing its claim on this note.

(b) Second Canadian Bank agrees to accept land in exchange for relinquishing its claim on this note. This land had a cost of $1,900,000 on Downunder's books but its current fair value is $2,300,000.

(c) Second Canadian Bank agrees to modify the terms of the note, indicating that Downunder does not have to pay any interest on the note over the three-year period. Apply the accounting treatment that assumes this is a change in terms of the existing debt.

(d) Second Canadian Bank agrees to reduce the principal balance due to $2,000,000 and requires interest to be at a rate of 12%. Apply the accounting treatment that assumes this is a new obligation.

*E15-18 **(Premium Amortization for Serial Bonds: Bonds Outstanding Method)** McLeod Inc. sells a 10% serial bond issue in the amount of $2,000,000 to underwriters for $2,080,000. The bonds are dated January 1, 1996 and mature in the amount of $400,000 on January 1 of each year beginning January 1, 1998.

Instructions

Compute the premium to be amortized during each of the years in which any of the bonds are outstanding, using the bonds outstanding method.

PROBLEMS

P15-1 The following amortization and interest schedule reflects the issuance of 10-year bonds by Roadmaster Inc. on January 1, 1998 and the subsequent interest payments and charges. The company's year-end is December 31, and financial statements are prepared once yearly.

AMORTIZATION SCHEDULE

Year	Cash	Interest	Amount Unamortized	Carrying Value
1/1/98			$5,651	$ 94,349
1998	$11,000	$11,322	5,329	94,671
1999	11,000	11,361	4,968	95,032
2000	11,000	11,404	4,564	95,436
2001	11,000	11,452	4,112	95,888
2002	11,000	11,507	3,605	96,395
2003	11,000	11,567	3,038	96,962
2004	11,000	11,635	2,403	97,597
2005	11,000	11,712	1,691	98,309
2006	11,000	11,797	894	99,106
2007	11,000	11,894		100,000

Instructions

(a) Indicate whether the bonds were issued at a premium or a discount and how you can determine this fact from the schedule.

(b) Indicate whether the amortization schedule is based on the straight-line method or the effective interest method and how you can determine which method is used.

(c) Determine the stated interest rate and the effective interest rate.

(d) On the basis of the schedule, prepare the journal entry to record the issuance of the bonds on January 1, 1998.

(e) On the basis of the schedule, prepare the journal entries to reflect the bond transactions and accruals for 1998.

(f) On the basis of the schedule, prepare the journal entries to reflect the bond transactions and accruals for 2005.

P15-2 Assume the same situation as presented in P15-1 above, except that the bonds, although dated January 1, 1998, weren't issued until May 1, 1998. The bonds were sold to yield the same rate of interest as in P15-1.

Instructions

(a) Calculate the issue price and prepare the journal entry to record the issuance of the bonds on May 1, 1998.

(b) Prepare the journal entries required on December 31, 1998 and January 1, 1999.

In 1997, Jasper Tent Co. Ltd. was considering the issuance of bonds as of January 1, 1998, as follows:

P15-3

Plan 1: $2,000,000 par value 11%, first mortgage, 20-year bonds, due December 31, 2017, at 95, with interest payable annually.

Plan 2: $2,000,000 par value 11%, first mortgage, 20-year bonds, due December 31, 2017, at 100, with provision for payment of a 5% ($100,000) premium at maturity, interest payable annually.

Costs of issue such as printing and lawyers' fees may be ignored for the purpose of answering this question. Discount or premium is to be allocated to accounting periods on a straight-line basis.

Instructions

Give two separate sets of journal entries with appropriate explanations showing the accounting treatment that the foregoing plans of bond issues would necessitate, respectively:

(a) At time of issue.

(b) Yearly thereafter.

(c) On payment at date of maturity.

Hydro Corp. sells 10% bonds having a maturity value of $1,500,000 for $1,391,862. The bonds are dated and sold on January 1, 1998 and mature January 1, 2003. Interest is payable annually on January 1.

P15-4

Instructions

(a) 1. Calculate the effective rate of interest the bonds will yield.

2. Set up a schedule of interest expense and discount amortization under:

i) the effective interest method, and

ii) the straight-line method.

(b) If the bonds had sold at $1,558,342:

1. Calculate the effective rate of interest the bonds will yield.

2. Set up a schedule of interest expense and premium amortization under:

i) the effective interest method, and

ii) the straight-line method.

Seek Inc. issued its 9%, 25-year mortgage bonds in the principal amount of $5,000,000 on January 2, 1983 at a discount of $200,000, which it proceeded to amortize by charges to expense over the life of the issue on a straight-line basis. The indenture securing the issue provided that the bonds could be called for redemption in total but not in part at any time before maturity at 104% of the principal amount, but it did not provide for any sinking fund.

P15-5

On December 18, 1997, the company issued its 11%, 20-year debenture bonds in the principal amount of $6,000,000 at 101, and the proceeds were used to redeem the 9%, 25-year mortgage bonds on January 2, 1998 (15 years after their issuance). The indenture securing the new issue did not provide for any sinking fund or for retirement before maturity.

Instructions

(a) Prepare journal entries to record the issuance of the 11% bonds and the retirement of the 9% bonds.

(b) Indicate the income statement treatment of the gain or loss from retirement and any accompanying note disclosure. Assume: 1998 income before the gain or loss, extraordinary items, and income taxes of $3,200,000; a weighted average number of shares outstanding of 1,500,000; and an income tax rate of 40%.

In each of the following independent cases the company closes its books on December 31.

P15-6

1. Blacken Corp. sells $250,000 of 10% bonds on February 1, 1997. The bonds pay interest on February 1 and August 1. The due date of the bonds is August 1, 2000. The bonds yield 12%. Give entries through December 31, 1998.

2. Blue Ltd. sells $600,000 of 12% bonds on June 1, 1997. The bonds pay interest on June 1 and December 1. The due date of the bonds is June 1, 2001. The bonds yield 10%. On September 1, 1998, Blue Ltd. buys back and cancels $120,000 maturity value of bonds for $126,000 (includes accrued interest). Give entries through December 1, 1999.

Instructions

For the two cases, prepare all of the relevant journal entries from the time of sale until the date indicated. Use the effective interest method for discount or premium amortization (construct amortization tables where applicable). Amortize premium or discount on interest dates and at year end. Assume that no reversing entries are made. (Round to the nearest dollar.)

P15-7   Presented below are selected transactions of B. Good Corporation.

May 1, 1997   Bonds payable with a par value of $700,000, which are dated January 1, 1997, are sold at 105 plus accrued interest. They are coupon bonds, bear interest at 12% (payable annually at January 1), and mature January 1, 2007.

Dec. 31   Adjusting entries are made to record the accrued interest on the bonds and the amortization of the premium. (Use straight-line amortization.)

Jan. 1, 1998   Interest on the bonds is paid.

April 1   Bonds of par value of $420,000 that were sold May 1, 1997 are purchased at 102 plus accrued interest, and retired.

Dec. 31   Adjusting entries are made to record the accrued interest on the bonds and the amortization of the premium.

Instructions

Prepare journal entries for the transactions above.

P15-8   On April 1, 1997, Beck Inc. sold 12,000 of its 12%, 15-year, $1,000 face value bonds at 97. Interest payment dates are April 1 and October 1, and the company uses the straight-line method of bond discount amortization. On March 1, 1998, Beck took advantage of favourable prices of its shares to raise sufficient cash to extinguish 3,000 of the bonds. 100,000 no-par value common shares were sold for $31 each on March 1, 1998.

Instructions

Prepare the journal entries needed on the books of Beck Inc. to record the following:

(a) April 1, 1997: issuance of the bonds.

(b) October 1, 1997: payment of semiannual interest.

(c) December 31, 1997: accrual of interest expense.

(d) March 1, 1998: extinguishment of 3,000 bonds.

P15-9   On January 1, 1995, Brock Inc. sold $150,000 (face value) of bonds. The bonds are dated January 1, 1995 and will mature on January 1, 2000. Interest is paid annually on December 31. The bonds are callable after December 31, 1997 at 101. Issue costs related to these bonds amounted to $3,000, and these costs are being amortized by the straight-line method. The following amortization schedule was prepared by the accountant for the first two years of the life of the bonds:

Date	Cash	Interest	Amortization	Carrying Value of Bonds
1/1/95				$139,186
12/31/95	$15,000	$16,702	$1,702	140,888
12/31/96	15,000	16,907	1,907	142,795

Instructions

On the basis of the information above, answer the following questions (round your answers to the nearest dollar or percent):

(a) What is the nominal or stated rate of interest for this bond issue?

(b) What is the effective or market rate of interest for this bond issue?

(c) Present the journal entry to record the sale of the bond issue, including the issue costs.

(d) Present the appropriate entry(ies) at December 31, 1997.

(e) Present the disclosure of this bond issue on the December 31, 1997 balance sheet. Balance sheet subheadings are to be given.

(f) On June 30, 1998, $100,000 of the bond issue was redeemed at the call price. Present the journal entry for this redemption.

(g) Present the effects of the bond redemption on the 1998 income statement. The income tax rate was 40%. Income from operations before the effect of the redemption and income taxes was $40,000, and the weighted average number of common shares outstanding during the year was 18,000.

P15-10   Gucci Leather Inc. reported the following:

Jan. 1, 1997   Bonds payable (coupon bonds) in the amount of $1,500,000, and bearing interest at the rate of 10% payable semiannually on January 1 and July 1, due January 1, 2013 (i.e., 16 years from issuance date), are issued at 96.

June 15 The Commerce Bank has been engaged as trustee to handle the payment of interest to individual bondholders. A cheque for the interest due July 1, 1997 is sent to the trustee. (Note: Transfer from the Cash account to a Bond Interest Fund until bondholders have been paid.)

30 Record the interest expense for the first six months of 1997. Bond discount is to be amortized only at the end of each year by the straight-line method.

July 20 The trustee returns to the company cancelled interest coupons paid in the amount of $68,000 and reports that trustee's expenses charged against the account amounted to $645.

Dec. 15 A cheque for the interest due January 1, 1998 and for the July 20 reported expenses is sent to the trustee.

31 Record the interest expense for the six months ended December 31, and amortize the discount for the year.

Jan. 21, 1998 The trustee returns to the company cancelled interest coupons paid in the amount of $73,000.

Mar. 1 Bonds of par value of $200,000 are bought on the market at 95 plus accrued interest and retired. All interest coupons dated before July 1, 1998 have been removed.

Instructions

(a) Prepare journal entries on the books of Gucci Leather Inc. for the transactions given above. Present answers to nearest dollar amount.

(b) What will be the amount of the cheque to the trustee for the interest for the first six months of 1998?

(c) What will be the amount, to the nearest dollar, of the discount amortized on December 31, 1998?

On December 31, 1997, Waterloo Inc. acquired computers from Laurier Corporation by issuing a $400,000 noninterest-bearing note, payable in full on December 31, 2001. Waterloo's credit rating permits it to borrow funds from its several lines of credit at 10%. The computers are expected to have a five-year life and a $40,000 residual value. **P15-11**

Instructions

(a) Prepare the journal entry for the purchase on December 31, 1997.

(b) Prepare any necessary adjusting entries relative to depreciation (use straight-line) and amortization (use effective interest method) on December 31, 1998.

(c) Prepare any necessary adjusting entries relative to depreciation and amortization on December 31, 1999.

Swift Clean Inc. purchased machinery on December 31, 1996, paying $10,000 down and agreeing to pay the balance in four equal instalments of $30,000 payable each December 31. An assumed interest of 12% is implicit in the purchase price. **P15-12**

Instructions

Prepare the journal entries to record the purchase of the machine on December 31, 1996 and the payments and interest on December 31, 1997 through 2000.

Presented below are five independent situations: **P15-13**

1. On March 1, 1998, Red Dye Corp. issued at 104 plus accrued interest $3,000,000, 9% bonds. The bonds are dated January 1, 1998 and pay interest semiannually on July 1 and January 1. In addition, Red Dye Corp. incurred $27,000 of bond issuance costs. Compute the net amount of cash received by Red Dye Corp. as a result of the issuance of these bonds.

2. On January 1, 1998, Electric Co. Ltd. issued 9% bonds with a face value of $500,000 for $469,280 to yield 10%. The bonds are dated January 1, 1998 and pay interest annually. What amount is reported for interest expense in 1998 related to these bonds, assuming that Electric used effective interest method for amortizing bond premium and discount?

3. Cherub Corp. has a number of long-term bonds outstanding at December 31, 1998. These long-term bonds have the following requirements for sinking fund balances and to pay bond maturities for the next six years.

	Sinking Fund	Maturities
1999	$100,000	$100,000
2000	200,000	250,000
2001	300,000	100,000
2002	200,000	—
2003	200,000	150,000
2004	200,000	100,000

Indicate how this information should be reported in the financial statements at December 31, 1998.

4. Bip Inc., on February 1, 1995, issued 12%, $4,000,000 face amount, 10-year bonds at 98 plus accrued interest. The bonds are dated November 1, 1994, and interest is payable on May 1 and November 1. On May 1, 1998, Bip decided to defease (legally, not in-substance) this debt because interest rates had dropped, and the bonds were defeased at a cost of $3,650,000. Ignoring the income tax effect, at what amount and where would Bip's defeasance be reported on the financial statements? (Use straight-line amortization.)

5. In the long-term debt structure of Happy-time Inc., the following three bonds were reported: mortgage bonds payable $10,000,000; collateral trust bonds $5,000,000; bonds maturing in instalments, secured by plant equipment $4,000,000. Determine the total amount, if any, of debenture bonds outstanding.

P15-14 Moonbeam Inc. has been producing quality children's apparel for more than 25 years. The company's fiscal year runs from April 1 to March 31. The following information relates to the obligations of Moonbeam as of March 31, 1998.

Bonds Payable

Moonbeam issued $5,000,000 of 11% bonds on July 1, 1992 at 96, which yielded proceeds of $4,800,000. The bonds will mature on July 1, 2002. Interest is paid semiannually on July 1 and January 1. Moonbeam uses the straight-line method to amortize the bond discount.

Notes Payable

Moonbeam has signed several long-term notes with financial institutions and insurance companies. The maturities of these notes are given in the schedule below. The total unpaid interest for all of these notes amounts to $310,000 on March 31, 1998.

Due Date	Amount Due
April 1, 1998	$ 200,000
July 1, 1998	150,000
October 1, 1998	150,000
January 1, 1999	150,000
April 1, 1999–March 31, 2000	500,000
April 1, 2000–March 31, 2001	500,000
April 1, 2001–March 31, 2002	700,000
April 1, 2002–March 31, 2003	1,400,000
April 1, 2003–March 31, 2004	500,000
	$4,250,000

Estimated Warranties

Moonbeam has a one-year product warranty on some selected items in its product line. The estimated warranty liability on sales made during the 1996–97 fiscal year and still outstanding as of March 31, 1997 amounted to $84,000. The warranty costs on sales made from April 1, 1997 through March 31, 1998 are estimated at $200,000. The actual warranty costs incurred during the current 1997–98 fiscal year are as follows:

Warranty claims honoured on 1996–97 sales	$ 84,000
Warranty claims honoured on 1997–98 sales	95,000
Total warranty claims honoured	$179,000

Other Information

1. *Trade payables.* Accounts payable for supplies, goods, and services purchased on open account amount to $550,000 as of March 31, 1998.

2. *Payroll-related items.* Outstanding obligations related to Moonbeam's payroll as of March 31, 1998 are:

Accrued salaries and wages	$155,000
CPP and EI payable	18,000
Income taxes withheld from employees	25,000
Other payroll deductions	5,000

3. *Taxes.* The following taxes incurred but not due until the next fiscal year are:

Income taxes	$305,000
Property taxes	125,000
Sales taxes (not offset by input credits)	182,000

4. *Miscellaneous accruals.* Other accruals not separately classified amount to $75,000 as of March 31, 1998.

5. *Dividends*. On March 15, 1998 Moonbeam's Board of Directors declared a cash dividend of $.40 per common share on its 3,000,000 outstanding shares. This dividend was to be distributed on April 12, 1998 to the common shareholders of record at the close of business on March 31, 1998.

Instructions

Prepare the liability sections of Moonbeam Inc.'s March 31, 1998 balance sheet and appropriate accompanying notes.   (CMA adapted)

Sorenson Ltd. issued 500,000 preferred shares to Ace Venture Capitalists, Inc. on December 1, 1998 to help fund the   **P15-15** development of new products. The preferred shares are redeemable for $4,000,000 cash on December 1, 2008 at the option of the preferred shareholders. The preferred annual dividend is $.60 per share payable December 1, 1999 and each December 1 up to and including December 1, 2008, and the entire issue netted the company $4,240,000.

Instructions

(a) Assuming company management determined that the preferred shares are financial liabilities in substance, prepare journal entries needed on the following dates, using straight-line amortization if applicable:

1. December 1, 1998.

2. December 31, 1998.

3. December 1, 1999.

4. December 1, 2008, assuming the shares are redeemed.

(b) Calculate the balances in all accounts related to the issuance of the preferred shares as at December 31, 1998, and identify where each is reported on Sorenson's December 31, 1998 financial statements.

(c) If Sorenson Ltd. repurchased half the preferred shares on the open market on December 1, 2000 (after payment of the annual dividend) at a price of $7.95 per share and cancelled the shares, calculate any "gain" or "loss" on the repurchase and identify where Sorenson would report this amount on their December 31, 2000 financial statements.

Santiago Saddles Limited, having outgrown their existing premises, found a property they were interested in   **P15-16** acquiring that would suit their needs over the next 10 to 20 years. The land and building could be purchased for $250,000, and another $100,000 would need to be spent to get the property into condition for efficient use of the facilities. The company's bankers agreed to provide a mortgage for 70% of the expected costs based on cash flow projections provided by Santiago's VP Finance.

The 8%, five-year term, $245,000 mortgage note payable signed by the company on September 1, 1998 called for blended payments of principal and interest every three months beginning December 1, 1998, based on a 10-year amortization.

Instructions

(a) Determine the amount of the quarterly payment required to be paid by Santiago Saddles Limited.

(b) Prepare a mortgage amortization schedule for the period September 1, 1998 to March 1, 2000.

(c) Prepare the journal entries to record the mortgage payment on December 1, 1998, the interest accrual on December 31, 1998 (Santiago's year end), and the mortgage payment on March 1, 1999.

(d) Calculate the mortgage interest expense to be reported on the company's income statement for the year ended December 31, 1999.

(e) Indicate how the mortgage liability will be reported on the December 31, 1998 balance sheet.

On December 31, 1995, Emma Ltd. sold an 11% serial bond issue in the amount of $3,200,000 for $3,402,116. The   ***P15-17** bonds mature in the amount of $400,000 on December 31 of each year, beginning December 31, 1996, and interest is payable annually. On December 31, 1996 and 1997, the company retired the $400,000 of bonds due on these dates and in addition, on December 31, 1997, purchased at 102 and retired bonds in the amount of $200,000 that were due on December 31, 1999. (Hint: The unamortized premium on the $200,000 retired bonds using the bonds outstanding method was $5,614.33 at December 31, 1997.)

Instructions

(a) For 1996, prepare entries to record the payment of interest, amortization of the premium for the year using the bonds outstanding method, and redemption of $400,000 of bonds.

(b) Prepare entries to record the redemption of the bonds of $600,000 that were retired on December 31, 1997.

(c) Discuss the disclosures that are required relative to the bond transactions in 1997.

(d) What amount of premium would be amortized for the year 1998 under the bonds outstanding method?

(e) Prepare entries for 1996, 1997, and 1998 to record the transactions above using the effective interest method, assuming the bonds were sold for $3,419,127 to yield 9%.

CASES

C15-1 The Good Tire Company has completed a number of transactions during 1998. In January the company purchased under contract a machine at a total price of $1,000,000, payable over five years with instalments of $200,000 per year. The seller is accounting for the transaction by using the instalment method with the title transferring to Good Tire at the time of the final payment.

On March 1, 1998, Good Tire issued $10 million of general revenue bonds priced at 99 with a coupon rate of 10% payable July 1 and January 1 of each of the next 10 years. The July 1 interest was paid, and on December 30 the company transferred $1,000,000 to the trustee, Country Trust Company, for payment of the January 1, 1999 interest.

Due to the depressed market for the company's common shares, Good Tire purchased $500,000 maturity value of its 6% convertible bonds for a price of $450,000. Management expects to resell the bonds when the share price has recovered.

As the accountant for Good Tire Company, you prepared the balance sheet and presented it to the president of the company. The president then asked you the following questions:

1. Why has depreciation been charged on the machine purchased under the long-term instalment contract? Title has not passed to the company and, therefore, it is not our asset. Why shouldn't the company just show only the amount paid to date on the asset side of the balance sheet instead of showing the full contract price with the unpaid portion on the liability side?

2. What is a bond discount? As a debit balance, why shouldn't it be classified among the assets?

3. Bond interest payable is shown as a current liability. Did we not pay our trustee the full amount of interest due this period?

4. Treasury bonds are shown as a deduction from bonds payable issued. Why should they not be shown as an asset, since they can be sold again? Are they the same as bonds of other companies that we hold as investments?

Instructions
Provide answers to these questions, including a brief explanation to justify your conclusions.

C15-2 The following paraphrases and condenses an article in a business newspaper:

Bond Markets

Provincial Telephone Corporation Issue Hits Resale Market With $70 Million Left Over

SASKATOON—Provincial Telephone Corporation's slow-selling new 5¼% bonds were tossed onto the resale market at a reduced price with about $70 million still available from the $200 million offered Thursday, dealers said.

The utility's bonds originally had been priced at 99.803, to yield 5.3%. They were marked down yesterday the equivalent of about $5.50 for each $1,000 face amount, to about 99.25, where their yield jumped to 5.45%.

Instructions
(a) How will the development above affect the accounting for the utility's bond issue?
(b) Provide several possible explanations for the markdown and the slow sale of the bonds.

C15-3 On January 1, 1998, Central Corp. issued for $1,075,230 its 20-year, 13% bonds that have a maturity value of $1,000,000 and pay interest semiannually on January 1 and July 1. Therefore, the yield rate was 12%. Bond issue costs were not material in amount. Below are three presentations of the long-term liability section of the balance sheet that might be used for these bonds at the issue date:

1. Bonds payable (maturing January 1, 2018)	$1,000,000
Unamortized premium on bonds payable	75,230
Total bond liability	$1,075,230
2. Bonds payable—principal (face value $1,000,000 maturing January 1, 2018)	$ 97,220ᵃ
Bonds payable—interest (semiannual payment $65,000)	978,010ᵇ
Total bond liability	$1,075,230
3. Bonds payable—principal (maturing January 1, 2018)	$1,000,000
Bonds payable—interest ($65,000 per period for 40 periods)	2,600,000
Total bond liability	$3,600,000

ᵃThe present value of $1,000,000 due at the end of 40 (six-month) periods at the yield rate of 6% per period.
ᵇThe present value of $65,000 per period for 40 (six-month) periods at the yield rate of 6% per period.

Instructions

(a) Discuss the conceptual merit(s) of each of these date-of-issue balance sheet presentations.

(b) Explain why investors would pay $1,075,230 for bonds that have a maturity value of only $1,000,000.

(c) Assuming that a discount rate is needed to compute the carrying value of the obligations arising from a bond issue at any date during the life of the bonds, discuss the conceptual merit(s) of using for this purpose:

    1. The coupon or nominal rate.

    2. The effective or yield rate at date of issue.

(d) If the obligations arising from these bonds are to be carried at their present value computed by means of the current market rate of interest, how would the bond valuation at dates subsequent to the date of issue be affected by an increase or a decrease in the market rate of interest? (AICPA adapted)

C15-4

On March 1, 1998, Pueblo Corp. sold its five-year, $1,000 face value, 6% bonds dated March 1, 1998 at an effective annual interest rate (yield) of 7%. Interest is payable semiannually, and the first interest payment date is September 1, 1998. Pueblo uses the effective interest method of amortization. Bond issue costs of a material amount were incurred in preparing and selling the bond issue. The bonds can be called by Pueblo at 101 at any time on or after March 1, 1999.

Instructions

(a) 1. How would the selling price of the bonds be determined?

    2. Specify how all items related to the bonds would be presented in a balance sheet prepared immediately after the bond issue was sold.

(b) What items related to the bond issue would be included in Pueblo's 1998 income statement, and how would each be determined?

(c) Would the amount of bond discount amortization using the effective interest method of amortization be lower in the second or third year of the life of the bond issue? Explain.

(d) Assuming that the bonds were called in and retired on March 1, 1999, how would the retirement of the bonds affect the 1999 income statement? (AICPA adapted)

C15-5

The following is a footnote prepared by Plover Company for its 1998 annual report:

On December 30, 1998, the Company entered into agreements with a trustee that facilitated in-substance defeasance of its 5% and 5¼% capital note issues. Government securities costing $10,063,000 were deposited in an irrevocable trust, the principal and interest of which will be sufficient to pay the scheduled principal and interest on the 5% and 5¼% capital note issues of the Company. Proceeds from the sale of certain short-term liquid assets of the Company were used to purchase these securities. The 5% capital notes require principal payments of $500,000 on January 1 in each of the years 1999 through 2005 and the balance of $7,500,000 in 2006. The 5¼% cpital notes require principal payments of $262,500 in each of the years 1999 through 2007 and the balance of $1,750,000 due in 2008. Interest on both issues is payable on January 1 and July 1 of each year that the notes remain outstanding. In December 1998, the Company prepaid the principal and interest payments on both issues due January 1, 1999.

The Company recognized a gain in the 1998 income statement as the excess of the current principal outstanding on the note issues over the cost of the securities placed in the defeasance trusts, plus related trustee costs. The gain on the in-substance defeasance of both note issues of $2,732,000 is equivalent to a gain of $0.57 per common share.

Instructions

(a) What is in-substance defeasance?

(b) Discuss alternative accounting methods that might be used for this type of transaction.

(c) What is the treatment under GAAP?

C15-6

In its December 31, 1995 financial statements, Noranda Inc. reported an outstanding issuance of $150 million of convertible, unsecured, subordinated debenture bonds due in 2007. These bonds bear an interest rate that is the greater of 5% or 1% plus the percentage that two times the common share dividend paid in the previous six months is of the conversion price. Subject to certain conditions, Noranda may satisfy the interest requirement through the issue of common shares. These debentures are convertible at the holder's option into common shares at a conversion price of $35 per common share on or before the last business day prior to the maturity date of the debentures or the last business day prior to redemption. Noranda has the option of redeeming the debentures for common shares.

Instructions

Provide your recommendations on how these debentures and any related interest should be reported in Noranda Inc.'s financial statements. Justify your recommendations.

C15-7   Interest rate and currency swaps have been identified as a form of off-balance-sheet financing. Below is an extract from the note on long-term debt in the 1995 financial statements of Canadian Pacific Limited with reference to the long-term debt of two of its subsidiaries, PanCanadian Petroleum Limited and Marathon Realty Company Limited.

> PanCanadian Petroleum Limited (PanCanadian), through a series of swap transactions, converted $100 million of medium term notes with a fixed interest rate of 8.4% into US $73.1 million with a fixed interest rate of approximately 6.33%.
>
> Marathon Realty Company Limited's bank term loans of $122.7 million which bear interest at rates which fluctuate with bank prime or money market rates have been fixed by way of interest rate swaps for periods of one to six years effectively fixing the interest rate at a weighted average rate of approximately 9.6%.

Instructions

(a) What is meant by off-balance-sheet financing, and why would a company engage in such financing?

(b) What is an interest rate and a currency swap, why are they forms of off-balance-sheet financing, and why would Canadian Pacific Limited's subsidiaries enter into such financial arrangements?

C15-8   A common account found on the financial statements of smaller private corporations is "Advances from Owners." The account represents amounts loaned by shareholders, it is often noninterest-bearing, and its repayment is usually subordinated to the repayment of other liabilities.

Instructions

Discuss the classification of this account on the statement of financial position under the requirements of *Handbook* Section 3860 on financial instruments.

C15-9   Erindale Enterprises Incorporated (EEI) is in the process of a major expansion into the United States market. For the past 10 years, since the company started up, its founder and owner focussed solely on the Canadian market. In 1998 however, on the advice of the company's outside consultants, EEI decided to raise a significant amount of funds and expand into the United States.

The funds were raised by the issuance of two distinctly different financial instruments. The first was a preferred share issue that was issued on the Toronto Stock Exchange and resulted in a wide shareholder base. The second was a perpetual debt instrument that was issued to two major institutional investors, a major pension fund and a mid-sized mutual fund investment company. Since the expansion into the United States would take a few years to show a profit, EEI had planned that the funding be of a more long-term nature, hence the legal form of the debt (i.e., perpetual). When the deal was done, both the pension fund and the investment company acknowledged that they were looking to longer-term horizons for a return on their money.

The terms of the perpetual debt are as follows.

- The debt does not have a repayment schedule and is due upon windup or liquidation of the company. Since it is secured by a mortgage on the assets of the U.S. operations, it ranks in preference on liquidation.
- Interest is due at 8%, which is equal to market rates at the time of issue for similar debt with similar risk. After 10 years, the return will increase to include 1% of after-tax profits of the U.S. operations.
- The debt is repayable at the option of the lender on 60 days' notice and at face value.

The terms of the preferred shares are as follows.
- The shares are redeemable at the option of EEI after Year 2.
- The shares carry a dividend of 6% (of invested share capital) that increases after Year 5 by 1% per year to Year 15. Therefore, in Year 10, the dividend rate would be 11%. The dividends are cumulative.

By early 1999, the investment company that held part of the debt had run into cash flow difficulties and had scheduled a meeting with EEI to dicuss the early repayment option on the debt. Interest rates had risen precipitously and were now 13%. Although this was causing much uncertainty in the markets, many financial analysts were expecting the rates to decline to more reasonable levels in the short to medium term.

Instructions

Adopt the role of EEI's chief financial accountant and discuss the financial reporting issues surrounding the reporting of the preferred shares and the perpetual debt.

(Irene Wiecek)

*C15-10   Chrysis Corp. has recently fallen into financial difficulties. To help Chrysis avert bankruptcy, Dominion Bank has given Chrysis a break. Chrysis owes Dominion Bank $2,000,000, payable in 10 years. The interest rate on the loan is 10%, the market rate when the monies were first advanced. Dominion, wishing to minimize its losses, has agreed to reduce the interest rate to 5% per year.

Mr. Walters, Dominion's controller, sees no need for any journal entries to record this deal. Since Chrysis still owes $2,000,000, he feels that there is no need for a writedown of this loan and a recognition of a loss. Likewise, he sees no need for a journal entry on the books of Chrysis in recognition of this event.

Mr. Mocha, controller for Chrysis, however, would not do it this way. He points out that the $1,385,544 present value of Chrysis's restructured obligations to Dominion (discounted at the currently prevailing 10% market interest rate for similar loans) is considerably less than the $2,000,000 present value of the obligation before the interest rate was reduced. He feels that this provides a basis for recognition of a gain by Chrysis and, correspondingly, a loss by Dominion.

Instructions

(a) What are possible arguments that you might expect from Dominion Bank and Chrysis Corp. to support their respective views on how the loan restructure should be accounted for?

(b) What entries would be recorded regarding the recognition of the loan restructure on the books of each company under the accounting treatment preferred by:

1. Dominion Bank.

2. Chrysis Corp.

(c) What is the treatment under current GAAP?

USING YOUR JUDGEMENT

FINANCIAL REPORTING PROBLEM

Refer to the financial statements of Moore Corporation Limited presented in Appendix 5A and answer the following questions.

1. To what extent has Moore Corp. financed its investments in assets by using long-term debt? State your answer in the form of a percentage. Is this a high percentage or a low one? How do you know?

2. How are the rest of the assets financed? Is Moore Corp. highly leveraged? What are the benefits and the limitations of being highly leveraged?

3. Has Moore Corp. provided all the disclosure that is required by the *CICA Handbook* section on long-term debt?

4. Has Moore Corp. engaged in any off-balance-sheet financing? Comment.

5. Prepare a summary comment on the level of risk associated with this company's level of debt and use of derivatives.

ETHICS CASE

In the United States, in-substance defeasance allows a company to remove debt from the balance sheet as long as it places risk-free securities or cash in an irrevocable trust, such that these new assets will be used to satisfy the full value of the original debt. Following this accounting rule, Exxon was permitted to remove $515 million of its bonds payable by placing only $313 million of government securities in an irrevocable trust, which resulted in a large extraordinary gain on the "supposed" redemption of bonds, recorded as follows:

Bonds Payable	$515,000,000	
Gain on Redemption of Bonds (Extraordinary)		$202,000,000
Cash		$313,000,000

Instructions

(a) What are the ethical implications of in-substance defeasance and off-balance sheet financing to users of financial statement information?

(b) How does Exxon benefit from the accounting rule on in-substance defeasance and, in particular, its ability to remove long-term liabilities from the balance sheet?

(c) Who could be harmed by Exxon's ability to remove $515 million of bonds payable from the balance sheet, keeping in mind that it is still legally obligated to pay the original debtors?

part 4

SHAREHOLDERS' EQUITY, DILUTIVE SECURITIES, AND EARNINGS PER SHARE

chapter 16

SHAREHOLDERS' EQUITY: ISSUANCE AND REACQUISITION OF SHARE CAPITAL

CHAPTER

16

Shareholders' Equity:
Issuance and Reacquisition of Share Capital

Learning Objectives

After studying this chapter, you should be able to:

1. Understand the nature of shareholders' equity and know its key components or sources.

2. Know and be able to discuss the characteristics of the corporate form of organization.

3. Identify the rights of shareholders.

4. Describe and understand the major features of preferred shares.

5. Account for the issuance of shares for cash or receivables, in combination with the sale of other securities, and in nonmonetary transactions.

6. Explain how to account for share issue costs.

7. Account for the acquisition and cancellation of shares previously outstanding.

8. Explain what treasury shares are and how to account for them under the single-transaction method.

9. Identify the disclosure requirements for share capital.

10. Account for the issue and reacquisition of par value shares (Appendix 16A).

In your first exposure to financial accounting you were probably taught that the equity side of the balance sheet represents the sources of enterprise assets. Liabilities represent the amount of assets that were financed by borrowing, and shareholders' equity represents (1) the amount that was contributed by the shareholders; and (2) the portion of assets generated from earnings that have been retained by the enterprise.

In recent years the creation of a variety of financial instruments, together with innovative investment practices, have blurred this simple distinction between liabilities and equities. As a result, the AcSB has issued *CICA Handbook* recommendations on the classification of financial instruments.[1] One of the major contributions of this document is its attempt to clarify the distinction between financial liabilities and equity instruments.

As discussed in Chapter 15, the classification on the issuer's balance sheet is governed by the substance of the financial instrument, not its legal form. Obviously, whether a particular financial instrument is classified as a liability or an equity item affects the content of the balance sheet and the ratios of assets to equity and of debt to equity. But, more critically, the line between liabilities and equity affects the measurement of income. Income is defined to include changes in equity during a period other than those resulting from transactions with owners of an enterprise's equity instruments. Income is a return *on* equity capital and includes only inflows in excess of the amount needed to maintain

---

[1] *CICA Handbook* (Toronto: CICA), Section 3860, "Financial Instruments—Disclosure and Presentation," issued September, 1995.

capital. Without a distinction between the claims of creditors and those of owners, measurement of income is not possible. Even with the guidance offered by Section 3860, professional judgement is needed to determine the appropriate classification for specific financial instruments.

This and the next two chapters cover the shareholders' equity section. Chapter 16 introduces the basic legal aspects of corporate ownership and covers accounting for the issue of shares to shareholders and the effects of any subsequent acquisition of its shares by the corporation. Chapter 17 is devoted almost entirely to retained earnings and the legal and accounting requirements for the distribution of assets to shareholders by way of dividends. This chapter describes other commonly found shareholders' equity accounts and explains the accounting for financial reorganizations in which the Retained Earnings/Deficit account of a company can be set back to zero. Chapter 18 completes the shareholders' equity section by looking at securities that can dilute the interests of existing common shareholders, including executive compensation arrangements related to shares of the company, and the calculation of the only statistic reported in the financial statements, that of earnings per share.

THE NATURE OF SHAREHOLDERS' EQUITY

OBJECTIVE 1
Understand the nature of shareholders' equity and know its key components or sources.

Although the owners of an enterprise ultimately bear the risks and uncertainties of the business, they also receive the benefits of enterprise operations. Their interest is measured by the difference between the assets and the liabilities of the enterprise. **Owners'** or **shareholders' equity** or interest in a business enterprise is a *residual interest*. It ranks after liabilities as a claim to or interest in the assets of an enterprise. Shareholders' equity represents the cumulative net contributions by shareholders plus recorded earnings that have been retained. As a residual interest, shareholders' equity has no existence apart from the assets and liabilities of the enterprise—shareholders' equity equals net assets. Shareholders' equity is not a claim to specific assets, but is instead a claim against a portion of the total assets. Its amount is not specified or fixed; it depends on the enterprise's profitability. Shareholders' equity grows if the enterprise is profitable and shrinks or may disappear entirely if the enterprise is unprofitable.

SOURCES OF SHAREHOLDERS' EQUITY

Accounting for shareholders' equity is greatly influenced by tradition and corporate law. Although the legal aspects of equity must be respected and disclosed, legal requirements need not be the only accounting basis for classifying and reporting the components of equity. *The two primary sources from which owners' equity is derived are (1) contributions by shareholders; and (2) income (earnings) retained by a corporation.* These two components should be accounted for and reported by every corporation. Illustration 16-1 depicts the two major sources of changes in total shareholders' equity.[2]

Changes in total shareholders' equity may also occur by conversion of debt into equity and through capital donations to a corporation. In addition, changes within components of, but not the total of, shareholders' equity are brought about by stock dividends and conversion of preferred shares into common shares. The comprehensive revaluation of assets and liabilities in a financial reorganization can result in a change in both

---

[2] Adapted from "Elements of Financial Statements of Business Enterprises," *Statement of Financial Accounting Concepts No. 3* (Stamford, CT: FASB, 1980), p. 23.

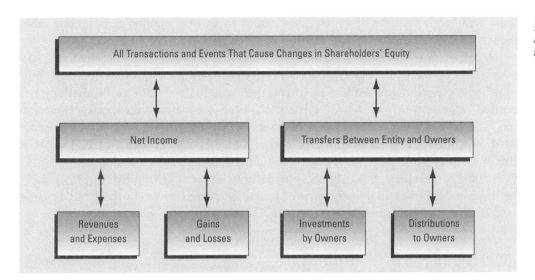

ILLUSTRATION 16-1
Major Sources of Changes in Shareholders' Equity

the components and total of shareholders' equity. These types of changes are examined in Chapters 17 and 18.

WHAT IS CAPITAL?

To this point, the authors have used the terms "shareholders' equity" or "owners' equity" to denote the total of ownership capital of an enterprise. It is important to understand the many different meanings attached to the word **capital**, because the word often is construed differently by various groups. In corporate finance, for example, capital commonly represents the total assets of the enterprise. In law, capital is considered that portion of shareholders' equity that is required by statute to be retained in the business for the protection of creditors. Generally, **legal capital (stated capital)** is the full price received for shares issued as specified by the Canada Business Corporations Act and most provincial incorporation acts. In some jurisdictions, ownership shares may have a par value, in which case that amount is considered to be the legal capital.

Accountants for the most part define capital more broadly than legal capital, but more narrowly than total assets. ***When accountants refer to capital, they usually mean shareholders' or owners' equity.*** They then subclassify shareholders' equity into various components, the primary ones being share capital, contributed surplus, and retained earnings. **Share capital** (or **capital stock**) represents the legal or stated capital of a corporation as defined in the previous paragraph. **Contributed surplus** includes items such as donations from owners and other sources, gains on forfeited shares, credits arising when the company's own shares are reacquired and cancelled at a cost less than their issue price, and amounts received in excess of par value when such shares are issued. Share capital and contributed surplus constitute **contributed capital**. **Retained earnings** represents the **earned capital** of an enterprise and consists of all undistributed income that remains invested in the enterprise. A comprehensive illustration of the shareholders' equity section of a balance sheet is given in Chapter 17 on page 852, which shows how these categories may be presented and provides examples of what they may include.

TERMINOLOGY

The terminology used to report shareholders' equity varies from company to company. While share capital or capital stock, contributed surplus, and retained earnings are terms used to categorize sources of shareholders' equity by many Canadian corporations, other names for these categories are sometimes used.[3]

A particular concern of the accounting profession has been the use of the term "surplus" in corporate reporting. The concern is derived from the belief that the word "surplus" connotes to many readers of financial statements a residue or "something not needed." Consequently, the word "surplus" has been eliminated in most cases. For example, "retained earnings" has replaced the heading "earned surplus," which was formerly used. Whenever the word "surplus" is used in contemporary reports, the CICA suggests that it be in conjunction with a descriptive adjective,[4] as in, for example, the heading "Contributed Surplus." A widely accepted term to replace Contributed Surplus has not yet been used in financial statements of Canadian corporations. In the United States, "Additional Paid-In Capital" is the frequently used heading for this category.

CORPORATE FORM OF ENTITY

OBJECTIVE 2
Know and be able to discuss the characteristics of the corporate form of organization.

Of the *three primary forms of business organization—the proprietorship, the partnership, and the corporation—*the corporate form is dominant. In terms of the aggregate amount of resources controlled, goods and services produced, and people employed, the corporation is by far the leader. Nearly all of the largest business organizations are corporations. Although the corporate form has a number of advantages (as well as disadvantages) over the other two forms, a principal factor contributing to its present dominant role is the ability to attract and accumulate large amounts of capital.

Various types of corporations exist, distinguished by the nature of their ownership, their purpose, and the type of legislation under which they have been created. The following are common in Canada.

1. **Profit-oriented corporations** engage in activities with the intent of making a financial return for their owners. Ownership may be widely traded and distributed (often called **publicly held corporations**) or held by a small number of shareholders with restrictions on the transferability of shares (often referred to as **privately held corporations**).

2. **Not-for-profit corporations**, organizations in which there is normally no transferable ownership interest, are created to provide educational, charitable, recreational, or similar services for their members or society in general.

3. **Crown corporations** are created by special government statutes to provide services to the public, such as the Canadian Broadcasting Corporation and Canada Post.

The profit-oriented corporation is the type examined in this book.

Among the special characteristics of the corporate form that affect accounting are:

1. Influence of corporate law.

2. Use of the share capital or capital stock system.

3. Development of a variety of ownership interests.

---

[3] *Financial Reporting in Canada—1995* (Toronto: CICA, 1995) indicated that in 1994: (a) Share Capital was used by 100 of 300 companies surveyed and Capital Stock was used by 158 companies, while other headings used were Common Shares or Preferred Shares (18 companies), Stated Capital (7); (b) Contributed Surplus was used by 60 of 65 companies reporting such items, while the remaining companies used such headings as Premium on Shares Issued (1), Capital Surplus (1), Paid-in Surplus (2); (c) Retained Earnings was used by 234 of the 300 companies, Deficit by 54, while other headings included Reinvested Earnings, Retained Income, and Earnings Reinvested in the Business; (d) Shareholders' Equity was used by 280 companies as the title for the balance sheet section with 6 using Common Shareholders' Equity, and 13 using different titles.

[4] *CICA Handbook,* Section 3250, par. .02.

4. Limited liability of shareholders.

5. Formality of profit distribution.

CORPORATE LAW

In Canada, a corporation may be established provincially or federally by submitting the required documentation to the appropriate government office. If incorporated provincially, the company would be subject to the requirements and provisions of the respective province's business corporations act. Federally incorporated companies are created and operated under the provisions of the **Canada Business Corporations Act** (CBCA). While the provisions of most business corporations acts are reasonably similar, differences do exist. These differences create difficulties when trying to make generalizations in a discussion of shareholders' equity. Consequently, the CBCA will be the focal point when discussing legal aspects of accounting for shareholders' equity in this book.

Under the CBCA, one or more individuals over 18, of sound mind and not bankrupt, are entitled to incorporate. To do so, incorporators develop, sign, and send **articles of incorporation**[5] to the Director, Department of Consumer and Corporate Affairs. The Director, who is responsible for the administration of the CBCA, will issue a **certificate of incorporation** after ensuring that the incorporating documents are appropriately completed. Incorporation is essentially a right under the CBCA because the Director has no discretion to refuse documents that are in order. When a certificate of incorporation is issued, the resulting business becomes a separate legal entity entitled to act in the capacity of a natural person when conducting its affairs. As with any person, it is bound by the laws of the country. In addition, the corporation (unless a particular exemption is explicitly granted) must act in accordance with all of the provisions of the CBCA. These provisions have significant implications regarding accounting for corporations in general and for shareholders' equity in particular, as will be discussed throughout this and the next chapter.

First, however, one important accounting aspect of the CBCA should be emphasized: the *CBCA Regulations state that financial statements are to be prepared in accordance with the standards set out in the* **CICA Handbook**. This provision gives the *Handbook* a legal status, a fact that significantly contributes to the self-regulating nature of the Canadian accounting profession, as the authors of the *Handbook* are primarily members of the accounting profession. This privilege and responsibility of the profession does not exist in most other countries in which governmental influences are significant to the determination of accounting practices and standards.[6]

SHARE CAPITAL OR CAPITAL STOCK SYSTEM

The share capital of a corporation is generally made up of a large number of units or shares. For a given class of shares (stock), each share is exactly equal to every other share. Each owner's interest is determined by the number of shares possessed. If a company has only one class of stock divided into 1,000 shares, a person owning 500 shares controls one-half the ownership interest of the corporation; one holding 10 shares has a one-hundredth interest.

---

[5] The articles of incorporation must specify such things as the name of the company (which must use the word "Incorporated" or "Limited" or "Corporation" or its abbreviation or a French equivalent as part of the name), place of registered office, classes and any maximum number of shares authorized, restrictions on rights to transfer shares, number of directors, and any restrictions on the corporation's business.

[6] Chapter 1 examined the process by which Canadian accounting standards in the *CICA Handbook* are developed, and considered some of the implications to the profession resulting from the legal status conferred on the *CICA Handbook*.

Each share has certain rights and privileges that can be restricted only by provisions in the articles of incorporation. In the absence of restrictive provisions, each share carries the following **basic** or **inherent rights**:

1. To *share proportionately in profits and losses*.
2. To *share proportionately in management* (the right to vote at shareholder meetings).
3. To *share proportionately in corporate assets upon liquidation*.

In addition to these three rights, the CBCA allows a corporation to assign a **pre-emptive right** to any or all classes of shares through appropriate specification in the articles of incorporation. A pre-emptive right means that existing shareholders of a class of shares have a right to acquire additional shares of any new issue of that class in proportion to their existing holdings before the new issue of shares can be offered to others.

The pre-emptive right protects existing shareholders from involuntary dilution of ownership interest. Without this right, shareholders with a given percentage interest might find their interest reduced by the issuance of additional shares without their knowledge and at prices that were not favourable to them. Because assigning the pre-emptive right makes it inconvenient for a corporation to make large issuances of additional shares, as is frequently done when acquiring other companies, it has not been used by many corporations.

The great advantage of the share system is the ease with which an interest in the business may be transferred from one individual to another. Generally, individuals owning shares in a corporation may sell them to others at any time and at any price without obtaining the consent of the company or other shareholders. Each share is the personal property of the owner and may be disposed of at will.

The corporation is required to maintain a list or subsidiary ledger of shareholders as a basis for dividend payments, or issuance of share rights or voting proxies. A share or stock certificate book and a share or stock transfer book are included among the special corporate records involved in accounting for shares. A share certificate book is similar to a cheque-book in that printed share certificates are enclosed. A share transfer book simply tells who owns the shares at a given point in time. Obviously the corporation must be able to obtain at any time a list of the current shareholders so that dividend payments, notices of annual shareholder meetings, and voting proxies may be sent to the appropriate persons.

Because shares are frequently transferred, it is necessary for the corporation to revise the subsidiary ledger of shareholders periodically, generally in advance of every dividend payment or shareholders' meeting. As the number of shareholders grows, the need may develop for a more efficient system that can handle large numbers of share transactions. Also, the major stock exchanges require controls that the typical corporation finds uneconomic to provide. Thus many corporations avoid the problems concerned with handling share capital sales and transfers by engaging an organization that specializes in this type of work to serve as a **registrar and transfer agent**. Trust companies frequently serve in this capacity, keeping all the necessary records. The corporation is provided, upon request, with a list of registered shareholders for such purposes as mailing dividend cheques or voting proxies.

While a corporation's shares may be continuously traded in the stock market, only the amount received by the corporation when the shares were originally issued is reported on the financial statements as part of shareholders' equity.

VARIETY OF OWNERSHIP INTERESTS: COMMON AND PREFERRED SHARES

Corporations may issue shares of various classes. Each class would have specified rights, privileges, restrictions, and conditions attached to it as stated in the company's articles of incorporation. The CBCA simply refers to the possible existence of classes of shares without specifying what they should be called. Consequently, the name corporations give to different classes of shares can be varied.

Typical practice is to identify classes by a letter (i.e., Class A, Class B), followed by a brief description of the nature of rights or restrictions attached to each share in the class. However, the rights and restrictions of Class A shares for one corporation can be quite different from those of Class A shares for another corporation. Therefore, the only means by which one can identify the rights and restrictions of a class of shares for a particular corporation is to examine the description that applies to that class.

In every corporation, one class of shares must represent the basic ownership interest. This class is called common shares. **Common shares** are the residual corporate interest that bears the ultimate risk of loss and receives the benefits of success. They are guaranteed neither dividends nor assets upon dissolution, but common shareholders generally control the management of the corporation and tend to profit most if the company is successful. In the event that a corporation has only one authorized issue of shares, that issue is considered to be common shares, whether so designated or not.

To appeal to all types of investors, corporations may offer two or more share classes, each with different rights or privileges. The preceding section emphasized that each share of a given class has the same rights as other shares of the same class and that there are three rights inherent in every share (to share in profits, management, and assets upon liquidation). By specification in the articles of incorporation, certain of these rights may be sacrificed, usually in return for other special rights or privileges. We will be using the terms common shares and **preferred shares** in this book as a means to differentiate between basic ownership interest shares and shares that have specific privileges or restrictions regarding the rights identified in the previous section.

Preferred shareholders typically have a prior claim on earnings. They are assured a dividend, usually a stated amount, before any dividend may be distributed to the common shareholders. In return for this preference, the preferred shareholders may sacrifice the right to a voice in management or the right to share in profits beyond the stated amount.

A company may accomplish a variety of objectives by issuing more than one class of shares. For example, one company created two classes, A and B, when it decided to issue shares to the public several years ago. Both Class A and Class B participate equally (per share) in all dividend payments and have the same claim on assets on dissolution. The differences are that Class A is voting and Class B is not; Class B is traded publicly while Class A, which is "family owned," must be sold privately; and Class A shares are convertible, one for one, into Class B shares but not vice versa. By issuing two classes of shares, the Class A owners obtained a ready market for the company's shares and yet provided an effective shield against outside takeover.[7]

An additional example of the variety of shares that may be issued is provided by Rogers Communications Inc., which has nine series of preferred shares that vary in their terms of redemption, retraction, conversion, and dividend amounts. There are also two classes labelled as common shares—Class A, with voting rights, and Class B, without voting rights but which receive a minimum dividend before dividends may be paid on Class A shares.

LIABILITY OF SHAREHOLDERS

Shareholders of a corporation contribute cash, other property, or services to the enterprise in return for ownership shares. The amount invested in the enterprise is the extent of a shareholder's possible loss. That is, if the corporation sustains losses to such an extent

---

[7] Ironically, the voting class (which would necessarily be concerned about an unfriendly takeover) often gains the most if an acquisition does take place. That is, the acquirer is willing to pay a substantial premium for the voting shares, but not for the nonvoting ones.

that remaining assets are insufficient to pay creditors, no recourse can be held by the creditors against the personal assets of the individual shareholders. In a partnership or proprietorship, personal assets of the owners can be called upon to satisfy unpaid claims against the enterprise. Ownership interests in a corporation are legally protected against such a contingency; *the shareholders may lose their investment but they cannot lose more than their investment.*[8]

While the corporate form of organization grants the protective feature of limited liability to the shareholders, it also requires that withdrawal of the amount of shareholders' investment represented by amounts in share capital accounts not occur unless all prior claims on corporate assets have been paid. The corporation must maintain this capital until dissolution. Upon dissolution, it must satisfy all prior claims before distributing any amounts to the shareholders. In a proprietorship or partnership, the owners can withdraw amounts at will because all their personal assets may be called upon to protect creditors from loss.

Under the CBCA, all shares must be *without a nominal or par value*. This simply means that all proceeds from the corporation's issuance of shares must be credited to the appropriate share capital account.

Prior to the implementation of the CBCA, federally incorporated companies could have **par value** shares; some provincial acts continue to permit par value shares to be issued. Par value is simply an amount per share determined by the company's incorporators and stated as such in the articles of incorporation. From an accounting point of view, par value is the amount credited to the appropriate share capital account when shares are issued. This par value amount represents **legal capital**, an amount that cannot be used as a basis for dividend distributions. As an arbitrary amount designated by incorporators, par value has little to do with the market value of shares issued. Because shares with par value are a rapidly diminishing phenomenon for companies incorporated in Canada, the accounting for shares without par value is the focus of this book. However, since par value shares continue to have limited applicability in Canada and are common in many other countries, matters related to them are covered in Appendix 16A at the end of this chapter.[9]

FORMALITY OF PROFIT DISTRIBUTION

Generally, the directors of an enterprise (elected by shareholders) determine what is to be done with the additional net assets generated through profitable operations. Profits may be left in the business to permit expansion or merely to provide a margin of safety, or they may be withdrawn and divided among the owners. In a proprietorship or partnership, this decision is made by the owner or owners informally and requires no specific action. In a corporation, however, profit distribution is controlled by certain legal restrictions.

First, *no amounts may be distributed among the owners unless the corporate capital is maintained intact*. This reflects the presumption that sufficient net assets or security must be left in a corporation to satisfy the liability holders after any assets have been distributed to shareholders as dividends. Various tests of corporate solvency have been used over the years. Under the CBCA, dividends may not be declared or paid if there are reasonable grounds for believing that (1) the corporation is, or would be after the dividend,

---

[8] While share ownership in a corporation does provide limited liability, this advantage may be lost, particularly for smaller private corporations that have a single or few shareholders, because of contractual agreements. For example, a bank usually requires the owner of an owner-operated corporation to personally guarantee any loans by the bank to the corporation.

[9] *Financial Reporting in Canada—1995* reported that 18 of 300 companies surveyed in 1994 disclosed the existence of a par value or stated value (similar to par value) for one class of shares issued, often in circumstances where a company had many share classes outstanding. The United States is an example of a country that uses par value shares extensively.

unable to pay its liabilities as they become due; or (2) the realizable value of the corporation's assets would, as the result of the dividend, be less than the total of its liabilities and stated (legal) capital for all classes of shares.

Second, *distributions to shareholders must be formally approved by the board of directors and recorded in the minutes of their meetings*. As the top executive body in the corporation, the board of directors must make certain that no distributions are made to shareholders that are not justified by profits. Directors are generally held liable to creditors if liabilities cannot be paid because company assets have been illegally paid out to shareholders.

Third, *dividends must be in full agreement with the share capital provisions as to preferences, participation, and the like*. Once the corporation has created specific stipulations regarding the rights of various classes of shareholders, these stipulations must be observed.

CHARACTERISTICS OF PREFERRED SHARES

As previously stated, preferred shares are a special class of shares because they possess certain preferences or restrictions not possessed by common shares. The following characteristics are most frequently associated with preferred share issues:

OBJECTIVE 4
Describe and understand the major features of preferred shares.

- Preference as to dividends (rights regarding priority, and whether or not they are cumulative and/or participating).
- Preference as to assets in the event of liquidation.
- Convertible into common shares.
- Callable (redeemable) at the option of the corporation.
- Retractable at the option of the shareholder.
- Nonvoting.

NATURE OF RIGHTS IN PREFERRED SHARES

A corporation may attach whatever preferences or restrictions in whatever combination it desires to a preferred share issue so long as it does not violate its incorporation law. Also, more than one class of preferred shares may be issued by a company. The features that distinguish preferred from common shares may be of a more restrictive and negative nature than preferences; for example, the preferred shares may be nonvoting, noncumulative, and nonparticipating. Unless specifically prohibited, however, all of the inherent rights of ownership apply to preferred shares.

A dividend on shares without par value is usually expressed as a *specific dollar amount per share*. A *preference as to dividends is not an assurance that dividends will be paid*; it is merely assurance that the stated dividend applicable to the preferred shares must be paid before dividends can be paid on common shares.

In addition to a preference as to the priority of payment of dividends, various other features may be attributed to a class of preferred shares:

1. **Cumulative.** Dividends not paid in any year must be made up in a later year before any dividends can be distributed to common shareholders. If the directors fail to declare a dividend at the normal date for dividend action, the dividend is said to have been "passed." Any passed dividend on cumulative preferred shares constitutes a **dividend in arrears**. *Because no liability exists until the board of directors declares a dividend, a dividend in arrears is not recorded as a liability but is disclosed in a note to the financial statements.* (In common law, if the corporation articles are silent about the cumulative feature, preferred shares are considered to be cumulative.) Because a passed dividend is lost forever on noncumulative preferred shares, they are not attractive to investors and, consequently, are seldom issued.

2. **Participating.** Holders of participating preferred shares share proportionately with the common shareholders in any profit distributions beyond the prescribed amount. That is, $5 preferred shares, if fully participating, will receive not only their $5 return but also, after a proportional amount per share is paid to common shareholders, additional dividends at the same level as those paid to common shareholders. Also, participating preferred shares may not always be fully participating as described, but partially participating. For example, provisions may be made that $5 preferred shares will be participating up to a maximum total amount of $10 per share, after which they cease to participate in additional profit distributions. Although participating rights are not used very often, Rogers Communications Inc.'s Class B shares are entitled to an annual dividend of $.05 per share and then participate equally in dividends with Class A shares after the Class A shares have also been paid a $.05 per share dividend.

3. **Convertible.** The shareholders may, at their option, exchange their preferred shares for common shares at a predetermined ratio and specified time. The convertible preferred shareholder not only enjoys a prior claim on dividends but also has the option of converting into a common shareholder with unlimited participation in earnings. Convertible preferred shares have been widely used in the past two decades, especially in consummating business combinations, and are favoured by investors who are attracted by the preferred dividend feature and the possibility of sharing in the long-term success of the company. The accounting problems related to convertible securities are discussed in Chapter 18.

4. **Callable (redeemable).** The issuing corporation can call or redeem at its option the outstanding preferred shares at specified future dates and at stipulated prices. Many preferred issues are callable. The call or redemption price is ordinarily set slightly above the original issuance price. The callable feature permits the corporation to use the capital obtained through the issuance of such shares until the need has passed or it is no longer advantageous. The existence of a call price or prices tends to set a ceiling on the market value of the preferred shares unless they are convertible into common shares. When cumulative preferred shares are called for redemption, any dividends in arrears must be paid. For many decades some preferred share issues contained provisions for redemption at some future date through sinking funds or other means. More recently, some preferred share issues have provided for mandatory redemption within five or 10 years of issuance.

5. **Retractable.** Holders of retractable preferred shares may, at their option, have the issuing company buy them back, usually at a specified price and at a specified time.

Preferred shares are often issued instead of debt because a company's debt-to-equity ratio has become too high. In other instances, issuances are made through private placements with other corporations at a lower than market dividend rate because the acquiring corporation receives some tax advantages.

PREFERRED SHARES WITH DEBT CHARACTERISTICS

With the right combination of features (i.e., fixed return, no vote, redeemable), preferred shares may possess more of the characteristics of debt than of ownership equity. Preferred shares generally have no maturity date, but the preferred shareholder's relationship with the company may be terminated if the corporation exercises its call privileges. Despite these debt characteristics, preferred shares in the past have traditionally been accounted for as an equity instrument and reported in the shareholders' equity section of the balance sheet. This accounting emphasizes the legal form of such securities in that they do not have priority over claims of unsecured creditors, and payments to owners are likely to be governed by legal restrictions related to the solvency position of the corporation.

CICA Handbook Section 3860, "Financial Instruments—Disclosure and Presentation," released in 1995, requires a different approach to determining whether a financial instrument should be classified as a liability or equity item. This section requires companies to present financial instruments based on their economic substance rather than legal form. As such, preferred shares having the same characteristics as debt have to be presented in the balance sheet as debt rather than shareholders' equity, and dividends on these shares are treated as if they were interest expense. Gains and losses on the redemption and cancellation of such shares are reported in the income statement.

Section 3860 identifies the existence of a contractual obligation on the issuer's part to deliver cash or other financial asset to the holder as the critical feature in differentiating between a financial liability and an item of equity. If such a contractual obligation exists as when "a preferred share provides for mandatory redemption by the issuer for a fixed or determinable amount at a fixed or determinable future date or gives the holder the right to require the issuer to redeem the share at or after a particular date for a fixed or determinable amount, the instrument meets the definition of a financial liability and is classified as such."[10] Chapter 15 provides a more detailed consideration of these issues.

ACCOUNTING FOR THE ISSUANCE OF SHARES

From the preceding discussion it can be seen that a corporation obtains funds from its shareholders through a series of events and transactions. After establishing the authorized classes of shares in the articles of incorporation, the shares are offered for sale, contracts for sale are entered into, amounts paid for shares are collected, and the shares are issued. The accounting involved in this process is discussed under the following topics:

OBJECTIVE 5
Account for the issuance of shares for cash or receivables, in combination with the sale of other securities, and in nonmonetary transactions.

1. Accounting for shares without par value.

2. Accounting for shares sold on a subscription basis.

3. Accounting for shares issued in combination with other securities.

4. Accounting for shares issued in nonmonetary transactions.

5. Accounting for shares issued financed by company loans.

6. Accounting for expenses related to issuance.

ACCOUNTING FOR SHARES WITHOUT PAR VALUE

The CBCA requires that all authorized shares issued by companies incorporated under it be without par or nominal value, and that the stated capital account be credited for the fair value of the shares issued.[11] **Authorized shares** simply represent the classes and

---

[10] *CICA Handbook*, Section 3860, par. .22. A financial liability is defined in par. .05 as "any liability that is a contractual obligation: (i) to deliver cash or another financial asset to another party; or (ii) to exchange financial instruments with another party under conditions that are potentially unfavourable." As an equity instrument is defined as a residual interest in assets after deducting liabilities, the definition of equity is determined by the definition of a financial liability.

[11] The CBCA, in Section 26, subsection 3, states that, after November 8, 1977, shares issued in non-arm's-length transactions (in the meaning of that term in the Income Tax Act) may have the whole or any part of the consideration received in exchange added to the stated capital amounts for the shares of the class. As such, assigning an amount less than that deemed to be received for shares is possible under this Act, but the circumstances under which such a treatment would be permitted pertain to tax issues and occur infrequently. When this does happen, the excess of the amount received over the value assigned to the shares would be credited to a Contributed Surplus account.

nature of shares that a company is entitled to issue. These would be specified in its articles of incorporation. The CBCA allows but does not require a corporation to specify a number of authorized shares for each class.

Assume that Video Electronics Ltd. is incorporated under the CBCA with 10,000 authorized common shares without par value. No entry, other than a memorandum entry, need be made for the authorization as no economic transaction is involved. A memorandum entry or notation simply means that a Common Shares account would be created and the number of shares authorized (10,000) and their nature (without par value) would be noted. Entries into this account would be made as share transactions between the company and investors take place. By having such a notation in the account, one can readily determine the number of unissued but authorized shares by deducting the number issued from the authorized number.

When shares without par value are issued, the full amount of the proceeds received is credited to the appropriate share capital account. If 500 common shares of Video Electronics Ltd. are sold for cash at $10 each, the entry would be:

Cash	5,000	
Common Shares		5,000

If another 500 shares are sold at a later date for $11 per share, the entry would be:

Cash	5,500	
Common Shares		5,500

The price received for a share is governed by the marketplace. In determining market price, investors assess the share relative to other shares and financial instruments in terms of rights, future earnings, and risk.

Entries for the sale of preferred shares without par value are the same as illustrated for common shares except that a Preferred Shares account is credited. The accounts titled Common Shares or Preferred Shares may alternatively be titled Common Stock or Preferred Stock, or Class A Shares or Class B Shares if so designated.

SHARES SOLD ON A SUBSCRIPTION BASIS

The preceding discussion assumed that the shares were sold for cash, but they may also be sold on a **subscription basis**. MacMillan Bloedel Limited, Suncor Inc., and Falconbridge Ltd. serve as examples of companies that have had subscription or instalment issues. When shares are sold on a subscription basis, the full price is not received immediately. Normally only a partial payment is made initially, and the shares are not issued, nor rights associated with the shares given, until the full subscription price is received.

In some cases, **instalment receipts** are issued that trade on the stock exchanges. These represent partially paid shares whose owner on the date of record for the second (or later) instalment is required to pay the instalment due. When fully paid, the instalment receipts are withdrawn and common shares are issued. To enhance the marketability of the shares, some issues come with full dividend rights as soon as the first instalment is paid.

Accounting for Subscribed Shares. Two new accounts are used when shares are sold on a subscription basis. The first, **Common** (or **Preferred**) **Shares Subscribed**, indicates the corporation's obligation to issue shares upon payment of final subscription balances by those who have subscribed. This account thus signifies a commitment against the unissued capital shares. Once the subscription price is fully paid, the Common (or Preferred) Shares Subscribed account is debited and the Common (or Preferred) Shares account is credited. ***Shares Subscribed accounts are presented in the Shareholders' Equity section below the respective Common or Preferred Shares accounts.***

The second account, Subscriptions Receivable, indicates the amount yet to be collected before subscribed shares will be issued. Controversy exists concerning the presentation of Subscriptions Receivable on the balance sheet. Some argue that Subscriptions Receivable should be reported in the Current Asset section (assuming that payment on the receivable will be received within the operating cycle or one year, whichever is longer). They note that it is similar to Trade Accounts Receivable, but that it differs in conception. Trade Accounts Receivable grow out of sales transactions in the ordinary course of business; Subscriptions Receivable relate to the issuance of a concern's own shares and represent capital contributions not yet paid to the corporation.

Others argue that Subscriptions Receivable should be reported as a deduction from Common (or Preferred) Shares Subscribed in the Shareholders' Equity section. Their reasoning is based on a concern that doing otherwise may result in users of financial statements misunderstanding the share capital accounts (i.e., not realizing that some shares are only partially paid for), and the fact that subscribers cannot be forced to pay the unpaid balance of a subscription receivable.

It should be emphasized that there is no right answer to this classification issue. Judgement must therefore be exercised. In the United States, practice generally follows the contra-equity approach, which is required in reports to the Securities Exchange Commission. A similar rule does not exist in Canada.

The journal entries for handling shares sold on a subscription basis are illustrated by the following example. Lakehead Corp. offers 500 no-par value common shares on a subscription basis at a price of $20 per share. Various individuals accept the company's offer and agree to pay 40% down and the remaining 60% at the end of six months. At the date the subscriptions are received, the entries are:

Subscriptions Receivable	10,000	
Common Shares Subscribed		10,000
To record receipt of subscriptions for 500 shares.		

Cash	4,000	
Subscriptions Receivable		4,000
To record receipt of first instalment representing 40% of total due on subscribed shares.		

Assuming that Lakehead Corp. had 10,000 common shares authorized, and had previously issued 5,000 shares for a total of $75,000, the receivable and subscribed accounts after the subscription was received could be shown as follows using the contra-equity approach.

EXHIBIT 16-1 LAKEHEAD CORP.

PARTIAL BALANCE SHEET

Shareholders' Equity		
Share Capital		
Common shares, no-par value,		
10,000 authorized, 5,000 issued		$75,000
Common shares subscribed (500 shares)	$10,000	
Less: Subscriptions receivable	(6,000)	4,000
Total share capital		$79,000

Alternatively, the $6,000 subscription receivable could be shown as a current asset and the Common Shares Subscribed amount would be shown at the gross amount ($10,000) in Shareholders' Equity.

When the final payment is received and the shares are issued, the entries are:

Cash	6,000	
Subscriptions Receivable		6,000
To record receipt of final instalment on subscribed shares.		

Common Shares Subscribed	10,000	
Common Shares		10,000
To record issuance of 500 shares upon receipt of final instalment from subscribers.		

Defaulted Subscription Accounts. Sometimes a subscriber is unable to pay all instalments and defaults on the agreement. The question is then what to do with the balance of the subscription account as well as the amount already paid in. The answer depends on the terms of the subscription contract, corporate policy, and any applicable law of the jurisdiction of incorporation. The possibilities include returning the amount already paid by the subscriber (possibly after deducting some expenses), treating the amount paid as forfeited and therefore transferred to a Contributed Surplus account, or issuing shares to the subscriber equivalent to the number that previous subscription payments would have paid in full.

For example, assume that a subscriber to 50 Lakehead Corp. common shares defaulted on the final payment. If the subscription contract stated that amounts paid by a defaulting subscriber would be refunded, Lakehead Corp. would make the following entry when the default occurs, assuming the cash is paid at a later date:

Common Shares Subscribed	1,000	
Subscriptions Receivable		600
Due to Defaulting Subscriber		400
To record default on 50 shares subscribed for at $20 each and on which 40% had been paid and for which the subscriber will be given a refund.		

If the amount paid by the subscriber was forfeited, there would be a $400 credit to a Contributed Surplus—Forfeited Shares account instead of to the Due to Defaulting Subscriber account.

SHARES ISSUED IN COMBINATION WITH OTHER SECURITIES (LUMP SUM SALES)

Generally, corporations sell classes of shares separately from one another so that the proceeds relative to each class, and even relative to each lot, are known. Occasionally, two or more classes of securities are issued for a single payment or lump sum. It is not uncommon for more than one type or class of security to be issued in the acquisition of another company. The accounting problem in a lump sum issuance is to determine the allocation of the proceeds between the various classes of securities. The two methods of allocation available for accountants are (1) the proportional method, also called the relative market value method; and (2) the incremental method.

Proportional Method. If the fair market value or another sound basis for determining relative value is available for each class of security, *the lump sum received is allocated between the classes of securities on a proportional basis*—that is, the ratio of each to the total. For instance, if 1,000 common shares having a market value of $20 each and 1,000 preferred shares having a market value of $12 each are issued for a lump sum of $30,000, the allocation of the $30,000 between the two classes would be as shown in Exhibit 16-2.

EXHIBIT 16-2

Fair market value of common (1,000 × $20)		=	$20,000
Fair market value of preferred (1,000 × $12)		=	12,000
Aggregate fair market value			$32,000
Allocated to common:	$\frac{\$20,000}{\$32,000} \times \$30,000$	=	$18,750
Allocated to preferred:	$\frac{\$12,000}{\$32,000} \times \$30,000$	=	$11,250
Total allocation			$30,000

Incremental Method. In instances *where the fair market value of all classes of securities is not determinable, the incremental method may be used*. The market value of the securities is used as a basis for those classes that are known, and the remainder of the lump sum is allocated to the class for which the market value is not known. For instance, if 1,000 common shares having a market value of $20 each and 1,000 preferred shares having no established market value are issued for a lump sum of $30,000, the allocation of the $30,000 to the two classes would be as follows.

EXHIBIT 16-3

Lump sum receipt	$30,000
Allocated to common (1,000 shares × $20 fair market value)	20,000
Balance allocated to preferred	$10,000

If fair market value is not determinable for any of the classes of shares involved in a lump sum exchange, the allocation may have to be arbitrary. If it is known that one or more of the classes of securities issued will have a determinable market value in the near future, the arbitrary basis may be used with the intent to make an adjustment when the future market value is established. If a market value is unlikely to be determinable for any of the share classes in the near future, the shares involved may be left in a single account until a separate market value can be established.

SHARES ISSUED IN NONMONETARY TRANSACTIONS

It is not uncommon for a corporation to issue shares in exchange for property, services, or other forms of nonmonetary assets,[12] which raises a problem of valuation. *The general rule to be applied in such situations is the cost principle, which states that the transaction should be recorded at the fair market value of what is given up, or what is acquired, if the latter is clearer.*

If the fair market value of only the property or services received, or of only the shares issued, is determinable, it is used as the basis for recording the exchange. If both are readily determinable and the transaction is the result of an arm's-length exchange, there will probably be little difference in their fair market values. In such cases it should not matter which value is regarded as the basis for valuing the exchange. If the fair market value of the shares being issued and the property or services being received are not readily determinable, the value to be assigned is generally established by management or the board of

---

[12] *CICA Handbook*, Section 3830 covers the accounting for nonmonetary transactions. It defines monetary assets and liabilities as "money or claims to future cash flows, that are fixed or determinable in amount and timing by contract or other arrangement."

directors, usually with the assistance of independent appraisers. The use of book values as a basis of valuation for these transactions should be avoided, if at all possible.

When shares are issued for personal services provided by employees or outsiders, the fair value of the services as of the date of the contract for such services, rather than the date of issuance of the shares, should be the basis for valuation because the contract is viewed in an accounting sense as a subscription. In these exchanges, however, the fair market value of the shares issued may be more readily determinable.

The following illustrates how to record the issuance of 10,000 common shares for a patent under various circumstances:

1. The fair market value of the patent is not readily determinable but the fair market value of the shares is known to be $140,000.

Patent	140,000	
Common Shares		140,000

2. The fair market value of the shares is not readily determinable, but the fair market value of the patent is determined to be $150,000.

Patent	150,000	
Common Shares		150,000

3. Neither the fair market value of the share nor the patent is readily determinable. An independent consultant values the patent at $125,000, and the board of directors agrees with that valuation.

Patent	125,000	
Common Shares		125,000

Care should be taken in assigning fair market values to shares based on values established by previous sales. Large blocks of shares may trade at different values than a small number of shares, and share values change over time, making recent prices more relevant than those in the distant past.

In corporate law, the board of directors is granted the power to set the value of non-cash transactions. In some instances, this power has been abused. The issuance of shares for property or services has resulted in cases of overstated corporate capital through intentional overvaluation of the property or services received. The overvaluation of the shareholders' equity resulting from inflated asset values creates what is referred to as **watered stock**. The "water" can be eliminated from the corporate structure by writing down the overvalued assets.

If, as a result of the issuance of shares for property or services, the recorded assets are undervalued, **secret reserves** are created. A secret reserve may also be achieved by excessive depreciation or amortization charges, by expensing capital expenditures, by excessive write-downs of inventories or receivables, or by any other understatement of assets or overstatement of liabilities. An example of a liability overstatement is an excessive provision for estimated product warranties that correspondingly results in an understatement of owners' equity, thereby creating a secret reserve.

SHARES ISSUED FINANCED BY COMPANY LOANS

As will be discussed in Chapter 18, many companies provide stock option or stock appreciation plans to top management as part of their total compensation package. Other companies provide loans to individual managers or other employees to enable them to purchase company shares. The shares are pledged as security for the loans and often the annual dividend is sufficient to cover the interest charges on the loan. Because the shares are paid for by the company's own assets (until the loans are repaid), the outstanding receivables from the employees should be reported as a contra account to the capital stock account.[13]

Leon's Furniture Limited—Meubles Leon Ltée reports the balance owed by employees for share purchase loans in this manner as illustrated in the following excerpt from note 8 to their December 31, 1995 balance sheet:

EXHIBIT 16-4 LEON'S FURNITURE LIMITED-MEUBLES LEON LTÉE

8. Capital Stock

The company's capital stock consists of the following:

(*$ in thousands*)		1995		1994
Authorized				
Unlimited common shares				
Unlimited convertible, non-voting, series 1990 shares				
Unlimited convertible, non-voting, series 1994 shares				
Issued				
19,825,912 [1994-19,758,400] common shares	$	4,053	$	3,554
719,039 [1994-786,551] convertible, non-voting, series 1990 shares		5,321		5,820
78,150 [1994-89,400] convertible, non-voting, series 1994 shares		995		1,138
Less employee share purchase loans		(6,263)		(6,647)
	$	4,106	$	3,865

Costs of Issuing Shares

The costs associated with the acquisition of corporate capital from the issuance of securities include lawyers' fees, public accountants' fees, underwriters' fees and commissions, expenses of printing and mailing certificates and registration statements, clerical and administrative expenses of preparation, and costs of advertising the issue.

OBJECTIVE 6
Explain how to account for share issue costs.

While *CICA Handbook* Section 3610 identifies these costs as **capital transactions** and recommends that they be excluded from the determination of net income, in practice there are at least three methods of accounting for initial issue costs.

The first and predominantly used method treats issue costs as a reduction of the amounts paid in. This treatment, used in the United States, has the result of simply reducing the amount credited to the share capital account. This treatment is based on the premise that issue costs are unrelated to corporate operations and thus are not properly chargeable against earnings from operations; issue costs are viewed as a reduction of proceeds of the financing activity.

The second method treats issue costs as an organization cost that is charged neither to current earnings nor to corporate capital; such costs are capitalized and classified as a deferred charge. They would be amortized over an arbitrary time period not to exceed 40 years. This treatment is based on the premise that amounts paid in as invested capital should not be violated, and that issue costs benefit the corporation over a long period of time or so long as the invested capital is used. This method is also consistent with the accounting treatment accorded issue costs of debt.

The third method charges issue costs directly against retained earnings. This accomplishes the objectives of maintaining the total amount received for shares in share capital accounts and not charging issue costs against earnings from operations.

In addition to the costs of issuing shares, corporations annually incur costs for maintaining the shareholders' records and handling ownership transfers. These recurring costs, primarily registrar and transfer agents' fees, should be charged as expense to the period in which incurred.

---

[13] See *EIC-44* (CICA, April 20, 1993) for a fuller discussion of share purchase loans.

ACQUISITION BY A COMPANY OF ITS OWN SHARES

It is not unusual for corporations to buy back their own shares. Corporations first obtain approval for such action from the stock exchange on which the shares are listed, and then proceed to purchase their own shares. Imasco Limited, AGF Management, and Cogico Cable are examples of corporations that have acquired their own shares through buybacks.

Corporations purchase their outstanding shares for a variety of reasons. Rogers Communications Inc. bought a total of 14.2 million shares to reduce its foreign ownership so that it would not lose its eligibility for Canadian broadcasting licences. More general reasons for buybacks include:

- To have enough shares on hand to meet employee stock option contracts.
- To reduce the shares outstanding in hopes of increasing earnings per share.
- To buy out a particular ownership interest.
- To attempt to make a market in the company's shares.
- To reduce the operations of the business.
- To meet the share needs of a potential merger.
- To change the debt-to-equity ratio.
- To settle a debt.
- To provide a psychological boost to shareholders.
- To fulfil the terms of a contract.
- To satisfy a claim of a dissenting shareholder.
- To change from public to private corporation status.

Whether or not a corporation may purchase its own shares and what it may do with them depends on the terms and conditions of its articles of incorporation, and the legal constraints imposed by the Act under which it is incorporated and the stock exchange on which its shares are registered.

Assuming that a corporation may purchase or otherwise acquire its own shares, they may be either (1) retired (cancelled); or (2) held in treasury for reissue.

ACQUISITION AND RETIREMENT

OBJECTIVE 7
Account for the acquisition and cancellation of shares previously outstanding.

The CBCA and acts of various provinces permit a corporation to purchase or redeem its shares by special resolution of its board of directors as long as such an action would not result in the insolvency of the corporation. Insolvency under the CBCA would result if, after acquisition, the corporation was unable to pay its liabilities or if the realizable value of its assets was less than its liabilities and stated capital. *The CBCA generally requires that acquired shares be cancelled or, if the articles have an authorized limit on the number of shares, restored to the status of authorized but unissued shares.*

When shares are purchased or redeemed by the issuing corporation, it is likely that the price paid will differ from the amount received for the shares when they were issued. It would be incorrect to treat any differences as a gain or loss shown in the income statement, owing to the capital nature of the transaction.[14] Consequently, when shares are purchased or redeemed and cancelled, shareholders' equity accounts are adjusted. The accounts adjusted and the nature of the adjustments are specified in the *CICA Handbook* as follows:

> Where a company redeems its own shares, or cancels its own shares that it has acquired, and the cost of such shares is equal to or greater than their par, stated or assigned value, the cost should be allocated as follows:

---

[14] *CICA Handbook*, Section 3240, par. .06.

(a) To share capital, in an amount equal to the par, stated, or assigned value of the shares;

(b) Any excess, to contributed surplus to the extent that contributed surplus was created by a net excess of proceeds over cost on cancellation or resale of shares of the same class;

(c) Any excess, to contributed surplus in an amount equal to the pro rata share of the portion of contributed surplus that arose from transactions, other than those in (b) above, in the same class of shares;

(d) Any excess, to retained earnings.[15]

In the case where the cost to purchase shares is less than the par, stated, or assigned value, the cost is allocated as follows:

(a) To share capital in an amount equal to the par, stated, or assigned value of the shares;

(b) The difference, to contributed surplus.[16]

These specifications are written to apply to both par and no-par value shares. *For shares without par value, the amount of the acquisition cost to be charged against the share capital account is an assigned value equal to the average per share amount in the account for that class of shares at the transaction date.*[17]

For no-par value shares, acquisition and cancellation at a cost in excess of assigned value would, following the steps in the *Handbook*, normally result in simply debiting share capital Step (a) and retained earnings Step (d). Exceptions to this procedure would occur if a prior cancellation of some shares of this class had resulted in the creation of contributed surplus (that is, if the cost of the shares purchased was less than their assigned value at that earlier time) or if other contributed surplus accounts existed related to the same class of shares. In the former case, purchase for cancellation at a cost in excess of assigned value would result in a reduction of the Share Capital account for the assigned value Step (a), the Contributed Surplus account created by the prior transaction Step (b), and the Retained Earnings account if necessary Step (d).

In the latter case, the same step-by-step process is followed except that prior to debiting Retained Earnings for any residual in Step (d), other related Contributed Surplus accounts are reduced in proportion to the number of shares being cancelled relative to the total number outstanding before the redemption Step (c).

To illustrate the application of the accounting procedures for the purchase and cancellation of no-par shares, assume the following composition of shareholders' equity for Waterloo Corp. as a starting point.

EXHIBIT 16-5 WATERLOO CORP.

SHAREHOLDERS' EQUITY
December 31, 1997

Share capital:	
Class A, 10,500 shares issued and outstanding, no-par value	$ 63,000
Class B, 50,000 shares issued and outstanding, no-par value	100,000
Total share capital	$163,000
Retained earnings	300,000
Total shareholders' equity	$463,000

---

[15] *CICA Handbook*, Section 3240, par. .15.

[16] *Ibid.*, par. .17.

[17] *Ibid.*, par. .18.

On January 30, 1998, Waterloo Corp. purchased and cancelled 500 Class A shares at a cost of $4 per share. The required entry is:

Class A Shares [500($63,000/10,500)]	3,000	
Cash		2,000
Contributed Surplus—Excess of Assigned Value		
Over Acquisition Cost		1,000

This entry is derived by following the allocation procedure when the cost to purchase is less than the assigned value of shares cancelled.

On September 10, 1998, the company purchased and cancelled an additional 1,000 Class A shares. The purchase cost was $8 per share. This transaction is recorded as follows:

Class A Shares [1,000($60,000/10,000)]	6,000	
Contributed Surplus—Excess of Assigned		
Value Over Acquisition Cost	1,000	
Retained Earnings	1,000	
Cash		8,000

This entry is derived by following the steps for the situation where the cost of the shares purchased is greater than their assigned value. Specifically, the procedure is as follows:

Step (a): Remove from share capital the assigned value of the Class A shares cancelled. The assigned value is the amount in the Class A shares account ($60,000, which is the $63,000 on December 31 less the $3,000 debit for the acquisition on January 30) divided by the number of shares issued and outstanding (10,000, which is the 10,500 on December 31 less the 500 acquired on January 30) at the date of the transaction.

Step (b): If there is any contributed surplus arising from previous cancellations of the same share class (i.e., when the cost of purchased shares was less than their assigned value), it is reduced by a debit to that account. The amount debited is limited only by the account balance. (Contributed surplus accounts cannot have debit balances.) From the cancellation of Class A shares on January 30, 1998, such a Contributed Surplus account resulted in a $1,000 balance. Since the purchase cost of the present cancellation was $2,000 greater than the assigned value, the full $1,000 balance in this Contributed Surplus account is debited.

Step (c): If, after Steps (a) and (b), there is still an excess of cost to be accounted for, this excess is charged against any Contributed Surplus account—other than that in (b)—that arose from transactions in the same class of shares. The maximum that can be charged to such accounts is the pro rata share of the account balance. The pro rata share is determined by dividing the number of shares acquired by the number of shares issued prior to the acquisition and multiplying the result by the balance in the Contributed Surplus account. There are no such Contributed Surplus accounts in this example, and they would be rare in the case of no-par value shares (Contributed Surplus on Forfeited Shares would be an example). Such accounts exist for par value shares in which the proceeds received in excess of par value are credited to a Contributed Surplus account.

Step (d): Since there is still an excess of $1,000 after Steps (a) to (c), this amount is charged against Retained Earnings.

While this example illustrated calculations associated with all steps in the process, it would not be necessary to continue through steps beyond those required to allocate the total purchase cost of the shares cancelled. For example, if the cost had been only $6,700, the full amount would be accounted for by debiting the Class A Shares for $6,000 and the Contributed Surplus—Excess of Assigned Value Over Acquisition Cost account for $700. If there are no accounts in Contributed Surplus arising from transactions in the class of shares involved, Steps (b) and (c) would be omitted.

TREASURY SHARES

Treasury shares or treasury stock are a company's own shares that have been purchased but have not been cancelled—they are being held for reissue.

OBJECTIVE 8
Explain what treasury shares are and how to account for them under the single-transaction method.

While Canadian corporate law has allowed companies to issue redeemable preferred shares for some time, it was not until 1971 that corporations were permitted to purchase other types of their own shares. At that time, Ontario's incorporation act allowed for such transactions for the first time in a Canadian jurisdiction. Since then, the CBCA and provincial acts have allowed corporations to acquire their own shares. Legislation varies, however, in terms of what companies may do with such shares. As previously stated, the CBCA requires that purchased shares be cancelled and, if the articles limit the number of authorized shares, be restored to the status of authorized but unissued shares. Two exceptions allowed by the CBCA are (1) when acting in the capacity of a legal representative not receiving any beneficial interest from the shares; and (2) when such shares are held as security for purposes of ordinary business transactions that involve the lending of money.

Consequently, with rare exception, there can be no such thing as treasury shares for companies incorporated under the CBCA. Alternatively, many countries (e.g., the United States) and some provincial jurisdictions do permit such treasury shares to exist.[18] Clearport Petroleums Ltd. is an example of a Canadian company that has disclosed treasury shares. Treasury shares are considered to be issued shares, but because they are not outstanding in the hands of shareholders, voting rights and dividend declarations do not usually apply to them, nor are they included as outstanding in the calculation of earnings per share.

The *CICA Handbook* states that the **single-transaction method** should be used to account for treasury shares.[19] The presumption underlying this method is that the purchase and sale of treasury shares are essentially two parts of a single procedure being used by a corporation. In essence, the acquisition of treasury shares is the initiation of a transaction that is consummated when the shares are resold. Consequently, the holding by a company of its own shares is viewed as a transition phase between the beginning and end of a single activity.

When shares are purchased under the single-transaction method, the total cost is debited to a Treasury Shares account. There are no reductions of any individual shareholders' equity accounts. The balance in the Treasury Shares account is shown as a deduction from the total of the components of shareholders' equity in the balance sheet.[20] An example of such disclosure follows.

EXHIBIT 16-6

Shareholders' equity:	
Common shares, no-par value; authorized	
24,000,000 shares; issued 19,045,870 shares	
of which 209,750 are in treasury	$ 27,686,000
Retained earnings	253,265,000
Total	$280,951,000
Less: Cost of treasury shares (209,750 shares)	(7,527,000)
Total shareholders' equity	$273,424,000

---

[18] *Financial Reporting in Canada—1995* reported that of the 300 companies surveyed in 1994, nine disclosed the acquisition of their own common shares. Also, 30 companies disclosed cancellations of common shares purchased.

[19] *CICA Handbook,* Section 3240, pars. .10 and .11. Another method, called the two-transaction method, exists and is an acceptable alternative to the single-transaction method in other countries such as the United States. The presumption associated with the two-transaction method is that the purchase by a company of its own shares terminates the relationship between the company and the shareholder. Such an acquisition therefore represents a completed, independent transaction in terms of the company's capital. Essentially, the acquisition of shares under this method is recorded as if the shares were retired. A subsequent resale of the acquired shares is also viewed as a separate, independent transaction. Therefore, these two transactions (purchase and sale of shares) would be recorded independently of each other.

[20] *Ibid.,* par. .11.

When the shares are sold, the Treasury Shares account is credited for their cost. If they are sold for more than their cost, the excess is credited to a Contributed Surplus account. If they are sold at less than their cost, the difference is debited to any balance in a Contributed Surplus account resulting from the resale or cancellation of shares of the same class; any remaining difference is charged against Retained Earnings.[21]

To illustrate the accounting entries under the single-transaction method, assume as a starting point the information regarding the shareholders' equity of Waterloo Corp. as at December 31, 1997 as shown on page 799. Now assume that on January 15, 1998, the company acquired as treasury shares 1,000 Class A shares paying $7 per share. This would be recorded as follows:

Treasury Shares, Class A	7,000	
Cash		7,000

On February 15, 1998, all treasury shares were sold for $8 per share. The journal entry would be:

Cash	8,000	
Treasury Shares, Class A		7,000
Contributed Surplus—Excess of Sale Price of Class A Treasury Shares Over Cost		1,000

If the treasury shares recorded under the single-transaction method are subsequently retired (cancelled), then the procedure for cancelling shares is applied, with the balance in the Treasury Shares account being eliminated. For example, if Waterloo Corp. decided to cancel instead of sell the treasury shares on February 15, the entry would be:

Class A Shares	6,000	
Retained Earnings	1,000	
Treasury Shares, Class A		7,000

DISCLOSURE OF SHARE CAPITAL

OBJECTIVE 9
Know the requirements regarding disclosures for share capital.

The *CICA Handbook* recommends that various disclosures be made regarding a corporation's share capital. Basic disclosures regarding authorized share capital, issued share capital, and changes in share capital since the last balance sheet date are required.[22] Note disclosure is the usual means of meeting these requirements. In such notes, each share class is described in terms of:

(1) the authorized number of shares (or stating there is no authorized limit),

(2) the existence of unique rights (e.g., dividend preference and amount of such dividends, redemption and/or retraction privileges, conversion rights, whether or not they are cumulative),

(3) the number of shares issued and the amount received,

(4) if they are no-par value or par value shares,

(5) the amount of any dividends in arrears, and

(6) amounts and other details about changes during the year (e.g., new issuances, redemptions, and resale of treasury shares).

Section 3860 of the *Handbook*, in addition to making recommendations on the classification of equity instruments with debt characteristics, requires disclosure of any signifi-

---

[21] *CICA Handbook*, Section 3240, par. .20.

[22] *Ibid.*, pars. .02 to .05.

cant terms and conditions of equity instruments that might affect the amount, timing, and uncertainty of future cash flows.[23]

Exhibit 16-7 provides an example of note disclosure regarding share capital. This note was cross-referenced to the Capital Stock section of Shareholders' Equity in Loblaw's December 30, 1995 balance sheet, which simply contained two line items—one for total preferred shares and the other for total common shares.

EXHIBIT 16-7 LOBLAW COMPANIES LIMITED

NOTES TO CONSOLIDATED FINANCIAL STATEMENTS
52 Weeks Ended December 30, 1995

9. Capital Stock

	Number of shares issued			Paid-up-capital (in millions of dollars)		
	1995	1994	1993	**1995**	1994	1993
First preferred shares						
First series	**432,752**	437,952	439,652	**$ 21.6**	$ 21.9	$ 22.0
Second preferred shares						
Fourth series		120	120		60.0	60.0
Total preferred shares	**432,752**	438,072	439,772	**21.6**	81.9	82.0
Common shares	**80,039,946**	79,821,346	79,425,426	**236.6**	232.8	228.1
Total capital stock				**$258.2**	$314.7	$310.1

Share Description:

First preferred shares (authorized – 1,000,000) First series – $2.40 cumulative dividend redeemable at $50.

Second preferred shares (authorized – unlimited) Fourth series – cumulative dividend with a fixed rate of 7.75% to March 1, 1995. These shares were redeemed according to their terms at $500,000 each on March 1, 1995.

Common shares (authorized – unlimited) In 1995, the Company issued 218,600 (1994 – 395,920) common shares for cash consideration of $3,782,084 (1994 – $4,672,814) on exercise of employee stock options.

As at December 30, 1995, there were outstanding stock options, which were granted at the market price on the day preceding the grant, to purchase 2,840,990 common shares at prices ranging from $15.50 to $23.375 with a weighted average price of $21.02. In 1995, stock options for 45,500 shares were cancelled. Options expire on dates ranging from March 8, 1997 to December 17, 2000, with no options expiring in 1996.

The exercise of the stock options would not materially dilute net earnings per common share.

Chapter 17 continues the study of shareholders' equity by covering the accounting requirements for the other components of this major accounting element, primarily that of retained earnings.

[23] *CICA Handbook,* Section 3860, par. .52.

NOT EVERYTHING IN BLACK AND WHITE MAKES SENSE

The accounting treatment of shareholders' equity items varies greatly among countries, as does the manner in which they are presented in annual reports. Not only does the appearance differ: concepts underlying the accounting methods can differ, as does much of the terminology. The following excerpt is from the *Group Balance Sheet* as included in the *Report and Accounts* of **Guinness PLC** for 1996:

EQUITY

	Notes	1996 £m	1995 £m
Capital and Reserves			
Called up share capital	21(B)	483	506
Share premium account	21(B)	590	569
		1,073	1,075
Other reserves	22(A)	2,141	2,069
Profit and loss account	22(A)	2,236	2,440
Goodwill	22(B)	(1,298)	(1,298)
Shareholders' funds		4,152	4,286
Minority Interest (equity)		95	111
Total Equity		4,247	4,397

Presentation under the rules of the United Kingdom and Ireland differs in several important respects from Canadian accounting pronouncements. *Called up share capital* and the *share premium account* have counterparts in Canadian financial reports. However, the term reserve is no longer used in Canadian practice, yet is widely used in other countries to refer to items of equity arising from a variety of sources. In Britain, disclosure of certain, specified reserves is required, under the Companies Act. These include, for example, the *profit and loss account, other reserves,* and (in certain cases) a *goodwill reserve.*

For **Guinness PLC**, the category *other reserves* includes:

- a *Revaluation Reserve,* arising from restatement of various balance sheet items, in accordance with alternative accounting rules as provided under the Act;

- a *Capital Redemption Reserve,* being the nominal value of shares reacquired by the company from shareholders, in accordance with Companies Act provisions; and

- a *Merger Reserve,* an alternative to a share premium account, credited when shares are issued in a merger, and the fair value exceeds the nominal value of those shares.

The term *profit and loss account,* nomenclature considered archaic in Canada, is required under the British Companies Act; this item is analogous to the retained earnings account in Canadian practice. The *Goodwill* reserve, with a debit balance, arises from intercorporate investments. For Guinness PLC, this amount is not amortized. In Canada, such an amount would be carried as an asset and systematically amortized to income in accordance with *CICA Handbook* provisions.

Even a cursory examination of a foreign financial statement will indicate that differences from Canadian practice are both widespread and possibly difficult to understand. Provisions of the *CICA Handbook* apply within Canada, but have no applicability beyond Canadian jurisdiction. The applicable rules and other reference sources must be consulted to fully understand reports prepared elsewhere.

Contributed by: Peter Secord, St. Mary's University

Summary of Learning Objectives

1. **Understand the nature of shareholders' equity and know its key components or sources.** Shareholders' equity represents that portion of a company's assets that accrues to its owners. It is a residual interest, and is comprised primarily of amounts contributed by shareholders and the undistributed increase in net assets due to profitable operations.

2. **Know and be able to discuss the characteristics of the corporate form of organization.** A corporation is a separate legal entity operating under the provisions of federal or provincial or territorial companies' legislation. Ownership of a corporation is evidenced by shares carrying basic rights; various classes of shares may exist, each with specific rights and restrictions. Shareholders' liability to others outside the entity is limited to their ownership interest in the corporation.

3. **Identify the rights of shareholders.** The basic rights of shareholders are to have proportionate voting rights at shareholder meetings and to share proportionately in profits (and losses) and in the residual assets at dissolution.

4. **Describe and understand the major features of preferred shares.** Preferred shares have preference over common shares in relation to their interest in profits and residual assets on dissolution. Preferred shares may be converted into common shares and be retracted or redeemed at the holder's option. They may be nonvoting and may be called or redeemed at the company's option.

5. **Account for the issuance of shares for cash or receivables, in combination with the sale of other securities, and in nonmonetary transactions.** The cost principle applies in recording the issuance of shares; that is, recognize the transaction at the fair value of what is given up (the shares) or what is acquired, if clearer. Where amounts remain owing to the company for the purchase of shares, the share capital should be reported net of amounts receivable. In this way, shareholders' equity is increased only by the increase in the company's assets.

6. **Explain how to account for share issue costs.** Share issue costs can be treated as a reduction of the amounts paid in for the shares, deferred as an organization cost and amortized, or charged directly against retained earnings. Recognition of share issue costs as a capital transaction precludes the second option.

7. **Account for the acquisition and cancellation of shares previously outstanding.** When shares are acquired at a price less than their par, stated, or assigned value and are subsequently cancelled, the "gain" is recorded as an item of contributed surplus. Where the acquisition price exceeds the par, stated, or assigned value, the "loss" first is charged against any previously recorded "gain" in the same class of shares in contributed surplus; second, the "loss" reduces on a proportionate basis any other contributed surplus accounts related to the same class of shares; and third, if any "loss" remains to be absorbed, it is charged against retained earnings.

KEY TERMS

articles of incorporation, 785

authorized shares, 791

basic rights, 786

callable, 790

Canada Business Corporations Act, 785

capital, 783

capital stock, 783

capital transactions, 797

certificate of incorporation, 785

CICA Handbook, 785

common shares, 787

common shares subscribed, 792

contributed capital, 783

contributed surplus, 783

convertible, 790

Crown corporations, 784

cumulative, 789

dividend in arrears, 789

earned capital, 783

inherent rights, 786

instalment receipts, 792

legal capital, 788

not-for-profit corporations, 784

owners' equity, 782

participating, 790

par value, 788

pre-emptive right, 786

preferred shares, 787

preferred shares subscribed, 792

privately held corporations, 784

profit-oriented corporations, 784

8. **Explain what treasury shares are and how to account for them under the single-transaction method.** Treasury shares are a company's own shares that have been purchased and not cancelled. They are *issued*, but not *outstanding* shares. Treasury shares are accounted for in a separate "inventory of treasury shares" account that is debited for the cost of treasury shares purchased and credited for the cost of treasury shares subsequently resold. None of the original capital stock accounts are affected by the purchase of treasury shares. "Gains" are reported as items of contributed surplus, and "losses" are charged first against contributed surplus accounts resulting from the resale or cancellation of shares of the same class and then to retained earnings.

9. **Identify the disclosure requirements for share capital.** Disclosure requirements for share capital ensure that readers are informed of the rights and restrictions associated with each class of share and the activity in each shareholders' equity account over the reporting period.

APPENDIX 16A

Accounting for Par Value Shares

As indicated in the chapter, par value is an arbitrary amount per share determined by the incorporators of a company and stated as such in the articles of incorporation. When a par value exists today, it is usually very low ($1, $5, $10 per share), which contrasts dramatically with the situation in the early 1900s when practically all shares had a par value of $100. The reason for having low par values is to permit the original sale of shares at low amounts per share and to avoid the contingent liability of shareholders associated with shares sold below par. Shares with a low par value are rarely, if ever, sold by the issuing company below par value (i.e., at a discount). Indeed, such an action is generally not permitted in Canadian jurisdictions allowing for par value shares. A par value has nothing to do with the market value of the share. The accounting significance of par value is that it is the amount per share issued that is credited to the Share Capital account. Amounts received above par value are credited to other accounts, as will be illustrated shortly.

Par value shares were common in Canada prior to the mid-1980s. In 1975, the Canada Business Corporations Act (CBCA) decreed that par value shares were no longer permitted for companies incorporated under it. Such enterprises had five years from January 1, 1976 to file for continuance under the CBCA—that is, to switch from the requirements of the predecessor Canada Corporations Act to those of the CBCA. Most provincial incorporation acts followed the example of the CBCA in requiring that share capital be of no-par value. The development of consistent regulations across all Canadian jurisdictions and the necessary conversion by companies from old to new requirements have taken considerable time. *Financial Reporting in Canada—1995* indicates that in 1994, of the 300 companies surveyed, 112 disclosed that all share classes were without par value, 18 disclosed a par value (or a stated value) for at least one class of shares, 26 indicated no-par value for one share class with no reference to other classes, and 144 made no reference to either par or no-par value. The large number making no reference to par or no-par value was stated to be a reflection of the fact that certain corporations acts require all shares to be without par value. Consequently, it would appear safe to conclude that Canadian corporations predominantly issue shares without par value, although some still have par value shares.

While the authors have chosen to follow the CBCA requirements regarding the issuance of shares without par value throughout this book, they recognize that some may wish to consider the accounting aspects related to par value shares to a greater extent than is possible from the limited references to it in the chapter. Also, a more comprehensive examination of such accounting may be beneficial to understanding financial statements that incorporate par value shares (i.e., those of companies that operate in jurisdictions permitting par value, or are incorporated in countries such as the United States that permit par value shares). For these reasons, we have provided the material in this appendix. Accounting for par value shares is examined under the following headings:

- Issuance of par value shares for cash.
- Par value shares sold on a subscription basis.
- Acquisition and retirement of par value shares.
- Treasury shares having a par value.

ISSUANCE OF PAR VALUE SHARES FOR CASH

OBJECTIVE 10
Account for the issue and reacquisition of par value shares.

To show the required information for issuance of par value shares, accounts must be kept for each class of shares as follows:

1. **Preferred Shares or Common Shares.** Reflects the par value of the corporation's issued shares. These accounts are credited for the par value when the shares are originally issued. No additional entries are made in these accounts unless additional shares are issued or shares are retired.

2. **Contributed Surplus in Excess of Par or Premium on Common (or Preferred) Shares.** Indicates any excess over par value paid by shareholders in return for the shares issued to them. Once paid, the excess over par becomes a part of the corporation's contributed surplus and the individual shareholder has no greater claim on the excess paid than all other holders of the same class of shares.

To illustrate how these accounts are used, assume that Hamilton Corporation sold 100 common shares with a par value of $5 per share for a total of $1,100. The entry to record the issuance is as follows.

Cash	1,100	
Common Shares		500
Contributed Surplus in Excess of Par		600
(or Premium on Common Shares)		

While this entry reflects the receipt of cash for the shares, such shares could be issued in combination with other securities (lump sum sales) or for noncash consideration. In such situations, the basic issue is to determine the amount (fair value) received for the shares. Solutions to these issues are the same as those stated in the chapter regarding shares without par value. Once the amount received for par value shares has been determined, the appropriate Share Capital account is credited for its par value and the excess is credited to a Contributed Surplus account.

PAR VALUE SHARES SOLD ON A SUBSCRIPTION BASIS

The journal entries for handling par value shares sold on a subscription basis are illustrated by the following example. Mercury Ltd. offers 500 common shares of $5 par value on a subscription basis at a price of $20 per share. Various individuals accept the company's offer and agree to pay 50% down and the remaining 50% at the end of six months.

At date of subscription

Subscriptions Receivable	10,000	
Common Shares Subscribed		2,500
Contributed Surplus in Excess of Par		7,500
To record receipt of subscriptions for 500 shares.		

Cash	5,000	
Subscriptions Receivable		5,000
To record receipt of first instalment representing 50% of total due on subscribed shares.		

When the final payment is received and the shares are issued, the entries are:

Six months later

Cash	5,000	
Subscriptions Receivable		5,000
To record receipt of final instalment on subscribed shares.		

Common Shares Subscribed	2,500	
Common Shares		2,500
To record issuance of 500 shares upon receipt of final instalment from subscribers.		

ACQUISITION AND RETIREMENT FOR PAR VALUE SHARES

To illustrate accounting procedures for the purchase and cancellation of par value shares, we will draw upon the Waterloo Corp. example presented on page 799 regarding the acquisition and retirement of no-par value shares.. This will allow for comparison of accounting between par value and no-par value shares. Two modifications to the original shareholders' equity section are made: Class A shares issued for $63,000 had a $5 par value resulting in a **Premium on Class A Shares**, which is a Contributed Surplus account. Therefore, the starting point for this par value shares illustration is as follows:

EXHIBIT 16A-1   WATERLOO CORP.

SHAREHOLDERS' EQUITY

December 31, 1997

Share capital	
Class A, 10,500 shares issued and outstanding, $5 par value	$ 52,500
Class B, 50,000 shares issued and outstanding, no-par value	100,000
Total share capital	$152,500
Contributed surplus	
Premium on Class A shares	10,500
Retained earnings	300,000
Total shareholders' equity	$463,000

On January 30, 1998, Waterloo Corp. purchased and cancelled 500 Class A shares. The purchase cost was $4 per share. The required entry would be:

Class A Shares (500 × $5)	2,500	
Cash		2,000
Contributed Surplus—Excess of Par Value Over		
Acquisition Cost, Class A		500

This entry is derived by following the *CICA Handbook* allocation procedure as identified in Chapter 16 when the cost to purchase is less than the par value of shares cancelled.

On September 10, 1998, the company purchased and cancelled an additional 1,000 Class A shares at a cost of $8 each. This transaction would be recorded as:

Class A Shares (1,000 × $5)	5,000	
Contributed Surplus—Excess of Par Value Over		
Acquisition Cost, Class A	500	
Contributed Surplus—Premium on Class A Shares	1,050	
Retained Earnings	1,450	
Cash		8,000

This entry is derived by following the steps in the *CICA Handbook* for situations where the cost of the shares purchased is greater than their par or assigned value. Specifically, the procedure is as follows:

Step (a): Remove from share capital the par value of the Class A shares cancelled. This is equal to the par value ($5) multiplied by the number of shares cancelled (1,000).

Step (b): If there is any contributed surplus arising from previous cancellations of the same share class (i.e., when the cost of purchased shares was less than their par value), it is reduced by a debit to that account. The amount is the lesser of the account's total balance or the amount by which the purchase cost exceeds the par value of the cancelled shares. From the cancellation of Class A shares on January 30, 1998, such a Contributed Surplus account resulted in a $500 balance. Since the purchase cost of the present cancellation was $3,000 greater than the par value, the Contributed Surplus account is debited for the full $500 balance. Contributed surplus accounts cannot have debit balances.

Step (c): If, after Steps (a) and (b), there is still an excess of cost to be accounted for, the excess is charged against any Contributed Surplus account—other than that in (b)—that arose from transactions in the same class of shares. In this example, Premium on Class A Shares is such an account. The maximum that can be charged to such an account is a pro rata portion of the account balance. The pro rata share is determined by dividing the number of shares purchased (1,000) by the number of shares issued prior to the purchase (10,500 from December 31 less 500 retired on January 30 equals 10,000) and multiplying the result (0.1) by the balance in the Premium account ($10,500). This maximum amount so determined of $1,050 is debited to the Premium on Class A Shares account, because there is an excess of cost over allocations made in Steps (a) and (b) of $2,500.

Step (d): Since there is still an excess of $1,450 of the cost over allocations made in Steps (a), (b), and (c), this amount is charged against Retained Earnings.

If the cost to acquire the shares had been only $5,300, the full amount would be accounted for by debiting the Class A Shares for $5,000 and the Contributed Surplus—Excess of Par Value Over Acquisition Cost account for $300.

TREASURY SHARES HAVING A PAR VALUE

The basic concepts of accounting for treasury shares under the single-transaction method were specified in Chapter 16 and continue to apply for par value shares. Again, for purposes of comparison between par value and no-par value shares accounting, the example of the Shareholders' Equity section of Waterloo Corp. at December 31, 1997 is used as a starting point. The events related to treasury share transactions are:

January 15, 1998—The company acquired 1,000 treasury shares of Class A $5 par value shares by paying $7 per share.

February 15, 1998—The treasury shares were sold for $8 per share.

Using the single-transaction method, the following entries would be made:

January 15

Treasury Shares, Class A	7,000	
Cash		7,000

February 15

Cash	8,000	
Treasury Shares, Class A		7,000
Contributed Surplus—Excess of Sale Price		
of Class A Treasury Shares Over Cost		1,000

If the treasury shares were reissued on February 15 for less than their cost of $7 per share, the deficiency would be charged first against any Contributed Surplus from the resale or cancellation of the same class of shares, and then to Retained Earnings.

If, instead of selling the treasury shares on February 15, Waterloo Corp. used the single-transaction method to record the purchase and then decided to cancel them, the entry at the time of that decision would be:

Class A Shares	5,000	
Premium on Class A Shares	1,000*	
Retained Earnings	1,000	
Treasury Shares, Class A		7,000

*Pro rata share allocation = (1,000 shares/10,500 shares) × $10,500 = $1,000

Summary of Learning Objective for Appendix 16A

10. Account for the issue and reacquisition of par value shares. When par value shares are issued (or subscribed for), the proceeds must be allocated between the legal capital account, Common (or Preferred) Shares, and an account that accumulates the amount received in excess of the shares' par value. This latter account is a contributed surplus account commonly referred to as Premium on Common (or Preferred). Entries to record the acquisition and retirement of par value shares and to account for treasury shares follow the same steps identified in the chapter for no-par value shares. The major difference in the case of par value shares is that it is likely there will be a Contributed Surplus account to absorb, on a pro rata basis, any "loss" on cancellation of the shares.

KEY TERMS

premium on shares, 809

Note: Any *asterisked* Exercises, Problems or Cases, relate to material in the appendix to the chapter.

EXERCISES

(Recording the Issuance of Common and Preferred Shares) Aaronville Corporation was organized on January 1, 1998. It was authorized to issue 10,000 shares of $8 dividend, no-par value preferred shares, and 500,000 no-par common shares. The following share transactions were completed during the first year.

E16-1

January	10	Issued 80,000 common shares for cash at $3 per share.
March	1	Issued 5,000 preferred shares for cash at $108 per share.
April	1	Issued 24,000 common shares for land. The asking price of the land was $90,000; the fair market value of the land was $80,000.
May	1	Issued 80,000 common shares for cash at $7 per share.
August	1	Issued 10,000 common shares to attorneys to pay their bill of $50,000 for services rendered in organizing the company.
September	1	Issued 10,000 common shares for cash at $9 per share.
November	1	Issued 1,000 preferred shares for cash at $112 per share.

Instructions

Prepare the journal entries to record the above transactions.

*E16-2 **(Subscribed Shares: No-Par Value and Par Value Shares)** Joe Sharron Inc. intends to sell shares to raise additional capital to allow for expansion in the rapidly growing service industry. The corporation decides to sell the shares through a subscription basis, and publicly notifies the investment world. The stock is no-par value and 30,000 shares are offered at $25 a share. The terms of the subscription are 40% down and the balance at the end of six months. All shares are subscribed for during the offering period, and all collections are made as anticipated.

Instructions

(a) Give the journal entries for the original subscription, the collection of the down payments, the collection of the balance of the subscription price, and the issuance of the common shares.

(b) Prepare all required journal entries assuming the shares were $10 par value instead of no-par value shares.

E16-3 **(Shares Issued for Nonmonetary Assets)** Jibbeau Products Inc. was formed to operate a manufacturing plant in Gentown. The events for the formation of the corporation include the following:

1. 5,000 no-par common shares were issued to investors at $20 per share.

2. 8,000 common shares were issued to acquire used equipment, which had a depreciated book value to the seller of $120,000.

3. In order to attract the manufacturing plant to Gentown and stimulate employment in the area, the town council agreed to convey title to land and a building to Jibbeau. In return, Jibbeau agreed to sign a $75,000 mortgage contract for these assets. The fair market value of the land was $45,000 and $90,000 for the building.

Instructions

Prepare journal entries to record the above transactions.

E16-4 **(Subscribed Shares with Defaulting Subscriber)** On January 1, 1998, Eggson Inc. received authorization to issue an additional 40,000 common shares of no-par value. Subscribers have contracted to purchase all the shares at the subscription price of $100 per share with terms of 30% down in cash and the remaining 70% at the end of six months.

Instructions

(a) Give Eggson's journal entry for the situation above on the date of subscription.

(b) Assume that John Blue has subscribed to 200 of the shares but defaults after paying his 30% down payment. Assume also that the subscription contract affords the subscriber the right to receive shares on a pro rata basis in the event of default. Give Eggson's journal entry for the disposition of the balances in the accounts related to Mr. Blue.

E16-5 **(Subscribed Shares with Defaulting Subscriber)** Binney Corp. is authorized to issue 300,000 no-par value common shares. On November 30, 1997, 60,000 shares were subscribed for at $33 per share. A 25% down payment was made on the subscribed shares. On January 30, 1998, the balance due on the subscribed shares was collected, except for a subscriber of 5,000 shares who defaulted on her subscription. The 5,000 shares were sold on February 28, 1998 at $36 per share and the defaulting subscriber's down payment was returned.

Instructions

Prepare the required journal entries for the transactions above.

E16-6 **(Lump Sum Sale of Shares with Bonds)** The Van Ross Corp. sells units of its equity. Each unit consists of a $500 maturity value, 12% debenture bond and 10 of the company's common no-par shares. Van Ross has issued 10,000 units, with the investment broker retaining 400 units as the underwriting fee. The remaining 9,600 units were sold to investors for cash of $950 per unit. Prior to this sale the two-week average asking price of common was $40 per share. The 12% interest is a reasonable yield for the debentures.

Instructions

(a) Prepare the journal entry to record the above transaction by employing:

1. The incremental method, assuming the interest rate on the debentures is the best market measure.

2. The proportional method.

(b) In your opinion, which is the better method? Explain.

(Lump Sum Sale of Common and Preferred Shares) Kelly Corp. was organized with 50,000 preferred shares of no-par value, $9 dividend, and 100,000 no-par value common shares. During the first year, 1,000 preferred shares and 1,000 common shares were issued for a lump sum price of $180,000.

E16-7

Instructions
What entry should be made to record this transaction under each of the following independent conditions?
(a) Shortly after the transaction described above, 500 preferred shares were sold at $115.
(b) The market value per common share was $75.
(c) At the date of issuance, the preferred shares had a market price of $136 each and the common shares had a market price of $46 each.

(Lump Sum Sale of Par Value Shares) Assume the same situation as described in E16-7 except that the preferred shares are $100 par value and the common shares have a $10 par value each.

E16-8*

Instructions
Prepare the journal entries to record the lump sum sale of the preferred and common shares for $180,000 under each of the independent conditions described above.

(Share Issuances, Issuance Costs, and Repurchase) Carras Corporation is authorized to issue 50,000 no-par value common shares. During 1998, the company's first year of operation, Carras took part in the following transactions:

E16-9 ⁓

1. Issued 5,000 shares at $45 per share, less costs related to the issuance of the shares totalling $7,000.
2. Issued 1,000 shares for land appraised at $50,000. The shares were actively traded on a national stock exchange at approximately $46 per share on the date of issuance. Carras paid $300 in connection with the issue of these shares.
3. Purchased 500 shares at $46 per share and restored them to the status of authorized but unissued shares.

Instructions
(a) Prepare journal entries to record the above transactions, assuming the issue costs are treated as a reduction of amounts paid in for the shares.
(b) Prepare journal entries to record the above transactions, assuming the issue costs are treated as organization costs.
(c) Discuss the subsequent accounting treatment of the organization costs recorded in (b).

(Substance of a Preferred Share Issue) Crush Corporation acquired all of the common shares of Brush Inc. through the issuance of Series A preferred shares valued at $400 per share. The Series A indenture provides the following: no-par value and dividends of $35 per share, payable annually. The issue is cumulative, nonparticipating, preferred over common shares and other preferred share series as to both dividends and assets. The shares are nonvoting and not convertible to common shares but are callable at the discretion of the board of directors and must be redeemed at $400 plus any cumulative dividends in arrears by the end of year 10.

E16-10

Instructions
(a) Should this issue of preferred shares be reported as a liability or as equity? Substantiate your response.
(b) Provide partial financial statements indicating where and how Crush Corporation should report the shares and dividends.

(Effect of Treasury Share Transactions on Financial Statements) At December 31, 1997, Horne Company has 40,000 no-par value common shares outstanding, which were issued at an average price of $30 per share. The only other shareholders' equity account is retained earnings.
  The following transactions took place during 1998.

E16-11 ⁓

1. Purchased 5,000 treasury shares at $34 per share.
2. Sold 2,000 of the treasury shares at $35 per share.
3. Sold 500 of the treasury shares at $33 per share.
4. Retired the remaining treasury shares.

Instructions
(a) Prepare journal entries to record the treasury stock transactions.
(b) Complete the following table, indicating the effect of each transaction on the financial statement categories provided. Use **I** for Increase, **D** for Decrease, and **NE** for No Effect.

Item	Assets	Liabilities	Owners' Equity	Share Capital	Other Contributed Capital	Retained Earnings
(1)						
(2)						
(3)						
(4)						

E16-12   **(Reacquisition and Subsequent Sale of Shares)** Vogue Ltd. has outstanding 35,000 no-par value common shares, all of which had been issued at $25 per share. On July 5, 1998, Vogue purchased 1,000 of these shares at $39 per share.

Instructions

(a) Assuming the company is incorporated under the Canada Business Corporations Act, what entry would be made on July 5 to record the acquisition?

(b) Assuming the acquired shares were to be held as treasury shares, what entry would be made on July 5 under Canadian GAAP?

(c) Vogue Ltd., after having purchased its shares on July 5, 1998 and accounted for them as in (b), sold the shares on July 30, 1998. What entries would be made under the single-transaction method if these treasury shares were sold for $42 per share? for $33 per share?

E16-13   **(Employee Share Purchase Plan)** The Kingmore Company has developed a strategic plan aimed at increasing its market share, reducing its production costs, and increasing employee satisfaction. Among other initiatives, Kingmore introduced an employee share purchase plan whereby each of its 120 employees is eligible to borrow money from the company to finance up to 90% of the cost of their purchase of Kingmore Company shares. The loans are repayable in five equal annual instalments beginning one year after the share purchase.

On June 30, 1998, 79 employees each acquired 100 newly issued no-par value common shares at a price of $36 per share. Under the terms of the share purchase plan, the company advanced, by way of loan, 90% of the purchase price to these employees.

Instructions

Assuming the company had 426,000 common shares outstanding before this transaction at an average issue price of $30 per share, prepare the Share Capital section of Kingmore Company's balance sheet after the June 30, 1998 transaction.

E16-14   **(Balance Sheet Presentation of Shareholders' Equity)** Aragonite Corporation's articles authorized 100,000 common shares of no-par value, and 30,000, $6 dividend, cumulative and nonparticipating preferred shares of no-par value. Aragonite Corporation engaged in the following share transactions through December 31, 1998: issued 30,000 common shares for cash of $350,000, and 12,000 preferred shares for machinery valued at $1,450,000. Subscriptions for 4,500 common shares have been taken, and 40% of the subscription price of $16 per share have been collected. The shares will be issued upon collection of the subscription price in full. Treasury shares consisting of 1,000 common shares have been purchased for $15 each. The Retained Earnings balance is $180,000, on which there is a restriction in terms of availability for dividends in an amount equal to the cost of treasury shares.

Instructions

Prepare the Shareholders' Equity section of the balance sheet as at December 31, 1998.

*E16-15   **(Reacquisition and Subsequent Sale of Par Value Shares)** On November 15, 1998, Municipal Leisure Corp. acquires 3,000 of its own $10 par value common shares in the market at a cost of $40 per share. All shares issued by the company had originally sold for $34 each.

Instructions

(a) Prepare Municipal's journal entry to record the acquisition of treasury shares.

(b) Assume that Municipal sells the acquired shares on December 20, 1998 for the market price of $48 per share. Prepare the journal entry to record this sale.

(c) Prepare journal entries to record the acquisition and subsequent sale of shares if the shares had been cancelled and restored to the status of authorized but unissued shares.

(Correcting Entries for Equity Transactions) Basalt Ltd. recently hired a new accountant with extensive experience in accounting for partnerships. Because of the pressure of the new job, the accountant was unable to review what he had learned earlier about corporation accounting. During the first month, he made the following entries for the company's share capital. ***E16-16**

May 2	Cash		192,000	
	Common Shares			192,000
	Issued 12,000 shares of $10 par value common stock at $16 per share.			
May 15	Common Shares		15,000	
	Cash			15,000
	Purchased 1,000 shares of common stock for the treasury at $15 per share.			
May 31	Cash		8,500	
	Common Shares			5,000
	Gain on Sale of Common Shares			3,500
	Sold 500 shares of treasury stock at $17 per share.			

Instructions

On the basis of the explanation for each entry, prepare the entries that should have been made for the share transactions and the required entries to correct the accounts.

(Analysis of Equity Data and Preparation of Shareholders' Equity Section) For a recent two-year period, the balance sheet of Cinnabar Company showed the following Shareholders' Equity section data (in thousands). **E16-17**

	1998	1997
Common shares	$ 545	$ 540
Other contributed surplus	923	817
Retained earnings	7,167	5,226
Treasury shares	1,562	910
Total shareholders' equity	7,073	5,673
Number of common shares issued	218	216
Number of shares authorized	500	500
Number of treasury shares	34	27

Instructions

(a) Was the cost of acquiring treasury shares higher in 1998 or in 1997?

(b) What was the average issue price for the common shares?

(c) What is the book value per common share?

(d) Prepare the Shareholders' Equity section of the 1998 balance sheet.

PROBLEMS

On January 5, 1998, Masek Corporation began operations with authorized capital of 5,000 no-par value, $8 dividend, cumulative and nonparticipating preferred shares, and 50,000 common shares of no-par value. It then completed the following transactions. **P16-1** ✓

January	11	Accepted subscriptions to 20,000 common shares at $16 per share; 40% down payments accompanied the subscriptions.
February	1	Issued to Parsons Corp. 4,000 preferred shares for the following assets: machinery with a fair market value of $50,000; a factory building with a fair market value of $110,000; and land with an appraised value of $270,000.
March	16	Other machinery, with a fair market value of $210,000, was donated to the company. (Assume credited to Contributed Surplus—Donated Machinery.)
April	15	Collected the balance of the subscription price on the common shares and issued the shares.

May	21	Acquired 1,800 of its own common shares at $19 per share and cancelled them by restoring them to the status of authorized but unissued shares.
August	10	Sold 1,500 common shares at $14 per share.
August	26	Declared a 10% stock dividend on the common shares. The shares were selling at $16 each on the day of the declaration; this amount was used to record the stock dividend (the increase in common shares to be issued as a stock dividend is charged to Retained Earnings and credited to a Common Stock Dividend Distributable account until distributed).
September	15	Distributed the stock dividend.
December	31	Declared a $0.25 per share cash dividend on common and declared the required preferred dividend.
December	31	Closed the Income Summary account. There was a $125,300 net income.

Instructions

(a) Record the journal entries for the transactions listed above.

(b) Prepare the Shareholders' Equity section of Masek's balance sheet as of December 31, 1998.

P16-2 Mary Ellen Company has two classes of shares outstanding: $1.60 no-par value preferred, and no-par value common. At December 31, 1997, the following accounts were included in shareholders' equity.

Preferred shares: 100,000 shares outstanding	$ 2,100,000
Common shares: 2,000,000 shares outstanding	37,500,000
Contributed Surplus—Excess of Assigned Value Over Acquisition Cost, Common	500,000
Retained earnings	3,500,000

The following transactions affected shareholders' equity during 1998.

January	1	25,000 preferred shares were issued at $22 per share.
February	1	40,000 common shares were issued at $20 per share.
June	1	2-for-1 stock split (number of common shares doubled; market value reduced by one-half).
July	1	30,000 shares of common treasury shares were purchased at $8 per share.
September	15	10,000 shares of common treasury shares were reissued at $11 per share.
December	31	Net income of $2,100,000 is reported.
December	31	The preferred dividend is declared, and a common dividend of $.50 per share is declared.

Instructions

Prepare the Shareholders' Equity section of Mary Ellen Company's balance sheet at December 31, 1998. Show all supporting calculations.

P16-3 Karen Corporation's charter authorized issuance of 100,000 common shares of no-par value, and 50,000 preferred shares of no-par value. The following transactions involving the issuance of shares were completed. Each transaction is independent of the others.

1. Issued a $10,000, 9% bond payable for the par value and gave as a bonus one preferred share, which was selling for $105 a share at that time.

2. Issued 500 common shares for machinery. The machinery had been appraised at $6,700; the seller's book value was $6,200. The most recent market price of the common shares was $15 a share.

3. Issued 375 common shares and 100 preferred shares for a lump sum amounting to $12,625. The common had been selling at $14 and the preferred at $95.

4. Issued 200 common shares and 50 preferred shares for furniture and fixtures. The common had a fair market value of $16 per share and the furniture and fixtures were appraised at $6,100.

Instructions

Record the transactions listed above in journal entry form.

P16-4 At the beginning of its 1998 fiscal period, Jonrowe Corporation's general ledger reflected the following account balances.

Common shares, no-par value, 9,000 shares	$360,000
Retained earnings	80,000

Instructions
(a) Record the 1998 transactions given below under the assumption that Jonrowe Corporation is incorporated under the Canada Business Corporations Act.

1. Purchased 380 shares at $39 a share.

2. Purchased 300 shares at $41 a share.

3. Sold 1,000 common shares at $44 a share, incurring issue costs of $260.

4. Sold 800 shares at $45 a share, incurring issue costs of $190.

5. Purchased 400 shares at $42 a share.

Jonrowe Corporation treats share issue costs as a reduction of the proceeds received on the shares.

(b) Prepare the Shareholders' Equity section of the balance sheet at the completion of Jonrowe's 1998 fiscal period, and any required note disclosures.

Share transactions of Husky Corp. are as follows.

P16-5

April 1	Subscriptions to 500 common shares of no-par value are received, together with cheques from the various subscribers to cover a 25% down payment. The shares were subscribed at a price of $120 per share. The remainder of the subscription price is to be paid in three equal monthly instalments.
May 1	First instalments are collected from all subscribers.
June 1	Second instalments are received from all subscribers except Susan Boucher, who had subscribed for 100 shares.
5	In reply to correspondence, Ms. Boucher states that she is unable to complete her instalment payments and authorizes the company to dispose of the shares subscribed for by her.
17	The shares subscribed for by Ms. Boucher are sold for cash of $105 each. Expenses of $125 were incurred in disposing of these shares. Expenses and deficiencies between the subscription price and amounts received are charged against the amount due to the subscriber and the subscriber is then given a refund.
25	A cheque is mailed to Ms. Boucher equal to the refund due her.
July 1	The final instalments are collected on all open subscription accounts and the shares are issued.

Instructions
Prepare entries in journal form to record these transactions and events.

The Shareholders' Equity section of the CanAir Inc. balance sheet at December 31, 1997 was as follows.

P16-6

Common shares—no-par value; 50,000 authorized; 17,500 shares issued and outstanding	$1,750,000
Contributed Surplus—Donated Land	230,000
Retained Earnings	1,210,000
	$3,190,000

On January 2, 1998, the company had idle cash and repurchased 1,000 of its outstanding shares for $114,500. These shares were handled in the manner specified in the *Canada Business Corporations Act*, the legislation under which the company was incorporated. During the year, CanAir sold some of these shares, as they had been restored to the status of authorized but unissued shares. The first such sale was on April 15, at which time the company received $117 per share for 300 shares. The second sale was made on August 13 when another 200 shares were sold for $110 per share.

Instructions
(a) Prepare the journal entries for the transactions identified for 1998.

(b) Assuming net income for 1998 was $57,800, prepare the Shareholders' Equity section of CanAir's balance sheet as at December 31, 1998.

Magic Thongs Inc. (MTI) is a closely held toy manufacturer. You have been engaged as the independent public accountant to perform the first audit of MTI. It is agreed that only current-year (1998) financial statements will be prepared.

P16-7

The following shareholders' equity information has been developed from MTI records on December 31, 1997:

Common shares, no-par value:	
authorized 30,000 shares; issued 9,000 shares	$405,000
Retained earnings	180,000

The following transactions took place during 1998:

1. On March 15, MTI issued 7,000 common shares to Mary Lyon for $62 per share.
2. On March 31, MTI acquired 4,000 shares from Emma Gold (MTI's founder) for $75 per share. These shares were cancelled upon receipt.

For the year 1998, MTI reported net income of $110,000.

Instructions

(a) How should the shareholders' equity information be reported in the MTI financial statements for the year ended December 31, 1998?

(b) How would your answer to Part (a) be altered if MTI had treated the acquired shares as treasury shares under the single-transaction method?

P16-8   Taconite Company has the following shareholders' equity accounts at December 31, 1997:

Common Shares—no-par value; authorized, 10,000	
shares; issued, 4,800 shares	$480,000
Retained Earnings	294,000

Instructions

(a) Prepare journal entries to record the following transactions, which took place during 1998:

1. 240 of the issued shares were acquired for $96 per share and cancelled.
2. A $20 per share cash dividend was declared.
3. The dividend declared above was paid.
4. 240 common shares were sold for $102 per share.
5. 500 common shares were acquired for a total of $51,500, then cancelled.
6. 120 additional outstanding shares were acquired at $97 per share, then cancelled.
7. 330 common shares were sold for $99 per share.

(b) Prepare the Shareholders' Equity section of Taconite Company's balance sheet after giving effect to these transactions, assuming that the net income for 1998 was $93,000.

P16-9   Mica Corporation is a publicly owned company. At December 31, 1997, Mica had 60,000,000 common shares of no-par value authorized, of which 30,000,000 shares were issued and outstanding; and 500,000, $8 cumulative, no-par value preferred shares authorized, none of which have been issued.

The shareholders' equity accounts at December 31, 1997 had the following balances:

Common shares	$540,000,000
Retained earnings	150,000,000

During 1998, Mica entered into the following transactions:

1. On February 1, a secondary distribution of 4,000,000 common shares was completed. The shares were sold to the public at $21.50 per share and share offering costs came to $0.50 per share.
2. On February 15, Mica issued at $120 per share (net of $1.25 per share issue costs), 100,000 preferred shares.
3. On March 1, Mica acquired 40,000 common shares for $23 per share, and they were cancelled.
4. On March 15, when the common shares were trading for $21 per share, a major shareholder donated 10,000 shares to the company, which were subsequently cancelled.
5. On March 31, Mica declared a semiannual cash dividend on the common shares of $0.15 per share, payable on April 30, to shareholders of record on April 10.
6. On April 30, Mica issued share purchase loans totalling $2,000,000 to 10 top managers to enable them to purchase 100,000 shares of the company at $20 per share. The shares were issued on this date.

7. On May 31, when the market price of the common shares was $22 per share, Mica declared a 2% stock dividend distributable on July 1 to shareholders of record on June 1. The stock dividend is recorded using the market price with the increase in the common shares being charged to the Retained Earnings account.

8. On June 30, Mica sold 400,000 common shares for $23 per share.

9. On September 30, Mica declared a semiannual cash dividend on the common shares of $0.25 per share and the yearly dividend on preferred shares, both payable on October 30, to shareholders of record on October 10.

10. On December 31, as required by the share purchase loan agreement, the 10 managers paid a total of $100,000 on their loans.

Net income for 1998 was $90,000,000.

Instructions

Prepare a work sheet to be used to summarize, for each transaction, the changes in Mica's shareholders' equity accounts for 1998. The columns on this work sheet should have the following headings:

> Date of transaction (or beginning date)
> Common shares—number of shares
> Common shares—amount
> Preferred shares—number of shares
> Preferred shares—amount
> Contributed surplus*
> Retained earnings
> Share purchase loans receivable

*While there may be several individual accounts that would be recognized in contributed surplus, use this column to record the effects of transactions on the total amount of contributed surplus.

Show supporting computations in good form.   (AICPA adapted)

Transactions of Gypsum Company are as follows: ***P16-10**

1. The company is incorporated with authorized capital of 15,000 preferred shares of $100 par value and 15,000 common shares with a par value of $10.

2. 8,000 common shares are issued to founders of the corporation for land valued by the board of directors at $210,000.

3. 4,200 preferred shares are sold for cash at $110 each.

4. 600 common shares are sold to an officer of the corporation for $42 a share.

5. 300 of the preferred shares outstanding are purchased for cash at par and are immediately cancelled.

6. 400 of the preferred shares outstanding are purchased for cash of $98 a share and are held as treasury shares.

7. 500 of the common shares outstanding are purchased for $49 a share and are held as treasury shares.

8. 200 of the purchased preferred shares in treasury are reissued for $102 each.

9. 2,100 previously unissued preferred shares are issued for $103 each.

10. 400 of the acquired common shares in treasury are reissued for $39 a share.

11. 200 common shares are purchased for $30 a share and are cancelled.

Instructions

(a) Prepare journal entries to record the transactions listed above. No other transactions affecting the share capital accounts have occurred. (Round to the nearest dollar where necessary.)

(b) Assuming that the company has retained earnings of $112,000 before these transactions, prepare the Shareholders' Equity section of its balance sheet after considering all the transactions given.

The following information is drawn from the records of the Nova Scotia Company Limited as at December 31:   ***P16-11**

Preferred shares authorized ($100 par value)	$800,000
Common shares authorized ($10 par value)	600,000
Unissued preferred shares	300,000
Unissued common shares	180,000
Subscriptions receivable, common	18,000

Subscriptions receivable, preferred	21,500
Preferred shares subscribed	28,000
Common shares subscribed	43,000
Treasury shares, preferred (1,230 shares)	120,540
Contributed surplus (excess of amount paid in over par value of common shares)	153,400

Instructions

Use the above information to determine the following:

(a) Total authorized share capital.

(b) Total unissued share capital.

(c) Total issued share capital.

(d) Share capital subscribed.

(e) Share capital available for sale.

(f) Total share capital and contributed surplus.

CASES

C16-1 Garcia Computer Ltd. is a small, closely held corporation. 80% of the issued shares are held by Andy Garcia, President; of the remainder, 10% are held by members of his family and 10% by Lori Boudreau, a former officer who is now retired. The balance sheet of the company at June 30, 1998 was substantially as shown below.

Assets		Liabilities and Shareholders' Equity	
Cash	$ 22,000	Current liabilities	$150,000
Other	600,000	Share capital	300,000
		Retained earnings	172,000
	$622,000		$622,000

Additional authorized share capital of 15,000 no-par value shares had never been issued. To strengthen the cash position of the company, Mr. Garcia issued 5,000 shares to himself, paying $100,000 cash. At the next shareholders' meeting, Ms. Boudreau objected and claimed that her interests had been injured. All shares previously issued were for the same price of $20 per share.

Instructions

(a) What shareholder's right may have been ignored in the issue of shares to Mr. Garcia?

(b) How may any damage to Ms. Boudreau's interests be repaired most simply?

(c) If Andy Garcia offered Lori Boudreau a personal cash settlement and they agreed to employ you as an impartial arbitrator to determine the amount based only on the information provided, what settlement would you propose? Present your calculations with sufficient explanation to satisfy both parties.

C16-2

ALTOONA INDUSTRIES INC.

	1998	1997
	(in thousands)	
Series A first preferred shares—subject to mandatory redemption ($4,062,500 liquidation value in 1998 and 1997); no-par value; authorized 100,000 shares; issued, 40,625 shares in 1998 and 1997 (note 6)	$ 3,250	$ 3,250
Common shareholders' equity:		
Common shares, no-par value; authorized 20,000,000 shares; issued, 5,522,602 shares (5,280,602 in 1997)	552	528
Contributed surplus	463	460
Retained earnings	34,610	20,891
Common shareholders' equity	$35,625	$21,879

Notes to Consolidated Financial Statements

6. Redeemable Preferred Shares:

The Company's preferred shares consist of 250,000 authorized shares of no-par value First Preferred Shares of which 40,625 shares of Series A First Preferred Shares were outstanding at December 31, 1998. The Series A First Preferred Shares, which are not convertible, were sold for $80.00 per share. The shares are entitled to cumulative dividends of $12.70 annually ($3.175 per quarter) per share and must be redeemed at 10% per year commencing on December 31, 2001 at $100.00 per share plus accrued and unpaid dividends. The Company, at its option, may, in 1999 or any subsequent year, redeem any number of shares at that price plus a premium amounting to $3.55 per share. This premium will decline proportionately in each year after 1999 through 2007, after which there will be no premium. Altoona had total debt of $85,979 in 1998. A restrictive covenant on some of the debt prohibits Altoona from additional borrowing if the debt-to-equity ratio exceeds 2.5 or if retained earnings falls below $17,000.

Instructions

From the information provided, answer the following questions:

(a) Are the Series A preferred shares an equity instrument or a financial liability?

(b) What are the GAAP requirements for reporting all aspects of the preferred shares on the financial statements for the year ended December 31, 1998?

(c) Assume the company redeems 5% of the outstanding preferred shares in 1999 at a time when all dividends are up-to-date. Identify how this transaction would be reported on the financial statements for the year ended December 31, 1999.

(d) Is Altoona in violation of its debt covenants in 1998, based on the reported numbers above? Discuss.

C16-3

It has been said that the accounting practices that help create "secret reserves" include: (1) the use of the FIFO inventory method during an extended period of declining prices; and (2) the expensing of all human-resource costs.

Instructions

(a) What is a secret reserve? How can secret reserves be created or enlarged?

(b) What is the basis for saying that the two specific practices cited above tend to create secret reserves?

(c) Is it possible to create a secret reserve in connection with accounting for a liability? If so, explain and give an example.

(d) What are the objections to the creation of secret reserves?

(e) It has also been said that "watered stock" is the opposite of a secret reserve. What is watered stock?

(f) Describe the general circumstances in which watered stock can arise.

(g) What steps can be taken to eliminate "water" from a capital structure? (AICPA adapted)

C16-4

J. Trevino Corporation sold 50,000 shares of its no-par value common stock on a subscription basis for $40 per share. By December 31, 1998, collections on these subscriptions totalled $1,200,000. No subscriptions have yet been paid in full.

Instructions

(a) Discuss the meaning of the account Common Shares Subscribed and indicate how it is reported in the financial statements.

(b) Discuss the arguments in favour of reporting Subscriptions Receivable as a current asset.

(c) Discuss the arguments in favour of reporting Subscriptions Receivable as a contra equity account.

(d) Discuss the similarity(ies) between accounting for subscribed shares and shares issued and fully paid for under a company-sponsored share purchase loan program.

C16-5

Smits Corporation is planning to issue 3,000 shares of its own common stock for 2 ha of land to be used as a building site.

Instructions

(a) What general rule should be applied in determining the amount at which the land should be recorded?

(b) Under what circumstances should this transaction be recorded at the fair market value of the land?

(c) Under what circumstances should this transaction be recorded at the fair market value of the shares issued?

C16-6   Olmos Corporation purchased $160,000 worth of equipment in 1998 for $100,000 cash and a promise to deliver an indeterminate number of common shares having a market value of $20,000 on January 1 of each year for the next four years. Hence, $80,000 in "market value" of shares will be required to discharge the $60,000 balance due on the equipment.

Instructions
(a) Discuss the propriety of recording the equipment at:
   1. $100,000 (the cash payment).
   2. $160,000 (the cash price of the equipment).
   3. $180,000 (the $100,000 cash payment plus the $80,000 market value of the shares that must be transferred to the vendor in order to settle the obligation according to the terms of the agreement).
(b) Discuss the arguments for treating the balance due as
   1. A liability.
   2. Common shares subscribed.

C16-7   Lakeview Powerboat Limited (LPL) is a privately owned Canadian powerboat manufacturer that makes fibreglass powerboats ranging in size from 5 to 10 m. LPL was federally incorporated in 1978 by three brothers, John, Mark, and Harry Smith. Each brother initially contributed $200,000 in return for a one-third interest in the voting common shares. The $600,000 was used to purchase land, a building, and some equipment.

The partner in charge at Simon & King, a public accounting firm, convinced the brothers several years ago that they needed a shareholders' agreement to allow for the retirement of the original owners and the succession of control. The brothers agreed unanimously that control should pass to John Smith's son, Bill, who had expressed an interest in owning and running LPL. Bill was young and aggressive with some exciting plans for LPL.

The shareholders' agreement was drawn up by a lawyer and signed by the brothers. In addition to specifying that control would pass to Bill, the agreement provided for a buy/sell arrangement regarding the repurchase of shares from any of the brothers. On September 30, 1998, Harry Smith formally notified LPL in writing that he wanted LPL to repurchase his common shares by January 15, 1999.

The Smith brothers decided that the time had come to hand over the reins to Bill. He will now take over as president in mid-November. John and Mark will stay on as managers for five more years, and then they too will retire. After several discussions attended by LPL's lawyers, John, Mark, and Bill signed a letter of intent in October, 1998 that contains the following agreement in principle:

   1. John and Mark will "freeze" the value of their equity, measured in accordance with the shareholders' agreement, based on the financial statements for the fiscal year ended September 30, 1998.
   2. All subsequent appreciation or depreciation in the value of LPL will accrue to Bill Smith.
   3. John and Mark are flexible as to the form that their equity interest will take, but they insist on retaining voting control until their equity is withdrawn from LPL in the form of cash. The withdrawal shall take place no sooner than October 1, 2003.
   4. John and Mark will continue to receive their salary from LPL until their retirement at the end of the 2003 fiscal year.

Instructions
Advise the Smith brothers on how to achieve the spirit of the above agreement through share capital structuring (i.e., classes and rights of shares).

(CICA UFE adapted)

USING YOUR JUDGEMENT

FINANCIAL REPORTING PROBLEM

Refer to the financial statements of Moore Corporation Limited presented in Appendix 5A and answer the following questions.
   1. What rights and conditions are attached to Moore Corporation's common and preferred shares?
   2. Summarize the reasons for the increase in Moore's share capital over the three-year period ending December 31, 1995.

3. Moore Corporation's common shares traded on the Toronto Stock Exchange at prices ranging between 23⅞ and 27⅜ during the October 1 to December 31, 1995 period, and traded for as much as 32¼ during 1995. What was the book value per common share on December 31, 1995? Why is there a difference between the book value and market value per share?

4. Moore Corporation Limited has a Dividend Reinvestment and Share Purchase Plan. Explain briefly how this plan works. Suggest reasons why the company operates such a plan.

ETHICS CASE

Maureen Lester is the accounting manager of LBC, which is a closely held and rapidly growing retail sporting equipment concern with 30 stores located throughout British Columbia and Alberta. Maureen has been asked by the CFO, Curtis Morgan, to review two agreed-upon alternatives for the purchase of a newly constructed warehouse facility located in Calgary, Alberta:

Option 1:

New Building	$1,500,000	
LBC Common Shares (no-par value)		$1,500,000

Option 2:

New Building	$1,350,000	
Notes Payable (with contractor)		$1,200,000
Cash		150,000

In addition to the above facts and figures, Maureen knows that LBC would probably prefer the first option because Curtis told her earlier that, "the company is experiencing tough working capital problems due to its rapid expansion in recent years."

Instructions

(a) Assuming the value of the new warehouse was independently appraised by a real estate consulting firm at $1.5 million, what are the ethical implications that should be considered by Maureen when considering both options?

(b) Assuming that the value of the new warehouse was independently appraised by a real estate consulting firm at $1.35 million, what are the ethical implications that should be considered by Maureen when considering both options?

(c) Who could be harmed if LBC chose to inflate its asset values in a "watered stock" transaction?

(d) Explain how your answers to the above questions would change if LBC was a publicly traded corporation.

chapter 17

SHAREHOLDERS' EQUITY: CONTRIBUTED SURPLUS AND RETAINED EARNINGS

CONTRIBUTED SURPLUS

RETAINED EARNINGS

DIVIDEND POLICY

TYPES OF DIVIDEND

STOCK SPLITS

LIQUIDATING DIVIDENDS

DIVIDEND PREFERENCES

RESTRICTIONS ON RETAINED EARNINGS

OTHER COMPONENTS OF SHAREHOLDERS' EQUITY

FINANCIAL REORGANIZATIONS

REPORTING SHAREHOLDERS' EQUITY

CHAPTER 17

Shareholders' Equity:
Contributed Surplus and Retained Earnings

Learning Objectives

After studying this chapter, you should be able to:

1. Explain the nature of contributed surplus, sources from which it may be derived, and how it is reported on the balance sheet.

2. Identify common causes of changes in retained earnings.

3. Describe the factors to consider when determining if dividends are to be distributed.

4. Identify the various forms of dividend distributions and explain how to account for them.

5. Explain the nature of stock dividends and how they are accounted for.

6. Distinguish between stock splits and stock dividends and identify the accounting consequences of each.

7. Distinguish between liquidating and regular dividends.

8. Allocate dividend distributions between preferred and common shareholders.

9. Identify reasons for restrictions on retained earnings and properly disclose them in financial statements.

10. Explain the issues regarding accounting for self-insurance.

11. Identify other components of shareholders' equity and explain their nature.

12. Explain what a financial reorganization is, and how it is accounted for and disclosed in financial statements.

13. Prepare statements or schedules to report changes in retained earnings, contributed surplus, share capital, or total shareholders' equity.

The following three categories most frequently appear as part of shareholders' equity in a corporation's financial statements:

1. Share Capital or Capital Stock (legal or stated capital).

2. Contributed Surplus.

3. Retained Earnings or Deficit.

The first two categories, Share Capital and Contributed Surplus, constitute **contributed capital**. Retained Earnings represents the **earned capital** of the enterprise. The distinction between contributed capital and earned capital has a legal origin, but at present it serves the useful purpose of indicating the different sources from which a corporation has obtained its **equity capital**.

The first category—Share Capital—was discussed in Chapter 16. The objective of this chapter is to examine the accounting for and disclosure of the other components of shareholders' equity. Within the discussion of Retained Earnings, this chapter covers the accounting for various types of dividends and examines the nature of and accounting for restrictions on Retained Earnings. While these three categories represent the most common components of shareholders' equity, other categories may appear. Examples include Appraisal Increase Credits, Cumulative Translation Adjustments from the translation of the accounts of foreign operations, Revaluation Adjustments resulting from a financial reorganization, and Treasury Shares, a contra-equity account, which was discussed in Chapter 16.

CONTRIBUTED SURPLUS

OBJECTIVE 1
Explain the nature of contributed surplus, sources from which it may be derived, and how it is reported on the balance sheet.

The *CICA Handbook* states that there can be only two sources of surplus within a corporation, these being amounts received by way of contributions and amounts earned in the conduct of the business. In order to provide readers of financial statements with an adequate view of a company's affairs, it is necessary to report information about these two basic sources separately.[1]

Contributed surplus may be derived from a variety of transactions and events, as indicated in the following summary.[2]

EXHIBIT 17-1

CONTRIBUTED SURPLUS ACCOUNTS

Arising from:

	Excess of consideration received over par value	
• The issue of par value shares.	— Pro rata reduction on retirement of par value shares (see Chapter 16); or — Liquidating dividend.	— Premium, or excess of proceeds over par value of shares issued.

	Donated capital	
• Capital donations.	— Liquidating dividend.	— Donations of land, shares, etc.

	Excess of proceeds on treasury shares over cost	
• Treasury stock transactions.*	— Proceeds on sale of treasury shares below cost. — Liquidating dividend.	— Proceeds on sale of treasury shares in excess of cost.

	Excess of assigned value over acquisition cost	
• Purchase and retirement or cancellation of shares.*	— Excess of acquisition cost over par, stated, or assigned value of shares. — Liquidating dividend.	— Excess of par, stated, or assigned value over acquisition cost of shares.

---

[1] *CICA Handbook* (Toronto: CICA), Section 3250, par. .04. "Surplus" is used in the accounting sense of being the excess of net assets over the total share capital of a corporation (Section 3250, par. .01).

[2] *Ibid.*, par. .05, serves as the basic source of the items listed. Each item represents a potential source for a debit or credit to the Contributed Surplus control account, however, debit balances are not permitted in any Contributed Surplus account. Par. .11 indicates that charges against (debits to) specific Contributed Surplus accounts should be restricted to cases such as direct opposites to amounts previously credited, and charges resulting from a reorganization.

EXHIBIT 17-1 (Continued)

CONTRIBUTED SURPLUS ACCOUNTS

Revaluation adjustment

• Financial reorganizations. [Note: Balance may be closed to other shareholders' equity account, or left as contributed surplus.]	– Net write-down of net assets. – Transfer from other shareholders' equity account. – Liquidating dividend.	– Net write-up of net assets. INVALID – Transfer from other shareholders' equity account. – Additional capital provided.

Stock options/warrants outstanding

• Issue of stock rights and warrants (see Chapter 18). [Note: If expired, balance is transferred to a lapsed or expired stock options/warrants account.]	– Transfer to share capital on exercise of stock rights, warrants, and options.	– Amounts attributed to stock rights, warrants, and options.

Conversion rights

• Issue of convertible debt (see Chapter 18). [Note: If expired, balance is transferred to a lapsed or expired conversion rights account.]	– Transfer to share capital on conversion of debt.	– Value assigned to conversion feature on issue of convertible debt.

- Other types of contributed surplus accounts may exist, such as on the forfeiture of amounts received on shares subscribed but not paid for in full, or additional assessments on shareholders, etc.

*See Chapter 16 for situations where debits exceed the existing credit balance.

An interesting aspect of the *Canada Business Corporations Act* (**CBCA**) is that, because of its requirements to have no-par value shares and to cancel reacquired shares, it eliminates the source of most contributed surplus items. However, companies incorporated under acts permitting these or that had these items in their accounts before filing for continuance under the CBCA could carry the items forward.[3]

No operating gains or losses or extraordinary gains and losses are debited or credited to Contributed Surplus. The profession has long discouraged by-passing net income and retained earnings through the write-off of losses (e.g., write-offs of bond discount, goodwill, or obsolete plant and equipment) to contributed surplus or other capital accounts.

A subsidiary ledger or separate general ledger accounts may be kept of the different sources of contributed surplus. Maintaining such separate records greatly facilitates disclosure of changes in contributed surplus during a period, as is required by the *CICA Handbook*.[4] On the balance sheet, only one account (Contributed Surplus) and one amount (which is the total of all contributed surplus accounts) need appear.

RETAINED EARNINGS

Retained earnings is sometimes a difficult concept to grasp as the account itself has no "substance:" it represents the accumulated increase in net assets from generating profits

---

[3] *Financial Reporting in Canada—1995* (Toronto: CICA, 1995) reports that of the 300 companies surveyed, 65 in 1994 and 68 in 1993 disclosed the existence of contributed surplus items. In more than 90% of these cases, the items were labelled simply as Contributed Surplus in shareholders' equity.

[4] *CICA Handbook*, Section 3250, par. .13. *Financial Reporting in Canada—1995* indicates that where contributed surplus changed in a period, the nature of the change was predominantly disclosed in notes to the financial statements. Other means of disclosure were by a statement of changes in contributed surplus or inclusion of the change in a statement of changes in shareholders' equity.

OBJECTIVE 2

Identify common causes of changes in retained earnings.

(net income) in excess of distributions to shareholders as dividends. Net income is derived from a variety of sources. These include the main operations of the enterprise (such as manufacturing and selling a given product); any ancillary activities (such as disposing of scrap or renting out unused space); financing decisions (interest income); the results of discontinued operations; and extraordinary items. Shareholders assume the greatest risk in enterprise operations and bear any losses or share in any profits resulting from enterprise activities. Any income not distributed among the shareholders becomes additional shareholders' equity. The more common items that either increase (credit) or decrease (debit) the Retained Earnings account are expressed in account form below.

EXHIBIT 17-2

Retained Earnings

1. Net loss.	1. Net income.
2. Retroactive adjustments that may result from changes in accounting principles or error corrections.	2. Retroactive adjustments that may result from changes in accounting principles or error corrections.
3. Cash dividends.	
4. Stock dividends.	
5. Property dividends.	
6. Transactions involving share reacquisitions as discussed in Chapter 16.	

In Chapter 4 it was pointed out that, under the all-inclusive concept of income, the results of unusual and extraordinary transactions should be reported in the income statement, not in the statement of retained earnings. Changes in accounting policies that are applied retroactively and corrections of errors of prior years should be reported as adjustments to beginning retained earnings, by-passing completely the current period's income statement. The Retained Earnings account form above illustrates that *it can be increased only by earnings* (and adjustments/corrections of prior year's earnings), but that it can be reduced by other capital charges.

DIVIDEND POLICY

When retained earnings exist within a corporation, there are two possible alternatives regarding its disposition: the credit balance can be (1) reduced by a distribution of assets (a dividend) to the shareholders; or (2) left intact and the offsetting assets used in the operations of the business.

Very few companies pay dividends in amounts equal to the retained earnings legally available for dividends. The major reasons for this are as follows.

1. Lack of sufficient cash.

2. Agreements (bond covenants) with specific creditors to retain all or a portion of the earnings (in the form of assets) to build up additional protection against possible loss for those creditors.

3. Desire to retain assets that would otherwise be paid out as dividends, to finance growth or expansion. This is sometimes called **internal financing**, reinvesting earnings, or "ploughing" the profits back into the business.

4. Desire to smooth out dividend payments from year to year by accumulating assets through earnings in good years and using such accumulated earnings as a basis for dividends in bad years.

5. Desire to build up a cushion or buffer against possible losses.

6. Legal restrictions included in the acts under which a company is incorporated. For example, a dividend may not be paid if it would render a corporation insolvent even if retained earnings exist. Also, in circumstances permitting treasury shares, the law may require that retained earnings equivalent to the cost of such shares be restricted against dividend declarations.

No particular explanation is required for any of these except the last. The laws of most jurisdictions require that the corporation's stated capital (legal capital) be restricted from distribution to shareholders so that it may serve as a protection against loss to creditors. If, for example, the corporation buys its own outstanding shares, it reduces its stated and outstanding capital and distributes assets to shareholders. Therefore, the corporation could, by purchasing shares at any price desired, return to the shareholders their investments and leave creditors with little or no protection against loss. Consequently, restricting dividends to the extent that retained earnings will not fall below the cost of the reacquired shares is a way to overcome this problem.

Companies usually pay dividends that represent a distribution of profits (and therefore retained earnings) to their shareholders, but dividends that are a distribution of contributed capital are also permitted. While dividends charged to Retained Earnings are a return *on* the capital invested by shareholders, dividends charged to Contributed Surplus are a return *of* the capital invested. This distinction is recognized by the tax authorities and the investment community, as the former is treated as income in the shareholders' hands whereas the latter dividend reduces the cost of the investment to the shareholder.

If a company is considering declaring a dividend, two preliminary questions must be asked:

OBJECTIVE 3
Describe the factors to consider when determining if dividends are to be distributed.

1. Is the condition of the corporation such that a dividend is *legally permissible*?

2. Is the condition of the corporation such that a dividend is *economically sound*?

LEGALITY OF DIVIDENDS

The legality of a dividend can be determined only by reviewing the applicable incorporation law. Even then the law may not be clear, and a decision may require recourse to the courts. Usually, to reduce the possibility of legal misinterpretation, the company's lawyer is consulted. For most general dividend declarations, the following guidelines are adequate:

1. The balance in the Retained Earnings account, unless legally restricted in some manner, is usually the correct basis for dividend distributions.

2. In some jurisdictions, assets generated through contributed surplus may be used as a basis for dividends.

3. Deficits must be eliminated before the payment of any dividends.

4. In most jurisdictions that allow treasury shares, dividends may not reduce retained earnings below the cost of treasury shares held.

The CBCA prohibits the declaration or payment of dividends if there are reasonable grounds for believing that such an action would make the company **insolvent**, that is: (1) result in the corporation being unable to pay its liabilities when they become due; or (2) result in the realizable value of the corporation's assets being less than the total of its liabilities and stated (legal) capital of all share classes. Adhering to the legal requirements associated with dividends is critical to a corporation's directors because, if such requirements are judged to have been violated, the directors can be held jointly and severally liable for the entire debts and obligations of the company.

FINANCIAL CONDITION AND DIVIDEND DISTRIBUTIONS

Corporations are generally required to have a credit balance in Retained Earnings before assets can be distributed as dividends. From the standpoint of good management, attention must be given to other conditions as well. Particularly important is the liquidity of the corporation. If we assume an extreme situation such as the following, these considerations become apparent.

EXHIBIT 17-3

BALANCE SHEET

Plant assets	$500,000	Share capital	$400,000
		Retained earnings	100,000
	$500,000		$500,000

This company has a retained earnings credit balance and, unless it is restricted, may legally declare a dividend of $100,000. However, because all its assets are plant assets and used in operations, payment of a cash dividend of $100,000 requires the sale of plant assets or borrowing.

Even if we assume a balance sheet showing current assets, there is still the further question of whether those assets are needed for other purposes.

EXHIBIT 17-4

BALANCE SHEET

Cash	$100,000	Current liabilities		$ 60,000
Plant assets	460,000	Share capital	$400,000	
		Retained earnings	100,000	500,000
	$560,000			$560,000

The existence of current liabilities implies very strongly that some of the cash is needed to meet current debts as they mature. Furthermore, day-by-day cash requirements for payroll and other expenditures not included in current liabilities will also require cash.

Thus, before a dividend is declared, management and directors must consider the *availability of funds to pay the dividend*. Other demands for cash should be identified, perhaps by preparing a cash forecast. A dividend should not be paid unless both the present and future financial position appear to warrant the distribution.

Directors and management must also consider the effect of inflation and replacement costs on reported income. During a period of rising prices, some costs charged to expense under historical cost accounting are understated in a comparative purchasing power sense. Income is thereby "overstated" because certain costs have not been adjusted for inflation. As an example, at one time a company reported conventional net income of $179 million but, when the dollars reported were adjusted for inflation, net income was reduced to $68 million. Yet the company paid cash dividends of $72 million. Were cash dividends paid excessive? This subject is discussed in Chapter 25.

The conclusion regarding a decision to declare a dividend is clear. While the existence of nonrestricted retained earnings is a necessity, many other factors are important. No corporate director should ever recommend a dividend based on the existence of retained earnings alone. The legal requirements as well as the present and expected future financial position must also be considered.

TYPES OF DIVIDEND

Dividend distributions are based on either accumulated profits—that is, retained earnings—or, in some cases, contributed surplus accounts. The natural expectation of any shareholder who receives a dividend is that the corporation has operated successfully and that he or she is receiving a share of the increased assets generated by profitable operations. Any dividend not based on retained earnings (a liquidating dividend) should be adequately described in the accompanying message to the shareholders so that there will be no misunderstanding of its source.

OBJECTIVE 4
Identify the various forms of dividend distributions and explain how to account for them.

Dividends representing a distribution of earnings can be of the following types:[5]

1. Cash dividends.

2. Property dividends.

3. Scrip dividends.

4. Stock dividends.

Dividends are commonly paid in cash but occasionally in shares, scrip, or some other asset. *Any dividend other than a stock dividend reduces the shareholders' equity in the corporation*. The equity is reduced either through an immediate or promised future distribution of assets. When a stock dividend is declared, the corporation does not pay out assets or incur a liability. It issues additional shares to each shareholder and nothing more.

CASH DIVIDENDS

The board of directors votes on the declaration of dividends, and if the resolution is approved, the dividend is declared. Before it is paid, a current list of shareholders must be prepared. For this reason there is usually a time lag between declaration and payment. A dividend approved at the January 10 (**date of declaration**) meeting of the board of directors might be declared payable February 5 (**date of payment**) to shareholders of record on January 25 (**date of record**).

The period from January 10 to January 25 gives time for any transfers in process to be completed and registered with the transfer agent. The time from January 25 to February 5

---

[5] *Financial Reporting in Canada—1995* indicates that for 1994, 64% of the 300 survey companies disclosed the declaration or payment of a dividend, predominantly a cash dividend.

provides an opportunity for the transfer agent or accounting department, depending on who does this work, to prepare a list of shareholders as of January 25 and to prepare and mail dividend cheques.

A declared dividend, except for a stock dividend, is a liability and, because payment is generally required soon, it is usually a current liability. The following entries are required to record the declaration and payment of a dividend payable in cash. This example assumes that on June 10 a corporation declares a cash dividend of $0.50 a share on 1.8 million shares, payable July 16 to all shareholders of record on June 24.

At date of declaration (June 10):		
Retained Earnings (Cash Dividends Declared)	900,000	
Dividends Payable		900,000
At date of record (June 24):		
No entry		
At date of payment (July 16):		
Dividends Payable	900,000	
Cash		900,000

When dividends are declared, companies debit either Retained Earnings directly or an account called Cash Dividends Declared, which is closed to Retained Earnings at the end of the year. However, *companies with preferred shares that are financial liabilities in substance* (see **Chapters 15 and 16**) *should charge (i.e., debit) dividends declared on these shares to a separate account that is given the same accounting treatment as interest on long-term debt*.[6] These dividends are a deduction in determining net income for the period rather than a direct reduction of retained earnings, and the amount of such dividends should be disclosed.

Dividend declarations are made as a stated amount per share for no-par value shares[7] *and are paid only on shares that are issued and outstanding*. Dividends are not paid on treasury or other shares that have not been cancelled or on shares subscribed for but not fully paid.[8]

Dividend Reinvestment. Some companies provide their shareholders with a **dividend reinvestment option** whereby the shareholder can elect to have an amount equal to the dividend retained by the company and reinvested in additional shares of stock. Shareholders who are interested in the growth of their equity holdings rather than in regular cash flows are primary users of this option, especially as the shares generally are purchased at a small discount from market value with no fees or commissions charged. Companies benefit from a cash flow perspective and from increased shareholder loyalty. The entries to record the dividend illustrated above when 5% of the shareholdings are covered by a dividend reinvestment plan are as follows.

At date of declaration (June 10):		
Retained Earnings (Cash Dividends Declared)	900,000	
Dividends Payable [.95(900,000)]		855,000
Common Stock Distributable [.05(900,000)]		45,000
At date of payment (July 16):		
Dividends Payable	855,000	
Common Stock Distributable	45,000	
Cash		855,000
Common Stock		45,000

---

[6] *CICA Handbook*, Section 3860, par. .31.

[7] For par value shares, dividends may be declared as a certain percentage of the par value.

[8] *CICA Handbook*, Section 3240, par. .22.

Dividend policies vary among corporations. Some older, well-established companies take pride in a long, unbroken string of quarterly or annual dividend payments.[9] They would lower or pass the dividend only if forced to do so by a sustained decline in earnings or a critical shortage of cash.

The percentage of annual earnings distributed as cash dividends, the **payout ratio**, depends somewhat on the stability and trend of earnings, with 25% to 75% of earnings being paid out by many well-established corporations. Growth companies, on the other hand, pay little or no cash dividends because their policy is to expand as rapidly as internal and external financing permit. For example, the following statement appears in the annual reports of Newbridge Networks Corporation regarding its common shares on which no dividends have ever been paid.

EXHIBIT 17-5 NEWBRIDGE NETWORKS CORPORATION

COMMON SHARE INFORMATION

The Company has not paid cash dividends on its Common Shares, and it presently intends to continue this policy for the foreseeable future in order to retain earnings for the development of the Company's business.

Shareholders in companies that pay small or no dividends hope the price of their shares will appreciate so that they will realize a profit when they sell the shares. Newbridge Networks shares, for example, traded under $5 in the late 1980s, yet rose to almost $100 per share in 1993—*after* a two-for-one stock split that halved the value of each share. The company split their shares again on a two-for-one basis in mid-1993!

Knowledge of the dividend policy for a particular corporation may be gained from an analysis of its successive financial statements. While no explicit recommendation regarding disclosure of dividend policy exists in Canada, the Ontario Securities Commission requires disclosure of dividend history in an annual information return; companies often also provide a statement of their dividend policy in the return. In the United States the SEC encourages companies that have earnings but fail to pay dividends, or companies that do not expect to pay dividends in the foreseeable future, to report this information in their annual report. In addition, companies that have had a consistent pattern of paying dividends are encouraged to indicate whether they intend to continue this practice in the future.

PROPERTY DIVIDENDS

Dividends payable in assets of the corporation other than cash are called **property dividends** or **dividends in kind**. Property dividends may be in whatever form the board of directors designates; for example, merchandise, real estate, or investments. Because of the obvious difficulties of divisibility of units and delivery to the shareholders, the usual property dividend is in the form of securities of other companies that the distributing corporation holds as an investment.

A property dividend is a **nonreciprocal transfer** *of nonmonetary assets between an enterprise and its owners.*[10] *CICA Handbook* Section 3830 on "Non-Monetary Trans-

---

[9] The Bank of Montreal and the Bank of Nova Scotia have been paying dividends since 1829 and 1833, respectively!

[10] A nonreciprocal transfer is a transfer of assets or services in one direction, either from an enterprise to its owners or another entity or from owners or another entity to the enterprise, without consideration.

actions" recommends that nonreciprocal transfers such as property dividends be *recorded at the fair value of the asset given up*.[11]

The **fair value** of the nonmonetary asset distributed is the amount that would be agreed upon by informed and willing parties dealing at arm's length in an open and unrestricted market.[12] Such an amount could be determined by referring to estimated realizable values in cash transactions of the same or similar assets, quoted market prices, independent appraisals, and other available evidence.

The failure to recognize the fair value of nonmonetary assets transferred may both misstate the dividend and fail to recognize gains and losses on assets that have already been earned or incurred by the enterprise. Recording the dividend at fair value permits future comparisons of dividend rates. If cash must be distributed to some shareholders in place of the nonmonetary asset, determination of the amount to be distributed is simplified.

When a property dividend is declared, the corporation should restate at fair value the property to be distributed, recognizing any gain or loss as the difference between the fair value and carrying value of the property at the date of declaration. The declared dividend may then be recorded as a debit to Retained Earnings (or Property Dividends Declared) and a credit to Property Dividends Payable at an amount equal to the fair value of the property to be distributed. Upon distribution of the dividend, Property Dividends Payable is debited, and the account containing the distributed asset (restated at fair value) is credited.

For example, Inuit Inc. transferred some of its investments in marketable securities costing $1,250,000 to shareholders by declaring a property dividend on December 18, 1997, to be distributed on January 30, 1998 to shareholders of record on January 15, 1998. At the date of declaration the securities had a market value of $2,000,000. The entries are as follows.

At date of declaration (December 18, 1997):		
Investment in Securities	750,000	
Gain on Appreciation of Securities		750,000
Retained Earnings (Property Dividends Declared)	2,000,000	
Property Dividends Payable		2,000,000
At date of distribution (January 30, 1998):		
Property Dividends Payable	2,000,000	
Investment in Securities		2,000,000

Spin-offs. An exception to this accounting treatment occurs when the shares of a subsidiary company of the corporation are distributed in total to the shareholders of the corporation. Such an event is called a **spin-off**. The shareholders now *directly* own the shares of the subsidiary company instead of *indirectly* owning the subsidiary through ownership of the shares of the parent company. While a spin-off results in giving property (i.e., the corporation's investment in the subsidiary) to the corporation's shareholders, the transfer is measured at the carrying value, not the fair value, of the shares distributed.[13] The rationale for this treatment is that there has been no change in substance as a result of the transaction: the company's shareholders originally owned the subsidiary through their share ownership of the parent company, and subsequent to the spin-off they continue to own the spun-off company, but now directly. There is no basis for a change in the valuation of the spun-off shares.

---

[11] *CICA Handbook*, Section 3830, par. .05.

[12] *Ibid.*, par. .04.

[13] *Ibid.*, par. .11.

SCRIP DIVIDENDS

A dividend payable in **scrip** means that the corporation, instead of paying the dividend now, has elected to pay it at some later date. *The scrip issued to shareholders as a dividend is merely a special form of note payable.* Scrip dividends may be declared when the corporation has a sufficient retained earnings balance but is short of cash. The recipient of the scrip dividend may hold it until the due date, if one is specified, and collect the dividend or sell it to obtain immediate cash.

When a scrip dividend is declared, the corporation debits Retained Earnings (or Scrip Dividend Declared) and credits Scrip Dividend Payable, reporting the payable as a liability on the balance sheet. Upon payment, Scrip Dividend Payable is debited and Cash credited. If the scrip bears interest, the interest portion of the cash payment is debited to Interest Expense and not treated as part of the dividend.

As an example, Berg Canning Co. Ltd., when short of cash, avoided missing its eighty-fourth consecutive quarterly dividend by declaring on May 6, 1998 a scrip dividend in the form of two-month promissory notes (from the date of record) amounting to $0.80 a share on 2,545,000 shares outstanding. The date of record was May 27, 1998 and scrip notes were sent to shareholders on May 30. The notes had an interest rate of 10% per annum with a maturity (payment) date of July 27. The entries related to this scrip dividend are as follows.

At date of declaration (May 6, 1998):

Retained Earnings (Scrip Dividend Declared)	2,036,000	
Notes Payable to Shareholders ($0.80 × 2,545,000)		2,036,000

At date of payment (July 27, 1998):

Notes Payable to Shareholders	2,036,000	
Interest Expense ($2,036,000 × 61/365 × .10)*	34,026	
Cash		2,070,026

* The interest runs from the date of record to the date of payment.

STOCK DIVIDENDS

A **stock dividend** occurs when the board of directors of a company declares that a dividend will be paid to shareholders in the form of a company's own shares (of the same or different class).[14] This may occur because the board wishes to capitalize part of the earnings (i.e., reclassify amounts from earned to contributed capital) and thus retain earnings in the business on a permanent basis. Alternatively, a stock dividend may be declared because the board, unwilling or unable to pay a cash dividend, may still desire to provide the shareholders with something tangible for their interest in the company. Many would argue, however, that a stock dividend, while it may provide some psychological benefit to the shareholder, does not provide any real economic benefits. This is because, in a stock dividend, *no assets are distributed*, and *each shareholder has exactly the same proportionate interest in the corporation and the same total book value after the stock dividend as before the dividend.* Of course, *the book value per share is lower because an increased number of shares are outstanding.*

Accounting for a stock dividend of no-par value shares results in transferring an amount from Retained Earnings to the appropriate share capital account. The question to be answered is "What amount should be transferred?" The *CICA Handbook* does not con-

OBJECTIVE 5
Explain the nature of stock dividends and how they are accounted for.

---

[14] *Financial Reporting in Canada—1995* indicated that of 300 companies surveyed, 12 in 1994 and 14 in 1993 disclosed the distribution of a stock dividend in a note to the financial statements or in the retained earnings statement.

tain a recommendation regarding this. The CBCA states that, for stock dividends, the declared amount of the dividend shall be added to the stated capital account. The CBCA does not allow shares to be issued until they are fully paid for in an amount not less than the fair equivalent of money that the corporation would have received if the shares had been issued for cash. Therefore, *the fair market value must be used* for companies incorporated under this legislation.

Ordinarily, *the fair value to be used is the market price of the shares on the date of the dividend declaration*. This is reasonable given the assumption that the market price will not change materially as a result of the stock dividend. When the market price is significantly affected (e.g., when a relatively large number of shares are being issued), it would be more appropriate to account for the event as a stock split (as described later), even though it may be called a stock dividend.

While the corporation issuing a stock dividend transfers the fair value of the no-par value shares issued from Retained Earnings to appropriate share capital accounts, an interesting question is whether those receiving the stock dividend should consider it as income, as they would consider a cash dividend.[15] Conceptually, the answer would be no. The stock dividend is not income to shareholders because it merely distributes the recipient's equity over a larger number of shares. Theoretically, while the number of shares held increases, the underlying worth of the total number of shares held does not change because the net assets of the corporation do not change. If, however, the market price per share does not decline in direct proportion to the increased number of shares now issued (i.e., the market does not respond perfectly), the recipients of the stock dividend could be better off. To realize their gain, however, they would have to sell their shares.

Given the direction in the CBCA, this chapter illustrates the *accounting for stock dividends using the market value of the shares issued at the date of declaration as the appropriate measurement*.

Entries for Stock Dividends. Assume that a corporation has outstanding 1,000 common shares of no-par value issued for $100,000 and a retained earnings balance of $50,000. If it declares a 10% stock dividend, it issues 100 additional shares to existing shareholders. Assuming the fair market value per share was $130 at the time of the stock dividend declaration, the entry would be:

Retained Earnings (Stock Dividend Declared)	13,000	
Common Stock Dividend Distributable		13,000

Note from the entry above that *no asset or liability has been affected*. The entry merely reflects a reclassification within shareholders' equity. If a balance sheet is prepared between the dates of declaration and distribution, the Common Stock Dividend Distributable account should be shown in the Shareholders' Equity section as an addition to share capital, whereas cash or property dividends payable are shown as current liabilities.[16]

When the shares are issued the entry would be:

Common Stock Dividend Distributable	13,000	
Common Shares		13,000

No matter what the fair value is at the time of the stock dividend, each shareholder retains the same proportionate interest in the corporation. Exhibit 17-6 shows that the

---

[15] For Canadian income tax purposes, at the time of this writing, the recipient of a stock dividend has to treat it in the same manner as a cash dividend, measured at the "paid up capital" (legal capital, which would be the fair market value for no-par shares) of the shares received. As such, the stock dividend would be taxable, an aspect that may contribute to the downward trend in the number of companies issuing stock dividends in recent years.

[16] Some argue that no entry need be made at the declaration date since court decisions have allowed for stock dividends to be revoked after declaration. Nevertheless, the declaration should be disclosed in financial statements. Journalizing at the time of declaration and disclosing in the statements as indicated is appropriate. A note could also be used.

total net worth of each shareholder (A, B, and C) does not change as a result of a stock dividend, and that each shareholder owns the same proportion of the total shares outstanding after as before the stock dividend.

EXHIBIT 17-6

Before dividend:

Share capital, 1,000 common shares of no-par value	$100,000
Retained earnings	50,000
Total shareholders' equity	$150,000

Shareholders' interests:

A—400 shares, 40% interest, book value	$ 60,000
B—500 shares, 50% interest, book value	75,000
C—100 shares, 10% interest, book value	15,000
	$150,000

After declaration but before distribution of 10% stock dividend:

If fair market value per share ($130) is used as the basis for entry

Share capital, 1,000 shares	$100,000
Common stock dividend distributable, 100 shares	13,000
Retained earnings ($50,000 − $13,000)	37,000
Total shareholders' equity	$150,000

After distribution of 10% stock dividend:

Share capital, 1,100 shares	$113,000
Retained earnings ($50,000 − $13,000)	37,000
Total shareholders' equity	$150,000

Shareholders' interests:

A—440 shares, 40% interest, book value	$ 60,000
B—550 shares, 50% interest, book value	75,000
C—110 shares, 10% interest, book value	15,000
	$150,000

For shareholders owning a quantity of shares not evenly divisible by 10 (unlike this case), companies will issue either fractional shares or cash equal to the proportion of a share to which they are entitled. For example, if Shareholder A owned 323 of the 1,000 shares of the company in the illustration, this shareholder is entitled to 32.3 additional shares as a result of the 10% stock dividend.

If fractional share entitlements are payable in cash and the company records indicate an equivalent of five fractional shares as a result of the stock dividend, the following entries would be made to record the declaration and payment of the dividend.

Retained Earnings (Stock Dividend Declared)	13,000	
Common Stock Dividend Distributable (95 × $130)		12,350
Dividend Payable (5 × $130)		650
Common Stock Dividend Distributable	12,350	
Dividend Payable	650	
Common Shares		12,350
Cash		650

STOCK SPLITS

If a company has not distributed earnings over several years and a sizable balance in retained earnings has accumulated, it is likely that the market value of its outstanding shares has increased. Shares that were issued at prices less than $50 can easily increase to market values in excess of $200 a share. The higher the market price of a share, the less readily shares can be purchased by most people (particularly given that shares are sold in lots, not individually). The managements of many corporations believe that for better public relations, broad ownership of a corporation's shares is desirable. They wish, therefore, to have a market price sufficiently low to be within range of the majority of potential investors. To reduce the market value of shares, the device of a **stock split** may be employed. For example, the now notorious Bre-X Minerals common shares were selling for over $200 each in early 1996 before being split 10-for-one. Bre-X shares closed at $234.00 on May 21, 1996, and traded at a high of $24.30 and a low of $22.35 before closing at $22.40 on May 22, the effective date of the split. The company's intent was to improve the marketability of its shares.[17] Examples of companies that have recently had stock splits include Imasco Ltd. (two-for-one), Heinz (three-for-two), and Harley-Davidson, whose two-for-one stock split in 1994 was the third since its initial public offering in 1986.

From an accounting standpoint, *no entry is recorded for a stock split*; a memorandum note, however, is made to indicate that the number of shares outstanding has increased.[18] The absence of any other changes in shareholders' equity is indicated in the following illustration for a two-for-one stock split on 1,000 no-par value common shares.

EXHIBIT 17-7

Shareholders' Equity Before Two-for-One Split		Shareholders' Equity After Two-for-One Split	
Common, **1,000 shares,**		Common, **2,000 shares,**	
no-par value	$100,000	no-par value	$100,000
Retained earnings	50,000	Retained earnings	50,000
	$150,000		$150,000

STOCK SPLITS AND STOCK DIVIDENDS DIFFERENTIATED

OBJECTIVE 6
Distinguish between stock splits and stock dividends and identify the accounting consequences of each.

A stock split is distinguished from a stock dividend in that *a stock split results in an increase* (or decrease in a reverse stock split) *in the number of shares outstanding with no change in the share capital or retained earnings amounts, whereas a stock dividend results in an increase in both the number of shares outstanding and the share capital amount and a decrease in retained earnings. Neither,* however, *results in any change to net assets or total shareholders' equity.*

A stock dividend, like a stock split, may be used to increase the marketability of the shares, although marketability is often a secondary consideration. If the stock dividend is so large that the principal consideration appears to be a desire to reduce the price of the shares, the action results in a stock split, regardless of the form it may take. The AICPA Committee on Accounting Procedures stated that whenever additional shares are issued for the purpose of reducing the unit market price, then the distribution more closely resembles a stock split than a stock dividend. This effect usually results only if the num-

---

[17] Some companies use reverse stock splits. A **reverse stock split** reduces the number of shares outstanding, which increases the price per share. This technique is used when the share price is unusually low or when management wishes to take control of the company. For example, MTC Electronic Technologies Co. Ltd. had a one-for-four reverse split. As a dramatic example of the use of a reverse split, two officers of Metropolitan Maintenance Co. took control of the company several years ago by forcing a 1-for-3,000 reverse stock split on their shareholders. But anyone who had fewer than 3,000 shares received only cash for his or her shares. Only the two officers owned more than 3,000 shares, so they then owned all the shares. A nice squeeze play! (*Forbes*, November 19, 1984, p. 54.)

[18] If shares have a par value, the memorandum note would indicate that the par value had changed as well as the number of shares outstanding.

ber of shares issued is more than 20% or 25% of the number of shares previously outstanding.[19] While no clear rules have been specified for the Canadian practitioner, the Toronto Stock Exchange views 25% as the maximum stock dividend.

The following table summarizes and compares the accounting consequences of cash dividends, stock dividends, and stock splits. The accounting consequences of property and scrip dividends are the same as for cash dividends.

EXHIBIT 17-8

| | Declaration and Payment of a Cash Dividend | Declaration and Distribution of | |
| | | Stock Dividend | Stock Split |
Effect on:			
Net assets (Assets — Liabilities)	Decrease	-0-	-0-
Total shareholders' equity	Decrease	-0-	-0-
Retained earnings	Decrease	Decrease*	-0-
Share capital	-0-	Increase*	-0-
Number of shares outstanding	-0-	Increase	Increase
*Market value of shares issued			

LIQUIDATING DIVIDENDS

Some corporations have used contributed surplus as a basis for dividends. Without proper disclosure of this fact, shareholders may erroneously believe the corporation has been operating at a profit. A further result could be subsequent sale of additional shares by the corporation at a higher price than is warranted. This type of deception, intentional or unintentional, can be avoided by providing a clear statement of the basis of dividends accompanying the dividend cheque.

Dividends based on other than retained earnings are sometimes described as **liquidating dividends**, thus implying that they are a return of the shareholder's investment rather than of assets generated from profits. In fact, the distribution may be based on contributed surplus that resulted from donations by outsiders or other shareholders and not be a return of the given shareholder's contribution. But, in a more general sense, *any dividend not based on earnings must be a reduction of corporation capital and, to that extent, it is a liquidating dividend.*[20] We noted in Chapter 12 that companies in the extractive industries may pay dividends equal to the total of accumulated income and depletion. The portion of these dividends in excess of accumulated income represents a return of part of the shareholders' investment.

For example, McChesney Mines Inc. issued a dividend to its common shareholders of $1,200,000. The cash dividend announcement noted that $900,000 should be considered income and the remainder a return of capital. The entries are:

At date of declaration:

Retained Earnings	900,000	
Contributed Surplus	300,000	
Dividends Payable		1,200,000

OBJECTIVE 7
Distinguish between liquidating and regular dividends.

[19] American Institute of Certified Public Accountants, *Accounting Research and Terminology Bulletin No. 43* (New York: AICPA, 1961), par. 13. The U.S. SEC has added more precision to the 20 to 25% rule. Specifically, the SEC indicates that distributions of 25% or more should be considered a "split-up effected in the form of a dividend." Distributions of less than 25% should be accounted for as a stock dividend.

[20] *The Globe and Mail*, February 21, 1996, p. B15 reported that 62.5 cents of each $1 of Mackenzie Industrial Income Fund's "dividend" in 1995 was a return of capital and that over the five years ending June 30, 1995, $2.25 of the total distributions per unit of $5.00 was a repayment of the investors' own money. The article notes that although the Fund discloses this to investors, some investment dealers may not realize and spell out to investors that a significant portion of the $1.00 annual distribution is not a return on the investment.

At date of payment:

Dividends Payable	1,200,000	
Cash		1,200,000

DIVIDEND PREFERENCES

OBJECTIVE 8
Allocate dividend distributions between preferred and common shareholders.

In Chapter 16, it was indicated that various rights and privileges may be given to particular classes of shares. In most cases, these rights and privileges pertain to dividends and reflect various combinations regarding cumulative and participating arrangements. The examples given below illustrate the effect of various provisions on dividend distributions to common and preferred shareholders. Assume that $50,000 is to be distributed as cash dividends, and that outstanding share capital consists of $400,000 received for 8,000 common shares of no-par value and $100,000 received for 1,000, $6 dividend, no-par value preferred shares. Dividends would be distributed to each class according to the assumptions stated for each situation.[21]

A. Assumption—the preferred shares are noncumulative and nonparticipating.

EXHIBIT 17-9

	Preferred	Common	Total
$6 × 1,000 shares	$6,000		$ 6,000
The remainder to common		$44,000	44,000
Totals	$6,000	$44,000	$50,000

B. Assumption—the preferred shares are cumulative and nonparticipating, and dividends have not been paid on them in the preceding two years.

EXHIBIT 17-10

	Preferred	Common	Total
Dividends in arrears, $6 × 1,000 shares for two years	$12,000		$12,000
Current year's dividend, $6 × 1,000 shares	6,000		6,000
The remainder to common		$32,000	32,000
Totals	$18,000	$32,000	$50,000

C. Assumption—the preferred shares are noncumulative and fully participating. Participation is in terms of the proportionate (percentage) relationship of the amounts paid for the shares (i.e., the amounts in the share capital accounts). Participation takes place after the stipulated preferred dividend is satisfied and common shareholders have been allocated an equal rate on their share capital.

---

[21] The terms and bases for determining participating dividends can be different from those shown in illustrations C and D. The specific details related to how participating dividend amounts are determined are described in the issuing corporation's articles of incorporation. For example, Canadian Utilities Limited has Class A non-voting shares and Class B common shares that share equally, on a share-for-share basis, in all dividends declared by the company.

EXHIBIT 17-11

	Preferred	Common	Total
Current year's dividend—preferred	$ 6,000	—	$ 6,000
Current year's dividend—common	—	$ 24,000	24,000
Participating dividend—pro rata	4,000	16,000	20,000
	$10,000	$ 40,000	$50,000

The amounts are determined as follows:

	Preferred	Common	Total
Current year's dividend			
Preferred ($6 × 1,000 shares)		$ 6,000	
Common (Preferred rate × common share capital)			
[($6,000/$100,000) × $400,000)]		24,000	$30,000
Amount available for participation		$ 20,000	
Total share capital ($100,000 + $400,000)		500,000	
Rate of participation			
$\frac{\text{Amount available}}{\text{Total share capital}} = \frac{\$\ 20,000}{\$500,000}$		4%	
Participating dividend			
Preferred (4% × $100,000)			$ 4,000
Common (4% × $400,000)			16,000
			$20,000

An alternative to calculating these amounts would be:

(a) Determine the percentage of the total amount available for dividends to total share capital:

$$\frac{\$\ 50,000}{\$500,000} = 10\%$$

(b) If this rate is greater than the rate committed to preferred for the year (6% = $6,000/ $100,000) then it can be applied to the share capital for each class to determine their respective total dividend:

To preferred (10% × $100,000)	$10,000
To common (10% × $400,000)	40,000
Total	$50,000

(c) If the rate is less than the rate committed to preferred, the preferred are given their full amount ($6,000) if available, with the remainder, if any, going to the common shareholders.

D. Assumption—the preferred shares are cumulative and fully participating, and dividends have not been paid in the preceding two years. In this case, the dividends in arrears are allocated to the preferred shareholders and the balance available is allocated according to the procedures illustrated in Assumption C. Therefore, the distribution is as follows.

EXHIBIT 17-12

	Preferred	Common	Total
Preferred dividends in arrears			
(2 years × $6 × 1,000 shares)	$12,000		$12,000
Current year's dividend			
(6% of share capital)	6,000	$24,000	30,000
Participating dividend			
($8,000/$500,000) × share capital	1,600	6,400	$ 8,000
Totals	$19,600	$30,400	$50,000

RESTRICTIONS ON RETAINED EARNINGS

OBJECTIVE 9

Identify reasons for restrictions on retained earnings and properly disclose them in financial statements.

In general, assets equal to the balance of retained earnings are considered to be available for distribution as dividends. For various reasons, however, *restrictions may be placed on retained earnings so that a specified amount is not available for dividend distribution*. The causes for such **restrictions** arise from:

1. *Statutory or contractual obligations.* For example, a bond indenture may contain a requirement that a specified minimum amount of retained earnings be maintained by a company over the life of the bond.

2. *Discretionary action by management and the board of directors.* For example, management may have intentions for future plant expansion to be financed internally. As a consequence, an amount of retained earnings may be voluntarily excluded from being available for dividends. Other reasons for such voluntary restrictions may be because of possible future losses (e.g., for declines in inventory prices or from lawsuits or unfavourable contractual obligations), a desire to maintain a strong working capital position, or to provide for general contingencies.

While the first cause represents a legal requirement that cannot be avoided, the necessity for formally establishing discretionary restrictions is debatable. Establishing and disclosing a discretionary restriction does reflect a legitimate attempt to inform statement users that, for a particular reason, part of retained earnings is not available for dividends. A consequence, however, may be that such users wonder why the unrestricted retained earnings have not been distributed as dividends. In a sense, all earnings not distributed as dividends are "implicitly restricted" for a variety of reasons. Generally, perhaps to help avoid confusion or because there is no need to do so, companies seldom establish discretionary restrictions.

The *existence of a contractual or discretionary restriction on retained earnings in no way results in the automatic creation of a cash fund that is available for use for the reasons related to the restriction* (e.g., to pay bonds or to carry out a plant expansion). Should such a cash fund be required or desired, actions apart from restricting retained earnings must be taken. Also, restricting retained earnings is not a substitute way to account for loss contingencies (discussed in Chapter 5).

When there is a condition restricting or affecting the distribution of retained earnings, the details should be disclosed.[22] This may be accomplished through notes to the financial statements or a more formal accounting procedure for recognizing appropriations of retained earnings.

DISCLOSURE OF RESTRICTIONS IN NOTES

Most restrictions on the distribution of retained earnings are disclosed by note, which provides a medium for extended explanations of restrictions such as those imposed by bond indentures and loan agreements.[23] The type of detail revealed by such notes includes identification of the source of the restriction, pertinent provisions, and the amount of retained earnings subject to restriction, or the amount not so restricted. The Consumers Packaging Inc. and Canadian Utilities Limited examples from recent annual reports illustrate note disclosure relating to restrictions on retained earnings and dividends.

---

[22] *CICA Handbook*, Section 3250, par. .10.

[23] *Financial Reporting in Canada—1995* stated that in 1994, 40 of the 300 surveyed companies made such note disclosures (35 giving details) compared with 41 in 1993. Between 1987 and 1990, only two surveyed companies disclosed restrictions by formally appropriating retained earnings, and between 1991 and 1994, all used note disclosure.

EXHIBIT 17-13   CONSUMERS PACKAGING INC.

Note 7 (in part)

e) Dividend Restrictions
Under the terms of the Credit Agreement, the declaration or payment of a dividend on its Series C Preferred Shares or Common Shares would be an event of default.

EXHIBIT 17-14   CANADIAN UTILITIES LIMITED

Note 7 (in part)

Retained earnings

The debenture trust indenture places certain limitations on the Corporation which include restrictions on the payment of dividends on Class A and Class B shares. Consolidated retained earnings in the amount of $167.2 million are free from such restrictions.

When there is more than one type of restriction relating to a particular contract, disclosure of the amount of retained earnings so restricted would be based on the most restrictive covenants. This is sufficient because restrictions seldom, if ever, pyramid in amount.

DISCLOSURE OF RESTRICTIONS THROUGH APPROPRIATIONS

Appropriations (also called **reserves**[24]) of retained earnings are nothing more than reclassifications of retained earnings, temporarily or perhaps even permanently established to reflect restrictions on the availability of retained earnings for dividends. *Appropriations are created by transferring amounts from the unappropriated retained earnings account to an appropriated retained earnings account. When the appropriation is no longer necessary, the appropriated amount is returned to unappropriated retained earnings.* The purpose of an appropriation is to show in the body of the balance sheet that a portion of retained earnings is not available for dividend distributions.

As soon as the board of directors has approved an appropriation of retained earnings, it is necessary to record it in the accounts. For example:

(a) An Appropriation for Plant Expansion is to be created by transfer from Retained Earnings of $400,000 a year for five years. The entry for each year would be:

Retained Earnings	400,000	
Retained Earnings Appropriated for Plant Expansion		400,000

(b) At the end of five years, the appropriation account would have a balance of $2,000,000. If the expansion plan has been completed, the appropriation is no longer required and can be returned to retained earnings by making the following entry.

Retained Earnings Appropriated for Plant Expansion	2,000,000	
Retained Earnings		2,000,000

Return of such an appropriation to retained earnings has the effect of increasing unappropriated retained earnings without affecting the assets, total shareholders' equity,

---

[24] The *CICA Handbook* limits the use of the term "reserve" to appropriations of retained earnings or other surplus (Section 3260, par. .01).

or total retained earnings. In effect, over the five years the company has expanded by reinvesting assets acquired through the earnings process.

Reporting appropriations in financial statements is accomplished simply by categorizing total retained earnings into two components: appropriated and unappropriated. For example, if total retained earnings consisted of $800,000 appropriated for plant expansion and $2,200,000 unappropriated, this would be reported in the Shareholders' Equity section of the balance sheet as follows.

EXHIBIT 17-15

Shareholders' Equity:		
Share capital		$1,000,000
Retained earnings:		
Appropriated for plant expansion	$ 800,000	
Unappropriated	2,200,000	3,000,000
Total shareholders' equity		$4,000,000

While restrictions on retained earnings are usually reported through note disclosure, the appropriation of retained earnings is acceptable practice, provided that it is shown as part of shareholders' equity and is clearly identified as to the source from which it was created.[25]

ACCOUNTING AND REPORTING FOR SELF-INSURANCE

OBJECTIVE 10
Explain the issues regarding accounting for self-insurance.

A company may insure against many contingencies such as fire, flood, storm, and accident by taking out insurance policies and paying premiums to insurance companies. Some contingencies, however, are not insurable or the rates may be judged as being prohibitively high in the circumstances. In such situations, some companies may adopt a policy referred to as **self-insurance**. Self-insurance appears especially valid when a company's physical or operating characteristics permit application of probability analysis as used by insurance companies. Whenever the risk of loss can be spread over a large number of possible loss events that individually would be small in relation to the total potential loss, self-insurance is a temptation. It is based on the belief that the losses will cost fewer dollars over an extended period of time than the premiums that would be paid to insure against such losses. The company thus avoids paying the insurance company's overhead costs including the insurance agent's commission. Examples of self-insurance situations are a car rental company with hundreds of cars in different locations or a grocery chain with many stores scattered geographically.

In the past, many companies accounted for such a policy by estimating a hypothetical amount of annual insurance expense, charging it to the income statement, and crediting a liability account such as Liability for Self-Insurance Risks or Liability for Uninsured Losses. When actual casualty losses occurred they were charged against the liability account. Because there is no actual obligation, and because the effect is to arbitrarily smooth income and, therefore, give a perception of lower risk than that to which the company is actually exposed, this method is no longer permitted under GAAP.

GAAP requires that uninsured losses be charged against revenues in the period in which the losses are sustained. This results in a higher variability of reported income than the accounting methods previously used and this better reflects the increased risks to which a self-insurer is exposed. Some companies who self-insure appropriate retained earnings each period in an amount approximating the premium cost of adequate insurance covering the risk or a prorated allocation of anticipated losses. The balance of the

---

[25] *CICA Handbook*, Section 3260, par. .04.

appropriation account would not exceed the maximum expected loss at any one time. The intent of this appropriation is to indicate to shareholders why assets must be retained in the corporation rather than be paid out as dividends.

OTHER COMPONENTS OF SHAREHOLDERS' EQUITY

APPRAISAL INCREASE CREDITS

The *CICA Handbook* generally requires that all capital assets be recorded at cost.[26] Prior to the inclusion of the revised Section 3060 in the *Handbook* in 1990, assets could be written up to an appraised value above their cost in limited circumstances (e.g., a reorganization or to recognize discovery value). When an asset's appraisal value was in excess of its book value and this fact was recognized in the accounts, the credit was made to a shareholders' equity account such as Excess of Appraised Value of Fixed Assets Over Depreciated Cost or simply Appraisal Increase. Such **appraisal increase credit** accounts that existed prior to the new Section 3060 were, and continue to be, shown as a separate item in shareholders' equity, with disclosure of the basis of valuation of the underlying assets and the date of the appraisal.[27] An appraisal increase account should be amortized to retained earnings each period in amounts equal to the realization of the appreciation through sale or depreciation provisions, and the depreciation expense on the appraised asset that is charged to income should be based on the appraised value.[28]

OBJECTIVE 11
Identify other components of shareholders' equity and explain their nature.

CUMULATIVE TRANSLATION ADJUSTMENTS

When corporations consolidate the financial statements of self-sustaining foreign subsidiaries with those of the parent company, all accounting elements must be remeasured in current Canadian dollars.[29] As the exchange rate used changes from period to period, the Canadian dollar equivalent of the subsidiary's net assets changes as well. The accumulated adjustment, which can be either a debit or a credit balance, is disclosed in the parent company's Shareholders' Equity section as a separate item entitled **Cumulative Translation Adjustment** or Foreign Currency Translation Adjustment.[30] Consistent with other shareholders' equity items, companies are required to disclose the significant elements giving rise to changes in the exchange gains and losses accumulated in this account during the period.

FINANCIAL REORGANIZATIONS

A corporation that consistently suffers net losses accumulates negative retained earnings, or a **deficit**. Corporate laws typically provide that no dividends may be declared and paid so long as a corporation's contributed capital (share capital and contributed surplus) has been impaired by a deficit. In these cases, a corporation with a debit balance of

OBJECTIVE 12
Explain what a financial reorganization is, and how it is accounted for and disclosed in financial statements.

---

[26] *CICA Handbook*, Section 3060, par. .18. Excluded from coverage by this section (par. .02) of the *Handbook* are goodwill and special circumstances when a comprehensive revaluation of all assets and liabilities occurs as a result of a financial reorganization.

[27] *CICA Handbook*, Section 3060, par. .64.

[28] *Financial Reporting in Canada—1995* reports that of the 300 companies surveyed, only 4 in 1994 and 5 in 1993 reported appraisal increases as a separate item in shareholders' equity.

[29] A self-sustaining foreign operation is one where the parent company's exposure to risk of loss (or gain) from changes in the exchange rate is limited to its investment in the subsidiary's net assets. Further discussion of this issue is deferred to an advanced accounting course.

[30] *Financial Reporting in Canada—1995* reports that of the 300 companies surveyed in 1994, 136 disclosed the existence of this type of account (127 companies in 1993).

retained earnings must accumulate sufficient profits to offset the deficit before dividends are possible.

This situation may be a real hardship on a corporation and its shareholders. A company that has operated unsuccessfully for several years and accumulated a deficit may have finally "turned the corner." Development of new products and new markets, a new management team, or improved economic conditions may promise much-improved operating results. But, if the law prohibits dividends until the deficit has been replaced by accumulated earnings, the shareholders must wait until such profits have been earned, which may take a considerable period of time. Furthermore, future success may depend on obtaining additional funds through the sale of shares. If no dividends can be paid for some time, however, the market price of any new share issue is likely to be low, if such shares can be marketed at all. Additionally, if a corporation in financial difficulty has non-equity interests (e.g., bondholders), it is quite likely that meeting interest and/or principal payments is in jeopardy.

Thus, a company with every prospect of a successful future may be prevented from accomplishing its plans because of past financial difficulties that created the deficit, although present management may have had nothing whatever to do with the years over which the problems occurred. To permit the corporation to proceed with its plans might well be to the advantage of all interests in the enterprise; to require it to eliminate the deficit through profits might actually force it to liquidate.

A procedure that enables a company that has gone through financial difficulty to proceed with its plans without the encumbrance of having to recover from a deficit is called a **financial reorganization**. A financial reorganization is defined as *a substantial realignment of the equity and non-equity interests of an enterprise such that the holders of one or more of the significant classes of non-equity interests and the holders of all of the significant classes of equity interests give up some (or all) of their rights and claims upon the enterprise.*[31]

A financial reorganization results from negotiation and the reaching of an eventual agreement between non-equity and equity holders in the corporation. These negotiations may take place under the provisions of a legal act (e.g., Companies' Creditors Arrangement Act) or a less formal process.[32]

ACCOUNTING FOR A FINANCIAL REORGANIZATION

When a financial reorganization occurs *where the same party does not control the company both before and after the reorganization, and where new costs are reasonably determinable*, the assets and liabilities of the company should undergo a **comprehensive revaluation**.[33] This entails three accounting objectives: first, to record the changes in debt and equity interests as negotiated in the reorganization agreement; second, to assign appropriate going concern values to all assets and liabilities; and third, to bring the deficit balance to zero as if the company were starting anew. The consequence is that the company is given a "fresh start" for purposes of financial reporting.

To account for a financial reorganization, the following occur:

1. The balance in the Retained Earnings (Deficit) account is brought up to date. In addition to closing any open income statement accounts (i.e., the reorganization date is not the same as the year end), any asset write-downs related to circumstances that existed prior to the reorganization must be accounted for (see Chapter 12).

---

[31] *CICA Handbook*, Section 1625, par. .03.

[32] *Ibid.*, par. .15.

[33] *Ibid.*, pars. .04 and .05.

2. The updated balance of Retained Earnings (Deficit) is reclassified to either Share Capital, Contributed Surplus, or a separately identified account within shareholders' equity, and the Retained Earnings or Deficit account is given a zero balance.

3. The assets and liabilities of the enterprise are comprehensively revalued. This means that values for assets and liabilities established in the negotiations among the equity and non-equity interests (or fair values if no negotiated values are established) become the new costs to be accounted for subsequent to the reorganization. The difference between the carrying values before the reorganization and these new values is accounted for as a **revaluation adjustment**. The revaluation adjustment and any costs directly incurred to carry out the financial reorganization are accounted for as capital transactions and are closed to either Share Capital, Contributed Surplus, or a separately identified account within shareholders' equity.[34]

To illustrate, consider the following based on the appendix to *Handbook* Section 1625.

EXHIBIT 17-16   HOPEFUL CO. LTD.

(in 000s)

	Balance Prior to Financial Reorganization	Adjustments to Reflect Write-Downs Before Reorganization	Revaluation Adjustment from Reorganization	Balance After Financial Reorganization
Assets:				
Current assets	$1,000			$1,000
Property, plant, and equipment (net)	5,000	$(400)ᵃ	$ (600)ᶜ	4,000
Goodwill	300	(300)ᵃ		—
Patents	—		100ᶜ	100
	$6,300	$(700)	$ (500)	$5,100
Liabilities and Shareholders' Equity:				
Current liabilities	$2,400			$2,400
Bonds payable	1,000		($500)ᶜ	500
Preferred shares				
• 4,000 no-par, $20 dividend, two years in arrears	400		(400)ᶜ	—
Common shares				
• Issued prior to reorganization, 100,000 shares	4,000			2,200
• Issued on financial reorganization to bondholders, 60,000 shares and to preferred shareholders, 45,000 shares			(2,200)ᵇ 400ᶜ	
Deficit	(1,500)	(700)ᵃ	2,200ᵇ	—
	$6,300	$(700)	$ (500)	$5,100

This work sheet reflects the following accounting consequences of a financial reorganization.

(a) Property, plant, and equipment is written down by $400,000, and the $300,000 goodwill is eliminated in order to reflect circumstances that existed prior to the reorgani-

---

[34] *Ibid.*, pars. .39 to .49. If the result is a negative shareholders' equity, share capital is disclosed as a nominal amount and the balance is disclosed as a Capital Deficiency Resulting from Financial Reorganization.

zation. These write-downs relate to income of the period prior to the reorganization and are, therefore, sources for additions to the deficit prior to the reorganization. The work sheet column "Adjustments to Reflect Write-Downs Before Reorganization" shows the results of the write-downs on balance sheet accounts. The following journal entry incorporates these write-downs in the accounting records:

Deficit	700,000	
Property, Plant, and Equipment		400,000
Goodwill		300,000

(b) The Deficit account balance prior to the reorganization is now $2,200,000. This is reclassified as share capital, contributed surplus, or a separately identified account within the Shareholders' Equity section. The following entry brings the deficit to zero by reclassifying it to share capital, as is shown in the work sheet:

Common Shares	2,200,000	
Deficit		2,200,000

(c) The assets and liabilities are comprehensively revalued such that Property, Plant, and Equipment is reduced by a further $600,000 (i.e., after the write-down for circumstances prior to the reorganization), and previously unrecognized Patents developed by the company are recorded at $100,000. Bondholders have agreed to exchange one-half of their bonds for 60,000 common shares and preferred shareholders relinquish all their shares and dividends in arrears in exchange for 45,000 common shares. The entry to recognize these facts, with the resulting revaluation adjustment being recorded as share capital, is as follows.

Patents	100,000	
Bonds Payable	500,000	
Preferred Shares	400,000	
Property, Plant, and Equipment		600,000
Common Shares (revaluation adjustment)		400,000

Note that the $400,000 credit to Common Shares in the last entry is determined by the book value of the bonds ($500,000) and the preferred shares ($400,000) exchanged, reduced by the write-off of Property, Plant and Equipment ($600,000) and increased by the value of the Patent recognized ($100,000). Each of these adjustments could have been accumulated in a Revaluation Adjustment account that subsequently is closed to the Common Shares account.

This illustration is an example of a situation where a comprehensive revaluation of assets and liabilities is permitted by GAAP. There has been a change in the control of the company as the original common shareholders now own only 100,000 (i.e., less than 50%) of the 205,000 shares outstanding, and new values were reasonably determinable. *Where companies reorganize without a change in control*, GAAP does not allow asset values to be increased or nonrecorded assets to be recognized, although realignments of debt and equity interests, net asset write-downs, and the Retained Earnings or Deficit account can be adjusted.

FINANCIAL STATEMENT DISCLOSURE OF A FINANCIAL REORGANIZATION

Given that comprehensive revaluation of assets and liabilities has taken place as the result of a financial reorganization, the *CICA Handbook* requires that certain disclosures be made.

In financial statements for the period in which the reorganization takes place, the date of the reorganization, a description of the reorganization, and the amount of change in each major class of assets, liabilities, and shareholders' equity resulting from the reorganization must be disclosed. Financial statements for at least three years after the reorganization must disclose the date of reorganization, the revaluation adjustment amount and the shareholders' equity account in which it was recorded, and the amount of retained earnings (deficit) reclassified on the reorganization as well as the account to which it was reclassified. Additionally, the measurement bases used to revalue assets and liabilities should be disclosed for as long as the revalued amounts are significant.[35]

When a company reorganizes without a change in control of its equity interests, the elimination of any deficit against share capital or contributed surplus, or other financial rearrangement requires that Retained Earnings be "dated" for a period of at least three years.[36] Mitel Corporation, for example, in the Shareholders' Equity section of its March 25, 1994 balance sheet reported the following.

EXHIBIT 17-17   MITEL CORPORATION[37]

	1994	1993
Retained earnings (deficit), after capital reduction of $136.3 during 1992	$3.4	$(13.7)

REPORTING SHAREHOLDERS' EQUITY

The *CICA Handbook* recommends that changes in each of contributed surplus, retained earnings, and appropriations of retained earnings (reserves) during the period be disclosed.[38] Also, disclosure of the details of transactions affecting share capital is required.[39] While either notes to the financial statements or statements of changes in these shareholder equity categories may be presented to accomplish this, the basic format reconciles the beginning balance previously reported with the balance at the end of the period by providing information to explain the additions to and deductions from each account.

The following examples in Exhibits 17-18 and 17-19 indicate how such disclosure may be accomplished.

OBJECTIVE 13
Prepare statements or schedules to report changes in retained earnings, contributed surplus, share capital or total shareholders' equity.

EXHIBIT 17-18   DOMAN INDUSTRIES LIMITED

Consolidated Balance Sheets (in part)

ASSETS

	December 31,	
	1995	1994
	($000's)	
Shareholders' equity		
Share capital (Note 9(a))		
Preferred shares	112,309	112,309
Common and non-voting shares	196,376	196,376
	308,685	308,685
Retained earnings	127,097	86,034
	435,782	394,719

---

[35] *CICA Handbook*, Section 1625, pars. .50 to .52.

[36] *CICA Handbook*, Section 3250, par. .12. *Financial Reporting in Canada—1995* reports that 3 of its surveyed companies in 1994 (5 in 1993) indicated that a deficit was eliminated or reduced by reduction of share capital and/or transfer from contributed surplus. 14 companies (13 in 1993) indicated that a deficit had been eliminated or reduced in previous years.

[37] Reprinted with permission from Mitel Corporation's 1994 Annual Report ©(1994) Mitel Corporation.

[38] *CICA Handbook*, Sections 3250, par. .13 and 3260, par. .05.

[39] *CICA Handbook*, Section 3240, par. .05.

EXHIBIT 17-18   DOMAN INDUSTRIES LIMITED (Continued)

Consolidated Statements of Retained Earnings

	Years Ended December 31,	
	1995	1994
	($000's)	
Retained Earnings, beginning of year	$ 86,034	$42,747
Net earnings	53,192	55,794
	139,226	98,541
Deduct		
Dividends (Note 9(d))	12,129	12,437
Share issue expenses (net of deferred income taxes of $55,000 in 1994)	—	70
	12,129	12,507
Retained Earnings, end of year	$127,097	$86,034

Note 9. Share Capital (in part)

(c) *Changes in Issued Shares*

(i) Preferred shares

	Number of Shares				
	Class A, Series 2	Class A, Series 3	Class A, Series 4	Total	Amount
					($000's)
Balance, December 31, 1993	556,103	964,660	1,281,526	2,802,289	$126,212
Conversions	(549,033)	—	—	(549,033)	(13,726)
Redemption	(7,070)	—	—	(7,070)	(177)
Balance, December 31, 1994 and 1995	—	964,660	1,281,526	2,246,186	$112,309

(ii) Common and non-voting shares

	Number of Shares			
	Class A	Class B, Series 2	Total	Amount
				($000's)
Balance, December 31, 1993	5,656,795	26,110,576	31,767,371	$129,737
Issued for cash	—	3,000,000	3,000,000	52,500
Issued for cash on exercise of stock options	—	39,000	39,000	413
Conversions	(567,773)	2,327,468	1,759,695	13,726
Balance, December 31, 1994	5,089,022	31,477,044	36,566,066	196,376
Conversions	(17,833)	17,833	—	—
Balance, December 31, 1995	5,071,189	31,494,877	36,566,066	$196,376

EXHIBIT 17-19   NEWBRIDGE NETWORKS CORPORATION

APRIL 30, 1996 AND 1995

(Canadian dollars in thousands)

Consolidated Balance Sheets (in part)

	1996	1995
Share capital (Note 11)		
Common shares - 84,338,140 outstanding (1995 - 82,257,308 outstanding)	290,170	262,446
Accumulated foreign currency translation adjustment	1,285	3,832
Retained earnings	611,231	408,367
	902,686	674,645
	$1,093,417	$827,163

EXHIBIT 17-19   NEWBRIDGE NETWORKS CORPORATION (Continued)

APRIL 30, 1996 AND 1995

(Canadian dollars in thousands)

11. Share Capital (in part)

Authorized

An unlimited number of Common Shares.

An unlimited number of participating preferred shares, ranking in priority upon distribution of assets over Common Shares, may be issued in series with additional provisions as fixed by the Board of Directors.

CONSOLIDATED STATEMENTS OF SHAREHOLDERS' EQUITY

Years Ended April 30, 1996 and 1995 (in part)
(Canadian dollars in thousands)

	Common Shares		Accumulated Foreign Currency Adjustment	Retained Earnings	Shareholders' Equity
	Number	Amount			
At April 30, 1994	80,782,468	247,362	6,233	219,977	473,572
Exercise of employees' and directors' options	1,574,840	12,079			12,079
Purchase of Company's shares	(100,000)	(4,674)			(4,674)
Income tax benefit related to stock options		7,679			7,679
Effect of foreign currency translation ..			(2,401)		(2,401)
Net earnings				188,390	188,390
At April 30, 1995	82,257,308	262,446	3,832	408,367	674,645
Exercise of employees' and directors' options	2,580,832	50,068			50,068
Purchase of Company's shares	(500,000)	(28,209)			(28,209)
Income tax benefit related to stock options		5,865			5,865
Effect of foreign currency translation ..			(2,547)		(2,547)
Net earnings				202,864	202,864
At April 30, 1996	84,338,140	$290,170	$1,285	$611,231	$902,686

The following presentation is an example of a Shareholders' Equity section of a balance sheet. It includes most of the equity items discussed in Chapters 16 and 17, but the notes that would normally provide more details on the items have been omitted.

EXHIBIT 17-20   MODEL CORPORATION

SHAREHOLDERS' EQUITY

December 31, 1998

Share Capital:		
Class A, preferred, $9 dividend, cumulative, no-par value,		
30,000 shares authorized, issued, and outstanding		$ 3,150,000
Class B, common, no-par value, no authorized limit,		
400,000 shares issued and 398,000 outstanding as		
2,000 are in treasury		4,000,000
Class B common stock dividend distributable, 20,000 shares		200,000
Total share capital		7,350,000 (1)
Contributed Surplus:		
Excess of assigned value over cost of common shares		
purchased and cancelled	$ 10,000	
Donated land	830,000	
Total contributed surplus		840,000
		8,190,000 (2)
Retained Earnings:		
Appropriated for plant expansion	$2,100,000	
Unappropriated	2,160,000	
Total retained earnings		4,260,000
Total contributed capital and retained earnings		12,450,000
Excess of appraised value of fixed assets over		
depreciated cost		100,000
Cumulative translation adjustment		137,500
Total		12,687,500
Less cost of treasury shares (2,000 Class B common shares)		(75,500)
Total shareholders' equity		$12,612,000

(1) legal capital
(2) total contributed capital

Summary of Learning Objectives

1. **Explain the nature of contributed surplus, sources from which it may be derived, and how it is reported on the balance sheet.** Contributed surplus generally comprises all items of shareholders' equity in excess of the corporation's legal capital and earned surplus. It is derived, for example, from amounts paid for shares in excess of their par or stated value, donations to the company of assets or shares, and net "gains" (excess of assigned values over purchase price) from reacquired and cancelled shares or from treasury stock transactions. Although there may be several types of contributed surplus accounted for in separate accounts according to source, contributed surplus is usually reported as a single line item on the balance sheet.

2. **Identify common causes of changes in retained earnings.** Retained earnings can be increased only by net income or adjustments to the income of specific prior years, but is reduced by net losses, dividends, "losses" (excess of purchase price over assigned values) on reacquired and cancelled shares and treasury stock transactions, and other capital transactions.

3. **Describe the factors to consider when determining if dividends are to be distributed.** Before dividends are declared, it must be determined whether they are legally permitted and whether it is economically sound for the company to distribute assets. A company must have a positive retained earnings balance, must not contravene any agreements, and must not be insolvent as a result of the dividend. In addition, the company must assess its current and future cash requirements, and the signal that any change in dividend policy would send to the capital markets.

4. **Identify the various forms of dividend distributions and explain how to account for them.** Dividends can be in the form of cash, other assets, or company shares. If there is a significant time lag before the date of payment (a scrip dividend), interest may accrue on the outstanding balance. If dividends are paid with nonmonetary assets, the assets should be brought to their fair market value and any gain or loss recognized before distribution. A stock dividend is not a distribution of company assets to shareholders. It is simply the distribution of more shares representing the same proportionate ownership interest to existing shareholders. Dividends representing the distribution of assets generated by profitable operations, as well as stock dividends, are charged against retained earnings when declared.

5. **Explain the nature of stock dividends and how they are accounted for.** Stock dividends result in the capitalization of retained earnings, as the fair value of the shares issued is transferred from earned surplus to share capital accounts. In effect, it shifts retained earnings amounts to the permanent capital of the firm. There is no transfer of company assets to shareholders and each shareholder has the same proportionate interest in the company after the share distribution as before the dividend.

6. **Distinguish between stock splits and stock dividends and identify the accounting consequences of each.** Stock dividends and stock splits usually differ according to the company's motivation and size, and the effect dividends and splits can have on the individual components of shareholders' equity. A stock dividend results in a transfer of amounts from retained earnings to share capital, whereas a stock split does not affect the balance in any account. A stock split merely multiplies (reduces, in a reverse split) the number of shares authorized, issued, and outstanding, and changes the par value (if any) proportionately. Both theoretically affect the market price in direct proportion to the extent of the dividend or split.

7. **Distinguish between liquidating and regular dividends.** A regular dividend represents the distribution to shareholders of company assets generated by the profitable operation of the company, whereas a liquidating dividend represents a return to shareholders of assets originally invested in or contributed to the company.

8. **Allocate dividend distributions between preferred and common shareholders.** There is a clear order to follow in the allocation of dividends between common and preferred shareholders, governed by the stated features of each type of share. Dividends in arrears on cumulative preferred shares must be paid first. The stated dividend for the current year on preferred shares comes next in the allocation. The common shareholders are then entitled to a dividend at the same rate as that paid on preferred shares for the current period. Any remaining dividend distribution is allocated between the common and preferred shares according to any participation features. If preferred shares are nonpartic-

dividends in kind, 833

earned capital, 825

equity capital, 825

fair value, 834

financial reorganization, 846

insolvent, 830

internal financing, 828

liquidating dividends, 839

nonreciprocal transfer, 833

payout ratio, 833

property dividends, 833

reserves, 843

restrictions, 842

retained earnings, 827

revaluation adjustment, 847

reverse stock split, 838

scrip, 835

self-insurance, 844

spin-off, 834

stock dividend, 835

stock split, 838

ipating, the common claims the residual. If the preferred shares are fully participating, the common and preferred share the remainder at the same rate. If the preferred shares are partially participating, they are allocated a dividend up to the agreed rate and the residual accrues to the common shareholders.

9. **Identify reasons for restrictions on retained earnings and properly disclose them in financial statements.** Restrictions on the distribution of dividends, and therefore retained earnings, are often imposed by creditors of the firm who want to restrict the outflow of company resources to owners in order to safeguard their position. Companies' legislation also imposes restrictions on the payment of dividends when company assets have been used to reacquire company shares. In addition, there may be internal restrictions imposed by management. Note disclosure of these restrictions is most common, although some companies still report this information by a formal appropriation of retained earnings.

10. **Explain the issues regarding accounting for self-insurance.** The basic accounting issue is whether companies who self-insure should accrue an estimated insurance expense and liability each period, or whether uninsured losses should be charged against income when the losses actually occur. GAAP no longer permits the former treatment because it artificially smoothes income and requires recognizing a liability that does not exist. The issue for this chapter is that companies who self-insure often appropriate or otherwise restrict retained earnings in order to advise shareholders that the company needs to conserve assets to cover possible losses.

11. **Identify other components of shareholders' equity and explain their nature.** The most common account reported in shareholders' equity aside from contributed capital and retained earnings is the Cumulative Translation Adjustment account. This represents the accumulated deferred exchange gains and losses on the translation of the foreign currency denominated accounts of self-sustaining foreign subsidiaries. Appraisal Increase Credits still appear in the Shareholders' Equity section of companies who, prior to revised *Handbook* Section 3060, recognized the appreciation in the value of specific capital assets. This account will disappear over time as it is taken to income to offset the higher depreciation charges on the appreciated assets.

12. **Explain what a financial reorganization is, and how it is accounted for and disclosed in financial statements.** A financial reorganization is a significant realignment of creditor and equity interests. Where a financial reorganization results in a change in control of the organization, GAAP requires the company's assets and liabilities to be comprehensively revalued assuming new values can be reasonably determined. The objective is to give the organization a fresh start from an accounting perspective, usually resetting the retained earnings or deficit balance to zero. Where there is a reorganization, but a change in control does not take place, a company can still reflect the changes in owner and creditor interests, the write-down (but not write-up or recognition of unrecorded values) of overvalued assets, and an adjustment to its retained earnings or deficit balance. In both cases, the retained earnings balance is "dated" for a period of at least three years, and significant information must be provided about the reorganization.

13. **Prepare statements or schedules to report changes in retained earnings, contributed surplus, share capital, or total shareholders' equity.** One overriding objective in reporting shareholders' equity is the need for financial statement readers to be informed of all changes in equity over the reporting period. For this reason, changes in each component of equity are required to be disclosed.

EXERCISES

(Classification of Equity Items) Shareholders' equity on the balance sheet is composed of the following major sections: 1. Share Capital; 2. Contributed Surplus; 3. Retained Earnings; and 4. Other. **E17-1**

Instructions
Classify each of the following items as affecting one of the four sections above or as 5, an item not to be included in shareholders' equity.

(a) Retained earnings appropriated for plant expansion.

(b) Cumulative translation adjustment.

(c) Sinking fund.

(d) Employee share purchase loans receivable.

(e) Contributed capital—forfeit of cash received on preferred shares subscribed but not paid for in full.

(f) Excess of proceeds over purchase cost of treasury shares.

(g) Common shares subscribed.

(h) Stock split

(i) Revaluation adjustment on financial reorganization.

(j) Cash dividends declared.

(Equity Items on the Balance Sheet) The following are selected transactions that may affect shareholders' equity. **E17-2**

1. Recorded the sale of merchandise on account.

2. Declared a cash dividend.

3. Paid the cash dividend declared in Item 2.

4. Recorded an increase in value of an investment that will be distributed as a property dividend.

5. Declared a property dividend (see Item 4).

6. Distributed the property dividend to shareholders (see Items 4 and 5).

7. Recorded salaries accrued to the balance sheet date.

8. Declared a stock dividend.

9. Distributed the stock dividend declared in Item 8.

10. Declared and paid a dividend on preferred shares that meet the definition of a financial liability.

11. Declared and distributed a stock split.

12. Recorded a retained earnings appropriation.

Instructions
In a table like the following, indicate the effect each of the 12 transactions has on the financial statement elements listed. Use the following codes.

I = Increase   D = Decrease   NE = No Effect

Item	Assets	Liabilities	Shareholders' Equity	Share Capital	Retained Earnings	Net Income
1.						
2.						
etc.						

(Cash Dividend and Liquidating Dividend) Western Corporation has 2 million common shares issued and outstanding. On July 1 the board of directors voted a $0.75 per share cash dividend to shareholders of record as of July 14, payable July 31. **E17-3**

Instructions
(a) Prepare the journal entry for each of the dates above assuming the dividend represents a distribution of earnings.

(b) How would the entry differ if the dividend was a liquidating dividend?

E17-4   **(Preferred Dividends)** Kilmarnock Company's ledger shows the following balances on December 31, 1998:

Preferred shares—no-par value, $0.70 dividend, outstanding 20,000 shares	$ 200,000
Common shares—no-par value, outstanding 30,000 shares	3,000,000
Retained earnings	630,000

Instructions

Assuming that the directors decide to declare total dividends in the amount of $334,000, determine how much each class of shares would receive under each of the conditions stated below. Dividends on the preferred shares were not paid in the previous year.

(a) The preferred shares are cumulative and fully participating based on the proportion of share capital amounts for each class.

(b) The preferred shares are noncumulative and nonparticipating.

(c) The preferred shares are noncumulative and are to participate in distributions in excess of a 10% dividend rate on the common shares.

E17-5   **(Preferred Dividends)** The outstanding share capital of Lochmaben Corporation consists of (1) 2,000 preferred shares with no-par value and with a stated dividend of $8 for which $200,000 was received when all were sold; and (2) 5,000 common shares of no-par value for which $250,000 was received.

Instructions

Assuming that the company has cash and retained earnings of $86,000, all of which is to be paid out in dividends, and that preferred dividends were not paid during the two years preceding the current year, state how much each class of shares would receive under each of the following conditions.

(a) The preferred shares are noncumulative and nonparticipating.

(b) The preferred shares are cumulative and nonparticipating.

(c) The preferred shares are cumulative and participating, with participation based on the proportion of share capital amounts for each class.

E17-6   **(Stock Split and Stock Dividend)** The common shares of Troon Inc. are currently selling at $120 per share. The directors wish to reduce the share price and increase share volume prior to a new issue. The book value per share is $70. One million shares are issued and outstanding.

Instructions

Prepare the necessary journal entries assuming:

(a) The board votes a two-for-one stock split.

(b) The board votes a 100% stock dividend.

Briefly discuss the accounting and securities market differences between these two methods of increasing the number of shares outstanding.

E17-7   **(Stock Dividends)** Swansea Ltd. has 500,000 shares issued and outstanding. The book value per share is $32 and the market value per share is $39.

Instructions

(a) Prepare the necessary journal entries for the date of declaration and date of issue assuming a 20% stock dividend is declared.

(b) If Swansea has 50,000 shares of treasury stock, should the stock dividend be applied to the treasury shares? Explain.

(c) What is the amount of the corporation's liability for the period from the declaration date to the distribution date?

E17-8   **(Dividend Entries)** The following data were taken from the balance sheet accounts of Tiverton Corporation on December 31, 1997.

Current assets	$540,000
Investments	624,000
Common shares no-par value, no authorized limit, 50,000 shares issued and outstanding	500,000
Contributed surplus—donated land	150,000
Retained earnings	840,000

Instructions

Prepare the required journal entries for the following unrelated items.

(a) A 5% stock dividend is declared and distributed at a time when the market value of a share is $38.

(b) A scrip dividend of $75,000 is declared.

(c) The shares are split five-for-one.

(d) A property dividend is declared January 5, 1998, and paid January 25, 1998, in bonds held as an investment; the bonds have a book value of $100,000 and a fair market value of $130,000.

(Dividend Entries with Par Value Shares) Refer to Exercise 17-8. Assume that the common shares are $10 par value instead of no-par value shares.

E17-9

Instructions

Prepare the required journal entries to record the unrelated items in Parts (a) to (d).

(Retained Earnings Appropriations and Disclosures) At December 31, 1997, the Retained Earnings account of Thrapston Inc. had a balance of $320,000. There were no appropriations at this time. During 1998, net income was $235,000. Cash dividends declared during the year were $50,000 on preferred shares and $68,000 on common. A stock dividend on common shares resulted in a $70,000 charge to retained earnings. At December 31, 1998, the board of directors decided to create an appropriation for contingencies of $100,000 because of an outstanding lawsuit that did not meet the criteria for accrual.

E17-10

Instructions

(a) Prepare the journal entry to record the appropriation at December 31, 1998.

(b) Prepare a statement of unappropriated retained earnings for 1998.

(c) Prepare the Retained Earnings section of the December 31, 1998 balance sheet.

(d) Assume that in May 1999, the lawsuit is settled and Thrapston agrees to pay $88,000. At this time, the board of directors also decides to eliminate the appropriation. Prepare all necessary entries.

(e) Assume in (a) that Thrapston decided to disclose the appropriation through a note at December 31, 1998 instead of preparing a formal journal entry. Prepare the necessary note.

(Computation of Retained Earnings) The following information has been taken from the ledger accounts of St. Albans Corporation.

E17-11

Total reported income since incorporation	$300,000
Total cash dividends paid	60,000
"Gains" from treasury stock transactions	40,000
Total value of stock dividends distributed	30,000
Retroactive adjustment to correct an error in undercalculation of depreciation in a prior period	20,000
Unamortized discount on bonds payable	32,000
Appropriated for plant expansion	70,000

Instructions

Determine the current balance of unappropriated retained earnings.

(Appropriations for Self-Insurance) Colin Booth, president of Redcar Inc., has decided against purchasing casualty insurance to cover the company's four plants. Recognizing the possibility of casualty losses, he has appropriated $60,000 a year as a reserve for such contingencies; the first appropriation was made in 1995. In 1998 a fire completely destroys one of his plants. The plant had a 30-year life, no salvage value, and an original cost of $270,000 when it was constructed 12 years ago (straight-line depreciation). After the fire in 1998, Colin Booth changes his mind, buys insurance, pays an annual premium of $25,000 on January 2, 1999, and eliminates his casualty reserve.

E17-12

Instructions

Prepare the entries to journalize the insurance and casualty transactions and events of 1995, 1998, and 1999.

E17-13 **(Participating Preferred, Stock Dividend, and Share Reacquisition)** The following is the Shareholders' Equity section of Rennes Corp. at December 31, 1998.

Common shares, no-par, authorized 200,000 shares; issued 90,000 shares	$ 4,800,000
Preferred shares,* no-par, authorized 100,000 shares; issued 15,000 shares	750,000
Total share capital	5,550,000
Contributed surplus	150,000
Total share capital and contributed surplus	5,700,000
Retained earnings	5,213,000
Total shareholders' equity	$10,913,000

*Each preferred share has a $6 dividend, is cumulative, and is participating in any distribution in excess of a $3 dividend per share on the common shares. Participation is based on the proportion of share capital for each class of shares.

Instructions
(a) No dividends have been paid in 1996 or 1997. On December 31, 1998 Rennes wants to pay a cash dividend of $4 a share to common shareholders. How much cash would be needed for the total amount paid to preferred and common shareholders?

(b) Instead, Rennes will declare a 10% stock dividend on the outstanding common shares. The market value is $103 per common share. Prepare the entry on the date of declaration.

(c) Instead, Rennes will acquire and cancel 7,500 common shares. The current market value is $103 per share. Prepare the entry to record the retirement, assuming the contributed surplus arose from previous cancellations of common shares.

E17-14 **(Dividends and Shareholders' Equity Section)** Moulins Company reported the following amounts in the Shareholders' Equity section of its December 31, 1997 balance sheet:

Preferred shares, $10 dividend, no-par, 10,000 shares authorized, 2,000 shares issued	$200,000
Common shares, no-par, 100,000 shares authorized, 20,000 shares issued	200,000
Contributed surplus	25,000
Retained earnings	450,000
Total	$875,000

During 1998, Moulins took part in the following transactions concerning shareholders' equity.

1. Paid the annual 1997 $10 dividend on preferred shares and a $1 dividend on common shares. These dividends had been declared on December 28, 1997.

2. Issued 500 preferred shares at $106 each.

3. Declared a 10% stock dividend on the outstanding common shares when they were selling for $39 each.

4. Issued the stock dividend.

5. Under the terms of an employee share purchase plan, advanced loans totalling $25,000 to 10 employees for the purpose of purchasing common shares at a time when the share price was $40 per share, and issued the shares.

6. Declared the annual 1998 $10.00 dividend on preferred shares and a $1.50 dividend on common shares. These dividends are payable in 1999. Of the $1.50 common dividend, $0.50 represents a return of capital (contributed surplus) to the shareholders.

Instructions
(a) Prepare journal entries to record the transactions.

(b) Prepare the December 31, 1998 Shareholders' Equity section. Assume 1998 net income was $305,000. Provide note disclosure regarding changes in share capital during 1998. Support the retained earnings amount by a statement of retained earnings for the year.

(c) Assume the preferred shares identified in the Shareholders' Equity section of the December 31, 1997 balance sheet were term preferred shares that meet the definition of a financial liability. How would your answers to Parts (a) and (b) differ, if at all, as a result of this information? Explain briefly.

E17-15 **(Shareholders' Equity Section)** Bordeaux Corporation's post-closing trial balance at December 31, 1998 was as follows.

BORDEAUX CORPORATION
Post-Closing Trial Balance
December 31, 1998

	Dr.	Cr.
Accounts payable		$ 310,000
Accounts receivable	$ 480,000	
Accumulated depreciation—building and equipment		185,000
Allowance for doubtful accounts		30,000
Appropriated retained earnings—plant expansion		100,000
Bonds payable		300,000
Building and equipment	1,450,000	
Cash	190,000	
Common shares		1,200,000
Contributed surplus		310,000
Dividends payable on preferred shares—cash		4,000
Inventories	560,000	
Land	400,000	
Preferred shares		500,000
Prepaid expenses	40,000	
Retained earnings		181,000
Totals	$3,120,000	$3,120,000

At December 31, 1998, Bordeaux had the following number of no-par value common and preferred shares.

	Common	Preferred
Authorized	600,000	60,000
Outstanding	140,000	10,000

The dividend on a preferred share is $4 cumulative. In addition, a preferred share has a preference in liquidation of $50 per share.

Instructions

(a) Prepare the Shareholders' Equity section of Bordeaux's balance sheet at December 31, 1998.

(b) Assuming there are no preferred dividends in arrears, what is the amount of the common shareholders' equity in Bordeaux's net assets? What is the book value per common share?

(c) Assuming preferred dividends have not been paid for two years, what is the book value of the common shareholders' equity? What is the book value per common share? (AICPA adapted)

(Financial Reorganization: Entries) The following condensed balance sheets reflect Morecambe Company immediately before and one year after it completed a financial reorganization.   **E17-16**

	Before Reorganization	One Year After			Before Reorganization	One Year After
Current assets	$ 300,000	$ 420,000		Common shares	$2,400,000	$1,550,000
Plant assets (net)	1,700,000	1,290,000		Contributed surplus	220,000	
				Retained earnings	(620,000)	160,000
	$2,000,000	$1,710,000			$2,000,000	$1,710,000

For the year following the financial reorganization, Morecambe reported net income of $190,000, which included depreciation expense of $80,000, and paid a cash dividend of $30,000. No purchases or sales of plant assets and no share transactions occurred in the year following the financial reorganization.

The company wrote down inventories by $120,000 in order to reflect circumstances that existed prior to the reorganization. Also, the deficit and any revaluation adjustment was accounted for by charging the amounts against contributed surplus until it was eliminated, with any remaining amounts being charged against the common shares. The common shares are widely held and there is no controlling interest.

Instructions

(a) Prepare all the journal entries made at the time of the financial reorganization.

(b) Does this reorganization qualify for a comprehensive revaluation of assets and liabilities under *Handbook* Section 1625? Explain.

(c) Provide the note to the financial statements regarding the required disclosure for the year in which the financial reorganization took place.

E17-17 **(Financial Reorganization: Balance Sheet)** Cognac Corporation has just undergone a financial reorganization. Immediately prior to the reorganization, the company had the following balances in its accounts.

Cash	$ (5,000)	Accounts payable	$ 450,000
Accounts receivable	320,000	Notes payable	605,000
Inventory	450,000	Taxes and wages payable	60,000
Equipment	860,000	Mortgage payable	150,000
Accumulated depreciation	(525,000)	Common shares	50,000
Intangibles	80,000	Retained earnings	(135,000)
Total	$1,180,000	Total	$1,180,000

The non-equity and equity holders accepted the following financial reorganization agreement. Revaluation of the assets was by the following amounts.

Accounts receivable	$ 80,000 write-down.
Inventory	$170,000 write-down.
Intangibles	$ 80,000 write-off.
Equipment	$100,000 write-up.

The trade creditors (accounts payable) will reduce their claim by 30%, accept one-year notes for 50% of the amount due, and retain their current claim for the remaining 20%. The bank overdraft, tax, wage, and mortgage claims will remain unchanged. The current common shares will be surrendered to the corporation and cancelled. In consideration thereof, the current shareholders shall be held harmless from any possible personal liability. The current holder of the note payable shall receive 1,000 shares of no-par common stock in full satisfaction of the note payable. The deficit will be eliminated and, after accounting for the revaluations, the only shareholders' equity item will be the 1,000 common shares held by the former holder of the note payable.

Instructions

(a) Does this reorganization qualify to have its assets and liabilities comprehensively revalued? Explain.

(b) Prepare a classified balance sheet that reflects the financial position of the company immediately after the financial reorganization.

PROBLEMS

P17-1 As the newly appointed controller for Zeeland Company, you are interested in analysing the Additional Capital account of the company in terms of what it includes and its appropriateness. Your assistant, Kevin Utrecht, who has maintained the account from the inception of the company, submits the following summary:

Additional Capital Account

	Debits	Credits
Excess of assigned value over acquisition cost of shares retired		$ 10,000
Cash dividends—preferred	$ 119,000	
Cash dividends—common	340,000	
Net income		780,000
Appraisal increase credit for land, appropriately recognized prior to 1990		430,000
Retroactive effect of a change in accounting principle from FIFO to weighted average	91,000	
Extraordinary gain		22,500
Donated building		270,000
Extraordinary loss	98,500	
Correction of a prior period error	55,000	
	$ 703,500	$1,512,500
Credit balance of Additional Capital account	809,000	
	$1,512,500	$1,512,500

Instructions

(a) Prepare a journal entry to close the Additional Capital account and establish appropriate accounts. Indicate how you derive the balance of each new account.

(b) If generally accepted accounting principles had been followed, what amount would have been reported as total net income?

The balance sheet of Jambes Inc. shows $400,000 share capital, consisting of 4,000 common shares, and retained earnings of $144,000. As controller of the company, you find that Ann Twerp, the assistant treasurer, is $83,000 short in her accounts and has concealed this shortage by adding the amount to the inventory. She owns 740 of the company's shares and, in settlement of the shortage, offers these shares at their book value. The offer is accepted; the company pays her the excess value and distributes the 740 shares thus acquired to the other shareholders. Assume that the addition to the Inventory account took place after the income had been properly calculated and closed to the retained earnings.

P17-2

Instructions

(a) What amount should Jambes Inc. pay Ann Twerp?

(b) By what journal entries should the foregoing transactions be recorded? (Assume the acquired shares were cancelled by being restored to the status of authorized but unissued shares and that their redistribution was as a stock dividend with the market value equal to the book value.)

(c) What is the total shareholders' equity after the share distribution?

Andorra Inc. began operations in January 1994 and had the following reported net income or loss for each of its five years of operations:

P17-3

1994	$ 225,000 loss
1995	140,000 loss
1996	180,000 loss
1997	422,500 income
1998	1,500,000 income

At December 31, 1998, the company's share capital accounts were as follows:

Common, no-par value, authorized 200,000 shares, issued and outstanding 50,000 shares	$ 750,000
$8, nonparticipating, noncumulative preferred, no-par value; authorized, issued, and outstanding 5,000 shares	500,000
$5, fully participating, cumulative preferred, no-par value; authorized, issued, and outstanding 10,000 shares	1,500,000

Andorra has never declared a cash or stock dividend. There has been no change in the share capital accounts since Andorra began operations. The incorporation law permits dividends only from retained earnings provided their payment will not result in insolvency. The participation formula for the preferred shares is based on relative capital contributions by each class of shares.

Instructions

Prepare a work sheet showing the retained earnings amount available for dividends on December 31, 1998 and how it would be distributable to the holders of the common shares and each of the preferred shares. Show supporting computations in good form. (AICPA adapted)

On December 1, 1998, the board of directors of Nyborg Corp. declared a 4% stock dividend on the outstanding no-par value common shares of the corporation, payable on December 28, 1998, to the holders of record at the close of business December 15, 1998. They stipulated that cash dividends were to be paid in lieu of issuing any fractional shares. They also directed that the amount to be charged against retained earnings should be equal to the market value per share on the declaration date multiplied by the total of (a) the number of shares issued as a stock dividend; and (b) the number of shares on which cash is paid in place of the issuance of fractional shares. The following facts are given.

P17-4

1. At the dividend date:

(a) Shares of common issued and outstanding	3,048,750
(b) Shares of common included in (a) held by persons who will receive cash in lieu of fractional shares	222,750
(c) Shares of common held in treasury	1,100

2. Values of Nyborg common were as follows:

Market value at December 1st	$25
Book value at December 1st	$14

Instructions

Prepare entries and explanations to record the payment of the dividend.   (AICPA adapted)

P17-5   The books of Fitzgerald Inc. carried the following account balances as of December 31, 1997:

Cash	$ 195,000
Preferred shares, $0.60 cumulative dividend, nonparticipating, no-par value, 15,000 shares issued	750,000
Common shares, no-par value, 300,000 shares issued, no authorized limit	1,500,000
Retained earnings	105,000

The preferred shares have dividends in arrears for the past year (1997).

The board of directors, at their annual meeting on December 21, 1998, declared the following: "The current year dividends shall be $0.60 per share on the preferred and $0.25 per share on the common; the dividends in arrears shall be paid by issuing one common share for each 10 shares of preferred held."

The preferred is currently selling at $80 per share and the common at $6 per share. Net income for 1998 is estimated at $64,000.

Instructions

(a) Prepare the journal entries required for the dividend declaration and payment, assuming that they occur simultaneously.

(b) Could Fitzgerald Inc. give the preferred shareholders two years' (1997 and 1998) dividends and common shareholders a $0.25 per share dividend, all in cash? Explain the factors to be considered in reaching your decision.

(c) Assume the preferred shares are determined to be financial liabilities. Discuss how this would change the accounting for and reporting of the dividends in Part (a).

P17-6   MacLaren Ltd. has outstanding 2,500 preferred shares of no-par value, $6 dividend, which were issued for $250,000, and 15,000 common shares of no-par value for which $150,000 was received. The schedule below shows the amount of dividends paid out over the last four years.

Instructions

Allocate the dividends to each class of shares under assumptions (a) and (b). Express your answers in per-share amounts, using the following format.

		Assumptions			
		(a) Preferred, noncumulative, and nonparticipating		(b) Preferred, cumulative, and fully participating*	
Year	Paid Out	Preferred	Common	Preferred	Common
1995	$12,500				
1996	$26,000				
1997	$57,000				
1998	$72,000				

*Based on relative amounts of contributed capital.

P17-7   Zabbar Company has the following shareholders' equity accounts:

	Issued Shares	Amount
Preferred shares, no-par value	2,200	$220,000
Common shares without par value	3,600	118,800
Retained earnings		494,640

In view of the large retained earnings, the board of directors resolves: (1) "to pay a 20% stock dividend on all shares outstanding, capitalizing amounts of retained earnings equal to the average issue price of the preferred and common shares outstanding" respectively, and thereafter (2) "to pay a cash dividend of $6 on preferred shares and a cash dividend of $2 a share on common."

Instructions

(a) Prepare entries in journal form to record the declaration of these dividends.

(b) Prepare the Shareholders' Equity section of the balance sheet for Zabbar after declaration but before distribution of these dividends.

Some of the account balances of Timothy Corp. at December 31, 1997 are shown below:

P17-8

$6 cumulative preferred shares, no-par, 2,000 shares authorized, 2,000 issued	$ 200,000
Common, no-par, 100,000 shares authorized, 50,000 issued	600,000
Unappropriated retained earnings	304,000
Retained earnings appropriated for contingencies	75,000
Retained earnings appropriated for fire insurance	95,000

The price of the company's common shares has been increasing steadily on the market; it was $21 on January 1, 1998, advanced to $23 by July 1, and by the end of 1998 was $27.

The preferred shares are not openly traded, but were appraised at $120 per share during 1998. Because they are required to be redeemed by December 31, 2008, they are deemed to be financial liabilities instead of equity.

Instructions

(a) Give the journal entries for each of the following transactions or events in 1998.

   (1) The company incurred a fire loss of $54,000 to its warehouse.

   (2) The company declared a property dividend on April 1. Each Timothy Corp. common shareholder was to receive one Beja Ltd. share for every 10 shares held. Timothy Corp. owned 8,000 Beja Ltd. shares (2% of total outstanding shares), which were purchased as an investment in 1995 for $68,400. The market value of Beja Ltd. shares was $16 each on April 1. Record appreciation only on the shares distributed.

   (3) On June 18, Timothy Corp. purchased 800 of its preferred shares from the estate of a deceased shareholder, paying the appraised value of $120 per share. The shares were subsequently cancelled.

   (4) On July 1, the company declared a 5% stock dividend to the common shareholders, payable in common shares.

   (5) The city of Kirkland, in an effort to persuade the company to expand into that locality, donated to Timothy Corp. land with an appraised value of $36,000.

   (6) In early December, the annual dividend on the preferred shares was declared and paid.

   (7) At the annual board of directors' meeting, the board resolved to set up an appropriation of retained earnings for the future construction of a new plant. Such appropriation will be $150,000 per year. Also, it was resolved to increase the appropriation for contingencies by $25,000 and to eliminate the appropriation for fire insurance and begin purchasing such insurance from Chaves Insurance Company.

(b) Prepare the Shareholders' Equity section of Timothy Corp. December 31, 1998 balance sheet in good form assuming a 1998 net income of $74,500. Show all supporting calculations.

The Shareholders' Equity section of Horton Corp.'s balance sheet on January 1 of the current year is as follows:

P17-9

Share Capital		
Common shares, no-par, 20,000 shares authorized, 10,000 shares issued		$1,400,000
Retained Earnings		
Unappropriated	$300,000	
Appropriated for plant expansion	120,000	
Total retained earnings		420,000
Total Shareholders' Equity		$1,820,000

The following selected transactions occurred during the year.

   1. Paid cash dividends of $1.20 per share on the common shares. The dividend had been properly recorded when declared last year.

2. Declared a 10% stock dividend on the common shares when the shares were selling at $112 each in the market.

3. Corrected an error of $60,000 (net of tax) that overstated net income in the previous year. The error was the result of an overstatement of ending inventory. The applicable tax rate was 30%.

4. Issued the certificates for the stock dividend.

5. The board appropriated $40,000 of retained earnings for plant expansion, and declared a cash dividend of $1.65 per share on the common shares.

6. The company's net income was $210,000 for the year (incorporating the inventory error referred to in Item 3).

Instructions

(a) Prepare journal entries for the selected transactions above.

(b) Prepare a statement of unappropriated retained earnings for the current year.

(c) Assume, after making all entries in (a), that the company decided to account for appropriations through note disclosure. Prepare the required journal entry(ies) to account for this change in method of disclosure. How would this affect your answer to Part (b)?

P17-10 On December 15, 1997, the directors of Malaga Corporation voted to appropriate $90,000 of retained earnings and to retain in the business assets equal to the appropriation for use in expanding the corporation's factory building. This was the fourth of such appropriations; after it was recorded, the Shareholders' Equity section of Malaga's balance sheet appeared as follows.

Shareholders' equity		
Common shares, no-par value, 300,000 shares authorized, 200,000 shares issued and outstanding		$5,600,000
Retained earnings		
Unappropriated	$1,800,000	
Appropriated for plant expansion	360,000	
Total retained earnings		2,160,000
Total shareholders' equity		$7,760,000

On January 9, 1998, the corporation entered into a contract for the construction of the factory addition for which the retained earnings were appropriated. On November 1, 1998, the addition was completed and the contractor was paid the contract price of $322,500.

On December 14, 1998, the board of directors voted to return the balance of the Retained Earnings Appropriated for Plant Expansion account to Unappropriated Retained Earnings. They also voted a 25,000 share stock dividend distributable on January 23, 1999 to the January 15, 1999 shareholders of record. The corporation's shares were selling at $46 in the market on December 14, 1998. Malaga reported net income for 1997 of $525,000 and for 1998 of $600,000.

Instructions

(a) Prepare the appropriate journal entries for Malaga Corporation for the information above (December 15, 1997 to January 23, 1999, inclusive).

(b) Prepare the Shareholders' Equity section of the balance sheet for Malaga Corporation at December 31, 1998.

P17-11 Borneo Corp. has outstanding 2,000,000 common shares of no-par value that were issued at $10 each. The balance in its Retained Earnings account at January 1, 1998 was $24,000,000. During 1998 the company's net income was $5,600,000. A cash dividend of $0.50 a share was paid June 30, 1998, and a 6% stock dividend was distributed on December 30 to shareholders of record at the close of business on December 15, 1998 (declaration date was November 30). You have been asked to advise on the appropriate accounting treatment for the stock dividend.

The existing shares of the company are quoted on a stock exchange. The market price per share has been as follows.

October 31, 1998	$31
November 30, 1998	33
December 15, 1998	38
December 31, 1998	37
Average price over the past two-month period	35

Instructions

(a) Prepare a journal entry to record the cash dividend.

(b) Prepare a journal entry to record the stock dividend.

(c) Prepare a statement of retained earnings for the year ended December 31, 1998 and the Shareholders' Equity section of the balance sheet of Borneo Corp. for the year ended December 31, 1998, on the basis of the foregoing information. Draft a memo to the controller of Borneo Corp. setting forth the basis of the accounting for the stock dividend and provide appropriate comments or explanations regarding the basis chosen.

On June 30, 1998, the Shareholders' Equity section of the balance sheet of Puma Company Inc. appears as follows: **P17-12**

Shareholders' equity			
$8, cumulative preferred shares			
Authorized and issued,			
3,000 shares, no-par value	$300,000		
Common shares			
Authorized 30,000 shares of no-par value,			
issued, 13,600 shares	680,000	$980,000	
Retained earnings (deficit)		(320,000)	$660,000

A note to the balance sheet points out that preferred share dividends are in arrears in the amount of $96,000.

At a shareholders' meeting on July 3, 1998, a new group of officers was voted into power, and a financial reorganization plan proposed by the new officers to be effective July 1 was accepted by the shareholders. The short-term creditors' position was not to be changed and the company had no long-term debt. The terms of this plan were as follows:

1. Preferred shareholders are to cancel their claim against the corporation for dividends in arrears.
2. Certain depreciable properties and inventories owned by the company are to be revalued downward $90,000 and $30,000, respectively, to reflect circumstances that existed prior to the reorganization.
3. The company owned a patent on a new product it had just developed. It was not shown as an asset on the June 30, 1998 balance sheet. However, it was to be recorded at its fair value of $60,000 as a result of a comprehensive revaluation of assets and liabilities regarding the financial reorganization.
4. The deficit prior to the reorganization was to be reclassified to common share capital and any revaluation adjustment was to be accounted for through common share capital.

Instructions
(a) Discuss whether this situation qualifies under *Handbook* Section 1625 for a comprehensive revaluation of its assets and liabilities.
(b) Assuming *Handbook* Section 1625 applies, and that the various steps in the financial reorganization plan are effectively carried out as of July 1, 1998:
   (1) Prepare journal entries to record the reorganization.
   (2) Prepare the Shareholders' Equity section of the balance sheet as June 30, 1999, assuming the company earned a net income of $40,000 and paid the stated preferred dividend.
(c) How would your answer to (b) differ if it was not appropriate to comprehensively revalue the company's assets and liabilities? Be specific.

Micmac Ltd.'s shares are traded on the over-the-counter market. At December 31, 1997, Micmac had 5,000,000 **P17-13** authorized common shares of no-par value, of which 1,500,000 shares were issued and outstanding. The shareholders' equity accounts at December 31, 1997 had the following balances.

Common shares	$15,000,000
Retained earnings	5,700,000

Transactions during 1998 and other information relating to the shareholders' equity accounts were as follows:

1. On January 5, 1998, Micmac issued at $108 per share, 100,000, $8, cumulative preferred shares. Micmac had 600,000 authorized preferred shares. The preferred shares have a liquidation value of $100 each.
2. On February 1, 1998, Micmac reacquired 20,000 common shares for $16 per share. These shares were cancelled by being restored to the status of authorized but unissued.
3. On April 30, 1998, Micmac sold 500,000 common shares to the public at $17 per share.
4. On June 18, 1998, Micmac declared a cash dividend of $1 per common share, payable on July 11, to shareholders of record on July 1, 1998.
5. On November 10, 1998, Micmac sold 10,000 common shares for $21 per share.

6. On December 14, 1998, Micmac declared the yearly cash dividend on preferred shares, payable on January 14, 1999, to shareholders of record on December 31, 1998.

7. On January 20, 1999, before the books were closed for 1998, Micmac became aware that the ending inventory at December 31, 1997 was understated by $300,000 (after-tax effect on 1997 net income was $180,000). The appropriate correction entry was recorded.

8. After correcting the beginning inventory, net income for 1998 was $3,600,000.

Instructions

(a) Prepare a statement of retained earnings for the year ended December 31, 1998. Assume that only single-period financial statements for 1998 are presented.

(b) Prepare the Shareholders' Equity section of Micmac's balance sheet at December 31, 1998.

(c) Of the total shareholders' equity or book value of Micmac Ltd., determine the entitlement of the preferred shareholders to the company's net assets.

(d) What is the entitlement of the common shareholders to the net assets? What is the book value per share of the common stock?

(AICPA adapted)

P17-14 Van Ltd. was formed on July 1, 1996. It was authorized to issue 300,000 common shares of no-par value and 100,000 preferred shares, $2 dividend, no-par value, and cumulative. Van has a June 30 fiscal year end.

The following information relates to the shareholders' equity accounts of Van Ltd.

Common Shares

Prior to the 1997–98 fiscal year, Van had 110,000 common shares outstanding, issued as follows.

1. 95,000 shares were issued for cash on July 1, 1996, at $30 per share.

2. On July 24, 1996, 5,000 shares were exchanged for a plot of land that cost the seller $70,000 in 1990 and had an estimated market value of $220,000 on July 24, 1996.

3. 10,000 shares were issued on March 1, 1997; the shares had been subscribed for $42 per share on October 31, 1996.

During the 1997–98 fiscal year, the following transactions regarding common shares took place:

October 1, 1997	Subscriptions were received for 10,000 shares at $46 per share. Cash of $92,000 was received in full payment for 2,000 shares and share certificates were issued. The remaining subscriptions for 8,000 shares were to be paid in full by September 30, 1998, at which time the certificates were to be issued.
November 30, 1997	Van purchased 2,000 of its own shares on the open market at $48 per share. These shares were restored to the status of authorized but unissued shares.
December 15, 1997	Van declared a 5% stock dividend for common shareholders of record on January 15, 1998, to be issued on January 31, 1998. Van was having a liquidity problem and could not afford a cash dividend at the time. Van's common shares were selling at $52 per share on December 15, 1997.
June 20, 1998	Van sold 500 common shares for $22,500.

Preferred Shares

Van issued 30,000 preferred shares for $43 each on July 1, 1996.

Cash Dividends

Van has followed a schedule of declaring cash dividends in December and June with payment being made to shareholders of record in the following month. The cash dividends that have been declared since inception of the company through June 30, 1998, are shown below:

Declaration Date	Common Shares	Preferred Shares
12/15/96	$.10 per share	$1.00 per share
6/15/97	$.10 per share	$1.00 per share
12/15/97	—	$1.00 per share

No cash dividends were declared during June 1998 due to the company's liquidity problems.

Retained Earnings

As of June 30, 1997, Van's Retained Earnings account had a balance of $670,000. For the fiscal year ending June 30, 1998, Van reported net income of $40,000.

In March 1998, Van received a term loan from the Dominion Bank. The bank requires Van to establish a sinking fund and restrict retained earnings for an amount equal to the sinking fund deposit. The annual sinking fund payment of $50,000 is due on April 30 each year; the first payment was made on schedule on April 30, 1998.

Instructions

Prepare the Shareholders' Equity section of the balance sheet, including appropriate notes, for Van Ltd. as of June 30, 1998.

(CMA adapted)

P17-15

Todd Corporation is a publisher of children's books. The company was started as a family business in 1949 and is still closely held. For its fiscal year ended May 31, 1998, Todd had net income of $900,000 on sales of $10,625,000. The net income included a loss of $350,000, net of tax, that resulted from the discontinuance of a segment of the business. The board of directors of Todd will be meeting on June 25, 1998 to review the company's financial condition. One of the agenda items for this meeting is to re-examine Todd's dividend policy and draft the dividend plans for the 1998–99 fiscal year.

Debra Oickle, Assistant Controller of Todd Corporation, is responsible for the preparation of the company's financial statements for both internal and external reporting purposes. She is also responsible for preparing any reports and statements to be reviewed by the board of directors. Of the material specifically requested by the Board for its June 25 meeting, the only report not yet prepared is the statement of retained earnings. To assist in this preparation, Oickle listed the account balances for Todd's equity accounts as of May 31, 1997, and gathered, from the corporation's books, pertinent information that affected Todd's equity accounts during the 1997–98 fiscal year. These data are presented below.

Account Balances as of May 31, 1997

Unappropriated retained earnings	$1,255,000
Appropriation for plant expansion (appropriation is 100% of cost)	425,000
Appropriation for bond sinking fund	300,000
Preferred shares, $8, cumulative, no-par value, 20,000 shares authorized, 10,000 shares issued and outstanding	1,040,000
Common shares, no-par value, 220,000 shares authorized, 174,000 shares issued and outstanding	3,420,000
Contributed surplus—treasury stock transactions	11,000

Additional Information

1. Dividend activity for the year was as follows.

   (a) A cash dividend of $0.50 per share was paid June 10, 1997. The dividend was declared May 10, 1997 to all common shareholders of record May 25, 1997.

   (b) A cash dividend of $1.25 per share was declared on November 1, 1997 to all common shareholders of record on November 15, 1997. This dividend was paid on November 25, 1997.

   (c) A 10% stock dividend was declared May 15, 1998 to all common shareholders of record on May 25, 1998. This dividend was to be paid from authorized but unissued common shares on June 15, 1998. The per share market price on May 15, 1998 was $27.

   (d) The required preferred dividend was paid on May 31, 1998 to all preferred shareholders of record.

2. On June 1, 1997, Todd sold an additional 5,000 preferred shares for $102 per share.

3. The fiscal year addition to the bond sinking fund and the appropriation for the sinking fund was $25,000.

4. On January 1, 1998, 10,000 common shares were sold for $24 each.

5. Todd's plant expansion program was now 60% complete, and a proportionate share of the appropriation for this purpose was returned to retained earnings at May 31, 1998.

6. During the year, depreciation expense for the fiscal year ended May 31, 1997 was discovered to be understated by $25,000. This was considered an error that required an adjustment to the previous year's earnings.

7. Todd Corporation was subject to an effective income tax rate of 30% for the fiscal years ended May 31, 1997 and 1998.

Instructions

(a) Todd Corporation's board of directors requested the statement of retained earnings in order to determine the retained earnings available for dividends as of May 31, 1998. Prepare the statement of retained earnings for the year ended May 31, 1998, showing:

   1. Total (appropriated and unappropriated) retained earnings as of May 31, 1997.

   2. Adjustments, additions, and deductions that occurred during the 1997–98 fiscal year.

   3. Total (unappropriated and appropriated) retained earnings as of May 31, 1998.

   4. Appropriations of retained earnings by restriction as of May 31, 1998.

   5. Retained earnings available for dividends as of May 31, 1998.

(b) Discuss how each of the following items would have an impact on the board of directors' decision regarding Todd Corporation's dividend policy.

1. The disposal of the segment during the 1997–98 fiscal year that resulted in a $350,000 net-of-tax loss.
2. The forecasted earnings for the next three fiscal years.
3. The declaration of the stock dividends to all common shareholders of record that took place on May 15, 1998, and the declaration of any additional stock dividends to common shareholders in the future.

(c) Explain why most companies do not distribute all their available retained earnings.

CASES

C17-1 *CICA Handbook*, Section 1000, on "Financial Statement Concepts" sets forth financial accounting and reporting objectives and concepts that are to be used by the Accounting Standards Board in developing standards. Included in Section 1000 are definitions of various elements of financial statements, some of which are expanded upon in Section 3860 on "Financial Instruments—Disclosure and Presentation."

Instructions
Answer the following questions based on Sections 1000 and 3860 of the *CICA Handbook*.
(a) Define and discuss the element "equity."
(b) What transactions or events change owners' equity?
(c) Define "investments by owners" and provide examples of this type of transaction. Are all investments by owners reported in shareholders' equity? Explain. What financial statement element other than equity is typically affected by owner investments?
(d) Define "distributions to owners" and provide examples of this type of transaction. What financial statement element other than equity is typically affected by distributions?
(e) What are examples of changes within owners' equity that do not change the total amount of owners' equity?

C17-2 The directors of Agatha Ltd. are considering the issuance of a stock dividend. They have asked you to discuss the proposed action by answering the following questions.

Instructions
(a) What is a stock dividend? How is a stock dividend distinguished from a stock split, from an accounting standpoint?
(b) For what reasons does a corporation usually declare a stock dividend? A stock split?
(c) Discuss the amount, if any, of retained earnings to be capitalized in connection with a stock dividend.
(d) Discuss the case against considering a stock dividend as income to the recipient.
(e) Discuss the case both for and against distributing a stock dividend to shares held in treasury.   (AICPA adapted)

C17-3 Sun Inc., a large retail chain company, has stores throughout Canada. Due to the stores' many different locations, the president thinks it would be advantageous to self-insure the company's stores against the risk of any future loss or damage from fire or other natural causes. From past experience and by applying appropriate statistical and actuarial techniques, the president feels the amount of future losses can be predicted with reasonable accuracy.

Instructions
The president has asked you how Sun should record this type of contingency and on what basis the current period should be allocated a portion of the estimated losses. What would you tell the president?

C17-4 The Retained Earnings section of Travel Products Inc.'s balance sheet was presented as follows.

Retained Earnings	
Appropriation for plant expansion	$ 9,000,000
Appropriation for contingencies	3,000,000
Appropriation regarding bond indenture contract	1,000,000
Total appropriated	$13,000,000
Unappropriated (see Note 7)	17,000,000
Total retained earnings	$30,000,000

Note 7: The board of directors has restricted $8,000,000 of this amount, given that there is presently litigation proceedings against the company claiming this as a maximum amount for damages.

Pat Green, a common shareholder in the company, was recently quoted as saying, "I think appropriations mean that dividends can't be declared out of such amounts. Unfortunately, something must have gone wrong with the company's accounting because a special cash account for each of these appropriations was not shown in the Asset section of the balance sheet. Also, I don't really understand why an appropriation was not set up for the $8,000,000 regarding litigation proceedings. The fact this was disclosed by a note must mean that the restriction is of a second-class nature to the listed appropriations. Furthermore, at the next shareholders' meeting, I think we should really get after management as they don't appear to want to give us our fair amount of dividends. Even accepting the appropriations and restriction as being reasonable, that leaves $9,000,000 that should have been paid as dividends because management has given no reasons why it should be kept in the company."

Instructions

Discuss Mr. Green's points regarding his understanding of the reported information.

Primates Ltd., a medium-sized manufacturer, has experienced losses for the five years it has been doing busi- **C17-5** ness. Although the operations for the year just ended resulted in a loss, several important changes resulted in a profitable fourth quarter, and the future operations of the company are expected to be profitable. The treasurer, Harriet Carter, suggests that there be a financial reorganization to (1) eliminate the accumulated deficit of $750,000; (2) write up the $500,000 carrying value of operating land and buildings to their fair value; and (3) set up an asset of $120,000 representing the estimated future tax benefit of the losses accumulated to date as they could be offset against future income thereby reducing future taxes payable. Primates Ltd. has the following liabilities and shareholders' equity items at this time:

Current liabilities	$ 50,000
Long-term notes payable	75,000
Preferred shares	200,000
Common shares (widely held)	1,000,000
Deficit	750,000

Instructions

(a) What is the purpose of a financial reorganization?

(b) Identify the requirements and accounting necessary for a financial reorganization to result in a "fresh start" for the company.

(c) Identify and discuss issues regarding the treasurer's proposals to:

1. Eliminate the deficit of $750,000.

2. Write up the $500,000 carrying value of the operating land and buildings to their fair value.

3. Set up an asset of $120,000 representing the estimated future tax benefit of the losses accumulated to date.

USING YOUR JUDGEMENT

FINANCIAL REPORTING PROBLEM

Refer to the financial statements of Moore Corporation Limited in Appendix 5A and respond to the following questions.

1. Identify the authorized share capital of Moore and what conditions or rights accrue to each type.

2. The company has not issued any of its preferred shares. Suggest reasons for this.

3. Review the Consolidated Statement of Retained Earnings and the notes to the financial statements. Does Moore Corporation follow a policy of appropriating retained earnings? Are there any restrictions on the ability of the company to pay out dividends equal to its Retained Earnings balance? Discuss.

4. What is Moore Corporation's dividend payout ratio for 1995? For 1994?

5. Note 14 to the financial statements discusses and provides information about the continuity of a restructuring reserve. What is the nature of this reserve? Where do you think the remaining reserve balance of $21 million at December 31, 1995 is reported on the December 31, 1995 balance sheet? Explain.

6. Comment on the company's use of the term "reserve."

ETHICS CASE

"You can't write up assets," said Al Schick, Internal Audit Director of Rhuland International, to his boss, Jim Gaa, Vice President and Chief Financial Officer. "Nonsense," said Jim, "I can do this as part of a financial reorganization of our company." For the last three years, Rhuland International, a farm equipment manufacturer, has experienced a downturn in its profits resulting from stiff competition with U.S. and overseas firms and increasing labour costs. Though the prospects are still gloomy, the company is hoping to turn a profit by modernizing its property, plant, and equipment. This will require Rhuland to raise serious money.

Over the past few months, Jim has tried to raise funds from various financial institutions. They are unwilling to consider lending capital, however, because the company's net book value of capital assets on the balance sheet, based on historic cost, was not ample enough to sustain major funding. Jim attempted to explain to bankers and investors that these assets were more valuable than their recorded amounts, given that the company used accelerated depreciation methods and tended to underestimate the useful lives of assets. Jim also believes that the company's land and buildings are substantially undervalued because of rising real estate prices over the past several years.

Jim's idea is a simple one: First, declare a large dividend to shareholders of the company, such that Retained Earnings would have a large debit balance. Then, write up the capital assets of Rhuland to an amount equal to the deficit in the Retained Earnings account.

Instructions

(a) What are the ethical implications of Jim Gaa's creative accounting scheme?

(b) Who could be harmed if the accounting reorganization were implemented and Rhuland International received additional funding?

(c) Why can't a company write up assets when the fair value of these assets exceeds their original cost?

chapter 18

DILUTIVE SECURITIES AND EARNINGS PER SHARE CALCULATIONS

SECTION 1: DILUTIVE SECURITIES AND COMPENSATION PLANS

ACCOUNTING FOR CONVERTIBLE DEBT

CONVERTIBLE PREFERRED SHARES

STOCK WARRANTS

STOCK COMPENSATION PLANS

SECTION 2: COMPUTING EARNINGS PER SHARE

SUMMARY

CHAPTER 18

Dilutive Securities and Earnings Per Share Calculations

Learning Objectives

After studying this chapter, you should be able to:

1. Describe the accounting for the issuance, conversion, and retirement of convertible securities.
2. Explain the accounting for convertible preferred shares.
3. Contrast the accounting for stock warrants and stock warrants issued with other securities.
4. Describe the accounting for stock compensation plans.
5. Compute earnings per share on a simple capital structure.
6. Compute earnings per share in a complex capital structure.

The urge to merge that dominated the business scene in the 1960s developed into merger mania in the 1980s. One consequence of heavy merger activity is an increase in the use of securities such as convertible bonds, convertible preferred shares, share purchase warrants, and contingent shares. They are called **dilutive securities** because a reduction—dilution—in earnings per share often results when these securities become common shares.

During the sixties, corporate officers recognized that the issuance of dilutive securities in a merger did not have the same immediate adverse effect on earnings per share as the issuance of common shares. In addition, executives found that issuance of convertible securities did not seem to upset common shareholders, even though the common shareholders' interests were substantially diluted when these securities were later converted or exercised.

As a consequence of this step-up in merger activity during the 1980s, the presence of dilutive securities on corporate balance sheets is now very prevalent. Also increasing is the usage of stock option plans, which are dilutive in nature. These option plans are used mainly to attract and retain executive talent and to provide tax relief for executives in high tax brackets.

The widespread use of different types of dilutive securities has led the accounting profession to examine accounting in this area closely. Specifically, the profession has directed its attention to accounting for these securities at date of issuance, and to the presentation of earnings per share figures that recognize their effect. The following discussion includes consideration of convertible securities, warrants, stock options, and contingent shares. The second section of the chapter indicates how these securities are used in earnings per share computations.

SECTION 1: DILUTIVE SECURITIES AND COMPENSATION PLANS

ACCOUNTING FOR CONVERTIBLE DEBT

If bonds can be converted into other corporate securities during some specified period of time after issuance, they are called **convertible bonds**. A convertible bond *combines the benefits of a bond with the privilege of exchanging it for shares at the holder's option*. It is purchased by investors who desire the security of a bond holding—guaranteed interest—plus the added option of conversion if the value of the shares appreciates significantly.

Corporations issue convertibles for two main reasons. One is the desire to raise equity capital without giving up more ownership control than is necessary. To illustrate, assume that a company wants to raise $1,000,000 at a time when its common shares are selling at $45 each. Such an issue would require the sale of approximately 22,222 shares (ignoring issue costs). By selling 1,000 bonds at $1,000 par, with each bond convertible into 20 common shares, the enterprise may raise $1,000,000 by committing only 20,000 common shares.

A second reason why many companies issue convertible securities is to obtain common equity financing at cheaper rates. Many enterprises could issue debt only at high interest rates unless a convertible covenant were attached. The conversion privilege entices the investors to accept a lower interest rate than would normally be the case on a straight debt issue. A company might have to pay 10% for a straight debt obligation but it can issue a convertible at 8%. For this lower interest rate, the investor receives the right to acquire the company's common shares at a fixed price until maturity, which is often 10 years.

Accounting for convertible debt involves reporting issues at the time of (1) issuance; (2) conversion; and (3) retirement.

OBJECTIVE 1
Describe the accounting for the issuance, conversion, and retirement of convertible securities.

AT TIME OF ISSUANCE

As discussed in Chapter 15, convertible bonds are defined as compound financial instruments; that is, a single security that is composed partly of a liability and partly of an equity. Recording convertible bonds at the date of issue requires apportioning the proceeds received between the liability and equity components and recording these amounts in the books. Measurement of the amounts to be allocated to each component may be accomplished by using either (1) the "incremental" method; or (2) "proportional" methods.

Incremental Method. Under the "incremental" method the value of the most easily measured component is determined and deducted from the total issue proceeds to determine the value of the remaining component. For example, assume that Chatham Ltd. issued 1,000 five-year convertible bonds at 10% with a $1,000 par value, and that the corporation received net proceeds of $1,079,854 (i.e., a yield of 8%). The bond indenture stipulates that bondholders may convert each $1,000 bond into five common shares. The company's investment bankers estimated that the bonds would have sold at par value (i.e., yielding 10%) without the conversion feature. Under the incremental approach the amounts allocated to each security would be as follows.

Proceeds received for compound instrument		$1,079,854
Present value of bond principal at 10% ($1,000,000 × .62092)	$620,920	
Present value of interest ($100,000 × 3.79079 rounded $1)	379,080	
Fair value of liability		1,000,000
Residual allocated to conversion rights		$ 79,854

Receipt and allocation of the cash proceeds would be recorded as follows.

Cash	1,079,854	
Bonds Payable		1,000,000
Conversion Rights		79,854

Proportional Method. The proportional method may be used when values for both the liability and equity components are determinable. The liability component, as shown above, is valued at present value using the rate of interest appropriate to a similar debt without a conversion feature. A fair value for the equity component may be approximated by using various option pricing models.[1] If the Chatham Ltd. conversion rights are estimated to be worth $16.50 each, then the total fair value of the equity component would be $82,500 (1,000 × 5 × $16.50). The total proceeds from the issue would be allocated as follows.

Fair value of bonds	$1,000,000
Fair value of conversion rights	82,500
Fair value of the compound instrument	$1,082,500
Allocation of Proceeds:	
Bonds [$1,079,854 × (1,000,000/1,082,500)]	$ 997,556
Conversion rights [$1,079,854 × (82,500/1,082,500)]	82,298
Total	$1,079,854

The entry to record the issue would be as follows.

Cash	1,079,854	
Discount on Bonds Payable ($1,000,000 − $997,556)	2,444	
Bonds Payable		1,000,000
Conversion Rights		82,298

The $2,444 discount resulting from the issuance of the convertible bonds should be amortized on the assumption that the bonds will be held to maturity because it is difficult to predict when, if at all, conversion will occur.

AT TIME OF CONVERSION

If bonds are converted into other securities, the principal accounting problem is to determine the amount at which to record the securities exchanged for the bond. For example, three years after Chatham Ltd. issued the convertible bonds, assume that all the bonds were

---

[1] Various option pricing models may be used to compute the fair value of the conversion rights. This involves calculations beyond the scope of this book. Most finance textbooks contain detailed procedures for pricing stock options and rights.

converted to no-par value common shares (i.e., 5,000 shares exchanged for 1,000, $1,000 bonds). At the time of conversion the unamortized bond discount is $978 ($2,444 × 2/5), the bonds are selling at par, and the shares are quoted on the market at $200. Two possible methods of determining the issue price of the shares could be used.

1. The **market price** of the shares or bonds, or $1,000,000.

2. The **book values** of the bonds and conversion rights (as valued using the proportional method), or $1,081,320 [($1,000,000 − $978) + $82,298].

Market Value Approach. Recording the shares issued using their **market price at the issue date** is a theoretically sound method. If 5,000 common shares could be sold for $1,000,000, share capital of $1,000,000 should be recorded. Since bonds and conversion rights having a book value of $1,081,320 are converted, a gain of $81,320 ($999,022 − 1,000,000) + $82,298) on the bond conversion occurs.[2] The entry would be:

Bonds Payable	1,000,000	
Conversion Rights	82,298	
Gain on Redemption of Bonds Payable		81,320
Discount on Bonds Payable		978
Common Shares		1,000,000

Using the bond's market price can be supported on similar grounds. If the market price of the shares is not determinable, but the bonds can be purchased at $1,000,000, a good argument can be made that the shares have an issue price of $1,000,000.

Book Value Approach. From a practical point of view, if the market price of the shares or the bonds is not determinable, then the **book value of the bonds and conversion rights** offers the best available measurement of the issue price. Indeed, many accountants contend that even if market quotations are available, they should not be used. The common shares are merely substituted for the bonds and conversion rights and, therefore, should be recorded at the carrying amounts of the converted bonds and rights.

Supporters of this view argue that an agreement was established at the date of issuance to pay either a stated amount of cash at maturity or to issue a stated number of shares of equity securities. Therefore, when the debt is converted to equity in relation to pre-existing contract terms, no gain or loss is recognized upon conversion. To illustrate the specifics of this approach, the entry for the foregoing transaction of Chatham Ltd. would be:

Bonds Payable	1,000,000	
Conversion Rights	82,298	
Common Shares		1,081,320
Discount on Bonds Payable		978

The book value method of recording convertible bonds is the method used in practice[3] and should be used in homework unless the problem specifies otherwise.

---

[2] These calculations are based on the assumption that market price changes are attributed only to the liability. If changes in value are associated with the equity component, then the entry would become much more complex. Showing the conversion rights retired at more or less than issue price would result in entries to contributed surplus or retained earnings, as explained in Chapter 17.

[3] Convertible bonds have become less desirable recently because leveraged buyouts diminish the bondholders' rights. In addition, issuance of bonds may place excessive demands on the issuer's cash flow, which may depress share prices and discourage conversion.

Induced Conversions. Sometimes the issuer wishes to induce prompt conversion of its convertible debt to equity securities to reduce interest cost or improve its debt-to-equity ratio. As a result, the issuer may offer some form of additional consideration (cash, common shares) called a "sweetener" to **induce conversion**. An amount equal to the fair value of the additional securities or other consideration given should be reported as an expense of the current period.

Assume that three years after issuing the convertible bonds described in the previous illustration, management of Chatham Ltd. wishes to reduce its interest cost. To do so, Chatham Ltd. agrees to pay the holders of the convertible bonds an additional $80,000 if they will convert. Assuming conversion occurs and Chatham used the proportional method to value the conversion rights, the following entry is made.

Debt Conversion Expense	80,000	
Bonds Payable	1,000,000	
Conversion Rights	82,298	
Common Shares		1,081,320
Discount on Bonds Payable		978
Cash		80,000

The additional $80,000 is recorded as an expense of the current period and not as a reduction of equity. Some argue that the cost of a conversion inducement is a cost of obtaining equity capital. Others believe that since the transaction involves both the issuance of equity and also the retirement of debt, it should be reported as an expense.[4] Since there are no provisions for either treatment in Canada, firms may wish to follow the FASB requirement that consideration given to bondholders to induce conversion within a given time be reported as an expense.

AT TIME OF RETIREMENT OF CONVERTIBLE DEBT

The retirement of the liability component of convertible debt is treated the same as non-convertible bonds as explained in Chapter 15. The equity component requires reclassification since it no longer represents outstanding conversion rights. The amount originally assigned to Conversion Rights is added to "Contributed Surplus from Expired Conversion Rights."

CONVERTIBLE PREFERRED SHARES

OBJECTIVE 2
Explain the accounting for convertible preferred shares.

The major difference in accounting for a convertible bond and a convertible preferred share at the date of issue is that convertible bonds are considered part liability and part equity, while **convertible preferreds** (unless mandatory redemption exists) are considered a part of shareholders' equity.

In addition, when preferred share conversion privileges are exercised, there is no theoretical justification for recognition of a gain or loss. No gain or loss is recognized when the entity deals with its shareholders in their capacity as business owners. *The book value method is employed*: Preferred Share Capital is decreased and Common Share Capital is increased by the same amount.

Assume Host Enterprises issued 1,000 no-par common shares upon conversion of 1,000 no-par preferred shares that were originally issued for $1,200. The entry would be:

---

[4] "Induced Conversions of Convertible Debt," *Statement of Financial Accounting Standards No. 84* (Stamford, Conn.: FASB, 1985).

Convertible Preferred Shares	1,200	
Common Shares		1,200

If part of the original issuance price of the convertible preferred shares had been credited to other shareholders' equity accounts such as Contributed Surplus, then these related amounts should be cleared in the entry to record the conversion.

STOCK WARRANTS

Warrants are certificates that entitle the holder to acquire shares at a specified price within a stated period. This option is similar to the conversion privilege because warrants, if exercised, become common shares and usually have a dilutive effect (reduce earnings per share) similar to that of the conversion of convertible securities. However, a substantial difference between convertible securities and stock warrants is that upon exercise of the warrants, the holder has to pay a certain amount of money to obtain the shares.

The issuance of warrants or options to buy additional shares normally arises under three situations.

OBJECTIVE 3
Contrast the accounting for stock warrants and stock warrants issued with other securities

1. When issuing different types of securities, such as bonds or preferred shares, warrants are often included to make the *security more attractive,* to provide an "equity kicker" as an inducement for investors.

2. Upon the issuance of additional common shares, existing shareholders may have a *pre-emptive right to purchase common shares* first. Warrants may be issued to evidence that right.

3. Warrants, often referred to as stock options, are given as *compensation to executives and employees*.

The problems in accounting for stock warrants are complex and present many difficulties, some of which remain unresolved.

STOCK WARRANTS ISSUED WITH OTHER SECURITIES

Warrants issued with other securities are basically long-term options to buy common shares at a fixed price. Although some perpetual warrants are traded, generally their life is 5 years, or occasionally 10 years.

A warrant works like this: Tenneco Ltd. offers a unit comprised of one share and one detachable warrant exercisable at $24.25 per share and good for five years. The unit sells for $22.75. Given that the price of the common share the day before the sale was $19.88, a price of $2.87 for the warrant is suggested.

In this situation, the warrants have an apparent value of $2.87, even though it would not be profitable at present for the purchaser to exercise the warrant and buy the shares since the price of the shares is far below the exercise price of $24.25.[5] The investor pays for the warrant to receive a possible future call on the shares at a fixed price when the price has risen significantly. For example, if the price of the shares rises to $30, the investor has gained $2.88 ($30 minus $24.25 minus $2.87) on an investment of $2.87, a 100% increase! But if the price never rises, the investor loses the full $2.87.[6]

---

[5] Later in this discussion it will be shown that the value of the warrant is normally determined on the basis of a relative market value approach because of the difficulty of imputing a warrant value in any other manner.

[6] Trading in warrants is often referred to as licensed gambling. From the illustration, it is apparent that buying warrants can be an "all or nothing" proposition.

The proceeds from the sale of debt with **detachable stock warrants** should be allocated between the two securities.[7] Two separable instruments are involved, that is: (1) a bond; and (2) a warrant that gives the holder the right to purchase common shares at a certain price. Warrants that are detachable can be traded separately from the debt and, therefore, a market value can be determined. The amounts allocated to the debt and equity components may be determined by using either the proportional method or the incremental method.

Proportional Method. AT & T's offering of detachable five-year warrants to buy one common share at $25 (at a time when a share was selling for approximately $50) enabled it to price its offering of bonds at par with a moderate 8¾% yield. To place a value on the two securities one would determine (1) the value of the bonds without the warrants; and (2) the value of the warrants. For example, assume that AT & T's bonds (par $1,000) sold for 99 without the warrants soon after they were issued. The market value of the warrants at that time would have been $30. Prior to sale the warrants will not have a market value. The allocation is based on an estimate of market value, generally as established by an investment dealer or on the relative market value of the bonds and the warrants soon after they are issued and traded. The price paid for 10,000, $1,000 bonds with the warrants attached was par or $10,000,000. The allocation between the bonds and warrants would be made as follows.

Fair market value of bonds (without warrants) ($10,000,000 × .99)	=	$ 9,900,000
Fair market value of warrants (10,000 × $30)	=	300,000
Aggregate fair market value		$10,200,000
Allocated to bond: $\frac{\$9,900,000}{\$10,200,000}$ × $10,000,000 =		$9,705,882
Allocated to warrants: $\frac{\$300,000}{\$10,200,000}$ × $10,000,000 =		294,118*
Total allocation		$ 10,000,000
*rounded		

In this situation the bonds sell at a discount and are recorded as follows.

Cash	9,705,882	
Discount on Bonds Payable	294,118	
Bonds Payable		10,000,000

In addition, the company sells warrants that are credited to Contributed Surplus. The entry is as follows.

Cash	294,118	
Contributed Surplus—Stock Warrants		294,118

The entries may be combined if desired; they are shown separately here to indicate that the purchaser of the bond is buying not only a bond, but also a possible future claim on common shares.

Assuming that all 10,000 warrants are exercised (one warrant per one share), the following entry would be made.

Cash (10,000 × $25)	250,000	
Contributed Surplus—Stock Warrants	294,118	
Common Shares		544,118

---

[7] A detachable warrant means that the warrant can sell separately from the bond. *APB Opinion No. 14* makes a distinction between detachable and nondetachable warrants because nondetachable warrants must be sold with the security as a complete package; thus, no allocation is permitted.

What if the warrants are not exercised? Contributed Surplus—Stock Warrants is debited for $294,118 and Contributed Surplus from Expired Warrants is credited for a like amount. The contributed surplus reverts to the former shareholders.

Incremental Method. In instances where the fair values of either the warrants or the bonds are not determinable, the incremental method used in lump sum security purchases (explained in Chapter 15) may be used. That is, the security for which the market value is determinable is used and the remainder of the purchase price is allocated to the security for which the market value is not known. Assume that the market price of the AT&T warrants was known to be $300,000, but that the market price of the bonds without the warrants could not be determined. In this case, the amount allocated to the warrants and the shares would be as follows.

Lump sum receipt	$10,000,000
Allocated to the warrants	300,000
Balance allocated to bonds	**$ 9,700,000**

RIGHTS TO SUBSCRIBE TO ADDITIONAL SHARES

If the directors of a corporation decide to issue new shares, the old shareholders generally have the right (pre-emptive privilege) to purchase newly issued shares in proportion to their holdings. The privilege, referred to as a **stock right**, saves existing shareholders from suffering a dilution of voting rights without their consent, and it may allow them to purchase shares somewhat below their market value. The warrants issued in these situations are of short duration, unlike the warrants issued with other securities.

The certificate representing the stock right states the number of shares the holder of the right may purchase, as well as the price at which the new shares may be purchased. Each share ordinarily gives the owner one stock right. The price is normally less than the current market value of such shares, which gives the rights a value in themselves. From the time rights are issued until they expire, they may be purchased and sold like any other security.

No entry is required when rights are issued to existing shareholders. Only a memorandum entry is needed to indicate the number of rights issued to existing shareholders and to ensure that the company has additional unissued shares registered for issuance in case the rights are exercised. No formal entry is made at this time because no shares have been issued and no cash has been received.

If the rights are exercised, usually a cash payment of some type is involved. The appropriate Share Capital account is credited with the amount of cash received.

STOCK COMPENSATION PLANS

Another form of the warrant arises in stock compensation plans that are used to pay and motivate employees. The warrant is a **stock option**, which gives selected employees the option to purchase common shares at a given price over an extended period of time. Stock options are very popular because they meet the objectives of an effective compensation program.

Effective compensation has been a subject of considerable interest lately. A consensus of opinion is that effective compensation programs are ones that (1) motivate employees to high levels of performance; (2) help retain executives and allow for recruitment of new talent; (3) base compensation on employee and company performance; (4) maximize the employee's after-tax benefit and minimize the employer's after-tax cost; and (5) use performance criteria over which the employee has control. Although straight cash compensation plans (salary and, perhaps, bonus) are an important part of any compensation program, they are oriented to the short run. Many companies recognize that a more long-run compensation plan is often needed in addition to a cash component.

Long-term compensation plans attempt to develop in the executive a strong loyalty toward the company. An effective way to accomplish this goal is to give the employees "a piece of the action"—that is, an equity interest based on changes in long-term measures such as increases in earnings per share, revenues, share prices, or market share. These plans, generally referred to as **stock option plans**, come in many different forms. Essentially, they provide the executive with the opportunity to receive shares or cash in the future if the performance of the company (however measured) is satisfactory.

THE MAJOR ACCOUNTING ISSUE

To illustrate the most contentious accounting issue related to stock option plans, suppose that you are an employee of Hurdle Ltd. and that you are granted options to purchase 10,000 shares of the firm's common shares as part of your compensation. *The date you receive the options* is referred to as the **grant date**. The options are good for 10 years; the market price and the exercise price for the shares are both $20 at the grant date. What is the value of the compensation you just received?

Some believe you have not received anything; that is, the difference between the market price and the exercise price is zero and therefore no compensation results. Others argue these options have value: if the share price goes above $20 any time over the next 10 years and you exercise these options, substantial compensation results. For example, if at the end of the fourth year the market price is $30 per share and you exercise your options, you will have earned $100,000 [10,000 options × ($30 − $20)], ignoring income taxes.

How should the granting of these options be reported by Hurdle Ltd.? In most companies the compensation cost is measured by the excess of the market price of the shares over its exercise price at the grant date. Hurdle would therefore not recognize any compensation expense related to your options because at the grant date the market price and exercise price were the same.

ACCOUNTING FOR STOCK COMPENSATION PLANS

OBJECTIVE 4
Describe the accounting for stock compensation plans.

Accounting for stock option plans presents difficulties. The following three questions must be resolved:

1. How should compensation expense be determined?
2. Over what periods should compensation expense be allocated?
3. What types of plans are used to compensate officers and key executives?

Determination of Compensation Expense. Total compensation expense is computed as the *excess of the market price of the shares over the option price on the measurement date*. The **measurement date** is the first date on which are known both (1) the number of shares that an individual employee is entitled to receive; and (2) the option or purchase price. The measurement date for many plans is the date an *option is granted* to an employee (i.e., the grant date). The measurement date may be later than the grant date in plans with variable terms (that is, either the number of shares or option price or both are not known) that depend on events after date of grant. Usually the measurement date for plans with variable terms is the **date of exercise**.

If the number of shares or the option price, or both, are unknown, compensation expense may have to be estimated on the basis of assumptions as to what will be the final number of shares and the option price.

Allocation of Compensation Expense. Compensation expense is recognized *in the period(s) in which the employee performs the services* (often referred to as the **service period**). The total compensation expense is determined at the measurement date and allocated to the appropriate periods benefited by the employee's services. In practice, it is often difficult to specify the period of service, and considerable judgement is exercised in this determination. If the service period cannot be clearly defined, the general rule followed is that any method that is systematic and rational is appropriate. Assuming the measurement date is the date of grant, many enterprises recognize the compensation expense over an arbitrary period; others amortize it from the grant date to the date the option may be first exercised; and still others record it as a current expense.

TYPES OF PLANS

Many types of plans are used to compensate key executives. In all these plans the amount of the reward is dependent upon future events. Consequently, continued employment is a necessary element in almost all types of plans. The popularity of a given plan usually depends on prospects in the stock market and tax considerations. For example, if it appears that appreciation will occur in the price of a company's shares, a plan that offers the option to purchase shares is attractive to an executive. Conversely, if it appears that price appreciation is unlikely, then compensation might be tied to some performance measure such as an increase in book value or earnings per share. Three common plans that illustrate different accounting issues are:

1. Stock option plans.

2. Stock appreciation rights plans.

3. Performance-type plans.

We'll look at the accounting for each type of plan.

Stock Option Plans. To illustrate the accounting for a stock option plan, assume that on November 1, 1997 the shareholders of Scott Company approve a plan that grants the company's five executives options to purchase 2,000 shares each of the company's no-par value common shares. The options are granted on January 1, 1998 and may be exercised at any time within the next 10 years. The option price per share is $60, and the market price of the shares at the date of grant is $70 per share. The total compensation expense is computed below. (Note that January 1, 1998 is the measurement date because the number of shares each executive can purchase and the option price are known on this date, which coincides with the beginning of the fiscal period.)

Market value of 10,000 shares at date of grant ($70 per share)	$700,000
Option price of 10,000 shares at date of grant ($60 per share)	600,000
Total compensation expense	**$ 100,000**

As indicated earlier, the value of the option should be recognized as an expense in the period(s) in which the employee performs services. In the case of Scott Company, assume that documents associated with issuance of the options indicate that the expected period of benefit is two years, starting with the grant date. The entry to record the total compensation expense at the date of grant is as follows.

Deferred Compensation Expense	100,000	
Contributed Surplus—Stock Options		100,000

The deferred compensation expense (a contra shareholders' equity account) then is amortized to expense over the period of service involved (two years).[8] The credit balance in the Contributed Surplus—Stock Options account is treated as an element of shareholders' equity. On December 31, 1998 and on December 31, 1999 the following journal entry is recorded to recognize the compensation cost for the year attributable to the stock option plan.

Compensation Expense	50,000	
Deferred Compensation Expense		50,000

At December 31, 1998 the Shareholders' Equity section would be presented as follows, assuming that 1,000,000 no-par value shares were issued.

Shareholders' equity		
Common shares, no-par value, 1,000,000 shares		
issued and outstanding		$1,000,000
Contributed surplus—stock options	$100,000	
Less: Deferred compensation expense	**50,000**	50,000
Total shareholders' equity		$ 1,050,000

If 20% or 2,000 of the 10,000 options were exercised on June 1, 2000 (three years and five months after date of grant), the following journal entry would be recorded.

Cash (2,000 × $60)	120,000	
Contributed Surplus—Stock Options (20% of $100,000)	20,000	
Common Shares		140,000

If the remaining stock options are not exercised before their expiration date, the balance in the Contributed Surplus—Stock Options account should be transferred to a more properly titled contributed surplus account, such as Contributed Surplus from Expired Stock Options. The entry to record this transaction at the date of expiration would be as follows.

Contributed Surplus—Stock Options (80% of $100,000)	80,000	
Contributed Surplus from Expired Stock Options		80,000

The fact that a stock option is not exercised does not nullify the propriety of recording the costs of services received from the executives and attributable to the stock option plan. Compensation expense is, therefore, not adjusted upon expiration of the options. However, if a stock option is forfeited because *an employee fails to fulfil an obligation* (i.e., leaves employment), the estimate of compensation expense recorded in the current period should be adjusted (as a change in estimate). This change in estimate would be recorded by debiting Contributed Surplus—Stock Options and crediting Compensation Expense, thereby decreasing compensation expense in the period of forfeiture.

---

[8] The rationale for using a contra equity account is that deferred compensation expense represents an unearned compensation amount and is better reported as contra equity than as an asset. An alternative to this entry is to record no formal entry at the date of grant but to accrue compensation expense at the end of each period as incurred. We will use the approach illustrated above for problem material because this method formalizes in the records the compensation element of these plans.

Stock Appreciation Rights Plans. In a **stock appreciation rights** (SAR) plan, the executive is given the right to receive **share appreciation**, which is defined as the excess of the market price of the shares at the date of exercise over a pre-established price. This share appreciation may be paid in cash, shares, or a combination of both. The major advantage of SARs is that the executive often does not have to make a cash outlay at the date of exercise, but receives a payment for the share appreciation that may be used to pay related income taxes. Unlike shares acquired under a stock option plan, the shares that constitute the basis for computing the appreciation in a SARs plan are not issued. The executive is awarded only cash or shares having a market value equivalent to the appreciation.

As indicated earlier, the usual date for measuring compensation related to stock compensation plans is the date of grant. However, with SARs, the final amount of cash or shares (or a combination of the two) to be distributed is not known until the date of exercise—the measurement date. Therefore total compensation cannot be measured until this date.

How then should compensation expense be recorded during the interim periods from the date of grant to the date of exercise? Such a determination is not easy because it is impossible to know what total compensation cost will be until the date of exercise, and the service period will probably not coincide with the exercise date. The best estimate of total compensation cost for the plan at any interim period is the difference between the **current market price** of the shares and **option price** multiplied by the number of stock appreciation rights outstanding. This total estimated compensation cost is then allocated over the service period to record an expense (or a decrease in expense if market price falls) in each period. At the end of each interim period, total compensation expense reported to date should equal the percentage of the total service period that has elapsed multiplied by the estimated compensation cost.

For example, if at an interim period the service period is 40% complete and total estimated compensation is $100,000, then total compensation expense reported to date should equal $40,000 ($100,000 times 40%). As another illustration, in the first year of a four-year plan, the company charges one-fourth of the appreciation to date; in the second year, it charges off two-fourths or 50% of the appreciation to date less the amount already recognized in the first year. In the third year, it charges off three-fourths of the appreciation to date less the amount recognized previously, and in the fourth year it charges off the remaining compensation expense. We will refer to this method as the **percentage approach** for allocating compensation expense.

A special problem arises when the exercise date is later than the service period. In the previous example, if the SARs were not exercised at the end of four years it would be necessary to account for the difference between the market price and the option price in the fifth year. In this case, compensation expense is adjusted whenever a change in market price of the shares *occurs in subsequent reporting periods until the rights expire or are exercised, whichever comes first.*

Increases or decreases in the market value of these shares between the date of grant and the exercise date, therefore, result in a change in the measure of compensation. Some periods will have credits to compensation expense if the quoted market price of the shares falls from one period to the next; the credit to compensation expense, however, cannot exceed previously recognized compensation expense. In other words, *cumulative compensation expense arising from the plan cannot be negative.*

To illustrate, assume that Bigger Hotels Ltd. establishes a SARs program on January 1, 1998 that entitles executives to receive cash at the date of exercise (anytime in the next five years) for the difference between the market price of the shares and the pre-established price of $10 on 10,000 SARs; the market price on December 31, 1998 is $13 per share, and the service period runs for two years (1998–1999). The following schedule indicates the amount of compensation expense to be recorded each period, assuming that the executives hold the SARs for three years, at which time the rights are exercised.

					Stock Appreciation Rights			
					Schedule of Compensation Expense			
(1)	(2)	(3)	(4)	(5)	(6)			
Date	Market Price	Pre-established Price (10,000 SARs)	Cumulative Compensation Recognizable[b]	Percentage Accrued[b]	Cumulative Compensation Accrued to Date	Expense 1998	Expense 1999	Expense 2000
Dec. 31/98	$13	$10	$30,000	50%	$ 15,000	$15,000		
					55,000		$55,000	
Dec. 31/99	17	10	70,000	100%	70,000			
					(20,000)			$(20,000)
Dec. 31/00	15	10	50,000	100%	$ 50,000			

[a]Cumulative compensation for unexercised SARs to be allocated to periods of service.
[b]The percentage accrued is based upon a two-year service period (1998–1999).

In 1998, Bigger Hotels would record compensation expense of $15,000 because 50% of the $30,000 total compensation cost estimated at December 31, 1998 can be allocated to 1998. In 1999, the market price increases to $17 per share; therefore, the additional compensation expense of $55,000 ($70,000 minus $15,000) is recorded. The SARs are held through 2000, during which time the share price decreases to $15. The decrease is recognized by recording a $20,000 credit to Compensation Expense and a debit to Liability Under Stock Appreciation Plan. Note that after the service period ends, since the rights are still outstanding, the rights are adjusted to market at December 31, 2000. Any such credit to Compensation Expense cannot exceed previous charges to expense attributable to that plan.

As the compensation expense is recorded each period, the corresponding credit should be to a liability account if the stock appreciation is to be paid in cash. If shares are to be issued, then a more appropriate credit would be to Contributed Surplus. The entry to record compensation expense in the first year, assuming that the SAR ultimately will be paid in cash, is as follows.

Compensation Expense	15,000	
Liability Under Stock Appreciation Plan		15,000

The liability account would be credited again in 1999 for $55,000 and debited for $20,000 in 2000 when the negative compensation expense is recorded. The entry to record the negative compensation expense is as follows.

Liability Under Stock Appreciation Plan	20,000	
Compensation Expense		20,000

At December 31, 2000 executives receive $50,000; the entry removing the liability is as follows.

Liability Under Stock Appreciation Plan	50,000	
Cash		50,000

Because compensation expense is measured by the difference between the market price of the shares from period to period, multiplied by the number of SARs, compensation expense can increase or decrease substantially from one period to the next.

Many accountants are disturbed by the accounting for SARs because the amount of compensation expense to be reported each period is subject to fluctuations in the stock market. "Shouldn't earnings determine share prices, rather than share prices determine earnings?" ask some accountants. Even with this drawback, though, this type of plan is gaining in popularity because executives are required to make little, if any, cash outlay under these programs.

SARs are often issued in combination with compensatory stock options (referred to as **tandem** or **combination plans**) and the executives must then select which of the two sets of terms to exercise, thereby cancelling the other. The existence of alternative plans running concurrently poses additional problems from an accounting standpoint because the accountant must determine, on the basis of the facts available each period, which of the two plans has the higher probability of exercise and then account for this plan, and ignore the other.

Performance-Type Plans. Many executives have become disenchanted with stock compensation plans whose ultimate payment depends on an increase in the market price of the common shares. They do not like having their compensation and judgement of performance at the mercy of the stock market's erratic behaviour. As a result, there has been a substantial increase in the use of plans whereby executives receive common shares (or cash) if specified performance criteria are attained during the performance period (generally three to five years).

The **performance criteria** employed usually are increases in return on assets or equity, growth in sales, growth in earnings per share (EPS), or a combination of these factors. A performance-type plan's measurement date is the date of exercise because neither the number of shares that will be issued nor cash that will be paid out when performance is achieved is known at the date of grant. The compensation cost is allocated to the periods involved in the same manner as with stock appreciation rights; that is, the percentage approach is used.

Tandem or combination awards are popular with these plans. The executive has the choice of selecting between a performance or stock option award. In these cases, the executive has the best of both worlds: if either the share price increases or the performance goal is achieved, the executive gains. Sometimes, the executive receives both types of plans, so that the monies received from the performance plan can finance the exercise price on the stock option plan.

Noncompensatory Plans. In some companies, stock purchase plans permit all employees to purchase shares at a discounted price over a short period of time. These plans are usually classified as **noncompensatory**. Noncompensatory means that the primary purpose of the plan is not to compensate the employees but, rather, to enable the employer to secure equity capital or to induce widespread ownership of an enterprise's common shares among employees. Specifically, the profession has concluded that noncompensatory plans have the following characteristics:

1. Participation by all employees who meet limited employment qualifications.
2. Equal offers of shares to all eligible employees.
3. Limitation to a reasonable period of time permitted for exercise of an option or purchase right.
4. Discount from the market price of the shares no greater than would be reasonable in an offer of shares to shareholders or others.

For example, IBM has a stock purchase plan under which employees who meet minimal employment qualifications are entitled to purchase IBM shares at a 15% reduction from market price for a short period of time. Such a reduction from market price is not considered compensatory because the employer's objectives appear to be either to raise additional equity capital or to expand ownership of the enterprise's shares among the employees as a means of enhancing loyalty to the enterprise. This position is debatable because the employee is receiving a valuable fringe benefit. However, because it is difficult to determine the company's objectives, in practice the foregoing type of stock purchase plan is considered noncompensatory if the discount is in the amount of 10 to 15% of the market price.

It should be emphasized that plans that do not possess all of the above-mentioned four characteristics are classified as compensatory.

DISCLOSURE OF COMPENSATION PLANS

Disclosure plays an important role in helping users of the financial statements better understand compensation plans and their possible effects. Regardless of the basis used in valuing stock options, rights, and other types of awards, **full disclosure should be made** about the status of these plans at the end of the period, including the number of shares under option and the option price. As to options exercised during the period, disclosure should be made of the number of shares involved and the option price used for exercise.

Falconbridge Limited disclosed employee stock options as shown below.

EXHIBIT 18-1   FALCONBRIDGE LIMITED

8. Share capital

(a) Employee stock option plan

The Corporation has a stock option plan through which options have been granted to officers and various employees for the purchase of common shares. Options were granted at prices equal to the closing market value on the last trading day prior to the grant and are exercisable for five years from the date of vesting. Of the 766,000 options granted to executive officers in 1994, 20% vested on the date of the grant and 20% vest on each of the first four anniversaries of the date of the grant. Except for the above noted shares, all of the other options granted vested on the day of the grant.

The following options were outstanding at December 31:

Expiry date	Option price per share	Number of Shares		
		1996	1995	1994
1999	$18.50	119,600	159,900	315,500
2000	$22.75 to $28.75	102,500	102,500	—
2001	$29.90 to $30.85	201,000	—	—
2003	$18.50	334,500	490,000	766,000
		757,600	752,400	1,081,500

EXHIBIT 18-1 FALCONBRIDGE LIMITED (Continued)

Stock option transactions for the respective years were as follows:

	1996	1995	1994
Outstanding, beginning of year	752,400	1,081,500	–
Granted	201,000	102,500	1,081,500
Exercised	98,300	360,600	–
Cancelled	97,500	71,000	–
Outstanding, end of year	757,600	752,400	1,081,500

SUMMARY

A summary of these plans and their major characteristics is provided below.

Summary of Compensation Plans

Type of Plan	Measurement Date	Measurement of Compensation	Allocation Period	Allocation Method
Stock option	Grant	Market price less exercise price	Service	Percentage approach for service period
Stock appreciation rights	Exercise	Market price less exercise price	Service	Straight-line
Performance-type plan	Exercise	Market value of shares issued	Service	Percentage approach for service period

Conceptual Issues Involving Stock Compensation Plans. Much debate exists concerning the proper accounting and reporting for stock compensation plans. Two primary conceptual questions that must be resolved before acceptable accounting standards may be adopted are discussed below.

Alternative Dates. What date should be used to measure total compensation cost? Many accountants favour the date of grant because the company foregoes an alternative use of shares on that date. Other believe that some other date such as the date the option becomes vested or exercised is more appropriate.

The date the option becomes vested is favoured by some because at that date the employee has performed the option contract, and the company is obligated to issue shares at the option price.

Others state that the excess of the market price over the option price at the date the option becomes vested is still an incomplete valuation that understates the value of the option, particularly when this option may be held for several years before expiring. They believe that only at the date that the option is exercised is the final value of the employee's services recognizable. In short, the commitment to transfer cash or shares to employees under a plan is only a contingency until the date of exercise, when the amount of the transfer will be known.

Valuation. A second issue relates to how the option should be valued, assuming the measurement date is the date of grant. One group believes that an attempt should be made to value the option itself. They note that an option to buy shares at a price equal to or below the market price has value and cannot be considered worthless. Because there is no risk of loss to the executive and a possibility, if not a probability, of great gain, the option may possess value that is greater than the spread between the option price and the market price at the date of the grant. Similarly, others argue that although services are normally valued at the cost of the assets given in exchange for them, the fair value of the services received is also a proper and acceptable basis of valuation. Using this approach, an attempt is made to determine what type of cash trade-off the executives make receiving an option for shares in lieu of a straight cash distribution. By imputing this cash trade-off, the total amount of compensation may be determined.[9]

Others stress that the approaches described above are too subjective and argue for the approach adopted by the profession in the United States, namely, that compensation expense be measured by the difference between the market price and the option price at the date of grant. This argument is based on the premise that the only objective and verifiable amount that can be determined at the date of grant is the spread between the market and option prices. Many are unhappy with this approach because little or no compensation is recorded for many stock option plans (e.g., incentive stock option plans report zero compensation expense).

Finally, it is sometimes argued that no compensation expense should be reported at all because no cost to the entity results from the issuance of additional shares; the cost to the shareholders is the possible dilution of their interest in the entity, and accountants should ignore this factor in their accounting. In the authors' opinion, this does not appear to be a reasonable approach because a cost is involved to the existing shareholders that should be considered a cost of operating the enterprise.

SECTION 2: COMPUTING EARNINGS PER SHARE

Earnings per share information is frequently reported in the financial press and is widely used by shareholders and potential investors to evaluate the profitability of a company. **Earnings per share** indicates the income earned by each common share. Thus, *earnings per share is reported only for common shares*. For example, if Oscar Limited has net income of $300,000 and a weighted average of 100,000 common shares outstanding for the year, earnings per share is $3 ($300,000 ÷ 100,000).

Because of the importance of earnings per share information, most companies are required to report this information either in the income statement or in the notes. Exceptions to this rule include government-owned companies, wholly-owned subsidiaries, and companies with only a few shareholders. Generally, earnings per share information is reported below net income in the income statement. For Oscar Limited, the presentation would be as follows.

Net income	$300,000
Earnings per share	$ 3.00

When the income statement contains intermediate components of income, earnings per share should be disclosed for each component. The following is representative:

---

[9] For an interesting discussion of an attempt to value options, see Clifford W. Smith, Jr. and Jerold L. Zimmerman, "Valuing Employee Stock Option Plans Using Option Pricing Models," *Journal of Accounting Research* (Autumn, 1976), pp. 357–64.

Earnings per share:	
Income from continuing operations	**$4.00**
Loss from discontinued operations, net of tax	.60
Income before extraordinary item	**3.40**
Extraordinary gain, net of tax	1.00
Net income	**$4.40**

These disclosures enable the user of the financial statements to recognize the effects of income from continuing operations on EPS, as distinguished from income or loss from irregular items.[10]

EARNINGS PER SHARE—SIMPLE CAPITAL STRUCTURE

A corporation's capital structure is regarded as **simple** if it consists only of common shares or includes no potentially dilutive convertible securities, options, warrants, or other rights that upon conversion or exercise could in the aggregate dilute earnings per common share. A capital structure is regarded as **complex** if it includes securities that could have a dilutive effect on earnings per common share. The computation of earnings per share for a simple capital structure involves two items (other than net income): preferred dividends and the weighted-average number of common shares outstanding.

OBJECTIVE 5
Compute earnings per share on a simple capital structure.

Preferred Dividends. As indicated earlier, earnings per share relates to earnings per common share. When a company has both common and preferred shares outstanding, *the current year dividends on preferred shares are subtracted from net income to arrive at income available to common shareholders*. The formula for computing earnings per share is stated as follows.

$$\frac{\text{Net Income} - \text{Preferred Dividends}}{\text{Weighted Average of Shares Outstanding}} = \text{Earnings Per Share}$$

In reporting earnings per share information, preferred dividends should be subtracted from each of the intermediate components of income (income from continuing operations and income before extraordinary items) and finally net income to arrive at income available to common shareholders. If preferred dividends are declared and a net loss occurs, *the preferred dividend is added to the loss* for the purposes of computing the loss per share. If the preferred shares are cumulative and the dividend is not declared in the current year, *an amount equal to the dividend that should have been declared for the current year only* should be subtracted from net income or added to the net loss. Dividends in arrears for previous years should have been included in the previous year's computations.

Weighted-Average Number of Shares Outstanding. In all computations of earnings per share, the **weighted-average number of shares outstanding** during the period constitutes the basis for the per-share amounts reported. Shares issued or retired during the period affect the amount outstanding and must be *weighed by the fraction of the period in which they were outstanding*. The rationale for this approach is to find the equivalent

---

[10] Reporting per-share amounts for gain or loss on discontinued operations and gain or loss on extraordinary items is optional. The reason is that a financial statement user can determine these amounts if the other per-share data are provided.

number of whole shares outstanding for the year. To illustrate, assume that Stallone Limited has the following changes in its common shares outstanding for the period.

Date	Share Changes	Shares Outstanding
Jan. 1	Beginning balance	90,000
Apr. 1	Issued 30,000 shares for cash	30,000
		120,000
July 1	Purchased 39,000 shares	39,000
		81,000
Nov. 1	Issued 60,000 shares for cash	60,000
Dec. 31	Ending balance	141,000

To compute the weighted-average number of shares outstanding, the following computation is made.

	(A)	(B)	(C)
Dates Outstanding	Shares Outstanding	Fraction of Year	Weighted Shares (A × B)
Jan. 1–Apr. 1	90,000	3/12	22,500
Apr. 1–July 1	120,000	3/12	30,000
July 1–Nov. 1	81,000	4/12	27,000
Nov. 1–Dec. 31	141,000	2/12	23,500
Weighted average number of shares outstanding			**103,000**

As illustrated, 90,000 shares were outstanding for three months, which translated to 22,500 whole shares for the entire year. Because additional shares were issued on April 1, the shares outstanding change and these shares must be weighted for the time outstanding. When 39,000 shares were reacquired on July 1, the shares outstanding were reduced and again a new computation was made to determine the proper weighted shares outstanding.

Stock Dividends and Stock Splits. When **stock dividends** and **stock splits** occur, computation of the weighted-average number of shares requires restatement of the shares outstanding before the stock dividend or split. For example, assume that a corporation has 100,000 shares outstanding on January 1 and issued a 25% stock dividend on June 30. For purposes of computing a weighted average for the current year, the additional 25,000 shares outstanding as a result of the stock dividend are assumed to have been outstanding since the beginning of the year. Thus the weighted average for the year would be 125,000 shares.

The issuance of a stock dividend or stock split requires retroactive restatement, but the issuance or reacquisition of shares for cash does not. Why? The reason is that stock splits and stock dividends do not increase or decrease the net assets of the enterprise; only additional shares are issued and, therefore, the weighted-average shares must be restated. Conversely, the issuance or purchase of shares for cash changes the amount of net assets. As a result, the company either earns more or less in the future as a result of this change in net assets. Stated another way, *a stock dividend or split does not change the shareholders' total investment* — it only increases (unless it is a reverse split) the number of common shares representing the investment.

To illustrate how a stock dividend affects the computation of the weighted-average number of shares outstanding, assume that Rambo Limited has the following changes in its common shares during the year.

Date	Share Changes	Shares Outstanding
Jan. 1	Beginning balance	100,000
Mar. 1	Issued 20,000 shares for cash	20,000
		120,000
June 1	60,000 additional shares (50% stock dividend)	60,000
		180,000
Nov. 1	Issued 30,000 shares for cash	30,000
Dec. 31	Ending balance	210,000

The computation of the weighted-average number of shares outstanding would be as follows.

Dates Outstanding	(A) Shares Outstanding	(B) Restatement	(C) Fraction of Year	(D) Weighted Shares (A × B)
Jan. 1–Mar. 1	100,000	1.50	2/12	25,000
Mar. 1–June 1	120,000	1.50	3/12	45,000
June 1–Nov. 1	180,000		5/12	75,000
Nov. 1–Dec. 31	210,000		2/12	35,000
Weighted-average number of shares outstanding				**180,000**

The shares outstanding prior to the stock dividend must be restated. The shares outstanding from January 1 to June 1 are adjusted for the stock dividend, so that these shares are stated on the same basis as shares issued subsequent to the stock dividend. Shares issued after the stock dividend do not have to be restated because they are on the new basis. The stock dividend simply restates existing shares. The same type of treatment is required for a stock split.

If a stock dividend or stock split occurs after the end of the year, but before the financial statements are issued, the weighted-average number of shares outstanding for the year (and any other years presented in comparative form) must be restated. For example, assume that Hendricks Limited computes its weighted-average number of shares to be 100,000 for the year ended December 31, 1998. On January 15, 1999, before the financial statements are issued, the company splits its shares 3 for 1. In this case, the weighted-average number of shares used in computing earnings per share for 1998 would be 300,000 shares. If earnings per share information for 1997 is provided as comparative information, it also must be adjusted for the stock split.

Comprehensive Illustration. Bannerman Limited has income before extraordinary items of $580,000 and an extraordinary gain, net of tax, of $240,000. In addition it has declared a dividend on its 100,000 preferred shares of $1 each. Bannerman Limited also has the following changes on its common shares outstanding during 1998.

Date	Share Changes	Shares Outstanding
Jan. 1	Beginning balance	180,000
May 1	Purchased 30,000 shares for cash	30,000
		150,000
July 1	300,000 additional shares (3 for 1 stock split)	300,000
		450,000
Dec. 31	Issued 50,000 shares for cash	50,000
Dec. 31	**Ending balance**	**500,000**

To compute the earnings per share information, the weighted-average number of shares outstanding is determined as follows.

Dates Outstanding	(A) Shares Outstanding	(B) Restatement	(C) Fraction of Year	(D) Weighted Shares (A × B × C)
Jan. 1–May 1	180,000	3	4/12	180,000
May 1–Dec. 1	150,000	3	8/12	300,000
Weighted-average number of shares outstanding				**480,000**

In computing the weighted-average number of shares, the shares issued on December 31, 1998 are ignored because they have not been outstanding during the year. The weighted-average number of shares is then divided into income before extraordinary items and net income to determine earnings per share. Bannerman Limited's preferred dividends of $100,000 are subtracted from income before extraordinary items ($580,000) to arrive at income before extraordinary items available to common shareholders of $480,000 ($580,000 − $100,000). Deducting the preferred dividends from the income before extraordinary items has the effect of also reducing net income without affecting the amount of the extraordinary item. The final amount is referred to as income available to common shareholders.

	(A) Income Information	(B) Weighted Shares	(C) Earnings Per Share (A / B)
Income before extraordinary items available to common shareholders	$480,000*	480,000	$1.00
Extraordinary gain (net of tax)	240,000	480,000	.50
Income available to common shareholders	$720,000	480,000	$1.50

*$580,000–$100,000

Disclosure of the per-share amount for the extraordinary item is optional. Income and per-share information reported would be as follows.

Income before extraordinary item	$580,000
Extraordinary gain, net of tax	240,000
Net income	$820,000
Earnings per share:	
Income before extraordinary item	$1.00
Extraordinary item, net of tax	.50
Net income	**$1.50**

EARNINGS PER SHARE—COMPLEX CAPITAL STRUCTURE

One problem with a simple EPS computation is that it fails to recognize the potentially dilutive impact of dilutive securities on earnings per share. Dilutive securities present a serious problem in determining the proper earnings per share because conversion or exercise may have an adverse effect on earnings per share. This adverse effect can be significant and, more importantly, unexpected unless financial statements call attention to the potential dilutive effect in some manner.

OBJECTIVE 6
Compute earnings per share in a complex capital structure.

Because of the increasing use of dilutive securities in the 1960s, the profession can no longer ignore the significance of these securities and, therefore, has required additional earnings per share disclosures for firms having complex capital structures. A complex capital structure exists when a corporation has any debt or equity securities that may be converted, options, warrants, or other rights that upon conversion or exercise could dilute earnings per share.

A complex capital structure requires a **dual presentation** of earnings per share. These two presentations are referred to as "basic earnings per share" and "fully diluted earnings per share." **Basic earnings per share** is based on the number of common shares outstanding. **Fully diluted earnings per share** indicates the dilution of earnings per share that would have occurred if all contingent issuances of common shares that would have reduced earnings per share had taken place. Because of computational rules, fully diluted earnings per share are always less (less income per share or more loss per share) than basic EPS.

Materiality and Anti-dilution.   A company may have dilutive securities but still not have to report fully diluted earnings per share. Many corporations have potential dilution that is not material. In defining materiality some Canadian accountants use the **3% materiality threshold** applicable in the United States. Any corporation whose capital structure has potential dilution of less than 3% of earnings per common share reports only basic earnings per share.

To illustrate, Murphy Limited has basic earnings per share of $2.00, ignoring all dilutive securities in its capital structure. If the possible conversion or exercise of the dilutive securities in the aggregate reduces earnings per share to $1.94 (97% × $2) or below, it is necessary to present both basic and fully diluted earnings per share (dual presentation). Otherwise, the company reports basic earnings per share at $2.00 without additional disclosure. It is to be assumed that the weighted-average number of shares is the basis and that potential dilution, if any exists, is less than 3%. *In computing the 3% dilution factor, the aggregate of all dilutive securities should be considered.*

Whether the capital structure is simple or complex, earnings per share data should be shown before and after extraordinary items, where applicable. In addition, when the income statement includes a disposal of a business segment, the *Handbook* recommends reporting results of continuing operations separately from the results of operations of that segment.[11] Also, earnings per share amounts must be shown for all periods presented; all prior period earnings per share amounts presented should be restated for stock dividends and stock splits. When results of operations of a prior period have been restated as a result of a prior period adjustment, the earnings per-share data shown for the prior period should also be restated. The effect of the restatement, expressed in per- share terms, should be disclosed in the year of restatement.

---

[11] *CICA Handbook*, par. 3500.12.

Basic Earnings Per Share. Basic earnings per share must be computed and presented for all enterprises except for business enterprises that do not have share capital, government-owned companies, wholly-owned subsidiaries, and companies with only a few share-holders. If a corporation has more than one class of common shares (i.e., shares having equal participation rights after prescribed dividends), then it is necessary to compute and report separate basic earnings per share amounts for each class.

When common shares are issued on conversion of debt or senior shares, the shares issued are considered to have been outstanding from the date when interest or dividends cease to be legally due on the securities converted. For example, suppose a firm had 100,000 shares outstanding on January 1 and on August 1 an additional 10,000 shares were issued as a result of bond conversions. The bond indenture specifies that interest on bonds converted will be paid to the regular interest payment date (June 30 and December 31) preceding the date of conversion. In this case the weighted-average number of common shares for the year would be 105,000 (100,000 + 10,000/2).

Another case in which the date of issue of common shares may not be the same as the date used in determining the term outstanding involves shares issued to effect a merger or an acquisition. If common shares are issued to effect a merger or an acquisition that is accounted for as a purchase, the shares so issued are considered to be outstanding from the date that earnings of the investee first accrue to the investor. If the merger is accounted for as a pooling-of-interests, the shares issued will be treated as outstanding retroactive to the beginning of the period since the earnings are also included from that date.

Adjusted Basic Earnings Per Share. In the computation of basic earnings per share, common shares issued during the year as a result of conversions of senior shares or debt are considered to be outstanding for only that portion of the year subsequent to the termination of the firm's obligation for interest or dividends. When such conversions take place during a fiscal period, firms are required to provide an additional earnings per share amount. This additional per-share figure is known as "adjusted basic" earnings per share. Adjusted basic earnings per share is computed in the same way as basic earnings per share except that the shares issued in the conversion are treated as if they had been outstanding from the beginning of the year.

Income Available to Common Shares. As previously emphasized, earnings per share is computed by dividing the amount of net income (or loss) available to common shareholders by the weighted-average number of common shares outstanding. The **income available to common shareholders** is determined by deducting dividends on senior shares from the reported income. If the senior shares are noncumulative, dividends declared should be deducted from reported income. When senior shares include cumulative preferreds, it is necessary to deduct the amount of dividends prescribed, whether paid or not. For example, a firm reports $100,000 net income for a year during which it had 60,000 common shares outstanding, 10,000 $1.00 ordinary preferred and 20,000 $1.00 cumulative preferred. Assuming that dividends of $0.50 per share were paid on both ordinary and cumulative preferred shares, the amount of income available to common shareholders would be $75,000 ($100,000 minus $5,000 paid on ordinary preferred and $20,000 prescribed on the cumulative preferred).

Fully Diluted Earnings Per Share. Firms having complex capital structures must present appropriate fully diluted earnings per share amounts if the potential dilution is material. Potential earnings per share dilution exists whenever a firm has convertible senior shares or debt outstanding or has issued stock rights, options, or warrants. The purpose of reporting fully diluted earnings per share is to disclose the maximum possible reduction in earnings per share that could take place if all qualifying issuable common shares were issued.

Computing fully diluted earnings per share involves a hypothetical calculation. The weighted-average number of common shares used in this calculation includes both issued and contingently issuable common shares. Issuable common shares include only those that are issuable under outstanding conversion privileges and/or options and warrants within a 10-year period from the balance sheet date. The term during which these issuable common shares are considered to be outstanding is the shorter of the full fiscal period or, if less than one year, the term during which the underlying security or option has been outstanding.

In addition to changing the weighted-average number of common shares outstanding, it is necessary to recognize the "income effect" of the issuable common shares. If common shares are issuable as a result of outstanding convertible preferred, the income effect is equal to the dividends applicable to the convertible preferred. That is, if the holders of the convertible preferred shares converted their shares to common, the income available to common shareholders would now be increased by the amount of the dividends which would have otherwise been allocated to preferred shares. When the income effect involves an income statement item such as interest expense on convertible bonds, the amount of the adjustment is the amount by which the after-tax income would be increased. For example, if holders of convertible bonds exercised their conversion privilege, then income available to common shareholders would be increased by the amount of interest that would have been paid on the bonds less the amount by which income tax expense would be increased due to the reduction in interest expense.

Convertible Securities. Convertible securities that affect the calculation of fully diluted earnings per share include convertible senior shares and debt. Any outstanding rights to convert either senior shares or debt into common shares within a **10-year term** that would result in dilution (reduction) of earnings per share should be included in the calculation of fully diluted earnings per share. As emphasized above, the number of issuable common shares outstanding as a result of the related convertible security is included in the computation of the weighted-average number of common shares outstanding. Income is adjusted to reflect, on a pro forma basis, the changes that would occur if the conversion privileges had been exercised at the beginning of the year or date of issue, whichever is later.

As an example, Marshy Field Limited has net income for the year of $310,000 and an average number of common shares outstanding during the period of 100,000. The company has two convertible debenture bond issues outstanding. One (outstanding at the beginning of the current year) is a 10% issue sold at 100 (total of $1,000,000) and convertible into 40,000 common shares. The other is a 15% issue sold at 100 (total of $1,000,000) on April 1 of the current year and convertible into 64,000 common shares. In addition, the firm has 50,000 noncumulative $1.00 convertible (one preferred for one common) preferred shares outstanding. Due to a cash shortage, dividends of only $0.75 per share were declared and paid during the current year. Assume that the tax rate at present is 40%.

EXHIBIT 18-2 MARSHY FIELD LTD.

COMPUTATION OF EARNINGS PER SHARE

	Number of Shares	Net Income
Net income		$310,000
Common shares	100,000	
Deduct:		
Preferred dividends declared (50,000 × $0.75)		37,500
Income available to common	100,000	$272,500
Basic earnings per share ($272,500/100,000)		$2.73
From above	100,000	$272,500
Add assumed conversions:		
Convertible preferred		
Dividends (50,000 × $0.75)		37,500
Number of shares	50,000	
10% convertible debentures:		
Interest net of tax ($1,000,000 × [0.10 × 0.6])		60,000
Number of shares	40,000	
15% convertible debentures:		
Interest net of tax ($1,000,000 × [0.15 × 0.6]) × 9/12		67,500
Number of shares (64,000 × 9/12)	48,000	
Totals	238,000	$437,500
Fully diluted earnings per share		$1.84

Options and Warrants. Stock options and warrants outstanding and their equivalents (if exercisable within the 10-year limit) are included in fully diluted earnings per share computations unless their effect on EPS is antidilutive (i.e., increase EPS). Stock purchase contracts, stock subscriptions not fully paid, deferred compensation packages providing for the issuance of common shares, and convertible securities that allow or require the payment of cash at issuance are treated as options and warrants. The number of common shares issuable upon exercise of outstanding options, warrants, and their equivalents are included in the weighted-average number of common shares for the calculation of fully diluted earnings per share.

These calculations are based on the assumption that the options and/or warrants are exercised at the beginning of the year (or date of issue if later) and the proceeds from the exercise of the options and warrants are invested in operating assets of the firm. The amount assumed to be invested, in turn, earns an assumed return that would increase the amount of income available to the common shareholders. The appropriate rate of return (net of tax) is left to the professional judgement of the accountant.

To illustrate the computation of fully diluted earnings per share when stock options and/or warrants are outstanding at the year end, assume that Kubitz Industries Limited has net income for the period of $220,000. The average number of common shares outstanding for the period was 50,000 shares. Options to purchase 5,000 common shares at a price of $10 per share were outstanding at the end of the year. Of the 5,000 options, 4,000 were outstanding at the beginning of the year and 1,000 were issued on October 1 of the current year. Kubitz's average rate of return on assets over the past three years has been 25% before income taxes of 40%.

EXHIBIT 18-3 KUBITZ INDUSTRIES LIMITED

COMPUTATION OF EARNINGS PER SHARE

		Number of Shares	Net Income
Net income			$220,000
Common shares		50,000	
Basic earnings per share			$4.40
From above		50,000	$220,000
Issuable common shares—stock options:			
Outstanding one year 4,000 × 1		4,000	
Outstanding three months 1,000 × 3/12		250	
Imputed earnings on option proceeds:			
Proceeds 4,000 × $10	$40,000		
Imputed earnings $40,000 × 0.25	10,000		
Less income taxes @ 40%	4,000		6,000
Proceeds 1,000 × $10	$10,000		
Imputed earnings $10,000 × 0.25	2,500		
Less income taxes @ 40%	1,000		
Net earnings for 12 months	1,500		
Imputed earnings for 3 months			
$1,500 × 3/12			375
Totals		54,250	$226,375
Fully diluted earnings per share			$4.17

In most cases, holders of convertible securities, options, rights, and warrants are protected against a dilution of the number of shares to which they are entitled in the event of either a stock split or a stock dividend. This protection is an antidilution clause that provides for a proportionate increase (decrease) in the conversion ratio or the number of shares that may be acquired with each option or warrant. For example, a convertible bond with an original exchange ratio of 20 common shares for each $1,000 bond would, if so specified in an antidilution clause, have an exchange ratio of 40 to one after a two for one stock split.

Anti-dilution. When determining whether fully diluted earnings per share should be reported, all dilutive securities must be considered. In addition, any of the securities that are antidilutive should be excluded and cannot be used to offset dilutive securities. **Antidilutive securities** are securities that would create an increase in earnings per share (or a reduction in net **loss per share**). For example, convertible debt is antidilutive whenever interest (net of tax) on the debt expressed in per-share terms (based upon the number of common shares issuable upon conversion) is greater than basic earnings per share. With options or warrants, whenever the imputed earnings (net of tax) expressed in per-share terms (number of shares issuable under the associated options or warrants) are greater than basic earnings per share, they are considered antidilutive. A test for antidilution must be made before including any item in the fully diluted earnings per share calculation. This test involves simply comparing the per-share effect of each potentially dilutive item with the basic earnings per share. If the per-share amount of the potentially dilutive item is greater than the basic earnings per share (less than net loss per share) then the item is antidilutive and must be omitted from the fully diluted earnings per share.

To illustrate, assume that the conversion ratio for Marshy Field's preferred shares is four preferred for each common. The number of issuable common shares would be 12,500 (50,000 ÷ 4) and the income effect would remain $37,500. The per-share effect of the preferred would be $3.00 ($37,500 ÷ 12,500). Since this amount ($3.00) is greater than the basic earnings per share ($2.73)(see page 896), including these convertible preferred shares in the calculation of fully diluted earnings per share would increase rather than reduce earnings per share. Such securities (antidilutive) should be omitted from the computation of fully diluted earnings per share. The test for antidilution is more complex than implied by the above illustration and is discussed later in this chapter.

Pro Forma Earnings Per Share. When transactions affecting common shares occur subsequent to the date of the balance sheet, earnings per share figures previously computed may not be relevant to users' needs. In these cases, pro forma earnings per share amounts must be disclosed in a note to the financial statements. Pro forma basic earnings per share should be computed following any one of the following three kinds of transactions occurring subsequent to the date of the balance sheet.[12]

(a) Issuance of common shares when the proceeds are to be used to retire senior shares or debt outstanding at the date of the balance sheet.

(b) Common shares issued on the conversion of senior shares or debt outstanding at the balance sheet.

(c) When common shares are issued in a reorganization.

The effect of the foregoing transaction on basic earnings per share is given retroactive recognition to the beginning of the current period or at the date of issuance of the senior shares or debt if later.

Type (b) transactions would have been anticipated in fully diluted earnings per share and therefore are not used in computing pro forma fully diluted earnings per share. However, if type (a) or (c) transactions occur, then pro forma fully diluted earnings per share must be computed and disclosed in a note to the financial statements. Neither pro forma basic nor pro forma fully diluted earnings per share need to be reported for any prior periods. In addition, it is not necessary to report pro forma earnings figures that are not materially different from the basic and fully diluted earnings per share amounts.

Earnings Per Share Presentations and Disclosures. If a corporation's capital structure is complex, the earnings per share presentations would be as follows.

Net Income per Common Share	
Basic	$3.30
Fully diluted	$2.70

When the income of a period includes special transactions, per-share amounts (where applicable) should be shown for income before extraordinary items and net income. Reporting per-share amount for gain or loss on extraordinary items is optional. A presentation reporting extraordinary items follows.

[12] *CICA Handbook*, Section 3500, par. 39.

Net Income per Common Share	
Basic earnings per common share:	
Income before extraordinary item	$3.80
Extraordinary item	0.80
Net income	$3.00
Fully diluted earnings per common share:	
Income before extraordinary item	$3.35
Extraordinary item	0.65
Net income	$2.70

Earnings per share amounts must be shown for all periods presented and all prior period earnings per share amounts presented should be restated for stock dividends and stock splits. When the results of operations of a prior period have been restated as a result of a correction of errors, the earnings per share data shown for the prior periods should be restated. The effect of the restatement should be disclosed in the year of restatement.

Some Canadian firms are required to report in jurisdictions outside of Canada. In these cases, the firms must disclose the earnings per share amounts required in Canada as well as those, if different, required in the foreign country.

Comprehensive Illustration. The following comprehensive illustration demonstrates how the methods for computing earnings per share would be handled in a complex situation. The following section of the balance sheet of Rhode Limited is presented for analysis; assumptions related to the capital structure follow.

EXHIBIT 18-4 RHODE LIMITED

SELECTED BALANCE SHEET INFORMATION
AT DECEMBER 31, 1998

Long-term debt:		
Notes payable, 7.2%	$ 500,000	
4% Convertible debentures	1,500,000	
5% Convertible debentures	2,500,000	$ 4,500,000
Shareholders' equity:		
$5 cumulative convertible preferred, no-par value, authorized 100,000 shares, issued 25,000 shares	2,500,000	
Common shares, no-par value, authorized 5,000,000 shares, issued 500,000 shares	500,000	
Contributed surplus	2,500,000	
Retained earnings (includes 1998 income of $1,000,000)	$9,000,000	14,500,000
		$19,000,000

Notes and Assumptions
December 31, 1998

1. Options, exercisable at any time after July 1, 2001 were granted to purchase 50,000 common shares at $20 per share on July 2, 1998.

2. Warrants to purchase 100,000 common shares at $25 per share were issued in 1996. These warrants may be exercised at any time after January 1, 2003.

3. 4% and 5% convertible debentures are convertible into common shares at $25 per share (40 shares for each $1,000 bond).

4. $5 cumulative convertible preferred shares are convertible at the rate of four shares of common for each share of preferred ($25 conversion price).

5. All debt was issued at face value and all preferred was issued at $100 per share.

6. Except for the stock options in item 1 and the convertible debentures in item 11, all debt and securities were outstanding at the beginning and end of the year.

EXHIBIT 18-4 RHODE LIMITED (Continued)

7. The average applicable income tax rate is 40%.

8. 25,000 common shares were issued January 25, 1999 for $26 per share. The proceeds of this issue were used to retire 550 $1,000 5% convertible debentures.

9. On February 10, 1999 prior to issuance of the financial statements, directors of Rhode Limited voted to split the common shares two for one.

10. Net income for the year of $1,000,000 did not include any extraordinary items.

11. Holders of 1000 4% convertible debentures exercised their conversion rights on September 30, 1998.

12. Rhode earns approximately 8% after taxes on net assets.

13. All options, warrants, and convertible securities have legal protection against dilution as a result of stock dividends and stock splits.

The computation of earnings per share amounts in accordance with Section 3500 of the *CICA Handbook* is as follows.

Computation of Earnings Per Share	No. of Shares	Income	Per-Share Amount
Basic earnings per share (Exhibit 18-5(A))	940,000	$ 875,000	$0.93
Dilutive securities:			
4% convertible debentures (Exhibit 18-5(B))	180,000	54,000	0.30
5% convertible debentures (Exhibit 18-5(C))	200,000	75,000	0.375
Convertible preferred shares (Exhibit 18-5(D))	200,000	125,000	0.625
Stock options (Exhibit 18-5(E))	—	—	—
Stock warrants (Exhibit 18-5(F))	—	—	—
Fully diluted earnings per share	1,520,000	$1,129,000	$0.74
Adjusted basic earnings per share (Exhibit 18-5(J))	1,000,000	$ 893,000	$0.89

The following exhibits illustrate the computations for arriving at basic and fully diluted earnings per share. Exhibit 18-5(A) shows the calculation of basic earnings per share.

EXHIBIT 18-5(A)

COMPUTATION OF BASIC EARNINGS PER SHARE

Net income as reported	$1,000,000
Deduct dividends prescribed on cumulative preferred shares (25,000 × $5.00)	125,000
Income attributed to common shares	$ 875,000
Common shares outstanding:	
For 12 months (500,000 − 40,000)	460,000
For three months (1,000 × $1,000)/$25 = 40,000	
40,000 × 3/12 =	10,000
Total	470,000
Adjustment for two for one stock split	× 2
Weighted-average number of common shares outstanding	940,000
Basic earnings per share ($875,000/940,000)	$ 0.93

Exhibit 18-5(B) illustrates the calculation of the earnings per share effect of the 4% convertible debentures.

EXHIBIT 18-5(B)

4% CONVERTIBLE DEBENTURES

Pro forma income effect of conversion:

Interest expense reduction ($1,500,000 × 0.04) + [($1,000,000 × 0.04) × 9/12]	$ 90,000
Less income tax expenses increase ($90,000 × 0.4)	36,000
Net increase in net income that would have occurred had conversion occurred Jan. 1, 1998	$ 54,000
Number of common shares issuable upon conversion ($1,500,000/$25) + ($1,000,000/$25 × 9/12)	90,000
Adjustment for two for one stock split	× 2
Total issuable common shares	180,000
Earnings per share effect of possible conversion ($54,000/180,000)	$ 0.30

Exhibit 18-5(C) presents the calculations of the pro forma earnings per share effect of the conversion of the 5% convertible debentures at January 1, 1998.

EXHIBIT 18-5(C)

5% CONVERTIBLE DEBENTURES

Pro forma income effect of conversion:

Interest expense reduction ($2,500,000 × 0.05)	$125,000
Less income tax expense increase ($125,000 × 0.4)	50,000
Net increase in net income that would have occurred had conversion taken place January 1, 1998	$ 75,000
Number of common shares issuable upon conversion ($2,500,000/$25)	100,000
Adjustment for two for one stock split	× 2
Total issuable common shares	200,000
Pro forma earnings per share effect of conversion ($75,000/200,000)	$ 0.375

Exhibit 18-5(D) illustrates the computation of the pro forma earnings per share effect of the conversion of the convertible preferred shares.

EXHIBIT 18-5(D)

CONVERTIBLE PREFERRED SHARES

Income effect of conversion: Dividends prescribed (25,000 × $5.00)	$125,000
Number of common shares issuable upon conversion: (25,000 × 4)	100,000
Adjustment for two for one stock split	× 2
Issuable common shares	200,000
Earnings per share effect of conversion ($125,000/200,000)	$0.625

Exhibit 18-5(E) shows the earnings per share effect of the exercise of the stock options on the date of issue (July 1, 1998).

EXHIBIT 18-5(E)

STOCK OPTIONS

Income that would have been earned on the proceeds from exercise of the options from date of issue to December 31, 1998 (50,000* × $20* × .08 × 6/12)	$40,000
Issuable common shares 50,000 × 6/12	25,000
Adjustable for two for one stock split	× 2
Issuable common shares	50,000
Earnings per share effect of exercise of stock options ($40,000/50,000)	$ 0.80

*At the time of the stock split, the number of shares issuable under the options would be increased proportionately and the option price would be reduced to prevent dilution of the value of the options. (Options would be increased to 100,000 shares and the price would be reduced to $10 per share.)

Exhibit 18-5(F) illustrates the calculation of the earnings per share effect of potential issuance of shares to holders of stock warrants. Notice that these are considered potentially dilutive securities since they may be exercised within the 10-year limit.

EXHIBIT 18-5(F)

STOCK WARRANTS

Imputed income on proceeds from exercise of stock warrants ($12.50* × 200,000*) × 0.08	$200,000
Number of common shares issuable upon exercise of warrants	100,000
Adjustment for stock split	× 2
Total number of shares issuable	200,000
Earnings per share effect of exercise of stock warrants ($200,000/200,000)	$ 1.00

*Adjusted for stock split

Exhibits 18-5(A) to 18-5(F) show the calculations of the per-share effect of various potentially dilutive securities. Only those that cause reductions to basic earnings per share should be included in the calculation of fully diluted earnings per share. In order to determine which dilutive securities to include in the fully diluted earnings per share amount, it is necessary to rank the pro forma per-share effects starting with the most dilutive. Fully diluted earnings per share is then computed by progressively including the dilutive securities until the lowest per-share amount is determined. Any dilutive securities that cause this lowest possible amount to increase should be omitted from the calculation when determining the fully diluted earnings per share to be reported in the financial statements. This procedure is illustrated in Exhibit 18-5(G).

EXHIBIT 18-5(G)

FULLY DILUTED EARNINGS PER SHARE

	No. of Shares	Income	Earnings Per Share
Basic earnings per share (Exhibit 18-5(A))	940,000	$ 875,000	$0.93
4% debentures (Exhibit 18-5(B))	180,000	54,000	
Subtotal	1,120,000	929,000	0.829
5% debentures (Exhibit 18-5(C))	200,000	75,000	
Subtotal	1,320,000	1,004,000	0.761
Convertible preferred (Exhibit 18-5(D))	200,000	125,000	
Subtotal	1,520,000	1,129,000	0.743
Stock options (Exhibit 18-5(E))	50,000	40,000	
Subtotal	1,570,000	1,169,000	0.745*
Stock warrants (Exhibit 18-5(F))	200,000	200,000	
Total	1,770,000	$1,369,000	0.773*

*Earnings per share increases; therefore, stock options and warrants are antidilutive and should be omitted from calculation of fully diluted earnings per share.

The issuance of common shares subsequent to the end of the fiscal period and the proceeds used to retire debt necessitates computation and disclosure of pro forma basic and fully diluted earnings per share. These calculations are illustrated in Exhibits 18-5(H) and 18-5(I).

EXHIBIT 18-5(H)

PRO FORMA BASIC EARNINGS PER SHARE

Net income attributed to common shares (Exhibit 18-5(A))		$875,000
Add: Interest expense reduction from debt retired January 25, 1999 ($550,000 × 0.05)	$27,500	
Less income tax (27,500 × 0.4)	11,000	16,500
Pro forma income available to common shares		$891,500
Weighted-average number of common shares outstanding (Exhibit 18-5(A))		940,000
Add: Common shares issued January 25, 1999		50,000
Pro forma weighted-average number of common shares outstanding during 1998		990,000
Pro forma basic earnings per share ($891,500/990,000)		$0.90

EXHIBIT 18-5(I)

PRO FORMA DILUTED EARNINGS PER SHARE

Pro forma available to common (Exhibit 18-5(H))		$ 891,500
Add: Income attributed to assumed conversions		
4% convertible debentures (Exhibit 18-5(B))		54,000
5% convertible debentures (Exhibit 18-5(C))	$ 75,000	
Less after-tax interest on debentures retired January 25, 1999 (Exhibit 18-5(H))	16,500	58,500
Convertible preferred shares (Exhibit 18-5(D))		125,000
Total		$1,129,000
Weighted-average number of common shares Pro forma basic (Exhibit 18-5(H))		990,000
4% convertible debentures (Exhibit 18-5(B))		180,000
5% convertible debentures (Exhibit 18-5(C))	200,000	
Less debentures retired January 25, 1999 (550,000/25 adjusted for stock split)	44,000	156,000
Convertible preferred shares (Exhibit 18-5(D))		200,000
Total		1,526,000
Pro forma fully diluted earnings per share ($1,129,000/1,526,000)		$0.74

When conversions of senior shares or debt occur during the fiscal period, adjusted basic earnings per share should be calculated as though the conversion had taken place at the beginning of the period. This calculation is presented in Exhibit 18-5(J).

EXHIBIT 18-5(J)

ADJUSTED BASIC EARNINGS PER SHARE

Income attributed to common shares (Exhibit 18-5(A))		$ 875,000
Add income effect of shares issued September 30 on conversion of 4% debentures (1,000,000 × 0.04 × 9/12)		30,000
Deduct increases in income tax ($30,000 × 0.4)		(12,000)
Net income available to common shareholders		$ 893,000
Weighted-average number of common shares outstanding (Exhibit 18-5(A))		940,000
Add shares issued September 30 on conversion restated to January 1 (40,000 × 9/12)	30,000	
Adjustment for stock split	× 2	60,000
Weighted-average number of common shares for adjusted basic earnings per share		$1,000,000
Adjusted basic earnings per share ($893,000/1,000,000)		$0.89

SUMMARY

Computation of earnings per share has become a complex issue. Many accountants take a strong exception to some of the arbitrary rules contained in Section 3500 of the Handbook. The situation facing accountants in this area is a difficult one because many securities, although technically not common shares, have the basic characteristics of common shares. In addition, many companies have issued these types of securities rather than common shares in order to avoid an adverse effect on the earnings per share figure. Section 3500 of the *Handbook* was issued as an attempt to develop credibility in reporting earnings per share data.

Summary of Learning Objectives

1. **Describe the accounting for the issuance, conversion, and retirement of convertible securities.** The method for recording convertible bonds at the date of issue requires allocating the proceeds between the liability and equity components. The amount to be assigned to each component may be determined by using either the incremental or proportional method. Under the incremental method a value is assigned to the most easily measured element and the remaining residual of issue proceeds assigned to the other element. When a fair value can be computed for both elements of the instrument, the proportional method may be used. The value assigned to each component is equal to the proceeds multiplied by the proportion that the component is of total fair value. If bonds are converted into other securities, the principal accounting problem is to determine the amount at which to record the securities exchanged for the bond. Two possible methods of determining the issue price of the shares could be used: (1) the market value approach; or (2) the book value approach. The book value of the bonds and conversion rights is the method most commonly used in practice. The retirement of convertible debt is considered a debt retirement, and the difference between the carrying amount of the retired convertible debt and the cash paid should result in a charge or credit to income.

2. **Explain the accounting for convertible preferred shares.** When convertible preferred shares are converted, the book value method is employed; Preferred Shares, along with any related Contributed Surplus, is debited, and Common Shares is credited.

3. **Contrast the accounting for stock warrants and stock warrants issued with other securities.** Stock rights: No entry is required when rights are issued to existing shareholders. Only a memorandum entry is needed to indicate the number of rights issued to existing shareholders and to ensure that the company has additional unissued shares registered for issuance in case the rights are exercised. Stock warrants: The proceeds from the sale of debt with detachable stock warrants should be allocated between the two securities. Warrants that are detachable can be traded separately from the debt, and therefore, a market value can be determined. The two methods of allocation available are the proportional method and the incremental method. Nondetachable warrants also require an allocation in the same manner as conversion rights.

KEY TERMS

antidilutive securities, 897

basic earnings per share, 893

complex capital structure, 889

convertible bond, 873

convertible preferred shares, 876

date of exercise, 880

detachable stock warrants, 878

dilutive securities, 872

earnings per share, 888

fully diluted earnings per share, 893

grant date, 880

income available to common shareholders, 894

induced conversion, 876

measurement date, 880

noncompensatory plans, 885

service period, 881

share appreciation, 883

simple capital structure, 889

stock appreciation rights, 883

stock option, 879

stock option plans, 880

stock right, 879

tandem (combination) plans, 885

3% materiality test, 893

4. **Describe the accounting for stock compensation plans.** (1) Incentive stock option plans: The market price and exercise price on the grant date must be equal. Because there is no compensation expense, there is no allocation problem. (2) Compensatory stock option plans: Compensation is the difference between the market price and exercise price on the grant date. Compensation expense is allocated by the straight-line method during the service period. (3) Stock appreciation rights: The compensation is measured by the difference between market price on the exercise date. The compensation expense is allocated by the percentage approach over the service period, then marked to market. (4) Performance-type plan: Compensation is measured by the market value of the shares issued on the exercise date. Compensation expense is allocated by the percentage approach over the service period, then marked to market.

5. **Compute earnings per share in a simple capital structure.** When a company has both common and preferred shares outstanding, the current year preferred share dividend is subtracted from net income to arrive at income available to common shareholders. The formula for computing earnings per share is net income less preferred share dividends divided by the weighted average of shares outstanding.

6. **Compute earnings per share in a complex capital structure.** A complex capital structure may require dual presentation of earnings per share. These two presentations are referred to as basic earnings per share and fully diluted earnings per share. Basic earnings per share is based on the number of common shares outstanding. Fully diluted earnings per share indicates the dilution of earnings per share that would have occurred if all contingent issuances of common shares that would have reduced earnings per share had taken place.

EXERCISES

E18-1 **(Conversion of Bonds)** Aurora, Ltd. issued $4,000,000 of 10%, 10-year convertible bonds on June 1, 1997 at 98 plus accrued interest. The bonds were dated April 1, 1997 with interest payable April 1 and October 1. Bond discount was amortized semiannually on a straight-line basis. Bonds without the conversion privilege would have sold at 97 plus accrued interest.

On April 1, 1998, $1,500,000 of these bonds were converted into 30,000 no-par value common shares. Accrued interest was paid in cash at the time of conversion.

Instructions

(a) Prepare the entry to record the interest expense at October 1, 1997. Assume that accrued interest payable was credited when the bonds were issued. (Round to the nearest dollar.)

(b) Prepare the entry(ies) to record the conversion on April 1, 1998. (Book value method is used.) Assume that the incremental method was used to determine the amounts allocated to the bond and conversion rights and that the entry to record amortization of the bond discount and interest payment has been made.

E18-2 **(Issuance and Conversion of Bonds)** For each of the unrelated transactions described below, present the entry(ies) required and record each transaction.

1. Thornhill Ltd. issued $20,000,000 par value 10% convertible bonds at 99. If the bonds had not been convertible, the company's investment banker estimates they would have been sold at 95. Expenses of issuing the bonds were $70,000.

2. Vernon Limited issued $20,000,000 par value 10% bonds at 98. One detachable stock purchase warrant was issued with each $100 par value bond. At the time of issuance the warrants were selling for $4.

3. On July 1, 1998 Stratford Company called its 11% convertible debentures for retirement. The $10,000,000 par value bonds were converted into 1,000,000 no-par value common shares. On July 1, there was $150,000 of unamortized discount applicable to the bonds, and a balance of $200,000 in an account called "Conversion Rights." The company paid an additional $75,000 to the bondholders to induce conversion of all the bonds. The company recorded the conversion using the book value method.

(Conversion of Bonds) Linwood Ltd. has bonds payable outstanding in the amount of $500,000, the Premium on Bonds Payable account has a balance of $5,000, and the Conversion Rights account has a balance of 4,000. Each $1,000 bond is convertible into 20 no-par preferred shares.

E18-3

Instructions
(a) Assuming that the bonds are quoted on the market at 102 and that the preferred shares may be sold on the market at $50.75, make the entry to record the conversion of the bonds to preferred shares. (Use the market value approach.)
(b) Assuming that the book value method is used, what entry would be made?

(Conversion of Bonds) On January 1, 1997, when its no-par value common shares were selling for $80 per share, Delta Ltd. issued $10,000,000 of 8% convertible debentures due in 20 years. The conversion option allowed the holder of each $1,000 bond to convert the bond into five no-par common shares of the corporation's. The debentures were issued for $10,800,000. The present value of the bond payments at the time of issuance was $8,500,000 and the corporation believed the difference between the present value and the amount paid was attributable to the conversion feature. On January 1, 1998 the corporation's common shares were split 2 for 1. On January 1, 1999, when the corporation's shares were selling for $135 per share, holders of 30% of the convertible debentures exercised their conversion options. The corporation used the straight-line method for amortizing any bond discounts or premiums.

E18-4

Instructions
(a) Prepare in general journal form the entry to record the original issuance of the convertible debentures.
(b) Prepare in general journal form the entry to record the exercise of the conversion option, using the book value method. Show supporting computations in good form.

(Conversion of Bonds) The December 31, 1997 balance sheet of Havelock Ltd. includes the following:

E18-5

10% Callable, Convertible Bonds Payable (semiannual interest dates April 30 and October 31; convertible into 6 no-par value common shares per $1,000 of bond principle; maturity date April 30, 2003)	$500,000	
Discount on Bonds Payable	10,240	$489,760
Conversion Rights		9,000

On March 5, 1998 Havelock Ltd. called all of the bonds as of April 30 for the principal plus interest through April 30. By April 30 all bondholders had exercised their conversion rights as of the interest payment date. Consequently, on April 30, Havelock Ltd. paid the semiannual interest and issued common shares for the bonds. The discount was amortized on a straight-line basis. Havelock used the book value method.

Instructions
Prepare the entry(ies) to record the interest expense and conversion on April 30, 1998. Reversing entries were made on January 1, 1998. (Round to the nearest dollar.)

(Conversion of Bonds) On January 1, 1997 Hawkesbury Ltd. issued $4,000,000 of 10-year, 8% convertible debentures at 104. Investment bankers believe that the debentures would have sold at 102 without the conversion privilege. Interest is to be paid semiannually on June 30 and December 31. Each $1,000 debenture can be converted into eight of Hawkesbury's no-par common shares after December 31, 1998.

E18-6

On January 1, 1999 $400,000 of debentures are converted into common shares, which were then selling at $110. An additional $400,000 of debentures are converted on March 31, 1999. The market price of the common shares is then $115. Accrued interest at March 31 will be paid on the next interest date.

Bond premium is amortized on a straight-line basis.

Instructions
Make the necessary journal entries for:
(a) December 31, 1998.   (b) January 1, 1999.
(c) March 31, 1999.   (d) June 30, 1999.
Record the conversions under both the fair market value method and the book value method.

E18-7 **(Issuance of Bonds with Warrants)** Thornhill Inc. has decided to raise additional capital by issuing $170,000 face value of bonds with a coupon rate of 10%. In discussions with their investment consultants, it was determined that to help the sale of the bonds, detachable stock warrants should be issued at the rate of 10 warrants for each $1,000 bond sold. The value of the bonds without the warrants is considered to be $136,000, and the value of the warrants in the market is $24,000. The bonds sold in the market at issuance for $152,000.

Instructions
(a) What entry should be made at the time of the issuance of the bonds and warrants?
(b) If the warrants were nondetachable, would the entries be different? Discuss.

E18-8 **(Issuance of Bonds with Detachable Warrants)** On September 1, 1998 Quadeville Limited sold at 104 (plus accrued interest) 4,000 of its 9%, 10-year, $1,000 face value, nonconvertible bonds with detachable stock warrants. Each bond carried two detachable warrants; each warrant was for one share of no-par common, at a specified option price of $15 per share. Shortly after issuance the warrants were quoted on the market for $3 each. No market value could be determined for the bonds above. Interest was payable on December 1 and June 1. Bond issue costs of $30,000 were incurred.

Instructions
Prepare in general journal format the entry to record the issuance of the bonds.   (AICPA adapted)

E18-9 **(Use of Proportional and Incremental Method)** Presented below are two independent situations.
1. On March 15, 1998 Fenwick Limited issued $3,000,000 of 11% nonconvertible bonds at 105 plus accrued interest. Each $1,000 bond was issued with 50 detachable stock warrants, each of which entitled the bondholder to purchase, for $48, one of Fenwick's no-par common shares. On March 15, 1998 the market value of Fenwick's common was $41 per share and the market value of each warrant was $5. Prepare the journal to record this transaction.

2. On February 1, 1998 Sombra Ltd. issued $4,000,000, 10-year, 12% bonds for $4,080,000. Each $1,000 bond had a detachable warrant permitting the purchase of one of Sombra's no-par common shares for $62. Immediately after the bonds were issued, Sombra's securities had the following market values:

Common shares, no-par value	$ 58
Warrant	10
12% bond without warrant	1,040

Instructions
Prepare the journal entry to record this transaction. (Round all computations to the nearest dollar.)

E18-10 **(Issuance and Exercise of Stock Options)** On November 1, 1996 Ompah Company adopted a stock option plan that granted options to key executives to purchase 30,000 shares of the company's no-par value common shares. The options were granted on January 2, 1997 and were exercisable two years after date of grant if the grantee was still an employee of the company; the options expired six years from date of grant. The option price was set at $40; market price at the date of the grant was $47 a share.

All of the options were exercised during the year 1999: 20,000 on January 3 when the market price was $67 and 10,000 on May 1 when the market price was $77 a share.

Instructions
(a) Compute the value of the stock option and the corresponding amount of executive compensation.
(b) Prepare journal entries relating to the stock option plan for the years 1997, 1998, and 1999. Assume that the employee performs services equally in 1997 and 1998.

E18-11 **(Issuance, Exercise, and Termination of Stock Options)** On January 1, 1996 Thomasburg Inc. granted stock options to officers and key employees for the purchase of 20,000 of the company's no-par value common shares at $25 each.

The options were exercisable within a five-year period beginning January 1, 1998 by grantees still in the employ of the company, and they expire December 31, 2002. The market price of Thomasburg's common was $33 per share at the date of grant. Thomasburg prepared a formal journal entry to record this award. The service period for this award was two years.

On April 1, 1997, 2,000 option shares were terminated when the employees resigned from the company. The market value of the common was $35 per share on this date.

On March 31, 1998, 12,000 option shares were exercised when the market value of common was $40 per share.

Instructions
Prepare journal entries to record issuance of the stock options, termination of the stock options, exercise of the stock options, and charges to compensation expense for the years ended December 31, 1996, 1997, and 1998.

(AICPA adapted)

(Issuance, Exercise, and Termination of Stock Options) On November 2, 1994 the shareholders of Caledonia Limited voted to adopt a stock option plan for Caledonia's key officers. According to terms of the option agreement, the officers of the company could purchase 40,000 shares of no-par common during 1997 and 54,000 shares during 1998. The shares that were purchasable during 1997 represented executive compensation for 1995 and 1996, and those purchasable during 1998 represented such compensation for 1995, 1996, and 1997. If options for shares were not exercised during either year, they lapsed as of the end of that year. **E18-12**

Options were granted to the officers of Caledonia on January 1, 1995, and at that time the option price was set for all shares at $30. During 1997, all options were exercised. During 1998, however, options for only 27,000 shares were exercised. The remaining options lapsed because the executives decided not to exercise. The market prices of Caledonia common at various dates are as follows:

Dates	Market Price of Caledonia's Common
Option agreement accepted by shareholders	$33
Options granted	36
Options exercised in 1996	38
Options exercised in 1997	34

Instructions
Make any necessary journal entries related to this stock option for the years 1994 through 1998. (Caledonia closes its books on December 31.)

(Stock Appreciation Rights) On December 31, 1996 Petawawa Limited issues 150,000 stock appreciation rights to its officers entitling them to receive cash for the difference between the market price of its shares and a pre-established price of $10. **E18-13**

The market price fluctuates as follows: 12/31/97—$14; 12/31/98—$8; 12/31/99—$20; 12/31/2000—$18. The service period is four years and the exercise period is seven years.

Instructions
(a) Prepare a schedule that shows the amount of compensation expense allocable to each year affected by the stock appreciation rights plan.
(b) Prepare the entry at 12/31/2000 to record compensation expense, if any, in 2000.
(c) Prepare the entry on 12/21/2000 assuming that all 150,000 SARs are exercised by all of the eligible officers.

(Stock Appreciation Rights) Concord Limited establishes a stock appreciation rights program that entitles its new president, Shari Fano, to receive cash for the difference between the market price of the shares and a pre-established price of $30 (also market price) on December 31, 1997 on 30,000 SARs. The date of grant is December 31, 1997 and the required employment (service) period is four years. President Fano exercises all of the SARs in 2003. The market value of the stock fluctuates as follows: 12/31/98—$36; 12/31/99—$39; 12/31/2000—$45; 12/31/2001—$36; 12/31/2002—$48. **E18-14**

Instructions
(a) Prepare a five-year (1998–2002) schedule of compensation expense pertaining to the 30,000 SARs that were granted to President Fano.
(b) Prepare the journal entry for compensation expense in 1998, 2001, and 2002 relative to the 30,000 SARs.

E18-15 **(Weighted-Average Number of Shares)** Minesing Ltd. uses a calendar year for financial reporting. The company is authorized to issue 9,000,000 no-par value common shares. At no time has Minesing issued any potentially dilutive securities. Listed below is a summary of Minesing's common share activities.

1. Number of common shares issued and outstanding at December 31, 1996	2,000,000
2. Shares issued as a result of a 10% stock dividend on September 30, 1997	200,000
3. Shares issued for cash on March 31, 1998	2,000,000
Number of common shares issued and outstanding at December 31, 1998	4,200,000

4. A 2-for-1 stock split of Minesing's common shares took place on March 31, 1999.

Instructions

(a) Compute the weighted-average number of common shares used in computing earnings per common share for 1997 on the 1998 comparative income statement.

(b) Compute the weighted-average number of common shares used in computing earnings per common share for 1998 on the 1998 comparative income statement.

(c) Compute the weighted-average number of common shares to be used in computing earnings per common share for 1998 on the 1999 comparative income statement.

(d) Compute the weighted-average number of common shares to be used in computing earnings per common share for 1999 on the 1999 comparative income statement.

(CMA adapted)

E18-16 **(EPS: Simple Capital Structure)** On January 1, 1998 the Renfrew Corp. had 480,000 shares of common stock outstanding. During 1998, it had the following transactions that affected the common share account.

February 1	Issued 120,000 shares
March 1	Issued a 10% stock dividend
May 1	Acquired 100,000 treasury shares
June 1	Issued a 3-for-1 stock split
October 1	Reissued 60,000 shares of treasury stock

Instructions

(a) Determine the weighted-average number of shares outstanding as of December 31, 1998.

(b) Assume that Renfrew Corp. earned net income of $3,456,000 during 1998. In addition, it had 100,000 of shares of $9, no-par nonconvertible, noncumulative preferred stock outstanding for the entire year. Because of liquidity considerations, however, the company did not declare and pay a preferred dividend in 1998. Compute earnings per share for 1998 using the weighted-average number of shares determined in part (a).

(c) Assume the same facts as in part (b), except that the preferred stock was cumulative. Compute earnings per share for 1998.

(d) Assume the same facts as in part (b), except that net income included an extraordinary gain of $864,000 and a loss from discontinued operations of $432,000. Both items are net of applicable income taxes. Compute earnings per share for 1998.

E18-17 **(EPS: Simple Capital Structure)** Jarvis Limited had 200,000 common shares outstanding on December 31, 1998. During the year 1999 the company issued 8,000 shares on May 1 and retired 14,000 shares on October 31. For the year 1999 Jarvis Limited reported net income of $249,690 after a casualty loss of $40,600 (net of tax).

Instructions

What earnings per share data should be reported in the financial statements, assuming that the casualty loss is extraordinary?

E18-18 **(EPS: Simple Capital Structure)** Lisle, Inc. presented the following data:

Net income	$2,500,000
Preferred shares: 50,000 no-par shares outstanding,	
$8 cumulative, not convertible	5,000,000
Common shares: Shares outstanding, Jan. 1	750,000
Issued for cash, May 1	300,000
Acquired treasury shares for cash, Aug. 1	150,000
2-for-1 stock split, Oct. 1	

Instructions
Compute earnings per share.

(EPS: Simple Capital Structure) A portion of the combined statement of income and retained earnings of Markstay   **E18-19**
Ltd. for the current year follows.

Income before extraordinary item		$15,000,000
Extraordinary loss, net of applicable income tax (Note 1)		1,340,000
Net income		13,660,000
Retained earnings at the beginning of the year		83,250,000
		96,910,000
Dividends declared:		
On preferred shares—$6.00 per share	$ 300,000	
On common shares—$1.75 per share	14,875,000	15,175,000
Retained earnings at the end of the year		$81,735,000

Note 1. During the year, Markstay Ltd. suffered a major casualty loss of $1,340,000
after applicable income tax reduction of $1,200,000.

At the end of the current year, Markstay Ltd. has outstanding 8,500,000 shares of no-par common and 50,000 shares of $6 preferred.

On April 1 of the current year, Markstay Ltd. issued 1,000,000 common shares for $32 per share to help finance the casualty.

Instructions
Compute the earnings per share on common for the current year as it should be reported to shareholders.

(EPS: Simple Capital Structure) On January 1, 1998 Grimsby Industries had shares outstanding as follows.   **E18-20**

$6 Cumulative preferred, no-par value, issued and outstanding 10,000 shares	$1,000,000
Common no-par value, issued and outstanding 200,000 shares	2,000,000

To acquire the net assets of three smaller companies, Grimsby authorized the issuance of an additional 160,000 common shares. The acquisitions took place as follows:

Date of Acquisition	Shares Issued
Company A April 1, 1998	50,000
Company B July 1, 1998	80,000
Company C October 1, 1998	30,000

On May 14, 1998 Grimsby realized a $90,000 (before taxes) gain on the expropriation of investments originally purchased in 1987.

On December 31, 1998 Grimsby recorded net income of $300,000 before tax and exclusive of the gain.

Instructions
Assuming a 50% tax rate, compute the earnings per share data that should appear on the financial statements of Grimsby Industries as of December 31, 1998. Assume that the expropriation is extraordinary.

(EPS: Simple Capital Structure) At January 1, 1998 Lowbanks Company's outstanding shares included: **E18-21**

280,000 shares of no-par value, $3.50 cumulative preferred
900,000 shares of no-par value common

Net income for 1998 was $2,530,000. No cash dividends were declared or paid during 1998. On February 15, 1999, however, all preferred dividends in arrears were paid, together with a 5% stock dividend on common shares. There were no dividends in arrears prior to 1998.

On April 1, 1998, 450,000 common shares were sold for $10 per share and on October 1, 1998, 110,000 common shares were purchased for $20 per share and held as treasury shares.

Instructions

Compute earnings per share for 1998. Assume that financial statements for 1998 were issued in March, 1999.

E18-22   **(EPS with Convertible Bonds, Various Situations)** In 1997, Barrie Enterprises issued, at par, 60, $1,000, 8% bonds. Each bond was convertible into 100 common shares. Barrie had revenues of $15,750 and expenses other than interest and taxes of $8,400 for 1998 (assume that the tax rate is 40%). Throughout 1998, 2,000 common shares were outstanding; none of the bonds were converted or redeemed.

Instructions

(a) Compute earnings per share for 1998.

(b) Assume the same facts as those assumed for Part (a), except that the 60 bonds were issued on September 1, 1998 (rather than in 1997), and none had been converted or redeemed.

(c) Assume the same facts as assumed for Part (a), except that 20 of the 60 bonds were actually converted on July 1, 1998.

E18-23   **(EPS with Convertible Bonds)** On June 1, 1996 Mattawa Limited and Sparta Limited merged to form Lunenburg Ltd. A total of 800,000 shares were issued to complete the merger. The new corporation reports on a calendar-year basis.

On April 1, 1998 the company issued an additional 400,000 shares for cash. All 1,200,000 shares were outstanding on December 31, 1998.

Lunenburg Ltd. also issued $600,000 of 20-year, 8% convertible bonds at par on July 1, 1998. Each $1,000 bond converts to 40 common shares at any interest date. None of the bonds has been converted to date.

Lunenburg Ltd. is preparing its annual report for the fiscal year ending December 31, 1998. The annual report will show earnings per share figures based upon a reported after-tax net income of $1,435,000 (the tax rate is 40%).

Instructions

Determine for 1998:

1. The number of shares to be used for calculating:

    (a) Basic earnings per share.

    (b) Fully diluted earnings per share.

2. The earnings figures to be used for calculating:

    (a) Basic earnings per share.

    (b) Fully diluted earnings per share.   (CMA adapted)

E18-24   **(Basic and Fully Diluted EPS)** The Staffa Corporation issued 10-year, $5,000,000 par, 8% callable convertible subordinated debentures on January 2, 1998. The bonds have a par value of $1,000 with interest payable annually. The current conversion ratio is 14:1, and in two years it will increase to 18:1. At the date of issue, the bonds were sold at 98. Bond discount is amortized on a straight-line basis. Staffa's effective tax is 35%. Net income in 1998 was $9,500,000, and the company had 2,000,000 common shares outstanding during the entire year.

Instructions

(a) Prepare a schedule to compute basic and fully diluted earnings per share.

(b) Discuss how the schedule would differ if the security was convertible preferred shares.

E18-25   **(EPS with Options, Various Situations)** Paisley Limited's net income for 1998 is $60,000. The only potentially dilutive securities outstanding were 1,000 options issued during 1997, each exercisable for one share at $6. None has been exercised, and 10,000 common shares were outstanding during 1998. Paisley earns 15% after tax on its assets.

Instructions

(a) Compute the earnings per share (round to nearest cent).

(b) Assume the same facts as those assumed for Part (a), except that the 1,000 options were issued on October 1, 1998 (rather than in 1997).

E18-26   **(EPS with Options)** Southwold Ltd. indicates that its net income for 1998 is $17,748,000, which includes a gain on casualty (net of tax) of $1,566,000. Its capital structure includes some common shares reserved under employee stock options (109,000 shares). The common shares outstanding for the year remain at 5,800,000. The controller, Jennifer Kyncl, asks your advice concerning the earnings per share figure that they should present.

Instructions

What would you tell the controller? (Assume that the gain is extraordinary.)

(EPS with Contingent Issuance Agreement) Palgrave Ltd. recently purchased Vittoria Limited, a large home painting corporation. One of the terms of the merger was that if Vittoria's income for 1998 was $110,000 or more, 10,000 additional shares would be paid to Vittoria's shareholders in 1999. Vittoria's income for 1997 was $120,000.   **E18-27**

Instructions

(a) Would the contingent shares have to be considered in Palgrave's 1997 earnings per-share computations?

(b) Assume the same facts, except that the 10,000 shares were contingent on Vittoria's achieving a net income of $130,000 in 1998. Would the contingent shares have to be considered in Palgrave's earnings per share computations?

(EPS with Warrants) Barwick Corporation earned $360,000 during a period when it had an average of 100,000 common shares outstanding. The company earns 15% after tax on its assets. Also outstanding were 15,000 warrants that could be exercised to purchase one common share for $10 for each warrant exercised.   **E18-28**

Instructions

(a) Are the warrants dilutive?

(b) Compute basic earnings per share.

(c) Compute fully diluted earnings per share.

PROBLEMS

The shareholders' equity section of Fingal Ltd. at the beginning of the current year appears below.   **P18-1**

Common shares, no-par value, authorized 1,000,000 shares, 300,000 shares issued and outstanding	$3,600,000
Retained earnings	570,000

During the current year the following transactions occurred:

1. The company issued to the shareholders 200,000 rights. Ten rights are needed to buy one share at $32. The rights were void after 30 days. The market price of the shares at this time was $34 per share.

2. The company sold to the public a $200,000, 10% bond issue at par. The company also issued with each $100 bond one detachable stock purchase warrant, which provided for the purchase of common at $30 per share. Shortly after issuance, similar bonds without warrants were selling at 96 and the warrants at $8.

3. All but 20,000 of the rights issued in (1) were exercised in 30 days.

4. At the end of the year, 80% of the warrants in (2) had been exercised, and the remaining were outstanding and in good standing.

5. During the current year, the company granted stock options for 5,000 common shares to company executives. The market price of the shares on that date was $40 and the option price was $30. The options were to expire at year end and were considered compensation for the current year.

6. All but 1,000 shares related to the stock option plan were exercised by year end. The expiration resulted because one of the executives failed to fulfil an obligation related to the employment contract.

Instructions

(a) Prepare general journal entries for the current year to record the transactions listed above.

(b) Prepare the Shareholders' Equity section of the balance sheet at the end of the current year. Assume that retained earnings at the end of the current year was $750,000.

Walkerton Ltd. issued $1,500,000 of convertible 10-year bonds on July 1, 1997 at 98. Investment advisers estimate that without the conversion privilege the bonds would have sold at 97. The bonds provide for 12% interest payable semiannually on January 1 and July 1. The discount in connection with the issue is being amortized monthly on a straight-line basis.   **P18-2**

The bonds are convertible after one year into eight shares of Walkerton Ltd.'s no-par value common shares for each $1,000 of bonds.

On August 1, 1998, $150,000 of bonds were turned in for conversion into common shares. Interest has been accrued monthly and paid as due. At the time of conversion any accrued interest on bonds being converted was paid in cash.

Instructions (Round to nearest dollar)
Prepare the journal entries to record the conversion, amortization, and interest in connection with the bonds as of:

(a) August 1, 1998 (assume the book value method is used).

(b) August 31, 1998.

(c) December 31, 1998, including closing entries for end-of-year.   (AICPA adapted)

P18-3   MAAN Company adopted a stock option plan on November 30, 1996 that designated 70,000 shares of no-par value common as available for the granting of options to officers of the corporation at a price of $8 a share. The market value was $12 a share on November 30, 1996.

On January 2, 1997 options to purchase 28,000 shares were granted to President Don Pedro—15,000 for services to be rendered in 1997 and 13,000 for services to be rendered in 1998. Also on that date, options to purchase 14,000 shares were granted to Vice-President Beatrice Leonato—7,000 for services to be rendered in 1997 and 7,000 for services to be rendered in 1998. The market value was $14 a share on January 2, 1997. The options were exercisable for a period of one year following the year in which the services were rendered.

In 1998 neither the president nor the vice-president exercised their options because the market price of the shares was below the exercise price. The market value was $7 a share on December 31, 1998 when the options for 1997 services lapsed.

On December 31, 1999 both President Pedro and Vice-President Leonato exercised their options for 13,000 and 7,000 shares, respectively, when the market price was $16 a share.

Instructions

(a) Prepare the necessary journal entries in 1996 when the stock option plan was adopted, in 1997 when options were granted, in 1998 when options lapsed, and in 1999 when options were exercised.

(b) What disclosure of the stock option plan should appear in the financial statements at December 31, 1996? At December 31, 1997? Assume that the stock options outstanding or exercised at any time are a significant financial item.

P18-4   Marion Kasawal, controller at Norwich Pharmaceutical Industries, a public company, is currently preparing the calculation for basic and fully diluted earnings per share and the related disclosure for Norwich's external financial statements. Below is selected financial information for the fiscal year ended June 30, 1998.

NORWICH PHARMACEUTICAL INDUSTRIES
Selected Statement of
Financial Position Information
June 30, 1998

Long-term debt	
Notes payable, 10%	$ 1,000,000
7% convertible bonds payable	5,000,000
10% bonds payable	6,000,000
Total long-term debt	$12,000,000
Shareholders' equity	
Preferred shares, $4.25 cumulative, no-par value,	
100,000 shares authorized, 25,000 shares issued and outstanding	$ 1,250,000
Common shares, no-par value, 10,000,000 shares	
authorized, 1,000,000 shares issued and outstanding	4,500,000
Contributed surplus — conversion rights	500,000
Retained earnings	6,000,000
Total shareholders' equity	$12,250,000

The following transactions have also occurred at Norwich.

1. Options were granted in 1996 to purchase 100,000 shares at $15 per share. Although no options were exercised during 1998, the average price per common share during the fiscal year 1998 was $20 per share, and the market price on June 30, 1998, was $25 per share.

2. The 7% bonds were issued at 110. The bonds would have sold at par without the conversion privilege. The convertible bonds will convert into common shares at 50 shares per $1,000 bond. The conversion privilege is exercisable after five years and was issued in 1997.

3. The preferred shares were issued in 1996.

4. There are no preferred dividends in arrears; however, preferred dividends were not declared in fiscal year 1998.

5. The 1,000,000 common shares were outstanding for the entire 1998 fiscal year.

6. The net income for fiscal year 1998 was $1,500,000 after an extraordinary loss (net of tax) of $400,000. In addition, the company discontinued certain operations at an after-tax gain of $150,000. The company's rate of return has been 25% before income taxes of 40%.

Instructions

(a) For the fiscal year ended June 30, 1998, calculate Norwich's:

1. Basic earnings per share.

2. Fully diluted earnings per share.

(b) Describe the appropriate disclosure required for earnings per share for Norwich Pharmaceutical Industries for the fiscal year ended June 30, 1998.

As auditor for Burford & Associates, you have been assigned to check Denfield Corporation's computation of earnings per share for the current year. The controller, Shari Smith, has supplied you with the following computations. **P18-5**

Net income	$3,374,960
Common shares issued and outstanding:	
Beginning of year	1,285,000
End of year	1,200,000
Average	1,242,500
Earnings per share	

$$\frac{\$3,374,960}{1,242,500} = \$2.72 \text{ per share}$$

You have developed the following additional information:

1. There are no other equity securities in addition to the common shares.

2. There are no options or warrants outstanding to purchase common shares.

3. There are no convertible debt securities.

4. Activity in common shares during the year was as follows.

Outstanding Jan. 1	1,285,000
Treasury shares acquired, Oct. 1	(250,000)
	1,035,000
Shares reissued, Dec. 1	165,000
Outstanding, Dec. 31	1,200,000

Instructions

(a) On the basis of the information above, do you agree with the controller's computation of earnings per share for the year? If you disagree, prepare a revised computation of earnings per share.

(b) Assume the same facts as those in (a), except that options had been issued to purchase 140,000 shares of common at $10 per share. These options were outstanding at the beginning of the year and none had been exercised or cancelled during the year. The company earns a rate of return of 12% after taxes. Prepare a computation of earnings per share.

√P18-6   Harrow Corporation is preparing the comparative financial statements for the annual report to its shareholders for fiscal years ended May 31, 1997 and May 31, 1998. The income from operations for each year was $1,800,000 and $2,500,000, respectively. In both years, the company incurred a 10% interest expense on $2,400,000 of debt, an obligation that requires interest-only payments for five years. The company experienced a loss of $500,000 from a fire in its Sudbury facility in February 1998, which was determined to be an extraordinary loss. The company uses a 40% effective tax rate for income taxes.

The capital structure of Harrow Corporation on June 1, 1996 consisted of 2 million common shares outstanding and 20,000 $4 cumulative preferred shares of no-par value. There were no preferred dividends in arrears, and the company had not issued any convertible securities, options, or warrants.

On October 1, 1997, Harrow sold an additional 500,000 common shares at $20 per share. Harrow distributed a 20% stock dividend on the common shares outstanding on January 1, 1998. On December 1, 1998, Harrow was able to sell an additional 800,000 common shares at $22 per share. These were the only common share transactions that occurred during the two fiscal years.

Instructions

(a) Identify whether the capital structure at Harrow Corporation is a simple or complex capital structure, and explain why.

(b) Determine the weighted-average number of shares that Harrow Corporation would use in calculating earnings per share for the fiscal year ended:

1. May 31, 1997.

2. May 31, 1998.

(c) Prepare, in good form, a Comparative Income Statement, beginning with income from operations, for Harrow Corporation for the fiscal years ended May 31, 1997 and May 31, 1998. This statement will be included in Harrow's annual report and should display the appropriate earnings per share presentations.   (CMA adapted)

P18-7   Kenneth Geis of the controller's office of Lefroy Corporation is given the assignment of determining the basic and fully diluted earnings per share values for the year ending December 31, 1998. Geis has compiled the information listed below.

1. The company is authorized to issue 8,000,000 no-par value common shares. As of December 31, 1997, 3,000,000 shares had been issued and were outstanding.

2. A total of 700,000 shares of an authorized 1,200,000 convertible preferred shares had been issued on July 1, 1997. The shares were issued at $25 each, and they have a cumulative dividend of $3 per share. The shares are convertible into common at the rate of one share of convertible preferred for one share of common. The rate of conversion is to be automatically adjusted for stock splits and stock dividends. Dividends are paid quarterly on September 30, December 31, March 31, and June 30.

3. Lefroy Corporation is subject to a 40% income tax rate.

4. The after-tax net income for the year ended December 31, 1998 was $13,550,000.

The following specific activities took place during 1998.

1. January 1—A 5% common stock dividend was issued. The dividend had been declared on December 1, 1997 to all shareholders of record on December 29, 1997.

2. April 1—A total of 200,000 shares of the $3 convertible preferred was converted into common. The company issued new common shares and retired the preferred shares. This was the only conversion of the preferred during 1998.

3. July 1—A 2-for-1 split of common became effective on this date. The Board of Directors had authorized the split on June 1.

4. August 1—A total of 300,000 common shares were issued to acquire a factory building.

5. November 1—A total of 24,000 common shares were purchased on the open market at $9 per share. These shares were to be held as treasury shares and were still in the treasury as of December 31, 1998.

6. Cash dividends to common shareholders—Cash dividends to common shareholders were declared and paid as follows:
   April 15—$.30 per share
   October 15—$.20 per share

7. Cash dividends to preferred shareholders—Cash dividends to preferred shareholders were declared and paid as scheduled.

Instructions

(a) Determine the number of shares used to compute basic earnings per share for the year ended December 31, 1998.

(b) Determine the number of shares used to compute fully diluted earnings per share for the year ended December 31, 1998.

(c) Compute the adjusted net income to be used as the numerator in the basic earnings per share calculation for the year ended December 31, 1998.

Cayuga Ltd. is preparing the comparative financial statements to be included in the annual report to shareholders. **P18-8** Cayuga employs a fiscal year ending May 31.

Income from operations before income taxes for Cayuga was $1,400,000 and $660,000, respectively, for fiscal years ended May 31, 1998 and 1997. Cayuga experienced an extraordinary loss of $500,000 because of an earthquake on March 3, 1998. A 40% combined income tax rate pertains to any and all of Cayuga's profits, gains, and losses.

Cayuga's capital structure consists of preferred and common shares. The company has not issued any convertible securities or warrants and there are no outstanding stock options.

Cayuga issued 50,000 no-par value, $6 cumulative preferred shares in 1984. All of these shares are outstanding and no preferred dividends are in arrears.

There were 1,500,000 no-par value common shares outstanding on June 1, 1996. On September 1, 1996, Cayuga sold an additional 400,000 common shares at $17 each. Cayuga distributed a 20% stock dividend on the common shares outstanding on December 1, 1997. These were the only common share transactions during the past two fiscal years.

Instructions

(a) Determine the weighted-average number of common shares that would be used in computing earnings per share on the current comparative income statement for:

1. The year ended May 31, 1997.
2. The year ended May 31, 1998.

(b) Starting with income from operations before income taxes, prepare a comparative income statement for the years ended May 31, 1998 and 1997. The statement will be part of Cayuga Limited's annual report to shareholders and should include appropriate earnings per share presentation.

(c) The capital structure of a corporation is the result of its past financing decisions. Furthermore, the earnings per share data presented on a corporation's financial statements are dependent upon the capital structure.

1. Explain why Cayuga Limited is considered to have a simple capital structure.
2. Describe how earnings per share data would be presented for a corporation that has a complex capital structure.

The controller of Powassan Corporation has requested assistance in determining income, basic earnings per share, **P18-9** and fully diluted earnings per share for presentation in the company's income statement for the year ended September 30, 1998. As currently calculated, the company's net income is $830,000 for fiscal year 1997–1998. The controller has indicated that the income figure might be adjusted for the following transactions that were recorded by charges or credits directly to retained earnings (the amounts are net of applicable income taxes):

1. The sum of $300,000, applicable to a breached 1994 contract, was received as a result of a lawsuit. Prior to the award, legal counsel was uncertain about the outcome of the suit.
2. A gain of $270,000 was realized from an expropriation of property (extraordinary).
3. A "gain" of $165,000 was realized on the sale of treasury shares.
4. A special inventory writeoff of $200,000 was made, of which $140,000 applied to goods manufactured prior to October 1, 1997.

Your working papers disclose the following opening balances and transactions in the company's share capital accounts during the year:

1. Common shares (at October 1, 1997, average issue price $10, authorized 450,000 shares; effective December 1, 1997, authorized 900,000 shares):

> Balance, October 1, 1997—issued and outstanding 100,000 shares
> December 1, 1997—100,000 shares issued in a 2-for-1 stock split
> December 1, 1997—420,000 shares issued at $39 per share

2. Treasury shares—common:

> March 1, 1998—purchased 60,000 shares at $37.25 per share
> April 1, 1998—sold 60,000 shares at $40 per share

3. Stock purchase warrants, Series A (initially, each warrant was exchangeable with $60 for one common share; effective December 1, 1997, each warrant became exchangeable for two common shares at $30 per share):

October 1, 1997—40,000 warrants issued at $6 each.

4. Stock purchase warrants, Series B (each warrant is exchangeable with $45 for one common share):

April 1, 1998—30,000 warrants authorized and issued at $10 each

5. First mortgage bonds, 9%, due 2013 (nonconvertible; priced to yield 8% when issued):

Balance, October 1, 1997—authorized, issued, and outstanding—the face value of $2,100,000

6. Convertible debentures, 7%, due 2017 (initially, each $1,000 bond was convertible at any time until maturity into 12 ½ common shares; effective December 1, 1997, the conversion rate became 25 shares for each bond):

October 1, 1997—authorized and issued at their face value (no premium or discount) of $3,600,000

Instructions

(a) Prepare a schedule computing net income as it should be presented in the company's income statement for the year ended September 30, 1998.

(b) Assuming that net income after income taxes for the year was $4,125,000 and that there were no extraordinary items, prepare a schedule computing (1) the basic earnings per share and (2) the fully diluted earnings per share that should be presented in the company's income statement for the year ended September 30, 1998. A supporting schedule computing the numbers of shares to be used in these computations should also be prepared. (Assume an income tax rate of 40% and that the company earns 20% after tax on assets.)   (AICPA adapted)

P18-10   The shareholders' equity section of Redbridge Company's balance sheet as of December 31, 1998 contains the following.

$2 cumulative convertible preferred shares (no-par value authorized 1,500,000 shares, issued 1,400,000, converted to common 750,000, and outstanding 650,000 shares; liquidation value, $30 a share, aggregating $19,500,000)	$16,250,000
Common shares (authorized 15,000,000 shares issued and outstanding 9,200,000 shares)	2,300,000
Contributed surplus	30,500,000
Retained earnings	45,050,000
Total shareholders' equity	$94,100,000

On April 1, 1998 Redbridge Company acquired the business and assets and assumed the liabilities of Geraldton Corporation in a transaction accounted for as a pooling of interests. For each of Geraldton Corporation's 2,400,000 common shares outstanding, the owner received one Redbridge common share.

(*Hint:* In a pooling of interests, shares are considered outstanding for the entire year.)

Included in the liabilities of Redbridge Company are 10% convertible subordinated debentures issued at their face value of $20,000,000 in 1997. The debentures are due in 2014 and until then are convertible into Redbridge Company common at the rate of five common shares for each $100 debenture. To date none of these has been converted.

On April 2, 1998 Redbridge Company issued 1,400,000 convertible preferred shares at $40 per share. Quarterly dividends to December 31, 1998 have been paid on these shares. The preferred shares are convertible into common at the rate of two common shares for each preferred share. On October 1, 1998, 150,000 shares and on November 1, 1998, 600,000 preferred shares were converted into common.

During July, 1997 Redbridge Company granted options to its officers and key employees to purchase 610,000 of the company's common shares at a price of $20 a share. The options do not become exercisable until 1999.

Redbridge Company's consolidated net income for the year ended December 31, 1998 was $11,360,000. The provision for income taxes was computed at a rate of 48%. The company earns 20% after tax on its assets.

Instructions

(a) Prepare a schedule that shows for 1998 the computation of:

1. The weighted-average number of shares for computing basic earnings per share.

2. The weighted-average number of shares for computing fully diluted earnings per share.

(b) Prepare a schedule that shows for 1998 the computation to the nearest cent of:

1. Basic earnings per share.

2. Fully diluted earnings per share.

(AICPA adapted)

On February 1, 1998, when your audit and report are nearly complete, Carol McEachern, the president of Huntsville **P18-11** ✓
Ltd., asks you to prepare statistical schedules of comparative financial data for the past five years for inclusion in the company's annual report. Your working papers reveal the following information.

1. Income statements show net income amounts as follows:

> 1993 — $ 40,000
> 1994 — (39,000) loss
> 1995 — 49,000
> 1996 — 76,000
> 1997 — 100,000

2. On January 1, 1993 there were 2,000 common shares outstanding and 1,000 $3 cumulative preferred shares.

3. A 6% dividend was paid in common shares to common shareholders on December 31, 1994. The fair market value of the common was $145 per share at the time.

4. Nine hundred common shares were issued on March 31, 1995 to purchase another company. (The transaction was accounted for as a purchase, not a pooling of interests. Earnings of the purchased company began to accrue to Huntsville on March 31, 1995.)

5. A dividend of cumulative preferred shares was distributed to common shareholders on July 1, 1995. One preferred share was distributed for every five common shares held. The fair market value of the preferred was $57 per share before the distribution and $54 per share immediately after the distribution.

6. The common shares were split 2-for-1 on December 31, 1996, and again on December 31, 1997.

7. Cash dividends are paid on the preferred shares on June 30, and again on December 31. Preferred share dividends were paid in each year except 1994; the 1994 and 1995 dividends were paid in 1995.

8. Cash dividends on common shares are paid on June 30 and December 31. Dividends paid per common share outstanding at the respective dates were:

	June 30	Dec. 31
1993	$ .50	$ .50
1994	None	None
1995	.50	.75
1996	1.00	.50ª
1997	.75	.75ᵇ

ªAfter 2-for-1 split.
ᵇBefore 2-for-1 split.

Instructions

(a) In connection with your preparation of the statistical schedule of comparative data for the past five years:

1. Prepare a schedule that computes the number of common and preferred shares outstanding as of the respective year-end dates.

2. Prepare a schedule that computes the current equivalent of common shares outstanding as of the respective year-end dates. The current equivalent shares means the weighted-average number of shares outstanding in the respective prior periods after restatement for stock splits and stock dividends.

3. Compute the total cash dividends paid to holders of preferred shares and to holders of common shares for each of the five years.

(b) Prepare a five-year summary of financial statistics to be included in the annual report. The summary should show by years "Net Income (or Loss)," Earnings Per Share," Cash Dividends Per Common Share." The per-share figures should be computed on the basis of current equivalent shares.

(AICPA adapted)

CASES

C18-1 Incurring long-term debt with an arrangement whereby lenders receive an option to buy common shares during all or a portion of the time the debt is outstanding is a frequent corporate financing practice. In some situations the result is achieved through the issuance of convertible bonds; in others the debt instruments and the warrants to buy shares are separate.

Instructions

(a) Describe the differences (if any) that exist in current accounting for original proceeds of the issuance of convertible bonds (compound financial instruments) and of debt instruments with separate warrants to purchase common shares.

(b) At the start of the year, Belmont Limited issued $18,000,000 of 12% notes along with warrants to buy 1,200,000 shares of its no-par value common shares at $18 each. The notes mature over the next 10 years starting one year from the date of issuance with annual maturities of $1,800,000. At the time, Belmont had 9,600,000 common shares outstanding and the market price was $23 per share. The company received $20,040,000 for the notes and the warrants. For Belmont Company, 12% was a relatively low borrowing rate. If offered alone, at this time, the notes would have been issued at a 22% discount. Prepare the journal entry (or entries) for the issuance of the notes and warrants for the cash consideration received. (AICPA adapted)

C18-2 On February 1, 1995 Acton Company sold its five-year, $1,000 par value, 8% bonds, which were convertible at the option of the investor into Acton Company common shares at a ratio of 10 shares for each bond. The convertible bonds were sold by Acton Company at a discount. Interest is payable annually each February 1. On February 1, 1998 Hagersville Company, an investor in the Acton Company convertible bonds, tendered 1,000 bonds for conversion into 10,000 of Acton Company's common shares that had a market value of $120 per share at the date of the conversion.

Instructions

How should Acton Company account for the conversion of the convertible bonds into common shares under both the book value and market value methods? Discuss the rationale for each method. (AICPA adapted)

C18-3 For various reasons a corporation may issue warrants to purchase common shares at specified prices that, depending on the circumstances, may be less than, equal to, or greater than the current market price. For example, warrants may be issued:

1. To existing shareholders on a pro rata basis.
2. To certain key employees under an incentive stock option plan.
3. To purchasers of the corporation's bonds.

Instructions

For each of the three examples of how stock warrants are used:

(a) Explain why they are used.

(b) Discuss the significance of the price (or prices) at which the warrants are issued (or granted) in relation to (1) the current market price of the company's shares; and (2) the length of time over which they can be exercised.

(c) Describe the information that should be disclosed in financial statements, or notes thereto, that are prepared when stock warrants are outstanding in the hands of the three groups listed above. (AICPA adapted)

C18-4 In 1995 Cobden Ltd. adopted a plan to give additional incentive compensation to its dealers to sell its principal product, fire extinguishers. Under the plan, Cobden transferred 9,000 shares of no-par value common shares to a trust with the provision that Cobden would have to forfeit interest in the trust and no part of the trust fund could ever revert to Cobden. Shares were to be distributed to dealers on the basis of their share of fire extinguisher purchases from Cobden (above certain minimum levels) over the three-year period ending June 30, 1998.

In 1995 the shares were closely held. The book value of the shares was $7.90 per share as of June 30, 1995, and in 1995 additional shares were sold to existing shareholders for $8 per share. On the basis of this information, market value of the shares was determined to be $8 each.

In 1995, when the shares were transferred to the trust, Cobden charged Prepaid Expenses for $72,000 ($8 per share market value) and credited Share Capital for $72,000. The prepaid expense was charged to operations over a three-year period ended June 30, 1998.

Cobden sold a substantial number of its shares to the public in 1997 at $60 per share.

In July, 1998 all shares in the trust were distributed to the dealers. The market value of the shares at date of distribution from the trust had risen to $110 per share. Cobden obtained a tax deduction equal to that market value for the tax year ended June 30, 1999.

Instructions

(a) How much should be reported as selling expense in each of the years noted above?

(b) Cobden is also considering other types of option plans, such as a stock appreciation rights (SARs) plan. What is a stock appreciation rights plan? What is a potential disadvantage of a SARs plan from the viewpoint of the company?

On December 12, 1995 the board of directors of Mactier Company authorized a grant of options to company executives for the purchase of 20,000 common shares at $50 anytime during 1998 if the executives are still employed by the company. The closing price of Mactier common shares was $55 on December 12, 1995, $51 on January 2, 1998, and 49\frac{1}{8}$ December 31, 1998. None of the options was exercised. **C18-5**

Instructions

(a) Prepare a schedule that presents the computation of the compensation cost that should be attributed to the options of Mactier Company.

(b) Assume that the market price of Mactier common rose to $58 (instead of declining to $51) on January 2, 1998, and that all options were exercised on that date. Would the company incur a cost for executive compensation? Why?

(c) Discuss the arguments for measuring compensation from executive stock options in terms of the spread between:

1. Market price and option price when the grant is made.
2. Market price and option price when the options are first exercisable.
3. Market price and option price when the options are exercised.
4. Cash value of the executives' services estimated at date of grant and the amount of their salaries.

(AICPA adapted)

"Earnings per share" (EPS) is the most featured single financial statistic about modern corporations. Daily published quotations of stock prices have recently been expanded to include, for many securities, a "times earnings" figure that is based on EPS. Stock analysts often focus their discussions on the EPS of the corporations they study. **C18-6**

Instructions

(a) Explain how dividends or dividend requirements on any class of preferred shares that may be outstanding affect the computation of EPS.

(b) The calculation of various EPS amounts requires the identification of issuable common shares.

1. What items are considered issuable common shares?
2. Describe the circumstances under which the potential impact of an outstanding convertible security on EPS would not be included in the calculation. (AICPA adapted)

Earnings per share (EPS) amounts were calculated and reported in various ways on an optional basis prior to 1969. *CICA Handbook*, Section 3500, "Earnings Per Share," issued in 1970, required that EPS be reported and prescribed how these amounts would be computed and disclosed. **C18-7**

The Accounting Standards Committee requires that firms having a simple capital structure present a single EPS amount and those with complex capital structures provide a dual EPS presentation.

Instructions

(a) Explain why the existence of convertible securities and other financing instruments necessitated the reporting requirements for EPS prescribed by *CICA Handbook*, Section 3500.

(b) Much of the effort involved in reporting EPS concerns the identification of issuable common shares.

1. What items are considered issuable common shares?
2. Describe the circumstances under which a convertible security would not be assumed to be converted in the computation of EPS. (CMA adapted)

C18-8 Duart Corporation, a new audit client of yours, has not reported earnings per share data in its annual reports to shareholders in the past. The treasurer, Jean Dunbar, requested that you furnish information about the reporting of earnings per share data in the current year's annual report in accordance with generally accepted accounting principles.

Instructions

(a) Define the term "earnings per share" as it applies to a corporation with a capitalization structure composed of only one class of common shares. Explain how earnings per share should be computed, and how the information should be disclosed in the corporation's financial statements.

(b) Discuss the treatment, if any, that should be given to each of the following items in computing earnings per common share for financial statement reporting:

1. Outstanding preferred shares issued at $46 with a $40 liquidation right.

2. The exercise at a price below market value but above book value of a common stock option issued during the current fiscal year to officers of the corporation.

3. The replacement of a machine immediately prior to the close of the current fiscal year at a cost 20% above the original cost of the replaced machine. The new machine will perform the same function as the old machine that was sold for its book value.

4. The declaration of current dividends on cumulative preferred shares.

5. The acquisition of some of the corporation's outstanding common shares during the current fiscal year. The shares were classified as treasury shares.

6. A 2-for-1 stock split of common shares during the current fiscal year.

7. An appropriation created out of retained earnings for a contingent liability from a possible lawsuit.

USING YOUR JUDGEMENT

FINANCIAL REPORTING PROBLEM

Refer to the financial statements and notes of Moore Corporation presented in Appendix 5A and answer the following questions.

1. At December 31, 1995 Moore Corporation had 1,496,000 options granted under a Long-Term Incentive Plan outstanding. How might these options affect the calculation of various earnings per share amounts?

2. Explain how the lapsing of 73,500 options during 1995 would affect expense and shareholders' equity.

3. How many options were granted in 1995? How would the granting of these options affect income for the year?

ETHICS CASE

The executive officers of Veryshrewd Corporation have a performance-based compensation plan. The performance criteria of this plan is linked to growth in earnings per share. When annual earnings per share growth is 12%, executives earn 100% of the shares; if growth is 16%, executives earn 125%. If earnings per share growth is lower than 8%, executives receive no additional compensation.

In 1998, Kate Padua, the controller of Veryshrewd, reviews year-end estimates of bad debts expense and warranty expense. She calculates the EPS growth at 15%. Vince Lucentio, a member of the executive group, remarks over lunch that the estimate of bad debt expense might be decreased so that EPS growth will be 16.1%. Padua is not sure that she should do this because she believes that the current estimate of bad debts is sound. On the other hand, she recognizes that a great deal of subjectivity is involved in the computations.

Instructions

(a) What, if any, is the ethical dilemma for Padua?

(b) Should Padua's knowledge of the compensation plan be a factor that influences her estimate?

(c) How would you respond to Lucentio's request?

ISSUES RELATED TO SELECTED TOPICS

part 5

chapter 19

ACCOUNTING FOR CORPORATE INCOME TAXES

CHAPTER 19

Accounting for Corporate Income Taxes

Learning Objectives

After studying this chapter, you should be able to:

1. Explain the difference between accounting income and taxable income.

2. Explain what a taxable temporary difference is and why a future tax liability is recognized.

3. Explain what a deductible temporary difference is and why a future tax asset is recognized.

4. Explain why the future income tax asset account is reassessed at the balance sheet date.

5. Identify timing and permanent differences.

6. Prepare analyses and related journal entries to record income tax expense when there are multiple temporary differences.

7. Explain the effect of various tax rates and tax rate changes on future income tax accounts.

8. Apply accounting procedures for a tax loss carryback.

9. Apply accounting procedures and disclosure requirements for a tax loss carryforward.

10. Identify evidence to consider in determining if future taxable income is likely to be available.

11. Explain the need for and be able to apply intraperiod tax allocation.

12. Identify the reporting and disclosure requirements for corporate income taxes.

13. Identify outstanding issues within the liability method.

14. Identify alternatives to and present arguments for and against comprehensive interperiod tax allocation using the liability approach (Appendix 19A).

"Here we go again! The Accounting Standards Board gears up for another run at corporate income taxes."[1] As this article title indicates, the determination of GAAP in relation to accounting for income taxes has been anything but straightforward.

The basic approach in *CICA Handbook* Sections 3470 and 3471 that is known generally as comprehensive tax allocation has been required since 1967. While there have been minor changes since then, the fundamental approach has remained unchanged. An *Exposure Draft* released in 1988 proposed revisions to Section 3470, but the Accounting Standards Committee concluded in 1990 that there was not sufficient consensus on the

[1]Patsy Willett, "Here We Go Again! The Accounting Standards Board Gears Up for Another Run at Corporate Income Taxes", *CA Magazine*, September, 1993, p. 56.

issues to warrant the issue of revised *Handbook* recommendations. At that time, Canadian attempts to resolve accounting for income taxes were frustrated and made more complex by concurrent U.S. and international (IASC) processes.

In 1992, the Financial Accounting Standards Board issued *Statement of Financial Accounting Standards No. 109,* "Accounting for Income Taxes," a replacement for *SFAS No. 96* issued five years earlier. *SFAS No. 96* never gained the support of the business community due to its complexity and failure to recognize certain future tax benefits. With the U.S. position substantially resolved, the Canadian standard setters felt the time was appropriate to revisit the corporate income tax area, and an *Exposure Draft* entitled "Income Taxes" was issued in 1996. In 1997, new *Handbook* Section 3465 was approved by the Accounting Standards Board. Section 3465 requirements are effective for fiscal periods beginning on or after January 1, 2000, at which time it replaces Sections 3470 and 3471.

This chapter examines the nature of problems associated with accounting for corporate income taxes and how the profession has resolved them. Specifically, the chapter explains how to apply interperiod tax allocation using the liability approach as required by new *Handbook* Section 3465.

The objective of **interperiod tax allocation** is to recognize not only income tax expense (or benefit) and income taxes payable (or refundable) for the current year, but also the future tax consequences of transactions and events that have been recognized in the financial statements or tax returns to the balance sheet date. As a result, future tax liabilities and assets are recognized on the balance sheet and income tax expense (benefit) includes a future component.

The **liability,** or **asset-liability, method** as it is sometimes called, specifies that the future income tax expense (or benefit) is determined by measuring the change in the net future income tax liability or asset account. The future tax liability or asset accounts are adjusted to reflect changes in income tax rates as the rates expected to apply in the future change. The asset-liability approach is believed to be the method most consistent with the conceptual framework identified in *Handbook* Section 1000.

This represents a significant change from the **income statement** or **revenue-expense approach** used in Section 3470. Under that approach, the amount of income tax expense or benefit was measured based on timing differences in the year between income reported on the income statement and that reported for tax purposes. The deferred tax asset or liability accounts were adjusted by amounts needed to bring the income statement expense or benefit to the desired balance. Because the tax asset or liability accounts in this situation were merely "leftovers" from the matching process and not considered real economic resources or obligations, no adjustments were made to them as tax rates changed.

Alternative approaches and methods exist to account for corporate income taxes. These are discussed in Appendix 19A, which considers some of the conceptual aspects of interperiod tax allocation and the reasons for the AcSB's conclusion to support the comprehensive, liability approach.

INTRODUCTION TO INCOME TAXES

CASH IMPACT OF INCOME TAXES

Income of an incorporated business, similar to income earned by individuals, is generally subject to federal and provincial income taxes.[2] Few business decisions are made without considering the often substantial tax effects that accompany alternatives faced by man-

---

[2]Proprietorships and partnerships are not subject to income taxes as separate legal entities. Instead, the income of a proprietorship or partnership is taxable in the hands of the proprietor or partners as individuals.

agement. Because most revenue earned by a corporation is taxable revenue, each dollar of revenue earned does not generate one dollar of cash. If the tax rate is 30%, only 70 cents of cash flows in from that revenue. On the other hand, most expenses are deductible by a company when it determines the amount of income on which it must pay tax. Wherever the tax legislation permits one dollar of expense to be deducted in calculating taxable income, the cash outflow to the organization is only 70 cents: the one dollar spent on the expense less the 30 cent savings in taxes that would otherwise have been payable.

In addition, because money has time value, management plans its taxation strategies to defer the payment of taxes to the future wherever possible.

ACCOUNTING INCOME AND TAXABLE INCOME

Differences often exist between the income reported on the income statement (GAAP income, or pretax **accounting income**[3]) and income computed for the tax return in accordance with prescribed tax regulations and rules, or **taxable income**. In computing income taxes payable to governmental units, corporations must complete tax returns, including a statement that reconciles the amount of income reported on the financial statements with the amount of income subject to tax.

OBJECTIVE 1
Explain the difference between accounting income and taxable income.

Income reported on the financial statements is measured in accordance with generally accepted accounting principles, where the objective is to provide a measure of the economic performance of the organization, reporting revenues earned during the period and reporting expenses incurred in generating that revenue. The objectives of, and many of the rules for, measuring taxable income are different from those for measuring income for financial statement purposes. For example, one general principle that underlies tax legislation is that the taxability or deductibility should correspond closely with the cash impact of the revenue or expense on the organization. Examples of differences between taxable and accounting income include:

1. Revenue is generally recognized on the accrual (sale) basis for financial reporting purposes, but may be recognized on the instalment basis for tax purposes.

2. Depreciation may be computed on a straight-line basis for financial reporting purposes, but capital cost allowance (CCA) that must be used for tax purposes is based on a declining balance method (the CCA method was discussed in Chapter 12).

3. For financial reporting purposes, warranty expenses are recognized in advance of actual problems with products sold so the costs can be matched with the related sales revenue. For tax purposes, warranty expenses are not deductible until actual costs are incurred to remedy product problems.

Differences between taxable income and income reported on the financial statements may be related to many of the topics examined throughout this text such as leases, pension plans, research and development costs, and intangibles. Because most revenues and expenses are taxable and deductible, respectively, in the same accounting period as they are reported on the income statement, corporations do not prepare a "tax income statement," but instead provide to the tax authorities a reconciliation of income reported on the income statement to taxable income.

To illustrate how these differences affect taxable income and therefore income tax payable, assume that Chelsea Inc. in 1998, its first year of operations, has revenues of $130,000 for accounting purposes and $100,000 for tax purposes and has expenses of $60,000 for both. The $30,000 difference in revenues arises because Chelsea recognizes

---

[3]The term "accounting income" has a precise meaning according to *CICA Handbook* Section 3470. In this chapter, it is used in its general sense and it is presumed to be a pretax amount.

revenue on the accrual basis for financial reporting purposes, but reports revenues as cash is collected for tax purposes. Chelsea's accounting income, taxable income, and income taxes payable (assuming a 40% tax rate) for 1998 are determined as follows:

EXHIBIT 19-1 CHELSEA INC.	
Revenues per financial statements	$130,000
Expenses per financial statements	60,000
Accounting income, 1998	**70,000**
Deduct 1998 revenue not taxable in 1998	(30,000)
Taxable income, 1998	**$ 40,000**
Tax rate	40%
Current income tax expense, and income tax payable for 1998: $40,000 × 40%	$ 16,000

Income Tax Payable is classified as a current liability on the balance sheet, and the expense is reported as *current income tax expense* for 1998. The **cost (benefit) of current income taxes** or **current income tax expense (benefit)** is the amount of income tax payable (recoverable) in respect of the current period.[4]

TEMPORARY DIFFERENCES AND FUTURE INCOME TAX BALANCE SHEET ACCOUNTS

Because revenues and expenses are defined as increases and decreases in economic resources, or as inflows and outflows of assets and liabilities, differences in the taxability and deductibility of items on the income statement will also result in differences between the carrying values of assets and liabilities on the balance sheet and their tax values. The measurement of future income tax assets and liabilities and future income tax expense or benefit is based on these differences.

A fundamental principle in preparing and interpreting financial statements is that assets are reported at no more than the future economic benefits (usually cash) that will be realized from their use or sale; and that liabilities are reported at the amount of assets or economic benefits (usually cash) that will be given up to settle them.

When recovering an amount equal to the carrying value of an asset results in an increase in future income taxes payable, the future economic benefit or cash flow from that asset is less than its carrying amount. Therefore, a tax liability—a *future tax liability*—should be recognized on the balance sheet to adjust the accounts to the net economic benefit to be realized from the asset.

When settling a liability for its carrying amount results in a decrease in future income taxes payable, the net resources used are less than the carrying amount of the liability. In this case, a tax asset—a *future tax asset*—should be recognized on the balance sheet to adjust the accounts to the net economic resources needed to settle the obligation.

The situations described above occur only when there are differences between the carrying amounts of the assets and liabilities on the balance sheet and their tax bases. These are known as **temporary differences**, and are discussed in greater detail in the following section.

---

[4] *CICA Handbook,* Section 3465, par. .09(g).

TAXABLE TEMPORARY DIFFERENCES

To illustrate the concept of **taxable temporary differences**, i.e., the temporary differences that will result in taxable amounts included in taxable income of future periods when the carrying amount of an asset is recovered or liability is settled,[5] the Chelsea Inc. example introduced earlier is continued.

OBJECTIVE 2
Explain what a taxable temporary difference is and why a future tax liability is recognized.

After income tax payable (the amount owed to the government) is computed, the next question is whether any other taxes have to be recognized for financial reporting purposes. The answer depends on whether there are any temporary differences between the amounts reported for tax and those reported for accounting purposes.

In Chelsea Inc.'s situation, the only difference between the carrying amount and tax basis of the assets and liabilities relates to accounts receivable that arose from revenue recognized for financial reporting purposes. Although Accounts Receivable are reported at $30,000 on the December 31, 1998 GAAP balance sheet, the receivables have a tax basis of zero, as illustrated below.

EXHIBIT 19-2 CHELSEA INC.			
Carrying Value	12/31/98	Tax Basis	12/31/98
Accounts receivable	$30,000	Accounts receivable	$ –0–

The **tax basis of an asset** is defined as *the amount, determined with reference to the rules established by the taxation authorities, that could be deducted in the determination of taxable income if the asset were recovered for its carrying value.*[6] For accounting purposes, as the $30,000 is recovered the receivable is eliminated and no part of the $30,000 is reported in future income; it was reported in income when the receivable was recognized. For tax purposes, as the $30,000 carrying value is recovered the full $30,000 will be added to taxable income; no part of it can be deducted or withheld in determining the taxable amount. Its tax value is therefore zero.

What will happen to this $30,000 temporary difference that originated in 1998 for Chelsea Inc.? Assuming that Chelsea expects to collect $20,000 of the receivable in 1999 and $10,000 in 2000, this collection will result in future taxable amounts of $20,000 in 1999 and $10,000 in 2000. These future taxable amounts will cause taxable income to exceed the accounting income in both 1999 and 2000, with a resulting increase in future taxes payable and an outflow of resources.

Because the Accounting Standards Board has indicated that an objective of accounting for income taxes includes the recognition in the balance sheet of the future income tax consequences of realizing an asset or settling a liability for its carrying amount, accrual accounting requires that the GAAP balance sheet recognize, in the current period, the future tax consequences of temporary differences. That is, the amount of income taxes that will be payable (or refundable) when the reported amounts of the assets are recovered and the liabilities are settled must be given recognition on the balance sheet. Illustration 19-1 illustrates the existence of the temporary difference at the end of 1998 and its reversal, with the resulting taxable amounts, in future periods.

Because taxable amounts will arise in the future as a result of temporary differences that exist at the end of the current year (1998), the future income tax consequences of these taxable amounts are recognized currently (in 1998) as a liability and as a future income tax component of 1998 income tax expense.

---

[5] *CICA Handbook*, Section 3465, par. .09(c)(ii).

[6] *Ibid.*, par. .11.

ILLUSTRATION 19-1

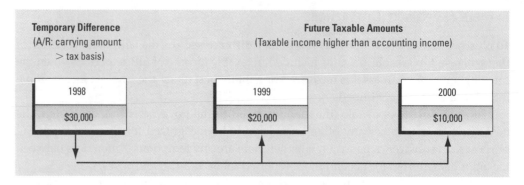

Future Income Tax Liabilities. **Future income tax liabilities** exist when future income tax effects that are attributable to existing temporary differences result in net taxable amounts in future years. They are measured as the amount of income tax that arises from the taxable temporary differences.[7] In essence, because of temporary differences that currently exist, income tax payable in future years will be greater than the amount calculated by multiplying the accounting income of those years by the appropriate tax rate. Consequently, a liability for these future taxes should be recognized in the current year. Recognition of a future tax liability also results in recognition of the **cost of future income taxes** on the income statement as a component of income tax expense. When the future income tax expense is added to the current income tax expense, *the result is the income tax expense for the current year to be reported on the income statement*. These two components require separate disclosure, either on the face of the income statement or in a note to the financial statements.

To illustrate the future income tax liability, the Chelsea example is continued. Recall that income tax payable was computed as $16,000 ($40,000 × 40%) in 1998. In addition, at the end of 1998 a temporary difference exists because the revenue and related accounts receivable are reported differently for accounting and tax purposes. The carrying value of accounts receivable is $30,000 and the tax basis is zero. Thus, the total future tax liability at the end of 1998 is $12,000, computed as follows.

EXHIBIT 19-3 CHELSEA INC.	
Carrying amount of accounts receivable, end of 1998	$30,000
Tax basis of accounts receivable, end of 1998	–0–
Temporary difference at the end of 1998	30,000
Tax rate expected to apply for 1999 and 2000	40%
Future tax liability at end of 1998	$12,000

Another way to compute the future tax liability is to prepare a schedule as illustrated below that indicates the taxable amounts scheduled for the future as a result of existing temporary differences. Such a schedule is particularly useful when the computations become more complex, such as when different tax rates are expected to apply in future years.

EXHIBIT 19-4 CHELSEA INC.			
	1999	2000	Total
Future taxable amounts	$20,000	$10,000	
Tax rate expected to apply	40%	40%	
Future income tax liability, at end of 1998	$ 8,000	$ 4,000	$12,000

---

[7] *CICA Handbook*, Section 3465, par. .09(e).

Because it is the first year of operations for Chelsea, there is no future tax liability at the beginning of the year. The income tax expense for 1998 is computed as shown below. Note that, as expected, an increase in the tax liability (as with liabilities in general) results in an increase in the amount of expense recognized.

EXHIBIT 19-5 CHELSEA INC.	
Future tax liability at end of 1998	$12,000
Future tax liability at beginning of 1998	–0–
Future tax expense for 1998	12,000
Current tax expense for 1998	16,000
Income tax expense (total) for 1998	**$28,000**

This computation illustrates the point made earlier that income tax expense has two components: the current tax expense, which is the income tax payable in respect of the period; and the **future income tax expense**, which is the increase in the net future tax liability during the accounting period. Taxes due and payable are credited to Income Tax Payable, and the increase in future income taxes is credited to a Future Income Tax Liability account. For Chelsea Inc., the following entries are made at the end of 1998.[8]

Current Income Tax Expense	16,000	
Income Tax Payable		16,000
Future Income Tax Expense	12,000	
Future Income Tax Liability		12,000

At the end of 1999, the second year, the difference between the carrying amount and the tax basis of the accounts receivable is $10,000. This difference is multiplied by the tax rate expected to apply when the $10,000 increases taxable income to arrive at the future tax liability of $4,000 ($10,000 3 40%) to be reported at the end of 1999. Assuming that income tax payable for 1999 is $19,000, the income tax expense for 1999 is as shown below. A reduction in the future tax liability (as with liabilities in general) results in the recognition of a benefit or reduced expense in the current period.

EXHIBIT 19-6 CHELSEA INC.	
Future tax liability at end of 1999 ($10,000 × 40%)	$ 4,000
Future tax liability at beginning of 1999	12,000
Future tax expense (benefit) for 1999	(8,000)
Current tax expense for 1999 (given)	19,000
Income tax expense (total) for 1999	**$11,000**

The journal entries to record income tax expense, the change in the future income tax liability, and income tax payable for 1999 are as follows.

Current Income Tax Expense	19,000	
Income Tax Payable		19,000
Future Income Tax Liability	8,000	
Future Income Tax Benefit		8,000

---

[8] These two entries could have been combined with one debit to Income Tax Expense of $28,000. Because disclosure is required of the amount of the current and the future expense (benefit), entries in this chapter use separate accounts to assist in "keeping track" of the amounts of each.

In the entries to record income taxes at the end of 2000, the Future Income Tax Liability is reduced by $4,000. The Future Income Tax Liability account appears as follows at the end of 2000, with a zero balance.

Future Income Tax Liability			
		1998	12,000
1999	8,000		
2000	4,000		

Some analysts dismiss future tax liabilities when assessing the financial strength of a company. One of the common complaints about *Handbook* recommendations in Section 3470 on deferred income taxes is that the resulting balance sheet account reported is merely a "leftover" from the matching process. The changes incorporated in new Section 3465 base the measurement of the future tax liability on the difference between the carrying amounts and tax values of balance sheet accounts and, in general, treat the account as a real obligation of the entity. The future tax liability meets the definition of a liability established in Section 1000 of the *CICA Handbook* because:

1. *It is a present obligation.* Taxable income in future periods will be higher than accounting income as a result of this temporary difference. Thus, a present obligation exists.

2. *It arises from past transactions or events.* In the Chelsea example, services were performed for customers and revenue was recognized in 1998 for financial reporting purposes although revenue was deferred for tax purposes.

3. *It will require the use of assets or relinquishment of economic benefits in the future.* Taxable income and taxes due in future periods will result, requiring the transfer of company assets in the future.

Also note that the balance sheet at the end of each accounting period reports the cash impact of recovering the carrying value of the account receivable. The following table illustrates the relationship between the future economic benefits accruing to Chelsea and the net assets reported on the balance sheet.

	End of 1998	End of 1999
As carrying amount is recovered:		
Future cash to be collected on the receivable	$30,000	$10,000
Future cash outflow for related income tax	12,000	4,000
Net future cash inflow	$18,000	$ 6,000
Impact on balance sheet:		
Account receivable	$30,000	$10,000
Future income tax liability	12,000	4,000
Net asset reported	$18,000	$ 6,000

If the future tax liability was not recognized at the end of 1998, assets (and net assets) of $30,000 would be reported on the balance sheet, which would generate only $18,000 of future economic benefits. At the end of 1999, net assets would be overstated by $4,000.

DEDUCTIBLE TEMPORARY DIFFERENCES

OBJECTIVE 3
Explain what a deductible temporary difference is and why a future tax asset is recognized.

The previous discussion examined the financial accounting consequences of a temporary difference that results in taxable amounts in the future. In other situations, temporary differences result in amounts that will be deducted in calculating taxable income in the future. These are known as **deductible temporary differences**.

Assume that during 1998, Cunningham Inc. estimates its warranty costs related to the sale of microwave ovens to be $500,000 and that $300,000 of these costs will be incurred in 1999 and $200,000 in the year 2000. For accounting purposes, in 1998 Cunningham reports warranty expense and a related estimated liability for warranties of $500,000 in its financial statements. For tax purposes, *the warranty tax deduction is not allowed until actual warranty costs are incurred*; therefore, the tax basis of the warranty liability is zero.

The **tax basis of a liability** is its carrying amount less any amount that will be deductible for income tax purposes in respect of that liability in future periods.[9] In this case, the $500,000 carrying amount, less the amount deductible for tax purposes in future periods of $500,000 as the costs are incurred, results in a tax value of zero. Thus, the balance sheet difference at the end of 1998 is as follows.

EXHIBIT 19-7 CUNNINGHAM INC.

Carrying Value	12/31/98	Tax Basis	12/31/98
Estimated liability for warranties	$500,000	Estimated liability for warranties	$ –0–

When the warranty liability is settled by incurring costs to repair or replace the microwave products, a deductible expense will be allowed for tax purposes. Because deductible amounts will arise in the future as a result of temporary differences at the end of 1998, the future income tax consequences (benefits) of these deductible amounts are recorded by Cunningham as a future income tax asset on the December 31, 1998 balance sheet and as a component of income tax expense. The following diagram illustrates the existence of the temporary difference at the end of 1998 and its reversal, with the resulting deductible amounts, in future periods.

ILLUSTRATION 19-2

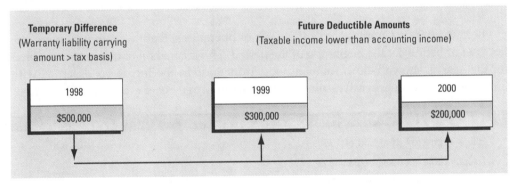

Future Income Tax Assets. **Future income tax assets** *are the future tax benefits attributable to deductible temporary differences.* In other words, a future income tax asset represents and is measured as the tax savings in future years as a result of deductible temporary differences existing at the end of the current year.[10] Future income tax assets should be recognized *only to the extent that it is more likely than not that the future income tax asset will be realized.* This is contingent on earning sufficient taxable income in the future against which the temporary differences can be deducted. Section 3465 defines **more likely than not** as a probability of greater than 50%.[11]

Recognition of a future tax asset also results in recognition of the benefit of the future income tax reduction on the income statement, as a component of income tax expense.

---

[9] *CICA Handbook*, Section 3465, par. .13.

[10] *Ibid.*, par. .09(d). Future income tax assets also include the income tax benefits that arise in respect of the carry-forward of unused tax losses and unused income tax reductions, excluding investment tax credits. These are discussed later in the chapter.

[11] *Ibid.*, par. .09(i).

When the future income tax benefit is deducted from the current income tax expense, the result is the income tax expense for the current year.

To illustrate the determination and recognition of the future tax asset and income tax benefit, the Cunningham example is continued. Assume that 1998 is the company's first year of operations and that income tax payable is $600,000. The computation of the future income tax asset at the end of 1998, assuming a 40% tax rate, is shown below.

EXHIBIT 19-8 CUNNINGHAM INC.	
Carrying amount of warranty liability, end of 1998	$500,000
Tax basis of warranty liability, end of 1998	–0–
Deductible temporary difference, end of 1998	$500,000
Tax rate expected to apply for 1999 and 2000	40%
Future income tax asset, end of 1998	$200,000

Another way to compute the future income tax asset is to prepare a schedule as illustrated below that indicates the deductible amounts scheduled for the future as a result of deductible temporary differences at the end of 1998.

EXHIBIT 19-9 CUNNINGHAM INC.			
	Future Years		
	1999	2000	Total
Future deductible amounts	$300,000	$200,000	
Tax rate expected to apply	40%	40%	
Future income tax asset, end of 1998	$120,000	$ 80,000	$200,000

Because 1998 is Cunningham's first year of operations, there was no future income tax asset or liability at the beginning of the period. The calculation of income tax expense for the year is shown below. As expected, an increase in the future tax asset (as with increases in assets in general) results in the recognition of a benefit or reduced expense.

EXHIBIT 19-10 CUNNINGHAM INC.	
Future income tax asset, end of 1998	$200,000
Future income tax asset, beginning of 1998	–0–
Future tax expense (benefit) for 1998	(200,000)
Current tax expense for 1998 (given)	600,000
Income tax expense (total) for 1998	$400,000

The future income tax benefit results from the increase in the future income tax asset from the beginning to the end of the period and it reduces income tax expense. The total income tax expense of $400,000 on the income statement for 1998 is comprised of two elements: current tax expense of $600,000 and a future tax benefit of $200,000. For Cunningham Inc. the following journal entries are made at the end of 1998 to record income tax expense, the change in the future income tax asset, and income tax payable.

Current Income Tax Expense	600,000	
Income Tax Payable		600,000
Future Income Tax Asset	200,000	
Future Income Tax Benefit		200,000

At the end of the second year, 1999, the difference between the carrying amount of $200,000 and the tax basis of zero is $200,000. Therefore, the future tax asset at this date is 40% of $200,000, or $80,000. Assuming that income tax payable for 1999 is $440,000, the computation of income tax expense for 1999 is as shown below. As expected, a reduction in the tax asset account (as with assets in general) results in an increase in the expense recognized.

EXHIBIT 19-11 CUNNINGHAM INC.

Future income tax asset, end of 1999	$ 80,000
Future income tax asset, beginning of 1999	200,000
Future tax expense (benefit) for 1999	120,000
Current tax expense for 1999 (given)	440,000
Income tax expense (total) for 1999	$560,000

The journal entries to record income taxes for 1999 follow.

Current Income Tax Expense	440,000	
Income Tax Payable		440,000
Future Income Tax Expense	120,000	
Future Income Tax Asset		120,000

The total income tax expense of $560,000 on the income statement for 1999 is comprised of two elements: current tax expense of $440,000, and future tax expense of $120,000.

Note that the future income tax expense of $120,000 recognized in 1999 *is not related to future events at all*: It represents the using up or reversal of a future income tax benefit recognized at the end of the preceding year. While a third component of income tax expense for the current year such as Utilization of Previously Recognized Future Tax Assets or Reduction in Future Income Tax Assets could be given separate recognition, the authors have chosen to incorporate this as a component of future tax expense or benefit. The future income tax expense or benefit is a measure of the change in the net income tax liability or asset account over the period. As such, it is a combination of increased future tax liabilities, reversals of taxable temporary differences, recognition of future tax assets, and the utilization of future tax benefits recognized in the past.

At the end of 2000, the Future Income Tax Asset is further reduced by $80,000, as shown in the T account below. Future income tax expense in 2000 is $80,000.

Future Income Tax Liability

1998	200,000		
		1999	120,000
		2000	80,000

A key issue in accounting for income taxes is whether a future tax asset should be recognized in the accounts. Because of the changes introduced in Section 3465, the future tax asset account has all three characteristics of an asset as defined in *CICA Handbook* Section 1000 on financial statement concepts:

1. ***It will contribute to future net cash flows.*** Taxable income is higher than accounting income in the current year (1998). However, in the next year the opposite occurs, with taxable income being lower than income reported for financial statement purposes. Because this deductible temporary difference reduces taxes payable in the future, a future benefit exists at the end of the year.

2. *Access to the benefits are controlled by the entity.* Cunningham Inc. has the ability to obtain the benefit of existing deductible temporary differences by reducing its taxes payable in the future. The company has the exclusive right to that benefit and can control others' access to it.

3. *It results from a past transaction or event.* In the Cunningham Inc. example, the sale of the product with the two-year warranty is the past event that gives rise to a future deductible temporary difference.

Note that when the future tax asset is recognized, the balance sheet at the end of each accounting period reports the economic resources needed to settle the warranty liability. The following table illustrates this relationship.

	End of 1998	End of 1999
Economic resources needed to settle the obligation:		
Future resources needed to settle the liability	$500,000	$200,000
Future tax savings as liability is settled	200,000	80,000
Net future economic resources needed	$300,000	$120,000
Impact on balance sheet:		
Warranty liability	$500,000	$200,000
Future income tax asset	200,000	80,000
Net liability reported	$300,000	$120,000

In the absence of interperiod tax allocation, that is, if the future income tax asset is not recognized at the end of 1998, liabilities (and net liabilities) of $500,000 would be reported on the balance sheet, which require only $300,000 of economic resources to settle. Similarly, net liabilities would be overstated by $80,000 at the end of 1999.

OBJECTIVE 4
Explain why the future income tax asset account is reassessed at the balance sheet date.

Reassessment of the Future Income Tax Asset Account. Consistent with the reporting of all other types of assets, the Future Income Tax Asset account must be reviewed to ensure that the carrying amount is appropriate. Where it is more likely than not that insufficient taxable income will be generated in the future to allow the benefit of the future tax asset to be realized, the future tax asset must be recalculated based on a judgement about the extent to which it will be realized. The carrying value of the account is then written down.[12] This "affirmative judgement" approach differs from the "impairment approach" recommended by FAS 109, which requires recognition of a future income tax asset for *all* deductible temporary differences, unused tax losses and income tax reductions offset by an impairment allowance for the portion of the asset deemed more likely than not to *not* be realized. Because there is no substantive difference between the results of applying the two approaches, Section 3465 permits the use of the valuation allowance approach.[13] The approach preferred by the AcSB, however, recognizes only assets that are expected to be realized and eliminates the complexity of valuation of the asset and separate allowance, particularly where the tax rates and laws for the periods of realization are required.

Assume Jensen Co. has a deductible temporary difference of $1,000,000 at the end of its first year of operations. Its tax rate is 40% and a future tax asset of $400,000 ($1,000,000 × 40%) is recognized on the basis that it is more likely than not that sufficient taxable income will be generated in the future. The journal entry to record the future income tax benefit and the change in the future tax asset is:

Future Income Tax Asset	400,000	
Future Income Tax Benefit		400,000

---

[12] *CICA Handbook,* Section 3465, par. .31(a).

[13] *Ibid.,* par. .30.

If, at the end of the next period, the deductible temporary difference remains at $1,000,000 but now only $750,000 is more likely than not to be utilized, the future tax asset expected to be realized is recalculated to be 40% of $750,000, or $300,000. The following entry is made to adjust the asset account.

Future Income Tax Expense	100,000	
Future Income Tax Asset		100,000

All available evidence, both positive and negative, should be carefully considered in determining the appropriate value for the future tax account. For example, if the company expects to experience a series of loss years, a reasonable assumption is that the benefit of the future deductible amounts may be lost. Other conditions are discussed later in the chapter.

Section 3465 also recommends that the future tax asset account be reviewed to determine whether it is more likely than not that taxable income will be available to allow the benefit of a *previously unrecognized future income tax asset* to be used. If so, a future income tax asset should be recognized to the extent it is more likely than not to be realized.[14] The future income tax benefit is recognized in the same period.

TAX BASIS OF ASSETS AND LIABILITIES

Unlike *CICA Handbook* Section 3470, in which recommendations are based on recognizing *timing* and *permanent* differences between income reported on the income statement and taxable income, the recommendations of Section 3465 are based on *temporary* differences between the carrying values of assets and liabilities on the balance sheet and the tax values of those assets and liabilities. The tax basis of an asset or liability is determined by reference to tax legislation.

TAX BASIS OF AN ASSET

Section 3465 defines the tax basis of an asset as the amount that could be deducted in the determination of taxable income if the asset were recovered for its carrying amount. Guidance is provided to clarify this definition.

1. If amounts related to an asset are deductible in calculating taxable income over one or more years, its tax basis is that amount less all amounts already deducted in determining taxable income to date. For example, a capital asset with an original tax basis of $10,000 and on which $2,500 of capital cost allowance has been claimed has a tax basis of $7,500.

2. If amounts related to an asset are deductible when the asset is disposed of or withdrawn from use, its tax basis is that amount. For example, land purchased for $35,000 has a tax basis of that amount.

3. If the carrying value of an asset is not tax deductible, and the proceeds from its disposition are not taxable, the tax basis of the asset is its carrying value. For example, the tax basis of dividends receivable from taxable Canadian corporations is equal to their carrying value because the receipt of the dividend has no tax impact.[15]

---

[14] *CICA Handbook*, Section 3465, par. .30(b).

[15] *CICA Handbook*, Section 3465, par. .12. This paragraph also indicates that when the amount of tax-deductible costs varies with whether the asset is used or sold, the higher amount should be identified as the tax basis.

TAX BASIS OF A LIABILITY

The tax basis of a liability is its carrying value less any amounts deductible for tax purposes in future periods. Where salaries payable of $4,000 are recognized, for example, all of which has been deducted in calculating taxable income in the current period, the liability has a tax basis of $4,000 less $0, or $4,000. Other guidance includes:

1. For revenues received in advance, the tax basis of the liability account is its carrying value less amounts that are not taxable in the future. An Unearned Rental Revenue account with a carrying amount of $1,200, $1,000 of which was taxable in the current year, has a tax basis of $200, or $1,200 less $1,000.

2. For liabilities whose settlement has no tax consequences, the tax basis is equal to the carrying amount. For example, a $5,000 payable for golf club dues has a tax basis of $5,000. Golf club dues are not considered deductible expenses under existing tax law; therefore, the settlement of the liability has no tax consequences. Other examples include the principal amounts of most indebtedness because the principal portions of loan repayments have no tax effects.[16]

Some assets and liabilities may have a tax value, but not appear on the balance sheet because of a zero carrying amount. Examples include research costs expensed for financial reporting purposes but deferred for later deduction for tax purposes; or revenues taken into income for accounting purposes but deferred for tax. In these cases, the deferred research costs and unearned income have carrying amounts of zero, but positive tax values. It is important to identify the temporary differences in these situations.

Where the tax basis of an asset or liability is not clear, the fundamental principles underlying the recommendations should be considered: the purpose for recognizing the tax effects of temporary differences on the balance sheet is to offset the carrying values of the assets and liabilities with the related tax consequence so that the net amount of future economic benefit expected from or used to settle the reported asset or liability is reported on the statement of financial position.[17]

CALCULATION OF TAXABLE INCOME

TIMING AND PERMANENT DIFFERENCES

OBJECTIVE 5
Identify timing and permanent differences.

To calculate income taxes currently payable, companies must first calculate taxable income. As indicated earlier in the chapter, this is done by beginning with the income reported on the income statement and adjusting this number to the amount that is taxable.

---

[16] *CICA Handbook*, Section 3465, par. .13.

[17] *Ibid.* Par. .43, for consistency, requires that when the tax basis of an asset acquired (other than in a business combination) is less than its cost, the cost of future income taxes should be added to the cost of the asset with an offset to a future tax liability account; and when the tax basis is greater than its cost, that the benefit related to future income taxes should be deducted from the asset's cost on the balance sheet with the difference attributed to a future tax asset. The reasons for this are twofold: the cost of the asset reported on the balance sheet better reflects the consideration paid for the asset; and the resulting future income tax expense (benefit) is recognized over the life of the asset instead of being given immediate recognition.

The major reasons for differences between accounting and taxable income, most of which result in or affect the amount of a temporary difference, are provided below.

(A) *Revenues or gains are taxable after they are recognized in accounting income.* An asset such as a receivable or an investment may be recognized on the balance sheet as revenues or gains are recognized on the income statement; however, amounts are not included in taxable income until future years when the asset is recovered or realized. Examples include:
1. Instalment sales accounted for on the accrual basis for financial reporting purposes and on the cash basis for tax purposes.
2. Contracts accounted for under the percentage-of-completion method for financial reporting purposes with a portion of the related gross profit deferred for tax purposes.

(B) *Expenses or losses are deductible after they are recognized in accounting income.* A liability (or contra asset) may be recognized on the balance sheet when expenses or losses are recognized for financial reporting purposes; however, amounts are not deductible in calculating taxable income until future periods when the liability is settled. Examples include:
1. Product warranty liabilities.
2. Estimated losses and liabilities related to discontinued operations and restructurings.
3. Litigation accruals.
4. Accrued pension costs in excess of amounts funded.

(C) *Revenues or gains are taxable before they are recognized in accounting income.* A liability may be recognized for an advance payment for goods or services to be provided in future years. For tax purposes, the advance payment may be included in taxable income on the receipt of cash. When the entity recognizes revenue in the future as the goods or services are provided that settle the liability, these amounts are deductible in calculating taxable income in those years. Examples include:
1. Subscriptions, royalties, and rentals received in advance.
2. Sales and leasebacks including the deferral of profit on the sale for financial reporting purposes, but reported as realized for tax purposes.

(D) *Expenses or losses are deductible before they are recognized in accounting income.* The cost of an asset may be deducted faster for tax purposes than expensed for financial reporting purposes. If future amounts received as the asset is realized are equal to the carrying value of the asset, the amounts recovered in excess of the tax value result in taxable amounts in future years. Examples include:
1. Depreciable property and depletable resources.
2. Deductible pension funding exceeding pension expense recognized.
3. Prepaid expenses that are deducted in calculating taxable income in the period paid.

(E) *Permanent differences.* Some differences between taxable income and accounting income are permanent. **Permanent differences** are caused by items that (1) enter into accounting income but never into taxable income; or (2) enter into taxable income but never into accounting income. Since permanent differences affect only the period in which they occur, they do not give rise to future taxable or deductible amounts. As a result, there are no future tax consequences to be recognized. Examples of permanent differences include:

1. Items that enter into accounting income but never into taxable income. These include non-tax-deductible expenses such as fines and penalties, golf and social club dues, and expenses related to the earning of non taxable revenue; and non taxable revenue, such as dividends from taxable Canadian corporations, and proceeds on life insurance policies carried by the company on key officers or employees.

2. Items that enter into taxable income but never into accounting income, such as depletion allowance of natural resources in excess of their cost.

The differences identified in (A) to (D) above are known as **timing differences**.[18] Their accounting treatment and tax treatment is the same, but the timing of when they are included in accounting income and taxable income differs. Timing differences are generally related to temporary differences in that timing differences cause the balance of a temporary difference to change. An **originating timing difference** is the cause of the initial difference between the carrying value and the tax basis of an asset or liability, or of an increase in the temporary difference, regardless of whether the tax basis of the asset or liability exceeds or is exceeded by the carrying amount of the asset or liability. A **reversing timing difference**, on the other hand, causes a temporary difference at the beginning of the period to decrease, and the related tax effect is removed from the future income tax account.

For example, assume that Sharp Co. has tax depreciation (CCA) in excess of accounting depreciation of $2,000 in each of 1994, 1995, and 1996, and that it has an excess of accounting depreciation over CCA of $3,000 in 1997 and in 1998 for the same asset. Assuming a tax rate of 30% for all years involved, the Future Income Tax Liability account would reflect the following activity.

Future Income Tax Liability

			1994	600	}	Tax effects
			1995	600	}	of
Tax effects			1996	600	}	Originating Differences
of	{ 1997	900				
Reversing Differences	{ 1998	900				

The originating differences for Sharp in each of the first three years would be $2,000, and the related tax effect of each originating difference would be $600. The reversing differences in 1997 and 1998 would each be $3,000, and the related tax effect of each would be $900.

OBJECTIVE 6

Prepare analyses and related journal entries to record income tax expense when there are multiple temporary differences.

Multiple Differences Illustrated. To illustrate the computations used when multiple differences exist, assume that the Bio-Tech Company reports accounting income of $200,000 in each of the years 1997, 1998, and 1999. The company is subject to a 30% tax rate that is expected to continue into the future, and has the following differences between income reported on the financial statements and taxable income:

1. An instalment sale of $18,000 in 1997 is reported for tax purposes over an 18-month period at a constant amount each month as it is collected, beginning January 1, 1998. The entire sale and related profit is recognized for financial reporting purposes in 1997.

2. Premium paid for life insurance carried by the company on key officers is $5,000 in 1998 and 1999. This is not deductible for tax purposes, but is expensed for accounting purposes.

3. A warranty was provided on sales in 1997 and an associated expense of $30,000 was recognized in the same year. It was expected that $20,000 of the warranty work would be performed in 1998 and $10,000 in 1999.

---

[18] The accounting requirements in *CICA Handbook* Section 3470 were based on the tax effects of timing differences. Section 3465 is concerned mainly with temporary differences.

The first and third items are timing differences that result in temporary differences. The second item is a permanent difference with no future tax consequences. The reconciliation of Bio-Tech's accounting income to taxable income and the computation of income tax payable is as follows.

EXHIBIT 19-12	BIO-TECH COMPANY		
	1997	1998	1999
Accounting income	$200,000	$200,000	$200,000
Adjustments:			
Instalment sale	(18,000)	12,000	6,000
Warranty expense	30,000	(20,000)	(10,000)
Nondeductible expense	—	5,000	5,000
Taxable income	$212,000	$197,000	$201,000
Tax rate	30%	30%	30%
Income tax payable	$ 63,600	$ 59,100	$ 60,300

Note that the calculations work toward the taxable amount; therefore, revenue items not taxable until a future period are deducted, and expenses not deductible in the year are added back. Conversely, revenue items not included in accounting income but taxable in the period must be added and expenses not included in accounting income but deductible in the year are subtracted.

All differences between accounting income and taxable income are considered in reconciling the income reported on the financial statements to taxable income. Only those resulting in temporary differences, however, are considered when calculating future income tax amounts for the balance sheet. When multiple differences exist, a schedule should be prepared of the balance sheet accounts that have a carrying value and tax basis that differ.

Bio-Tech Company's analysis and calculation of net temporary differences, the net future income tax asset or liability, and the future income tax expense or benefit for 1997 is shown below.

In 1997, Bio-Tech has two originating timing differences that result in temporary differences. The journal entries to record income taxes for 1997 based on the above analyses are:

EXHIBIT 19-13	BIO-TECH COMPANY — 1997		
	Carrying Amount	Tax Basis	Taxable (Deductible) Temporary Differences
Assets			
Accounts receivable	$18,000	–0–	$18,000
Liabilities			
Liability for warranties	$30,000	–0–	(30,000)
Net deductible temporary difference			($12,000)
Future income tax liability $18,000 at 30%			$ 5,400
Future income tax asset $30,000 at 30%			(9,000)
Net future income tax asset, December 31, 1997			(3,600)
Less opening net future income tax asset			–0–
Future income tax expense (benefit) — 1997			($ 3,600)

Current Income Tax Expense	63,600	
Income Tax Payable		63,600
Future Income Tax Asset	3,600	
Future Income Tax Benefit		3,600

At the end of 1998, the following analysis is made of the temporary differences at December 31 in order to calculate the change in the net future tax asset or liability. The two types of temporary differences that originated in 1997 have begun to reverse and the tax effect on the change in temporary differences is the future income tax expense or benefit component of income tax expense for 1998.

EXHIBIT 19-14   BIO-TECH COMPANY — 1998

	Carrying Amount	Tax Basis	Taxable (Deductible) Temporary Differences
Assets			
Accounts receivable	$ 6,000	–0–	$ 6,000
Liabilities			
Liability for warranties	$10,000	–0–	(10,000)
Net deductible temporary difference			$(4,000)
Future income tax liability $6,000 at 30%			$ 1,800
Future income tax asset $10,000 at 30%			(3,000)
Net future income tax asset, December 31, 1998			(1,200)
Less opening net future income tax asset			(3,600)
Future income tax expense (benefit) — 1998			$ 2,400

The journal entries to record income taxes at December 31, 1998 are:

Current Income Tax Expense	59,100	
Income Tax Payable		59,100
Future Income Tax Expense	2,400	
Future Income Tax Asset		2,400

At the end of 1999, all temporary differences have reversed, leaving no temporary differences between balance sheet amounts and tax values.

EXHIBIT 19-15   BIO-TECH COMPANY — 1999

	Carrying Amount	Tax Basis	Taxable (Deductible) Temporary Differences
Assets			
Accounts receivable	$ –0–	$ –0–	$ –0–
Liabilities			
Liability for warranties	$ –0–	$ –0–	$ –0–
Net taxable (deductible) temporary difference			$ –0–
Net future income tax liability (asset), December 31, 1999			$ –0–
Less opening net future income tax asset			(1,200)
Future income tax expense (benefit) — 1999			1,200

The journal entries at December 31, 1999 reduce the Future Income Tax Asset account to zero and recognize the $1,200 future income tax expense as part of the income tax expense for the current 1999 year.

Current Income Tax Expense	60,300	
Income Tax Payable		60,300
Future Income Tax Expense	1,200	
Future Income Tax Asset		1,200

Note that there is no future tax amount associated with the difference caused by the nondeductible insurance expense because it is does not result in a temporary difference.

Based on the above entries, total income tax expense reported in 1997, 1998, and 1999 is $60,000, $61,500, and $61,500, respectively. Although the statutory (enacted) rate of 30% applies for all three years, the effective rate is 30% for 1997 ($60,000 /$200,000 = 30%) and 30.75% for 1998 and 1999 ($61,500/$200,000 = 30.75%). The **effective tax rate** is computed by dividing total income tax expense for the period by the pretax income reported on the financial statements. The difference between the enacted and effective rates in this case is caused by the nondeductible insurance expense.

TAX RATE CONSIDERATIONS

In the previous illustrations, the enacted tax rate did not change from one year to the next. Therefore, to compute the future income tax amount to be reported on the balance sheet, the temporary difference is simply multiplied by the current tax rate which is expected to apply to future years as well. Using Bio-Tech as an example, the temporary difference related to the instalment sale of $18,000 is multiplied by the enacted rate of 30% to arrive at a future tax liability of $5,400 ($18,000 × 30%), and the difference of $30,000 relative to warranty expenses is multiplied by the same rate to compute the future tax asset.

OBJECTIVE 7
Explain the effect of various tax rates and tax rate changes on future income tax accounts.

FUTURE TAX RATES

What happens if tax rates are different for future years? *Handbook* Section 3465 takes the position that the income tax rates that are expected to apply when the tax liabilities are settled or tax assets are realized should be used. These would normally be those enacted at the balance sheet date.[19] The accounting standard does recognize, however, that situations may exist where a substantively enacted rate may be more appropriate.[20] The rates expected to apply are used in measuring future tax assets and liabilities. For example, assume that Warlen Co. at the end of 1997 has the following temporary difference of $300,000, computed as follows.

EXHIBIT 19-16 WARLEN CO.	
Carrying amount of depreciable assets	$1,000,000
Tax basis of depreciable assets	700,000
Temporary difference	$ 300,000

Furthermore, assume that the $300,000 will reverse and result in taxable amounts in the following years when the tax rates expected to apply are as provided on the schedule that follows. As indicated, the total future income tax liability at the end of 1997 is $108,000.

---

[19] *CICA Handbook*, Section 3465, par. .56. Note that this covers changes in tax laws as well as tax rates.

[20] *Ibid.*, par. .58. Use of a substantively enacted rate would require persuasive evidence that the government is able and committed to enacting the proposed change in the foreseeable future. This would usually require that the legislation or regulation has been drafted in an appropriate form and tabled in Parliament or presented in Council.

EXHIBIT 19-17 WARLEN CO.

	1998	1999	2000	2001	2002	Total
Future taxable amounts	$80,000	$70,000	$60,000	$50,000	$40,000	$300,000
Tax rate expected to apply	40%	40%	35%	30%	30%	
Future income tax liability	$32,000	$28,000	$21,000	$15,000	$12,000	$108,000

Because the Canadian tax system provides incentives in the form of reductions in the income tax rates applied to taxable income, it is recommended that the tax rate used to compute the future tax amounts incorporate the tax rate reductions, provided it is more likely than not that the company will qualify for the rate reductions in the periods of reversal.[21] The general principle is to use the expected average or effective tax rate of the period in which the temporary differences are expected to reverse, provided it is enacted or substantively enacted at the balance sheet date.

Section 3465, consistent with the U.S. standard in FAS 109 and the international standard in IAS 12 (revised), prohibits the discounting of future income tax assets and liabilities.[22] The issue of discounting remains a contentious one that requires resolution on a broader level.

REVISION OF FUTURE TAX RATES

When a change in the tax rate is enacted (or substantively enacted) into law, its effect on the existing future income tax asset and liability accounts should be recorded immediately as an adjustment to income tax expense in the period of the change.

Assume that on December 10, 1997 a new income tax rate is enacted that lowers the corporate rate from 40% to 35%, effective January 1, 1999. If Hostel Co. has one temporary difference at the beginning of 1997 related to $3 million of excess capital cost allowance, then it has a Future Income Tax Liability account with a balance of $1,200,000 ($3,000,000 × 40%) at January 1, 1997. If taxable amounts related to this difference are scheduled to occur equally in 1998, 1999, and 2000, the future tax liability at the end of 1997 is $1,100,000, as computed below.

EXHIBIT 19-18 HOSTEL CO.

	1998	1999	2000	Total
Future taxable amounts	$1,000,000	$1,000,000	$1,000,000	$3,000,000
Tax rate	40%	35%	35%	
Future income tax liability	$ 400,000	$ 350,000	$ 350,000	$1,100,000

An entry is made at the end of 1997 to recognize the decrease of $100,000 ($1,200,000 − $1,100,000) in the future tax liability.

Future Income Tax Liability	100,000	
Future Income Tax Benefit		100,000

Separate disclosure of this component of future income tax expense is suggested, but not required by Section 3465.

---

[21] Examples of tax incentives include the small business deduction, the manufacturing and processing profits deduction, and the resource allowance deduction.

[22] *CICA Handbook*, Section 3465, par. .57.

Basic corporate tax rates do not change often and, therefore, the current rate will usually be employed. However, provincial rates, foreign tax rates and surcharges on all levels of income affect the effective rate and may require adjustments to the future tax accounts.

ACCOUNTING FOR INCOME TAX LOSS CARRYOVER BENEFITS

A **loss for income tax purposes** or **tax loss** occurs in a year when tax-deductible expenses and losses exceed taxable revenues and gains. An inequitable tax burden would result if companies were taxed during profitable periods without receiving any tax relief during periods of losses. Therefore, a company pays no income taxes for a year in which it incurs a tax loss. In addition, the tax laws permit taxpayers to use a tax loss of one year to offset taxable income of other years. This tax-averaging is accomplished through the tax loss carryback and carryforward provisions of income tax legislation, which allows taxpayers to benefit from tax losses either by recovering taxes previously paid or by reducing taxes that will otherwise be payable.

A corporation may elect to carry the tax loss back against taxable income of the immediately preceding three years, which is a **loss carryback.** Alternatively, it may elect to carry it forward to the seven years that immediately follow the loss, which is a **loss carryforward.** Or, it may elect to do both. The following diagram illustrates the carryover periods, assuming a tax loss is incurred in 1998.

ILLUSTRATION 19-3

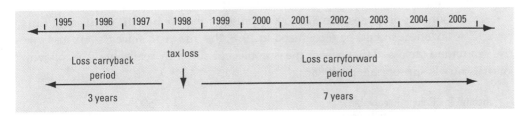

If a loss is carried back, it must be applied against the earliest available income. The benefit from a loss carryback is the recovery of some or all of the taxes paid in those years. The tax returns for the preceding years are refiled, the current year tax loss is deducted from the previously reported taxable income, and a revised amount of income tax payable for each year is determined. This is compared with the taxes paid for each applicable preceding year, and the government is asked to refund the difference.

If a corporation elects to carry the loss forward instead, or if the full amount of the loss could not be absorbed in the carryback period, the tax loss can be used to offset taxable income in the future—thereby reducing or eliminating taxes that would otherwise be payable in those years.

The decision on how to use a tax loss will depend on factors such as its size, results of the previous years' operations, past and anticipated future tax rates, and other factors in which management sees the greatest tax advantage.

Operating losses are relatively common and can be substantial.[23] Companies that have suffered substantial losses are often attractive merger candidates because, in certain cases, the acquirer may use these losses to reduce its taxable income and, therefore, its income taxes. In a sense, a company that has suffered substantial losses may find itself worth more "dead" than "alive" because of the economic value related to the tax benefit that may be derived from its losses by another company.

The following sections discuss the accounting treatment of loss carrybacks and carryforwards recommended in *CICA Handbook* Section 3465.

---

[23] *Financial Reporting in Canada — 1995* indicates that of the 300 companies surveyed from 1991 to 1994, between 25 and 60 companies each year disclosed tax recoveries from the carryback of current year's losses. As well, for each of these years, between 104 and 117 companies disclosed potential tax recoveries due to loss carryforwards.

LOSS CARRYBACK ILLUSTRATED

OBJECTIVE 8
Apply accounting procedures for a tax loss carryback.

To illustrate the accounting procedures for tax loss carrybacks, assume that Groh Inc. experienced the following.

EXHIBIT 19-19 GROH INC.

Year	Taxable Income or (Loss)	Tax Rate	Tax Paid
1994	$ 75,000	30%	$22,500
1995	50,000	35%	17,500
1996	100,000	30%	30,000
1997	200,000	40%	80,000
1998	(500,000)	—	–0–

The taxable incomes and tax loss were the same as the amounts reported on the income statement in each year: that is, there were no temporary differences at any year end. In 1998, Groh Inc. incurred a tax loss that it elects to carry back. The carryback is applied first to 1995, the *third year preceding the loss year*. Any remaining unused loss can then be applied to 1996 and then to 1997. Accordingly, Groh would file amended tax returns for each of the years 1995, 1996, and 1997, receiving refunds for $127,500 ($17,500 + $30,000 + $80,000) of taxes paid in those years.

For accounting purposes, the $127,500 represents the **tax benefit of the loss carryback**. This tax effect should be recognized in 1998, the loss year, since the tax loss gives rise to a refund (an asset) that is both measurable and currently realizable. The following journal entry is appropriate for 1998.

Income Tax Refund Receivable	127,500	
Current Income Tax Benefit		127,500

The Income Tax Refund Receivable is reported on the balance sheet as a current asset at December 31, 1998. The tax benefit is reported on the income statement for 1998 as follows.

EXHIBIT 19-20 GROH INC.

PARTIAL INCOME STATEMENT FOR 1998

Loss before income taxes	$(500,000)
Income tax benefit	
Current benefit due to loss carryback	127,500
Net loss	$(372,500)

If the tax loss carried back to the three preceding years is less than the taxable income of those three years, the only entry required is the one indicated above. In the Groh Inc. example, however, the $500,000 tax loss for 1998 exceeds the $350,000 total taxable income from the three preceding years; the remaining $150,000 loss therefore remains to be carried forward.

OBJECTIVE 9
Apply accounting procedures and disclosure requirements for a tax loss carryforward.

LOSS CARRYFORWARD ILLUSTRATED

If a tax loss is not fully absorbed through a carryback, or if it is decided not to carry the loss back, it can be carried forward for up to seven years. Because carryforwards are used to offset future taxable income, the **tax benefit associated with a loss carryforward** is represented by future tax savings, reductions in taxes in the future that would otherwise be payable. Realization of the future tax benefit is dependent upon the existence of future taxable income, the prospect of which may be highly uncertain.

The accounting issue, then, is whether the tax effect of a loss carryforward should be recognized in the loss year when the potential benefits arise, or in future years when the benefits are actually realized. The AcSB, in Section 3465, takes the position that the potential benefit associated with unused tax losses meets the definition of an asset and that the benefit should be recognized to the extent that it is more likely than not that future taxable income will be available against which the losses and reductions can be utilized.[23]

When it is determined that a tax loss carryforward is more likely than not to result in economic benefits in the future, it should be accounted for as if it were a deductible temporary difference: a future income tax asset should be recognized that is equal to the expected benefit.

Future Taxable Income More Likely Than Not. To illustrate the accounting for an income tax loss carryforward, the Groh Inc. example is continued. In 1998, after carrying back as much of the loss as possible to the three preceding years, the company has a $150,000 tax loss available to carry forward. Assuming the company determines it is more likely than not that it will generate sufficient taxable income in the future so that the benefit of the loss can be realized, Groh records a future tax asset to recognize the benefit of the loss. If a rate of 40% is expected to apply to future years, the amount of the asset recognized is $60,000 ($150,000 × 40%). The 1998 journal entries to record the benefits of the carryback and carryforward are as follows.

To recognize benefit of loss carryback

Income Tax Refund Receivable	127,500	
Current Income Tax Benefit		127,500

To recognize benefit of loss carryforward

Future Income Tax Asset	60,000	
Future Income Tax Benefit		60,000

The income tax refund receivable of $127,500 will be realized soon after the tax return is filed as a refund of taxes paid in the past. The Future Income Tax Asset account is a measure of the benefit of the future tax savings. The two accounts credited are contra income tax expense items, which appear on the income statement as shown below.

EXHIBIT 19-21 GROH INC.

PARTIAL INCOME STATEMENT FOR 1998

Loss before income taxes		$(500,000)
Income tax benefit		
Current benefit due to loss carryback	$127,500	
Future benefit due to loss carryforward	60,000	187,500
Net loss		$(312,500)

The $127,500 *current tax benefit* is the income tax refundable for the year. The $60,000 is the *future tax benefit* for the year that results from an increase in the future tax asset.

---

[23] *CICA Handbook*, Section 3465, par. .24. This represents a significant change from the requirements of Section 3470, which require "virtual certainty" of future realization before the benefit of a tax loss carryforward can be recognized as an asset.

For 1999, assume that Groh Inc. returns to profitability and has taxable income of $200,000 from the year's operations, subject to a 40% tax rate. In 1999 Groh Inc. realizes the benefits of the entire $150,000 tax loss carryforward, which was recognized for accounting purposes in 1998. The income tax payable for 1999 is computed as follows.

EXHIBIT 19-22 GROH INC.

Taxable income prior to loss carryforward	$200,000
Loss carryforward deduction	(150,000)
Taxable income for 1999	50,000
Tax rate	40%
Income tax payable for 1999	$ 20,000

The journal entries to record income taxes in 1999 are as follows.

Current Income Tax Expense	20,000	
Income Tax Payable ($50,000 × 40%)		20,000
Future Income Tax Expense	60,000	
Future Income Tax Asset ($150,000 × 40%)		60,000

The first entry records the income taxes payable for 1999 and is the basis for current income tax expense. The second entry records the utilization of the future income tax asset.

The 1999 income statement below illustrates that the 1999 income tax expense is based on 1999's reported income. The benefit of the tax loss is not reported in 1999; the benefit was reported previously in 1998.

EXHIBIT 19-23 GROH INC.

PARTIAL INCOME STATEMENT FOR 1999

Income before income taxes		$200,000
Income tax expense		
Current	$20,000	
Future	60,000	80,000
Net income		$120,000

Future Taxable Income Not Likely. Return to the Groh Inc. example and 1998. A tax asset (Income Tax Refund Receivable) was recognized in 1998 because the ability to carry back the loss and recover income taxes paid in the past provides evidence that benefits related to $350,000 of the loss will be realized. Assume now that the future of the company is uncertain and it is determined at December 31, 1998 that there is insufficient evidence about the availability of future taxable income to recognize an income tax asset and benefit related to the remaining $150,000 of income tax losses. In this case, the only 1998 income tax entry is as follows.

Income Tax Refund Receivable	127,500	
Current Income Tax Benefit		127,500

The presentation in the following income statement indicates that only the benefit related to the loss carryback is recognized. The unrecognized potential tax benefit and related unrecognized future income tax asset associated with the remaining $150,000 of tax losses is relevant information for financial statement readers and therefore the amounts and expiry dates of unrecognized income tax assets related to the carryforward of unused tax losses must be disclosed. Such information is useful as it makes readers aware of the possibility of future benefits (reduced future income tax outflows) from the loss, even though the likelihood of realization of these benefits was not sufficient to be accorded formal recognition in the body of the statements.

EXHIBIT 19-24 GROH INC.

PARTIAL INCOME STATEMENT FOR 1998

Loss before income taxes	$(500,000)
Income tax benefit	
Current benefit due to loss carryback	127,500
Net loss	$(372,500)

In 1999, assume the company performs better than expected, generating taxable income of $200,000 from its annual operations. After applying the $150,000 loss carryforward, tax is payable on only $50,000 income. With a tax rate of 40%, the following entry is made:

Current Income Tax Expense	20,000	
Income Tax Payable ($50,000 × 40%)		20,000

This entry recognizes the taxes currently payable in the year. Because the potential tax benefit associated with the loss carryforward was not recognized in 1998 as an asset (a future income tax asset), the tax benefit is recognized in 1999, the year it is realized. The $20,000 current tax expense is made up of two components: income taxes of $80,000 accrued on the 1999 income of $200,000, and a $60,000 tax benefit due to realization of the unrecorded loss carryforward. Separate disclosure of these components is suggested by Section 3465, but is not required.

The 1999 income statement reporting the components of current income tax expense is illustrated below.

EXHIBIT 19-25 GROH INC.

PARTIAL INCOME STATEMENT FOR 1999

Income before income taxes		$200,000
Income tax expense		
Current expense	$ 80,000	
Current benefit due to loss carryforward	(60,000)	20,000
Net income		$180,000

If 1999's taxable income had been less than $150,000, only a portion of the unrecorded and unused tax loss could have been applied. The entry to record 1999 income taxes would have been similar to the entry above. A note to the financial statements would be provided to disclose the remaining amount and expiry date of the unused loss.

Section 3465 requires that the carrying amount of all future income tax assets (including those with zero balances) be reviewed. Where it is no longer likely that taxable income will be available in the future to allow the recorded benefit of the tax loss to be realized, the future tax asset should be written down. Where it is determined that taxable income will be available in the future to allow a company to benefit from previously unrecognized tax losses, a future tax asset should be recorded.[25]

---

[25] *CICA Handbook*, Section 3465, par. .31(b).

RECOGNITION OF FUTURE TAX ASSETS

OBJECTIVE 10
Identify evidence to consider in determining if future taxable income is likely to be available.

Section 3465 recommends the recognition of a future income tax asset for all deductible temporary differences and for the carryforward of unused tax losses and income tax reductions, *to the extent that it is more likely than not that the future income tax asset will be realized, i.e., that taxable income will be available against which the deductible temporary differences, unused tax losses, or income tax reductions can be utilized.*[26] Guidance is provided on how to determine if it is more likely than not that future taxable income will be available, and the need to exercise judgement in weighing the impact of evidence is emphasized.

All positive and negative information should be considered in determining the extent to which a future tax asset should be recognized. The following possible *sources of taxable income* may be available under the tax law to realize a tax benefit for deductible temporary differences and tax loss carryovers.[27]

EXHIBIT 19-26

TAXABLE INCOME SOURCES

a. Future reversals of existing taxable temporary differences.

b. Future taxable income exclusive of reversing temporary differences and loss carryforwards.

c. Taxable income in prior carryback years.

d. **Tax-planning strategies** that would, if necessary, be implemented to realize a future income tax asset. Tax strategies are actions that are prudent, feasible, and that would be applied.

Forming a conclusion to recognize a future tax asset is difficult when there is negative evidence such as cumulative losses in recent years. Other examples of negative evidence include, but are not limited to:[28]

EXHIBIT 19-27

NEGATIVE EVIDENCE

a. A history of tax losses or income tax reductions expiring unused.

b. Losses expected in early future years (by a presently profitable entity).

c. Unsettled circumstances that, if unfavourably resolved, would adversely affect future operations and profit levels on a continuing basis in future years.

d. A carryback, carryforward period that is so brief that it would limit realization of tax benefits, particularly if the enterprise operates in a traditionally cyclical business.

---

[26] *CICA Handbook*, Section 3465, par. .24. Three exceptions are identified: temporary differences arising from the transfer of assets within a consolidated group, those arising from the translation of the dollar cost of the net non-monetary assets of an integrated foreign operation, and those arising from investments in subsidiaries and joint ventures where it is apparent that the differences will not reverse in the foreseeable future.

[27] *Ibid.*, pars. .25 and .26. The value assigned to the future tax asset would take into account the cost of implementing the tax strategy.

[28] *Ibid.*, par. .27.

Examples of positive evidence that might support a conclusion to recognize a future tax asset when there is negative evidence include the following.[29]

EXHIBIT 19-28

POSITIVE EVIDENCE

a. Sufficient existing taxable temporary differences that would result in taxable amounts against which tax losses or reductions can be applied.

b. Existing contracts or firm sales backlog that will produce more than enough taxable income to realize the future tax asset based on existing sale prices and cost structures.

c. An excess of fair value over the tax basis of the entity's net assets in an amount sufficient to realize the future tax asset.

d. A strong earnings history exclusive of the loss that created the future deductible amount coupled with evidence indicating that the loss is an aberration rather than a continuing condition.

INTRAPERIOD TAX ALLOCATION

OBJECTIVE 11
Explain the need for and be able to apply intraperiod tax allocation.

Another objective of accounting for income taxes is identified in Section 3465.07: to reflect the cost or benefit related to income tax assets and liabilities in a manner consistent with the transaction or event giving rise to the asset or liability. In general, this refers the fact that the cost or benefit of current and future income taxes of the current period related to discontinued operations, extraordinary items, adjustments reported in retained earnings, and capital transactions should be reported with the item to which it relates. Otherwise, the cost or benefit should be included before income or loss before discontinued operations and extraordinary items, as should any future tax expense or benefit resulting from a change in the net future income tax asset or liability due to changes in tax rates.[30] This approach to allocating taxes *within* the financial statements of the current period is referred to as **intraperiod tax allocation**. *Interperiod tax allocation*, on the other hand, reflects the allocation of taxes *between years*.

To illustrate, assume that Copy Doctor Inc. has an ordinary loss from continuing operations of $500,000. The tax rate is 35%. In addition, the company has an extraordinary gain of $900,000, of which $210,000 is not taxable. Accounting and taxable income, and income taxes payable are computed below.

EXHIBIT 19-29   COPY DOCTOR INC.

	Ordinary Income (Loss)	Extraordinary Gain (Loss)	Total
Accounting income (loss)	($500,000)	$ 900,000	$ 400,000
Less nontaxable gain	—	(210,000)	(210,000)
Taxable income (loss)	($500,000)	$ 690,000	$ 190,000
Tax rate	35%	35%	
Income tax payable	($175,000)	$ 241,500	$ 66,500

---

[29] *CICA Handbook*, Section 3465, par. .28.

[30] *Ibid.*, pars. .63 and .64.

Income taxes are reported in the income statement as shown below.

EXHIBIT 19-30 COPY DOCTOR INC.	
Loss before income taxes and extraordinary item	($5,00,000)
Current income tax benefit from operating loss	175,000
Loss before extraordinary item	(325,000)
Extraordinary gain (net of $241,500 tax)	658,500
Net income	$333,500

FINANCIAL STATEMENT PRESENTATION AND DISCLOSURE REQUIREMENTS

BALANCE SHEET PRESENTATION

OBJECTIVE 12
Identify the reporting and disclosure requirements for corporate income taxes.

Income tax assets and income tax liabilities are required to be reported separately from other assets and liabilities on the balance sheet, and current tax assets and liabilities are reported separately from future tax assets and liabilities.[31]

Where an entity differentiates between current and noncurrent assets and liabilities on its statement of financial position, future income tax assets and liabilities (related to the same taxable entity and taxation authority) should be classified and reported as one net current amount and one net noncurrent amount. *An individual future tax liability or asset is classified as current or noncurrent based on the classification of the related asset or liability for financial reporting purposes; those not related to a liability or asset, such as a future tax asset related to a tax loss carryforward, should be classified according to the expected reversal date of the temporary difference or the date on which the benefit is expected to be realized.*[32]

Most companies engage in a large number of transactions that give rise to future income taxes. The balances in the future income tax accounts should be analyzed and classified on the balance sheet in two categories: one for the *net current amount*, and one for the *net noncurrent amount*. This procedure is summarized as follows.

1. *Classify the amounts as current or noncurrent.* If they are related to a specific asset or liability, they should be classified in the same manner as the related asset or liability. If not so related, they should be classified on the basis of the expected reversal date.

2. *Determine the net current amount* by summing the various future tax assets and liabilities classified as current. If the net result is an asset, report on the balance sheet as a current asset; if a liability, report as a current liability.

3. *Determine the net noncurrent amount* by summing the various future tax assets and liabilities classified as noncurrent. If the net result is an asset, report on the balance sheet as a noncurrent asset included with "Other Assets"; if a liability, report as a long-term liability.

To illustrate, assume that K. Scott Company has four future tax items at December 31, 1998. An analysis reveals the following.

---

[31] *CICA Handbook*, Section 3465, par. .86.

[32] *Ibid.*, pars. .87 and .88.

EXHIBIT 19-31   K. SCOTT COMPANY

Temporary Difference	Resulting Future Tax (Asset)	Liability	Related Balance Sheet Account	Classification
1. Rent collected in advance: recognized when earned for accounting purposes and when received for tax purposes.	$(42,000)		Unearned Rent	Current
2. Use of straight-line depreciation for accounting purposes and accelerated depreciation for tax purposes.		$214,000	Equipment	Noncurrent
3. Recognition of profits on instalment sales during period of sale for accounting purposes and during period of collection for tax purposes.		45,000	Instalment Accounts Receivable	Current
4. Warranty liabilities: recognized for accounting purposes at time of sale; for tax purposes at time paid.	(12,000)		Estimated Liability Under Warranties	Current
Totals	$(54,000)	$259,000		

The future taxes to be classified as current net to a $9,000 asset ($42,000 + $12,000 − $45,000), and the future taxes to be classified as noncurrent net to a $214,000 liability. Consequently, future income taxes appear on the December 31, 1998 balance sheet as shown below.

EXHIBIT 19-32   K. SCOTT COMPANY

Current assets	
Future income tax asset	$ 9,000
Long-term liabilities	
Future income tax liability	$214,000

As indicated earlier, a future tax asset or liability *may not be related* to an asset or liability for financial reporting purposes. One example is research costs that are recognized as expenses when incurred for financial reporting purposes, but that are deferred and deducted in later years for tax purposes. Another example is a realizable tax loss carryforward. In both cases, a future tax asset is recorded, but there is no related, identifiable asset or liability for financial reporting purposes. In these situations, future income taxes should be classified according to the *expected reversal date* of the temporary difference *or the date the tax benefit is expected to be realized*. That is, the tax effect of the temporary differences expected to reverse or be realized next year should be classified as current and the remainder should be reported as noncurrent.

Income tax payable is reported as a current liability on the balance sheet. Because corporations are required to make instalment payments to Revenue Canada through the year, a debit balance may result in this account, which is reported as a current asset called Prepaid Income Taxes. Income Tax Refund Receivable, resulting from carrying the current year's tax loss back against previous years' taxable income, is also reported as a current asset. Current income tax liabilities and current income tax assets would ordinarily be netted.[33]

---

[33] *CICA Handbook*, Section 3465, par. . 88. Offsetting is permitted only if they relate to the same taxable entity and the same taxation authority. This issue has greater significance for consolidated financial statements.

INCOME STATEMENT PRESENTATION

In addition to requiring the total income tax expense related to income or loss before discontinued operations and extraordinary items to be presented on the face of the income statement, the following items require separate disclosure.

1. Current income tax expense, and the future income tax expense related to income or loss before discontinued operations and extraordinary items; and

2. Income tax expense related to discontinued operations and to extraordinary items.

Disclosure of the following major components of income tax expense included in income or loss before discontinued operations and extraordinary items may be useful to financial statement readers, but is not required.

1. Current income tax expense before any reduction for previously unrecognized income tax reductions;

2. Future income tax expense before any components identified below;

3. The amount of future income tax expense related to changes in income tax rates and laws or the imposition of new taxes;

4. The reduction in income tax expense from the recognition of a previously unrecognized tax loss, tax credit, or temporary difference;

5. Future income tax expense arising from the write-down of a future income tax asset when it is no longer more likely than not that future taxable income will be available.[34]

OTHER DISCLOSURES

For all entities, separate disclosure is required of the cost of current and future income tax expense related to items charged or credited to equity, the amount and expiry date of unused tax losses and reductions, and the amount of deductible temporary differences for which no future income asset has been recognized.[35]

For entities with debt or equity securities traded in a public market (a stock exchange or over-the-counter market) that are required to file financial statements with a securities commission, entities that provide financial statements in connection with the issue of securities in a public market, life insurance companies, deposit-taking institutions, and cooperative business enterprises, the following additional disclosures are required.

1. The nature and tax effect of the temporary differences, unused tax losses, and unused tax reductions that give rise to future income tax assets and future income tax liabilities, with disclosure of significant offsetting items included in the future tax asset and liability balances;

2. The major components of income tax expense included in the determination of net income or loss for the period before discontinued operations and extraordinary items;

3. A reconciliation of the income tax expense related to net income or loss for the period before discontinued operations and extraordinary items, to the statutory income tax rate or dollar amount, including the nature and amount using percentages or dollar amounts of each significant reconciling item. Significant offsetting items should be disclosed even if there is no variation from the statutory rate.[36]

---

[34] *CICA Handbook*, Section 3465, pars. .85 and .93.

[35] *Ibid.*, par. .91.

[36] *Ibid.*, par. .92.

These latter disclosures are required for several reasons, some of which are discussed below.

Assessment of Quality of Earnings. Investors seeking to assess the quality of a company's earnings are interested in the reconciliation of pretax accounting income to taxable income. Earnings that are enhanced by a favourable tax effect should be examined carefully, particularly if the tax effect is nonrecurring.

Better Predictions of Future Cash Flows. Examination of the future portion of income tax expense provides information as to whether taxes payable are likely to be higher or lower in the future. A close examination may disclose the company's policy regarding capitalization of costs, recognition of revenue, and other policies giving rise to a difference between income on the financial statements and taxable income. As a result, it may be possible to predict upcoming reductions in future liabilities leading to a loss of liquidity because actual tax payments will be higher than the tax expense reported on the income statement.

Input in Setting Government Policy. Understanding the amount companies currently pay and the effective tax rate is helpful to government policymakers. In the early 1970s when the oil companies were believed to have earned excess profits, many politicians and other interested parties attempted to determine their effective tax rates. Unfortunately, at that time such information was not available in published reports.

Section 3465 concludes by requiring that entities that are not subject to income tax because income is taxed directly to their owners must disclose this fact and, if public enterprises, report their net temporary differences at the balance sheet date.

The recommendations included in *Handbook* Section 3465 represent a significant change in approach and terminology from the requirements of Sections 3470 and 3471. Because the new requirements are not effective until the year 2000, no Canadian examples exist to illustrate their application. The income tax disclosures provided below of the U.S. company PepsiCo, Inc. for its year ended December 31, 1995, however, are similar to those that will be required in Canada in the near future. Notice that *SFAS No. 109* uses the term **deferred income tax** instead of **future income tax**. These terms have almost identical meanings.

EXHIBIT 19-33 PEPSICO, INC.

Note 11 – Income Taxes
The details of the provision for income taxes on income before cumulative effect of accounting changes are set forth below:

		1995	1994
Current:	Federal	$ 706	$642
	Foreign	154	174
	State	77	131
		937	947
Deferred:	Federal	(92)	(64)
	Foreign	(18)	(2)
	State	(1)	(1)
		(111)	(67)
		$ 826	$880

In 1993, a charge of $30 million ($0.04 per share) was recorded to increase net deferred tax liabilities as of the beginning of 1993 for a 1% statutory income tax rate increase under 1993 U.S. Federal tax legislation.

A reconciliation of the U.S. Federal statutory tax rate to PepsiCo's effective tax rate is set forth below:

	1995	1994
U.S. Federal statutory tax rate	35.0%	35.0%
State income tax, net of Federal tax benefit	2.0	3.2
Effect of lower taxes on foreign income (including Puerto Rico and Ireland)	(3.0)	(5.4)
Adjustment to the beginning-of-the-year deferred tax assets valuation allowance	–	(1.3)
Reduction of prior years' foreign accruals	–	–
Settlement of prior years' audit issues	(4.1)	–
Effect of 1993 tax legislation on deferred income taxes	–	–
Effect of adopting SFAS 121	1.4	–
Nondeductible amortization of U.S. goodwill	1.0	0.8
Other, net	1.7	0.7
Effective tax rate	34.0%	33.0%

EXHIBIT 19-33 (Continued)

The details of the 1995 and 1994 deferred tax liabilities (assets) are set forth below:

	1995	1994
Intangible assets other than nondeductible goodwill	$ 1,631	$ 1,628
Property, plant and equipment	496	506
Safe harbor leases	165	171
Zero coupon notes	100	111
Other	257	337
Gross deferred tax liabilities	2,649	2,753
Net operating loss carryforwards	(418)	(306)
Postretirement benefits	(248)	(248)
Casualty claims	(119)	(71)
Various accrued liabilities and other	(790)	(637)
Gross deferred tax assets	(1,575)	(1,262)
Deferred tax assets valuation allowance	498	319
Net deferred tax liability	$ 1,572	$ 1,810
Included in		
Prepaid expenses, taxes and other current assets	$ (313)	$ (167)
Other current liabilities	–	4
Deferred income taxes	1,885	1,973
	$ 1,572	$ 1,810

The valuation allowance related to deferred tax assets increased by $179 million in 1995, primarily resulting from additions related to current year operating losses in a number of state and foreign jurisdictions and the adoption of SFAS 121.

Net operating loss carryforwards totaling $2.3 billion at year-end 1995 are available to reduce future tax of certain subsidiaries and are related to a number of state and foreign jurisdictions. Of these carryforwards, $16 million expire in 1996, $2.1 billion expire at various times between 1997 and 2010 and $173 million may be carried forward indefinitely.

SOME CONCEPTUAL QUESTIONS

OBJECTIVE 13
Identify outstanding issues within the liability method.

The asset-liability method is the approach that the AcSB deems most appropriate to record future income taxes. However, some conceptual questions remain. Three important issues are identified below.

1. *Failure to discount.* Without discounting the asset or liability, that is, failing to consider its present value, financial statements do not indicate the appropriate benefit of tax deferral or the burden of tax prepayment. Thus, comparability of the financial statements is impaired because a dollar related to short-term deferral appears to be of the same value as a dollar of longer-term deferral. In addition, the measurement of tax assets and liabilities is not consistent with that of other assets and liabilities with delayed payment terms.

2. *Classification issue.* Consistent with the asset-liability approach, future tax assets and liabilities should be classified on the balance sheet based on when they will be realized or settled rather than based on the classification of the asset or liability to which they relate. Many believe that future taxes related to temporary differences that reverse in the next period should be reported as current.

3. ***Dual criteria for recognition of future income tax asset.*** Some accountants believe that future deductible amounts that arise from tax loss carryforwards are different from future deductible amounts that arise from normal operations. One rationale provided is that a future tax asset that arises from normal operations results in a tax prepayment—a prepaid tax asset. In the case of loss carryforwards, no tax prepayment has been made.

Others argue that realization of a loss carryforward is less likely—and thus should require a more severe test—than for a net deductible amount that arises from normal operations. Some have suggested that the test be changed to a test more stringent than "more likely than not," while others have suggested that future income tax assets should never be established for loss carryforwards.

The above controversies assume that the asset-liability approach is used. Others argue that completely different types of approaches should be used to report future income taxes. These approaches are discussed in Appendix 19A to this chapter.

COMPREHENSIVE ILLUSTRATION OF INTERPERIOD TAX ALLOCATION

The basics of comprehensive interperiod tax allocation applying the liability approach have been explained and illustrated in this chapter. A comprehensive illustration is now provided that follows a company with several temporary differences through two complete years. Careful study of this material should enrich your understanding of the concepts and procedures presented earlier.

First Year — 1998

Allman Company, which began operations at the beginning of 1998, produces various products on a contract basis. Each contract generates a gross profit of $80,000. Some of Allman's contracts provide for the customer to pay on an instalment basis whereby one-fifth of the contract revenue is collected in the year of the sale and in each of the following four years. Gross profit is recognized in the year of completion for financial reporting purposes (accrual basis) and in the year cash is collected for tax purposes (instalment basis).

Presented below is information related to Allman's operations for 1998.

1. In 1998, the company completed seven contracts that allow the customer to pay on an instalment basis. The related gross profit of $560,000 on instalment sales of $1,500,000 (to be collected at $300,000 per year beginning in 1998) is recognized for financial reporting purposes, whereas only $112,000 of gross profit on instalment sales is reported on the 1998 tax return. The related accounts receivable in the accounting records and for tax purposes, and future taxable amounts covering the five-year period, are summarized below.

EXHIBIT 19-34

| | Accounting | | Tax | | | |
| | Gross Profit | Receivable | Gross Profit | Deferred | Receivable | Net |
Year	Recognized	Balance	Recognized	Gross Profit	Balance	Receivable
1998	$560,000	$1,200,000	$112,000	$(448,000)	$1,200,000	$752,000
1999	—	900,000	112,000	(336,000)	900,000	564,000
2000	—	600,000	112,000	(224,000)	600,000	376,000
2001	—	300,000	112,000	(112,000)	300,000	188,000
2002	—	—	112,000	—	—	—
	$560,000		$560,000			

2. At the beginning of 1998, Allman Company purchased depreciable assets with a cost of $540,000. For financial reporting purposes, Allman depreciates these assets using the straight-line method over a six-year service life. For tax purposes, the assets fall into capital cost allowance (CCA) Class 8, permitting a 20% rate, and for the first year the half-year rule is applied. The depreciation and net value schedules for both financial reporting and tax purposes follow.

EXHIBIT 19-35

| | Accounting | | Tax | |
Year	Depreciation	Carrying Value, End of Year	CCA	Undepreciated Capital Cost, End of Year
1998	$ 90,000	$450,000	$ 54,000	$486,000
1999	90,000	360,000	97,200	388,800
2000	90,000	270,000	77,760	311,040
2001+	270,000	—	311,040	—
	$540,000		$540,000	

3. The company guarantees its product for two years from the date of completion of the contract. During 1998, the product warranty liability accrued for financial reporting purposes was $200,000 and the amount paid for the satisfaction of the warranty liability was $44,000. The remaining $156,000 is expected to be settled by expenditures of $56,000 in 1999 and $100,000 in 2000.

4. At December 31, 1998 the company accrued nontaxable dividends receivable of $28,000, the only dividend revenue reported for the year.

5. During 1998 nondeductible fines and penalties of $26,000 were paid.

6. Accounting income for 1998 before the provision for income taxes is $412,000.

7. The enacted tax rate for 1998 is 50%, and for 1999 and future years is 40%.

8. Allman Company has a December 31 year end.

9. The company is expected to have taxable income in all future years.

1998 Taxable Income, Income Tax Payable, and Current Income Tax Expense. The first step in determining Allman Company's income tax payable for 1998 is to calculate its taxable income. The computation—which starts with the income reported on the income statement—is reconciled to taxable income. The taxes levied on the taxable amount are the taxes payable and the current income tax expense for the year.

EXHIBIT 19-36

Accounting income, 1998	$412,000
Adjustments:	
Excess gross profit per books ($560,000 − $112,000)	(448,000)
Excess depreciation per books ($90,000 − $54,000)	36,000
Excess warranty expense per books ($200,000 − $44,000)	156,000
Nontaxable revenue—dividends	(28,000)
Nondeductible expenses—fines and penalties	26,000
Taxable income, 1998	$154,000
Income tax payable (current tax expense) for 1998	
$154,000 × 50%	$ 77,000

Future Income Tax Assets and Liabilities at December 31, 1998, and 1998 Future Income Tax Expense. Because the future income tax component of income tax expense for the current year is the difference between the opening and closing balance of the net future tax asset or liability account, the next step is to calculate the future tax asset and liability amounts. These represent the tax effects of the temporary differences at December 31, 1998. The following illustration identifies those assets and liabilities with a tax basis that differs from their carrying values and determines the net temporary difference. From this, the net future income tax asset or liability is calculated and compared with the opening balance. The difference is the future income tax expense or benefit for the current year.

EXHIBIT 19-37

	Carrying Value	Tax Basis	Taxable (Deductible) Temporary Difference
Receivables (net)	$1,200,000	$752,000	$448,000
Dividends receivable	28,000	28,000	—
Depreciable assets	450,000	486,000	(36,000)
Liability for warranties	(156,000)	—	(156,000)
Net taxable temporary difference			$256,000
Future tax liability: $448,000 at 40%			$179,200
Future tax asset: ($36,000 + $156,000) at 40%			(76,800)
Net future tax liability, December 31,1998			102,400
Less: Opening future tax liability			–0–
Future income tax expense (benefit) —1998			$102,400

For the instalment receivables, the tax basis is $752,000, equal to the uncollected balance of $1,200,000 reduced by the deferred or unrecognized gross profit of $448,000 as shown in Exhibit 19-37. When the carrying amount of the receivable is recovered in the future at its carrying value of $1,200,000, $448,000 will have to be added into future taxable income. This is a taxable temporary difference that requires the payment of income tax in the future.

The difference between the carrying value of the dividend receivable of $28,000 and its tax value of $28,000 is zero. When the cost of the asset is not deductible in determining taxable income, and any proceeds on disposal are not included in taxable income, the tax basis of the asset is equal to the carrying amount. When the $28,000 receivable is recovered, no amount will be added to taxable income because the dividend is not taxable.

The $450,000 carrying value of the depreciable assets is less than the $486,000 undepreciated capital cost, indicating that if $450,000 is recovered from the asset, for tax purposes an additional $36,000 would be deductible in determining the taxable amount. This is a deductible temporary difference that results in the recognition of a future tax asset.

The only temporary difference between the carrying and tax values of liabilities relates to the warranty liability recognized for accounting purposes but not for tax. When the liability is settled in the future for $156,000, this amount will be deductible in calculating future taxable income. The associated benefit or tax asset is recognized in the accounting records in the current period.

The temporary differences for receivables, capital assets, and the warranty liability are combined to produce a net taxable temporary difference of $256,000. The associated future tax liability of $179,200 and future tax asset of $76,800 net to a future tax liability of $102,400. A 40% tax rate is used to calculate the net future tax liability as this is the enacted (or substantively enacted) rate that is expected to apply in future periods when the temporary differences reverse. Because a single tax rate is involved for all future years, the 40% rate can be applied to all temporary differences. If the 40% rate applied only to 1999 and a 38% rate, for example, applied thereafter, a schedule detailing the temporary difference amounts expected to reverse in 1999 would have to be prepared separately from the 2000 and beyond reversals.

When the required December 31, 1998 net future income tax liability of $102,400 is compared to the net balance at the beginning of the year of $0, the difference is the measure of the future income tax component of 1998's income tax expense. An increase in the net tax liability over the period results in an additional expense, whereas a reduction in the net liability would be recognized as a benefit in the current year.

Income Tax Expense and the Accounting Entry for 1998. The total income tax expense for 1998 is calculated by combining the current and future amounts.

EXHIBIT 19-38	
Current tax expense for 1998	$ 77,000
Future tax expense for 1998	102,400
Income tax expense (total) for 1998	$179,400

The journal entries to record income tax payable, the change in the net future tax liability, and income tax expense are as follows.

Current Income Tax Expense	77,000	
Income Tax Payable		77,000
Future Income Tax Expense	102,400	
Future Income Tax Liability		102,400

Financial Statement Presentation. Future tax assets and liabilities are classified as current and noncurrent on the balance sheet based on the classifications of related assets and liabilities. When there is more than one category of future taxes, they are classified into one net current and one net noncurrent amount. The classification of Allman's future tax account at the end of 1998 is shown below.

EXHIBIT 19-39

Balance Sheet Account	Temporary Difference	Resulting Future Tax (Asset)	Liability	Related Account Classification
Instalment receivables	$448,000		$179,200	Current
Depreciable assets	(36,000)	(14,400)		Noncurrent
Liability for warranties	(156,000)	(62,400)		Current
		$(76,800)	$179,200	

For the first temporary difference, the related asset on the balance sheet is the instalment accounts receivable. That asset is classified as a current asset because the company has a trade practice of selling to customers on an instalment basis; hence, the resulting future tax liability is classified as a current liability. The plant assets are classified as noncurrent; therefore, the resulting future tax asset is classified as noncurrent. Since Allman's operating cycle is at least four years in length, the entire $156,000 warranty obligation is classified as a current liability and the related future tax asset of $62,400 is classified as current.[37]

The balance sheet at the end of 1998 reports the following amounts.

EXHIBIT 19-40

Other (noncurrent) assets	
Future income tax asset	$14,400
Current liabilities	
Income tax payable	$77,000
Future income tax liability ($179,200 − $62,400)	116,800

The 1998 income statement reports the following.

EXHIBIT 19-41

Income before income tax		$412,000
Income tax expense		
Current	$ 77,000	
Future	102,400	179,400
Net income		$232,600

[37] If Allman's operating cycle was less than one year in length and the instalment receivables and warranty obligation were classified on the balance sheet partially as current and partially as noncurrent items, then the future tax amounts would have to be allocated between current and noncurrent. A reasonable basis on which to allocate the future tax amounts is to recognize as current assets and liabilities the tax effects of that portion of the temporary differences that will reverse in the next year. The remainder is considered noncurrent. For example, in Allman's case, since $112,000 of the temporary difference related to the instalment receivables is expected to reverse in 1999, the current portion of the related future tax liability is $112,000 × 40% = $44,800; and the noncurrent portion is $179,200 − $44,800 = $134,400. Alternatively, the allocation could be based on the proportion of the asset or liability classified as current and long-term. In this case, $300,000/$1,200,000 or ¼ of $179,200 = $44,800 would be classified as current, the same as the alternative suggested above. Different amounts would result where the temporary differences reverse on a basis different than the method used for the balance sheet classification of the asset or liability.

SECOND YEAR — 1999

1. During 1999 the company collected one-fifth of the sales price from customers for the receivables arising from contracts completed in 1998. Recovery of the remaining receivables is still expected to result in taxable amounts of $112,000 in each of the following three years.

2. In 1999 the company completed four new contracts with a total selling price of $1,000,000 (to be paid in five equal instalments beginning in 1999) and gross profit of $320,000. For financial reporting purposes the full $320,000 is recognized in 1999, whereas for tax purposes the gross profit is deferred and taken into taxable income as the cash is received; that is, one-fifth in 1999 and one-fifth in each of 2000 to 2003. The following table summarizes the differences between what is recorded in the accounting records and what is recognized for tax purposes for the instalment receivables.

EXHIBIT 19-42

	Accounting		Tax			
	Gross Profit	Receivable	Gross Profit	Deferred	Receivable	Net
Year	Recognized	Balance	Recognized	Gross Profit	Balance	Receivable
1998–1998 sales	$560,000	$1,200,000	$112,000	$(448,000)	$1,200,000	$ 752,000
1999–1998 sales	—	900,000	112,000	(336,000)	900,000	564,000
−1999 sales	320,000	800,000	64,000	(256,000)	800,000	544,000
	320,000	1,700,000	176,000	(592,000)	1,700,000	1,108,000
2000–1998 sales	—	600,000	112,000	(224,000)	600,000	376,000
−1999 sales	—	600,000	64,000	(192,000)	600,000	408,000
	—	1,200,000	176,000	(416,000)	1,200,000	784,000
2000 to 2003						
−1998 sales	—	—	224,000	—	—	—
−1999 sales	—	—	192,000	—	—	—
	—	—	416,000	—	—	—

3. During 1999 Allman continued to depreciate the assets acquired in 1998 according to the depreciation and CCA schedules that appear on page 958. Therefore, depreciation expense amounted to $90,000 and CCA of $97,200 was claimed for tax purposes.

4. An analysis at the end of 1999 of the product warranty liability account showed the following activity:

EXHIBIT 19-43

	Accounting				Tax
	Liability,	Expense	Payments under	Liability,	Liability,
	January 1	Recognized	Warranty	December 31	December 31
1998	—	$200,000	$ 44,000	$156,000	—
1999					
−re 1998 sales	$156,000	—	62,000	94,000	—
−re 1999 sales	—	180,000	50,000	130,000	—
	$156,000	$180,000	$112,000	$224,000	$ —

The warranty lapses on the 1998 warranties in 2000 and it is expected that $94,000 of expenditures will be made relative to these warranties in 2000. Of the $130,000 liability relating to 1999 warranties, $50,000 is expected to be disbursed in 2000 and $80,000 in 2001.

5. During 1999, nontaxable dividend revenue was $24,000, none of which was outstanding at year end.

6. A loss of $172,000 was accrued for financial reporting purposes because of pending litigation. This amount is not tax deductible until the period the loss is realized, which is estimated to be 2004.

7. Accounting income for 1999 is $504,800.

8. The tax rate in effect for 1999 is 40%; tax rate increases have been enacted for 2000 and subsequent years at 42%.

1999 Taxable Income, Income Tax Payable, and Current Income Tax Expense. The computation of taxable income, income tax payable, and current income tax expense for 1999 is illustrated below.

EXHIBIT 19-44

Accounting income, 1999		$ 504,800
Adjustments:		
Instalment sales—re 1998 sales	$112,000	
—re 1999 sales ($320,000 − $64,000)	(256,000)	(144,000)
Excess CCA over depreciation ($97,000 − $90,000)		(7,200)
Warranties —re 1998 sales ($62,000 − 0)	(62,000)	
—re 1999 sales ($50,000 − $180,000)	130,000	68,000
Litigation loss accrued		172,000
Nontaxable dividend revenue		(24,000)
Taxable income, 1999		$ 569,600
Income tax payable (current tax expense) for 1999		
$569,600 × 40%		$ 227,840

Future Income Tax Assets and Liabilities at December 31, 1999, and 1999 Future Income Tax Expense. The next step is to list all the assets and liabilities at the end of the year with carrying amounts that differ from their tax bases. From these, temporary differences are identified that are the basis for determining the balance of the net future income tax asset or liability; the change in this amount from the opening balance is the future tax expense or benefit for the current year. These steps are illustrated in Exhibit 19-45 for 1999.

The carrying and tax values are taken from the analysis of each item that starts on page 961. The future tax liability and future tax asset at December 31, 1999 are measured using 42%, the tax rate enacted for 2000 and subsequent years when the temporary differences will reverse. The net future tax liability of $70,224 is lower than the net future tax liability at the end of the preceding year, which results in a future income tax *benefit* of $32,176 being recognized in 1999.

As the major components of income tax expense are required to be disclosed in some cases and are desirable in others, a further analysis can determine how much of the future

EXHIBIT 19-45

	Carrying Value	Tax Basis	Taxable (Deductible) Temporary Difference
Receivables (net)	$1,700,000	$1,108,000	$592,000
Depreciable assets	360,000	388,800	(28,800)
Liability for warranties	(224,000)	—	(224,000)
Loss accrual	(172,000)	—	(172,000)
Net taxable temporary difference			$ 167,200
Future tax liability $592,000 at 42%			$248,640
Future tax asset ($28,800 + $224,000 + $172,000) at 42%			(178,416)
Net future tax liability, Decmeber 31,1999			70,224
Less: Opening future tax liability $256,000 at 40%			(102,400)
Future income tax expense (benefit) –1999			$(32,176)

tax expense is due to a change in the rate of tax used to measure the net future tax liability and how much is due to a change in temporary differences. Because the tax rate for measuring the net future tax liability increased from 40% to 42%, the change in rate results in an increase in the future tax expense. The analysis to explain the $32,176 benefit is as follows.

EXHIBIT 19-46

Future income tax expense (benefit) due to:

- Increase in tax rate:

Opening future tax liability at 40%	$102,400	
Opening future tax liability at 42% ($256,000 × .42)	107,520	$5,120

- Originating and reversing timing differences during 1999:

Opening future tax liability at 42%	107,520	
Ending future tax liability at 42%	70,224	
Decrease in net future tax liability		(37,296)
Change in future income tax liability and future income tax expense (benefit) for 1999		$(32,176)

Income Tax Expense and the Accounting Entry for 1999. The total income tax expense for 1999 of $195,664 is the net of the current tax expense of $227,840 and the future tax benefit of $32,176 as calculated above. The journal entries to record the expense, the payable, and the change in the future tax liability are as follows.

Current Income Tax Expense	227,840	
Income Tax Payable		227,840
Future Income Tax Liability	32,176	
Future Income Tax Benefit		32,176

If information is required on the components of total income tax expense, the following details would be provided.

EXHIBIT 19-47

Future tax expense due to increase in future tax rate	$ 5,120
Future tax benefit from originating and reversing timing differences in 1999	(37,296)
Future tax benefit for 1999	(32,176)
Current tax expense for 1999	227,840
Income tax expense (total) for 1999	$195,664

Financial Statement Presentation. The classification of Allman's future tax accounts at the end of 1999 is as follows.

EXHIBIT 19-48

Balance Sheet Account	Temporary Difference	Resulting Future Tax (Asset)	Liability	Related Account Classification
Instalment receivables	$ 592,000		$248,640	Current
Depreciable assets	(28,800)	(12,096)		Noncurrent
Liability for warranties	(224,000)	(94,080)		Current
Loss accrual	(172,000)	(72,240)		Noncurrent
	$ 167,200	$(178,416)	$248,640	

The new temporary difference introduced in 1999 due to the litigation loss accrual results in a litigation obligation that is classified as a long-term liability. Therefore, the related future tax asset is noncurrent. The balance sheet at December 31, 1999 reports the following amounts.

EXHIBIT 19-49

Other (noncurrent) assets	
Future income tax asset ($12,096 + $72,240)	$ 84,336
Current liabilities	
Income tax payable	$227,840
Future income tax liability ($248,640 − $94,080)	$154,560

The 1999 income statement reports the following.

EXHIBIT 19-50

Income before income tax		$504,800
Income tax expense		
Current	$227,840	
Future	(32,176)*	195,664
Net income		$309,136
*Components may be disclosed		

AND WHAT ABOUT GERMANY?

Accounting for income taxes may differ in other countries. Germany is of particular interest because of its socioeconomic environment which favours conservatism and where the commercial balance sheet is used as a basis for computing taxable income. As a result, most corporations will prepare only one set of financial statements and will record no deferred or future tax on their balance sheet.

In Germany, the so-called "Massgeblichkeitsprinzip" has had great influence on the development and practice of the accounting profession. This principle states that, except for special recognitions and valuation options which are specifically provided for by tax regulations, the treatment of a transaction shall be the same in the tax financial statements as that in the commercial accounts. In addition, some tax benefits may be allowed only if they are also reflected in the commercial financial statements. Therefore, the reported profits and the valuation of assets and liabilities shall be the same for financial statements and for income tax purposes. This interaction between financial reporting and taxation may be linked to the basic objectives of accounting principles in Germany.

As a rule, the continental European principles of accounting favour conservatism as compared to the Anglo-Saxon principles which emphasize the matching of revenues and expenses. This principle of prudence is of particular importance in Germany where corporations are generally financed by banks. As a result, financial statements are characterized by the importance given to the protection of the creditors and the preservation of capital. The presentation of financial statements recognizes that a corporation must meet its credit obligations and should remain a going concern. All risks and losses should be accounted for by recording anticipated liabilities. In addition, income is recognized only when determined as being sufficiently certain and dividends are limited to distributable profits.

The German tax authorities have accepted the principle of prudence in the measurement of income for tax purposes. This is to the advantage of a corporation which will compute a moderate income that will result in a lower tax liability.

Because of the strong influence of tax rules and tax-motivated decisions, the users of the financial information may have a negative perception of the business potential of German published corporations since the financial information/statements are unduly conservative. The finance community must interpret in an individual manner future prospects of the businesses, causing a higher degree of risk. Taking into account the growing importance of international investors and the influence of the Anglo-Saxon based accounting standards, the group Daimler-Benz AG has chosen to publish its financial statements according to U.S. GAAP.

Contributed by: Lucie Laliberté, Bishop's University

Summary of Learning Objectives

1. **Explain the difference between accounting income and taxable income.** Accounting income (or income reported on the income statement before income taxes) is computed in accordance with generally accepted accounting principles. Taxable income is computed in accordance with prescribed tax regulations. Because tax regulations and GAAP have different objectives, accounting income and taxable income frequently differ.

2. **Explain what a taxable temporary difference is and why a future tax liability is recognized.** A taxable temporary difference is the difference between the carrying value of an asset or liability and its tax basis such that when the asset is recovered or liability is settled in the future for an amount equal to its carrying value, taxable amounts will be included in taxable income of that future period. Because taxable amounts will arise in the future as a result of temporary differences existing at the balance sheet date, the future tax consequences of these taxable amounts must be given current accounting recognition as a tax liability.

3. **Explain what a deductible temporary difference is and why a future tax asset is recognized.** A deductible temporary difference is the difference between the carrying value of an asset or liability and its tax basis such that when the asset is recovered or a liability is settled in the future for an amount equal to its carrying value, tax-deductible amounts will be deducted in determining taxable income of that future period. Because deductible amounts will arise in the future as a result of temporary differences existing at the balance sheet date, the future tax consequences of these deductible amounts must be given current accounting recognition as a tax asset.

4. **Explain why the future income tax asset account is reassessed at the balance sheet date.** Consistent with asset valuation principles in general, every asset must be reassessed to ensure it is not reported at an amount in excess of the economic benefits expected to be received from the use or sale of the asset. The economic benefit to be received from the future income tax asset is the reduction in future income taxes payable. If it is unlikely that sufficient taxable income will be generated in the future to allow the entity to benefit from future deductible amounts, the income tax asset may have to be written down.

5. **Identify timing and permanent differences.** General categories of timing differences that result in assets and liabilities having carrying amounts different from tax values are: (1) revenues or gains that are taxable after they are recognized in accounting income; (2) expenses or losses that are deductible for tax purposes after they are recognized in accounting income; (3) revenues or gains that are taxable before they are recognized in accounting income; (4) expenses or losses that are deductible for tax purposes before being charged against income in the financial statements. Permanent differences usually result in the carrying value and tax value of an asset or liability being the same, where the recovery or settlement of the asset or liability in the future at the carrying amount will not result in taxable or deductible amounts. These differences result primarily from items recognized for financial reporting purposes but not for tax purposes, and items recognized in calculating taxable income that have no GAAP counterpart.

KEY TERMS

accounting income, 927

asset-liability method, 926

benefit of current income taxes, 928

benefit of future income taxes, 928

cost of current income taxes, 928

cost of future income taxes, 930

current income tax benefit, 928

current income tax expense, 928

deductible temporary differences, 932

effective tax rate, 943

future income tax assets, 933

future income tax expense, 931

future income tax liability, 930

income statement approach, 926

interperiod tax allocation, 926

intraperiod tax allocation, 951

liability method, 926

loss carryback, 945

loss carryforward, 945

loss for income tax purposes, 945

more likely than not, 933

originating timing difference, 940

permanent differences, 939

revenue-expense approach, 926

reversing timing difference, 940

6. **Prepare analyses and related journal entries to record income tax expense when there are multiple temporary differences.** With multiple differences, the following steps should be followed: (1) calculate taxable income and taxes payable; (2) identify all temporary differences between carrying and tax values at the balance sheet date; (3) calculate the net future income tax asset or liability; (4) compare the opening income tax asset or liability with that at the balance sheet date, the difference being the future income tax expense component of the current year's tax provision; (5) prepare the journal entries based on the tax payable (which is also the current income tax expense) and the change in the amount of the net future tax asset or liability (which is the future income tax expense).

7. **Explain the effect of various tax rates and tax rate changes on future income tax accounts.** Tax rates other than the current rate may be used only when the future tax rates have been enacted into legislation or substantively enacted. When there is a change in the future tax rate, its effect on the future income tax accounts should be recognized immediately. The effects are reported as an adjustment to future income tax expense in the period of the change.

8. **Apply accounting procedures for a tax loss carryback.** A company may carry a taxable loss back three years and receive refunds to a maximum of the income taxes paid in those years. Because the economic benefits related to the losses carried back are certain, they are recognized in the period of the loss as a tax benefit on the income statement and as an asset, Income Tax Refund Receivable, on the balance sheet.

9. **Apply accounting procedures and disclosure requirements for a tax loss carryforward.** A taxable loss can be carried forward and applied against the taxable incomes of the succeeding seven years. If the economic benefits related to the tax loss are more likely than not to be realized because of the likelihood of generating sufficient taxable income during the carryforward period, they can be recognized in the period of the loss as a tax benefit in the income statement and as a future tax asset on the balance sheet. If the economic benefits are not more likely than not to be realized, they should not be recognized in the financial statements. Instead, disclosure is required of the amounts of tax loss carryforwards and their expiry dates. If previously unrecorded tax losses are subsequently used to benefit a future period, the benefit is recognized in that future period.

10. **Identify evidence to consider in determining if future taxable income is likely to be available.** Determining whether taxable income will be available to enable future tax assets to be realized is a matter of professional judgement. A history of taxable incomes, the ability to reverse existing temporary differences, taxable income in carryback periods, and specific tax planning strategies are all indications of taxable income sources. In the absence of such concrete indicators, other positive and negative evidence should be considered.

11. **Explain the need for and be able to apply intraperiod tax allocation.** Because the income statement is classified into income before discontinued operations and extraordinary items, discontinued operations, and extraordinary items, the income taxes associated with each component should be reported with that component. Taxes related to items reported in retained earnings and those associated with share capital should also be reported with the related item in the financial statements.

12. **Identify the reporting and disclosure requirements for corporate income taxes.** Income taxes currently payable (or receivable) are reported as a current liability (or current asset) on the balance sheet. Future income tax assets and liabilities are classified as one net current and one net noncurrent amount based on the classification of the asset or liability to which the temporary difference relates. If a future tax asset or liability arose from other than an existing balance sheet account, it is classified according to when the temporary differences are expected to reverse. On the income statement, current and future tax expense must be disclosed for income before discontinued operations and extraordinary items. Separate disclosure is required of the amounts and expiry dates of unused tax losses, the amount of deductible temporary differences for which no future tax asset has been recognized, and any tax expense related to items charged or credited to equity. For companies who seek financing in public markets, additional disclosures are required about temporary differences and unused tax losses, about the major components of income tax expense, and the reasons for the difference between the expected statutory tax rate and the effective rate indicated on the income statement.

13. **Identify outstanding issues within the liability method.** Those who agree with the liability method of comprehensive tax allocation are not all agreed on issues related to whether the future tax amounts should be measured at their discounted present values, the basis on which future tax assets and liabilities are classified, and the degree of certainty that should exist before the benefits of future deductible amounts and tax losses should be given accounting recognition.

APPENDIX 19A

Conceptual Aspects of Interperiod Tax Allocation

OBJECTIVE 14
Identify alternatives to and present arguments for and against comprehensive interperiod tax allocation using the liability approach.

The desirability of recognizing future income tax consequences of temporary differences (i.e., interperiod tax allocation) is not unanimously agreed upon. Some believe that the appropriate tax expense to be reported on the income statement is the tax actually levied in that year. In short, this group, often referred to as the **nonallocation** (or **tax payable** or **flow-through**) **method** proponents, does not believe that the recognition of future income taxes provides useful information to users of the financial statements, or at least benefits in excess of cost. They note that the nature of the credit balance in a future income tax liability account is not clear. They contend that it is not a liability at the time the account is established because it is not payable to anyone. The payment of additional tax in the future is contingent upon the earning of future taxable income: if taxable income does not occur in the future, there is no liability. Similar arguments are advanced against the recognition of future tax assets.

Others argue that income taxes are more like a dividend than an expense and therefore should not be allocated between accounting periods. These proponents say that taxes are a distribution of income earned, not an expense or determinant of income.

Despite these arguments, the AcSB justifies the recognition of future income taxes on the basis of asset and liability recognition concepts and the matching principle. Income taxes are seldom paid completely in the period to which they relate. However, the operations of a business entity are expected to continue on a going-concern basis in the absence of evidence to the contrary and income taxes are expected to continue to be assessed in the future. Recognition of deferred or future income taxes is needed to report the future taxes expected to be paid or recovered and to appropriately match tax expense to related accounting income, because the tax return treatment for various items is different from their financial statement treatment.

Although the predominant view holds that recognition of future income taxes is appropriate, there are two approaches regarding the extent to which it should be applied: (1) comprehensive allocation; and (2) partial allocation.

COMPREHENSIVE ALLOCATION VERSUS PARTIAL ALLOCATION

Under **comprehensive allocation**, recognition of future income taxes is applied to *all temporary differences*. Supporters of this view believe that reported future income taxes should reflect the tax effects of all temporary differences regardless of the period in which the related income taxes are actually paid or recovered. This view recognizes that the amount of income tax currently payable is not necessarily the income tax expense reported in the financial statements relating to the current period. Consequently, future income taxes should be recognized when temporary differences originate, even if it is virtually certain that their reversal in future periods will be offset by new originating differences at that time. As a practical matter, therefore, recurring differences between taxable income and accounting income give rise to an indefinite postponement of tax.

An example of a recurring timing difference is the use of accelerated depreciation (capital cost allowance) for tax purposes by a company that uses straight-line depreciation for accounting purposes. This results in the accumulation of future income tax liabilities that will not be paid as long as the company is acquiring depreciable assets faster than it is retiring them. Although the future income tax associated with specific assets does indeed reverse, the aggregate balance of a future income tax liability remains stable or continues to grow because of the purchases of additional assets.

Supporters of **partial allocation** contend that unless future income tax amounts are expected to be paid or recovered within a relevant period of time, they should not affect reported income. Consequently, recognition of future income taxes is not appropriate for temporary differences resulting from *recurring timing differences that result in an indefinite postponement of tax*. Under this view, the presumption is that reported tax expense for a period should generally be the same as the tax payable for the period. Accordingly, only temporary differences that result from *nonrecurring*, material timing differences should be subject to recognition. These should be recognized only if they are reasonably expected to be paid or recovered within a relatively short period of time not exceeding, for example, three years. An example is an *isolated* instalment sale in which the receivable and related gross profit are reported for accounting purposes at the date of sale and for tax purposes when cash is collected.

The supporters of comprehensive allocation contend that partial allocation is a departure from accrual accounting because it emphasizes cash outlays, whereas comprehensive allocation results in a more thorough and consistent recognition of assets and liabilities, and the related income tax expense or benefit. As recommended in new Section 3465 and as previously recommended in 3470, *GAAP requires application of comprehensive allocation, subject to the modification that future income tax assets are not recognized in certain cases* (e.g., nonrecoverability).

ALTERNATIVE METHODS OF INTERPERIOD TAX ALLOCATION

The preceding viewpoints—ranging from no allocation, to partial allocation, to comprehensive allocation—represent different approaches to the problem of identifying those transactions for which the recognition of future income taxes is appropriate. The three views differ as to *whether accounting recognition should be given to the future tax effects of temporary differences.* Because tax rates change over time, additional questions relate to what method of tax allocation should be used in accounting for tax effects, and how those effects should be presented in the financial statements. Three different methods of tax allocation or reporting have been proposed: (1) the deferral method; (2) the liability (or asset-liability) method; and (3) the net-of-tax method.

Deferral Method. Under the **deferral method**, the amount of future income tax is based on the tax rate in effect during the year when a temporary difference originates. The balance in the future income tax account is not adjusted to reflect subsequent changes in tax rates or the imposition of new taxes. Essentially, adjustments to balance sheet and income statement accounts to reflect the effect of income taxes in the current year are determined by multiplying the difference between accounting income (adjusted for permanent differences) and taxable income for the year by the tax rate for the year. As such, this method emphasizes an income statement perspective: it determines what income tax expense should be reported, the result of which is "plugged" into balance sheet accounts. This contrasts with the liability method (sometimes called a balance sheet perspective) that emphasizes determination of a future income tax liability or asset, the result of which becomes an adjustment to income tax expense. Consequently, under the deferral method, a balance in a future income tax balance sheet account may not represent the actual amount of taxes payable or refundable in future periods when temporary differences reverse because it is not based on tax rates that will be in effect when the reversals occur.

With the deferral method, taxes calculated on originating timing differences are recorded in a Deferred Income Taxes (DIT) account, not a future income tax liability or asset account. Any credit or debit to a DIT account for an originating difference is matched by a corresponding debit or credit to the year's income tax expense (tax rate applied to accounting income) to be reported. A credit balance in a DIT account is technically not a liability because it is not measured appropriately as a future obligation: its balance is based on the amount of taxes that would have been paid if originating timing differences were taxed at the rate in effect in the year of origination, not the year of reversal. For similar reasons, a debit balance in a DIT account is technically not an asset as defined in the conceptual framework. Because of this, classification of a DIT account in the balance sheet is a problem. If a DIT account has a credit balance, many classify it as a unique item between total liabilities and shareholders' equity. Others may simply ignore the rigour of the definition of a liability and show such a DIT balance within the applicable (current or noncurrent) liability category. A debit balance in a DIT account, while not meeting the definition of an asset, would likely be classified as such (current and/or noncurrent), or is shown in a separate category in the asset section labelled "Deferred Amounts."

The deferral method, using a comprehensive approach, was the method required for Canadian practice up to the time of adoption of *CICA Handbook* Section 3465. This is effective for year ends beginning on or after January 1, 2000, although earlier adoption is encouraged.

Liability Method. Under the **liability method** (also called the **asset-liability** or **accrual method**), *the amount of future income tax is based on the tax rates that will be in effect during the periods in which the timing differences reverse.* Advocates of this method believe that the initial computation of future taxes is a tentative estimate that is subject to future adjustment if the tax rate changes or new taxes are imposed. Ordinarily, the most reasonable assumption about future tax rates is that the current tax rate will continue. However, if a rate change is known (enacted or substantively enacted) at the time of the initial computation, the expected rate is used under the liability method. Also, since the initial computation is an estimate, it is subject to future adjustment if tax rates change or new taxes are imposed. (The FASB requires that the rate change be *enacted* before adjustments are permitted to the "deferred" tax accounts.) Under this method, future taxes are viewed as economic liabilities for tax payable or assets for prepaid tax. The concepts and procedures related to the liability method, using a comprehensive approach, were examined in the chapter.

Net-of-Tax Method. Under the **net-of-tax method** (or valuation account method) *no Future Income Tax Liability or Asset account is reported on the balance sheet.* Further, the amount of income tax expense reported on the income statement is the same as the taxes currently payable. The tax effects of temporary differences (determined by either the deferral or liability method) are not reported separately. Instead, they are reported as *adjustments to the carrying amounts of specific assets or liabilities and the related revenues or expenses.* This view recognizes that future taxability and tax deductibility are important factors in the valuation of individual assets and liabilities. For example, depreciation is said to reduce the value of an asset both because of a decline in economic usefulness and because of the loss of a portion of future tax deductibility; capital cost allowance uses up this latter portion of the asset value more rapidly than does straight-line depreciation. Under this view, depreciation expense reported on the income statement would include, in addition to an amount for straight-line depreciation, an amount equal to the current tax effect of the excess of CCA over accounting depreciation. On the balance sheet the related cumulative tax effect is reported as a reduction of the specific asset rather than as a future income tax liability. Under this method asset, liability, revenue, and expense accounts are presented "net-of-tax." This method has been rejected because of its highly complex form of presentation, which mixes tax effects with underlying transactions: understandability would be a problem and any benefits of the method may be outweighed by its cost.

ILLUSTRATION OF THE DIFFERENT METHODS OF TAX ALLOCATION

To illustrate the differences in these three methods of interperiod tax allocation, assume that on January 1, 1998 Orange Inc. acquires for $100,000 equipment that has a five-year useful life and no salvage value. Straight-line depreciation is used for financial reporting purposes. Capital cost allowance for 1998 is $25,000. The tax rate for 1998 is 40%, but the tax rate (enacted into law) for future years is 50%. Tax payable for 1998, assuming that income before depreciation and taxes is $200,000, is computed below.

EXHIBIT 19A-1

Income before depreciation and income taxes	$200,000
Depreciation for tax purposes (capital cost allowance)	25,000
Taxable income	175,000
Tax rate	40%
Income tax payable	$ 70,000

An abbreviated income statement for 1998 under the three methods is as follows.

EXHIBIT 19A-2

	Deferral	Liability	Net-of-Tax
Income before depreciation and income taxes	$200,000	$200,000	$200,000
Depreciation	20,000	20,000	22,000
Income before income taxes	180,000	180,000	178,000
Current tax expense	70,000	70,000	70,000
Deferred or future tax expense	2,000	2,500	—
Total income tax expense	72,000	72,500	70,000
Net income	$108,000	$107,500	$108,000

Under the *deferral method,* the deferred (future) portion of income taxes is computed as follows.

EXHIBIT 19A-3

Depreciation for tax purposes (capital cost allowance)	$25,000
Depreciation for accounting purposes (20% × $100,000)	20,000
Difference	5,000
Tax rate	40%
Increase in deferred income tax credit account	$ 2,000

Under the *liability method,* the computation of the future portion of income taxes is essentially the same except that the future tax rate is used instead of the current rate.

EXHIBIT 19A-4

Equipment, tax basis ($100,000 − $25,000)	$75,000
Equipment, carrying value ($100,000 − $20,000)	80,000
Taxable temporary difference	5,000
Tax rate expected to apply	50%
Increase in future tax liability, and balance of future tax liability, December 31,1998	$ 2,500

Under the *net-of-tax method* the computation is more complicated. As indicated earlier, depreciation expense reported on the income statement would include, in addition to an amount for straight-line depreciation, an amount equal to the current tax effect of the excess of tax depreciation over accounting depreciation. This computation is as follows.[38]

EXHIBIT 19A-5

Depreciation for accounting purposes (20% × $100,000)	$20,000
Tax effect of excess depreciation [($25,000 − $20,000) × 40%]	2,000
Depreciation expense	$22,000

Thus, under the net-of-tax method, depreciation expense and accumulated depreciation are higher by $2,000.

Note that in the example both the deferral method and the net-of-tax method report the same net income. The difference between these two methods relates to the classification of the expense and whether a deferred tax account is created. The liability method uses a different—and, in this case, higher—tax rate than the deferral and net-of-tax methods; net income is therefore lower. If the future tax rate had been used in the net-of-tax method (i.e., if it applied the measurement rule of the liability method) the resulting net income would be the same as that determined under the liability method.

KEY TERMS

Summary of Learning Objective for Appendix 19A

14. Identify alternatives to and present arguments for and against comprehensive interperiod tax allocation using the liability approach. Alternatives to the current generally accepted methods of accounting for income taxes include the nonallocation and partial allocation approaches, and the deferral and net-of-tax methods.

---

[38] Conceptually, under the net-of-tax method we assume that a company purchases two items when it purchases an asset; one item is its service potential and the other is its tax deductibility feature. In the case above, the service potential feature is $60,000 ($100,000 × 60%), and the tax deductibility feature is $40,000 ($100,000 × 40%). In the first year, the service potential feature depreciates at a 20% rate, whereas the tax deductibility feature depreciates at a 25% rate. Total depreciation would, therefore, be computed as follows.

Depreciation of service potential feature ($60,000 × 20%)	$12,000
Depreciation of tax deductibility feature ($40,000 × 25%)	10,000
Depreciation expense	$22,000

Note: All *asterisked* Exercises, Problems, or Cases relate to material contained in the appendix to the chapter.

EXERCISES

(Future Taxable Amount, No Beginning Future Tax Account) Canadian Grant Corporation has one temporary difference at the end of 1998 that will reverse and cause taxable amounts of $55,000 in 1999, $60,000 in 2000, and $60,000 in 2001. The company's income reported on the 1998 income statement is $300,000 and the tax rate is 30% for all years. There were no future taxes at the beginning of 1998.

E19-1

Instructions

(a) Compute taxable income and income taxes payable for 1998.

(b) Prepare the journal entry(ies) to record income tax expense, future income taxes, and income tax payable for 1998.

(c) Prepare the Income Tax Expense section of the income statement for 1998, beginning with the line "income before income taxes."

(Future Deductible Amount, No Beginning Future Tax Account) Schuyler Colfax Corporation has one temporary difference at the end of 1998 that will reverse and cause deductible amounts of $50,000 in 1999, $65,000 in 2000, and $40,000 in 2001. The company's income reported on the 1998 income statement is $200,000, and the tax rate is 30% for all years. There were no future tax accounts at the beginning of 1998, and Schuyler Colfax expects profitable operations to continue in the future.

E19-2

Instructions

(a) Compute taxable income and income taxes payable for 1998.

(b) Prepare the journal entry(ies) to record income tax expense, future income taxes, and income taxes payable for 1998.

(c) Prepare the Income Tax Expense section of the income statement for 1998, beginning with the line "income before income taxes."

(One Future Taxable Amount, Beginning Future Taxes) Julia Dent Company began 1998 with a $90,000 balance in the Future Income Tax Liability account. At the end of 1998, the related temporary difference amounts to $350,000, and it will reverse evenly over the next two years. Accounting income for 1998 is $525,000. The tax rate for all years is 40%, and taxable income for 1998 is $400,000.

E19-3

Instructions

(a) Compute income taxes payable for 1998.

(b) Prepare the journal entry(ies) to record income tax expense, future income taxes, and income taxes payable for 1998.

(c) Prepare the Income Tax Expense section of the income statement for 1998, beginning with the line "income before income taxes."

(Three Differences, Entry for Taxes) The Bateman Company reports accounting income of $70,000 for 1998. The following items cause taxable income to be different from accounting income.

E19-4

   1. Capital cost allowance exceeds depreciation by $18,000.

   2. Rent collected and reported on the tax return is greater than rent earned by $22,000.

   3. Fines for pollution (non-tax-deductible) appear as an expense of $11,000 on the income statement.

Bateman's tax rate is 30% for all years and the company expects to report taxable income in all future years. There are no future taxes at the beginning of 1998.

Instructions

(a) Compute taxable income and income taxes payable for 1998.

(b) Prepare the journal entry(ies) to record income tax expense, future income taxes, and income taxes payable for 1998.

(c) Prepare the Income Tax section of the 1998 income statement, beginning with the line "income before income taxes."

(d) Compute the effective tax rate for 1998. Why does it differ from the enacted rate?

E19-5   **(Two Differences, Beginning Future Taxes)** The following facts relate to William Wheeler Corporation.

1. Future tax liability, January 1, 1998, $40,000.
2. Future tax asset, January 1, 1998, $0.
3. Taxable income for 1998, $95,000.
4. Accounting income for 1998, $180,000.
5. Temporary difference at December 31, 1998 giving rise to future taxable amounts, $220,000.
6. Temporary difference at December 31, 1998 giving rise to future deductible amounts, $35,000.
7. Tax rate for all years, 40%.
8. The company is expected to operate profitably in the future.

Instructions

(a) Compute income taxes payable for 1998.

(b) Prepare the journal entry(ies) to record the income tax expense, future income taxes, and income taxes payable for 1998.

(c) Prepare the Income Tax section of the 1998 income statement, beginning with the line "income before income taxes."

E19-6   **(Identify Timing or Permanent Differences)** Listed below are items that are commonly accounted for differently for financial reporting purposes than they are for tax purposes.

Instructions
For each item, indicate whether it involves:

1. A timing difference that will result in future deductible amounts and, therefore, will usually give rise to a future income tax asset.
2. A timing difference that will result in future taxable amounts and, therefore, will usually give rise to a future income tax liability.
3. A permanent difference.

Use the appropriate number to indicate your answer for each.

_____ (a) The capital cost allowance method is used for tax purposes, and the straight-line depreciation method is used for accounting purposes for some plant assets.

_____ (b) A landlord collects some rents in advance. Rents received are taxable in the period when they are received.

_____ (c) Instalment sales are accounted for by the accrual method for financial reporting purposes and the instalment method for tax purposes.

_____ (d) Interest is received on an investment in tax-exempt government bonds.

_____ (e) Costs of guarantees and warranties are estimated and accrued for financial reporting purposes.

_____ (f) Expenses are incurred in obtaining tax-exempt income.

_____ (g) Proceeds are received from a life insurance company because of the death of a key officer (the company carries a policy on key officers).

_____ (h) For some assets, straight-line depreciation is used for both financial reporting purposes and tax purposes, but the assets' lives are shorter for tax purposes.

_____ (i) The tax return reports no revenue for the dividends received from a Canadian corporation. The cost method is used to account for the related investments for financial reporting purposes, with cash dividends received being treated as income.

_____ (j) Estimated losses on pending lawsuits and claims are accrued for financial reporting purposes. These losses are tax deductible in the period(s) when the related liabilities are settled.

E19-7   **(Terminology, Relationships, Computations, Entries)**

Instructions
Complete the following statements by filling in the blanks.

(a) In a period in which a taxable temporary difference reverses, the reversal will cause taxable income to be _____ (less than, greater than) accounting income.

(b) If a $60,000 balance in Future Income Tax Asset was computed by use of a 40% rate, the underlying temporary difference amounts to $_____.

(c) Future taxes _____ (are, are not) recorded to account for permanent differences.

(d) If a taxable temporary difference originates in 1998, it will cause taxable income of 1998 to be _____ (less than, greater than) accounting income for 1998.

(e) If total tax expense is $50,000 and future tax expense is $70,000, then the current portion of the expense computation is referred to as current tax _____ (expense, benefit) of $_____.

(f) If a corporation's tax return shows taxable income of $100,000 for Year 2 and a tax rate of 40%, how much will appear on the December 31, Year 2 balance sheet for "Income Tax Payable" if the company has made estimated tax payments of $37,000 for Year 2? $_____

(g) An increase in the Future Tax Liability account on the balance sheet is recorded by a _____ (debit, credit) to the Income Tax Expense account.

(h) An income statement that reports current tax expense of $82,000 and future tax benefit of $21,000 will report total income tax expense of $_____.

(i) The future income tax asset account must be remeasured whenever it is judged to be _____ that a portion of a previously recognized future tax asset _____ (will be, will not be) realized.

(j) If the tax return shows total taxes due for the period of $75,000 but the income statement shows total income tax expense of $55,000, the difference of $20,000 is referred to as future tax _____ (expense, benefit).

(One Temporary Difference Through Three Years, One Rate) Kenyon Company reports the following amounts in   **E19-8**
its first three years of operations:

	1998	1999	2000
Taxable income	160,000	142,000	140,000
Accounting income	200,000	120,000	125,000

The difference between taxable income and accounting income is due to one timing difference. The tax rate is 40% for all years and the company expects to continue with profitable operations in the future.

Instructions

(a) For each year: (1) identify the amount of the timing difference originating or reversing during that year; and (2) indicate the amount of the temporary difference at the end of the year.

(b) Indicate the balance in the related future tax account at the end of each year and identify it as either a future tax asset or liability.

(Carryback and Carryforward of Taxable Loss) The accounting income (or loss) figures for the T. Crowell   **E19-9**
Company are as follows.

1993	$160,000
1994	250,000
1995	80,000
1996	(160,000)
1997	(380,000)
1998	120,000
1999	100,000

Accounting income (or loss) and taxable income (loss) were the same for all years involved. Assume a 50% tax rate for 1993 and 1994 and a 40% tax rate for the remaining years.

Instructions

Prepare the journal entries for the years 1995 to 1999 to record income tax expense and the effects of the tax loss carrybacks and carryforwards assuming T. Crowell elects to use the carryback provision to its fullest extent before considering carryforwards. All income and losses relate to normal operations and the company assumes that future profitable operations are likely at the end of each year.

(Loss Carryback and Carryforward, No Temporary Differences, Entries and Income Statement) Charles Tupper   **E19-10**
Corporation reports accounting income (or loss) equal to taxable income (or loss) from 1990 through 1998 as follows.

	Income (Loss)	Tax Rate
1990	$ 29,000	30%
1991	40,000	30%
1992	17,000	20%
1993	48,000	50%
1994	(150,000)	40%
1995	60,000	40%
1996	30,000	40%
1997	105,000	40%
1998	(60,000)	45%

Accounting income (loss) and taxable income (loss) were the same for all years since Tupper has been in business. Assume the carryback elective is employed for taxable losses to its fullest extent before considering carryforwards. In recording the benefits of a loss carryforward, assume it is more likely than not that the related benefits will be realized.

Instructions

(a) What entry(ies) for income taxes should be recorded in 1994?

(b) Prepare the income tax section of the 1994 income statement, beginning with "loss before income taxes."

(c) What entry(ies) for income taxes should be recorded in 1995?

(d) How should the income tax section of the 1995 income statement appear?

(e) What entry(ies) for income taxes should be recorded in 1998?

(f) How should the income tax section of the 1998 income statement appear?

E19-11   (Three Differences, Classify Future Taxes) At December 31, 1997 Orange Company had a net future income tax liability of $350,000. An explanation of the items that compose this balance is as follows.

Reason for Temporary Differences	Resulting Balances in Future Taxes
1. Excess of CCA over depreciation.	$200,000
2. Accrual, for accounting purposes, of estimated loss contingency from pending lawsuit that is expected to be settled in 1998. The loss will be deducted on the tax return when paid.	(50,000)
3. Percentage-of-completion method used for book purposes and completed contract for tax purposes.	200,000
	$350,000

In analysing the temporary differences, you find that $10,000 of the capital cost temporary difference will reverse in 1998 and $100,000 of the temporary difference due to the construction revenue will reverse in 1998. The tax rate for all years is 40%.

Instructions

Indicate the manner in which future income taxes should be presented on Orange Company's December 31, 1997 balance sheet.

E19-12   (Two Temporary Differences, Beginning Future Taxes) The following facts relate to Hiram Company.

1. Future tax liability, January 1, 1998, $60,000.

2. Future tax asset, January 1, 1998, $20,000.

3. Taxable income for 1998, $105,000.

4. Temporary difference at December 31, 1998, giving rise to future taxable amounts, $225,000.

5. Temporary difference at December 31, 1998, giving rise to future deductible amounts, $80,000.

6. Tax rate for all years, 40%. No other differences exist between accounting and taxable income.

7. The company is expected to operate profitably in the future.

Instructions

(a) Compute the amount of accounting income.

(b) Prepare the journal entry(ies) to record income tax expense, future income taxes, and income taxes payable for 1998.

(c) Prepare the income tax expense section of the 1998 income statement, beginning with the line "income before income taxes."

(d) Compute the effective tax rate for 1998.

(One Difference, Multiple Rates, No Beginning Balance, and Beginning Balance of Future Taxes) At the end of **E19-13** 1997, Berger Corporation has $180,000 of temporary differences that will result in reporting future taxable amounts as follows.

1998	$ 60,000
1999	20,000
2000	70,000
2001	30,000
	$180,000

Tax rates enacted as of the beginning of 1996 are:

1996 and 1997	40%
1998 and 1999	30%
2000 and later	25%

Berger's taxable income for 1997 is $320,000. Taxable income is expected in all future years.

Instructions

(a) Prepare the journal entry(ies) for Berger to record income taxes payable, future income taxes, and income tax expense for 1997, assuming that there were no future taxes at the end of 1996.

(b) Prepare the journal entry(ies) for Berger to record income taxes payable, future income taxes, and income tax expense for 1997, assuming that there was a balance of $22,000 in a Future Tax Liability account at the end of 1996.

(Future Tax Asset—Different Amounts To Be Realized) Bouchard Corp. has a future tax asset account with a bal- **E19-14** ance of $150,000 at the end of 1997 due to a single temporary difference of $375,000. At the end of 1998 this same temporary difference has increased to $450,000. Taxable income for 1998 is $850,000. The tax rate is 40% for all years.

Instructions

(a) Record income tax expense, future income taxes, and income taxes payable for 1998, assuming that it is more likely than not that the future tax asset will be realized.

(b) Assuming that it is more likely than not that $20,000 of the future tax asset will not be realized, prepare the journal entry(ies) at the end of 1998 to record income taxes for the period.

(Future Deductible Amounts Deemed More Likely Than Not To Be Realized on Reassessment) Dan Abbey **E19-15** Limited was incorporated early in 1996. The operating results for 1996 and 1997 were at a break-even level with no taxes payable in either year. Because of poor results, Dan Abbey took no capital cost allowance for tax purposes, although $18,000 depreciation expense was reported over the two-year period. Because it was questionable whether sufficient future taxable income would be generated, Dan Abbey's accountant did not recognize the future tax effects of this deductible temporary difference.

In 1998, the company reported income before taxes of $70,000 after deducting depreciation expense of $10,000. CCA deducted for tax purposes in 1998 is $14,000. The outlook for the company improved significantly this year and the accountant now judges that it is more likely than not that the tax benefits associated with all temporary differences will be realized.

The tax rate enacted for all years is 38%.

Instructions

Prepare the journal entry(ies) to record income taxes for the year ended December 31, 1998.

(Future Tax Liability, Change in Tax Rate, Partial Income Statement) P.A. Fitzgerald Inc.'s only temporary differ- **E19-16** ence at the beginning and end of 1997 is caused by a $3 million deferred gain for tax purposes for an instalment sale of a plant asset, and the related receivable (only half of which is classified as a current asset) is due in equal instalments in 1998 and 1999. The related future tax liability at the beginning of the year is $1,200,000. In the third quarter of 1997, a new tax rate of 30% is enacted into law and is scheduled to become effective for 1999. Taxable income for 1997 is $5,000,000 and taxable income is expected in all future years.

Instructions

(a) Determine the amount reported as a future tax liability at the end of 1997. Indicate proper classification(s).

(b) Prepare the journal entry (if any) necessary to adjust the future tax liability when the new tax rate is enacted into law.

(c) Draft the Income Tax Expense portion of the 1997 income statement, beginning with the line "income before income taxes."

E19-17 **(Two Temporary Differences, Three Years, Multiple Rates)** Taxable income and accounting income would be identical for Parkinson Corp. except for its treatment of gross profit on instalment sales and estimated costs of warranties. The following income computations have been prepared.

Taxable income	1997	1998	1999
Excess of revenues over expenses (excluding two timing differences)	$160,000	$210,000	$90,000
Instalment gross profit collected	7,000	7,000	7,000
Expenditures for warranties	(5,000)	(5,000)	(5,000)
Taxable income	$162,000	$212,000	$92,000
Accounting income			
Excess of revenues over expenses (excluding two timing differences)	$160,000	$210,000	$90,000
Instalment gross profit earned	21,000	-0-	-0-
Estimated cost of warranties	(15,000)	-0-	-0-
Income before taxes	$166,000	$210,000	$90,000

The tax rates in effect are: 1997, 40%; 1998 and 1999, 45%. All tax rates were enacted into law on January 1, 1997. No future income tax accounts existed at the beginning of 1997. Taxable income is expected in all future years.

Instructions

Prepare the journal entry(ies) to record income tax expense, future income taxes, and income tax payable for 1997, 1998, and 1999.

E19-18 **(Two Differences, No Beginning Future Taxes, Multiple Rates)** The following data pertain to the Suzanne Foster Company.

1. At December 31, 1997 the company has a $30,000 liability reported for estimated litigation claims. This $30,000 balance represents amounts that have been charged to income but that are not tax deductible until they are paid. The company expects to pay the claims and thus have tax-deductible amounts in the future in the following manner.

Year	Payments
2000	$ 5,000
2001	23,000
2002	2,000
	$30,000

2. The company uses different depreciation methods for accounting and tax purposes. Consequently, at December 31, 1997 the company has a temporary difference due to depreciable property of $80,000. This $80,000 temporary difference due to depreciation is to result in taxable amounts in future years in the following manner.

Year	Amount
1998	$16,000
1999	16,000
2000	16,000
2001	16,000
2002	16,000
	$80,000

3. The tax rates enacted at the beginning of 1996 are as follows.

1997 and 1998	50%
1999 and 2000	40%
2001 and later	30%

4. Taxable income for 1997 is $80,000. Foster expects to report taxable income for at least the next five years.

5. No temporary differences existed at the end of 1996.

Instructions

(a) Prepare the journal entry(ies) for Foster to record income tax payable, future income taxes, and income tax expense for 1997.

(b) Prepare the Income Tax Expense section of the income statement, beginning with the line "income before income taxes."

(Two Differences, One Rate, Accounting Loss) Granville, Inc., in its first year of operations, has an accounting loss even though it has taxable income. A reconciliation between these two amounts for the calendar year 1998 is as follows.

E19-19

Accounting loss	$ (50,000)
Estimated expenses that will be deductible for tax purposes when paid	2,000,000
Excess of CCA over depreciation	(1,200,000)
Taxable income	$ 750,000

At the end of 1998, the reported amount of Granville's depreciable assets in the financial statements is $3 million, and the tax basis of these assets is $1.8 million. Future recovery of the depreciable assets will result in $1,200,000 of taxable amounts ($300,000 per year in years 1999 to 2002) over the four-year remaining life of the assets. Also, a $2,000,000 estimated liability for litigation expenses has been recognized in the financial statements in 1998, but the related expenses will be deductible on the tax return in 2001 when the liability is expected to be settled. Granville expects to report taxable income in the next few years.

Instructions
Prepare the journal entries (if any) to record income tax expense, income tax payable, and future income taxes for 1998, assuming a tax rate of 30% for all periods.

(Depreciation Difference, Effect of Expectation for Future Income Versus Future Losses) Thomas Riley Inc. began operations at the beginning of 1998. Plant assets costing $2,400,000 were placed into service on January 2, 1998. Presented below is a schedule of depreciation and capital cost allowance to be taken by the company.

E19-20

	Depreciation	Capital Cost Allowance	Difference
1998	$ 240,000	$ 300,000	$ (60,000)
1999	240,000	510,000	(270,000)
2000	240,000	530,000	(290,000)
2001	240,000	530,000	(290,000)
2002	240,000	530,000	(290,000)
2003	240,000		240,000
2004	240,000		240,000
2005	240,000		240,000
2006	240,000		240,000
2007	240,000		240,000
	$2,400,000	$2,400,000	$ -0-

Assume that the tax rates are 50% for 1998 through 2002, 40% in 2003, and 30% in 2004 and later years. All rates were enacted by the end of 1998.

Instructions

(a) Compute the future income taxes to be reported for Thomas Riley Inc. at the end of 1998, 1999, and 2000 assuming taxable income is expected in each of the next 10 years. Explain how they would appear on the balance sheet.

(b) Compute the future taxes to be reported for Thomas Riley Inc. at the end of 1998, 1999, and 2000. Assume there is zero taxable income for 1998. Taxable losses are expected for the next five years, and large amounts of taxable income are expected for all subsequent years.

E19-21 **(Three Differences, Multiple Rates, Future Taxable Income)** During 1998, Alexander Company's first year of operations, the company reports accounting income of $250,000. Alexander's tax rate is 50% for 1998 and 40% for all later years. Alexander expects to have taxable income in each of the next five years. The effects on future tax returns of temporary differences existing at December 31, 1998, are summarized below.

	Future Years					
	1999	2000	2001	2002	2003	Total
Future taxable (deductible) amounts:						
Instalment sales	$32,000	$32,000	$32,000			$ 96,000
Depreciation	(30,000)	(30,000)	30,000	$30,000	$30,000	30,000
Unearned rent	(50,000)	(50,000)				(100,000)

Instructions

(a) Calculate the amount of the net future income tax asset or liability at December 31, 1998.

(b) Compute taxable income for 1998.

(c) Prepare the journal entry(ies) to record income tax payable, future income taxes, and income tax expense for 1998.

E19-22 **(One Temporary Difference, Multiple Rates, Beginning Future Tax Balance)** Hamby Ltd.'s taxable income for 1997 is $350,000. Hamby's noncurrent future income tax liability balance at December 31, 1996 was $85,000. At the end of 1997, Hamby Ltd. has a $220,000 temporary difference that will result in reporting future taxable amounts as follows.

1998	$ 50,000
1999	40,000
2000	60,000
2001	70,000
	$220,000

Tax rates enacted at the beginning of 1996 are as follows:

1996 and 1997	50%
1998 and 1999	40%
2000 and later	30%

Hamby is expected to report taxable income through 2001. All future taxes relate to a single temporary difference.

Instructions

(a) Calculate the amount of future income taxes that should be reported on Hamby's balance sheet at December 31, 1997. Indicate the proper classification(s) of the amount determined.

(b) Prepare the journal entry(ies) to record income taxes for 1997.

(c) Draft the Income Tax Expense section of the 1997 income statement beginning with the line "income before income taxes," assuming accounting income is $354,000.

E19-23 **(Two Differences, No Beginning Future Taxes, Multiple Rates)** Aaron Morton Inc., in its first year of operations, has the following differences between the carrying value and tax basis of its assets and liabilities at the end of 1997.

	Carrying Amount	Tax Basis
Equipment (net)	$400,000	$340,000
Estimated warranty liability	$200,000	$ -0-

It is estimated that the warranty liability will be settled in 1998. The difference in equipment (net) will result in taxable amounts of $20,000 in 1998, $30,000 in 1999, and $10,000 in 2000. The company has taxable income of $550,000 in 1997. As of the beginning of 1997, its enacted tax rate is 34% for 1997–1999, and 30% for 2000. Aaron Morton expects to report taxable income through 2000.

Instructions

(a) Prepare the journal entry(ies) to record income tax expense, future income taxes, and income tax payable for 1997.

(b) Indicate how future income tax amounts will be reported on the balance sheet at the end of 1997.

(Capital Asset Temporary Difference over Three Years) Caroline Davis Co. purchased depreciable assets costing $900,000 on January 2, 1998. For financial reporting purposes, the company uses straight-line depreciation over five years. For tax purposes, the asset falls into a capital cost allowance class that has a rate of 30%. The enacted tax rate for all years is 34%. The depreciation difference is the only temporary difference the company has. Assume that Davis has taxable income of $240,000 in each of the years 1998 to 2000.

E19-24

Instructions

Determine the amount of the future income tax asset or liability and indicate where it should be reported in the balance sheet for 1998, 1999, and 2000.

(Two Temporary Differences, Multiple Rates) Garret Hobart Inc. has two temporary differences at the end of 1997. The first difference stems from instalment sales and the second one results from the accrual of a loss contingency. Hobart's accounting department has developed a schedule of future taxable and deductible amounts related to these temporary differences as follows:

E19-25

	1998	1999	2000	2001
Taxable amounts	$40,000	$ 50,000	$ 60,000	$80,000
Deductible amounts		(15,000)	(19,000)	
	$40,000	$ 35,000	$ 41,000	$80,000

As of the beginning of 1997, the enacted tax rate is 34% for 1997 and 1998 and 40% for 1999 to 2002. At the beginning of 1997 the company had no future income taxes on its balance sheet. Taxable income for 1997 is $500,000. Taxable income is expected in all future years.

Instructions

(a) Prepare the journal entry(ies) to record income tax expense, future income taxes, and income taxes payable for 1997.

(b) Indicate how future income taxes would be classified on the balance sheet at the end of 1997.

(Two Differences, One Rate, First Year) The differences between the carrying value and tax basis of the assets and liabilities of Niles Corporation at the end of 1997 are presented below.

E19-26

	Carrying Amount	Tax Basis
Accounts receivable	$50,000	$-0-
Litigation liability	10,000	-0-

It is estimated that the litigation liability will be settled in 1998. The difference in accounts receivable will result in taxable amounts of $30,000 in 1998 and $20,000 in 1999. The company has taxable income of $350,000 in 1997 and is expected to have taxable income in each of the following two years. Its enacted tax rate is 34% for all years. This is the company's first year of operations. The operating cycle of the company is two years.

Instructions

(a) Prepare the journal entry(ies) to record income tax expense, future income taxes, and income tax payable for 1997.

(b) Indicate how the future income taxes will be reported on the balance sheet at the end of 1997.

(Loss Carryback and Carryforward, Different Values for the Loss Carryforward Benefit) Konchalski Inc. reports the following income (loss) for both accounting purposes and tax purposes (assume the loss is carried back to the fullest extent before being carried forward).

E19-27

Year	Income (Loss)	Tax Rate
1996	$120,000	34%
1997	90,000	34%
1998	(280,000)	40%
1999	220,000	40%

The tax rates listed were all enacted by the beginning of 1996.

Instructions

(a) Prepare the journal entries for the years 1996 to 1999 to record income tax expense (benefit) and income tax payable (refundable) and the tax effects of the loss carryback and carryforward, assuming that at the end of 1998 the benefits of the loss carryforward are judged more likely than not to be realized in the future.

(b) Using the assumption in (a), prepare the Income Tax section of the 1998 income statement beginning with the line "loss before income taxes."

(c) Prepare the journal entries for 1998 and 1999, assuming that based on the weight of available evidence, it is more likely than not that one-fourth of the benefits of the carryforward will not be realized.

(d) Using the assumption in (c), prepare the Income Tax section of the 1998 income statement beginning with the line "loss before income taxes."

E19-28   **(Loss Carryback and Carryforward, Benefit Not Fully Realizable)** The Ozmon Company reports the following income (loss) for both book and tax purposes, and applies all losses back to the maximum allowed before carrying losses forward.

Year	Income (Loss)	Tax Rate
1996	$120,000	40%
1997	90,000	40%
1998	(280,000)	50%
1999	120,000	50%

The tax rates listed were all enacted at the beginning of 1996.

Instructions

(a) Prepare the journal entries for the years 1996 to 1999 to record income tax expense (benefit) and income tax payable (refundable) and the tax effects of the loss carryback and carryforward assuming that, based on the weight of available evidence, it is more likely than not that one-half of the benefits of the loss carryforward will not be realized.

(b) Prepare the Income Tax section of the 1998 income statement beginning with the line "loss before income taxes."

(c) Prepare the Income Tax section of the 1999 income statement beginning with the line "income before income taxes."

E19-29   **(Intraperiod Allocation, One Rate)** In 1998 Stanfield Company has a loss from continuing operations of $200,000 and an extraordinary gain of $280,000, only 75% of which is taxable. There are no temporary differences. The tax rate is 40%.

Instructions

Indicate how income taxes would be reported on the income statement for 1998 by drafting the bottom portion of the statement, beginning with the line "loss before income taxes and extraordinary items."

PROBLEMS

P19-1   At December 31, 1997 the Versailles Corporation had a temporary difference (related to depreciation) and reported a related future tax liability of $40,000 on its balance sheet. At December 31, 1998, Versailles has four temporary differences. An analysis of these reveals the following.

Temporary Difference	1999	2000	Later Years
	Future Taxable (Deductible) Amounts		
1. Use of straight-line depreciation for accounting purposes and accelerated depreciation for tax purposes	$ 80,000	$110,000	$380,000
2. Royalties collected in advance; recognized when earned for accounting purposes and when received for tax purposes	(190,000)	—	—
3. Various expenses accrued when incurred for accounting purposes; recognized for tax purposes when paid	(45,000)	—	—
4. Recognition of profits on instalment sales during the period of sale for accounting purposes and during the period of collection for tax purposes	138,000	105,000	—
	$ (17,000)	$215,000	$380,000

The tax rate for all years is 40%. Assume the company has income taxes of $180,000 due per the tax return for 1998. The instalment receivable collectible in 2000 is classified as noncurrent.

Instructions

(a) Indicate the manner in which future income taxes should be presented on Versailles Corporation's December 31, 1998 balance sheet.

(b) Compute taxable income for 1998.

(c) Compute accounting income for 1998.

(d) Draft the Income Tax section of the 1998 income statement, beginning with the line "income before income taxes."

The accounting income of Alice Company differs from its taxable income throughout each of the last four years as follows. **P19-2**

Year	Pretax Financial Income	Taxable Income	Tax Rate
1998	$280,000	$180,000	34%
1999	320,000	225,000	40%
2000	350,000	270,000	40%
2001	420,000	580,000	40%

Accounting income for each year includes a nondeductible expense of $30,000 (never deductible for tax purposes). The remainder of the difference between income reported on the financial statements and taxable income in each period is due to one depreciation timing difference. No future income taxes existed at the beginning of 1998.

Instructions

(a) Prepare journal entries to record income taxes in all four years. Assume that the change in the tax rate to 40% was not enacted until the beginning of 1999.

(b) Draft the Income Tax section of the 1999 income statement.

The following information has been obtained for the VanSnick Corporation. **P19-3**

1. Prior to 1997, taxable income and accounting income were identical.

2. Accounting income is $1,700,000 in 1997 and $1,400,000 in 1998.

3. On January 1, 1997, equipment costing $1,000,000 is purchased. It is to be depreciated at a 20% CCA rate for tax purposes and over eight years on a straight-line basis for financial reporting purposes.

4. Dividends of $60,000 were received from taxable Canadian corporations and included in accounting income in 1998. (Intercompany dividends are not taxable.)

5. Included in 1998 accounting income is an extraordinary gain of $200,000, which is fully taxable.

6. The tax rate is 40% for all periods.

7. Taxable income is expected for all future periods.

Instructions

(a) Compute taxable income and income tax payable for 1998.

(b) Prepare the journal entry(ies) to record 1998 income taxes.

(c) Prepare the bottom portion of VanSnick's 1998 income statement, beginning with "income before income taxes and extraordinary items."

(d) Indicate how future income taxes should be presented on the December 31, 1998 balance sheet.

P19-4   Panama Company started operations in 1997. A reconciliation of its accounting income to its taxable income for 1997 is as follows.

Accounting income	$ 24,000,000
Litigation accrual for book purposes	8,000,000
Excess CCA over depreciation	(3,000,000)
Taxable income	$ 29,000,000

As of the beginning of 1997, enacted tax rates are 34% for 1997 and 1998, and 40% for all subsequent years. It is estimated that the litigation accrual will be settled in 2002 and that the temporary difference due to the excess CCA will reverse equally over the three-year period from 1998 to 2000.

Instructions

(a) Determine the income tax payable, future income taxes, and income tax expense to be reported for 1997 assuming that taxable income is expected in all future years.

(b) Classify the future income taxes computed in (a) into current and noncurrent components. Explain where the future taxes should appear on the balance sheet.

(c) Determine the income tax payable, future income taxes, and income tax expense for 1997 assuming that operating losses are expected to appear on tax returns for 1998 through 2002 and taxable income is very likely for 2003 and later years.

(d) Classify the future income taxes computed in (c) into current and noncurrent components. Explain where the future taxes should appear on the balance sheet.

P19-5   Grant Inc. reported the following accounting income (loss) and related tax rates during the years 1993 to 1999.

	Income (Loss)	Tax Rate	
1993	$ 40,000	30%	
1994	25,000	30%	7500
1995	60,000	30%	18000
1996	80,000	45%	36000
1997	(200,000)	50%	
1998	60,000	40%	24000
1999	90,000	20%	

Accounting income (loss) and taxable income (loss) were the same for all years since Grant began business. The taxes from 1996 to 1999 were enacted in 1996.

Instructions

(a) Prepare the journal entries for the years 1997 to 1999 to record income tax payable (refundable), income tax expense (benefit), and the tax effects of the loss carryback and carryforward. Assume that Grant elects to use the carryback possibilities to their fullest extent before considering carryforwards.

(b) Indicate the effect the 1997 entry(ies) have on the December 31, 1997 balance sheet.

(c) Indicate how the bottom portion of the 1997 income statement would be reported, starting with the line "loss before income taxes."

(d) Indicate how the bottom portion of the 1998 income statement would be reported, starting with the line "income before income taxes."

The following facts apply to the Roderick Company.

1. 1997 is Roderick's first year of operations.
2. Tax rates enacted by the end of 1997 are as follows.

1997	35%
1998 and 1999	30%
2000 and later	25%

3. For 1997, Roderick has accounting income of $80,000 and taxable income of $60,000.
4. Temporary differences existing at the end of 1997 are as follows.

Instalment sale difference (taxable in 1998)	$ 30,000
Depreciation difference (see details below)	10,000
Estimated expenses (deductible in 2003)	(20,000)
Net temporary difference	$ 20,000

5. The temporary difference related to depreciable assets will result in the following future taxable (deductible) amounts.

1998	$(90,000)
1999	60,000
2000	40,000
	$ 10,000

Instructions

(a) Compute the amount of future income taxes to appear on the balance sheet at December 31, 1997 and indicate the appropriate classification(s) (current versus noncurrent and asset versus liability).

(b) Compute the total income tax expense for 1997. Indicate the portion that is current and the portion that is due to future income tax expense or benefit.

(c) Prepare the journal entry(ies) to record income tax payable, future income taxes, and income tax expense for 1997.

Presented below are two independent situations related to future taxable and deductible amounts resulting from temporary differences existing at December 31, 1997.

1. Helen Herron Co. has developed the following schedule of future taxable and deductible amounts.

	1998	1999	2000	2001	2002
Taxable amounts	$300	$300	$300	$ 300	$300
Deductible amounts	—	—	—	(1,400)	—

2. Cherry Blossom Co. has the following schedule of future taxable and deductible amounts:

	1998	1999	2000	2001
Taxable amounts	$300	$300	$ 300	$300
Deductible amounts	—	—	(2,000)	—

Both Herron and Blossom have taxable income of $3,000 in 1997 and expect to have taxable income in all future years. The tax rates enacted as of the beginning of 1997 are 30% for 1997 to 2000 and 40% for years thereafter. All of the underlying temporary differences relate to noncurrent assets and liabilities.

Instructions

For each of these two situations, compute the amount of net future income taxes to be reported at the end of 1997 and indicate how it should be shown on the balance sheet.

Perfecto Gusto Inc. sold an investment on an instalment basis. The total gain of $60,000 was reported on the financial statements in the period of the sale. The company qualifies to use the instalment method for tax purposes. The instalment period is three years; one-third of the sale price is collected in the period of sale. The tax rate was 34% in 1997, and 30% in 1998 and 1999. The 30% tax rate was enacted into law in 1998. The accounting and tax data for the three years is shown below.

	Financial Accounting	Tax Return
1997 (34% tax rate)		
Income before timing difference	$ 70,000	$70,000
Timing difference	60,000	20,000
Income	$130,000	$90,000
1998 (30% tax rate)		
Income before timing difference	$ 70,000	$70,000
Timing difference	-0-	20,000
Income	$ 70,000	$90,000
1999 (30% tax rate)		
Income before timing difference	$ 70,000	$70,000
Timing difference	-0-	20,000
Income	$ 70,000	$90,000

Instructions

(a) Prepare the journal entries to record the income tax expense, future income taxes, and the income tax payable at the end of each year. No future income taxes existed at the beginning of 1997.

(b) Explain how the future taxes will appear on the balance sheet at the end of each year, assuming the instalment receivable is classified as a current asset.

(c) Draft the Income Tax Expense section of the income statement for each year, beginning with the line "income before income taxes."

P19-9 Dean Corp. began operations at the beginning of Year 1. At the beginning of Year 1, Dean Corp. purchased a truck with a cost of $180,000. For accounting purposes, Dean finds it appropriate to depreciate the asset by the straight-line method over a six-year service life. For tax purposes, Dean uses capital cost allowance rates. The depreciation and CCA schedules follow.

Year	Depreciation for Accounting Purposes	CCA for Tax Purposes	Difference
1	$ 30,000	$ 36,000	$ (6,000)
2	30,000	57,600	(27,600)
3	30,000	34,560	(4,560)
4	30,000	20,736	9,264
5	30,000	20,736	9,264
6	30,000	10,368	19,632
	$180,000	$180,000	$ -0-

The difference in depreciation accounting is the only difference Dean has between accounting income and taxable income for the six years involved. Tax rates enacted as of the beginning of Year 1 are 40% for Year 1, 30% for Years 2 and 3, and 25% for Year 4 and later years.

Instructions

(a) Compute the temporary difference at the end of each of the six years.

(b) Assuming taxable income of $40,000 for Year 1 and expectations of taxable income for all future years, compute the amount of net future taxes to be reported on Dean's balance sheet at the end of Year 1. (Indicate whether the amount is to be classified as an asset or a liability.)

(c) Assuming taxable income of $40,000 for Year 1, expectations of losses for tax purposes for Years 2 and 3 (the benefits of which are expected to be realized through the carryback provision), and expectations of taxable income for Year 4 and later years, compute the amount of net future income taxes to be reported on Dean's balance sheet at the end of Year 1. Indicate the proper classification of the future taxes calculated.

(d) Assuming zero taxable income for Year 1, expectations of losses for tax purposes for Years 2 and 3, and expectations of taxable income for Years 4 and later, compute the amount of net future taxes to be reported on Dean's balance sheet at the end of Year 1.

The following information was disclosed during the audit of the Conrad Corporation. **P19-10**

1.

Year	Amount Due Per Tax Return
1997	$130,000
1998	102,000

2. On January 1, 1997, equipment costing $400,000 is purchased. For accounting purposes, the company uses straight-line depreciation over a five-year life. For tax purposes, the company uses CCA at a 25% rate.

3. In January 1998, $225,000 is collected in advance for the rental of a building for a three-year period. The entire $225,000 is reported as taxable income in 1998, but $150,000 of the $225,000 is reported as unearned revenue in 1998 for financial reporting purposes. The remaining amount of unearned revenue is to be earned equally in 1999 and 2000.

4. The tax rate is 40% in 1997 and all subsequent periods.

5. No temporary differences existed at the end of 1996. Conrad expects to report taxable income in each of the next five years.

Instructions
(a) Determine the amount to report for future income taxes at the end of 1997 and indicate how it should be classified on the balance sheet.
(b) Prepare the journal entry(ies) to record income taxes for 1997.
(c) Draft the Income Tax section of the 1997 income statement beginning with the line "income before income taxes." (Hint: You must compute taxable income and then combine that with changes in the temporary differences to arrive at accounting income.)
(d) Determine the future income taxes at the end of 1998 and indicate how they should be classified on the balance sheet.
(e) Prepare the journal entry(ies) to record income taxes for 1998.
(f) Draft the Income Tax section of the 1998 income statement beginning with the line "income before income taxes."

CASES

The amount of income taxes due to the government for a period of time is rarely the amount reported on the income statement for that period as income tax expense. **C19-1**

Instructions
(a) Explain the objectives of accounting for income taxes in general purpose financial statements.
(b) Explain the basic principles that are applied in accounting for income taxes at the date of the financial statements to meet the objectives discussed in (a).
(c) List the steps in the annual computation of future tax liabilities and assets.

The J. Howe Company appropriately uses the asset-liability method to record future income taxes. J. Howe reports **C19-2**
depreciation expense for certain machinery purchased this year using the capital cost allowance system for tax purposes and the straight-line basis for financial reporting purposes. The tax deduction is the larger amount this year.

J. Howe received rent revenues in advance this year. These revenues are included in this year's taxable income. However, for financial reporting purposes, these revenues are reported as unearned revenues, a current liability.

Instructions
(a) What are the principles of the asset-liability approach?
(b) How would J. Howe account for the temporary differences?
(c) How should J. Howe classify the future tax consequences of the temporary differences on its balance sheet?

C19-3   The asset-liability approach for recording future income taxes is a widely accepted method of accounting for inter-period tax allocation. The application of intraperiod tax allocation (within a period) is also required.

Instructions
(a) Explain the need for intraperiod tax allocation.
(b) Indicate whether each of the following independent situations results in a temporary difference in interperiod tax allocation and explain why or why not.
   1. Estimated warranty costs (covering a three-year warranty) are expensed for accounting purposes at the time of sale but deducted for income tax purposes when paid.
   2. Depreciation for accounting and income tax purposes differs because of different bases of carrying the related property, which was acquired in a trade-in. The different bases are a result of different rules used for accounting and tax purposes to compute the cost of assets acquired in a trade-in.
   3. A company properly uses the equity method to account for its 30% investment in another company. The investee pays nontaxable dividends that are about 10% of its annual earnings.
(c) Discuss the nature of the future income tax accounts and possible classifications in a company's balance sheet. Indicate the manner in which these accounts are to be reported.

C19-4   Listed below are 15 items that are treated differently for accounting purposes than they are for tax purposes.
   1. Excess of charge to accounting records (allowance method) over charge to tax return (direct write-off method) for uncollectible receivables.
   2. Excess of accrued pension expense over amount paid.
   3. Receipt of dividends from a Canadian corporation treated as income for accounting purposes, but which are not subject to tax.
   4. Instalment sales are accounted for on the accrual basis for financial reporting purposes and on the cash basis for tax purposes.
   5. Expenses incurred in obtaining tax-exempt income.
   6. A trademark acquired directly from the government is capitalized and amortized over subsequent periods for accounting purposes and expensed for tax purposes.
   7. Prepaid advertising expense is deferred for accounting purposes and is deducted as an expense for tax purposes.
   8. Premiums paid on life insurance of officers (corporation is the beneficiary).
   9. Penalty for filing a late tax return.
   10. Proceeds of life insurance policies on lives of officers.
   11. Estimated future warranty costs are recognized in determining accounting income.
   12. Fine for polluting, not tax deductible.
   13. Excess of CCA over accounting depreciation.
   14. Tax-exempt interest revenue.
   15. Excess depletion for accounting purposes over amount taken for tax purposes.

Instructions
For each item above:
(a) Indicate if it is:
   1. A timing difference, or
   2. A permanent difference.
(b) Indicate if it will:
   1. Create future taxable amounts, or
   2. Create future deductible amounts, or
   3. Not affect any future tax returns.

(c) Indicate if it usually will:
   1. Result in reporting a future tax liability, or
   2. Result in reporting a future tax asset, or
   3. Not result in reporting any future taxes.

Part A   **C19-5**

This year the Joyce Company has each of the following items in its income statement:
   1. Gross profit on instalment sales.
   2. Revenues on long-term construction contracts.
   3. Estimated costs of product warranty contracts.
   4. Premiums on officers' life insurance with Joyce as beneficiary.

Instructions

(a) Under what conditions would future income taxes need to be reported in the financial statements?

(b) Specify when future income taxes would need to be recognized for each of the items above, and indicate the rationale for such recognition.

Part B

Joyce Company's president has heard that future income taxes can be classified in different ways in the balance sheet.

Instructions

Identify the conditions under which future income taxes would be classified as a noncurrent item in the balance sheet. What justification exists for such classification?   (AICPA adapted)

At December 31, 1998 Carol Loughery Corporation has one temporary difference that will reverse and cause taxable   **C19-6**
amounts in 1999. In 1998 new tax regulations set taxes equal to 50% for 1998, 40% for 1999, and 35% for 2000 and
years thereafter.

Instructions

Explain what circumstances would call for Carol Loughery to compute its future tax liability at the end of 1998 by multiplying the temporary difference by:

(a) 50%.

(b) 40%.

(c) 35%.

Michael Layton and Lara Morrison are discussing accounting for income taxes. They are currently studying a sched-   **C19-7**
ule of taxable and deductible amounts that will arise in the future as a result of existing temporary differences. The
schedule is as follows:

	Current Year	Future Years			
	1998	1999	2000	2001	2002
Taxable income	$700,000				
Taxable amounts		$300,000	$300,000	$ 300,000	$300,000
Deductible amounts				(2,000,000)	
Enacted tax rate	50%	45%	40%	35%	30%

Instructions

(a) Explain the concept of future taxable amounts and future deductible amounts as illustrated in the schedule.

(b) How do the carryback and carryforward provisions affect the reporting of future tax assets and future tax liabilities?

USING YOUR JUDGEMENT

FINANCIAL REPORTING PROBLEM

Refer to the financial statements of Moore Corporation Limited presented in Appendix 5A and answer the following questions.

1. In its 1995 Statement of Earnings, Moore reported $123,738,000 of income tax expense. This provision was equivalent to a 31.6% effective income tax rate for the year. What were the factors that caused Moore's effective tax rate to deviate from the combined federal and provincial statutory income tax rate of 43.8%?

2. In Note 21 to the financial statements, Moore discloses the main items included in deferred income taxes under United States GAAP. Noting that Section 3465 uses the term *future income taxes* instead of *deferred income taxes*, and that this *Handbook* section brings the Canadian position closer to that of the United States, provide explanations for the $165,974,000 of future income tax assets that would appear on Moore's balance sheet under the U.S. and Section 3465 requirements.

3. How has Moore classified its deferred income tax accounts on the December 31, 1995 balance sheet? Explain the rationale for the classifications used.

4. Moore Corporation incurred a loss in 1993. Did the company report income tax expense in this year? Explain fully.

ETHICS CASE

Nona Anderson, CMA, is the newly hired director of corporate taxation for Major Electric Limited (ME), which is a publically traded corporation. Nona's first job with ME was the review of the company's accounting practices on deferred (future) income taxes. In carrying out her review, she noticed differences between tax and accounting depreciation methods that resulted in ME reporting a sizable future tax liability on its balance sheet, but no income taxes payable in respect of the current period. Nona also discovered that ME has an explicit policy of selling off capital assets before they reversed in the future income tax account. This policy, coupled with the rapid expansion of its capital asset base, allowed ME to "defer" all income taxes payable for several years, even though it has always reported positive earnings and an increasing EPS. Nona checked with the legal department and found the policy to be legal, but she's concerned with the ethics of it.

Instructions
(a) Why would Major Electric have an explicit policy of selling assets before they reversed in the future income tax account?
(b) What are the ethical implications of Major Electric's "deferral" of income taxes?
(c) Who could be harmed by Major Electric's ability to "defer" income taxes payable for several years, despite positive earnings?
(d) As a CMA, what are Nona Anderson's professional responsibilities in a situation such as this?

chapter 20

PENSIONS AND OTHER EMPLOYEES' FUTURE BENEFITS

Pensions and Other Employees' Future Benefits

Learning Objectives

After studying this chapter, you should be able to:

1. Describe a defined benefit plan with service related benefits.

2. Identify types of pension plans and their characteristics.

3. Distinguish between accounting for the employer's pension costs and accounting for the pension plan.

4. Explain alternatives for measuring the pension obligation.

5. Identify the major components of pension expense.

6. Define projected benefit obligation and identify events that affect its balance.

7. Define plan assets and identify events that affect their balance.

8. Explain the usefulness of—and be able to complete—a work sheet to support the employer's pension expense entries.

9. Explain the pension accounting treatment of past service costs.

10. Explain the pension accounting treatment of actuarial gains and losses, including corridor amortization.

11. Identify the differences between pensions and post-retirement health care benefits.

12. Identify the financial reporting and disclosure requirements for defined benefit plans with service related benefits.

13. Identify the accounting and disclosure requirements for defined benefit plans whose benefits are not service related.

14. Identify the accounting and disclosure requirements for defined contribution plans.

15. Differentiate between plan settlements and plan curtailments (Appendix 20A).

16. Explain why there is a limit on the accrued benefit asset recognized on the balance sheet (Appendix 20A).

17. Differentiate between termination benefits that are part of an existing plan and special termination benefits (Appendix 20A).

Since the late 1800s, many business organizations have been concerned with providing for the retirement of their employees. During recent decades a marked increase in this concern has resulted in the establishment of private pension and other benefit plans in companies of all sizes. By the mid 1990s, gross assets held by trusteed pension funds in Canada exceeded $300 billion, more than triple the value of 10 years earlier. The substantial growth of pension plans, both in numbers of employees covered and in dollar amounts of retirement benefits, has increased the significance of pension costs in relation to a company's financial position, results of operations, and cash flows. Generally accepted accounting principles for pension accounting by employers have been provided in Section 3460 of the *CICA Handbook* for many years, but the accounting for pensions has been—and continues to be—a much debated topic; some aspects are still controversial.[1] Increasingly, in addition to providing pensions to employees, companies are committing to other retirement benefits, post-employment benefits, compensated absences, and termination benefits.

In an attempt to ensure that different types of employees' future benefits are accounted for using similar principles, and to eliminate, where possible, differences between U.S. and Canadian practice, the AcSB of the CICA has begun the process of revising *Handbook* Section 3460. In June, 1997 an *Exposure Draft* entitled "Employees' Future Benefits" was issued. Because the current standard-setting climate in Canada supports the elimination of U.S./Canadian GAAP differences wherever possible, and because the authors hold the opinion that the major aspects of the *Exposure Draft* will find general acceptance, this chapter is based on the June, 1997 *Exposure Draft* proposals.

Part 1 of this chapter covers the accounting for defined benefit pension plans and other future benefits that are related to the amount of service provided by employees. The costs of these future benefits are accrued by the company as the benefits are earned. Part 2 looks at accounting for the costs of future benefits where the level of benefits provided is the same for all employees regardless of years of service. The "event accrual" method of accounting deemed appropriate for the costs related to this type of benefit is explained in this segment. Part 3 discusses defined contribution and other future benefit plans where the cash basis is recommended as the appropriate method of accounting for the costs. Complexities related to settlements and curtailments, limitations on the amount of benefit asset to be recognized, and termination benefits are the subject of Appendix 20A.

Benefits such as salaries, wages, bonuses, occasional sick days that do not accumulate, and other fringe benefits that employees earn in the current year and that are provided shortly thereafter are addressed in Chapter 14. Stock options and share purchase plans are covered in Chapter 18.

PART 1: DEFINED BENEFIT PLANS— SERVICE RELATED FUTURE BENEFITS

INTRODUCTION

The first and most complex type of benefit plan is one that provides defined benefits that depend on, or are increased by, the length of an employee's service.[2] Accounting for the cost of such benefits follows full accrual accounting in that the expense and liability are recognized over the periods in which the related services are provided.

A **defined benefit plan** is "a plan that specifies either the benefits to be received by employees, for example, $100,000 of life insurance, semi-private hospital accommodation, or the method for determining those benefits, for example, a pension equal to 1.5% of the average of five years salary times the total years of service, 80% of the cost of prescriptions, and so forth. Any benefit plan that is not a defined contribution plan is a defined benefit plan."[3]

OBJECTIVE 1
Describe a defined benefit plan with service related benefits.

---

[1] Note that this chapter takes the perspective of accounting by the employer company, not the perspective of the pension or other benefit plan itself.

[2] CICA *Exposure Draft*, "Employees' Future Benefits" (June, 1997) par. .006(h) defines a **benefit plan** as "any arrangement,...whereby an entity undertakes to provide its current and former employees with benefits after active service in exchange for their services." The plan may be in writing or implied from past practice or oral representations.

[3] *Ibid.*, par. .006(j).

The second characteristic, that the future benefits depend upon or are increased by the length of service, requires further explanation. Employees' rights to *pension benefits* usually vest after they work a specified number of years, and the amount of the benefit generally increases with the length of service provided. **Vesting** occurs when the right to receive future benefits is conferred on an employee, whether or not the employee remains in the service of the entity.[4] The rights to most *other retirement benefits*, such as supplementary health insurance, usually accrue to employees who have been employed for a required length of time and/or who have reached a specified age. Some *post-employment benefits* and *compensated absences* are service related as well. Examples in which the rights to the benefits are earned by providing services include sick leave that accumulates and is paid out without an illness-related absence and long-term disability that increases with length of service. Either the employee must work for a specified period of time before the benefits vest, or the benefit increases or accumulates with the length of service provided.[5]

In each of these cases the benefits are earned by the employees as they provide services. The expense should therefore be recognized over the same periods. It is important to correctly identify the accounting periods to which the benefits should be attributed. The matching principle is applied in the *Exposure Draft* by requiring that *the cost of the future benefits be attributed to the periods beginning with the date of hire and ending with the date on which the employee obtains full eligibility for the benefits.*[6]

Accounting for defined benefit plans with service related future benefits is explained below as it relates to a common employee future benefit: a defined benefit pension plan.

DEFINED BENEFIT PENSION PLANS

BACKGROUND

OBJECTIVE 2
Identify types of pension plans and their characteristics.

A **pension plan** is an arrangement whereby an employer promises to provide benefits (payments) to employees after they retire for services they provided while employed. The two most common types of pension arrangements are defined contribution plans and defined benefit plans.

In a **defined contribution plan**, the employer agrees to contribute to a pension trust a certain sum each period based on a formula. The formula may consider factors such as age, length of employee service, employer's profits, and compensation levels, but *only the employer's contribution to the fund is defined*. No promise is made regarding the ultimate benefits to be paid out to the employees. Because the size of the pension benefit that the employee finally collects under this type of plan depends on the amounts originally contributed, the income accumulated on the funds invested, the treatment of forfeitures of funds caused by early terminations of other employees, and the economic conditions prevailing at retirement, the employee assumes the economic risk. The employer's responsibility is limited to making a contribution each year based on the formula established in the plan.

A **defined benefit plan**, in contrast, defines the amount of pension the employee will receive at the time of retirement. The formula that is typically used provides for the pension benefit to be a function of the employee's years of service and the employee's compensation level when he or she nears retirement. In order to match the pension expense with the accounting period that benefits from the employee service, it is necessary to determine what the cost is today to meet the pension benefit commitments that will be paid after retirement.

While the employees are the beneficiaries of a defined contribution plan or trust, *the employer is the beneficiary of a defined benefit trust*. The trust's primary purpose under

---

[4] CICA *Exposure Draft*, "Employees' Future Benefits" (June, 1997), par. .006(r).

[5] *Ibid.*, pars. .029 and .031.

[6] *Ibid.*, par. .043.

a defined benefit plan is to safeguard the assets and to invest them so that there will be enough to pay the employer's obligation to the employees when they retire. *In form*, the trust is a separate entity; *in substance*, the trust assets and liabilities belong to the employer. That is, *as long as the plan continues, and without regard to what happens in the trust, the employer is responsible for the payment of the defined benefits*. Any shortfall in the accumulated assets held by the trust must be made up by the employer. Any excess accumulated in the trust can be recaptured by the employer, either through reduced future funding or through a reversion of funds.[7]

With a defined benefit plan, the employer assumes the economic risks: the employee is secure because the benefits to be paid upon retirement are predefined, but the employer is at risk because the cost is uncertain. The cost depends on factors such as employee turnover, mortality, length of service, and compensation levels as well as investment returns earned on pension fund assets, inflation, and other economic conditions over long periods of time.

Because the cost to the company is subject to a wide range of uncertain future variables, *accounting for a defined benefit plan is complex*. Measurement of the pension expense and liability to be recognized each period as the employees provide services to earn their pension entitlement is not a simple task. In addition, an appropriate funding pattern must be established to assure that enough funds are available at retirement to provide the benefits promised. Note that the expense to be recognized each period is not necessarily equal to the cash funding contribution, just as the depreciation expense recognized on the use of a capital asset is not defined in terms of how the asset is paid for or financed!

The accounting issues related to defined benefit plans are complex. The discussion in the following sections therefore deal primarily with this type of plan.[8]

EMPLOYER VERSUS PLAN ACCOUNTING

The subject of pension accounting may be divided and treated separately as *accounting for the employer* and *accounting for the pension plan*. The company or employer is the organization that sponsors the pension plan. It incurs the costs and makes contributions to the pension fund. The plan is the entity that receives the contributions from the employer, administers the pension assets, and makes the benefit payments to the pension recipients (retired employees). The diagram below shows the three entities involved in a pension plan and indicates the flow of cash among them.

OBJECTIVE 3
Distinguish between accounting for the employer's pension costs and accounting for the pension plan.

ILLUSTRATION 20-1

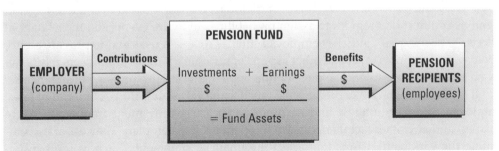

---

[7] The ownership of pension fund surpluses has been the subject of much recent litigation. The courts have increasingly determined that pension fund surpluses or a significant portion of them should accrue to the benefit of the employee group.

[8] **Multi-employer benefit plans**, plans sponsored by two or more different employers, are often negotiated as part of labour union contracts in a variety of industries. They are characterized by the pooling of plan assets so that those contributed by one entity are not restricted to providing benefits to its employees alone. Although such a plan may have the characteristics of a defined benefit plan, every employer may not have access to necessary actuarial information, in which case the employer would account for the costs of the benefits as if they were a defined contribution plan.

The preceding pension plan is being **funded**: that is, the employer company sets funds aside for future pension benefits by making payments to a funding agency that is responsible for accumulating the assets of the pension plan and for making payments to the recipients as the benefits become due.[9] In an insured plan, the funding agency is an insurance company; in a trust fund plan, the funding agency is a trustee.

In **contributory plans**, the employees bear part of the cost of the stated benefits or voluntarily make payments to increase their benefits, whereas the employer bears the entire cost in **noncontributory plans**. Companies generally design **registered pension plans** in accordance with income tax requirements that permit them to deduct contributions to the pension fund (within certain limits) and exclude earnings on the pension fund assets from taxable income.

The need for proper administration of and sound accounting for pension plans becomes apparent when one appreciates the size of these funds. For example, the companies listed below recently had pension fund assets and related shareholders' equity as follows.

EXHIBIT 20-1

Company	Pension Fund Assets (millions)	Total Shareholders' Equity (millions)
Canadian Pacific Limited	$4,117	$5,847
MacMillan Bloedel Limited (salaried employees only)	$ 602	$1,998
Royal Bank of Canada	$3,158	$9,414

The plan should have a separate legal and accounting identity for which a set of books is maintained. General purpose financial statements for pension plans are prescribed by the *CICA Handbook* in Section 4100. This chapter is concerned with the pension accounting and reporting problems of the employer as the sponsor of a pension plan rather than the reporting by the pension plan itself.

THE ROLE OF ACTUARIES

Because the problems associated with many benefit plans involve complicated actuarial considerations, actuaries are engaged to ensure that the plan is appropriate for the employee group covered. **Actuaries** are individuals who are trained through a long and rigorous certification program to assign probabilities to future events and their financial effects.[10] The insurance industry employs actuaries to assess risks and to provide advice about what premiums to set and other aspects of insurance policies. Employers rely heavily on actuaries for assistance in developing, implementing, and funding pension plans.

It is actuaries who make predictions, called **actuarial assumptions**, of mortality rates, employee turnover, interest and earnings rates, early retirement frequency, future salaries, and any other factors necessary to operate a pension plan. They assist by computing the various measures that affect the financial statements, such as the pension

---

[9] When used as a verb, "fund" means to pay to a funding agency (as to fund future pension benefits or to fund pension costs). Used as a noun, it refers to assets accumulated in the hands of a funding agency or trustee for the purpose of meeting future benefits when they become due.

[10] An actuary's primary purpose is to ensure that the company has established an appropriate funding pattern to meet its pension obligations. This computation entails the development of a set of assumptions and continued monitoring of these assumptions to assure their realism. That the general public has little understanding of what an actuary does is illustrated by the following excerpt from *The Wall Street Journal*: "A polling organization once asked the general public what an actuary was and received among its more coherent responses the opinion that it was a place where you put dead actors."

obligation, the annual cost of servicing the plan, and the cost of amendments to the plan. In summary, accounting for defined benefit pension plans is highly reliant upon information and measurements provided by actuaries.

THE PENSION OBLIGATION (LIABILITY)

In accounting for pensions, the question eventually arises: "What is the amount of the employer's liability, and what is the amount of pension obligation to report in the financial statements?" Attempting to answer this question has produced much controversy for at least two reasons. First, a variety of approaches exists to the measurement of the obligation, and second, even if agreement were reached on its measurement, there is disagreement about whether the full obligation should be recognized or whether the company's liability should be limited by relating it to the amount of pension expense recognized.

OBJECTIVE 4
Explain alternatives for measuring the pension obligation.

An employer's **pension obligation** is the deferred compensation obligation it has to the employees for their service under the terms of the pension plan. However, there are two actuarial valuation approaches that could be used to determine the liability and the cost of pension benefits for a period. **Level contribution methods** estimate the final cost of providing all future benefits and allocate this to accounting periods in equal amounts or as a constant percentage of salary. **Accrued benefit methods**, on the other hand, attribute a distinct unit of future benefit to each year of credited service, with the present value of that benefit computed separately for the period in which it is presumed to accrue. Because the accrued benefit approach provides a better matching of cost to the period when employee services are rendered, the accrued benefit method is recommended for defined benefit plans.[11] However, there are a variety of ways to measure the cost of the accrued benefits under this approach.

Alternative Measures of the Liability and Benefit Cost. One possible measure of the obligation is to limit it to the cost of the benefits vested to the employees. Vested benefits are those that the employee is entitled to receive even if the employee renders no additional services under the plan. Under most pension plans a specific minimum number of years of service to the employer is required before an employee achieves vested benefits status. The **vested benefits pension obligation** is computed *using current salary levels and includes only vested benefits*.

Another measure bases the computation of the deferred compensation amount *on all years of service performed by employees under the plan—both vested and nonvested—using current salary levels*. This measurement of the pension obligation is called the **accumulated benefit obligation**.

A third possibility bases the computation of the deferred compensation amount *on both vested and nonvested service using future salaries*. This measurement of the pension obligation is called the **projected benefit obligation**. Because future salaries are expected to be higher than current salaries, this approach results in the largest measure of the pension obligation. Within this method, two different approaches exist. One, the projected benefit method *pro rated on salaries*, allocates the cost to each period based on the percentage of total estimated career compensation earned by the employee in that period. Because salaries are expected to increase over time, relatively low amounts are attributed to the employees' early years and large amounts to later years. The projected benefit method *pro rated on services* allocates an equal portion of the cost of the total estimated benefit to each year of an employee's service.[12] The result of this method is an accrual of a more equal charge each period.

---

[11] CICA *Exposure Draft*, "Employees' Future Benefits" (June, 1997), pars. .006(b) and .039.

[12] *Ibid.*, par. .006(b)(ii) and (iii).

The choice among these measures is critical because it affects the amount of the pension liability and the annual pension expense reported. Regardless of the approach used, the estimated future benefits to be paid are discounted to their present value.[13]

Which of these methods does the *Exposure Draft* propose? Consistent with existing *Handbook* Section 3460, **the Exposure Draft** *recommends the accrued benefit method for all defined benefit plans, and where future salary levels affect the amount of the future benefits, that the projected benefit method pro rated on services be used to determine the obligation.*[14]

Those critical of the projected benefit obligation argue that using future salary levels is tantamount to adding future obligations to existing ones. Those in favour of the projected benefit obligation contend that a promise by an employer to pay benefits based on the employees' future salary is far different from a promise to pay benefits based on their current salary, and such a difference should be reflected in the measure of the liability and the expense.

CAPITALIZATION VERSUS NONCAPITALIZATION

Another fundamental choice in accounting for pensions and other future benefits is whether a capitalization or noncapitalization approach should be taken. The major issue in this case is whether the full obligation should be recognized as a liability, or whether the amount recorded should be restricted and related to the amount of expense recognized.

Under a **capitalization approach**, pension plan assets and full pension obligations are reported as assets and liabilities on the employer company's balance sheet. This portrays the economic substance of the pension plan arrangement, since the employer has a clear obligation to pay pension benefits for employee services already performed. As the employees work, pension expense is incurred and the employer's liability increases. The pension liability and the pension assets are both reduced through the payment of benefits to retired employees. Funding the plan is recognized on the balance sheet by the transfer of company assets into a separate category of asset set aside for the pension fund, *but the funding has no effect on the amount of the liability*

A **noncapitalization approach**, on the other hand, is more consistent with the legal form of pension arrangements whereby the plan is considered a separate legal and accounting entity. *Cash and investments set aside to fund pension obligations are considered assets of the pension plan, not of the employer company; therefore, neither the pension assets nor the obligation are recognized on the employer's balance sheet.* Under this approach, the employer accrues a pension liability equal to the pension expense recognized, and as long as the employer's contribution to the trustee of the fund is the same as the pension expense, the balance sheet reports no asset or liability related to the pension plan. If the funding exceeds the expense recognized, a prepaid expense is included on the balance sheet; if the funding is less than the expense, a pension liability is recorded. When the trustee pays benefits to retirees, the employer records no entries because the company's recorded assets and liabilities are not reduced. This approach is often referred to as a method of **off-balance-sheet financing** because the over- or underfunding of the plan itself for which the employer is ultimately responsible is not recognized on the company's balance sheet.

---

[13] When the phrase "present value of benefits" is used throughout this chapter, it means the actuarial present value of benefits. Actuarial present value is the amount payable adjusted to reflect the time value of money and the probability of payment (by means of decrements for events such as death, disability, withdrawals, or retirement) between the present date and the expected date of payment. For simplicity, the term "present value" instead of "actuarial present value" is used.

[14] CICA *Exposure Draft*, "Employees' Future Benefits" (June, 1997), par. .039.

The Accounting Standards Board adopted a noncapitalization approach as a compromise position in *Handbook* Section 3460, and this has been carried forward to the 1997 *Exposure Draft*.

MAJOR COMPONENTS OF PENSION EXPENSE

There is broad agreement that pension costs should be accounted for on the accrual basis and be matched with the accounting period that benefits from the employees' service. The profession recognizes that *accounting for pension plans requires measurement of the cost and its identification with appropriate time periods*. The determination of pension expense for a particular period, however, is complex. The following illustration summarizes the major components and the effect of each on pension expense.

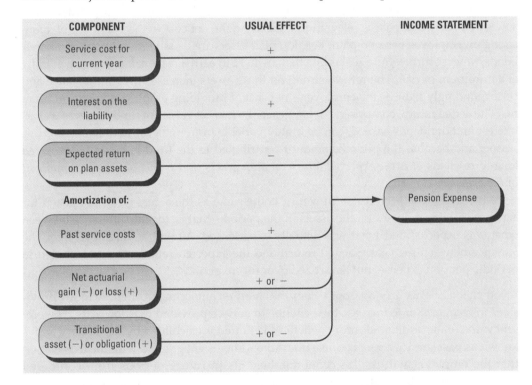

ILLUSTRATION 20-2
Components of Annual Pension Expense

Service Cost.   The **service cost** is the cost of the benefits provided in exchange for employees' services rendered in the period. The actuary predicts the additional benefits that must be paid under the plan's benefit formula as a result of the employees' current year's service and then discounts the cost of these benefits to their present value.

OBJECTIVE 5
Identify the major components of pension expense.

As indicated earlier, for defined benefit plans where future benefits depend on or are increased by the length of service, the actuary should base his or her calculations on future salary levels and attribute the cost of the future benefits to the accounting periods beginning at the date of hire and ending when the employee obtains full eligibility for benefits.[15] The AcSB supports the projected benefit actuarial method because it provides a more realistic measure on a going concern basis of the employer's obligation under the plan and, therefore, of determining current service cost.

Interest on the Liability.   The second component of pension expense is **interest on the liability**. Because a pension is a deferred compensation arrangement whereby this element of wages is deferred and an obligation is created, the time value of money becomes a factor. Because the obligation is not paid until maturity, it is measured on a discounted basis

---

[15] CICA *Exposure Draft*, "Employees' Future Benefits" (June, 1997), pars. .069(a), .039, and .043.

and accrues interest with the passage of time. *Interest expense accrues each year on the projected benefit obligation just as it does on any discounted debt, with interest computed as the expected increase in the benefit obligation to recognize the effects of the passage of time.*

What interest rate should be used? Section 3460 currently requires that the discount rate reflect management's best estimates, and, while suggesting that they take into account the long-term nature of the plan and expected long-term future events, it does permit the use of a current rate. The *Exposure Draft*, consistent with the U.S. standard for pensions, requires the use of a **current market rate**, such as the current yield on high-quality debt instruments. Alternatively, entities could use a current **settlement rate**, the rate implied in an insurance contract that could be purchased to effectively settle the pension obligation.[16]

Expected Return on Plan Assets. The return earned by the accumulated pension fund assets in a particular year is relevant in measuring the net cost to the employer of sponsoring an employee pension plan. Pension plan assets are usually investments in shares, bonds, other securities, and real estate that are held to earn a reasonable return, generally at a minimum of risk. The return earned on these assets increases the fund balance and correspondingly reduces the employer's net cost of providing employees' pension benefits. The actual return, comprised of changes in the market values of fund assets as well as interest and dividends earned, can be highly variable from one year to the next. For this reason, and because the periodic amount contributed to the fund is based on expected long-term yields, *it is the expected return on plan assets that is included as a component of the expense.*

Note that the **expected rate of return** is the same as the actual return, adjusted for experience gains or losses on the assets in the period—that is, for the difference between what was expected and what was actually experienced. As will be discussed later, the variance between the yearly actual return and the expected return may be included in periodic pension expense, but amortized over future periods.

Amortization of Past Service Costs. Plan initiation or amendment often includes provisions to recognize or to increase the benefits for service provided in prior years. The present value of the additional future benefits so granted is calculated by the actuary and is known as **past service costs**. Because plan amendments are granted with the expectation that the employer will realize economic benefits in future periods from continued employee service, the past service cost is generally allocated to pension expense in the future, normally over the expected period to full eligibility of the affected employee group.[17]

Amortization of the Net Actuarial Gain or Loss. **Actuarial gains and losses** arise from two sources: (1) a change in actuarial assumptions—that is, assumptions as to the occurrence of future events that affect the measurement of employees' future benefit costs and obligations; and (2) **experience gains and losses**—the difference between what has occurred and the previous actuarial assumptions as to what was expected.[18] When assumptions are proven to be inaccurate by later events, adjustments are needed. The net accumulated actuarial gain or loss, if significant, is amortized over future periods using a "corridor approach" described later in the chapter.

---

[16] The difference in discount rates is not insignificant. In 1994, each one percentage point change in rate for General Motors would change the pension obligation by close to U.S.$5 billion.

[17] CICA *Exposure Draft*, "Employees' Future Benefits" (June, 1997), par. .077.

[18] *Ibid.*, pars. .006(d) and (e). Examples of actuarial assumptions underlying pension plans include those about rates of return on plan assets, termination rates, disability claims, retirement age, mortality, dependency status, discount rates, and future salary levels.

Amortization of Transitional Asset or Obligation. The amendments to Section 3460 in the late 1980s involved significant changes in pension accounting as will the 1997 *Exposure Draft* proposals, particularly with respect to post-retirement benefits other than pensions. When companies apply the new requirements for the first time, the excess or deficiency of the projected benefit obligation over the fair value of the plan assets at that time has to be determined. Where recommendations (of Section 3460 in the past or of the finalized *Exposure Draft* in the future) are applied prospectively, the net **transitional asset** or **transitional obligation** is amortized to expense rather than given immediate recognition. Both Section 3460 and the *Exposure Draft* call for amortization of this transitional balance in a systematic and rational basis over an appropriate period of time, which normally is the expected average remaining service life of the employee group covered by the plan. The **expected average remaining service life** of an employee group, known as **EARSL**, is the total number of years of future service expected to be rendered by that group divided by the number of employees in the group.[19]

Other Components. Four other components of expense for the period are identified in the 1997 *Exposure Draft*, including gains and losses on plan settlements and curtailments, termination benefits, and amounts recognized as a valuation allowance. These aspects are discussed in Appendix 20A to this chapter.

PROJECTED BENEFIT OBLIGATION AND PLAN ASSETS

Although not recognized on the employer's balance sheet as liabilities and assets, the projected benefit obligation and plan assets lie at the heart of accounting for pension costs. Understanding the nature of the obligation and fund assets and the transactions and events that affect their measurement clarifies the study of accounting for benefit plans.

The following illustration summarizes the **projected benefit obligation**, or **PBO**, from the perspective of the transactions and events that change it. At any point in time, the PBO represents the actuarial present value of the benefits accumulated by employees for services rendered to date. This increases as employees render further services, as interest is added, and as plans are amended to increase future benefits related to past service. Payments to retirees reduce the liability, and changed assumptions either increase or decrease the liability balance. Actuaries provide most of the necessary measurements related to the PBO.

OBJECTIVE 6
Define projected benefit obligation and identify events that affect its balance.

EXHIBIT 20-2

PROJECTED BENEFIT OBLIGATION (PBO) CONTINUITY SCHEDULE

PBO, beginning of period

+ Current service cost

+ Interest cost

+ Past service costs of plan amendments during period

− Benefits paid to retirees

± Actuarial gains (−) or losses (+) during period on the PBO

= PBO, end of period

---

[19] CICA *Exposure Draft*, "Employees' Future Benefits" (June, 1997), par. .006(l).

OBJECTIVE 7
Define plan assets and identify events that affect their balance.

The plan assets are the other major element. As can be seen from the exhibit below, the assets increase as a result of contributions from the employer (and employee, if the plan is contributory) and from the actual return generated on the assets invested. Payments to retirees reduce the pool of assets. The relationship between the actual and expected return is also illustrated, indicating that the actual return is made up of what was expected and the difference between what was expected and what actually happened. The plan trustee provides most of this information.

EXHIBIT 20-3

PLAN ASSETS CONTINUITY SCHEDULE

Plan assets, fair value at beginning of period

+ Contributions from employer company, and employees, if applicable

+ Expected return

+ Experience gain
    or   or $\pm$ Actual return

− Experience loss

− Benefits paid to retirees

= Plan assets, fair value at end of period

The difference between the projected benefit obligation and the fair value of the pension assets at any point in time is known as the plan's **funded status**. A plan with liabilities that exceed assets is underfunded; a plan with accumulated assets in excess of the related obligation is said to be overfunded.

Before covering the more complex pension expense components in detail, we will illustrate the basic accounting entries for the first three components: service cost, interest, and expected return on plan assets.

ILLUSTRATION

Among the compromises the AcSB made when Section 3460 was issued (and carried forward to the 1997 *Exposure Draft*) was the nonrecognition (noncapitalization) in the financial statements of several significant items related to the pension plan. These include the following items.

1. Projected benefit obligation.

2. Pension plan assets.

3. Unrecognized past service cost.

4. Unrecognized net actuarial gain or loss.

5. Unrecognized transitional balance.

OBJECTIVE 8
Explain the usefulness of—and be able to complete—a work sheet to support the employer's pension expense entries.

As discussed later, the employer is required to disclose many of these balances in the notes to the financial statements, but the balances are not recognized in the body of the financial statements. Their exact amounts must be known at all times because they are used in the computation of annual pension expense. Therefore, in order to track these off-balance-sheet pension items, supplementary information has to be maintained outside the formal general ledger accounting system. As an example of how this could be done, a work sheet unique to pension accounting will be used to record both the formal entries and the memo entries to keep track of all the employer's relevant pension plan items and components.[20]

The format of the work sheet follows.

---

[20] The use of this pension entry work sheet is recommended and illustrated by Paul B.W. Miller, "The New Pension Accounting (Part 2)," *Journal of Accountancy*, February, 1987, pp. 86–94.

EXHIBIT 20-4

PENSION WORK SHEET

	General Journal Entries			Memo Record	
Items	Annual Pension Expense	Cash	Prepaid/ Accrued Cost	Projected Benefit Obligation	Plan Assets

---

The left-hand "General Journal Entries" columns of the work sheet indicate entries needed in the formal general ledger accounts. The right-hand "Memo Record" columns maintain balances on the unrecognized (noncapitalized) pension items. On the first line of the work sheet, the beginning balances are recorded. Subsequently, transactions and events related to the pension plan are recorded, using debits and credits and using both sets of records as if they were one for recording the entries. For each transaction or event, the debits must equal the credits.

1998 Entries and Work Sheet. To illustrate the use of the work sheet and how it helps in accounting for a pension plan, assume that on January 1, 1998 Zarle Company adopts *Handbook* Section 3460 to account for its defined benefit pension plan. The following facts apply to the pension plan for the year 1998.

1. Plan assets, January 1, 1998 are $100,000 and at December 31, 1998 are $111,000.

2. Projected benefit obligation, January 1, 1998 is $100,000 and at December 31, 1998 is $112,000.

3. Annual service cost for 1998 is $9,000, accrued as of the end of 1998.

4. Interest (discount) rate on the liability for 1998 is 10%.

5. Expected and actual earnings on plan assets for 1998 is 10%.

6. Contributions (funding) in 1998 are $8,000, remitted at the end of 1998.

7. Benefits paid to retirees in 1998 are $7,000, paid at the end of 1998.

Using the data presented above, the following work sheet presents the beginning balances and all of the pension entries recorded by Zarle Company in 1998.

EXHIBIT 20-5 ZARLE COMPANY

PENSION WORK SHEET: 1998

	General Journal Entries			Memo Record	
Items	Annual Pension Expense	Cash	Prepaid/ Accrued Cost	Projected Benefit Obligation	Plan Assets
Balance, Jan. 1, 1998				100,000 Cr.	100,000 Dr.
(a) Service cost	9,000 Dr.			9,000 Cr.	
(b) Interest cost	10,000 Dr.			10,000 Cr.	
(c) Expected return	10,000 Cr.				10,000 Dr.
(d) Contributions		8,000 Cr.			8,000 Dr.
(e) Benefits paid				7,000 Dr.	7,000 Cr.
Expense entry, 1998	9,000 Dr.		9,000 Cr.		
Contribution, 1998		8,000 Cr.	8,000 Dr.		
Balance, Dec. 31,1998			1,000 Cr.	112,000 Cr.	111,000 Dr.

The beginning balances for the projected benefit obligation and the pension plan assets are recorded on the first line of the work sheet in the memo record. They are not recorded in the formal general journal and, therefore, are not reported as a liability and an asset in the financial statements of Zarle Company. These two significant pension items are therefore examples of off-balance-sheet amounts that affect pension expense but are not recorded as assets and liabilities in the employer's books.

Entry (a) recognizes the service cost component, which increases pension expense $9,000 and increases the liability (projected benefit obligation) $9,000. Entry (b) accrues the interest expense component, which increases both the PBO and the pension expense $10,000 (the beginning projected benefit obligation multiplied by the interest rate of 10%). Entry (c) records the expected return on plan assets, which increases the plan assets and decreases the pension expense. Entry (d) reflects Zarle Company's contribution (funding) of assets to the pension fund; cash is decreased $8,000 and plan assets are increased $8,000. Entry (e) records the benefit payments made to retirees, which results in equal $7,000 decreases to the plan assets and the projected benefit obligation.

The adjusting journal entry on December 31, 1998 to formally record the pension expense for the year is as follows.

| Pension Expense | 9,000 | |
| Prepaid/Accrued Pension Cost | | 9,000 |

When Zarle Company issued its $8,000 cheque to the pension fund trustee, the following entry was made.

| Prepaid/Accrued Pension Cost | 8,000 | |
| Cash | | 8,000 |

The credit balance in the Prepaid/Accrued Pension Cost account of $1,000 represents the difference between the 1998 pension expense of $9,000 and the amount funded of $8,000. Because the full amount recognized as expense was not funded, a Prepaid/Accrued Pension Cost account credit balance remains. This account is usually reported as Accrued Pension Cost and is included with long-term liabilities. If the amount funded exceeds the pension expense recognized, the account would have a debit balance, be described as Deferred Pension Expense, and be included in the balance sheet with the deferred charges. Separate disclosure of this balance sheet account, the pension expense, and the employer's contribution is proposed in the 1997 Exposure Draft.[21]

The Prepaid/Accrued Pension Cost account balance of $1,000 also equals the net of the balances in the memo accounts. A reconciliation of the off-balance-sheet items with the accrued pension cost liability reported in the balance sheet is shown below.

EXHIBIT 20-6

RECONCILIATION SCHEDULE: DECEMBER 31, 1998

Projected benefit obligation (Credit)	$(112,000)
Plan assets at fair value (Debit)	111,000
Funded status—net liability (Credit)	**$ (1,000)**
Accrued pension cost liability (Credit)	$ (1,000)

[21] CICA Exposure Draft, "Employees' Future Benefits" (June, 1997), par. .138(e)–(g).

If the net of the balances in the memo record accounts is a credit, then the reconciling amount in the Prepaid/Accrued Cost column will also be a credit that is equal in amount. If the net of the memo record balances is a debit, the Prepaid/Accrued Cost account will also be a debit that is equal in amount. The work sheet is designed to highlight the relationships among these accounts, information that will be useful later in preparing the notes related to pension disclosures.

AMORTIZATION OF UNRECOGNIZED PAST SERVICE COST

OBJECTIVE 9
Explain the pension accounting treatment of past service costs.

When a defined benefit plan is either initiated (adopted) or amended, credit is often given to employees for years of service provided prior to the date of initiation or amendment. As a result of these credits for past services, the actuary remeasures the projected benefit obligation, which is usually greater than it was before. The cost of the retroactive benefits is the increase in the projected benefit obligation at the date of initiation or amendment. This increase is often substantial.

One question that arises is whether the expense and related liability for these past service costs should be fully recognized at the time the plan is initiated or amended. The AcSB has taken the position that no expense for these costs should be recognized at the time of the plan's adoption or amendment. The Board's rationale is that the employer would not provide credit for past years of service unless it expected to receive benefits in the future. As a result, the 1997 *Exposure Draft* specifies that *the cost of the retroactive benefits should be recognized on a straight-line basis over an appropriate period of time, which normally would be the expected period to full eligibility of the employee group covered by the plan.*[22] This accounting treatment has the effect of smoothing the amount of pension expense from year to year.

To illustrate the amortization of unrecognized past service cost, assume that Zarle Company amends its defined benefit pension plan on January 1, 1999 to grant past service benefits to certain employees. The Company's actuaries determine that the increase that results in the projected benefit obligation is $80,000. The affected employees are grouped according to expected remaining years of service to full eligibility and the expected remaining service period is computed as follows.

EXHIBIT 20-7

Group	Number of Employees	Expected Remaining Years of Service to Full Eligibility	Total
A	40	1	40
B	20	2	40
C	40	3	120
D	50	4	200
E	20	5	100
	170		500

Expected period to full eligibility = 500 ÷ 170 = 2.94

Note: FASB prefers a "years-of-service" amortization method similar to a units-of-production computation. In the first year, for example, 170 service years are worked by employees. Therefore, 170/500 of the past service cost is recognized in the first year.

[22] CICA *Exposure Draft*, "Employees' Future Benefits." (June, 1977), par. .077. This approach represents a change from existing Section 3460. Section 3460 recommends that past service costs be amortized in a rational and systematic manner over an appropriate period of time, which normally is the expected average remaining service life (EARSL) of the employee group covered by the plan.

The annual amortization of the unrecognized past service cost to be recognized in pension expense each year is $27,211 ($80,000 ÷ 2.94) in 1999, $27,211 in 2000, and the remainder of $25,578 in 2001. Note that although the projected benefit obligation is increased as soon as the company amends the plan on January 1, 1999, the expense and associated liability are recognized on the books of Zarle over a three-year period, 1999 to 2001. At the end of 1999 and 2000, therefore, a portion of the increased obligation has not been recognized in the financial statements, but is an off-balance-sheet amount.

If full capitalization of all elements of the pension plan had been adopted, the increase in the company's obligation would have been given accounting recognition immediately as a credit to the liability and a charge (debit) to an intangible asset. The intangible asset treatment assumes that the cost of additional pension benefits increases loyalty and productivity and reduces turnover among the affected employees. This account would be amortized over its useful life.

However, past service cost is accounted for off-balance-sheet initially and may be called **unrecognized past service cost**. Although not recognized on the balance sheet immediately, past service cost is a factor in computing pension expense.

1999 Entries and Work Sheet. Continuing the Zarle Company illustration into 1999, we note that the January 1, 1999 amendment to the pension plan grants to employees past service benefits having a present value of $80,000. The annual amortization of $27,211 for 1999 as computed in the previous section is carried forward in this illustration. The following facts apply to the pension plan for the year 1999.

1. On January 1, 1999 Zarle Company grants past service benefits having a present value of $80,000.

2. Annual service cost for 1999 is $9,500.

3. Interest on the pension obligation (PBO) is 10%.

4. Expected and actual return on plan assets is 10%.

5. Annual contributions (funding) are $20,000.

6. Benefits paid to retirees in 1999 are $8,000.

7. Amortization of past service cost (PSC) is $27,211.

8. At December 31, 1999 the PBO is $212,700 and plan assets are $134,100.

In all chapter examples and end-of-chapter problem material, unless otherwise specified, it is assumed that current service cost is credited at year end and that contributions to the fund and benefits paid to retirees are year-end cash flows.

Exhibit 20-8 presents all of the pension entries and information recorded by Zarle Company in 1999. The first line of the work sheet shows the beginning balances of the Accrued Pension Cost liability account and the memo accounts. Entry (f) records Zarle Company's granting of past service benefits by adding $80,000 to the projected benefit obligation and to the unrecognized (noncapitalized) past service cost. Entries (g), (h), (i), (k), and (l) are similar to the corresponding entries in 1998. Entry (j) recognizes the 1999 amortization of unrecognized past service cost by including $27,211 in Pension Expense, reducing the Unrecognized Past Service Cost memo account by the same amount.

The journal entry on December 31, 1999 to formally record the pension expense for the year is as follows.

Pension Expense	44,811	
Prepaid/Accrued Pension Cost		44,811

EXHIBIT 20-8   ZARLE COMPANY

PENSION WORK SHEET: 1999

	General Journal Entries			Memo Record		
Items	Annual Pension Expense	Cash	Prepaid/ Accrued Cost	Projected Benefit Obligation	Plan Assets	Unrecognized Past Service Cost
Balance, Dec. 31,1998			1,000 Cr.	112,000 Cr.	111,000 Dr.	
(f) Past service cost				80,000 Cr.		80,000 Dr.
Balance, Jan. 1, 1999			1,000 Cr.	192,000 Cr.	111,000 Dr.	80,000 Dr.
(g) Service cost	9,500 Dr.			9,500 Cr.		
(h) Interest cost	19,200 Dr.			19,200 Cr.		
(i) Expected return	11,100 Cr.				11,100 Dr.	
(j) Amortization of PSC	27,211 Dr.					27,211 Cr.
(k) Contributions		20,000 Cr.			20,000 Dr.	
(l) Benefits paid				8,000 Dr.	8,000 Cr.	
Expense entry, 1999	44,811 Dr.		44,811 Cr.			
Contribution, 1999		20,000 Cr.	20,000 Dr.			
Balance, Dec. 31,1999			25,811 Cr.	212,700 Cr.	134,100 Dr.	52,789 Dr.

When the company made its contributions to the pension fund, the following entry was recorded.

Prepaid/Accrued Pension Cost	20,000
Cash	20,000

Because the expense exceeds the funding, the Accrued Pension Cost liability account increases by the $24,811 difference ($44,811 less $20,000). In 1999, as in 1998, the balance of the Prepaid/Accrued Pension Cost account ($25,811) is equal to the net of the balances in the memo accounts as shown in the following reconciliation schedule.

EXHIBIT 20-9

RECONCILIATION SCHEDULE: DECEMBER 31, 1999

Projected benefit obligation (Credit)	$ (212,700)
Plan assets at fair value (Debit)	134,100
Funded status—net liability (Credit)	(78,600)
Unrecognized past service cost (Debit)	52,789
Accrued pension cost liability (Credit)	$(25,811)

ACTUARIAL GAINS AND LOSSES

Of great concern to companies that have pension plans are the uncontrollable and unexpected swings in pension expense that could be caused by (1) large and sudden changes in the market value of plan assets; and (2) changes in actuarial assumptions that affect the

OBJECTIVE 10
Explain the pension accounting treatment of actuarial gains and losses, including corridor amortization.

amount of the projected benefit obligation. If these gains or losses were to impact fully in the financial statements in the period of realization or incurrence, substantial fluctuations in pension expense would result. Therefore, the profession decided to reduce the volatility associated with pension expense by using smoothing techniques that dampen the fluctuations.

Asset Gains and Losses. The return on plan assets is a component of pension expense that normally reduces the amount of the expense. A significant change in the actual return can substantially affect pension expense for the year. Assume a company has used 8% as an expected return on plan assets while the actual return experienced is 40%. Should this substantial and perhaps one-time event affect current pension expense?

Actuaries ignore current fluctuations when they develop a funding pattern to pay expected benefits in the future. They develop an expected rate of return and multiply it by an asset value weighted over a reasonable period of time to arrive at an expected return on plan assets. This return is then used to determine its funding pattern.

The Board adopted the actuaries' approach in order to avoid recording wide swings that might occur in the actual return: use of the *expected return* on plan assets is required as a component of pension expense. To achieve this goal, the expected rate of return (the actuary's rate) is multiplied by the market-related values of plan assets at the beginning of the year adjusted by additional contributions and payments to retirees during the year. The **market-related value of plan assets** is either the fair value of the assets or a calculated value that recognizes changes in fair value in a systematic and rational manner over no more than five years.[23] Throughout our Zarle Company illustrations, market-related value and fair value of plan assets are assumed equal.

The difference between the expected return and the actual return is referred to as an **asset experience gain or loss.** A gain occurs when the actual return is greater than the expected return and a loss occurs when actual returns are less than expected.

The annual amount of asset gain or loss is determined at the end of each year by comparing the calculated expected return with the actual return earned. In the preceding example, the expected return on Zarle's pension fund assets for 1999 was $11,100. If the actual return on the plan assets for the year 1999 was $12,000, then an experience gain of $900 ($12,000 − $11,100) exists. Plan assets are increased by $12,000, annual expense is credited with $11,100, and an unrecognized actuarial gain of $900 is included in the memo accounts.

Liability Gains and Losses. In estimating the projected benefit obligation (the liability), actuaries make assumptions about such items as mortality rate, retirement rate, turnover rate, disability rate, and salary amounts. Any difference between these assumed rates and amounts and those actually experienced changes the amount of the projected benefit obligation. Seldom does actual experience coincide exactly with actuarial predictions. Such an unexpected gain or loss that results in a change in the projected benefit obligation is referred to as a **liability experience gain or loss.** Actuarial gains and losses also arise when the assumptions used by the actuary in computing the PBO are revised, causing a change in the amount of the obligation. An example is the effect on the calculated obligation of a change in the interest rate used to discount the pension cash flows. Because experience gains and losses are similar to and affect the PBO in the same way as actuarial gains and losses, both types are referred to as actuarial gains and losses.

To illustrate, assume that the expected projected benefit obligation of Zarle Company was $212,700 at December 31, 1999. If the company's actuaries, using December 31, 1999 estimates, compute a projected benefit obligation of $213,500, then the company has suffered

---

[23] CICA *Exposure Draft*, "Employees' Future Benefits" (June, 1997), par. .074. Different ways of calculating market-related value may be used for different classes of assets. For example, an employer might use fair value for bonds and a five-year-moving-average for equities, but the manner of determining market-related value should be applied consistently from year to year for each asset class.

an actuarial loss of $800 ($213,500 − $212,700). If the actuary computes a reduced obligation, an actuarial gain results. The PBO is adjusted to its correct balance and the difference is included in the memo accounts as an unrecognized actuarial gain or loss.

CORRIDOR AMORTIZATION

Because the asset gains and losses and the liability gains and losses can offset each other, the accumulated total unrecognized net gain or loss may not grow very large. But it is possible that no offsetting will occur and the balance in the Unrecognized Net Gain or Loss account will continue to grow. To limit its growth, a **corridor approach** has been proposed for amortizing the net unrecognized gain or loss. Under this approach, *the unrecognized net gain or loss balance is considered too large and must be amortized only when it exceeds the arbitrarily selected criterion of 10% of the larger of the beginning balances of the projected benefit obligation or the market-related value of the plan assets.*

To illustrate the corridor approach, assume data on the projected benefit obligation and the plan assets over a period of six years as shown in the schedule below.

EXHIBIT 20-10

Beginning-of-the-Year Balances	Projected Benefit Obligation	Market-Related Asset Value	Corridor* +/− 10%
1996	**$1,000,000**	$ 900,000	$100,000
1997	**1,200,000**	1,100,000	120,000
1998	1,300,000	**1,700,000**	170,000
1999	1,500,000	**2,250,000**	225,000
2000	1,700,000	**1,750,000**	175,000
2001	**1,800,000**	1,700,000	180,000

*The corridor becomes 10% of the larger (in boldface) of the projected benefit obligation or the market-related plan asset value.

If the balance of the net Unrecognized Gain or Loss account stays within the limits of the corridor each year, no amortization is required—the unrecognized net gain or loss is carried forward unchanged.

If amortization is required, the minimum amortization is the excess divided by the average remaining service period of the employee group.[24] Any systematic method of amortization may be used in lieu of the amount determined under this approach, provided it is greater than the minimum and is used consistently for both gains and losses, and is disclosed. The corridor approach to amortization of actuarial gains and losses, consistent with the U.S. requirements, represents a change in Canadian practice.[25]

Illustration. In applying the corridor approach, amortization of the excess unrecognized net gain or loss should be included as a component of pension expense only if, *at the beginning of the year*, the unrecognized net gain or loss exceeded the corridor. If no unrecognized net gain or loss exists at the beginning of the period, no recognition of gains or losses can result in that period.

---

[24] CICA *Exposure Draft*, "Employees' Future Benefits" (June, 1997), par. .083.

[25] Under existing *Handbook* recommendations in Section 3460, the requirement is to amortize the gain or loss in a rational and systematic manner over an appropriate period of time, usually the EARSL. Also, actuarial gains and losses that occur in the current year are, under existing 3460, permitted to be recognized in the current year or deferred until the following year.

To illustrate the amortization of unrecognized net gains and losses, assume the following information for Soft-White, Inc.

	1998	1999	2000
Projected benefit obligation, beginning of year	$2,100,000	$2,600,000	$2,900,000
Market-related asset value, beginning of year	2,600,000	2,800,000	2,700,000
Unrecognized net loss, beginning of year	0	400,000	300,000

If the average remaining service life of the employee group is five and one-half years, the schedule to amortize the unrecognized net loss is as follows.

EXHIBIT 20-11

Year	Projected Benefit Obligation[a]	Plan Assets[a]	Corridor[b]	Cumulative Unrecognized Net Loss[a]	Minimum Amortization of Loss (For Current Year)
1998	$2,100,000	$2,600,000	$260,000	$ –0–	$ –0–
1999	2,600,000	2,800,000	280,000	400,000	21,818[c]
2000	2,900,000	2,700,000	290,000	678,182[d]	70,579[d]

[a]All as of the beginning of the period.

[b]10% of the greater of projected benefit obligation or plan assets market-related value.

[c]$400,000 − $280,000 = $120,000; $120,000 ÷ 5.5 = $21,818

[d]$400,000 − $21,818 + $300,000 = $678,182; $678,182 − $290,000 = $388,182; $388,182 ÷ 5.5 = $70,579.

As indicated in the illustration above, the $400,000 loss at the beginning of 1999 increased pension expense in 1999 by $21,818. This amount is small in comparison with the total loss of $400,000 and indicates that the corridor approach dampens the effects (reduces volatility) of these gains and losses on pension expense. The rationale for the corridor is that gains and losses result from refinements in estimates as well as real changes in economic value and that over time some of these gains and losses should not be recognized fully as a component of pension expense in the period in which they arise.

Note that these gains and losses are subject to triple smoothing. First, the asset gain or loss is smoothed by using the expected return. Then the unrecognized gain or loss at the beginning of the year is not amortized unless it is greater than the corridor. Finally, the excess is spread over the remaining service life of existing employees.

2000 Entries and Work Sheet. Continuing the Zarle Company illustration into 2000, the following facts apply to the pension plan.

1. Annual service cost for 2000 is $13,000.

2. Interest on accrued benefits is 10%.

3. Expected return on plan assets is 10% or $13,410.

4. Actual return on plan assets is $12,000.

5. Market-related and fair values of plan assets at December 31, 2000 are $159,600.

6. Amortization of past service cost in 2000 is $27,211.

7. Annual contributions (funding) are $24,000.

8. Benefits paid to retirees in 2000 are $10,500.

9. Changes in actuarial assumptions establish the end-of-year PBO at $265,000.

The work sheet shown below presents all of the pension entries and information recorded by Zarle Company in 2000. The beginning balances that relate to the pension plan are recorded on the first line of the work sheet. In this case, the beginning balances for Zarle Company are the ending balances from the 1999 pension work sheet on page 1005.

EXHIBIT 20-12   ZARLE COMPANY

PENSION WORK SHEET: 2000

	General Journal Entries			Memo Record			
Items	Annual Pension Expense	Cash	Prepaid/ Accrued Cost	Projected Benefit Obligation	Plan Assets	Unrecognized Past Service Cost	Unrecognized Actuarial Gain or Loss
Balance, Dec. 31,1999			25,811 Cr.	212,700 Cr.	134,100 Dr.	52,789 Dr.	
(m) Service cost	13,000 Dr.			13,000 Cr.			
(n) Interest cost	21,270 Dr.			21,270 Cr.			
(o) Expected return	13,410 Cr.				13,410 Dr.		
(p) Amortization of PSC	27,211 Dr.					27,211 Cr.	
(q) Contributions		24,000 Cr.			24,000 Dr.		
(r) Benefits paid				10,500 Dr.	10,500 Cr.		
(s) Liability loss				28,530 Cr.			28,530 Dr.
(t) Asset loss					1,410 Cr.		1,410 Dr.
Expense entry, 2000	48,071 Dr.		48,071 Cr.				
Contribution, 2000		24,000 Cr.	24,000 Dr.				
Balance, Dec. 31, 2000			49,882 Cr.	265,000 Cr.	159,600 Dr.	25,578 Dr.	29,940 Dr.

Entries (m), (n), (o), (p), (q), and (r) are similar to the corresponding entries explained in 1998 or 1999. Entries (o) and (t) are related. The recording of the expected return in entry (o) has been illustrated in 1998 and 1999. In both these years, it was assumed that the actual return on plan assets was equal to the expected return. In 2000 the expected return of $13,410 (the expected rate of 10% times the beginning-of-the-year market-related value of the plan assets of $134,100) is higher than the actual return of $12,000. The resulting asset loss of $1,410 ($13,410 − $12,000) is not recognized in the company's accounts in 2000.

Entry (s) records the change in the projected benefit obligation that results from a change in actuarial assumptions. As indicated, the actuary has now computed the ending balance to be $265,000. Given that the memo record balance at December 31 is $236,470 ($212,700 + $13,000 + $21,270 − $10,500), a difference of $28,530 ($265,000–$236,470) is indicated. This $28,530 increase in the employer's obligation is an actuarial loss that is deferred by debiting it to the Unrecognized Actuarial Gain or Loss account.

No amortization of the net actuarial loss is recognized in 2000 because the amortization is based on the net actuarial gain or loss that existed at the first of the year.

The journal entry on December 31, 2000 to formally record pension expense for the year is as follows.

Pension Expense	48,071	
Prepaid/Accrued Pension Cost		48,071

The company has already recorded the $24,000 contribution during the year as follows.

Prepaid/Accrued Pension Cost	24,000	
Cash		24,000

As illustrated for the 1998 and 1999 work sheets, the credit balance of the Prepaid/Accrued Pension Cost account at December 31, 2000 of $49,882 is equal to the net of the balances in the memo accounts as shown below.

EXHIBIT 20-13

RECONCILIATION SCHEDULE
DECEMBER 31, 2000

Projected benefit obligation (Credit)	$(265,000)
Plan assets at fair value (Debit)	159,600
Funded status—net liability (Credit)	(105,400)
Unrecognized past service cost (Debit)	25,578
Unrecognized net actuarial loss (Debit)	29,940
Accrued pension cost liability (Credit)	$ (49,882)

DEFINED BENEFIT PLANS OTHER THAN PENSIONS THAT HAVE SERVICE RELATED FUTURE BENEFITS

Seagram Co. Ltd. announced early in 1993 that it was taking a onetime U.S.$1.4 billion charge against income for its year ended January 31, 1993. Most of this charge flowed through from its 24.5% interest in E.I. DuPont de Nemours & Co., a U.S. investment accounted for by the equity method, and resulted from the adoption of the new FASB accounting standard on post-retirement benefits.[26] A month later, General Motors announced a U.S.$20.8 billion charge against its 1992 earnings for the same reason. What was this new standard and how does it compare with Canadian GAAP?

After much study, the FASB in 1990 issued *Statement No. 106*, "Employers' Accounting for Postretirement Benefits Other Than Pensions." It was this standard that accounts for health care and other welfare benefits provided to retirees, their spouses, dependents, and beneficiaries, that was the cause of the large charges to income.[27]

For 95% of U.S. companies, the new standard required a change from the widely used practice of accounting for post-retirement benefits on a pay-as-you-go cash basis to an accrual basis. Similar to pension accounting, the accrual basis necessitates measurement of the employer's obligation to provide future benefits and accrual of the cost during the years that the employee provides service. The pay-as-you-go basis is still the predominant method in Canada, a situation that will be reversed assuming the June, 1997

---

[26] As Seagram's shares trade on the New York Stock Exchange, the company was required to comply with U.S. GAAP. For Canadian reporting, the change in accounting policy was given retroactive treatment, reducing retained earnings directly instead of net income.

[27] The "other welfare benefits" include life insurance offered outside a pension plan, dental and eye care, legal and tax services, tuition assistance, day care, and housing assistance. These "post-retirement benefits" exclude "post-employment benefits" related to severance pay, wage continuation, and continuance of health and life insurance benefits for disabled, terminated, or laid-off employees or their beneficiaries. These latter benefits are the subject of *SFAS* No. 112.

Exposure Draft on "Employees' Future Benefits" is accepted. This *Exposure Draft* requires Canadian companies to account for all such plans where the future benefits are service related on the same basis as they account for defined benefit pension plans, and on the same basis as *SFAS* No. 106.[28] Some of the larger Canadian companies with reporting requirements south of the border moved to adopt the FASB standard soon after it was issued. These requirements are illustrated below.

Unlike pension benefits, companies tend not to prefund their other post-employment benefit plans. One reason is because payments to prefund health care costs (for example), unlike contributions to a pension trust, are not tax deductible. Another reason is because such benefits were once perceived as low-cost employee benefits that could be changed or eliminated at will and, therefore, were not a legal liability. The accounting definition of a liability now goes beyond the notion of a legally enforceable claim to encompass equitable or constructive obligations, making it clear that many future benefit promises are liabilities. In addition, the costs and liabilities are increasing as the population ages and as new expensive drugs and technology expand what is possible.

DIFFERENCES BETWEEN PENSION BENEFITS AND POST-RETIREMENT HEALTH CARE BENEFITS

Although these two types of retirement benefits appear similar, there are some significant differences, as shown in the exhibit below.

OBJECTIVE 11
Identify the differences between pensions and post-retirement health care benefits.

EXHIBIT 20-14

DIFFERENCES BETWEEN PENSIONS AND POST-RETIREMENT HEALTH CARE BENEFITS

Item	Pensions	Health Care Benefits
Funding	Generally funded.	Generally NOT funded.
Benefit	Well defined and level dollar amount	Generally uncapped and great variability.
Beneficiary	Retiree (maybe some benefit to surviving spouse).	Retiree, spouse, and other dependants.
Benefit Payable	Monthly.	As needed and used.
Predictability	Variables are reasonably predictable.	Utilization difficult to predict. Level of cost varies geographically and fluctuates over time.

Because many plans do not set a limit on health care benefits and the level of health care benefit utilization and health care costs is difficult to predict, the employer's obligation for future payments for health care benefit plans is much more difficult to estimate than for pension plans. The *Exposure Draft* proposals indicate that actuarial assumptions about medical costs should consider anticipated changes in the cost of medical services due to general inflation, changes in specific prices on medical services, and changes in medical practices and technology.[29]

The basic concepts, accounting terminology, and measurement methodology applicable to defined benefit pensions are equally applicable to the requirements for other retirement benefits that are based on or related to service provided by employees. The

---

[28] The impact of such a change in Canada will not be as significant as in the U.S. because we have more government health coverage, although this is decreasing. A recent Financial Executives Institute Canada (FEI) study estimated a total Canadian unreported liability of $52 billion, almost entirely unfunded.

[29] CICA *Exposure Draft*, "Employees' Future Benefits" (June, 1997), par. .065.

recognition and measurement criteria for the obligation and plan assets are the same, as is the actuarial valuation method, the attribution period, and the calculation of the current cost of benefits.

One area where there is likely to be a difference in the variables that affect the calculation of the current expense is in the relative size of the transitional amount. When a company begins to apply the recommendations of the new proposals to future benefits such as post-retirement health care and life insurance, a large transitional liability will likely result. This is caused by significant unrecognized liabilities and negligible plan assets due to the common practice of not funding these plans. Where the change in policy is accounted for on a prospective basis, the net unrecorded obligation is amortized in a rational and systematic manner, normally over the expected average remaining service life of the employee group covered by the plan.[30] The amortization is a component of the current benefit expense.

In other respects, accounting for the costs of the benefits is similar to that illustrated for defined benefit pensions.

Illustration. Assume that on January 1, 1998 Quest Company adopts the new accounting standards to account for its retirement health care benefit plan. The following facts apply to this plan for the following year, 1999.

1. Plan assets at fair value (also market-related value) on January 1, 1999 are $10,000.

2. PBO, January 1, 1999, is $426,000.

3. Unrecognized transition liability at January 1, 1999 is $336,000 (original amount of $352,000; amortization period of 22 years).

4. Unrecognized net actuarial loss at January 1, 1999 is $48,000.

5. Accrued benefit liability at January 1, 1999 is $32,000.

6. Actual return on plan assets in 1999 is $600.

7. Expected return on plan assets in 1999 is $800.

8. Discount rate is 8%.

9. Increase in PBO, December 31, 1999, due to change in actuarial assumptions is $20,000.

10. Service cost for 1999 is $26,000.

11. Contributions (funding) to plan in 1999 are $50,000.

12. Benefit payments to employees in 1999 are $35,000.

13. Expected average remaining service life (EARSL), January 1, 1999, is 24 years.

The following work sheet presents all of the entries and information recorded by Quest Company in 1999.

---

[30] CICA *Exposure Draft*, "Employees' Future Benefits" (June, 1997), par. .149. The Emerging Issues Committee has provided guidance to Canadian companies who move to the accrual method of recognizing post-retirement benefits other than pensions in *EIC-49*, issued October 15, 1993. The Committee concluded that prospective treatment with amortization of the transition amount over EARSL was appropriate, consistent with the transitional provisions for pensions in *CICA Handbook* Section 3460. The Committee noted that the transition balance could also be accounted for retroactively as a change in accounting policy. This has the effect of charging the accumulated transition costs to the opening balance of retained earnings rather than to current income as in the U.S. standard. The transitional provisions in the 1997 *Exposure Draft* are consistent with *EIC-49*.

EXHIBIT 20-15   QUEST COMPANY

WORK SHEET: 1999

Items	General Journal Entries			Memo Record			
	Annual Expense	Cash	Prepaid/ Accrued Cost	PBO	Plan Assets	Unrecognized Transition Amount	Unrecognized Net Actuarial Gain or Loss
Balance, Jan. 1, 1999			32,000 Cr.	426,000 Cr.	10,000 Dr.	336,000 Dr.	48,000 Dr.
(a) Service cost	26,000 Dr.			26,000 Cr.			
(b) Interest cost	34,080 Dr.			34,080 Cr.			
(c) Expected return	800 Cr.				800 Dr.		
(d) Experience loss					200 Cr.		200 Dr.
(e) Contributions		50,000 Cr.			50,000 Dr.		
(f) Benefits paid				35,000 Dr.	35,000 Cr.		
(g) Amortization: Transition liability	16,000 Dr.					16,000 Cr.	
(h) Inc. in PBO—loss				20,000 Cr.			20,000 Dr.
(i) Amortization: Unrecognized net actuarial loss	225 Dr.						225 Cr.
Expense entry, 1999	75,505 Dr.		75,505 Cr.				
Contribution, 1999		50,000 Cr.	50,000 Dr.				
Balance, Dec. 31, 1999			57,505 Cr.	471,080 Cr.	25,600 Dr.	320,000 Dr.	67,975 Dr.

Entry (a) records the service cost component, which increases the retirement health benefit expense by $26,000 and the liability (PBO) by $26,000. Entry (b) accrues the interest expense, which increases both the liability (PBO) and the expense by $34,080—the weighted-average PBO multiplied by the discount rate of 8%. Because the service cost, benefits paid, and actuarial loss are all assumed to take place at the end of the year, the weighted-average balance of the PBO for the year is the opening balance of $426,000.

Entries (c) and (d) are related. The expected return of $800 is higher than the actual return of $600. The expected return is calculated by applying the expected long-term rate of return on plan assets to the weighted-average market-related value of plan assets. In this example, the payments to retirees and contributions received from the employer are assumed to be year-end transactions. The weighted-average market-related value for 1999, therefore, is the opening balance at January 1, 1999. The amount of the expected return of $800 is given in this case. To smooth the expense, the expected return is used in its computation and the experience loss of $200 ($800 − $600) is deferred by debiting Unrecognized Net Actuarial Gain or Loss.

Entry (e) records Quest Company's contribution (funding) of assets to the retirement health care benefit fund. Entry (f) records the benefit payments made for the benefit of retirees, which results in equal $35,000 decreases to the plan assets and the liability (PBO). Entry (g) records the amortization of the unrecognized transition obligation. It is amortized over the expected average remaining service life of the employee group on January 1, 1998 of 22 years. The amortization of $16,000 ($352,000/22) increases the expense and decreases the unrecognized costs associated with the transition obligation. If Quest Company had treated the transition costs as a change in accounting policy instead, recognizing the entire transition liability when the accrual method was first used, the transition obligation would have been given full accounting recognition as a liability with the accumulated costs recognized as an adjustment to the January 1, 1998 balance of retained earnings. As the full transition balance is recognized, there would be no future amortization required.

Entry (h) records the change in the PBO that results from a change in actuarial assumptions. This $20,000 increase in the employer's accumulated liability is an actuarial loss that is deferred by debiting it to Unrecognized Net Actuarial Gain or Loss.

The last adjustment, entry (i), records the minimum amortization of the unrecognized net actuarial loss. The $225 amortization is determined as follows.

Corridor amount — 10% of the greater of the January 1, 1999 balance of the PBO ($426,000) and the market-related value of the plan assets ($10,000): $426,000 × 10%		$42,600
Unamortized net actuarial loss, January 1, 1999		$48,000
Excess of unamortized loss over corridor amount, January 1, 1999: $48,000 − $42,600		$5,400
Minimum amortization required: $5,400/24		$225

Quest Company could use a different method of amortization, but the minimum amount that must be amortized in 1999 is $225. This increases the current retirement health care benefit expense and reduces the unrecognized net actuarial loss.

During 1999, Quest Company would have recorded the cash disbursement to the benefit fund as follows.

Prepaid/Accrued Retirement Health Cost	50,000	
Cash		50,000

All that remains is to record the December 31, 1999 adjusting journal entry to recognize the annual retirement health benefit expense.

Retirement Health Benefit Expense	75,505	
Prepaid/Accrued Retirement Health Cost		75,505

The balance of the Accrued Retirement Health Cost account at December 31, 1999 of $57,505 is equal to the net of the balances in the memo accounts as shown in the following reconciliation.

EXHIBIT 20-16

RECONCILIATION SCHEDULE DECEMBER 31, 1999

Retirement health benefit PBO (Credit)	$(471,080)
Plan assets at fair value (Debit)	25,600
Funded status—net liability (Credit)	(445,480)
Unrecognized transition amount (Debit)	320,000
Unrecognized net actuarial loss (Debit)	67,975
Accrued retirement health cost liability (Credit)	$ (57,505)

Other Post-Employment Benefits and Compensated Absences. Full accrual accounting is also appropriate for post-employment benefits and compensated absences where the benefits either vest in the employee or accumulate with the length of service provided.

The June 1997 *Exposure Draft* proposes that the same recognition and measurement principles as applied above for pensions and other retirement benefits should be used, subject to the standard recognition caveats that (1) the amount of the liability and expense can be reasonably estimated; and (2) payment of the benefits is probable.[31]

Assume an employee benefit plan that provides a cash bonus of $500 per year of service on termination of employment or retirement from the company provided the employee has been employed for a minimum period of 10 years. Because the right to the benefit is earned by rendering service and the amount increases with the length of service provided, the cost and related liability should be accrued from the date of employment. The measurement of the obligation and expense would take into consideration the probabilities related to employee turnover. The fact that the benefits do not vest for 10 years does not eliminate the need to recognize the cost and liability over the first 10 years of employment.

As explained in Chapter 14, sick leave that accumulates with service but that does not vest in the employee should, in theory, be accrued as the employee provides service. In practical terms, the difficulty in determining a reasonable estimate of the amount, coupled with its relative immateriality, means that the cost is often not accrued.

FINANCIAL REPORTING AND DISCLOSURE REQUIREMENTS

Information about employee benefit plans is frequently important to an understanding of the financial position, results of operations, and cash flows of a company. However, prior to the 1997 *Exposure Draft* proposals, the disclosure requirements for defined benefit plans were few.

OBJECTIVE 12
Identify the financial reporting and disclosure requirements for defined benefit plans with service related benefits.

For defined benefit pension plans, *the only required disclosure* in *Handbook* Section 3460 up to 1998 is found in par. .60:

For defined benefit pension plans, an enterprise should disclose separately the actuarial present value of accrued pension benefits attributed to services rendered up to the reporting date and the value of pension fund assets.

Consistent with the noncapitalization approach adopted in Section 3460, this disclosure is found in the notes to the financial statements. Air Canada's financial statements for its year ended December 31, 1996 provide an illustration of the minimum disclosure requirements.

EXHIBIT 20-17   AIR CANADA

($ MILLIONS)

13. Pension Plans

The Corporation and its subsidiaries maintain several defined benefit pension plans. Based on the latest actuarial reports prepared as at December 31, 1994 using management's assumptions, the estimated present value of the accrued pension benefits as at December 31, 1996 amounted to $3,670 and the net assets available to provide these benefits were $4,065 calculated on a four year moving average market value basis.

Section 3460, par. .61 suggests additional information that may be useful in assessing the impact of a defined benefit plan on the financial statements.[32] These details may be disclosed at the discretion of management.

[31] CICA *Exposure Draft*, "Employees' Future Benefits" (June, 1997), par. .029.

[32] These include a general description of the plan, significant matters affecting the comparability of information, the amount of pension expense for the period and the deferred charge or accrual for pension costs on the balance sheet, the basis of valuing fund assets, salary and interest rate assumptions, the methods and periods used to amortize unrecognized balances, and the date of the most recent actuarial revaluation.

The Emerging Issues Committee in *EIC-5*, "Post Retirement Benefits Other Than Pensions," determined that employers that sponsored such plans should provide a general description of the post-retirement benefits provided and the accounting policies followed. *EIC-49*, "Post Retirement Benefits Other Than Pensions—Transitional Balance," states that an entity should disclose the method used to account for the transitional balance.

The June, 1997 *Exposure Draft* "Employees' Future Benefits" significantly expands the disclosures that are required for service related future benefits associated with defined benefit plans. It proposes that entities disclose the following information for plans that provide pension benefits, with separate disclosure for plans that provide other employee benefits:[33]

1. A description of the benefit plans. This includes the type of plan and whether it is contributory or noncontributory, the benefit formula, whether the plan is funded, the extent of employee groups covered, and a description of the benefits.

2. The method used to determine the market-related value of plan assets (needed in calculating asset experience gains and losses), and the method of recognizing net actuarial gains and losses.

3. The total plan obligation, the fair value of plan assets, and the resulting surplus or deficit.

4. The unamortized amounts, separately disclosing the unamortized past service costs, the unamortized net actuarial gain or loss, and the unamortized transition balance.

5. The amount of the accumulated benefit liability or asset in the balance sheet, the expense for the period in the income statement, and the employer contributions for the period.

6. Major assumptions underlying the measurement of the benefit obligation, including the discount rate, the rate of increase in compensation levels, and the assumed health care cost trend rate for health care benefits; and the expected long-term rate of return on plan assets.

7. In situations where the amount cannot be reasonably estimated, that the obligation for post-employment benefits and compensated absences that vest or accumulate is not accrued.

Note disclosures vary significantly in practice from the pre–*Exposure Draft* minimal presentation of pension assets and the projected benefit obligation as illustrated in Exhibit 20-17 for Air Canada, to very detailed descriptions and schedules. Many Canadian companies take the disclosures further than suggested in Section 3460 and provide the details required by U.S. companies that report under FASB standards. Major differences include information on the components of pension expense and a schedule that reconciles the funded status of the plan with amounts reported in the employer's balance sheet. This expanded disclosure is illustrated in Exhibit 20-18 in the Royal Bank of Canada's note to its consolidated financial statements for the year ended October 31, 1996.

The June, 1997 *Exposure Draft* disclosure proposals go a long way toward the provision of better information for users to assess the amounts and likelihood of cash flows associated with future benefits, the relationship between cash flows and pension and other benefits expense, the impact of employee benefits on the income statement, and the reasonableness of the assumptions that underlie the liability, fund assets, and current expense. Information about unrecognized amounts informs readers of the extent to which obligations to employees to date will impact on future earnings.

---

[33] CICA *Exposure Draft*, "Employees' Future Benefits" (June, 1997), pars. .130–.135, .138–.142.

EXHIBIT 20-18   ROYAL BANK OF CANADA

($ MILLIONS)

Note 14. Postretirement Benefits

A reconciliation of the funded status of the bank's pension plans to the "prepaid pension cost" included in "Other assets" is as follows:

FUNDED STATUS OF PENSION PLANS FOR WHICH ASSETS EXCEED ACCUMULATED BENEFIT OBLIGATION	1996	1995
Accumulated benefit obligation:		
Vested	$2,230	$2,041
Non-vested	65	51
	2,295	2,092
Effect of future salary increases	368	339
Projected benefit obligation	2,663	2,431
Pension fund assets, at adjusted market values*	2,952	2,684
Funding excess	289	253
Net unrecognized gains	(48)	(33)
Unrecognized transition funding excess	(8)	(15)
Other items, net	18	24
Prepaid pension cost	$ 251	$ 229

* *Pension fund assets are carried at adjusted market values, with adjustments to bring the value of the assets to market value being made over a three year period. The actual market value of the assets at October 31, 1996 was $3,158 million (1995 – $2,741 million). Pension fund assets at October 31, 1996 were comprised of equity securities (55%), bonds and debentures (41%), short-term investments (2%), and other investments (2%).*

The transition funding excess and net unrecognized gains are amortized to pension expense on a straight-line basis over the expected average remaining service lives of the employees covered by the plans. Assumptions, unchanged from 1995 and 1994, used to determine the present value of the projected benefit obligation included a weighted-average discount rate of 8.0% and a weighted-average rate of future salary increases of 5.1%. The assumed weighted-average rate of return on pension fund assets was 8.0%.

PENSION EXPENSE	1996	1995	1994
Cost of benefits accrued during the year	$ 68	$ 64	$ 61
Interest expense on projected benefit obligation	185	171	158
Actual return on pension fund assets	(387)	(33)	(387)
Net amortization and deferral	192	(146)	212
Net pension expense	$ 58	$ 56	$ 44

Postretirement health and dental care and life insurance benefits expense was $9 million in 1996 (1995 – $8 million; 1994 – $7 million).

PART 2: DEFINED BENEFIT PLANS — NON-SERVICE RELATED FUTURE BENEFITS

POST-EMPLOYMENT BENEFITS AND COMPENSATED ABSENCES

Some post-employment benefits and compensated absences are available to all employees regardless of the length of service provided. Entitlement to these benefits is not dependent upon or increased by length of service, nor do the benefits vest or accumulate. Examples of this type of benefit include parental (maternity and paternity) leave and long-term disability benefits. Another class of benefits with similar characteristics, known as termination benefits, is covered in the Appendix to this chapter.

For practical reasons, the June, 1997 *Exposure Draft* proposes that an entity should recognize a liability and expense for this type of benefit when (a) the event obligating the entity to provide the benefit has occured; (b) the payment of the benefit is probable; and (c) the amount can be reasonably estimated.[34] Thus, when an employee applies for mater-

OBJECTIVE 13
Identify the accounting and disclosure requirements for defined benefit plans whose benefits are not service related.

---

[34] CICA *Exposure Draft*, "Employees' Future Benefits" (June, 1997), par. .030.

nity leave or when an employee becomes disabled, the total estimated liability and expense associated with the event is recognized at that point as follows.

Employee Benefit Expense	xxx	
Maternity Leave Benefits Payable		xxx
or		
Estimated Disability Liability		xxx

As the compensated absences are taken, the liability is reduced.

In theory, the liability for and cost of the benefits should be accrued as employees provide services. Practical difficulties in measuring the liability and the relative immateriality of the amounts involved lie behind the proposal to defer recognition until an event occurs that obligates the company to provide the benefit. Thus, this method of accounting has been referred to as the "event accrual" method.

As discussed in Part 1 of this chapter, similar measurement problems may exist with sick leave that accumulates but does not vest. The "event accrual" method is proposed as appropriate in this circumstance as well.[35]

DISCLOSURE REQUIREMENTS

Where material, a company should disclose information that allows financial statement readers to assess the impact of the benefit plans on current and future operations and cash flows. A brief description of the plans should be provided and, where obligations for post employment benefits and compensated absences have not been accrued as recommended due to measurement problems, this fact should be disclosed.

PART 3: DEFINED CONTRIBUTION PLANS

ACCOUNTING FOR DEFINED CONTRIBUTION PLANS

OBJECTIVE 14
Identify the accounting and disclosure requirements for defined contribution plans.

A **defined contribution plan** is a plan that specifies how contributions are determined rather than the benefits the individual is to receive or the method of determining those benefits. The plan also attributes the contributions to specific individuals.[36] The contribution may be a fixed sum, for example $200 per year, or be related to salary, such as 6% of regular plus overtime earnings. The most common defined contribution plans are pension plans. Under the new proposals for employees' future benefits, the requirements for accounting for defined contribution plans will not change significantly.

Because the contribution is defined, *the accounting for a defined contribution plan is straightforward*: the employer's annual cost (expense) is the amount that it is obligated to contribute in exchange for the employees' services provided. A liability is reported on the employer's balance sheet if the contribution has not been made in full, and an asset is reported if more than the required amount has been contributed. The employer assumes no further obligation or risk relative to this plan. The accounting method used, therefore, is the *cash basis* or what is known as **pay-as-you-go** accounting.[37]

When a defined contribution plan is initiated or amended, the employer may be obligated to make contributions for employee services rendered prior to the date of the

---

[35] CICA *Exposure Draft*, "Employees' Future Benefits" (June, 1997), par. .035.

[36] *Ibid.*, par. .006(k).

[37] *Ibid.*, par. .010 recommends, however, that if a defined contribution plan provides for the employer to continue to make contributions after an employee retires or terminates employment, the additional cost should be estimated and accrued during the employee's service period.

initiation or amendment. Similar to defined benefit plans, this obligation is referred to as past service cost. Amounts arising as past service costs are amortized in a rational and systematic manner as part of the annual benefit expense, usually over the expected average remaining service life of the employee group covered by the plan.[38] Any difference between the cumulative amounts expensed to the balance sheet date and the funding to that point is reported as either a deferred charge (asset) or an accrual for pension costs (liability).

DISCLOSURE REQUIREMENTS

Information about plans that provide pension benefits should be reported separately from those that provide other employee benefits. The following disclosures are proposed in the 1997 *Exposure Draft*.[39]

1. A description of the plan, including whether it is contributory or noncontributory, whether the plan is funded, the extent of the employee groups covered, and a description of the benefits.

2. The amount of the net accrued benefit reported on the balance sheet.

3. The present value of required future contributions in respect of past service. The benefit expense for the period may be disclosed, and if so, it should be reported separately from the expense related to defined benefit plans.

CONCLUDING NOTE

The June, 1997 *Exposure Draft*, "Employees' Future Benefits," not only proposes changes to the existing recommendations for accounting for pensions in *CICA Handbook* Section 3460, but also sweeps in accounting recommendations for other retirement benefits, post-employment benefits, compensated absences, and termination benefits. The proposals were motivated by four objectives: (1) to provide under one umbrella an accounting standard for pensions and other employees' future benefits; (2) to ensure consistent standards for similar situations; (3) to eliminate existing Canadian/U.S. GAAP differences in pension accounting, and; (4) to reduce the potential for differences in new standards for other employee benefits when there is no substantive reason for a difference.

The new proposals result in recommendations for ***full accrual accounting*** when the benefits are related to the service provided, the rights to the benefits vest or accumulate, and the recognition criteria of measurability and probability of payment are met. The ***event accrual method*** is recommended when full accrual cannot be used due to measurement problems, for situations where the benefits are not related to service provided, and where the benefits do not vest or accumulate. The ***cash basis*** is recommended for benefit costs that are defined in terms of the required contribution.

The single largest impact in accepting the *ED*'s proposals will be the change from pay-as-you-go to the full accrual method of accounting for post-retirement benefits other than pensions. Within defined benefit pension accounting, the major changes include:

1. A change in the attribution period for current service costs *from* the service life of the employee (generally interpreted as the date of hire to expected retirement) *to* a period beginning at the date of hire to the date at which the employee obtains full eligibility for benefits.

---

[38] CICA *Exposure Draft*, "Employees' Future Benefits" (June, 1997), par. .012.
[39] *Ibid.*, pars. .130 to .137.

2. A change in the amortization period for past service costs *from* EARSL *to* the expected period to full eligibility of the employee group covered, consistent with the change for current service costs.

3. A change in the discount rate *from* management's expected long-term interest rate, often equal to the return on pension assets (this is implied) *to* a requirement for an interest rate determined with reference to current market rates.

4. A change in the amortization of net actuarial gains and losses *from* a rational and systematic method, usually over the EARSL, *to* the amortization of a minimum amount (which may be zero) as determined using the corridor approach. The current method may be used as long as the amount of amortization exceeds the minimum as defined.

5. A change in the requirements for settlements, curtailments, and termination benefits, as well as a limitation on the net pension asset reported. These are addressed in the Appendix to this chapter.

6. A significant increase in the disclosure requirements *from* a requirement to report the PBO and fund assets *to* the provision of much more information to allow users to assess the impact of benefit plans on current and future operations, financial position, and cash flows.

Critics still abound—from those who prefer the capitalization approach where the recognition of past service costs, actuarial gains and losses, and transition amounts would be immediate instead of delayed, to those who think the numbers that underlie estimates of the costs and obligations (for example, forecasted health care costs, changes in government programs, rate of pre-65 retirement, etc.) are too "soft" for inclusion in accounting reports.

Those who drafted the U.S. requirements concluded in *SFAS No. 106* that "the obligation to provide post retirement benefits meets the definition of a liability, is representationally faithful, is relevant to statement users, and can be measured with sufficient reliability at a justifiable cost."[40] This conclusion appears to be shared by Canadian standard setters.

HOW ORDINARY CANADIANS ARE MAKING THEIR PRESENCE FELT IN BOARDROOMS ACROSS CANADA

Who owns Canada's public companies and who makes the key operating investing and financing decisions?

Traditionally, in Canada, ownership has rested with corporate managers and several of Canada's wealthier families.[1] More recently, however, through ownership in shares of mutual funds and through pension plan investments, ordinary Canadians are becoming significant shareholders and beginning to influence key corporate decisions.

Take for example the Ontario Municipal Employees Retirement System ("OMERS"). OMERS was established in 1962 as a multi-employer pension plan for Ontario municipal employees and presently has over 185,000 members. According to the 1996 financial statements of the plan, OMERS has over $25.6 billion dollars, much of which is invested in shares of Canadian companies, and the fund continues to grow.

The impact of this is more far reaching than might first be expected. In many instances, this gives OMERS and pension plans like OMERS influence over the decisions made by the companies in which investments are held. A case in point involves the Ontario Teachers Pension Plan ("OTPP") and Maple Leaf Foods Inc. ("MLF"). In September of 1997, MLF was negotiating a new three-year contract with its union, the United Foods and Commercial Workers union (which represents about 6,800 MLF workers). The talks

[40] "Employers' accounting for Postretirement Benefits Other Than Pensions," *Statement of Financial Accounting Standards No. 106* (Norwalk, CT: FASB, 1990), par. .163.

stalled and MFL allegedly locked out workers at a plant in Saskatchewan. The issues apparently centred on wage and benefit concerns.[2] The head of the Ontario Teachers Federation "OTF", Eileen Lennon, felt that teachers should not invest in firms that did not respect employee rights and brought this to the attention of Claude Lamoureux, President of the Board of the OTPP.[3]

Mr. Lamoureux is quoted in the Financial Post as saying that the OTPP . . ."is very happy with the management of MLF and our investment in the company". Lamoureux felt that OTPP should retain the investmentt since it made "financial sense"[4]. OTPP has 22.5% of the voting shares of the company.[5]

Even though the OTPP made the preliminary decision to hold on to the shares for financial reasons, the union was encouraged by the OTF stance taken.

This is an example of how the members of the pension plan were made their opinion heard through OTPP and as a shareholder of MLF. It will be interesting to watch the role of mutual funds and pension plans in Canada as increasingly significant institutional investors as they continue to grow in size over the next decade.

[1] Toronto Star Sunday April 15, 1995 "The big gorilla of pensions funds"

[2] Financial Post September 6, 1997 "Maple Leaf warned of November strike"

[3] Financial Post September 1997 "Ontario teachers stand firm on Maple Leaf Holding"

[4] *Ibid*

[5] Toronto Star September 9, 1997 "Teachers to review Maple Leaf Stake"

Contributed by: Irene Wiecek, University of Toronto

Summary of Learning Objectives

1. **Describe a defined benefit plan with service related benefits.** A defined benefit plan is a plan that specifies the benefits the employee is to receive or the method to determine the benefits. The benefits are service related when the entitlement to the benefit depends on or is increased by the length of service. This includes situations where the rights to the benefits are earned by working a specified period of time and/or reaching a specified age while employed.

2. **Identify types of pension plans and their characteristics.** Pension plans are either defined contribution or defined benefit plans. Under a defined contribution plan, the employer company's responsibility is limited to the setting aside of funds for each individual equal to a formula in the pension plan agreement based on known salary and service information. The employer takes no responsibility for the amount of the pension benefits to be paid on retirement. The employer's pension expense is based on the required contributions. Under a defined benefit plan, the employer is responsible for the retirement benefits to be paid according to the pension formula in the pension agreement. In this case the formula is based on future salary and years of service on retirement. The uncertainty of the variables that affect the accumulation of sufficient funds to meet the estimate of the company's obligation means the employer assumes the risk associated with this type of plan. The calculation of pension expense in this case is complex.

3. **Distinguish between accounting for the employer's pension costs and accounting for the pension plan.** Because the pension plan is a separate legal and accounting entity that reports on the accumulated assets set aside to fund pension benefits under a specific agreement, the employer company includes neither these assets nor the accumulated obligation to pay pension benefits on

KEY TERMS

accrued benefit methods, 999

accumulated benefit obligation, 999

actuarial assumptions, 998

actuarial gains and losses, 1002

actuaries, 998

asset experience gain or loss, 1010

benefit plan, 995

capitalization approach, 1000

contributory plans, 998

corridor approach, 1011

defined benefit plan, 995

defined contribution plan, 996

expected average remaining service life (EARSL), 1003

expected rate of return, 1002

experience gains and losses, 1002

funded, 998

its balance sheet. The employer's objective in accounting for pensions is to charge the cost of pension benefits earned by employees for services rendered in the current period against current income, and to report on the extent to which amounts recognized as expense have been funded.

4. **Explain alternatives for measuring the pension obligation.** The employer's obligation under the pension agreement at any point in time theoretically could be based on any one of at least three amounts. First, it could be calculated on current salary levels for only those employees who have worked long enough that they have an unconditional right to receive benefits, that is, the vested benefits pension obligation. Second, it could be calculated for all employees whether the benefits have vested or not, based on current salary levels. This is the accumulated benefit obligation. Third, it can be calculated for all employees based on the salary levels they are expected to attain on retirement and on which the pension benefits will be determined—the projected benefit obligation. Section 3460 requires the third option.

5. **Identify the major components of pension expense.** Pension expense is made up of the service cost for the current year increased by the interest on the projected benefit obligation, reduced by the expected return on plan assets, and increased or decreased by the amortization of the delayed recognition items related to past service cost, actuarial gains and losses, and transitional balances. Additional items that might affect pension expense are gains or losses from plan settlements or curtailments, costs of termination benefits, and adjustments to the valuation allowance associated with an accrued benefit asset.

6. **Define projected benefit obligation and identify events that affect its balance.** The projected benefit obligation is the actuarial present value of the accumulated pension benefits earned for employee services provided to date based on the pension formula, incorporating expected future salaries. The balance of the PBO is increased by the pension benefits earned by employees for services provided in the current period, by the interest cost on the outstanding obligation, by plan amendments that usually increase employee entitlements for prior services, and by actuarial losses . The balance is reduced by the payment of pension benefits and by actuarial gains. The PBO is also affected by plan settlements and curtailments and by enhanced benefits offered for early retirement.

7. **Define plan assets and identify events that affect their balance.** Plan assets are the cash and investments set aside for the purpose of meeting retirement benefit payments when they become due. They are measured at fair value. Plan assets are increased by company contributions and the actual return earned on fund assets (that is, the expected return plus the asset experience gain or minus the asset experience loss), and are reduced by pension benefits paid to retirees.

8. **Explain the usefulness of—and be able to complete—a work sheet to support the employer's pension expense entries.** A pension work sheet accumulates all the information needed to calculate pension expense, including continuity schedules for the off-balance-sheet projected benefit obligation, fund assets, unrecognized past service costs, unrecognized actuarial gains and losses, and unrecognized transition amount. By completing the changes in the off-balance-sheet memo accounts and pulling out information that affects the calculation of pension expense, year-end balances are determined. The balances in the memo accounts reconcile to the reported prepaid or accrued pension cost account on the company's balance sheet.

9. **Explain the pension accounting treatment of past service costs.** Past service costs arise from giving credit to employees for service provided prior to the date of initiation or amendment of a pension plan and, for defined benefit plans, are measured as the increase in the projected benefit obligation as a result of such change. Because the increased pension benefits are expected to benefit the employer as the employee group covered provides service to the company in the future, past service costs are amortized to pension expense over the expected period to full eligibility of the affected employee group.

10. **Explain the pension accounting treatment of actuarial gains and losses, including corridor amortization.** Actuarial gains and losses represent the difference between the expected return on plan assets and the actual return earned, the change in the projected benefit obligation due to the difference between expected variables and actual outcomes, and changes in actuarial assumptions. If these changes were taken into pension expense each year in their entirety, reported pension expense would fluctuate widely. Because the actuary uses long-term rates to project amounts necessary to fund the estimated pension obligation, the expected long-term rates are used in the calculation of pension expense. The net actuarial gain or loss is amortized into pension expense when it grows to an amount in excess of 10% of the greater of the PBO and the market-related value of the fund assets. The excess amount is required to be amortized over the EARSL of the employee group.

11. **Identify the differences between pensions and post-retirement health care benefits.** Post-retirement health care benefits are more difficult to measure than pension benefits due mainly to the uncertainties associated with the changing health care environment and the variability of usage by those eligible for benefits.

12. **Identify the financial reporting and disclosure requirements for defined benefit plans with service related benefits.** At the time of writing, the only required disclosures for defined benefit pension plans under Section 3460 are the actuarial present value of accrued pension benefits attributed to services rendered up to the reporting date and the value of pension fund assets. Disclosures proposed in the 1997 *Exposure Draft* are much more extensive. They include, among others, information about the plan(s), major assumptions that underlie the measurement of the projected benefit obligation and plan assets, disclosure of unrecognized balances that will affect future income statements, and disclosure of the amounts reported in the current balance sheet and income statement.

13. **Identify the accounting and disclosure requirements for defined benefit plans whose benefits are not service related.** In this case, the "event accrual" method is applied: when the event obligating the employer to provide the benefit occurs, the total estimated expense and liability are recognized. According to the 1997 *Exposure Draft*, the entity should provide a description of the plan(s) and disclose situations where such benefits have not been accrued because of measurement uncertainties.

14. **Identify the accounting and disclosure requirements for defined contribution plans.** Defined contribution plans are accounted for on a cash basis. Companies should provide a description of such plans, the amount of any balance sheet accounts related to the net accrued benefits, and the present value of any remaining payments required due to past service costs.

APPENDIX 20A

Settlements and Curtailments, Accrued Benefit Asset Limitation, and Termination Benefits

SETTLEMENTS AND CURTAILMENTS

OBJECTIVE 15
Differentiate between plan settlements and plan curtailments.

Some employees believe that employers treat pension plans like company piggy banks, to be raided at will. This refers to the practice by some companies when their pension plan assets exceed projected benefit obligations: they pay off the obligation and pocket the difference. Generally, provincial laws prevent companies from recapturing excess assets unless they pay participants what is owed to them and then terminate the plan. As a result, companies sometimes buy annuities to pay off the pension claimants and use the excess funds for other corporate purposes.[41] Plans can be terminated through settlements or curtailments.

SETTLEMENTS

A **plan settlement** occurs when an employer substantially discharges all or part of the obligation for accrued benefits. This can be effected, for example, by irrevocably transferring assets to the beneficiaries of the plan, or by purchasing an insurance contract, or by otherwise transferring the obligation to an unrelated third party. In each case, the obligation is settled as far as the employer is concerned, but the employees continue to work for the company and/or continue to earn benefits.

According to the 1997 *Exposure Draft*, the settlement gain or loss included in the calculation of current expense is made up of three components:

1. The gain or loss as a result of the remeasurement of the plan assets and benefit obligation at the time of settlement;

2. The pro rata share (based on the percentage reduction in the obligation) of any unrecognized actuarial gain or loss; and

3. The pro rata share of any unrecognized transitional asset.

Where the benefit plan being settled is not a pension plan, a settlement gain must first be applied to reduce any unrecognized transitional liability.[42]

The unrecognized actuarial gain or loss is included as part of the settlement gain or loss because the obligation is settled, precluding the possibility of future offsetting gains and losses on the obligation and related assets in the future. Any unrecognized past service costs, however, are not written off and recognized as part of the settlement gain or loss. This is because the employees who are covered by the plan amendments or initiation continue to provide service to the employer.

---

[41] A real question exists as to whom the pension fund money belongs; that is, some argue that the excess funds are for the employees, not for the employer. In addition, given that the funds have been reverting to the employer, critics charge that cost-of-living increases and the possibility of other increased benefits in the future will be reduced, because companies will be reluctant to use those excess funds to pay for such increases.

[42] CICA *Exposure Draft*, "Employees' Future Benefits" (June, 1997), pars. .098 and .099.

CURTAILMENTS

A **plan curtailment** occurs when the expected years of future service to be rendered by current employees is reduced significantly or when the accrual of defined benefits for some or all of their future services is eliminated for a significant number of current employees.[43] Unlike a plan settlement, employees are terminated or benefits are curtailed, but the obligation for benefits earned to date remains. Curtailments are usually the result of decreased business activity; the closing of a production unit, for example, may result in the termination of additional benefits being earned by employees.

The calculation of the curtailment gain or loss included in current expense proposed by the 1997 *Exposure Draft* is complex. In general terms, the net curtailment gain or loss for defined benefit plans includes:

1. The loss calculated as the pro rata portion of the unrecognized past service costs and unrecognized transition obligation; and

2. The gain or loss that results from the change in the PBO caused by the curtailment. This gain or loss is further adjusted by amounts related to unamortized transitional assets and/or unamortized actuarial gains or losses.[44]

Because past service costs are amortized over the future service lives of the employee group affected and a curtailment results in the termination of future service for at least a portion of the employee group, any unamortized amounts related to the affected employee group are taken into income as part of the gain or loss on curtailment. No future economic benefit will be received from this group. On the other hand, the company retains the benefit obligation, and future actuarial gains and losses will continue to affect the measurement of the obligation and fund assets.

The 1997 *Exposure Draft* recommends that the amount of any settlement or curtailment gains or losses recognized during the period and the nature of the underlying event be disclosed.[45]

ACCRUED BENEFIT ASSET LIMITATION

OBJECTIVE 16
Explain why there is a limit on the accrued benefit asset recognized on the balance sheet.

For defined benefit plans, there is a limitation on the carrying value of an accrued benefit asset, often referred to as the **EIC-1 limit**. The carrying value limitation received this name as the Emerging Issues Committee of the CICA dealt with the topic of pension surplus recognition in *EIC-1*. What is the issue?

An employer with a defined benefit pension plan may be in a position where fund assets are significantly greater than accumulated benefit obligations. As a result, the company may recognize net pension benefits in income and have a pension asset instead of an accrued pension liability on the balance sheet. This is not a problem if the employer has full access to the assets that underlie the pension surplus, but in situations where the employer's access to pension fund assets is restricted, there is a question as to the amount of the pension asset that should be recognized on the company's balance sheet.[46] To the extent the company is unable to benefit from the surplus assets, the measurement of the pension asset on the balance sheet should be restricted.

[43] CICA *Exposure Draft*, "Employees' Future Benefits" (June, 1997), par. .104.

[44] *Ibid.*, par. .106.

[45] *Ibid.*, par. .144.

[46] Some provinces prohibit the withdrawal of pension surplus by employers; significant litigation has also clouded the rights of employers to these assets. In 1997 when the T. Eaton Co. Ltd. was reorganizing under the Companies' Creditors Arrangement Act, the insolvent company negotiated to share pension surpluses to provide them with $190 million. The agreement specified that all pension monies would revert to the employees if the restructuring plan failed.

The Emerging Issues Committee determined that it is legitimate to recognize a pension asset even if the employer is not permitted to withdraw assets from the fund because benefits can also be obtained by reduced or waived pension contributions. The 1997 *Exposure Draft* echoes *EIC-1* by proposing that "for a defined benefit plan, an entity should limit the carrying value of any accrued benefit asset, through a valuation allowance, to the amount of the expected future benefit."[47] The expected future benefit can arise as the benefit asset reverses through the normal application of the accounting recommendations for defined benefit plans. For example, the existence of a net unamortized liability related to transitional balances, past service costs, and net actuarial gains and losses indicates that some portion of the accounting surplus will be realized as these are taken into income.

To agree on how much more of the pension asset should be accorded accounting recognition is more difficult. The *EIC-1* position was to set the maximum value of the asset as the amount that, when invested, would yield an amount equal to the annual service cost for current employees. The *Exposure Draft* proposals permit a higher limit—one based on the current number of employees and demographic composition that also reflects salary escalation. The calculation of the cap for the pension asset is a contentious issue and one that may change before the final recommendations are approved.

TERMINATION BENEFITS

OBJECTIVE 17
Differentiate between termination benefits that are part of an existing plan and special termination benefits.

Termination benefits, currently dealt with in *EIC-23* "Special Termination Benefits" and *EIC-60* "Liability Recognition for Costs to Exit an Activity (including Certain Costs Incurred in a Restructuring)," are also addressed in the 1997 *Exposure Draft* on "Employees' Future Benefits." Proposals are made for two types of termination benefits: termination benefits that are part of an existing plan, and special benefits, either for voluntary terminations or involuntary terminations. Examples of termination benefits include severance pay, salary continuation, supplemental unemployment benefits, and job training and counselling. If the employees are also covered by a defined benefit pension or other post-retirement benefit plan, termination benefits may include increased entitlements. In this latter case it is common for plan curtailments to take place as well.

TERMINATION BENEFITS THAT ARE PART OF AN EXISTING PLAN

Termination benefits are defined as benefits required to be paid to employees under the existing terms of a benefit plan that are payable only in the event of employees' involuntary termination of service if a specified event, such as a plant closing, occurs.[48] The benefits could be lump-sum payments or periodic payments or both.

The major accounting issue for termination benefits is the timing of recognition of the related costs in income. Often, there is a significant amount of time between the decision to look at a plant closure until the closure actually takes place and the benefits are paid. The 1997 proposals call for the cost and liability associated with the termination benefits provided under the terms of existing plans to be recognized *when it is probable that employees will be entitled to the benefits and the amount can be reasonably estimated.*[49] If delayed payment terms are involved, the cost should be based on the present value of the flows.

---

[47] CICA *Exposure Draft*, "Employees' Future Benefits" (June, 1997), par. .113.

[48] *Ibid.*, par. .006(q).

[49] *Ibid.*, par. .125.

SPECIAL TERMINATION BENEFITS

Special termination benefits are those offered to employees for a short period of time in exchange for employees' voluntary or involuntary termination of service.[50] Unlike the guidance in the EIC material but consistent with the U.S. position, the 1997 *Exposure Draft* recommends different expense recognition points for voluntary and involuntary terminations.

The cost of special termination benefits associated with employees who leave *on a voluntary* basis should be accrued and recognized when the affected employees sign the offer, provided the amount can be reasonably estimated. This postpones expense and liability recognition until quite late in the staff reduction planning process.

The cost of special termination benefits associated with employees who leave *involuntarily* is required to be recognized earlier in the planning process. In this case, the costs should be recognized in income in the period in which management approves the termination plan, providing certain criteria are met. These criteria include:

1. Management at an appropriate level must have committed the entity to the plan and set out the benefits employees will receive.

2. The arrangements have been communicated to employees in sufficient detail that they can determine the benefits to which they will be entitled.

3. The number of employees, their job classifications, and locations are identified.

4. The plan will come into effect and be completed in a relatively short period of time, making significant changes to the plan unlikely.[51]

Companies that provide special termination benefits are required to disclose information about the nature of the underlying event and the amount of expense recognized during the period.

Summary of Learning Objectives

15. **Differentiate between plan settlements and plan curtailments.** A plan settlement is one in which a company discharges its obligation for employees' future benefits under a defined benefit plan. The employees continue to work for the company and may continue to earn new benefits. A plan curtailment, on the other hand, results in a continuing obligation on the part of the employer for the benefits earned by the employees to date, but the earning of new benefits by the employees is curtailed, usually due to plant closures or downsizing in general.

16. **Explain why there is a limit on the accrued benefit asset recognized on the balance sheet.** Because the definition of an asset includes the requirement that it contribute directly or indirectly to future net cash flows, an accrued benefit asset should be recognized only to the extent that future benefits can be obtained. If an employer cannot use the surplus assets in a pension fund, the amount of pension asset the company reports on its balance sheet may be restricted.

KEY TERMS

EIC-1 limit, 1029

plan curtailment, 1029

plan settlement, 1028

special termination benefits, 1031

termination benefits, 1030

---

[50] CICA *Exposure Draft*, "Employees' Future Benefits" (June, 1997), par. .006(p).

[51] *Ibid.*, par. .124.

17. **Differentiate between termination benefits that are part of an existing plan and special termination benefits.** Termination benefits included in the provisions of an existing benefit plan usually require payments in the event of an involuntary reduction in workforce necessitated by division, plant, or similar closures. Following general recognition criteria, the expense and related liabilities should be recognized when it is probable that the employees will be entitled to the benefits and when the amount can be reasonably estimated. Special termination benefits are provided under short-term offers and the benefits payable to those who volunteer to end their employment are often different from the benefits available for those who are later required to leave. The costs related to involuntary terminations are accrued when sufficient evidence exists about management's commitment to the staff reduction plan; costs related to voluntary terminations are recognized as employees accept the employer's offer.

Note: All *asterisked* Exercises, Problems, and Cases relate to material contained in the appendix to the chapter. Unless otherwise specified, current service benefits are assumed to be credited at the end of the year, and contributions paid into plan funds and benefits paid to retirees are assumed to be end-of-year transactions.

EXERCISES

E20-1 **(Defined Contribution Plan)** Colin Corporation's defined contribution pension plan requires the company to deduct 4% of each employee's gross salary from each paycheque as the employee contribution to the plan, to be matched by an equal contribution from the employer. Colin Corporation remits the contributions to the fund trustee on the 15th of the following month.

Instructions

(a) Assuming December, 1998's payroll reported gross salaries and wages of $236,500, prepare the entry(ies) to record pension expense for the month of December, 1998.

(b) What amount(s) will be reported on the company's December 31, 1998 balance sheet in relation to the pension plan?

(c) How would a January, 1998 plan amendment that gave benefits for past services affect the amount of pension expense and the disclosure requirements for this company?

E20-2 **(Computation of Pension Expense)** Tony Ltd. provides the following information about its defined benefit pension plan for the year 1998:

Service cost	$ 80,000
Projected benefit obligation at Jan. 1, 1998	700,000
Actual and expected return on plan assets	16,000
Amortization of past service cost	10,000
Amortization of actuarial loss	2,000
Interest on liability	10%

Instructions
Compute the pension expense for the year 1998.

E20-3 **(Computation of Pension Expense)** Quality Print Ltd. provides the following information about its noncontributory defined benefit pension plan for the year 1998:

Service cost	$ 90,000
Contribution to the plan	105,000
Past service cost amortization	10,000
Actual and expected return on plan assets	60,000
Benefits paid	40,000
Accrued pension cost liability at Jan. 1, 1998	7,000
Plan assets at Jan. 1, 1998	643,000
Projected benefit obligation at Jan. 1, 1998	800,000
Unrecognized past service cost balance at Jan. 1, 1998	150,000
Interest on pension obligation	10%

Instructions

Compute the pension expense for the year 1998.

(Preparation of Pension Work Sheet) Using the information in E20-3, prepare a pension work sheet. Insert January 1, 1998 balances, indicate December 31, 1998 balances, and prepare the journal entry that records pension expense.   E20-4

(Basic Pension Work Sheet) The following facts apply to the pension plan of Browning Ltd. for the year 1998.   E20-5

Plan assets, Jan. 1, 1998	$490,000
Projected benefit obligation, Jan. 1, 1998	490,000
Interest and expected earnings rate	8.5%
Annual pension service cost	40,000
Contributions (funding)	30,000
Actual return on plan assets	48,605
Benefits paid to retirees	23,400

Instructions

Using the preceding data, compute pension expense for the year 1998. As part of your solution, prepare a pension work sheet that shows the journal entry for pension expense for 1998 and the year-end balances in the related pension accounts.

(Calculation of EARSL and Amortization) James McInnes Company has five employees who participate in its defined benefit pension plan. Expected years of future service for these employees at the beginning of 1998, also equal to the period to full eligibility, are as follows: E20-6

Employee	Future Years of Service
Tom	2
Carole	3
Greg	5
Kate	5
Mike	5

On January 1, 1998 the company amended its pension plan which increased its projected benefit obligation by $60,000.

Instructions

Compute the amount of past service cost amortization for the years 1998, 1999, 2000, 2001, and 2002 using the straight-line method.

(Computation of Actual Return) Bateman Importers provides the following pension plan information.

E20-7

Fair value of pension plan assets, Jan. 1, 1998	$2,300,000
Fair value of pension plan assets, Dec. 31, 1998	2,500,000
Contributions to the plan in 1998	250,000
Paid to retirees in 1998	350,000

Instructions

From the data above, compute the actual return on the plan assets for 1998.

E20-8 **(Basic Pension Work Sheet)** The following defined benefit pension data of J.B. Hobbs Ltd. apply to the year 1998.

Projected benefit obligation, 1/1/98 (before amendment)	$548,800
Plan assets, 1/1/98	546,200
Prepaid/accrued pension cost (credit)	2,600
On Jan. 1, 1998, J. B. Hobbs Ltd., through plan amendment, grants past service benefits having a present value of	100,000
Expected rate of return on plan assets and discount rate	9%
Annual pension service cost	58,000
Contributions (funding)	55,000
Actual return on plan assets	52,280
Benefits paid to retirees	40,000
Past service cost amortization for 1998	17,000

Instructions

(a) Prepare a continuity schedule for the PBO for the year 1998.

(b) Prepare a continuity schedule for the plan assets for the year 1998.

(c) Determine 1998 pension expense and provide the journal entry to record the expense.

(d) Identify the year-end balances in all pension-related accounts, both those reported on the balance sheet and those that are off-balance-sheet accounts.

E20-9 **(Application of the Corridor Approach)** Ernest Basler Limited has beginning-of-the-year present values for its projected benefit obligation and market-related values for its pension plan assets as follows.

	Projected Benefit Obligation	Plan Assets Value
1996	$2,000,000	$1,900,000
1997	2,400,000	2,500,000
1998	2,900,000	2,600,000
1999	3,600,000	3,000,000

The average remaining service life per employee in 1996 and 1997 is 10 years and in 1998 and 1999 is 12 years. The actuarial gain or loss that occurred during each year is as follows: 1996, $280,000 loss; 1997, $70,000 loss; 1998, $10,000 loss; and 1999, $25,000 gain.

Instructions

Using the corridor approach, compute the minimum amount of the net actuarial gain or loss to be amortized and charged to pension expense in each of the four years, setting up an appropriate schedule.

E20-10 **(Pension Expense and Reconciliation)** Round Table Enterprises provides the following information relative to its defined benefit pension plan.

Balances or Values at December 31, 1998	
Projected benefit obligation	$2,733,000
Fair value of plan assets	2,278,329
Unrecognized past service cost	205,000
Unrecognized actuarial loss (Jan. 1, 1998 balance, -0-)	45,680
Accrued pension cost liability	203,991
Other pension plan data:	
Service cost for 1998	90,000
Unrecognized past service cost amortization for 1998	45,000
Actual return on plan assets in 1998	130,000
Expected return on plan assets in 1998	175,680
Interest on Jan. 1, 1998 projected benefit obligation	253,000
Contributions to the plan in 1998	92,329
Benefits paid	140,000

Instructions

(a) Prepare a note to comply with the disclosure requirements of the pre-1998 *Handbook* Section 3460.

(b) Prepare the note(s) to provide the disclosures proposed in the 1997 *Exposure Draft* "Employees' Future Benefits."

(c) Prepare a schedule that reconciles the funded status of the plan with the amounts reported in the December 31, 1998 financial statements.

(Pension Work Sheet with Reconciliation, Contributory, and Noncontributory Plans) Larry D. Beaty Ltd. sponsors a noncontributory defined benefit pension plan for its employees. On January 1, 1998, the following balances relate to this plan.

Plan assets	$480,000
Projected benefit obligation	605,000
Prepaid/accrued pension cost (credit)	25,000
Unrecognized past service cost	100,000

As a result of the operation of the plan during 1998, the following additional data are provided by the actuary.

Service cost for 1998	$90,000
Discount rate	9%
Actual return on plan assets in 1998	57,000
Amortization of past service cost	19,000
Expected return on plan assets	52,000
Unexpected loss from change in projected benefit obligation, due to change in actuarial predictions	76,000
Contributions in 1998	99,000
Benefits paid retirees in 1998	85,000

Instructions

(a) Using the data above, compute pension expense for Larry D. Beaty Ltd. for the year 1998 by preparing a pension work sheet that shows the journal entry for pension expense and the year-end balances in the related pension accounts.

(b) At December 31, 1998, prepare a schedule that reconciles the funded status of the plan with the pension amount reported on the balance sheet.

(c) Assume the pension plan is a contributory plan and that employees provide $35,000 of the $99,000 contribution in 1998 by way of payroll deductions. How would this affect your answer to (a) and (b) above? Be specific.

(Pension Expense, Entries, Funded Status) The Rocky Pizza Company sponsors a defined benefit pension plan for its employees. The following data relate to the operation of the plan for the year 1998.

1. The actuarial present value of future benefits earned by employees for services rendered in 1998 amounted to $50,000.
2. The company's funding policy requires a contribution to the pension trustee amounting to $145,000 for 1998.
3. As of January 1, 1998, the company had a projected benefit obligation of $1,000,000 and an unrecognized past service cost of $400,000. The fair value of the pension assets (also the market-related value) was $600,000. The expected return on plan assets and the interest rate for the accrued benefits were both 9%. The actual return on plan assets was $54,000.
4. Amortization of unrecognized past service cost was $40,000 in 1998.
5. No benefits were paid in 1998.

Instructions

(a) Determine the amounts of the components of pension expense that should be recognized by the company in 1998.

(b) Prepare the journal entries to record pension expense and the employer's contribution to the pension trustee in 1998.

(c) Determine the funded status of the plan and reconcile this to the prepaid/accrued pension cost on the December 31, 1998 balance sheet.

(Pension Expense, Entries, Statement Presentation) Golden Ltd. received the following information from its pension plan trustee concerning the operation of the company's defined benefit pension plan for the year ended December 31, 1998.

	January 1, 1998	December 31, 1998
Projected benefit obligation	$2,000,000	$2,075,000
Market-related and fair value of pension assets	800,000	1,130,000
Actuarial (gains) losses	-0-	(200,000)

The service cost component of pension expense for employee services rendered in the current year amounted to $75,000 and the amortization of unrecognized past service cost was $115,000. The company's actual funding of the plan in 1998 amounted to $250,000. The expected return on plan assets and the actual rate were both 10%, and the discount rate was 10%. No prepaid or accrued pension cost existed on January 1, 1998. Assume no benefits were paid in 1998.

Instructions

(a) Determine the pension expense that should be recognized by the company in 1998.

(b) Prepare the journal entries to record pension expense and the employer's contribution to the pension plan in 1998.

E20-14 **(Computation of Actual Return, Gains and Losses, Corridor Test, Past Service Cost, Pension Expense, and Reconciliation)** James Reynolds Company sponsors a defined benefit pension plan. The corporation's actuary provides the following information about the plan.

	January 1, 1998	December 31, 1998
Projected benefit obligation	$2,800	$3,650
Plan assets (market-related and fair value)	1,700	2,600
Interest rate and expected rate of return		10%
Prepaid/(Accrued) pension cost	-0-	?
Unamortized past service cost	1,100	?
Service cost for the year 1998		400
Contributions (funding) in 1998		800
Benefits paid in 1998		200

The average remaining service life and period to full eligibility is 20 years.

Instructions

(a) Compute the actual return on the plan assets in 1998.

(b) Compute the amount of the net actuarial gain or loss as of December 31, 1998 (assume the January 1, 1998 balance was zero).

(c) Compute the amount of actuarial gain or loss amortization for 1998 using the corridor approach. How will 1999's expense be affected, if at all?

(d) Compute the amount of past service cost amortization for 1998.

(e) Compute the pension expense for 1998.

(f) Prepare a schedule reconciling the plan's funded status with the amounts reported on the December 31, 1998 balance sheet.

E20-15 **(Work Sheet for E20-14)** Using the information in E20-14 about James Reynolds Company's defined benefit pension plan, prepare a 1998 pension work sheet with supplementary schedules of computations. Prepare the journal entry at December 31, 1998 to record pension expense.

E20-16 **(Pension Expense, Entries)** Fitzgerald Workshop Inc. initiated a noncontributory-defined benefit pension plan for its 100 employees on January 1, 1997. Employment levels have remained constant and are expected to be stable in the future. All these employees are expected to receive benefits under the plan. It is calculated that the expected average remaining service life (as well as the expected period to full eligibility) of the employees is 25 years. On December 31, 1997, the company's actuary submitted the following information.

Present value of future benefits attributed by the pension plan formula to employee services rendered in the current year	$120,000
Accumulated benefit obligation	100,000
Projected benefit obligation	120,000
Employer's funding contribution for 1997 (made on Dec. 31, 1997)	130,000
Interest rate used in actuarial computations	8%
Actual and expected return on plan assets	8%

During 1998, the company amended the pension plan by granting credit for past services performed prior to January 1, 1998, the date of the plan amendment. The plan amendment increased unrecognized past service cost by $110,000. The company's accountants calculated the pension expense that is to be recognized in 1998 at $167,662.

Instructions
(Round to the nearest dollar)
(a) Calculate the amount of the pension expense to be recognized in 1997. Explain.
(b) Prepare the journal entries to record pension expense and the employer's funding contribution for 1997. Do not prepare a work sheet.
(c) Describe how the company's accountants calculated the $167,662 as the pension expense to be recognized in 1998. Indicate each of the five components that make up the total amount to be recognized. Assume that market-related and fair value of the plan assets are the same.

(Reconciliation, and Unrecognized Loss) Presented below is partial information related to Sharon Costume **E20-17**
Company at December 31, 1998.

Market-related and fair value of plan assets	$700,000
Projected benefit obligation	930,000
Past service cost not yet recognized in pension expense	120,000
Unamortized actuarial gains and losses	-0-

Instructions
(a) Present a schedule that reconciles the funded status with the asset/liability reported on the balance sheet.
(b) Assume the same facts as in (a) except that Sharon Costume Company has an experience loss of $16,000 during 1998.
(c) Explain the rationale for the treatment of the unrecognized loss and the past service cost not yet recognized in pension expense.

(Amortization of Net Actuarial Gain or Loss, Corridor Approach) The actuary for the pension plan of Bailey **E20-18**
Limited calculated the following net actuarial gains and losses.

Net Gain or Loss	
Incurred During the Year	(Gain) or Loss
1998	$300,000
1999	480,000
2000	(210,000)
2001	(290,000)

Other information about the company's pension obligation and plan assets is as follows.

As of January 1	Projected Benefit Obligation	Plan Assets
1998	$4,000,000	$2,400,000
1999	4,520,000	2,200,000
2000	4,980,000	2,600,000
2001	4,250,000	3,040,000

Bailey Limited has a stable labour force of 400 employees who are expected to receive benefits. It is anticipated that the expected average remaining service life is 13 years. The beginning balance of unrecognized net actuarial gain or loss is zero on January 1, 1998. The market-related value and fair value of plan assets are the same for the four-year period. (Assume the EARSL remains constant over time.)

Instructions
Prepare a schedule that reflects the minimum amount of net unamortized actuarial gain or loss amortized as a component of net periodic pension expense for each of the years 1998, 1999, 2000, and 2001.

(Amortization of Unrecognized Net Actuarial Gain or Loss, Corridor Approach) Trainor Company sponsors a **E20-19**
defined benefit pension plan for its 600 employees. The company's actuary provided the following information about the plan.

	January 1, 1997	December 31, 1997	1998
Projected benefit obligation	$2,800,000	$3,650,000	$4,400,000
Plan assets at market-related and fair value	1,700,000	2,900,000	2,100,000
Unrecognized net (gain) or loss (for purposes of the corridor calculation)	-0-	101,000	(24,000)
Discount rate		11%	8%
Actual and expected asset return rate		10%	10%

The company anticipates that the expected average remaining service life and the expected period to full eligibility of the employees is 10.5 years. The service cost component of net periodic pension expense for employee services rendered amounted to $400,000 in 1997 and $475,000 in 1998. At January 1, 1997 the only unrecognized amounts (of $1,100,000) related to past service costs. No benefits have been paid.

Instructions

(Round to the nearest dollar)

(a) Compute the amount of unrecognized past service costs to be amortized for each of the years 1997 and 1998.

(b) Prepare a schedule that reflects the amount of unrecognized actuarial gain or loss to be amortized as a component of net periodic pension expense for 1997 and 1998.

(c) Determine the total amount of net periodic pension expense to be recognized by the company in 1997 and 1998.

E20-20 (Post-Retirement Benefit Expense Computation) Toby Coffin Inc. provides the following information related to its post-retirement benefits for the year 1998.

Accumulated benefit obligation at January 1, 1998	$810,000
Actual and expected return on plan assets	30,000
Unrecognized past service cost amortization	21,000
Amortization of transition amount (loss)	3,000
Discount rate	10%
Service cost	88,000

Instructions

Compute post-retirement expense for 1998.

E20-21 (Post-Retirement Benefit Expense Computation) Michael Layton Co. provides the following information about its post-retirement benefit plan for the year 1998.

Service cost	$ 90,000
Past service cost amortization	3,000
Contribution to the plan	16,000
Actual and expected return on plan assets	62,000
Benefits paid	40,000
Plan assets at January 1, 1998	710,000
Accumulated benefit obligation at January 1, 1998	800,000
Unrecognized past service cost balance at January 1, 1998	20,000
Amortization of transition amount (loss)	5,000
Unrecognized transition amount at January 1, 1998	70,000
Discount rate	9%

Instructions

(a) Compute the post-retirement expense for 1998.

(b) Prepare the disclosures required to be reported by the 1997 Exposure Draft.

E20-22 (Post-Retirement Benefit Work Sheet) Using the information in E20-21 prepare a work sheet. Insert January 1, 1998 balances, show December 31, 1998 balances, and prepare the journal entry to record post-retirement expense for the year.

PROBLEMS

On January 1, 1998 Bob Blunden Company had the following defined benefit pension plan balances.   **P20-1**

Projected benefit obligation	$4,200,000
Fair value of plan assets	$4,200,000

The interest rate applicable to the pension obligation is 6%. On January 1, 1999 the company amends its pension agreement so that past service costs of $500,000 are created. Other data related to the pension plan are:

	1998	1999
Service costs	$140,000	$180,000
Unrecognized past service cost amortization	-0-	90,000
Contributions (funding) to the plan	140,000	184,658
Benefits paid	200,000	280,000
Actual return on plan assets	252,000	260,000
Expected return on plan assets	6%	8%

Instructions

(a) Prepare a pension work sheet for the pension plan for 1998 and 1999.

(b) As of December 31, 1999, prepare a schedule reconciling the funded status with the reported accrued pension cost.

Van Snick Company reports the following January 1, 1998 balances for its defined benefit pension plan: plan assets,   **P20-2**
$200,000; projected benefit obligation, $200,000. Other data relative to three years of operation of the plan are as follows.

	1998	1999	2000
Annual service cost	$16,000	$ 19,000	$ 26,000
Interest rate on accrued benefits and fund assets	10%	10%	10%
Actual return on plan assets	18,000	22,000	24,000
Annual funding (contributions)	16,000	40,000	48,000
Benefits paid	14,000	16,400	21,000
Unrecognized past service cost (plan amended Jan. 1, 1999)		160,000	
Amortization of unrecognized past service cost		21,500	21,500
Change in actuarial assumptions establishes a Dec. 31, 2000 projected benefit obligation of:			520,000
EARSL	10 years	10 years	10 years

Instructions

(a) Prepare a pension work sheet that presents pension balances and activities for all three years.

(b) Prepare the journal entries to reflect all pension plan transactions and adjustments at December 31 of each year.

(c) At December 31 each year, prepare a schedule that reconciles the funded status of the plan with the pension amounts reported in the financial statements.

Samuels Company sponsors a noncontributory defined benefit plan for its 100 employees. On January 1, 1997 the   **P20-3**
company's actuary provided the following information.

Unrecognized past service cost	$150,000
Pension plan assets (market-related and fair value of plan assets)	200,000
Accumulated benefit obligation	260,000
Projected benefit obligation	350,000

The average remaining service life for the participating employees is 10.5 years. All employees are expected to receive benefits under the plan. On December 31, 1997 the actuary calculated that the present value of future benefits earned for employee services rendered in the current year amounted to $50,000; the projected benefit obligation was $450,000; and the market-related and fair value of plan assets is $275,000. The expected return on plan assets and interest on the accrued benefits were both 10%. The actual return on plan assets is $10,000. The company's current year's contribution to the pension plan amounted to $65,000. No benefits were paid during the year.

Instructions

(Round to the nearest dollar)

(a) Determine the components of pension expense that the company will recognize in 1997. (Because only one year is involved, you need not prepare a work sheet.)

(b) Prepare the journal entries to record the pension expense and the company's funding of the pension plan in 1997.

(c) Compute the amount of the 1997 increase/decrease in unrecognized actuarial gains or losses and the minimum amount to be amortized in 1997 and 1998.

(d) Prepare a schedule that reconciles the funded status of the plan with the pension amounts reported in the financial statements as of December 31, 1997.

P20-4 Sara K. Smith Company sponsors a defined benefit pension plan for its 50 employees. On January 1, 1998 the company's actuary calculated the following:

Projected benefit obligation	$1,200,000
Plan assets (at market-related and fair value)	800,000
Unamortized past service cost	400,000

The average remaining service life of the participating employees is 13 years, while the expected period to full eligibility is 10 years. All employees are expected to receive benefits under the plan. The actuary calculated the present value of future benefits attributed to employees' services in the current year to be $65,000. A 10% interest rate (settlement rate) is assumed for the actuarial computations. The expected return on plan assets is 11%. The company's funding contribution to the pension plan for 1998 was $125,000. The status of the pension plan's operations at December 31, 1998 is as follows.

Projected benefit obligation	$1,310,000
Pension plan assets (at fair value)	930,000
Pension plan assets (at market-related value)	900,000
Benefit payments	-0-

Instructions

(Round to the nearest dollar; do not prepare a work sheet.)

(a) Determine the amounts of the components of pension expense that should be recognized by the company in 1998.

(b) Prepare the journal entries to record pension expense and the employer's funding contribution for 1998.

(c) Indicate the pension-related amounts that would be reported on the company's income statement and balance sheet for the year 1998.

(d) Compute the amount of the 1998 increase/decrease in unamortized actuarial gains or losses and the minimum amount to be amortized in 1998 and 1999.

(e) Prepare a schedule that reconciles the funded status of the plan with the pension amounts reported in the financial statements as of December 31, 1998.

P20-5 Bluemint Toothpaste Company initiates a defined benefit pension plan for its 50 employees on January 1, 1998. The insurance company that administers the pension plan provides the following information for the years 1998, 1999, and 2000.

	For Year Ended December 31		
	1998	1999	2000
Plan assets (fair value)	$50,000	$ 85,000	$170,000
Projected benefit obligation	55,000	200,000	320,000
Unrecognized net actuarial (gain) loss in the year		(24,500)	84,500
Employer's funding contribution (made at end of year)	50,000	60,000	95,000

There were no balances as of January 1, 1998 when the plan was initiated. The actual and expected return on plan assets was 10% over the three-year period, but the interest rate used in computing the projected benefit obligation was 13% in 1998, 11% in 1999, and 8% in 2000. The service cost component of net periodic pension expense amounted to the following: 1998, $55,000; 1999, $85,000; and 2000, $115,000. The average remaining service life of the employee group was 13 years. No benefits were paid in 1998; $30,000 benefits were paid in 1999, $18,500 benefits were paid in 2000 (all benefits paid at end of year).

Instructions
(Round to the nearest dollar)

(a) Calculate the amount of net periodic pension expense the company will recognize in 1998, 1999, and 2000.

(b) Prepare the journal entries to record pension expense and the employer's funding contributions for the years 1998, 1999, and 2000.

Ansong Ltd. has sponsored a noncontributory defined benefit pension plan for its employees since 1983. Prior to **P20-6** 1998 cumulative net pension expense recognized equaled cumulative contributions to the plan. Other relevant information about the pension plan on January 1, 1998 is as follows.

1. The company has 200 employees who are expected to receive benefits under the plan. The expected period to full eligibility of the employees is 13 years with an EARSL of 15 years.

2. The projected benefit obligation amounted to $5,000,000 and the market-related and fair value of plan assets was $3,000,000. Unamortized past service cost was $2,000,000.

On December 31, 1998 the projected benefit obligation was $4,750,000. The fair value of the pension plan assets was $3,900,000 and the market-related value of plan assets was $3,790,000 at the end of the year. A 10% interest rate and a 10% expected asset return rate was used in the actuarial present value computations in the pension plan. The present value of benefits attributed by the pension benefit formula to employee service in 1998 amounted to $200,000. The employer's contribution to the plan assets amounted to $575,000 in 1998. No payments to retirees were made.

Instructions
(Round all amounts to the nearest dollar)

(a) Prepare a schedule that shows the unrecognized past service cost that should be amortized as a component of pension expense for 1998, 1999, and 2000.

(b) Compute pension expense for the year 1998.

(c) Prepare the journal entries required to account for the company's pension plan for 1998.

(d) Compute the amount of the 1998 increase or decrease in unrecognized net actuarial gains or losses and the minimum amount to be amortized in 1998 and 1999.

(e) Prepare a schedule that reconciles the funded status of the plan with the pension amounts reported in the financial statements as of December 31, 1998.

P. Secord Corp. sponsors a defined benefit pension plan for its employees. On January 1, 1998, the following bal- **P20-7** ances relate to this plan.

Plan assets (fair value)	$520,000
Projected benefit obligation	710,000
Prepaid/accrued pension cost (credit)	18,000
Unamortized past service cost	81,000
Unamortized net actuarial gain or loss (debit)	91,000

As a result of the operation of the plan during 1998, the actuary provided the following additional data at December 31, 1998.

Service cost for 1998	$108,000
Expected return on assets	10%
Actual return on assets in 1998	48,000
Amortization of past service cost	25,000
Market-related asset value, January 1, 1998	550,000
Contributions in 1998	138,000
Benefits paid retirees in 1998	85,000
Average remaining service life of active employees	10 years
Interest rate on obligation	9%

Instructions

Compute pension expense for P. Secord Corp. for the year 1998 by preparing a pension work sheet that incorporates the journal entry to record pension expense.

P20-8 Emerson Limited sponsors a defined benefit pension plan for its employees. The following data relate to the operation of the plan for the years 1998 and 1999.

	1998	1999
Projected benefit obligation, Jan. 1	$650,000	
Plan assets (market-related and fair value), Jan. 1	410,000	
Prepaid/Accrued pension cost (credit), Jan. 1	80,000	
Unamortized past service cost, Jan. 1	160,000	
Service cost	40,000	$ 58,000
Expected rate of return and discount rate	10%	10%
Actual return on plan assets	36,000	66,000
Amortization of past service cost	70,000	55,000
Annual contributions	72,000	81,000
Benefits paid retirees	31,500	54,000
Increase in projected benefit obligation due to changes in actuarial assumptions	87,000	-0-
Average service life of all employees		20 years
Vested benefit obligation at Dec. 31		464,000

Instructions

(a) Prepare a pension work sheet for 1998 and 1999, and present all accompanying computations.

(b) Prepare the journal entries to reflect all pension plan transactions and adjustments at December 31 of each year.

(c) At December 31, 1999, prepare a schedule that reconciles the funded status of the pension plan with the pension amounts reported in the financial statements.

P20-9 Tammy Gorman was recently promoted to assistant controller of Haber Corporation, having previously served Haber as a staff accountant. One of the responsibilities of her new position is to prepare the annual pension accrual. Barry Crowell, the corporate controller, provided Gorman with last year's workpapers and information from the actuary's annual report. The pension work sheet for the prior year is presented below.

	Journal Entry			Memo Records		
	Pension Expense	Cash	Prepaid (Accrued) Cost	Projected Benefit Obligation	Plan Assets	Unamortized Past Service Cost
6-1-96[1]				($20,000)	$20,000	
Service cost[1]	$1,800			(1,800)		
Interest[2]	1,200			(1,200)		
Actual return[3]	(1,600)				1,600	
Contribution[1]		$(1,000)			1,000	
Benefits paid[1]				900	(900)	
Past service cost[4]				(2,000)		$2,000
Journal entry	$1,400		$(1,400)			
Funding entry		$(1,000)	$ 1,000			
May 31, 1997 balance			$(400)	$(24,100)	$21,700	$2,000

[1]Per actuary's report.
[2]Beginning projected benefit obligation x discount rate of 6%.
[3]Expected return was $1,600 (beginning plan assets x expected return of 8%).
[4]A plan amendment that granted employees retroactive benefits for work performed in earlier periods took effect on May 31, 1997. The amendment increased the May 31, 1997 projected benefit obligation by $2,000. No amortization was recorded in the fiscal year ended May 31, 1997.

Pertinent information from the actuary's report for the year ended May 31, 1998 follows. The report indicated no actuarial gains or losses in the fiscal year ended May 31, 1998.

Contribution	$ 100
Service cost	$ 3,000
Interest on obligation	6%
Expected return	8%
Accumulated benefits obligation 5-31-97	$21,000
Accumulated benefits obligation 5-31-98	$27,000
Actual return on plan assets	$ 1,736
Benefits paid	$ 500
Expected period to full eligibility	10 years
Expected average remaining service life	12 years
Fair value plan assets 5-31-97	$21,700
Fair value plan assets 5-31-98	$23,036

Instructions

(a) Prepare the pension work sheet for Haber Corporation for the year ended May 31, 1998.

(b) Prepare the journal entries required to reflect the accounting for Haber Corporation's pension plan for the year ended May 31, 1998. (CMA adapted)

P20-10

A. Bailey Foods Inc. sponsors a post-retirement medical and dental benefit plan for its employees. The company adopts the accrual method of accounting for this plan beginning January 1, 1998. The following balances relate to the plan on this date.

Plan assets	$200,000
Accumulated post-retirement benefit obligation	860,000
No prior service costs exist.	

As a result of the plan's operation during 1998, the following additional data are provided by the actuary.

Service cost for 1998 is $70,000
Discount rate is 9%
Contributions to the plan in 1998 are $60,000
Expected return on plan assets is $9,000
Actual return on plan assets is $15,000
Benefits paid to retirees from plan are $44,000
Average remaining service to full eligibility: 20 years
Average remaining service to expected retirement: 22 years
Transition amount is to be amortized

Instructions

(a) Compute the net periodic post-retirement benefit cost for 1998 by preparing a work sheet that shows the journal entry for post-retirement expense and the year-end balances in the related memo accounts. Assume that contributions and benefits are paid at the end of the year.

(b) At December 31, 1998, prepare a schedule that reconciles the funded status of the plan with the post-retirement amount reported on the balance sheet.

Rice Western Ltd.'s (RWL) controller raised the following issues at the company's most recent financial managers' meeting as a result of the release of the 1997 *Exposure Draft* on "Employees' Future Benefits."

*P20-11

Situation 1
RWL provides a contributory long-term disability program for its employees through an insurance company. For an annual premium the insurance company takes on the responsibility of providing salary continuation on a long-term basis after a three-month waiting period, during which time RWL continues to pay the employee at full salary. For its year ended December 31, 1998, RWL paid a $20,000 premium on the insurance policy and recovered $5,000 from employee withholdings as their contribution to the cost of the benefit package. Jeff Kavanagh, a department manager earning $4,000 per month, was injured in late October and not expected to be able to return to work for at least one year.

Instructions

(a) Identify whether this benefit plan is a defined benefit or a defined contribution plan; whether the benefits are service related or not; and the accounting method recommended by the 1997 *Exposure Draft*.

(b) Prepare all entries required to be made by RWL in 1998.

Situation 2

Akes & Paynes Ltd., a subsidiary of RWL, determined that it had to reduce its costs in order to remain competitive. Top management decided, therefore, to merge two divisions into one in order to save the long-run administration costs associated with a multi-division structure. The restructuring is to be effective January 31, 1999. Rather than choose which divisional manager would be terminated, Akes & Paynes offered two years' salary (at $65,000 per year) to whichever manager volunteered to leave the company. Management felt certain that one of the two long-term employees would take up this offer. On January 5, 1999, Bill Acton agreed to the two-year package.

Instructions

(a) Identify the type of employee future benefit Akes & Paynes has offered.

(b) Prepare any entries that Akes & Paynes must record for their year ended December 31, 1998. State any assumptions necessary.

Situation 3

RWL's new HiTek division tries to attract the most knowledgeable and creative employees it can find. To help in this regard, it offers to a special group of technology employees the right to a fully paid sabbatical leave after every five years of continuous service. Three such employees were hired effective January 1, 1998 at an annual salary of $50,000 each per year.

Instructions

(a) Explain briefly how this employee future benefit should be accounted for.

(b) What additional information is needed before HiTek's accountant can make any accounting entries relative to this benefit?

(c) Prepare skeleton journal entries (that is, without numbers) required in each of the years 1998 to 2003 (if any) to account for the sabbatical benefit.

CASES

C20-1 Many business organizations have been concerned with providing for the retirement of employees since the late 1800s. During recent decades, a marked increase in this concern has resulted in the establishment of private pension and other retirement benefit plans in most companies of any size.

The substantial growth of these plans, both in numbers of employees covered and in the types and amounts of retirement benefits, has increased the significance of employees' future benefit costs in relation to the financial position and results of operations of many companies. In examining the costs of benefit plans, an accountant encounters certain terms. The elements of benefit costs that the terms represent must be dealt with appropriately if generally accepted accounting principles are to be reflected in the financial statements of entities with such plans.

Instructions

(a) Define a private benefit plan. How does a contributory pension plan differ from a noncontributory plan?

(b) Differentiate between "accounting for the employer" and "accounting for the benefit plan."

(c) Explain the terms "funded" and "benefit liability" as they relate to:

   1. The benefit plan.

   2. The employer.

(d) 1. Discuss the theoretical justification for accrual recognition of future benefit costs.

   2. Discuss the theoretical justification for "event accrual" accounting for future benefit costs.

   3. Discuss the relative objectivity of the measurement process of full accrual versus event accrual versus cash (pay-as-you-go) accounting for annual benefit costs.

(e) Distinguish among the following as they relate to pension plans.

   1. Service cost.

   2. Past service costs.

   3. Actuarial funding methods.

   4. Vested benefits.

The following items have appeared on Chesley Company's financial statements over the past few years. **C20-2**

1. Under the caption Assets: Deferred pension cost
2. Under the caption Liabilities: Accrued pension cost
3. On the Income Statement: Pension expense

Instructions

Explain the significance of each of the items above on corporate financial statements.

In examining the costs of pension plans, an accountant encounters certain terms. The elements of pension costs that **C20-3** the terms represent must be dealt with appropriately if generally accepted accounting principles are to be reflected in the financial statements of entities with pension plans.

Instructions

(a) 1. Discuss the theoretical justification for accrual recognition of pension costs.
    2. Discuss the relative objectivity of the measurement process of accrual versus cash (pay-as-you-go) accounting for annual pension costs.
(b) Explain the following terms as they apply to accounting for pension plans.
    1. Market-related asset value.
    2. Actuarial funding methods.
    3. Projected benefit obligation.
    4. Capitalization approach.
    5. Corridor approach.
(c) What information is required to be disclosed about a company's pension plans in its financial statements, including its notes? Comment.

Marion Burke, president of Express Mail Ltd., is discussing the possibility of developing a pension plan for its **C20-4** employees with Mark Sullivan, controller, and James Salamon, assistant controller. Their conversation is as follows.

MARION BURKE: If we are going to be competitive, we must have a pension plan to attract talented employees.

MARK SULLIVAN: I must warn you, Marion, that a pension plan will take a large bite out of our income. The only reason we have been so profitable is the lack of a pension cost in our income statement. In some of our competitors' cases, pension expense is 30% of pretax income.

JAMES SALAMON: Why do we have to worry about a pension cost now anyway? Benefits do not vest until after 10 years of service. If they do not vest, then we are not liable. We should not have to report an expense until we are legally liable to provide benefits.

MARION BURKE: But James, the employees would also want credit for past service with full vesting 10 years after starting service, not 10 years after the plan. How would we allocate the large past service cost?

JAMES SALAMON: Well, I believe that the past service cost is a cost of providing a pension plan for employees forever. It is an intangible asset that will not diminish in value because it will increase the morale of our present and future employees and provide us with a competitive edge in acquiring future employees.

MARION BURKE: I hate to disagree, but I believe the past service cost is a benefit only to the present employees. This past service is directly related to the composition of the employee group at the time the plan is initiated and is in no way related to any intangible benefit received by the company because of the plan's existence. Therefore, I propose that the past service cost be amortized over the expected average remaining service life (EARSL) of the existing employee group.

MARK SULLIVAN (Somewhat perturbed): But what about the income statement? You two are arguing theory without consideration of our income figure.

MARION BURKE: Settle down, Mark.

MARK SULLIVAN: Sorry, perhaps James' approach to resolving this problem is the best one. I am just not sure.

Instructions

(a) Assuming that Express Mail Ltd. establishes a pension plan, how should their liability for pensions be computed in the first year?
(b) How should their liability be computed in subsequent years?
(c) How should pension expense be computed each year?
(d) Assuming that the pension fund is set up in a trustee relationship, should the assets of the fund be reported on the books of Express Mail Ltd.? Explain.

(e) What interest rate factor should be used in the present value computations?

(f) How should actuarial gains and losses be reported?

C20-5 Barlex Corporation is a medium-sized manufacturer of paperboard containers and boxes. The corporation sponsors a noncontributory, defined benefit pension plan that covers its 250 employees. Alex Nowicki has recently been hired as president of Barlex Corporation. While reviewing last year's financial statements with Susan Kimpton, controller, Nowicki expressed confusion about several of the items in the footnote to the financial statements that relates to the pension plan. In part, the footnote reads as follows.

> **Note J.** The company has a defined benefit pension plan that covers substantially all of its employees. The benefits are based on years of service and the employee's compensation during the last four years of employment. The company's funding policy is to contribute annually the maximum amount allowed under the federal tax law. Contributions are intended to provide for benefits expected to be earned in the future as well as those earned to date.

Effective for the year end December 31, 1988, Barlex Corporation adopted the provisions of *CICA Handbook*, Section 3460—Pension Costs and Obligations. The net periodic pension expense on Barlex Corporation's comparative income statement was $36,000 in 1998 and $28,840 in 1997.

The following are selected figures from the plan's funded status and amount recognized in the Barlex Corporation's balance sheet at December 31, 1998 ($000 omitted).

Actuarial present value of benefit obligations:	
Accumulated benefit obligation	
(including vested benefits of $318)	$(435)
Projected benefit obligation	$(600)
Plan assets at fair value	525
Projected benefit obligation in	
excess of plan assets	$ (75)

Given that Barlex Corporation's workforce has been stable for the last six years, Nowicki could not understand the increase in the net periodic pension expense. Kimpton explained that the net periodic pension expense consists of several elements, some of which may decrease the net expense.

Instructions

(a) The determination of the net periodic pension expense is a function of six major elements. List and briefly describe each of the elements.

(b) Describe the major difference and the major similarity between the accumulated benefit obligation and the projected benefit obligation.

(c) Explain why actuarial gains and losses are not recognized on the income statement in the period in which they arise. Briefly describe how these gains and losses are recognized. (CMA adapted)

C20-6 Sally Groft and Kathy Dahl have to do a class presentation on employees' future benefits, particularly those related to pensions and other post-retirement benefits. In developing the class presentation, they decided to provide the class with a series of questions related to these benefits, and then to discuss the answers in class. Given that the class has all read the 1997 *Exposure Draft* on "Employees' Future Benefits," they felt that this approach would provide a lively discussion. Here are the situations:

1. In an article in *The Financial Post*, it was reported that the discount rates used by the largest 200 companies for pension reporting ranged from 5% to 11%. How can such a situation exist, and will the *Exposure Draft* proposals alleviate this problem?

2. An article indicated that when *Handbook* Section 3460 became effective, it caused an increase in the liability reported for pensions for approximately 20% of companies. Why might this situation occur? What is expected to happen when the *Exposure Draft* proposals become finalized in *Handbook* form?

3. A recent article noted that while "smoothing" is not necessarily an accounting virtue, pension accounting has long been recognized as an exception—an area of accounting in which at least some dampening of market swings is appropriate. This is because pension plans are managed so that their performance is insulated from the extremes of short-term market swings. A pension expense that reflects the volatility of market swings might, for that reason, convey information of little relevance. Are these statements true?

4. Funds of many companies hold assets twice as large as they need to fund their pension plans. Are these assets reported on the balance sheet of these companies? If not, where are they reported?

5. Understanding the impact of pension and retirement health care accounting and reporting on a company requires detailed information about its benefit plans and an analysis of the relationship of many factors, particularly:

   (a) the transition amount and the date of initial application.

   (b) the type of plan(s) and any significant amendments.

   (c) the plan participants.

   (d) the funding status.

   (e) the actuarial funding method and assumptions currently used.

   What impact will each of these items have on financial statement presentation under the *Exposure Draft* proposals?

6. An article noted that the corridor approach to amortizing actuarial gains and losses is recommended in the proposals. What is the corridor method and what is its purpose?

Instructions

What answers do you believe Sally and Kathy gave to each of these questions?

C20-7

A *Globe & Mail* article discussed the billions of dollars of unrecorded liabilities on the balance sheets of Canadian companies for post-retirement benefit costs, particularly those related to post-retirement health care and life insurance. As financial vice-president and controller for Alco, Inc., you found this article interesting because the president recently expressed concern about the company's rising health costs. The president was particularly concerned about health care premiums paid on behalf of retired employees. He wondered what charge Alco, Inc. will have to take to its income statement for its post-retirement benefit program when the accounting standards in this area are finalized.

Instructions

As financial vice-president and controller of Alco, Inc., explain to the president what the company will have to do relative to post-retirement benefits (other than pensions), assuming that the AcSB finalizes the proposals recommended in the 1997 *Exposure Draft* on "Employees' Future Benefits." Identify any alternative treatments available.

C20-8*

"Accounting for ongoing pensions is complex enough without having to deal with plan settlements and curtailments!" exclaimed Jennifer Ho after reading the AcSB's 1997 proposals for these issues. "However, there is some logic in how gains and losses are calculated. For example, the settlement gain or loss includes the write-off of a pro rata portion of any unrecognized net actuarial gain or loss, but not the unrecognized past service cost. The curtailment gain or loss, on the other hand, includes a pro rata share of the unrecognized past service cost, but not generally the unrecognized net actuarial gain or loss."

Instructions

Explain the logic that underlies the proposed requirements for calculating settlement and curtailment gains and losses to which Jennifer refers.

USING YOUR JUDGEMENT

FINANCIAL REPORTING PROBLEM

Refer to the financial statements and other documents of Moore Corporation Limited presented in Appendix 5A and answer the following questions.

1. What kinds of pension plans does Moore offer to its employees? How are the funding policies determined for each of these pension plans?

2. What were the amounts of Moore's prepaid pension cost or accrued pension cost at the end of 1994 and 1995? How did the Corporation report the prepaid and accrued pension cost?

3. What were the amounts of net periodic pension expense for Moore's pension plans for the years 1995 and 1994? What discount rate was used to determine the projected benefit obligation for 1995? What was the expected long-term rate of return for plan assets?

4. Were Moore Corporation's pension plans over- or underfunded at December 31, 1995? At December 31, 1994? Explain. Prepare a summary reconciliation of the funded status with the amounts reported on the December 31, 1995 balance sheet.

5. What policy does Moore Corporation follow in accounting for post-retirement benefits other than pensions? What dollar difference would it have made to 1994 and 1995 net income if the company had used the alternative policy?

ETHICS CASE

John Gardner, Chief Executive Officer of Apex Dynamics Corp., a large defence-contracting firm, is considering ways to improve the company's financial position after several years of sharply declining profitability. One way to do this is to reduce or completely eliminate AD's commitment to present and future retirees with coverage on full medical and dental benefits. Despite fiscal problems, however, AD is still committed to providing excellent pension benefits.

Instructions

(a) What factors should John Gardner consider before making his decision to cut post-retirement health benefits?

(b) Does your answer to the above question change if Apex Dynamics was paying John Gardner, CEO, a salary of $20 million per year?

(c) In your opinion, how does the profession's requirements to accrue such post-retirement benefits influence the commitment of many organizations to their employees?

chapter 21

ACCOUNTING FOR LEASES

Learning Objectives

After studying this chapter, you should be able to:

1. Explain the nature, economic substance, and advantages of lease transactions.

2. Identify and explain the accounting criteria and procedures for capitalizing leases by the lessee.

3. Identify the lessee's disclosure requirements for capital leases.

4. Identify the lessee's accounting and disclosure requirements for an operating lease.

5. Contrast the operating and capitalization methods of recording leases.

6. Calculate the lease payment required for the lessor to earn a given return.

7. Identify the classifications of leases for the lessor.

8. Describe the lessor's accounting for direct financing leases.

9. Describe the lessor's accounting for sales-type leases.

10. Describe the lessor's accounting for operating leases.

11. Identify the lessor's disclosure requirements.

12. Describe the effect of residual values, guaranteed and unguaranteed, on lease accounting.

13. Describe the effect of bargain purchase options on lease accounting.

14. Describe the lessor's accounting treatment for initial direct costs.

15. Describe the lessee's accounting for sale-leaseback transactions.

16. Explain the classification and accounting treatment accorded leases that involve land as well as buildings and equipment (Appendix 21A).

OBJECTIVE 1
Explain the nature, economic substance, and advantages of lease transactions.

Over the past three decades, leasing has grown tremendously in popularity and today it is the fastest-growing form of capital investment. Instead of borrowing money to buy an airplane, a computer, a nuclear core, or a satellite, a company leases it. Even the gambling casinos lease their slot machines. Airlines and railroads lease huge amounts of equipment, many hotel and motel chains lease their facilities, and most retail chains lease the bulk of their retail premises and warehouses.

A **lease** is a contractual agreement between a **lessor** and a **lessee** that gives the lessee the right to use specific property owned by the lessor for a specific period of time in return for stipulated, and generally periodic, cash payments (rents). An essential element of the lease agreement is that the lessor conveys less than the total interest in the property. Because of the financial, operating, and risk advantages that the lease arrangement provides, many businesses and other types of organizations lease substantial amounts of property, both real and personal, as an alternative to ownership.

The increased significance and prevalence of lease arrangements in recent years have intensified the need for uniform accounting and complete informative reporting of these transactions.[1] This chapter provides background for your study of leases, and explains the accounting and disclosure requirements set out in *CICA Handbook* Section 3065. Appendix 21A identifies issues related to leases involving land; Appendix 21B replicates the AcSB's decision trees on accounting for capital, sales-type and direct financing leases; and Appendix 21C illustrates the application of Section 3065 to specific situations.

LEASE PROVISIONS

Because a lease is a contract, the provisions agreed to by the lessor and lessee may vary widely and may be limited only by their ingenuity. The duration or term of the lease may be from a few moments to the entire expected economic life of the asset. The **rental payments** may be level from year to year, increasing in amount, or decreasing. The rents may be predetermined or may vary with sales, the prime interest rate, the consumer price index, or some other factor. In most cases the rent is set to enable the lessor to recover its investment in the asset plus a fair return over the life of the lease.

The executory costs or obligations for taxes, insurance, and maintenance may be assumed by either the lessor or the lessee, or they may be divided. Restrictions comparable to those in bond indentures may limit the lessee's activities relative to dividend payments or the incurrence of further debt and lease obligations. The lease contract may be noncancellable or may grant the right to early termination upon payment of a set scale of prices plus a penalty. In case of default, the lessee may be liable for all future payments at once, receiving title to the property in exchange, or the lessor may enjoy the prerogative to sell and to collect from the lessee all or a portion of the difference between the sale price and the lessor's unrecovered cost.

Alternatives open to the lessee at termination of the lease range from none, to the right to purchase the leased asset at its fair market value, to the right to renew or buy it at a nominal price.

ADVANTAGES OF LEASING

Although the lease arrangement is not without its disadvantages, the growth in its use suggests that leasing often has a genuine advantage over owning property. Some of the commonly discussed advantages of leasing to the lessee and lessor include the following.

1. **100% *financing at fixed rates.*** Leases are often executed without requiring any money down from the lessee, which helps to conserve scarce cash—an especially desirable feature for new and developing companies. In addition, lease payments often remain fixed, which protects the lessee against inflation and increases in the cost of money. The following comment regarding a conventional loan is typical: "Our local bank finally came up to 80% of the purchase price but wouldn't go any higher,

---

[1] The popularity and general applicability of leasing are evidenced by the fact that 230 of 300 companies surveyed by the CICA in 1994 disclosed either capitalized or noncapitalized lease data. *Financial Reporting in Canada—1995* (Toronto: CICA, 1995).

and they wanted a floating interest rate. We just couldn't afford the down payment and we needed to lock in a final payment rate we knew we could live with."

From the lessor's point of view, financial institutions and leasing companies find leasing attractive because it provides competitive interest margins.

2. **Protection against obsolescence.** Leasing equipment reduces risk of obsolescence to the lessee, and in many cases passes the risk in residual value to the lessor. For example, Syntex Corp. (pharmaceutical maker) leased Wang computers. Syntex was permitted under the lease agreement to turn in an old computer for a new model at any time, cancelling the old lease and writing a new one. The cost of the new lease was added to the balance due on the old lease, less the old computer's trade-in value.

   On the other hand, the lessor can benefit from the reversion of the property at the end of the lease term. Residual values can produce very large profits. For example, Citicorp at one time assumed that the commercial aircraft it was leasing to the airline industry would have a residual of 5% of its purchase price. It turned out that the planes were worth 150% of their cost — a handsome price appreciation. However, three years later these same planes slumped to 80% of their cost, a residual value far greater than the projected 5%.

3. **Flexibility.** Lease agreements may contain less restrictive provisions than other debt agreements. Innovative lessors can tailor a lease agreement to the lessee's special needs. For instance, rental payments can be structured to meet the timing of cash revenues generated by the equipment, so that payments are made when the equipment is productive.

4. **Less costly financing for lessee, tax incentives for lessor.** Some companies find leasing cheaper than other forms of financing. For example, start-up companies in depressed industries or companies in low tax brackets may lease as a way of claiming tax benefits that might otherwise be lost. Investment tax credits and capital cost allowance deductions are of no benefit to companies that have little if any taxable income. Through leasing, these tax benefits are used by the leasing companies or financial institutions, which can pass some of these tax benefits back to the user of the asset in the form of lower rental payments.

5. **Off-balance-sheet financing.** Certain leases do not add debt on a balance sheet or affect financial ratios, and may add to borrowing capacity.[2] **Off-balance-sheet financing** is critical to some companies. For instance, the balance sheet of Chart House, Inc., which operated over 500 restaurants in the United States, showed long-term debt of $127 million and total shareholders' equity of $88 million, resulting in a high but manageable debt-to-equity ratio of 1.4 to 1. If the company's future rental payments of $125 million related to noncancellable leases were required to be capitalized and added to its long-term debt, Chart House's debt-to-equity ratio would have climbed to well over 2 to 1.

CONCEPTUAL NATURE OF A LEASE

If Echo Bay Mines Ltd. borrows $15,000,000 on a 10-year note from the Royal Bank of Canada to purchase a Boeing 727 jet plane, it is clear that an asset and related liability should be reported on Echo Bay's balance sheet at that amount. If Echo Bay purchases the 727 jet for $15,000,000 directly from Boeing through an instalment purchase over 10 years, it is equally clear that an asset and related liability should be reported. However, if Echo

---

[2] As demonstrated later in this chapter, certain types of lease arrangements need not be capitalized on the balance sheet. The Liability section is frequently relieved of large future lease commitments that, if recorded, would adversely affect the debt-to-equity ratio. The reluctance to record lease obligations as liabilities is one of the primary reasons that capitalized lease accounting is resisted and circumvented by lessees.

Bay leases the Boeing 727 for 10 years through a noncancellable lease transaction with payments of the same amount as the instalment purchase transaction, differences of opinion start to develop over how this and other types of lease transactions should be reported. The various views of accounting for leases can be summarized as follows.

Do not capitalize any leased assets. Because the lessee does not have ownership of the property, capitalization is considered inappropriate. Furthermore, a lease is an **executory contract** requiring continuing performance by both parties. Because other executory contracts, such as purchase commitments and employment contracts, are not capitalized, leases should not be capitalized.

Capitalize those leases that are similar to instalment purchases. Accountants should report transactions in accordance with their economic substance; therefore, if instalment purchases are capitalized, so also should leases that have similar characteristics. In the illustration above, Echo Bay is committed to the same payments over a 10-year period for either a lease or an instalment purchase; lessees simply make rental payments, while owners make mortgage payments. Why shouldn't the financial statements report these transactions in the same manner?

Capitalize all long-term leases. Under this approach, the long-term right to use property justifies its capitalization. This property rights approach capitalizes all long-term leases.

Capitalize firm leases where the penalty for nonperformance is substantial. A final approach is to capitalize only firm, noncancellable contractual rights and obligations. "Firm" means that it is unlikely that performance under the lease can be avoided without a severe penalty.[3]

In short, the various viewpoints range from no capitalization to capitalization of all leases. The CICA standard is consistent with the approach that capitalizes leases that are similar to an instalment purchase, noting that *a lease that transfers substantially all of the benefits and risks of ownership of property should be capitalized.*

This viewpoint implies three basic conclusions: (1) the characteristics that indicate that substantially all of the benefits and risks of ownership have been transferred must be identified; (2) the same characteristics should apply consistently to the lessee and the lessor; and (3) those leases that do *not* transfer substantially all the benefits and risks of ownership should not be capitalized but rather should be accounted for as rental payments and receipts.

By capitalizing the present value of the future rental payments, *the lessee* records an asset and a liability at an amount generally representative of the asset's market value or purchase price. *The lessor*, having transferred substantially all the benefits and risks of ownership, removes the asset from its balance sheet, replacing it with a receivable. The typical journal entries for the lessee and the lessor, assuming equipment is leased and is capitalized, appear as shown below.

EXHIBIT 21-1

Lessee			Lessor		
Leased Equipment	XXX		Lease Receivable (net)	XXX	
Lease Obligation		XXX	Equipment		XXX

Having capitalized the asset, the lessee recognizes the depreciation. The lessor and lessee treat the rental payments as the receipt and the payment, respectively, of interest and principal.

---

[3] Yuji Ijiri, "Recognition of Contractual Rights and Obligations," *Research Report* (Stamford, CT: FASB, 1980).

If the lease is not capitalized, no asset is recorded by the lessee and no asset is removed from the lessor's books. When a lease payment is made, the lessee records rental expense and the lessor recognizes rental revenue.

The remainder of this chapter presents the different types of leases and the specific criteria, accounting rules, and disclosure requirements set forth by the CICA in accounting for leases.

ACCOUNTING BY LESSEES

OBJECTIVE 2
Identify and explain the accounting criteria and procedures for capitalizing leases by the lessee.

From the standpoint of the lessee, all leases are classified for accounting purposes as either an operating lease or a capital lease. Where the risks and benefits of ownership are transferred from the lessor to the lessee, the lease must be accounted for as a capital lease (**capitalization method**); otherwise, it is accounted for as an operating lease (**noncapitalization method**).

CAPITALIZATION CRITERIA

CICA Handbook Section 3065, par. .06 specifies that if, at the inception of a lease, *any one of the following criteria is met*, the risks and benefits of ownership are assumed to be transferred to the lessee, and the lessee should classify and account for the arrangement as a **capital lease**.

1. There is reasonable assurance that the lessee will obtain ownership of the leased property by the end of the lease term. If there is a bargain purchase option in the lease, it is assumed that the lessee will exercise it and obtain ownership.

2. The lease term is such that the lessee will receive substantially all of the economic benefits expected to be derived from the use of the leased property over its life span. This is usually assumed to occur if the lease term is 75% or more of the economic life of the leased property.

3. The lease allows the lessor to recover its investment in the leased property and to earn a return on the investment. This is assumed to occur if the present value of the minimum lease payments (excluding executory costs) is equal to substantially all (usually 90% or more) of the fair value of the leased property.

A lease that does not meet any one of the three criteria listed above is classified and accounted for by the lessee as an **operating lease**. The flowchart below illustrates this decision. The criteria, however, are controversial and can be difficult to apply in practice.

ILLUSTRATION 21-1

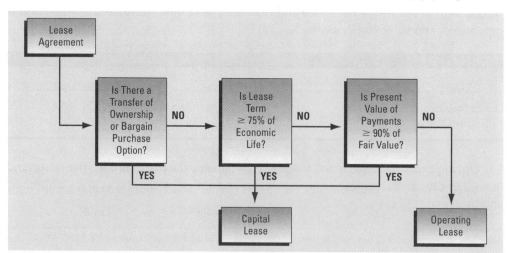

TRANSFER OF OWNERSHIP TEST

If the lease transfers ownership of the asset to the lessee by the end of the lease term, it is a capital lease. This criterion is not controversial and is easily implemented in practice.

The transfer of ownership may be facilitated at the end of the lease term without additional consideration or through a bargain purchase option. A **bargain purchase option** is a provision allowing the lessee to purchase the leased property for a price that is significantly lower than the property's expected fair value at the date the option becomes exercisable. At the inception of the lease, the difference between the option price and the expected fair value must be large enough to make exercise of the option reasonably assured.[4]

For example, assume that you are to lease a car for $350 per month for 40 months with an option to purchase it for $100 at the end of the 40-month period. If the estimated fair value of the car is $4,000 at the end of 40 months, the $100 option to purchase is clearly a bargain and, therefore, capitalization is required. In other cases, the criterion may not be as easy to apply, and to determine now that a certain future price is a bargain can be difficult.

ECONOMIC LIFE TEST

If the lease period equals or exceeds 75% of the asset's economic life, it follows that most of the risks and rewards of ownership are transferred to the lessee. However, determining the **lease term** and economic life of the asset may be troublesome.

The lease term is generally considered the fixed, noncancellable term of the lease. However, this period can be extended if a bargain renewal option is provided in the lease agreement. A **bargain renewal option** is a provision allowing the lessee to renew the lease for a rental that is lower than the expected fair rental at the date the option becomes exercisable. At the inception of the lease, the difference between the renewal rental and the expected fair rental must be great enough to make the exercise of the option to renew reasonably assured.

For example, if a computer is leased for three years at a rental of $100 per month, and then subsequently can be leased for $10 per month for another two years when the fair rental at that time is $75 per month, it clearly is a bargain renewal option and the lease term is considered to be five years. However, as with bargain purchase options, it is sometimes difficult to determine what is a bargain.[5]

Determining estimated economic life can also pose problems, especially if the leased asset is a specialized item or has been used for a significant period of time. For example, determining the economic life of a nuclear core is extremely difficult because it is subject to much more than normal wear and tear.

RECOVERY OF INVESTMENT BY LESSOR TEST

If the present value of the minimum lease payments equals or exceeds 90% of the fair value of the asset, then the leased asset should be capitalized. The rationale for this test is that if the present value of the minimum lease payments is reasonably close to the market

---

[4] The Emerging Issues Committee of the CICA, in *EIC–30*, concluded that the ultimate test is whether there is reasonable assurance that the lessee will obtain ownership by the end of the lease. A situation, for example, where there is no bargain purchase option but other lease provisions make it probable that the lessee will acquire the leased property for its fair value at the end of the lease term are sufficient to classify the transaction as a capital lease.

[5] The original lease term is also extended for leases that exhibit the following: substantial penalties for nonrenewal; periods for which the lessor has the option to renew or extend the lease; renewal periods preceding the date a bargain purchase option becomes exercisable; and renewal periods during which the lessee guarantees the lessor's debt related to the leased property.

price of the asset, the lessor is recovering its investment in the asset through the lease arrangement and the asset is being purchased by the lessee.

In determining the present value of the minimum lease payments, three important concepts are involved: minimum lease payments, executory costs, and the discount rate.

Minimum Lease Payments. In general, the minimum lease payments are those that the lessee is obligated to make or can be expected to make in connection with the leased property. **Minimum lease payments** *from the lessee's point of view* are defined as including:[6]

1. *Minimum rental payments.* Minimum payments the lessee is obligated to make to the lessor under the lease agreement, excluding executory costs (defined below). The minimum rental payments may be equal to the minimum lease payments. However, the minimum lease payments also include the guaranteed residual value, penalty for failure to renew, or bargain purchase option, if incorporated in the agreement.

2. *Guaranteed residual value.* The **residual value** is the estimated fair value of the leased property at the end of the lease term. The lessor often transfers the risk of loss to the lessee or to a third party by requiring a guarantee of the estimated residual value. The **guaranteed residual value** is (1) the amount at which the lessor has the right to require the lessee to purchase the asset; or (2) the amount the lessee or the third-party guarantor guarantees the lessor will realize. The **unguaranteed residual value**, that portion of the residual value that is not guaranteed or is guaranteed solely by a party related to the lessor, is not included in the definition of minimum lease payments.

3. *Penalty for failure to renew or extend the lease.* The amount payable by the lessee if the agreement specifies that the lease must be extended or renewed and the lessee fails to do so.

4. *Bargain purchase option.* As indicated earlier, an option given to the lessee to purchase the equipment at the end of the lease term at a price that is sufficiently below the expected fair value so that, at the inception of the lease, purchase appears to be reasonably assured. Ordinarily, if a bargain purchase option (BPO) is included in the lease agreement, a guaranteed residual value and penalty would not apply.

Executory Costs. Like most assets, leased tangible assets require the incurrence of insurance, maintenance, and tax expenses (called **executory costs**) during their economic life. If the lessor retains responsibility for the payment of these ownership-type costs, any portion of each lease payment that represents the recovery of executory costs from the lessee *should be excluded* in computing the present value of the minimum lease payments. This portion of the lease payment does not represent payment on or a reduction of the capitalized obligation. If the portion of the lease payment representing executory costs is not determinable from the provisions of the lease, an estimate of the amount must be made. Many lease agreements, however, specify that these executory costs be assumed by the lessee; in these cases the rental payments can be used without adjustment in the present value computation.

Discount Rate. The lessee computes the present value of the minimum lease payments using the lessee's **incremental borrowing rate**, which is defined as the interest rate that, at the inception of the lease, the lessee would have incurred to borrow, over a similar term and with similar security for the borrowing, the funds necessary to purchase the leased asset.[7] For example, assume that Mortensen Ltd. decides to lease computer equipment for

[6] *CICA Handbook* (Toronto: CICA), Section 3065, par. .03(q).

[7] *Ibid.*, par. .03(p).

a five-year period at a cost of $10,000 per year. To determine whether the present value of these payments is less than 90% of the fair value of the property, the lessee discounts the lease payment using its incremental borrowing rate. The determination of the incremental borrowing rate often requires judgement because it is based on a hypothetical purchase of property.

There is one exception to the use of this rate. If (1) the lessee knows the **implicit rate** used by the lessor in calculating the amount of the lease payments; and (2) it is less than the lessee's incremental borrowing rate, then the lessee must use the implicit rate. The interest rate implicit in the lease is the discount rate that, when applied to the minimum lease payments and the unguaranteed residual value accruing to the lessor, causes the aggregate present value to be equal to the fair value of the leased property to the lessor.[8] In other words, it is the lessor's internal rate of return implied by the lease variables.

The purpose of this exception is twofold. First, the implicit rate of the lessor is generally a more realistic rate to use in determining the amount, if any, to report as the asset and related liability for the lessee. Second, the guideline is provided to ensure that the lessee does not use an artificially high incremental borrowing rate *that would cause the present value of the minimum lease payments to be less than 90% of the fair value of the property and thus make it possible to avoid capitalization of the asset and related liability*. The lessee may argue that it cannot determine the implicit rate of the lessor and therefore the higher rate should be used. In most cases, however, the implicit rate used by the lessor is disclosed or can be approximated. The determination of whether or not a reasonable estimate can be made requires judgement, particularly where the result from using the incremental borrowing rate comes close to meeting the 90% test. Because *the leased property cannot be capitalized at more than its fair value*, the lessee is prevented from using an excessively low discount rate.

ACCOUNTING FOR A CAPITAL LEASE

Asset and Liability Recorded. *In a capital lease transaction, the lessee uses the lease as a source of financing.* The lessor provides the leased asset to the lessee and finances the transaction by accepting instalment payments. The lessee treats the transaction as if an asset was purchased and a long-term liability was created. Over the life of the property leased, the rental payments made by the lessee to the lessor constitute a repayment of principal and interest.

The lessee recognizes the asset and liability at the lower of (1) the present value of the minimum lease payments, as defined above; and (2) the fair value of the leased asset at the inception of the lease. The rationale for this approach is that, like all other assets, a leased asset cannot be recorded at more than its fair value.

Amortization Period and Method. One troublesome aspect of accounting for the depreciation of the capitalized leased asset relates to the **amortization period**. For example, if the lease agreement transfers ownership of the asset to the lessee or contains a bargain purchase option, the leased asset is depreciated in a manner consistent with the lessee's normal depreciation policy for owned assets, *using the economic life of the asset.*

On the other hand, if the lease does not transfer ownership or contain a bargain purchase option, the leased asset is depreciated *over the term of the lease*, because the leased asset reverts to the lessor after this point.

The lessee depreciates the leased asset by applying conventional depreciation methods: straight-line, sum-of-the-years'-digits, declining balance, units of production, etc. The CICA uses the term "amortization" more frequently than the term "depreciation" in recog-

---

[8] *CICA Handbook*, Section 3065, par. .03(m).

nition of intangible leased property rights. We prefer the widely used term "depreciation" as a description of the write-off of the costs of the expired services of a tangible asset.

Effective Interest Method. Although the amount initially capitalized as an asset and recorded as an obligation are computed at the same present value, the *subsequent depreciation of the asset and the discharge of the obligation are independent accounting processes*.

Over the term of the lease, the **effective interest method** is used to allocate each lease payment between principal and interest. This method produces a constant rate of interest in each period on the obligation's outstanding balance. The discount rate used by the lessee in determining the present value of the minimum lease payments is used by the lessee in applying the effective interest method to capital leases.

Capital Lease Illustrated. Lessor Company and Lessee Company sign a lease agreement that calls for Lessor Company to lease equipment to Lessee Company beginning January 1, 1998. The lease agreement contains the following terms and provisions.

1. The term of the lease is five years, and the lease agreement is noncancellable, requiring equal rental payments of $25,981.62 at the beginning of each year (annuity due basis).

2. The equipment has a fair value at the inception of the lease of $100,000, an estimated economic life of five years, and no residual value.

3. Lessee Company pays all of the executory costs directly except for the property taxes of $2,000 per year, which are included in the annual payments to the lessor.

4. The lease contains no renewal options and the equipment reverts to Lessor Company at the termination of the lease.

5. Lessee Company's incremental borrowing rate is 11% per year.

6. Lessee Company depreciates similar equipment it owns on a straight-line basis.

7. Lessor Company set the annual rental to ensure a rate of return on its investment of 10% per year; this fact is known to Lessee Company.

The lease meets the criteria for classification as a capital lease because (1) the lease term of five years, being equal to the equipment's estimated economic life of five years, satisfies the 75% test; or because (2) the present value of the minimum lease payments ($100,000 as computed below) exceeds 90% of the fair value of the property ($100,000).

The minimum lease payments are $119,908.10 ($23,981.62 × 5) and the amount capitalized as leased assets is $100,000, the present value of the minimum lease payments determined as follows.

EXHIBIT 21-2

Capitalized amount = ($25,981.62 − $2,000) × present value of an annuity due of
$1 for 5 periods at 10% (Table A-5)

= $23,981.62 × 4.16986

= **$100,000**

The lessor's implicit interest rate of 10% is used instead of the lessee's incremental borrowing rate of 11% because (1) it is lower, and (2) the lessee has knowledge of it. [9]

---

[9] If Lessee Company had an incremental borrowing rate of 9% (lower than the 10% rate used by Lessor Company) and it had not known the rate used by Lessor Company, the present value computation would yield a capitalized amount of $101,675.35 ($23,981.62 × 4.23972). Because this amount exceeds the $100,000 fair value of the equipment, Lessee Company would capitalize the $100,000 and use 10% as its effective rate for recognition of interest on the lease obligation.

The entry to record the capital lease on Lessee Company's books on January 1, 1998 is:

Leased Equipment Under Capital Leases	100,000	
Obligations Under Capital Leases		100,000

The journal entry to record the first lease payment on January 1, 1998 is:

Property Tax Expense	2,000.00	
Obligations Under Capital Leases	23,981.62	
Cash		25,981.62

Each rental payment of $25,981.62 consists of three elements: (1) a reduction in the principal of the lease obligation; (2) a financing cost (interest expense); and (3) executory costs (property taxes). The total financing cost or interest expense over the term of the lease is the difference between the present value of the lease payments ($100,000) and the actual cash disbursed, net of executory costs ($119,908.10), or $19,908.10. The annual interest expense is a function of the outstanding obligation, as illustrated in the following schedule.

EXHIBIT 21-3 LESSEE COMPANY

LEASE AMORTIZATION SCHEDULE

(Annuity due basis)

Date	Annual Lease Payment	Interest (10%) on Unpaid Obligation	Reduction of Lease Obligation	Balance of Lease Obligation
	(a)	(b)	(c)	(d)
Jan. 1/98				$100,000.00
Jan. 1/98	$ 23,981.62	-0-	$ 23,981.62	76,018.38
Jan. 1/99	23,981.62	$ 7,601.84	16,379.78	59,638.60
Jan. 1/00	23,981.62	5,963.86	18,017.76	41,620.84
Jan. 1/01	23,981.62	4,162.08	19,819.54	21,801.30
Jan. 1/02	23,981.62	2,180.32*	21,801.30	-0-
	$119,908.10	$19,908.10	$100,000.00	

(a) Lease payment as required by lessor, excluding executory costs.
(b) 10% of the preceding balance of (d) except for January 1, 1998; since this is an annuity due, no time has elapsed at the date of the first payment and no interest has accrued.
(c) (a) minus (b).
(d) Preceding balance minus (c).
*Rounded by 19 cents.

At Lessee Company's fiscal year-end, December 31, 1998, accrued interest is recorded as follows.

Interest Expense	7,601.84	
Interest Payable		7,601.84

Depreciation of the leased equipment over its lease term of five years, applying Lessee Company's normal depreciation policy (straight-line method), results in the following entry on December 31, 1998.

Depreciation Expense—Leased Equipment	20,000	
Accumulated Depreciation—Leased Equipment ($100,000 ÷ 5)		20,000

At December 31, 1998 the assets recorded under capital leases are separately identified on the lessee's balance sheet. Similarly, the related obligations are separately identified. The principal portion due within one year or the operating cycle, whichever is longer, is classified with current liabilities and the rest with noncurrent liabilities. For example, the current portion of the December 31, 1998 total obligation of $76,018.38 in the lessee's amortization schedule is the amount of the reduction in the principal of the obligation in 1999, or $16,379.78. The liability section as it relates to lease transactions at

---

EXHIBIT 21-4

Current Liabilities	
Interest Payable	$ 7,601.84
Obligations Under Capital Leases	16,379.78
Noncurrent Liabilities	
Obligations Under Capital Leases	$59,638.60

December 31, 1998 appears as follows.

The journal entry to record the lease payment of January 1, 1999 is as follows.

Property Tax Expense	2,000.00	
Interest Payable[10]	7,601.84	
Obligations Under Capital Leases	16,379.78	
Cash		25,981.62

Entries through 2002 follow the pattern above. Other executory costs (insurance and maintenance) assumed by Lessee Company are recorded in a manner similar to that used to record operating costs incurred on other assets owned by Lessee Company.

Upon expiration of the lease, the amount capitalized as leased equipment is fully amortized and the lease obligation is fully discharged. If not purchased, the equipment is returned to the lessor, and the leased equipment and related accumulated depreciation accounts are removed from the books. If the equipment is purchased for $5,000 at the termination of the lease, and the estimated total life of the equipment is changed from five to seven years, the following entry would be made.

Equipment ($100,000 + $5,000)	105,000	
Accumulated Depreciation—Capital Leases	100,000	
Leased Equipment Under Capital Leases		100,000
Accumulated Depreciation—Equipment		100,000
Cash		5,000

OBJECTIVE 3

Identify the lessee's disclosure requirements for capital leases.

Reporting and Disclosure Requirements for Capital Leases. Consistent with the recognition of a capital asset and a long-term liability, most of the required disclosures are similar to those required in *Handbook* Sections 3060 and 3210 for these two balance sheet items. *CICA Handbook* Section 3065, pars. .21 to .28, identify the following required disclosures.

---

[10] This entry assumes the company does not prepare reversing entries. If reversing entries are used, the Interest Expense account would be debited for this amount.

1. The gross amount of assets recorded under capital leases and related accumulated amortization as of the date of each balance sheet presented, in aggregate and preferably by major category.

2. Depreciation expense on leased assets may be disclosed separately or as part of depreciation and amortization expense for fixed assets, and the methods and rates of amortization should be disclosed.

3. Separate disclosure of lease obligations from other long-term obligations, with separate disclosure of related details about interest rates, expiry dates, and any significant restrictions imposed as a result of the lease agreements.

4. The portion, if any, of the lease obligations payable within one year out of current funds should be reported as a current liability.

5. Future minimum lease payments as of the date of the balance sheet, in the aggregate and for each of the five succeeding fiscal years, with a separate deduction for amounts included in the minimum lease payments representing executory costs and imputed interest. The resulting net amount is the total lease obligation reported on the balance sheet.

6. Periodic interest expense related to lease obligations may be disclosed separately or included in interest on long-term indebtedness.

7. Although not required, it may be appropriate to disclose separately total contingent rentals (rentals based on a factor other than the passage of time) as well as the amount of future minimum rentals receivable from noncancellable sub-leases.

Disclosure Example. The following excerpts from the financial statements of Mark's Work Wearhouse for the year ended January 27, 1996 illustrate the disclosure by a lessee of capital leases.

EXHIBIT 21-5 MARK'S WORK WEARHOUSE

CONSOLIDATED FINANCIAL STATEMENTS
52 Weeks Ended January 27, 1996

Consolidated Balance Sheets (partial)   ($000s)

Capital assets (Note 6)	11,853
Current portion of long-term debt (Note 8)	249
Long-term debt (Note 8)	4,025

Notes to Consolidated Financial Statements

Note 1 Significant Accounting Policies

D. **CAPITAL ASSETS** – Depreciation is designed to amortize capital assets on a straight line basis over their estimated useful lives at the following annual rates:

Leasehold improvements	Term of the lease
Furniture, fixtures and equipment	20%
Capital leases	Term of the lease

EXHIBIT 21-5 MARK'S WORK WEARHOUSE (Continued)

CONSOLIDATED FINANCIAL STATEMENTS (Continued)

Note 6 Capital Assets (partial)

	1996	
	COST	NET BOOK VALUE
Leasehold improvements	$ 4,760	$ 2,310
Furniture, fixtures and equipment	16,000	8,497
Equipment under capital lease	1,174	1,046
	$21,934	$11,853

Note 8 Long-Term Debt (partial)

	1996
8% Convertible subordinated debentures	$ 3,000
Capital lease obligations — 1996,	
9.1% average interest rate over 52 months	1,274
Total	4,274
Less: amount due within one year	249
	$ 4,025

The aggregate repayments of principal required to meet long-term debt obligations are as follows:

1997	$ 249
1998	3,271
1999	300
2000	305
2001	19
Thereafter	130

OBJECTIVE 4

Identify the lessee's accounting and disclosure requirements for an operating lease.

ACCOUNTING FOR AN OPERATING LEASE

Under an operating lease, neither the leased asset nor the obligation to make lease payments is given accounting recognition. Instead, the lease payments are treated as rent expense, assigned to the accounting periods benefitting from the use of the leased asset.[11] Appropriate accruals or deferrals are made if the accounting period ends between cash payment dates.

---

[11] *EIC–21, Accounting for Lease Inducements by the Lessee* (CICA: January 21, 1991) provides guidance on accounting for the benefits of lease inducements such as an up-front cash payment to the lessee, initial rent-free periods, etc. It is recommended that such benefits be taken into income over the term of the lease on a straight-line or other basis that is representative of the pattern of benefits from the leased property.

Assume the capital lease illustrated above does not qualify as a capital lease and, by default, is accounted for as an operating lease. The charge to the income statement for rent expense in each year is $25,981.62, the amount of the rental payment. The journal entry to record the payment each January 1 is as follows.

Prepaid Rent	25,981.62	
Cash		25,981.62

At each December 31 fiscal year end, the following entry is made, assuming adjusting entries are prepared only annually.

Rent Expense	25,981.62	
Prepaid Rent		25,981.62

Required Disclosures for Operating Leases. While disclosure of the amount of operating lease rentals charged against income and other details related to operating lease agreements may be desirable, the required disclosures are few.

1. The future minimum lease payments, in total and for each of the next five years.

2. A description of the nature of other commitments under such leases.[12]

These disclosures allow readers to assess the impact of such agreements on the organization.

Disclosure Example. Note 9 to the financial statements of Mark's Work Wearhouse for the 52 weeks ended January 27, 1996 follows, and illustrates the lessee's disclosures related to operating leases.

EXHIBIT 21-6 MARK'S WORK WEARHOUSE

52 WEEKS ENDED JANUARY 27, 1996

9. COMMITMENTS

The Company has entered into operating lease agreements terminating at various dates to 2008.

The minimum annual rentals, excluding tenant operating costs, under these agreements are as follows:

1997	$ 11,641
1998	10,500
1999	9,112
2000	8,329
2001	7,558
Thereafter	30,312

In addition to minimum annual rentals, contingent rentals may be payable under certain store leases on the basis of sales in excess of stipulated amounts.

COMPARISON OF CAPITAL LEASE WITH OPERATING LEASE

As indicated above, if the lease had been accounted for as an operating lease, the first-year charge to operations would have been $25,981.62, the amount of the rental payment. Treating the transaction as a capital lease, however, resulted in a first-year charge of $29,601.84: straight-line depreciation of $20,000, interest expense of $7,601.84, and execu-

OBJECTIVE 5
Contrast the operating and capitalization methods of recording leases.

---

[12] *CICA Handbook*, Section 3065, pars. .31 to .33.

tory expenses of $2,000. The schedule below shows that while the *total* charges to operations are the same over the lease term whether the lease is accounted for as a capital lease or as an operating lease, the charges are higher in the earlier years and lower in the later years under the capital lease treatment.[13]

EXHIBIT 21-7 LESSEE COMPANY

SCHEDULE OF CHARGES TO OPERATIONS
CAPITAL LEASE VS. OPERATING LEASE

Year	Capital Lease Charges				Operating Lease Charge	Difference
	Depreciation	Executory Costs	Interest	Total Charge		
1998	$ 20,000	$ 2,000	$ 7,601.84	$ 29,601.84	$ 25,981.62	$3,620.22
1999	20,000	2,000	5,963.86	27,963.86	25,981.62	1,982.24
2000	20,000	2,000	4,162.08	26,162.08	25,981.62	180.46
2001	20,000	2,000	2,180.32	24,180.32	25,981.62	(1,801.30)
2002	20,000	2,000	—	22,000.00	25,981.62	(3,981.62)
	$100,000	$10,000	$19,908.10	$129,908.10	$129,908.10	$ -0-

If an accelerated method of depreciation is used, the differences between the amount charged to operations under the two methods would be even larger in the earlier and later years.

In addition, the capital lease approach results in an asset and related liability of $100,000 being initially reported on the balance sheet whereas no such asset or liability is reported under the operating method. A capital lease therefore has the following effects on the financial statements: (1) the amount of reported debt (both short-term and long-term) is higher; (2) the amount of total assets (specifically long-lived assets) is higher; and (3) income, and therefore retained earnings, is lower early in the life of the lease. It is not surprising that the business community resists capitalizing leases as the resulting higher debt-to-equity ratio, reduced total asset turnover, and reduced rate of return on total assets are perceived to have a detrimental effect on the company.

Whether this resistance is well founded is a matter of conjecture. From a cash flow point of view, the company is in the same position whether the lease is accounted for as an operating or a capital lease. The reasons managers often give when arguing against capitalization are (1) it can more easily lead to violation of loan covenants; (2) it can affect the amount of compensation received (for example, a stock compensation plan tied to earnings); and (3) it can lower rates of return and increase debt-to-equity relationships, thus making the company less attractive to present and potential investors.[14]

---

[13] The higher charges in the early years are one reason lessees are reluctant to classify leases as capital leases. Lessees claim that it is not more costly to operate the leased asset in the early years than in the later years; thus, they advocate an even charge similar to that produced by the operating method.

[14] A study indicated that management's behaviour did change as a result of the profession's requirements to capitalize certain leases. For example, many companies restructured their leases to avoid capitalization, while others increased their purchases of assets instead of leasing, and still others, faced with capitalization, postponed their debt offerings or issued stock instead. However, it is interesting to note that the study found no significant effect on stock or bond prices as a result of capitalization of leases. A. Rashad Abdel-Khalik, "The Economic Effects on Leases of FASB Statement No. 13, Accounting for Leases," *Research Report* (Stamford, CT: FASB, 1981).

ACCOUNTING BY LESSORS

DETERMINING THE LEASE PAYMENT

How does the lessor determine the periodic lease or rental amount? The primary variable is the rate of return, that is, the implicit rate the lessor needs to earn to justify leasing the asset. The factors considered in establishing the rate of return are the credit standing of the lessee, the length of the lease, the status of the residual value (guaranteed versus unguaranteed), and so on. In the Lessor Company/Lessee Company example that starts on page 1058, the lessor wanted a 10% return, the fair value of the equipment was $100,000 (also the lessor's cost), and the estimated residual value was zero. Lessor Company determined the amount of the rental payment in the following manner.

OBJECTIVE 6
Calculate the lease payment required for the lessor to earn a given return.

EXHIBIT 21-8

Fair value of leased equipment	$100,000.00
Less present value of amount to be recovered through bargain purchase option or residual value at termination of lease	-0-
Present value of amount to be recovered by lessor through lease payments	$100,000.00

Lease payments: $i = 10$, $n = 5$ (Annuity due)
$= \$100{,}000 \div 4.16986$ (Table A-5)
$= \$23{,}981.62$

If a bargain purchase option or other residual value is involved, the lessor does not have to recover as much through the rental payments. Therefore, the present value of these amounts is deducted before determining the lease payment. This is illustrated later in the chapter in more detail.

CLASSIFICATION OF LEASES BY THE LESSOR

From the standpoint of the *lessor*, all leases are classified for accounting purposes as follows.

OBJECTIVE 7
Identify the classifications of leases for the lessor.

(a) Operating leases.

(b) Direct financing leases or sales-type leases

Similar to the lessee's decision, where the risks and benefits of ownership related to the leased property are transferred from the lessor to the lessee, the lessor accounts for the lease as either a direct financing or a sales-type lease. Where the risks and benefits are retained for the most part by the lessor, the lessor accounts for the agreement as an operating lease.[15]

Whether a lease is a direct financing or a sales-type lease depends on the situation. Some companies enter into lease agreements as a means of selling their products (usually a sales-type lease) while other companies are in business to facilitate the financing of a variety of assets in order to generate financing income (usually a direct financing lease).

CAPITALIZATION CRITERIA

If at the inception of the lease agreement the lease meets *one or more* of the following Group I criteria and *both* of the following Group II criteria, the lessor classifies and

---

[15] *CICA Handbook*, Section 3065, pars. 09 and .10.

accounts for the arrangement as a **direct financing lease** or a **sales-type lease**. Note that the Group I criteria are identical to the criteria on page 1054 that must be met for a lease to be classified as a capital lease by a lessee.

Group I

1. There is reasonable assurance that the lessee will obtain ownership of the leased property by the end of the lease term. If there is a bargain purchase option in the lease, it is assumed that the lessee will exercise it and obtain ownership.

2. The lease term is such that the lessee will receive substantially all of the economic benefits expected to be derived from the use of the leased property over its life span. This is usually assumed to occur if the lease term is 75% or more of the economic life of the leased property.

3. The lease allows the lessor to recover its investment in the leased property and to earn a return on the investment. This is assumed to occur if the present value of the minimum lease payments (excluding executory costs) is equal to substantially all (usually 90% or more) of the fair value of the leased property.

Group II

1. The credit risk associated with the lease is normal when compared to the risk of collection of similar receivables.

2. The amounts of any unreimbursable costs that are likely to be incurred by the lessor under the lease can be reasonably estimated.[16]

Why the Group II requirements? The answer is that the profession wants to make sure that the lessor has really transferred the risks and benefits of ownership. If collectibility of payments is not reasonably assured or if performance by the lessor is incomplete, then it is inappropriate to remove the leased asset from the lessor's books. In short, the Group II criteria are standard revenue recognition criteria applied to a lease situation.

Computer leasing companies at one time used to buy IBM equipment, lease it, and remove the leased assets from their balance sheets. In leasing the asset, the computer lessors stated that they would substitute new IBM equipment if obsolescence occurred. However, when IBM introduced a new computer line, IBM refused to sell it to the computer leasing companies. As a result, a number of computer leasing companies could not meet their contracts with their customers and were forced to take back the old equipment. What the computer leasing companies had taken off the books now had to be reinstated. Such a case demonstrates one reason for Group II requirements.

The difference for the lessor between a direct financing lease and a sales-type lease is the presence or absence of a manufacturer's or dealer's profit (or loss). A sales-type lease incorporates a manufacturer's or dealer's profit, but a direct financing lease does not. The profit (or loss) to the lessor is the difference between the fair value of the leased property at the inception of the lease, and the lessor's cost or carrying amount (book value). Normally, sales-type leases arise when manufacturers or dealers use leasing as a means of marketing their products. For example, a computer manufacturer will lease its computer equipment to businesses and institutions. Direct financing leases generally result from arrangements with lessors that are primarily engaged in financing operations, such as lease-finance companies, banks, insurance companies, and pension trusts. However, a lessor need not be a manufacturer or dealer to realize a profit (or loss) at the inception of the lease that requires application of sales-type lease accounting.

---

[16] *Ibid.*, par. .07.

All leases that do not qualify as direct financing or sales-type leases are classified and accounted for by the lessors as operating leases. The following flowchart shows the circumstances under which a lease is classified as operating, direct financing, or sales-type for the lessor.

ILLUSTRATION 21-2

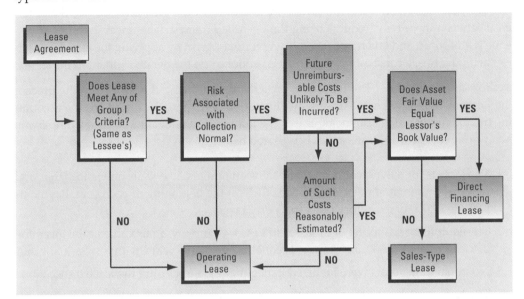

It is possible that a lessor that does not meet both Group II criteria will classify a lease as an *operating* lease while the lessee will classify the same lease as a *capital* lease. In such an event, both the lessor and lessee carry the asset on their books and both depreciate the capitalized asset.

DIRECT FINANCING METHOD

Leases that are in substance the financing of an asset purchase by a lessee require the lessor to remove the asset from its books and replace it with a receivable. The information necessary to record a direct financing lease is as follows.

OBJECTIVE 8
Describe the lessor's accounting for direct financing leases.

EXHIBIT 21-9

DIRECT FINANCING LEASE TERMS

1. **Gross Investment (Lease Payments Receivable).** The minimum lease payments plus any unguaranteed residual value accruing to the lessor at the end of the lease term.
2. **Unearned Finance (Interest) Revenue.** The difference between the gross investment (the receivable) and the cost, or carrying amount, if different, of the leased property. In most cases, cost or carrying amount is equal to fair value.
3. **Net Investment.** The gross investment (the receivable) less the unearned interest (finance) revenue included therein; the present value of the gross investment.

The computation of the gross investment (lease payments receivable) is often confusing because of uncertainty about how to account for residual values. Remember that the term "minimum lease payments" includes:

1. Rental payments, excluding any executory costs.
2. Bargain purchase option, if any.
3. Guaranteed residual value, if any.
4. Penalty for failure to renew, if any.

When "lease payments receivable" is defined as minimum lease payments plus unguaranteed residual value, it simply means that *residual value, whether guaranteed or unguaranteed, is included as part of the gross investment* if it is relevant to the lessor (that is, if the lessor expects to get the asset back).

The net investment is the calculated present value of the gross investment, the difference between these two accounts being the unearned interest. The unearned interest revenue is amortized and taken into income over the lease term by applying the effective interest method. Thus, a constant rate of return is produced on the net investment in the lease.

Illustration: Annuity Due. The following presentation, utilizing the data from the preceding Lessor Company/Lessee Company illustration on page 1058, illustrates the accounting treatment for a direct financing lease. The information relevant to Lessor Company in accounting for the lease transaction is repeated below.

1. The lease is for a five-year term that begins on January 1, 1998, is noncancellable, and requires equal rental payments of $25,981.62 at the beginning of each year. Payments include $2,000 of executory costs (property taxes).

2. The equipment has a cost of $100,000 to Lessor Company, a fair value at the inception of the lease of $100,000, an estimated economic life of five years, with no residual value.

3. No initial direct costs were incurred in negotiating and closing the lease transaction.

4. The lease contains no renewal options; the equipment reverts to Lessor Company at the termination of the lease.

5. Collectibility is reasonably assured and no additional costs, with the exception of the property taxes that are being reimbursed by the lessee, are to be incurred by Lessor Company.

6. Lessor Company set the annual rentals to ensure a rate of return of 10% (implicit rate) on its investment as shown previously on page 1065.

The lease meets the criteria for classification as a direct financing lease because (1) the lease term exceeds 75% of the equipment's estimated economic life; or (2) the present value of the minimum lease payments exceeds 90% of the equipment's fair value; and (3) the credit risk is normal relative to similar receivables; and (4) there are no further unreimbursable costs to be incurred by Lessor Company. It is not a sales-type lease because there is no dealer profit between the fair value ($100,000) of the equipment and the lessor's cost ($100,000).

The lease payments receivable (gross investment) is calculated as follows.

EXHIBIT 21-10

Lease payments receivable = Minimum lease payments plus unguaranteed residual value
= [($25,981.62 − $2,000) × 5] + $0
= $119,908.10

The unearned interest income is computed as the difference between the lease payments receivable and the lessor's cost or carrying amount of the leased asset, as shown below.

EXHIBIT 21-11

Unearned interest income = Lease payments receivable minus asset cost or carrying value
= $119,908.10 − $100,000
= $ 19,908.10

The net investment in this direct financing lease is the present value of the minimum lease payments of $100,000, or the gross investment of $119,908.10 minus the unearned interest revenue of $19,908.10.

The transfer of the asset, the resulting receivable, and the unearned interest income are recorded on January 1, 1998 as follows.

Lease Payments Receivable	119,908.10	
Equipment		100,000.00
Unearned Interest Revenue—Leases		19,908.10

The unearned interest income is classified on the balance sheet as a contra account to the receivable account. Generally, the lease payments receivable, although *recorded* at the gross investment amount, is *reported* in the balance sheet at the "net investment" amount (gross investment less unearned interest revenue) and entitled "net investment in capital leases." It is classified as current or noncurrent, depending on when the net investment is to be recovered.

The leased equipment with a cost of $100,000, representing Lessor Company's investment, is replaced with a net lease receivable. In a manner similar to the lessee's treatment of interest, Lessor Company applies the effective interest method and recognizes interest revenue as a function of the unrecovered net investment, as illustrated in Exhibit 21-12.

EXHIBIT 21-12   LESSOR COMPANY

LEASE AMORTIZATION SCHEDULE

(Annuity due basis)

Date	Annual Lease Payment	Interest (10%) on Net Investment	Reduction of Net Investment	Balance of Net Investment
	(a)	(b)	(c)	(d)
Jan. 1/98				$100,000.00
Jan. 1/98	$ 23,981.62	-0-	$ 23,981.62	76,018.38
Jan. 1/99	23,981.62	$ 7,601.84	16,379.78	59,638.60
Jan. 1/00	23,981.62	5,963.86	18,017.76	41,620.84
Jan. 1/01	23,981.62	4,162.08	19,819.54	21,801.30
Jan. 1/02	23,981.62	2,180.32*	21,801.30	-0-
	$119,908.10	$19,908.10	$100,000.00	

(a) Rental payment as required by lessor, excluding executory costs.
(b) 10% of the preceding balance of (d) except for January 1, 1998.
(c) (a) minus (b).
(d) Preceding balance minus (c).
*Rounded by 19 cents.

On January 1, 1998 the journal entry to record receipt of the first year's lease payment is as follows.

Cash	25,981.62	
Lease Payments Receivable		23,981.62
Property Tax Expense		2,000.00

On December 31, 1998 the interest revenue earned during the first year is recognized through the following entry.

Unearned Interest Revenue—Leases	7,601.84	
Interest Revenue—Leases		7,601.84

T accounts for the lease receivable and the unearned interest contra account after these entries appear as follows.

EXHIBIT 21-13

	Lease Payments Receivable		Unearned Interest Revenue		Net Investment in Lease
Jan. 1/98	$119,908.10			$19,908.10	$100,000.00
Jan. 1/98		23,981.62			(23,981.62)
	95,926.48			19,908.10	76,018.38
Dec. 31/98			7,601.84		7,601.84
	95,926.48			12,306.26	83,620.22

The net investment at December 31, 1998 is $83,620.22, which is the balance at January 1, 1998 of $76,018.38 plus interest receivable for 1998 of $7,601.84. The current portion is $23,981.62 (the net investment to be recovered in 1999, which is $16,379.78 plus the interest accrued to the balance sheet date of $7,601.84). The remaining $59,638.60 (lease payments receivable of $71,944.86 [$23,981.62 × 3] minus unearned interest Revenue of $12,306.26 [$5,963.86 + $4,162.08 + $2,180.32]) should be reported in the non-current asset section.

The asset section as it relates to lease transactions to December 31, 1998 appears as follows.

EXHIBIT 21-14

Current assets:

Net investment in capital leases $23,981.62

Noncurrent assets (investments):

Net investment in capital leases $59,638.60

The following entries record receipt of the second year's lease payment and recognition of the interest earned.

January 1, 1999

Cash   25,981.62
    Lease Payments Receivable   23,981.62
    Property Tax Expense   2,000.00

December 31, 1999

Unearned Interest Revenue—Leases   5,963.86
    Interest Revenue—Leases   5,963.86

Journal entries through 2002 follow the same pattern except that no entry is recorded in the last year, 2002, for earned interest. Because the receivable is fully collected by January 1, 2002, no investment balance is outstanding during 2002 to which Lessor Company could attribute any interest. Upon expiration of the lease, whether an ordinary annuity or an annuity due, the gross receivable and the unearned interest revenue are fully written off. Because the leased asset was removed from the accounts at the inception of the lease, *Lessor Company records no depreciation*. If the equipment is sold to Lessee Company for $5,000 on expiration of the lease, Lessor Company would recognize the disposition of the equipment as follows.

Cash	5,000	
Gain on Sale of Equipment Leased		5,000

Illustration: Ordinary Annuity. The classification of the lease obligation/net investment was presented in previous sections in an annuity due situation. As indicated on page 1058, the lessee's current liability is the payment on the lease obligation of $23,981.62 to be made on January 1 of the next year. Similarly, on page 1058, the lessor's current asset is the amount to be collected on the lease receivable of $23,981.62 on January 1 of the next year. In both of these annuity due instances, the balance sheet date is December 31 and the due date of the lease payment is one day later on January 1, so that the present value of the next payment ($23,981.62) is the same as the rental payment ($23,981.62).

What happens if the lease is an *ordinary annuity* rather than an *annuity due*? For example, assume that the rent is to be paid each December 31 rather than January 1. *CICA Handbook* Section 3065 does not indicate how to measure the current and noncurrent amounts; it requires that "any portion of lease obligations payable within a year out of current funds should be included in current liabilities."[17] The most common method of measuring the current liability portion in ordinary annuity leases is the *change in the present value* method.[18]

To illustrate the change in the present value method, assume an ordinary annuity situation with the same facts as the Lessee Company/Lessor Company case, excluding the $2,000 of executory costs. Because the rents are paid at the end of the period instead of at the beginning, the five rents are set at $26,379.73 to have an effective interest rate of 10%. The ordinary annuity amortization schedule appears as follows.

EXHIBIT 21-15   LESSEE COMPANY/LESSOR COMPANY

LEASE AMORTIZATION SCHEDULE

(Ordinary annuity basis)

Date	Annual Lease Payment	Interest (10%)	Reduction of Principal	Balance of Lease Obligation/ Net Investment
Jan. 1/98				$100,000.00
Dec. 31/98	$ 26,379.73	$10,000.00	$ 16,379.73	83,620.27
Dec. 31/99	26,379.73	8,362.03	18,017.70	65,602.57
Dec. 31/00	26,379.73	6,560.26	19,819.47	45,783.10
Dec. 31/01	26,379.73	4,578.31	21,801.42	23,981.68
Dec. 31/02	26,379.73	2,398.05	23,981.68	-0-
	$131,898.65	$31,898.65	$100,000.00	

The current portion of the lease obligation/net investment under the change in the present value method as of December 31, 1998 is $18,017.70 ($83,620.27 − $65,602.57); and as of December 31, 1999 it is $19,819.47 ($65,602.57 − $45,783.10). The portion of the lease obligation/net investment that is noncurrent, that is $65,602.57, is classified as such at December 31, 1998.

Thus, both the annuity due and the ordinary annuity situations report the reduction of principal for the next period as a current liability/current asset along with any interest accrued but unpaid to the balance sheet date. In the annuity due situation, interest is

---

[17] *CICA Handbook*, Section 3065, par. .23.

[18] For additional discussion on this approach and possible alternatives, see R.J. Swieringa, "When Current Is Noncurrent and Vice Versa!" *The Accounting Review* (January, 1984), pp. 123–130.

accrued during the year but is not paid until the next period. As a result, in the annuity due situation a current liability/current asset arises for both the principal reduction and the interest that was incurred/earned to the balance sheet date.

In the ordinary annuity example, the interest accrued to December 31 is paid up to the balance sheet date; consequently, only the subsequent year's principal reduction is shown as a current liability/current asset. *Where the lease payment date is other than December 31, any interest accrued to the balance sheet date must also be included in current liabilities.*

SALES-TYPE METHOD ILLUSTRATED

OBJECTIVE 9
Describe the lessor's accounting for sales-type leases.

Accounting for a sales-type lease is very similar to accounting for a direct financing lease. The major difference is that the lessor in the sales-type lease usually has manufactured or otherwise acquired the leased asset for resale and is looking, through the lease agreement, to recover the selling price of the asset through the lease payments. The cost or carrying value on the lessor's books is usually less than the asset's fair value to the customer. The lessor, therefore, must record a sale and the cost of goods sold for the leased asset.

The same data from the Lessor Company/Lessee Company example beginning on page 1058 is used to illustrate the accounting for a sales-type lease. There is one exception: Instead of the leased asset having a cost of $100,000 to Lessor Company, assume that Lessor Company manufactured the asset and that it is in Lessor's inventory at a cost of $85,000. Lessor's regular selling price for this asset, its fair value, is $100,000, and it is this amount that the company recovers through the lease payments.

The following terms apply for a sales-type lease.

EXHIBIT 21-16

SALES-TYPE LEASE TERMS

1. **Gross Investment** (also "lease payments receivable"). The minimum lease payments plus any unguaranteed residual value.

2. **Unearned interest revenue.** The gross investment less the fair market value of the asset.

3. Sales price of the asset. The present value of the minimum lease payments. Note: This excludes any unguaranteed residual value.

4. **Cost of goods sold.** The cost of the asset to the lessor, less the present value of any unguaranteed residual value, if applicable.

The lessor's accounting entries to record the lease transactions are the same as those illustrated earlier for a direct financing lease with the exception of the entry at the inception of the lease. Sales and cost of goods sold must be recorded in a sales-type lease. The entries are as follows.

	January 1, 1998		
Lease Payments Receivable		119,908.10	
Unearned Interest Revenue—Leases			19,908.10
Sales			100,000.00
Cost of Goods Sold		85,000.00	
Inventory			85,000.00
Cash		25,981.62	
Lease Payments Receivable			23,981.62
Property Tax Expense			2,000.00
	December 31, 1998		
Unearned Interest Revenue—Leases		7,601.84	
Interest Revenue—Leases			7,601.84

Compare the January 1, 1998 entries for the two types of lease. The direct financing lease removes the leased asset, the net investment the lessor wants to recover, from the lessor's books. The sales-type lease recognizes that what is being recovered is the selling price of the asset and therefore records a sale. The cost of the inventory is transferred to cost of goods sold. The lessor recognizes a gross profit from the sale reported *at the inception of the lease*, and interest or finance income *over the period of the lease* until the lease payments receivable is no longer outstanding. A lessor with a direct financing lease reports only financing income.

OPERATING LEASE

OBJECTIVE 10
Describe the lessor's accounting for operating leases.

Under an operating lease, each rental receipt of the lessor is recorded as rental revenue. The leased asset is depreciated by the lessor in the normal manner, with the depreciation expense of the period matched against the rental revenue. The amount of revenue recognized in each accounting period is a level amount (straight-line basis) regardless of the lease provisions, unless another systematic and rational basis is more representative of the pattern in which benefits are derived from the leased asset. In addition to the depreciation charge, maintenance costs and the costs of any other services rendered under the provisions of the lease that pertain to the current accounting period are charged to expense.

Illustration. To illustrate the accounting for an operating lease, assume that the Lessor Company/Lessee Company example above does not meet the capitalization criteria and is therefore classified as an operating lease. The entry to record the cash rental payment, assuming the $2,000 is for property tax expense, is as follows.

Cash	25,981.62	
Rental Revenue		25,981.62

Depreciation is recorded by the lessor as follows (assuming the straight-line method, a cost basis of $100,000, and a five-year life).

Depreciation Expense—Leased Buildings	20,000.00	
Accumulated Depreciation—Leased Buildings		20,000.00

If property taxes, insurance, maintenance, and other operating costs during the year are the obligation of the lessor, they are recorded as expenses chargeable against the gross rental revenues.

If the lessor owns plant assets that it uses in addition to those leased to others, the leased buildings are separately classified in an account such as Property Leased to Others or Investment in Leased Property. If significant in amount or in terms of activity, the rental revenues and accompanying expenses are separated in the income statement from sales revenue and cost of goods sold.

REPORTING AND DISCLOSURE REQUIREMENTS FOR THE LESSOR

OBJECTIVE 11
Identify the lessor's disclosure requirements.

The *Handbook* requires lessors to disclose on the balance sheet their net investment in direct financing and sales-type leases, appropriately segregated between current and long-term categories. In addition, the amount of finance income from these types of lease and how the investment in leases has been calculated for purposes of income recognition must be disclosed.[19]

---

[19] *CICA Handbook,* Section 3065, par. .54.

The list of desirable disclosures is longer, with the AcSB suggesting that the total future minimum lease payments receivable, unguaranteed residual values, unearned finance income, executory costs included in minimum lease payments, contingent rentals taken into income, lease terms, and the amounts of minimum lease payments receivable for each of the next five years would be useful information.[20]

The objective of the required disclosures for operating leases is to enable users to assess the extent of resources committed to this activity and the resulting cash flows generated. For operating leases, lessors must report the cost and related accumulated depreciation of property held for leasing purposes and the amount of rental income from such leases. Further disclosure concerning minimum future rentals and contingent rentals included in income is at the discretion of management.[21]

Disclosure Examples. Excerpts from the financial statements of BC Telecom Inc. for its year ended December 31, 1995 are reproduced in Exhibit 21-17 to provide a good example of the disclosures provided by a lessor for direct financing or sales-type leases.

Finning Ltd., a Canadian-based international company that sells, finances, and provides customer service for a full line of heavy equipment, discloses the information shown in Exhibit 21-18 related to its operating lease activities as the lessor.

EXHIBIT 21-17   BC TELECOM INC.

December 31 (Millions)	1995	1994
On the balance sheet:		
Current Assets		
Accounts receivable (NOTE 6)	455.7	469.3
Other Assets		
Leases receivable	27.1	25.8
On the income statement:		
Other income (NOTE 3)	52.9	11.9

Notes to Consolidated Financial Statements

I. SUMMARY OF SIGNIFICANT ACCOUNTING POLICIES

(h) Leases (in part)

Where the Company is the lessor, the majority of capital leases are through its subsidiary Telecom Leasing Canada (TLC) Limited, which acts as a financing intermediary. The long-term leases receivable represent the present value of future lease payments receivable due beyond one year. Finance income derived from these financing leases is recorded so as to produce a constant rate of return over the terms of the leases.

3. OTHER INCOME (in part)

Lease finance income	$	8.6	$	7.9

6. ACCOUNTS RECEIVABLE (in part)

Current portion of leases receivable	34.4	33.8

---

[20] *CICA Handbook*, Section 3065, par. .54.
[21] *Ibid.*, pars. .57 to .59.

EXHIBIT 21-18   FINNING LTD.

AS AT DECEMBER 31, 1995

Excerpts from the Consolidated Balance Sheets	1995	1994
	(dollars in thousands)	
Equipment leased to customers (Note 4)..............................	**213,018**	171,888

Notes to the Financial Statements

1. Summary of Significant Accounting Policies

Revenue Recognition   (in part)

Revenue from sales of products and services is recognized at the time of shipment of products to, and performance of services for, customers. Equipment lease and rental revenue is recognized over the term of the lease or rental.

4. Equipment Leased to Customers

	1995	1994
	(dollars in thousands)	
Cost...	**$307,066**	$245,435
Less accumulated depreciation	**(94,048)**	(73,547)
	$213,018	$171,888

Under the terms of the lease agreements in effect at December 31, 1995, $71,728,000 of the above costs will be recovered in 1996 (1995 - $36,477,000).

Depreciation of equipment leased to customers for the year ended December 31, 1995 was $55,736,000 (1994 - $45,510,000).

SPECIAL ACCOUNTING PROBLEMS

Lease arrangements that provide unique accounting problems include:

1. Residual values.
2. Bargain purchase options.
3. Initial direct costs of the lessor.

RESIDUAL VALUES

To this point, there has been little discussion of residual values so that the basic accounting issues related to lessee and lessor accounting could be developed. Accounting for residual values is complex, but follows a reasoned approach.

The **residual value** is the estimated fair value of the leased asset at the end of the lease term. Frequently, a significant residual value exists, especially when the economic life of the leased asset exceeds the lease term. If title does not pass automatically to the lessee or a bargain purchase option (Criterion 1) does not exist, the lessee returns physical custody of the asset to the lessor at the end of the lease term.[22]

OBJECTIVE 12
Describe the effect of residual values, guaranteed and unguaranteed, on lease accounting.

---

[22] When the lease term and the economic life are not the same, the residual value and the salvage value of the asset will probably differ. Salvage value refers to the estimated value at the end of the asset's economic life.

The residual value may be unguaranteed or guaranteed by the lessee. If the lessee, for example, agrees to make up any deficiency below a stated amount at the end of the lease term, that stated amount is the **guaranteed residual value**.

The guaranteed residual value is employed in lease arrangements for two reasons. One is a business reason: It protects the lessor against any loss in estimated residual value, thereby ensuring the lessor of the desired rate of return on investment. The second, discussed more fully later in the chapter, relates to how the lease is classified by the lessor and lessee.

Effect on Lease Payments. A guaranteed residual value has more assurance of realization than does an unguaranteed residual value. As a result, the lessor may reduce the implicit rate of return, and therefore the rental rate, because the certainty of recovery is increased. It makes no difference from an accounting point of view whether the residual value is guaranteed or unguaranteed as the net investment recorded by the lessor, once the rate is set, will be the same.

Assume the same data as in the continuing Lessee Company/Lessor Company illustrations except that a residual value of $5,000 is estimated at the end of the five-year lease term. The lessor, whether a sales-type or direct financing lease, wants to recover a net investment of $100,000 and earn an ROI of 10%.[23] Whether the residual value is guaranteed or unguaranteed, Lessor Company computes the amount of the lease payments as follows.

EXHIBIT 21-19

LESSOR'S COMPUTATION OF LEASE PAYMENTS (10% ROI)
ANNUITY DUE BASIS
GUARANTEED OR UNGUARANTEED RESIDUAL VALUE

Fair value of leased asset	$100,000.00
To be recovered through residual value, end of year 5	
Present value of residual value : $5,000 × 0.62092 (Table A-2)	(3,104.60)
Amount to be recovered by lessor through lease payments	$ 96,895.40
Five periodic lease payments ($96,895.40 ÷ 4.16986, Table A-5)	**$ 23,237.09**

Contrast the amount of this lease payment with the lease payment of $23,981.62 computed on page 1070 when no residual value existed. The payments are less because a portion of the lessor's net investment of $100,000 is recovered through the residual value. Because the residual value is not received for five years, its present value is used in this calculation.

Lessee Accounting for Residual Values. Whether the estimated residual value is guaranteed or unguaranteed is of economic *and* accounting consequence to the lessee. The accounting difference is the fact that the term *minimum lease payments*, the basis for capitalization, includes the guaranteed residual value but excludes the unguaranteed residual value. Since the lessee assumes no responsibility for the condition of the leased asset upon termination of the lease when the residual value is unguaranteed, no liability is recorded.

Guaranteed Residual Value. A guaranteed residual value affects the lessee's computation of the minimum lease payments and, therefore, the amounts capitalized as a leased asset and a

---

[23] Technically the rate of return demanded by the lessor would be different, depending on whether the residual value was guaranteed or unguaranteed. We are ignoring this difference in subsequent sections to simplify the illustrations.

lease obligation. In effect, it is an additional lease payment that will be paid in property or cash, or both, at the end of the lease term. Using the rental payments as computed by the lessor above, the minimum lease payments (excluding executory costs) are $121,185.45 ([$23,237.09 × 5] + $5,000). The capitalized present value of the minimum lease payments is computed below.

EXHIBIT 21-20

LESSEE'S CAPITALIZED AMOUNT (10% RATE)
ANNUITY DUE BASIS—GUARANTEED RESIDUAL VALUE

Present value of five annual rental payments of $23,237.09	
$23,237.09 × 4.16986 (Table A-5)	$ 96,895.40
Present value of guaranteed residual value of $5,000 due five years after date of	
inception: ($5,000 × 0.62092, Table A-2)	3,104.60
Lessee's capitalized amount	**$100,000.00**

Lessee Company's schedule of interest expense and amortization of the $100,000 lease obligation results in a $5,000 guaranteed residual value final payment at the end of five years, as shown below.

EXHIBIT 21-21   LESSEE COMPANY

LEASE AMORTIZATION SCHEDULE
ANNUITY DUE BASIS—GUARANTEED RESIDUAL VALUE

Date	Lease Payment	Interest (10%) on Unpaid Obligation	Reduction of Lease Obligation	Lease Obligation
	(a)	(b)	(c)	(d)
Jan. 1/98				$100,000.00
Jan. 1/98	$ 23,237.09	$ -0-	$ 23,237.09	76,762.91
Jan. 1/99	23,237.09	7,676.29	15,560.80	61,202.11
Jan. 1/00	23,237.09	6,120.21	17,116.88	44,085.23
Jan. 1/01	23,237.09	4,408.52	18,828.57	25,256.66
Jan. 1/02	23,237.09	2,525.67	20,711.42	4,545.24
Dec. 31/02	5,000.00*	454.76**	4,545.24	-0-
	$121,185.45	$21,185.45	$100,000.00	

(a) Lease payment as required by lease, excluding executory costs.
(b) Preceding balance of (d) × 10%, except January 1, 1998.
*Represents the guaranteed residual value.

(c) (a) minus (b).
(d) Preceding balance minus (c).
**Rounded by 24 cents.

The journal entries (page 1080) to record the leased asset and obligation, depreciation, interest, property tax, and lease payments are made on the basis that the residual value is guaranteed. The format of these entries is the same as illustrated earlier, but the amounts are different because of the capitalized residual value. The leased asset is recorded at $100,000 and is depreciated over five years. Assuming that the straight-line method is used, the depreciation expense each year is $19,000 ([$100,000 − $5,000] × 1/5).

At the end of the lease term, before the lessee transfers the asset to the lessor, the leased asset and obligation accounts have the following balances.

EXHIBIT 21-22

Leased equipment under capital leases	$100,000	Obligations under capital leases	$5,000
Less accumulated depreciation—capital leases	95,000		
	$ 5,000		

If the fair value of the leased property is less than $5,000 at the end of the lease, Lessee Company will record a loss. Assume that Lessee Company depreciated the leased asset down to its residual value of $5,000 but that the fair market value of the asset at December 31, 2002 is $3,000. In this case, Lessee Company records the following journal entry, assuming cash is paid to make up the residual value deficiency, and reports a loss of $2,000.

Loss on Capital Lease	2,000.00	
Interest Expense	454.76	
Obligations Under Capital Lease	4,545.24	
Accumulated Depreciation—Capital Lease	95,000.00	
Leased Equipment Under Capital Lease		100,000.00
Cash		2,000.00

If the fair value exceeds $5,000, a gain may or may not be recognized. Gains on guaranteed residual values may be apportioned to the lessor and lessee in whatever ratio the parties initially agreed.

If the lessee *had* depreciated the total $100,000 cost of the asset, a misstatement would occur; that is, the carrying amount of the asset at the end of the lease term would be zero, but the obligation under the capital lease would be stated as $5,000. If the asset is worth $5,000, the lessee would report a gain of $5,000 at the time the asset is transferred to the lessor. As a result, depreciation would be overstated and net income understated in 1998 through 2001, but in the last year (2002) net income would be overstated.

Unguaranteed Residual Value. An unguaranteed residual value from the lessee's viewpoint is the same as no residual value in terms of its effect on the lessee's computation of the minimum lease payments and the capitalization of the leased asset and the lease obligation. Assume the same facts as those above except that the $5,000 residual value is *unguaranteed.* The annual lease payment is the same ($23,237.09) because whether the residual value is guaranteed or unguaranteed, Lessor Company's amount to be recovered though lease rentals is the same: $96,895.40. Lessee Company's minimum lease payments are $116,185.45 ($23,237.09 × 5), and the company capitalizes the following amount.

EXHIBIT 21-23

LESSEE'S CAPITALIZED AMOUNT (10% RATE)
ANNUITY DUE BASIS—UNGUARANTEED RESIDUAL VALUE

Present value of five annual lease payments of $23,237.09	
$23,237.09 × 4.16986 (Table A-5)	$96,895.40
Present value of unguaranteed residual value of $5,000 not capitalized by lessee	-0-
Lessee's capitalized amount	**$96,895.40**

Lessee Company's schedule of interest expense and amortization of the lease obligation of $96,895.40, assuming an unguaranteed residual value of $5,000 at the end of five years, is shown on page 1079.

EXHIBIT 21-24   LESSEE COMPANY

LEASE AMORTIZATION SCHEDULE (10%)
ANNUITY DUE BASIS—UNGUARANTEED RESIDUAL VALUE

Date	Annual Lease Payments	Interest (10%) on Unpaid Obligation	Reduction of Lease Obligation	Lease Obligation
	(a)	(b)	(c)	(d)
Jan. 1/98				$96,895.40
Jan. 1/98	$ 23,237.09	-0-	$23,237.09	73,658.31
Jan. 1/99	23,237.09	$ 7,365.83	15,871.26	57,787.05
Jan. 1/00	23,237.09	5,778.71	17,458.38	40,328.67
Jan. 1/01	23,237.09	4,032.87	19,204.22	21,124.45
Jan. 1/02	23,237.09	2,112.64*	21,124.45	-0-
	$116,185.45	$19,290.05	$96,895.40	

(a) Annual lease payment as required by lease, excluding executory costs.
(b) Preceding balance of (d) × 10% except January 1, 1998
(c) (a) minus (b).
(d) Preceding balance minus (c).
*Rounded by 19 cents.

The journal entries (page 1080) to record the leased asset and obligation, depreciation, interest, property tax, and payments on the lease obligation are made on the basis that the residual value is unguaranteed. The format of these entries is the same as illustrated earlier. Note that the leased asset is recorded at $96,895.40 and is depreciated over five years. Assuming that the straight-line method is used, the depreciation expense each year is $19,379.08 ($96,895.40 × 1/5). At the end of the lease term, before the lessee transfers the asset to the lessor, the following balances in the accounts result.

EXHIBIT 21-25

Leased equipment under capital leases	$96,895	Obligations under capital lease	$-0-
Less accumulated depreciation—capital leases	96,895		
	$ -0-		

Assuming a residual value of $3,000, no entry is required at the end of the lease term except to remove the asset from the books, and no loss is reported.

If the lessee *had* depreciated the asset down to its estimated — but unguaranteed — residual value, a misstatement would occur; that is, the carrying amount of the leased asset would be $5,000 at the end of the lease, but the obligation under the capital lease would be zero before the transfer of the asset. Thus, the lessee would end up reporting a loss of $5,000 when it transferred the asset to the lessor. Depreciation would be understated and net income overstated in 1998 through 2001, but in the last year (2002) net income would be understated because of the loss recorded.

The entries by Lessee Company for both a guaranteed and an unguaranteed residual value follow in comparative form.

EXHIBIT 21-26	LESSEE COMPANY

ENTRIES FOR GUARANTEED AND UNGUARANTEED RESIDUAL VALUES

Guaranteed Residual Value			Unguaranteed Residual Value		
Capitalization of Lease Jan. 1/98					
Leased Equipment Under			Leased Equipment Under		
Capital Leases	100,000.00		Capital Leases	96,895.40	
Obligations Under Capital Leases		100,000.00	Obligations Under Capital Leases		96,895.40
First Payment Jan. 1/98					
Property Tax Expense	2,000.00		Property Tax Expense	2,000.00	
Obligations Under Capital Leases	23,237.09		Obligations Under Capital Leases	23,237.09	
Cash		25,237.09	Cash		25,237.09
Adjusting Entry for Accrued Interest Dec. 31/98					
Interest Expense	7,676.29		Interest Expense	7,365.83	
Interest Payable		7,676.29	Interest Payable		7,365.83
Entry to Record Depreciation Dec. 31/98					
Depreciation Expense—Capital Leases	19,000.00		Depreciation Expense—Capital Leases	19,379.08	
Accumulated Depreciation—			Accumulated Depreciation—		
Capital Leases		19,000.00	Capital Leases		19,379.08
([$100,000 − $5,000] ÷ 5 years)			($96,895.40 ÷ 5 years)		
Second Payment Jan. 1/99					
Property Tax Expense	2,000.00		Property Tax Expense	2,000.00	
Obligations Under Capital Leases	15,560.80		Obligations Under Capital Leases	15,871.26	
Interest Payable	7,676.29		Interest Payable	7,365.83	
Cash		25,237.09	Cash		25,237.09

Lessor Accounting for Residual Values: Direct Financing Lease. As indicated earlier, the lessor works on the assumption that the residual value will be realized at the end of the lease term whether guaranteed or unguaranteed. The lease payments required by the lessor to earn a certain return on investment are the same ($23,237.09) whether the residual value is guaranteed or not.

Using the Lessee Company/Lessor Company data and assuming a residual value (either guaranteed or unguaranteed) of $5,000 and the classification of the lease as a direct financing lease, the following amounts are computed.

EXHIBIT 21-27	
Gross investment	= ($23,237.09 × 5) + $5,000 = $121,185.45
Net investment:	= $23,237.09 × 4.16986 (Table A-5)
PV of lease payments + PV of residual value, or	+ $5,000 × .62092 (Table A-2) = $100,000
amount to be recovered	
Unearned interest revenue	= $121,185.45 − $100,000.00 = $21,185.45

The amortization schedule with a guaranteed or unguaranteed residual value is identical as shown at the top of the next page.

Lessor Company's entries during the first year for this direct financing lease are shown in Exhibit 21-29. These entries should be compared to those of Lessee Company above.

Lessor Accounting for Residual Values: Sales-Type Lease. As already indicated, the primary difference between a direct financing and a sales-type lease is the existence of a manufacturer's or dealer's profit (or loss). The gross investment and the unearned interest revenue account are the same for both types of leases whether a guaranteed or an unguaranteed residual value is involved.

EXHIBIT 12-28   LESSOR COMPANY

LEASE AMORTIZATION SCHEDULE

ANNUITY DUE BASIS—GUARANTEED OR UNGUARANTEED RESIDUAL VALUE

Date	Lease Payment	Interest (10%) on Net Investment	Net Investment Recovery	Net Investment
	(a)	(b)	(c)	(d)
Jan. 1/98				$100,000.00
Jan. 1/98	$ 23,237.09	-0-	$ 23,237.09	76,762.91
Jan. 1/99	23,237.09	$ 7,676.29	15,560.80	61,202.11
Jan. 1/00	23,237.09	6,120.21	17,116.88	44,085.23
Jan. 1/01	23,237.09	4,408.52	18,828.57	25,256.66
Jan. 1/02	23,237.09	2,525.67	20,711.42	4,545.24
Dec. 31/02	5,000.00*	454.76**	4,545.24	-0-
	$121,185.45	$21,185.45	$100,000.00	

(a) Lease payment as required by lease, excluding executory costs.
(b) Preceding balance of (d) × 10%, except January 1, 1998.
(c) (a) minus (b).
(d) Preceding balance minus (c).
*Represents the residual value.
**Rounded by 24 cents.

EXHIBIT 21-29   LESSOR COMPANY

GUARANTEED OR UNGUARANTEED RESIDUAL VALUE—DIRECT FINANCING LEASE

Inception of Lease Jan. 1/98

Lease Payments Receivable	121,185.45	
Equipment		100,000.00
Unearned Interest Revenue—Leases		21,185.45

First Payment Received Jan. 1/98

Cash	25,237.09	
Lease Payments Receivable		23,237.09
Property Tax Expense/Property Tax Payable		2,000.00

Adjusting Entry for Accrued Interest Dec. 31/98

Unearned Interest Revenue—Leases	7,676.29	
Interest Revenue—Leases		7,676.29

When recording sales revenue and cost of goods sold, however, there is a difference in accounting for guaranteed and unguaranteed residual values. The guaranteed residual value can be considered part of sales revenue because the lessor knows that the entire amount will be realized. There is uncertainty, however, that any unguaranteed residual portion of the asset has been "sold" (i.e., will be realized); therefore, sales and cost of goods sold are recognized only for the portion of the asset for which realization is assured. *The gross profit amount on the sale of the asset is the same*, however, whether a guaranteed or unguaranteed residual value is involved as the present value of any unguaranteed residual is withheld from the calculation of both sales and cost of goods sold amounts.

To illustrate a sales-type lease with a guaranteed residual value and a sales-type lease with an unguaranteed residual value, assume the same facts as in the preceding direct financing lease situation (page 1080). The estimated residual value is $5,000 (the present value of which is $3,104.60), the annual lease payments are $23,237.09 (the present value of which is $96,895.40), and the leased equipment has an $85,000 cost to the dealer, Lessor Company. At the end of the lease term assume that the fair value of the leased asset is $3,000. The amounts relevant to a sales-type lease are computed as shown below.

EXHIBIT 21-30

SALES-TYPE LEASE

	Guaranteed Residual Value	Unguaranteed Residual Value
Gross Investment	$121,185.45 ([$23,237.09 × 5] + 5,000)	Same
Unearned Interest revenue	$21,185.45 ($121,185.45 − [$96,895.40 + $3,104.60])	Same
Sales	$100,000.00 ($96,895.40 + $3,104.60)	$96,895.40
Cost of goods sold	$85,000.00	$81,895.40 ($85,000.00 − $3,104.60)
Gross profit	$15,000.00 ($100,000 − $85,000)	$15,000.00 ($96,895.40 − $81,895.40)

The profit recorded by Lessor Company at the point of sale is the same, $15,000, whether the residual value is guaranteed or unguaranteed, but the sales revenue and cost of goods sold amounts are different.

The 1998 entries and the entry to record the return of the asset at the end of the lease term are as follows.

EXHIBIT 21-31 LESSOR COMPANY

ENTRIES FOR GUARANTEED AND UNGUARANTEED RESIDUAL VALUES

Guaranteed Residual Value			Unguaranteed Residual Value		
To record sales-type lease at inception (January 1, 1998):					
Cost of Goods Sold	85,000.00		Cost of Goods Sold	81,895.40	
Lease Payments			Lease Payments		
Receivable	121,185.45		Receivable	121,185.45	
Sales Revenue		100,000.00	Sales Revenue		96,895.40
Unearned Interest Revenue		21,185.45	Unearned Interest Revenue		21,185.45
Inventory		85,000.00	Inventory		85,000.00
To record receipt of the first lease payment (January 1, 1998):					
Cash	25,237.09		Cash	25,237.09	
Lease Payments Receivable		23,237.09	Lease Payments Receivable		23,237.09
Property Tax Expense/Property Tax Payable		2,000.00	Property Tax Expense/Property Tax Payable		2,000.00
To recognize interest revenue earned during the first year (December 31, 1998):					
Unearned Interest			Unearned Interest		
Revenue	7,676.29		Revenue	7,676.29	
Interest Revenue		7,676.29	Interest Revenue		7,676.29
To record return of leased asset at end of the lease term (December 31, 2002):					
Inventory	3,000.00		Inventory	3,000.00	
Cash	2,000.00		Loss on Capital Lease	2,000.00	
Lease Payments Receivable		5,000.00	Lease Payments Receivable		5,000.00

The estimated unguaranteed residual value in sales-type and direct financing leases must be reviewed periodically. If the estimate of the unguaranteed residual value declines, the accounting for the transaction must be revised using the changed estimate. The decline represents a reduction in the lessor's net investment and is recognized as a loss in the period in which the residual estimate is reduced. Upward adjustments in estimated residual values are not recognized.

BARGAIN PURCHASE OPTIONS

OBJECTIVE 13
Describe the effect of bargain purchase options on lease accounting.

A bargain purchase option allows the lessee to purchase the leased property for a future price that is substantially lower than the property's expected future fair value. The price is so favourable at the lease's inception that the exercise of the option at the end of the lease term is reasonably assured. If a bargain purchase option exists, the lessee's accounting assumes it will be exercised and the title to the leased property will be transferred to the lessee. Therefore, ***the lessee must include the present value of the option price in the calculation of the minimum lease payments in determining the amount to capitalize.***

For example, assume that Lessee Company in the illustration on p1058 has an option to buy the leased equipment for $5,000 at the end of the five-year lease term when the fair value is expected to be $18,000. The significant difference between the option price and the estimated fair value indicates this is a bargain purchase option, and exercising the option is reasonably assured. The following computations are affected by a bargain purchase option in the same way as they were by a guaranteed residual value. (1) The amount of the five lease payments necessary for the lessor to earn a 10% return on net investment. (2) The amount of the minimum lease payments. (3) The amount capitalized as leased assets and lease obligation. (4) The amortization of the lease obligation. Therefore, the computations and amortization schedule necessary for a $5,000 *bargain purchase option* are identical to those shown previously for the lessee and lessor for a $5,000 *guaranteed residual value.*

The only difference between the accounting treatment given a bargain purchase option and a guaranteed residual value of identical amounts and circumstances is in the computation of the annual depreciation. In the case of a guaranteed residual value, the lessee depreciates the asset over the life of the lease because the asset will revert to the lessor. In the case of a bargain purchase option, the lessee uses the economic life of the asset and its estimated salvage value because it is assumed that the lessee will acquire title to the asset by exercising the option.

NOTE

INITIAL DIRECT COSTS OF THE LESSOR

Initial direct costs are defined in paragraph .03(l) of Section 3065 of the *CICA Handbook* as:

OBJECTIVE 14
Describe the lessor's accounting treatment for initial direct costs.

> those costs incurred by the lessor that are directly associated with negotiating and executing a specific leasing transaction. Such costs include commissions, legal fees and costs of preparing and processing documents for new leases. Such costs do not include supervisory and administrative costs, promotion and lease design costs intended for recurring use, costs incurred in collection activities and provisions for uncollectible rentals.

The costs directly related to an employee's time spent on a specific lease transaction may also be considered initial direct costs.

In a *direct financing lease*, initial direct costs should be expensed as incurred and the lessor should offset this expense by taking into income an equal amount of the unearned interest income. At the inception of the lease, therefore, the net effect on income is zero; however, the amount of the net investment in the lease (the gross investment less the unearned interest income) is increased.

For example, if the Lease Payments Receivable (gross investment in the lease) account is $600,000 with unearned interest income at the inception of the lease of $200,000, the net investment is $400,000. If initial direct costs of $35,000 are incurred and expensed and $35,000 of the unearned interest is recognized as earned, the net investment is increased to $435,000 ($600,000 − [$200,000 − $35,000]).

Because the finance income earned on the net investment should be recognized at a constant rate of return each period, the lessor must recalculate the effective rate[24] (it will be lower) for purposes of amortizing the net investment. In this way, the initial costs are recognized over the term of the lease in the form of reduced interest income each period.

In a *sales-type lease* transaction, the lessor expenses the initial direct costs in the year of incurrence; that is, they are expensed in the period in which the profit on the sale is recognized.

For *operating leases*, the lessor should defer initial direct costs and allocate them over the lease term in proportion to the recognition of rental income.

SALE-LEASEBACK TRANSACTIONS

OBJECTIVE 15
Describe the lessee's accounting for sale-lease-back transactions.

Sale-leaseback describes a transaction in which the owner of property (the seller-lessee) sells the property to another party (the purchaser-lessor) and simultaneously leases it back from the new owner. The use of the property is generally continued without interruption.

For example, a company buys land, constructs a building to its specifications, sells the property to an investor, and then immediately leases it back. The advantage of a sale and leaseback from the seller's viewpoint usually involves financing considerations. If the purchase of equipment has already been financed, a sale-leaseback can allow the seller to refinance at lower rates if rates have decreased, or a sale-leaseback can provide additional working capital when liquidity is tight.

To the extent the seller-lessee's use of the asset sold continues after the sale, *the sale-leaseback is really a change in the form of financing only* and, therefore, no gain or loss should be recognized on the transaction. In substance, the seller-lessee is simply borrowing funds. On the other hand, if the seller-lessee gives up the right to the use of the asset sold, the transaction is in substance a sale, and gain or loss recognition is appropriate. Trying to ascertain when the lessee has given up the use of the asset is difficult, however, and complex rules have been formulated to identify this situation.[25] The profession's basic position in this area is that the lease should be accounted for as a capital, direct financing, or operating lease, as appropriate, by the seller-lessee and by the purchaser-lessor.[26]

---

[24] To calculate the effective or implied rate of interest in a lease when it isn't given, students are referred to page A-12, "Illustration: Computation of the Interest Rate" in Appendix: Accounting and the Time Value of Money. In short, "*i*" is the internal rate of return. It is a matter of solving for "*i*" when the present value amount, the annuity amount, and "*n*" are all known. The interest rate is the rate that equates the present value amount (in this case the net investment) with the annuity payments. It may have to be computed using a "trial and error" method.

[25] Guidance is provided in *EIC–25* (CICA, April 22, 1991) for situations where the leaseback relates to only a portion of the property sold by the seller-lessee. A discussion of the issues related to these transactions and others such as real estate sale-leaseback transactions are beyond the scope of this textbook.

[26] *CICA Handbook*, Section 3065, par. .66.

LESSEE ACCOUNTING

If the lease meets one of the three criteria for treatment as a capital lease, *the seller-lessee accounts for the lease as a capital lease.* Any profit or loss experienced by the seller-lessee from the sale of the assets that are leased back under a capital lease should be deferred and amortized over the lease term (or the economic life if Criterion 1 is satisfied) in proportion to the amortization of the leased assets. If the leased asset is land only, the amortization is on a straight-line basis over the lease term.[27] If Lessee, Inc. sells equipment having a book value of $580,000 and a fair value of $623,110 to Lessor, Inc. for $623,110 and leases the equipment back for $50,000 per year for 20 years, the profit of $43,110 is amortized over the 20-year period at the same rate that the $623,110 is depreciated.

If not one of the capital lease criteria is satisfied, *the seller-lessee accounts for the transaction as a sale and the lease as an operating lease.* Under an operating lease, such profit or loss is deferred and amortized in proportion to the rental payments over the period of time the assets are expected to be used by the lessee.[28]

The profession requires, however, that when there is a legitimate loss on the sale of the asset, that is, when the fair value of the asset *is less than* the book value (carrying amount), the loss must be recognized immediately. For example, if Lessee, Inc. sells equipment having a book value of $650,000 and a fair value of $623,110, the difference of $26,890 is charged directly to a loss account.[29]

LESSOR ACCOUNTING

If the lease meets one of the criteria in Group I and both the criteria in Group II (see page 1066), the purchaser-lessor records the transaction as a purchase and a direct financing lease. If the lease does not meet the criteria, the purchaser-lessor records the transaction as a purchase and an operating lease. The criteria for a sales-type lease would not be met in a sale-leaseback transaction.

ILLUSTRATION

To illustrate the accounting treatment accorded a sale-leaseback transaction, assume that Lessee Corp. on January 1, 1998 sells aircraft, a capital asset having a carrying amount on its books of $75,500,000, to Lessor Corp. for $80,000,000, and immediately leases the aircraft back under the following conditions.

1. The lease is for a term of 15 years, noncancellable, and requires equal rental payments of $10,487,443 at the beginning of each year.

2. The aircraft has a fair value of $80,000,000 on January 1, 1998 and an estimated economic life of 15 years.

3. Lessee Corp. pays all executory costs.

4. Lessee Corp. depreciates similar aircraft that it owns on a straight-line basis over 15 years.

5. The annual payments assure the lessor a 12% return, the same as Lessee's incremental borrowing rate.

6. The present value of the minimum lease payments is $80,000,000, or $10,487,443 × 7.62817 (Table A-5: $i = 12, n = 15$).

---

[27] *CICA Handbook,* Section 3065, par. .68.

[28] *Ibid.,* par. .69.

[29] *Ibid.,* par. .70.

This lease is a capital lease to Lessee Corp. because the lease term exceeds 75% of the estimated remaining life of the aircraft and the present value of the lease payments exceeds 90% of the fair value of the aircraft. Assuming that collectibility of the lease payments is reasonably assured and no important uncertainties exist in relation to unreimbursable costs yet to be incurred by the lessor, Lessor Corp. should classify this lease as a direct financing lease.

The journal entries to record the transactions related to this lease for both Lessee Corp. and Lessor Corp. for the first year are presented below.

EXHIBIT 21-32

ENTRIES FOR SALE-LEASEBACK

Lessee Corp.			Lessor Corp.		

Sale of Aircraft by Lessee to Lessor Corp., Jan. 1, 1998, and Leaseback Transaction

Cash	80,000,000		Aircraft	80,000,000	
Aircraft (net)		75,500,000	Cash		80,000,000
Unearned Profit on Sale-Leaseback		4,500,000			
			Lease Payments Receivable	157,311,645	
Leased Aircraft Under Capital Leases	80,000,000		Aircraft		80,000,000
Obligations Under Capital Lease		80,000,000	Unearned Interest Revenue—Leases		77,311,645
			($10,487,443 × 15 = $157,311,645)		

First Lease Payment, Jan. 1, 1998

| Obligations Under Capital Leases | 10,487,443 | | Cash | 10,487,443 | |
| Cash | | 10,487,443 | Lease Payments Receivable | | 10,487,443 |

Incurrence and Payment of Executory Costs by Lessee Corp. Throughout 1998

| Insurance, Maintenance, Taxes, etc. Expense | XXX | | (No entry) | | |
| Cash or Accounts Payable | | XXX | | | |

Depreciation Expense for 1998 on the Aircraft, Dec. 31, 1998

Depreciation Expense	5,333,333		(No entry)		
Accumulated Depreciation—					
Capital Leases		5,333,333			
($80,000,000 ÷ 15)					

Amortization of Deferred Profit on Sale-Leaseback by Lessee Corp., Dec. 31, 1998

Unearned Profit on Sale-Leaseback	300,000				
Depreciation Expense		300,000			
($4,500,000 ÷ 15)					

Note: A case might be made for crediting Revenue instead of Depreciation Expense.

Interest for 1998, Dec. 31, 1998

| Interest Expense—Capital Leases | 8,341,507[a] | | Unearned Interest Revenue | 8,341,507 | |
| Interest Payable | | 8,341,507 | Interest Revenue—Leases | | 8,341,507[a] |

[a]Partial Lease Amortization Schedule

Date	Annual Rental Payment	Interest (12%)	Reduction of Balance	Balance
Jan. 1/98				$80,000,000
Jan. 1/98	$10,487,443	-0-	$10,487,443	69,512,557
Jan. 1/99	10,487,443	$8,341,507	2,145,936	67,366,621

Although there are no specific disclosure requirements for a sale-leaseback transaction other than those required for leases in general, the following is an example of how Mark's Work Wearhouse Ltd. reported such a transaction.

EXHIBIT 21-33   MARK'S WORK WEARHOUSE

52 WEEKS ENDED JANUARY 27, 1996
NOTE 6 TO THE FINANCIAL STATEMENTS (PARTIAL)

Effective August 1, 1991, the Company sold and leased back its corporate office and warehouse facility. The gain realized on the sale has been deferred and is being amortized as a reduction of occupancy expense over the 128-month term of the lease. The deferred gain balance at January 27, 1996 is $366,000 (January 28, 1995, $399,000 and January 29, 1994, $435,000).

LEASE ACCOUNTING: THE UNSOLVED PROBLEM

As indicated at the beginning of this chapter, lease accounting is a much abused area in which strenuous efforts are made to circumvent *CICA Handbook* Section 3065. In practice, the accounting rules for capitalizing leases have been rendered partially ineffective by the strong desires of lessees to resist capitalization. Leases generally involve large dollar amounts that, when capitalized, materially increase reported liabilities and adversely affect the debt-to-equity and other ratios. Lease capitalization is also resisted because charges to expense made in the early years of the lease term are higher under the capital lease method than under the operating method, frequently without tax benefit. As a consequence, much effort has been devoted to beating the profession's lease capitalization rules.[30]

To avoid asset capitalization, lease agreements are designed, written, and interpreted so that none of the three criteria is satisfied from the lessee's viewpoint. Devising lease agreements in such a way has not been too difficult when the following specifications are met.

1. Make certain that the lease does not specify the transfer of title to the property to the lessee.

2. Do not include a bargain purchase option.

3. Set the lease term at something less than 75% of the estimated economic life of the leased property.

4. Arrange for the present value of the minimum lease payments to be less than 90% of the fair value of the leased property.

But the real challenge lies in disqualifying the lease as a capital lease to the lessee while having the same lease qualify as a capital (sales or financing) lease to the lessor.

---

[30] Richard Dieter, "Is Lessee Accounting Working?" *The CPA Journal* (August 1979), pp. 13–19. This article provides interesting examples of abuses of U.S. Statement No. 13, discusses the circumstances that led to the current situation, and proposes a solution.

Unlike lessees, lessors try to avoid having lease arrangements classified as operating leases.[31]

Avoiding the first two criteria is relatively simple, but it takes a little ingenuity to avoid the "90% recovery test" for the lessee while satisfying it for the lessor. Two factors involved in this effort are (1) the use of the incremental borrowing rate by the lessee when it is higher than the implicit interest rate of the lessor, by making information about the implicit rate unavailable to the lessee; and (2) residual value guarantees.

The lessee's use of the higher interest rate is probably the more popular subterfuge. While lessees are knowledgeable about the fair value of the leased property and, of course, the rental payments, they generally are not aware of the estimated residual value used by the lessor. Therefore the lessee does not know exactly the lessor's implicit rate and is therefore free to use its own incremental borrowing rate.

The residual value guarantee is the other popular device used by lessees and lessors. In fact, a whole new industry has emerged to circumvent symmetry between the lessee and the lessor in accounting for leases. The residual value guarantee has spawned numerous companies whose principal function is to guarantee the residual value of leased assets. For a fee, these "third-party guarantors" (insurers) assume the risk of deficiencies in leased asset residual values.

Because the guaranteed residual value is included in the minimum lease payments for the lessor, the 90% recovery of fair market value test is satisfied and the lease is a nonoperating lease to the lessor. Because the residual value is guaranteed by a third party, the minimum lease payments of the lessee do not include the guarantee. Thus by merely transferring some of the risk to a third party, lessees can alter substantially the accounting treatment by converting what would otherwise be capital leases to operating leases.

Much of this circumvention is encouraged by the nature of the criteria used, and accounting standard-setting bodies, both domestic and international, continue to have poor experience with arbitrary size and percentage criteria, such as "90% of," "75% of," etc.

This situation provided the motivation for a study and the subsequent publication of a paper on a new approach to lease accounting.[32] The authors took an approach that, because all noncancellable lease contracts result in the lessee acquiring an asset and a liability as defined under the conceptual frameworks of the standard-setting bodies represented, and because the recognition criteria identified in those conceptual frameworks are met, all finance and most, if not all, operating leases qualify for recognition as assets and liabilities.

The study group hopes that the paper will generate discussion of the issues involved and lead to the development of improved and harmonized accounting standards for leases.

---

[31] The reason is that most lessors are financial institutions and do not want these types of assets on their balance sheets. Furthermore, the capital lease transaction from the lessor's standpoint provides higher income flows in the earlier periods of the lease.

[32] Warren McGregor, Principal Author, *Accounting for Leases: A New Approach—Recognition by Lessees of Assets and Liabilities Arising under Lease Contracts*, (FASB, 1996). The working group from whose efforts the paper emerged consisted of Board members and senior staff of the standard-setting bodies of Australia, Canada, New Zealand, the United Kingdom, and the USA, and the staff of the IASC.

Summary of Learning Objectives

1. **Explain the nature, economic substance, and advantages of lease transactions.** A lease is a contract between two parties whereby the lessee is granted the right to use property owned by the lessor. In situations where the lessee obtains the use of the majority of the economic benefits inherent in a leased asset, the transaction is similar in substance to the acquisition of an asset. Therefore, the lessee incurs a liability and the lessor transfers the asset. The major advantages of leasing for the lessee relate to the cost and flexibility of the financing and protection against obsolescence, and for the lessor to the attractiveness of the finance income.

2. **Identify and explain the accounting criteria and procedures for capitalizing leases by the lessee.** Where the risks and benefits of ownership of the leased asset are transferred to the lessee as evidenced by either the transfer of title, the use of the majority of the asset services inherent in the leased asset, or the recovery by the lessor of its investment in the leased asset plus a return on that investment, the asset should be capitalized on the lessee's balance sheet and a liability recognized for the obligation owing to the lessor. The amount capitalized is the present value of the minimum lease payments, an amount based on that for which the lessee has accepted responsibility in the lease agreement. The lessee accounts for the leased asset and lease liability as it would any other capital asset and obligation by recording depreciation and interest expense. Lease payments reduce the liability, including any accrued interest.

3. **Identify the lessee's disclosure requirements for capital leases.** Lessees must disclose information similar to the required disclosures for capital assets and long-term debt in general. In addition, the total future minimum lease payments and those required in each of the next five years must be reported with a separate deduction for executory and interest costs to reconcile the total owing to the obligation reported on the balance sheet.

4. **Identify the lessee's accounting and disclosure requirements for an operating lease.** A lessee recognizes the lease payments made as rent expense in the period covered by the lease, usually on a time proportion basis. The lessee must disclose the future minimum lease payments in total and for each of the next five years, and the nature of any other commitments under such leases.

5. **Contrast the operating and capitalization methods of recording leases.** Over the term of a lease, the total amount charged to expense is the same whether the lease has been treated as a capital lease or as an operating lease. The difference relates to the timing of recognition for the expense (more is charged in the early years for a capital lease), the type of expense charged (depreciation and interest expense for a capital lease versus rent expense for an operating lease), and the recognition for a capital lease versus nonrecognition for an operating lease of the leased asset and obligation on the balance sheet over the term of the lease.

6. **Calculate the lease payment required for the lessor to earn a given return.** The lessor determines the investment it wants to recover from a leased asset. If the lessor has acquired an asset for the purpose of leasing it, it is usually the asset's cost the lessor wants to recover. If the lessor participates in leases as a means of selling its product, it is usually the sales price it wants to recover. The lessor's

KEY TERMS

amortization period, 1057

bargain purchase option, 1055

bargain renewal option, 1055

capital lease, 1054

capitalization method, 1054

direct financing lease, 1066

effective interest method, 1058

executory contract, 1053

executory costs, 1056

guaranteed residual value, 1056, 1076

implicit rate, 1057

incremental borrowing rate, 1056

initial direct costs, 1083

lease, 1050

lease term, 1055

lessee, 1050

lessor, 1050

minimum lease payments, 1056

noncapitalization method, 1054

off-balance-sheet financing, 1052

operating lease, 1054

rental payments, 1051

residual value, 1056

sale-leaseback, 1084

sales-type lease, 1066

unguaranteed residual value, 1056

investment in the cost or selling price can be recovered in part through the estimated residual value of the asset if it is to be returned to the lessor, or through a bargain purchase price expected to be paid by the lessee, if part of the lease agreement. Other than from these sources, the lessor recovers its investment through the lease payments. The periodic lease payment, therefore, is the annuity amount whose present value exactly equals the amount to be recovered through lease payments.

7. **Identify the classifications of leases for the lessor.** If a lease in substance transfers the risks and benefits of ownership of the leased asset to the lessee (decided in the same way as for the lessee) *and* revenue recognition criteria related to collectibility and ability to estimate any remaining costs are met, the lessor accounts for the lease as either a direct financing or a sales-type lease. The existence of a manufacturer's or dealer's profit on the amount to be recovered from the lessee differentiates the sales-type lease from a direct financing lease where the objective is to generate only finance income. If either the capitalization or revenue recognition criteria are not met, the lessor accounts for the lease as an operating lease.

8. **Describe the lessor's accounting for direct financing leases.** The lessor removes the leased asset from its books and replaces it with its net investment in the lease. This is made up of two accounts: (1) the gross investment or Lease Payments Receivable, which captures the dollars to be received through lease payments (excluding executory costs); and (2) estimated residual values or bargain purchase options, offset by the portion of these amounts that represents unearned interest. The net investment, therefore, represents the present value of the lease payments and the residual value or bargain purchase option amounts. Looked at another way, this also represents the cost of the leased asset to the lessor. As the lease payments are received, the receivable is reduced. As time passes, the unearned interest is taken into income on the basis of the implicit rate of return applied to the net investment.

9. **Describe the lessor's accounting for sales-type leases.** The lessor records sales revenue offset by the net investment in the lease. Again, the net investment is made up of two accounts: (1) the gross investment or lease payments receivable; and (2) the contra account representing the unearned interest included in the lease payments receivable. In addition, the lessor transfers the cost of the leased asset from inventory to cost of goods sold. In the period of the inception of the lease the lessor reports a gross profit on sale and over the lease term recognizes finance income earned based on the net investment.

10. **Describe the lessor's accounting for operating leases.** The lessor records the lease payments received from the lessee as rental revenue in the period covered by the lease payment. Because the leased asset remains on the lessor's books, the lessor records depreciation expense.

11. **Identify the lessor's disclosure requirements.** For direct financing and sales-type leases, the lessor must disclose its net investment in the leases, segregated according to current and noncurrent asset categories, and how the investment was calculated for purposes of income recognition. The amount of finance income recognized must also be disclosed. For operating leases, separate disclosure is required of the cost and accumulated depreciation of property held for leasing purposes, and the amount of rental income earned.

12. **Describe the effect of residual values, guaranteed and unguaranteed, on lease accounting.** When a *lessee* guarantees a residual value, it is obligated to return either the leased asset or cash or a combination of both equal to that guaranteed value. This amount is therefore included in the lease obligation and leased asset value. The lessee depreciates the asset to this value by the end of the lease term. If the residual is unguaranteed, the lessee takes no responsibility for the residual and it is excluded from the lessee's calculations. From the lessor's viewpoint in a *direct financing lease*, it makes no difference whether or not the residual is guaranteed. The expected residual is included in the lessor's calculations as the best estimate of what will be returned at the end of the lease. In a *sales-type lease*, the gross investment, net investment, and unearned finance income are not affected by whether or not the residual is guaranteed. The only difference is that when the residual is unguaranteed, the uncertainty associated with whether or not the full sales amount will be realized dictates that sales revenue and cost of goods sold accounts be reduced by the present value of the unguaranteed residual. There is no difference, however, in the amount of gross profit recognized on the sales-type lease.

13. **Describe the effect of bargain purchase options on lease accounting.** In a lease with a bargain purchase option , it is assumed that the *lessee* will exercise the option and that the title to the leased asset will be transferred to the lessee. The present value of the bargain purchase option is therefore included in the amount capitalized as the asset and lease liability. Because the assumption is that the lessee will acquire title, the asset is depreciated over its economic life. The *lessor*, whether a direct financing lease or a sales-type lease, includes the bargain purchase option in the gross investment and its present value in the net investment in the leased asset.

14. **Describe the lessor's accounting treatment for initial direct costs.** In all cases, the initial direct costs are matched with the revenue generated from the incurrence of the costs. For an operating lease, they are deferred and recognized over the same period as the rental revenue is recognized; for a sales-type lease, they are deducted in the same period as the gross profit on sale is recognized; and for a direct financing lease, they are amortized over the term of the lease because they reduce the unearned finance income contra account, which increases the "net investment" and reduces the implicit interest rate required to amortize the net investment.

15. **Describe the lessee's accounting for sale-leaseback transactions.** A sale and leaseback is accounted for by the lessee as if the two transactions are related. Any gain or loss, with the exception of a "real" loss, must be deferred by the lessee and recognized in income over the lease term. If it is an operating lease, the seller-lessee takes the deferred gain or loss into income in proportion to the rental payments made; if it is a capital lease, the deferred gain or loss is taken into income over the same period and basis as the amortization of the leased asset.

APPENDIX 21A

Real Estate Leases

OBJECTIVE 16
Explain the classification and accounting treatment accorded leases that involve land as well as buildings and equipment.

When a capital lease involves land whose ownership will not be transferred to the lessee, capitalization of the land on the lessee's balance sheet would result in no depreciation or other similar expense being recognized over the term of the lease, and a loss equal to the capitalized value of the land being recognized when it reverts to the lessor. For this reason, special guidance is given for leases that involve land.

LAND

If land is the sole item of property leased, the *lessee* should account for the lease as a capital lease only if Criterion 1 is met; that is, if the lease transfers ownership of the property or contains a bargain purchase option. Otherwise it is accounted for as an operating lease. Although the lease is classified as a capital lease when ownership of the land is expected to pass to the lessee, this is an asset that is not normally depreciated. The *lessor* accounts for a land lease either as a sales-type or direct financing lease, whichever is appropriate, provided the lease transfers ownership or contains a bargain purchase option and meets both the collectibility and uncertainties tests—otherwise the operating method is used.

LAND AND BUILDING

If both land and building are involved and the lease transfers ownership or contains a bargain purchase option, the capitalized value of the land and the building should be separately classified by the *lessee*. The present value of the minimum lease payments is allocated between land and building in proportion to their fair values at the inception of the lease. The *lessor* accounts for the lease as a single unit, as a sales-type, direct financing, or operating lease, as appropriate.

    When both land and building are involved and the lease does not transfer ownership or contain a bargain purchase option, the accounting treatment is dependent upon the proportion of land to building. If the fair value of the land is minor in relation to the total fair value of the leased property, both lessee and lessor consider the land and the building as a single unit. However, if the fair value of the land at the inception of the lease is significant in relation to the total fair value of the leased property, the land and building are considered separately by both lessee and lessor. The lessee accounts for the building as a capital lease and the land as an operating lease if one of Criteria 2 and 3 is met. If none of the criteria is met, the lessee uses the operating method for the land and building. The lessor accounts for the building as a sales-type or direct financing lease as appropriate, and treats the land element separately as an operating lease.

REAL ESTATE AND EQUIPMENT

If a lease involves both real estate and equipment, the portion of the lease payments applicable to the equipment should be estimated by whatever means are appropriate and reasonable. The equipment should then be treated separately for purposes of applying the criteria and accounted for separately according to its classification by both lessees and lessors.

Summary of Learning Objective for Appendix 21A

16. **Explain the classification and accounting treatment accorded leases that involve land as well as buildings and equipment.** Because the capitalization of land by the lessee in a capital lease that does not transfer title would result in an unwanted and unintended effect on the lessee's financial statements, the portion of such leases that relates to land should be accounted for as operating leases. If the relative value of the land is minor, however, the minimum lease payments are fully capitalized as building and/or equipment.

APPENDIX 21B

Flowcharts—Accounting for Leases

Appendix B to *CICA Handbook* Section 3065 provides decision trees to illustrate the classification and accounting decisions required in applying its recommendations. Those related to accounting for a capital lease, a sales-type lease, and a direct financing lease are reproduced on the following pages. The CICA cautions that these should be read and applied in conjunction with Section 3065 recommendations .

MLP = Net minimum lease payments
MRP = Net minimum rental payments called for over the lease term

ILLUSTRATION 21B-2
*Accounting for a
Sales-Type Lease*

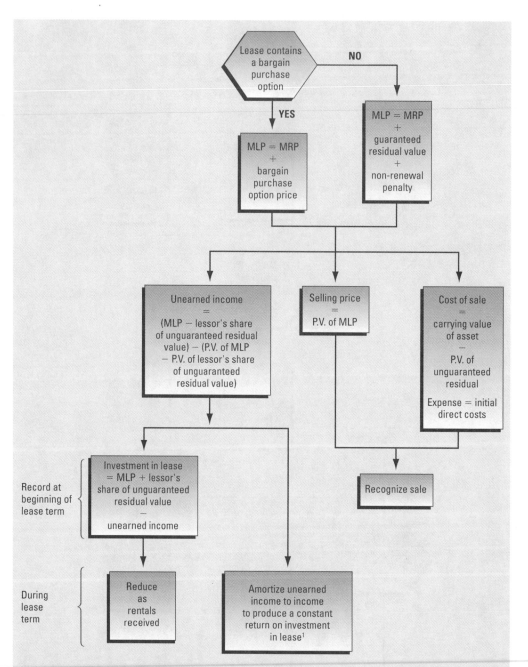

MLP = Net minimum lease payments
MRP = Net minimum rental payments called for over the lease term
P.V. = Present value

[1]Investment in lease for purposes of income recognition:
(a) when income tax factors taken into consideration for accounting purposes = MLP + lessor's share of unguaranteed
    residual value − unearned income − deferred taxes − investment tax credit; or
(b) when income tax factors not taken into consideration for accounting purposes = MLP + lessor's share of
    unguaranteed residual value − unearned income.

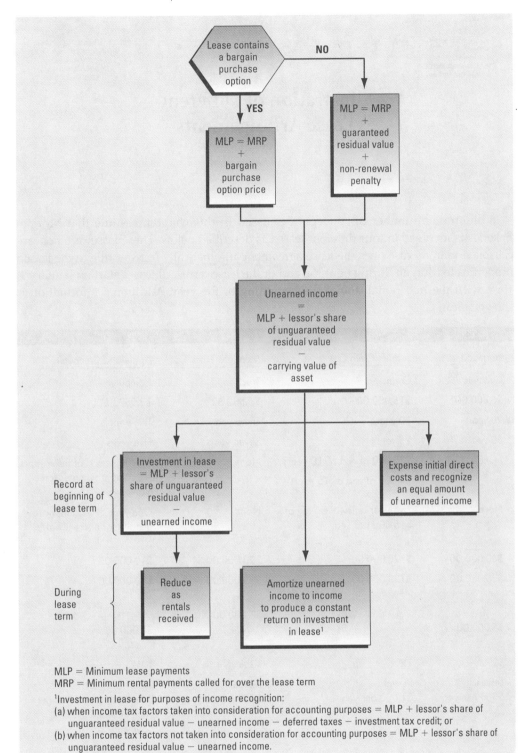

MLP = Minimum lease payments
MRP = Minimum rental payments called for over the lease term

[1]Investment in lease for purposes of income recognition:
(a) when income tax factors taken into consideration for accounting purposes = MLP + lessor's share of
     unguaranteed residual value − unearned income − deferred taxes − investment tax credit; or
(b) when income tax factors not taken into consideration for accounting purposes = MLP + lessor's share of
     unguaranteed residual value − unearned income.

APPENDIX 21C

Illustration of Different Lease Arrangements

To illustrate a number of concepts discussed in this chapter, assume that Morgan Bakeries is involved in four different leases as described below. These leases are noncancellable and in no case does the lease agreement automatically transfer title to the leased properties to Morgan during or at the end of the lease term. All leases start on January 1, 1998, with the first rental due at the beginning of the year. Additional information is shown below.

EXHIBIT 21C-1

Lessor	Harmon Ltd.	Arden's Oven Co.	Mendota Truck Co.	Appleland Computer
Type of property	Cabinets	Oven	Truck	Computer
Yearly rental	$6,000.00	$15,000.00	$5,582.62	$3,557.25
Lease term	20 years	10 years	Three years	Three years
Estimated economic life	30 years	25 years	Seven years	Five years
Purchase option	None	$75,000 at end of 10 years $4,000 at end of 15 years	None	$3,000 at end of three years, which approximates fair market value.
Renewal option	None	Five-year renewal option at $15,000 per year	None	One year at $1,500; no penalty for nonrenewal
Fair market value at inception of lease	$60,000.00	$120,000.00	$20,000.00	$10,000.00
Cost of asset to lessor	$60,000.00	$120,000.00	$15,000.00	$10,000.00
Residual value				
Guaranteed	-0-	-0-	$7,000.00	-0-
Unguaranteed	$5,000.00	-0-	-0-	$3,000.00
Incremental borrowing rate of lessee	12%	12%	12%	12%
Executory costs paid by	Lessee $300 per year	Lessee $1,000 per year	Lessee $500 per year	Lessor Estimated to be $500 per year, included in rental payment
Present value of minimum lease payments				
Using incremental borrowing rate of lessee	$50,194.68	$115,153.35	$20,000.00	$8,224.16
Using implicit rate of lessor	Not known	Not known	Not known	Known by lessee: $8,027.48
Fair market value at end of lease	$5,000.00	$80,000 at end of 10 years $60,000 at end of 15 years	Not available	$3,000
Credit risk of lease	Normal	Normal	Normal	Normal
Lessor's unreimbursable costs can be estimated?	Yes	Yes	Yes	Yes

Harmon Ltd.

The following is an analysis of the Harmon Ltd. lease.

1. *Transfer of title.* In lease? No. Bargain purchase option? No.

2. *Economic life test (75% test).* The lease term is 20 years and the estimated economic life is 30 years. Thus it does not meet the 75% test.

3. *Recovery of investment test (90% test).*

Fair value	$60,000	Rental payments	$ 6,000
Rate	90%	PV of annuity due for 20 years at 12%	× 8.36578
90% of fair value	$54,000	PV of minimum lease payments	$50,194.68

Because the present value of the minimum lease payments is less than 90% of the fair value, the 90% test is not met. Both Morgan and Harmon should account for this lease as an operating lease as indicated by the entries shown below for January 1, 1998.

Morgan Bakeries (Lessee)			Harmon Ltd. (Lessor)	
Rental Expense	6,000		Cash	6,000
Cash		6,000	Rental Revenue	6,000

Alternatively, Morgan might debit Prepaid Rent (Harmon might credit Unearned Rental Revenue) and charge (credit) the $6,000 to income at $500 per month.

Arden's Oven Co.

The following is an analysis of the Arden's Oven Co. lease.

1. *Transfer of title.* In lease? No. Bargain purchase option? The $75,000 option at the end of 10 years does not appear to be sufficiently lower than the expected fair value of $80,000 to be reasonably assured that it will be exercised. However, the $4,000 at the end of 15 years when the fair value is $20,000 does appear to be a bargain.

2. *Economic life test (75% test).* Given that a bargain purchase option exists, the lease term is the initial lease period of 10 years plus the 5-year renewal option since it precedes a bargain purchase option. Even though the lease term is now 15 years, this test is still not met because 75% of the economic life of 25 years is 18.75 years.

3. *Recovery of investment test (90%) test.*

Fair value	$120,000	Rental payments (1–15)	$ 15,000.00
Rate	90%	PV of annuity due for 15 years at 12%	× 7.62817
90% of fair value	$108,000	PV of rental payments	$114,422.55
		PV of bargain purchase option:	
		$4,000 × .18270 =	$ 730.80
		PV of rental	114,422.55
		PV of minimum lease payments	$115,153.35

The present value of the minimum lease payments is greater than 90% of the fair value; therefore, the 90% test *is* met. Morgan Bakeries should account for this as a capital lease because both criteria 1 and 2 are met. Assuming that Arden's implicit rate is the same as Morgan's incremental borrowing rate, the following entries are made on January 1, 1998.

Morgan Bakeries (Lessee)		Arden's Oven Co. (Lessor)		
Leased Asset—Oven	115,153.35	Lease Payments		
Obligation Under		Receivable	$229,000*	
Capital Lease	115,153.35	Asset—Oven		120,000
		Unearned Interest		
		Revenue		109,000
		*([$15,000 × 15] + $4,000)		

Morgan Bakeries would depreciate the leased asset over its economic life of 25 years because it is assumed that the lessee will acquire title to the asset through the bargain purchase option. Arden does not use sales-type lease accounting because the fair value and the cost of the asset are the same at the inception of the lease.

MENDOTA TRUCK CO.

The following is an analysis of the Mendota Truck Co. lease.

1. *Transfer of title. In lease?* No. Bargain purchase option? No.

2. *Economic life test (75% test).* The lease term is three years and the estimated economic life is seven years. Thus it does *not* meet the 75% test.

3. *Recovery of investment test (90% test).*

Fair value	$20,000	Rental payments	$ 5,582.62
Rate	90%	PV of annuity due for three years at 12%	× 2.69005
90% of fair value	$18,000	PV of rental payments	$15,017.54
		Guaranteed residual value	$ 7,000.00
		PV of 1 for three years at 12%	× .71178
		PV of guaranteed residual value	$ 4,982.46
		PV of rental payments	$15,017.54
		PV of guaranteed residual value	4,982.46
		PV of minimum lease payments	$20,000.00

The present value of the minimum lease payments is greater than 90% of the fair value; therefore, the 90% test *is* met. Assuming that Mendota Truck Co.'s implicit rate is the same as Morgan's incremental borrowing rate, the following entries are made on January 1, 1998.

Morgan Bakeries (Lessee)		Mendota Truck (Lessor)		
Leased Asset	20,000.00	Lease Payments		
Lease Obligation	20,000.00	Receivable	$23,747.86*	
		Cost of Goods Sold	15,000.00	
		Inventory—Truck		15,000.00
		Sales		20,000.00
		Unearned Interest		
		Revenue		3,747.86
		*([$5,582.62 × 3] + $7,000)		

The leased asset is depreciated over three years to its guaranteed residual value.

APPLELAND COMPUTER

The following is an analysis of the Appleland Computer lease.

1. *Transfer of title.* In lease? No. Bargain purchase option? No. The option to purchase at the end of three years at fair value is clearly not a bargain.

2. *Economic life test (75% test).* The lease term is three years and no bargain renewal period exists. Therefore the 75% test is not met.

3. *Recovery of investment test (90% test).*

Fair value	$10,000	Rental payments	$3,557.25
Rate	90%	Less executory costs	500.00
90% of fair value	$ 9,000		$3,057.25
		PV of annuity due for three years at 12% ×2.69005	
		PV of minimum lease payments	$8,224.16

The present value of the minimum lease payments using the incremental borrowing rate is $8,224.16; using the implicit rate it is $8,027.48. The lessee uses the higher $8,224.16 when comparing to 90% of fair value because the lessor's implicit rate must be higher than the lessee's rate to generate a lower present value amount. In any case, the present value of the minimum lease payments is lower than the 90% cut-off, and therefore the recovery of investment test is *not* met.

The following entries are made on January 1, 1998, indicating an operating lease.

Morgan Bakeries (Lessee)			Appleland Computer (Lessor)		
Rental Expense	3,557.25		Cash	3,557.25	
Cash		3,557.25	Rental Revenue		3,557.25

Note: If the lease payments had been $3,557.25 with no executory costs included, this lease would qualify for capital lease accounting treatment. If the renewal option of $1,500 for Year 4 is considered a bargain renewal option, the present value of the minimum lease payments (as shown below) is closer, but still below the 90% cut-off, and an operating lease treatment is still appropriate.

PV of minimum lease payments, years 1 to 3 (as above)	$8,224.16
Add PV of beginning of year 4 payment	
$1,500 – $500 = $1,000 × .71178	711.78
PV of minimum lease payments	$8,935.94

Note: All *asterisked* Exercises, Problems, or Cases relate to material contained in the appendices to the chapter.

EXERCISES

(Lessee Entries: Basic Capital Lease) Zephyr Company enters into a lease agreement on July 1, 1998 for the pur- **E21-1** pose of leasing a machine to be used in its manufacturing operations. The following data pertain to this agreement:

1. The term of the noncancellable lease is three years, with no renewal option and no residual value at the end of the lease term. Payments of $102,356.39 are due on July 1 of each year, beginning July 1, 1998.
2. The fair value of the machine on July 1, 1998 is $300,000. The machine has a remaining economic life of five years, with no salvage value. The machine reverts to the lessor on the termination of the lease.
3. Zephyr Company elects to depreciate the machine on the straight-line method.
4. Zephyr Company's incremental borrowing rate is 10% per year, and it has no knowledge of the implicit rate computed by the lessor.

Instructions
Prepare the journal entries on the books of the lessee that relate to the lease agreement through June 30, 2001. The accounting period of Zephyr Company ends on December 31. (Assume that reversing entries are made.)

E21-2 **(Lessee Computations and Entries: Capital Lease with Guaranteed Residual Value)** Piper Company leases an automobile with a fair value of $7,850 from Austin Motors, Inc. on the following terms:

1. Noncancellable term of 50 months.

2. Rental of $180 per month (at end of each month; present value at 1% per month is $7,055).

3. Estimated residual value after 50 months is $1,060 (the present value at 1% per month is $645). Piper Company guarantees the residual value of $1,060.

4. Estimated economic life of the automobile is 60 months.

5. Piper Company's incremental borrowing rate is 12% per year (1% per month). Austin's implicit rate is unknown.

Instructions

(a) What is the nature of this lease to Piper Company? Explain.

(b) What is the present value of the minimum lease payments?

(c) Record the lease on Piper Company's books at the date of inception.

(d) Record the first month's depreciation on Piper Company's books (assume the straight-line method).

(e) Record the first month's lease payment.

E21-3 **(Lessee Entries: Capital Lease with Executory Costs and Unguaranteed Residual Value)** On January 1, 1998 Morrow Paper Co. signs a 10-year, noncancellable lease agreement to lease a storage building from Sheffield Storage Company. The following information pertains to this lease agreement:

1. The agreement requires equal annual rental payments of $70,000 beginning January 1, 1998.

2. The fair value of the building on January 1, 1998 is $440,000.

3. The building has an estimated economic life of 12 years with an unguaranteed residual value of $10,000. Morrow Paper Co. depreciates similar buildings on the straight-line method.

4. The lease is nonrenewable. At the termination of the lease, the building reverts to the lessor.

5. Morrow Paper's incremental borrowing rate is 12% per year. The lessor's implicit rate is not known by Morrow Paper Co.

6. The yearly rental payment includes $470.51 of executory costs related to taxes on the property.

Instructions

Prepare the journal entries on the lessee's books to reflect the signing of the lease agreement and to record the payments and expenses related to this lease for the years 1998 and 1999. Morrow Paper's corporate year end is December 31.

E21-4 **(Lessor Entries: Direct Financing Lease with Option to Purchase)** Castle Leasing Company signs a lease agreement on January 1, 1998 to lease electronic equipment to Perry Company. The term of the noncancellable lease is two years and payments are required at the end of each year. The following information relates to this agreement:

1. Perry Company has the option to purchase the equipment for $8,000 on termination of the lease.

2. The equipment has a cost of $160,000 to Castle Leasing Company; the useful economic life is two years, with a salvage value of $8,000.

3. Perry Company is required to pay $5,000 each year to the lessor for executory costs.

4. Castle Leasing Company wants to earn a return of 10% on its investment.

5. Collectibility of the payments is reasonably predictable, and there are no important uncertainties surrounding the costs yet to be incurred by the lessor.

Instructions

(a) Prepare the journal entries on the books of Castle Leasing to reflect the payments received under the lease, and to recognize income for the years 1998 and 1999.

(b) Assuming that Perry Company exercises its option to purchase the equipment on December 31, 1999, prepare the journal entry to reflect the sale on Castle's books.

E21-5 **(Type of Lease: Amortization Schedule)** Perch Leasing Company leases a new machine that has a cost and fair value of $92,000 to Clyde Corporation on a three-year noncancellable contract. Clyde Corporation agrees to assume all risks of normal ownership, including such costs as insurance, taxes, and maintenance. The machine has a three-year useful life and no residual value. The lease was signed on January 1, 1998 and Perch Leasing Company expects to earn a 9% return on its investment. Annual rentals are payable on each December 31.

Instructions

(a) Discuss the nature of the lease arrangement and the accounting method each party to the lease should apply.

(b) Prepare an amortization schedule that is suitable for both lessor and lessee and covers all the years involved.

(Lessor Entries: Sales-Type Lease) Dutch Company leases a car to T. Crowell on January 1, 1998. The term of the noncancellable lease is four years. The following information about the lease is provided: **E21-6**

1. Title to the car passes to the lessee on termination of the lease. Residual value is estimated at $1,000 at the end of the lease.

2. The fair value of the car is $21,188. The car is carried in Dutch's inventory at $17,000. The car has an economic life of five years.

3. Dutch Company wants a rate of return of 9% on its investment.

4. Collectibility of the lease payments is reasonably predictable. There are no important uncertainties about the amount of costs yet to be incurred by the lessor.

5. Equal annual lease payments are due at the beginning of each lease year.

Instructions

(a) What type of lease is this? Discuss.

(b) Prepare a lease amortization schedule for Dutch Company for the four-year lease term.

(c) Prepare the journal entries for 1998, 1999, and 2000 to record the lease agreement, the receipt of lease payments, and the recognition of income.

(Lessee Entries with Bargain Purchase Option) The following facts pertain to a noncancellable lease agreement between Shetland Leasing Company and Falabella Company, a lessee: **E21-7**

Inception date	May 1, 1998
Annual lease payment due at the beginning of each year, beginning with May 1, 1998	$20,987.83
Bargain purchase option price at end of lease term	$4,000.00
Lease term	5 years
Economic life of leased equipment	10 years
Lessor's cost	$65,000.00
Fair value of asset at May 1, 1998	$90,000.00
Lessor's implicit rate	10%
Lessee's incremental borrowing rate	10%

The collectibility of the lease payments is reasonably predictable, and there are no important uncertainties relative to the costs yet to be incurred by the lessor. The lessee assumes responsibility for all executory costs.

Instructions

(a) Discuss the nature of this lease to Falabella Company.

(b) Discuss the nature of this lease to Shetland Company.

(c) Prepare a lease amortization schedule for Falabella Company for the five-year lease term.

(d) Prepare the journal entries on the lessee's books to reflect the signing of the lease agreement and to record the payments and expenses related to this lease for the years 1998 and 1999. Falabella's annual accounting period ends on December 31. Reversing entries are not used by Falabella.

(Lessor Entries with Bargain Purchase Option) Refer to the lease agreement between Shetland Leasing Company and Falabella Company described in E21-7. **E21-8**

Instructions

Perform the following tasks for the lessor:

(a) Compute the amount of gross investment at the inception of the lease.

(b) Compute the amount of net investment at the inception of the lease.

(c) Prepare a lease amortization schedule for Shetland Leasing Company for the five-year term.

(d) Prepare the journal entries to reflect the signing of the lease agreement and to record the receipts and income related to this lease for the years 1998, 1999, and 2000. The lessor's accounting period ends on December 31. Reversing entries are not used by Shetland.

(Computation of Rental: Journal Entries for Lessor) Morgan Leasing Company signs an agreement on January 1, 1998 to lease equipment to Shire Company. The following information relates to this agreement: **E21-9**

1. The term of the noncancellable lease is six years with no renewal option. The equipment has an estimated economic life of six years.

2. The cost of the asset to the lessor is $250,000. The fair value of the asset at January 1, 1998 is $250,000.

3. The asset will revert to the lessor at the end of the lease term, at which time the asset is expected to have a residual value of $52,480, none of which is guaranteed.

4. Shire Company assumes direct responsibility for all executory costs.

5. The agreement requires equal annual rental payments, beginning on January 1, 1998.

6. Collectibility of the lease payments is reasonably predictable. There are no important uncertainties surrounding the amount of costs yet to be incurred by the lessor.

Instructions

(a) Assuming the lessor desires a 10% rate of return on its investment, calculate the amount of the annual rental payment required. Round to the nearest dollar.

(b) Prepare an amortization schedule that would be suitable for the lessor for the lease term.

(c) Prepare all of the journal entries for the lessor for 1998 and 1999 to record the lease agreement, the receipt of lease payments, and the recognition of income. Assume the lessor's annual accounting period ends on December 31.

E21-10 **(Amortization Schedule, Journal Entries, and Disclosure for Lessee)** Hockey Leasing Company signs an agreement on January 1, 1998 to lease equipment to Cob Company. The following information relates to this agreement:

1. The term of the noncancellable lease is five years with no renewal option. The equipment has an estimated economic life of five years.

2. The fair value of the asset at January 1, 1998 is $80,000.

3. The asset will revert to the lessor at the end of the lease term, at which time the asset is expected to have a residual value of $7,000, none of which is guaranteed.

4. Cob Company assumes direct responsibility for all executory costs, which include the following annual amounts: $1,200 to Mountain Insurance Company for insurance, $800 to Queens County for property taxes.

5. The agreement requires equal annual rental payments of $18,142.95 to the lessor, beginning January 1, 1998.

6. The lessee's incremental borrowing rate is 12%. The lessor's implicit rate is 10% and is known to the lessee.

7. Cob Company uses the straight-line depreciation method for all equipment.

8. Cob uses reversing entries when appropriate.

Instructions

(a) Prepare an amortization schedule that is suitable for the lessee for the lease term.

(b) Prepare all of the journal entries for the lessee for 1998 and 1999 to record the lease agreement, the lease payments, and all expenses related to this lease. Assume the lessee's annual accounting period ends on December 31.

(c) Prepare a partial balance sheet at December 31, 1999 with appropriate disclosure of all items related to this lease.

E21-11 **(Accounting for an Operating Lease)** On January 1, 1998 Trake Co. leased a building to Suffolk Inc. The relevant information related to the lease is as follows:

1. The lease arrangement is for 10 years.

2. The leased building cost $4,200,000 and was purchased for cash on January 1, 1998.

3. The building is depreciated on a straight-line basis. Its estimated economic life is 50 years.

4. Lease payments are $200,000 per year and are made at the end of the year.

5. Property tax expense of $45,000 and insurance expense of $10,000 on the building were incurred by Trake in the first year. Payment on these two items was made at the end of the year.

6. Both the lessor and the lessee are on a calendar-year fiscal basis.

Instructions

(a) Prepare the journal entries that Trake Co. should make in 1998.

(b) Prepare the journal entries that Suffolk Inc. should make in 1998.

(c) If Trake paid $30,000 to a real estate broker on January 1, 1998 as a fee for finding the lessee, how much should be reported as an expense for this item in 1998 by Trake Co.?

(Accounting and Disclosure for an Operating Lease) On January 1, 1998 a machine was purchased for $900,000 by Red River Co. The machine is expected to have an eight-year life with no salvage value. It is to be depreciated on a straight-line basis. The machine was leased to St. Sauveur Inc. on January 1, 1998 at an annual rental of $210,000. Other relevant information is as follows: **E21-12**

1. The lease term is for three years.
2. Red River incurred maintenance and other executory costs of $25,000 in 1998 related to this lease.
3. The machine could have been sold by Red River for $940,000 instead of leasing it.
4. St. Sauveur is required to pay a rent security deposit of $35,000 and to prepay the last month's rent of $17,500.

Instructions
(a) How much should Red River Co. report as income before income tax on this lease for 1998?
(b) What amount should St. Sauveur Inc. report for rent expense for 1998 on this lease?
(c) What financial statement disclosures are required for both companies' December 31, 1998 year ends, relative to this lease?

(Operating Lease for Lessee and Lessor) On February 20, 1998 Andes, Inc. purchased a machine for $1,500,000 for the purpose of leasing it. The machine is expected to have a 10-year life, with no residual value, and will be depreciated on a straight-line basis. The machine was leased to Ural Company on March 1, 1998 for a four-year period at a monthly rental of $17,500. There is no provision for the renewal of the lease or purchase of the machine by the lessee at the expiration of the lease term. Andes paid $30,000 of commissions associated with negotiating the lease in February 1998. **E21-13**

Instructions
(a) What expense should Ural record as a result of the facts above for the year ended December 31, 1998? Show supporting computations.
(b) What income or loss before income taxes should Andes record as a result of the facts above for the year ended December 31, 1998?. (AICPA adapted)

(Sale and Leaseback) On January 1, 1998 Breton Corporation sells a computer to Liquidity Finance Co. for $680,000 and immediately leases the computer back. The relevant information is as follows: **E21-14**

1. The computer was carried on Breton's books at a value of $580,000.
2. The term of the noncancellable lease is 10 years; title will transfer to Breton.
3. The lease agreement requires equal rental payments of $110,666.81 at the end of each year.
4. The incremental borrowing rate of Breton Corporation is 12%. Breton is aware that Liquidity Finance Co. sets the annual rental to ensure a rate of return of 10%.
5. The computer has a fair value of $680,000 on January 1, 1998 and an estimated economic life of 10 years.
6. Breton pays executory costs of $5,000 per year.

Instructions
Prepare the journal entries for both the lessee and the lessor for 1998 to reflect the sale and leaseback agreement. No uncertainties exist, and collectibility is reasonably certain.

(Lessee–Lessor, Sale-Leaseback) Presented below are four independent situations. **E21-15**

1. On December 31, 1998 Hilary Inc. sold computer equipment to Cowdy Co. and immediately leased it back for 10 years. The sale price of the equipment was $500,000, its carrying amount was $400,000, and its estimated remaining economic life was 12 years. Determine the amount of deferred gain to be reported from the sale of the computer equipment on December 31, 1998.
2. On December 31, 1998 Berber Co. sold a machine to Crown Co. and simultaneously leased it back for one year. The sale price was $480,000, the carrying amount was $435,000, and the machine had an estimated remaining useful life of 14 years. The present value of the rental payments for the one year is $35,000. At December 31, 1998, how much should Berber report as deferred gain from the sale of the machine?
3. On January 1, 1998 Bard Corp. sold an airplane with an estimated useful life of 10 years. At the same time, Bard leased back the plane for 10 years. The sale price of the airplane was $500,000; the carrying amount $390,000; and the annual rental $73,975.22. Bard intends to depreciate the leased asset using the sum-of-the-years'-digits method. Discuss how the gain on the sale should be reported at the end of 1998 in the financial statements.

4. On January 1, 1998 Oxford Co. sold equipment with an estimated useful life of five years. At the same time, Oxford leased back the equipment for two years under a lease classified as an operating lease. The sale price (fair value) of the equipment was $212,700, the carrying amount was $310,000, the monthly rental under the lease was $6,000, and the present value of the rental payments was $115,753. For the year ended December 31, 1998, determine which items would be reported on Oxford's income statement for the sale-leaseback transaction.

PROBLEMS

P21-1 Fell, Inc. agrees to rent Country Winery Corporation the equipment that it requires to expand its production capacity to meet customers' demands for its products. The lease agreement calls for five annual lease payments of $90,000 at the end of each year. On the date the capital lease begins, the lessee recognizes the existence of leased assets and the related lease obligation at the present value of the five annual payments discounted at a rate of 12%, or $324,430.20. The lessee uses the effective-interest method of reducing lease obligations. The leased equipment has an estimated useful life of five years and no residual value. Country Winery uses the sum-of-the-years'-digits method on similar equipment that it owns.

Instructions

(a) What would be the total amount of the reduction in the lease obligation of the lessee during the first year? The second year?

(b) Prepare the journal entry made by Country Winery Corporation (lessee) on the date the lease begins.

(c) Prepare the journal entries to record the lease payment and interest expense for both the first and second years.

(d) Prepare the journal entry at the end of the first full year to recognize depreciation of the leased equipment.

P21-2 Synergetics Company leased a new crane to Alpha Construction Company under a five-year noncancellable contract starting January 1, 1998. Terms of the lease require payments of $21,000 each January 1 starting January 1, 1998. Synergetics will pay insurance, taxes, and maintenance charges on the crane, which has an estimated life of 12 years, a fair value of $160,000, and a cost to Synergetics Company of $160,000. The estimated fair value of the crane is expected to be $45,000 at the end of the lease term. No bargain purchase or renewal options are included in the contract. Both Synergetics and Alpha adjust and close books annually at December 31. Collectibility is reasonably certain and no uncertainties exist relative to unreimbursable lessor costs. Alpha's incremental borrowing rate is 10% and Synergetics' implicit interest rate of 9% is unknown to Alpha.

Instructions

(a) Identify the type of lease involved and give reasons for your classification. Discuss the accounting treatment that should be applied by both the lessee and the lessor.

(b) Prepare all the entries related to the lease contract and leased asset for the year 1998 for the lessee and the lessor, assuming insurance costs of $1,700, taxes of $240, maintenance of $650, a straight-line depreciation policy, and an estimated salvage value of $10,000.

(c) Identify what should be presented in the balance sheet and income statement and related notes of both the lessee and the lessor at December 31, 1998.

P21-3 Cascade Railroad and Addison Corporation enter into an agreement that requires Addison to build three diesel-electric engines to Cascade's specifications. Upon completion of the engines, Cascade has agreed to lease them for a period of 10 years and to assume all costs and risks of ownership. The lease is noncancellable, becomes effective on January 1, 1998, and requires annual rental payments of $620,000 due each January 1, beginning in 1998.

Cascade's incremental borrowing rate is 10%, and the implicit interest rate used by Addison and known to Cascade is 8%. The total cost of building the three engines is $3,900,000, and, under normal pricing policies, would sell for $4,493,072. The economic life of the engines is estimated to be 10 years, with residual value set at zero. The railroad depreciates similar equipment on a straight-line basis. At the end of the lease, the railroad assumes title to the engines. Collectibility is reasonably certain and no uncertainties exist relative to unreimbursable lessor costs.

Instructions

(Round all numbers to the nearest dollar.)

(a) Discuss the nature of this lease transaction from the viewpoint of both lessee and lessor.

(b) Provide proof that Addison's implicit interest rate is 8%.

(c) Prepare the journal entry or entries to record the transaction on January 1, 1998 on the books of Cascade Railroad.

(d) Prepare the journal entry or entries to record the transaction on January 1, 1998 on the books of Addison Corporation.

(e) Prepare the journal entries for both the lessee and the lessor to record the first rental payment on January 1, 1998.

(f) Prepare the journal entries to record interest expense (revenue) for both the lessee and the lessor at December 31, 1998. (Prepare a two-year lease amortization schedule.)

(g) Show the items and amounts that would be reported on the balance sheet (not notes) at December 31, 1998 for both the lessee and the lessor.

The following facts pertain to a noncancellable lease agreement between Omuto Leasing Company and Sylvan Electronics Company, a lessee, for a computer system.   **P21-4**

Inception date	September 1, 1998
Lease term	six years
Economic life of leased equipment	six years
Fair value of asset at September 1, 1998	$200,000.00
Residual value at end of lease term	–0–
Lessor's implicit rate	10%
Lessee's incremental borrowing rate	10%
Annual lease payment due at the beginning of each year, beginning with September 1, 1998	$41,746.77

The collectibility of the lease payments is reasonably predictable, and there are no important uncertainties surrounding the costs yet to be incurred by the lessor. The lessee assumes responsibility for all executory costs, which amount to $4,000 per year and are to be paid each September 1, beginning September 1, 1998. (This $4,000 is not included in the rental payment of $41,746.77.) The asset will revert to the lessor at the end of the lease term. The straight-line depreciation method is used for all equipment.

The following amortization schedule has been prepared correctly for use by both the lessor and the lessee in accounting for this lease. The lease is to be accounted for properly as a capital lease by the lessee and as a direct financing lease by the lessor.

Date	Annual Lease Payment/ Receipt	Interest (10%) on Unpaid Obligation/ Net Investment	Reduction of Lease Obligation/ Net Investment	Balance of Lease Obligation/ Net Investment
9/01/98				$200,000.00
9/01/98	$ 41,746.77		$ 41,746.77	158,253.23
9/01/99	41,746.77	$15,825.32	25,921.45	132,331.78
9/01/00	41,746.77	13,233.18	28,513.59	103,818.19
9/01/01	41,746.77	10,381.82	31,364.95	72,453.24
9/01/02	41,746.77	7,245.32	34,501.45	37,951.79
9/01/03	41,746.77	3,794.98*	37,951.79	–0–
	$ 250,480.62	$50,480.62	$200,000.00	

*Rounding error is 20 cents.

Instructions

(a) Assuming the lessee's accounting period ends on August 31, answer the following questions with respect to this lease agreement:

1. What items and amounts will be shown on the lessee's income statement for the year ending August 31, 1999?

2. Where and what items and amounts will be shown on the lessee's balance sheet at August 31, 1999?

3. What items and amounts will be shown on the lessee's income statement for the year ending August 31, 2000?

4. Where and what items and amounts will be shown on the lessee's balance sheet at August 31, 2000?

(b) Assuming the lessee's accounting period ends on December 31, answer the following questions with respect to this lease agreement:

1. What items and amounts will be shown on the lessee's income statement for the year ending December 31, 1998?

2. Where and what items and amounts will be shown on the lessee's balance sheet at December 31, 1998?

3. What items and amounts will be shown on the lessee's income statement for the year ending December 31, 1999?

4. Where and what items and amounts will be shown on the lessee's balance sheet at December 31, 1999?

P21-5 Assume the same information as for Problem 21-4.

Instructions

(a) Assuming the lessor's accounting period ends on August 31, answer the following questions with respect to this lease agreement:

1. What items and amounts will be shown on the lessor's income statement for the year ending August 31, 1999?

2. Where and what items and amounts will be shown on the lessor's balance sheet at August 31, 1999?

3. What items and amounts will be shown on the lessor's income statement for the year ending August 31, 2000?

4. Where and what items and amounts will be shown on the lessor's balance sheet at August 31, 2000?

(b) Assuming the lessor's accounting period ends on December 31, answer the following questions with respect to this lease agreement:

1. What items and amounts will be shown on the lessor's income statement for the year ending December 31, 1998?

2. Where and what items and amounts will be shown on the lessor's balance sheet at December 31, 1998?

3. What items and amounts will be shown on the lessor's income statement for the year ending December 31, 1999?

4. Where and what items and amounts will be shown on the lessor's balance sheet at December 31, 1999?

P21-6 The following facts pertain to a noncancellable lease agreement between Watson Leasing Company and Erwin Company, a lessee.

Inception date	January 1, 1998
Annual lease payment due at the beginning of each year, beginning with January 1, 1998	$81,915.24
Residual value of equipment at end of lease term, guaranteed by the lessee	$45,000.00
Lease term	six years
Economic life of leased equipment	six years
Fair value of asset at January 1, 1998	$400,000.00
Lessor's implicit rate	12%
Lessee's incremental borrowing rate	12%

The lessee assumes responsibility for all executory costs, which are expected to amount to $4,000 per year. The asset will revert to the lessor at the end of the lease term. The lessee uses the straight-line depreciation method for all equipment.

Instructions

(a) Provide proof that the lessor's implicit interest rate is 12%.

(b) Prepare an amortization schedule that is suitable for the lessee for the lease term.

(c) Prepare all of the journal entries for the lessee for 1998 and 1999 to record the lease agreement, the lease payments, and all expenses related to this lease. Assume the lessee's annual accounting period ends on December 31 and reversing entries are used when appropriate.

P21-7 Chretien Steel Company signed a lease agreement as lessee for equipment for five years, beginning December 31, 1997. Annual rental payments of $32,000 are to be made at the beginning of each lease year (December 31). The taxes, insurance, and the maintenance costs are the obligation of the lessee. The interest rate used by the lessor in setting the payment schedule is 10%; Chretien's incremental borrowing rate is 12%. Chretien is unaware of the rate being used by the lessor. At the end of the lease, Chretien has the option to buy the equipment for $1, considerably below its then estimated fair value. The equipment has an estimated useful life of eight years. Chretien uses the straight-line method of depreciation on similar owned equipment.

Instructions

(Round all numbers to the nearest dollar.)

(a) Prepare the journal entry or entries, with explanations, that should be recorded on December 31, 1997 by Chretien.

(b) Prepare the journal entry or entries, with explanations, that should be recorded on December 31, 1998 by Chretien. (Prepare the lease amortization schedule for all five payments.)

(c) Prepare the journal entry or entries, with explanations, that should be recorded on December 31, 1999 by Chretien.

(d) What amounts would appear on the December 31, 1999 balance sheet of Chretien relative to the lease arrangement?

P21-8

On January 1, 1998 Mason Holdings Company contracts to lease equipment for five years, agreeing to make a payment of $86,000 (including the executory costs of $6,000) at the beginning of each year, starting January 1, 1998. The taxes, insurance, and maintenance costs, estimated at $6,000 per year, are obligations of the lessee. The leased equipment is to be capitalized at $333,589. The asset is to be amortized on a double-declining balance basis and the obligation is to be reduced on an effective-interest basis. Mason Holdings' incremental borrowing rate is 12%, and the implicit rate in the lease is 10%, which is known by Mason Holdings. Title to the equipment transfers to Mason when the lease expires. The asset has an estimated useful life of five years and no residual value.

Instructions
(Round all numbers to the nearest dollar.)

(a) Explain the probable relationship of the $333,589 amount to the lease arrangement.

(b) Prepare the journal entry (or entries) that should be recorded on January 1, 1998 by Mason Holdings Company.

(c) Prepare the journal entry to record depreciation of the leased asset for the year 1998.

(d) Prepare the journal entry to record the interest expense for the year 1998.

(e) Prepare the journal entry to record the lease payment of January 1, 1999, assuming reversing entries are not made.

(f) What amounts will appear on the lessee's December 31, 1998 balance sheet relative to the lease contract?

P21-9

Chambers, Inc. was incorporated in 1997 to operate as a computer software service firm with an accounting fiscal year ending August 31. Chambers' primary product is a sophisticated on-line inventory-control system; its customers pay a fixed fee plus a usage charge for using the system.

Chambers has leased a large, Alpha-3 computer system from the manufacturer. The lease calls for a monthly rental of $60,000 for the 144 months (12 years) of the lease term. The estimated useful life of the computer is 15 years.

Each scheduled monthly rental payment includes $5,000 for full-service maintenance on the computer to be performed by the manufacturer. All rentals are payable on the first day of the month beginning with August 1, 1998, the date the computer was installed and the lease agreement was signed.

The lease is noncancellable for its 12-year term, and it is secured only by the manufacturer's chattel lien on the Alpha-3 system. Chambers can purchase the Alpha-3 system from the manufacturer at the end of the 12-year lease term for 75% of the computer's fair value at that time.

This lease is to be accounted for as a capital lease by Chambers, and it will be depreciated by the straight-line method with no expected salvage value. Borrowed funds for this type of transaction would cost Chambers 12% per year (1% per month). Following is a schedule of the present value of $1 for selected periods discounted at 1% per period when payments are made at the beginning of each period.

Periods (months)	Present Value of $1 per Period Discounted at 1% per Period
1	1.000
2	1.990
3	2.970
143	76.658
144	76.899

Instructions
Prepare, in general journal form, all entries Chambers should make in its accounting records during August 1998 relating to this lease. Give full explanations and show supporting computations for each entry. August 31, 1998 is the end of Chambers' fiscal accounting period and it will be preparing financial statements on that date. Do not prepare closing entries.

(AICPA adapted)

P21-10

Morgan Dairy leases its milking equipment from Murdoch Finance Company under the following lease terms:

1. The lease term is 10 years, is noncancellable, and requires equal rental payments of $25,250 due at the beginning of each year starting January 1, 1998.

2. The equipment has a fair value at the inception of the lease (January 1, 1998) of $185,078, an estimated economic life of 10 years, and a residual value (which is guaranteed by Morgan Dairy) of $20,000.

3. The lease contains no renewal options and the equipment reverts to Murdoch Finance Company upon termination of the lease.

4. Morgan Dairy's incremental borrowing rate is 9% per year; the implicit rate is also 9%.

5. Morgan Dairy depreciates similar equipment that it owns on a straight-line basis.

6. Collectibility of the lease payments is reasonably predictable and there are no important uncertainties surrounding the costs yet to be incurred by the lessor.

Instructions

(a) Describe the nature of the lease and, in general, discuss how the lessee and lessor should account for the lease transaction.

(b) Prepare the journal entries at January 1, 1998 for both parties.

(c) Prepare the journal entries at December 31, 1998 (both the lessee's and the lessor's year end).

(d) Prepare the journal entries at January 1, 1999 for the lessor and the lessee. (Assume reversing entries are not recorded.)

(e) What would have been the amount to be capitalized by the lessee upon the inception of the lease if:

    1. The residual value of $20,000 had been guaranteed by a third party, not the lessee?

    2. The residual value of $20,000 had not been guaranteed at all?

(f) On the lessor's books, what would be the amount recorded as the net investment at the inception of the lease assuming:

    1. Murdoch Finance had incurred $1,200 of direct costs in processing the lease?

    2. The residual value of $20,000 had been guaranteed by a third party?

    3. The residual value of $20,000 had not been guaranteed at all?

(g) Suppose the useful life of the milking equipment had been 20 years. How large would the residual value have to be at the end of 10 years in order for the lessee to qualify for the operating method? (Assume that the residual value would be guaranteed by a third party.) Hint: The lessee's annual payments will be appropriately reduced as the residual value increases.

P21-11 Brady Company manufactures a desk-type computer with an estimated economic life of 12 years and leases it to National Airlines for a period of 10 years. The normal selling price of the equipment is $210,485, and its unguaranteed residual value at the end of the lease term is estimated to be $20,000. National will make annual payments of $30,000 at the beginning of each year and will pay all maintenance, insurance, and taxes. Brady incurred costs of $180,000 in manufacturing the equipment and $5,000 in negotiating and closing the lease. Brady has determined that the collectibility of the lease payments is reasonably predictable, that no additional costs will be incurred, and that the implicit interest rate is 10%.

Instructions
(Round all numbers to the nearest dollar.)

(a) Discuss the nature of this lease in relation to the lessor and compute the amount of each of the following items:

    1. Gross investment.   3. Sales.

    2. Unearned income.   4. Cost of sales.

(b) Prepare a 10-year lease amortization schedule.

(c) Prepare all of the lessor's journal entries for the first year of the lease, assuming the lessor's fiscal year end is eight months into the lease. Reversing entries are not used.

(d) Determine the current and noncurrent portion of the net investment eight months into the lease at the lessor's fiscal year end.

(e) Assume the $20,000 residual value is guaranteed by the lessee. Identify the changes necessary to parts (a) to (d) to reflect this situation.

P21-12 Assume the same data as in Problem 21-11, ascribing to National Airlines an incremental borrowing rate of 10%.

Instructions
(Round all numbers to the nearest dollar.)

(a) Discuss the nature of this lease in relation to the lessee and compute the amount of the initial obligation under capital leases.

(b) Prepare a 10-year lease amortization schedule.

(c) Prepare all of the lessee's journal entries for the first year, assuming the lease year and National's fiscal year are the same.

P21-13

During 1998, Roth Leasing Co. began leasing equipment to small manufacturers. Below is information regarding the leasing arrangements:

1. Roth Leasing Co. leases equipment with terms from three to five years, depending on the useful life of the equipment. At the expiration of the lease, the equipment will be sold to the lessee at 10% of the lessor's cost, the expected salvage value of the equipment.

2. The amount of the lessee's monthly payment is computed by multiplying the lessor's cost of the equipment factor applicable to the term of lease.

Term of lease	Payment factor
Three years	3.32%
Four years	2.63%
Five years	2.22%

3. The excess of the gross contract receivable for equipment rentals over the cost (reduced by the estimated salvage value at the termination of the lease) is recognized as revenue over the term of the lease under the straight-line method.

4. The following leases were entered into during 1998:

Machine	Dates of Lease	Period of Lease	Machine Cost
Die	7/1/98–6/30/02	Four years	$150,000
Press	9/1/98–8/31/01	Three years	$100,000

Instructions

(a) Prepare a schedule of gross contracts receivable for equipment rentals at the dates of the lease for the die and press machines.

(b) Prepare a schedule of unearned lease income at December 31, 1998 for each lease.

(c) Prepare a schedule computing the present dollar value of lease payments receivable (gross investment) for equipment rentals at December 31, 1998. (The present dollar value of the "lease receivables for equipment rentals" is the outstanding amount of the gross lease receivables less the unearned lease income included therein.) Without prejudice to your solution to part (b), assume that the unearned lease income at December 31, 1998 was $52,000.

(AICPA adapted)

P21-14

In 1997 UVC Trucking Company negotiated and closed a long-term lease contract for newly constructed truck terminals and freight storage facilities. The buildings were erected to the company's specifications on land owned by the company. On January 1, 1998 UVC Trucking Company took possession of the leased properties. On January 1, 1998 and 1999 the company made cash payments of $1,050,000 that were recorded as rental expenses.

Although the terminals have a composite useful life of 40 years, the noncancellable lease runs for 20 years from January 1, 1998 with a bargain purchase option available upon expiration of the lease.

The 20-year lease is effective for the period January 1, 1998 through December 31, 2017. Advance rental payments of $900,000 are payable to the lessor on January 1 of each of the first 10 years of the lease. Advance rental payments of $320,000 are due on January 1 for each of the last 10 years of the lease. The company has an option to purchase all of these leased facilities for $1 on December 31, 2017. It also must make annual payments to the lessor of $50,000 for property taxes and $100,000 for insurance. The lease was negotiated to assure the lessor a 6% rate of return.

Instructions

(Round all computations to the nearest dollar.)

(a) Prepare a schedule to compute for UVC Trucking Company the discounted present value of the terminal facilities and related obligation at January 1, 1998.

(b) Assuming that the discounted present value of terminal facilities and related obligation at January 1, 1998 was $9,000,000, prepare journal entries for UVC Trucking Company to record the:

1. Cash payment to the lessor on January 1, 2000.

2. Amortization of the cost of the leased properties for 2000 using the straight-line method and assuming a zero salvage value.

3. Accrual of interest expense at December 31, 2000.

   Selected present value factors are as follows:

Periods	For an Ordinary Annuity of $1 at 6%	For $1 at 6%
1	0.943396	0.943396
2	1.833393	0.889996
8	6.209794	0.627412
9	6.801692	0.591898
10	7.360087	0.558395
19	11.158117	0.330513
20	11.469921	0.311805

(AICPA adapted)

P21-15 Riel Corporation, a lessor of office machines, purchased a new machine for $600,000 on December 31, 1998 that was delivered the same day (by prior arrangement) to O'Hara Company, the lessee. The following information relating to the lease transaction is available:

1. The leased asset has an estimated useful life of five years, which coincides with the lease term.

2. At the end of the lease term, the machine will revert to Riel, at which time it is expected to have a residual value of $60,000 (none of which is guaranteed by O'Hara).

3. Riel's implicit interest rate (on its net investment) is 8%, which is known by O'Hara.

4. O'Hara's incremental borrowing rate is 10% at December 31, 1998.

5. Lease rentals consist of five equal annual payments, the first of which is paid on December 31, 1998.

6. The lease is appropriately accounted for as a direct financing lease by Riel and as a capital lease by O'Hara. Both lessor and lessee are calendar-year corporations and depreciate all fixed assets on the straight-line basis.

Instructions
(Round all numbers to the nearest dollar.)

(a) Compute the annual rental under the lease.

(b) Compute the amounts of the gross lease rentals receivable and the unearned interest revenue that Riel should disclose at the inception of the lease on December 31, 1998.

(c) What expense should O'Hara record for the year ended December 31, 1999?   (AICPA adapted)

P21-16 Laurel Inc. manufactures an X-ray machine with an estimated life span of 12 years and leases it to Grace Hospital for a period of 10 years. The normal selling price of the machine is $343,734 and its guaranteed residual value at the end of the lease term is $15,000. The hospital will pay rents of $50,000 at the beginning of each year and all maintenance, insurance, and taxes. Laurel Inc. incurred costs of $280,000 in manufacturing the machine and $6,000 in negotiating and closing the lease. Laurel Inc. has determined that the collectibility of the lease payments is reasonably predictable, no additional costs will be incurred, and the implicit interest rate is 10%.

Instructions
(Round all numbers to the nearest dollar.)

(a) Discuss the nature of this lease in relation to the lessor and compute the amount of each of the following items:
   1. Gross investment   3. Sales.
   2. Unearned interest revenue.   4. Cost of sales.

(b) Prepare a 10-year lease amortization schedule.

(c) Prepare all of the lessor's journal entries for the first year.

(d) Identify the balance sheet and income statement amounts to be reported on Laurel's first-year balance sheet and income statement, and prepare any required note disclosures.

(e) Assume instead that the residual value is not guaranteed. Identify what changes are necessary in parts (a) to (d) to reflect this situation.

P21-17 Assume the same data as in Problem 21-16 and that Grace Hospital has an incremental borrowing rate of 10%.

Instructions
(Round all numbers to the nearest dollar.)

(a) Discuss the nature of this lease in relation to the lessee and compute the amount of the initial obligation under capital leases.

(b) Prepare a 10-year lease amortization schedule.

(c) Prepare all of the lessee's journal entries for the first year.

(d) Prepare any note disclosures required at the end of Year 1 and determine the balance sheet and income statement amounts that will be reported at the end of the first year.

New Brunswick Electronics Limited (NBEL) recently expanded its local operations by leasing a property in a new industrial park. The site was designed to be attractive to employees and customers, and the modern building was situated on a large landscaped lot. ***P21-18**

On August 1, 1998 NBEL signed a 10-year noncancellable lease for the property. The lease required quarterly payments of $14,098.41, beginning August 1, 1998. At the end of the lease term, the property reverts to the lessor, RL Limited, which estimates a residual value (unguaranteed) for the property of $100,000 at that time. The real estate leased to NBEL was part of a larger development project carried out by the lessor, and the costs allocated to the property on RL's books were $75,000 for land and $250,000 for the building.

In mid-1998, RL estimates the fair value of the property to be $400,000, with the land making up the same proportion of the total value as its cost is to the total costs recorded. RL wants to earn a 10% rate of return on the lease, and this is known to NBEL.

Instructions

(a) Provide calculations to show how RL determined the amount of the lease payment.

(b) Is this a capital lease or an operating lease to NBEL? Explain.

(c) Assume NBEL classifies this as a capital lease and capitalizes the land and building in separate accounts in proportion to their relative costs to RL.

1. How much interest expense and depreciation expense will NBEL report over the 10-year lease?

2. What entry will NBEL make when the property reverts to the lessor?

(d) Assume NBEL accounts for the leased land and building according to Section 3065 of the *Handbook*.

1. How much expense, and of what type, will NBEL recognize and report over the lease term?

2. What entry will NBEL make when the property reverts to the lessor?

(e) Compare your answers to (c) and (d). Discuss.

CASES

On January 1, 1998 Grishell Company entered into a noncancellable lease for a machine to be used in its manufacturing operations. The lease transfers ownership of the machine to Grishell by the end of the lease term. The term of the lease is eight years. The minimum lease payment made by Grishell on January 1, 1998 was one of eight equal annual payments. At the inception of the lease, the criteria established for classification as a capital lease by the lessee were met. **C21-1**

Instructions

(a) What is the theoretical basis for the accounting standard that requires certain long-term leases to be capitalized by the lessee? Do not discuss the specific criteria for classifying a specific lease as a capital lease.

(b) How should Grishell account for this lease at its inception and determine the amount to be recorded?

(c) What expenses related to this lease will Grishell incur during the first year of the lease, and how will they be determined?

(d) How should Grishell report the lease transaction on its December 31, 1998 balance sheet?   (AICPA adapted)

A recent study approached lease accounting from the perspective of whether the lease agreement resulted in the lessee having acquired an asset and liability as defined in the conceptual frameworks of standard-setting bodies such as Canada's. This contrasts with our existing approach that tests whether the benefits and risks associated with ownership were deemed to be transferred from the lessor to the lessee. **C21-2**

Instructions

(a) How would noncancellable operating leases under existing *Handbook* Section 3065 be accounted for under such an approach?

(b) Referring to *Handbook* Section 1000, what support can you find for this approach? Explain.

Amiro Corp. entered into a lease arrangement with Barth Leasing Corporation for a certain machine. Barth's primary business is leasing; it is neither a manufacturer nor a dealer. Amiro will lease the machine for a period of three **C21-3** years, which is 50% of the machine's economic life. Barth will take possession of the machine at the end of the initial three-year lease and lease it to another smaller company that does not need the most current version of the machine. Amiro does not guarantee any residual value for the machine and will not purchase the machine at the end of the lease term.

Amiro's incremental borrowing rate is 16% and the implicit rate in the lease is 14.5%. Amiro has no way of knowing the implicit rate used by Barth. Using either rate, the present value of the minimum lease payments is between 90% and 100% of the fair value of the machinery at the date of the lease agreement.

Amiro has agreed to pay all executory costs directly, and no allowance for these costs is included in the lease payments.

Barth is reasonably certain that Amiro will pay all lease payments. Because Amiro has agreed to pay all executory costs, there are no important uncertainties regarding costs to be incurred by Barth. Assume that no indirect costs are involved.

Instructions

(a) With respect to Amiro (the lessee), answer the following:

1. What type of lease has been entered into? Explain the reason for your answer.

2. How should Amiro compute the appropriate amount to be recorded for the lease or asset acquired?

3. What accounts will be created or affected by this transaction, and how will the lease or asset and other costs related to the transaction be matched with earnings?

4. What disclosures must Amiro make regarding this lease or asset?

(b) With respect to Barth (the lessor), answer the following:

1. What type of leasing arrangement has been entered into? Explain the reason for your answer.

2. How should this lease be recorded by Barth, and how are the appropriate amounts determined?

3. How should Barth determine the appropriate amount of earnings to be recognized from each lease payment?

4. What disclosures must Barth make regarding this lease? (AICPA adapted)

C21-4 On January 1, Barnaby Company, a lessee, entered into three noncancellable leases for brand-new equipment: Lease J, Lease K, and Lease L. None of the three leases transfers ownership of the equipment to Barnaby at the end of the lease term. For each of the three leases, the present value at the beginning of the lease term of the minimum lease payments, excluding that portion of the payments representing executory costs such as insurance, maintenance, and taxes to be paid by the lessor, is 75% of the fair value of the equipment.

The following information is peculiar to each lease:

1. Lease J does not contain a bargain purchase option; the lease term is equal to 80% of the estimated economic life of the equipment.

2. Lease K contains a bargain purchase option; the lease term is equal to 50% of the estimated economic life of the equipment.

3. Lease L does not contain a bargain purchase option; the lease term is equal to 50% of the estimated economic life of the equipment.

Instructions

(a) How should Barnaby Company classify each of the three leases above, and why? Discuss the rationale for your answer.

(b) What amount, if any, should Barnaby record as a liability at the inception of the lease for each of the three leases above?

(c) Assuming that the minimum lease payments are made on a straight-line basis, how should Barnaby record each minimum lease payment for each of the three leases above? (AICPA adapted)

C21-5 Part 1. Capital leases and operating leases are the two classifications of leases described in the CICA Handbook from the standpoint of the lessee.

Instructions

(a) Describe how a capital lease would be accounted for by the lessee both at the inception of the lease and during the first year of the lease, assuming the lease transfers ownership of the property to the lessee by the end of the lease.

(b) Describe how an operating lease would be accounted for by the lessee both at the inception of the lease and during the first year of the lease, assuming equal monthly payments are made by the lessee at the beginning of each month of the lease. Describe the change in accounting, if any, when rental payments are not made on a straight-line basis.

Do *not* discuss the criteria for distinguishing between capital leases and operating leases.

Part 2. Sales-type leases and direct financing leases are two of the classifications of leases described in the *CICA Handbook* from the standpoint of the *lessor*.

Instructions

Compare and contrast a sales-type lease with a direct financing lease as follows:

(a) Gross investment in the lease.

(b) Amortization of unearned interest revenue.

(c) Manufacturer's or dealer's profit.

Do *not* discuss the criteria for distinguishing between the leases described above and operating leases.

(AICPA adapted)

Albert Corporation is a diversified company with nationwide interests in commercial real estate developments, bank- **C21-6**
ing, copper mining, and metal fabrication. The company has offices and operating locations in major cities throughout Canada. Corporate headquarters for Albert Corporation is located in a metropolitan area of a western province, and executives connected with various phases of company operations travel extensively. Corporate management is currently evaluating the feasibility of acquiring a business aircraft that can be used by company executives to expedite business travel to areas not adequately served by commercial airlines. Proposals for either leasing or purchasing a suitable aircraft have been analysed; a leasing proposal is considered to be more desirable than purchasing the aircraft.

The proposed lease agreement involves a twin-engine turboprop Viking that has a fair market value of $900,000. This plane would be leased for a period of 10 years beginning January 1, 1998. The lease agreement is cancellable only upon accidental destruction of the plane. An annual lease payment of $127,600 is due on January 1 of each year; the first payment is to be made January 1, 1998. Maintenance operations are strictly scheduled by the lessor, and Albert Corporation will pay for these services as they are performed. Estimated annual maintenance costs are $6,200. The lessor will pay all insurance premiums and local property taxes, which amount to a combined total of $3,600 annually and are included in the annual lease payment of $127,600. On expiration of the 10-year lease, Albert Corporation can purchase the Viking for $40,000. The estimated useful life of the plane is 15 years, and its salvage value in the used plane market is estimated to be $100,000 after 10 years. The salvage value probably will never be less than $75,000 if the engines are overhauled and maintained as prescribed by the manufacturer. If the purchase option is not exercised, possession of the plane will revert to the lessor, and there is no provision for renewing the lease agreement beyond its termination on December 31, 2007.

Albert Corporation can borrow $900,000 under a 10-year term loan agreement at an annual interest rate of 12%. The lessor's implicit interest rate is not expressly stated in the lease agreement, but this rate appears to be approximately 8% based on 10 net rental payments of $124,000 per year and the initial market value of $900,000 for the plane. On January 1, 1998 the present value of all net rental payments and the purchase option of $40,000 is $800,000, using the 12% interest rate. The present value of all net rental payments and the $40,000 purchase option on January 1, 1998 is $920,000, using the 8% interest rate implicit in the lease agreement. The financial vice-president of Albert Corporation has established that this lease agreement is a capital lease as defined in Section 3065 of the *CICA Handbook*, "Accounting for Leases."

Instructions

(a) What is the appropriate amount that Albert Corporation should recognize for the leased aircraft on its balance sheet after the lease is signed?

(b) How was the 8% implicit interest rate determined?

(c) Without prejudice to your answer in part (a), assume that the annual lease payment is $127,600 as stated in the question, that the appropriate capitalized amount for the leased aircraft is $900,000 on January 1, 1998, and that the interest rate is 9%. How will the lease be reported in the December 31, 1998 balance sheet and related income statement? (Ignore any income tax implications.) (CMA adapted)

On January 1, 1998 Simon Company sold equipment for cash and leased it back. As seller-lessee, Simon retained the **C21-7**
right to substantially all of the remaining use of the equipment.

The term of the lease is eight years. There is a gain on the sale portion of the transaction. The lease portion of the transaction is classified appropriately as a capital lease.

Instructions

(a) What is the theoretical basis for requiring lessees to capitalize certain long-term leases? Do not discuss the specific criteria for classifying a lease as a capital lease.

(b) 1. How should Simon account for the sale portion of the sale-leaseback transaction at January 1, 1998?

2. How should Simon account for the leaseback portion of the sale-leaseback transaction at January 1, 1998?

(c) How should Simon account for the gain on the sale portion of the sale-leaseback transaction during the first year of the lease? Why? (AICPA adapted)

USING YOUR JUDGEMENT

FINANCIAL REPORTING PROBLEM

Mark's Work Wearhouse Ltd. (MWW) reported net income of $3,117,000 and sales for its company-owned stores of $198,262,000 for the 52 weeks ended January 27, 1996. The following balances (summarized) appeared on its January 27, 1996 balance sheet:

Assets	(000s)	Equities	(000s)
Capital assets	$11,853	Current liabilities	$32,769
Other assets	59,204	Long-term debt and deferred credits	6,134
		Shareholders' equity	32,154
	$71,057		$71,057

Aside from a small balance reported as equipment under capital lease and capital lease obligations (averaging a 9.1% interest rate), the company has significant commitments under operating leases as illustrated in Exhibit 21-6 of this chapter. Assume you want to compare a competitor's position and performance with that of MWW. The competitor's operations are similar except that it follows a policy of purchasing property instead of leasing it. You therefore want to capitalize MWW's operating leases for comparison purposes.

Instructions

(a) Calculate the following ratios for MWW based on the published financial statements:

1. Debt-to-equity ratio.

2. Capital asset turnover.

3. Total asset turnover.

4. Return on investment (net income to total assets).

(b) How would the financial statements as presented be affected if MWW capitalized the operating leases? Be specific. State the assumptions underlying your calculations.

(c) Recalculate the ratios from part (a) using the revised numbers determined in part (b). Briefly discuss.

ETHICS CASE

Opcy Corporation entered into a lease agreement for 10 photocopy machines for its corporate headquarters. The lease agreement qualifies as an operating lease in all terms except there is a bargain purchase option. After the five-year lease term, the corporation can purchase each copier for $1,000, when the anticipated market value is $2,500.

Mark Althaus, the financial vice-president, thinks the financial statements must necessarily recognize the lease agreement as a capital lease because of the bargain purchase agreement. The controller, Alicia Greenberg, disagrees: "Although I don't know much about the copiers themselves, there is a way to avoid recording the lease liability." She argues that the corporation might claim that copier technology advances rapidly and that by the end of the lease term the machines will most likely not be worth the $1,000 bargain price.

Instructions

(a) What ethical issue is at stake?

(b) Should the controller's argument be accepted if she does not really know much about copier technology? Would it make a difference if the controller was knowledgeable about the pace of change in copier technology?

(c) What would you do?

chapter 22

ACCOUNTING CHANGES AND ERROR ANALYSIS

Accounting Changes and Error Analysis

Learning Objectives

After studying this chapter, you should be able to:

1. Identify the types of accounting changes.

2. Describe the accounting for changes in accounting policy.

3. Understand how to account for retroactive-with-restatement type of accounting changes.

4. Understand how to account for retroactive-without-restatement type of accounting changes.

5. Understand how to account for prospective-type accounting changes.

6. Describe the accounting for changes in estimates.

7. Identify changes in a reporting entity.

8. Describe the accounting for correction of errors.

9. Identify economic motives for changing accounting methods.

10. Analyse the effect of errors.

Readers of the financial press regularly see headlines such as the following which announce accounting changes and related events:

> "Accounting change aids White Farm."
> "Aeronautical company revises estimates of service lives of Boeing 747s."
> "Deficit would have been $20 million more if firm hadn't altered accounting."
> "AT&T hit by accounting change."
> "Thompson taking $170-million charge."

Why do these changes in accounting occur? First, the accounting profession may *mandate* the use of a new accounting method or principle. For example, in 1996 the CICA for the first time prescribed accounting methods for financial instruments. Second, *changing economic conditions* may cause a company to change its methods of accounting. Third, *changes in technology* and in operations may require a company to revise the service lives, depreciation method, or expected residual value of depreciable assets. AT&T changed both its estimates and its depreciation methods as a result of the changes in its competitive environment and in telecommunications technology.

The accountant also faces the need to make accounting changes when accounting errors are discovered. How should such errors be corrected and disclosed so that the usefulness of the financial information is enhanced? In this chapter we discuss the different types of accounting changes and error corrections, and the procedures for handling them in the financial statements.

ACCOUNTING CHANGES

Before the issuance of *CICA Handbook* Section 1506, "Accounting Changes," in 1980, companies had considerable flexibility and were able to use alternative accounting treatments for essentially equivalent situations. When steel companies changed their methods of depreciating plant assets from accelerated depreciation to straight-line depreciation, the effect of the change was presented in many different ways. The cumulative difference between the depreciation charges that had been recorded and those that would have been recorded under the new method could have been reported in the income statement of the period of the change. Or, the change could have been ignored, and the undepreciated asset balance simply depreciated on a straight-line basis in the future. Or, companies could simply have restated the prior periods on the basis that the straight-line approach had always been used.

TYPES OF ACCOUNTING CHANGES

When alternatives exist, comparability of the statements between periods and between companies is diminished and useful historical trend data are obscured. The profession's first step to clarify this area was to establish four categories for the different types of changes and corrections that occur in practice.[1] Three of the categories deal with types of accounting changes, which are:

> **OBJECTIVE 1**
> Identify the types of accounting changes.

1. *Change in accounting policy.* A change from one generally accepted accounting principle to another generally accepted accounting principle; for example, a change in the method of depreciation from declining balance to straight-line depreciation of plant assets.
2. *Change in accounting estimate.* A change that occurs as a result of new information or as additional experience is acquired. An example is a change in the estimate of the service lives of depreciable assets.
3. *Change in reporting entity.* A change from reporting as one type of entity to another; for example, changing specific subsidiaries that constitute the group of companies for which consolidated financial statements are prepared.

The fourth category also necessitates changes in the accounting, but is not classified as an accounting change.

4. *Reporting the Correction of an Error.* Errors occur as a result of mathematical mistakes, mistakes in the application of accounting principles, or oversight or misuse of facts that existed at the time financial statements were prepared. An example is the incorrect application of the retail inventory method for determining the final inventory value.

Changes were classified into these four categories because the individual characteristics of each category necessitate different methods of recognition in the financial statements. Each of these items is discussed separately to investigate its unusual characteristics and to determine how each item should be reported in the accounts and how the information should be disclosed in comparative statements.

---

[1] *CICA Handbook*, Section 1506.

CHANGES IN ACCOUNTING POLICY

A change in accounting policy *involves a change from one generally accepted accounting principle to another.* For example, a company might change the basis of inventory pricing from average cost to LIFO. Or it might change the method of depreciation on plant assets from accelerated to straight-line, or vice versa. Yet another change might be from the completed-contract to percentage of completion method of accounting for construction contracts.

A careful examination must be made in each circumstance to ensure that a change in principle has actually occurred. *A change in accounting principle is not considered to result from the adoption of a new principle in recognition of events that have occurred for the first time or that were previously immaterial.* For example, when a depreciation method that is adopted for *newly* acquired plant assets is different from the method or methods used for previously recorded assets of a similar class, a change in accounting principle has **not occurred.** Certain marketing expenditures that were previously immaterial and expensed in the period incurred may now be material and acceptably deferred and amortized without a change in accounting principle.

Finally, *if the accounting principle previously followed was not acceptable, or if the principle was applied incorrectly, a change to a generally accepted accounting principle is considered a correction of an error.* A switch from the cash basis of accounting to the accrual basis is considered a correction of an error. If the company deducted residual value when computing declining-balance depreciation on plant assets, and later recomputed depreciation without deduction of estimated residual, an error is corrected.

Three approaches have been suggested for reporting changes in accounting policies in the accounts.

1. **Retroactively.** The cumulative effect of the use of the new method on the financial statements at the beginning of the period is computed. A **retroactive adjustment** of the financial statement is then made, recasting the financial statements of prior years on a basis consistent with the newly adopted principle. Advocates of this position argue that only with restatement of prior periods can changes in accounting principles lead to comparable financial statements. If this approach is not used, the year previous to the change will be on the old method; the year of the change will reflect the entire cumulative adjustment in income; and the following year will present financial statements on the new basis without the cumulative effect of the change. Consistency is considered essential to providing meaningful earnings-trend data and other financial relationships necessary to evaluate the business.

2. **Currently.** The cumulative effect of the use of the new method on the financial statements at the beginning of the period is computed. This adjustment is then reported in the current year's income statement as a **special item** between the captions "Extraordinary items" and "Net income." Advocates of this position argue that restating financial statements for prior years results in a loss of confidence by investors in financial reports. How will a present or prospective investor react when told that the earnings computed five years ago are now entirely different? Restatement, if permitted, also might upset many contractual and other arrangements that were based on the old figures. For example, profit-sharing arrangements computed on the old basis might have to be recomputed and completely new distributions made, which might create numerous legal problems. Many practical difficulties also exist: the cost of restatement may be excessive, or restatement may be impossible on the basis of data available.

3. **Prospectively (in the future).** Previously reported results remain; no change is made. Opening balances are not adjusted, and no attempt is made to allocate charges or credits for prior events. Advocates of this position argue that once management presents

to investors and to others financial statements based on acceptable accounting principles, they are final; management cannot change prior periods by adopting a new principle. According to this line of reasoning, the cumulative adjustment in the current year is not appropriate because this approach would reflect in net income an amount that has little or no relationship to the current year's income or economic events.

Before the adoption of *Handbook* Section 1506, all three of these approaches were used. Section 1506, however, settled this issue by establishing guidelines for each type of change in accounting principle. We have classified these changes in accounting policy into three categories:

1. Retroactive-With-Restatement Type Accounting Change.

2. Retroactive-Without-Restatement Type Accounting Change.

3. Prospective-Type Accounting Change.

RETROACTIVE-WITH-RESTATEMENT TYPE ACCOUNTING CHANGE

The profession established the general requirement that the *retroactive method with restatement of prior periods be used to account for changes in accounting policy*. The general requirements are as follows.

OBJECTIVE 3
Understand how to account for retroactive-with-restatement type of accounting changes.

1. The newly-adopted accounting policy should be applied retroactively.

2. Financial statement amounts for prior periods included for comparative purposes should be restated to give effect to the new accounting policy.

3. The effect of the change on significant items such as net income, earnings per share, and working capital for the current year as well as for prior periods should be disclosed, along with a brief description of the change.

Illustration. Assume that Lang Ltd. decided at the beginning of 1998 to change from the declining-balance method of deprecation to the straight-line method for financial reporting on its plant assets (assume that this change is not being made as a result of changed circumstances, experience or new information). For tax purposes, the company has claimed capital cost allowance which is, coincidentally, equal to the amount of the declining-balance depreciation; this relationship will continue. The assets originally cost $120,000 in 1996 and have an estimated useful life of 10 years. The data assumed for this illustration are:

Year	Declining Balance Depreciation	Straight-Line Depreciation	Difference	Tax Effect 40%	Effect on Income (net of tax)
1996	$24,000	$12,000	$12,000	$4,800	$ 7,200
1997	$19,200	12,000	7,200	2,880	4,320
Cumulative effect			$19,200	$7,680	$11,520
1998	$15,360	$12,000	$ 3,360	$1,344	$ 2,016

The entry made to record this change in accounting policy in 1998 should be:

Accumulated Depreciation	19,200	
Future Tax Liability		7,680
Retained Earnings—Cumulative Effect of Change in Accounting Policy—Depreciation		11,520

The debit of $19,200 to Accumulated Depreciation is the excess of the declining-balance depreciation over the straight-line depreciation. The Future Tax Liability of $7,680 is recorded to reflect interperiod tax allocation procedures. Prior to the change in accounting principle, depreciation and capital cost allowance were the same. However, if the straight-line method had been employed for book purposes in previous years, the excess of capital cost allowance over book depreciation would have created credits to Future Tax Liability that totalled $11,520. The cumulative effect on retained earnings at the beginning of the year in which the change was made results from the difference between declining balance and straight-line depreciation, reduced by the tax on that difference.

The information presented in the **original** income statements prior to the change for 1996 and 1997 is summarized below.

EXHIBIT 22-1 LANG LTD.

SUMMARIZED COMPARATIVE INCOME STATEMENTS FOR THE YEARS 1997 AND 1996

	1997	1996
Income before extraordinary item (assumed)	$120,000	$111,000
Extraordinary item (assumed)	(30,000)	10,000
Net income	$ 90,000	$121,000
Earnings per share		
Basic earnings per share (100,000 shares)		
Income before extraordinary item	$1.20	$1.11
Extraordinary item	(0.30)	0.10
Net income	$0.90	$1.21

Lang's two-year comparative income statements for 1998 and 1997 that follow the change in depreciation method would appear as follows.

EXHIBIT 22-2 LANG LTD.

SUMMARIZED COMPARATIVE INCOME STATEMENTS FOR THE YEARS 1998 AND 1997

	1998	1997
Income before extraordinary item (assumed)	$135,000	$124,320*
Extraordinary item (assumed)	18,000	(30,000)
Net income	$153,000	$ 94,320
Earnings per share		
Basic earnings per share (100,000 shares)		
Income before extraordinary item	$1.35	$1.24
Extraordinary item	0.18	(0.30)
Net income	$1.53	$0.94

*restated ($120,000 + $4,320)

The Statement of Retained Earnings for 1997 would reflect the portion of the cumulative effect of the accounting change not included in the 1997 comparative income statement (the portion attributed to 1996). The same would be true for 1998. This is illustrated in the following comparative statement of retained earnings for 1998.

EXHIBIT 22-3 LANG LTD.

COMPARATIVE STATEMENT OF RETAINED EARNINGS FOR THE YEARS 1998 AND 1997

	1998	1997
Balance at beginning of year As previously reported (assumed)	$483,800	$450,000
Retroactive change in accounting policy (Note 2)	11,520	7,200
As restated	$495,320	$457,200
Net income	153,000	94,320
	$648,320	$551,520
Dividends (assumed)	63,000	56,200
Balance at end of year	$585,320	$495,320

Note 2—Change in Depreciation Method for Plant Assets. In 1998, depreciation of plant equipment is computed by use of the straight-line method. In prior years, beginning in 1996, depreciation of plant and equipment was computed by the declining-balance method. The straight-line method has been applied retroactively to equipment acquisitions of prior years. The effect of the change in 1998 was to increase net income by approximately $2,016 (or two cents per share). The 1997 comparative income statement has been retroactively restated to reflect the effect of the change on 1997 net income (an increase of $4,320, or approximately four cents per share). Income for 1997 and prior periods would have been increased by $11,520, or 12 cents per share.

It should be noted that only the financial statements presented for comparison purposes are restated to show the effect of the change and that any change attributable to those periods prior to the earliest comparative period presented is shown as an adjustment to beginning retained earnings. Other balance sheet accounts affected by the change should also be restated.

RETROACTIVE-WITHOUT-RESTATEMENT TYPE ACCOUNTING CHANGE

Retroactive restatement requires the use of information that may, in some cases, be unreasonably difficult to obtain. For example, if a construction firm wishes to change from the completed-contract method of accounting for long-term projects to the percentage-of-completion method, it would be necessary to obtain the estimated completion costs for each uncompleted project at various preceding year ends. In such cases where the total cumulative effect of a change in accounting policy may be determined but the effect on individual prior periods cannot be reasonably determined, the *Handbook* permits retroactive adjustment without restatement of prior periods' financial statements.

To illustrate the retroactive without restatement method, assume that Denson Construction Limited has accounted for its income from long-term construction contracts using the completed-contract method. In 1998, the company changed to the percentage-of-completion method because management believed it provided a more appropriate measure of the income earned. For tax purposes (assume a 40% rate), the company has employed the completed-contract method and plans to continue using this method in the future.

OBJECTIVE 4 Understand how to account for retroactive-without restatement type of accounting changes.

The following information is available for analysis:

| | Pretax Income from | | Difference in Income | | |
Year	Percentage-of-Completion	Completed Contract	Difference	Tax Effect 40%	Income Effect (net of tax)
Prior to 1997	$600,000	$400,000	$200,000	$80,000	$120,000
In 1997	180,000	160,000	20,000	8,000	12,000
Total at beginning of 1998	$780,000	$560,000	$220,000	$88,000	$132,000
in 1998	$200,000	$190,000	$ 10,000	$ 4,000	$ 6,000

The entry to record the change in 1998 would be:

Construction in Progress	220,000	
Future Tax Liability		88,000
Retained Earnings		132,000

The Construction in Progress account is increased by $220,000, representing the increase in the inventory under the new method. The Future Tax Liability account is used to recognize interperiod tax allocation. If, in previous years, the percentage-of-completion method had been employed for accounting purposes while the completed-contract method was used for tax purposes, a difference of $220,000 between book income and taxable income would have developed, on which $88,000 of tax would have been deferred.

The adjustment for the cumulative effect of the accounting change would be reported in the statement of retained earnings as follows.

EXHIBIT 22-4 DENSON CONSTRUCTION LIMITED

STATEMENT OF RETAINED EARNINGS

	1998	1997
Balance at beginning of year, as previously reported	$1,696,000	$1,600,000
Add: adjustment for the cumulative effect on prior years of applying retroactively the new method accounting for long-term contracts (Note A)	132,000	120,000
Balance at beginning of year, as restated	$1,828,000	1,720,000
Net income (assumed)	120,000	108,000
Balance at end of year	$1,948,000	$1,828,000

Note A—Change in Method of Accounting for Long-Term Contracts. The company has accounted for revenue and costs for long-term contracts by the percentage-of-completion method in 1998, whereas in all prior years revenue and costs were determined by the completed contract method. The new method of accounting for long-term contracts was adopted to recognize (state justification for change in accounting policy) and financial statements of prior periods have not been restated to apply the new method retroactively. For income tax purposes, the completed contract method has been continued. The effect of the accounting change on income of 1998 was an increase of $6,000 net of related taxes and on income of prior periods an increase of $132,000 net of related taxes.

Note that the foregoing example is similar to the case involving restatement of prior periods' financial statements. The journal entries to record the accounting change are similar since the cumulative effect of the change on Retained Earnings is recorded as an adjustment to beginning Retained Earnings. The only difference between retroactive adjustment with restatement and without restatement is in the printed financial statements. Restatement provides financial statement readers with amounts which would have been reported had the new policy been adopted at an earlier date. On the other hand, retroactive adjustment without restatement leaves the comparative financial statements as originally reported and presents the cumulative effect of the change as an adjustment to beginning Retained Earnings. In both examples, as required by Section 1506 of the *Handbook*, the effect of the change on the current year's income is disclosed in the note.

PROSPECTIVE-TYPE ACCOUNTING CHANGE

Retroactive application of a change in an accounting policy may not be possible in some cases because it would be extremely difficult to obtain the necessary financial data. This situation could arise, for example, on the adoption of a new *Handbook* recommendation or legislative requirement of such a nature that the cumulative effect of the necessary accounting change could not be determined without incurring unreasonable cost or using imprecise data. In these rare circumstances, it is permissible to make the required or desired accounting change in the current year without restating the beginning Retained Earnings.

OBJECTIVE 5
Understand how to account for prospective-type accounting changes.

As an example, suppose that a new *Handbook* section requires capitalization of interest on certain long-term construction projects. Those firms with assets that have been constructed in the past and that now qualify for interest capitalization would find it extremely difficult to determine the adjusted cost and accumulated depreciation necessary to apply the method retroactively. In these cases, the *Handbook* permits prospective application of the accounting change. That is, the new accounting policy would be applied in the current and future years.

CHANGES IN ACCOUNTING ESTIMATE

The preparation of financial statements requires an estimate of the effects of future conditions and events. Future conditions and events and their effects cannot be perceived with certainty; therefore, estimating requires the exercise of judgement. Accounting estimates will change as new events occur, as more experience is acquired, or as additional information is obtained. The following are examples of items that require estimates.

OBJECTIVE 6
Describe the accounting for changes in estimates.

1. Uncollectible receivables.

2. Inventory obsolescence.

3. Useful lives and residual values of assets.

4. Periods benefitted by deferred costs.

5. Liabilities for warranty costs and income taxes.

6. Recoverable mineral reserves.

Changes in estimates must be handled prospectively.[2] That is, no changes should be made in previously reported results. Opening balances are not adjusted, and no attempt is made to "catch up" for prior periods. Financial statements of prior periods are not restated and pro forma amounts for prior periods are not reported. Instead, the effects of all changes in estimates are accounted for in (1) the period of change if the change affects that period only; or (2) the period of change and future periods if the change affects both. When changes in estimates are viewed as ***normal recurring corrections and adjustments***, the natural result of the accounting process, retroactive treatment is prohibited.

---

[2] *CICA Handbook*, Section 1506, par. 25.

The circumstances related to a change in estimate are different from those surrounding a change in accounting policy. If changes in estimates were handled on a retroactive basis, or catch-up basis, continual adjustments of prior years' income would occur. It seems proper to accept the view that because new conditions or circumstances exist, the revision fits the new situation and should be handled in the current and future periods.

To illustrate, Salamon Ltd. purchased a building for $300,000 which was originally estimated to have a life of 15 years and no residual value. Depreciation has been recorded for five years on a straight-line basis. On January 1, 1998 the estimate of the useful life of the asset is revised so that the asset is considered to have a total life of 25 years. Assume, for simplicity, that depreciation and capital cost allowance are the same. The amounts at the beginning of the sixth year are as follows.

Building	$300,000
Less: Accumulated Depreciation—Building	100,000
Book value of building	$200,000

The entry to record depreciation for the year 1998 is:

Depreciation Expense	10,000	
Accumulated Depreciation—Building		10,000

The $10,000 depreciation charge is computed as follows.

$$\text{Depreciation charge} = \frac{\text{Book Value of Asset}}{\text{Remaining Service Life}} = \frac{\$200,000}{25 \text{ years} - 5 \text{ years}}$$

The disclosure of a change in estimated accrued revenue appeared in the 1996 Annual Report of Spar Aerospace Limited.

EXHIBIT 22-5 SPAR AEROSPACE LIMITED

12. Writedown of accrued incentive revenue

On an annual basis, the company reviews the present value of estimated future cash receipts related to satellite incentives. Such reviews include the consideration of anticipated insurance premiums and allowances for performance failure. The 1995 review resulted in a writedown of accrued ANIK E incentive revenue in the amount of $4 million.

Differentiating between a change in estimate and a change in accounting policy is sometimes difficult. Is it a change in policy or a change in estimate when a company changes from deferring and amortizing certain marketing costs to recording as an expense as incurred because future benefits of the cost have become doubtful? In such a case, *whenever it is difficult to determine whether a change in policy or a change in estimate has occurred, the change should be considered a change in estimate.* The profession has clarified this problem slightly by recommending that whenever a change is attributed to "changed circumstances, experience or new information" it should be treated as a change in estimate.[3]

A similar problem occurs in differentiating between a change in estimate and a correction of an error, although the answer is more clear cut. How do we determine whether the information was overlooked in earlier periods (an error) or whether the information

---

[3] *CICA Handbook*, Section 1506, par. 23.

is now available for the first time (change in estimate)? Proper classification is important because corrections of errors have a different accounting treatment from changes in estimates. The general rule is that *careful estimates that later prove to be incorrect should be considered changes in estimate.* Only when the estimate was obviously computed incorrectly because of lack of expertise or in bad faith should the adjustment be considered an error. There is no clear demarcation line here and the accountant must use good judgement in light of all the circumstances.

CHANGES IN REPORTING ENTITY

Accounting principles pertaining to a change in the reporting entity are included in various sections of the Handbook. Circumstances often arise such that the entity's financial statements for the current period actually represent the activities of a different entity from that reported on in the prior period. As examples, when two firms merge to form a single continuing entity as a result of a transaction known as a *pooling of interests* or when a *significant business segment is discontinued,* the continuing entity is different from the reporting entity of the prior year. Such circumstances are collectively referred to in this book as a **change in the reporting entity.**[4]

OBJECTIVE 7

Identify changes in a reporting entity.

An accounting change resulting in financial statements that are actually the statements of a different entity should be reported by (1) restating the financial statements of all prior periods presented to show the financial information for the new reporting entity for all periods (retroactive-with-restatement); or (2) reporting the activities of the new entity prospectively from the date of acquisition (disposal) and presenting supplementary pro forma information in a note (prospective).

When a business combination transaction is accounted for as a pooling of interest, "the results of operations for the period in which the combination occurs and for all prior periods should be reflected on a combined basis."[5] Thus, a change in the reporting entity caused by a pooling of interests must be disclosed by retroactive application with restatement of all prior periods.

When an acquisition of another firm has been accounted for as a purchase transaction and the financial statements are consolidated following the acquisition, the resulting change in the reporting entity is disclosed on a prospective basis. That is, the statements of the current and future periods reflect the effect of the change. In addition, if the acquisition takes place on a date other than the beginning of the fiscal period, the acquiring firm must present supplementary information showing on pro forma basis the amount of income that would have been earned had the acquisition taken place at the beginning of the fiscal period.

If a firm disposes of an investment in a firm previously included in the consolidated financial statements, then income from the remaining or continuing operations should be presented on a pro forma basis. The reason for this requirement is that projections of future income are facilitated by data about the earnings of that portion of the accounting entity which is expected to continue operations in the future.

In summary, a change in a reporting entity attributed to a pooling of interests requires retroactive restatement of the financial statements, while a change in a reporting entity that results from either an acquisition or a disposal of subsidiaries is disclosed on a prospective basis with supplementary pro forma information containing the full year's earnings of the continuing entity.

---

[4] The *CICA Handbook* does not define a change in a reporting entity. However, Sections 1580, 1590, 1600, 3050, and 3475 prescribe reporting and disclosure procedures for circumstances in which there has been a substantial change in the entity.

[5] *CICA Handbook,* Section 1580, par.69.

REPORTING THE CORRECTION OF AN ERROR

OBJECTIVE 8
Describe the accounting for correction of errors.

Handbook Section 1506 also discusses how a **correction of an error** should be handled in the financial statements. No business, large or small, is immune from errors. The risk of material errors, however, may be reduced through the installation of good internal controls and the application of sound accounting procedures.

The following are examples of accounting errors.

1. A change from an accounting principle that is **not** generally accepted to an accounting principle that is acceptable. The rationale is that the prior periods were incorrectly presented because of the application of an improper accounting principle. Example: a change from the cash basis of accounting to the accrual basis.

2. Mathematical mistakes that result from adding, subtracting, and so on. Example: the incorrect totalling of the inventory count sheets in computing the inventory value.

3. Changes in estimates that occur because the estimates are not prepared in good faith. Example: the adoption of a clearly unrealistic depreciation rate.

4. An oversight such as the failure to accrue or defer certain expenses and revenues at the end of the period.

5. A misuse of facts, such as the failure to use residual value in computing the depreciable base for the straight-line approach.

6. The incorrect classification of a cost as an expense instead of an asset and vice versa.

As soon as they are discovered, errors must be corrected by proper entries in the accounts and reflected in the financial statements. *The profession requires that corrections of errors in prior period financial statements should be accounted for retroactively,* and be reported in the financial statements as an adjustment to the beginning balance of retained earnings. If comparative statements are presented, the prior statements affected should be restated to correct for the error. The disclosures need not be repeated in the financial statements of subsequent periods.

To illustrate, in 1998 the bookkeeper for Selectric Company discovered that in 1997 the company failed to record in the accounts $20,000 of depreciation expense on a newly constructed building. The capital cost allowance is correctly included in the tax return. Because of numerous timing differences, reported net income for 1997 was $150,000 and taxable income was $110,000. The following entry was made for income taxes (assume a 40% effective tax rate in 1997).

Income Tax Expense	60,000	
Income Tax Payable		44,000
Future Tax Liability		16,000

As a result of the $20,000 omission error in 1997:

Depreciation expense (1997) was understated	$20,000
Accumulated depreciation is understated	20,000
Income tax expense (1997) was overstated ($20,000 × 40%)	8,000
Net income (1997) was overstate	12,000
Future tax liability is overstated ($20,000 × 40%)	8,000

The entry made in 1998 to correct the omission of $20,000 of depreciation in 1997 would be:

1998 Correcting Entry

Retained Earnings	12,000	
Future Tax Liability	8,000	
Accumulated Depreciation—Buildings		20,000

The journal entry to record the correction of the error is the same whether single-period or comparative financial statements are prepared; however, presentation on the financial statements will differ. If single-period (noncomparative) statements are presented, the error should be reported as an adjustment to the opening balance of retained earnings of the period in which the error is discovered, as shown below.

Retained earnings, January 1, 1998:		
As previously reported		$350,000
Correction of an error (depreciation)	$20,000	
Less applicable income tax reduction	8,000	(12,000)
Adjusted balance of retained earnings, January 1, 1998		338,000
Add net income 1998		400,000
Retained earnings, December 31, 1998		$738,000

If comparative financial statements are prepared, adjustments should be made to correct the amounts for all affected accounts reported in the statements for all periods reported. The data for each year being presented should be restated to the correct basis, and any catch-up adjustment should be made to the opening balance of retained earnings for the earliest period being reported. For example, in the case of Selectric Company, the error of omitting the depreciation of $20,000 in 1997, which was discovered in 1998, results in the restatement of the 1997 financial statements when presented in comparison with those of 1998. The following accounts in the 1997 financial statements (presented in comparison with those of 1998) would have been restated.

In the balance sheet:

Accumulated depreciation—buildings	$20,000 increase
Future tax liability	$ 8,000 decrease
Retained earnings, ending balance	$12,000 decrease

In the income statement:

Depreciation expense—buildings	$20,000 increase
Tax expense	$ 8,000 decrease
Net income	$12,000 decrease

In the statement of retained earnings:

Retained earnings, ending balance (due to lower net income for the period)	$12,000 decrease

The 1998 financial statements in comparative form with those of 1997 are prepared as if the error had not occurred. As a minimum, such comparative statements in 1998 would include a note calling attention to restatement of the 1997 statements and disclosing the effect of the correction on income before extraordinary items, net income, and the related per share amounts.

SUMMARY OF ACCOUNTING CHANGES AND CORRECTIONS OF ERRORS

The development of guidelines in reporting accounting changes and corrections has helped to resolve several significant and long-standing accounting problems. Yet, because of diversity in situations and characteristics of the items encountered in practice, the application of professional judgement is of paramount importance. In applying these guides, the primary objective is to serve the user of the financial statements; achieving such service requires accuracy, full disclosure, and an absence of misleading implications. The principal distinction and treatments presented in the earlier discussion are summarized below.

CHANGE IN ACCOUNTING POLICY.

General Rule. Employ the retroactive-with-restatement approach by:

1. Reporting current and future results on the new basis.

2. Restating all prior-period financial statements presented for comparison.

3. Providing note disclosure that describes the change and its effect on the current period's financial statements.

Exceptions. Employ the retroactive-without-restatement approach by:

1. Reporting the current and future results on the new basis.

2. Reporting the cumulative effect of the adjustment in the statement of retained earnings as an adjustment to the beginning balance.

3. Providing a description of the change and the effect of the change on the current year's net income.

EMPLOY THE PROSPECTIVE APPROACH BY:

1. Reporting the current and future results on the new basis.

2. Disclosing the effect of the change on the current year's income.

CHANGE IN ACCOUNTING ESTIMATE.

Employ the prospective approach by:

1. Reporting current and future results on the new basis.

2. Presenting prior-period financial statements as previously reported.

3. Making no adjustment to current period opening balances for purposes of catch-up, and making no pro forma presentations.

CHANGE IN REPORTING ENTITY.

Employ the retroactive-with-restatement approach by:

1. Restating the financial statements of all prior periods presented.

2. Disclosing in the year of change the effect on net income for all prior periods presented.

3. Providing a note that describes details of the entity disposed of or acquired.

Employ the prospective approach with pro forma information (purchases or disposals of subsidiaries) by:

1. Reporting current financial statements on the new basis.

2. Providing pro forma supplementary information of the new income for the full year from the continuing entity.

REPORTING THE CORRECTION OF AN ERROR.

Employ the retroactive-with-restatement approach by:

1. Correcting all prior-period statements presented.

2. Restating the beginning balance of retained earnings for the first period presented when the error effects extend to a period prior to that one.

3. Providing a note that describes the error and restates its effect on the current and prior year financial statements, and that restates prior period financial statements.

Changes in accounting principles are considered appropriate when the enterprise considers the newly adopted generally accepted accounting principle to be **preferable** to the existing one. Preferability among accounting principles should be determined on the basis of whether the new principle constitutes an *improvement in financial reporting,* not on the basis of its effect on income and taxes alone. But it is not always easy to determine what is an improvement in financial reporting. *How does one measure preferability or improvement?* One enterprise might argue that a change in accounting principle from FIFO to LIFO inventory valuation better matches current costs and current revenues. Conversely, another enterprise might change from LIFO to FIFO because it wishes to report a more realistic balance sheet amount for inventory. How does an accountant determine which is the better of these two arguments? It appears that the auditor should have some "standard" or "objective" as a basis for determining the method that is preferable. Because no universal standard or objective is generally accepted, the problem of determining preferability continues to be a difficult one.

MOTIVATIONS FOR CHANGE

Difficult as it is to determine which accounting standards have the strongest conceptual support, other complications make the process even more complex. These complications stem from the fact that managers (and others) have a self-interest in how the financial statements make the company look. Managers naturally wish to show their financial performance in the best light. A favourable profit picture can influence investors, and a strong liquidity position can influence creditors. **Too** favourable a profit picture, however, can provide union negotiators with ammunition during collective bargaining negotiations. Also, if the federal government has established price controls, managers might believe that lower-trending profits might persuade the regulatory authorities to grant their company a price increase. Hence, managers might have varying profit motives depending on economic times and whom they seek to impress.

OBJECTIVE 9

Identify economic motives for changing account methods.

Research has provided additional insight into why companies may prefer certain accounting methods. Some of these reasons are as follows.

1. **Political Costs.** As companies become larger and more politically visible, politicians and regulators devote more attention to them. Many suggest that these politicians and regulators can "feather their own nests" by imposing regulations on these organizations for the benefit of their own constituents. Thus the larger the firm, the more likely it is to become subject to regulations such as the anti-combines regulation and the more likely it is required to pay higher taxes. Therefore, companies that are politically visible may attempt to report income numbers that are low to avoid the scrutiny of regulators. By reporting low income numbers, companies hope to reduce their exposure to the perception of monopoly power. In addition, other constituents such as labour unions may be less willing to ask for wage increases if reported income is low. Thus, researchers have found that the larger the company, the more likely it is to adopt approaches that decrease income when they select accounting methods.[6]

2. **Capital Structure.** A number of studies have indicated that the capital structure of the company can affect the selection of accounting methods. For example, a company

[6] Ross Watts and Jerold Zimmerman, "Towards a Positive Theory of the Determination of Accounting Standards," *The Accounting Review* (January 1978).

with a high debt-to-equity ratio is more likely to be constrained by debt covenants. That is, a company may have a debt covenant that indicates that it cannot pay any dividends if retained earnings fall below a certain level. As a result, this type of company is more likely to select accounting methods that will increase net income. For example, one group of writers indicated that a company's capital structure affected its decision whether to expense or capitalize interest.[7] Others indicated that full cost accounting was selected instead of successful efforts by companies that have high debt-to-equity ratios.[8]

3. **Bonus Payments**. If bonus payments paid to management are tied to income, it has been found that management will select accounting methods that maximize their bonus payments. Thus, in selecting accounting methods, management does concern itself with the effect of accounting income changes on their compensation plans.[9]

4. **Smooth Earnings**. Substantial increases in earnings attract the attention of politicians, regulators, and competitors. In addition, large increases in income create problems for management because the same results are difficult to achieve the following year. Compensation plans may adjust to these higher numbers and therefore make it difficult for management to achieve its profit goals and receive its bonus compensation the following year. Conversely, large decreases in earnings might be viewed as a signal that the company is in financial trouble. Furthermore, substantial decreases in income raise concerns on the part of shareholders, lenders, and other interested parties about the competency of management. Thus, companies have an incentive to manage earnings. Management typically believes that steady growth of 10% per year is much better than 30% growth one year followed by a 10% decline the next.[10] In other words, management usually prefers a gradually increasing income report (often referred to as income smoothers) and sometimes changes accounting methods to ensure such a result.

Management pays careful attention to the accounting it follows and often changes accounting methods not for conceptual reasons, but rather for economic reasons. As indicated throughout this textbook, such arguments have come to be known as "economic consequences arguments" since they focus on the supposed impact of accounting on the behaviour of investors, creditors, competitors, governments, and the managers of the reporting companies themselves, rather than address the conceptual justification for accounting standards.[11]

To counter these pressures, standards setters have declared, as part of their conceptual framework, that they will assess the merits of proposed standards from a position of neutrality. That is, the soundness of standards should not be evaluated on the grounds of their possible impact on behaviour. It is not the Accounting Standards Board's place to

---

[7] R.M. Bowen, E.W. Noreen, and J.M. Lacy, "Determinants of the Corporate Decision to Capitalize Interest," *Journal of Accounting and Economics* (August 1981).

[8] See, for example, Dan S. Dhaliwal, "The Effects of the Firm's Capital Structure on the Choice of Accounting Methods," *The Accounting Review* (January 1980); and W. Bruce Johnson and Ramachandran Ramanan, "Discretionary Accounting Changes from "Successful Efforts" to "Full Cost Methods; 1970-76" *The Accounting Review* (January 1988). The latter study found that firms that changed to full cost were more likely to exhibit higher levels of financial risk (leverage) than firms that retained successful efforts.

[9] See, for example, Mark Zmijewski and Robert Hagerman, "An Income Strategy Approach to the Positive Theory of Accounting Standard Setting/Choice." *Journal of Accounting and Economics* (1985).

[10] O. Douglas Moses, "Income Smoothing and Incentives: Empirical Test Using Accounting Changes," *The Accounting Review* (April 1987). Finding provide evidence that smoothers are associated with firm size, the existence of bonus plans, and the divergence of actual earnings from expectations.

[11] Economic consequences arguments—and there are many of them—are manipulation through the use of lobbying and other forms of pressure brought on standard setters. We have seen examples of these arguments in the oil and gas industry about successful efforts versus full cost, in the technology area with the issue of mandatory expensing of all research and most development cost, and so on.

choose standards according to the kinds of behaviour they wish to promote and the kinds they wish to discourage. At the same time, it must be admitted that some standards **will** often have the effect of influencing behaviour. Yet their justification should be conceptual, not behavioural.

ERROR ANALYSIS

OBJECTIVE 10
Analyse the effect of errors.

As indicated earlier, material errors are unusual in large corporations because internal control procedures coupled with the diligence of the accounting staff are ordinarily sufficient to find any major errors in the system. Smaller businesses may face a different problem. These enterprises may not be able to afford an internal audit staff, nor implement the control procedures necessary to ensure that accounting data are always recorded accurately.[12]

In practice, firms do not correct for errors discovered that do not have a significant effect on the presentation of the financial statements. For example, the failure to record accrued wages of $5,000 when the total payroll for the year is $1,750,000 and net income is $940,000 is not considered significant, and no correction is made. Obviously, defining materiality is difficult, and accountants must rely on their experience and judgement to determine whether adjustment is necessary for a given error. All errors discussed in this section are assumed to be material and to require adjustment. Also, all of the tax effects are ignored in this section.

The accountant must answer three questions in error analysis:

1. What type of error is involved?
2. What entries are needed to correct the error?
3. How are financial statements to be restated once the error is discovered?

As indicated earlier, the profession requires that errors be treated retroactively with restatement and reported in the current year as adjustments to the beginning balance of Retained Earnings. If comparative statements are presented, the prior statements affected should be restated to correct for the error.

Three types of errors can occur: balance sheet, income statement, and balance sheet and income statement errors. Because each type has its own peculiarities, it is important to differentiate among them.

BALANCE SHEET ERRORS

These errors affect only the presentation of an asset, liability, or shareholders' equity account. Examples are the classification of a short-term receivable as part of the investment section; the classification of a note payable as an account payable; and the classification of plant assets as inventory. Reclassification of the item to its proper position is needed when the error is discovered. If comparative statements that include the error year are prepared, the balance sheet for the error year is restated correctly.

INCOME STATEMENT ERRORS

These errors affect only the presentation of the nominal accounts in the income statement. Errors involve the improper classification of revenues or expenses, such as recording interest revenue as part of sales; purchases as bad debt expense; and depreciation

---

[12] See Mark L. DeFord and James Jiambalvo, "Incidence and Circumstances of Accounting Errors," *The Accounting Review* (July 1991) for examples of different type of errors and why these errors might have occurred.

expense as interest expense. An income statement error has no effect on the balance sheet and no effect on net income; a reclassification entry is needed when the error is discovered, if it is discovered in the year it is made. If the error occurred in prior periods, no entry is needed at the date of discovery because the accounts for the current year are correctly stated and accounting records have been closed for the previous years. If comparative statements that include the error year are prepared, the income statement for the error year is restated correctly.

BALANCE SHEET AND INCOME STATEMENT ERRORS

The third type of error involves both the balance sheet and income statement. For example, assume that accrued wages payable were overlooked by the bookkeeper at the end of the accounting period. The effect of this error is to understate expenses, understate liabilities, and overstate net income for that period of time. This type of error affects both the balance sheet and the income statement and is classified in the following two ways—counterbalancing and noncounterbalancing.

Counterbalancing errors are errors that will be offset or corrected over two periods. In the previous illustration, the failure to record accrued wages is considered a counterbalancing error because over a two-year period the error will no longer be present. In other words, the failure to record accrued wages in the previous period means: (1) wages expense is understated; (2) net income for the first period is overstated; and (3) accrued wages payable (a liability) is understated. In the next period, net income is understated; accrued wages payable (a liability) is correctly stated; and wages expense is overstated. For the *two years combined:* (1) total wage expense is correct; (2) net income is correct; and (3) accrued wages payable at the end of the second year is correct. Most errors in accounting that affect both the balance sheet and income statement are counterbalancing errors.

Noncounterbalancing errors are errors that are not offset in the next accounting period. The failure to capitalize equipment that has a useful life of five years is an example. If this asset is expensed immediately, expenses will be overstated in the first period but understated in the next four periods. At the end of the second period, the effect of the error is not fully offset. Net income is correct in the aggregate only at the end of five years, because the asset is fully depreciated at this point. Thus, *noncounterbalancing errors are those that take longer than two periods to correct themselves.*

Only in rare circumstances is an error never reversed, such as when land is initially expensed. Because land is not depreciable, theoretically the error is never offset unless the land is sold.

Counterbalancing Errors. The usual types of counterbalancing errors are illustrated on the following pages. In studying these illustrations, a number of points should be remembered. First, determine whether or not the books have been closed for the period in which the error is found.

1. **The books have been closed**.
   (a) If the error is already counterbalanced, no entry is necessary.
   (b) If the error is not yet counterbalanced, an entry is necessary to adjust the present balance of retained earnings and the other balance sheet account(s) affected.

2. The books have not been closed.
   (a) If the error is already counterbalanced and we are in the second year, an entry is necessary to correct the current period income statement item(s) and to adjust the beginning balance of Retained Earnings.
   (b) If the error is not yet counterbalanced, an entry is necessary to adjust the beginning balance of Retained Earnings and to correct the current period income statement item and any other balance sheet account(s) affected.

Second, if comparative statements are presented, restatement of the amounts for comparative purposes is necessary. ***Restatement is necessary even if a correcting journal entry is not required*** To illustrate, assume that Sanford's Cement Co. failed to accrue income in 1995 when earned, but recorded the income in 1996 when received. The error was discovered in 1998. No entry is necessary to correct for this error because the effects have been counterbalanced by the time the error was discovered in 1998. However, if comparative financial statements for 1995 through 1998 are presented, the accounts and related amounts for the years 1995 and 1998 should be restated correctly for financial reporting purposes.

Failure to Record Accrued Wages. On December 31, 1997 accrued wages in the amount of $1,500 were not recognized. The entry in 1998 to correct this error, assuming that the books have not been closed for 1998, is:

Retained Earnings	1,500	
Wages Expense		1,500

The rationale for this entry is as follows: (1) When the accrued wages of 1997 are paid in 1998, an additional debit of $1,500 is made to 1998 Wages Expense. (2) Wages Expense—1998 is overstated by $1,500. (3) Because 1997 accrued wages were not recorded as Wages Expense—1997, the net income for 1997 was overstated by $1,500. (4) Because 1997 net income was overstated by $1,500, the Retained Earnings account was overstated by $1,500 because net income is closed to Retained Earnings.

If the books have been closed for 1998, no entry would be made because the error was counterbalanced.

Failure to Record Prepaid Expenses. In January, 1997 Hurley Enterprises purchased a two-year insurance policy costing $1,000; Insurance Expense was debited and Cash was credited. No adjusting entries were made at the end of 1997.
The entry on December 31, 1998 to correct this error, assuming that the books were not closed for 1998, would be:

Insurance Expense	500	
Retained Earnings		500

If the books have been closed for 1998, no entry would be made because the error has been counterbalanced.

Understatement of Unearned Revenue. On December 31, 1997 Hurley Enterprises received $50,000 as a prepayment for renting certain office space for the following year. The entry made at the time of receipt of the rent payment was a debit to Cash and a credit to Rent

Revenue. No adjusting entry was made as of December 31, 1997. The entry on December 31, 1998 to correct this error, assuming that the books have not been closed for 1998, would be:

Retained Earnings	50,000	
Rent Revenue		50,000

If the books have been closed for 1998, no entry would be made because the error has been counterbalanced.

Overstatement of Accrued Revenue. On December 31, 1997 Hurley Enterprises accrued as interest revenue $8,000 that applied to 1998. The entry made on December 31, 1997 was to debit Accrued Interest Receivable and to credit Interest Revenue. The entry on December 31, 1998 to correct this error, assuming that the books have not been closed for 1998, would be:

Retained Earnings	8,000	
Interest Revenue		8,000

If the books have been closed for 1998, no entry would be made because the error has been counterbalanced.

Understatement of Ending Inventory. On December 31, 1997 the physical count of the inventory was understated by $25,000 because the inventory crew failed to count one warehouse of merchandise. The entry on December 31, 1998 to correct this error, assuming that the books have not been closed for 1998, would be:

Inventory (beginning-income statement)	25,000	
Retained Earnings		25,000

If the books have been closed for 1998, no entry would be made because the error has been counterbalanced.

Overstatement of Purchases. Hurley Enterprise's accountant recorded a purchase of merchandise for $9,000 in 1997 that applied to 1998. The physical inventory for 1997 was correctly stated. The entry on December 31, 1998 to correct this error, assuming that the books have not been closed for 1998, would be:

Purchases	9,000	
Retained Earnings		9,000

If the books have been closed for 1998, no entry would be made because the error has been counterbalanced.

Overstatement of Purchases and Inventories. Sometimes both the physical inventory and the purchases are incorrectly stated. Assume, as in the previous illustration, that purchases for 1997 were overstated by $9,000 and that inventory was overstated by the same amount. The entry on December 31, 1998 to correct this error, assuming that the books have not been closed for 1998, would be:

Purchases	9,000	
Inventory		9,000[a]

[a]The net income for 1997 is correctly computed because the overstatement of purchases was offset by the overstatement of ending inventory in the cost of goods sold computation.

If the books have been closed for 1998, no entry would made because the error is counterbalanced.

Noncounterbalancing Errors. Because such errors do not counterbalance over a two-year period, the entries are more complex and correcting entries are needed, even if the books have been closed.

Failure to Record Depreciation. Assume that Hurley Enterprises purchased a machine for $10,000 on January 1, 1997, and it had an estimated useful life of five years. The accountant incorrectly expensed this machine in 1997. The error was discovered in 1998. If we assume that the company desired to use straight-line depreciation on this asset, the entry on December 31, 1998 to correct this error, given that the books have not been closed, would be:

Machinery	10,000	
Depreciation Expense	2,000	
Retained Earnings		8,000[a]
Accumulated Depreciation		4,000[a]

[a]Computations:
Retained Earnings

Overstatement of expense in 1997	10,000	
Proper depreciation for 1997 (20% × $10,000)	(2,000)	
Retained earnings understated as of Dec. 31, 1997	$ 8,000	

Accumulated Depreciation

Accumulated depreciation (20% × $10,000 × 2)	$ 4,000

If the books have been closed for 1998, the entry is:

Machinery	10,000	
Retained Earnings		6,000[a]
Accumulated Depreciation		4,000

[a]Computations:
Retained Earnings

Retained earnings understated as of Dec. 31, 1997	$ 8,000
Proper depreciation for 1998 (20% × $10,000)	(2,000)
Retained earnings understated as of Dec. 31, 1998	$ 6,000

Failure to Adjust for Bad Debts. Companies sometimes use a specific charge-off method in accounting for bad debt expense when a percentage of sales is more appropriate. Adjustments are often made to change from the specific write-off to some type of allowance method. For example, assume that Hurley Enterprises has recognized bad debt expense because the debts have actually become uncollectible as follows:

	1997	1998
From 1997 sales	$550	$690
From 1998 sales		700

Hurley estimates that an additional $1,400 will be charged off in 1999, with $300 applicable to 1997 Sales and $1,100 to 1998 Sales. The entry on December 31, 1998, assuming that the books have not been closed for 1998 would be:

Bad Debt Expense	410[a]	
Retained Earnings	990[a]	
Allowance for Doubtful Accounts		1,400

[a]**Computations:**
Allowance for doubtful accounts—additional $300 for 1997 sales and $1,100 for 1998 sales.

Bad debts and retained earnings balance:

	1997	1998
Bad debts expense charged	$1,240[b]	$ 700
Additional bad debts anticipated	300	1,100
Proper bad debt expense	1,540	1,800
Charges currently made to each period	(550)	(1,390)
Bad debt adjustment	$ 990	$ 410

[b]$550 + $690 = $1,240

If the books have been closed for 1998, the entry would be:

Retained Earnings	1,400	
Allowance for Doubtful Accounts		1,400

Comprehensive Illustration: Numerous Errors. In some circumstances, a combination of errors rather than one error occur. A work sheet is therefore prepared to facilitate the analysis. To demonstrate the use of a work sheet, the following problem is presented for solution. The mechanics of the work sheet preparation should be obvious from the solution format.

The income statements of the Hudson Company for the three years ended December 31 in 1996, 1997, and 1998 indicate the following net incomes.

1996	$17,400
1997	20,200
1998	11,300

An examination of the accounting records of the Hudson Company for these years indicates that several errors were made in arriving at the net income amounts reported. The following errors were discovered.

1. Wages earned by workers but not paid at December 31 were consistently omitted from the records. The amounts omitted were:

December 31, 1996	$1,000
December 31, 1997	1,400
December 31, 1998	1,600

These amounts were recorded as expenses when paid in the year following that in which they were earned.

2. The merchandise inventory on December 31, 1996 was overstated by $1,900 as the result of errors made in the footings and extensions on the inventory sheets.

3. Unexpired insurance of $1,200, applicable to 1998, was expensed on December 31, 1997.

4. Interest receivable in the amount of $240 was not recorded on December 31, 1997.

5. On January 2, 1997 a piece of equipment costing $3,900 was sold for $1,800. At the date of sale, the equipment had accumulated depreciation pertaining to it of $2,400. The cash received was recorded as Miscellaneous Revenue in 1997. In addition, depreciation was recorded for this equipment in both 1997 and 1998 at the rate of 10% of cost.

The first step in preparing the work sheet is to prepare a schedule showing the corrected net income amounts for the years ended December 31, 1996, 1997, and 1998. Each correction of the amount originally reported is clearly labelled. The next step is to indicate the balance sheet accounts affected as of December 31, 1998. The completed work sheet for Hudson Company is as follows.

EXHIBIT 22-6 HUDSON COMPANY

WORK SHEET ANALYSIS

	Changes in Net Income				Balance Sheet Correction at December 31, 1998		
	1996	1997	1998	Totals	Debit	Credit	Account
Net income as reported	17,400	20,200	11,300	48,900			
Wages unpaid, Dec. 31/96	(1,000)	1,000		-0-			
Wages unpaid, Dec. 31/97		(1,400)	1,400	-0-			
Wages unpaid, Dec. 31/98			(1,600)	(1,600)		1,600	Wages Payable
Inventory overstatement, Dec. 31/96	(1,900)	1,900		-0-			
Unexpired insurance, Dec. 31/97		1,200	(1,200)	-0-			
Interest receivable, Dec. 31/97		240	(240)	-0-			
Correction for entry made upon sale of equipment, Jan. 2/97°		(1,500)		(1,500)	2,400	3,900	Accumulated Depreciation Machinery
Overcharge of depreciation, 1997		390		390	390		Accumulated Depreciation
Overcharge of depreciation, 1998			390	390	390		Accumulated Depreciation
Corrected net income	14,500	22,030	10,050	46,580			

°Cost	$ 3,900
Accumulated depreciation	2,400
Book value	1,500
Proceeds from sale	1,800
Gain on sale	300
Income reported	(1,800)
Adjustment	(1,500)

Correcting entries **if the books have not been closed** on December 31, 1998 would be:

1. 1996 error has been counterbalanced—no entry necessary

Retained Earnings	1,400	
Wages Expense		1,400

(To correct improper charge of 1997 wages to expense for 1998)

Wages Expense	1,600	
Wages Payable		1,600

(To record proper wages expense for 1998)

2. No entry—counterbalanced

3.
Insurance Expense	1,200	
Retained Earnings		1,200

(To record proper insurance expense for 1998)

4.
Interest Revenue	240	
Retained Earnings		240

(To correct improper credit to interest revenue in 1998)

5.
Retained Earnings	1,500	
Accumulated Depreciation	2,400	
Machinery		3,900

(To record write-off of machinery in 1997 and adjustment of retained earnings. Proceeds from sale $1,800 — gain $300.)

6.
Accumulated Depreciation	780	
Depreciation Expense		390
Retained Earnings		390

(To correct improper charge for depreciation expense in 1997 and 1998)

If the books have been closed:

1.
Retained Earnings	1,600	
Wages Payable		1,600

(To record proper wage expense for 1998)

2. 3. 4. No entry

5.
Retained Earnings	1,500	
Accumulated Depreciation	2,400	
Machinery		3,900

(To record write-off of machinery in 1997 and adjustment of retained earnings)

6.
Accumulated Depreciation	780	
Retained Earnings		780

(To correct improper charge for depreciation expense in 1997 and 1998)

PREPARATION OF COMPARATIVE STATEMENTS

Up to now, our discussion of error analysis has been concerned with identifying the type of error involved and accounting for its correction in the accounting records. The correction of the errors should be presented on comparative financial statements. In addition, five or 10-year summaries are often given for the interested financial reader. The work sheet in Exhibit 22-1 illustrates how a typical year's financial statements are restated given many different errors.

Dick & Wally's Outlet is a small retail outlet in the town of Prescott. Lacking expertise in accounting, they did not keep adequate records. As a result, numerous errors occurred in recording accounting information. The errors are listed below.

1. The bookkeeper inadvertently failed to record a cash receipt of $1,000 on the sale of merchandise in 1998.

2. Accrued wages expense at the end of 1997 was $2,500; at the end of 1998, $3,200. The company does not accrue for wages; all wages are charged to administrative expense.

3. The beginning inventory was understated by $5,400 because goods in transit at the end of last year were not counted. The proper purchase entry had been made.

4. No allowance had been set up for estimated uncollectible receivables. Dick and Wally decided to set up such an allowance for the estimated probable losses as of December 31, 1998 for 1997 accounts of $700, and for 1998 accounts of $1,500. It is also decided to correct the charge against each year so that it shows the losses (actual and estimated) relating to that year's sales. Accounts have been written off to bad debt expense (selling expense) as follows.

	In 1997	In 1998
1997 Accounts	$400	$2,000
1998 Accounts		1,600

5. Unexpired insurance not recorded at the end of 1997, $600; at the end of 1998, $400. All insurance expense is charged to Administrative Expense.

6. An account payable of $6,000 should have been a note payable.

7. During 1997, an asset that cost $10,000 and had a book value of $4,000 was sold for $7,000. At the time of sale, Cash was debited and Miscellaneous Revenue was credited for $7,000.

8. As a result of the last transaction, the company overstated depreciation expense (an administrative expense) in 1997 by $800 and in 1998 by $1,200.

9. In a physical count, the company determined the final inventory to be $40,000.

Presented below is a work sheet that begins with the unadjusted trial balance of Dick and Wally's Outlet; the correcting entries and their effect on the financial statements can be determined by examining the work sheet.

EXHIBIT 22-7   DICK & WALLY'S OUTLET

WORK SHEET ANALYSIS TO ADJUST
FINANCIAL STATEMENTS
FOR THE YEAR 1998

	Trial Balance Unadjusted		Adjustments		Income Statement Adjusted		Balance Sheet Adjusted	
	Debit	Credit	Debit	Credit	Debit	Credit	Debit	Credit
Cash	3,100		(1) 1,000				4,100	
Accounts Receivable	17,600						17,600	
Notes Receivable	8,500						8,500	
Inventories, Jan. 1, 1998	34,000		(3) 5,400		39,400			
Property, Plant and Equipment	112,000			(7) 10,000ᵃ			102,000	
Accumulated Depreciation		83,500	(7) 6,000ᵃ					
			(8) 2,000					75,500
Investments	24,300						24,300	
Accounts Payable		14,500	(6) 6,000					8,500
Notes Payable		10,000		(6) 6,000				16,000
Share Capital		43,500						43,500
Retained Earnings		20,000	(4) 2,700ᵃ	(3) 5,400				
			(7) 4,000ᵃ	(5) 600				
			(2) 2,500	(8) 800				17,600
Sales		94,000		(1) 1,000		95,000		
Purchases	21,000				21,000			
Selling Expenses	22,000			(4) 500ᵇ	21,500			
Administrative Expenses	23,000		(2) 700	(5) 400				
			(5) 600	(8) 1,200	22,700			
Totals	265,500	265,500						
Wages Payable				(2) 3,200				3,200
Allowance for Doubtful Accounts				(4) 2,200ᵇ				2,200
Unexpired Insurance			(5) 400				400	
Inventory, Dec. 31, 1998						(9) 40,000	(9) 40,000	
Net Income					30,400			30,400
Totals			31,300	31,300	135,000	135,000	196,900	196,900

Computations:

ᵃMachinery			ᵇBad Debts	1997	1998
Proceeds from sale	$7,000		Bad debts charged for	$2,400	$1,600
Book value of machinery	4,000		Additional bad debts anticipated	700	1,500
Gain on sale	3,000			3,100	3,100
Income credited	7,000		Charges currently made to each year	(400)	(3,600)
Retained earnings adjustment	$4,000		Bad debt adjustment	$2,700	$ (500)

Summary of Learning Objectives

1. **Identify the types of accounting changes.** The three different types of accounting changes are: (1) change in accounting policy: a change from one generally accepted accounting principle to another generally accepted accounting principle; (2) change in accounting estimate: a change that occurs as a result of new information or as additional experience is acquired; (3) change in reporting entity: a change from reporting as one type of entity to another type of entity.

2. **Describe the accounting for changes in accounting policy.** A change in accounting policy involves a change from one generally accepted accounting principle to another. A change in accounting policy is not considered to result from the adoption of a new principle in recognition of events that have occurred for the first time or that were previously immaterial. If the accounting principle previously followed was not acceptable, or if the principle was applied incorrectly, a change to a generally accepted accounting principle is considered a correction of an error.

3. **Understand how to account for retroactive-with-restatement type of accounting changes.** The general requirement for changes in accounting policy is that the cumulative effect of the change (net of tax) be shown as an adjustment to the beginning retained earnings. Income statements of the affected prior periods presented for comparative purposes are restated to show, on a retroactive basis, the effects of the new accounting policy.

4. **Understand how to account for retroactive-without-restatement type of accounting changes.** When the effects of a change in accounting policy on particular prior periods cannot be readily determined, the cumulative effect of the change (net of tax) is shown as an adjustment to the beginning retained earnings. Comparative financial statements of prior periods presented for comparison are not restated.

5. **Understand how to account for prospective-type accounting changes.** When accounting changes affect only the current and future fiscal periods, the change is accounted for currently and in all future periods. The financial statements should contain a note explaining the nature of the change.

6. **Describe the accounting for changes in estimates.** Changes in estimates must be handled prospectively; that is, no changes should be made in previously reported results. Opening balances are not adjusted. Financial statements of prior periods are not restated, and pro-forma amounts for prior periods are not reported.

7. **Identify changes in a reporting entity.** An accounting change that results in financial statements that are actually the statements of a different entity as a result of a pooling of interests should be reported by restating the financial statements of all prior periods presented, to show the financial information for the new reporting entity for all periods. When there has been a substantial change in the reporting entity as a result of the purchase or disposition of another entity during a fiscal period, pro forma disclosure is required.

8. **Describe the accounting for correction of errors.** As soon as they are discovered, errors must be corrected by proper entries in the accounts and reported in the financial statements. The profession requires that corrections of errors must

be treated as prior period adjustments, be recorded in the year in which the error was discovered, and be reported in the financial statements as an adjustment to the beginning balance of retained earnings. If comparative statements are presented, the prior statements affected should be restated to correct for the error. The disclosures need not be repeated in the financial statements of subsequent periods.

9. **Identify economic motives for changing accounting methods.** Managers might have varying profit motives depending on economic times and whom they seek to impress. Some of the reasons for changing accounting methods are: (1) political costs; (2) capital structure; (3) bonus payments; (4) smooth earnings.

10. **Analyse the effect of errors.** Error analysis involves identifying the type of error, making the proper correcting entries, and properly restating the prior period financial statements. Three types of errors can occur: (1) balance sheet errors: affect only the presentation of an asset, liability, or shareholders' equity account; (2) income statement errors: affect only the presentation of the nominal accounts in the income statement; (3) balance sheet and income statement effect: involves both the balance sheet and income statement. Errors are classified into two types: (1) counterbalancing errors: will be offset or corrected over two periods; (2) noncounterbalancing errors: are not offset in the next accounting period and take longer than two periods to correct themselves.

EXERCISES

E22-1 **(Error and Change in Policy—Depreciation)** Kinosota Ltd. purchased equipment on January 1, 1995 for $495,000. At that time it was estimated that the machine would have a 10-year life and no residual value. On December 31, 1998 the firm's accountant found that the entry for depreciation expense had been omitted in 1996. In addition, management informed the accountant that they plan to switch to straight-line depreciation, starting with the year 1998. At present, the company uses the double declining balance method for depreciating equipment.

Instructions
Assuming that this is a change in accounting policy, prepare the general journal entries the accountant should make at December 31, 1998. (Ignore tax effects.)

E22-2 **(Change in Policy and Change in Estimate—Depreciation)** Komarno Inc. acquired the following assets in January of 1995:

Equipment, estimated service life of, 5 years; residual value, $15,000	$525,000
Building, estimated service life of 30 years; no residual value	$693,000

The equipment has been depreciated using the double declining balance method for the first three years, for financial reporting purposes. In 1998, the company decided to change the method of computing depreciation to the straight-line method for the equipment, but no change was made in the estimated service life or residual value. It was also decided to change the total estimated service life of the building from 30 years to 45 years, with no change in the estimated residual value. The building is depreciated on the straight-line method.

The company has 100,000 common shares outstanding. Results of operations for 1998 and 1997 are shown below:

	1998	1997
Net Income (depreciation for 1998 has been computed on the straight-line basis for both the equipment and buildings[a])	$375,000	$400,000
Income per share	$3.75	$4.00

[a]It should be noted that the computation for depreciation expense for 1998 and 1997 for the building was based on the original estimate of service life of 30 years.

Instructions

(a) Compute the effect of the change in accounting principle to be reported in the restated statement of retained earnings for 1998, and prepare the journal entry to record the change. (Ignore tax effects.)

(b) Present comparative data for the years 1997 and 1998, starting with the income before the effect of accounting change. Prepare pro forma data. Do not prepare the footnote. (Ignore tax effects.)

(Change in Policy and Change in Estimate—Depreciation) Hilbre Corporation owns equipment that originally cost $400,000 and had an estimated useful life of 20 years. The equipment had no expected residual value. **E22-3**
    The two requirements below are independent and must be considered as entirely separate from each other.

Instructions

(a) After using the double-declining balance method for two years, the company decided to switch to the straight-line method of depreciation. Prepare the general journal entry(ies) necessary in the third year to properly account for (1) the change in accounting principle; and (2) depreciation expense. (Ignore income tax effects and assume that this is a change in policy and not a change in estimate.)

(b) After using the straight-line method for two years, the company determined that the useful life of the equipment is 27 years (seven more than the original estimate). Prepare the general journal entry(ies) necessary to properly account for the depreciation expense in the third year.

(Change in Estimate—Depreciation) Morden Co. purchased equipment for $460,000 which was estimated to have   **E22-4**
a useful life of 10 years with a residual value of $10,000 at the end of that time. Depreciation has been entered for seven years on a straight-line basis. In 1998, it was determined that the total estimated life should be 15 years with a residual value of $5,000 at the end of that time.

Instructions

(a) Prepare the entry (if any) to correct the prior years' depreciation.

(b) Prepare the entry to record depreciation for 1998.

(Change in Policy—Depreciation) Killarney Industries changed from the double-declining balance to the straight-   **E22-5**
line method in 1998 on all its plant assets. For tax purposes, assume that the amount of CCA is higher than the double-declining balance depreciation for each of the three years. The appropriate information related to this change is as follows:

Year	Double-Declining Balance Depreciation	Straight-Line Depreciation	Difference
1996	$250,000	$125,000	$125,000
1997	225,000	125,000	100,000
1998	202,500	125,000	77,500

Net income for 1997 was reported at $270,000 and for 1998 was reported at $300,000, excluding any adjustment for the effect of a change in depreciation methods. The straight-line method of depreciation was employed in computing net income for 1998. (Assume that this may be accounted for as a change in policy.)

Instructions

(a) Assuming a tax rate of 30%, what is the amount of the cumulative effect adjustment in 1998?

(b) Prepare the journal entry(ies) to record the cumulative effect adjustment in the accounting records.

(Change in Policy— Depreciation) At the end of the fiscal year 1998, management of Kelwood Manufacturing   **E22-6**
Company has decided to change its depreciation method from the double-declining balance method to the straight-line method for financial reporting purposes. For federal income taxes the company must continue to use the CCA method. The income tax rate for all years is 30%. At the end of fiscal 1998, the company has 200,000 common shares issued and outstanding. Information regarding depreciation expense and income after income taxes is as follows:
    Depreciation expense to date under:

	Straight-Line	Double-Declining Balance
Pre-1997	$400,000	$950,000
1997	150,000	260,000
1998	160,000	275,000

Reported income after income taxes:

1997		$1,200,000
1998		1,450,000

Instructions

(a) Prepare the journal entries to record the change in accounting method in 1998 and indicate how the change in depreciation method would be reported in the 1998 statement of retained earnings. Also indicate how earnings per share would be disclosed. (Hint: adjust Deferred Income Tax account.)

(b) Show the amount of depreciation expense to be reported in 1998.

E22-7 (Change in Policy—Long-term Contracts) Kleefeld Construction Company changed from the completed-contract to the percentage-of-completion method of accounting for long-term construction contracts during 1998. For tax purposes, the company employs the completed-contract method and will continue this approach in the future. The appropriate information related to this change is as follows:

	Pretax Income from:		
	Percentage-of-Completion	Completed-Contract	Difference
1997	$780,000	$590,000	$190,000
1998	700,000	480,000	220,000

Instructions

(a) Assuming that the tax rate is 40%, what is the amount of net income that would be reported in 1998?

(b) What entry(ies) are necessary to adjust the accounting records for the change in accounting policy?

E22-8 (Various Changes in Policy—Inventory Methods) Below is the net income of Libau Instrument Co., a private corporation, computed under the two inventory methods using a periodic system.

	FIFO	Average Cost
1995	$25,000	$23,000
1996	30,000	25,000
1997	29,000	27,000
1998	34,000	30,000

Instructions

(a) Assume that in 1998 Libau decided to change from the FIFO method to the average cost method of pricing inventories. Prepare the journal entry necessary for the change that took place during 1998, and show all the appropriate information needed for reporting on a comparative basis.

(b) Assume that in 1998 Libau, which had been using the average cost method since incorporation in 1995, changed to the FIFO method of pricing inventories. Prepare the journal entry necessary for the change, and show all the appropriate information needed for reporting on a comparative basis.

E22-9 (Change in Policy— FIFO to Average Cost) Manitou Industries utilizes periodic inventory procedures and on Dec. 31, 1998 decides to change from FIFO to average cost. The following information is available in the company records:

		Units	Unit Cost
1997:	Beginning Inventory	3,000	$21
	Purchases: #1	5,000	24
	#2	4,000	30
	#3	6,000	32
	#4	5,000	34
	#5	5,000	36
	Ending Inventory	8,000	
1998:	Beginning Inventory	8,000	
	Purchases: #1	2,000	45
	#2	5,000	47
	#3	5,000	50
	#4	7,000	54
	#5	3,000	56
	Ending Inventory	11,000	

Instructions

(a) State the value at which Manitou Industries reports the ending inventory for 1998.

(b) Indicate what additional disclosures are necessary for this change (both within the body of the financial statements and in notes). Assume a 40% tax rate.

(Error Correction Entries) The first audit of the books of Lundar Company was made for the year ended December 31, 1998. In examining the books, the auditor found that certain items had been overlooked or incorrectly handled in the last three years. These items are: **E22-10**

1. At the beginning of 1996, the company purchased a machine for $510,000 (residual value of $30,000) that had a useful life of six years. The bookkeeper used straight-line depreciation, but failed to deduct the residual value in computing the depreciation base for the three years.

2. At the end of 1997, the company failed to accrue sales salaries of $42,000.

3. A tax lawsuit that involved the year 1996 was settled late in 1998. It was determined that the company owed an additional $80,000 in taxes related to 1996. The company did not record a liability in 1996 or 1997 because the possibility of loss was considered remote, and charged the $80,000 to a loss account in 1998.

4. Lundar Company purchased another company early in 1996 and recorded goodwill of $440,000. Lundar had not amortized goodwill since its value had not diminished.

5. In 1998, the company changed its basis of inventory pricing from FIFO to average cost. The cumulative effect of this change decreased the income of prior years by $68,000. The company debited this cumulative effect to Retained Earnings. Average cost was used in computing income in 1998.

6. In 1998, the company wrote off $84,000 of inventory considered to be obsolete; this loss was charged directly to Retained Earnings.

Instructions

Prepare the journal entries necessary in 1998 to correct the books, assuming that the books have not been closed. The proper amortization period for goodwill is 40 years. Disregard effects of corrections on income tax.

(Change in Policy and Error; Financial Statements) Presented below are the comparative statements for Lorette Company Ltd. **E22-11**

	1998	1997
Sales	$340,000	$270,000
Cost of sales	200,000	142,000
Gross profit	140,000	128,000
Expenses	88,000	50,000
Net income	$ 52,000	$ 78,000
Retained earnings (Jan. 1)	$125,000	$ 72,000
Net income	52,000	78,000
Dividends	(30,000)	(25,000)
Retained earnings (Dec. 31)	$147,000	$125,000

The following additional information is provided:
1. In 1998, Lorette Inc. decided to switch its depreciation method from sum-of-the-years'- digits to the straight-line method. The differences in the two depreciation methods for the assets involved are as follows:

	1998	1997
Sum-of-the-years'-digits	$50,000ᵃ	$40,000
Straight-line	25,000	25,000

ᵃThe 1998 income statement contains depreciation expense of $50,000.

2. In 1998, the company discovered that the ending inventory for 1997 was overstated by $28,000; ending inventory for 1998 was correctly stated.

Instructions
(a) Prepare the revised income and retained earnings statement for 1997 and 1998, assuming comparative statements (ignore income tax effects). Do not prepare notes or pro forma amounts.
(b) Prepare the revised income and retained earnings statement for 1998, assuming a noncomparative presentation (ignore income tax effects). Do not prepare footnotes.

E22-12   (Error Analysis and Correcting Entry) You have been engaged to review the financial statements of Thornhill Corporation. In the course of your examination, you conclude that the bookkeeper hired during the current year is not doing a good job. You notice a number of irregularities as follows:

1. Year-end wages payable of $2,300 were not recorded because the bookkeeper thought that "they were immaterial."

2. Accrued vacation pay for the year of $32,600 was not recorded because the bookkeeper "never heard that you should to do it."

3. Insurance for a 12-month period purchased on November 1 of this year was charged to insurance expense in the amount of $2,160 because "the amount of the cheque is about the same every year."

4. Reported sales revenue for the year is $2,120,000. This includes all sales taxes collected for the year. The sales tax rate is 6%. Because the sales tax is forwarded to the Provincial Minister of Revenue, the Sales Tax Expense account is debited because the bookkeeper thought that "the sales tax is a selling expense." At the end of the current year, the balance in the Sales Tax Expense account is $103,400.

Instructions
Prepare the necessary correcting entries (assuming that Thornhill uses a calendar-year basis).

E22-13   (Error Analysis and Correcting Entry) The reported net incomes for the first two years of Oakbank Products, Inc. were as follows: 1997—$147,000; 1998—$185,000. Early in 1999, the following errors were discovered:
1. Depreciation of equipment for 1997 was overstated $9,000.
2. Depreciation of equipment for 1998 was understated $38,500.
3. December 31, 1997 inventory was understated $50,000.
4. December 31, 1998 inventory was overstated $16,200.

Instructions
Prepare the correcting entry necessary when these errors are discovered. Assume that the books are closed. Ignore income tax considerations.

E22-14   (Error Analysis) Moosehorn Tool Company's December 31 year-end financial statements contained the following errors:

	December 31, 1997	December 31, 1998
Ending inventory	$9,600 understated	$8,100 overstated
Depreciation expense	$2,300 understated	—

An insurance premium of $60,000 was prepaid in 1997 that covered the years 1997, 1998 and 1999. The entire amount was charged to expense in 1997. In addition, on December 31, 1998, fully depreciated machinery was sold for $15,000 cash, but the entry was not recorded until 1999. There were no other errors during 1997 or 1998, and no corrections have been made for any of the errors. Ignore income tax considerations.

Instructions

(a) Compute the total effect of the errors on 1998 net income.

(b) Compute the total effect of the errors on the amount of Moosehorn's working capital at December 31, 1998.

(c) Compute the total effect of the errors on the balance of Moosehorn's Retained earnings at December 31, 1998.

(Error Analysis; Correcting Entries) A partial trial balance of Ninga Corporation is as follows on December 31, 1998:   **E22-15**

	Dr.	Cr.
Supplies on hand	$ 2,700	
Accrued salaries and wages		$ 1,500
Accrued interest on investments	5,100	
Prepaid insurance	90,000	
Unearned rental income		-0-
Accrued interest payable		15,000

Additional adjusting data:

1. A physical count of supplies on hand on December 31, 1998 totalled $1,200.

2. Through oversight, the accrued salaries and wages account was not changed during 1998. Accrued salaries and wages on 12/31/98 amounted to $4,200.

3. The accrued interest on investments account was also left unchanged during 1998. Accrued interest on investments amounts to $4,300 on 12/31/98.

4. The unexpired portions of the insurance policies totalled $74,500 as of December 31, 1998.

5. $26,000 was received on January 1, 1998 for the rent of a building for both 1998 and 1999. The entire amount was credited to rental income.

6. Depreciation for the year was erroneously recorded as $2,500 rather than the correct figure of $25,000.

7. A further review of depreciation calculations of prior years revealed that depreciation of $6,200 was not recorded. It was decided that this oversight should be corrected by a prior period adjustment.

Instructions

(a) Assuming that the books have not been closed, what are the adjusting entries necessary at December 31, 1998? Ignore income tax considerations.

(b) Assuming that the books have been closed, what are the adjusting entries necessary at December 31, 1998? Ignore income tax considerations.

(Error Analysis) The before-tax income for Sarto Co. was $98,000 for 1997 and $75,400 for 1998. However, the accountant noted that the following errors had been made: **E22-16**

1. Sales for 1997 included amounts of $38,200 which had been received in cash during 1997, but for which the related products were delivered in 1998. Title did not pass to the purchaser until 1998.

2. The inventory on December 31, 1997 was understated by $8,640.

3. The bookkeeper, in recording interest expense for both 1997 and 1998 on bonds payable, made the following entry on an annual basis:

Interest Expense	15,000	
Cash		15,000

The bonds have a face value of $250,000 and pay a stated interest rate of 6%. They were issued at a discount of $15,000 on January 1, 1997 to yield an effective interest rate of 7%. (Assume that the effective yield method should be used.)

4. Ordinary repairs to equipment had been erroneously charged to the Equipment account during 1997 and 1998. Repairs in the amount of $8,500 in 1997 and $9,400 in 1998 were so charged. The company applies a rate of 10% to the balance in the Equipment account at the end of the year in its determination of depreciation charges.

Instructions

Prepare a schedule that shows the determination of corrected net income for 1997 and 1998.

E22-17 (**Error Analysis**) When the records of Cromer Corporation were reviewed at the close of 1998, the errors listed below were discovered. For each item indicate by a check mark in the appropriate column whether the error resulted in an overstatement, an understatement, or had no effect on net income for the years 1997 and 1998.

Item	1997			1998		
	Over-statement	Under-statement	No Effect	Over-statement	Under-statement	No Effect
1. Failure to record amortization of patent in 1998.						
2. Failure to record the correct amount of ending 1997 inventory. The amount was understated because of an error in calculation.						
3. Failure to record merchandise purchased in 1997. Merchandise was also omitted from ending inventory in 1997 but was not yet sold.						
4. Failure to record accrued interest on notes payable in 1997; amount was recorded when paid in 1998.						
5. Failure to reflect supplies on hand on balance sheet at end of 1997.						

E22-18 (**Error and Changes in Policy and Estimate—Entries**) Presented below is the net income related to Souris Inc.:

1998	1997	1996
$186,000	$142,000	$224,000

Assume that depreciation entries for 1998 have not been recorded. The following information is also available.

1. Souris purchased a truck on January 1, 1995 for $50,000 with a $5,000 residual value and a five-year life. The company debited an expense account and credited cash on the purchase date.

2. During 1998, Souris changed from the straight-line method of depreciation for its building to the double-declining method. The following computations present depreciation using both approaches. (Assume a change in policy.)

	1998	1997	1996
Straight-line	$30,000	$30,000	$30,000
Double-declining	54,150	57,000	60,000

3. Early in 1998, Souris determined that a piece of equipment purchased in January, 1995 at a cost of $27,000 with an estimated life of five years and residual value of $2,000 is now estimated to continue in use until December 31, 2002 with a $1,000 residual value. Souris has been using straight-line depreciation.

4. Souris won a court case in 1998 related to a patent infringement in 1995. Souris will collect its $20,000 settlement of the suit in 1999. The company had not recorded any entries related to this suit in previous periods.

5. Souris, in reviewing its provision for uncollectibles during 1998, has determined that 1% of sales is the appropriate amount of bad debt expense to be charged to operations. The company had used 1/2 of 1% as its rate in 1997 and 1996 when the expense had been $10,000 and $7,000, respectively. The company would have recorded $9,000 of bad debt expense on December 31, 1998 under the old rate. An entry for bad debt expense in 1998 has not been recorded.

Instructions

For each of the foregoing accounting changes, errors, or prior period adjustments, present the journal entry(ies) Souris would have made to record them during 1998, assuming that the books have not been closed. If no entry is required, write "none." Ignore income tax considerations.

PROBLEMS

P22-1

Sifton Company reported net income of $640,000 for 1997. Its preliminary calculations of net income for 1998 shows $900,000. The books are still open for 1998. Additional information is as follows:

1. On January 1, 1997 Sifton purchased equipment for $880,000. Sifton estimated its useful life to be 10 years with a zero residual value. Sifton uses double declining balance depreciation. On the basis on new information available at the end of 1998, Sifton now estimates the asset's useful life to be eight years. Depreciation expense based on a 10-year useful life has already been recorded in 1998.

2. In reviewing the December 31, 1998 inventory, Sifton discovered errors in its inventory-taking procedures which caused inventories for the last three years to be incorrect. Inventory at the end of 1996 was overstated by $11,000; at the end of 1997, it was overstated by $20,000; and at the end of 1998, it was understated by $19,000. Sifton uses a periodic inventory system and does not have a Cost of Goods Sold account. All information used to compute cost of goods sold is compiled in the Income Summary account. At the end of 1998, entries were made to remove the beginning inventory amount from the Inventory account (with a corresponding debit to Income Summary) and to establish the ending inventory amount in the Inventory account (with a corresponding credit to Income Summary). The Income Summary account is still open.

3. Sifton has failed to accrue wages payable at the end of each of the last three years, as follows:

December 31, 1996	$1,600
December 31, 1997	3,000
December 31, 1998	2,400

4. Sifton has two large blast furnaces that it uses in its manufacturing process. These furnaces must be periodically relined. Furnace A was relined in January 1992 at a cost of $300,000 and again in January 1997 at a cost of $400,000. Furnace B was relined for the first time in January 1998 at a cost of $450,000. All these costs were charged to Maintenance Expense as incurred.

5. Since a relining will last for five years, a better matching of revenues and expenses would have resulted if the cost of the relining was capitalized and depreciated over five years on a straight-line basis. A full year's depreciation will be taken in the year of relining. This change meets the requirements for a change in accounting principle.

Instructions

(a) Prepare the journal entries necessary at December 31, 1998 to record the corrections and changes above. The books are still open for 1998. Income tax effects may be ignored.

(b) Sifton plans to issue comparative (1998 and 1997) financial statements. Starting with $900,000 for 1998 and $640,000 for 1997, prepare a schedule to derive the correct net incomes for 1998 and 1997 to be shown in these statements. Income tax effects may be ignored.

P22-2

On December 31, 1998, before the books were closed, the management and accountants of Hilbre, Inc. made the following determinations about three depreciable assets:

1. Depreciable asset A was purchased January 2, 1995. It originally cost $495,000 and, for depreciation purposes, the straight-line method was originally chosen. The asset was expected to be useful for 10 years and to have a zero residual value. In 1998, the decision was made to change the depreciation method from straight-line to double declining balance, and the estimates relating to useful life and residual value remained unchanged (assume a change in policy).

2. Depreciable asset B was purchased January 3, 1994. It originally cost $120,000 and, for depreciation purposes, the straight-line method was chosen. The asset was expected to be useful for 15 years and to have a zero residual value. In 1998, the decision was made to shorten the total life of this asset to nine years and to estimate the residual value at $8,000.

3. Depreciable asset C was purchased January 5, 1994. The asset's original cost was $70,000, and this amount was entirely expensed in 1994. This particular asset has a 10-year useful life and no residual value. The straight-line method was chosen for depreciation purposes.

Additional data:

1. Income in 1998 before depreciation expense amounted to $410,000.
2. Depreciation expense on assets other than A, B, and C totalled $55,000 in 1998.
3. Income in 1997 was reported at $380,000.
4. Ignore all income tax effects.
5. 100,000 common shares were outstanding in 1997 and 1998.

Instructions

(a) Prepare all necessary entries in 1998 to record these determinations.
(b) Prepare comparative income statements for Hilbre, Inc. for 1997 and 1998.
(c) Prepare comparative retained earnings statements for Hilbre, Inc. for 1997 and 1998. The company had retained earnings of $200,000 at December 31, 1996.

P22-3 Ninga Ltd. was organized in early 1995 to manufacture and sell hosiery. At the end of its fourth year of operation, the company has been fairly successful, as indicated by the following reported net incomes.

| 1995 | $180,000ᵃ | 1997 | 245,000 |
| 1996 | 200,000ᵇ | 1998 | 316,000 |

ᵃIncludes a $12,000 increase because of change in bad debt experience rate.
ᵇIncludes an extraordinary gain of $40,000.

The company has decided to expand operations and has applied for a sizable bank loan. The bank officer has indicated that the records should be audited and presented in comparative statements to facilitate analysis by the bank. Ninga, therefore, hired the auditing firm of Check, Doublecheck & Co. and has provided the following additional information:

1. In early 1996, Ninga changed their estimate from 2% to 1% on the amount of bad debt expense to be charged to operations. Bad debt expense for 1995, if a 1% rate had been used, would have been $12,000. The company, therefore, restated its net income of 1995.
2. In 1998, the auditor discovered that the company had changed its method of inventory pricing from average cost to FIFO. The effect on the income statements for the previous years is as follows:

	1995	1996	1997	1998
Net income unadjusted— average cost basis	$180,000	$200,000	$245,000	$316,000
Net income unadjusted— FIFO basis	195,000	205,000	255,000	300,000
	$ 15,000	$ 5,000	$ 10,000	($ 16,000)

3. In 1996, the company changed its method of depreciation from the accelerated method to the straight-line approach. The company used the straight-line method in 1996. The effect on the income statement for the previous year is as follows:

	1995
Net income unadjusted (accelerated method)	$180,000
Net income unadjusted (straight-line method)	187,000
	$ 7,000

4. In 1998, the auditor discovered that:

(a) The company incorrectly overstated the ending inventory by $11,000 in 1997.
(b) A dispute developed in 1996 with Revenue Canada over the deductibility of entertainment expenses. In 1995, the company was not permitted these deductions, but a tax settlement was reached in 1998 that allowed these expenses. As a result of the court's finding, tax expenses in 1998 were reduced by $60,000.

Instructions

(a) Indicate how each of these changes or corrections should be handled in the accounting records. Ignore income tax considerations.

(b) Present comparative income statements for the years 1995 to 1998, starting with income before extraordinary items. Ignore income tax considerations.

The management of Lenore Instrument Company has concluded, with the concurrence of its independent auditors, that results of operations would be more fairly presented if Lenore changed its method of pricing inventory from first-in, first-out (FIFO) to average cost in 1998. Given below is the five-year summary of income and a schedule of what the inventories might have been if stated on the average cost method.

P22-4

LENORE INSTRUMENT COMPANY
Statement of Income and Retained Earnings
For the Years Ended May 31

	1994	1995	1996	1997	1998
Sales	$13,964	$15,506	$16,673	$18,221	$18,898
Cost of goods sold					
Beginning inventory	1,000	1,100	1,000	1,115	1,237
Purchases	13,000	13,900	15,000	15,900	17,100
Ending inventory	(1,100)	(1,000)	(1,115)	(1,237)	(1,369)
Total	12,900	14,000	14,885	15,778	16,968
Gross profit	1,064	1,506	1,788	2,443	1,930
Administrative expenses	700	763	832	907	989
Income before taxes	364	743	956	1,536	941
Income taxes (50%)	182	372	478	768	471
Net income	182	371	478	768	470
Retained earnings—beginning	1,206	1,388	1,759	2,237	3,005
Retained earnings—ending	$ 1,388	$ 1,759	$ 2,237	$ 3,005	$ 3,475
Earnings per share	$ 1.82	$ 3.71	$ 4.78	$ 7.68	$ 4.70

Schedule of Inventory Balances Using Average Cost Method
Year Ended May 31

1993	1994	1995	1996	1997	1998
$950	$1,124	$1,101	$1,270	$1,490	$1,699

Instructions
Prepare comparative statements for the five years, assuming that Lenore changed its method of inventory pricing to average cost. Indicate the effects on net income and earnings per share for the years involved. (All amounts except EPS are rounded up to the nearest dollar.)

Hartney Corporation has decided that in the preparation of its 1998 financial statements two changes will be made from the methods used in prior years:

P22-5

1. *Depreciation.* Hartney has always used the CCA method for tax and financial reporting purposes but has decided to change during 1998 to the straight-line method for financial reporting only. Assume that the CCA method for tax and reporting purposes has been the same in the past. The effect of this change is as follows:

Excess of CCA Depreciation
Over Straight-line Depreciation

Prior to 1997	$1,365,000
1997	106,050
1998	103,950
	$1,575,000

Depreciation is charged to cost of sales and to selling, general, and administrative expenses on the basis of 75% and 25%, respectively.

2. *Bad debt expense.* In the past, Hartney has recognized bad debt expense equal to 1.5% of net sales. After careful review it has been decided that a rate of 1.75% is more appropriate for 1998. Bad debt expense is charged to selling, general, and administrative expenses.

The following information is taken from preliminary financial statements, prepared before giving effect to the two changes:

HARTNEY CORPORATION
Condensed Balance Sheet
December 31, 1998
With Comparative Figures for 1997

	1998	1997
Assets		
Current assets	$43,561,000	$43,900,000
Plant assets, at cost	45,792,000	43,974,000
Less accumulated depreciation	23,761,000	22,946,000
	$65,592,000	$64,928,000
Liabilities and Shareholders' Equity		
Current liabilities	$21,124,000	$23,650,000
Long-term debt	15,154,000	14,097,000
Share Capital	11,620,000	11,620,000
Retained earnings	17,694,000	15,561,000
	$65,592,000	$64,928,000

HARTNEY CORPORATION
Income Statement
For the Year Ended December 31, 1998
With Comparative Figures for 1997

	1998	1997
Net sales	$80,520,000	$78,920,000
Cost of goods sold	(54,847,000)	(53,074,000)
	25,673,000	25,846,000
Selling, general, and administrative expenses	(19,540,000)	(18,411,000)
	6,133,000	7,435,000
Other income (expense), net	(1,198,000)	(1,079,000)
Income before income taxes	4,935,000	6,356,000
Income taxes	(2,368,800)	(3,050,880)
Net income	$ 2,566,200	$ 3,305,120

There have been no timing differences between any book and tax items prior to the changes above. The tax rate is 48%.

Instructions
For the items listed below, compute the amounts that would appear on the comparative (1998 and 1997) financial statements of Hartney Corporation after adjustment for the two accounting changes. Show amounts for both 1998 and 1997 and prepare supporting schedules as necessary.
(a) Accumulated depreciation.
(b) Deferred income taxes (cumulative).
(c) Selling, general, and administrative expenses.
(d) Current portion of federal income tax expense.
(e) Deferred portion of federal income tax expense.
(f) Retained earnings.
(g) Net income.

P22-6 You have been assigned to examine the financial statements of Kenville Company for the year ended December 31, 1998. You discover the following situations:

1. Depreciation of $2,900 for 1998 on delivery vehicles was not recorded.

2. The physical inventory count on December 31, 1997 improperly excluded merchandise costing $18,000 that had been temporarily stored in a public warehouse. Kenville uses a periodic inventory system.

3. The physical inventory count on December 31, 1998 improperly included merchandise with a cost of $7,000 that had been recorded as a sale on December 27, 1998, and held for the customer to pick up on January 4, 1999.

4. A collection of $5,200 on account from a customer received on December 31, 1998 was not recorded until January 2, 1999.

5. In 1998, the company sold for $3,200 fully depreciated equipment that originally cost $22,000. The company credited the proceeds from the sale to the Equipment account.

6. During November 1998, a competitor filed a patent-infringement suit against Kenville claiming damages of $220,000. The company's legal counsel has indicated that an unfavourable verdict is likely and a reasonable estimate of the court's award to the competitor is $120,000. The company has not reflected or disclosed this situation in the financial statements.

7. Kenville has a portfolio of temporary investments reported as a short-term investment at the lower of cost and market. Information on cost and market value is as follows:

	Cost	Market
December 31, 1997	$84,000	$86,000
December 31, 1998	$84,000	$82,000

8. At December 31, 1998 an analysis of payroll information showed accrued salaries of $12,400. The Accrued Salaries Payable account had a balance of $16,000 at December 31, 1998, which was unchanged from its balance at December 31, 1997.

9. A large piece of equipment was purchased on January 3, 1998 for $24,000 and was charged to Repairs Expense. The equipment is estimated to have a service life of eight years and no residual value. Kenville normally uses the straight-line depreciation method for this type of equipment.

10. A $12,000 insurance premium paid on July 1, 1997 for a policy that expires on June 30, 2000 was charged to insurance expense.

11. A trademark was acquired at the beginning of 1997 for $40,000. No amortization has been recorded since its acquisition. The maximum allowable amortization period is to be used.

Instructions

Assume that the trial balance has been prepared but that the books have not been closed for 1998. Assuming all amounts are material, prepare journal entries that show the adjustments that are required. Ignore income tax considerations.

P22-7 Lyleton Company is in the process of adjusting and correcting its books at the end of 1998. In reviewing its records, the following information is compiled:

1. On January 1, 1997 Lyleton implemented a stock appreciation right (SAR) plan for its top executives. The plan was to run from January 1, 1996 to December 31, 1998. This period was the intended service period and the date of exercise was December 31, 1998. At December 31, 1998 (the measurement date), the executives were to receive in cash the appreciation in the market value of the shares over the three-year period. Using the market prices of the shares at the end of 1996 and 1997 respectively, Lyleton estimated compensation expense of $30,800 for 1996 and $49,700 for 1997. At December 31, however, the market price of the stock was below its price at January 1, 1996.

2. Lyleton has failed to accrue sales commissions payable at the end of each of the last two years, as follows:

December 31, 1997	$4,000
December 31, 1998	$2,600

3. In reviewing the December 31, 1998 inventory, Lyleton discovered errors in its inventory taking procedures which have caused inventories for the last three years to be incorrect, as follows:

December 31, 1996 Understated	$16,000
December 31, 1997 Understated	$21,000
December 31, 1998 Overstated	$ 6,000

Lyleton has already made an entry to establish the incorrect December 31, 1998 inventory amount.

4. At December 31, 1998 Lyleton decided to change its depreciation method on its office equipment from double-declining balance to straight line. Assume that tax CCA is higher than the double-declining depreciation taken for each period. The following information is available (the tax rate is 30%):

	Double-Declining Balance	Straight Line	Pre-Tax Difference	Tax Effect	Difference, Net of Tax
Prior to 1998	$70,000	$40,000	$30,000	$9,000	$21,000
1998	12,000	10,000	2,000	600	1,400

Lyleton has already recorded the 1998 depreciation expense using the double-declining balance method.

5. Before 1998, Lyleton accounted for its income from long-term construction contracts on the percentage-of-completion basis (while using the completed-contract method for tax purposes). Early in 1998, Lyleton changed to the completed-contract basis on its books so it would be using the same method for its books as it uses for tax purposes. Income for 1998 has been recorded using the completed-contract method. The income tax rate is 30%. The following information is available:

	Pretax Income	
	Percentage of Completion	Completed Contract
Prior to 1998	$150,000	$100,000
1998	60,000	20,000

Instructions

Prepare the journal entries necessary at December 31, 1998 to record the above corrections and changes. The books are still open for 1998. Lyleton has not yet recorded its 1998 income tax expense and payable amounts so current year tax effects may be ignored. Prior year tax effects must be considered in items 4 and 5.

P22-8 On March 5, 1998 you were hired by Sprague Inc., a closely held company, as a staff member of its newly created internal auditing department. While reviewing the company's records for 1996 and 1997, you discover that no adjustments have yet been made for the items listed below.

Items

1. Interest income of $13,600 was not accrued at the end of 1996. It was recorded when received in February 1997.

2. A word processor costing $ 8,000 was expensed when purchased on July 1, 1996. It is expected to have a four-year life with no residual value. The company typically uses straight-line depreciation for all fixed assets.

3. Research costs of $30,000 were incurred early in 1996. They were capitalized and were to be amortized over a three-year period. Amortization of $10,000 was recorded for 1996 and $10,000 for 1997.

4. On January 2, 1996 Sprague leased a building for five years at a monthly rental of $8,000. On that date, the company paid the following amounts, which were expensed when paid.

Security deposit	$27,000
First month's rent	8,000
Last month's rent	8,000
	$43,000

5. The company received $33,000 from a customer at the beginning of 1996 for services that it is to perform evenly over a three-year period beginning in 1996. None of the amount received was reported as unearned revenue at the end of 1996.

6. Merchandise inventory costing $17,500 was in the warehouse at December 31, 1996, but was incorrectly omitted from the physical count at that date.

Instructions

Indicate the effect of any errors on the net income figure reported on the income statement for the year ending December 31, 1996, and the retained earnings figure reported on the balance sheet at December 31, 1997. Assume all amounts are material and ignore income tax effects. Using the following format, enter the appropriate dollar amounts in the appropriate columns. Consider each item independently of other items. It is unnecessary to total the columns on the grid.

Item	Net Income for 1996		Retained Earnings at 12/31/97	
	Understated	Overstated	Understated	Overstated

(CICA adapted)

Neepawa Corporation has used the accrual basis of accounting for several years. A review of the records, however, **P22-9** indicates that some expenses and revenues have been handled on a cash basis because of errors made by an inexperienced bookkeeper. Income statements prepared by the bookkeeper reported $31,000 net income for 1997 and $40,000 net income for 1998. Further examination of the records reveals that the following items were handled improperly.

1. Rent was received from a tenant in December 1997; the amount, $1,200, was recorded as income at that time even though the rental pertained to 1998.

2. Wages payable on December 31 have been consistently omitted from the records of that date and have been entered as expenses when paid in the following year. The amounts of the accruals recorded in this manner were:

December 31, 1996	$1,100
December 31, 1997	1,500
December 31, 1998	940

3. Invoices for office supplies purchased have been charged to expense accounts when received. Inventories of supplies on hand at the end of each year have been ignored, and no entry has been made for them.

December 31, 1996	$1,300
December 31, 1997	740
December 31, 1998	1,420

Instructions
Prepare a schedule that will show the corrected net income for the years 1997 and 1998. All items listed should be labelled clearly.

Fraserwood Corporation is in the process of negotiating a loan for expansion purposes. Fraserwood's books and **P22-10** records have never been audited and the bank has requested that an audit be performed. Fraserwood has prepared the following comparative financial statements for the years ended December 31, 1998, and 1997:

FRASERWOOD CORPORATION
Balance Sheet
As of December 31, 1998 and 1997

	1998	1997
Assets		
Current assets		
Cash	$163,000	$ 82,000
Accounts receivable	392,000	296,000
Allowance for doubtful accounts	(37,000)	(18,000)
Marketable securities, at cost	78,000	78,000
Merchandise inventory	207,000	202,000
Total current assets	$803,000	$640,000
Plant assets		
Property, plant, and equipment	167,000	169,500
Accumulated depreciation	(121,600)	(106,400)
Total fixed assets	45,400	63,100
Total assets	$848,400	$703,100

Liabilities and Shareholders' Equity		
Liabilities		
Accounts payable	$121,400	$196,100
Shareholders' equity		
Common shares, no-par value, authorized 50,000 shares, issued and outstanding 20,000 shares	260,000	260,000
Retained earnings	467,000	247,000
Total shareholders' equity	727,000	507,000
Total liabilities and shareholders' equity	$848,400	$703,100

Statement of Income
For the Years Ended December 31, 1998 and 1997

	1998	1997
Sales	$1,000,000	$900,000
Cost of sales	430,000	395,000
Gross profit	570,000	505,000
Operating expenses	210,000	205,000
Administrative expenses	140,000	105,000
Total expenses	350,000	310,000
Net income	$ 220,000	$195,000

During the course of the audit, the following additional facts were determined:

1. An analysis of collections and losses on accounts receivable during the past two years indicates a drop in anticipated losses due to bad debts. After consultation with management it was agreed that the loss experience rate on sales should be reduced from the recorded 2% to 1%, beginning with the year ended December 31, 1998.

2. An analysis of temporary investments revealed that this portfolio consisted entirely of short- term investments in marketable equity securities that were acquired in 1997. The total market valuation for these investments as of the end of each year was as follows:

December 31, 1997	$82,000
December 31, 1998	$65,000

3. The merchandise inventory at December 31, 1997 was overstated by $8,900 and the merchandise inventory at December 31, 1998 was overstated by $13,200.

4. On January 2, 1997 equipment that cost $30,000 (estimated useful life of 10 years and residual value of $5,000) was incorrectly charged to operating expenses. Fraserwood records depreciation on the straight-line method. In 1998 fully depreciated equipment (with no residual value) that originally cost $17,500 was sold as scrap for $2,800. Fraserwood credited the proceeds of $2,800 to the equipment account.

5. An analysis of 1997 operating expenses revealed that Fraserwood charged to expense a four- year insurance premium of $4,240 on January 15, 1997.

Instructions

(a) Prepare the journal entries to correct the books at December 31, 1998. The books for 1998 have not been closed. Ignore income taxes.

(b) Prepare a schedule that shows the computations of corrected net income for the years ended December 31, 1998 and 1997, assuming that any adjustments are to be reported on comparative statements for the two years. The first items on your schedule should be the net income for each year. Ignore income taxes. (Do not prepare financial statements.)

(AICPA adapted)

P22-11   You have been asked by a client to review the records of Rosenort Company, a small manufacturer of precision tools and machines. Your client is interested in buying the business, and arrangements have been made for you to review the accounting records.
    Your examination reveals the following:

1. Rosenort Company commenced business on April 1, 1995 and has been reporting on a fiscal year ending March 31. The company has never been audited, but the annual statements prepared by the bookkeeper reflect the following income before closing and before deducting income taxes:

Year Ended March 31	Income Before Taxes
1996	$ 73,600
1997	114,400
1998	107,580

2. A relatively small number of machines have been shipped on consignment. These transactions have been recorded as ordinary sales and billed as such. On March 31 of each year, machines billed and in the hands of consignees amounted to:

1996	$ 6,500
1997	none
1998	5,590

Sales price was determined by adding 30% to cost. Assume that the consigned machines are sold the following year.

3. On March 30, 1997 two machines were shipped to a customer on a C.O.D. basis. The sale was not entered until April 5, 1997 when cash was received for $6,100. The machines were not included in the inventory at March 31, 1997. (Title passed on March 30, 1997.)

4. All machines are sold subject to a five-year warranty. It is estimated that the expense ultimately to be incurred in connection with the warranty will amount to 1/2 of 1% of sales. The company has charged an expense account for warranty costs incurred.
Sales per books and warranty costs were:

| Year Ended March 31 | Sales | Warranty Expense for Sales Made in | | | Total |
		1996	1997	1998	
1996	$ 940,000	$760			$ 760
1997	1,010,000	360	$1,310		1,670
1998	1,795,000	320	1,620	$1,910	3,850

5. A review of the corporate minutes reveals the manager is entitled to a bonus of 1/2 of 1% of the income before deducting income taxes and the bonus. The bonuses have never been recorded or paid.

6. Bad debts have been recorded on a direct write-off basis. Experience of similar enterprises indicates that losses will approximate 1/4 of 1% of sales. Bad debts written off were:

| | Bad Debts Incurred on Sales Made In | | | |
	1996	1997	1998	Total
1996	$750			$ 750
1997	800	$ 520		1,320
1998	350	1,800	$1,700	3,850

7. The bank deducts 6% on all contracts financed. Of this amount, 1/2% is placed in a reserve to the credit of Rosenort Company that is refunded to Rosenort as finance contracts are paid in full. The reserve established by the bank has not been reflected in the books of Rosenort. The excess of credits over debits (net increase) to the reserve account with Rosenort on the books of the bank for each fiscal year were as follows:

1996	$ 3,000
1997	3,900
1998	5,100
	$12,000

8. Commissions on sales have been entered when paid. Commissions payable on March 31 of each year were:

1996	$1,400
1997	800
1998	1,120

Instructions

(a) Present a schedule that shows the revised income before taxes for each of the years ended March 31, 1996, 1997, and 1998. Make computations to the nearest whole dollar.

(b) Prepare the journal entry or entries you would give the bookkeeper to correct the books. Assume the books have not yet been closed for the fiscal year ended March 31, 1998. Disregard correction of income taxes.

(AICPA adapted)

CASES

C22-1   Napinka Ltd. has recently hired a new independent auditor who says she wants "to get everything straightened out." Consequently, she has proposed the following accounting changes in connection with Napinka's 1998 financial statements:

1. At December 31, 1997 the client had a receivable of $900,000 from KapKim Inc. on its balance sheet. KapKim Inc. has gone bankrupt, and no recovery is expected. The client proposes to write off the receivable as a prior period item.

2. The client proposes the following changes in depreciation policies:

   (a) For office furniture and fixtures, it proposes a change from a 10-year useful life to an eight-year life. If this change had been made in prior years, retained earnings at December 31, 1997 would have been $250,000 less. The effect of the change on 1998 income alone would be a reduction of $50,000.

   (b) For its manufacturing assets, the client proposes to change from double-declining balance depreciation to straight-line. If straight-line depreciation had been used for all prior periods, retained earnings would have been $380,800 greater at December 31, 1997. The effect of the change on 1998 income alone would be a reduction of $4,800.

   (c) For its equipment in the leasing division the client proposes to adopt the sum-of-the- years'-digits depreciation method. The client had never used SYD before. The first year the client operated a leasing division was 1998. If straight-line depreciation were used, 1998 income would be $90,000 greater.

3. In preparing its 1997 statements, one of the client's bookkeepers overstated ending inventory by $250,000 because of a mathematical error. The client proposes to treat this item as a prior period adjustment.

4. In the past, the client has spread preproduction costs in its furniture division over five years. Because its latest furniture is of the "fad" type, it appears that the largest volume of sales will occur during the first two years after introduction. Consequently, the client proposes to amortize preproduction costs on a per-unit basis, which will result in expensing most of such costs during the first two years after the furniture's introduction. If the new accounting method had been used prior to 1998, retained earnings at December 31, 1997 would have been $400,000 less.

5. For the nursery division, the client proposes to switch from FIFO to average cost inventories as it is believed that average cost will provide a better matching of current costs with revenues. The effect of making this change on 1998 earnings would be an increase of $310,000. The client says that the effect of the change on December 31, 1997 retained earnings cannot be determined.

6. To achieve a better matching of revenues and expenses in its building construction division, the client proposes to switch from the completed-contract method of accounting to the percentage-of-completion method. Had the percentage-of-completion method been employed in all prior years, retained earnings at December 31, 1997 would have been $1,250,000 greater.

Instructions

(a) For each of the changes described above decide whether:

   1. The change involves an accounting principle, accounting estimate, or correction of an error.

   2. Restatement of opening retained earnings is required.

(b) What would be the proper adjustment to the December 31, 1997 retained earnings? What would be the effect of the new policies on the 1998 income statement?

Various types of accounting changes can affect the financial statements of a business enterprise differently. Assume that the following list describes changes that have a material effect on the financial statements for the current year of your business enterprise.

   C22-2

1. A change from the completed-contract method to the percentage-of-completion method of accounting for long-term construction-type contracts.
2. A change in the estimated useful life of previously recorded fixed assets based on newly acquired information.
3. A change from deferring and amortizing preproduction costs to recording such costs as an expense when incurred because future benefits of the costs have become doubtful. The new accounting method was adopted in recognition of the change in estimated future benefits.
4. A change from including the employer share of CPP premiums with Payroll Expenses to including it with "Retirement Benefits" on the income statement.
5. Correction of a mathematical error in inventory pricing made in a prior period.
6. A change from prime costing to full absorption costing for inventory valuation.
7. A change from presentation of statements of individual companies to presentation of consolidated statements.
8. A change in the method of accounting for leases for tax purposes to conform with the financial accounting method. As a result, both deferred and current taxes payable changed substantially.
9. A change from the FIFO method of inventory pricing to the average cost method of inventory pricing.

Instructions

Identify the type of change that is described in each item above and indicate whether the prior year's financial statements should be restated when presented in comparative form with the current year's statements. Ignore possible pro forma effects.

Listed below are three independent, unrelated sets of facts relating to accounting changes.

   C22-3

Situation I.

    Pinawa Company is in the process of having its first audit. The company's policy with regard to recognition of revenue is to use the instalment method. However, Handbook Section 3400 permits the use of the instalment method of revenue recognition in circumstances which are not present here. Pinawa's president, Dan Cornish, is willing to change to an acceptable method.

Situation II.

A company decides in January, 1998 to adopt the straight-line method of depreciation for plant equipment. The straight-line method will be used for new acquisitions as well as for previously acquired plant equipment for which depreciation had been provided on an accelerated basis.

Situation III.

    A company determined that the depreciable lives of its fixed assets are too long at present to fairly match the cost of the fixed assets with the revenue produced. The company decided at the beginning of the current year to reduce the depreciable lives of all of its existing fixed assets by five years.

Instructions

For each of the situations described, provide the information indicated below:
(a) Type of accounting change.
(b) Manner of reporting the change under current generally accepted accounting principles including a discussion, where applicable, of how amounts are computed.
(c) Effect of the change on the balance sheet and income statement.

Katherine Mitchell, controller of Laurier Corp., is aware that there is a handbook section on accounting changes. After reading the section, she is confused and is not sure what action should be taken on the following items related to Laurier Corp. for the year 1998:

   C22-4

1. In 1998, Laurier decided to change the company's policy on accounting for certain marketing costs. Previously, the company had chosen to defer and amortize all marketing costs over at least five years because Laurier believed that a return on these expenditures did not occur immediately. Recently, however, the time differential has considerably shortened, and Laurier is now expensing the marketing costs as incurred.
2. In 1998, the company examined its entire policy relating to the depreciation of plant equipment. Plant equipment had normally been depreciated over a 15-year period, but recent experience has indicated that the company was incorrect in its estimates and that the assets should be depreciated over a 20-year period.

3. One division of Laurier Corp., Mafeking Ltd. has consistently shown an increasing net income from period to period. On closer examination of their operating statement, it is noted that bad debt expense and inventory obsolescence charges are much lower than in other divisions. In discussing this with the controller of this division, it is learned that the controller has increased his net income each period by knowingly making low estimates related to the write-off of receivables and inventory.

4. In 1998, the company purchased new machinery that should increase production dramatically. The company has decided to depreciate this machinery on an accelerated basis, even though other machinery is depreciated on a straight-line basis.

5. All equipment sold by Laurier is subject to a three-year warranty. It has been estimated that the expense ultimately to be incurred on these machines is 1% of sales. In 1998, because of a production breakthrough, it is now estimated that 1/2 of 1% of sales is sufficient. In 1996 and 1997, warranty expense was computed as $55,000 and $60,000, respectively. The company now believes that these warranty costs should be reduced by 50%.

6. In 1998, the company decided to change its method of inventory pricing from average cost to the FIFO method. The effect of this change on prior years is to increase 1996 income by $60,000 and increase 1997 income by $20,000.

Instructions

Katherine Mitchell has come to you, her accountant, for advice about the situations above. Indicate the appropriate accounting treatment that should be given each of these situations.

C22-5 Waskada Manufacturing is preparing its year-end financial statements. The controller, Judy Forest, is confronted with several decisions about statement presentation with regard to the following items:

1. The Vice-President of Sales has indicated that one product line has lost its customer appeal and will be phased out over the next three years. Therefore, a decision has been made to lower the estimated lives on related production equipment from the remaining five years to three years.

2. Estimating the lives of new products in the Leisure Products Division has become very difficult due to the highly competitive conditions in this market. Therefore, the practice of deferring and amortizing preproduction costs has been abandoned in favour of expensing such costs as they are incurred.

3. The Hightone Building was converted from a sales office to offices for the Accounting Department at the beginning of this year. Therefore, the expense related to this building will now appear as an administrative expense rather than a selling expense on the current year's income statement.

4. When the year-end physical inventory adjustment was made for the current year, the prior year's physical inventory sheets for an entire warehouse were discovered to have been mislaid and excluded from last year's count.

5. The method of accounting used for financial reporting purposes for certain receivables has been approved for tax purposes during the current tax year by Revenue Canada. This change for tax purposes will cause both deferred and current taxes payable to change substantially.

6. Management has decided to switch from the FIFO inventory valuation method to the average cost inventory valuation method for all inventories.

7. Waskada's Custom Division manufactures large-scale custom designed machinery on a contract basis. Management decided to switch from the completed-contract method to the percentage-of-completion method of accounting for long-term contracts.

Instructions

(a) CICA Handbook Section 1506, "Accounting Changes," identifies three types of accounting changes: changes in accounting policy, changes in accounting estimates, and changes due to error. For each of these three types of accounting changes:

1. Define the type of change.

2. Explain the general accounting treatment required according to Handbook Section 1506 with respect to the current year and prior years' financial statements.

3. Discuss the impact of the changes on the external auditor's report.

(b) For each of the seven changes Waskada Manufacturing has made in the current year, identify and explain whether the change is a change in accounting principle, in estimate, in entity, or due to error. If any of the changes is not one of these four types, explain why.

(CMA adapted)

USING YOUR JUDGEMENT

FINANCIAL REPORTING PROBLEM

Using the financial statements and accompanying notes from Moore Corporation's 1995 Annual Report as presented in Appendix 5A, answer the following questions or instructions.

1. Identify changes in accounting policy, if any, reported by Moore Corporation during the three years covered by its income statements (1993 - 1995).

2. For each change in accounting policy, identify, if possible, the effect on opening retained earnings and operating results in the year of change. If it is not possible to determine the effect of the change(s), describe how the change(s) would affect opening retained earnings and income.

3. Identify any significant estimates made by Moore Corporation during 1993 - 1995. Have these estimates been revised?

ETHICS CASE

Andy Stahl is an audit senior of a large public accounting firm who has just been assigned to the Carman Corporation's annual audit engagement, which has been a client of Andy's firm for many years. Carman is a fast-growing business in the commercial construction industry. In reviewing the fixed asset ledger, Andy discovered a series of unusual accounting changes, in which the useful lives of assets, depreciated using the straight-line method, were substantially lowered near the midpoint of the original estimate. For example, the useful life of one dump truck was changed from 10 years to 6 years during the fifth year of service. Upon further investigation, Andy was told by Fred Martin, Carman's accounting manager, "I don't really see your problem. After all, it is perfectly legal to change an accounting estimate. Besides, our CEO likes to see big earnings!"

Instructions

(a) What are the ethical issues concerning Carman's practice of changing the useful lives of fixed assets?

(b) Who could be harmed by Carman's unusual accounting changes?

(c) What should Andy Stahl do in this situation?

PREPARATION AND ANALYSIS OF FINANCIAL STATEMENTS

part

6

chapter 23

STATEMENT OF CASH FLOWS

CHAPTER 23

Statement of Cash Flows

Learning Objectives

After studying this chapter, you should be able to:

1. Describe the evolution and objectives of the statement of cash flows.

2. Define cash and cash equivalents.

3. Identify the major classifications of cash flows and explain the significance of each type.

4. Identify how business transactions and events are classified and reported on the statement of cash flows.

5. Contrast the direct and indirect methods of calculating net cash flow from operating activities.

6. Differentiate between net income and net cash flows from operations.

7. Prepare a statement of cash flows.

8. Identify the financial reporting and disclosure requirements for the statement of cash flows.

9. Use a worksheet to prepare a statement of cash flows (Appendix 23A).

10. Use T-accounts to prepare a statement of cash flows (Appendix 23A).

INTRODUCTION TO CASH FLOW STATEMENTS

Will the company continue to be able to pay dividends? Where will it get the cash to meet the debt coming due? How did Imperial Oil Ltd. finance the large investment it made to acquire Texaco Canada? How did Campeau Corp. finance the $6.58 billion required to purchase Federated Department Stores Inc.? How did Gandalf Technologies finance its operations while reporting large accumulated deficits? How did The Molson Companies Limited end up in such an enviable cash position in 1996 after reporting such a significant loss that year?

These are the types of questions often asked by investors, creditors, and internal managers who are interested in the financial operations of a business enterprise. An examination of the balance sheet, income statement, and statement of retained earnings, however, often fails to provide ready answers to such questions. That is why companies are required to prepare a fourth primary financial statement—the statement of cash flows.

EVOLUTION OF THE STATEMENT OF CASH FLOWS

The history of the statement of cash flows is an interesting example of how accounting evolves to meet the needs of financial statement users. The statement originated as a simple analysis called the "Where-Got and Where-Gone Statement" that consisted of nothing more than a list of the increases and decreases in the company's balance sheet items. After

OBJECTIVE 1
Describe the evolution and objectives of the statement of cash flows.

some years, the title of this statement was changed to the "funds statement." In 1961, the AICPA, recognizing the significance of this statement, sponsored research in this area that resulted in the publication of *Accounting Research Study No. 2*: " 'Cash Flow' Analysis and the Funds Statement."[1] This study recommended that the funds statement be included in all annual reports to the shareholders and that it be covered by the auditor's opinion.

Prior to 1974 in Canada, this statement was known as the "Statement of Source and Application of Funds." In 1974, the CICA revised and expanded Section 1540 of the *Handbook*, changing the statement's title to "Statement of Changes in Financial Position." The objective for this statement was to provide information on how the activities of the enterprise had been financed and how its financial resources had been used during the period covered by the statement. Accordingly, the statement summarized the sources and uses of funds, and provided details of how funds were acquired by the company (through borrowings, sales of assets, etc.) and how they were used (to retire debt, purchase assets, etc.). Companies were permitted to use various definitions of "funds"; *working capital* — the excess of current assets over current liabilities — was the most common.

In 1985, an important revision to Section 1540 was released that changed the objective of the statement. It was now intended to provide information about the operating, financing, and investing activities of the entity, and the effects of these activities on its cash resources. The change in emphasis from providing information about changes in *financial resources* to providing information about changes in *cash resources* had important implications for accountants.

Why the change from an emphasis on working capital to one on cash? The answer lies in what was happening in the financial reporting environment. One major reason was that investors and analysts were concerned that *accrual accounting had become far removed from the underlying cash flows of the enterprise.*[2] They contended that accountants were using too many arbitrary allocation devices (deferred taxes, depreciation, amortization of intangibles, accrual of revenues, etc.) and were therefore computing a net income figure that no longer provided an acceptable indicator of the enterprise's earning power. Similarly, *because financial statements take no cognizance of inflation, many looked for a more concrete standard, such as cash flow, to evaluate operating success or failure.* In addition, others contended that the *working capital basis does not provide as useful information about liquidity and financial flexibility as does the cash basis.* Frequently, receivable and inventory mismanagement leads to a lack of liquidity that a statement focusing on working capital would not uncover.[3]

Finally, a statement of cash flows was determined to be more useful to management and short-term creditors in *assessing the enterprise's ability to meet cash operating needs.* The chairman of one bank noted, "Well, assets give you a warm feeling, but they don't generate cash. The first question I would ask any borrower these days is, 'What is your break-even cash flow?' That's the one thing we can't find out from your audit reports and it is the single most important question we ask."

The change in focus to reporting cash flows in the statement of changes in financial position was widely accepted by preparers and users of financial statements and standard setters in most countries around the world. Differing jurisdictions, however, recom-

---

[1] Perry Mason, "'Cash Flow' Analysis and the Funds Statement," *Accounting Research Study No. 2* (New York: AICPA, 1961).

[2] See "Where's the Cash?" *Forbes,* April 8, 1985, p. 120. Three reasons cited for the rising importance of cash flow analysis were: (1) the high and continuing debt levels of many companies; (2) the trend over the previous 20 years toward capitalizing and deferring more expenses; and (3) a wave of corporate bankruptcies in the early 1980s.

[3] The classic example of such a problem is W.T. Grant (a large U.S. retailer), which reported reasonable amounts of working capital provided by operations. However, too much of its working capital was tied up in receivables and inventories. A review of its net cash flow from operating activity would have shown the significant lack of liquidity and financial flexibility that eventually caused the company's bankruptcy.

mended different accounting and reporting treatment of such aspects as the definition of cash and cash equivalents; the treatment of noncash financing and investing activities; the classification of cash flows among the operating, investing, and financing categories; how to report cash flows from operations; and specific disclosure requirements. Because of the significant number of Canadian companies that raised capital in the United States and other major countries, and the increased globalization of world capital markets in general, the commitment of the CICA and its AcSB to the harmonization of accounting standards through their membership in the International Accounting Standards Committee (IASC) grew.

In 1996, the AcSB issued an exposure draft that proposed to adopt IAS 7, "Cash Flow Statements," as a replacement for the existing requirements of *Handbook* Section 1540.[4] The acceptance of IAS 7 by the U.S. Securities and Exchange Commission for cash flow statements provided by foreign registrants and the endorsement of IAS 7 by the International Organization of Securities Commissions influenced the AcSB decision to put the international standard forward as the recommended Canadian position. The exposure draft clarifies and changes some of the existing requirements, and makes compulsory the inclusion of a cash flow statement in any set of financial statements prepared according to GAAP.[5]

At the time of writing, the final standard had not yet been approved by the Accounting Standards Board. The following discussion assumes that the positions articulated in the 1996 *Exposure Draft* are carried forward to a revised *Handbook* Section 1540.

OBJECTIVES OF THE STATEMENT OF CASH FLOWS

Regardless of the type of entity, organizations need cash to carry out their operations, to meet their obligations, and to provide returns to their investors. Investors and creditors, in making economic decisions related to an entity, need information to allow them to evaluate the organization's ability to generate cash, and to assess the timing and the degree of certainty of those cash flows. Financial statement users must also evaluate the needs of the organization for cash and the purposes to which it will be put. To this end, the objective of Section 1540 is to require the provision of information about the historical changes in cash (and cash equivalents) of an enterprise by means of a cash flow statement. This statement classifies cash flows during the period according to whether they flow from operating, investing, or financing activities.[6]

According to the Accounting Standards Board, the information provided in a cash flow statement, when used with related disclosures and information in the other financial statements, should help investors, creditors, and others to:

1. Evaluate changes in the net assets of an enterprise and in its financial structure, including its liquidity and solvency.

2. Evaluate the organization's ability to affect the amounts and timing of cash flows in order to adapt to changing circumstances and opportunities.

3. Assess the ability of an enterprise to generate cash, which enables users to develop models to compare the present value of the future cash flows of different enterprises. Historical cash flow information is often useful as an indicator of the amount, the timing, and the certainty of future cash flows.

---

[4] Except for minor changes to reflect existing Canadian standards and terminology, the *Exposure Draft* mirrors the international standard.

[5] Although the 1985 changes to *Handbook* Section 1540 did not explicitly require all firms to present a statement of changes in financial position with their financial statements, it was required of companies that operated under the jurisdiction of the Canada Business Corporations Act.

[6] CICA *Exposure Draft* (May 1996) on Cash Flow Statements to replace *Handbook Section* 1540, par. .01.

4. Compare the reporting of operating performance across companies by eliminating the effects of using different accounting treatments for the same transactions and events.

5. Check the accuracy of past assessments of future cash flows.

6. Examine the relationship between profitability and net cash flow, and the impact of changing prices.[7]

Because the statement of cash flows reports cash receipts, cash payments, and the net change in cash that results from the operating, investing, and financing activities of an enterprise during a period, in a format that reconciles the beginning and ending cash balances, the statement helps to explain how it is possible to report a net loss and still make a large capital expenditure or pay dividends. It will indicate whether the company issued or retired debt or shares, or both, permitting a quick assessment of any change in capital structure during the period.

Reporting the net increase or decrease in cash is considered useful because investors, creditors, and other interested parties want to know and can generally comprehend what is happening to a company's most liquid resource — its cash. A cash flow statement is useful because it provides answers to the following simple but important questions about the enterprise:

1. Where did the cash come from during the period?

2. For what purpose was the cash used during the period?

3. What was the change in the cash balance during the period?

WHAT IS CASH?

As part of a company's cash management system, short-term investments are often held instead of cash, thereby allowing the company to earn a return on cash balances in excess of its immediate needs. Also, it is common for an organization to have an agreement with the bank that permits the cash balance to fluctuate between a positive balance and an overdraft. Because an entity's cash activity and position are more appropriately described by the inclusion of these other cash management activities, the AcSB recommends that **cash flows** be defined as inflows and outflows of cash and cash equivalents.[8]

OBJECTIVE 2
Define cash and cash equivalents.

Cash is defined as cash on hand and demand deposits. **Cash equivalents** are short-term, highly liquid investments that are readily convertible to known amounts of cash and which are subject to an insignificant risk of changes in value.[9] Nonequity investments acquired with short maturities and bank overdrafts repayable on demand, both of which result from and are an integral part of an organization's cash management policies, would be included in cash and cash equivalents.[10]

Throughout the discussion and illustrations in this chapter, the use of the term "cash" should be interpreted to mean "cash and cash equivalents."

CLASSIFICATION AND INTERPRETATION OF CASH FLOW INFORMATION

OBJECTIVE 3
Identify the major classifications of cash flows and explain the significance of each type.

The cash flows reported on a cash flow statement should be classified according to the three major activities in which the management of an organization engages: operating, investing, and financing activities. Transactions and events characteristic of each kind of activity and the significance of each type of cash flow are as follows.

---

[7] *Ibid.*, pars. .04 and .05.

[8] *Ibid.*, par. .06(c).

[9] *Ibid.*, pars. .06(a) and (b).

[10] *Ibid.*, par. .07 suggests a maturity "of, say, three months or less from the date of acquisition." Examples of cash equivalents are treasury bills, commercial paper, and money market funds purchased with cash that is in excess of immediate needs.

1. **Operating activities** are the principal revenue-producing activities of the enterprise and other activities that are not investing or financing activities.[11] Operating flows generally involve the cash effects of transactions that enter into the determination of net income and usually affect current asset and current liability (i.e., working capital) accounts: collections from customers on accounts receivable; and payments to suppliers on accounts payable, to Revenue Canada on income taxes payable, and to employees on salaries and wages payable.

   The level of cash provided from or used in operations is a key indicator for users of the financial statements. Like blood flowing through the veins and arteries of our bodies, operating cash flows—derived mainly from receipts from customers—are needed to maintain the organization's systems: to meet payrolls, to pay suppliers, to cover rentals and insurance, and to pay taxes. In addition, surplus flows from operations are needed to repay loans, to take advantage of new investment opportunities, and to pay dividends without having to seek new external financing.

   Users must exercise care in interpreting operating cash flows, however. Companies in a developmental or growth stage will usually use more cash in their operating activities than they generate from customers, a situation that should reverse as the life cycle of the business matures. Users of financial statements should also look beyond the amount of cash generated or used in operations, and analyse the reasons for the cash flows. Were collections on accounts receivable at an all-time high and accounts payable stretched to their limits? If so, the operating cash flows in the period under review may not be indicative of replicable operating cash flows.

2. **Investing activities** cover the acquisition and disposal of long-term assets and other investments not included in cash equivalents.[12]

   The use of cash in investment activities tells the financial statement reader whether the entity is ploughing cash back into additional long-term assets that will generate profits and increased cash flows in the future, or whether the stock of long-term productive assets is being decreased by conversion into cash. Information about the type of investment being made is useful to readers as well, as it makes a difference to the future of a company whether it is investing in productive operating assets or in more passive types of investments.

3. **Financing activities** are activities that result in changes in the size and composition of the equity capital and borrowings of the enterprise.[13] They affect liability and owners' equity items and include (a) obtaining cash through the issuance of debt and repaying the amounts borrowed; and (b) obtaining capital from owners and providing them with a return of their investment through share redemptions.

   Details of the cash flows related to financing activities allow readers to assess the potential for future claims to the organization's cash and to identify major changes in the form of financing, especially between debt and equity. Companies in a growth stage will usually report significant amounts of cash generated from financing activities, financing that is needed to handle increased investment activity. As growth levels off and operations begin to generate positive cash flows, the financing flows tend to reverse as debt is repaid and, if appropriate, shares are redeemed.

The following schedule identifies typical examples of operating, investing, and financing cash receipts and payments. *Note that the operating cash flows are related almost entirely to current asset and current liability accounts, the investing cash flows generally involve long-term asset items, and the financing flows are derived principally from long-term liability and shareholders' equity accounts.*

OBJECTIVE 4
Identify how business transactions and events are classified and reported on the statement of cash flows.

---

[11] *Ibid.*, par. .06(d).

[12] *Ibid.*, par. .06(e).

[13] *Ibid.*, par. .06(f).

EXHIBIT 23-1

OPERATING FLOWS

Cash Inflows	Cash Outflows
From cash sales	To suppliers, paying on account for purchases
From customers paying on account for sales of goods and services	of goods and services
From cash receipts for royalties, fees, and other revenue	To and on behalf of employees for salaries and wages
	To government for taxes
	To others for expenses

INVESTING FLOWS

Cash Inflows	Cash Outflows
From sales of property, plant, and equipment	To acquire property, plant and equipment
From sales of intangibles and other long-term assets	To acquire intangibles and other long-term assets
From sales of equity or debt instruments of other enterprises	To acquire equity or debt instrumetns of other enterprises
From repayment of advances and loans made to other parties	To other parties as advances or for loans

FINANCING FLOWS

Cash Inflows	Cash Outflows
From sales of equity securities	To acquire or redeem outstanding shares
From the issuance of bonds, notes, and other debt securities	To repay amounts borrowed
	To reduce capital lease obligations

The AcSB allows some flexibility in the reporting of cash flows from interest and dividends received and paid, although it requires consistent reporting from period to period.[14] Dividends and interest received may be reported as investment cash flows as they represent returns earned on investments held. Alternatively, they could be reported as operating flows because they are included in the calculation of income, consistent with the returns on holding and operating long-term productive assets.

Interest and dividends paid are financing costs, therefore justifying disclosure as financing cash flows. Alternatively, as interest expense is included in the determination of net income and because it is useful for users to be able to assess the ability of the organization to cover its financing costs from operating cash flows, both interest and dividends paid may be reported as outflows of cash from operating activities.

In the examples and illustrations provided in this chapter, the authors classify all interest and dividends received and paid as operating cash flows. This approach means the Investing and Financing Cash Flow sections report only on the cash impact of changes in the stock of investments and financial instruments.[15]

Some items, although reported on the income statement, relate very directly to investing and financing activities. For example, the cash received from the sale of property, plant, and equipment is properly classified as an investing cash inflow. The amount of the gain or loss, although reported in the income statement, must be excluded in deter-

---

[14] *Ibid.*, par. .31.

[15] FASB's SFAS 95 requires dividends paid to be reported as a financing flow, and dividends and interest received to be reported as operating flows. The CICA *Exposure Draft* to revise Section 1540 is permissive in relation to interest and dividends paid and received. This is an area where the final recommendations may be more restrictive than those in the *Exposure Draft*.

mining cash flows from operating activities. Similarly, a gain or loss on the repayment (extinguishment) of debt is not an operating cash flow. The cash outflow to redeem the debt, not the amount of the gain or loss, is the actual cash flow and the repayment is clearly a financing activity. The cash flows associated with extraordinary items are required to be classified as arising from operating, investing, or financing activities as appropriate and be separately disclosed.

Income taxes present another complexity. While income tax expense is identifiable with specific operating, investing, and financing transactions, the related cash payments are difficult to identify and often fall in a different accounting period than the cash flows of the underlying activity attracting the tax. For this reason, it is recommended that income tax payments be classified as operating cash flows unless they can be specifically identified with financing and investing activities.[16]

How should **significant noncash transactions** that affect the asset and capital structure of an organization be handled? Examples of the more common of these noncash transactions include the following:

1. Acquisition of assets by assuming liabilities (including capital lease obligations) or by issuing equity securities.

2. Exchanges of nonmonetary assets.

3. Conversion of debt or preferred shares to common shares.

4. Issuance of equity securities to retire debt.

Because the statement reports only the effects of activities in terms of cash flows, any significant investing and financing transactions that do not affect cash should be excluded from the cash flow statement and should be disclosed elsewhere in the financial statements.[17]

FORMAT OF THE STATEMENT OF CASH FLOWS

The three activities discussed in the preceding section constitute the general format of the statement of cash flows. The Operating Activities section normally appears first, followed by the Investing and Financing activities sections. Also, the gross amounts of cash receipts and cash payments related to investing and financing activities are reported separately. Thus, the cash outflow from the purchase of property, plant, and equipment is reported separately from the cash inflow from the sale of property, plant, and equipment. Similarly, the cash inflow from the issuance of debt securities is reported separately from the cash outflow for the retirement of debt. Not reporting them separately obscures the investing and financing activities of the enterprise and makes it more difficult to assess future cash flows.

Exceptions to this general rule are permitted in limited circumstances. Cash flows may be netted where the inflow and outflow were made on behalf of a customer, and they reflect the activities of the customer rather than the reporting entity. A property management firm, for example, might collect rentals on behalf of a property owner client, turning the rentals over to the owners and earning a fee for the collection activities. Another exception covers situations where the cash receipt and payment amounts are large, the maturities are short, and the turnover is quick. A company with revolving

---

[16] CICA *Exposure Draft* (May 1996) on Cash Flow Statements to replace *Handbook* Section 1540, par. .35.

[17] *Ibid.*, par. .43. Note that prior to the issuance of the expected standard on the statement of cash flows, significant noncash transactions were included in the statement because of their effect on the asset and capital structure of the entity. This difference illustrates the change in focus from a statement of changes in financial position to a statement of cash flows.

short-term borrowings would net the many receipts and payments into one net financing inflow or outflow.[18]

The skeleton format of a statement of cash flows is illustrated below.

EXHIBIT 23-2

COMPANY NAME
STATEMENT OF CASH FLOWS
PERIOD COVERED

Cash flows from operating activities		
Net income		XX
Adjustments to reconcile net income to net cash provided		
by (used in) operating activities: list of individual adjustments	XX	XX
Net cash flow from (used in) operating activities		XX
Cash flows from investing activities		
List of individual inflows and outflows	XX	
Net cash provided (used) by investing activities		XX
Cash flows from financing activities		
List of individual inflows and outflows	XX	
Net cash provided (used) by financing activities		XX
Net increase (decrease) in cash		XX
Cash at beginning of period		XX
Cash at end of period		XX

OBJECTIVE 5
Contrast the direct and indirect methods of calculating net cash flow from operating activities.

Exhibit 23-2 derives the net cash flow from operating activities indirectly by making the necessary adjustments to the net income reported on the income statement. This is referred to as the **indirect method** (or **reconciliation method**). The cash flow from operating activities alternatively could be calculated directly by identifying the sources of the cash receipts and payments. This approach is referred to as the **direct method** and is illustrated below.

EXHIBIT 23-3

Cash flows from operating activities	
Cash receipts from customers	XX
Cash receipts from other revenue sources	XX
Cash payments to suppliers for goods and services	(XX)
Cash payments to and on behalf of employees	(XX)
Cash payments of income taxes	(XX)
Net cash flow from (used in) operating activities	XX

The use of the direct method is encouraged because of the additional information it provides, but its use is not mandatory.[19]

---

[18] CICA *Exposure Draft* (May 1996) on Cash Flow Statements to replace *Handbook* Section 1540, pars. .21 to .24 contain additional details on reporting cash flows on a net basis.

[19] Prior to the expected revisions to Section 1540 in 1997, companies were permitted to use either method. *Financial Reporting in Canada — 1995* (Toronto: CICA, 1995) reported that 299 of the 300 surveyed companies in 1994 used the indirect method.

PREPARATION OF THE CASH FLOW STATEMENT

SOURCES OF INFORMATION AND STEPS IN THE PROCESS

The statement of cash flows was previously called the Statement of Changes in Financial Position—for good reason. By analysing the changes in all noncash accounts on the statement of financial position, or balance sheet, from one period to the next, the sources of all cash receipts and all cash disbursements can be identified and summarized. Exhibit 23-4 illustrates why this is so.

EXHIBIT 23-4

$$A = L + OE$$
$$\Delta A = \Delta(L + OE)$$
$$\Delta A = \Delta L + \Delta OE$$
$$\Delta(\text{Cash} + \text{noncash A}) = \Delta L + \Delta OE$$
$$\Delta \text{Cash} + \Delta \text{noncash A} = \Delta L + \Delta OE$$
$$\Delta \text{Cash} = \Delta L + \Delta OE - \Delta \text{noncash A}$$

Note: Δ is a symbol meaning "change in."

Therefore, unlike the other major financial statements that are prepared from the adjusted trial balance, the statement of cash flows is prepared by analysing the changes in the balance sheet accounts over the accounting period. Information to prepare this statement usually comes from the following three sources.

- *Comparative balance sheets.* These provide the opening and closing balances of the assets, liabilities, and equities and, therefore, the change in each account from the beginning to the end of the period.

- *Current income statement.* This provides details about the change in the balance sheet retained earnings account, and provides information to help the preparer determine the amount of cash provided by, or used in, operations during the period.

- *Selected transaction data.* Details from the general ledger about selected transactions provide input necessary to determine how, and how much, cash was provided or used during the period.

Preparing the statement of cash flows from the data sources above involves four major steps:

1. *Determine the change in cash.* This procedure is straightforward because the difference between the beginning and the ending cash and cash equivalents balances can easily be computed from an examination of the comparative balance sheets. Explaining this change is the objective of the subsequent analysis.

2. *Record information from the income statement on the statement of cash flows.* This is the starting point for the calculation of cash flows from operating activities and it provides part of the explanation for the change in retained earnings on the balance sheet over the period.

   Preparers of cash flow statements know that income calculated on the accrual basis of accounting and cash flows from operations are not equal, but use the income statement information as a starting point. Whenever subsequent analyses indicate that the operating cash flow and the amount reported on the income statement differ, the numbers originally recognized are adjusted.

OBJECTIVE 6
Differentiate between net income and net cash flows from operations.

Most adjustments fit into one of three categories.

(a) *Category 1.* Amounts reported as revenue and expense are not the same as cash received from customers and cash paid to the suppliers of goods and services. Companies receive cash from customers for work done and revenue reported in a previous year and do not receive cash for all the revenue reported as earned in the current period. Similarly, cash payments are made in the current period to suppliers for goods and services acquired, used, and recognized as expense in a preceding period. In addition, not all amounts recognized as expenses in the current year are paid for by year end. Most of these adjustments are related to receivables, payables, and other working capital accounts.

(b) *Category 2.* Some expenses, such as depreciation, represent the amortization of previously incurred and deferred costs. While there was a cash flow associated with the original acquisition of the asset (an investing flow), there is no cash flow associated with amortizing this cost over the period of use.

(c) *Category 3.* Amounts reported as gains or losses on the income statement are not usually the same as the cash flow associated with the underlying transaction and, in most cases, the underlying activity is not an operating transaction. For example, gains and losses on the disposal of long-term assets and the early retirement of long-term debt are reported on the income statement. These result, respectively, from an investing and a financing transaction and the cash flow amounts are the proceeds on disposal of the asset and the payment to retire the debt, not the amount of the reported gain or loss.

3. *Analyse the change in each balance sheet account, identify any cash flows associated with a change in the account balance, and record the effect on the statement of cash flows.* This analysis identifies all investing and financing cash flows, and all adjustments needed to convert income reported on the income statement to cash flows from operations. Analyse the balance sheet accounts one at a time until all the changes in each account have been explained and the related cash flows are identified.

4. *Complete the statement of cash flows.* Calculate subtotals for operating, investing and financing activities and ensure the change in cash thus determined is equal to the actual change in cash for the period.[20]

ILLUSTRATION OF THE BASICS OF STATEMENT PREPARATION

OBJECTIVE 7
Prepare a statement of cash flows.

To illustrate the basic steps in the preparation of a statement of cash flows, we will use the first year of operations for Tax Consultants Limited. The company started on January 1, 1998, when it issued 10,000 no-par value common shares for $60,000 cash. The company rented its office space and furniture and equipment and performed tax consulting services throughout the year. The comparative balance sheets at the beginning and end of 1998 and the income statement and additional information for Tax Consultants Limited are shown in Exhibits 23-5 and 23-6 respectively.

---

[20] On occasion, even experienced accountants get to this step and find the statement does not balance! Don't despair. Determine the amount of your error and review your analysis until found.

EXHIBIT 23-5 TAX CONSULTANTS LIMITED

COMPARATIVE BALANCE SHEETS

Assets	Dec. 31, 1998	Jan. 1, 1998	Change Increase/Decrease
Cash	$49,000	$–0–	$49,000 Increase
Accounts receivable	36,000	–0–	36,000 Increase
Total	$85,000	$–0–	
Liabilities and Shareholders' Equity			
Accounts payable	$ 5,000	$–0–	5,000 Increase
Common shares	60,000	–0–	60,000 Increase
Retained earnings	20,000	–0–	20,000 Increase
Total	$85,000	$–0–	

EXHIBIT 23-6 TAX CONSULTANTS LIMITED

INCOME STATEMENT
FOR THE YEAR ENDED DECEMBER 31, 1998

Revenues	$125,000
Operating expenses	85,000
Income before income taxes	40,000
Income tax expense	6,000
Net income	$ 34,000

Additional Information
Examination of selected data indicates that a dividend of $14,000 was declared during the year.

Step 1. Determine the change in cash. To prepare a statement of cash flows, the first step, determining the change in cash, is a simple computation. Tax Consultants Limited had no cash on hand at the beginning of 1998, but $49,000 was on hand at the end of 1998; therefore, the change in cash for 1998 was an increase of $49,000. The other steps are more complex and involve additional analysis.

Step 2. Record information from the income statement on the statement of cash flows. As the bulk of the cash activity in any organization is related to operating cash flows, the second step takes information from the statement of operations (the income statement) and reports it on the cash flow statement under the heading "Cash flows from operating activities." This information will be converted from the accrual basis to the cash basis by adjustments arising from the analysis described in Step 3.

What specific information is taken from the income statement and reported on the cash flow statement in this step differs depending on whether the indirect method or the direct approach is used.

Indirect Method. In determining the amount of cash generated by or used in operations, the indirect approach (or **reconciliation method**) begins by transferring the net income amount reported on the income statement to the operations section of the cash flow statement. This is illustrated below for Tax Consultants Limited where net income of $34,000 is reported under the heading "Cash flows from operating activities."

EXHIBIT 23-7 TAX CONSULTANTS LIMITED

INDIRECT APPROACH

Cash flows from operating activities

    Net income   +34,000
    Adjustments:

Cash flows from investing activities

Cash flows from financing activities

Whenever any analysis in Step 3 indicates an operating cash inflow or outflow that is not equal in amount to the revenue or expense captured in the net income figure, an adjustment is made to the net income number to "correct" it to the operating cash impact.

Direct Method. Under this approach, skeleton headings similar to those illustrated in Exhibit 23-3 are set up under "Cash flows from operating activities." The number and description of these headings may vary from company to company. Amounts reported on the income statement are then transferred on a line-by-line basis to the heading that comes closest to representing the type of cash flow, until all components of net income have been transferred.

Exhibit 23-8 indicates that three headings are appropriate initially for Tax Consultants Limited. Because all income statement amounts are transferred to the Operating Activities section of the statement of cash flows, the amount transferred is equal to net income, the same amount as under the indirect approach.

EXHIBIT 23-8 TAX CONSULTANTS LIMITED

DIRECT APPROACH

Cash flows from operating activities

Cash receipts from customers	+125,000
Cash payments to suppliers	− 85,000
Cash payments of income taxes	− 6,000
	+ 34,000

Cash flows from investing activities

Cash flows from financing activities

As you proceed through Step 3 using the direct approach, an adjustment is made to the appropriate line item within the Operating Cash Flow section whenever your analysis indicates an operating cash inflow or outflow that is not equal in amount to the revenue or expense reported on the income statement. Revenues of $125,000 will be converted into cash receipts from customers; operating expenses of $85,000 will be adjusted to an amount that represents the cash payments made to suppliers; and income tax expense of $6,000 becomes income tax payments remitted to the government.

Under this approach, each specific revenue and expense is adjusted. Under the indirect method discussed above, it is only the bottom-line net income number that is adjusted.

Step 3. Analyse the change in each balance sheet account, identify any cash flows associated with a change in the account balance, and record the effect on the statement of cash flows. By analysing the change in each balance sheet account, transactions that involve cash can be identified, and the effects recorded on the cash flow statement.

Because the change in each balance sheet account has to be explained, it is reasonable to begin with the first noncash asset and work down through each asset, liability and equity account in turn. The results of this step are illustrated in Exhibit 23-9, where each item is referenced to the analysis below.

EXHIBIT 23-9 TAX CONSULTANTS LIMITED

Cash flows from operating activities

INDIRECT METHOD

Net income	+34,000
Adjustments: Increase in accounts receivable	−36,000(a)
Increase in accounts payable	+ 5,000(b)
Dividends paid	−14,000(d)
	−11,000

DIRECT METHOD

Cash receipts from customers	+125,000	−36,000(a)	+89,000
Cash payments to suppliers	−85,000	+ 5,000(b)	−80,000
Cash payments of income taxes	− 6,000		− 6,000
Cash dividends paid		−14,000(d)	−14,000
	+ 34,000		−11,000

Cash flows from investing activities	—
Cash flows from financing activities	
Proceeds from issue of common shares	+60,000(c)
	+60,000
Increase in cash	+49,000

(a) **Accounts Receivable.** During the year, Tax Consultants' receivables increased by $36,000. Because the Accounts Receivable account is increased by the amount of revenue recognized and decreased by the cash received from customers paying on account, the cash received from customers must have been $36,000 less than the revenue reported on the 1998 income statement. This requires an adjustment to the income statement numbers within the Operating Activities section of the cash flow statement. Under the indirect method, where net income is adjusted to cash flows from operations, $36,000 is deducted from the net income number because $36,000 less cash came in than is included in the revenue component of the net income reported. Using the direct method, the revenue number is reduced directly.

(b) **Accounts Payable.** Because the Accounts Payable account is increased by purchases of goods and services and decreased by payments on account, Tax Consultants' purchases must have exceeded cash payments by $5,000 during 1998. An adjustment of $5,000 is required to convert the purchases to the amount of the cash outflow.

Using the indirect method, $5,000 is added back to net income to reflect the fact that the amounts previously deducted as expense did not use an equivalent amount of cash. Under the direct approach, the $5,000 adjustment is made to the operating expense line where the cost of the goods and services purchased were charged. This adjusts the expense to the cash outflow for the purchases—to the cash payments to suppliers.

(c) Common Shares. The $60,000 increase in this account is the result of the issue of shares:

| Cash | 60,000 | |
| Common Shares | | 60,000 |

The $60,000 inflow of cash is a financing flow and is reported as such in the statement of cash flows.

(d) Retained Earnings. An amount of $34,000 of the increase in retained earnings is explained by net income. This was recognized on the cash flow statement as the starting point in calculating cash flows from operations. The remainder of the change in the account is explained by the following entry:

| Retained Earnings | 14,000 | |
| Cash | | 14,000 |

The entry indicates a cash outflow of $14,000 for the payment of dividends. While dividends paid could be reported as either a financing flow or an operating flow, they are recognized as operating outflows throughout this chapter. The dividend is deducted in calculating cash flows from operations under the indirect method. It is listed as a separate cash outflow if the direct approach is used.

If only part of the dividend had been paid, there would be a Dividend Payable account. An analysis of the change in that account identifies the extent to which cash was paid out for dividends relative to the dividends declared. Because Tax Consultants Limited does not have a Dividends Payable account, the entire dividend must have resulted in an equivalent cash outflow.

The changes in all balance sheet accounts have been explained, all information required for preparation of the statement of cash flows has been identified, and the statement can now be completed.

Step 4. Complete the statement of cash flows. To complete the statement, subtotals are calculated for each of the operating, investing, and financing sections of the statement. From the subtotals, the change in cash during the year as a result of the analysis is determined. This is compared with the change identified in Step 1. The $49,000 increase in Tax Consultants' cash balance during 1998 has been explained.

The completed statement illustrating both the indirect and the direct method is provided in Exhibit 23-10.

The $49,000 increase in cash was generated by financing inflows from the sale of common shares ($60,000) in excess of the net cash used in operations during the year ($11,000). The indirect method explains how the company could report a healthy income of $34,000 yet have a net operating outflow of cash of $11,000. The main reason is that $36,000 of the revenue reported has not yet been collected; the other major factor is the $14,000 cash dividend paid.

The direct method provides different insights into operating cash flows. The reason for the $11,000 shortfall in cash from operations is explained by the fact that while cash collections from customers ($89,000) were sufficient to cover operating cash outflows to suppliers and to the government for taxes ($80,000 + $6,000), they could not cover the dividend payment ($14,000).

EXHIBIT 23-10   TAX CONSULTANTS LIMITED

STATEMENT OF CASH FLOWS
YEAR ENDED DECEMBER 31, 1998

Indirect Method			Direct Method		
Cash flows from (used in) operations			Cash flows from (used in) operations		
Net income	$ 34,000		Cash received from customers		$89,000
Less: Increase in			Less cash payments:		
accounts receivable	(36,000)		To suppliers	$80,000	
dividends paid	(14,000)		For income taxes	6,000	
Add: Increase in accounts payable	5,000		For dividends	14,000	100,000
	(11,000)				(11,000)
Cash flows from investing activities	–0–		Cash flows from investing activities		–0–
Cash flows from financing activites			Cash flows from financing activities		
Proceeds on issue of			Proceeds on issue of		
common shares	60,000		common shares		60,000
Increase in cash during year	49,000		Increase in cash during year		49,000
Opening cash balance	–0–		Opening cash balance		–0–
Cash, December 31, 1998	$49,000		Cash, December 31, 1998		$49,000

STATEMENT PREPARATION WITH ADDED COMPLEXITY

To illustrate the preparation of a more complex statement of cash flows, we will use the operations of Eastern Window Products Limited (EWPL) for its 1998 year. EWPL has been in operation for a number of years, and the comparative balance sheets of the company at December 31, 1998 and 1997 and its statement of income and retained earnings for the year ended December 31, 1998 are illustrated below.

EXHIBIT 23-11   EASTERN WINDOW PRODUCTS LIMITED

BALANCE SHEETS—DECEMBER 31

	1998 $	1997 $	Change Increase/Decrease $
Cash	37,000	59,000	22,000 Dec
Accounts receivable	46,000	56,000	10,000 Dec
Inventory	82,000	73,000	9,000 Inc
Prepaid expense	6,000	7,500	1,500 Dec
Land	70,000	—	70,000 Inc
Building	200,000	—	200,000 Inc
Accumulated depreciation—building	(6,000)	—	6,000 Inc
Equipment	68,000	63,000	5,000 Inc
Accumulated depreciation—equipment	(19,000)	(10,000)	9,000 Inc
	484,000	248,500	

EXHIBIT 23-11   EASTERN WINDOW PRODUCTS LIMITED (Continued)

BALANCE SHEETS—DECEMBER 31

	1998 $	1997 $	Change Increase/Decrease $
Accounts payable	70,000	59,100	10,900 Inc
Income taxes payable	4,000	1,000	3,000 Inc
Wages payable	2,000	2,700	700 Dec
Mortgage payable	152,400	—	152,400 Inc
Bonds payable	50,000	40,000	10,000 Inc
Common shares	80,000	72,000	8,000 Inc
Retained earnings	125,600	73,700	51,900 Inc
	484,000	248,500	

STATEMENT OF INCOME AND RETAINED EARNINGS
YEAR ENDED DECEMBER 31, 1998

Sales revenue		$ 592,000
Less: Cost of goods sold		355,000
Gross profit		237,000
Salaries and wages expense	$55,000	
Interest expense	16,200	
Depreciation expense	15,000	
Other operating expenses	51,000	137,200
Income before income tax		99,800
Income tax expense		39,900
Net income		59,900
Retained earnings, January 1		73,700
Dividends declared		(8,000)
Retained earnings, December 31		$125,600

Step 1. Determine the change in cash. In the case of EWPL, cash decreased by $22,000 from a balance of $59,000 at the first of the year to $37,000 at the end of the year. The objective of the remaining steps in the preparation of the statement is to identify why the cash balance decreased by $22,000, and to classify the reasons according to whether the flows were operating, investing, or financing in nature.

Step 2. Record information from the income statement on the statement of cash flows. The indirect approach begins by transferring the $59,900 net income reported on the income statement to the Operations section of the cash flow statement. Whenever any analysis in Step 3 indicates an operating cash inflow or outflow that is not equal in amount to the revenue or expense captured in the $59,900 net income, it is adjusted to reflect the operating cash impact.

Under the direct approach, skeleton headings that indicate the types of cash flows involved are set up under "Cash flows from operations." Exhibit 23-12 indicates that six headings are appropriate initially for EWPL, including an "Other expenses/losses" section that includes income statement items such as depreciation expense that do not fall under the other headings. Because all income statement amounts are transferred to the Operating Activities section of the statement of cash flows, the amount transferred is equal to net income, the same amount as under the indirect approach.

As you proceed through Step 3 using the direct approach, sales revenue of $592,000 will be converted into cash received from customers; cost of goods sold of $355,000 and other operating expenses of $51,000 will be adjusted to an amount that represents the cash payments made to suppliers for goods and services acquired; salaries and wages expense of $55,000 will become cash payments made to and on behalf of employees; interest expense of $16,200 becomes interest payments made; and income tax expense of $39,900 becomes income tax payments remitted to the government. Under this approach, each specific revenue and expense is adjusted, unlike the indirect method where only the bottom-line net income number is adjusted.

Step 3. Analyse the change in each balance sheet account, identify any cash flows associated with a change in the account balance, and record the effect on the statement of cash flows. This step requires analytical skills and knowledge of accounting procedures for all asset, liabilities and shareholders' equity items. By analysing the change in each balance sheet account, transactions that involve cash can be identified and the effects recorded on the cash flow statement. Again, it is reasonable to begin with the first noncash asset and work down through each asset, liability, and equity account. The results of this step are illustrated in Exhibit 23-12, where each item is referenced to the analysis below.

(a) Accounts Receivable. During the year, EWPL's receivables decreased by $10,000. Because the Accounts Receivable account is increased by the amount of revenue recognized and decreased by cash received from customers, the cash inflow from customers must have been $10,000 greater than the revenue reported on the 1998 income statement. Under the indirect method, where net income is adjusted to cash flows from operations, $10,000 is added to the net income number because $10,000 more cash came in than is included in the revenue component of the net income reported. Using the direct method, the revenue number is increased directly.

(b) Inventory. Inventory increased by $9,000 in 1998. Because the Inventory account is increased by the purchase of goods and is reduced by transferring costs to cost of goods sold, EWPL must have purchased $9,000 more inventory than it sold and, therefore, $9,000 more than the costs included in cost of goods sold on the income statement. The first part of this analysis does not tell us how much cash was paid for the purchases, but merely converts cost of goods sold to the cost of purchases in the year. This preliminary step is needed because it is the payables that arise from ***purchases*** that require operating cash outflows. The analysis of accounts payable (see (h) below) converts the amount purchased to the amount of cash payments to suppliers.

Cost of goods sold of $355,000 was deducted on the income statement in calculating net income. Under the indirect method, net income must be further reduced by $9,000 to adjust for the additional $9,000 of goods purchased, but not yet sold. Under the direct method, the $9,000 adjustment is made to cost of goods sold directly to adjust it to the cost of goods purchased.

(c) Prepaid Expenses. Prepaid expenses decreased from $7,500 at the first of the year to $6,000 at the end of 1998. Because this account is increased by the acquisition of goods and services in advance of use and decreased by transferring the cost of the goods and services used up to expense—the same as for inventory—EWPL must have recognized $1,500 more expense than the amount purchased. The expenses reported on the income statement, therefore, must be reduced by $1,500 to correspond to the cost of goods and services purchased. Using the indirect method, $1,500 is added back to the income reported. Under the direct method, the appropriate expense is reduced directly for the $1,500. When the Accounts Payable account is analysed, the purchases are adjusted to cash payments to suppliers.

(d) Land, Building. The comparative balance sheets reflect an increase in land of $70,000 and an increase in building of $200,000, suggesting an investing cash outflow of $270,000. The investment in real property, however, is often financed by the assumption of a mortgage note payable that results in a lower net cash outflow. If a review of the records indicates that EWPL assumed a $155,000 mortgage in acquiring the land and building, *the actual investing cash outflow is only $115,000* (the $270,000 cost of the land and building less the financing provided by the mortgage of $155,000). Because the mortgage financing covers the acquisition of both land and building, the statement of cash flows reports a single cash outflow for this investing activity.

It is often useful to prepare the underlying journal entry to help analyse the changes in balance sheet accounts. In this case the entry is:

Land	70,000	
Building	200,000	
Mortgage Payable		155,000
Cash		115,000

This entry explains the change in the Land and the Building accounts on the balance sheet; it explains part of the change in the Mortgage payable account (see item (k) below); and it identifies the actual outflow of cash of $115,000.[21] This amount is reported under investing cash flows on the cash flow statement.

(e) Accumulated Depreciation, Building. The $6,000 increase in this account is due entirely to the recognition of depreciation expense for the year. The underlying journal entry is:

Depreciation expense	6,000	
Accumulated depreciation, building		6,000

The entry records a noncash event. However, because depreciation expense was deducted in calculating net income, an adjustment is required within the Operating section of the cash flow statement to adjust the reported income to reflect the noncash nature of this expense. Under the indirect approach, $6,000 is added back to net income because depreciation expense did not require the use of cash. Under the direct approach, depreciation expense is adjusted directly.

(f) Equipment. EWPL purchased $5,000 of equipment during 1998, changing its Equipment account from a cost of $63,000 to $68,000. This resulted in an investing outflow of cash of $5,000.

(g) Accumulated Depreciation, Equipment. The $9,000 increase in this account is due to depreciation expense for the year. As explained above in item (e), the operating activities section of the statement must be adjusted for this noncash expense.

(h) Accounts Payable. The Accounts Payable account is increased by purchases and decreased by payments on account. EWPL's purchases of goods and services, therefore, must have exceeded cash payments by $10,900 during 1998. In steps (b) and (c) above, cost of goods sold and other expenses were adjusted to convert them to the cost of goods and services purchased during the year. Therefore, the adjusted statement now reflects

---

[21] Prior to the expected changes to *Handbook* Section 1540 in 1997, this transaction could have been reported in two parts: as an investing outflow of $270,000, and as a financing inflow of $155,000. The expected revisions to Section 1540 specifically exclude this treatment.

the purchases of goods and services. A further adjustment of $10,900 is required to convert the purchases to the amount of the cash outflow.

Using the indirect method, $10,900 is added back to net income to reflect the fact that the amounts previously deducted for purchases did not use an equivalent amount of cash. Under the direct approach, the $10,900 adjustment reduces the amounts representing the purchases of goods and services to an amount equal to the cash outflow for these purchases.

(i) Income Taxes Payable. This account is increased by the expense reported and decreased by payments to the government. The increase in the account balance, therefore, reflects the fact that income tax expense exceeded payments by $3,000.

Under the indirect method, the $3,000 difference is added back to net income because the cash paid out was not as great as the expense deducted. The direct method adjusts the income tax expense itself by reducing it to the cash payments for taxes.

(j) Wages Payable. Similar to other current payables, this account is increased by amounts recognized as expense and decreased by payments, in this case, to employees. The $700 decrease in the Wages Payable account indicates that cash outflows were $700 greater than wages expense.

Using the indirect method, an additional $700 is deducted from the reported income. Salaries and wages expense is adjusted directly to convert it to payments made to employees under the direct approach.[22]

(k) Mortgage Payable. The cash flow associated with part of the change in this account was identified above in item (d). A $155,000 mortgage was assumed on the purchase of land and building, reducing what would otherwise have been a $270,000 investing cash outflow to a $115,000 cash outflow.

If the account increased by $155,000 on the assumption of the mortgage, principal payments of $2,600 must have been made to reduce the balance to $152,400. The entry underlying this transaction is:

Mortgage Payable	2,600	
Cash		2,600

The outflow of $2,600 is recognized on the cash flow statement as a financing activity.

(l) Bonds Payable. The increase in this account is explained by the following journal entry.

Cash	10,000	
Bonds Payable		10,000

The $10,000 inflow of cash is recognized on the cash flow statement as a financing cash flow.

(m) Common Shares. The $8,000 increase in this account is the result of the issue of shares:

Cash	8,000	
Common shares		8,000

The $8,000 inflow of cash is a financing flow.

---

[22] For all current asset and current liability account changes that adjust accrual basis net income to cash flows from operations, a simple check should be made. The adjustment for all increases in current asset accounts should have the same effect within the Operating Activities section of the cash flow statement. All decreases in current asset accounts should have the same effect. All increases and decreases in current liability accounts should have the opposite effect of increases and decreases, respectively, in current asset accounts. This is a useful mechanical procedure to double-check your adjustments.

EXHIBIT 23-12   EASTERN WINDOW PRODUCTS LIMITED

Cash flows from operating activities

INDIRECT METHOD

Net income		+59,900
Adjustments: Decrease in accounts receivable		+10,000 (a)
Increase in inventory		− 9,000 (b)
Decrease in prepaid expenses		+ 1,500 (c)
Depreciation expense, building		+ 6,000 (e)
Depreciation expense, equipment		+ 9,000 (g)
Increase in accounts payable		+10,900 (h)
Increase in income taxes payable		+ 3,000 (i)
Decrease in wages payable		− 700 (j)
Dividends paid		− 8,000 (n)
		+82,600

DIRECT METHOD

Cash receipts from customers	+592,000	+10,000 (a)	+602,000
Cash payments to suppliers for goods and services	−355,000	− 9,000 (b)	
	− 51,000	+ 1,500 (c)	−402,600
		+10,900 (h)	
Cash payments to employees	− 55,000	− 700 (j)	− 55,700
Cash interest payments	− 16,200		− 16,200
Cash payments of income taxes	− 39,900	+ 3,000 (i)	− 36,900
Other expenses/losses—depreciation	− 15,000	+ 6,000 (e)	
		+ 9,000 (g)	—
Dividends paid		− 8,000 (n)	− 8,000
	+ 59,900		+ 82,600

Cash flows from investing activities		
Land and building		−270,000 ⌐115,000 (d)
Equipment		− 5,000 (f)
		−120,000
Cash flows from financing activities		
Mortgage payable		152,400 ≠ 2,600 (k)
Bonds issued		+ 10,000 (l)
Shares issued		+ 8,000 (m)
		+ 15,400
Change in cash		− 22,000

(n) Retained Earnings. An amount of $59,900 of the increase in retained earnings is explained by net income. This was recognized on the cash flow statement already as the starting point in calculating cash flows from operations. The remainder of the change in the account is explained by the following entry:

Retained Earnings	8,000	
Cash		8,000

The entry indicates a cash outflow of $8,000 for the payment of dividends. This is reported as an operating outflow in this chapter.

The changes in all balance sheet accounts have now been explained, all information required for preparation of the statement of cash flows has been identified, and the statement can be completed.

Step 4. Complete the statement of cash flows. Subtotals are calculated for each section of the statement and the change in cash during the year that results is determined. This is compared with the change calculated in Step 1. Both show a $22,000 decrease in EWPL's cash balance during 1998.

The cash flow statement that results from Steps 3 and 4 can be considered a rough draft. A statement in good form should be prepared using more appropriate descriptions and explanations, such as shown below, where the indirect method is illustrated.

EXHIBIT 23-13   EASTERN WINDOW PRODUCTS LIMITED

STATEMENT OF CASH FLOWS
YEAR ENDED DECEMBER 31, 1998

Cash provided by (used in) operations:		
Net income		$ 59,900
Add back noncash expense—depreciation		15,000
Add (deduct) changes in noncash working		
capital*—accounts receivable	$10,000	
inventory	(9,000)	
prepaid expenses	1,500	
accounts payable	10,900	
income taxes payable	3,000	
wages payable	(700)	15,700
Less dividends paid		(8,000)
		82,600
Cash provided by (used in) investing activities:		
Purchase of capital assets		(120,000)
Cash provided by (used in) financing activities:		
Payment on mortgage payable	(2,600)	
Proceeds on issue of bonds	10,000	
Proceeds on issue of common shares	8,000	15,400
Decrease in cash		(22,000)
Cash balance, beginning of year		59,000
Cash balance, end of year		$37,000

Notes: 1. Cash consists of cash on hand and balances with banks.
2. Cash outflows during the year for interest and income taxes were $16,200 and $36,900, respectively.
3. During the year, capital assets were acquired at a total cost of $275,000 (land $70,000; building $200,000; equipment $5,000) of which $155,000 was financed directly by the assumption of a mortgage.

*Many companies provide only the subtotal on the statement of cash flows and report the details in a note to the financial statements.

Where the direct method is preferred, the operating section of the cash flow statement would appear as follows.

EXHIBIT 23-14	
Cash provided by (used in) operations:	
Received from customers	$ 602,000
Payments to suppliers	(402,600)
Payments to and on behalf of employees	(55,700)
Interest payments	(16,200)
Income taxes paid	(36,900)
Dividends paid	(8,000)
	$ 82,600

FINANCIAL REPORTING AND DISCLOSURE REQUIREMENTS

OBJECTIVE 8
Identify the financial reporting and disclosure requirements for the statement of cash flows.

In addition to requiring that cash flows be reported according to operating, investing, and financing classifications, revised CICA *Handbook* Section 1540 will require separate disclosure of the following.

1. Cash flows associated with extraordinary items, classified as operating, investing, or financing, as appropriate.

2. Interest and dividend cash inflows and interest and dividend cash outflows, each classified on a consistent basis from period to period as either operating, investing or financing.

3. Cash flows related to income taxes, classified as operating cash flows unless specifically identifiable with investing or financing activities.

4. The components of cash and cash equivalents, with a reconciliation of the amounts reported on the cash flow statement with the amounts reported on the balance sheet.

5. The amount of cash and cash equivalents held that are not available for use, if significant, with an explanatory commentary by management.

The recommendations leave the choice between the direct and indirect method up to the preparer, although the AcSB encourages reporting operating cash flows under the direct approach.[23] The principal advantage of the direct method is that *it shows operating cash receipts and payments.* That is, it is more consistent with the objective of a statement of cash flows—to provide information about cash receipts and cash payments—than the indirect method, which does not report operating cash receipts and payments.

Supporters of the direct method contend that knowledge of the specific sources of operating cash receipts and the purposes for which operating cash payments were made in past periods is useful in estimating future operating cash flows. Furthermore, information about amounts of major classes of operating cash receipts and payments is more use-

---

[23] In the United States, the FASB encourages the use of the direct method but permits use of the indirect method. If the direct method is used, a reconciliation of net income to net cash flow from operating activities must be provided in a separate schedule. At the time of writing, such a reconciliation is not a requirement of the proposed revised *Handbook* section.

ful than information about only their arithmetic sum—the net cash provided (used) by operating activities—in assessing an enterprise's ability to generate sufficient cash from internal sources, repay debt obligations, reinvest, and make distributions to its owners.

Many corporate providers of financial statements say that they do not currently collect information in a manner that allows them to determine directly from their accounting systems amounts such as cash received from customers or cash paid to suppliers. Supporters of the direct method contend that the incremental cost of assimilating such operating cash receipts and payments data is not significant.

The principal advantage of the indirect method is that *it focuses on the difference between net income and net cash flow from operating activities.* That is, it provides a useful link between the cash flow statement, the income statement, and the balance sheet. Many providers of financial statements contend that it is less costly to adjust net income to net cash flow from operating activities (indirect) than it is to report gross operating cash receipts and payments (direct). Because the indirect method has been used almost exclusively in the past, users are more familiar with it. Supporters of the indirect method also state that the direct method, which effectively reports income statement information on a cash basis rather than an accrual basis, may erroneously suggest that net cash flow from operating activities is as good as, or better than, net income as a measure of performance.

The recommendations also require the reporting of gross cash inflows and outflows from investing and financing activities rather than netted amounts, and separate disclosure elsewhere in the financial statements about investing and financing transactions that did not generate or use cash resources. Other requirements related to financial institutions, foreign currency cash flows, and business combinations and disposals are left to a course in advanced financial accounting.

The AcSB's recommendations suggest that other information may be useful in helping users understand the liquidity and financial position of an organization. For example, reporting investing outflows that are used to maintain the entity's operating capacity separately from those used to increase operating capability, and reporting cash flows by industry and geographic segment, allows users to better assess future cash prospects. The usefulness is further enhanced by management's discussion of the additional information.

COMPREHENSIVE ILLUSTRATION OF STATEMENT PREPARATION

Having covered the basic preparation and reporting requirements for a statement of cash flows, the next step is to see how the same principles are applied to more complex situations. Some of these complexities are illustrated below for Yoshi Corporation, using the same approach as used earlier in the chapter. Those who prefer a more structured method of accumulating the information for the cash flow statement should refer to the appendix to this chapter, in which the work sheet and T-account methods are illustrated for the same Yoshi Corporation example.

The comparative balance sheets of Yoshi Corporation at December 31, 1998 and 1997, the statement of income and retained earnings for the year ended December 31, 1998, and selected additional information are provided in the exhibits that follows.

Step 1. Determine the change in cash. Because Yoshi's cash and cash equivalents include temporary holdings of money market instruments as well as cash balances, *the change in cash to be explained is a decrease of $7,000*. This is the difference between the opening cash and cash equivalents of $66,000, made up of cash of $32,000 and short-term investments of $34,000, and the ending cash and cash equivalents of $59,000, comprised of cash of $20,000 and short-term investments of $39,000.

EXHIBIT 23-15   YOSHI CORPORATION

COMPARATIVE BALANCE SHEETS
DECEMBER 31, 1998 AND 1997

	1998 $	1997 $	Change Increase/Decrease $
Assets			
Cash	20,000	32,000	12,000 Dec
Short-term investments	39,000	34,000	5,000 Inc
Accounts receivable	106,500	52,700	53,800 Inc
Allowance for doubtful accounts	(2,500)	(1,700)	800 Inc
Inventories	303,000	311,000	8,000 Dec
Prepaid expenses	16,500	17,000	500 Dec
Investment in shares of Porter Co.	18,500	15,000	3,500 Inc
Deferred development costs	190,000	30,000	160,000 Inc
Land	131,500	82,000	49,500 Inc
Equipment	187,000	142,000	45,000 Inc
Accumulated depreciation, equipment	(29,000)	(31,000)	2,000 Dec
Buildings	262,000	262,000	—
Accumulated depreciation, buildings	(74,100)	(71,000)	3,100 Inc
Goodwill	7,600	10,000	2,400 Dec
Total assets	1,176,000	884,000	
Liabilities			
Accounts payable	130,000	131,000	1,000 Dec
Dividends payable, term preferred shares	2,000	—	2,000 Inc
Accrued liabilities	43,000	39,000	4,000 Inc
Income taxes payable	3,000	16,000	13,000 Dec
Bonds payable	100,000	100,000	—
Premium on bonds payable	7,000	8,000	1,000 Dec
Term preferred shares	60,000	—	60,000 Inc
Future income tax liability	9,000	6,000	3,000 Inc
Total liabilities	354,000	300,000	
Shareholders' Equity			
Common shares	247,000	88,000	159,000 Inc
Retained earnings	592,000	496,000	96,000 Inc
Treasury shares	(17,000)	—	17,000 Inc
Total shareholders' equity	822,000	584,000	
Liabilities and Shareholders' Equity	1,176,000	884,000	

Step 2. Record information from the income statement on the statement of cash flows. The specific information taken from the income statement depends on whether the direct or the indirect method is used. The net dollar amount transferred is identical regardless of the approach used; it is the degree of detail that differs.

EXHIBIT 23-16   YOSHI CORPORATION

STATEMENT OF INCOME AND RETAINED EARNINGS
YEAR ENDED DECEMBER 31, 1998

	$	$
Net sales		924,500
Equity in earnings of Porter Co.		5,500
		930,000
Expenses:	$	
Cost of goods sold	395,400	
Salaries and wages	200,000	
Selling and administrative	137,000	
Depreciation	14,600	
Interest	10,000	
Other expenses and losses	12,000	769,000
Income before income tax and extraordinary item		161,000
Income tax: Current	47,000	
Future	3,000	50,000
Income before extraordinary item		111,000
Extraordinary item: Gain on expropriation of land, net of tax of $2,500		8,000
Net income		119,000
Retained earnings, January 1		496,000
Less: Cash dividends, common shares	6,000	
Stock dividends, common shares	15,000	
Excess of cost of treasury shares over reissue price	2,000	23,000
Retained earnings, December 31		592,000

EXHIBIT 23-17   YOSHI CORPORATION

ADDITIONAL INFORMATION

1. Short-term investments represent temporary holdings of money market instruments.

2. During 1998, bad debts written off amounted to $1,450.

3. Yoshi accounts for its 22% interest in Porter Co. using the equity method. Porter Co. paid a dividend in 1998.

4. During 1998, Yoshi incurred $200,000 of market development costs, which met the criteria for deferral. $40,000 of deferred costs were amortized in the year.

5. Land in the amount of $54,000 was purchased through the issue of term preferred shares. In addition, the municipality expropriated a parcel of land resulting in a gain of $10,500 before tax.

EXHIBIT 23-17   YOSHI CORPORATION (Continued)

ADDITIONAL INFORMATION

6. An analysis of the Equipment account and related accumulated depreciation indicates the following:

Equipment:	Balance, January 1, 1998	$142,000
	Cost of equipment purchased	53,000
	Cost of equipment sold (sold at a loss of $1,500)	(8,000)
	Balance, December 31, 1998	$187,000
Accumulated depreciation:		
	Balance, January 1,1998	$31,000
	Accumulated depreciation on equipment sold	(2,500)
	Depreciation expense, 1998	11,500
	Major repair charged to accumulated depreciation	(11,000)
	Balance, December 31, 1998	$ 29,000

7. An analysis of the common shares account discloses the following:

Balance, January 1, 1998	$ 88,000
Issuance of a 2% stock dividend	15,000
Sale of shares for cash	144,000
Balance, December 31, 1998	$247,000

8. During 1998, Yoshi purchased common treasury shares in the market at a cost of $34,000. Later in the year, half of these shares were reissued for proceeds of $15,000.

9. Changes in other balance sheet accounts resulted from usual transactions and events.

Indirect Method. In calculating the cash generated by or used in operations, the net income of $119,000 is "slotted in" as the starting point in the operating section of the cash flow statement, as illustrated in Exhibit 23-18. Whenever subsequent analysis indicates that the actual operating cash flows differ from the numbers that make up the net income amount, an adjustment will be made to the $119,000.

Direct Method. Under this approach, skeleton headings that cover each type of cash flow—from receipts from customers to the extraordinary gain—are set up within the Operating Activities section of the cash flow statement, as illustrated in Exhibit 23-18. The description of each line may differ from situation to situation, but the income statement provides clues as to the types of operating cash flows and how they should be described. For example, the equity basis income from the investment in Porter Co. is not a cash flow, but will be replaced after adjustment with any dividends received from the investment, assuming this is reported as an operating flow.

Each amount making up the net income of $119,000 is then transferred to the most appropriate skeleton heading on the cash flow statement. Amounts reported as cost of goods sold, selling and administrative expense, and other expenses and losses form the base for what will eventually be "cash paid to suppliers for goods and services." Income tax expense on income before extraordinary items and the income tax expense on the extraordinary gain are both included on the line that will be adjusted to income taxes paid. The extraordinary item must be handled on a before-tax basis since the tax is reported separately.

Whenever subsequent analysis indicates an operating cash flow that differs from the line item amount reported, the appropriate line item is adjusted directly.

Step 3. Analyse the change in each balance sheet account, identify any cash flows associated with a change in the account balance, and record the effect on the statement of cash flows. Because each balance sheet account must be analysed to identify the sources, uses, and amounts of all cash flows, it is reasonable to begin with the first noncash asset and analyse each asset, liability, and equity account in turn. The analysis begins with accounts receivable, because in this example the short-term investments are considered cash equivalents.

(a) Accounts Receivable. Unlike the previous illustrations, where there were no allowances for doubtful accounts, Yoshi reports both the receivable and its contra allowance account. The receivable control account is increased by sales on account and reduced by the total of cash received from customers and accounts written off. During 1998, the receivable account increased by $53,800, indicating that the sales reported on the income statement exceeded the total of cash received on account and the accounts written off by $53,800. Because accounts written off explain $1,450 of the difference, the actual cash inflow from customers must have been $55,250 less than the sales revenue reported (i.e., $53,800 plus $1,450). Prepare a T account to verify this reasoning:

Accounts Receivable

Jan.1	52,700			
Sales	924,500	1,450		Accounts written off (given)
		?		Cash receipts
Dec. 31	106,500			

The cash receipts must have been $869,250, an amount $55,250 less than the revenue reported on the income statement. Using the indirect approach, $55,250 is deducted from the net income reported because the cash received from customers was $55,250 less than the revenue incorporated in the net income number. Under the direct method, the revenue of $924,500 is adjusted directly to convert it to cash received from customers.

(b) Allowance for Doubtful Accounts. The allowance account started the year with a balance of $1,700, was increased by the bad debt expense recognized for the year, was reduced by the accounts written off, and ended the year at $2,500. Because the amount of the accounts written off was $1,450, bad debt expense must have been $2,250 ($1,700 + bad debt expense − $1,450 = $2,500; or prepare a T account to determine this). Although there is no cash inflow or outflow as a result of these events, the noncash bad debt expense of $2,250 was deducted when net income was determined and, therefore, an adjustment is required to the income number reported on the cash flow statement.

Under the indirect method, $2,250 is added back to net income because no cash was paid out for this expense. Under the direct method, $2,250 reduces the expense line that includes bad debt expense. In this case, it is assumed that bad debt expense is included with the selling expenses.

Note that the only time it is necessary to analyse the Accounts Receivable and the allowance account separately is when the direct method is used for reporting cash flows from operations. This is because one adjustment corrects the revenue reported ($55,250) and the other corrects the noncash requiring bad debt expense ($2,250).

When the indirect method is used, both adjustments correct the net income number. The analysis is easier, therefore, if you zero in on the change in the net accounts receivable and make one adjustment to the net income number. For Yoshi Corporation, net receivables went from $51,000 ($52,700 − $1,700) at the beginning of the year to $104,000 ($106,500 − $2,500) at December 31, 1998, an increase of $53,000. The increase means that $53,000 of income was recognized that did not result in a corresponding cash flow. An adjustment is needed within the Operating Activities section of the cash flow statement to reduce net income by this amount.

EXHIBIT 23-18   YOSHI CORPORATION

Cash flows from operating activities

INDIRECT METHOD

Net income		+119,000
Adjustments: Increase in accounts receivable, net of write-offs		− 55,250 (a)
Bad debt expense		+ 2,250 (b)
Decrease in inventories		+ 8,000 (c)
Decrease in prepaid expenses		+ 500 (d)
Equity method investment income		− 5,500 (e)
Dividend from equity method investment		+ 2,000 (e)
Amortization of market development costs		+ 40,000 (f)
Extraordinary gain on expropriation of land		− 10,500 (g)
Loss on disposal of equipment		+ 1,500 (h)
Depreciation expense, equipment		+ 11,500 (h)
Depreciation expense, buildings		+ 3,100 (i)
Amortization expense, goodwill		+ 2,400 (j)
Decrease in accounts payable		− 1,000 (k)
Increase in dividends payable on term preferred shares		+ 2,000 (l)
Increase in accrued liabilities		+ 4,000 (m)
Decrease in income taxes payable		− 13,000 (n)
Increase in future income tax liability		+ 3,000 (q)
Dividends paid on common shares		− 6,000 (s)
		+108,000

DIRECT METHOD

Receipts from customers	+924,500	−55,520 (a)	+869,250
Received from investment in Porter Co.	+ 5,500	− 5,500 (e)	
		+ 2,000 (e)	+ 2,000
Payments for goods and services	−395,400	+ 2,250 (b)	
	−137,000	+ 8,000 (c)	
	− 12,000	+ 500 (d)	
		+40,000 (e)	−490,750
		+ 1,500 (h)	
		+ 2,400 (j)	
		− 1,000 (k)	
Payments to employees	−200,000	+ 4,000 (m)	−196,000
Interest payments	− 10,000	+ 2,000 (l)	− 8,000
Income taxes paid	− 50,000	−13,000 (n)	− 62,500
	− 2,500	+ 3,000 (q)	
Other items:			
Depreciation expense	− 14,600	+11,500 (h)	—
		+ 3,100 (i)	
Extraordinary gain, before tax	+ 10,500	−10,500 (g)	—
Common dividends paid		− 6,000 (s)	− 6,000
	+119,000		+108,000

EXHIBIT 23-18 YOSHI CORPORATION (Continued)		
Cash flows from investing activities		
Market development costs incurred	−200,000	(f)
Proceeds on expropriation of land (extraordinary item)	+ 15,000	(g)
Purchase of equipment	− 53,000	(h)
Proceeds on sale of equipment	+ 4,000	(h)
Major repair costs incurred	− 11,000	(h)
	−245,000	
Cash flows from financing activities		
Payment of principal on bonds payable, premium amortization	− 1,000	(o)
Proceeds on issue of term preferred shares	+ 6,000	(p)
Proceeds on issue of common shares	+144,000	(r)
Proceeds on reissue of treasury shares	+ 15,000	(s)
Payment to acquire treasury shares	− 34,000	(s)
	−130,000	
Change in cash	− 7,000	

(c) Inventories. The objective of the analysis of the Inventory account is to convert cost of goods sold into cost of goods purchased. (The analysis of the accounts payable account in (k) completes the analysis by converting cost of goods purchased to payments for purchases.) Because the Inventory account is increased by the cost of goods purchased and decreased by the transfer of costs to cost of goods sold, the $8,000 decrease in the Inventory account indicates that cost of goods sold exceeded purchases by $8,000. Using the indirect approach, $8,000 is added back to the net income number because the cost of goods sold that was deducted to determine net income was higher than the purchases made in the year. The direct approach adjusts cost of goods sold directly to convert it to the cost of goods purchased.

(d) Prepaid Expenses. The $500 decrease in this account resulted because the costs charged to the income statement were $500 greater than the costs incurred in acquiring prepaid goods and services in the year. For reasons similar to the inventory analysis in step (c), $500 is either added back to net income under the indirect approach, or adjusts the expense line associated with the prepaid expense under the direct approach. It is assumed in this case that the prepaid expenses were charged to selling and administrative expenses when they were used.

(e) Investment in Shares of Porter Co. Sufficient information has been provided to prepare the journal entries that explain how this account increased from $15,000 at the beginning of the year to $18,500 at the end.

Investment in Porter Co.	5,500	
Equity in earnings of Porter Co.		5,500

To record investment income in Porter Co. using the equity method.

Cash	2,000	
Investment in Porter Co.		2,000

To record the dividend received from Porter Co.

The amount of the investment income was provided on the income statement and the amount of the dividend was deduced from the change in the account balance. There was no cash impact as a result of the first entry. However, because $5,500 of revenue that did not generate $5,500 of cash was credited on the income statement, an adjustment is needed to the income number on the cash flow statement. Under the indirect method, the $5,500 is deducted to offset the $5,500 included in net income; under the direct approach, the $5,500 adjustment is made to the specific revenue line.

The second entry indicates a cash inflow of $2,000. Because the authors have opted to treat the return **on** investments as an operating flow, an adjustment is needed to the net income number reported that does not now include the dividend amount. Using the indirect method, $2,000 is added to net income; under the direct approach, $2,000 is added to the same line as the $5,500 deduction above.

(f) Deferred Development Costs.

Two types of transactions affected this account in the current year, summarized in the following journal entries.

Deferred development costs	200,000	
Cash		200,000

To record capitalized development costs.

Market development expenses	40,000	
Deferred development costs		40,000

To record the amortization of deferred development costs.

The first entry indicates a cash outflow of $200,000. This is an investing cash flow because it increases the balance of a noncurrent asset; it is therefore recognized under the investing activities section on the cash flow statement.

The second entry did not affect cash; however, as explained earlier, it is necessary to be alert to noncash events that affect the income statement. This entry records a $40,000 expense that did not require the use of cash; an adjustment is therefore needed within the Operating Activities section of the statement. Under the indirect approach, the $40,000 is added back to net income. Under the direct method, the adjustment is made to the specific expense, in this case, to the selling and administrative expense line.

(g) Land.

The Land account increased by $49,500 during 1998. Because land was purchased at a cost of $54,000 during the year, there must have been a disposal of land that cost $4,500. The entries that affect this account in 1998, therefore, were as follows.

Land	54,000	
Term preferred shares		54,000

To record the purchase of land through the issue of term preferred shares.

Cash	15,000	
Land		4,500
Gain on disposal of land (extraordinary item)		10,500

To record the appropriation of land costing $4,500 by the municipality.

The first entry indicates that there were no cash flows associated with either the acquisition of the land nor with the issue of the term preferred shares. Although this transaction is not reported in the statement of cash flows, there is a requirement that information about significant noncash investing and financing transactions that affect the asset and capital structure of the firm be disclosed elsewhere in the financial statements.

The second transaction entry identifies a cash inflow of $15,000 on the disposal of land. This is an investing inflow because it affects the stock of noncurrent assets in which the company has invested. This flow is included on the cash flow statement and is separately disclosed as the cash effect of an extraordinary item.

The second entry also results in a before-tax gain on the income statement of $10,500. By including all net income numbers in the Operating Cash Flow section of the statement initially in Step 2, the $10,500 gain is included in income as if the gain had generated $10,500 of operating cash flows. This is incorrect for two reasons. First, the cash inflow was $15,000, not $10,500. Second, the cash flow was an investing, not an operating, flow. An adjustment is needed, therefore, to deduct $10,500 from the income reported using the indirect method or from the extraordinary item if the direct method is used.

(h) Equipment and Accumulated Depreciation, Equipment. All information needed to replicate the entries made to both these accounts over the 1998 year is provided.

Equipment	53,000	
Cash		53,000
Cash	4,000	
Loss on disposal of equipment	1,500	
Accumulated depreciation, equipment	2,500	
Equipment		8,000
Depreciation expense	11,500	
Accumulated depreciation		11,500
Accumulated depreciation, equipment	11,000	
Cash		11,000

The first entry indicates a cash outflow of $53,000 due to the purchase of equipment, an investing activity. The second entry records the disposal of an asset that cost $8,000 with accumulated depreciation of $2,500. For an asset with a net book value of $5,500 to have been sold at a loss of $1,500, the proceeds on disposal must have been $4,000. The analysis of this item is similar to the analysis of the disposal of land in step (g). The cash impact is an inflow of $4,000. This is an investing inflow because it affects the stock of investment in noncurrent assets. The entry explains part of the change in the asset and accumulated depreciation accounts and recognizes a loss of $1,500 that is reported on the 1998 income statement. Because an outflow of $1,500 was not the cash effect (it was an inflow of $4,000) and because this was not an operating flow (it was an investing flow), an adjustment is needed in the Operating Cash Flow section. This is accomplished by adding back the $1,500 loss to net income under the indirect method, or to the appropriate line (other expenses and losses) under the direct approach.

The third entry reflects the annual depreciation expense on the equipment. As there is neither a debit nor a credit to cash in the entry, this event did not generate or use cash. However, because depreciation expense was deducted on the income statement, an adjustment is needed to the income number to correct it for the proper amount of cash flow from operations. Under the indirect method, $11,500 is added back to net income, and under the direct method, the depreciation line is corrected.

The fourth entry records the outflow of $11,000 for major repairs. Because the repairs result in "recouping" past depreciation, the company charged them to accumulated depreciation instead of to the asset account itself. The $11,000 cash flow is an investing outflow because it affects the stock of investment in noncurrent assets.

(i) Buildings and Accumulated Depreciation, Buildings. There was no change in the asset account during the year and, in the absence of additional information, the increase in the accumulated depreciation account must have been due entirely to the depreciation expense recorded for the year. For the same reasons as discussed above for depreciation expense on the equipment, the $3,100 noncash expense is adjusted in the Operating Activities section.

(j) Goodwill. The $2,400 decrease in Goodwill is assumed to be the result of the following entry.

| Amortization expense | 2,400 | |
| Goodwill | | 2,400 |

Recognition of this expense did not affect cash; therefore, an adjustment is required within the Operating Activities section similar to those for depreciation expense. Under the indirect method, $2,400 is added back to net income; under the direct approach, the selling and administrative expense line that includes the amortization expense is reduced.

(k) Accounts Payable. Because the Accounts Payable account is increased by purchases on account for operations and decreased by payments to suppliers, cash outflows to suppliers must have exceeded purchases by $1,000 during 1998. Previous cash flow statement adjustments, such as those resulting from the inventory analysis, converted expenses reported on the income statement to the amount of purchases of goods and services. The analysis of accounts payable completes this by converting the purchases amount to the cash paid for purchases. Because payments were $1,000 greater than purchases, the indirect method adjustment deducts an additional $1,000 from the net income reported, while the direct method adjusts the expense line to convert it to the amount of the cash outflow for goods and services.

(l) Dividends Payable on Term Preferred Shares. The $2,000 increase in this account indicates that cash dividends paid were $2,000 less than the dividends declared on these shares. Therefore, an adjustment to the dividends reported must be made to adjust them to the actual cash impact. Because the term preferred shares are reported within the Liability section of the balance sheet they must be, in substance, a financial liability. The dividends on these shares must be treated as if they were interest on debt and, in this case, they have been deducted on the income statement as interest expense.

The $2,000 adjustment, therefore, is made to the net income number under the indirect approach and is added back because the cash outflow was less than the interest reported. Under the direct approach, the line item that includes the dividend as interest expense is reduced.

(m) Accrued Liabilities. This account is increased by expenses accrued and decreased by payments of the amounts accrued. During 1998, the payments must have been $4,000 less than the expenses reported; $4,000 must therefore be added back to net income in the Operating section of the cash flow statement under the indirect method. Using the direct approach, a determination must be made as to which expenses should be adjusted. If it was interest expense that was accrued and paid, the interest expense line is adjusted; if wages and salaries payable, the salaries and wages expense is adjusted. On Exhibit 23-18, it is assumed that the accruals relate to payroll costs accrued to the balance sheet date.

(n) Income Taxes Payable. This account is increased by recognizing tax expense, and decreased by payments made to the tax authorities. The $13,000 reduction in this account in 1998 indicates that the cash outflows were $13,000 greater than the expense recognized. A $13,000 decrease in the net income reported in the Operating Activities section is therefore required. Using the direct method, the income tax line is adjusted directly.

Did the cash paid in excess of the expense recognized result from the extraordinary investing inflow from the expropriation of the land, or from tax on ordinary operating income? The difficulty in answering this question is the reason why the recommendations specify that all income tax cash flows be classified as operating cash flows unless it is clear that they relate to specific investing or financing activities.

(o) Bonds Payable, and Premium on Bonds Payable. Although there was no change in the Bonds Payable account, an understanding of how the Emerging Issues Committee of the CICA views this account is necessary to understand the adjustments for premiums and discounts on the statement of cash flows.[24] The EIC views the amount originally received for the interest-bearing instrument as the principal amount of the debt and, therefore, as the amount reported as a financing inflow when the security is first issued.

For a bond sold at a premium, the proceeds—including the premium—are the original financing inflow. The subsequent accounting entry made to record interest is:

Interest expense	xx	
Premium on bonds payable	x	
Cash		xxx

The cash payment for the interest is viewed as two distinct types of activity: a payment for interest expense, usually treated as an operating outflow, and a reduction of the principal of the bond equal to the reduction in premium, a financing outflow. In preparing the cash flow statement, no adjustment is needed to the interest expense as the amount of the expense on the income statement corresponds exactly with the portion of the cash flow assumed to be an operating outflow. The portion of the cash flow deemed to be a reduction of the principal (the amortization of the premium, which reduces the carrying value of the bond) must be reported on the statement as a financing outflow. Note that when the bond matures, the repayment of the maturity value is a financing outflow as well. Therefore, the original amount received when the bond was first issued was a financing inflow, which is matched with an equal amount of financing outflows — the premium amortization amounts over the life of the bond and the face value of the bond at maturity.

A similar rationale applies to a bond issued at a discount. The original amount received for the bond when it is issued, net of the discount, is a financing inflow. The subsequent entry to record interest expense each period is as follows.

Interest expense	xxx	
Discount on bond payable		x
Cash		xx

In this case the interest expense reported does not correspond with the operating cash outflow, so an adjustment is needed to add back to net income the difference between the expense reported and the cash amount paid, i.e., the discount amortization. No further amounts are reported on that period's cash flow statement. Note that when the bond is redeemed at maturity for its face value, the cash outflow at that time must be classified partly as a financing outflow (equal to the repayment of the original principal received when the bond was issued) and partly as an operating outflow equal to the total original discount representing additional interest to the investor that is now being paid.

Yoshi Corporation paid out $1,000 over and above the interest expense reported, reducing the premium and the carrying value of the bond payable. This $1,000 is, in effect, a reduction in the principal of the bond and is reported as a financing outflow on the statement of cash flows in Exhibit 23-18.

(p) Term Preferred Shares. Term preferred shares of $60,000 were issued during the year, $54,000 of which were issued in exchange for land. Information about this noncash investing and financing transaction is disclosed elsewhere in the financial statements. The remaining issue of shares, in the absence of information to the contrary, must have been for cash:

---

[24] *EIC-47, Interest Discount or Premium in the Statement of Changes in Financial Position,* CICA, October 15, 1993. The authors assume that the *EIC* will continue to apply to the revised statement of cash flows.

Cash	6,000	
Term preferred shares		6,000

This cash inflow is reported in the Financing Activities section of the cash flow statement.

(q) Future Income Tax Liability: The increase in this account's credit balance must have been a result of the following entry:

Income tax expense	3,000	
Future income tax liability		3,000

This entry resulted in a noncash expense that was reported on the income statement. Because this portion of income tax expense did not require the use of cash, an adjustment must be made within the Operating Activities section of the cash flow statement. $3,000 is added back to net income under the indirect method or the income tax line is adjusted directly under the direct approach.

(r) Common Shares. The following entries summarize the changes to this account in 1998.

Retained earnings	15,000	
Common shares		15,000
Cash	144,000	
Common shares		144,000

The first entry records the stock dividend, which neither required nor generated cash. The transaction did not change the capital and asset structure of the company and therefore does not need to be reported under cash flow statement requirements. The second entry records a $144,000 inflow of cash as a result of issuing shares, a financing activity. This is reported on the cash flow statement.

(s) Retained Earnings. The statement of income and retained earnings explains the $96,000 change in this account. The $119,000 increase due to net income and the cash flows associated with it already have been included in the Operating Activities section of the cash flow statement. The $6,000 decrease due to dividends paid on the common shares is reported on the cash flow statement as an operating cash outflow, although it could equally well have been included as a financing outflow. The $15,000 decrease due to the stock dividend was analysed above as having no cash flow implications.

The remaining $2,000 decrease due to the excess of cost of treasury shares over the issue price needs to be examined more closely. The entry underlying this transaction is:

Cash	15,000	
Retained earnings	2,000	
Treasury shares ($34,000 × 1/2)		17,000

This indicates there was a cash inflow of $15,000 on the reissue of treasury shares, which is reported as a financing activity on the statement of cash flows.

(t) Treasury Shares. The $17,000 increase in this account during the year resulted from the purchase by the company of its common shares as recorded in the entry below, and the subsequent sale of treasury shares as analysed in step (s) above.

Treasury shares	34,000	
Cash		34,000

The purchase is reported as a $34,000 financing outflow of cash. The cash inflows from the reissue of half these shares have been recognized on the cash flow statement already.

The changes in all balance sheet accounts have now been analysed and those with cash implications have been recorded on the cash flow statement. The following general statements summarize how to approach the analysis.

1. For most current asset and current liability accounts, zero in on what increases and what decreases each account. Compare the impact on the income statement with the

amount of the related cash flow and adjust the income number(s) slotted in on the cash flow statement to the cash flow effect accordingly.

2. For noncurrent asset and noncurrent liability accounts, reconstruct summary journal entries that explain how and why each account changed. For each entry in turn:
   (a) Identify debits and credits to cash as the cash impact. Include these as investing or financing cash flows on the cash flow statement.
   (b) Identify all debits or credits to income statement accounts where the operating cash impact is not equal to the amount of the revenue, gain, expense, or loss reported in the year. Each of these requires an adjustment to the net income number(s) originally reported in the operating activities classification.

While the transactions entered into by Yoshi Corporation represent a good cross section of common business activities, they do not encompass all possible situations. The general principles and approaches used in the above analysis, however, can be applied to most other transactions and events.

Step 4. Complete the statement of cash flows. Determine subtotals for each major classification of cash flow and ensure that the statement reconciles to the actual change in cash that was identified in Step 1.

Again, the rough draft prepared in Exhibit 23-18 should be presented with more appropriate descriptions and complete disclosure to enable readers to better interpret the information. Exhibit 23-19 illustrates the completed statement of cash flows, using the direct method to present the operating flows.

EXHIBIT 23-19	YOSHI CORPORATION

STATEMENT OF CASH FLOWS
YEAR ENDED DECEMBER 31, 1998

Cash provided by (used in) operations:		
Received from customers		$869,250
Dividends received on long-term investments		2,000
Payments to suppliers		(490,750)
Payments to and on behalf of employees		(196,000)
Payments for interest, and dividends on term preferred shares		(8,000)
Income taxes paid		(62,500)
		114,000
Dividends paid on common shares		(6,000)
		108,000
Cash provided by (used in) investing activities:		
Investment in development costs	($200,000)	
Purchase of equipment	(53,000)	
Major repairs incurred	(11,000)	
Proceeds on expropriation of land, an extraordinary item	15,000	
Proceeds on sale of equipment	4,000	(245,000)
Cash provided by (used in) financing activities:		
Proceeds on issue of common shares	144,000	
Proceeds on issue of term preferred shares	6,000	
Purchase of treasury shares	(34,000)	
Proceeds on reissue of treasury shares	15,000	
Principal repayment on bonds	(1,000)	130,000
Decrease in cash and cash equivalents		(7,000)
Cash and cash equivalents, January 1		66,000
Cash and cash equivalents, December 31		$ 59,000

For those who prefer the indirect method of reporting operating cash flows, Exhibit 23-20 illustrates how the Operating Activities section of the statement might look.

EXHIBIT 23-20   YOSHI CORPORATION

Cash provided by (used in) operations:		
Net income		$119,000
Add back noncash expenses:		
Depreciation	$ 14,600	
Amortization of goodwill	2,400	
Bad debts	2,250	
Amortization of development costs	40,000	59,250
Equity in income of Porter Co. in excess of dividends received		(3,500)
Deduct nonoperating gains (net)		
Extraordinary gain on land	(10,500)	
Loss on disposal of equipment	1,500	(9,000)
Deferral of income tax liability to future periods		3,000
Changes in noncash working capital accounts (see Note A)		(54,750)
Dividends paid on common shares		(6,000)
		108,000
Note A—changes in noncash working capital:		
Accounts receivable	($55,250)	
Inventory	8,000	
Prepaid expenses	500	
Accounts payable	(1,000)	
Dividends payable, term preferred shares	2,000	
Accrued liabilities	4,000	
Income taxes payable	(13,000)	
	$(54,750)	

There is considerable flexibility in how the information is summarized and reported in the cash flow statement. The way in which information is summarized and described can enhance the information content and help users interpret and understand the significance of the cash flow data.

The Yoshi Corporation cash flow statement in Exhibits 23-19 and 23-20 provides valuable information to readers of the financial statements. Cash receipts from customers and dividends from investments generated $114,000 more cash than needed to pay operating costs, leaving the company in a healthy position to cover the dividend to common shareholders. The excess operating cash flows allowed Yoshi to internally finance $108,000 of the $245,000 of increased investment, most of it spent on developmental activities.

The remainder of cash required for investment purposes was generated mainly through financing activities, eating into existing cash balances only marginally to the extent of $7,000. The majority of new financing was achieved through the issue of common equity. This is reasonable given that the funds were invested in development costs, assets difficult to finance through debt. A more detailed analysis of cash flows is left to a course on financial management.

FINANCIAL REPORTING EXAMPLE

The consolidated statement of cash flows for Crestar Energy Inc.'s year ended December 31, 1996 is reproduced in Exhibit 23-21. Note the inclusion of cash flow per share information at the bottom of the statement. While cash flow per share information is not permitted to be reported under U.S. accounting standards, the Emerging Issues Committee of the CICA, in EIC-34, determined that it could be presented on the cash flow statement or in notes to the financial statements, but not on the income statement. Sufficient information must be disclosed to allow readers of the statements to determine the basis for the calculations.

EXHIBIT 23-21   CRESTAR ENERGY INC.

Consolidated Statement of Cash Flow

Year ended December 31 (millions of dollars, except per share data)	1996	1995 (As restated, see note 2)
OPERATING ACTIVITIES		
Net income	$ 51.6	$ 18.3
Add (deduct) items not involving cash:		
Depletion and depreciation	181.5	143.6
Deferred income taxes	29.9	(6.6)
Foreign exchange amortization on long term debt	1.1	1.9
Other	(1.0)	(0.5)
Foreign exchange loss on repayment of long term debt	–	8.9
Cash flow from operations	263.1	165.6
Net changes in working capital, excluding cash	(7.3)	(6.7)
Deferred revenue drawdowns	(0.3)	(0.4)
	255.5	158.5
FINANCING ACTIVITIES		
Issue of long term debt	164.9	318.0
Repayment of long term debt	(173.8)	(111.7)
Issue of common shares	55.1	93.1
Increase (decrease) in other liabilities	(2.2)	6.1
	44.0	305.5
Cash available for investing activities	299.5	464.0
INVESTING ACTIVITIES		
Net corporate assets acquired *(note 3)*	86.6	271.8
Expenditures on property, plant and equipment	229.8	186.2
Proceeds on disposition of property, plant and equipment	(30.1)	(3.4)
Expenditures on abandonment and restoration	5.2	2.5
Other	0.9	–
	292.4	457.1
INCREASE IN CASH AND SHORT TERM INVESTMENTS	7.1	6.9
Cash and short term investments, beginning of year	7.1	0.2
CASH AND SHORT TERM INVESTMENTS, END OF YEAR	$ 14.2	$ 7.1
CASH FLOW FROM OPERATIONS PER SHARE		
Basic	$ 5.47	$ 3.96
Fully diluted	$ 5.31	$ 3.86

ACCRUAL ACCOUNTING AND CASH FLOWS—WHERE THE TWO CONCEPTS MEET

On February 27, 1997, The T. Eaton Company Limited ("Eaton's") filed for protection from their creditors under the Companies' Creditors Arrangement Act (the "CCAA"). In the months following, all of Canada has watched with "baited breath" to see if the decades-old Canadian institution would survive (as well as the thousands of jobs along with it).

As part of the restructuring plans put in place to help the ailing retailer get back on its feet, the company proposed to tap into the pension plan surplus that existed in its employee pension plan. In note 9 to its unaudited financial statements dated January 25, 1997, the company showed a pension fund surplus of $2733 million, $154 million of which was reflected in the balance sheet as an asset. The surplus represented 10% of the total reported assets of the company. Under current accounting rules, companies do not show the full pension plan surplus or deficit in the balance sheet and are allowed to defer recognition of a part of the surplus or deficit and recognize it over time. The amount for Eaton's of the unrecognized surplus was just under $120 million.

On May 21, 1997, Eaton's and its employees reached a deal to share the surplus—then pegged at $290 million. For Eaton's this gave them much needed cash, and for the employees, it allowed them to contribute to Eaton's chances of staying solvent and hence their own job security, without putting their pension fund at risk.

What is interesting to note here is the inexactness or softness of the actual surplus number. The surplus is calculated by deducting the pension plan obligations from the fair market value of the plan assets. Depending on the type of plan assets held, the estimated value may be reasonably easy to determine. The same does not hold true for the estimate of the obligation however, which involves numerous significant assumptions regarding mortality, turnover and future salary rates. A big variable is the discount rate used to calculate the present value of the potential future pension payments under the plan. Normally, users of financial statements are aware of how soft this number is and take this into account in investing and other decisions. In Eaton's case, the number was a net asset and so there was even less concern over its exactness especially since it was a long-term asset. All this is part of measurement risk and accountants have generally felt that it was better to try to estimate the number and disclose it than not to provide the information at all. After all, it is an accrual number and doesn't usually affect cash flows in the short or medium term.

In the case of Eaton's, there was a direct cash flow impact, since the employees and Eaton's agreed to liquidate the surplus and share the cash! Indeed this estimate and plan to cash in the surplus would have a more profound impact on the company and its liquidity position than the normally important "cash used in or supplied by operations" reported on the cash flow statement. The importance of using the "best estimate assumptions" in this case would have been paramount since it would have a direct and immediate cash flow impact on the company!

This is an excellent example of the importance of accrual accounting and how accrual accounting can help predict future cash flows.

Contributed by: Irene Wiecek, University of Toronto

Summary of Learning Objectives

1. **Describe the evolution and objectives of the statement of cash flows.** The funds flow statement has evolved over the years from its origin as a summary of the changes in the balance sheet accounts, to one that described the sources and application of working capital during the year, to a statement that explained both the sources and uses of cash resources and changes in the capital and asset structure of the enterprise. Most recently, the AcSB recommended that a cash flow statement replace the statement of changes in financial position. The objective of this statement is to provide information about historical changes in the cash of an enterprise so that investors and creditors can assess the amount, timing, and degree of certainty of an entity's future cash flows, as well as the needs of the organization for cash and how it will be used.

2. **Define cash and cash equivalents.** The definition of cash to be used for the cash flow statement is related to an organization's cash management activities. Cash and cash equivalents include cash on hand, demand deposits, short-term, highly liquid non-equity investments that are convertible to known amounts of cash with insignificant risk of changes in value, reduced by bank overdrafts that are repayable on demand.

3. **Identify the major classifications of cash flows and explain the significance of each type.** Cash flows can be classified into those resulting from operating, investing, and financing activities. The ability of a company to generate operating cash flows affects its capacity to pay dividends to shareholders, to take advantage of investment opportunities, to provide internal financing for growth, and to meet obligations when they fall due. The level of cash spent in investing activities affects the future cash flows of an organization. Cash invested in increased levels of productive assets forms the basis for operating cash inflows in the future. Financing cash activities affect the capital structure of the firm and, therefore, the requirements for cash outflows in the future.

4. **Identify how business transactions and events are classified and reported on the statement of cash flows.** Operating cash flows encompass the cash inflows from customers and other revenue sources, and the outflows to suppliers, employees, government, and others for operating costs. Investing flows relate to the cash spent on and derived from the investment in the stock of noncurrent assets. Financing flows, in general, capture the changes in cash due to the borrowing and repayment of debt and issue and redemption of shares. Flexibility is permitted for both interest and dividends paid and received. The return to investors and creditors in the form of dividends and interest may be considered as financing or operating outflows, while interest and dividends received on investments may be reported as investing or as operating inflows.

5. **Contrast the direct and indirect methods of calculating net cash flow from operating activities.** The direct method, which discloses major classes of gross cash receipts and gross cash payments, begins with the individual line items reported on the income statement and adjusts these to the cash flow associated with each line item. The indirect method, in contrast, begins with the net income number and adjusts it for all situations where the operating cash impact differs from the revenue or expense incorporated in the net income number.

KEY TERMS

cash, 1170

cash equivalents, 1170

cash flows, 1170

direct method, 1179, 1192

financing activities, 1171

indirect method, 1174, 1177

investing activities, 1171

operating activities, 1171

reconciliation method, 1174, 1177

significant noncash transactions, 1173

6. **Differentiate between net income and net cash flows from operations.** The calculation of net income is the direct result of the accrual-based accounting model, which recognizes revenues when earned and matches expenses with those revenues. Cash flow from operations differs from net income in three major respects: (1) cash inflows from customers and outflows to suppliers do not necessarily fall in the same accounting period as the associated revenues and expenses; (2) some expenses, such as depreciation and amortization, do not have corresponding operating cash outflows but result instead from investing outflows of previous periods; and (3) net income includes gains and losses on the disposal and retirement of noncurrent assets and liabilities that do not equal the cash flows of the underlying transaction and that are investing and financing flows in nature.

7. **Prepare a statement of cash flows.** The preparation of a statement of cash flows involves determining the change in cash and cash equivalents during the period, slotting in either the net income (indirect method) or line items from the income statement (direct method) as the starting point within the Operating Activities section of the statement, and analysing the change in each balance sheet account to identify all transactions with a cash impact. Transactions with a cash impact are recorded on the cash flow statement. To ensure that all cash flows have been identified, the results recorded on the statement are compared with the change in cash during the period. The formal statement is then prepared, complete with appropriate descriptions and disclosures.

8. **Identify the financial reporting and disclosure requirements for the statement of cash flows.** Separate disclosure is required of cash flows associated with extraordinary items, interest and dividends received and paid, the components of cash and cash equivalents reconciled to the amounts reported on the balance sheet, and the amount of and explanation for cash and cash equivalents not available for use. All income tax cash flows should be reported as operating flows unless they can be linked directly to investing or financing flows. Gross amounts should be reported except in specifically permitted circumstances, and noncash investing and financing transactions should be excluded from the cash flow statement with details reported elsewhere on the financial statements.

APPENDIX 23A

The Work Sheet and T-Account Methods

USE OF A WORK SHEET IN THE PREPARATION OF A CASH FLOW STATEMENT

When numerous adjustments are necessary or other complicating factors are present, many accountants prefer to use the **work sheet method** to assemble and classify the data that will appear on the statement of cash flows. The work sheet or spreadsheet, when using computer software, is merely a device that aids in the preparation of the statement; its use is optional. The skeleton format of the work sheet for preparation of the statement of cash flows using the indirect approach is shown in Exhibit 23A-1.

EXHIBIT 23A-1   XYZ LIMITED

STATEMENT OF CASH FLOWS FOR THE YEAR ENDED ...

Balance Sheet Accounts	End of Last Year Balances	Reconciling Items Debits	Reconciling Items Credits	End of Current Year Balances
Debit balance accounts	XX	XX	XX	XX
	XX	XX	XX	XX
Totals	XX			XXX
Credit balance accounts	XX	XX	XX	XX
	XX	XX	XX	XX
Totals	XX			XXX
Cash Flows				
Operating activities				
Net income		XX		
Adjustments		XX	XX	
Investing activities				
Receipts (dr.) and payments (cr.)		XX	XX	
Financing activities				
Receipts (dr.) and payments (cr.)		XX	XX	
Totals		XXX	XXX	
Increase (decrease) in cash		(XX)	XX	
Totals		XXX	XXX	

The following guidelines are important in using a work sheet:

1. In the Balance Sheet Accounts section, accounts with debit balances are listed separately from those with credit balances. This means, for example, that Accumulated Depreciation is listed under credit balances and not as a contra account with the

OBJECTIVE 9
Use a work sheet to prepare a statement of cash flows.

assets. The beginning and ending balances of each account are entered in the appropriate columns. The transactions that caused the change in the account balance during the year are entered as the analysis proceeds so that each line pertaining to a balance sheet account should balance. That is, the beginning balance plus or minus the reconciling item(s) must equal the ending balance. When this agreement exists for all balance sheet accounts, all changes in account balances have been identified and reconciled.

2. The bottom portion of the work sheet consists of space to record the operating, investing, and financing cash flows. It provides the detail for the change in the cash balance during the period, information that is necessary to prepare the formal statement of cash flows. Inflows of cash are entered as debits in the reconciling columns; outflows of cash are entered as credits in the reconciling columns. Thus, in this section, the sale of equipment for cash at book value is entered as a debit under inflows of cash from investing activities. Similarly, the purchase of land for cash is entered as a credit under outflows of cash from investing activities.

3. The reconciling items shown in the work sheet are not entered in any journal or posted to any account. They do not represent either adjustments or corrections of the balance sheet accounts. They are used only to facilitate the preparation of the cash flow statement.

PREPARATION OF THE WORK SHEET

The preparation of a work sheet involves a series of prescribed steps. The steps in this case are:

1. Enter the balance sheet accounts and their beginning and ending balances in the balance Sheet Accounts section.

2. Enter the debits and credits from the summary entries that explain the changes in each balance sheet account (other than cash), identify all that affect cash, and enter these amounts in the reconciling columns at the bottom of the worksheet.

3. After the analysis is complete and the changes in all balance sheet accounts have been explained, enter the increase or decrease in cash on the cash line (or lines, if cash equivalents) and at the bottom of the work sheet. This entry should enable the totals of the reconciling columns to be in agreement.

To illustrate procedures for preparing the work sheet, the same comprehensive illustration used in the chapter for the Yoshi Corporation is presented. The indirect method serves initially as the basis for the computation of net cash provided by operating activities. An illustration of the use of the direct method is provided later in the appendix. The financial statements and other data related to Yoshi Corporation for its year ended December 31, 1998 are presented in Exhibits 23-15, 16, and 17. Most of the analysis has been performed within the chapter and additional explanations related to preparation of the work sheet are provided throughout the discussion that follows.

ANALYSIS OF TRANSACTIONS

Before the analysis begins, the balance sheet accounts of Yoshi are transferred to the opening and ending balance columns of the work sheet. The following discussion provides an explanation of the individual adjustments that appear on the work sheet in Exhibit 23A-2. It assumes you are familiar with the analysis of the Yoshi illustration in the chapter.

EXHIBIT 23A-2   **YOSHI CORPORATION**

WORK SHEET FOR PREPARATION OF STATEMENT OF CASH FLOWS
YEAR ENDED DECEMBER 31, 1998

	Balance 12/31/97	Reconciling Items—1998 Debits	Reconciling Items—1998 Credits	Balance 12/31/98
Debits				
Cash	32,000		(23) 12,000	20,000
Short-term investments	34,000	(23) 5,000		39,000
Accounts receivable	52,700	(2) 55,250	(2) 1,450	106,500
Inventories	311,000		(3) 8,000	303,000
Prepaid expenses	17,000		(4) 500	16,500
Investment in shares of Porter Co.	15,000	(5) 5,500	(5) 2,000	18,500
Deferred development costs	30,000	(6) 200,000	(6) 40,000	190,000
Land	82,000	(7) 54,000	(7) 4,500	131,500
Equipment	142,000	(8) 53,000	(8) 8,000	187,000
Buildings	262,000			262,000
Goodwill	10,000		(9) 2,400	7,600
Treasury shares	–	(10) 34,000	(10) 17,000	17,000
Total debits	987,700			1,298,600
Credits				
Allowance for doubtful accounts	1,700	(2) 1,450	(11) 2,250	2,500
Accumulated depreciation, equipment	31,000	(8) 2,500	(12) 11,500	29,000
Accumulated depreciation, buildings	71,000	(12) 11,000	(13) 3,100	74,100
Accounts payable	131,000	(14) 1,000		130,000
Dividends payable, term preferred shares	–		(15) 2,000	2,000
Accrued liabilities	39,000		(16) 4,000	43,000
Income taxes payable	16,000	(17) 13,000		3,000
Bonds payable	100,000			100,000
Premium on bonds payable	8,000	(18) 1,000		7,000
Term preferred shares	–		(7) 54,000	60,000
			(19) 6,000	
Future income tax liability	6,000		(20) 3,000	9,000
Common shares	88,000		(21) 15,000	247,000
			(21) 144,000	
Retained earnings	496,000	(10) 2,000	(1) 119,000	592,000
		(21) 15,000		
		(22) 6,000		
Total credits	987,700			1,298,600
Cash Flows				
Operating activities:				
Net income		(1) 119,000		
Increase in accounts receivable			(2) 55,250	
Decrease in inventories		(3) 8,000		
Decrease in prepaid expenses		(4) 500		
Equity in earnings of Porter Co.			(5) 5,500	
Dividend from Porter Co.		(5) 2,000		

EXHIBIT 23A-2   YOSHI CORPORATION (Continued)

WORK SHEET FOR PREPARATION OF STATEMENT OF CASH FLOWS
YEAR ENDED DECEMBER 31, 1998

	Balance 12/31/97	Reconciling Items—1998 Debits	Reconciling Items—1998 Credits	Balance 12/31/98
Cash Flows				
Operating activities: (continued)				
Amortization, deferred development costs		(6) 40,000		
Gain on expropriation of land			(7) 10,500	
Loss on disposal of equipment		(8) 1,500		
Amortization expense, goodwill		(9) 2,400		
Bad debt expense		(11) 2,250		
Depreciation expense, equipment		(12) 11,500		
Depreciation expense, buildings		(13) 3,100		
Decrease in accounts payable			(14) 1,000	
Dividend, term preferred shares		(15) 2,000		
Increase in accrued liabilities		(16) 4,000		
Decrease in income taxes payable			(17) 13,000	
Future income tax liability		(20) 3,000		
Cash dividends, common shares			(22) 6,000	
Investing activities:				
Development costs incurred			(6)200,000	
Proceeds on disposal of land		(7) 15,000		
Purchase of equipment			(8) 53,000	
Proceeds on sale of equipment		(8) 4,000		
Major repair costs incurred			(12) 11,000	
Financing activities:				
Purchase of treasury shares			(10) 34,000	
Proceeds on reissue of treasury shares		(10) 15,000		
Payment of principal, bonds payable			(18) 1,000	
Proceeds on issue of term preferred shares		(19) 6,000		
Proceeds on sale of common shares		(21)144,000		
		842,950	849,950	
Decrease in cash		(23) 7,000		
		849,950	849,950	

1. **Net income.** Because so much of the analysis requires adjustments to convert accrual basis income to the cash basis, the net income number is usually the first reconciling item put in the work sheet. The entry to reflect this and the balance sheet account affected is:

Net income (operating cash inflow)	119,000	
Retained earnings		119,000

The credit to retained earnings explains part of the change in that account. We know that net income did not generate $119,000 of cash, so this number is considered a tentative one that will be adjusted whenever the subsequent analysis identifies revenues and expenses whose cash impact differs from the revenue and expense amounts incorporated in the net income number. It is a starting point only.[25]

2. **Accounts receivable.** Because the entire bottom of the work sheet when completed will provide the explanation for the change in cash (defined as cash and short-term investments in this case), and because all balance sheet accounts have to be analysed, accounts receivable is a logical starting point. The following two entries summarize the net change in this account and identify the other accounts affected.

Accounts receivable	55,250	
Revenue		55,250
Allowance for doubtful accounts	1,450	
Accounts receivable		1,450

Accounts receivable increased by $53,800 during the year after writing off accounts totalling $1,450. The gross increase due to reporting revenue in excess of cash receipts therefore must have been $55,250.

The first entry above explains an increase in accounts receivable of $55,250 and indicates that there was $55,250 of revenue reported in net income in excess of cash receipts. This requires an adjustment to the net income reported in the operating Activities section of the work sheet. The other entry explains changes in two balance sheet accounts with no cash impact.

3. **Inventories.** The entry to explain the net change in the Inventory account is as follows.

Cost of goods sold	8,000	
Inventories		8,000

The credit to inventories explains the change in that account. The debit is an expense of $8,000 that was deducted in calculating net income, but which did not use cash. This requires a debit column adjustment to the net income in the Operating Activities section.[26]

4. **Prepaid expenses.** Assuming the prepaid expenses were selling and administrative in nature, the following entry summarizes the change in this account during the year.

Selling and administrative expense	500	
Prepaid expenses		500

The credit entry explains the change in the Prepaid Expenses account. The debit represents a noncash expense deducted on the income statement and requires an adjustment to the net income reported within the operating activity category.

5. **Investment in shares of Porter Co.** Entries explaining the change in this account are:

Investment in shares of Porter Co.	5,500	
Equity in earnings of Porter Co.		5,500
Cash	2,000	
Investment in shares of Porter Co.		2,000

---

[25] Some accountants prefer to slot in the "income before extraordinary items" within the Operating Activities section and the "extraordinary item" within the Investing or Financing Activity section, as appropriate. In the Yoshi example, the extraordinary item is an investing activity. Regardless, the transaction underlying the extraordinary item must be revisited in the subsequent analysis and be further adjusted. For this reason, the authors prefer to begin with the net income and adjust for the extraordinary item later in the analysis.

[26] This analysis is consistent with that earlier in the chapter. If $8,000 of cost of goods sold came from a reduction in inventory levels, purchases for the year must have been $8,000 less than cost of goods sold. Therefore the analysis equally well converts cost of goods sold to the level of purchases in the year.

The first entry explains part of the change in the investment account and identifies a noncash generating revenue that was included in net income. Because a $5,500 cash inflow debit is incorporated in the net income number we started the work sheet with, the entry to adjust for the fact it was not a cash inflow must be a $5,500 credit.

The second entry credit explains the remainder of the change in the balance sheet Investment account. The debit portion of the entry represents an operating inflow of cash that is not included in the net income number. The Operating Activities section needs to be adjusted to reflect this $2,000 cash inflow.[27]

6. **Deferred development costs.** Noting that the development costs relate to marketing activities, the entries to summarize the changes in this account are as follows.

Deferred development costs	200,000	
Cash		200,000
Selling and administrative expense	40,000	
Deferred development costs		40,000

The first entry explains part of the change in the Deferred Development Costs account and identifies an outflow of cash related to the investment in this noncurrent asset, an investing flow. The second entry recognizes the amortization of these deferred costs that results in a noncash expense being reported in net income. Because this expense—which was deducted in determining net income—did not use cash, the adjustment adds back (debits) $40,000 to the net income number and the cash generated from it.

7. **Land.** The entries affecting the Land account are as follows.

Land	54,000	
Term preferred shares		54,000
Cash	15,000	
Land		4,500
Gain on disposal of land (extraordinary item)		10,500

The first entry explains changes in both the Land and Term Preferred Shares accounts, a noncash transaction. The second entry identifies a $15,000 investing inflow of cash, a reduction of $4,500 in the Land account, and a gain reported in net income that does not correspond to the actual cash flow, and which results from an investing transaction. Net income is adjusted.

8. **Equipment.** Entries affecting the Equipment account are reproduced below.

Equipment	53,000	
Cash		53,000
Cash	4,000	
Loss on disposal of equipment	1,500	
Accumulated depreciation, equipment	2,500	
Equipment		8,000

The first entry explains part of the change in the asset account and identifies a $53,000 investing outflow of cash. The second entry explains the remainder of the change in the asset account and part of the change in the Accumulated Depreciation account, reports a $4,000 investing inflow of cash, and a $1,500 noncash loss reported in net income that needs to be adjusted.

9. **Goodwill.** Goodwill decreased by $2,400 due to the amortization recorded.

Amortization expense	2,400	
Goodwill		2,400

---

[27] This cash flow could equally well have been reported as an investing inflow.

Similar to depreciation expense, the amortization of goodwill is a noncash charge to the income statement. It therefore requires an adjustment to the net income included in the Operating Activities section.

10. **Treasury shares.** The change in this account is explained in two entries.

Treasury shares	34,000	
Cash		34,000
Cash	15,000	
Retained earnings	2,000	
Treasury shares ($34,000 × 1/2)		17,000

The first entry explains part of the change in the account and identifies a $34,000 financing outflow of cash for the acquisition of treasury shares. The second entry explains the remainder of the change in the Treasury Shares account, part of the change in retained earnings, and recognizes a $15,000 inflow of cash from the reissue of the shares, a financing transaction.

11. **Allowance for doubtful accounts.** Part of the change in this account was explained previously. The remaining entry to this account recognizes bad debt expense.

Bad debt expense	2,250	
Allowance for doubtful accounts		2,250

This completes the explanation of changes to the Allowance account. In addition, it records a noncash expense of $2,250, which requires an adjustment to net income in the Operating Activities section.

12. **Accumulated depreciation, equipment.** One of the changes in the accumulated Depreciation account was explained previously. The remainder of the entries affecting this account are:

Depreciation expense	11,500	
Accumulated depreciation, equipment		11,500
Accumulated depreciation, equipment	11,000	
Cash		11,000

The first entry explains an increase in the Accumulated Depreciation account, recognizing an $11,500 noncash expense that requires an adjustment to net income and the cash flows from operations. The second entry explains the remainder of the change in the Accumulated Depreciation account, which results from an investing outflow of cash.

13. **Accumulated depreciation, buildings.** With no changes in the Buildings account during the year, the only entry needed to explain the change in the Accumulated Depreciation account is:

Depreciation expense	3,100	
Accumulated depreciation, buildings		3,100

This entry recognizes a $3,100 noncash expense, and necessitates an adjustment to the net income number in the Operating Activities section.

14. **Accounts payable.** The summary entry to explain the net change in this account is:

Accounts payable	1,000	
Cash		1,000

That is, a reduction in the payables balance must have resulted from paying out $1,000 more cash than purchases recorded. Cost of goods sold and other expenses have already been adjusted to represent the goods and services purchased, so a $1,000 credit adjustment is needed to convert the purchases amount to the amount paid, i.e., the operating cash outflow.

15. **Dividends payable on term preferred shares.** The summary entry explaining the net change in this account follows.

Dividends (income statement expense)	2,000	
Dividends payable on term preferred shares		2,000

The increase in the liability account is due to recognizing more dividends as a deduction on the income statement (these shares are a financial liability in substance) than dividends the company paid in the year. $2,000 must be added back to net income to adjust the operating cash flows for the dividends, reported as interest expense, that did not use cash.

16. **Accrued liabilities.** The $4,000 increase in this account was caused by recognizing $4,000 more expense than payments on accrued liabilities in the year.

Salaries and wages expense (assumed)	4,000	
Accrued liabilities		4,000

To correct net income for the cash effect of the operating expense, $4,000 must be added back or debited to the cash provided by net income as reported.

17. **Income taxes payable.** The decrease in this account during the year is because Yoshi Corporation paid out more cash than the expense reported.

Income taxes payable	13,000	
Cash		13,000

An adjustment is needed to recognize this additional cash outflow and to convert the income reported in the Operating Activity section to the amount of the operating cash flow. Since the expense reported has already been deducted from the income number, an additional $13,000 outflow must be deducted or credited on the worksheet.

18. **Premium on bonds payable.** Because there was no change in the bonds payable account itself, the change in the Premium account is explained by the following entry. It records the excess cash paid over and above the interest expense reported, as a reduction of the premium.

Premium on bonds payable	1,000	
Cash		1,000

The excess cash payment is treated as a reduction in the principal of the debt, a financing outflow.

19. **Term preferred shares.** $54,000 of the increase in this account has already been analysed. The remaining increase is assumed to have resulted from the following entry.

Cash	6,000	
Term preferred shares		6,000

This represents a $6,000 financing inflow.

20. **Future income tax liability.** The increase in this account is due to the deferral of the tax liability to future periods.

Income tax expense	3,000	
Future income tax liability		3,000

The change in the balance sheet account is explained, and the noncash portion of income tax expense is adjusted by adding back $3,000 to the net income number originally recognized.

21. **Common shares.** Two entries explain the change in this account over the year.

Retained earnings	15,000	
Common shares		15,000
Cash	144,000	
Common shares		144,000

The first entry records the stock dividend issued. As discussed in the chapter, this is a noncash activity that, although explaining the change in two balance sheet accounts, is not a part of the cash flow statement. The second entry records the inflow of cash for shares sold, a financing flow.

22. **Retained earnings.** Most of the changes in this account have already been dealt with above. One additional entry is needed to explain the remainder of the change.

Retained earnings (dividends)	6,000	
Cash		6,000

This entry records an operating outflow of cash for dividends on common shares.[28]

23. **Completion of the work sheet.** All that remains to complete the balance sheet portion of the work sheet is to credit the Cash account by $12,000 and debit the Short-Term investments by $5,000, netting to a $7,000 credit or decrease in cash. The $7,000 debit to balance this work sheet entry is inserted at the bottom of the work sheet. The debit and credit reconciling item columns are then totalled and balanced.

    If the direct method of determining cash flows from operating activities is preferred, one change is needed to the above procedures. Instead of debiting the net income of $119,000 and using this as the starting point to represent cash inflows from operations, the individual revenues, expenses, gains and losses *(netting to $119,000)* are transferred to the Operating Activities section on a line by line basis. The initial assumption is that all revenues and gains generated cash receipts equal to the revenues and gains reported, and all expenses and losses used cash equal to the expense or loss reported. Where this is not the case, adjustments are made to the specific income statement line item involved.

    It facilitates the analysis if items that will be reported together on the final statement are grouped together, and if all income tax amounts are grouped as well. This step and the adjustments needed in the Operating Activities section are illustrated in Exhibit 23A-3. The adjustments in the Operating Activities section are exactly the same as those made using the indirect approach, except that they are made directly to the line item that requires adjustment instead of to net income.

    The bottom part of the work sheet provides the necessary information to prepare the formal statement of cash flows illustrated in Exhibits 23-19 (direct method) and 23-20 (indirect method).

---

[28] This could be reported as a financing outflow instead of an operating flow.

EXHIBIT 23A-3

DIRECT METHOD

	Debits (inflow)	Credits (outflow)
Cash Flows		
Operating activities:		
Net sales	(1) 924,500	(2) 55,250
Equity in earnings of Porter Co.	(1) 5,500	(5) 5,500
	(5) 2,000	
Cost of goods sold	(3) 8,000	(1) 395,400
		(14) 1,000
Selling and administrative expense	(4) 500	(1) 137,000
	(6) 40,000	
	(9) 2,400	
	(11) 2,250	
Other expenses and losses	(8) 1,500	(1) 12,000
Salaries and wages expense	(16) 4,000	(1) 200,000
Interest expense	(15) 2,000	(1) 10,000
Income tax expense	(20) 3,000	(1) 50,000
		(1) 2,500
		(17) 13,000
Depreciation expense	(12) 11,500	(1) 14,600
	(13) 3,100	
Extraordinary gain, before tax	(1) 10,500	(7) 10,500
Common dividends paid		(22) 6,000

USE OF T ACCOUNTS IN THE PREPARATION OF A CASH FLOW STATEMENT

OBJECTIVE 10
Use T-accounts to prepare a statement of cash flows.

Some accountants prefer the **T-account method** of identifying the information needed to prepare a cash flow statement. This procedure provides a quick and systematic method to accumulate the appropriate information; its proponents contend that it is not as cumbersome and time-consuming as the development of a work sheet. Conceptually, the T-account method and work sheet approach are similar.

The work sheet approach requires reconciling debit and credit entries in the columns of a work sheet until all changes in balance sheet accounts have been explained and the cash effects have been identified on the bottom of the working paper. The T-account method requires debit and credit entries in balance sheet T accounts until all changes in account balances have been explained and the cash effects have been identified in one large master cash T account. *It should be noted that the T accounts used in this approach are not part of the general ledger or any other ledger; they are developed only for use in this process.*

The comprehensive Yoshi Corporation example used in the chapter and in explaining the work sheet method is used to illustrate the T-account approach.

T-ACCOUNT ILLUSTRATION

When the T-account approach is employed, the net change in cash and cash equivalents for the period is computed by comparing the beginning and ending balances of the Cash and Cash Equivalents accounts. One large T account for cash and cash equivalents is prepared and the net change is entered at the top of this account on the left (debit side) if the balance increased, and on the right (credit side) if it decreased. This is reflected as the $7,000 net change (decrease) in the Cash and Equivalents T account in Illustration 23A-1.

ILLUSTRATION 23A-1

Cash and cash equivalents				
Increases		**Decreases**		
		Net change		7,000
Operating activities:		Operating activities:		
(1) Net income	119,000	(2) Increase in accounts receivable		55,250
(3) Decrease in inventories	8,000	(5) Equity in earnings of Porter Co.		5,500
(4) Decrease in prepaid expenses	500	(7) Gain on disposal of land		10,500
(5) Dividend received, Porter Co.	2,000	(14) Decrease in accounts payable		1,000
(6) Amortization, deferred costs	40,000	(17) Decrease in income tax payable		13,000
(8) Loss on disposal of equipment	1,500	(22) Dividends paid, common shares		6,000
(9) Amortization expense, goodwill	2,400			91,250
(11) Bad debt expense	2,250			
(12) Depreciation expense, equipment	11,500			
(13) Depreciation expense, buildings	3,100			
(15) Dividends paid, term preferred shares	2,000			
(16) Increase in accrued liabilites	4,000			
(20) Increase in future income tax liability	3,000			
	199,250			
Investing activities:		Investing activities:		
(7) Proceeds, disposal of land	15,000	(6) Investment in development costs		200,000
(8) Proceeds, sale of equipment	4,000	(8) Purchase of equipment		53,000
	19,000	(12) Investment in major repairs		11,000
				264,000
Financing activities:		Financing activities:		
(10) Proceeds, reissue of treasury shares	15,000	(10) Purchase of treasury shares		34,000
(19) Proceeds, issue of term preferred shares	6,000	(18) Principal payment, bonds payable		1,000
(21) Proceeds, issue of common shares	144,000			35,000
	165,000			

This T account is then structured into six separate classifications: **Increases**—(1) Operating; (2) Investing; and (3) Financing, on the left; and **Decreases**—(4) Operating; (5) Investing; and (6) Financing, on the right. T accounts are then set up for all noncash items that have had activity during the period, with the net change entered at the top of each account. The objective of the T-account approach is to explain the net change in cash by examining the changes that have occurred in the noncash accounts. The master cash T account acts as a summarizing account. Most of the changes in the noncash items are explained through this account. Significant investing and financing transactions that did not affect cash are not recorded in the Cash account but are entered in their respective noncash accounts for purposes of reconciling the net changes in these accounts.

A complete version of the T-account approach is presented (indirect method) by working through the analysis of items 1 to 22 in the section of the appendix that dealt with the work sheet method. Each entry can be traced to the Cash and Cash Equivalents T account in Illustration 23A-1 and the noncash T accounts in Illustration 23A-2. The changes in the cash and noncash accounts are keyed to the same analysis and entries prepared for the work sheet approach.

ILLUSTRATION 23A-2

Accounts receivable

Change	53,800		
(2)	55,250	(2)	1,450

Inventories

		Change	8,000
		(3)	8,000

Investment in shares of Porter Co.

Change	3,500		
(5)	5,500	(5)	2,000

Land

Change	49,500		
(7)	54,000	(7)	4,500

Accumulated depreciation, equipment

Change	2,000		
(8)	2,500	(12)	11,500
(12)	11,000		

Goodwill

		Change	2,400
		(9)	2,400

Dividends payable, term pfd. shares

		Change	2,000
		(15)	2,000

Income taxes payable

Change	13,000		
(17)	13,000		

Term preferred shares

		Change	60,000
		(7)	54,000
		(19)	6,000

Common shares

		Change	159,000
		(21)	15,000
		(21)	144,000

Treasury shares

Change	17,000		
(10)	34,000	(10)	17,000

Allowance for doubtful accounts

		Change	800
(2)	1,450	(11)	2,250

Prepaid expenses

		Change	500
		(4)	500

Deferred development costs

Change	160,000		
(6)	200,000	(6)	40,000

Equipment

Change	45,000		
(8)	53,000	(8)	8,000

Accumulated depreciation, buildings

		Change	3,100
		(13)	3,100

Accounts payable

Change	1,000		
(14)	1,000		

Accrued liabilities

		Change	4,000
		(16)	4,000

Premium on bonds payable

Change	1,000		
(18)	1,000		

Future income tax liability

		Change	3,000
		(20)	3,000

Retained earnings

		Change	96,000
(10)	2,000	(1)	119,000
(21)	15,000		
(22)	6,000		

If the direct approach is used to determine cash flows from operations, the master T account would list all revenues and gains reported on the income statement as increases (debits) and all expenses and losses as decreases (credits). Each subsequent adjustment needed in the Operating Activities section is then entered on the appropriate revenue/gain or expense/loss line.

SUMMARY OF T-ACCOUNT APPROACH

Shortcuts are often used with the T-account approach. For example, journal entries may not be prepared because the transactions are few and their effects are obvious. Also, only the noncash T-accounts that have a number of changes, such as Equipment, Accumulated Depreciation—Equipment, and Retained Earnings, need be presented in T-account form. Other more obvious changes in noncash items can be determined simply by examining the comparative balance sheet and other related data.

The T-account approach provides certain advantages over the work sheet method in that (1) a statement of cash flows usually can be prepared much faster; and (2) the use of T-accounts helps in understanding the relationship between cash and noncash items. Conversely, when highly complex problems exist, the work sheet provides a more orderly and systematic approach to preparing the statement of cash flows. In practice, the work sheet is used to ensure proper accounting for all items.

To summarize, the following steps are used in the T-account approach.

1. Determine the increase or decrease in Cash and Cash Equivalents for the year.

2. Post the increase or decrease to the cash and cash equivalents T-account and establish six classifications within this account: Increases—Operating, Investing, and Financing, and Decreases—Operating, Investing, and Financing.

3. Determine and post the increase or decrease in each noncash account. Accounts that have no change can be ignored unless two transactions have occurred in the same account of the same amount, which is highly unlikely. A shortcut approach is to prepare T-accounts only for noncash accounts that have a number of transactions. All other changes can be immediately posted to the Cash account after examining additional information related to balance sheet changes.

4. Reconstruct entries in noncash accounts and post them to the noncash account affected.

5. Using the postings from the Cash T-account, prepare the formal statement of cash flows.

Summary of Learning Objectives for Appendix 23A

KEY TERMS

T-account method, 1216
work sheet method, 1207

9. **Use a work sheet to prepare a statement of cash flows.** A work sheet can be used to organize the analysis and cash flow information needed to prepare a statement of cash flows. This method accounts for all changes in the balances of noncash balance sheet accounts from the beginning of the period to the end of the period, identifying all operating, investing, and financing cash flows in the process. The cash flow statement is prepared from this cash flow information, which is accumulated at the bottom of the work sheet.

> 10. **Use T-accounts to prepare a statement of cash flows.** This approach to organizing the analysis and information required to prepare a statement of cash flows zeros in on analysing and explaining the changes in all noncash balance sheet accounts, represented by T-accounts. As the analysis proceeds, the operating, investing, and financing cash flows identified are summarized in a large master cash T-account. This is the information needed to prepare the formal cash flow statement.

Note: All *asterisked* Exercises, Problems, and Cases relate to material contained in the appendix to the chapter.

EXERCISES

E23-1 **(Classification of Transactions)** Jeffries Company had the following activity in its most recent year of operations.

1. Purchase of equipment
2. Sale of building
3. Depreciation
4. Exchange of equipment for furniture
5. Issuance of capital stock

6. Amortization of intangible assets
7. Issuance of bonds for land
8. Payment of dividends
9. Increase in interest receivable on note receivable
10. Pension expense exceeds amount funded

Instructions

Using the indirect method, classify the items as (a) operating—add to net income; (b) operating—deduct from net income; (c) investing; (d) financing; (e) significant noncash investing and financing activity; or (f) other.

E23-2 **(Analysis of Changes in Capital Asset Accounts and Related Cash Flows)** MacAskill Mills Limited engaged in the following activities in 1998.

1. The Land account increased by $50,000 over the year: Land that originally cost $12,000 was exchanged for another parcel of land valued at $30,000 and a lump sum cash receipt of $10,000. Additional land was acquired later in the year in a cash purchase.

2. The Furniture and Fixtures account had a balance of $67,500 at the beginning of the year and $62,000 at the end. The related Accumulated Depreciation account decreased over the same period from a balance of $24,000 to $15,200. Fully depreciated office furniture that cost $10,000 was sold to employees during the year for $1,000; fixtures that cost $3,000 with a net book value of $700 were written off; and new fixtures were acquired and paid for.

3. A five-year capital lease for specialized machinery was entered into halfway through the year whereby the company agreed to make five annual payments (in advance) of $25,000, after which the machinery will revert to the lessor. The present value of these lease payments at the 10% rate implicit in the lease (lower than the incremental borrowing rate) was $104,247. The first payment was made as agreed.

Instructions

For **each situation** described above:

(a) Prepare the underlying journal entries made by MacAskill Mills during 1998 to record all information related to the changes in each capital asset and associated accounts over the year.

(b) Identify the amount(s) of the cash flows that result from the transactions and events recorded, and determine the classification of each.

(c) Identify all charges (debits) or credits to the 1998 income statement that did not generate or use identical amounts of operating cash flows and that, therefore, require adjustments to the net income number(s) reported in the Operating Cash Flow section of the cash flow statement.

(Statement Presentation of Transactions—Indirect Method) Each of the following items must be considered in order to prepare a statement of cash flows (indirect method) for Rashid Inc. for the year ended December 31, 1998. **E23-3**

1. Plant assets that had cost $20,000 six years before and were being depreciated on a straight-line basis over 10 years with no estimated salvage value were sold for $6,000.

2. During the year, 10,000 no-par value common shares were issued for $40 a share.

3. Uncollectible accounts receivable in the amount of $24,000 were written off against the Allowance for Doubtful Accounts.

4. The company sustained a net loss for the year of $50,000. Depreciation amounted to $22,000, and a gain of $7,000 was realized on the sale of land for $38,000 cash.

5. A 60-day Government of Canada treasury bill was purchased for $100,000 on December 10, 1998.

6. Goodwill amortized for the year was $9,000.

7. The company exchanged common shares for a 40% interest in Tabasco Co. for $900,000.

Instructions
State where each item is to be shown in the statement of cash flows, if at all. If not included on the statement, explain why not.

(Preparation of Operating Activities Section—Direct Method) The income statement of Vancouver Company is shown below. **E23-4**

VANCOUVER COMPANY
Income Statement
For the Year Ended December 31, 1998

Sales		$6,900,000
Cost of goods sold		
Beginning inventory	$1,900,000	
Purchases	3,400,000	
Goods available for sale	5,300,000	
Ending inventory	1,600,000	3,700,000
Gross profit		3,200,000
Operating expenses		
Selling expenses	950,000	
Administrative expenses	1,200,000	2,150,000
Net income		$1,050,000

Additional information:

1. Administrative expenses include depreciation expense of $60,000.

2. Selling expenses include commissions and salaries of $300,000; administrative expenses include salaries of $500,000.

3. Accounts receivable decreased $350,000 during the year.

4. Prepaid expenses increased $150,000 during the year.

5. Accounts payable to suppliers decreased $300,000 during the year.

6. Accrued salaries payable decreased $40,000 during the year.

Instructions
Prepare the Operating Activities section of the statement of cash flows for the year ended December 31, 1998 for Vancouver Company, using the direct method.

(Preparation of Operating Activities Section—Indirect Method) Data for the Vancouver Company are presented in E23-4. **E23-5**

Instructions
Prepare the Operating Activities section of the statement of cash flows using the indirect method.

(Preparation of Operating Activities Section—Indirect Method) Flyer Company's income statement for the year ended September 30, 1998 contained the following condensed information. **E23-6**

Revenue from fees		$840,000
Operating expenses	$624,000	
Depreciation expense	60,000	
Loss on sale of equipment	26,000	710,000
Income before income taxes		130,000
Income tax expense		40,000
Net income		$ 90,000

Flyer's balance sheet contained the following comparative data at September 30.

	1998	1997
Accounts receivable	$37,000	$55,000
Accounts payable	41,000	33,000
Income taxes payable	4,000	9,000

Instructions

Prepare the Operating Activities section of the statement of cash flows using the indirect method.

E23-7 **(Preparation of Operating Activities Section—Direct Method)** Data for Flyer Company are presented in E23-6.

Instructions

Prepare the Operating Activities section of the statement of cash flows using the direct method.

E23-8 **(Computation of Operating Activities—Direct and Indirect Methods)** Presented below are two independent situations.

Situation A

Olajuwan Co. reports revenues of $200,000 and operating expenses of $110,000 in its first year of operations, 1998. Accounts receivable and accounts payable at year end were $70,000 and $32,000, respectively. Assume that the accounts payable relate only to operating expenses. Ignore income taxes.

Instructions

Compute net cash provided by operating activities using first the direct method, then the indirect method.

Situation B

The income statement for Ewing Company shows cost of goods sold of $310,000 and operating expenses, exclusive of depreciation, of $230,000. The comparative balance sheet for the year shows that inventory increased by $6,000, prepaid expenses decreased by $8,000, accounts payable (related to merchandise purchases only) decreased by $7,000, and accrued expenses payable (related to operating expenses only) increased by $11,000.

Instructions

Compute (a) cash payments to merchandise suppliers; and (b) cash payments for operating expenses.

E23-9 **(Schedule of Net Cash Flow from Operating Activities, Indirect Method)** Sekhon Ltd. reported $145,000 of net income for 1998. The accountant, in preparing the statement of cash flows, noted several items that might affect cash flows from operating activities. These items are listed below.

1. During 1998, Sekhon purchased 100 treasury shares at a cost of $20 per share. These shares were then resold at $25 per share.

2. During 1998, Sekhon sold 100 shares of IBM common at $200 per share. The acquisition cost of these shares was $150 per share. This investment was shown on Sekhon's December 31, 1997 balance sheet as a noncurrent asset at cost.

3. During 1998, Sekhon changed from the straight-line method to the double-declining balance method of depreciation for its machinery. The debit to the Retained Earnings account was $13,500.

4. During 1998, Sekhon revised its estimate for bad debts. Before 1998, Sekhon's bad debts expense was 1% of its net sales. In 1998, this percentage was increased to 2%. Net sales for 1998 were $500,000, and net accounts receivable decreased by $12,000 during 1998.

5. During 1998, Sekhon issued 500 of its no-par common shares for a patent. The market value of the shares on the date of the transaction was $23 per share.

6. Depreciation expense for 1998 is $48,000.

7. Sekhon Co. holds 40% of the Fargo Company's common shares as a long-term investment, which is accounted for using the equity method. Fargo Company reported $26,000 of net income for 1998.

8. Fargo Company paid a total of $5,000 of cash dividends in 1998.

9. A comparison of Sekhon's December 31, 1997 and December 31, 1998 balance sheet indicates that the credit balance in the Future Income Tax Liability account (classified as long-term) decreased by $4,000.

10. During 1998, Sekhon declared a 10% stock dividend. One thousand no-par value common shares were distributed. The market price at date of issuance was $20 per share.

Instructions
Prepare a schedule that shows net cash flow from operating activities using the indirect method. Assume no items other than those listed above affected the computation of 1998 net cash flow from operating activities.

(SCF—Direct Method) Flax Corp. uses the direct method to prepare its statement of cash flows. The company's   **E23-10**
trial balances at December 31, 1998 and 1997 are as follows:

	December 31	
	1998	1997
Debits		
Cash	$ 35,000	$ 32,000
Accounts receivable	33,000	30,000
Inventory	31,000	47,000
Property, plant, and equipment	100,000	95,000
Unamortized bond discount	4,500	5,000
Cost of goods sold	250,000	380,000
Selling expenses	141,500	172,000
General and administrative expenses	137,000	151,300
Interest expense	4,300	2,600
Income tax expense	20,400	61,200
	$756,700	$976,100
Credits		
Allowance for doubtful accounts	$ 1,300	$ 1,100
Accumulated depreciation	16,500	15,000
Accounts payable	25,000	17,500
Income taxes payable	21,000	27,100
Future income tax liability	5,300	4,600
Bonds payable, 8%	45,000	20,000
Common shares	59,100	47,500
Retained earnings	44,700	64,600
Sales	538,800	778,700
	$756,700	$976,100

Additional information:

1. Flax purchased equipment that cost $5,000 during 1998.

2. Flax allocated one-third of its depreciation expense to selling expenses and the remainder to general and administrative expenses.

Instructions
Determine what amounts Flax should report in its statement of cash flows for the year ended December 31, 1998 for the following:

(a) Cash collected from customers.

(b) Cash paid for goods and services.

(c) Cash paid for interest.

(d) Cash paid for income taxes.

(Convert Net Income to Operating Cash Flow—Indirect Method) Leung Limited reported net income of $6,500   **E23-11**
for its latest year ended October 31, 1998.

Instructions

For each situation below, calculate the cash flow from operations assuming the following balance sheet amounts.

	Accounts Receivable October 31		Inventory October 31		Accounts Payable October 31	
	1998	1997	1998	1997	1998	1997
(a)	$21,000	$20,500	$17,500	$16,900	$ 9,100	$ 9,000
(b)	20,000	23,000	20,300	17,500	10,600	14,200
(c)	20,000	—	12,000	—	7,000	—
(d)	21,500	19,000	15,500	19,600	11,200	10,100
(e)	24,500	21,000	14,900	12,000	10,300	13,300

E23-12 (SCF: Indirect and Direct Methods) Condensed financial data of Yarmouth Company for 1998 and 1997 are presented below.

Comparative Balance Sheet Data
As of December 31, 1998 and 1997

	1998	1997
Cash	$ 1,800	$ 1,150
Receivables	1,750	1,300
Inventory	1,600	1,900
Plant assets	1,900	1,700
Accumulated depreciation	(1,200)	(1,150)
Long-term investments	1,300	1,400
	$ 7,150	$ 6,300
Accounts payable	$ 1,200	$ 900
Accrued liabilities	200	300
Bonds payable	1,400	1,500
Share capital	1,900	1,700
Retained earnings	2,450	1,900
	$ 7,150	$ 6,300

Income Statement
For the Year Ended December 31, 1998

Sales		$ 6,900
Cost of goods sold		4,700
Gross margin		2,200
Operating expenses:		
Selling expense	$450	
Administrative expense	650	
Depreciation expense	50	1,150
Net income		1,050
Cash dividends		500
Income retained in business		$ 550

Additional information:

There were no gains or losses in any noncurrent transactions during 1998.

Instructions

(a) Prepare a statement of cash flows using the indirect method.

(b) Prepare a statement of cash flows using the direct method.

E23-13 (SCF: Indirect and Direct Methods) Condensed financial data of Lewis Company for the years ended December 31, 1998 and December 31, 1997 follow.

LEWIS COMPANY
Comparative Position Statement Data
As of December 31, 1998 and 1997

	1998	1997
Cash	$160,800	$ 38,400
Receivables	123,200	49,000
Inventories	112,500	61,900
Investments (long-term)	90,000	97,000
Plant assets	240,000	212,500
	$726,500	$458,800
Accounts payable	$100,000	$ 67,300
Mortgage payable	50,000	74,900
Accumulated depreciation	30,000	52,000
Common shares	175,000	131,100
Retained earnings	371,500	133,500
	$726,500	$458,800

Handwritten annotations in right margin:
122,400
74,200
50,600
(7,000)
27,500

32,700
(24,900)
(22,000)
43,900
238,000

LEWIS COMPANY
Income Statement
For the Year Ended December 31, 1998

Sales	$440,000	
Interest and other revenue	20,000	$460,000
Less:		
Cost of goods sold	130,000	
Selling and administrative expenses	10,000	
Depreciation	42,000	
Income taxes	5,000	
Interest expense	3,000	
Loss on sale of plant assets	12,000	202,000
Net income		258,000
Cash dividends		20,000
Income retained in business		$238,000

Additional information:
New plant assets that cost $105,000 were purchased during the year. Investments were sold at book value.

Instructions
(a) Prepare a statement of cash flows using the indirect method.
(b) Prepare a statement of cash flows using the direct method.

(SCF, Indirect and Direct Methods) Zeeland Limited, a greeting card company, had the following statements pre- **E23-14**
pared as of June 30, 1999.

ZEELAND LIMITED
Comparative Balance Sheet
As of June 30, 1999 and 1998

	6/30/99	6/30/98
Cash and cash equivalents	$ 41,000	$ 27,000
Accounts receivable	62,000	49,000
Inventories	40,000	60,000
Prepaid rent	5,000	4,000
Printing equipment	154,000	130,000
Accumulated depreciation—equipment	(35,000)	(25,000)
Goodwill	46,000	50,000
Total assets	$313,000	$295,000

Accounts payable	$ 46,000	$ 40,000
Income taxes payable	4,000	5,000
Wages payable	8,000	4,000
Short-term loans payable	8,000	10,000
Long-term loans payable	60,000	70,000
Common shares	130,000	130,000
Retained earnings	57,000	36,000
Total liabilities and equity	$313,000	$295,000

ZEELAND LIMITED
Income Statement
For the Year Ending June 30, 1999

Sales	$338,150
Cost of goods sold	175,000
Gross margin	163,150
Operating expenses	120,000
Operating income	43,150
Interest expense	9,400
Income before tax	33,750
Income tax expense	6,750
Net income	$ 27,000

Additional information:

1. Dividends in the amount of $6,000 were declared and paid during the year ended June 30, 1999.

2. Depreciation expense and amortization expense are included in operating expenses, as are salaries and wages expense of $75,000.

Instructions

(a) Prepare a statement of cash flows using the direct method.

(b) Prepare a statement of cash flows using the indirect method.

E23-15 **(SCF: Indirect Method)** Presented below are data taken from the records of Glooscap Company.

	December 31, 1998	December 31, 1997	
Cash	$ 15,000	$ 8,000	7,000
Current assets other than cash	85,000	55,000	30,000
Long-term investments	10,000	58,000	(48,000)
Plant assets	366,000	215,000	151,000
	$476,000	$336,000	
Accumulated depreciation	$ 20,000	$ 40,000	(20,000)
Current liabilities	35,000	22,000	13,000
Bonds payable	80,000	-0-	80,000
Share capital	254,000	214,000	40,000
Donated capital	42,000	-0-	42,000
Retained earnings	45,000	60,000	(15,000)
	$476,000	$336,000	

Additional information:

1. The net loss reported on the income statement for the year was $5,000.

2. Securities carried at a cost of $48,000 on December 31, 1997 were sold in 1998 for $39,000.

3. Plant assets that cost $50,000 and were 80% depreciated were sold during 1998 for $8,000.

4. Dividends paid amounted to $10,000.

5. Depreciation charged for the year was $20,000.

6. Land was donated to Glooscap Company by the city. The land was worth $42,000.

7. New shares of common stock were issued for cash.

Instructions
Prepare a statement of cash flows for the year 1998 using the indirect method.

(SCF: Indirect Method, and Balance Sheet) Tonopah Inc. had the following condensed balance sheet at the end of operations for 1997.   **E23-16**

TONOPAH INC.
Balance Sheet
December 31, 1997

Cash	$ 8,500	Current liabilities	$ 15,000
Current assets other than cash	29,000	Long-term notes payable	25,500
Investments	20,000	Bonds payable	25,000
Plant assets (net)	67,500	Share capital	75,000
Land	40,000	Retained earnings	24,500
	$165,000		$165,000

During 1998 the following occurred.
1. A tract of land was purchased for $4,450.
2. Bonds payable in the amount of $6,000 were retired at par.
3. An additional $10,000 in common shares was issued.
4. Dividends that totalled $9,375 were paid to shareholders.
5. Net income for 1998 was $35,250 after allowing for depreciation of $11,250.
6. Land was purchased through the issuance of $22,500 in bonds.
7. Tonopah Inc. sold part of its investment portfolio for $12,875. This transaction resulted in a gain of $875 for the firm.
8. Both current assets (other than cash) and current liabilities remained at the same amount.

Instructions
(a) Prepare a statement of cash flows for 1998 using the indirect method.
(b) Prepare the condensed balance sheet for Tonopah Inc. as it would appear at December 31, 1998.

(Partial SCF: Indirect Method) The accounts below appear in the ledger of Kitimat Company.   **E23-17**

Retained Earnings		Dr.	Cr.	Bal.
Jan. 1, 1998	Credit balance			$ 42,000
Aug. 15	Dividends (cash)	$18,000		24,000
Dec. 31	Net income for 1998		$12,000	36,000

Machinery		Dr.	Cr.	Bal.
Jan. 1, 1998	Debit balance			$140,000
Aug. 3	Purchase of machinery	$62,000		202,000
Sept. 10	Cost of machinery constructed	48,000		250,000
Nov. 15	Machinery sold		$56,000	194,000

Accumulated Depreciation— Machinery		Dr.	Cr.	Bal.
Jan. 1, 1998	Credit balance			$ 84,000
Apr. 8	Extraordinary repairs	$21,000		63,000
Nov. 15	Accumulated depreciation on machinery sold	25,200		37,800
Dec. 31	Depreciation for 1998		$16,800	54,600

Instructions
From the accounts provided, indicate how the transactions and events are reported on a statement of cash flows by preparing a partial statement of cash flows using the indirect method. The loss on sale of equipment on November 15 was $18,800.

*E23-18 **(Work Sheet Analysis of Selected Transactions)** The transactions below took place during the year 1998.

1. Convertible bonds payable of a par (and market) value of $250,000 were exchanged for unissued common shares with a market value of $250,000.

2. The net income for the year was $60,000.

3. Depreciation charged on the building was $24,000.

4. Organization costs in the amount of $10,000 were written off during the year as a charge to expense.

5. Used office equipment was traded in on the purchase of dissimilar office equipment. The following entry was made:

Office Equipment	5,000	
Accum. Depreciation, Office Equipment	3,000	
Office Equipment		4,000
Cash		3,400
Gain on Disposal of Plant Assets		600

6. Dividends in the amount of $18,000 were declared. They are payable in January, 1999.

7. The appropriations for bonded indebtedness in the amount of $400,000 was returned to retained earnings during the year because the bonds were retired during the year.

Instructions

Show by journal entries the adjustments and reconciling items that would be made on a work sheet for a statement of cash flows.

E23-19 **(Preparation of Cash Flow Statement)** Below is the comparative balance sheet for Roanoke Corporation.

	Dec. 31, 1998	Dec. 31, 1997	
Cash	$ 16,500	$ 20,000	(3500)
Marketable equity securities, short-term	25,000	20,000	5000
Accounts receivable	43,000	45,000	(2,000)
Allowance for doubtful accounts	(1,800)	(2,000)	200
Prepaid expenses	4,200	2,500	1,700
Inventories	81,500	65,000	16,500
Land	50,000	50,000	—
Buildings	125,000	73,500	51,500
Accumulated depreciation—buildings	(30,000)	(23,000)	7,000
Equipment	53,000	47,000	6,000
Accumulated depreciation—equipment	(19,000)	(16,500)	2,500
Delivery equipment	39,000	39,000	—
Accumulated depreciation—delivery equipment	(22,000)	(20,500)	1,500
Patents	15,000	-0-	15,000
	$379,400	$300,000	
Accounts payable	$ 26,000	$ 16,000	10,000
Short-term notes payable	4,000	6,000	(2,000)
Accrued payables	3,000	5,000	(2,000)
Mortgage payable	73,000	53,000	20,000
Bonds payable	50,000	62,500	(12,500)
Common shares	150,000	106,000	44,000
Retained earnings	73,400	51,500	21,900
	$379,400	$300,000	

Dividends in the amount of $10,000 were declared and paid in 1998.

Instructions

From this information, prepare a draft statement of cash flows, making reasonable assumptions as appropriate. You may prepare a work sheet, use T-accounts, or simply develop the cash flow information as your analysis proceeds.

PROBLEMS

At the beginning of their 1997 fiscal year, Discot Company issued four-year 8% bonds with a face value of $100,000 for $96,761. The bonds pay interest annually and were sold to yield 9%.

P23-1

At the same time, Primot Limited also issued four-year 8% bonds. These bonds had a face value of $100,000, paid interest annually, and were sold for $106,930 to yield a 6% return.

Both Discot and Primot use the effective interest method of amortizing discounts and premiums, both treat interest as an operating cash flow, and both repay the bonds at maturity on the last day of their fiscal year 2000.

Instructions
(a) Prepare bond amortization tables for Discot Company and Primot Limited from the date of issue to maturity.
(b) 1. For Discot Company, indicate the cash flows related to financing activities and operating activities on the cash flow statements for each year from 1997 to 2000. For the cash flows related to operating activities, begin with the interest expense reported in net income each year and adjust the interest expense if applicable.
   2. For Primot Limited, indicate the cash flows related to financing activities and operating activities on the cash flow statement for each year from 1997 to 2000. For the cash flows related to operating activities, begin with the interest expense reported in net income each year and adjust the interest expense if applicable.
(c) For each company, what was the total financing cash inflow over the four-year period? The total financing cash outflow? The total operating cash outflow?
(d) How is the four-year total operating cash outflow for each company related to the 8% nominal interest rate on the bonds? Explain.

The manager of Alexis Limited has reviewed the annual financial statements for the year 1998 and is unable to determine from a reading of the balance sheet the reasons for the cash flows during the year. You are given the following comparative balance sheet information of Alexis Limited.

P23-2

	12/31/98	12/31/97	Increase (Decrease)	
Land	$ 138,000	$ 218,000	$ (80,000)	INV
Machinery	485,000	200,000	285,000	"
Tools	40,000	70,000	(30,000)	INV.
Bond investment, long-term	20,000	15,000	5,000	FIN.
Inventories	157,000	207,000	(50,000)	OP.
Goodwill	-0-	14,000	(14,000)	N/A INVEST.
Buildings	810,000	550,000	260,000	INV
Accounts receivable	292,000	92,000	200,000	OP
Notes receivable—trade	96,000	176,000	(80,000)	OP
Cash in bank	-0-	8,000	(8,000)	BAL
Cash on hand	7,000	1,000	6,000	BAL
Unexpired insurance—machinery	700	1,400	(700)	OP
Unamortized bond discount	2,000	2,500	(500)	FIN.
	$2,047,700	$1,554,900		
Common shares	$ 900,000	$ 400,000	$ 500,000	FIN
Bonds payable	180,000	130,000	50,000	FIN
Accounts payable	36,000	32,000	4,000	OP
Bank overdraft (temporary)	3,000	-0-	3,000	BAL
Notes payable—trade	11,500	16,800	(5,300)	OP
Accrued interest payable	9,000	6,000	3,000	OP
Accrued taxes payable	4,000	3,000	1,000	OP
Allowance for doubtful accounts	4,700	2,300	2,400	OP CONTRA TO A/R
Accumulated depreciation	300,400	181,000	119,400	INV.
Retained earnings	599,100	783,800	(184,700)	FIN.
	$2,047,700	$1,554,900		

You are advised that the following transactions took place during the year.
   1. The income statement for the year 1998 was:

Sales (net)		$ 1,576,300
Operating charges:		
Material and supplies	$350,000	
Direct labour	210,000	
Manufacturing overhead	281,500	
Depreciation	158,900	
Selling expenses (includes commissions of $48,000)	245,000	
General expenses (includes salaries of $140,000)	330,000	
Interest expense (net)	15,000	
Other items:		
Write-off of goodwill	14,000	
Write-off of land	80,000	
Loss on machinery	6,600	1,691,000
Net loss		$ (114,700)

2. A 5% cash dividend was declared and paid on the outstanding shares at January 1, 1998.

3. There were no purchases or sales of tools. The cost of tools used is in depreciation.

4. Common shares were issued during the year at $90 per share, and a stock dividend was issued.

5. Machinery that cost $16,100 was scrapped and written off the books. Accumulated depreciation on this equipment was $9,500.

Instructions

(a) Prepare a statement of cash flows using the indirect method.

(b) Prepare the Operating Activities section of the cash flow statement assuming the direct method was used.

(c) Write a short report to the manager outlining the major aspects of the year's cash flow activities.

P23-3 The balance sheet of Shabbona Limited at December 31, 1997 is as follows.

SHABBONA LIMITED
Balance Sheet
December 31, 1997

Cash			$ 89,000
Receivables			258,000
Inventories			174,000
Prepaid expenses			28,000
Total current assets			549,000
Investments (long-term)			102,000
Land		$ 46,000	
Buildings	$570,000		
Less accumulated depreciation	110,000	460,000	
Equipment	385,000		
Less accumulated depreciation	180,000	205,000	711,000
Patents			121,000
			$1,483,000
Accounts payable			$ 60,000
Notes payable			120,000
Taxes payable			188,000
Total current liabilities			368,000
Bonds payable			500,000
Preferred shares		$300,000	
Common shares		300,000	
Retained earnings		15,000	615,000
			$1,483,000

Shabbona Company's management is budgeting the following transactions for the coming year.

Sales, on account	$5,000,000
Payments for salaries	1,650,000
Payments for purchases	2,500,000
Payments for interest	100,000
Payments for taxes	250,000
Decrease in prepaid expenses	7,000
Increase in receivables	110,000
Increase in inventories	35,000
Depreciation: Buildings	55,000
Depreciation: Equipment	80,000
Patent amortization	11,000
Increase in accounts payable	25,000
Increase in taxes payable	90,000
Reduction in bonds payable	500,000
Proceeds on sale of investments (all those held 12/31/97)	120,000
Issuance of common shares	100,000

Instructions

(a) Prepare a balance sheet as it will appear December 31, 1998 if all the budgeted transactions work out as expected.

(b) Prepare a statement of cash flows for 1998, assuming that the expected 1998 transactions are all completed. Use the indirect method.

(c) Compute net cash flow from operating activities, using the direct method.

The following is Omega Corporation's comparative balance sheet accounts at June 30, 1999 and 1998 with a column **P23-4** that indicates the increase or decrease from 1998 to 1999.

	June 30 1999	June 30 1998	Increase (Decrease)
Cash	$ 800,000	$ 700,000	$ 100,000
Accounts receivable	1,128,000	1,168,000	(40,000)
Inventories	1,850,000	1,715,000	135,000
Property, plant, and equipment	3,307,000	2,967,000	340,000
Accumulated depreciation	(1,165,000)	(1,040,000)	125,000
Investment in Belle Co.	305,000	275,000	30,000
Loan receivable	270,000	—	270,000
	$6,495,000	$5,785,000	
Accounts payable	$1,015,000	$ 955,000	$ 60,000
Income taxes payable	30,000	50,000	(20,000)
Dividends payable	80,000	90,000	(10,000)
Capital lease obligation	400,000	—	400,000
Common stock	2,000,000	2,000,000	—
Retained earnings	2,970,000	2,690,000	280,000
	$6,495,000	$5,785,000	

Additional information:

1. On June 30, 1998 Omega acquired 25% of Belle Company's common shares for $275,000. On that date, the carrying value of Belle's assets and liabilities, which approximated their fair values, was $1,100,000. Belle reported income of $120,000 for its year ended June 30, 1999. No dividend was paid on Belle common shares during the year.

2. During the 1999 fiscal year, Omega loaned $300,000 to Chase Company, an unrelated company. Chase made the first semiannual principal repayment of $30,000 plus interest at 10% on April 1, 1999.

3. On July 2, 1998 Omega sold equipment that cost $60,000, with a carrying amount of $35,000, for $40,000 cash.

4. On June 30, 1999 Omega entered into a capital lease for an office building. The present value of the annual lease payments is $400,000, which equals the fair value of the building. Omega made the first payment of $60,000 when due on July 2, 1999.

5. Omega reported net income for the year ended June 30, 1999 of $360,000.

6. Omega declared and paid cash dividends for the years ending June 30 as follows.

	1999	1998
Declared	June 15, 1999	June 15, 1998
Paid	August 31, 1999	August 31, 1998
Amount	$80,000	$90,000

Instructions

Prepare a statement of cash flows for Omega Corporation for the year ended June 30, 1999, using the indirect method.

P23-5 H. Kong Company had the following information available at the end of 1998.

H. KONG COMPANY
Comparative Balance Sheet

	12/31/98	12/31/97
Cash	$ 5,000	$ —
Investments in 60-day commercial paper	10,000	14,000
Short-term equity investments	20,000	30,000
Accounts receivable	17,500	12,950
Inventory	42,000	35,000
Prepaid rent	3,000	12,000
Prepaid insurance	2,100	900
Office supplies	1,000	750
Land	125,000	175,000
Building	350,000	350,000
Accumulated depreciation	(105,000)	(87,500)
Equipment	525,000	400,000
Accumulated depreciation	(130,000)	(112,000)
Patent	45,000	50,000
Total assets	$ 910,600	$ 881,100
Temporary bank overdraft	$ —	$ 10,000
Accounts payable	27,000	32,000
Taxes payable	5,000	4,000
Wages payable	5,000	3,000
Short-term notes payable	10,000	8,000
Long-term notes payable	60,000	72,000
Bonds payable	400,000	400,000
Premium on bonds payable	20,303	25,853
Common shares	260,000	237,500
Retained earnings	123,297	88,747
Total liabilities and equity	$ 910,600	$ 881,100

H. KONG COMPANY
Income Statement
For the Year Ended December 31, 1998

Sales revenue		$1,159,248
Cost of goods sold		(747,915)
Gross margin		411,333
Operating expenses		
Selling expenses	$ 29,200	
Administrative expenses	116,700	
Salaries and wages expense	90,000	
Depreciation/amortization expense	40,500	(276,400)
Income from operations		134,933
Other revenues/expenses		
Gain on sale of land	8,000	
Gain on sale of short-term investment	4,000	
Dividend revenue	2,400	
Interest expense	(51,750)	(37,350)
Income before taxes		97,583
Income tax expense		(39,033)
Net income		58,550
Dividends to common shareholders		(24,000)
Net addition to retained earnings		$ 34,550

Instructions

Prepare a statement of cash flows for H. Kong Company using the direct method. Prepare a separate reconciliation of net income to cash flows from operations.

The comparative balance sheets of Seneca Limited show the following information.

P23-6

	December 31	
	1998	1997
Cash	$ 38,500	$13,000
Accounts receivable	12,250	10,000
Inventory	12,000	9,000
Investments, long-term	–0–	3,000
Building	–0–	29,750
Equipment	40,000	20,000
Patent	5,000	6,250
Totals	$107,750	$91,000
Allowance for doubtful accounts	$ 3,000	$ 4,500
Accumulated depreciation on equipment	2,000	4,500
Accumulated depreciation on building	–0–	6,000
Accounts payable	5,000	3,000
Dividends payable	–0–	6,000
Notes payable, short-term (nontrade)	3,000	4,000
Long-term notes payable	31,000	25,000
Common shares	43,000	33,000
Retained earnings	20,750	5,000
	$107,750	$91,000

Additional data related to 1998 are as follows.

1. Equipment that had cost $11,000 and was 40% depreciated at time of disposal was sold for $2,500.
2. $10,000 of the long-term note payable was paid by issuing common shares.
3. Cash dividends paid were $6,000.
4. On January 1, 1998 the building was completely destroyed by a flood. Insurance proceeds on the building were $33,000, net of $4,000 of income tax.
5. Investments (long-term) were sold for $2,500 above their cost.
6. Cash of $15,000 was paid for the acquisition of equipment.
7. A long-term note for $16,000 was issued for the acquisition of equipment.
8. Interest of $2,000 and income taxes of $5,000 were paid in cash.

Instructions
Prepare a statement of cash flows for the year ended December 31, 1998 using the indirect method. Flood damage is unusual and infrequent in that part of the country.

Paso Inc. had the following information available at the end of 1998.

P23-7

PASO INC.
Comparative Balance Sheet
As of December 31, 1998 and 1997

	12/31/98	12/31/97
Cash	$ 46,000	$ 30,000
Accounts receivable	340,000	296,000
Short-term investments	350,000	325,000
Prepaid insurance	16,000	22,000
Merchandise inventory	400,000	350,000
Office supplies	4,000	7,000
Long-term investments (equity)	775,000	700,000
Land	650,000	500,000
Building	1,300,000	1,300,000
Accumulated depreciation—building	(400,000)	(360,000)
Equipment	500,000	550,000
Accumulated depreciation—equipment	(155,000)	(135,000)
Goodwill	63,000	65,000
Total assets	$ 3,889,000	$ 3,650,000

Accounts payable	$ 95,000	$ 70,000
Taxes payable	26,000	15,000
Accrued liabilities	47,000	40,000
Dividends payable	–0–	80,000
Long-term notes payable	45,000	50,000
Bonds payable	1,000,000	1,000,000
Discount on bonds payable	(50,750)	(64,630)
Preferred shares	720,000	600,000
Common shares	1,150,000	1,150,000
Retained earnings	876,750	749,630
Treasury shares (common, at cost)	(20,000)	(40,000)
Total liabilities and equity	$ 3,889,000	$ 3,650,000

PASO INC.
Income Statement
For the Year Ended December 31, 1998

Sales revenue		$1,007,500
Cost of goods sold		403,000
Gross profit		604,500
Selling/administrative expenses		222,087
Income from operations		382,413
Other revenues/expenses		
Long-term investment revenue	$ 115,000	
Interest on short-term investments	15,000	
Gain on sale of equipment	15,000	145,000
Interest expense		(98,880)
Income before taxes		428,533
Income tax expense		(171,413)
Net income		257,120
Dividends (current year)		(130,000)
Increase in retained earnings		$ 127,120

Additional information:

1. Short-term investments comprise holdings of 30- to 60-day treasury bills.

2. In early January, equipment with a book value of $45,000 was sold for a gain.

3. Long-term investments are carried under the equity method. Paso's share of investee income totalled $115,000 in 1998. Paso received dividends from its long-term investment totalling $40,000 during 1998.

4. Cost of goods sold includes $97,000 of direct labour, and selling and administrative expenses include $102,000 of salaries and wages.

Instructions
(a) Prepare a statement of cash flows using the direct method.
(b) Prepare a statement of cash flows using the indirect method.

P23-8 You have completed the field work in connection with your audit of Lang Limited for the year ended December 31, 1998. The following schedule shows the balance sheet accounts at the beginning and end of the year.

	Dec. 31, 1998	Dec. 31, 1997	Increase or (Decrease)
Cash	$ 267,900	$ 298,000	$ (30,100)
Accounts receivable	499,424	353,000	146,424
Inventory	741,700	610,000	131,700
Prepaid expenses	12,000	8,000	4,000
Investment in Marilla Company	110,500	—	110,500
Cash surrender value of life insurance	2,304	1,800	504
Machinery	187,000	190,000	(3,000)
Buildings	535,200	407,900	127,300

Land	52,500	52,500	—
Patents	69,000	64,000	5,000
Goodwill	40,000	50,000	(10,000)
Bond discount and expense	4,502	—	4,502
	$2,522,030	$2,035,200	
Accrued taxes payable	$ 95,250	$ 79,600	$ 15,650
Accounts payable	299,280	280,000	19,280
Dividends payable	70,000	-0-	70,000
Bonds payable—8%	125,000	-0-	125,000
Bonds payable—12%	-0-	100,000	(100,000)
Allowance for doubtful accounts	35,300	40,000	(4,700)
Accumulated depreciation—building	424,000	400,000	24,000
Accumulated depreciation—machinery	173,000	130,000	43,000
Premium on bonds payable	-0-	2,400	(2,400)
Common shares	1,280,200	1,453,200	(173,000)
Appropriation for plant expansion	10,000	-0-	10,000
Retained earnings—unappropriated	10,000	(450,000)	460,000
	$2,522,030	$2,035,200	

Statement of Retained Earnings

Jan. 1, 1998	Balance (deficit)	$ (450,000)
Mar. 31, 1998	Net income for first quarter of 1998	25,000
Apr. 1, 1998	Transfer from common shares	425,000
	Balance	-0-
Dec. 31, 1998	Net income for last three quarters of 1998	90,000
	Dividend declared—payable January 20, 1999	(70,000)
	Appropriation for plant expansion	(10,000)
	Balance	$ 10,000

Your working papers contain the following information.

1. On April 1, 1998 the existing deficit was written off against share capital created by reducing the stated value of the no-par shares.
2. 29,600 no-par shares were issued for $252,000 on November 1, 1998.
3. A patent was purchased for $15,000.
4. During the year, machinery that cost $16,400 and on which there was accumulated depreciation of $5,200 was sold for $7,000. No other plant assets were sold during the year.
5. The 12%, 20-year bonds were dated and issued on January 2, 1986. Interest was payable on June 30 and December 31. They were sold originally at 106. These bonds were retired at 102 plus accrued interest on March 31, 1998.
6. The 8%, 40-year bonds were dated January 1, 1998 and were sold on March 31 at 97 plus accrued interest. Interest is payable semiannually on June 30 and December 31. Issue costs were $839.
7. Lang Limited acquired a 40% ownership interest in Marilla Company on January 2, 1998 for $100,000. The income statement of this equity method investment for 1998 reports a net income of $26,250.
8. Extraordinary repairs to buildings of $7,200 were charged to Accumulated Depreciation, Building.
9. Interest paid in 1998 was $10,500 and income taxes paid were $34,000.

Instructions

(a) From the information above prepare a statement of cash flows using the indirect method. A work sheet or T-accounts are not necessary, but the principal computations should be supported by schedules or skeleton ledger accounts.

(b) Write a brief memo to the audit partner that summarizes relevant information about Lang Limited's cash activities for the year.

The following are comparative balance sheet accounts of Purba Corporation at December 31, 1998 and 1997.   **P23-9**

Assets	1998	1997	Increase or (Decrease)
Cash	$ 313,000	$ 195,000	$ 118,000
Marketable equity securities, at cost	175,000	175,000	—
Allowance to reduce marketable equity securities to market	(13,000)	(24,000)	(11,000)
Accounts receivable, net	418,000	450,000	(32,000)
Inventories	595,000	515,000	80,000
Land	390,000	170,000	220,000
Plant and equipment	765,000	690,000	75,000
Accumulated depreciation	(199,000)	(145,000)	54,000
Goodwill	57,000	60,000	(3,000)
Total assets	$ 2,501,000	$ 2,086,000	

Liabilities and Shareholders' Equity			
Current portion of long-term note	$ 150,000	$ 150,000	$ —
Accounts payable and accrued liabilities	594,000	475,000	119,000
Note payable, long-term	300,000	450,000	(150,000)
Future income tax	44,000	32,000	12,000
Bond payable	190,000	160,000	30,000
Common shares, no-par value	880,000	660,000	220,000
Contributed surplus from treasury stock transactions	9,000	—	9,000
Retained earnings	334,000	195,000	139,000
Treasury shares, at cost	—	(36,000)	(36,000)
Total liabilities and shareholders' equity	$ 2,501,000	$ 2,086,000	

Additional information:

1. On January 20, 1998 Purba issued 10,000 common shares for land having a fair value of $220,000.

2. On February 5, 1998 Purba reissued all of its treasury shares for $45,000.

3. On May 15, 1998 Purba paid a cash dividend of $58,000 on its common shares.

4. On August 8, 1998 equipment was purchased for $140,000.

5. 30 $1,000 bonds were issued at face value on September 1, 1998.

6. On September 30, 1998 equipment was sold for $40,000. The equipment cost $65,000 and had a carrying amount of $37,000 on the date of sale.

7. The future income tax liability represents temporary differences relating to the use of CCA for income tax reporting and the straight-line method for financial reporting.

8. Net income for 1998 was $197,000.

9. Income taxes paid were $70,000; interest paid was $63,000.

Instructions

Prepare a statement of cash flows using the indirect method.

P23-10   Presented below are the 1998 financial statements of Gunnison Corporation.

Balance Sheets

$ in millions	December 31	
	1998	1997
Assets		
Current assets:		
Cash	$ 20.4	$ 7.5
Receivables (net of allowance for doubtful accounts of $5.0 million in 1998 and $4.6 million in 1997)	241.6	213.2
Inventories:		
Finished goods	86.7	84.7

Raw materials and supplies	115.7	123.8
Prepaid expenses	6.2	6.7
Total current assets	470.6	435.9
Property, plant, and equipment:		
Plant and equipment	2,358.8	2,217.7
Less—accumulated depreciation	(993.4)	(890.1)
	1,365.4	1,327.6
Timberland—net	166.3	169.5
Total property, plant, and equipment—net	1,531.7	1,497.1
Other assets	74.7	34.7
Total assets	$2,077.0	$1,967.7

Liabilities and Shareholders' Equity

Current liabilities:		
Current maturities of long-term debt	$ 13.2	$ 10.5
Bank overdrafts (temporary)	25.5	20.2
Accounts payable	102.2	91.3
Accrued liabilities		
Payrolls and employee benefits	73.5	73.9
Interest and other expenses	44.3	29.4
Federal income taxes	17.4	12.7
Total current liabilities	276.1	238.0
Long-term liabilities:		
Future income taxes	333.6	280.0
4.75% to 11.25% revenue bonds with maturities to 2017	174.6	193.4
Other revenue bonds at variable rates with maturities to 2024	46.3	26.6
7 7/8% sinking fund debentures due 2005	19.5	21.0
8.70% sinking fund debentures due 2017	75.0	75.0
9 1/2% convertible subordinated debentures due 2018	—	38.9
9 3/4% notes due 2000	50.0	50.0
Promissory notes	—	60.2
Mortgage debt and miscellaneous obligations	25.7	21.7
Other long-term liabilities	21.8	—
Total long-term liabilities	746.5	766.8
Shareholders' investment:		
Common shares (60,000,000 shares authorized, 26,661,770 and 25,265,921 shares outstanding as of December 31, 1998 and 1997)	244.4	196.9
Reinvested earnings	810.0	766.0
Total shareholders' investment	1,054.4	962.9
Total liabilities and shareholders' investment	$2,077.0	$1,967.7

Statement of Income and Reinvested Earnings

	1998
$ in millions, except per share amounts	
Income	
Net sales	$ 2,039.2
Cost of sales	1,637.8
Gross margin	401.4
Selling, general, and administrative expense	(182.6)
Provision for reduced operations	(41.0)
Operating income	177.8
Interest on long-term debt	(33.5)
Other income—net	2.2
Pretax income	146.5
Income taxes	(61.2)
Net income	$ 85.3

Earnings per share	$ 3.20
Reinvested earnings	
Reinvested earnings at beginning of year	$ 766.0
Add—net income	85.3
	851.3
Deduct—dividends:	
Common shares ($1.57 a share in 1998)	41.3
Reinvested earnings at end of year	$ 810.0

Additional information:

1. Depreciation and cost of timberland harvested was $114.6 million.

2. The provision for reduced operations included a decrease in cash of $15.9 million.

3. Purchases of plant and equipment were $176.5 million, and purchases of timberland were $40 million.

4. Sales of plant and equipment resulted in cash inflows of $2.2 million. All sales were at book value.

5. The changes in long-term liabilities are summarized below.

Increase in future income tax liability	$ 53.6
New borrowings	63.2
Debt retired by cash payments	(86.5)
Debt converted into shares	(37.4)
Reclassification to current maturities	(13.2)
Decrease in long-term liabilities	$(20.3)

6. The increase in common shares results from the issuance of shares for debt conversion, $37.4 million, and shares issued for cash, $10.1 million.

7. Interest paid during 1998 was $21.2.

Instructions

(a) Prepare a statement of cash flows for the Gunnison Corporation using the indirect method.

(b) Prepare a brief memo that summarizes the company's cash activities during 1998. Ensure you explain how Gunnison was able to finance the significant investments in property, plant, and equipment during the year.

P23-11 Fairfax Company, a major retailer of bicycles and accessories, operates several stores and is a publicly traded company. The comparative Statement of Financial Position and the Income Statement for Fairfax as of May 31, 1998 are shown below. The company is preparing its Statement of Cash Flows.

FAIRFAX COMPANY
Comparative Statement of Financial Position

	5/31/98	5/31/97
Current assets		
Cash	$ 33,250	$ 20,000
Accounts receivable	80,000	50,000
Merchandise inventory	210,000	250,000
Prepaid expenses	9,000	7,000
Total current assets	332,250	327,000
Plant assets		
Plant assets	600,000	510,000
Less: Accumulated depreciation	150,000	125,000
Net plant assets	450,000	385,000
Total assets	$782,250	$712,000
Current liabilities		
Accounts payable	$123,000	$115,000
Salaries payable	47,250	72,000
Interest payable	27,000	25,000
Total current liabilities	197,250	212,000
Long-term debt		
Bonds payable	70,000	100,000

Total liabilities	267,250	312,000
Shareholders' equity		
Common shares	370,000	280,000
Retained earnings	145,000	120,000
Total shareholders' equity	515,000	400,000
Total liabilities and shareholders' equity	$782,250	$712,000

FAIRFAX COMPANY
Income Statement
For the Year Ended May 31, 1998

Sales	$1,255,250
Cost of merchandise sold	712,000
Total contribution	543,250
Expenses	
Salary expense	252,100
Interest expense	75,000
Other expenses	8,150
Depreciation expense	25,000
Total expenses	360,250
Operating income	183,000
Income tax expense	43,000
Net income	$ 140,000

The following is additional information concerning Fairfax's transactions during the year ended May 31, 1998.

1. Plant assets costing $90,000 were purchased by paying $40,000 in cash and issuing 5,000 common shares.
2. Prepaid expenses are related to the "other expenses."
3. All income taxes incurred during the year were paid during the year.
4. In order to supplement its cash, Fairfax issued 4,000 common shares at $10 each.
5. No penalties were assessed for the retirement of bonds.
6. Cash dividends of $115,000 were declared and paid at the end of the fiscal year.

Instructions
(a) Compare and contrast the direct method and the indirect method for reporting cash flows from operating activities.
(b) Prepare a statement of cash flows for Fairfax Company for the year ended May 31, 1998, using the direct method. Be sure to support the statement with appropriate calculations.
(c) Using the indirect method, calculate only the net cash flow from operating activities for Fairfax Company for the year ended May 31, 1998.

CASES

The following statement was prepared by Point Barrow Corporation's accountant.

C23-1

POINT BARROW CORPORATION
Statement of Sources and Application of Cash
For the Year Ended September 30, 1998

Sources of cash	
Net income	$ 85,000
Depreciation and depletion	70,000
Increase in long-term debt	189,000
Common shares issued under employee option plans	16,000
Changes in current receivables and inventories, less current liabilities (excluding current maturities of long-term debt)	14,000

	$374,000
Application of cash	
Cash dividends	$ 50,000
Expenditure for property, plant, and equipment	224,000
Investments and other uses	20,000
Change in cash	80,000
	$374,000

The following additional information relating to Point Barrow Corporation is available for the year ended September 30, 1998.

1. The corporation received $16,000 in cash from its employee stock option plans, and wage and salary expense attributable to the option plans was an additional $22,000.

2. Expenditures for property, plant, and equipment $250,000

   Proceeds from retirements of property, plant, and equipment   26,000

   Net expenditures $224,000

3. A stock dividend of 10,000 common shares was distributed to common shareholders on April 1, 1998 when the per-share market price was $7.

4. On July 1, 1998, when its market price was $6 per share, 16,000 Point Barrow Corporation common shares were issued in exchange for 4,000 preferred shares.

5. Depreciation expense $ 65,000

   Depletion expense   5,000

       $ 70,000

6. Increase in long-term debt $620,000

   Retirement of debt   431,000

   Net increase $189,000

Instructions

(a) In general, what are the objectives of a statement of the type shown above for the Point Barrow Corporation? Explain.

(b) Identify the weaknesses in the form or format of the Point Barrow Corporation's statement of cash flows without reference to the additional information.

(c) For each of the six items of additional information for the statement of cash flows, indicate the preferred treatment and explain why the suggested treatment is preferable.

(AICPA adapted)

C23-2   Linda Leung and Keith Vaughan are examining the following statement of cash flows for Agincourt's Clothing store, showing its first year of operations.

AGINCOURT'S CLOTHING STORE
Statement of Cash Flows
For the Year Ended January 31, 1999

Sources of cash	
From sales of merchandise	$362,000
From sale of share capital	440,000
From sale of all investments	80,000
From depreciation	70,000
From issuance of note for truck	30,000
From interest on investments	8,000
Total sources of cash	$990,000
Uses of cash	
For purchase of fixtures and equipment	$340,000
For merchandise purchased for resale	253,000
For operating expenses (including depreciation)	160,000
For purchase of investments	85,000
For purchase of truck by issuance of note	30,000
For purchase of treasury shares	10,000

For interest on note	3,000
Total uses of cash	881,000
Net increase in cash	$109,000

Linda claims that Agincourt's cash flow statement is an excellent portrayal of a superb first year with cash increasing $109,000. Keith replies that it was not a superb year, that the year was an operating failure, that the statement was incorrectly presented, and that $109,000 is not the actual increase in cash.

Instructions
(a) With whom do you agree, Linda or Keith? Explain your position.
(b) Using the data provided, prepare a statement of cash flows in proper indirect method form. The only noncash items in the income statement are depreciation and the loss from the sale of the investments.

Sedona Company is a young and growing producer of electronic measuring instruments and technical equipment. **C23-3**
You have been retained by Sedona as adviser in the preparation of a cash flow statement using the indirect method. For the fiscal year ended October 31, 1998 you have obtained the following information concerning certain events and transactions of Sedona.

1. The amount of reported earnings for the fiscal year was $800,000, which included a deduction for an extraordinary loss of $85,000 (see Item 5 below).
2. Depreciation expense of $325,000 was included in the earnings statement.
3. Uncollectible accounts receivable of $40,000 were written off against the allowance for doubtful accounts. Also, $48,000 of bad debts expense was included in determining income for the fiscal year, and the same amount was added to the allowance for doubtful accounts.
4. A gain of $6,000 was realized on the sale of a machine; it originally cost $75,000, of which $30,000 was undepreciated on the date of sale.
5. On April 1, 1998 lightning caused an uninsured building loss of $85,000 ($140,000 loss, less reduction in income taxes of $55,000). This extraordinary loss was included in determining income as indicated in Item 1 above.
6. On July 3, 1998 building and land were purchased for $600,000; Sedona gave in payment $75,000 cash, $200,000 market value of its unissued common shares, and signed a $325,000 mortgage note payable.
7. $800,000 face value of Sedona's 10% convertible debentures were converted into no-par value common shares on August 3, 1998. The bonds were originally issued at face value.
8. Sedona Company initiated a stock option plan for key personnel during the year. Options to acquire 10,000 shares at an option price of $10 were granted at a time when the shares were trading at $12 per share. The options are exercisable any time after May 1, 2000. Compensation expense of $5,000 was recognized for the year ended October 31, 1998 in relation to the options.

Instructions
Explain whether each of the eight numbered items is a source or use of cash, and explain how each should be reported in Sedona's cash flow statement for the fiscal year ended October 31, 1998. If any item is neither a source nor a use of cash, explain why it is not and indicate the disclosure, if any, that should be made of the item in Sedona's statement of cash flows for the fiscal year ended October 31, 1998.

Each of the following items must be considered in preparing a statement of cash flows for Havasu Fashions Inc. for **C23-4**
the year ended December 31, 1998.

1. Fixed assets that had cost $20,000 six and one-half years before and were being depreciated on a 10-year basis with no estimated residual value were sold for $6,250.
2. During the year, goodwill of $10,000 was completely written off to expense.
3. During the year, 500 common shares were issued for $32 a share.
4. The company sustained a net loss for the year of $2,100. Depreciation amounted to $2,000 and patent amortization was $400.
5. An appropriation for contingencies in the amount of $80,000 was created by a charge against Retained Earnings.
6. Uncollectible accounts receivable in the amount of $2,000 were written off against the allowance for doubtful accounts.
7. Long-term investments that cost $12,000 when purchased four years earlier were sold for $11,000.

8. Bonds payable with a par value of $24,000 on which there was an unamortized bond premium of $2,000 were redeemed at 103.

Instructions

For each item, state where it is to be shown in the statement and then illustrate how you would present the necessary information, including the amount. Consider each item independently of the others. Assume that correct entries were made for all transactions as they took place.

C23-5   In 1974, the CICA's Accounting Research Committee issued a replacement to *Handbook* Section 1540 on the Statement of Source and Application of Funds. The new section expanded the funds statement to include significant noncash exchanges affecting the asset and capital structure of the entity. The statement could show either changes in cash, working capital, or quick assets.

   In 1985, Section 1540 was revised again. This revision required that changes in cash and cash equivalents be reported. In addition, the statement should present information for operating activities, financing activities, and investing activities.

   Most recently, in 1997, new requirements were put in place for Section 1540. These changes completed the move from a statement of changes in financial position to one clearly focussed on cash flows.

Instructions

(a) By citing problems inherent in the statement of changes in financial position based on the source and application of funds, explain at least three reasons for developing the statement of cash flows.

(b) Explain the purposes of the cash flow statement.

(c) Identify and describe the three categories of activities that must be reported in the statement of cash flows.

(d) Identify two methods for reporting cash flows from operations. Are both permitted under GAAP? Explain.

(e) Describe the financial reporting requirements for noncash investing and financing transactions. Include in your description two examples of noncash investing and financing transactions.

USING YOUR JUDGEMENT

FINANCIAL REPORTING PROBLEMS

1. Refer to the financial statements and other documents of Moore Corporation Limited for the year ended December 31, 1995 presented in Appendix 5A, then answer the following questions.

   (a) How does Moore Corporation define cash? Is this consistent with the definition in the most recent recommendations? Explain.

   (b) Explain fully why the gain on sale of an investment and the decrease in pension reserves are deducted on the cash flow statement.

   (c) How has Moore Corporation handled dividends and interest paid, and dividends and interest received, on the cash flow statement? Suggest reasons to support this treatment. What alternative treatments could have been used? Which method do you prefer? Explain.

   (d) Which method of determining operating cash flows did the company use? To the extent possible, prepare the Operating Cash Flow section under the alternative method.

   (e) Write a memo that describes the company's major cash activities during its year ended December 31, 1995. Are these cash flows comparable (i.e., similar) to those in 1993 and 1994? Explain.

2. Write a memo to a colleague who is considering investing in Crestar Energy Inc. (see Exhibit 23-21) about the company's cash management activities. Ensure you address the following in your report.

   (a) Is the company liquid and solvent?

   (b) Explain why the 1996 cash flow from operations per share differs so much from the basic earnings per share of $1.07 ($0.44 in 1995) reported on the company's income statement.

   (c) What strategies did the company follow in 1996 to finance its extensive capital investment program? Is this consistent with 1995?

ETHICS CASE

Guthrie Guitar Company is in the business of manufacturing top-quality, steel-string folk guitars. In recent years the company has experienced working capital problems that resulted from the procurement of factory equipment, the unanticipated buildup of receivables and inventories, and the payoff of a balloon mortgage on a new manufacuring facility. The founder and president of the company, Jerry Guthrie, has attempted to raise cash from various financial institutions, but to no avail because of the company's poor performance in recent years. In particular, the company's bank is especially concerned about Guthrie's inability to maintain a positive cash position. The bank's commercial loan officer told Jerry, "I can't even consider your request for capital financing unless I see that your company is able to generate positive cash flows from operations."

Thinking about the banker's comment, Jerry came up with what he believes is a good plan: with a more attractive statement of cash flows, the bank might be willing to provide long-term financing. To "window dress" cash flows, Guthrie Guitars can sell its accounts receivable to factors and liquidate its raw material inventories. These rather costly transactions would generate lots of working capital. As the chief accountant for Guthrie Guitar, it is your job to tell Jerry what you think of his plan.

Instructions
(a) What are the ethical implications of Jerry's idea?
(b) As the chief accountant of Guthrie Guitar, what would you tell Jerry?

chapter 24

BASIC FINANCIAL STATEMENT ANALYSIS

CHAPTER 24

Basic Financial Statement Analysis

Learning Objectives

After studying this chapter, you should be able to:

1. Understand the role of financial statement analysis in helping various users of financial statements evaluate risk and reduce uncertainty regarding their decisions.

2. Appreciate the importance of an auditor's report, awareness of accounting policies used by a company, and having a logical approach when conducting financial statement analysis.

3. Identify major types of ratios and know what each is attempting to measure.

4. Identify liquidity ratios, know how they are calculated, and appreciate the questions they can help answer.

5. Identify activity ratios, know how they are calculated, and appreciate the questions they can help answer.

6. Identify profitability ratios, know how they are calculated, and appreciate the questions they can help answer.

7. Identify coverage ratios, know how they are calculated, and appreciate the questions they can help answer.

8. Describe and know how to apply comparative (trend) analysis.

9. Describe and know how to apply percentage (common-size) analysis.

10. Know sources of uncertainty for decision makers when using financial statement information and the related limitations of ratio analysis.

11. Recognize issues associated with the requirement that ratios be reported in financial statements.

As stated in Chapter 1, *the objective of financial statements* is to "communicate information that is useful to investors, creditors and other users in making resource allocation decisions and/or assessing management stewardship."[1] Thus far in this book we have examined (1) how accountants identify the economic transactions and events to be reported in financial statements; (2) how measurements are derived; and (3) how such items and measurements are disclosed in the body of the statements or related notes. Communication, however, means more than just preparing and sending out financial statements. *Communication* presumes understanding of the statements by users and accountants so that the information can be analysed and interpreted in a meaningful way. The objective of this chapter is to describe and illustrate some basic techniques of financial statement analysis as well as to consider the limitations of such analysis.[2]

---

[1] *CICA Handbook* (Toronto: CICA), Section 1000, par. .15.

[2] In some of the previous chapters (e.g., Chapter 8 on inventory and Chapter 12 on amortization) the implications of selecting particular methods for making accounting measurements on particular ratios have been considered.

ROLE OF FINANCIAL STATEMENT ANALYSIS IN DECISION MAKING

What would be important to you in studying a company's financial statements? In general you would probably want to know about the company's past performance and present condition in order to assess its future prospects. However, your particular answer would depend on your reasons for interest in the company — whether you are a creditor, shareholder, potential investor, manager, government agency, or labour leader. For example, *short-term creditors*, such as banks and suppliers, are primarily interested in a company's ability to pay its currently maturing obligations. *Bondholders* are concerned with the risk associated with the company's ability to pay the principal when due, as well as periodic interest. *Owners and financial analysts* also are interested in aspects of importance to creditors and bondholders. Additionally, they wish to assess a company's long-run profitability in order to evaluate their investment or recommendations for investment.[3] *Union leaders* need information to determine a company's "ability to pay" when negotiating wages and benefits.

A company's *management* has responsibility to these and other stakeholders. As such, it must carefully monitor and manage operations with which these groups are concerned. Also, the financial statements are a primary means by which management communicates financial information regarding the results of their decisions. Consequently, the possible results of a contemplated decision on financial statements and ratios developed from these statements are often important factors in making the decision.[4]

Regardless of the perspective or the type of decision, an underlying objective of a decision maker is to evaluate risk. **Risk** may be thought of as *the possibility of loss resulting from a decision.*[5] A major factor contributing to risk is uncertainty. **Uncertainty** is *the doubt experienced about the best action to take.*[6] It can be caused by factors such as naïveté, lack of information, or the simple fact that future events are unpredictable. Therefore:

> Risk is compounded by uncertainty, but reduced by decision-relevant information which enables enterprises, investors and creditors to take appropriate action to either avoid risky situations or obtain fair compensation for risk taking.[7]

> **OBJECTIVE 1**
>
> Understand the role of financial statement analysis in helping various users of financial statements evaluate risk and reduce uncertainty regarding their decisions.

---

[3] Two major viewpoints exist regarding the usefulness of financial statement (ratio) analysis to existing and potential shareholders of companies that trade shares through a well-organized market (i.e., stock exchange). The **capital market approach** is based on the hypothesis that such markets are efficient because a share's price incorporates all publicly available information (including that in financial statements) at any point in time. Therefore, analysing financial statements with the intent to identify over- or under-valued shares is not a useful exercise. Rather, investors should concentrate on the return from ownership of shares in an investment portfolio. Alternatively, the **fundamental analysis approach** assumes that financial statement analysis can provide information useful for identifying over- or under-valued shares. While considerable research had provided support for the capital markets approach, many believe that a combination of both approaches is useful. Even under the capital markets approach, someone (e.g., financial analysts) must analyse financial statement information in order to see that it is incorporated into market prices. Fundamental financial statement analysis also remains useful for investors in less than efficient market situations (e.g., private companies, proprietorships, partnerships) and for parties other than shareholders who have questions to be answered about a company. In this chapter, we consider financial statement analysis techniques associated with a fundamental analysis approach. Techniques and concepts of a capital market approach are commonly examined in finance or more advanced accounting courses.

[4] Management also can have its own unique interest in amounts reported in or ratios derived from financial statements when its compensation package includes bonus plans and stock options. In addition to annual financial statements, management typically has internal financial reports prepared regularly. Day-to-day information regarding cash flows, gross margins, variances form plans, etc., is used extensively for internal planning and control purposes.

[5] J.E. Boritz, *Approaches to Dealing with Risk and Uncertainty* (Toronto: CICA, 1990), p. XV. We have adapted the specific definition given by Boritz.

[6] *Ibid.*

[7] *Ibid.*

Acquisition and use of decision-relevant information is, therefore, an important factor in evaluating risk. Information about a particular company, the industry in which it operates, and the general state of the economy is all likely to have some relevance when making decisions about the company. Such information can come from a variety of sources, including financial magazines and newspapers, economic forecasts, speeches by top executives, credit rating organizations, financial analysts, reports filed with a securities commission, or personal or business acquaintances. Added to this list are financial statements. Therefore, while the authors concentrate on financial statement analysis as a means to derive decision-relevant information, it is important to appreciate that many other sources of such information are considered when making decisions.

A GENERAL PERSPECTIVE ON FINANCIAL STATEMENT ANALYSIS

OBJECTIVE 2

Appreciate the importance of an auditor's report, awareness of accounting policies used by a company, and having a logical approach when conducting financial statement analysis.

Financial statements include the balance sheet, income statement, statement of retained earnings, statement of cash flows, and cross-referenced notes to these statements. Generally, an auditor's report accompanies the statements. An **auditor's report** provides the opinion of an independent professional accountant as to whether the statements present information fairly and in accordance with generally accepted accounting principles. If the statements satisfy these requirements, an *unqualified opinion* is given. When the requirements of fairness and/or conformity to GAAP are not satisfied, the auditor must explain why. The seriousness of the problem determines whether a *qualified opinion, adverse opinion,* or *denial of opinion* will be given in the auditor's report. Consequently, when carrying out financial statement analysis, an initial action would be to examine the auditor's report to determine if there are any basic problems with the information in the financial statements. In some circumstances, an auditor's report may not accompany the financial statements. This fact should alert the user of the statements to discover why and to be particularly cautious when using the statements as a source of information for decision making.

Awareness of particular accounting policies and methods used by a company to recognize items and measure amounts reported is also important to interpreting and understanding the results of financial statement analysis. Examples of areas in which companies may choose different accounting policies include whether to capitalize or expense the interest related to financing asset construction or development of research, the method for amortizing long-lived assets, valuation of inventory, and the method used to recognize revenue on long-term contracts. The particular choice can have a significant effect on whether items and amounts are reported, how they are measured, where they are reported, and trends over time for a given company. Also, if the financial statement analysis involves intercompany comparison, the use of different policies by the companies must be taken into consideration.

Recognizing that awareness of accounting policies is important, the *CICA Handbook* requires that a "clear and concise description of significant accounting policies . . . should be included as an integral part of the financial statements."[8] Companies typically disclose these policies in the first note to the financial statements or in a separate summary. Therefore, in addition to examining the auditor's report, reading the disclosure regarding accounting policies is an important preparatory step to conducting financial statement analysis and interpreting the results.

Within this general context, specific information from financial statements can be obtained by examining relationships between items on the statements and identifying

---

[8] *CICA Handbook*, Section 1505, par. .04.

trends in these relationships. Relationships are expressed numerically in ratios and percentages, and trends are identified through comparative analysis.

A problem with learning how to analyse statements is that the means may become an end in itself. There are thousands of possible relationships that could be calculated and trends that could be identified. If one knows only how to calculate ratios and trends without understanding how such information can be used, little is accomplished. Therefore, a logical approach to financial statement analysis is necessary. Such an approach may consist of the following steps:

1. *Know the questions for which you want to find answers.* As indicated earlier, there are various groups with different types of interests in a company. Depending on the user, questions of particular interest to them can be identified.

2. *Know the questions that particular ratios and comparisons are to help answer.* These will be discussed in the remainder of this chapter.

3. *Match 1 and 2 above.* By such a matching, the statement analysis will have a logical direction and purpose.

Several caveats must be mentioned. *Financial statements report on the past.* As such, analysis of the data is an examination of the past. Whenever such information is incorporated into a decision-making (future-oriented) process, a critical assumption is that the past is a reasonable basis for predicting the future. This is usually a reasonable approach, but the limitations associated with it should be recognized.

Also, *while ratio and trend analyses will help identify strengths and weaknesses of a company, such analyses will not likely reveal why things are as they are.* Ratios and trends may serve as "red flags" to indicate problem areas. Finding answers about "why" usually requires an in-depth analysis and an awareness of many factors about a company that are not reported in the financial statements—for instance, the impact of inflation, actions of competitors, technological developments, or a strike at a major supplier's or buyer's business.

Another point is that a *single ratio by itself is not likely to be very useful.* For example, a current ratio of 2:1 (current assets are twice current liabilities) may be viewed as satisfactory. If, however, the industry average is 3:1, such a conclusion may be questioned. Even given this industry average, one may conclude that the particular company is doing well if the ratio last year was 1.5:1. Consequently, to derive meaning from ratios, some standard against which to compare them is needed. Such a standard may come from industry averages, past years' amounts, a particular competitor, or planned levels.

Finally, *awareness of the limitations of accounting numbers used in an analysis* is important. For example, the implications of different acceptable accounting policies on statements, ratios, and trends, particularly regarding comparability among companies and between a company and an industry average, must always be recognized. More will be said about some of the limitations and their consequences later in this chapter.

RATIO ANALYSIS

Various techniques are used in the analysis of financial statement data to bring out the comparative and relative significance of the financial information presented.[9] These include *ratio analysis, comparative analysis, percentage analysis, and examination of*

---

[9] *Using Ratios and Graphics in Financial Reporting*, CICA Research Study (Toronto: CICA, 1993). This study provides a comprehensive examination of the uses and limitations of ratio and graphical presentations to convey information to users of financial reports. It includes an extensive bibliography and a multitude of tables that identify the incidence of disclosures of ratios and graphics in annual reports of 200 companies.

related data (i.e., in notes and other sources). No one technique is more useful than another. Every situation faced by the analyst is different, and the answers needed are often obtained only on close examination of the interrelationships among all the data provided. Ratio analysis is a starting point in developing information desired by an analyst.

OBJECTIVE 3
Identify major types of ratios and know what each is attempting to measure.

A **ratio** is simply *an expression of the relationship between two numbers* drawn or derived from the financial statements. Ratios can be classified as shown in Exhibit 24-1.[10]

EXHIBIT 24-1

MAJOR TYPES OF RATIOS

Liquidity Ratios. Measures of the enterprise's short-run ability to pay its maturing obligations.

Activity Ratios. Measures of how efficiently the enterprise is using the assets employed.

Profitability Ratios. Measures of the degree of success or failure of a given enterprise or division for a given period of time.

Coverage Ratios. Measures of the degree of protection for long-term creditors and investors.

Generally, the liquidity ratios and coverage ratios reflect financial strength—ability to satisfy the financial requirements of non-ownership interests in the business. Assessing management's performance is a prime reason for examining activity and profitability ratios. From such assessment, investors formulate opinions about returns from future ownership interest.

The calculation[11] and use of individual ratios will be illustrated through a case example adopted from the annual report of a large concern that we have disguised under the name of Anetek Corporation. It is important, however, to look at ratios in a total context to be able to better understand the company's strengths and weaknesses. This will be done after the individual ratios are considered.

Anetek Corporation is a worldwide enterprise offering more than 1,400 products and services. Anetek employees number some 50,000 in 48 countries. The comparative consolidated income statement (Exhibit 24-2), balance sheet (Exhibit 24-3), and statement of cash flows (Exhibit 24-4) are the basis for the ratios to be calculated. The numbers used in the ratios, like the numbers used in the financial statements, are in thousands of dollars (i.e., have the last three digits (000) omitted).

LIQUIDITY RATIOS

OBJECTIVE 4
Identify liquidity ratios, know how they are calculated, and appreciate the questions they can help answer.

Liquidity ratios are primarily used to *help assess the ability of a firm to meet its current debts.* They are important in evaluating a company's short-term financial strength. For example, Anetek has current liabilities of $575,000. Can these current obligations be met when due? Certain basic ratios can be computed that provide some guidance for determining the enterprise's short-term debt-paying ability.

1. Current Ratio. The **current ratio** is the relationship of total current assets to total current liabilities. Although the quotient is the dollars of current assets available to cover each dollar of current debt, it is most frequently expressed as a coverage of so many

---

[10] Other terms may be used to categorize these ratios. For example, liquidity ratios are sometimes referred to as solvency ratios; activity ratios as turnover or efficiency ratios; and coverage ratios as leverage or capital structure ratios.

[11] The definitions and calculations for the various ratios to be illustrated are fairly commonly used. However, alternative definitions exist of what is included in any particular ratio. Consequently, when using ratios prepared by others (e.g., published industry averages being used for making comparisons to a company's calculated ratios), close attention should be given to the description of how these ratios were determined.

EXHIBIT 24-2 ANETEK CORPORATION

INCOME STATEMENT
FOR THE YEAR ENDED DECEMBER 31
(IN THOUSANDS OF DOLLARS)

	1998	1997
Sales and other revenue:		
Net sales	$1,600,000	$1,350,000
Interest revenue	25,000	20,000
Other revenue	50,000	30,000
Total revenue	$1,675,000	$1,400,000
Cost and other charges:		
Cost of goods sold	$1,000,000	$ 850,000
Depreciation and amortization	150,000	150,000
Selling and administrative expenses	225,000	150,000
Interest expense	50,000	25,000
Total	$1,425,000	$1,175,000
Income before taxes	$ 250,000	$ 225,000
Income taxes	100,000	75,000
Net income	$ 150,000	$ 150,000
Earnings per share*	$ 5.00	$ 5.00

*Additional information:
Weighted-average number of shares outstanding in 1998 is 30 million.
Market price of Anetek's shares at end of 1998 is $60 each.
Cash dividend per share in 1998 is $2.25.

EXHIBIT 24-3 ANETEK CORPORATION

BALANCE SHEET*
DECEMBER 31, 1998 AND 1997
(IN THOUSANDS OF DOLLARS)

	1998	1997
Assets		
Current assets:		
Cash	$ 40,000	$ 25,000
Marketable securities (at cost)	100,000	75,000
Accounts receivable	350,000	300,000
Inventories (at lower of cost and market)	310,000	250,000
Total current assets	$ 800,000	$ 650,000
Investments (at cost)	$ 300,000	$ 325,000
Capital assets:		
Property, plant, and equipment (at cost)	$2,000,000	$ 1,900,000
Less: accumulated depreciation	(900,000)	(800,000)
	$1,100,000	$ 1,100,000
Goodwill	$ 50,000	$ 25,000
Total assets	$2,250,000	$ 2,100,000

EXHIBIT 24-3 ANETEK CORPORATION (Continued)

	1998	1997
Liabilities and Shareholders' Equity		
Current liabilities:		
Accounts payable	$ 125,000	$ 50,000
Notes payable	250,000	250,000
Accrued and other liabilities	200,000	150,000
Total current liabilities	$ 575,000	$ 450,000
Long-term debt:		
Bonds and notes payable	725,000	782,500
Total liabilities	$1,300,000	$1,232,500
Shareholders' equity:		
Common shares	$ 150,000	$ 150,000
Contributed surplus	550,000	550,000
Retained earnings	250,000	167,500
Total shareholders' equity	$ 950,000	$ 867,500
Total liabilities and shareholders' equity	$2,250,000	$2,100,000

*The notes and some detail that accompanied this statement are excluded for purposes of simplicity and brevity.

EXHIBIT 24-4 ANETEK CORPORATION

STATEMENT OF CASH FLOWS*
FOR THE YEAR ENDED DECEMBER 31, 1998
(IN THOUSANDS OF DOLLARS)

Cash flows from operating activities:		
Net income		$ 150,000
Add (deduct) items not affecting cash		
Depreciation and amortization	$ 150,000	
Increase in accounts receivable	(50,000)	
Increase in inventory	(60,000)	
Increase in accounts payable	75,000	
Increase in accrued and other liabilities	50,000	165,000
Net cash flow from operating activities		$ 315,000
Cash flows from investing activities:		
Acquisition of property, plant, equipment	$(150,000)	
Acquisition of goodwill	(25,000)	
Sale of investments	25,000	
Net cash outflow from investing activities		(150,000)
Cash flows from financing activities:		
Reduction of bonds and notes payable	$ (57,500)	
Payment of dividends	(67,500)	
Net cash outflow from financing activities		(125,000)
Net increase in cash		$40,000
Cash, December 31,1997		(150,000)
Cash, December 31,1998		$(110,000)

*Cash and cash equivalents basis (cash + marketable securities − short-term notes payable)

times. Sometimes it is called the **working capital ratio**, because working capital is the excess of current assets over current liabilities. The computation of the 1998 current ratio for Anetek is shown in Exhibit 24-5.

EXHIBIT 24-5

CURRENT RATIO CALCULATION

$$\text{Current Ratio} \quad = \quad \frac{\text{Current Assets}}{\text{Current Liabilities}} \quad = \quad \frac{\$800,000}{\$575,000} \quad = \quad 1.39 \text{ times}$$

$$\text{Industry Average}^{12} \quad = 2.30 \text{ times}$$

The current ratio of 1.39 to 1 compared with the industry average of 2.3 to 1 indicates that Anetek's safety factor to meet maturing short-term obligations is noticeably low. Does the relatively low current ratio indicate the existence of a liquidity problem? Or, considering that the ratio is greater than 1 to 1, is the situation well in hand? The current ratio is only one measure of determining liquidity and it does not answer all of the liquidity questions. How liquid are the receivables and inventory? What effect does the omission of the inventory have on the analysis of liquidity? To help answer these and other questions, additional analysis of other related data is helpful.

2. **Acid-Test Ratio.** A satisfactory current ratio does not disclose the fact that a portion of the current assets may be tied up in slow-moving inventories. With inventories, especially raw material and work in process, there is a question of how long it will take to transform them into the finished product and what ultimately will be realized on the sale of the merchandise. Also, different companies may be using different inventory valuation methods. Elimination of the inventories, along with any prepaid expenses, from the current assets might provide better information for the short-term creditor. Many analysts favour a **quick** or **acid-test ratio** that relates the sum of cash, marketable securities, and net receivables to total current liabilities. The acid-test ratio is computed for Anetek as shown in Exhibit 24-6.

EXHIBIT 24-6

ACID-TEST RATIO CALCULATION

$$\text{Acid-Test Ratio} = \frac{\text{Cash} + \text{Marketable Securities} + \text{Net Receivables}}{\text{Current Liabilities}} = \frac{\$490,000}{\$575,000} = 0.85 \text{ times}$$

$$\text{Industry Average} = 1.20 \text{ times}$$

The acid-test ratio for Anetek is low when compared with the industry average. This confirms the signal given by the current ratio that Anetek may have difficulty in meeting its short-term obligations. Unless the firm is able to obtain additional current assets through conversion of some of its long-term assets, through additional financing, or through profitable operating results, it may have difficulty meeting its short-term obligations. Of particular concern is the fairly high amount of the short-term notes payable.

---

[12] The industry average ratios are taken from Dun and Bradstreet, Inc., *Key Business Ratios in 25 Lines*, and Leo Troy's *The Almanac of Business and Industrial Financial Ratios*. The industry average ratios provide a basis for comparison with other companies in the same industry.

3. **Defensive-Interval Ratio.** Neither the current ratio nor the acid-test ratio gives a complete explanation of the current debt-paying ability of the company. The matching of current assets with current liabilities assumes that the current assets will be employed to pay off the current liabilities. Some analysts argue that a better measure of liquidity is provided by the defensive-interval ratio. This ratio measures the time span a firm can operate on present liquid assets without resorting to funds that would be generated by future operations or other sources (e.g., sale of fixed assets, issuance of shares). The **defensive-interval ratio** is computed by dividing defensive assets (cash, marketable securities, and net receivables) by projected daily expenditures for operations. Projected daily expenditures are computed by dividing cost of goods sold plus selling and administrative expenses and other ordinary cash expenses by 365 days.[13] Exhibit 24-7 shows the defensive-interval measure for Anetek.

EXHIBIT 24-7

DEFENSIVE-INTERVAL RATIO CALCULATION

$$\text{Defensive-Interval Ratio} = \frac{\text{Defensive Assets}}{\substack{\text{Protected Daily Operational Expenditures} \\ \text{(based on past expenditures)} - \text{Noncash Charges}}}$$

$$= \$490,000 \div \left(\frac{\$1,525,000 - \$150,000}{365} \right)$$

$$= 130 \text{ days}$$

$$\text{Industry Average} = 80 \text{ days}$$

This ratio does not necessarily provide a better measure of liquidity than the current ratio or acid-test ratio. It does provide another useful tool for analysing the liquidity position of the enterprise. This ratio establishes a safety factor or margin for the analyst in determining the capability of the company to meet its basic operational costs. It would appear that 130 days provides the company with a relatively high degree of protection and tends to offset the weakness indicated by the low current and acid-test ratios. Despite this, an overall conclusion from the foregoing analysis would be that Anetek's management and creditors should be concerned about the company's liquidity position.

ACTIVITY RATIOS

OBJECTIVE 5
Identify activity ratios, know how they are calculated, and appreciate the questions they can help answer.

Activity ratios *express the relationship between the results of organizational activity (e.g., net sales) and the amount of an asset or combination of assets used to achieve the results.* Activity ratios are also called turnover ratios because the resulting number represents how many times a particular asset or combination of assets has been turned over during the period (i.e., how many times the inventory balance has sold).

Since an activity ratio is a measure of output (results) divided by a measure of input (resources), *it provides information regarding how efficiently an enterprise's management is utilizing its assets.* These ratios, particularly the ones that relate output to a current asset, also may be used as a way to assess liquidity — to determine how quickly

---

[13] Alternatively, and as shown in the example, projected daily expenditures may be determined by dividing 365 into total expenses reported, less any noncash charges such as depreciation and provisions for any known changes in planned operations from previous periods. Income tax expense has been included in the illustration to determine total expenses for the year.

certain assets can be turned into cash. How liquid, for example, are receivables and inventory?

4. Receivables Turnover. The **receivables turnover ratio** is computed by dividing net sales by average receivables outstanding during the year. Theoretically, the numerator should include only net credit sales. This amount is frequently not available, however, and if the relative amounts of charge and cash sales remain fairly constant, the trend indicated by the ratio will still be valid. Average receivables outstanding can be computed by dividing the total of beginning and ending balances of net trade receivables by 2.[14] This simple average is a reasonable reflection of the net receivables balance throughout the year unless seasonal factors are significant. Anetek's accounts receivable turnover ratio is computed as shown in Exhibit 24-8.

EXHIBIT 24-8

ACCOUNTS RECEIVABLE TURNOVER RATIO CALCULATION

$$\text{Accounts Receivable Turnover} = \frac{\text{Net Sales}}{\text{Average Trade Receivables (net)}}$$

$$= \$1,600,000 \div \left(\frac{\$350,000 + \$300,000}{2}\right)$$

$$= 4.92 \text{ times or every 74 days}[15] \ (365 \text{ days}/4.92)$$

$$\text{Industry Average} = 7.15 \text{ times or every 51 days}$$

This information provides an indication of the quality of the receivables and also an idea of how successful the firm is in collecting its outstanding receivables. The faster (higher) this turnover, the more credence the current ratio and acid-test ratio have in the financial analysis. For management purposes, an aging schedule should also be prepared to determine how long the receivables have been outstanding. It is possible that the receivables turnover is quite satisfactory, but this situation may have resulted because certain receivables have been collected quickly whereas others have been outstanding for a relatively long period.

In Anetek's case, the receivables turnover appears low. Dividing 365 days by the turnover provides a measure of the **average number of days to collect accounts receivable** (74 days for Anetek). The lower the turnover, the longer it takes to collect the receivables. As a general rule, the time allowed for payment (e.g., as established by the selling or credit granting department of a company) should not be exceeded by more than 10 or 15 days.

5. Inventory Turnover. Inventory turnover measures how quickly inventory is sold. It is computed by dividing the average inventory into the cost of goods sold. Dividing 365 days by the inventory turnover indicates the *average number of days it takes to sell inventory* (or *average number of days' sales for which inventory is on hand*). The inventory turnover ratio for Anetek is shown in Exhibit 24-9.

---

[14] If a beginning balance is not available, an average cannot be determined and, therefore, the ending balance is used to calculate the ratio.

[15] Often the receivables turnover is transformed to an average collection period. In this case, 4.92 is divided into 365 days to obtain 74 days. Several figures other than 365 could be used here; a common alternative is 360 days. Because the industry average was based on 365 days, we used this figure in our computations.

EXHIBIT 24-9

INVENTORY TURNOVER RATIO CALCULATION

$$\text{Inventory Turnover} = \frac{\text{Cost of Goods Sold}}{\text{Average Inventory}} = \frac{\$1,000,000}{\dfrac{\$310,000 + \$250,000}{2}}$$

$$= 3.57 \text{ times or every 102 days (365 days/3.57)}$$

Industry Average $= 4.62$ times or every 79 days

Generally, the higher the inventory turnover, the better the enterprise is performing. It is possible, however, that an enterprise is incurring high "stockout costs" because not enough inventory is available.

The inventory turnover ratio is useful because it provides a signal of possible problems, such as whether obsolete inventory is present or pricing problems exist. In Anetek's case, the turnover ratio is lower than the industry average, indicating that some slow-moving inventory exists. Remember that this ratio is an average, which means that many goods may be turning over quite rapidly whereas others may have failed to sell at all. In addition, it was assumed that an average of the beginning and ending inventory was representative of the average for the year. If this situation is not correct,[16] additional computations could be made by management but, because of the lack of information on fluctuations in inventory during the year, could not be made by others outside the organization.

Because inventory is stated at cost, it should be divided into cost of goods sold (a cost figure) instead of into net sales, which includes some margin of profit. Occasionally, analysts use net sales when the cost of goods sold is not reported. While such a calculation may reveal trends over time if the underlying gross margin rate is fairly stable, it is not a true inventory turnover. For example, it would not be useful for determining the number of days that inventory is on hand.

The method of inventory valuation can affect the computed inventory turnover and the current ratio. The analyst should be aware of the different valuations that can be used in costing inventory (i.e., FIFO, average-cost, LIFO) and the effect these different valuation procedures might have on the ratios.

From the accounts receivable and inventory turnover information, a total conversion period can be determined. The **total conversion period** is the average number of days it takes from the acquisition of inventory to the collection of cash from its sale.[17] It is calculated by adding the average number of days it takes to sell inventory to the average number of days to collect accounts receivable. For Anetek, the total conversion period is 176 days (102 + 74). Examining the conversion period and its two components can be useful in identifying differences between companies or between years for the same company when evaluating the efficiency of marketing, credit granting, and collection policies.

6. **Asset Turnover.** The **asset turnover ratio** is determined by dividing average total assets into net sales for the period. Exhibit 24-10 shows the asset turnover for Anetek.

If this turnover ratio is high, the implication is that the company is using its assets efficiently to generate sales. (A turnover of 0.74 indicates that for each $1 of assets, $0.74 of net sales revenue is earned.) If the turnover ratio is low, it could signal

---

[16] Year-end inventory may not be representative of that held during the year because the year end occurs at the low point in a company's annual operating cycle. Also, inventory clearance sales just prior to a year end can result in the year-end inventory amount being substantially lower than the normal amount during the year.

[17] The conversion period is sometimes referred to as the operating cycle, which is the span of time from the spending of cash to acquire inventory to the collection of cash from sales of that inventory. The operating cycle would, however, be shorter than the conversion period if inventory is bought on credit.

EXHIBIT 24-10

ASSET TURNOVER RATIO CALCULATION

$$\text{Asset Turnover} = \frac{\text{Net Sales}}{\text{Average Total Assets}} = \frac{\$1,600,000}{\dfrac{\$2,250,000 + \$2,100,000}{2}} = 0.74 \text{ times}$$

$$\text{Industry Average} = 0.94 \text{ times}$$

that the company's management should be considering how to use assets more efficiently or, possibly, that some should be disposed of.

A problem with this turnover is that it places a premium on using old assets because their book value is low. In addition, this ratio can be significantly affected by the depreciation method employed. For example, a company that uses an accelerated method of depreciation will have a higher turnover than a company that uses the straight-line method, all other factors being equal. For these reasons, this ratio should be interpreted in the context of the accounting policies being employed.

PROFITABILITY RATIOS

Profitability ratios *indicate how well the enterprise has operated during the year.* These ratios help to answer questions such as: Was the net income adequate? What rate of return does it represent? What is the rate of net income earned from assets invested in operating segments or other defined areas of activity? What percentage of income was paid in dividends? What amount was earned by different equity claimants? Generally, the ratios are computed on the basis of sales or on an investment base such as total assets. Profitability is frequently used as a significant test for evaluating management effectiveness.

OBJECTIVE 6
Identify profitability ratios, know how they are calculated, and appreciate the questions they can help answer.

7. **Profit Margin on Sales.** The **profit margin on sales** is computed by dividing net income by net sales for the period. Anetek's ratio is as shown in Exhibit 24-11.

This ratio indicates that Anetek is achieving an above-average rate of profit on

EXHIBIT 24-11

PROFIT MARGIN ON SALES CALCULATION

$$\text{Profit Margin on Sales} = \frac{\text{Net Income}}{\text{Net Sales}} = \frac{\$150,000}{\$1,600,000} = 9.4\%$$

$$\text{Industry Average} = 6.0\%$$

each dollar of sales. It provides some indication of the buffer available in case of higher costs or lower sales in the future.

8. **Rate of Return on Assets.** While the profit margin discloses useful information, it does not answer the important question of how profitable the enterprise was for the given time period. This can be examined by relating profit margin on each dollar of sales to the volume of sales per dollar invested in the company (asset turnover). The resulting relationship is called the **rate of return on assets,** and is determined as shown in Exhibit 24-12.

EXHIBIT 24-12

RATE OF RETURN ON ASSETS CALCULATION: MARGIN × TURNOVER

Rate of Return on Assets = Profit Margin on Sales × Asset Turnover

$$\text{Rate of Return on Assets} = \frac{\text{Net Income}}{\text{Net Sales}} \times \frac{\text{Net Sales}}{\text{Average Total Assets}}$$

$$= \frac{\$150,000}{\$1,600,000} \times \frac{\$1,600,000}{\dfrac{\$2,250,000 + \$2,100,000}{2}}$$

$$= 6.9\%$$

Industry Average = 5.6%

Rather than multiply the profit margin by the asset turnover, the rate of return on assets can be directly computed by dividing net income by average total assets, as Exhibit 24-13 indicates.

EXHIBIT 24-13

RATE OF RETURN ON ASSETS CALCULATION: DIRECT

$$\text{Rate of Return on Assets} = \frac{\text{Net Income}}{\text{Average Total Assets}}$$

$$= \$150,000 \div \left(\frac{\$2,250,000 + \$2,100,000}{2} \right)$$

$$= 6.9\%$$

Industry Average = 5.6%

While this calculation is a simpler and more direct means of determining the rate of return on assets, examining the profit margin and asset turnover components of the ratio is likely to reveal important information that is otherwise not evident. For example, Anetek's relatively high profit margin (compared with the industry) has more than offset its lower-than-average asset turnover, resulting in a rate of return on assets (6.9% under either calculation) that is above the average for the industry. Anetek's management appears to have established a policy of setting higher prices for its products (assuming costs are fairly similar across the industry) and accepting a lower volume of sales relative to assets invested.

Analysis of profit margin and asset turnover is, therefore, helpful in determining the particular strategies of companies within an industry when attempting to understand and evaluate rates of return on assets. Many enterprises have a small profit margin on sales and a high turnover (grocery and discount stores), whereas other enterprises have a relatively high profit margin but a low turnover (jewellery and furniture stores). Even companies in the same type of business follow different strategies. For example, in the restaurant business, McDonald's follows a strategy of charging relatively low prices to obtain a high volume of sales. An élite restaurant follows a strategy of charging higher prices, realizing volume may be lower than that generated by McDonald's. Both types of strategies can prove to be successful in terms of overall profitability. The significant point is that many factors contribute to the overall profitability of a company.

One of the more interesting applications of rate of return is called the du Pont system of financial control. In this system, ratios can be defined in enough detail to help explain the different effects leading to the rate of return on assets. The basic components of this system are shown in Illustration 24-1.

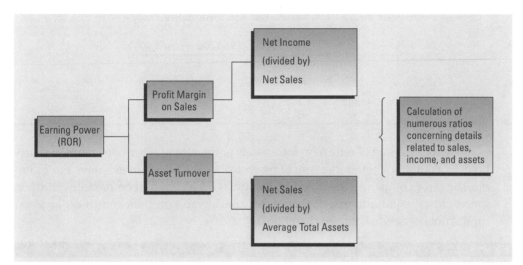

ILLUSTRATION 24-1
Du Pont System of Financial Control

Because of a belief that operating activities should be separated from financing activities when analysing a company, many analysts contend that a better measure of the rate of return on assets can be determined by using net income before subtraction of any interest charge.[18] This ratio is computed by dividing net income plus interest expense (net of tax) by average total assets. Interest expense (net of tax), including discount amortization, is added back to income because the interest represents a cost of financing the assets, not operating them. The result is a rate of return on assets that is independent of how they are financed. Exhibit 24-14 shows this ratio for Anetek.

EXHIBIT 24-14

RATE OF RETURN ON ASSETS AFTER ELIMINATING INTEREST

$$\text{Rate of Return on Assets (after eliminating interest expense and related tax savings)} = \frac{\text{Net Income} + \text{Interest Expense} - \text{Tax Savings}^{19}}{\text{Average Total Assets}}$$

$$= \frac{\$150,000 + \$50,000 - 0.40(\$50,000)}{\dfrac{\$2,250,000 + \$2,100,000}{2}}$$

$$= 8.3\%$$

9. **Rate of Return on Common Shareholders' Equity.** The **rate of return on common shareholders' equity** is a widely-used ratio. It is defined as net income minus preferred dividends (i.e., the income available specifically to common shareholders), divided by average common shareholders' equity. Anetek's ratio is computed as shown in Exhibit 24-15.

---

[18] For example, public utility companies often compute their rate of return using this approach.

[19] The tax savings is computed by multiplying the interest expense by the effective tax rate. The effective tax rate, if not reported, may be approximated by dividing the income tax expense by income before taxes.

EXHIBIT 24-15

RATE OF RETURN ON COMMON SHAREHOLDERS' EQUITY CALCULATION

$$\text{Rate of Return on Common Shareholders' Equity} = \frac{\text{Net Income} - \text{Preferred Dividends}}{\text{Average Common Shareholders' Equity}}$$

$$= \$150,000 \div \left(\frac{\$950,000 + \$867,500}{2}\right)$$

$$= 16.5\%$$

$$\text{Industry Average} = 9.5\%$$

Whether the rate of return on total assets or the rate of return on common shareholders' equity is a better measure of performance is difficult to evaluate. For example, the three companies identified in Exhibit 24-16 all have a comparable return on shareholders' equity; however, they differ considerably in their return on invested capital (total assets less current liabilities).[20]

EXHIBIT 24-16

COMPARISON OF DIFFERENT TYPES OF PROFITABILITY INDEXES

	Rate of Return	
	on Investment Capital	on Shareholders' Equity
Québecor Inc.	20.56%	20.65%
IBM Canada Inc.	14.64	21.83
DuPont Canada Inc.	28.33	20.35

If an analyst was to look at only one of these profitability ratios, the ranking of IBM Canada Inc. and DuPont Canada Inc. would be just the opposite to the ranking obtained from using the other ratio. Therefore, to evaluate the companies, both ratios should be considered. Additionally, the reason for the different rankings should be examined. In many cases, the differences are related to the degree of leverage (amount of debt in the capital structure) employed by the companies and the extent to which their trading on equity is favourable or unfavourable.

10. **Financial Leverage.** The expression "using **financial leverage**" or "**trading on the equity**" describes the practice of using borrowed money at fixed interest rates or issuing preferred shares with constant dividend amounts in hope of obtaining a higher rate of return from the use of the money acquired. Because these sources of financing are given a prior claim on some or all of the corporate assets, the advantage to common shareholders must come from borrowing at a lower rate of interest than the rate of return obtained by the corporation on its assets. If this can be done, the capital obtained from bondholders or preferred shareholders earns enough to pay the interest or preferred dividends and leave a margin for the common shareholders. When this condition exists, favourable use of financial leverage or trading on the equity at a profit occurs.

To illustrate, Anetek's rate of return on total assets is 6.9%, whereas the rate of return on the shareholders' equity is 16.5%. Anetek used financial leverage favourably. In essence, the overall cost of Anetek's liabilities was at a rate lower than

---

[20] *The Financial Post 500* (Toronto: The Financial Post, 1996), pp. 104–109.

6.9%. Anetek is a very highly leveraged company that has achieved an excellent rate of return on common equity by using its debt effectively. A word of caution: using financial leverage can be a two-way street. Just as a company's ownership gains can be magnified, so too can losses be magnified.

11. **Earnings Per Share.** **Earnings per share** is the only ratio that must be disclosed in the financial statements of most corporations.[21] It is one of the most frequently used ratios, yet it is one of the most deceptive. If no dilutive securities are present in the capital structure, then earnings per share is computed simply by dividing net income minus preferred dividends by the weighted-average number of common shares outstanding.[22] The computation for Anetek is shown in Exhibit 24-17.

EXHIBIT 24-17

BASIC EARNINGS PER SHARE CALCULATION

$$\text{Earnings Per Share} = \frac{\text{Net Income} - \text{Preferred Dividends}}{\text{Weighted-Average Number of Shares Outstanding}} = \frac{\$150,000 - 0}{30,000} = \$5.00$$

Because no dilutive securities that are common share equivalents or potentially dilutive securities are present in Anetek's capital structure, fully diluted earnings per share amounts are not calculated.

Certain problems exist when using the earnings per share ratio. For example, earnings per share can be increased simply by reducing the number of shares outstanding through purchase and cancellation. In addition, the earnings per share figure fails to recognize the probable increasing base of the shareholders' investment. That is, earnings per share, all other factors being equal, will probably increase year after year if the corporation reinvests earnings in the business because a larger earnings figure should be generated without a corresponding increase in the number of shares outstanding. Because even well-informed investors attach such importance to earnings per share, caution must be exercised and the figure should not be given more emphasis than it deserves. The basic concern is that the per-share figure draws the investor's attention away from the enterprise as a whole—which involves differing magnitudes of sales, costs, volumes, and invested capital—and concentrates too much attention on the single share.

12. **Price Earnings Ratio.** The **price earnings (P/E) ratio** is an oft-quoted statistic used by analysts in discussing the investment potential of a given enterprise. It is computed by dividing the market price of a share by the earnings per share. For Anetek, the ratio is derived as shown in Exhibit 24-18.

EXHIBIT 24-18

PRICE EARNINGS RATIO CALCULATION

$$\text{Price Earnings Ratio} = \frac{\text{Market Price Per Share}}{\text{Earnings Per Share}} = \frac{\$60}{\$5} = 12 \text{ times}$$

---

[21] *CICA Handbook*, Section 3500. par. .06. Excluded from this recommendation are businesses that do not have share capital, government-owned companies, wholly owned subsidiaries, and companies with few shareholders.

[22] See Chapter 18 for a discussion of how dilutive securities (e.g., convertible securities, stock options, warrants) should be handled to compute basic and fully diluted earnings per share.

Some companies have high P/E multiples, while others have low multiples. For instance, Encal Energy Ltd. in 1996 had a P/E ratio of 98.3, Algoma Steel Inc. had a P/E ratio of 2.8, and Moore Corporation Limited's P/E ratio was 5.2. The reason for such differences is linked to several factors: relative risk, stability of earnings, trends in earnings, and the market's perception of the company's growth potential. Generally, a steady drop in a company's price earnings ratio indicates that investors are wary of the firm's growth potential.

The inverse of the price earnings ratio (earnings per share divided by market price per share) provides a measure of the **rate of return on the market value of the share.** For Anetek, this would be 8.33%.

12. **Payout Ratio.** The **payout ratio** is the ratio of cash dividends to net income. If preferred shares are outstanding, this ratio is computed for common shareholders by dividing cash dividends paid to common shareholders by income available to common shareholders. Given that Anetek's cash dividends are $67,500, the payout ratio is as shown in Exhibit 24-19.

EXHIBIT 24-19

PAYOUT RATIO CALCULATION

$$\text{Payout Ratio} = \frac{\text{Cash Dividends}}{\text{Net Income} - \text{Preferred Dividends}} = \frac{\$67,500}{\$150,000 - 0} = 45\%$$

It is important to investors seeking continuous cash flow that a fairly substantial payout ratio exist; however, speculators view appreciation in the value of shares as more important. Generally, growth companies are characterized by low payout ratios because they reinvest most of their earnings. For example, Anetek has a relatively high payout ratio when compared with DuPont Canada Inc., which paid out approximately 21% of earnings in 1995, but a relatively low ratio when compared with Hudson's Bay Company's payout of approximately 156% of net earnings to common shareholders in 1995. The 1995 payout ratio for Moore Corporation Limited was approximately 35%.

Another closely related ratio that is often used is the **dividend yield**—the cash dividend per share, divided by the market price per share. The cash dividend per share for Anetek is $2.25, so the dividend yield is 3.75% ($2.25/$60). This ratio affords investors some idea of the rate of return that will be received in cash dividends from their investment. In 1996, Scott Paper Ltd. shareholders experienced a modest yield of 0.8%, while the Bank of Nova Scotia shareholders obtained a dividend yield of approximately 4.0%, and those of Moore Corporation Limited about 5.2%.

13. **Cash flow from Operations Per Share.** This is a popular yet not well understood ratio. **Cash flow from operations per share** is computed by dividing cash flow from operations by the number of common shares outstanding. The cash flow from operations per share for Anetek is shown in Exhibit 24-20.

EXHIBIT 24-20

CASH FLOW FROM OPERATIONS PER SHARE CALCULATION

$$\text{Cash Flow from Operations Per Share} = \frac{\text{Cash Flow from Operations}}{\text{Outstanding Shares}}$$

$$= \frac{\$315,000}{30,000} = \$10.50$$

This ratio is used to approximate the amount of cash flow generated internally. However, it has faults that *may* lead to its misinterpretation. A major concern is that cash flow per share may be used as an indicator of profitability. It does not reflect profitability (this is the purpose of earnings per share). Also, it does not provide a measure of all cash flowing through the organization since it incorporates only cash from operations. Finally, it has nothing to do with cash available to a shareholder at any point in time. Until the ratio is better understood and its usefulness is determined, employing it as an aspect of financial statement analysis must be done with care.

Many companies disclose a cash flow per share in the financial statements, although such disclosure is not required by the *CICA Handbook*. Recognizing that there are problems associated with this ratio, the CICA's Emerging Issues Committee issued an *Abstract* to guide presentation of cash flow per share information *if* it is provided.[23] The Committee concluded that the cash flow per share should be shown on the statement of changes in financial position or a note cross-referenced thereto. Not putting it on the income statement would help avoid any implication that it is a summary statistic reflecting profitability of the company. Additionally, information should be provided to clearly identify items from the statement of changes in financial position that are included in the cash flow when calculating the ratio. Our example used only cash flow from operations, but other sources of cash flow (i.e., from investing and financing decisions) could be used. To clarify the calculation for our example, we therefore specifically called the ratio cash flow from operations per share rather than cash flow per share. The Emerging Issues Committee clearly stated that the term "cash flow per share" should be used only if all cash flows from operating, investing, and financing activities are included.

14. **Cash Flow from Operations Payout Ratio.** The **cash flow from operations payout ratio** is determined by dividing cash dividends to common shareholders by the cash flow from operations available to these shareholders. For Anetek, this ratio is calculated as shown in Exhibit 24-21.

EXHIBIT 24-21

CASH FLOW FROM OPERATIONS PAYOUT RATIO CALCULATION

$$\text{Cash Flow from Operations Payout Ratio} = \frac{\text{Cash Dividends to Common Shareholders}}{\text{Cash Flow from Operations} - \text{Preferred Dividends}}$$

$$= \frac{\$67,500}{\$315,000 - 0}$$

$$= 21\%$$

The usefulness of this ratio is based on arguments similar to those for the payout ratio based on net income. The cash flow from operations payout ratio has additional benefit in that it reflects the fact that payment of dividends depends on the availability of cash, not just the earning of income. For example, if income is high but cash from operations is low, examination of this ratio may provide a possible explanation of why dividends are reduced or not declared.

---

[23] "Presentation of Cash Flow Per Share Information," *Abstract of Issue Discussed* by the Emerging Issues Committee (Toronto: CICA, November 20, 1992). In the United States, the FASB has a standard specifically stating that cash flow per share may not be presented in financial statements.

15. Cash Flow from Operations Versus Non-Operating Cash Flow. Decisions made to increase earnings (e.g., making capital expenditures) require cash. Such cash can come from operations or additional financing (long-term debt or equity). However, while increased sales and net income may result, a consequence may be a developing cash flow from operations problem—the increase in sales and absolute net income amounts also result in more dollars committed to noncash items and increased costs.

> ...the main culprit appears to be cyclical overexpansion. That could mean trouble ahead, since changes in cash flow tend to precede changes in earnings by several quarters.... Why the lag? While both income and OCF [operating cash flow] figures measure underlying operating performance, companies have more wiggle room in how they report income. Under generally accepted accounting principles, managers in a bind have plenty of leeway to massage income through "non-cash" items such as depreciation and amortization, and by the timing of when they book sales or expenses. Such finagling is far harder with OCF, so it's the first place trouble shows up.[24]

A means to identify if there is a cause for concern comes from examining cash flow from operations versus non-operating cash flow (from investing and financing activities). For example, if total non-operating cash outflow exceeded cash flow from operations over a period of years, a problem is signalled. If operating cash flow is falling or is negative and non-operating cash flows are providing amounts to offset the operating cash flow results, a problem is signalled.

The chart in Exhibit 24-22 shows the relationship between cash flow from operations (CFO) and non-operating cash flow (NOCF) for Anetek, and other possible hypothetical situations with an identification of whether a potential problem could exist if the relationship continued over time.

EXHIBIT 24-22

CASH FLOW FROM OPERATIONS AND NON-OPERATING CASH FLOW RELATIONSHIPS

	Anetek	Hypothetical Cases 1	2	3	4
CFO	+$315	+$315	+$100	−$100	−$100
NOCF	−$275	+ 100	− 275	− 275	+ 275
	+$ 40	+$415	−$175	−$375	+$175

Hypothetical cases 2, 3, and 4 signal problems if they are trends.

COVERAGE RATIOS

OBJECTIVE 7
Identify coverage ratios, know how they are calculated, and appreciate the questions they can help answer.

Coverage ratios are computed to **help predict the long-run solvency of a company**. These ratios are of interest primarily to bondholders and other long-term debtors who need some indication of the measure of protection available to them. In addition, they indicate part of the risk involved in investing in common shares. The more debt there is in a company's capital structure, the more uncertain is the return to common shareholders.

---

[24] "Are Profits Shakier Than They Look?" *Business Week*, August 5, 1996, p. 55.

16. **Debt to Total Assets.** The **debt (total liabilities) to total assets ratio** provides creditors with some idea of a corporation's ability to withstand losses without impairing the interests of creditors. From the creditor's point of view, a low ratio of debt to total assets is desirable. The lower this ratio the more "buffer" there is available to creditors before the corporation becomes insolvent. Exhibit 24-23 shows this ratio for Anetek.

EXHIBIT 24-23

DEBT TO TOTAL ASSETS RATIO CALCULATION

$$\text{Debt to Total Assets} = \frac{\text{Debt*}}{\text{Total Assets}} = \frac{\$1,300,000}{\$2,250,000} = 58\%$$

Industry Average = 38%

*Debt is equal to total liabilities in this ratio.

Other ratios provide similar information, such as the ratio of total debt to shareholders' equity, the ratio of shareholders' equity to the sum of total debt and shareholders' equity, or the ratio of long-term debt to total assets less current liabilities. Essentially, these ratios provide guidance to answer the question: How well protected are the creditors in the case of possible insolvency of the enterprise?[25] The information conveyed through these ratios can have a definite effect on the company's ability to obtain additional financing. Anetek is highly leveraged compared with the industry average. Further growth through debt financing could prove to be costly because debtors would require a high interest rate to compensate for the relatively higher risk.

17. **Times Interest Earned.** The **times interest earned ratio** is computed by dividing income (before interest charges and taxes) by the interest charge. This ratio stresses how important it is that a company can cover all interest charges. Note that the times interest earned ratio uses income before interest and income taxes because this amount represents the amount of income available to cover interest. Income taxes are paid only after interest charges have been met. The ratio for Anetek is computed as shown in Exhibit 24-24.

EXHIBIT 24-24

TIMES INTEREST EARNED RATIO CALCULATION

$$\text{Times Interest Earned} = \frac{\text{Income Before Taxes and Interest Charges}}{\text{Interest Charges}} = \frac{\$300,000}{\$50,000} = 6 \text{ times}$$

In this case Anetek's interest coverage appears to be adequate.

If a company pays preferred dividends, the number of times preferred dividends were earned is computed by dividing the net income for the year by the annual preferred dividend requirements.

---

[25] Additional protection, of course, is afforded through specified liens and collateral and through contractual restrictive covenants.

18. **Book Value Per Share.** A much-used basis for evaluating net worth is found in the book value or equity value per share. **Book value per share** is the amount each share would receive if the company were liquidated *on the basis of amounts reported on the balance sheet.* The figure loses much of its relevance if the valuations on the balance sheet do not approximate fair market value of the assets. It is computed by (1) allocating the shareholders' equity among the various classes of shares; and (2) dividing the amount allocated to a class by the number of shares outstanding in that class. Exhibit 24-25 shows the book value per common share for Anetek.

EXHIBIT 24-25

BOOK VALUE PER SHARE CALCULATION

$$\text{Book Value Per Share} = \frac{\text{Common Shareholders' Equity}}{\text{Outstanding Common Shares}} = \frac{\$950,000}{30,000} = \$31.67$$

Preferred shares are not a part of the capital structure of Anetek. When this type of security is present, an analysis of the covenants involving the preferred shares should be studied. If preferred dividends are in arrears, if preferred shares are participating, or if preferred shares have a redemption or liquidating value higher than their carrying amount, then retained earnings must be allocated between the preferred and common shareholders. To illustrate, assume the situation depicted in Exhibit 24-26.

EXHIBIT 24-26

BOOK VALUE PER SHARE: PREFERRED AND COMMON SHARES

Shareholders' equity	Preferred	Common
Preferred shares, $5 dividend per share	$300,000.00	
Common shares		$400,000.00
Contributed surplus		37,500.00
Retained earnings		162,582.00
Totals	$300,000.00	$600,082.00
Shares outstanding	3,000	4,000
Book value per share	$ 100.00	$ 150.02

In the computation, it is assumed that no preferred dividends are in arrears and that the preferred shares are not participating. Now assume that the same facts exist except that the $5 preferred is cumulative, participating up to $8 per share, and that dividends for the previous three years are in arrears. The book value of each class of shares is then computed as shown in Exhibit 24-27, assuming that no action has yet been taken concerning dividends for the current year.

EXHIBIT 24-27

BOOK VALUE PER SHARE: PREFERRED AND COMMON SHARES WHEN THERE ARE DIVIDENDS IN ARREARS AND PARTICIPATION RIGHTS

Shareholders' equity	Preferred	Common
Preferred shares,[26] $5	$300,000.00	
Common shares		$400,000.00
Contributed surplus		37,500.00
Retained earnings		
Dividends in arrears		
(3 years at $15,000 per year)	45,000.00	
Current year dividends		
($5 per share)	15,000.00	20,000.00
Participating—Additional $3 per share	9,000.00	12,000.00
Remainder to common		61,582.00
Totals	$369,000.00	$531,082.00
Shares outstanding	**3,000**	**4,000**
Book value per share	**$123.00**	**$132.77**

SUMMARY OF RATIOS AND IMPLICATIONS FROM ANALYSIS

A summary of the financial ratios examined in this chapter, their formulas, and their amounts for Anetek Corporation and the industry average is presented in Exhibit 24-28.

Given the preceding analysis and comparisons made to the industry averages, the following general conclusions may be reached regarding Anetek. The liquidity ratios signal that problems may exist in terms of the company's ability to pay creditors when due. Without addressing this potential problem, the company may defer paying creditors beyond due dates (e.g., the accounts payable increased from $50,000 to $125,000), and, possibly, be unable to take advantage of cash discounts. If the problem becomes serious, creditors may require down payments or security for their deliveries, or may not be willing to sell to Anetek.

A particular emergency may result if the holders of the short-term notes payable require quick payment. The activity ratios for receivables and inventory confirm possible liquidity problems, and the conversion period is considerably longer than the industry average. The turnover ratios indicate that, relative to sales, the company appears to have excess investment in receivables, inventory, and total assets. This suggests the company should address its credit granting and collection policies and determine if and why it may have more inventory than required. Increased efficiency in these areas could result in more cash being available to pay bills when due.

In terms of profitability, Anetek is doing relatively well. The apparent strategy of selling at a higher margin and incurring a lower asset turnover compared with the industry has

---

[26] If the preferred shares have a liquidating preference as to assets, this is considered in determining book value. For example, if the preferred shareholders receive $360,000 at liquidation instead of $300,000, an additional $60,000 is allocated to the preferred.

EXHIBIT 24-28

SUMMARY OF FINANCIAL RATIOS AND ANETEK'S RATIOS WITH INDUSTRY AVERAGE

Ratio	Formula for Computation	Anetek's Ratio	Industry Average
I. Liquidity			
1. Current ratio	$\dfrac{\text{Current assets}}{\text{Current liabilities}}$	1.39 times	2.30 times
2. Quick or acid-test ratio	$\dfrac{\text{Cash, marketable securities, and receivables}}{\text{Current liabilities}}$	0.85 times	1.20 times
3. Defensive-interval ratio	$\dfrac{\text{Defensive assets}}{\text{Projected daily expenditures minus noncash charges}}$	130 days	80 days
II. Activity			
4. Receivables turnover	$\dfrac{\text{Net Sales}}{\text{Average trade receivables (net)}}$	4.92 times, every 74 days	7.15 times, every 51 days
5. Inventory turnover	$\dfrac{\text{Cost of goods sold}}{\text{Average inventory}}$	3.57 times, every 102 days	4.62 times, every 79 days
6. Asset turnover	$\dfrac{\text{Net sales}}{\text{Average total assets}}$	0.74 times	0.94 times
III. Profitability			
7. Profit margin on sales	$\dfrac{\text{Net income}}{\text{Net sales}}$	9.4%	6.0%
8. Rate of return on assets	$\dfrac{\text{Net income}}{\text{Average total assets}}$	6.9%	5.6%
9. Rate of return on common shareholders' equity	$\dfrac{\text{Net income minus preferred dividends}}{\text{Average common shareholders' equity}}$	16.5%	9.5%
10. Earnings per share	$\dfrac{\text{Net income minus preferred dividends}}{\text{Weighted-average number of shares outstanding}}$	$5.00	—
11. Price earnings ratio	$\dfrac{\text{Market price per share}}{\text{Earnings per share}}$	12 times	—
12. Payout ratio	$\dfrac{\text{Cash dividends}}{\text{Net income}}$	45%	—
13. Cash flow per share	$\dfrac{\text{Cash flow from operations}}{\text{Outstanding shares}}$	$10.50	—
14. Cash flow from operations payout ratio	$\dfrac{\text{Cash dividends}}{\text{Cash flow from operations}}$	21%	—
15. Cash flow from operations versus non-operating cash flow	Cash flow from operations compared with non-operating cash flow	+$40,000	—
IV. Coverage			
16. Debt to total assets	$\dfrac{\text{Debt}}{\text{Total assets or equities}}$	58%	38%
17. Times interest earned	$\dfrac{\text{Income before interest charges and taxes}}{\text{Interest charges}}$	6 times	
18. Book value per share	$\dfrac{\text{Common shareholders' equity}}{\text{Outstanding shares}}$	$31.67	

resulted in a rate of return on assets above the industry average. Potential improvement may arise, however, if the company were able to reduce the investment in assets yet maintain the same margin on sales. The possibility of doing this is signalled by the ratio analysis, but actually achieving it requires considerable assessment of various possible actions by management.

Clearly the company is using leverage favourably. The coverage ratios indicate, however, that Anetek's use of debt to finance its assets is considerably in excess of the industry average. The shareholders' exposure to risk should profitability decline is, therefore, greater.

As these summary comments suggest, ratio analysis provides signalling information on financial strengths and weaknesses of a company. It does not provide answers as to why or what will be done to overcome the weaknesses and maintain the strengths. Also, the previous analysis considered only the ratios for one year. To appropriately derive a picture of a company's financial strength and assess management's performance, a comparative or trend analysis should be used.

COMPARATIVE (TREND) ANALYSIS

In **comparative trend analysis**, the same information for two or more different dates or periods is presented so that like items may be compared. Ratio analysis provides only a single snapshot, the analysis being for one given point in, or period of, time. In a comparative analysis, an analyst can concentrate on a given item and determine whether it appears to be growing or diminishing year by year and the proportion of such change to related items. Comparative analysis is the same thing as trend analysis.

The *CICA Handbook* states that "when it is meaningful, financial statements should be prepared on a comparative basis showing the figures for the corresponding preceding period."[27] Generally, companies present comparative financial statements.[28] In addition, many companies include in their annual reports five- or ten-year summaries of pertinent data that permit the reader to examine and analyse trends. An illustration of a five-year condensed statement with additional supporting data as presented by Anetek Corporation is shown in Exhibit 24-29. The summary for Moore Corporation Limited (Appendix 5A) covers an 11-year time frame.

OBJECTIVE 8
Describe and know how to apply comparative (trend) analysis.

EXHIBIT 24-29   ANETEK CORPORATION

CONDENSED COMPARATIVE STATEMENTS
(IN MILLIONS OF DOLLARS, EXCEPT WHERE NOTED)

Income	1998	1997	1996	1995	1994	10 Years Ago 1988	20 Years Ago 1978
Sales and other revenue:							
Net sales	$1,600.0	$1,350.0	$1,309.7	$1,176.2	$1,077.5	$636.2	$170.7
Other revenue	75.0	50.0	39.4	34.1	24.6	9.0	3.7
Total	$1,675.0	$1,400.0	$1,349.1	$1,210.3	$1,102.1	$645.2	$174.4

[27] *CICA Handbook*, Section 1500, par. .09.

[28] *Financial Reporting in Canada—1995* (Toronto: CICA, 1995) reported that all 300 of the surveyed companies provided comparative figures for the immediate preceding fiscal period in their 1994 financial statements.

EXHIBIT 24-29   ANETEK CORPORATION (Continued)

CONDENSED COMPARATIVE STATEMENTS
(IN MILLIONS OF DOLLAR, EXCEPT WHERE NOTED)

Income	1998	1997	1996	1995	1994	10 Years Ago 1988	20 Years Ago 1978
Costs and other charges:							
Cost of sales	$1,000.0	$ 850.0	$ 827.4	$ 737.6	$684.2	$386.8	$111.0
Depreciation and depletion	150.0	150.0	122.6	115.6	98.7	82.4	14.2
Selling and administrative expenses	225.0	150.0	144.2	133.7	126.7	66.7	10.7
Interest expense	50.0	25.0	28.5	20.7	9.4	8.9	1.8
Taxes on income	100.0	75.0	79.5	73.5	68.3	42.4	12.4
Total	$1,525.0	$1,250.0	$1,202.2	$1,081.1	$987.3	$587.2	$150.1
Net income for the year	$ 150.0	$ 150.0	$ 146.9	$ 129.2	$114.8	$ 58.0	$ 24.3
Other Statistics							
Earnings per share on common shares (in dollars)*	$ 5.00	$ 5.00	$ 4.90	$ 3.58	$ 3.11	$ 1.66	$ 1.06
Cash dividends per share paid to shareholders on common shares (in dollars)*	2.25	2.15	1.95	1.79	1.71	1.11	.25
Cash dividends declared on common shares	67.5	64.5	58.5	64.6	63.1	38.8	5.7
Stock dividend at approximate market value				46.8		27.3	
Taxes (major)	144.5	125.9	116.5	105.6	97.8	59.8	17.0
Wages paid	389.3	325.6	302.1	279.6	263.2	183.2	48.6
Cost of employee benefits	50.8	36.2	32.9	28.7	27.2	18.4	4.4
Number of employees at year end (thousands)	47.4	36.4	35.0	33.8	33.2	26.6	14.6
Additions to property	306.3	192.3	241.5	248.3	166.1	185.0	49.0

*Adjusted for stock splits and stock dividends.

PERCENTAGE (COMMON-SIZE) ANALYSIS

OBJECTIVE 9
Describe and know how to apply percentage (common-size) analysis.

Analysts also use percentage analysis to help them evaluate an enterprise. **Percentage (common-size) analysis** consists of converting a series of related amounts to a series of percentages of a given base. All items in an income statement are frequently expressed as a percentage of net sales; a balance sheet may be analysed on the basis of total assets. This conversion is helpful in evaluating the relative size of items in a given year's financial statements and can facilitate comparison of amounts or changes in amounts over time. It is also very helpful for comparing companies of different size. To illustrate, Exhibit 24-30 provides a comparative percentage analysis of the change in expenses in Anetek's income statement for the last two years. This approach, normally called **horizontal analysis**, indicates the proportionate change over a period of time. It is especially useful in evaluating a trend situation because absolute changes are often deceiving.

EXHIBIT 24-30

HORIZONTAL PERCENTAGE ANALYSIS

	1998	1997	Difference	% Change Inc. (Dec.)
Cost of sales	$1,000.0	$850.0	$150.0	17.6%
Depreciation and amortization	150.0	150.0	–0–	–0–
Selling and administrative expenses	225.0	150.0	75.0	50.0
Interest expense	50.0	25.0	25.0	100.0
Taxes	100.0	75.0	25.0	33.3

Another approach, called **vertical analysis**, is the proportional expression of each item on a financial statement in a given period to a base figure. For example, Anetek's income statement using this approach with net sales as the base figure appears in Exhibit 24-31.

EXHIBIT 24-31 ANETEK CORPORATION

VERTICAL PERCENTAGE ANALYSIS

	1998 Amount	Percentage of Total Revenue
Net sales	$1,600	100.0%
Other revenue	75	4.7
Total revenue	$1,675	104.7%
Less:		
Cost of goods sold	$1,000	62.5%
Depreciation and amortization	150	9.4
Selling and administrative expenses	225	14.1
Interest expense	50	3.1
Income tax	100	6.2
Total expenses	$1,525	95.3%
Net income	$ 150	9.4%

Reducing all the dollar amounts to a percentage of a base amount is frequently called **common-size analysis** because all of the statements and all of the years are reduced to a common size; that is, all of the elements within each statement are expressed in percentages of some common number.

For the balance sheet, common-size analysis answers such questions as: What is the distribution of financing between current liabilities, long-term debt, and owners' equity? What is the mix of assets (percentage-wise) with which the enterprise has chosen to conduct its business? What percentage of current assets is in inventory, receivables, and so forth?

The income statement lends itself to an analysis because each item in it is related to a common amount, usually net sales. It is instructive to know what proportion of each sales dollar is absorbed by the various costs and expenses incurred by the enterprise.

Common-size analysis may be used for comparing one company's statements over different years to detect trends not evident from the comparison of absolute amounts. Also, common-size analysis facilitates intercompany comparisons regardless of their size because the financial statements are recast into a comparable common-size format.

LIMITATIONS OF FINANCIAL STATEMENT ANALYSIS

Earlier, it was stated that an underlying objective of decision makers is to evaluate risk. Uncertainty is the major factor contributing to risk. Uncertainty is reduced and, therefore, awareness of risk is enhanced by decision-relevant information. We have argued that information in financial statements and ratio analysis based on this information can be decision-relevant and, consequently, useful in reducing uncertainty. Even so, a decision maker should be aware that there are significant limitations regarding financial statement information and ratio analysis.

OBJECTIVE 10
Know sources of uncertainty for decision makers when using financial statement information and the related limitations of ratio analysis.

A CICA *Research Study* identified the following four sources of uncertainty as being important when considering the usefulness of financial statement information to a decision maker.[29]

1. *Uncertainty about the nature and role of financial statements.* Misunderstanding the nature, purpose, terminology used, and method of preparation of financial statements can lead users to misinterpret and/or place inappropriate reliance on the information. An important component of the conceptual framework, discussed in Chapter 2, was the notion of user understandability to be assumed by preparers of financial statements. It is assumed that users have a reasonable understanding of business and economic activities and accounting, as well as a willingness to study information with reasonable diligence. This source of uncertainty indicates that accountants can have difficulty recognizing the problems for users to appropriately understand what is reported and/or how it is reported.

2. *Uncertainty about the nature of business operations portrayed in the financial statements.* The unpredictability of business activities due to factors such as economic environment, technology, and competitors' actions causes uncertainty. Knowledge of the type of business activities carried out is important in determining the extent of the uncertainties that characterize these activities. It is within such a knowledge base that analysis of financial information becomes most meaningful.

3. *Uncertainty due to limitations of financial statement measurements and disclosures.* The conceptual framework, *CICA Handbook* recommendations, and accounting practice dictate that various principles be followed and methods used. Uncertainty occurs when there is recognition that the resulting measurements and disclosures are not well understood or are thought to be incomplete or to lack relevance in a particular decision context. Ignoring or not being aware of these concerns can lead to inappropriate conclusions based on financial statement analysis.

4. *Uncertainty about management's motives and intentions.* Management is responsible for determining the accounting policies and methods used to prepare the finan-

---

[29] J.E. Boritz, *Approaches to Dealing with Risk and Uncertainty*, pp. 44–45.

cial statements. Choice of a policy or method should be based on reflecting underlying economic reality. This source of uncertainty suggests, however, that users may suspect that management's choices are more motivated by a need to report a smooth growth in income or to "bury" or not disclose information the users believe is important. To date, only the methods and policies chosen have to be disclosed in financial statements, not the reasons on which the choice is based.

Generally, the first, second, and fourth sources of uncertainty reflect an underlying limitation in that *there is a substantial amount of important information that is not provided in a company's financial statements.* Therefore, since ratio analysis is based on what is in financial statements, any conclusions from such analysis are subject to this limitation. Competitors' actions, technological developments, industry changes, management changes, union activities, government actions, and the state of the economic environment are examples of events that are often critical to the success of a company but are not necessarily disclosed in financial statements. They occur continuously, and information regarding them must come from careful analysis of reports in the media, speeches by knowledgeable persons, presentations in annual and other reports outside the financial statements, and other sources.

The third source of uncertainty—limitations regarding measurements and disclosures that are in financial statements—has a direct relationship to limitations of using ratios. Because a ratio can be computed precisely, it is easy to attach a high degree of reliability and significance to it. However, it must be remembered that ratios are only as good as the data on which they are based and the information with which they are compared.

One important limitation of ratios is that they are *based on historical cost, which can lead to distortions in measuring performance.* By failing to incorporate changing price information, some believe that inaccurate assessments of an enterprise's financial condition and performance result. To illustrate, Lytton Minerals Limited, in its 1994 statements, carried its investment in Glenmore Highlands Inc. at $2,475,525 although the fair market value of the investment was approximately $7,605,000. Such significant information tends to be obscured when computing and using ratios based on the historical cost amounts in the body of the statements.

Also, financial statement users must remember that *where estimated items (such as amortization, site restoration costs, bad debts) are significant, ratios lose some of their credibility.* In analysing ratios, the user should be cognizant of the uncertainty surrounding the computation of net income and the consequences on balance sheet amounts. "The physicist has long since conceded that the location of an electron is best expressed by a probability curve. Surely an abstraction like earnings per share is even more subject to the rules of probability and risk."[30]

Probably the greatest criticism of ratio analysis is the *difficult problem of achieving comparability among companies in a given industry.* Achieving comparability among companies that apply different accounting policies is difficult and requires that the analyst (1) identify basic differences existing in their accounting; and (2) adjust the balances to achieve comparability. Basic differences in accounting can involve any of the following areas.

1. Inventory valuation (FIFO, LIFO, average-cost; definition of market in the lower of cost and market application).

2. Amortization methods, particularly the use of straight-line versus accelerated methods.

---

[30] Richard E. Cheney, "How Dependable Is the Bottom Line?" *The Financial Executive,* January, 1971, p. 12.

3. Capitalization versus expensing of certain costs such as interest on self-constructed assets or development of research ideas.

4. Pooling versus purchase in accounting for business combinations.

5. Capitalization of leases versus noncapitalization.

6. Investments in common shares carried at cost, equity, and sometimes market.

7. Differing treatments of pension and other post-retirement costs.

8. Measurement and disclosure of off-balance-sheet financing and various financial instruments.

9. Questionable practices of defining discontinued operations, impairments, and extra-ordinary items.

The use of alternative but acceptable policies and methods can make a significant difference in the ratios computed. Several studies have analysed the impact of different accounting methods on financial statement analysis. The differences in income that can develop are staggering in some cases, depending on the company's accounting policies.[31] Decision makers may find it difficult to grasp all of these differences but must be aware of the potential problems if they are to be able to make the appropriate adjustments.

While differences in accounting policies create considerable difficulty in comparing companies, differences in estimates made to employ even a common policy necessarily enhance the difficulty. For example, differences in the estimated useful life and/or residual value of tangible capital assets can lead to substantial differences in reported amortization expense and carrying value of these assets, even if the companies being compared have the same assets and use the straight-line method.

In addition to these limitations, one should always be aware that "financial ratio analysis, as a quantitative approach, may appear to be easily learned and applied, but there are pitfalls to be avoided:"[32]

1. If historical analysis covers an insufficient number of years, the analyst may misinterpret trends and current performance.

2. Failing to use an average or weighted average where applicable can distort ratios.

3. Selecting an inappropriate comparison basis (e.g., noncomparable industries) can result in potentially misleading conclusions.

4. The nature and size of the business, geographic location, business practices, and other factors may introduce differences in the comparative analysis that may affect the result.

REPORTING RATIOS: SOME ISSUES

Computation of ratios requires that the necessary information be provided in the financial statements. For example, because rate of return on assets or shareholders' equity is often computed, it follows that sufficient data should be provided in the financial statements to enable its calculation. In fact, some argue that the profession should simply

---

[31] Examples of such studies ar: Curtis L. Norton and Ralph E. Smith, "A Comparison of General Price Level and Historical Cost Financial Statements in the Prediction of Bankruptcy, "*The Accounting Review,* January, 1979, pp. 72–87; and Thomas A. Nelson, "Capitalizing Leases—The Effect on Financial Ratios," *Journal of Accountancy,* July, 1963, pp. 49–58.

[32] Joseph E. Palmer, "Financial Ratio Analysis," *CPA/MAS Technical Consulting Practice Aid No. 3* (New York: AICPA, 1983), pp. 3–4.

require the reporting of the more common ratios in the financial statements rather than leaving the computation to the analyst. Many companies do report ratios in their five- or ten-year summaries of financial information, but this is not part of the formal financial statements.

Whether the Accounting Standards Board should establish standards for reporting of ratios is debatable. In fact, the *CICA Handbook* is already involved in establishing standards in the area of ratios, given its requirement that EPS information be disclosed. Because EPS is the only required ratio, many believe that undue emphasis is given to it. To discourage this emphasis and to enhance financial reporting, some argue that additional ratio information, such as rate of return on assets or equity, should be presented.

Others, however, believe that the AcSB should not be involved in developing standards related to the determination and presentation of ratios. A basic concern is how far the profession should go if such a responsibility were assumed. That is, where does financial reporting end and financial analysis begin? Another reason for the profession's reluctance to mandate disclosures is that research regarding the use and usefulness of summary indicators is still limited and, generally, inconclusive. For example, several studies using a combination of ratios to predict bankruptcy have been partially successful, whereas attempts to predict profitability from ratio analysis have met with failure. Ratios also have been used to predict other types of events, such as bank lending decisions, credit ratings, and mergers and acquisitions, although success has been limited in these areas.[33]

OBJECTIVE 11
Recognize issues associated with the requirement that ratios be reported in financial statements.

Summary of Learning Objectives

1. **Understand the role of financial statement analysis in helping various users of financial statements evaluate risk and reduce uncertainty regarding their decisions.** Decision makers want to evaluate risks associated with their alternative choices. Risk is compounded by uncertainty but reduced by decision-relevant information. Such information is available from a variety of sources, including that provided in financial statements and derived from related financial statement analysis.

2. **Appreciate the importance of an auditor's report, awareness of accounting policies used by a company, and having a logical approach when conducting financial statement analysis.** An auditor's report provides an independent opinion on whether the statements present information fairly and in accordance with generally accepted accounting principles. A company's choice of accounting policies can have a significant effect on amounts and totals reported in the financial statements relative to selecting other policies. Given this context, conducting a logical financial statement analysis involves knowing the questions for which you want answers, knowing the questions particular ratios are to help answer, and then matching the questions of interest to the ratios investigated.

KEY TERMS

acid-test ratio, 1253

activity ratios, 1254

asset turnover ratio, 1256

auditor's report, 1248

book value per share, 1266

cash flow from operations payout ratio, 1263

cash flow from operations per share, 1262

comparative (trend) analysis, 1269

coverage ratios, 1264

current ratio, 1250

debt (total liabilities) to total assets ratio, 1265

---

[33] Paul Frishkoff, "Reporting of Summary Indicators: An Investigation of Research and Practice," *Research Report* (Stamford, CT: FASB, 1981); William H. Beaver, "Financial Ratios as Predictors of Failure," Empirical Research in Accounting, Selected Studies, 1966, *Journal of Accounting Research*, pp. 71–127; E.B. Deakin, "Discriminate Analysis of Predictors of Business Failure," *Journal of Accounting Research*, Spring, 1972, pp. 167–179; Robert Libby, "Accounting Ratios and the Prediction of Failure: Some Behavioural Evidence," *Journal of Accounting Research*, Spring, 1975, pp. 150–161; and Edward I. Altman, *Corporate Financial Distress and Bankruptcy* (New York: John Wiley & Sons, 1993).

3. **Identify major types of ratios and know what each is attempting to measure.** A ratio is simply the expression of the relationship between two numbers. The major types of ratios are: liquidity ratios, activity ratios, profitability ratios, and coverage ratios. Liquidity and coverage ratios generally reflect the financial strength of a company. Activity and profitability ratios are usually associated with assessing management's performance.

4. **Identify liquidity ratios, know how they are calculated, and appreciate the questions they can help answer.** Liquidity ratios help assess the short-run ability of an enterprise to pay its maturing obligations. Liquidity ratios include the current ratio, acid-test ratio, and defensive-interval ratio.

5. **Identify activity ratios, know how they are calculated, and appreciate the questions they can help answer.** Activity ratios, also called turnover ratios, are designed to help assess how efficiently an enterprise is using its assets. Such ratios include the receivables turnover, inventory turnover, and asset turnover.

6. **Identify profitability ratios, know how they are calculated, and appreciate the questions they can help answer.** Profitability ratios help assess the degree of success or failure of an enterprise to generate revenues adequate to cover its costs of operations and provide a return on investment. Rate of return on assets and on common shareholders' equity are particularly relevant in this regard. Assessing rate of return in terms of profit margin and asset turnover reveals significant insight into an enterprise's strategy regarding profitability. Earnings per share, price earnings ratio, and payout ratio are other ratios used. While not based on profitability, ratios incorporating cash flow are receiving increasing attention as a means to help assess management's performance. Such information includes cash flow from operation (CFO) per share, CFO payout ratio, and examining CFO versus non-operating cash flow patterns.

7. **Identify coverage ratios, know how they are calculated, and appreciate the questions they can help answer.** Coverage ratios help assess the degree of protection for, and risk attached to, long-term creditors and investors. Coverage ratios include debt to total assets, times interest earned, book value per share, and cash flow from operations per share.

8. **Describe and know how to apply comparative (trend) analysis.** Comparative analysis is the comparison of like items for two or more accounting periods. From such analysis, trends in relationships are identified.

9. **Describe and know how to apply percentage (common-size) analysis.** Percentage analysis or common-size analysis consists of reducing a series of absolute dollar amounts to a series of percentages of a given base. Horizontal analysis provides the percentage change in an item over time, and vertical analysis expresses each item on a financial statement as a percentage of a base amount.

10. **Know sources of uncertainty for decision makers when using financial statement information and the related limitations of ratio analysis.** The usefulness of financial statement information is affected by uncertainty regarding understanding (1) the nature and role of financial statements; (2) the nature of the business operations portrayed in the statements; (3) the limitations of the measurements and disclosures made; and (4) the motives and intentions of management. Limitations regarding measurement and disclosures result in significant limitations of ratio analysis. For example, ratios are traditionally based on

historical cost numbers and many ratios use estimated amounts in their calculation. A significant criticism is that comparison of ratios between different enterprises is very difficult because each may be using different accounting policies and procedures.

11. **Recognize issues associated with the requirement that ratios be reported in financial statements.** With the exception of EPS amounts, ratios are not required as part of the financial statements. Because many ratios are voluntarily provided, some analysts believe that their calculation and disclosure should be standardized in order to improve comparability. Others contend that the AcSB should not establish such standards as there needs to be a clear separation between financial reporting and financial analysis.

EXERCISES

(Ratio Computation) Financial information for Dawn Inc. is presented below.   E24-1

Assets	12/31/98	12/31/97
Cash	$ 140,000	$ 165,000
Receivables (net)	340,000	198,000
Inventories	1,350,000	980,000
Short-term investments	200,000	600,000
Prepaid items	40,000	60,000
Land	580,000	400,000
Building and equipment (net)	2,000,000	1,760,000
	$4,650,000	$4,163,000

Equities		
Accounts payable	$ 730,000	$ 543,000
Notes payable	400,000	150,000
Accrued liabilities	100,000	100,000
Bonds payable due 2000	700,000	820,000
Common shares	2,000,000	2,000,000
Retained earnings	720,000	550,000
	$4,650,000	$4,163,000

DAWN INC.
Comparative Income Statement
Years Ended December 31, 1998 and 1997

	1998	1997
Sales	$4,400,000	$3,900,000
Cost of goods sold	3,250,000	3,100,000
Gross profit	$1,150,000	$ 800,000
Operating expenses	520,000	450,000
Net income	$ 630,000	$ 350,000

Instructions
From these data compute as many ratios presented in the chapter, for both years, as possible. Assume that the ending account balances for 1997 are representative of that year unless the information provided indicates differently. The beginning inventory for 1997 was $720,000.

E24-2   (Understanding Ratio Computations: Short Answers) Answer each of the questions in the following unrelated situations.

1. The current ratio of a company is 5:1 and its acid-test ratio is 1:1. If the inventories and prepaid items amount to $600,000, what is the amount of current liabilities?

2. A company had an average inventory last year of $200,000 and its inventory turnover was 5. If sales volume and unit cost remain the same this year as last and inventory turnover is 8 this year, what will average inventory have to be during the current year?

3. A company has current assets of $90,000 (of which $40,000 is inventory and prepaid items) and current liabilities of $30,000. What is the current ratio? What is the acid-test ratio? If the company borrows $15,000 cash from a bank on a 120-day loan, what will its current ratio be? What will the acid-test ratio be?

4. A company has current assets of $600,000 and current liabilities of $240,000. The board of directors declares a cash dividend of $180,000. What is the current ratio after the declaration, but before payment? What is the current ratio after the payment of the dividend?

5. A company's budgeted sales and budgeted cost of goods sold for the coming year are $144,000,000 and $90,000,000, respectively. Short-term interest rates on loans to finance inventory are expected to average 10%. If the company can increase inventory turnover from its present level of 9 times a year to a level of 12 times per year, compute its expected cost savings for the coming year.

E24-3   (Financial Leverage Analysis) Presented below is information related to Dali Inc.

Operating income	$ 532,150
Bond interest expense	135,000
	$ 397,150
Income taxes	182,689
Net income	$ 214,461
Bonds payable	$1,000,000
Common shares	875,000
Appropriation for contingencies	75,000
Retained earnings, unappropriated	300,000

Instructions
Is Dali Inc. using financial leverage favourably? Explain.

E24-4   (Ratio Computations, Analysis, and Effect of Transactions) Fine Arts Ltd.'s condensed financial statements provide the following information.

Balance Sheet

	Dec. 31, 1998	Dec. 31, 1997
Cash	$ 52,000	$ 60,000
Accounts receivable (net)	198,000	80,000
Marketable securities (short-term)	80,000	40,000
Inventories	440,000	360,000
Prepaid expenses	3,000	7,000
Total current assets	$ 773,000	$ 547,000
Property, plant, and equipment (net)	857,000	853,000
Total assets	$1,630,000	$1,400,000
Current liabilities	$ 240,000	$ 160,000
Bonds payable	400,000	400,000
Common shareholders' equity	990,000	840,000
Total liabilities and shareholders' equity	$1,630,000	$1,400,000

Income Statement
For the Year Ended 1998

Sales	$1,640,000
Cost of goods sold	(800,000)
Gross profit	$ 840,000
Selling and administrative expense	(440,000)
Interest expense	(40,000)
Net income	$ 360,000

Instructions

(a) Determine the following:

1. Current ratio at December 31, 1998.

2. Acid-test ratio at December 31, 1998.

3. Accounts receivable turnover for 1998.

4. Inventory turnover for 1998.

5. Rate of return on assets for 1998.

6. Rate of return on common shareholders' equity for 1998.

(b) Prepare a brief evaluation of the financial condition of Fine Arts Ltd. and of the adequacy of its profits.

(c) Indicate for each of the following transactions whether the transaction would improve, weaken, or have no effect on the current ratio of Fine Arts Ltd. at December 31, 1998.

1. Write off an uncollectible account receivable, $2,200.

2. Purchase some of the outstanding bonds payable for $30,000.

3. Pay $40,000 on notes payable (short-term).

4. Collect $23,000 on accounts receivable.

5. Buy equipment on account.

6. Give an existing creditor a short-term note in settlement of account.

(Ratio Analysis) As loan analyst for Mega Bank, you have been presented with the following information. **E24-5**

Assets

	Whiz Co. Ltd.	Magic Co. Ltd.
Cash	$ 120,000	$ 320,000
Receivables	220,000	302,000
Inventories	570,000	518,000
Total current assets	$ 910,000	$1,140,000
Other assets	500,000	612,000
Total assets	$1,410,000	$1,752,000

Liabilities and Shareholders' Equity

	Whiz Co. Ltd.	Magic Co. Ltd.
Current liabilities	$ 305,000	$ 350,000
Long-term liabilities	400,000	500,000
Share capital and retained earnings	705,000	902,000
Total liabilities and shareholders' equity	$1,410,000	$1,752,000
Annual sales	$ 930,000	$1,500,000
Rate of gross profit on sales	30%	40%

Each of these companies has requested a loan of $50,000 for six months, with no collateral offered. Only one of these loan requests is to be granted.

Instructions

Which of the two companies, as judged by the information given, would you recommend as the better risk, and why? Assume that the ending account balances are representative of the entire year.

E24-6 **(Analysis of Given Ratios)** WBM Co. Ltd. is a wholesale distributor of professional equipment and supplies. The company's sales have averaged about $900,000 annually for the three-year period 1996–1998. The firm's total assets at the end of 1998 amounted to $850,000.

The president of WBM has asked the controller to prepare a report that summarizes the financial aspects of the company's operations for the past three years. This report will be presented to the board of directors at its next meeting.

In addition to comparative financial statements, the controller has decided to present a number of financial ratios that can assist in the identification and interpretation of trends. At the request of the controller, the accounting staff has calculated the following ratios for the three-year period.

	1996	1997	1998
Current ratio	1.80	1.89	1.96
Acid-test (quick) ratio	1.04	0.99	0.87
Accounts receivable turnover	8.75	7.71	6.42
Inventory turnover	4.91	4.32	3.42
Percentage of total debt to total assets	51.0%	46.0%	41.0%
Percentage of long-term debt to total assets	31.0%	27.0%	24.0%
Sales divided by capital assets (capital asset turnover)	1.58	1.69	1.79
Sales as a percentage of 1996 sales	100.0%	103.0%	107.0%
Gross profit percentage	36.0%	35.1%	34.6%
Net income to sales	6.9%	7.0%	7.2%
Return on total assets	7.7%	7.7%	7.8%
Return on shareholders' equity	13.6%	13.1%	12.7%

In the preparation of her report, the controller has decided first to examine the financial ratios independently of any other data to determine if the ratios themselves reveal any significant trends over the three-year period.

Instructions

(a) The current ratio is increasing while the acid-test (quick) ratio is decreasing. Using the information provided, identify and explain the contributing factor(s) for this apparently divergent trend.

(b) In terms of the information provided, what conclusion(s) can be drawn regarding the company's use of financial leverage during the 1996–1998 period?

(c) Using the information provided, what conclusion(s) can be drawn regarding the company's net investment in capital assets?

(CMA adapted)

E24-7 **(Ratio Analysis)** Milltek is a manufacturer of electronic components and accessories with total assets of $20,000,000. Selected financial ratios for Milltek and the industry averages for firms of similar size are presented below.

	Milltek			1998 Industry Average
	1996	1997	1998	
Current ratio	2.09	2.27	2.51	2.24
Quick ratio	1.15	1.17	1.19	1.22
Inventory turnover	2.40	2.18	2.02	3.50
Net sales to shareholders' equity	2.71	2.80	2.99	2.85
Net income to shareholders' equity	0.14	0.15	0.17	0.11
Total liabilities to shareholders' equity	1.41	1.37	1.44	0.95

Milltek is being reviewed by several entities whose interests vary, and the company's financial ratios are a part of the data being considered. Each of the parties listed below must recommend an action based on its evaluation of Milltek's financial position.

1. Commerce Bank. The bank is processing Milltek's application for a new five-year term note. Commerce has been Milltek's banker for several years, but must re-evaluate the company's financial position for each major transaction.

2. HiRez Co. Ltd. HiRez is a new supplier to Milltek and must decide on the appropriate credit terms to extend to the company.

3. T&D Investors. As a brokerage firm specializing in the shares of electronics firms that are sold over-the-counter, T&D Investors must decide if it will include Milltek in a new fund being established for sale to its clients.

4. Working Capital Management Committee. This is a committee of Milltek's management personnel, chaired by the chief operating officer. The committee is charged with the responsibility of periodically reviewing the company's working capital position, comparing actual data against budgets, and recommending changes in strategy as needed.

Instructions

(a) Describe the analytical use of each of the six ratios identified.

(b) For each of the four entities described, identify two financial ratios from those ratios presented that would be most useful as a basis for its decision regarding Milltek.

(c) Discuss what the financial ratios presented in the question reveal about Milltek. Support your answer by citing specific ratio levels and trends as well as the interrelationships between these ratios. (CMA adapted)

(Discovering Reasons for Declining Return on Shareholders' Equity) The controller of DaVinci Company Ltd. **E24-8** finds that, although the company continues to earn about the same net income year after year, the rate of return on shareholders' equity is decreasing. Most of the profits remain in the business, so total assets are increasing year by year. As a recently hired accountant, you are requested to assist the controller in locating the difficulty and to suggest remedial measures. You obtain the following information.

	Inventory Dec. 31	Cost of Goods Sold
1995	$456,000	$3,120,000
1996	545,000	2,960,000
1997	601,000	3,000,000
1998	689,000	3,240,000

Instructions

(a) What conclusions can be reached on the basis of this information only?

(b) What further investigation does it suggest? State how you would proceed.

(c) If your conclusions are confirmed in the additional investigation, what recommendations would you make concerning remedial measures?

(Comparison of Alternative Forms of Financing) Shown below is the equity section of the balance sheet for Rock **E24-9** Inc. and Haven Inc. Each has assets totalling $4,200,000.

Rock Inc.		Haven Inc.	
Current liabilities	$ 300,000	Current liabilities	$ 600,000
Long-term debt, 10%	1,200,000	Common shares ($20 per share)	2,900,000
Common shares ($20 per share)	2,000,000	Retained earnings	700,000
Retained earnings	700,000		
	$4,200,000		$4,200,000

For the last two years each company has earned the same income before interest and taxes.

	Rock Inc.	Haven Inc.
Income before interest and taxes	$1,200,000	$1,200,000
Interest expense	120,000	-0-
	$1,080,000	$1,200,000
Income taxes (45%)	486,000	540,000
Net income	$ 594,000	$ 660,000

Instructions

(a) Which company is more profitable in terms of return on total assets?

(b) Which company is more profitable in terms of return on shareholders' equity?

(c) Which company has the greater net income per share? Why?

(d) From the point of view of income, is it advantageous to the shareholders of Rock Inc. to have the long-term debt outstanding? Why?

E24-10 **(Preparation of Working Capital Section of Balance Sheet from Ratios)** You have been engaged to perform management consulting services for Laurant Inc. One aspect of the engagement is to project working capital requirements. The sales forecast is $12 million for 1998. Target ratios for this year are as follows.

Cost of sales	55% of sales	Cash	4% of sales
Inventory turnover	6 times	Prepaid expenses	2% of sales
Receivables turnover	10 times	Accrued expenses	3% of sales

In addition, accounts payable are projected to be $550,000 at the end of 1998. Assume that the beginning and ending accounts receivable and inventory balances will not change.

Instructions

Prepare the projected working capital section of the balance sheet for December 31, 1998.

PROBLEMS

P24-1 Mint Corporation Ltd. was formed five years ago through a public subscription of common shares. Chris Lee, who owns 15% of the common shares, was one of the organizers of Mint and is its current president. The company has been successful but currently is experiencing a shortage of funds. On June 10, 1998 Lee approached the Cooperative Bank asking for a 24-month extension on two $35,000 notes, which are due on June 30, 1998 and September 30, 1998. Another note of $6,000 is due on December 31, 1999 but she expects no difficulty in paying this note on its due date. Lee explained that Mint's cash flow problems are due primarily to the company's desire to finance a $300,000 plant expansion over the next two fiscal years through internally generated funds.

    The commercial loans officer of the bank requested financial reports for the last two fiscal years. These reports are reproduced below.

MINT CORPORATION LTD.
Statement of Financial Position
March 31

Assets	1997	1998
Cash	$ 12,500	$ 18,200
Notes receivable	132,000	148,000
Accounts receivable (net)	125,500	131,800
Inventories (at cost)	50,000	95,000
Plant and equipment (net of depreciation)	1,420,500	1,449,000
Total assets	$1,740,500	$1,842,000

Liabilities and Shareholders' Equity	1997	1998
Accounts payable	$ 91,000	$ 69,000
Notes payable	61,500	76,000
Accrued liabilities	6,000	9,000
Common shares (130,000 shares issued and outstanding)	1,300,000	1,300,000
Retained earnings*	282,000	388,000
Total liabilities and shareholders' equity	$1,740,500	$1,842,000

*Cash dividends were paid at the rate of $1.00 per share in fiscal year 1997 and $2.00 per share in fiscal year 1998.

MINT CORPORATION LTD.
Income Statement
For the Fiscal Years Ended March 31

	1997	1998
Sales	$2,700,000	$3,000,000
Cost of goods sold*	1,425,000	1,530,000
Gross margin	$1,275,000	$1,470,000
Operating expenses	780,000	860,000
Income before income taxes	$ 495,000	$ 610,000
Income taxes (40%)	198,000	244,000
Net income	$ 297,000	$ 366,000

*Depreciation charges on the plant and equipment of $100,000 and $102,500 for fiscal years ended March 31, 1997 and 1998, respectively, are included in cost of goods sold.

Instructions
(a) Compute the following for Mint Corporation Ltd.
  1. Current ratio for fiscal years 1997 and 1998.
  2. Acid-test (quick) ratio for fiscal years 1997 and 1998.
  3. Inventory turnover for fiscal year 1998.
  4. Return on assets for fiscal years 1997 and 1998. (Assume total assets were $1,688,500 at 3/31/96.)
  5. Percentage change in sales, cost of goods sold, gross margin, and net income after taxes from fiscal year 1997 to 1998.
(b) Identify and explain what other financial reports and/or financial analyses might be helpful to the commercial loans officer in evaluating Lee's request for a time extension on Mint's notes.
(c) Assume that the percentage changes experienced in fiscal year 1998 as compared with fiscal year 1997 for sales, cost of goods sold, gross margin, and net income after taxes will be repeated in each of the next two years. Is Mint's desire to finance the plant expansion from internally generated funds realistic? Discuss.
(d) Should the Cooperative Bank grant the extension on Mint's notes, considering Lee's statement about financing the plant expansion through internally generated funds? Discuss.

(CMA adapted)

Twist Inc. is planning to invest $12,000,000 in an expansion program that is expected to increase income before inter- **P24-2** est and taxes by $2,200,000. The company currently is earning $2.40 per share on 1,000,000 common shares outstanding. The capital structure prior to the investment is:

Debt	$ 25,000,000
Equity	75,000,000
	$100,000,000

The expansion can be financed by sale of 300,000 shares at $40 net each or by issuing long-term debt at an 8% interest cost. The company's recent income statement was as follows.

Sales	$100,000,000
Variable costs	$ 65,000,000
Fixed costs	29,000,000
	$ 94,000,000
Income before interest and taxes	$ 6,000,000
Interest	2,000,000
Income before income taxes	$ 4,000,000
Income taxes (40%)	1,600,000
Net income	$ 2,400,000

Instructions

(a) Assuming that the company maintains its current income and achieves the anticipated income from the expansion, what will be the earnings per share (1) if the expansion is financed by debt? (2) if the expansion is financed by equity?

(b) At what level of income before interest and taxes will the earnings per share under either alternative be the same amount?

(c) The choice of financing alternatives influences the earnings per share. The choice might also influence the earnings multiple (price to earnings ratio) used by the "market." Discuss the factors inherent in the choice between the debt and equity alternatives that might influence the earnings multiple. Be sure to indicate the direction in which these factors might influence the earnings multiple.

(CMA adapted)

P24-3 Jigsaw Inc. has been operating successfully for a number of years. The balance sheet of the company as of December 31, 1998, is as follows.

JIGSAW INC.
Balance Sheet
December 31, 1998

Assets			Equities		
Current assets			Current liabilities		
Cash		$ 50,000	Notes payable		$ 80,000
Accounts receivable (net)		125,000	Accounts payable		97,000
Notes receivable		80,000	Taxes payable		61,000
Inventories		270,000	Total current liabilities		$ 238,000
Prepaid items		20,000			
Total current assets		$ 545,000	Long-term liabilities		
			Long-term bank loan, due		
Fixed assets			in 2002, 10% interest		190,000
Land	$ 30,000		Shareholders' equity		
Building (net)	256,000		Common shares		
Equipment (net)	400,000		(35,000 issued)	$350,000	
Total fixed assets		686,000	Retained earnings	453,000	803,000
		$1,231,000			$1,231,000

The balance sheet indicates that the bulk of the company's growth has been financed by the common shareholders, because $453,000 of past net income of the company has been retained and is now invested in various operating assets. For the last three years, the company has earned an average net income of $85,000 after interest ($21,000) and taxes ($48,000).

The board of directors has been considering an expansion of operations. Estimations indicate that the company can double its volume of operations with an additional investment of about $900,000. Of this amount, $600,000 would be used to add to the present building, to purchase new equipment, and to reorganize certain operations. The remaining amount would be needed for working capital—inventories and higher receivables. Competitive conditions are such that the added volume can probably be sold at the existing prices and that the total income from all operations before taxes and interest will be $320,000. The tax rate of about 36% on income after interest will continue. Three alternative plans for financing the expansion are under consideration:

1. Sell enough additional shares to raise $900,000. For this purpose, it is estimated that the shares would sell at $30 each.

2. Sell 20-year bonds at 12% interest, totalling $790,000. In addition, sell 10,000 shares at a price of $30 per share. Use part of the proceeds to pay off the present long-term bank loan.

3. Sell 20-year bonds at 12% interest, totalling $900,000. Use part of the proceeds to pay off the present long-term bank loan. The remaining funds are to be provided by short-term creditors. The cost of these remaining funds (in interest and discounts not taken) is estimated at $27,000 a year.

Assume that the financing alternative selected will take place immediately.

Instructions

(a) Compute the following for each plan:

1. Current ratio, comparing each ratio with the present current ratio.

2. Earnings per share, comparing each ratio with the present earnings per share.

3. Rate of return on common shareholders' equity, comparing each ratio with the present return.

4. Ratio of debt to total equity, comparing each ratio with the present ratio.

(b) Which alternative financing plan do you recommend? Why?

The transactions identified below relate to Hammel Inc. You are to assume that on the date on which each of the transactions occurred, the corporation's accounts showed only common shares outstanding, a current ratio of 2.7:1, and a substantial net income for the year to date (before giving effect to the transaction concerned). On that date, the book value per share was $151.53.

P24-4

Each numbered transaction is to be considered completely independently of the others, and its related answer should be based on the effect(s) of that transaction alone. Assume that all transactions occurred during 1998 and that the amount involved in each case was sufficiently material to distort reported net income if improperly included in the determination of net income. Assume further that each transaction was recorded in accordance with generally accepted accounting principles.

For each of the numbered transactions you are to decide whether it:

1. Increased the corporation's 1998 net income.

2. Decreased the corporation's 1998 net income.

3. Increased the corporation's total retained earnings directly (i.e., not via net income).

4. Decreased the corporation's total retained earnings directly.

5. Increased the corporation's current ratio.

6. Decreased the corporation's current ratio.

7. Increased each shareholder's proportionate share of total shareholders' equity.

8. Decreased each shareholder's proportionate share of total shareholders' equity.

9. Increased each shareholder's equity per share (book value).

10. Decreased each shareholder's equity per share (book value).

11. Had none of the foregoing effects.

Instructions

List the letters (a) through (h). Select as many numbers as you deem appropriate to reflect the effect(s) of each transaction as of the date of the transaction by printing beside the transaction letter the number(s) that identify that transaction's effect(s).

Transactions

(a) The corporation called in all its outstanding shares and exchanged them for new shares on a two-for-one basis.

(b) The corporation paid a cash dividend that had been recorded as a liability in the accounts at the time of declaration.

(c) Litigation involving Hammel Inc. as defendant was settled in the corporation's favour, with the plaintiff paying all court costs and legal fees. The corporation had appropriated retained earnings in 1995 as a special contingency for this court action, and the board directed abolition of the appropriation. (Indicate the effect of reversing the appropriation only.)

(d) The corporation received a cheque for the proceeds of an insurance policy from the company with which it was insured against theft of trucks. No entries concerning the theft had been made previously, and the proceeds reduced but did not completely cover the loss.

(e) The corporation sold, at a profit, land and a building that had been idle for some time. Under the terms of the sale, the corporation received a portion of the sales price in cash immediately, the balance maturing at six-month intervals.

(f) In January the board directed the write-off of certain patent rights that had suddenly and unexpectedly become worthless.

(g) The corporation wrote off all of the unamortized discount and issue expense applicable to bonds that it refinanced in 1998.

(h) The board of directors authorized the write-up of certain fixed assets to values established in a competent appraisal.

(AICPA adapted)

P24-5 Presented below are comparative balance sheets for Shoe Co. Ltd.

SHOE CO. LTD.
Comparative Balance Sheet
December 31, 1998 and 1997

Assets	1998	1997
Cash	$ 180,000	$ 275,000
Accounts receivable (net)	220,000	155,000
Investments	270,000	150,000
Inventories	960,000	980,000
Prepaid expenses	25,000	25,000
Capital assets	2,685,000	1,950,000
Accumulated amortization	(1,000,000)	(750,000)
	$3,340,000	$2,785,000
Liabilities and Shareholders' Equity		
Accounts payable	$ 50,000	$ 75,000
Accrued expenses	170,000	200,000
Bonds payable	500,000	190,000
Share capital	2,100,000	1,770,000
Retained earnings	520,000	550,000
	$3,340,000	$2,785,000

Instructions
(a) Prepare a comparative balance sheet of Shoe Co. Ltd. showing the percentage of each item to the total assets.
(b) Prepare a comparative balance sheet of Shoe Co. Ltd. showing the dollar change and the percentage change for each item.
(c) Of what value is the information provided in (a)?
(d) Of what value is the information provided in (b)?

P24-6 Jays Ltd. has, in recent years, maintained the following relationships among the data on its financial statements.

1. Gross profit rate on net sales	32%
2. Profit margin on net sales	8%
3. Rate of selling expenses to net sales	16%
4. Accounts receivable turnover	8 per year
5. Inventory turnover	10 per year
6. Acid-test ratio	2 to 1
7. Current ratio	3 to 1
8. Quick asset composition: 7% cash, 28% marketable securities, 65% accounts receivable	
9. Asset turnover	2 per year
10. Ratio of total assets to intangible assets	25 to 1
11. Ratio of accumulated depreciation to cost of tangible capital assets	1 to 4
12. Ratio of accounts receivable to accounts payable	2 to 1
13. Ratio of working capital to shareholders' equity	1 to 1.95
14. Ratio of total debt to shareholders' equity	1 to 3

The corporation had a net income of $520,000 for 1998 that resulted in earnings of $9.74 per common share. Additional information follows:

1. Share capital authorized, issued (all in 1990), and outstanding:
   Common, no-par value, issued at $11 per share.
   Preferred, $11 nonparticipating, no-par value, issued at $110 per share.
2. Market value per common share at December 31, 1998: $116.88
3. Preferred dividends paid in 1998: $33,000.

4. Times interest earned in 1998: 28.73.

5. The amounts of the following were the same at December 31, 1998, as at January 1, 1998: inventory, accounts receivable, 10% bonds payable—due 2000, and total shareholders' equity.

6. All purchases and sales were on account.

Instructions

(a) Prepare in good form the condensed (1) balance sheet and (2) income statement for the year ending December 31, 1998, presenting the amounts you would expect to appear on Jays' financial statements (ignoring income taxes). Major captions appearing on Jays' balance sheet are: Current Assets; Property, Plant, and Equipment; Intangible Assets; Current Liabilities; Long-Term Liabilities; and Shareholders' Equity. In addition to the accounts divulged in the problem, you should include accounts for Prepaid Expenses, Accrued Expenses, and Administrative Expenses.

(b) Compute the following for 1998 (show your computations).

1. Rate of return on common shareholders' equity.

2. Price earnings ratio for common shares.

3. Dividends paid per common share.

4. Dividends paid per preferred share.

5. Dividend yield on common shares.

(AICPA adapted)

C A S E S

As a consultant for Clipper Inc., you have been requested to develop some key ratios from the comparative financial statements. This information is to be used to convince creditors that Clipper Inc. is solvent (able to pay bills when due) and to support the use of going-concern valuation procedures in the financial statements. The data requested and the computations developed from the financial statements follow.   **C24-1**

	1998	1997
Current ratio	2.6 times	2.1 times
Acid-test ratio	0.8 times	1.3 times
Property, plant, and equipment to shareholders' equity	2.5 times	2.2 times
Sales to shareholders' equity	2.4 times	2.7 times
Net income	Up 32%	Down 9%
Earnings per share	$3.30	$2.50
Book value per share	Up 6%	Up 9%

Instructions

(a) Clipper's management asks you to prepare a list of brief comments stating how each of these items supports the solvency and going-concern valuation of the business. The management wishes to use these comments to support a presentation to its creditors. You are to prepare the comments as requested, giving the implications and the limitations of each item separately and then the collective inference that may be drawn from them about Clipper's solvency and going-concern potential.

(b) Having completed the requirement requested in (a), prepare a brief listing of additional ratio-analysis-type data for Clipper that you think its creditors are going to ask for to supplement the data provided in (a). Explain why you think the additional data will be helpful to these creditors in evaluating Clipper's solvency.

(c) What warnings should you offer these creditors about the limitations of ratio analysis for the purposes stated here?

While enjoying a beverage during a study break, you overheard two classmates discussing the usefulness of financial statement analysis based on single-year statements and comparative statements (e.g., presenting financial history for the last 10 years). The general direction of the discussion was leading to the conclusion that both approaches had inherent limitations and could be misleading. Noticing your interest, your classmates invited you to contribute to the assessment.   **C24-2**

Instructions

Provide an outline of the points you contribute regarding:

(a) The limitations of single-year statement analysis and the extent to which these limitations may be overcome by the availability of comparative statements.

(b) The factors or conditions that may contribute to misinterpretations when analysing a comparative (10-year) financial history.

Also, provide an identification of additional information and supplementary data that might be included in or provided with the statements to prevent misinterpretations.

C24-3 Foster Inc. went public three years ago (early 1996). The board of directors will be meeting shortly (early 1999) to decide on a dividend policy. In the past, growth has been financed primarily through the retention of earnings. A stock or a cash dividend has never been declared. Presented below is a brief financial summary of Foster Inc.'s operations.

	1998	1997	($000 omitted) 1996	1995	1994
Sales	$20,000	$16,000	$14,000	$6,000	$4,000
Net income	$ 2,900	$ 1,600	$ 800	$ 900	$ 250
Average total assets	$22,000	$19,000	$11,500	$4,200	$3,000
Current assets	$ 8,000	$ 6,000	$ 3,000	$1,200	$1,000
Working capital	$ 3,600	$ 3,200	$ 1,200	$ 500	$ 400
Common shares:					
Number of shares outstanding (000)	2,000	2,000	2,000	20	20
Average market price	$9	$6	$4	—	—

Instructions

(a) Identify at least 10 factors to be considered by the board of directors in establishing a dividend policy.

(b) Compute the rate of return on assets, profit margin on sales, earnings per share, price earnings ratio, and current ratio for each of the five years for Foster Inc.

(c) Comment on the appropriateness of declaring a cash dividend at this time, using the ratios computed in (b) as a major factor in your analysis.

C24-4 The Budget Committee of Anellio Limited was established to appraise and screen departmental requests for plant expansions and improvements at a time when these requests totalled $11,200,000. The committee then sought your advice and help in establishing the minimum performance standards that it should demand of these projects in the way of anticipated rates of return before interest and taxes.

Anellio Limited is a closely held family corporation in which the shareholders exert an active and unified influence on the management. At this date, the company has no long-term debt and has 1,000,000 common shares outstanding that were sold at $20 per share. It is currently earning $5 million (income before interest and taxes) per year. The applicable tax rate is 40%.

If the projects under consideration are approved, management is confident that the $11,200,000 of required funds can be obtained either:

1. By borrowing, via an issue of $11,200,000, 11%, 20-year bonds.

2. By equity financing, via an issue of 560,000 common shares to the general public. It is expected that the ownership of these 560,000 shares will be widely dispersed and scattered.

The company's after-tax net income of $3,000,000 per year provides slightly more than 14% return on a capitalized value (worth) per share of $21. The management and the dominant shareholders consider this rate of earnings to result in a fair price earnings ratio (7 times earnings) as long as the company remains free of long-term debt. A lowering of the price earnings ratio to 6 times earnings constitutes an adequate adjustment to compensate for the risk of carrying $11,200,000 of long-term debt. They believe that this reflects, and is consistent with, current market appraisals.

Instructions

(a) Determine the minimum earnings before interest and taxes required under each financing alternative so that the present capitalized value per share of $21 is maintained. (Hint: Begin with the capitalized value per share and work in reverse to determine the required earnings for each alternative.)

(b) What minimum rate of return before interest and taxes on new investment is necessary for each alternative to maintain the present capitalized value per share of $21?

(c) Which alternative financing plan would you recommend? Why? (Hint: Determine the rate of return before interest and taxes on shareholders' capitalized value of investment prior to any expansion and compare it with the answers to (b).)

(AICPA adapted)

C24-5

The owners of Max Inc., a closely held corporation, have offered to sell their 100% interest in the company's common shares at an amount equal to their book value. They will retain their interest in the company's preferred shares.

The president of Graff Ltd., your client, would like to combine the operations of Max Inc. with the Publishing Division, and she is seriously considering having Graff Ltd. buy the common shares of Max Inc. She questions the use of "book value" as a basis for the sale, however, and has come to you for advice.

Instructions

Draft a report to your client. Your report should include the following points.

(a) Explain the significance of book value in establishing a value for a business that is expected to continue in operation indefinitely.

(b) Why should your client consider Max Inc.'s accounting policies and methods in her evaluation of the company's reported book value? List the areas of accounting policy and methods relevant to this evaluation.

(c) What factors, other than book value, should your client recognize in determining a basis for the sale?

(AICPA adapted)

C24-6

TEDCO Limited is a manufacturer of highly specialized products for networking video-conferencing equipment. Production of specialized units are, to a large extent, performed under contract, with standard units manufactured to marketing projections. Maintenance of customer equipment is an important area of customer satisfaction. With the recent downturn in the computer industry, the video-conferencing equipment segment has suffered, causing a slide in TEDCO's performance. TEDCO's income statement for the fiscal year ended October 31, 1998 is presented below.

TEDCO LIMITED
Income Statement
For the Year Ended October 31, 1998
($000 omitted)

Net sales	
Equipment	$6,000
Maintenance contracts	1,800
Total net sales	$7,800
Expenses	
Cost of goods sold	$4,600
Customer maintenance	1,000
Selling expense	600
Administrative expense	900
Interest expense	150
Total expenses	$7,250
Income before income taxes	$ 550
Income taxes	220
Net income	$ 330

TEDCO's return on sales before interest and taxes was 9% in fiscal 1998, while the industry average was 12%. TEDCO's total asset turnover was three times, and its return on average assets before interest and taxes was 27%, both well below the industry average. To improve performance and raise these ratios nearer to, or above, industry averages, Betty Bowman, TEDCO's president, established the following goals for fiscal 1999.

1. Return on sales before interest and taxes   11%

2. Total asset turnover   4 times

3. Return on average assets before interest and taxes   35%

To achieve Bowman's goals, TEDCO's management team took into consideration the growing international video-conferencing market and proposed the following actions for fiscal 1999.

1. Increase equipment sales prices by 10%.

2. Increase the cost of each unit sold by 3% for needed technology and quality improvements, and increased variable costs.

3. Increase maintenance inventory by $250,000 at the beginning of the year and add two maintenance technicians at a total cost of $130,000 to cover wages and related travel expenses. These revisions are intended to improve customer service and response time. The increased inventory will be financed at an annual interest rate of 12%; no other borrowings or loan reductions are contemplated during fiscal 1999. All other assets will be held to fiscal 1998 levels.

4. Increase selling expenses by $250,000 but hold administrative expenses at 1998 levels.

5. The effective income tax rate for 1999 is expected to be 40%, the same as 1998.

It is expected that these actions will increase equipment unit sales by 6%, with a corresponding 6% growth in maintenance contracts.

Instructions

(a) Prepare a pro forma income statement for TEDCO Limited for the fiscal year ending October 31, 1999, on the assumption that the proposed actions are implemented as planned and that the increased sales objectives will be met. (All numbers should be rounded to the nearest thousand.)

(b) Calculate the following ratios for TEDCO Limited for fiscal year 1999 and determine whether Betty Bowman's goals will be achieved.

   1. Return on sales before interest and taxes.

   2. Total asset turnover.

   3. Return on average assets before interest and taxes.

(c) Discuss the limitations and difficulties that can be encountered in using ratio analysis, particularly when making comparisons to industry averages.

C24-7   Dye Co. Ltd. declared bankruptcy in 1998. The company's financial statements for the three most recent years are as follows.

Financial Statements (figures are in 000s)

Income Statement	1995	1996	1997
Sales	$5,000	$5,200	$5,500
Cost of goods sold	3,000	3,100	4,000
Gross profit	$2,000	2,100	1,500
Operating expenses	$1,150	$1,300	$1,400
Operating income	$ 850	$ 800	$ 100
Interest expense	150	250	400
Income before taxes	$ 700	$ 550	$ (300)
Income tax	210	150	-0-
Net income	$ 490	$ 400	$ (300)
Common share dividends	$ 200	$ 200	$ -0-

Balance Sheet			
Assets			
Cash	$ 500	$ 100	$ 10
Marketable securities	400	100	-0-
Accounts receivable	100	300	500
Inventories	300	210	100
Total current assets	$1,300	$ 710	$ 610
Land and buildings	$2,000	$3,000	$4,000
Machinery and equipment	500	800	1,500
Other	300	600	500
Less: Accumulated depreciation	1,000	1,400	1,800
Net fixed assets	$1,800	$3,000	$4,200
Total assets	$3,100	$3,710	$4,810

Liabilities and Shareholders' Equity

Accounts payable	$ 100	$ 50	$ 20
Notes payable	100	150	150
Accruals	200	100	180
Total current liabilities	$ 400	$ 300	$ 350
Long-term debt	$1,000	$1,510	$2,860
Common shares	$ 710	$ 710	$ 710
Contributed surplus	300	300	300
Retained earnings	690	890	590
Total shareholders' equity	$1,700	$1,900	$1,600
Total liabilities and shareholders' equity	$3,100	$3,710	$4,810

Instructions

(a) Using the financial statements provided, identify the causes of the firm's financial difficulties.

(b) Using the financial statements provided, explain how the company could have either avoided these financial difficulties or resolved the difficulties as they developed.

PART I Green Co. Ltd. and Blue Inc. both started their business operations on January 1, 1998. During 1998 both   **C24-8**
companies, by coincidence, had the same level of sales, expenses other than for cost of goods sold, amortization and income taxes, composition of debt, initial investment in capital assets, and share capital. For reasons of expediency each company paid income taxes based on the income before taxes determined on the income statement. The financial statements (amounts in thousands of dollars) for each company for 1998 were as follows.

Income Statement	Green Co. Ltd.	Blue Inc.
Revenues	$200	$200
Cost of goods sold	(85)	(95)
Amortization expense	(20)	(30)
Other expenses (includes $4,000 interest)	(70)	(70)
Income before income taxes	$ 25	$ 5
Income taxes (40%)	(10)	(2)
Net income	$ 15	$ 3

Balance Sheet		
Current assets	$ 50	$ 48
Capital assets net of amortization	100	90
Total assets	$150	$138
Current liabilities	$ 25	$ 25
Long-term debt	40	40
Common shares (30 outstanding)	70	70
Retained earnings	15	3
Total liabilities and shareholders' equity	$150	$138

Instructions

Using this financial statement information and justifying your answer:

(a) Which company appears to be in a stronger liquidity position?

(b) Which company appears to provide the greatest protection to long-term debtors?

(c) Which company appears to show the greater profitability?

(d) Which company appears to be using financial leverage most favourably to its shareholders?

PART II Examination of the notes to the financial statements of each of the above companies indicates that Green Co. Ltd. uses the FIFO inventory and the straight-line amortization methods whereas Blue Inc. uses the average-cost inventory and the accelerated amortization methods. Further investigation indicates that if Blue Inc. had used the FIFO inventory method, its ending inventory would have been $10,000 higher, and if it used the straight-line method its amortization expense would have been $10,000 lower.

Instructions

Given this information about the accounting policies of each company, provide and justify your answers to the same questions raised in the Instructions for Part I.

USING YOUR JUDGEMENT

FINANCIAL REPORTING PROBLEM

Twin Ricky Inc. (TRI) manufactures a variety of consumer products. The company's founders have run the company for 30 years and are now interested in retiring. Consequently, they are seeking a purchaser who will continue its operations. A group of investors, Donna Inc., is looking into the acquisition of TRI. To evaluate its financial stability and operating efficiency, TRI was requested to provide the latest financial statements and selected financial ratios. Summary information provided by TRI is as follows.

TRI
Statement of Income
For the Year Ended November 30, 1998
(in thousands)

Sales (net)	$30,500
Interest income	500
Total revenue	$31,000
Costs and expenses	
Cost of goods sold	$17,600
Selling and administrative expense	3,550
Depreciation and amortization expense	1,890
Interest expense	900
Total costs and expenses	$23,940
Income before taxes	$ 7,060
Income taxes	2,900
Net income	$ 4,160

Selected Financial Ratios

	TRI 1996	TRI 1997	Current Industry Average
Current ratio	1.62	1.61	1.63
Acid-test ratio	.63	.64	.68
Times interest earned	8.50	8.55	8.45
Profit margin on sales	12.1%	13.2%	13.0%
Total debt to shareholders' equity	1.02	.86	1.03
Total asset turnover	1.83	1.84	1.84
Inventory turnover	3.21	3.17	3.18

TRI
Statement of Financial Position
As of November 30
(in thousands)

	1998	1997
Cash	$ 400	$ 500
Marketable securities (at cost)	500	200
Accounts receivable (net)	3,200	2,900
Inventory	5,800	5,400
Total current assets	$ 9,900	$ 9,000
Property, plant, and equipment (net)	7,100	7,000
Total assets	$17,000	$16,000
Accounts payable	$ 3,700	$ 3,400
Income taxes payable	900	800
Accrued expenses	1,700	1,400
Total current liabilities	$ 6,300	$ 5,600
Long-term debt	2,000	1,800
Total liabilities	$ 8,300	$ 7,400
Common shares	$ 3,700	$ 3,700
Retained earnings	5,000	4,900
Total shareholders' equity	$ 8,700	$ 8,600
Total liabilities and shareholders' equity	$17,000	$16,000

Instructions

(a) Calculate a new set of ratios for the fiscal year 1998 for TRI based on the financial statements presented.

(b) Explain the analytical use of each of the seven ratios presented, describing what the investors can learn about TRI's financial strength and operating performance.

(c) Identify two major limitations of ratio analysis.

(CMA adapted)

ETHICS CASE

John Smoltz, the financial vice-president, and Scott Nagle, the controller, of Armbuster Manufacturing are reviewing the financial ratios of the company for the years 1997 and 1998. The financial vice-president notes that the profit margin on sales ratio has increased from 6% to 12%, a hefty gain. Smoltz is in the process of issuing a media release that emphasizes the efficiency of Armbuster Manufacturing in controlling cost. Scott Nagle knows that the difference in ratios is due primarily to an earlier company decision to reduce the estimates of warranty and bad expense for 1998. The controller, not sure of his supervisor's motives, hesitates to suggest to Smoltz that the company's improvement is unrelated to efficiency in control of cost. To complicate matters, the media release is scheduled to take place in a few days.

Instructions

(a) What, if any, is the ethical dilemma in this situation?

(b) Should Nagle remain silent? Give reasons for your answer.

(c) What stakeholders might be affected by Smoltz's media release?

(d) Give your opinion on the following statement and cite reasons: "Because Smoltz is most directly responsible for the media release, Nagle has no real responsibility in this matter."

chapter 25

FULL DISCLOSURE IN FINANCIAL REPORTING

25

Full Disclosure in
Financial Reporting

After studying this chapter, you should be able to:

1. Review the full disclosure principle and describe problems of implementation.

2. Explain the use of notes in financial statement preparation.

3. Describe the disclosure requirements for major segments of a business.

4. Describe the accounting problems associated with interim reporting.

5. Identify the major disclosures found in the auditor's report.

6. Understand other areas of the annual report.

7. Identify issues related to financial forecasts and projections.

8. Describe the profession's response to fraudulent financial reporting.

9. Understand and account for changing prices (Appendix 25A).

Accountants have long recognized that attempting to present all essential information about an enterprise in the four basic financial statements—balance sheet, income statement, statement of shareholders' equity, and statement of changes in financial position—is an extremely difficult task. *CICA Handbook* Section 1000 notes that although financial reporting and financial statements have essentially the same objectives, some useful information is better provided in the financial statements and some is better provided by other means. For example, earnings and cash flows are readily available in financial statements, but investors might do better to look at comparisons with other companies in the same industry. Information of this nature can be found in news articles or brokerage house reports.

Financial statements, notes to the financial statements, and supplementary information are areas directly affected by CICA and international standards. Other types of information found in the annual report, such as management's discussion and analysis, are not subject to either CICA or international standards.

FULL DISCLOSURE PRINCIPLE

As indicated in Chapter 2, the profession has adopted a **full disclosure principle** that calls for financial reporting of *any financial facts significant enough to influence the judgement of an informed reader*. In some situations, the benefits from disclosure may be apparent but the costs uncertain, whereas in other instances the costs may be certain but the benefits of disclosure not as apparent.

OBJECTIVE 1
Review the full disclosure principle and describe problems of implementation.

The costs of disclosure cannot be dismissed. For example, an article in a financial journal indicated that if segmented reporting were adopted, a company such as Fruehauf would have to increase its accounting staff 50%, from 300 to 450 individuals. In this case, the cost of disclosure is apparent but the benefits are less well defined. Some argue that reporting requirements are so detailed and substantial that users will have a difficult time absorbing the information; they charge the profession with engaging in **information overload.** Conversely, others contend that even more information is needed to assess an enterprise's financial position and earnings potential.

EXHIBIT 25-1

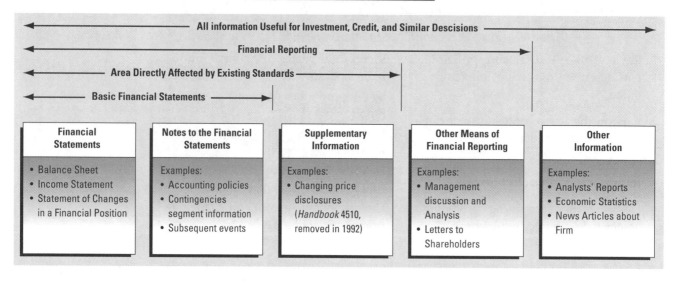

TYPES OF FINANCIAL INFORMATION[1]

The difficulty of implementing the full disclosure principle is highlighted by such financial disasters as White Farm, W.T. Grant, or Canadian Commercial Bank. Was the information presented about these companies not comprehensible? Was it buried? Was it too technical? Was it properly presented and fully disclosed as of the financial statement date, but the situation later deteriorated? Or was it simply not there? No easy answers are forthcoming.

One problem is that the profession is still in the process of developing guidelines on whether a given transaction should be disclosed and what format this disclosure should take. Different users want different information, and it becomes exceedingly difficult to develop disclosure policies that meet their varied objectives.[2]

INCREASE IN REPORTING REQUIREMENTS

Disclosure requirements have increased substantially in recent years. Each new *Handbook* section issued by the CICA, as illustrated throughout this textbook, has additional disclosure requirements for both financial and nonfinancial information. The reasons for this increase in disclosure requirements are varied; some of them are listed below.

Complexity of the Business Environment. The difficulty of distilling economic events into summarized reports has been magnified by the increasing complexity of business operations in such areas as derivatives, leasing, business combinations, pensions, financing

---

[1] Adapted from *Statement of Financial Accounting Concepts No. 5.*

[2] See, for example, Stephen Buzby, "The Nature of Adequate Disclosure," *The Journal of Accountancy* (April, 1974) for an interesting discussion of issues related to disclosure.

arrangements, revenue recognition, and deferred taxes. As a result, **notes to the financial statements** are used extensively to explain these transactions and their future effects.

Necessity for Timely Information. Today, more than ever before, users are demanding information that is current and predictive. For example, more complete **interim data** are required and published financial forecasts, long avoided and even feared by some accountants, have been recommended in a recent Research Study.[3]

Accounting as a Control and Monitoring Device. Federal and provincial governments, through statutes such as the Canada Business Corporations Act and Acts that regulate securities, require public disclosure of certain specific information in addition to that mandated in the *Handbook*. This leads in part toward **differential disclosure** of information to government agencies and to the public.

Information Needs of International Business and Investment. International accounting standards are being approved at a rapid pace by the International Accounting Standards Committee (IASC). Some of these standards require disclosure that is equivalent to or less than that required by the CICA. However, in some instances firms meeting international standards will disclose more or different information than would be necessary if the reports were to Canadian users only.

The purpose of this chapter is to acquaint you with (1) the general types of disclosure currently required; (2) some recent trends in financial reporting; and (3) the breadth of responsibility that has been placed on the accounting profession.

NOTES TO THE FINANCIAL STATEMENTS

As you know from your study of this textbook, notes are an integral part of the financial statements of a business enterprise. However, they are often overlooked because they are highly technical and often appear in small print. *Notes to the financial statements are the accountant's means of amplifying or explaining the items presented in the main body of the statements.* Information pertinent to specific financial statement items can be explained in qualitative terms and supplementary data of a quantitative nature can be provided to expand the information in the financial statements. Restrictions imposed by financial arrangements or basic contractual agreements can also be explained in notes. Although notes may be technical and difficult to understand, they provide meaningful information for the user of the financial statements.

OBJECTIVE 2
Explain the use of notes in financial statement preparation.

ACCOUNTING POLICIES

Accounting policies of a given entity are the specific accounting principles and methods currently employed and considered most appropriate to present fairly the financial statements of the enterprise. The profession, in *Handbook* Section 1505, concluded that information about the accounting policies a reporting entity adopts and follows is essential for financial statement users in making their economic decisions. It recommended that when financial statements are issued, *a statement identifying the accounting policies adopted and followed by the reporting entity should also be presented as an integral part of the financial statements.* The disclosure should be given in either a separate summary or as the first note to the financial statements. The Summary of Significant Accounting Policies should answer such questions as: What method of depreciation is used on plant assets? What valuation method is employed on inventories? What amortization policy is followed in regard to intangible assets?

Appendix 5A provides an illustration of note disclosure of accounting methods and other notes accompanying the audited financial statements of Moore Corporation Limited. An exhibit from Doman Industries Limited is provided on the following page.

---

[3] Robert H. Kidd, *Earnings Forecasts* (Toronto: CICA, 1976).

EXHIBIT 25-2 DOMAN INDUSTRIES LIMITED

Notes to the Consolidated Financial Statements

1. **Significant Accounting Policies**

These consolidated financial statements have been prepared in accordance with accounting principles generally accepted in Canada ("Canadian GAAP") and reflect the following significant accounting policies. Management has made assumptions and estimates that affect the reported amounts and other disclosures in these consolidated financial statements, and actual results may differ from those estimates.

In the case of Doman Industries Limited, Canadian GAAP differs in certain respects from accounting principles generally accepted in the United States ("U.S. GAAP") as explained in Note 15.

(a) *Basis of Consolidation*

These consolidated financial statements include the accounts of Doman Industries Limited and all of its subsidiaries (see Note 14(f)) (individually and collectively referred to as the "Company").

(b) *Inventories*

Inventories, other than supplies which are valued at cost, are valued at the lower of average cost and net realizable value.

(c) *Investments*

Investments in companies 20% to 50% owned where the Company has the ability to exercise significant influence are accounted for using the equity method whereby the Company's share of their earnings and losses is included in earnings and its investments therein adjusted by a like amount. Dividends received are credited to the investment accounts.

Other investments are accounted for using the cost method whereby income is included in earnings when received or receivable.

(d) *Property, Plant and Equipment*

Property, plant and equipment, including those under capital leases, are stated at cost, including capitalized interest and start-up costs incurred for major projects during the period of construction. Amortization of the pulp mills is provided on a unit-of-production basis over twenty-five years except for (i) the modernized portion of the Squamish mill which is over forty years and (ii) other major replacements and renewals which are over twelve years. Amortization of the sawmills and equipment is provided for the period of operations on a straight-line basis generally over fifteen to twenty years and over five to ten years, respectively. These rates reflect the estimated useful lives of the assets. Amortization of timberlands and logging roads is computed on the basis of the volume of timber cut.

(e) *Deferred Financing Costs*

These costs are being amortized on a straight-line basis over the term of the related debt. The amount of the amortization is included in interest on long-term debt.

(f) *Foreign Currency Translation*

Transactions denominated in U.S. dollars have been translated into Canadian dollars at the approximate rate of exchange prevailing at the time of the transaction. Monetary assets and liabilities have been translated into Canadian dollars at the year-end exchange rate. All exchange gains and losses are included directly in earnings, except for the unrealized exchange losses on translation of long-term debt which are deferred and amortized to earnings over the remaining life of the debt. Exchange gains and losses included in earnings that relate to long-term debt are considered to be an integral part of financing costs and accordingly, are included in interest expense.

(g) *Reforestation Obligation*

Timber is harvested under various licences issued by the Province of British Columbia. The future estimated reforestation obligation is accrued on the basis of the volume of timber cut. The non-current portion of this obligation is included in other liabilities.

(h) *Pension Costs*

Pension costs for hourly paid employees are charged to earnings as they accrue based on hours worked.

Pension costs for salaried employees are also charged to earnings as they accrue. In determining pension expense, the initial past service liability on implementation of these pension plans, adjustments arising from changes in actuarial assumptions, and experience gains and losses are amortized on a straight-line basis over the expected average remaining service life of the employee groups. The assets of these pension plans are valued at market values.

(i) *Income Taxes*

The Company uses the tax allocation method of accounting for income taxes whereby differences between the provision for income taxes on earnings for accounting purposes and the income taxes currently payable are shown as deferred income taxes.

(j) *Comparative Figures*

Certain of the 1994 comparative figures have been reclassified to conform with the classifications used in 1995.

Analysts examine carefully the Summary of Accounting Policy section to determine whether the company is using conservative or liberal accounting practices. For example, amortizing intangible assets over 40 years (the maximum) or depreciating plant assets over an unusually long period of time is considered liberal. On the other hand, expensing interest on funds borrowed for the construction of new plant and equipment might be considered conservative by some.

OTHER NOTES

Many of the notes to the financial statements are discussed throughout this textbook. Others will be discussed more fully in this chapter. The more common are as follows.

Inventory. The basis on which inventory amounts are stated (lower of cost and market) and the method used in determining cost (FIFO, average-cost, etc.) should also be reported. Manufacturers should report the inventory composition either in the balance sheet or in a separate schedule in the notes. Unusual or significant financing arrangements relating to inventories that may require disclosure include transactions with related parties, product financing arrangements, firm purchase commitments, and pledging of inventories as collateral.

Property, Plant, and Equipment. The basis of valuation for property, plant, and equipment should be stated; it is usually historical cost. Pledges, liens, and other commitments related to these assets should be disclosed. In the presentation of depreciation, the following disclosures should be made in the financial statements or in the notes: (1) depreciation expense for the period; (2) balances of major classes of depreciable assets, by nature and function, at the balance sheet date; (3) accumulated depreciation, either by major classes of depreciable assets or in total, at the balance sheet date; and (4) a general description of the method or methods used in computing depreciation with respect to major classes of depreciable assets.

Credit Claims. An investor normally finds it extremely useful to determine the nature and cost of creditorship claims. The Liability section in the balance sheet can provide the major types of liabilities outstanding only in the aggregate. Note schedules regarding such obligations provide additional information about how the company is financing its operations, the costs that will have to be borne in future periods, and the timing of future case outflows. Recall that the profession requires that financial statements disclose for each of the five years following the date of the financial statements the aggregate amount of maturities and sinking fund requirements for all long-term borrowings.

Equity Holders' Claims. Many companies present in the body of the balance sheet the number of shares authorized, issued, and outstanding for each type of equity security. Such data may also be presented in a note. Beyond that, the most common type of equity note disclosure relates to contracts and senior securities outstanding that might affect the various claims of the residual equity holders; for example, the existence of outstanding stock options, outstanding convertible debt, redeemable preferred shares, and convertible preferred shares. In addition, it is necessary to disclose to equity claimants certain types of restrictions currently in force. Generally, these types of restrictions involve the amount of earnings available for dividend distribution.

Contingencies and Commitments. An enterprise may have gain or loss contingencies that are not disclosed in the body of the financial statements. These contingencies may take a variety of forms such as litigation, debt and other guarantees, possible tax assessments, renegotiation of government contracts, sales of receivables with recourse, and so on. In addition, commitments that relate to dividend restrictions, purchase agreements (through-put and take-or-pay), hedge contracts, and employment contracts are also disclosed.

Deferred Taxes, Pensions, and Leases. Extensive disclosure is required in these areas. Chapters 19, 20, and 21 discuss each of these disclosures in detail. It should be emphasized that notes to the financial statements should be given a careful reading for information about off-balance-sheet commitments, future financing needs, and the quality of a company's earnings.

Changes in Accounting Policy. The profession defines various types of accounting changes and establishes guides for reporting each type. Either in the summary of significant accounting policies or in the other notes, changes in accounting principles (as well as material changes in estimates and corrections of errors) are discussed in Chapter 22.

Subsequent Events. Events or transactions that occur subsequent to the balance sheet date but prior to the issuance of the financial statements should be disclosed in the financial statements. Chapter 5 sets forth the criteria for the proper treatment of subsequent events.

The disclosures above have been discussed in earlier chapters. Three additional disclosures of significance (special transactions or events, segment reporting, and interim reporting) are illustrated in later sections of this chapter.

DISCLOSURE OF SPECIAL TRANSACTIONS OR EVENTS

Related party transactions, errors and irregularities, and subsequent events pose especially sensitive and difficult problems for the accountant. The accountant/auditor who has responsibility for reporting on these types of transactions has to be extremely careful that the rights of the reporting company and the needs of users of the financial statements are properly balanced.

Related party transactions arise when a business engages in transactions in which one of the transacting parties has the ability to influence significantly the policies of the other.[4] Transactions involving related parties cannot be presumed to be carried out on an arm's-length basis because the requisite conditions of competitive, free-market dealings may not exist. Transactions such as borrowing or lending money at abnormally low or high interest rates, real estate sales at amounts that differ significantly from appraisal values, exchanges of nonmonetary assets, and transactions involving enterprises that have no economic substance ("shell corporations") suggest that related parties may be involved.

The accountant is expected to report the economic substance rather than the legal form of these transactions and to make adequate disclosures. Section 3840 of the *CICA Handbook* requires the following disclosures of material related party transactions.

1. A description of the relationship between the transacting parties.

2. A description of the transactions.

3. The recorded amount of the transactions, classified by financial statement category.

4. The measurement basis used.

5. Amounts due to or from related parties as of the date of each balance sheet presented.

6. Contractual obligations with related parties.

7. Any contingencies involving related parties.[5]

An example of the disclosure of related party transactions is taken from the 1996 annual report of Infocorp Computer Solutions Ltd.

EXHIBIT 25-3 INFOCORP COMPUTER SOLUTIONS LTD.

12. Related party transactions

The company has paid management fees and marketing fees of $126,500 (1995: $98,586) to companies controlled by certain directors of the company.

---

[4] *CICA Handbook*, (Toronto: CICA) Section 3840.

[5] *Ibid.*, par. .13.

Errors are defined as unintentional mistakes, whereas **irregularities** (frauds) are intentional distortions of financial statements.[6] As indicated in earlier sections of this textbook, when errors are discovered, the financial statements should be corrected. The same treatment should be given to irregularities. The discovery of irregularities, however, gives rise to an entirely different set of suspicions, procedures, and responsibilities on the part of the accountant/auditor.

Many companies are involved in related party transactions; errors and irregularities, however, are the exception rather than the rule. Disclosure plays a very important role in these areas because the transaction or event is more qualitative than quantitative and involves more subjective than objective evaluation. The users of the financial statements must be provided with some indication of the existence and nature of these transactions, where material, through disclosures, modifications in the auditor's report, or reports of changes in auditors.

REPORTING FOR DIVERSIFIED (CONGLOMERATE) COMPANIES

In the last several decades business enterprises have at times had a tendency to diversify their operations. As a result, investors and investment analysts have sought more information concerning the details behind conglomerate financial statements. Particularly, they need income statement, balance sheet, and cash flow information on the **individual segments** that compose the ***total*** business income figure.

OBJECTIVE 3
Describe the disclosure requirements for major segments of a business.

An illustration of segmentation is presented in the following example of a hypothetical office equipment and auto parts company.

OFFICE EQUIPMENT AND AUTO PARTS COMPANY
Income Statement Data
(in millions)

	Consolidated	Office Equipment	Auto Parts
Net sales	$78.8	$18.0	$60.8
Manufacturing costs:			
Inventories, beginning	12.3	4.0	8.3
Materials and services	38.9	10.8	28.1
Wages	12.9	3.8	9.1
Inventories, ending	(13.3)	(3.9)	(9.4)
	50.8	14.7	36.1
Selling and administrative expense	12.1	1.6	10.5
Total operating expenses	62.9	16.3	46.6
Operating income	15.9	1.7	14.2
Income taxes	(9.3)	(1.0)	(8.3)
Net income	$ 6.6	$ 0.7	$ 5.9

If only the consolidated figures are available to the analyst, much information regarding the composition of these figures is hidden in aggregated totals. There is no way to tell from the consolidated data the extent to which the differing product lines ***contribute to the company's profitability, risk, and growth potential***.[7] For example, in the illustration above, if the office equipment segment is deemed to be a risky venture, the segmentation

---

[6] *CICA Handbook*, Section 5135, par. 02.

[7] One writer has shown that data provided on a segmental basis allows an analyst to predict future total sales and earnings better than data presented on a nonsegmental basis. See D.W. Collins, "Predicting Earnings with Sub-Entity Data: Some Further Evidence," *Journal of Accounting Research* (Spring, 1976).

provides useful information for purposes of making an informed investment decision regarding the whole company.

Companies have been somewhat hesitant to disclose segmented data for the reasons listed below.

1. Without a thorough knowledge of the business and an understanding of such important factors as the competitive environment and capital investment requirements, the investor may find the segment information meaningless or even draw improper conclusions about the reported earnings of the segments.

2. Additional disclosure may harm reporting firms because it may be helpful to competitors, labour unions, suppliers, and certain government regulatory agencies.

3. Additional disclosure may discourage management from taking intelligent business risks because segments reporting losses or unsatisfactory earnings may cause shareholder dissatisfaction with management.

4. The wide variation among firms in the choice of segments, cost allocation, and other accounting problems limits the usefulness of segment information.

5. The investor is investing in the company as a whole and not in the particular segments, and it should not matter how any single segment is performing if the overall performance is satisfactory.

6. Certain technical problems, such as classification of segments and allocation of segment revenues and cost (especially "common costs"), are formidable.

On the other hand, advocates of segmented disclosures offer these reasons in support of the practice.

1. Segment information is needed by the investor to make an intelligent investment decision regarding a diversified company.
   (a) Sales and earnings of individual segments are needed to forecast consolidated profits because of the differences between segments in growth rate, risk, and profitability.
   (b) Segment reports disclose the nature of a company's business and the relative size of the components as an aid in evaluating the company's investment worth.

2. The absence of segmented reporting by a diversified company may put its unsegmented, single-product-line competitors at a competitive disadvantage because the conglomerate may obscure information that its competitors must disclose.

The advocates of segment disclosure appear to have a much stronger case. Many users indicate that segment data are the most informative financial information provided, aside from the basic financial statements. As a result, the CICA has issued extensive reporting guidelines in this area.[8]

PROFESSIONAL PRONOUNCEMENTS

Recognizing the need for guidelines in the area of segment reporting, the profession issued *Handbook* Section 1700. This standard, however, applies only to enterprises whose securities are traded in a public market or that are required to file financial statements annually with a securities commission. The basic requirements of this pronouncement are discussed in the following sections.

---

[8] Professional bodies continue to study this area because of its importance. See, for example, John Boersema and Susan Van Weelden, "Financial Reporting for Segments," *Research Study* (CICA, 1992); and Paul Pacter, "Reporting Disaggregated Information by Business Enterprises," *Invitation to Comment* (Norwalk, Conn.: FASB, 1993)

Accounting Principle Selection. *Segment information required to be reported must be prepared on the same accounting basis as that used in the enterprise's consolidated financial statements.* An exception is intersegment sales that are eliminated for consolidated purposes but are shown when individual segments are presented. **Intersegment sales** are transfers of products or services among segments of the enterprise. An example of segment disclosures required by the profession for Inco Limited is shown below.

EXHIBIT 25-4 INCO LIMITED

Note 13. Segment information

The Company is engaged in two principal business segments, primary metals and alloys and engineered products, and has other interests which are included in a third segment, other business. In its primary metals business segment, the Company is a major producer of nickel and an important producer of copper, precious metals and cobalt. In its alloys and engineered products business segment, the Company is a major producer of high-nickel and other alloys and manufactures high-performance alloy components for aerospace and other industrial applications. The Company's other business segment includes the Company's venture capital program, its metals reclamation operations, its mining equipment operations and its lightweight aggregate operations. Other business also included the operations of TVX Gold Inc. until its sale by the Company in July 1993. Intersegment sales are generally made at prices used for sales to unaffiliated companies. Non-operating income (expenses) which are not allocated to business segments include interest expense, general corporate income and expenses, currency translation adjustments and, for 1993, the gain from the sale of TVX Gold Inc. Other assets which are not allocated to business segments consist of corporate assets, principally cash, securities, deferred pension charges, and certain receivables and fixed assets.

The principal geographic areas in which the Company operates are Canada, the United States and Europe. The Company also operates in other geographic areas including Indonesia, Japan and other Asian countries. Sales between geographic areas are generally made at prevailing market prices, except that sales of primary metals from Canada to other primary metals affiliates are net of discounts. Total net sales in Canada include exports to the United States of $745 million in 1995, $480 million in 1994 and $492 million in 1993, and exports to Europe of $898 million in 1995, $496 million in 1994 and $474 million in 1993. Net sales to customers in the Japan and other geographic area include sales in Japan of $441 million in 1995, $353 million in 1994 and $313 million in 1993 by the Company's primary metals operations in Japan.

Net sales to customers include sales at market prices to affiliates in Japan, Taiwan and South Korea aggregating $426 million in 1995, $193 million in 1994 and $298 million in 1993.

Identifiable assets in the Japan and other geographic area at December 31 include $769 million in 1995, $634 million in 1994 and $657 million in 1993 relating to the Company's primary metals nickel operations in Indonesia.

Financial data by business segment and geographic area follow:

Data by business segment

Year ended December 31	Primary metals			Alloys and engineered products			Other business			Eliminations			Total		
	1995	1994	1993	**1995**	1994	1993	**1995**	1994	1993	**1995**	1994	1993	**1995**	1994	1993
		(Restated)			(Restated)									(Restated)	
Net sales to customers	**$2,705**	1,874	1,568	**$707**	549	511	**$ 59**	61	51	**$ —**	—	—	**$3,471**	2,484	2,130
Intersegment sales	**150**	98	99	**2**	—	—	**4**	5	8	**(156)**	(103)	(107)	**—**	—	—
Total net sales	**$2,855**	1,972	1,667	**$709**	549	511	**$ 63**	66	59	**$(156)**	(103)	(107)	**$3,471**	2,484	2,130
Operating earnings (loss)	**$ 577**	82	(20)	**$ 50**	16	(28)	**$ 4**	(2)	9	**$ (12)**	(13)	10	**$ 619**	83	(29)
Non-operating income (expenses)													**(159)**	(123)	30
Earnings (loss) before income and mining taxes and minority interest													**$ 460**	(40)	1
Capital expenditures	**$ 290**	123	161	**$ 22**	13	18	**$ 14**	3	7	**$ —**	—	—	**$ 326**	139	186
Depreciation and depletion	**$ 222**	220	211	**$ 28**	28	31	**$ 5**	4	4	**$ —**	—	—	**$ 255**	252	246
Identifiable assets at December 31	**$3,884**	3,093	3,051	**$698**	626	585	**$116**	137	133	**$ (48)**	(44)	(29)	**$4,650**	3,812	3,740
Other assets													**43**	216	162
Total assets at December 31													**$4,693**	4,028	3,902

EXHIBIT 25-3 INCO LIMITED (Continued)

Data by geographic area

Year ended December 31	Canada 1995	1994	1993	United States 1995	1994	1993	Europe 1995	1994	1993	Japan and other 1995	1994	1993	Total after eliminations 1995	1994	1993
		(Restated)			(Restated)									(Restated)	
Net sales to customers	$ 324	277	230	$1,104	830	735	$ 948	658	595	$1,095	719	570	$3,471	2,484	2,130
Sales between geographic areas	1,975	1,226	1,169	59	42	41	231	57	46	—	—	—	—	—	—
Total net sales	$2,299	1,503	1,399	$1,163	872	776	$1,179	715	641	$1,095	719	570	$3,471	2,484	2,130
Operating earnings (loss)	$ 366	(26)	(77)	$ 48	23	(20)	$ 53	20	20	$ 142	69	35	$ 619	83	(29)
Identifiable assets at December 31	$2,736	2,096	2,161	$ 669	606	578	$ 384	313	292	$1,106	920	792	$4,650	3,812	3,740

Note that Inco Limited reports three segments: primary metals, alloys and engineered products, and other. Each segment follows the same accounting principles that are used to prepare the consolidated financial statements. *The profession also requires that the segment's revenues, operating profit (loss), and identifiable assets be reconciled to the consolidated financial statements. In addition, depreciation expense and the amount of capital expenditures must be reported for each segment.*

Selecting Reportable Segments. A number of methods might have been used by Inco Limited to identify its industry segments, such as the Statistics Canada Standard Industrial Classification Code, currently existing profit centres, or relating common risk factors to products or product groups. The CICA concluded that none of these methods by itself is universally applicable and that management should exercise its judgement in determining industry segments. The CICA, however, did indicate that there are three factors that should be seriously considered.[9]

1. *The nature of the product or service.* Related products or services have similar purposes or end uses. Thus, they may be expected to have similar rates of profitability, similar degrees of risk, and similar opportunities for growth.

2. *The nature of the production process.* Sharing of common or interchangeable facilities, equipment, labour force, or service group or use of the same or similar basic raw materials may suggest that products or services are related. Likewise, similar degrees of labour-intensiveness or similar degrees of capital-intensiveness may indicate a relationship among products or services.

3. *The nature of marketing methods.* Similarity of geographic marketing areas, types of customers, or marketing methods may indicate a relationship among products or services. The sensitivity of market price changes and to changes in general economic conditions may also indicate whether products or services are related or unrelated.

After the company decides on the segments it wishes to disclose, a quantitative test is made to determine whether the segment is significant enough to disclose. An industry segment is regarded as significant, and therefore identified as a reportable segment if it satisfies one or more of the following tests.

1. Its *revenue* (including both sales to unaffiliated customers and intersegment sales or transfers) is 10% or more of the combined revenue (sales to unaffiliated customers and intersegment sales or transfers) of all of the enterprise's industry segments.

---

[9] *CICA Handbook*, Section 1700, par. 17.

2. The absolute amount of its *operating profit or operating loss* is 10% or more of the greater, in absolute amount, of:
   (a) either the combined operating profit of all industry segments that did not incur an operating loss; or
   (b) the combined operating loss of all industry segments that did incur an operating loss.

3. Its *identifiable assets* are 10% or more of the combined identifiable assets of all industry segments.[10]

In applying these tests, two additional factors must be considered. First, segment data must explain a significant portion of the company's business. Specifically, the segmented results must equal or exceed 75% of the combined sales to unaffiliated customers for the entire enterprise. This test prevents a company from providing limited information on only a few segments and lumping all of the rest into one category.

Second, the profession recognized that reporting too many segments may overwhelm users with detailed information that may not be useful. Although the CICA did not issue any specific guidelines regarding how many segments are too many, this point is generally reached when a company has 10 or more reportable segments.

To illustrate these requirements, assume that a company has identified six possible reporting segments (000s omitted).

Segments	Total Revenue (Unaffiliated)	Operating Profit (Loss)	Identifiable Assets
A	$ 100	$10	$ 60
B	50	2	30
C	700	40	390
D	300	20	160
E	900	18	280
F	100	(5)	50
	$2,150	$85	$970

The respective tests may now be applied as follows:

Revenue test: 10% × 2,150 = $215; C, D, and E meet this test.

Operating profit (loss) test: 10% × 90 = $9 (note that the $5 loss is ignored): A, C, D, and E meet this test.

Identifiable assets test: 10% × 970 = $97; C, D, and E meet this test.

The reportable segments are therefore A, C, D, and E, assuming that these four segments have enough sales to meet the 75% of combined sales test. The 75% test is computed as follows.

75% of combined sales test: 75% × 2,150 = $1,612.50; the sales of A, C, D, and E total $2,000 ($100 + $700 + $300 + $900); therefore, the 75% test is met.

Information To Be Reported. As indicated above, the primary basis for segmenting the results of Inco Limited was by product line. The profession requires segmented information on other bases when appropriate. The three general areas are:

1. Service or product line.

2. Foreign geographic segments.

3. Export sales.

---

[10] *CICA Handbook,* Section 1700, par. 23.

Foreign operating income, revenues, and identifiable assets are reported when revenues of this type are 10% or more of total revenue or when total identifiable assets are more than 10% of the total assets of the business.

Similarly, a company must report export sales when the amounts are significant. **Export sales** are sales to customers in foreign countries; export sales information provides insight into the stability, risk, and growth potential of this revenue source.

CONTINUING CONTROVERSY

The area of segment reporting is controversial from a number of perspectives. One frequent complaint is that this information is costly to develop. As a result, the Accounting Standards Committee of the CICA decided that nonpublic companies are not required to disclose segmental data. Conversely, others argue that segment reporting should be extended to interim reports. The following issues, however, are still being hotly debated.

Definition of a Segment. A general view that seems to prevail among accountants is that the enterprise should be free to select the breakdown that best represents the underlying activities of the business. The problem with using this procedure is that a great deal of subjectivity is involved in selecting the segments, which can lead to a lack of comparability over a period of time.

In addition to the problem of determining the basis for identifying the segments, there is the question of what percentage to use. As indicated earlier, a 10% factor is applied to one of the following items: revenue, income or loss, or identifiable assets. But these criteria are still subject to interpretation. In general, however, the disclosure requirements associated with *Handbook* Section 1700 appear quite reasonable and the flexibility afforded management seems desirable. Management is in the best position to judge which is the most meaningful breakdown of its divisional data; with experimentation, useful information should be forthcoming.

Allocation of Common Costs. One of the critical problems in providing segmented income statements for conglomerate companies is the allocation of common costs. Common costs are those incurred for the benefit of more than one segment and whose interrelated nature prevents a completely objective division of costs among segments. For example, the president's salary is very difficult to allocate to various segments. One survey showed that the average ratio of common costs to net sales is greater than that of net income to net sales.

Many different bases for allocation have been suggested, such as sales, gross profit, assets employed, investment, and marginal income. The choice of basis is difficult because it can materially influence the relative profitability of the segments.

Transfer Pricing Problems. The practice of charging a price for goods "sold" between divisions or subsidiaries of a company is called **transfer pricing**. A transfer price system is used for several reasons, but the primary objective is to measure the performance and profitability of a given segment of the business in relation to other segments. In addition, a pricing system is needed to ensure control over the flow of goods through the enterprise.

Transfer pricing is not a problem of the same magnitude as common costs, but it still is very significant in many business enterprises. At present, different approaches to transfer pricing are used. Some firms transfer the goods at market prices; others use cost plus a fixed fee; and yet others use variable cost. In certain situations, the company lets the division bargain for the price of the item in question.

In evaluating a specific division, we must consider the transfer pricing problem. If, for example, Division A sells certain goods to Division B using a market price instead of cost, the operating results of both divisions are affected. Transfer pricing in many situations does not occur on an arm's-length basis and, therefore, the final results of a given division must be suspect. The basis of accounting for intersegment sales and transfers should be disclosed.

INTERIM REPORTS

One further source of information for the investor is interim reports. As noted earlier, **interim reports** are those reports that cover periods of less than one year. At one time, interim reports were referred to as the "forgotten reports"; such is no longer the case. The stock exchanges and the accounting profession have taken an active role in developing guidelines for the presentation of interim information. The CICA issued Section 1750 of the *Handbook*, which attempted to narrow the reporting alternatives related to interim reports. A recent annual report of Inco Limited illustrates the disclosure of selected quarterly data.

OBJECTIVE 4
Describe the accounting problems associated with interim reporting.

EXHIBIT 25-5 INCO LIMITED

(*$ in millions except per share amounts*)	First Quarter	Second Quarter	Third Quarter	Fourth Quarter	Year
	(Restated)				
1995					
Net sales	$ 881	$ 856	$ 830	$ 904	$ 3,471
Cost of sales and operating expenses	$ 674	$ 660	$ 665	$ 703	$ 2,702
Earnings before income and mining taxes and minority interest	$ 130	$ 113	$ 92	$ 125	$ 460
Net earnings	$ 68	$ 55	$ 44	$ 60	$ 227
Net earnings per common share	$ 0.57	$ 0.47	$ 0.33	$ 0.45	$ 1.82
Dividends per common share	$ 0.10	$ 0.10	$ 0.10	$ 0.10	$ 0.40

Because of the short-term nature of these reports, however, there is considerable controversy as to the general approach that should be employed. One group (which holds the **discrete view**) believes that each interim period should be treated as a separate accounting period; deferrals and accruals would therefore follow the principles employed for annual reports. Accounting transactions should be reported as they occur and expense recognition should not change with the period of time covered. Another group (which holds the **integral view**) believes that the interim report is an integral part of the annual report and that deferrals and accruals should take into consideration what will happen for the entire year. In this approach, estimated expenses are assigned to parts of a year on the basis of sales volume or some other activity base. At present, many companies follow the discrete approach for certain types of expenses and the integral approach for others.

INTERIM REPORTING REQUIREMENTS

Handbook Section 1750 requires that the same accounting principles used for annual reports should be employed for interim reports. Revenues should be recognized in interim periods on the same basis as they are for annual periods. For example, if the instalment sales method is used as the basis for recognizing revenue on an annual basis, then the instalment basis should also be applied to interim reports. Also, costs directly associated with revenues (product costs), such as material, labour and related fringe benefits, and manufacturing overhead, should be treated in the same manner for interim reports as for annual reports.

Companies generally should use the same inventory pricing methods (FIFO, weighted-average, etc.) for interim reports that they use for annual reports. Determination of the interim inventory valuation should include consideration of such factors as current market or replacement value as well as losses due to obsolescence, shrinkage, and theft. In addition, companies may use the retail inventory or gross profit methods of estimating interim inventory pricing.

Costs and expenses other than product costs, often referred to as *period costs*, are allocated among interim periods on the basis of an estimate of time expired, benefit received, or activity associated with the periods. Considerable latitude is exercised in accounting for these costs in interim periods, and many believe more definitive guidelines are needed.

Regarding disclosure, the following interim data should be reported as a minimum.

1. Sales or gross revenue, investment income, amount charged for depreciation and amortization, interest expense, income taxes, income before extraordinary items, extraordinary items (net of income taxes), and net income.

2. Basic and fully diluted earnings per share.

3. Details of any significant changes in financial position such as in working capital, fixed assets, long-term liabilities, and shareholders' equity.

4. Changes in accounting principles.

5. Subsequent events.

6. Other material matters not previously reported.[11]

The profession does not require companies to publish a balance sheet and a statement of cash flows. When this information is voluntarily presented, it should be presented in comparative form using consistent accounting policies. Thus, when accounting changes are made, retroactive restatement of both the current year's interim reports and any prior period interim data presented for comparison is required. To illustrate the type of summarized disclosure presented, an interim report for Industra Service Corporation for the first quarter for 1996 and 1995 is presented below.

EXHIBIT 25-6 INDUSTRA SERVICE CORPORATION

CONSOLIDATED STATEMENT OF INCOME

	Three Months Ended March 31,	
	1996	1995
Contract Income	$20,650,767	$13,811,505
Cost of Contracts	15,989,894	11,031,327
Gross Profit	4,660,873	2,780,178
General and Administrative Expenses	3,801,009	3,397,124
Depreciation and Amortization	324,020	288,104
Interest (Note)	106,328	8,042
	4,231,357	3,693,270
Operating Income (Loss)	429,516	(913,092)
Income Taxes (Recovery)	247,436	(81,633)
Income (Loss) Before Minority Interest	182,080	(831,459)
Minority Interest	93,615	18,120
Net Income (Loss)	$ 88,465	$ (849,579)
Earnings (Loss) Per Share		
Basic	$0.03	($0.24)
Fully Diluted	$0.03	($0.24)

The above statements have not been audited and are subject to year end adjustments.

---

[11] *CICA Handbook*, Section 1750, par. .06.

EXHIBIT 25-6 INDUSTRA SERVICE CORPORATION (Continued)

CONSOLIDATED SUMMARY BALANCE SHEET

| | as at March 31, | |
	1996	1995
Assets		
Current Assets	$21,584,909	$20,851,648
Other Assets	488,778	491,364
Property, Plant and Equipment	6,745,798	6,545,438
Intangible Assets	618,387	722,737
	$29,437,872	$28,611,187
Liabilities and Shareholders' Equity		
Current Liabilities	$11,194,261	$ 9,568,506
Long Term Liabilities	3,234,494	3,390,056
Minority Interest	499,174	236,572
Shareholders' Equity	14,509,943	15,416,053
	$29,437,872	$28,611,187

The above statements have not been audited and are subject to year end adjustments.

CONSOLIDATED STATEMENT OF CHANGES IN FINANCIAL POSITION

| | Three Months Ended March 31, | |
	1996	1995
Cash Provided By (Used In) Operating Activities		
Operations		
Net Income (Loss)	$ 88,465	$ (849,579)
Depreciation and Amortization	324,020	288,104
Deferred Income Taxes	(79,520)	(164,133)
Minority Interest	93,615	18,120
	426,580	(707,488)
Working Capital Items	(4,842,501)	(2,878,528)
	(4,415,921)	(3,586,016)
Cash Provided By (Used In) Financing Activities		
Dividends	0	(69,950)
Payments on Term Debt	(36,798)	(75,881)
Share Capital Issued	0	137,816
	(36,798)	(8,015)
Cash Provided By (Used In) Investing Activities		
Purchase of Property, Plant and Equipment	(244,063)	(635,148)
Loan to Related Party	659	627
Goodwill Arising on Acquisition of Subsidiaries	0	(149,664)
	(243,404)	(784,185)
Decrease in Cash	(4,696,123)	(4,378,216)
Bank Indebtedness at Beginning of Period	(401,782)	(1,216,116)
Bank Indebtedness at End of Period	$(5,097,905)	$(5,594,332)

The above statements have not been audited and are subject to year end adjustments.

EXHIBIT 25-6 INDUSTRA SERVICE CORPORATION *(Continued)*

NOTE TO CONSOLIDATED FINANCIAL STATEMENTS

| | Three Months Ended March 31, | |
	1996	1995
Interest On Revolving Demand Loan	$ 50,768	$ 83,535
Interest On Term Bank Loans	74,915	96,624
Interest And Other Income	(19,355)	(172,117)
Interest Expense	$106,328	$ 8,042

The above statements have not been audited and are subject to year end adjustments.

UNIQUE PROBLEMS OF INTERIM REPORTING

In *Handbook* Section 1750 the Committee indicated that it favoured the discrete approach. However, within this broad guideline, a number of unique reporting problems exist related to the following items.

Advertising and Similar Costs. The general guidelines are that costs such as advertising costs should be *deferred in an interim period if the benefits extend beyond that period; otherwise, they should be expensed as incurred.* But such a determination is difficult, and even if such costs are deferred, how should they be allocated between quarters? Because of the vague guidelines in this area, accounting for advertising varies widely. One method, for example, would involve charging advertising costs as a percentage of sales and adjusting to actual at year end, whereas under another acceptable method these costs would be charged to expense as incurred.

The same type of problem relates to such items as the employer's contributions to the Canada Pension Plan, research and development costs, major repairs, and tax loss carryback or carryforward. For example, should the company expense Canada Pension Plan contributions on the highly paid personnel early in the year, when paid, or allocate and spread them to subsequent quarters? Should a major repair that occurs later in the year be anticipated and allocated proportionately to earlier periods?

Expenses Subject to Year-End Adjustment. Bad debts, executive bonuses, pension costs, and inventory shrinkage are often not known with a great deal of certainty until year end. *These costs should be estimated and allocated in the best possible way to interim periods.* Companies use a variety of allocation techniques to accomplish this objective.

Income Taxes. Not every dollar of corporate taxable income is assessed at the same tax rate; the tax rate is progressive. This aspect of business income taxes poses a problem in preparing **interim financial statements**. Should the income to date be annualized and the proportionate income tax accrued for the period to date (**annualized approach**)? Or should the first amount of income earned be taxed at the lower rate of tax applicable to such income (**marginal principle approach**)? At one time, companies generally followed the latter approach and accrued the tax applicable to each additional dollar of income.

The marginal principal was especially applicable to businesses having a seasonal or uneven income pattern, because the interim accrual of tax was based on the actual results to date. However, firms are permitted to use either approach provided that it is used consistently from period to period.

Extraordinary Items. Extraordinary items consist of unusual and nonrecurring material gains and losses. In the past, they were handled in interim reports in one of three ways:

(1) absorbed entirely in the quarter in which they occurred; (2) prorated over the four quarters; or (3) disclosed only by note. *The required approach is to charge or credit the loss or gain in the quarter that it occurs instead of attempting some arbitrary multiple-period allocation.* This approach is consistent with the way in which extraordinary items are currently handled on an annual basis; no attempt is made to prorate the extraordinary items over several years.

Some accountants favour the omission of extraordinary items from the quarterly net income because they believe that the inclusion of extraordinary items that may be large in proportion to interim results naturally distorts the predictive value of interim reports. Many accountants, however, consider this approach inappropriate because it deviates from the actual situation.

Earnings Per Share. Interim reporting of earnings per share has all of the problems inherent in computing and presenting annual earnings per share, and more. If shares are issued in the third period, EPS for the first two periods will not be indicative of year-end EPS. If an extraordinary item is present in one period and new equity shares are sold in another period, the EPS figure for the extraordinary item will change for the year. On an annual basis, only one EPS figure is associated with an extraordinary item and that figure does not change; the interim figure is subject to change. *For purposes of computing earnings per share and making the disclosure determinations required by Section 1750, each interim period should stand alone; that is, all applicable tests should be made for that single period.*

Seasonality. Seasonality occurs when sales are compressed into one short period of the year while certain costs are fairly evenly spread throughout the year. For example, the natural gas industry has its heavy sales in winter months, as contrasted with the beverage industry, which has its heavy sales in summer months.

The problem of seasonality is related to the matching concept in accounting. Expenses should be matched against the revenues they create. In a seasonal business, wide fluctuations in profits occur because off-season sales may not absorb the company's fixed costs (e.g., manufacturing, selling, and administrative costs that tend to remain fairly constant regardless of sales or production).

To illustrate why seasonality is a problem, assume the following information.

Selling price per unit	$1
Annual sales for the period (projected and actual) 100,000 units @ $1.00	$100,000.00
Manufacturing costs:	
Variable	$0.10 per unit
Fixed	$0.20 per unit or $20,000.00 for the year
Nonmanufacturing costs:	
Variable	$0.10 per unit
Fixed	$0.30 per unit or $30,000.00 for the year

Sales for four quarters and the year (projected and actual) are as shown below.

		Percent of Sales
1st Quarter	$ 20,000	20%
2nd Quarter	5,000	5
3rd Quarter	10,000	10
4th Quarter	65,000	65
Total for the Year	$100,000	100%

Under the present accounting framework, the income statements for the quarters might be presented as follows.

	1st Qtr	2nd Qtr	3rd Qtr	4th Qtr	Year
Sales	$20,000	$5,000	$10,000	$65,000	$100,000
Manufacturing costs					
Variable	(2,000)	(500)	(1,000)	(6,500)	(10,000)
Fixed[a]	(4,000)	(1,000)	(2,000)	(13,000)	(20,000)
	14,000	3,500	7,000	45,500	70,000
Nonmanufacturing costs					
Variable	(2,000)	(500)	(1,000)	(6,500)	(10,000)
Fixed[b]	(7,500)	(7,500)	(7,500)	(7,500)	(30,000)
Net income	$ 4,500	($4,500)	($1,500)	$31,500	$ 30,000

[a]The fixed manufacturing costs are inventoried so that equal amounts of fixed costs do not appear during each quarter.

[b]The fixed nonmanufacturing costs are not inventoried so that equal amounts of fixed costs appear during each quarter.

An investor who uses the first quarter's results can be misled. If the first quarter's earnings are $4,500, should this figure be multiplied by four to predict annual earnings of $18,000? Or, as the analysis suggests, inasmuch as $20,000 in sales is 20% of the predicted sales for the year, net income for the year should be $22,500 ($4,500 × 5). Either figure is obviously wrong, and after the second quarter's results occur, the investor may become even more confused.

The problem with the conventional approach is that the fixed nonmanufacturing costs are not charged in proportion to sales. Some enterprises have adopted a way of avoiding this problem by making all fixed nonmanufacturing costs follow the sales pattern, as shown below.

	1st Qtr	2nd Qtr	3rd Qtr	4th Qtr	Year
Sales	$20,000	$5,000	$10,000	$65,000	$100,000
Manufacturing costs					
Variable	(2,000)	(500)	(1,000)	(6,500)	(10,000)
Fixed	(4,000)	(1,000)	(2,000)	(13,000)	(20,000)
	14,000	3,500	7,000	45,500	70,000
Nonmanufacturing costs					
Variable	(2,000)	(500)	(1,000)	(6,500)	(10,000)
Fixed	(6,000)	(1,500)	(3,000)	(19,500)	(30,000)
Net income	$ 6,000	$1,500	$3,000	$19,500	$ 30,000

This approach solves some of the problems of interim reporting; sales in the first quarter are 20% of total sales for the year, and net income in the first quarter is 20% of total income. In this case, as in the previous example, the investor cannot rely on multiplying any given quarter by four, but can use comparative data or rely on some estimate of sales in relation to income for a given period.

The greater the degree of **seasonality** experienced by a company, the greater the possibility for distortion. Because no definitive guidelines are available for handling such items as the fixed nonmanufacturing costs, variability in income can be substantial. To alleviate this problem, the profession recommends that companies should present comparative financial information using consistent methods.

The two illustrations above highlight the difference between the *discrete* and *integral* viewpoint. The fixed nonmanufacturing expenses would be expensed as incurred under the discrete viewpoint. They are charged to expense on the basis of some measure of activity under the integral method.

Continuing Controversy. The profession has developed some standards for interim reporting, but much still has to be done. As yet, it is unclear whether the discrete, integral, or some combination of these two methods will be proposed.

Discussion also persists concerning the independent auditor's involvement in interim reports. Many auditors are reluctant to express an opinion on interim financial information, arguing that the data are too tentative and subjective. Conversely, an increasing number of individuals advocate some type of examination of interim reports. A compromise may be a limited review of interim reports that provides some assurance that an examination has been conducted by an outside party and that the published information appears to be in accord with generally accepted accounting principles. An auditor may, upon request of the client, permit his or her name to be associated with the interim report if a limited review is made in accordance with Section 8200 of the *Handbook*.

Analysts want financial information as soon as possible, before it becomes old news. We may not be far from a continuous database system where corporate financial records can be accessed by microcomputer as often as desired and the information put into the required format. Thus investors could learn about sales slippage, cost increases, or earnings changes as they happen, rather than wait until after the quarter has ended.

A steady stream of information from the company to the investor could be very positive because it might alleviate management's continual concern with short-run interim numbers. Today, many contend that management is too short-run-oriented. The truth of this statement is echoed by the words of the president of a large company who decided to retire early: "I wanted to look forward to a year made up of four seasons rather than four quarters."

AUDITOR'S REPORT

Another important source of information that is often overlooked is the **auditor's report**. An **auditor** is an accounting professional who conducts an independent examination of the accounting data presented by the business enterprise. If the auditor is satisfied that the financial statements represent the financial position, results of operations, and changes in financial position fairly in accordance with generally accepted accounting principles, an unqualified opinion is expressed as shown below.[12]

OBJECTIVE 5
Identify the major disclosures found in the auditor's report.

EXHIBIT 25-7 METHANEX CORPORATION

Auditors' Report to the Shareholders

We have audited the consolidated balance sheets of Methanex Corporation as at December 31, 1995 and 1994 and the consolidated statements of earnings and retained earnings and changes in financial position for the years then ended. These financial statements are the responsibility of the Company's management. Our responsibility is to express an opinion on these financial statements based on our audits.

We conducted our audits in accordance with generally accepted auditing standards. Those standards require that we plan and perform an audit to obtain reasonable assurance whether the financial statements are free of material misstatement. An audit includes examining, on a test basis, evidence supporting the amounts and disclosures in the financial statements. An audit also includes assessing the accounting principles used and significant estimates made by management, as well as evaluating the overall financial statement presentation.

In our opinion, these consolidated financial statements present fairly, in all material respects, the financial position of the Company as at December 31, 1995 and 1994 and the results of its operations and the changes in its financial position for the years then ended in accordance with generally accepted accounting principles.

KPMG Peat Marwick Thorne

Chartered Accountants
Vancouver, Canada
February 8, 1996

---

[12] This auditor's report is in exact conformance with the specifications contained in "The Auditor's Standard Report," *CICA Handbook*, Section 5400.

In preparing this report, the auditor follows these reporting standards.

1. The report shall state whether the financial statements are presented in accordance with generally accepted accounting principles.

2. The report shall state whether such principles have been consistently observed in the current period in relation to the preceding period.

3. The report shall contain either an expression of opinion regarding the financial statements taken as a whole, or an assertion to the effect that an opinion cannot be expressed. When an overall opinion cannot be expressed, the reasons therefore should be stated. In all cases where an auditor's name is associated with financial statements, the report should contain a clear-cut indication of the character of the auditor's examination, if any, and the degree of responsibility being taken.

4. Informative disclosures in the financial statements are to be regarded as reasonably adequate unless otherwise stated in the report.

In most cases, the auditor issues a standard, **unqualified**, or **clean opinion**; that is, the auditor expresses the opinion that the financial statements present fairly, in all material respects, the financial position, results of operations, and its changes in financial position in conformity with generally accepted accounting principles. Certain circumstances, although they do not affect the auditor's unqualified opinion, may require the auditor to add a reservation to the audit report. Some of the more important circumstances are as follows.

1. *Departure from Generally Accepted Accounting Principles.* Occurs when one or more of the following three conditions arise:
   (a) Application of an inappropriate accounting policy.
   (b) An item in the financial statements is inappropriately valued.
   (c) Inadequate disclosure.

2. *Limitation in the scope of the audit.* Refers to circumstances under which the auditor has been unable to complete all of the tests and other audit procedures considered necessary.

The reservation may take the form of a **qualified** opinion, an **adverse** opinion, or a **denial** of opinion. The magnitude of the effect of the circumstances above on the financial statements is a primary factor used by auditors in determining the type of reservation that is appropriate.

A **qualified opinion** contains an exception to the standard opinion. Ordinarily the exception is not of sufficient magnitude to invalidate the statements as a whole; if it were, an adverse opinion would be rendered. A qualified opinion states that, except for the effects of the matter that the qualification relates, the financial statements present fairly, in all material respects, the financial position, results of operations, and changes in financial position in conformity with generally accepted accounting principles.

An **adverse opinion** is required in any report in which the exceptions to fair presentation are so material that in the independent auditor's judgement a qualified opinion is not justified. In such a case, the financial statements taken as a whole are not presented in accordance with generally accepted accounting principles. Adverse opinions are rare because most enterprises change their accounting to conform with the auditor's desires.

A **denial of an opinion** is appropriate when the auditor has gathered so little information on the financial statements that no opinion can be expressed. In this case the auditor would explain the circumstances that prevented him or her from obtaining the necessary information and then conclude the auditor's report with the following statement.

In view of the possible material effects on the financial statements of the matters described in the preceding paragraph, I am unable to express an opinion whether these financial statements are presented fairly in accordance with generally accepted accounting principles.[13]

The audit report should provide useful information to the investor. One investment banker noted, "Probably the first item to check is the auditor's opinion to see whether or not it is a clean one—in conformity with generally accepted accounting principles—or is qualified in regard to differences between the auditor and company management in the accounting treatment of some major item, or in the outcome of some major litigation."

OTHER AREAS IN THE ANNUAL REPORT

Some other areas in the annual report that merit special attention are as follows.

OBJECTIVE 6
Understand other areas of the annual report.

1. Management discussion and analysis

2. Management's report

3. Social Responsibility

MANAGEMENT DISCUSSION AND ANALYSIS

The **management discussion and analysis (MD&A)** section covers three financial aspects of an enterprise's business: liquidity, capital resources, and results of operations. Management highlights favourable or unfavourable trends and identifies significant events and uncertainties that may affect these three factors. This approach obviously involves a number of subjective estimates, opinions, and soft data. However, the Ontario, Quebec, and Saskatchewan Securities Commissions have mandated this disclosure.

How this section of the annual report can be made even more effective is the subject of continuing questions such as:

1. Is sufficient forward-looking information being disclosed under current MD&A requirements?

2. Should MD&A disclosures be changed to become more of a risk analysis?

3. Should the MD&A be audited by independent auditors?

MANAGEMENT'S REPORT

The public accounting profession has attempted for many years to educate the public to the fact that a company's management has the primary responsibility for the preparation, integrity, and objectivity of the company's financial statements. Only recently have management letters acknowledging such responsibility appeared in annual reports to shareholders.[14] Presented on the next page is the management statement that served as a prelude to the 1996 annual report of The Oshawa Group Limited.

---

[13] *CICA Handbook*, Section 5510.M.

[14] Accounting Guideline AcG-7 issued by the CICA in 1992 provides guidance as to the minimum content of the management report.

EXHIBIT 25-8 OSHAWA GROUP LIMITED

Responsibility for Financial Reporting

The management of The Oshawa Group Limited is responsible to the Board of Directors for the preparation and integrity of the consolidated financial statements and related information of the Company. These have been prepared in accordance with generally accepted accounting principles consistently applied and are based on management's best information and judgments.

To provide assurance in fulfilling its responsibilities, management maintains appropriate accounting records which incorporate sound systems of internal control designed to safeguard the Company's assets and ensure proper accounting of all of its business transactions.

In support of carrying out these responsibilities management and the Directors have the assistance of the internal audit department, the external auditors and the Audit Committee of the Board, all of whom review and report on such matters.

The Company's external auditors, Arthur Andersen & Co., conduct an independent examination of accounting records, policies, procedures and internal controls in accordance with generally accepted auditing standards and express their opinion on the consolidated financial statements.

The Audit Committee of the Board consisting entirely of outside Directors meets with both Arthur Andersen & Co. and the Director of Internal Audit to review their audit findings. The Committee reviews the audited consolidated financial statements and management discussion and analysis prior to their approval by the Board of Directors.

Allister P. Graham
Chairman and Chief Executive Officer

Robert E. Boyd, C.A.
Executive Vice President Finance
and Chief Financial Officer

SOCIAL RESPONSIBILITY

The social responsibility of business has received a great deal of public attention in recent years. The public and local, provincial, and federal governments have urged that businesses make a more adequate response to current issues of social concern than they have in the past.

The information related to social expenditures as presented in current annual reports is haphazard. Expenditures for the following types of items are generally considered "social awareness expenditures": assistance to educational institutions; grants to hospitals, health, and other community-related activities; aid to minority groups or enterprises; contributions to charitable foundations; aid to unemployed and related programs; and assistance in urban development.

Moore Corporation Limited, for example, disclosed the following regarding its social responsibility activities.

EXHIBIT 25-9 MOORE CORPORATION LIMITED

Environment

Moore, along with nine other companies, was selected by Australia's Environmental Protection Agency in 1995 to participate in a three-year project to help Australia adopt cleaner production techniques. The ten companies will be assisted by an environmental consultant to implement strategies for cleaner production such as minimizing the use of raw materials and energy, reducing waste, better housekeeping methods and innovative technology and management systems. Moore anticipates significant reductions in paper usage and energy.

Health and Safety

At Moore we believe that the health and safety of every person is more important than any job or objective. We are proud to report that the overall frequency and severity of injury continues on a steady decline. In 1995, we focused our attention on ergonomics issues in most business units. An ergonomics coordinator provided support to priority locations, concurrent with the development of an overall corporate ergonomics program.

Corporate Contributions

Donations

Moore Corporation believes strongly in our responsibility to be involved in the charitable and non-profit sector and has fulfilled this role for well over 100 years. We focus on four main areas: children and families, education, community services, and arts/culture. Our objective is to provide opportunities in communities where Moore employees and customers live and work.

Moore is also committed to assisting employees in their fundraising efforts. In 1995, in the wake of the Oklahoma City bombing, a group of Stillwater, Okla. plant employees joined together to raise funds, and asked other Moore plants to do the same. Moore matched the funds raised.

Sponsorships

Moore looks for new and innovative ways to get involved in corporate sponsorships. Through in-kind contributions this year, Moore focused on three key sponsorships which provided an opportunity to showcase our products and services, as well as assist in worthwhile events.

In 1995:

- Moore sponsored the World Veterans' Athletic Championships with 6,000 athletes and their families from more than 70 countries participating.

- Moore joined an elite group in sponsoring the G7 Economic Summit, where leaders of the world's most powerful nations met in Nova Scotia.

- Moore was the key sponsor of the business-to-business forum, *Japan: Still Profitable*, held in conjunction with the "Today's Japan" Festival in Toronto.

As yet, no standards or requirements have been proposed for the measurement and reporting of the social responsibilities assumed by individual enterprises. To some investors, it is a matter of importance whether a company is adopting affirmative policies with regard to environmental matters, or if it is simply doing the minimum to assure legal compliance. As indicated in Chapter 14, many companies have become concerned about the potentially large contingent liabilities related to hazardous waste because stricter laws are being enacted to control industrial waste.

REPORTING ON FINANCIAL FORECASTS AND PROJECTIONS

OBJECTIVE 7
Identify issues related to financial forecasts and projections.

In recent years, the investing public's demand for more and better information has focussed on disclosure of corporate expectations for the future.[15] These disclosures take one of two forms:[16]

A **forecast** is prospective financial results of operations, financial position, or changes in financial position, and reflects management's expectations and plans for the period involved.

A **projection** is prospective financial results of operations, financial position, or changes in financial position based on one or more hypothetical assumptions and a course of action that are not necessarily the most likely under the circumstances.

As indicated above, the difference between a forecast and a projection is that a forecast attempts to provide information on what is expected to happen, whereas a projection may provide information on what is not necessarily expected to happen.

Note that forecasts are the subject of intensive discussion with journalists, corporate executives, financial analysts, accountants, and others making their views known. Predictably, there are strong arguments on either side. The following are some of the arguments.

Arguments for requiring published forecasts:

1. Investment decisions are based on future expectations; therefore, information about the future facilitates better decisions.

2. Forecasts are already circulated informally, but are uncontrolled, frequently misleading, and not available equally to all investors. This confused situation should be brought under control.

3. Circumstances now change so rapidly that historical information is no longer adequate for prediction.

Arguments against requiring published forecasts:

1. No one can foretell the future. Therefore forecasts, while conveying an impression of precision about the future, will inevitably be wrong.

---

[15] Some areas in which companies are using financial information about the future are equipment lease versus buy analysis, analysis of a company's ability to successfully enter new markets, and examining merger and acquisition opportunities. In addition, forecasts and projections are also prepared for use by third parties in public offering documents (requiring financial forecasts), tax-oriented investments, and financial feasibility studies. Use of forward-looking data has been enhanced by the increased capability of the microcomputer to analyse, compare, and manipulate large quantities.

[16] "Future Data-Oriented Financial Information," *Re-exposure Draft* (Toronto: CICA Accounting Standards Committee, August, 1988).

2. Organizations will strive only to meet their published forecasts, not to produce results that are in the stockholders' best interest.

3. When forecasts are not proven to be accurate, there will be recriminations and probably legal actions.

4. Disclosure of forecasts will be detrimental to organizations because it will fully inform not only investors, but also competitors (foreign and domestic).[17]

The Accounting Standards Board has issued a standard (*Handbook* Section 4250) called "Future Oriented Financial Information." Three important components of this section are that it requires accountants to provide (1) a cautionary note stating that the actual results for the period may be different than the forecast; (2) a clear indication as to whether the information is a forecast or a projection; and (3) disclosure about the assumptions and hypotheses used.[18]

EXPERIENCE IN THE UNITED STATES AND THE UNITED KINGDOM

Great Britain has permitted financial forecasts for years, and the results have been fairly successful. A typical British forecast adapted from a construction company's report to support a public share offering is as follows.

> Profits have grown substantially over the past 10 years and directors are confident of being able to continue this expansion. . . While the rate of expansion will be dependent on the level of economic activity in Ireland and in England, the group is well structured to avail itself of opportunities as they arise, particularly in the field of property development, which is expected to play an increasingly important role in the group's future expansion.
>
> Profit before taxation for the half year ended 30th June 1992 was 402,000 pounds. On the basis of trading experiences since that date the present level of sales and completions, the directors expect that in the absence of unforeseen circumstances, the group's profits before taxation for the year to 31st December 1992 will be not less than 960,000 pounds. . . .
>
> No dividends will be paid in respect of the year December 31, 1992. In a full financial year, on the basis of the above forecasts (not including full year profits) it would be the intention of the board, assuming current rates of tax, to recommend dividends totalling 40% (of after-tax profits), of which 15% payable would be as an interest dividend in November 1993 and 25% as a final dividend in June 1994.

In the United States, the legal environment is not as favourable toward publication of financial forecasts. A general narrative-type forecast would be preferred over the more quantitative British forecast. The following illustrates a forecast that a U.S. company might issue.

> On the basis of promotions planned by the company for the second half of fiscal 1998, net earnings for that period are expected to be approximately the same as those for the first half of fiscal 1998, with net earnings for the third quarter expected to make the predominant contribution to net earnings for the second half of 1998.

QUESTIONS OF LIABILITY

What happens if a company does not meet its forecasts? Are the company and the auditor going to be sued? If a company, for example, projects an earnings increase of 15% and

---

[17] Joseph P. Cummings, *Financial Forecasts and the Certified Public Accountant* (New York: Peat, Marwick, Mitchell & Co., November 30, 1972).

[18] *CICA Handbook*, Section 1540, pars. .24 and .32.

achieves only 5%, should the shareholder be permitted to have some judicial recourse against the company? One possible solution to this problem would require passage of "safe harbour" legislation that would protect companies that have used "good faith" and "reasonable assumptions" in their forecasting.

In addition to the question of liability, several other issues must be resolved before earnings projections should be made mandatory. The role and responsibility of independent public accountants as attestors of forecasts must be determined. Should forecasts consist of general expectations or of detailed disclosures? Should a single value ($1.50) or a range of values ($1.50 ± $.20) be presented? What should be the length of the period forecast?

Financial forecasts provide such highly relevant investment information that the demand for them will not subside. Although there are some disadvantages to the requirement of forecasts, these are outweighed by the advantages. The authors believe that the publication of forecasts is a natural and inevitable extension of corporate disclosure.

FRAUDULENT FINANCIAL REPORTING

OBJECTIVE 8
Describe the profession's response to fraudulent financial reporting.

The system of financial reporting in Canada is generally considered to be among the best in the world. The importance of an effective financial reporting system cannot be understated, because it provides the financial information that ensures the proper functioning of the capital and credit markets. Unfortunately, the system does not always work as planned.

Frauds in financial reporting are unusual, but when they occur questions are raised about the financial reporting process. In order to enhance the credibility of audited financial statements, the AcSB issued *Handbook* Sections 5135 and 5136 in 1994. These sections specify audit procedures designed to reduce the risk of publishing audited statements containing misstatements due to fraud, error or illegal acts.

An important study of the financial reporting environment has been completed by a committee in the United States. The National Commission on Fraudulent Financial Reporting, chaired by James C. Treadway, Jr.—hereafter referred to as the **Treadway Commission**—identified causal factors that lead to fraudulent financial reporting and provided steps to reduce its incidence.[19]

The Commission defined **fraudulent financial reporting** as *"intentional or reckless conduct, whether act or omission, that results in materially misleading financial statements."* It also noted that fraudulent reporting can involve gross and deliberate distortion of corporate records (such as inventory count tags), or misapplication of accounting principles (failure to disclose material transactions).[20]

CAUSES OF FRAUDULENT FINANCIAL REPORTING

Fraudulent financial reporting usually occurs because of conditions in the internal or external environment.[21] Influences in the **internal environment** relate to poor systems of internal control, management's poor attitude toward ethics, or perhaps a company's liquidity or profitability. Those in the **external environment** may relate to industry conditions, overall business environment, or legal and regulatory considerations.

General incentives for fraudulent financial reporting are the desire to obtain a higher share price or debt offering, to avoid default on a loan covenant, or to make a personal

---

[19] "Report of the National Commission on Fraudulent Financial Reporting" (Washington, D.C., 1987).

[20] *Ibid*, page 2. Unintentional errors as well as corporate improprieties (such as tax fraud, employee embezzlements, and so on) that do not cause the financial statements to be misleading are excluded from the definition of fraudulent financial reporting.

[21] The discussion in this section is taken from the "Report of the National Commission on Fraudulent Financial Reporting," pp. 23–24.

gain of some type (additional compensation, promotion). Situational pressures on the company or an individual manager also may lead to fraudulent financial reporting. Examples of these situational pressures include:

1. Sudden decrease in revenue or market share. A single company or an entire industry can experience these decreases.

2. Unrealistic budget pressures, particularly for short-term results. These pressures may occur when headquarters arbitrarily determines profit objectives and budgets without taking actual conditions into account.

3. Financial pressure resulting from bonus plans that depend on short-term economic performance. This pressure is particularly acute when the bonus is a significant component of the individual's total compensation.

Opportunities for fraudulent financial reporting are present in circumstances when the fraud is easy to commit and when detection is difficult. Frequently these opportunities arise from:

1. *The absence of a Board of Directors or audit committee* that vigilantly oversees the financial reporting process.

2. *Weak or nonexistent internal accounting controls.* This situation can occur, for example, when a company's revenue system is overloaded as a result of a rapid expansion of sales, an acquisition of a new division, or the entry into a new, unfamiliar line of business.

3. *Unusual or complex transactions* such as the consolidation of two companies, the divestiture or closing of a specific operation, and agreements to buy or sell government securities under a repurchase agreement.

4. *Accounting estimates requiring significant subjective judgement* by company management, such as reserves for loan losses and the yearly provision for warranty expense.

5. *Ineffective internal audit staffs* resulting from inadequate staff size and severely limited audit scope.

A weak corporate ethical climate contributes to these situations. Opportunities for fraudulent financial reporting also increase dramatically when the accounting principles followed in reporting transactions are nonexistent, evolving, or subject to varying interpretations.

CRITERIA FOR MAKING ACCOUNTING AND REPORTING CHOICES

Throughout this textbook and especially in this chapter, we have stressed the need to provide information that is useful to predict the amount, timing, and uncertainty of future cash flows. To achieve this objective, accountants must make judicious choices between alternative accounting concepts, methods, and means of disclosure. You are probably surprised by the large number of choices among acceptable alternatives that accountants are required to make.

You should recognize, however, as indicated in Chapter 1, that accounting is greatly influenced by its environment. Because it does not exist in a vacuum, it seems unrealistic to assume that alternative presentations to certain transactions and events will be eliminated entirely. Nevertheless, we are hopeful that the profession, through the development of its conceptual framework, will be able to focus on the needs of financial statement users and to eliminate diversity where appropriate. The profession must continue its efforts to develop a sound foundation upon which accounting standards and practice can be built. As Aristotle said: "The correct beginning is more than half the whole."

SHOPPING FOR SHARES ON THE NET

Not so long ago, Canadians bought shares solely through stockbrokers, in person or over the telephone. Customers placed an order with the stockbroker who, for a commission, bought the shares on a recognized stock exchange such as the Vancouver Stock Exchange"VSE". Canada's major stock exchanges and the companies who have shares listed on these exchanges are monitored by the exchanges themselves and also by provincial securities commissions such as the Ontario Securities Commission ("OSC"). Brokers are also monitored for unscrupulous or unethical behaviour. This monitoring function is central to the whole process of keeping the markets to raise funds fair, and is very important, especially to protect smaller investors.

In the last couple of years there has been a dramatic increase in stock-related activity on the Internet. There are on-line brokers, chat rooms that promote stocks and even informal exchanges where stocks may be bought and sold directly (i.e., not through a formal stock exchange such as the VSE). Recently, the US Securities and Exchange Commission, the "SEC", authorized an Atlanta company to transmit "roadshows" for securities offering over the internet.[1] This is significant because it represents official recognition and validation of the option of using the Internet to promote the sale of shares.

A "roadshow" is an oral presentation made by a company who is trying to raise money through a share offering. Key management personnel from the company travel around the world and make presentations to potential investors. Often these investors are institutional investors such as insurance companies or pension plans. These presentations are generally not covered by securities laws that govern the distribution of prospectus material because they are made orally.[2]

The securities laws that govern the content and distribution of written prospectus material are very stringent in order to protect investors from promotional material that otherwise may not have any underlying substance or truth. Note that broadcasts on television and radio are regarded as prospectuses and are subject to the same strict laws as written material.[3]

What are the implications of this increased activity on the Internet for investors like you and me? As previously mentioned, the traditional system of using brokers, written prospectuses and formal stock exchanges, is heavily monitored by securities laws with the prime objective of protecting potential investors. A broker or company that steps out of line will be prohibited from engaging in trading activities. In the past, most companies have adhered strictly to the laws, rather than being denied access to public investment funds. Since the activity on the Internet does not fit into the more traditional categories for promoting stocks, it is potentially not covered by the securities laws. This means less protection for potential investors!

Where the securities commissions are involved, such as with the recent ruling by the SEC to allow roadshows, presumably, the laws to protect us will be enforced but what about the other areas where the securities commissions are not yet involved? What, if any, plans do the securities commissions have for protecting investors on the Internet?

The Toronto Stock Exchange, the"TSE", has set up a plan to monitor promotional activities on the Internet, planning to get a web crawler to look for and monitor information on the internet related to TSE companies.[4] NASDAQ, the second largest US stock market has plans and processes in place as does the Alberta Stock Exchange, to name a few examples. Other securities commissions have similar plans.

But until the various exchanges and commissions get completely on board, it is wise to be careful about what you see and read on the internet. As Barbara Barry, spokeswoman for the British Columbia Securities Commission is quoted as saying…"Never what you read in a chat room on the Internet. Would you believe what you heard at a cocktail party?"[5]

[1] Financial Post—September 10, 1997—"SEC approves Net Roadshows"

[2] *Ibid*

[3] *Ibid*

[4] *Financial Post* September 6, 1997—TSE set to beef up policing of Internet stock promotions"

[5] *Ibid*

Contributed by: Irene Wiecek, University of Toronto

Summary of Learning Objectives

1. **Review the full disclosure principle and describe problems of implementation.** The full disclosure principle calls for financial reporting of any financial facts significant enough to influence the judgement of an informed reader. Implementing the full disclosure principle is difficult, because the cost of disclosure can be substantial and the benefits difficult to assess. Disclosure requirements have increased because of (1) the growing complexity of the business environment; (2) the necessity of timely information; and (3) the use of accounting as a control and monitoring device.

2. **Explain the use of notes in financial statement preparation.** Notes are the accountant's means of amplifying or explaining the items presented in the main body of the statements. Information pertinent to specific financial statement items can be explained in qualitative terms, and supplementary data of a quantitative nature can be provided to expand the information in the notes.

Common note disclosures relate to such items as the following: accounting policies; inventories; property, plant, and equipment; credit claims; and contingencies and commitments.

3. **Describe the disclosure requirements for major segments of a business.** If only the consolidated figures are available to the analyst, much information regarding the composition of these figures is hidden in aggregated figures. There is no way to tell from the consolidated data the extent to which the differing product lines contribute to the company's profitability, risk, and growth potential. As a result, segment information is required by the profession in certain situations.

4. **Describe the accounting problems associated with interim reporting.** Interim reports cover periods of less than one year. Two viewpoints exist regarding interim reports. One view (discrete view) holds that each interim period should be treated as a separate accounting period. Another view (integral view) is that the interim report is an integral part of the annual report and that deferrals and accruals should take into consideration what will happen for the entire year.

    The same accounting principles used for annual reports should be employed for interim reports. A number of unique reporting problems develop related to the following items: (1) advertising and similar costs; (2) expenses subject to year-end adjustment; (3) income taxes; (4) extraordinary items; (5) changes in accounting; (6) earnings per share; and (7) seasonality.

5. **Identify the major disclosures found in the auditor's report.** If the auditor is satisfied that the financial statements present the financial position, results of operations, and cash flows fairly in accordance with generally accepted accounting principles, an unqualified opinion is expressed. A qualified opinion contains an exception to the standard opinion; ordinarily the exception is not of sufficient magnitude to invalidate the statement as a whole.

    An adverse opinion is required in any report in which the exceptions to fair presentation are so material that a qualified opinion is not justified. A disclaimer of opinion is appropriate when the auditor has gathered so little information on the financial statements that no opinion can be expressed.

6. **Understand other areas of the annual report.** Management's discussion and analysis section covers three financial aspects of an enterprise's business: liquidity, capital resources, and results of operations. Management has primary responsibility for the financial statements and this responsibility is often indi-

cated in a letter to the shareholders in the annual report. Companies often report on their socially responsible activities. As yet, no standards or requirements have been proposed by the AcSB for the measurement and reporting of the social responsibilities assumed by individual enterprises.

7. **Identify issues related to financial forecasts and projections.** Generally, companies in Canada are permitted (not required) to include profit forecasts in annual reports.

8. **Describe the profession's response to fraudulent financial reporting.** Fraudulent financial reporting is intentional or reckless conduct, whether act or omission, that results in materially misleading financial statements. Fraudulent financial reporting usually occurs because of poor internal control, management's poor attitude toward ethics, and so on. The profession has issued two auditing standards that address part of this problem.

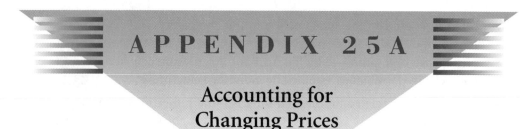

APPENDIX 25A

Accounting for Changing Prices

One assumption made in accounting is that the monetary unit remains stable over a period of time. But is that assumption realistic? Consider the classic story about the individual who went to sleep and woke up 10 years later. Hurrying to a telephone, she got through to her broker and asked what her formerly modest stock portfolio was worth. She was told that she was a multimillionaire—her Xerox Canada shares were worth $5 million and her BCE Inc. shares were up to $10 million. Elated, she was about to inquire about her other holdings, when the telephone operator cut in with "Your time is up. Please deposit $100,000 for the next three minutes."[22]

OBJECTIVE 9
Understand and account for changing prices.

What this little story demonstrates is that prices can and do change over a period of time, and that one is not necessarily better off when they do. Although the example above is extreme, consider some more realistic data that compare prices in 1988 with what was expected in 1998, assuming that prices increased either an average of 6% or 13% per year.

EXHIBIT 25A-1

EXAMPLES OF CHANGING PRICES

	1988	1998	
Assumed Average Price Increase		6%	13%
University, yearly average cost	$ 3,350.00	$ 6,000.00	$ 11,400.00
Average taxi ride, Toronto (before tip)	2.95	5.30	10.00
Slice of pizza	.65	1.20	2.25
First-class postage stamp	.30	.54	.93
Run-of-the-mill suburban $150,000 house, Vancouver	150,000.00	270,000.00	510,000.00
McDonald's milk shake	.75	1.35	2.55

Despite the inevitability of changing prices during a period of inflation, the accounting profession still follows the stable monetary unit assumption in the preparation of a company's primary financial statements. While admitting that some changes in prices do occur, the profession believes that the unit of measure (e.g., the dollar) has remained sufficiently constant over time to provide meaningful financial information.

The profession, however, at one time encouraged the disclosure of certain price-level adjusted data in the form of supplemental information. The two most widely used approaches that show the effects of changing prices on a company's financial statement are (1) constant dollar accounting; and (2) current cost accounting.

---

[22] Adapted from *Barron's*, January 28, 1980, p. 27.

CONSTANT DOLLAR ACCOUNTING

The real value of the dollar is determined by the goods or services for which it can be exchanged. This real value is commonly called **purchasing power**. As the company experiences **inflation** (rising price levels) **or deflation** (falling price levels), the amount of goods or services for which a dollar can be exchanged changes; that is, the purchasing power of the dollar changes from one period to the next.

Constant dollar accounting restates financial statement items into dollars that have equal purchasing power. As one executive of Shell Oil Company explained, "Constant dollar accounting is a restatement of the traditional financial information into a common unit of measurement." In other words, constant dollar accounting changes the unit of measurement; it does not, however, change the underlying accounting principles used to report historical cost amounts. Constant dollar accounting is cost-based.

Through constant dollar restatement, financial data are rendered comparable; thus, important trends can be detected. For example, a newspaper article recently lamented the fact that family income after taxes ($42,612) was only slightly higher than in 1976 ($42,495) after adjusting for inflation. This information suggests that the standard of living in Canada is holding constant at best.

PRICE-LEVEL INDICES

To restate financial information into constant dollars, it is necessary to measure a change in the price of a "basket of goods" from one period to the next. Developing this basket of goods is a complex process and involves judgement in selecting the most appropriate items to be part of this market basket. Fortunately, the government puts together a number of different baskets of goods and computes indices for them. One of the most popular, and the one that accountants use, is the Consumer Price Index (CPI). The CPI reflects the average change in the retail prices of a fairly broad group of consumer goods.

The procedure for restating reported historical cost dollars, which vary in purchasing power, to dollars of constant purchasing power is relatively straightforward. The restatement is accomplished by multiplying the amount to be restated by a fraction, the numerator of which is the index for current prices and the denominator of which is the index for prices that prevailed at the date related to the amount being restated. The denominator is often referred to as the base year. The formula is as follows.

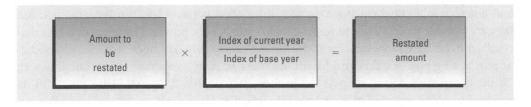

$$\text{Amount to be restated} \times \frac{\text{Index of current year}}{\text{Index of base year}} = \text{Restated amount}$$

To illustrate how this restatement process works, assume that land was purchased in 1991 for $100,000 and another parcel of land was purchased in 1995 for $80,000. If the price-level index was 100 in 1991, 120 in 1994, and 180 in 1998, the land parcels would be restated to the 1998 price level as follows.

$$1991 \text{ purchase } \$100,000 \times \frac{180}{100} = \$180,000$$

$$1995 \text{ purchase } \$\ 80,000 \times \frac{180}{120} = \underline{\ 120,000}$$

Land as restated $\underline{\underline{\$300,000}}$

The land is restated to $300,000 in terms of 1998 dollars using the 1998 index of 180 as the numerator for both parcels and the base year indices of 100 and 120 as the denominators. If historical cost dollars are not restated, dollars of different purchasing power are added together, and the total dollar amount is not meaningful.

MONETARY AND NONMONETARY ITEMS

In preparing constant dollar statements, it is essential to distinguish between monetary and nonmonetary items. **Monetary items** are contractual claims to receive or pay a fixed amount of cash. Monetary assets include cash, accounts and notes receivable, and investments that pay a fixed rate of interest and will be repaid at a fixed amount in the future. Monetary liabilities include accounts and notes payable, accruals such as wages and interest payable, and long-term obligations payable in a fixed amount of cash.

All assets and liabilities not classified as monetary items are classified as nonmonetary for constant dollar accounting purposes. **Nonmonetary items** are items whose prices in terms of the monetary unit change in proportion to changes in the general price level. Examples of nonmonetary assets are inventories; property, plant, and equipment; and intangible assets. Most liabilities are monetary items, while owners' equity items are usually nonmonetary.

The following chart indicates some major monetary and nonmonetary items.

Monetary Items	Nonmonetary Items
Cash	Inventories
Notes and accounts receivable	Investments in common shares
Investments that pay a fixed rate of interest	Property, plant, and equipment
	Intangible assets
Notes and accounts payable	Share capital

EFFECTS OF HOLDING MONETARY AND NONMONETARY ITEMS

Holders of monetary assets lose during inflation because a given amount of money buys progressively fewer goods and services. Conversely, liabilities such as accounts payable and notes payable held during a period of inflation become less burdensome because they are payable in dollars of reduced general purchasing power. The gains or losses that result from holding monetary items during periods of price changes are often referred to as **purchasing power gains and losses**. As one company explained in its annual report, "If the company's equity is invested in monetary assets, the purchasing power of its equity is gradually eroded at a rate equal to inflation."

To illustrate the effects of holding monetary and nonmonetary items in a period of inflation, assume that Helio Company has the following balance sheet at the beginning of the year.

HELIO COMPANY Balance Sheet (Beginning of Period) Price Index = 100			
Cash	$1,000	Share capital	$4,000
Inventory	3,000		
Total assets	$4,000	Total equity	$4,000

If the general price level doubles during the year and no transactions take place, then for the company to be in the same economic position at the end of the year as it was at the beginning, it should have the balance sheet shown below.

HELIO COMPANY
Balance Sheet
(Beginning of Period)
Price Index = 200

Cash	$2,000	Share capital	$8,000
Inventory	6,000		
Total assets	$8,000	Total equity	$8,000

As illustrated, all items should have doubled if the company is to be in the same economic position. However, only nonmonetary items (inventory and share capital) can be doubled. Helio still has only $1,000 in cash; therefore, it has experienced a purchasing power loss by holding cash during a period of inflation. Helio's balance sheet presented on a constant dollar basis would appear as follows.

HELIO COMPANY
Balance Sheet
(Beginning of Period)
Price Index = 200

Cash	$1,000	Share capital	$8,000
Inventory	6,000	Retained earnings	(1,000)
Total assets	$7,000	Total equity	$7,000

As noted, Helio Company has experienced a purchasing power loss of $1,000, which is shown as a reduction of retained earnings.

In summary, because monetary assets and liabilities are already stated in terms of current purchasing power in the historical cost balance sheet, they *appear at the same amounts in statements adjusted for general price-level changes.* The fact that the end-of-the-current-year amounts are the same in historical dollar statements as in constant dollar statements does not obscure the fact that purchasing power gains or losses result from holding them during a period of general price-level change. Conversely, *nonmonetary items are reported at different amounts in the constant dollar statements* than they are in the historical cost statements, when there is a change in the general price level. As a result, both the inventory and the share capital are adjusted to recognize changes in the purchasing power of the dollar.

CONSTANT DOLLAR ILLUSTRATION

To illustrate the preparation of financial statements on a constant dollar basis, assume that Hartley Company starts business on December 31, 1997 by issuing common shares for $190,000 cash. Land costing $80,000 is purchased immediately. During 1998, the company reports $190,000 of sales, cost of goods sold of $100,000, and operating expenses of $20,000. The income statement for Hartley Company on an historical cost basis is as follows.

HARTLEY COMPANY
Income Statement (Historical Cost)
For the Year Ended December 31, 1998

Sales	$190,000
Cost of goods sold	100,000
Gross profit	90,000
Operating expenses	20,000
Net income	$ 70,000

The comparative balance sheets on an historical cost basis are as follows.

HARTLEY COMPANY
Balance Sheet (Historical Cost)
December 31

Assets

	1998	1997
Cash	$145,000	$110,000
Inventory	35,000	—
Land	80,000	80,000
Total assets	$260,000	$190,000

Liabilities and Shareholders' Equity

Common shares	$190,000	$190,000
Retained earnings	70,000	—
Total liabilities and shareholders' equity	$260,000	$190,000

The relevant price indices for use in preparing constant dollar financial statements are presented below. These price indices are magnified here to illustrate their effect.

	Price Indices
December 31, 1997	100
1998 average	160
December 31, 1998	200

Constant Dollar Income Statement. When a constant dollar income statement is prepared, **revenues and expenses are restated to end-of-year dollars.** The difference between restated revenues and expenses is reported as income (loss) before purchasing power gain (loss). The purchasing power gain (loss) is then added (deducted) to produce "constant dollar net income (loss)."

Revenues and expenses are usually assumed to occur evenly throughout the period. Therefore, the historical dollar amounts are multiplied by the restatement ratio, of which the numerator is the end-of-year index and the denominator is the average index. The constant dollar income statement for Hartley Company follows (the explanations highlighted are not part of the formal statement; they are provided to explain how the statement is prepared).

HARTLEY COMPANY
Constant Dollar Income Statement
For the Year Ended December 31, 1998

Sales	$237,500	$190,000 × $\frac{200}{160}$
Cost of goods sold	125,000	$100,000 × $\frac{200}{160}$
Gross profit	112,500	
Operating expenses	25,000	$ 20,000 × $\frac{200}{160}$
Income before purchasing power loss	87,500	
Purchasing power loss	(118,750)	**(Per computation at bottom of page)**
Constant dollar net loss	$ (31,250)	

Restatement of the above items is explained below.

Sales. Because sales were spread evenly over the year, the average index is used in the computation to restate sales to end-of-year dollars.

Cost of Goods Sold. The cost of goods sold of $100,000 consists of two amounts: purchases of $135,000, less ending inventory of $35,000. Because the costs of purchases and ending inventories were spread evenly over the year, the average index is used in the computation to restate cost of goods sold to end-of-year dollars.

Operating Expenses. Because operating expenses were spread evenly over the year, the average index is used in the computation to restate operating expenses to end-of-year dollars.

Purchasing Power Loss. Computation of the purchasing power gain (loss) on monetary items requires a reconciliation of the beginning and ending balances of each monetary item for the period. A restatement ratio is then applied to the beginning balance and each reconciling amount. Hartley Company has only one monetary item: cash. Because prices are rising, it will experience a purchasing power loss for 1998. The computation of the loss is shown below.

Computation of Purchasing Power Loss

	1998 Historical	×	Restatement Ratio	=	Restated to 12/31/98 Dollars
Cash:					
Beginning balance	$110,000		$\frac{200}{100}$		$ 220,000
Add: Sales	190,000		$\frac{200}{160}$		237,500
Deduct: Purchases	(135,000)		$\frac{200}{160}$		(168,750)
Operating expenses	(20,000)		$\frac{200}{160}$		(25,000)
Total restated dollars					263,750
Ending balance	$145,000				145,000
Purchasing power loss					$(118,750)

The first column of this schedule provides a reconciliation of the beginning and ending cash balances. Note that the purchases amount is determined by adding ending inventory ($35,000) to cost of goods sold ($100,000) for Hartley Company. The restatement ratio for the beginning cash balance is based on the price index at the beginning of the year (100). The other ratios are based on the average price index during the year (160). The total restated dollars, $263,750, indicates how much cash the company should have to stay even with the price increases that have occurred. This amount is then compared with the historical cost ending balance to determine the amount of the purchasing power gain or loss. In this case, Hartley should have $263,750; it has only $145,000. Therefore, it has experienced a purchasing power loss of $118,750.

Constant Dollar Balance Sheet. When a constant dollar balance sheet is prepared, all monetary items are stated in end-of-year dollars and therefore do not need adjustment. Nonmonetary items, however, must be restated to end-of-year dollars. The constant dollar balance sheet for Hartley Company is provided below (the explanations highlighted are not part of the formal statement; they are provided to help you understand how the statement is prepared).

HARTLEY COMPANY
Constant Dollar Balance Sheet
December 31, 1998

Assets

Cash	$145,000	(Same as historical cost)
Inventory	43,750	$35,000 × $\frac{200}{160}$
Land	160,000	$80,000 × $\frac{200}{100}$
Total assets	$348,750	

Liabilities and Shareholders' Equity

Common shares	$380,000	$190,000 × $\frac{200}{100}$
Retained earnings	(31,250)	(See constant dollar income statement)
Total liabilities and shareholders' equity	$348,750	

Restatement of the preceding items is explained as follows.

Cash. Cash is a monetary item; therefore, no restatement is necessary.

Inventory. Inventory is a nonmonetary item and therefore must be restated. Because inventory was purchased evenly throughout the year, the $35,000 must be multiplied by the ratio of the ending index, 200, to the index at the time the inventory was purchased, which was the average for the year of 160.

Land. Land is a nonmonetary item; therefore, it must be restated. Because land was purchased at the end of the preceding year, the $80,000 must be multiplied by the ratio of the ending index to the index at the time the land was purchased, which was 100.

Common Shares. Share capital is a nonmonetary item; therefore, restatement is necessary. Because share capital was issued at the end of the preceding year, the $190,000 must be multiplied by the ratio of the ending index, 200, to the index at the time the shares were issued, which was 100.

Retained Earnings. Since no balance existed in retained earnings at the beginning of the year, the retained earnings in constant dollars includes only the constant dollar net loss for the current period of $31,250. Thus, Hartley Company on a constant dollar basis reports a negative retained earnings after its first year of operations.

ADVANTAGES AND DISADVANTAGES OF CONSTANT DOLLAR ACCOUNTING

Constant dollar financial statements have been discussed widely within both the accounting profession and the business and financial community and lauded by many as a means of overcoming reporting problems during periods of inflation or deflation. The following arguments have been submitted in support of preparing such statements.

1. Constant dollar accounting provides management with an *objectively* determined quantification of the impact of inflation on its business operations.

2. Constant dollar accounting eliminates the effects of inflation from financial information by requiring each enterprise to follow the same objective procedure and use the same price-level index, thereby *preserving comparability of financial statements between firms.*

3. Constant dollar accounting *enhances comparability between the financial statements of a single firm* by eliminating differences due to price-level changes and thereby improves trend analysis.

4. Constant dollar accounting eliminates the effects of price-level changes without having to develop a new structure of accounting; that is, it *preserves the historical cost-based accounting system* that is currently used and understood.

5. Constant dollar accounting *eliminates the necessity of and attraction to the "piece-meal" approaches* used in combating the effects of inflation on financial statements, namely, LIFO inventory costing and accelerated depreciation of property, plant, and equipment.

In spite of widespread publicity, discussion, and authoritative support both inside and outside the accounting profession, the preparation and public issuance of constant dollar financial statements up to this point has been negligible, probably because of the following disadvantages said to be associated with constant dollar financial statements.

1. The additional *cost* of preparing constant dollar statements is not offset by the benefit of receiving sufficient relevant information.

2. Constant dollar financial statements will cause *confusion* and will be misunderstood by users.

3. Restating the "value" of nonmonetary items at historical cost adjusted for general price-level changes *is no more meaningful than historical cost alone,* that is, it suffers all of the shortcomings of the historical cost method.

4. The reported purchasing power gain from monetary items is *misleading* because it does not necessarily represent successful management or provide funds for dividends, plant expansion, or other purposes.

5. Constant dollar accounting *assumes that the impact of inflation falls equally* on all business and on all classes of assets and costs, which is not true.

Probably the greatest deterrent to adoption of constant dollar accounting in the past has been *what it is not:* constant dollar accounting is not present value, not net realizable value, and not current cost accounting, and therein lies much of the opposition to its use.

CURRENT COST ACCOUNTING

The price of a specific item may be affected not only by general inflation, but also by individual market forces. For example, in a recent six-year period, certain items changed more or less than the general price level. To illustrate, during this period of time the cost of a local telephone call increased 150%, guaranteed overnight mail delivery increased 4,575%, a litre of gasoline decreased over 30%, and a flawless one-carat diamond decreased over 70%. Thus, changes in the specific price of items may be very different from the change in the general price level.

A popular means to measure the change in a specific price is current cost. **Current cost** is the cost of replacing the identical asset owned. Current cost may be approximated by reference to current catalogue prices or by applying a specific index to the book value of the asset. Unlike the constant dollar approach, which is simply a restatement of historical dollars into constant purchasing power, the current cost approach changes the basis of measurement from historical cost to current value.

Current Cost Adjustments

When current cost statements are prepared, it is also necessary to distinguish between monetary and nonmonetary items. Monetary items are stated at their current cost in the historical cost financial statements. As a result, no adjustment is necessary to items such as cash, accounts receivable, notes payable, or accounts payable when preparing a current cost balance sheet. A purchasing power gain or loss on the monetary items is not computed under current cost accounting because the measuring unit, the dollar, is not considered to have changed from one period to the next.

Conversely, nonmonetary items as a rule must be adjusted at year end. The current cost of nonmonetary items tends to change over time. For example, land held over a period of time will usually experience some type of price change. The same is true of other nonmonetary items such as inventory; property, plant, and equipment; and intangible assets.

When a nonmonetary item is restated, a holding gain or loss arises and must be reported on the financial statements. A **holding gain (loss)** is an increase or decrease in an item's value while it is held by the company. For example, if the current cost of land is $20,000 on January 1, 1998 and $32,000 on December 31, 1998, the company has a holding gain on this land of $12,000, computed as follows:

Current cost of land, December 31, 1998	$32,000
Current cost of land, January 1, 1998	20,000
Holding gain on land	$12,000

Revenues and expenses appearing on a current cost income statement are the same as the historical cost amounts, because at the time they are earned or incurred they represent current cost. A major exception is the cost of goods sold, which will be explained later.

To illustrate the preparation of financial statements on a current cost basis, assume that Sensor, Inc. started business on December 31, 1997 by selling common shares for $90,000. Land costing $40,000 was purchased immediately. During the next year, the company reported $160,000 of sales revenue, cost of goods sold of $75,000, and operating expenses of $25,000. The income statement for Sensor, Inc. on an historical cost basis appears as follows.

SENSOR, INC.
Income Statement (Historical Cost)
For the Year Ended December 31, 1998

Sales	$160,000
Cost of goods sold	75,000
Gross profit	85,000
Operating expenses	25,000
Net income	$ 60,000

The comparative balance sheets on an historical cost basis are as follows.

SENSOR, INC.
Balance Sheet (Historical Cost)
December 31

Assets

	1998	1997
Cash	$ 30,000	$50,000
Inventory	80,000	—
Land	40,000	40,000
Total assets	$150,000	$90,000

Liabilities and Shareholders' Equity

	1998	1997
Share capital	$ 90,000	$90,000
Retained earnings	60,000	—
Total liabilities and shareholders' equity	$150,000	$90,000

The relevant current cost amounts for the income statement and balance sheet items for 1998 are as follows.

Income Statement		Balance Sheet	
Sales	$160,000	Cash	$ 30,000
Cost of goods sold	95,000	Inventory	105,000
Operating expenses	25,000	Land	48,000
		Share capital	90,000

CURRENT COST INCOME STATEMENT

In a current cost income statement, two income numbers are reported. The first, **current cost income from operations**, is sales revenues less the current cost of goods sold plus operating expenses. This amount is the *income a company has earned after providing for the replacement of assets used in operations.*

The second income number, **current cost net income**, measures the *total income of a company from one period to the next.* Thus, holding gains (losses) are added (deducted) to current cost income from operations to arrive at this number. The current cost income statement for Sensor, Inc. follows. (The explanations highlighted are not part of the formal statement; they are provided to explain how the statement is prepared.)

SENSOR, INC.
Current Income Statement
For the Year Ended December 31, 1998

Sales	$160,000	(Same as historical cost)
Cost of goods sold	95,000	(Restated to current cost)
Gross profit	65,000	
Operating expenses	25,000	(Same as historical cost)
Current cost income from operations	40,000	
Holding gain	53,000	(Increase in current cost)
Current cost net income	$ 93,000	

The preceding items are explained below.

Sales and Operating Expenses. Sales and operating expenses are already stated at their current cost amounts on historical cost statements; therefore, no adjustment is needed for these items.

Cost of Goods Sold. Goods are sold at varying times of the year. At the time these goods are sold, the current cost of the inventory sold must be determined. The historical cost of goods sold and the current cost of goods sold are usually different.

Total Holding Gain. The holding gain for Sensor comprises three items, as shown below.

Current cost of goods sold	$ 95,000	
Historical cost of goods sold	75,000	
		$20,000
Current cost of inventory	105,000	
Historical cost of inventory	80,000	
		25,000
Current cost of land	48,000	
Historical cost of land	40,000	
		8,000
Total holding gain		$53,000

Recall that a holding gain is an increase in an item's value from one period to the next. If the item is sold during the period, however, the holding gain (loss) is computed only to the point of sale. Thus, the inventory sold, as reported in the current cost of goods sold amount, had increased $20,000. Also, inventory on hand and land experienced holding gains of $25,000 and $8,000, respectively. Holding gains or losses indicate how effective management is in acquiring and holding assets.

CURRENT COST BALANCE SHEET

The preparation of a current cost balance sheet is relatively straightforward. Monetary items are not adjusted because they are already stated at current cost. Similarly, capital equity is not adjusted because its balance represents the current cost of share capital. All other nonmonetary items must be adjusted to current cost. The current cost balance sheet for Sensor, Inc. follows (the explanations highlighted are not part of the formal statement; they are provided to explain how the statement is prepared).

SENSOR, INC.
Current Cost Balance Sheet
December 31, 1998

Assets

Cash	$ 30,000	(Same as historical cost)
Inventory	105,000	(Restated to current cost)
Land	48,000	(Restated to current cost)
Total assets	$183,000	

Liabilities and Shareholders' Equity

Share capital	$ 90,000	(Same as historical cost)
Retained earnings	93,000	(From current cost income statement)
Total liabilities and shareholders' equity	$183,000	

As indicated from the statement above, retained earnings is determined by adding the current cost net income amount to the beginning balance of retained earnings.

ADVANTAGES AND DISADVANTAGES OF CURRENT COST

A distinct advantage that current cost has over both historical cost and constant dollar accounting is that *specific changes (up and down) in individual items are considered.* While the general level of prices may be increasing, prices of specific items may be decreasing. Such items as calculators, tennis balls, watches, microwave ovens, and television sets, for example, have decreased in price, whereas the general level of prices has increased. Constant dollar accounting using a general price index does not make an allowance for these changes in prices as effectively as a current cost system does.

The major arguments for the use of a current cost approach are:

1. Current cost provides a *better measure of efficiency.* If, for example, depreciation is based on current costs, not historical costs, a better measure of operating efficiencies is obtained. For example, assume that you are a new manager in an operation that includes a number of assets purchased recently at current prices, and your performance is compared with that of someone in a similar job elsewhere who is using similar assets that were purchased five years ago when the prices were substantially lower. You probably would contend that the five-year-old assets should be revalued because the other manager will show a lower depreciation charge and higher net income than you will.

2. Current cost is an *approximation of the service potential* of the asset. It is difficult if not impossible to determine the present discounted values of specific cash flows that will occur from the use of certain assets, but current cost frequently is a reasonable approximation of this value. As the current cost increases, the implication is that the enterprise has a holding gain (an increase from one period to another in the current cost of that item) because the aggregate value of the asset's service potential has increased.

3. Current cost provides for the *maintenance of physical capital.* Assume that an asset is purchased for $1, sold for $2, and replaced for $2. How much income should be reported and how much tax should be paid? Under traditional accounting proce-

dures, $1 of income would be earned (which is subject to tax and a claim for dividend distribution). If current cost is used, however, no income exists to be taxed and claims for dividend distribution would probably be fewer.

4. Current cost provides an *assessment of future cash flows.* Information on current cost margins may be useful for assessing future cash flows when the selling price of a product is closely related to its current cost. In addition, reporting holding gains (losses) may help in assessing future cash flows.

The major arguments against current cost adjustments are:

1. The use of *current cost is subjective* because it is difficult to determine the exact current cost of all items at any point in time. A good second-hand market for all types of assets does not exist. In most cases, the asset is not replaced with an identical asset; it is replaced with a better one, a faster one, an improved one, an altogether different one, or not replaced at all.

2. *The maintenance of physical capital is not the accountant's function.* It is generally conceded that it is management's function to ensure that capital is not impaired.

3. *Current cost is not always an approximation of the fair market value.* An asset's value is a function of the future cash flows generated by it. Current cost, however, does not necessarily measure an increase in the service potential of that asset.

One final comment: Many of the arguments above also apply to a **current cost/constant dollar system** (a full illustration is not provided in the chapter). Additional arguments for a current cost/constant dollar system are (1) it stabilizes the measuring unit and provides current, comparable data; and (2) it provides more information than either system alone. Holding gains and losses adjusted for inflation or deflation are reported, as well as the purchasing power gain or loss on net monetary items. Its potential disadvantages are (1) cost of preparation; and (2) information is not always better information because it may confuse readers or lead to information overload.

PROFESSION'S POSITION ON CHANGING PRICE INFORMATION

In September, 1982 the CICA, in response to a perceived need for information on the effects of changing prices on financial statements, recommended that large publicly held companies disclose certain price-level-adjusted financial information. The required price-level-adjusted information was provided on an experimental basis and consisted of restated information from the primary financial statements to reflect changes in (1) general price levels (constant dollar data) and (2) specific price levels (current cost data).

A CICA survey of financial statement users, preparers, and auditors revealed that both the number of users and the extent of use of the data were limited. Many respondents commented that the price-level-adjusted data did not appear to have been used by the institutional investment community, bankers, or investors in general. Therefore, partly as a result of nonuse and partly as a result of prevailing low inflation rates, the accounting profession in 1987 was persuaded to cease requiring the disclosure of supplementary information on the effects of changing prices. Companies are now simply encouraged to disclose price-level-adjusted information and are not discouraged from experimenting with different forms of disclosure.

Summary of Learning Objectives
For Appendix 25A

9. **Understand and account for changing prices.** The two most widely used approaches to show the effects of changing prices are (1) constant dollar accounting; and (2) current cost accounting. Constant dollar accounting restates financial statement items into dollars that have equal purchasing power. Current cost is the cost of replacing the identical asset owned. Companies now are encouraged to disclose price-level-adjusted information and are not discouraged from experimenting with different forms of disclosure. Some companies include a discussion of inflation in the Management's Discussion and Analysis Section of the annual report.

Note: All *asterisked* Exercises, Problems, or Cases relate to material contained in the appendix to the chapter.

EXERCISES

(Constant Dollar Index Use) Kaleden Co. has made the following purchases of property, plant, and equipment since its formation in 1991.   *E25-1

Year	Price-Level Index	Item	Cost
1991	100	Land	$140,000
1991	100	Building	200,000
1991	100	Machinery	80,000
1993	120	Office Equipment	25,000
1995	125	Machinery	30,000
1997	140	Office Equipment	8,000

The price-level index for 1998 is 150.

Instructions
Restate the above items in terms of 1998 dollars. Round to two decimals.

(Constant Dollar Income Statement) Jaffray, Inc. had the following income statement data for 1998.   *E25-2

Sales	$250,000
Cost of goods sold	168,000
Gross profit	82,000
Operating expenses	34,000
Net income	$ 48,000

The following price levels were observed during the year:

	Price Index
December 31, 1998	150
1998 average	125
December 31, 1997	100

Instructions
Determine Jaffray's constant dollar income before purchasing power gain or loss for 1998.

*E25-3 **(Constant Dollar: Purchasing Power Computation)** Presented below is comparative financial statement informa-tion for Tofino Corp. for the years 1998 and 1997.

	December 31, 1998	December 31, 1997
Cash	$ 78,000	$ 57,000
Inventory	40,000	25,000
Sales	230,000	200,000
Cost of goods sold	150,000	132,000
Operating expenses	44,000	30,000

The following price level indexes were observed during the year:

	Price Index
December 31, 1998	140
1998 average	125
December 31, 1997	100

Instructions

Determine Tofino's purchasing power gain or loss for 1998. Assume that all transactions involved cash.

*E25-4 **(Constant Dollar Financial Statements)** Sicamous Corp. in its first year of operations reported the following finan-cial information for the year ended December 31, 1998, before closing.

Cash	$ 90,500	Retained earnings	$ 67,500
Inventory	42,000	Sales	220,000
Land	90,000	Cost of goods sold	122,500
Share capital	150,000	Operating expenses	25,000

The following price level indices were observed during the year:

	Price Index
December 31, 1998	121
1998 average	110
January 1, 1998	100

Sicamous experienced a purchasing power loss of $15,650 during 1998. Land was purchased and common shares issued on January 1, 1998. No inventory was on hand at the beginning of the year.

Instructions

Prepare the following financial statements for Sicamous Corp.:

(a) Constant dollar income statement for the year ended December 31, 1998.

(b) Constant dollar balance sheet on December 31, 1998.

*E25-5 **(Current Cost Income Statement)** Albion Co. reported the following financial information for 1998, its first year of operations:

ALBION CO.
Income Statement
for the Year Ended December 31, 1998

Sales	$290,000
Cost of goods sold	196,000
Gross profit	94,000
Operating expenses	41,300
Net income	$ 52,700

ALBION CO.
Balance Sheet
December 31, 1998

Assets		Liabilities and Shareholders' Equity	
Cash	$ 40,000	Common shares	$270,000
Inventory	95,000	Retained earnings	40,000
Land	175,000	Total liabilities and shareholders'	
Total assets	$310,000	equity	$310,000

Current cost information for 1998 is as follows:

Sales	$290,000	Inventory	$107,000
Cost of goods sold	215,000	Land	190,000
Operating expenses	41,300	Common shares	270,000
Cash	40,000		

Instructions
(a) Determine Albion's holding gain or loss for 1998 on a current cost basis.
(b) Prepare Albion's current cost income statement for 1998.

(Determine Current Cost Income Components) Cawston Chemical, Inc. is experimenting with the use of current costs. In 1998, the company purchased inventory that had a cost of $50,000, of which $30,000 was sold by year end at a sales price of $50,000. It was estimated that the current cost of the inventory at the date of sale was $35,000 and the current cost of the ending inventory at December 31, 1998 was $26,000. Operating expenses were $10,000.   *E25-6

Instructions
(a) Determine current cost income from operations.
(b) Determine current cost net income.

(Constant Dollar Purchasing Power Computation) Assume that the Falkland Company has the following net monetary assets (monetary assets less monetary liabilities) at the beginning and the end of 1998.   *E25-7

	1/1/98	12/31/98
Net monetary assets	$300,000	$200,000

Transactions causing a change in net monetary assets during the period were incurrence and payments of accounts payable, collections of accounts receivable, and purchases and sales of merchandise during the period. All of these transactions occurred evenly throughout the year.
Assume the following price-level indices:

January 1, 1998	125
Average for the year	150
December 31, 1998	175

Instructions
(Round all computations to the nearest dollar.)
(a) What is the amount of purchasing power gain or loss from holding the January 1 balance of net monetary items throughout the year?
(b) What is the amount of purchasing power gain or loss from holding net monetary items?
(c) Explain why the company had a purchasing power gain or loss.

(Constant Dollar Financial Statements) The income statement for 1998 and the balance sheet on December 31, 1998 for Canim Co. follow.   *E25-8

CANIM CO.
Income Statement
for the Year Ended December 31, 1998

Sales	$345,000
Cost of goods sold	246,000
Gross profit	99,000
Operating expenses	30,400
Net income	$ 68,600

CANIM CO.
Balance Sheet
December 31, 1998

Assets		Liabilities and Shareholders' Equity	
Cash	$ 59,000	Notes payable	$ 40,400
Accounts receivable	47,100	Accounts payable	61,000
Inventory	75,600	Common shares	300,000
Land	316,500	Retained earnings	96,800
		Total liabilities and shareholders'	
Total assets	$498,200	equity	$498,200

Additional Information

1. The relevant price indexes are as follows:

January 1, 1993	105
June 30, 1995	112
August 31, 1997	120
December 31, 1998	168
Average for 1998	140

2. The company was founded on January 1, 1993. All common shares were issued at that time.

3. One-fifth of the land was acquired on August 31, 1997; the remainder of the land was acquired on January 1, 1993.

4. A purchasing power loss of $20,400 was computed for 1998.

Instructions

(a) Prepare a constant dollar income statement for Canim for the year ended December 31, 1998.

(b) Prepare a constant dollar balance sheet for Canim on December 31, 1998. (Hint: Retained earnings is a balancing item.)

*E25-9 **(Current Cost Financial Statements)** The Lasqueti Co. income statement for 1998 and balance sheet dated December 31, 1998 (its first year of operations) are presented below.

LASQUETI CO.
Income Statement
For the Year Ended December 31, 1998

Sales	$795,000
Cost of goods sold	550,000
Gross profit	245,000
Operating expenses	57,000
Net income	$188,000

LASQUETI CO.
Balance Sheet
December 31, 1998

Assets		Liabilities and Shareholders' Equity	
Cash	$ 74,000	Notes payable	$ 42,000
Accounts receivable	91,000	Accounts payable	63,000
Inventory	187,000	Common shares	559,000
Land	450,000	Retained earnings	188,000
Goodwill	50,000	Total liabilities and shareholders'	
Total assets	$852,000	equity	$852,000

The current cost of the following items on December 31, 1998 is as follows:

Inventory	$200,000
Land	495,000
Goodwill	20,000
Cost of goods sold	585,000

Instructions

(a) Prepare a schedule to show the total holding gain (loss) for Lasqueti Co. for 1998.

(b) Prepare a current cost income statement for Lasqueti Co. for the year ended December 31, 1998.

(c) Prepare a current cost balance sheet for Lasqueti Co. on December 31, 1998.

(Current Cost Financial Statements) Gabriola Enterprises is considering the adoption of a current cost system. ***E25-10** Presented below is Gabriola's balance sheet based on historical cost at the end of its first year of operations.

GABRIOLA ENTERPRISES
Balance Sheet
December 31, 1998

Assets		Liabilities and Shareholders' Equity	
Cash	$25,000	Accounts payable	$ 9,000
Inventory	42,000	Common shares	50,000
Land	16,000	Retained earnings	24,000
	$83,000		$83,000

The following additional information is presented:

1. Cost of goods sold on an historical cost basis is $54,000; on a current cost basis, $58,000.

2. No dividends were paid in the first year of operations.

3. Ending inventory on a current cost basis is $46,000; land on a current cost basis is $22,000 at the end of the year.

4. Operating expenses for the first year were $25,000.

Instructions

(a) Prepare an income statement for the current year on (1) an historical cost basis; and (2) a current cost basis.

(b) Prepare a balance sheet for the current year on a current cost basis.

(c) Assume that the general price level at the beginning of the year was 100, the average for the year was 160, and the ending was 200. Also assume that revenues were earned and costs were incurred uniformly during the year. The land was purchased and the common shares were issued at the beginning of the year.

Determine the following:

1. Income before purchasing power gain or loss on a constant dollar income statement for 1998.

2. Amount reported for land on a constant dollar balance sheet at December 31, 1998.

3. Amount reported for cash on a constant dollar balance sheet at December 31, 1998.

*E25-11 (Current Value Accounting) During the first year of operations ended September 30, 1998 Atlantic Enterprises purchased 10,000 units of inventory for $6.00 each. Inventory purchases and sales were made uniformly throughout the year. During the year, 7,000 units of inventory were sold for $9.00 each. The replacement cost of the inventory is $6.40 per unit. The replacement cost on the date of sale is the same as at year end. The general price indices for the year were as follows:

Beginning of year	110
Average for the year	120
End of year	130

Instructions

(a) Using current value accounting, calculate the cost of goods sold for the year ending September 30, 1998.

(b) Using current value accounting, calculate the ending inventory as at September 30, 1998.

(c) Using constant dollar accounting, calculate the gross profit on sales for the year ending September 30, 1998, using average-year dollars as the unit of measure.

(d) Using constant dollar accounting, calculate the ending inventory as at September 30, 1998, using end-of-year dollars as the unit of measure.

(CGA adapted)

CASES

C25-1 Malahat Corporation is in the process of preparing its annual financial statements for the fiscal year ended April 30, 1998. The company manufactures plastic, glass, and paper containers for sale to food and drink manufacturers and distributors.

Malahat Corporation maintains separate control accounts for its raw materials, work-in-process, and finished goods inventories for each of the three types of containers. The inventories are valued at the lower of cost and market.

The company's property, plant, and equipment are classified in the following major categories: land, office buildings, furniture and fixtures, manufacturing facilities, manufacturing equipment, leasehold improvements. All fixed assets are carried at cost. The depreciation methods employed depend on the type of asset (its classification) and when it was acquired.

Malahat Corporation plans to present the inventory and fixed asset amounts in its April 30, 1998 balance sheet as shown below:

Inventories	$4,814,200
Property, plant, and equipment (net of depreciation)	$6,310,000

Instructions

What information regarding inventories and property, plant, and equipment must be disclosed by Malahat Corporation in the audited financial statements issued to shareholders, either in the body or the notes, for the 1997–98 fiscal year?

(CMA adapted)

C25-2 Rolla Inc. produces electronic components for sale to manufacturers of radios, television sets, and phonographic systems. In connection with her examination of Rolla's financial statements for the year ended December 31, 1998 Ann Neufeld, CA, completed field work two weeks ago. Ms. Neufeld is now evaluating the significance of the following items prior to preparing her auditor's report. Except as noted, none of these items has been disclosed in the financial statements or notes.

Item 1

A 10-year loan agreement, which the company entered into three years ago, provides that dividend payments may not exceed net income earned after taxes subsequent to the date of the agreement. The balance of retained earnings at the date of the loan agreement was $420,000. From that date through December 31, 1998 net income after taxes totalled $570,000 and cash dividends totalled $320,000. On the basis of these data, the staff auditor assigned to this review concluded that there was no retained earnings restriction at December 31, 1998.

Item 2

Recently, Rolla interrupted its policy of paying cash dividends quarterly to its shareholders. Dividends were paid regularly through 1997, discontinued for all of 1998 to finance equipment for the company's new plant, and resumed in the first quarter of 1999. In the annual report, dividend policy is to be discussed in the president's letter to shareholders.

Item 3
A major electronics firm has introduced a line of products that will compete directly with Rolla's primary line, now being produced in the specially designed new plant. Because of manufacturing innovations, the competitor's line will be of comparable quality but priced 50% below Rolla's line. The competitor announced its new line during the week following completion of field work. Ms. Neufeld read the announcement in the newspaper and discussed the situation by telephone with Rolla executives. Rolla will meet the lower prices, which are high enough to cover variable manufacturing and selling expenses, but will permit recovery of only a portion of fixed costs.

Item 4
The company's new manufacturing plant building, which cost $2,400,000 and has an estimated life of 25 years, is leased from Ancient National Bank at an annual rental of $600,000. The company is obligated to pay property taxes, insurance, and maintenance. At the conclusion of its 10-year noncancellable lease, the company has the option of purchasing the property for $1. In Rolla's income statement, the rental payment is reported on a separate line.

Instructions
For each of the items above, discuss any additional disclosures in the financial statements and footnotes that the auditor should recommend to her client. (The cumulative effect of the four items should not be considered.)

You are completing an examination of the financial statements of Fairmont Manufacturing Corporation for the year ended February 28, 1998. Fairmont's financial statements have not been examined previously. The controller of Fairmont has given you the following draft of proposed footnotes to the financial statements. **C25-3**

FAIRMONT MANUFACTURING CORPORATION
Notes to Financial Statements
Year Ended February 28, 1998

Note 1. With the approval of the Minister of Finance, the company changed its method of accounting for inventories from the first-in method to the average-cost method on March 1, 1997. In the opinion of the company, the effects of this change on the pricing of inventories and cost of goods manufactured were not material in the current year but are expected to be material in future years.

Note 2. The investment property was recorded at cost until December, 1997 when it was written up to its appraisal value. The company plans to sell the property in 1998 and an independent real estate agent in the area has indicated that the appraisal price can be realized. Pending completion of the sale the amount of the expected gain on the sale has been recorded in an unearned income account.

Note 3. The stock dividend described in our May 24, 1997 letter to shareholders has been recorded as a 110 for 100 stock split-up. Accordingly, there were no changes in the shareholders' equity account balances from this transaction.

Instructions
For each of the notes above, discuss the note's adequacy and needed revisions, if any, of the financial statements or the note.

You have completed your audit of Kemano Limited and its consolidated subsidiaries for the year ended December 31, 1998 and are satisfied with the results of your examination. You have examined the financial statements of Kemano Limited for the past three years. The corporation is now preparing its annual report to shareholders. The report will include the consolidated financial statements of Kemano Limited and its subsidiaries and your auditor's report. During your audit the following matters came to your attention: **C25-4**

1. A vice-president who is also a shareholder resigned on December 31, 1998 after an argument with the president. The vice-president is soliciting proxies from shareholders and expects to obtain sufficient proxies to gain control of the board of directors so that a new president will be appointed. The president plans to have a note to the financial statements prepared that will include information of the pending proxy fight, management's accomplishments over the years, and an appeal by management for the support of shareholders.

2. The corporation decides in 1998 to adopt the straight-line method of depreciation for plant equipment. The straight-line method will be used for new acquisitions as well as for previously acquired plant equipment for which depreciation had been provided on an accelerated basis.

3. Revenue Canada is currently examining the corporation's 1995 federal income tax return and is questioning the amount of a deduction claimed by the corporation's domestic subsidiary for a loss sustained in 1995. The examination is still in process, and any additional tax liability is indeterminable at this time. The corporation's tax counsel believes that there will be no substantial additional tax liability.

Instructions

(a) Prepare the notes, if any, that you would suggest for the preceeding items.

(b) State your reasons for not making disclosure by note for each of the listed items for which you do not prepare a note. (AICPA adapted)

C25-5 Presented below are three independent situations.

Situation I

A company offers a one-year warranty for the product that it manufactures. A history of warranty claims has been compiled and the probable amount of claims related to sales for a given period can be determined.

Situation II

Subsequent to the date of a set of financial statements, but prior to the issuance of the financial statements, a company enters into a contract that will probably result in a significant loss to the company. The amount of the loss can be reasonably estimated.

Situation III

A company has adopted a policy of recording self-insurance for any possible losses resulting from injury to others by the company's vehicles. The premium for an insurance policy for the same risk from an independent insurance company would have an annual cost of $4,000. During the period covered by the financial statements, there were no accidents involving the company's vehicles that resulted in injury to others.

Instructions

Discuss the accrual or type of disclosure necessary (if any) and the reason(s) why such disclosure is appropriate for each of the three independent sets of information above. (AICPA adapted)

C25-6 Presented below are excerpts from the financial statements of NQL Drilling Tools Inc.

Note 12. Segmented Information

During the year ended August 31, 1995 the company operated in Canada and the United States in two industry segments. Information by geographic segment for the year ended August 31, 1995 is as follows:

	Canada	United States	Corporate	Consolidated
Revenues	$15,835,709	$ 8,648,385	$ 8,471	$24,492,565
Operating profit	$ 6,559,006	$ 4,607,114	$ 8,471	$11,174,591
Amortization	$ 1,560,046	$ 1,188,861	$ 545,440	$ 3,294,347
Identifiable assets	$13,840,454	$10,317,175	$4,622,295	$28,779,924

Information by industry segments for the year ended August 31, 1995 is as follows:

	Downhole Drilling Motors	Vehicle Maintenance	Corporate	Consolidated
Revenues	$17,407,904	$7,076,190	$ 8,471	$24,492,565
Operating profit	$10,059,267	$1,106,853	$ 8,471	$11,174,591
Amortization	$ 2,344,260	$ 404,647	$ 545,440	$ 3,294,347
Identifiable assets	$23,514,336	$ 643,293	$4,622,295	$28,779,924

Instructions

(a) What criteria are used to determine whether a business segment for a product or service must be disclosed?

(b) What major items for products or services must be disclosed in reporting segments of a business?

(c) Comment on when segments of a business for a product or service do not have to be disclosed.

C25-7 In 1979 the Accounting Standards Committee issued guidelines for companies grappling with the problem of dividing up their businesses into industry segments for their annual reports. An industry segment may be defined as a part of an enterprise engaged in providing a product or service or a group of related products or services primarily to unaffiliated customers for a profit.

Although conceding that the process is a "subjective talk" that "to a considerable extent, depends on the judgment of management," the Accounting Standards Committee said companies should consider the nature of the products, the nature of their production, and their markets and marketing methods to determine whether products and services should be grouped together or in separate industry segments.

Instructions
(a) What does financial reporting for segments of a business enterprise involve?
(b) Identify the reasons for requiring financial data to be reported by segments.
(c) Identify the possible disadvantages of requiring financial data to be reported by segments.
(d) Identify the accounting difficulties inherent in segment reporting.

In the annual report of Bombardier Inc., the following was reported:

C25-8

Social Responsibility
"The Corporation fulfils its social and humanitarian responsibilities primarily through the J. Armand Bombardier Foundation, a nonprofit organization which receives funding equivalent to 3% of the Corporation's income before income taxes. Created by the Bombardier family to honour the founder's wishes, it continues the tradition of support to charitable causes that he established."

Instructions
(a) Do you believe that Bombardier should disclose information of this nature?
(b) How might an enterprise measure its socially responsible activities?

Kitimat Corporation, a publicly traded company, is preparing the interim financial data that it will issue to its shareholders and the Toronto Stock Exchange at the end of the first quarter of the 1997–98 fiscal year. Kitimat's financial accounting department has compiled the following summarized revenue and expense data for the first quarter of the year.

C25-9

Sales	$60,000,000
Cost of goods sold	36,000,000
Variable selling expenses	2,000,000
Fixed selling expenses	3,000,000

Included in the fixed selling expenses was a single lump sum payment of $2,000,000 for television advertisements for the entire year.

Instructions
(a) Kitimat Corporation must issue its quarterly financial statements in accordance with generally accepted accounting principles regarding interim financial reporting.
   1. Explain whether Kitimat should report its operating results for the quarter as if the quarter were a separate reporting period in and of itself or as if the quarter were an integral part of the annual reporting period.
   2. State how the sales, cost of goods sold, and fixed selling expenses would be reflected in Kitimat Corporation's quarterly report prepared for the first quarter of the 1997–98 fiscal year. Briefly justify your presentation.
(b) What financial information, as a minimum, must Kitimat Corporation disclose to its shareholders in its quarterly reports?
(CMA adapted)

The following statements have been excerpted from paragraphs .13 and .14 of *CICA Handbook* Section 1750, "Interim Financial Reporting to Shareholders."

C25-10

Interim financial reports should present information with respect to the results of operations of a company for a specified period rather than a proration of expected results for the annual period. Consistent with this position, the interim financial reports have to be prepared on the same basis as annual statements.
   The preparation of financial data should be based on accounting principles and practices consistent with those used in the preparation of annual financial statements.

Instructions
Following are six independent cases on how accounting facts might be reported on an individual company's interim financial reports. For each of these cases, state whether the method proposed to be used for interim reporting would be acceptable under generally accepted accounting principles applicable to interim financial data. Support each answer with a brief explanation.

1. R. King Company takes a physical inventory at year end for annual financial statement purposes. Inventory and cost of sales reported in the interim quarterly statements are based on estimated gross profit rates because a physical inventory would result in a cessation of operations. King Company does have reliable perpetual inventory records.

2. Florence Phillips Company is planning to report one-fourth of its pension expense each quarter.

3. Nancy Rice Company wrote inventory down to reflect the lower of cost and market in the first quarter. At year end the market exceeds the original acquisition cost of this inventory. Consequently, management plans to write the inventory back up to its original cost as a year-end adjustment.

4. W. DeWitt Company realized a large gain on the sale of investments at the beginning of the second quarter. The company wants to report one-third of the gain in each of the remaining quarters.

5. Alice Duckworth Company has estimated its annual audit fee. They plan to prorate this expense equally over all four quarters.

6. Lori Mitchell Company was reasonably certain they would have an employee strike in the third quarter. As a result, they shipped heavily during the second quarter but plan to defer the recognition of the sales in excess of the normal sales volume. The deferred sales would be recognized as sales in the third quarter, when the strike would likely be in progress. Mitchell Company management thought this was more nearly representative of normal second- and third-quarter operations.

C25-11 Recently, an accountant and a financial analyst were discussing the problem of corporate forecasts. The accountant noted that Section 4250 of the *CICA Handbook* established standards for reporting "future oriented financial information." Despite these standards, there is some concern among accountants over possible liability if forecasted results do not materialize.

The analyst responded by saying that "no one expects accountants to be able to forecast accurately" and that "the courts would certainly not hold them liable." In fact, a "safe harbour" rule would protect accountants, providing that the forecasts were made on a reasonable basis and in good faith.

Instructions
(a) What are the arguments for preparing profit forecasts?
(b) What is the purpose of a "safe harbour" rule?
(c) Why are corporations concerned about presenting profit forecasts?

C25-12 Baldonnel Manufacturing Company, a British Columbia corporation listed on the Vancouver Stock Exchange, budgeted activities for 1998 as follows:

	Amount	Units
Net sales	$9,000,000	1,000,000
Cost of goods sold	5,400,000	
Gross margin	$3,600,000	
Selling, general, and administrative expenses	2,100,000	
Operating income	$1,500,000	
Nonoperating revenues and expenses	-0-	
Income before income taxes	$1,500,000	
Estimated income taxes (current and deferred)	600,000	
Net income	$ 900,000	
Earnings per common share	$9.00	

Baldonnel has operated profitably for many years and has experienced a seasonal pattern of sales volume and production similar to those following forecasted for 1998. Sales volume is expected to follow a quarterly pattern of 10%, 20%, 35%, and 35% per quarter, respectively, because of seasonality of the industry. Also, owing to production and storage capacity limitations, it is expected that production will follow a pattern of 20%, 25%, 30%, and 25% per quarter, respectively.

At the conclusion of the first quarter of 1998, the controller of Baldonnel prepared and issued the following interim report for public release.

	Amount	Units
Net sales	$ 900,000	100,000
Cost of goods sold	540,000	100,000
Gross margin	$ 360,000	
Selling, general, and administrative		
expenses	412,500	
Operating loss	$ (52,500)	
Loss from warehouse fire	(262,500)	
Loss before income taxes	$(315,000)	
Estimated income taxes	-0-	
Net loss	$(315,000)	
Loss per common share		$(3.15)

The following additional information is available for the first quarter just completed but was not included in the public information released.

1. Assume that the warehouse fire loss met the conditions of an extraordinary loss. The warehouse had an undepreciated cost of $480,000; $217,500 was recovered from insurance on the warehouse. No other gains or losses are anticipated this year from similar events or transactions, and Baldonnel had no similar losses in preceding years; thus, the full loss will be deductible as an ordinary loss for income tax purposes.

2. The company uses a standard cost system in which standards are set at currently attainable levels on an annual basis. At the end of the first quarter, there was underapplied fixed factory overhead (volume variance) of $75,000 that was treated as an asset at the end of the quarter. Production during the quarter was 200,000 units, of which 100,000 were sold.

3. The selling, general, and administrative expenses were budgeted on a basis of $1,350,000 fixed expenses for the year plus $0.75 variable expenses per unit of sales.

4. The effective income tax rate is expected to average 40% of earnings before income taxes during 1998. There are no permanent differences between pretax accounting earnings and taxable income.

5. Earnings per share were computed on the basis of 100,000 common shares outstanding. Baldonnel has only one class of shares issued, no long-term debt outstanding, and no stock option plan.

Instructions
(a) Without reference to the specific situation described above, what are the standards of disclosure for interim financial data (published interim financial reports) for publicly traded companies? Explain.
(b) Identify the weaknesses in form and content of Baldonnel's interim report without reference to the additional information.
(c) For each of the five items of additional information, indicate the preferable treatment for each item for interim reporting purposes and explain why that treatment is preferable. (AICPA adapted)

Oliver Enterprises acquired a large tract of land in a small town approximately 10 km from Fleet City. The company **C25-13** executed a firm contract on November 15, 1997 for the construction of a 1 km race track, together with related facilities. The track and facilities were completed December 15, 1998. On December 31, 1998 a 15% instalment note of $210,000 was issued, along with other consideration in settlement of the construction contract. Instalments of $70,000 fall due on December 31 of each of the next three years. The company planned to pay the notes from cash received from operations and from sales of additional common shares.

The company adopted the double-declining balance method of computing depreciation. No depreciation was taken in 1998 because all racing equipment was received in December after the completion of the track and facilities.

The land on which the racing circuit was constructed was acquired at various dates for a total of $81,000, and its approximate market value on December 31, 1998 was $100,000.

Through the sale of tickets to spectators, parking fees, concession income, and income from betting, company officials anticipated that approximately $275,000 would be taken in during a typical year's racing season. Cash expenses for a racing season were estimated at $173,000.

You have made an examination of the financial condition of Oliver Enterprises as of December 31, 1998. The balance sheet as of that date and statement of operations follow.

OLIVER ENTERPRISES
Balance Sheet
December 31, 1998

Assets

Cash		$ 11,000
Accounts receivable		$ 12,000
Prepaid expenses		9,000
Property (at cost)		
Land	81,000	
Grading and track improvements	86,000	
Grandstand	200,000	
Buildings	76,000	
Racing equipment	56,000	499,000
Organization costs		1,000
Total assets		$532,000

Liabilities and Shareholders' Equity

Accounts payable	$ 32,000
Instalment note payable—15%	210,000
Shareholders' equity	
Common shares, no par value, authorized	
200,000, issued and outstanding 121,500 shares	121,500
Contributed surplus	188,500
Retained earnings (deficit)	(20,000)
Total liabilities and shareholders' equity	$532,000

OLIVER ENTERPRISES
Statement of Income
for the Period from Inception, December 1, 1995
to December 31, 1998

Income	
Profit on sales of land	$ 10,000
Other	2,000
	12,000
General and administrative expenses	32,000
Net loss for the period	$ 20,000

On January 15, 1999 legislation that declared betting to be illegal was enacted by the provincial government. A discussion with management on January 17 about the effect of the legislation revealed that revenue would be reduced to approximately $80,000 and cash expenses would be reduced to one-third the original estimate.

Instructions
(Disregard federal income tax implications.)
(a) Prepare the explanatory notes to accompany the balance sheet.
(b) What opinion do you believe the auditor should render? Discuss.   (AICPA adapted)

*C25-14   A business entity's financial statements could be prepared by using historical cost or current value as a basis. In addition, the basis could be stated in terms of unadjusted dollars or dollars restated for changes in purchasing power. The various permutations of these two separate and distinct areas are shown in the following matrix.

	Unadjusted Dollars	Dollars Restated for Changes in Purchasing Power
Historical cost	1	2
Current value	3	4

Block 1 of the matrix represents the traditional method of accounting for transactions in accounting today, wherein the absolute (unadjusted) amount of dollars given up or received is recorded for the asset or liability obtained (*relationship between resources*). Amounts recorded in the method described in block 1 reflect the original cost of the asset or liability and do not give effect to any change in value of the unit of measure (*standard of comparison*). This method assumes the validity of the accounting concepts of going concern and stable monetary unit. Any gain or loss (including holding and purchasing power gains or losses) resulting from the sale or satisfaction of amounts recorded under this method is deferred in its entirety until sale or satisfaction.

Instructions

For each of the remaining matrix blocks (2, 3, and 4), respond to the following questions. *Limit your discussion to nonmonetary assets only*.

(a) How will this method of recording assets affect the relationship between resources and the standard of comparison?

(b) What is the theoretical justification for using each method?

(c) How will each method of asset valuation affect the recognition of gain or loss during the life of the asset and ultimately from the sale or abandonment of the asset? Your response should include a discussion of the timing and magnitude of the gain or loss and conceptual reasons for any difference from the gain or loss computed using the traditional method. (AICPA adapted)

*C25-15 Lumby Corp., a wholesaler with large investments in plant and equipment, began operations in 1953. The company's history has been one of expansion in sales, production, and physical facilities. Recently, some concern has been expressed that the conventional financial statements do not provide sufficient information for decisions by investors. After consideration of proposals for various types of supplementary financial statements to be included in the 1998 annual report, management has decided to present a balance sheet as of December 31, 1998 and a statement of income and retained earnings for 1998, both restated for changes in the general price level.

Instructions

(a) On what basis can it be contended that Lumby's conventional statements should be restated for changes in the general price level?

(b) Distinguish between financial statements restated for general price-level changes and current value financial statements.

(c) Distinguish between monetary and nonmonetary assets and liabilities as the terms are used in constant dollar accounting. Give examples of each.

(d) Outline the procedures Lumby should follow in preparing the proposed supplementary statements.

(e) Indicate the major similarities and differences between the proposed supplementary statements and the corresponding conventional statements.

(f) Assuming that in the future Lumby will want to present comparative supplementary statements, can the 1998 supplementary statements be presented in 1998 without adjustment? Explain. (AICPA adapted)

*C25-16 The general purchasing power of the dollar has declined considerably because of inflation in recent years. To account for this changing value of the dollar, many accountants suggest that financial statements be adjusted for general price-level changes. Three independent, unrelated statements regarding general price-level-adjusted financial statements follow. Each statement contains some fallacious reasoning.

Statement I

The accounting profession has not seriously considered price-level-adjusted financial statements before because the rate of inflation usually has been so small from year to year that the adjustments would have been immaterial in amount. Price-level-adjusted financial statements represent a departure from the historical cost basis of accounting. Financial statements should be prepared on the basis of facts, not estimates.

Statement II

When adjusting financial data for general price-level changes, a distinction must be made between monetary and nonmonetary assets and liabilities that, under the historical cost basis of accounting, have been identified as "current" and "noncurrent." When using the historical cost basis of accounting, no purchasing power gain or loss is recognized in the accounting process; but when financial statements are adjusted for general price-level changes, a purchasing power gain or loss will be recognized on monetary and nonmonetary items.

Statement III

If financial statements were adjusted for general price-level changes, depreciation charges in the income statement would permit the recovery of dollars of current purchasing power and, thereby, equal the cost of new assets to replace the old ones. General price-level adjusted data would yield statement-of-financial-position amounts closely approximating values. Furthermore, management can make better decisions if constant dollar financial statements are published.

Instructions

Evaluate each of the independent statements and identify the areas of fallacious reasoning in each. Explain why the reasoning is incorrect. Complete your discussion of each statement before proceeding to the next statement.

(AICPA adapted)

C25-17 There are deficiencies in the use of consolidated financial statements due to details lost in the consolidation process. Section 1700 of the *CICA Handbook* requires large organizations to report additional information.

Instructions

(a) Explain what the main segments are that must be reported by certain large organizations under Section 1700.

(b) Assuming that a corporation meets the conditions requiring it to report under Section 1700, what are the conditions under which the specific segment information should be reported? (CGA adapted)

USING YOUR JUDGEMENT

FINANCIAL REPORTING PROBLEM

Refer to the financial statements and other documents of Moore Corporation Limited in Appendix 5A and answer the following questions.

1. What were the major operations Moore selected to report separately in its Notes to Financial Statements? What were the items reported?

2. Why did Moore report sales to foreign markets?

ETHICS CASE

Al Berta, the controller of Last Mountain Furniture Company, and Cal Gary, his assistant, are preparing the year-end financial statements. Cal wants to disclose the cost of available-for-sale securities as a parenthetical note on the balance sheet. Al—concerned about the decline in market value compared to the cost of these securities—does not want to call attention to this decline. He wants to "bury" the cost information in a note to the financial statements.

Instructions

(a) What ethical issue is posed by the choice between these two forms of disclosure?

(b) Are the interests of different stakeholders in conflict in the choice between the two methods of accounting reports?

(c) Which method would you choose, and why?

Appendix

ACCOUNTING AND THE TIME VALUE OF MONEY

APPLICATIONS OF TIME VALUE CONCEPTS

NATURE OF INTEREST

FUNDAMENTAL VARIABLES

SINGLE SUM PROBLEMS

ANNUITIES

COMPLEX SITUATIONS

INTERPOLATION OF TABLES TO DERIVE INTEREST RATES

FUNDAMENTAL CONCEPTS

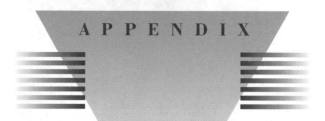

A P P E N D I X

Accounting and the
Time Value of Money

Learning Objectives

After studying this appendix, you should be able to:

1. Identify accounting topics where time value of money is relevant.

2. Distinguish between simple and compound interest.

3. Know how to use appropriate compound interest tables.

4. Identify variables fundamental to solving interest problems.

5. Solve future and present value of single sum problems.

6. Solve future amount of ordinary and annuity due problems.

7. Solve present value of ordinary and annuity due problems.

A prime purpose of financial accounting is to provide information that is useful in making business and economic decisions. Certainly the relationship between time and money is central to economic decision making. It would seem reasonable, then, to expect that any accounting system that has decision usefulness as a primary goal should have a rational basis for reflecting the time value of money in the values it assigns to assets and liabilities—that is, should provide monetary measurements that are interpretable in present value terms.[1]

Would you like to be a millionaire? If you are 20 years old now, can save $100 every month, and can invest those savings to earn an after-tax rate of return of 1% per month (more than 12% per year), you could be a millionaire before you are 59 years old. Alternatively, if you could invest $10,000 today at that same interest rate, you would have over a million dollars by age 59. Such is the power of *interest*, especially when it is energized with a generous dosage of *time*.[2]

Business enterprises both invest and borrow large sums of money. The common characteristic in these two types of transactions is the **time value of the money** (i.e., the interest factor involved). The timing of the returns on the investment has an important

---

[1] J. Alex Milburn, *Incorporating the Time Value of Money Within Financial Accounting* (Toronto: Canadian Institute of Chartered Accountants, 1988), p. 1. This is an excellent study regarding financial accounting and present value measurements. Its objective is to "develop proposals for reflecting the time value of money more fully within the existing financial accounting framework so as to enable a substantive improvement in the usefulness and credibility of financial statements" (p. 1). While we, the authors, accept the basic premise of this study, it is not our intention to examine the model and suggested changes to current financial accounting that are presented. The purpose of this appendix is more basic—to examine the time value of money and show how it can be incorporated in making measurements.

[2] As another example of how interest can multiply dollars quickly, Sidney Homer (author of *A History of Interest Rates*) indicated, "$1,000 invested at a mere 8% for 400 years would grow to $23 quadrillion—$5 million for every human on earth." But, "the first 100 years are the hardest." (*Forbes*, July 14, 1986).

effect on the worth of the investment (asset), and the timing of debt repayments has an effect on the value of the commitment (liability). Business people have become acutely aware of this timing factor and invest and borrow only after carefully analysing the relative values of the cash outflows and inflows.

Accountants are expected to make and understand the implications of value measurements. To do so, they must understand and be able to measure the *present value* of future cash inflows and outflows. This measurement requires an understanding of compound interest, annuities, and present value concepts. Therefore, the basic objectives of this appendix are to discuss and illustrate the essentials of these concepts, and to provide some accounting- and business-related examples in which they are applied.

APPLICATIONS OF TIME VALUE CONCEPTS

Compound interest, annuities, and application of present value concepts are relevant to making measurements and disclosures when accounting for various financial statement elements. The following are some examples examined in this book and the chapters in which they appear:

OBJECTIVE 1
Identify accounting topics where time value of money is relevant.

1. **Notes.** Valuing receivables and payables that carry no stated interest rate or a different than market interest rate (Chapters 7 and 15).

2. **Leases.** Valuing assets and obligations to be capitalized under long-term leases, and measuring the amount of the lease payments and annual leasehold amortization (Chapter 21).

3. **Amortization of Premiums and Discounts.** Measuring amortization of premium or discount on both bond investments and bonds payable (Chapters 10 and 15).

4. **Pensions and Other Post-Retirement Benefits.** Measuring service cost components of employers' post-retirement benefits expense and benefit obligations (Chapter 20).

5. **Capital Assets.** Determining the value of assets acquired under deferred-payment contracts (Chapter 11).

6. **Sinking Funds.** Determining the contributions necessary to accumulate a fund for debt retirement (Chapter 15).

7. **Business Combinations.** Determining the value of receivables, payables, liabilities, accruals, and commitments acquired or assumed in a "purchase" (Chapter 10).

8. **Depreciation.** Measuring depreciation charges under the sinking fund and the annuity methods (Chapter 12).

9. **Instalment Contracts.** Measuring periodic payments on long-term sales or purchase contracts (Chapters 6 and 15).

In addition to their accounting and business applications, compound interest, annuity, and present value concepts are applicable to personal finance and investment decisions. In purchasing a home, planning for retirement, and evaluating alternative investments, you must understand time value of money concepts.

NATURE OF INTEREST

Interest *is payment for the use of money*. It is the excess cash received or paid over and above the amount lent or borrowed (**principal**). For example, if the Toronto Dominion

Bank lends you $1,000 with the understanding that you will repay $1,150, the $150 excess over $1,000 represents interest expense to you and interest revenue to the bank.

The amount of interest to be paid is generally stated as a rate over a specific period of time. For example, if you use the $1,000 for one year before repaying $1,150, the rate of interest is 15% per year ($150/$1,000). The custom of expressing interest as a rate is an established business practice.[3]

The interest rate is commonly expressed as it is applied to a one-year time period. Interest of 12% represents a rate of 12% per year, unless otherwise stipulated. The statement that a corporation will pay bond interest of 12%, payable semiannually, means a rate of 6% every six months, not 12% every six months.

How is the *rate* of interest determined? One of the most important factors is the level of **credit risk** (risk of nonpayment). Other factors being equal, the higher the credit risk, the higher the interest rate. Every borrower's risk is evaluated by the lender. A low-risk borrower like Canadian Pacific Ltd. may obtain a loan at or slightly below the going market "prime" rate of interest. You or the neighbourhood delicatessen, however, will probably be charged several percentage points above the prime rate.

Another important factor is **inflation** (change in the general purchasing power of the dollar). Lenders want to protect the purchasing power of the future cash flows to be received (interest payments and return of the principal). If inflation is expected to be significant in the future, lenders will require a higher number of dollars (i.e., a higher interest rate) in order to offset their anticipation that the purchasing power of these dollars will be reduced.

In addition to receiving compensation for risk and expected inflation, lenders also desire a **pure** or **real return** for letting someone else use their money. This real return reflects the amount the lender would charge if there were no possibility of default or expectation of inflation.

The *amount* of interest related to any financing transaction is a function of three variables:

1. **Principal**—the amount borrowed or invested.
2. **Interest Rate**—a percentage of the outstanding principal.
3. **Time**—the number of years or portion of a year that the principal is outstanding.

SIMPLE INTEREST

OBJECTIVE 2
Distinguish between simple and compound interest.

Simple interest *is computed on the amount of the principal only*. It is the return on (or growth of) the principal for one time period. Simple interest[4] is commonly expressed as:

$$\text{Interest} = p \times i \times n$$

where

$$p = \text{principal}$$
$$i = \text{rate of interest for a single period}$$
$$n = \text{number of periods}$$

To illustrate, if you borrowed $1,000 for a three-year period, with a simple interest rate of 15% per year, the total interest to be paid would be $450, computed as follows:

---

[3] Federal and provincial legislation requires the disclosure of the effective interest rate on an *annual basis* in contracts. That is, instead of, or in addition to, stating the rate as "1% per month," it must be stated as "12% per year" if it is simple interest or "12.68% per year" if it is compounded monthly.

[4] Simple interest is also expressed as i (interest) = P(principal) $\times R$(rate) $\times T$(time).

$$\text{Interest} = (p)(i)(n)$$
$$= (\$1,000)(.15)(3)$$
$$= \$450$$

COMPOUND INTEREST

John Maynard Keynes, the legendary English economist, supposedly called it magic. Mayer Rothschild, the founder of the famous European banking firm, is said to have proclaimed it the eighth wonder of the world. Today people continue to extol its wonder and its power.[5] The object of their affection is compound interest.

Compound interest *is computed on the principal and any interest earned that has not been paid*. To illustrate the difference between simple interest and compound interest, assume that you deposit $1,000 in the Last Canadian Bank, where it earns simple interest of 9% per year. Assume that you deposit another $1,000 in the First Canadian Bank, where it earns annually compounded interest of 9%. Finally, assume that in both cases you do not withdraw any interest until three years from the date of deposit. The calculation of interest to be received is shown in Exhibit A-1.

EXHIBIT A-1

SIMPLE VS. COMPOUND INTEREST

	Last Canadian Bank			First Canadian Bank		
	Simple Interest Calculation	Simple Interest	Accumulated Year-End Balance	**Compound** Interest Calculation	Compound Interest	Accumulated Year-End Balance
Year 1	$1,000.00 × 9%	$ 90.00	$1,090.00	$1,000.00 × 9%	$ 90.00	$1,090.00
Year 2	1,000.00 × 9%	90.00	1,180.00	1,090.00 × 9%	98.10	1,188.10
Year 3	1,000.00 × 9%	90.00	1,270.00	1,188.10 × 9%	106.93	1,295.03
		$270.00	—— $25.03 Difference ——		$295.03	

Note that simple interest uses the initial principal of $1,000 to compute the interest in all three years, while compound interest uses the accumulated balance (principal plus interest to date) at each year end to compute interest in the succeeding year. Obviously, if you had a choice between investing at simple interest or at compound interest, you would choose compound interest, all other things—especially risk—being equal. In the example, compounding provides $25.03 of additional interest income.

Compound interest is generally applied in business situations. Financial managers view and evaluate their investment opportunities in terms of a series of periodic returns, each of which can be reinvested to yield additional returns. Simple interest is generally applicable only to short-term investments and debts that are due within one year.

---

[5] Here is an illustration of the power of time and compounding interest on money. In 1626, Peter Minuit bought Manhattan Island from the Manhattoe Indians for $24 worth of trinkets and beads. If the Indians had taken a boat to Holland, invested the $24 in Dutch securities returning just 6% per year, and kept the money and interest invested at 6%, by 1971 they would have had $13 billion, enough to buy back all the land on the island and still have a couple of billion dollars left (*Forbes*, June 1, 1971). By 1998, 372 years after the trade, the $24 would have grown to approximately $63 billion—$62 trillion had the interest rate been 8%.

COMPOUND INTEREST TABLES

Five different compound interest tables are presented at the end of this appendix (see pages A-29–A-33). These tables are the source for various "interest factors" used to solve problems that involve interest in this appendix and throughout the book. The titles of these five tables and their contents are:

OBJECTIVE 3
Know how to use appropriate compound interest tables.

1. **Future Amount of 1.** Contains the amounts to which $1.00 will accumulate if deposited now at a specified rate and left for a specified number of periods (Table A-1).

2. **Present Value of 1.** Contains the amounts that must be deposited now at a specified rate of interest to equal $1.00 at the end of a specified number of periods (Table A-2).

3. **Future Amount of an Ordinary Annuity of 1.** Contains the amounts to which periodic rents of $1.00 will accumulate if the rents are invested at the *end* of each period at a specified rate of interest for a specified number of periods (Table A-3).

4. **Present Value of an Ordinary Annuity of 1.** Contains the amounts that must be deposited now at a specified rate of interest to permit withdrawals of $1.00 at the *end* of regular periodic intervals for the specified number of periods (Table A-4).

5. **Present Value of an Annuity Due of 1.** Contains the amounts that must be deposited now at a specified rate of interest to permit withdrawals of $1.00 at the *beginning* of regular periodic intervals for the specified number of periods (Table A-5).

Exhibit A-2 shows the general format and content of these tables. It is from Table A-1, "Future Amount of 1," which indicates the amount to which a dollar accumulates at the end of each of five periods at three different rates of compound interest.

EXHIBIT A-2

FUTURE AMOUNT OF 1 AT COMPOUND INTEREST

(Excerpt from Table A-1)

Period	9%	10%	11%
1	1.09000	1.10000	1.11000
2	1.18810	1.21000	1.23210
3	1.29503	1.33100	1.36763
4	1.41158	1.46410	1.51807
5	1.53862	1.61051	1.68506

Interpreting the table, if $1.00 is invested for three periods at a compound interest rate of 9% per period, it will amount to $1.30 (1.29503 × $1.00), the **compound future amount.** If $1.00 is invested at 11%, at the end of four periods it amounts to $1.52. If the investment is $1,000 instead of $1.00, it will amount to $1,295.03 ($1,000 × 1.29503) if invested at 9% for three periods, or $1,518.07 if invested at 11% for four periods.

Throughout the foregoing discussion and the discussion that follows, the use of the term *periods* instead of *years* is intentional. While interest is generally expressed as an annual rate, the compounding period is often shorter. Therefore, the annual interest rate must be converted to correspond to the length of the period. To convert the "annual interest rate" into the "compounding period interest rate," ***divide the annual rate by the number of compounding periods per year***. In addition, the number of periods is determined by ***multiplying the number of years involved by the number of compounding periods per year***.

To illustrate, assume that $1.00 is invested for six years at 8% annual interest compounded quarterly. Using Table A-1, the amount to which this $1.00 will accumulate is determined by reading the factor that appears in the 2% column (8% ÷ 4) on the 24th row (6 years × 4), namely 1.60844, or approximately $1.61.

Because interest is theoretically earned every second of every day, it is possible to calculate continuously compounded interest. As a practical matter, however, most business transactions assume interest is compounded no more frequently than daily.

How often interest is compounded can make a substantial difference to the rate of return achieved. For example, 9% interest compounded daily provides a 9.42% annual yield, or a difference of .42%. The 9.42% is referred to as the **effective yield** or **rate**,[6] whereas the 9% annual interest rate is called the **stated**, **nominal**, **coupon**, or **face rate**. When the compounding frequency is greater than once a year, the effective interest rate is higher than the stated rate.

FUNDAMENTAL VARIABLES

The following four variables are fundamental to all compound interest problems:

1. **Rate of Interest.** This rate, unless otherwise stated, is an annual rate that must be adjusted to reflect the length of the compounding period if it is less than a year.

2. **Number of Time Periods.** This is the number of compounding periods for which interest is to be computed.

3. **Future Amount.** The value at a future date of a given sum or sums invested, assuming compound interest.

4. **Present Value.** The value now (present time) of a future sum or sums discounted, assuming compound interest.

OBJECTIVE 4
Identify variables fundamental to solving interest problems.

The relationship of these four variables is depicted in the *time diagram* in Illustration A-1.

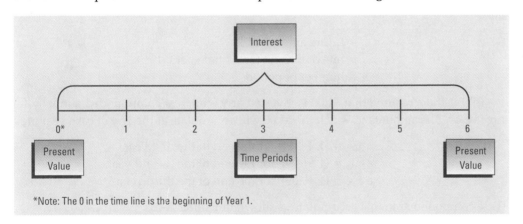

ILLUSTRATION A-1
Time diagram identifying four fundamental variables

*Note: The 0 in the time line is the beginning of Year 1.

In some cases all four of these variables are known, but in many business situations at least one is unknown. Frequently, the accountant is expected to determine the unknown amount or amounts. To do this, a time diagram can be very helpful in understanding the nature of the problem and finding a solution.

The remainder of the appendix covers the following six major time value of money concepts. Both formula and interest table approaches are used to illustrate how problems may be solved:

---

[6] The formula for calculating the effective rate in situations where the compounding frequency (*f*) is more than once a year is as follows:

$$\text{Effective rate} = (1 + i)^f - 1$$

where *i* = the interest rate per compounding period.

1. Future amount of a single sum.

2. Present value of a single sum.

3. Future amount of an ordinary annuity.

4. Future amount of an annuity due.

5. Present value of an ordinary annuity.

6. Present value of an annuity due.

SINGLE SUM PROBLEMS

OBJECTIVE 5
Solve future and present value of single sum problems.

Many business and investment decisions involve a single amount of money that either exists now or will exist in the future. Single sum problems can generally be classified into one of the following two categories:

1. Determining the *unknown future amount* of a known single sum of money that is invested for a specified number of periods at a specified interest rate.

2. Determining the *unknown present value* of a known single sum of money that is discounted for a specified number of periods at a specified interest rate.

FUTURE AMOUNT OF A SINGLE SUM

The **future amount** of a sum of money is the future value of that sum when left to accumulate for a certain number of periods at a specified rate of interest per period.

The amount to which 1 (one) will accumulate may be expressed as a formula:

$$a_{\overline{n}|\,i} = (1 + i)^n$$

where

$$a_{\overline{n}|\,i} = \text{future amount of 1}$$
$$i = \text{rate of interest for a single period}$$
$$n = \text{number of periods}$$

To illustrate, assume that $1.00 is invested at 9% interest compounded annually for three years. The amounts to which the $1.00 will accumulate at the end of each year are:

$$a_{\overline{1}|\,9\%} = (1 + .09)^1 \text{ for the end of the first year.}$$
$$a_{\overline{2}|\,9\%} = (1 + .09)^2 \text{ for the end of the second year.}$$
$$a_{\overline{3}|\,9\%} = (1 + .09)^3 \text{ for the end of the third year.}$$

These compound amounts accumulate as shown in Exhibit A-3.

EXHIBIT A-3

ACCUMULATION OF COMPOUND AMOUNTS

Period	Beginning-of-Period Amount	×	Multiplier (1 + i)	=	End-of-Period Amount*	Formula (1 + i)^n
1	1.00000		1.09		1.09000	$(1.09)^1$
2	1.09000		1.09		1.18810	$(1.09)^2$
3	1.18810		1.09		1.29503	$(1.09)^3$

*These amounts appear in Table A-1 in the 9% column.

To calculate the *future value of any single amount*, multiply the future amount of 1 factor by that amount.

$$a = p(a_{\overline{n}|\,i})$$

where

a = future amount
p = beginning principal or sum (present value)
$a_{\overline{n}|\,i} = (1 + i)^n$ = future amount of 1 for n periods at $i\%$.

For example, what is the future amount of $50,000 invested for five years at 11% compounded annually? In time-diagram form, this investment situation is indicated in Illustration A-2.

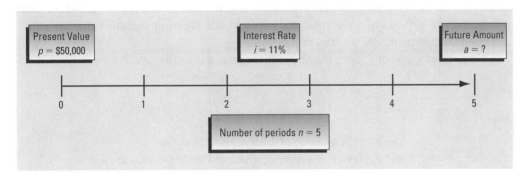

ILLUSTRATION A-2
Time diagram for future amount calculation

This investment problem is solved as follows.

$$
\begin{aligned}
a &= p(a_{\overline{n}|\,i}) \\
&= \$50,000(a_{\overline{5}|\,11\%}) \\
&= \$50,000\,(1.68506) \\
&= \$84,253.
\end{aligned}
$$

The future amount of 1 factor of 1.68506 is that which appears in Table A-1 in the 11% column and 5-period row.

To illustrate a more complex business situation, assume that at the beginning of 1998 Ontario Hydro Corp. deposits $250 million in an escrow account with Canada Trust Company as a commitment toward a small nuclear power plant to be completed December 31, 2001. How much will be on deposit at the end of four years if interest is compounded semiannually at 10%?

With a known present value of $250 million, a total of eight compounding periods (4 × 2), and an interest rate of 5% per compounding period (10% ÷ 2), this problem can be time-diagrammed and the future amount determined as indicated in Illustration A-3.

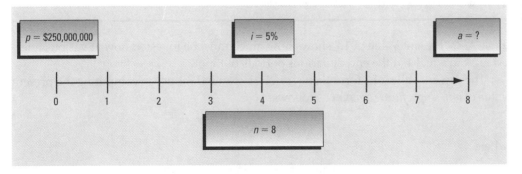

ILLUSTRATION A-3
Time diagram for future amount calculation

$$
\begin{aligned}
a &= \$250,000,000(a_{\overline{8}|\,5\%}) \\
&= \$250,000,000(1.47746) \\
&= \$369,365,000.
\end{aligned}
$$

The deposit of $250 million will accumulate to $369,365,000 by December 31, 2001. The future amount of 1 factor is found in Table A-1 (5% column and the 8-period row).

PRESENT VALUE OF A SINGLE SUM

A previous example showed that $50,000 invested at an annually compounded interest rate of 11% will be worth $84,253 at the end of five years. It follows that $84,253 to be received five years from now is presently worth $50,000, given an 11% interest rate (i.e., $50,000 is the present value of this $84,253). The **present value** is the amount that must be invested now to produce a known future amount. The *present value is always a smaller amount than the known future amount because interest is earned and accumulated on the present value to the future date*. In determining the future amount we move forward in time using a process of **accumulation**, while in determining present value we move backward in time using the process of **discounting**.

The present value of 1 (one) may be expressed as a formula:

$$p_{\overline{n}|i} = 1/a_{\overline{n}|i} = \frac{1}{(1 + i)^n}$$

where

$p_{\overline{n}|i}$ = present value of 1 for n periods at $i\%$.
$a_{\overline{n}|i} = (1 + i)^n$ = future amount of 1 for n periods at $i\%$.

To illustrate, assume that $1.00 is discounted for three periods at 9%. The present value of the $1.00 is discounted each period as follows.

$$p_{\overline{1}|9\%} = 1/(1 + .09)^1 \text{ for the first period}$$
$$p_{\overline{2}|9\%} = 1/(1 + .09)^2 \text{ for the second period}$$
$$p_{\overline{3}|9\%} = 1/(1 + .09)^3 \text{ for the third period}$$

Therefore, the $1.00 is discounted as shown in Exhibit A-4.

EXHIBIT A-4

PRESENT VALUE OF $1 DISCOUNTED AT 9% FOR THREE PERIODS

Discount Periods	Future Amount	÷	Divisor $(1 + i)^n$	=	Present Value*	Formula $1/(1 + i)^n$
1	1.00000		1.09		.91743	$1/(1.09)^1$
2	1.00000		$(1.09)^2$		.84168	$1/(1.09)^2$
3	1.00000		$(1.09)^3$		.77218	$1/(1.09)^3$

*These amounts appear in Table A-2 in the 9% column.

Table A-2, "Present Value of 1," shows how much must be invested now at various interest rates to equal 1 at the end of various periods of time.

The present value of 1 formula $p_{\overline{n}|i}$ can be expanded for use in computing the present value of *any single future amount* as follows.

$$p = a(p_{\overline{n}|i})$$

where

p = present value of a single future amount
a = future amount

$$p_{\overline{n}|i} = \frac{1}{(1 + i)^n} = \text{present value of 1 for } n \text{ periods at } i\%.$$

To illustrate, assume that your favourite uncle proposes to give you $4,000 for a trip to Europe when you graduate three years from now. He will finance the trip by investing a sum of money now at 8% compound interest that will accumulate to $4,000 upon your graduation. The only conditions are that you graduate and that you tell him how much to invest now.

To impress your uncle, you might set up a time diagram as shown in Illustration A-4 and solve the problem as follows.

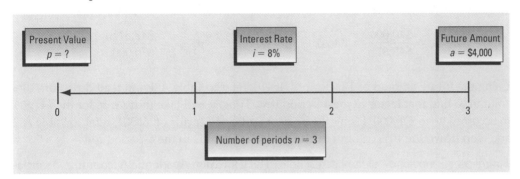

ILLUSTRATION A-4
Time diagram for present value calculation

$$p = \$4,000(p_{\overline{3}|\,8\%})$$
$$= \$4,000(.79383)$$
$$= \$3,175.32.$$

Advise your uncle to invest $3,175.32 now to provide you with $4,000 upon graduation. To satisfy your uncle's other condition, you must simply pass this course and many more. Note that the present value factor of .79383 is found in Table A-2 (8% column, 3-period row).

SINGLE SUM PROBLEMS: SOLVING FOR OTHER UNKNOWNS

In computing either the future amount or the present value in the previous single sum illustrations, both the number of periods and the interest rate were known. In business situations, both the future amount and the present value may be known, and either the number of periods or the interest rate may be unknown. The following two illustrations demonstrate how to solve single sum problems when there is either an unknown number of periods (n) or an unknown interest rate (i). These illustrations show that if any three of the four values (future amount, a; present value, p; number of periods, n; interest rate, i) are known, the one unknown can be derived.

Illustration: Computation of the Number of Periods. The local Big Sisters and Big Brothers associations in Regina want to accumulate $70,000 for the construction of a day-care centre. If at the beginning of the current year the associations are able to deposit $47,811 in a building fund that earns 10% interest compounded annually, how many years will it take for the fund to accumulate to $70,000?

In this situation, the present value ($47,811), future amount ($70,000), and interest rate (10%) are known. A time diagram of this investment is shown in Illustration A-5.

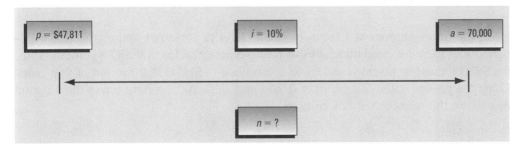

ILLUSTRATION A-5
Time diagram for number of periods calculation

The unknown number of periods can be determined using either the future amount or present value approaches, as shown below.

Future Amount Approach

$$a = p(a_{\overline{n}|\,10\%})$$

$$\$70{,}000 = \$47{,}811(a_{\overline{n}|\,10\%})$$

$$a_{\overline{n}|\,10\%} = \frac{\$70{,}000}{\$47{,}811} = 1.46410$$

Present Value Approach

$$p = a(p_{\overline{n}|\,10\%})$$

$$\$47{,}811 = \$70{,}000(p_{\overline{n}|\,10\%})$$

$$p_{\overline{n}|\,10\%} = \frac{\$47{,}811}{\$70{,}000} = .68301$$

Using the future amount of 1 factor of 1.46410, refer to Table A-1 and read down the 10% column to find that factor in the 4-period row. Thus, it will take four years for the $47,811 to accumulate to $70,000. Using the present value of 1 factor of .68301, refer to Table A-2 and read down the 10% column to also find that factor is in the 4-period row.

Illustration: Computation of the Interest Rate. The Canadian Academic Accounting Association wants to have $141,000 available five years from now to provide scholarships to individuals who undertake a PhD program. At present, the executive of the CAAA has determined that $80,000 may be invested for this purpose. What rate of interest must be earned on the investments in order to accumulate the $141,000 five years from now?

Illustration A-6 provides a time diagram of this problem.

ILLUSTRATION A-6

Time diagram for rate of interest calculation

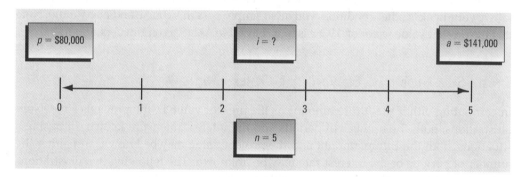

Given that the present value, future amount, and number of periods are known, the unknown interest rate can be determined using either the future amount or present value approaches, as shown below.

Future Amount Approach

$$a = p(a_{\overline{5}|\,i})$$

$$\$141{,}000 = \$80{,}000(a_{\overline{5}|\,i})$$

$$a_{\overline{5}|\,i} = \frac{\$141{,}000}{\$80{,}000} = 1.7625$$

Present Value Approach

$$p = a(p_{\overline{5}|\,i})$$

$$\$80{,}000 = \$141{,}000(p_{\overline{5}|\,i})$$

$$p_{\overline{5}|\,i} = \frac{\$80{,}000}{\$141{,}000} = 0.5674$$

Using the future amount of 1 factor of 1.7625, refer to Table A-1 and read across the 5-period row to find a close match of this future amount factor in the 12% column. Thus, the $80,000 must be invested at 12% to accumulate to $141,000 at the end of five years. Using the present value of 1 factor of 0.5674 and Table A-2, reading across the 5-period row shows this factor in the 12% column.

ANNUITIES

The preceding discussion involved only the accumulation or discounting of a single principal sum. Accountants frequently encounter situations in which a series of amounts are to be paid or received over time (e.g., when loans or sales are paid in instalments, invested funds are partially recovered at regular intervals, and cost savings are realized repeatedly). When a commitment involves a series of equal payments made at equal intervals of time, it is called an annuity. By definition, an **annuity** requires that (1) the *periodic payments or receipts* (called *rents*) *always be the same amount;* (2) the *interval between such rents always be the same*; and (3) the *interest be compounded once each interval.*

The **future amount of an annuity** *is the sum of all the rents plus the accumulated compound interest on them.* Rents may, however, occur at either the beginning or the end of the periods. To distinguish annuities under these two alternatives, an annuity is classified as an **ordinary annuity** *if the rents occur at the end of each period*, and as an **annuity due** *if the rents occur at the beginning of each period.*

FUTURE AMOUNT OF AN ORDINARY ANNUITY

One approach to calculating the future amount of an annuity is to determine the future amount of each rent in the series and then aggregate these individual future amounts. For example, assume that $1 is deposited at the *end* of each of five years (an ordinary annuity) and earns 12% interest compounded annually. The future amount can be computed as indicated in Illustration A-7 using the "Future Amount of 1" for each of the five $1 rents.

OBJECTIVE 6
Solve future amount of ordinary and annuity due problems.

ILLUSTRATION A-7
Solving for the future amount of an ordinary annuity

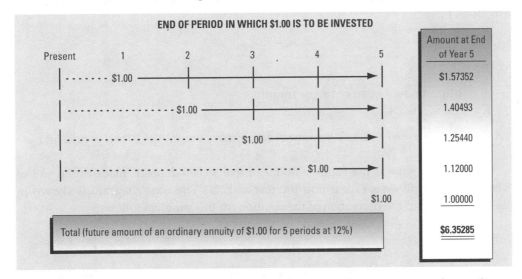

Although the foregoing procedure for computing the future amount of an ordinary annuity produces the correct answer, it is cumbersome if the number of rents is large. A more efficient way of determining the future amount of an ordinary annuity of 1 is to apply the following formula:

$$A_{\overline{n}|\,i} = \frac{(1 + i)^n - 1}{i}$$

where

$A_{\overline{n}|\,i}$ = future amount of an ordinary annuity of 1 for n periods at i rate of interest
n = number of compounding periods
i = rate of interest per period

Using this formula, Table A-3 has been developed to show the "Future Amount of an Ordinary Annuity of 1" for various interest rates and investment periods. Exhibit A-5 is an excerpt from this table.

EXHIBIT A-5

FUTURE AMOUNT OF AN ORDINARY ANNUITY OF 1

(excerpt from Table A-3)

Period	10%	11%	12%
1	1.00000	1.00000	1.00000
2	2.10000	2.11000	2.12000
3	3.31000	3.34210	3.37440
4	4.64100	4.70973	4.77933
5	6.10510	6.22780	6.35285*

*Note that this factor is the same as the sum of the future amounts of 1 factors shown in the previous schedule.

Interpreting the table, if $1.00 is invested at the end of each year for four years at 11% interest compounded annually, the amount of the annuity at the end of the fourth year will be $4.71 (4.70973 × $1.00). The $4.71 is made up of $4 of rent payments ($1 at the end of each of the 4 years) and compound interest of $0.71.

The $A_{\overline{n}|i}$ formula can be expanded to determine the future amount of an ordinary annuity as follows.

$$A = R(A_{\overline{n}|i})$$

where

A = future amount of an ordinary annuity.
R = periodic rents
$A_{\overline{n}|i} = \dfrac{(1 + i)^n - 1}{i}$ = future amount of an ordinary annuity of 1 for n periods at i%.

To illustrate, what is the future amount of five $5,000 deposits made at the end of each of the next five years, earning interest at 12%? The time diagram is shown in Illustration A-8 and the derivation of the solution for this problem follows.

ILLUSTRATION A-8
Time diagram for future amount calculation of an ordinary annuity

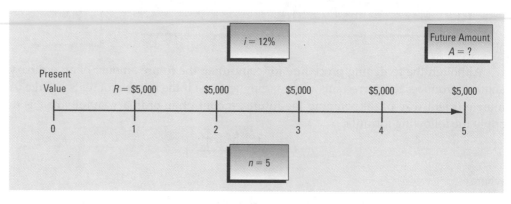

$$A = R(A_{\overline{n}|i})$$
$$= \$5,000(A_{\overline{5}|12\%})$$
$$= \$5,000(6.35285)$$
$$= \$31,764.25$$

The future amount of an ordinary annuity of 1 factor of 6.35285 is found in Table A-3 (12% column, 5-period row).

To illustrate these computations in a business situation, assume that Lightning Electronics Limited's management decides to deposit $75,000 at the end of each six-month period for the next three years for the purpose of accumulating enough money to meet debts that mature in three years. What is the future amount that will be on deposit at the end of three years if the annual interest rate is 10%?

The time diagram in Illustration A-9 and solution are as follows.

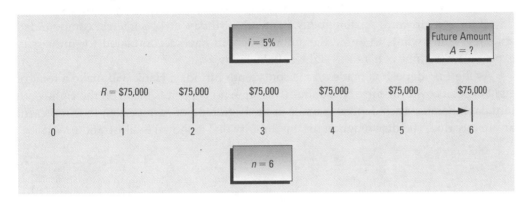

$$A = R(A_{\overline{n}|\,i})$$
$$= \$75{,}000(A_{\overline{6}|\,5\%})$$
$$= \$75{,}000(6.80191)$$
$$= \$510{,}143.25$$

Thus, six deposits of $75,000 made at the end of every six months and earning 5% per period will grow to $510,143.25 at the time of the last deposit.

FUTURE AMOUNT OF AN ANNUITY DUE

The preceding analysis of an *ordinary annuity* was based on the fact that the *periodic rents* occur at the *end* of each period. An **annuity due** is based on the fact that the *periodic rents* occur at the *beginning* of each period. This means an annuity due will accumulate interest during the first period whereas an ordinary annuity will not. Therefore, the significant difference between the two types of annuities is in the number of interest accumulation periods involved. The distinction is shown graphically in Illustration A-10.

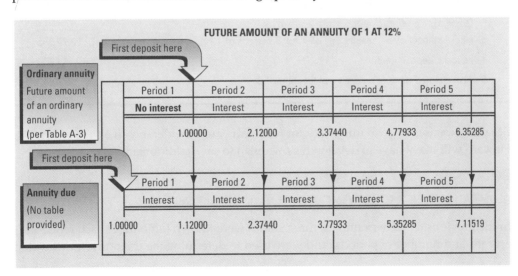

Because the cash flows from the annuity due come exactly one period earlier than for an ordinary annuity, the future value of the annuity due of 1 factor is exactly 12% higher than the ordinary annuity factor. Therefore, *to determine the future value of an annuity due of 1 factor, multiply the corresponding future value of the ordinary annuity of 1 factor by one plus the interest rate*. For example, to determine the future value of an annuity due of 1 factor for five periods at 12% compound interest, simply multiply the future value of an ordinary annuity of 1 factor for five periods (6.35285) by one plus the interest rate (1 + .12) to arrive at the future value of an annuity due of 1, 7.1152 (6.35285 × 1.12).

To illustrate, assume that Hank Lotadough plans to deposit $800 a year on each birthday of his son Howard, starting today, his tenth birthday, at 12% interest compounded annually. Hank wants to know the amount he will have accumulated for university expenses by the time of his son's eighteenth birthday.

As the first deposit is made on his son's tenth birthday, Hank will make a total of eight deposits over the life of the annuity (assume no deposit is made on the eighteenth birthday). Because each deposit is made at the beginning of each period, they represent an annuity due. The time diagram for this annuity due is shown in Illustration A-11.

ILLUSTRATION A-11
Time diagram for future amount calculation of an annuity due

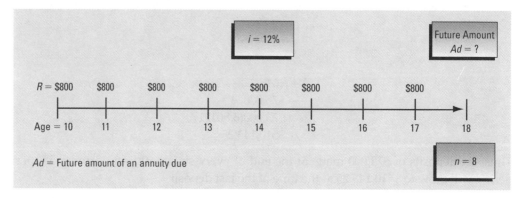

Referring to Table A-3, "Future Amount of an Ordinary Annuity of 1," for eight periods at 12%, a factor of 12.29969 is found. This factor is then multiplied by (1 + .12) to arrive at the future amount of an annuity due of 1 factor. As a result, the accumulated amount on his son's eighteenth birthday is computed as shown in Exhibit A-6.

EXHIBIT A-6

COMPUTATION OF THE FUTURE AMOUNT OF AN ANNUITY DUE

1. Future amount of an ordinary annuity of 1 for 8 periods at 12% (Table A-3)	12.29969
2. Factor (1 + .12)	× 1.12
3. Future amount of an annuity due of 1 for 8 periods at 12%	13.77565
4. Periodic deposit (rent)	× $800
5. Accumulated amount on son's eighteenth birthday	$11,020.52

Because expenses to go to university for four years are considerably in excess of $11,000, Howard will likely have to develop his own plan to save additional funds.

ILLUSTRATIONS OF FUTURE AMOUNT OF ANNUITY PROBLEMS

In the previous annuity examples, three values were known (amount of each rent, interest rate, and number of periods) and were used to determine the unknown fourth value (future amount). The following illustrations demonstrate how to solve problems when the unknown is (1) the amount of the rents; or (2) the number of rents in ordinary annuity situations.

Illustration: Computing the Amount of Each Rent. Assume that you wish to accumulate $14,000 for a down payment on a condominium five years from now and that you can earn an annual return of 8% compounded semiannually during the next five years. How much should you deposit at the end of each six-month period?

The $14,000 is the future amount of 10 (5 × 2) semiannual end-of-period payments of an unknown amount at an interest rate of 4% (8% ÷ 2). This problem is time-diagrammed in Illustration A-12.

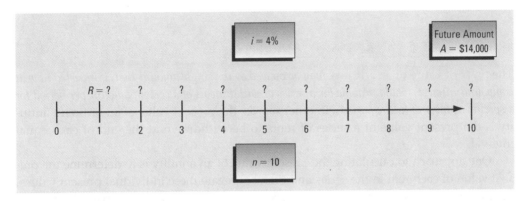

ILLUSTRATION A-12
Time diagram for calculating the semiannual payment of an ordinary annuity

Using the formula for the future amount of an ordinary annuity, the amount of each rent is determined as follows.

$$A = R(A_{\overline{n}|\,i})$$
$$\$14{,}000 = R(A_{\overline{10}|\,4\%})$$
$$\$14{,}000 = R(12.00611)$$
$$\frac{\$14{,}000}{12.00611} = R$$
$$R = \$1{,}166.07$$

Thus, you must make 10 semiannual deposits of $1,166.07 each in order to accumulate $14,000 for your down payment. The future amount of an ordinary annuity of 1 factor of 12.00611 is provided in Table A-3 (4% column, 10-period row).

Illustration: Computing the Number of Periodic Rents. Suppose that your company wants to accumulate $117,332 by making periodic deposits of $20,000 at the end of each year that will earn 8% compounded annually. How many deposits must be made?

The $117,332 represents the future amount of n(?) $20,000 deposits at an 8% annual rate of interest. Illustration A-13 provides a time diagram for this problem.

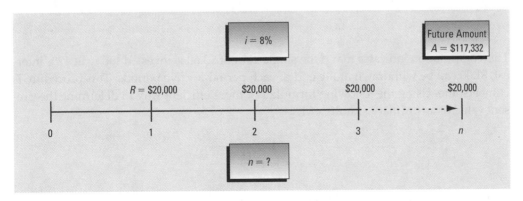

ILLUSTRATION A-13
Time diagram for number of periods calculation for an ordinary annuity

Using the future amount of an ordinary annuity formula, the factor of 1 is determined as follows.

$$A = R(A_{\overline{n}|\,i})$$
$$\$117,332 = \$20,000(A_{\overline{n}|\,8\%})$$
$$A_{\overline{n}|\,8\%} = \frac{\$117,332}{\$20,000} = 5.86660$$

Using Table A-3 and reading down the 8% column, 5.86660 is in the 5-period row. Thus, five deposits of $20,000 each must be made.

PRESENT VALUE OF AN ORDINARY ANNUITY

OBJECTIVE 7

Solve present value of ordinary and annuity due problems.

The **present value of an annuity** *may be viewed as the single amount that, if invested now at compound interest, would provide for a series of withdrawals of a certain amount per period for a specific number of future periods.* In other words, the present value of an ordinary annuity is the present value of a series of rents to be withdrawn at the end of each equal interval.

One approach to calculating the present value of an annuity is to determine the present value of each rent in the series and then aggregate these individual present values. For example, assume that $1.00 is to be received at the *end* of each of five periods (an ordinary annuity) and that the interest rate is 12% compounded annually. The present value of this annuity can be computed as shown in Illustration A-14 using Table A-2, "Present Value of 1," for each of the five $1 rents.

ILLUSTRATION A-14

Solving for the present value of an ordinary annuity

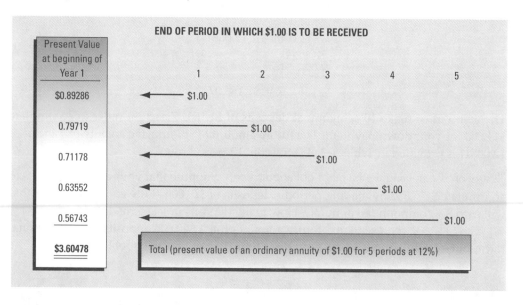

This computation indicates that if the single sum of $3.60 is invested today at 12% interest, $1.00 can be withdrawn at the end of each period for five periods. This procedure is cumbersome. Using the following formula is a more efficient way to determine the present value of an ordinary annuity of 1:

$$P_{\overline{n}|\,i} = \frac{1 - \dfrac{1}{(1 + i)^n}}{i}$$

Table A-4, "Present Value of an Ordinary Annuity of 1," is based on this formula. Exhibit A-7 is an excerpt from this table.

EXHIBIT A-7

PRESENT VALUE OF AN ORDINARY ANNUITY OF 1

(excerpt from Table A-4)

Period	10%	11%	12%
1	.90909	.90090	.89286
2	1.73554	1.71252	1.69005
3	2.48685	2.44371	2.40183
4	3.16986	3.10245	3.03735
5	3.79079	3.69590	**3.60478***

*Note that this factor is equal to the sum of the present value of 1 factors shown in the previous schedule.

The formula for the present value of any ordinary annuity of any rent value is as follows.

$$P = R(P_{\overline{n}|\,i})$$

where

P = present value of an ordinary annuity
R = periodic rent (ordinary annuity)

$$P_{\overline{n}|\,i} = \frac{1 - \dfrac{1}{(1+i)^n}}{i} = \text{present value of an ordinary annuity of 1 for } n \text{ periods at } i\%.$$

To illustrate, what is the present value of rental receipts of $6,000, each to be received at the end of each of the next five years when discounted at 12%? This problem is time-diagrammed in Illustration A-15 and the solution follows.

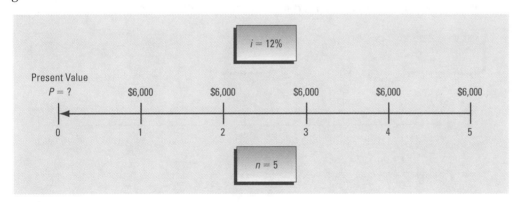

ILLUSTRATION A-15
Time diagram for present value calculation of an ordinary annuity

$$P = R(P_{\overline{n}|\,i})$$
$$= \$6,000(P_{\overline{5}|\,12\%})$$
$$= \$6,000(3.60478)$$
$$= \$21,628.68$$

The present value of the five ordinary annuity rental receipts of $6,000 each is $21,628.68. The present value of the ordinary annuity of 1 factor, 3.60478, is from Table A-4 (12% column, 5-period row).

PRESENT VALUE OF AN ANNUITY DUE

In the discussion of the present value of an ordinary annuity, the final rent was discounted back the same number of periods as there were rents. In determining the present value of an annuity due, there is one fewer discount periods. This distinction is shown graphically in Illustration A-16.

ILLUSTRATION A-16

Comparison of the present value of an ordinary annuity with that of an annuity due

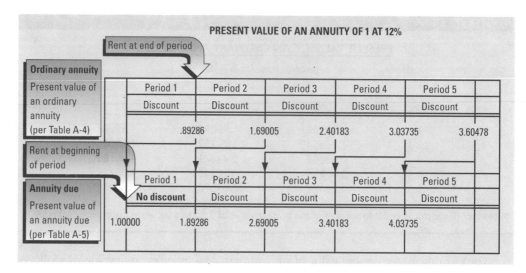

Because each cash flow (rent) comes exactly one period sooner in the present value of an annuity due, the present value of the cash flows is exactly 12% higher than the present value of an ordinary annuity. Thus, *the present value of an annuity due of 1 factor can be found by multiplying the present value of an ordinary annuity of 1 by one plus the interest rate.* For example, to determine the present value of an annuity due of 1 factor for five periods at 12% interest, take the present value of an ordinary annuity of 1 factor for five periods at 12% interest (3.60478) and multiply it by 1.12 to arrive at the present value of an annuity due of 1, which is 4.03735 (3.60478 × 1.12). Table A-5 provides present value of annuity due of 1 factors.

To illustrate, assume that Space Odyssey Inc. rents a communications satellite for four years with annual rental payments of $4.8 million to be made at the beginning of each year. Assuming an annual interest rate of 11%, what is the present value of the rental obligations?

This problem is time-diagrammed in Illustration A-17.

ILLUSTRATION A-17

Time diagram for present value calculation of an annuity due

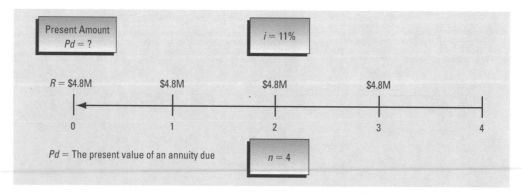

This problem can be solved as shown in Exhibit A-8.

EXHIBIT A-8

COMPUTATION OF PRESENT VALUE OF AN ANNUITY DUE

1. Present value of an **ordinary annuity** of 1 for 4 periods at 11% (Table A-4)	3.10245
2. Factor (1 + .11)	× 1.11
3. Present value of an **annuity due** of 1 for 4 periods at 11%	3.44371
4. Periodic deposit (rent)	×$4,800,000
5. Present value of payments	$ 16,529.808

Since Table A-5 gives present value of an annuity due of 1 factors, it can be used to obtain the required factor 3.44371 (in the 11% column, 4-period row).

ILLUSTRATIONS OF PRESENT VALUE OF ANNUITY PROBLEMS

The following illustrations show how to solve problems when the unknown is (1) the present value; (2) the interest rate; or (3) the amount of each rent for present value of annuity problems.

Illustration: Computation of the Present Value of an Ordinary Annuity. You have just won Lotto B.C. totalling $4,000,000. You will be paid the amount of $200,000 at the end of each of the next 20 years. What amount have you really won? That is, what is the present value of the $200,000 cheques you will receive over the next 20 years? A time diagram of this enviable situation is shown in Illustration A-18 (assuming an interest rate of 10%).

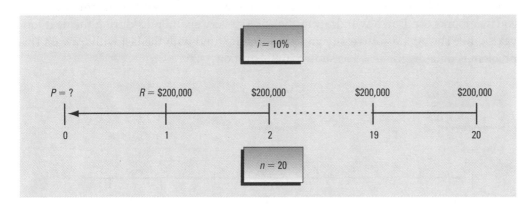

ILLUSTRATION A-18
Time diagram for present value calculation of an annuity due

The present value is determined as follows:

$$P = R(P_{\overline{n}|\, i})$$
$$= \$200,000(P_{\overline{20}|\, 10\%})$$
$$= \$200,00(8.51356)$$
$$= \$1,702,712$$

As a result, if Lotto B.C. deposits $1,702,712 now and earns 10% interest, it can draw $200,000 a year for 20 years to pay you the $4,000,000.

Illustration: Computation of the Interest Rate. Many shoppers make purchases by using a credit card. When you receive an invoice for payment, you may pay the total amount due or pay the balance in a certain number of payments. For example, if you receive an invoice from VISA with a balance due of $528.77 and are invited to pay it off in 12 equal monthly payments of $50.00 each with the first payment due one month from now, what rate of interest are you paying?

    The $528.77 represents the present value of the twelve $50 payments at an unknown rate of interest. This situation is time-diagrammed in Illustration A-19, which is followed by the determination of the interest rate.

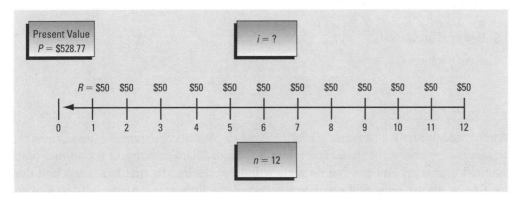

ILLUSTRATION A-19
Time diagram for rate of interest calculation of an ordinary annuity

$$P = R(P_{\overline{n}|\,i})$$
$$\$528.77 = \$50(P_{\overline{12}|\,i})$$
$$P_{\overline{12}|\,i} = \frac{\$528.77}{50} = 10.5754$$

Referring to Table A-4 and reading across the 12-period row, the 10.57534 factor is in the 2% column. Since 2% is a monthly rate, the nominal annual rate of interest is 24% (12 × 2%) and the effective annual rate is 26.82413% [(1 + .02)^{12} − 1]. At such a high rate of interest, you are better off paying the entire bill now if possible.

Illustration: Computation of a Periodic Rent. Vern and Marilyn have saved $18,000 to finance their daughter Dawn's university education. The money has been deposited with the National Trust Company and is earning 10% interest compounded semiannually. What equal amounts can Dawn withdraw at the end of every six months during the next four years while she attends university and exhausts the fund with the last withdrawal? This problem is time-diagrammed as shown in Illustration A-20.

ILLUSTRATION A-20

Time diagram for calculation of the withdrawal amount of an ordinary annuity

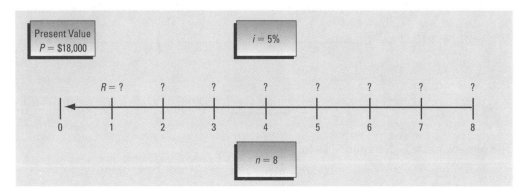

The answer is not determined simply by dividing $18,000 by 8 withdrawals because that ignores the interest earned on the money remaining on deposit. Given that interest is compounded semiannually at 5% (10% ÷ 2) for eight periods (4 years × 2) and using the present value of an ordinary annuity formula, the amount of each withdrawal is determined as follows:

$$P = R(P_{\overline{n}|\,i})$$
$$\$18,000 = R(P_{\overline{8}|\,5\%})$$
$$\$18,000 = R(6.46321)$$
$$R = \$2,784.99$$

COMPLEX SITUATIONS

It is often necessary to use more than one table to solve time value of money problems. Two common situations are illustrated to demonstrate this point:

1. Deferred annuities.

2. Bond problems.

DEFERRED ANNUITIES

A **deferred annuity** *is an annuity in which the rents begin a specified number of periods after the arrangement or contract is made.* For example, "an ordinary annuity of six annual rents deferred four years" means that no rents will occur during the first four years and that the first of the six rents will occur at the end of the fifth year. "An annuity due of six annual rents deferred four years" means that no rents will occur during the first four years, and that the first of six rents will occur at the beginning of the fifth year.

Future Amount of a Deferred Annuity. Determining the future amount of a deferred annuity is relatively straightforward. Because there is no accumulation or investment on which interest accrues during the deferred periods, the future amount of a deferred annuity is the same as the future amount of an annuity not deferred.

To illustrate, assume that Sutton Co. Ltd. plans to purchase a land site in six years for the construction of its new corporate headquarters. Because of cash flow problems, Sutton is able to budget deposits of $80,000 only at the end of the fourth, fifth, and sixth years, which are expected to earn 12% annually. What future amount will Sutton have accumulated at the end of the sixth year?

Illustration A-21 gives a time diagram of this situation.

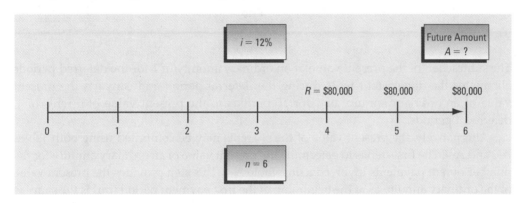

ILLUSTRATION A-21
Time diagram for calculation of the future amount of a deferred annuity

The amount accumulated is determined by using the standard formula for the future amount of an ordinary annuity:

$$A = R(A_{\overline{n}|\,i})$$
$$= \$80,000(A_{\overline{3}|\,12\%})$$
$$= \$80,000(3.37440)$$
$$= \$269,952$$

Present Value of a Deferred Annuity. In determining the present value of a deferred annuity, recognition must be given to the facts that no rents occur during the deferral period, and that the future actual rents must be discounted for the entire period.

For example, Shelly Hernandez has developed and copyrighted a software computer program that is a tutorial for students in introductory accounting. She agrees to sell the copyright to Campus Micro Systems for six annual payments of $5,000 each, the payments to begin five years from today. The annual interest rate is 8%. What is the present value of the six payments?

This situation is an ordinary annuity of six payments deferred four periods as is time-diagrammed in Illustration A-22.

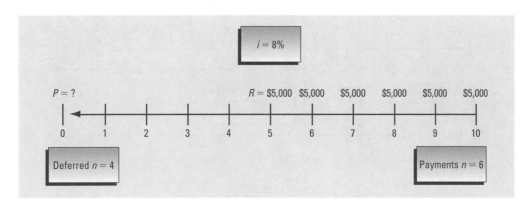

ILLUSTRATION A-22
Time diagram for calculation of the present value of a deferred annuity

Two options are available to solve this problem. The first is by using only Table A-4 and making the calculations shown in Exhibit A-9.

EXHIBIT A-9

COMPUTATION OF THE PRESENT VALUE OF A DEFERRED ANNUITY

1. Each periodic rent		$ 5,000
2. Present value of an ordinary annuity of 1 for total periods (10) [(number of rents (6) plus number of deferred periods (4)] at 8%	6.71008	
3. Less: Present value of an ordinary annuity of 1 for the number of deferred periods (4) at 8%	3.31213	
4. Difference		× 3.39795
5. Present value of 6 rents of $5,000 deferred 4 periods		$16,989.75

The subtraction of the present value of an ordinary annuity of 1 for the deferred periods eliminates the nonexistent rents during the deferral period and converts the present value of an ordinary annuity of 1 for 10 periods to the present value of 6 rents of 1, deferred 4 periods.

Alternatively, the present value of the six rents may be computed using both Tables A-2 and A-4. The first step is to determine the present value of an ordinary annuity for the number of rent payments involved using Table A-4. This step provides the present value of the ordinary annuity as at the beginning of the first payment period (this is the same as the present value at the end of the last deferral period). The second step is to discount the amount determined in Step 1 for the number of deferral periods using Table A-2. Application of this approach is as follows.

Step 1: $P = R(P_{\overline{n}|i})$
$= \$5,000(P_{\overline{6}|8\%})$
$= \$5,000(4.62288)$ Table A-4 (Present Value of an Ordinary Annuity)
$= \$23,114.40$

Step 2: $p = a(p_{\overline{n}|i})$ ("a" is the amount "P" determined in Step 1)
$= \$23,114.40 \ (p_{\overline{4}|8\%})$
$= \$23,114.40 \ (.73503)$ Table A-2 (Present Value of a Single Sum)
$= \$16,989.75$

A time diagram reflecting the completion of this two-step approach is shown in Illustration A-23.

ILLUSTRATION A-23
Time diagram reflecting the two-step approach for present value calculation of a deferred annuity

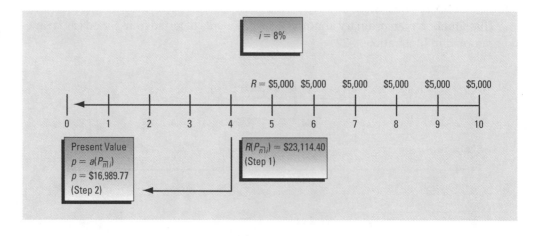

Applying the present value of an ordinary annuity formula discounts the annuity six periods, but because the annuity is deferred four periods, the present value of the annuity must be treated as a future amount to be discounted another four periods.

VALUATION OF LONG-TERM BONDS

A long-term bond provides two cash flows: (1) periodic interest payments during the life of the bond; and (2) the principal (face value) paid at maturity. At the date of issue, bond buyers determine the present value of these two cash flows using the market rate of interest.

The periodic interest payments represent an annuity while the principal represents a single sum. The current market value of the bonds is the combined present values of the interest annuity and the principal amount.

To illustrate, Servicemaster Inc. issues $100,000 of 9% bonds due in five years with interest payable annually at year end. The current market rate of interest for bonds of similar risk is 11%. What will the buyers pay for this bond issue?

The time diagram depicting both cash flows is shown in Illustration A-24.

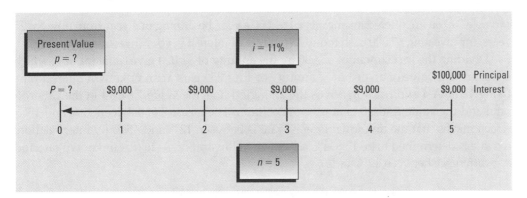

ILLUSTRATION A-24
Time diagram for valuation of long-term bonds

Exhibit A-10 shows how present value of the two cash flows is computed.

EXHIBIT A-10

COMPUTATION OF THE PRESENT VALUE OF AN INTEREST-BEARING BOND

1. Present value of the principal: $a(p\overline{\smash{5}}\rvert_{11\%}) = \$100,000(.59345) =$	$59,345.00
2. Present value of interest payments: $R(P\overline{\smash{5}}\rvert_{11\%}) = \$9,000(3.69590)$	33,263.10
3. Combined present value (market price)	$92,608.10

By paying $92,608.10 at date of issue, the buyers of the bonds will earn an effective yield of 11% over the 5-year term of the bonds.

INTERPOLATION OF TABLES TO DERIVE INTEREST RATES

Throughout the previous discussion, the illustrations were designed to produce interest rates and factors that could be found in the tables. Frequently it is necessary to interpolate to derive the exact or required interest rate. **Interpolation** is used to calculate a particular unknown value that lies between two values given in a table. The following examples illustrate interpolation using Tables A-1 and A-4.

Example 1. If $2,000 accumulates to $5,900 after being invested for 20 years, what is the annual interest rate on the investment?

Dividing the future amount of $5,900 by the investment of $2,000 gives $2.95, which is the amount to which $1.00 will grow if invested for 20 years at the unknown interest rate. Using Table A-1 and reading across the 20-period line, the value 2.65330 is found in the 5% column and the value 3.20714 is in the 6% column. The factor 2.95 is between 5% and 6%, which means that the interest rate is also between 5% and 6%. By interpolation, the rate is determined to be 5.536%, as shown in Illustration A-25 (i = unknown rate and d = difference between 5% and i).

ILLUSTRATION A-25
Interpolating to derive the rate of interest for an amount

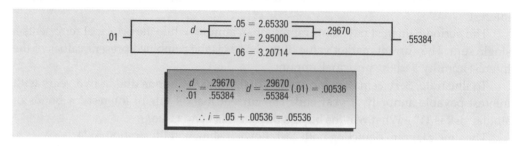

Example 2. You are offered an annuity of $1,000 a year, beginning one year from now for 25 years, for investing $7,000 cash today. What rate of interest is your investment earning?

Dividing the investment of $7,000 by the annuity of $1,000 gives a factor of 7, which is the present value of an ordinary annuity of 1 for 25 years at an unknown interest rate. Using Table A-4 and reading across the 25-period line, the value 7.84314 in the 12% column and the value 6.46415 is in the 15% column. The factor 7 is between 12% and 15%, which means that the unknown interest rate is between 12% and 15%. By interpolation, the rate is determined to be 13.834%, as shown in Illustration A-26 (i = unknown rate and d = difference between 12% and i):

ILLUSTRATION A-26
Interpolating to derive the rate of interest for an ordinary annuity

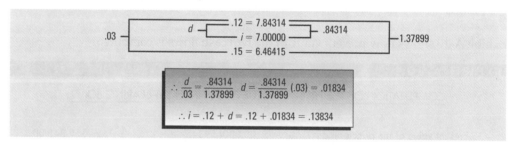

Interpolation assumes that the change between any two values in a table is linear. Although such an assumption is incorrect, the margin of error is generally insignificant if the table value ranges are not too wide.

Summary of Learning Objectives

1. **Identify accounting topics where the time value of money is relevant.** Some of the applications of time value of money measurements to accounting topics are: (1) notes; (2) leases; (3) amortization of premiums and discounts; (4) pensions and other post-retirement benefits; (5) capital assets; (6) sinking funds; (7) business combinations; (8) depreciation; and (9) instalment contracts.

2. **Distinguish between simple and compound interest.** See Fundamental Concepts following this Summary.

3. **Know how to use appropriate compound interest tables.** In order to identify the appropriate compound interest table to use of the five given, you must identify whether you are solving for (1) the future value of a single sum; (2) the present value of a single sum; (3) the future value of an annuity; or (4) the present value of an annuity. In addition, when an annuity is involved, you must identify whether these amounts are received or paid (1) at the beginning of each period (ordinary annuity); or (2) at the end of each period (annuity due).

4. **Identify variables fundamental to solving interest problems.** The following four variables are fundamental to all compound interest problems: (1) *Rate of interest:* unless otherwise stated, an annual rate that must be adjusted to reflect the length of the compounding period if less than a year. (2) *Number of time periods:* the number of compounding periods (a period may be equal to or less than a year). (3) *Future amount:* the value at a future date of a given sum or sums invested assuming compound interest. (4) *Present value:* the value now (present time) of a future sum or sums discounted assuming compound interest.

5. **Solve future and present value of single sum problems.** See Fundamental Concepts following this Summary, items 5(a) and 6(a).

6. **Solve future amount of ordinary and annuity due problems.** See Fundamental Concepts following this Summary, item 5(b).

7. **Solve present values of ordinary and annuity due problems.** See Fundamental Concepts following this Summary, item 6(b).

KEY TERMS

accumulation, A-10

annuity, A-13

annuity due, A-13

compound future amount, A-6

compound interest, A-5

deferred annuity, A-22

discounting, A-10

effective yield or rate, A-7

future amount, A-8

future amount of an annuity, A-13

interest, A-3

interpolation, A-25

ordinary annuity, A-13

present value, A-10

present value of an annuity, A-18

principal, A-3

simple interest, A-4

stated, nominal, coupon, or face rate, A-7

FUNDAMENTAL CONCEPTS

1. **Simple Interest.** Interest is computed only on the principal, regardless of interest that may have accrued in the past.

2. **Compound Interest.** Interest is computed on the unpaid interest of past periods, as well as on the principal.

3. **Rate of Interest.** Interest is usually expressed as an annual rate, but when the interest period is shorter than one year, the interest rate for the shorter period must be determined.

4. **Annuity.** A series of payments or receipts (called rents) that occur at equal intervals of time. The types of annuities are:
   (a) **Ordinary Annuity.** Each rent is payable (receivable) at the end of a period.
   (b) **Annuity Due.** Each rent is payable (receivable) at the beginning of a period.

5. **Future Amount.** Value at a later date of a given sum that is invested at compound interest.
   (a) **Future Amount of 1** (or amount of a given sum). The future value of $1.00 (or a single given sum), a, at the end of n periods at i compound interest rate (Table A-1).
   (b) **Future Amount of an Annuity.** The future value of a series of rents invested at compound interest; it is the accumulated total that results from a series of equal deposits at regular intervals invested at compound interest. Both deposits and interest increase the accumulation.

   1. **Future Amount of an Ordinary Annuity.** The future value on the date of the last rent (Table A-3).

   2. **Future Amount of an Annuity Due.** The future value one period after the date of the last rent. When an annuity due table is not available, use Table A-3 with the following formula:

   $$\begin{matrix} \text{Amount of annuity due} \\ \text{of 1 for } n \text{ rents} \end{matrix} = \begin{matrix} \text{Amount of ordinary annuity of 1} \\ \text{for } n \text{ rents} \times (1 + \text{interest rate}). \end{matrix}$$

6. **Present Value.** The value at an earlier date (usually now) of a given sum discounted at compound interest.
   (a) **Present Value of 1** (or present value of a single sum). The present value (worth) of $1.00 (or a given sum), p, due n periods hence, discounted at i compound interest (Table A-2).
   (b) **Present Value of an Annuity.** The present value (worth) of a series of rents discounted at compound interest; it is the present sum when invested at compound interest that will permit a series of equal withdrawals at regular intervals.

   1. **Present Value of an Ordinary Annuity.** The value now of $1.00 to be received or paid each period (rents) for n periods, discounted at i compound interest (Table A-4).

   2. **Present Value of an Annuity Due.** The value now of $1.00 to be received or paid at the beginning of each period (rents) for n periods, discounted at i compound interest (Table A-5). To use Table A-4 for an annuity due, apply this formula:

   $$\begin{matrix} \text{Present value of an annuity} \\ \text{due of 1 for } n \text{ rents} \end{matrix} = \begin{matrix} \text{Present value of ordinary annuity} \\ \text{of 1 for } n \text{ rents} \times (1 + \text{interest rate}). \end{matrix}$$

TABLE A-1

FUTURE AMOUNT OF 1

(Future Amount of a Single Sum)

$$a_{\overline{n}|i} = (1 + i)^n$$

(n) periods	2%	2½%	3%	4%	5%	6%	8%	9%	10%	11%	12%	15%
1	1.02000	1.02500	1.03000	1.04000	1.05000	1.06000	1.08000	1.09000	1.10000	1.11000	1.12000	1.15000
2	1.04040	1.05063	1.06090	1.08160	1.10250	1.12360	1.16640	1.18810	1.21000	1.23210	1.25440	1.32250
3	1.06121	1.07689	1.09273	1.12486	1.15763	1.19102	1.25971	1.29503	1.33100	1.36763	1.40493	1.52088
4	1.08243	1.10381	1.12551	1.16986	1.21551	1.26248	1.36049	1.41158	1.46410	1.51807	1.57352	1.74901
5	1.10408	1.13141	1.15927	1.21665	1.27628	1.33823	1.46933	1.53862	1.61051	1.68506	1.76234	2.01136
6	1.12616	1.15969	1.19405	1.26532	1.34010	1.41852	1.58687	1.67710	1.77156	1.87041	1.97382	2.31306
7	1.14869	1.18869	1.22987	1.31593	1.40710	1.50363	1.71382	1.82804	1.94872	2.07616	2.21068	2.66002
8	1.17166	1.21840	1.26677	1.36857	1.47746	1.59585	1.85093	1.99256	2.14359	2.30454	2.47596	3.05902
9	1.19509	1.24886	1.30477	1.42331	1.55133	1.68948	1.99900	2.17189	2.35795	2.55803	2.77308	3.51788
10	1.21899	1.28008	1.34392	1.48024	1.62889	1.79085	2.15892	2.36736	2.59374	2.83942	3.10585	4.04556
11	1.24337	1.31209	1.38423	1.53945	1.71034	1.89830	2.33164	2.58043	2.85312	3.15176	3.47855	4.65239
12	1.26824	1.34489	1.42576	1.60103	1.79585	2.01220	2.51817	2.81267	3.13843	3.49845	3.89598	5.35025
13	1.29361	1.37851	1.46853	1.66507	1.88565	2.13293	2.71962	3.06581	3.45227	3.88328	4.36349	6.15279
14	1.31948	1.41297	1.51259	1.73168	1.97993	2.26090	2.93719	3.34173	3.79750	4.31044	4.88711	7.07571
15	1.34587	1.44830	1.55797	1.80094	2.07893	2.39656	3.17217	3.64248	4.17725	4.78459	5.47357	8.13706
16	1.37279	1.48451	1.60471	1.87298	2.18287	2.54035	3.42594	3.97031	4.59497	5.31089	6.13039	9.35762
17	1.40024	1.52162	1.65285	1.94790	2.29202	2.69277	3.70002	4.32763	5.05447	5.89509	6.86604	10.76126
18	1.42825	1.55966	1.70243	2.02582	2.40662	2.85434	3.99602	4.71712	5.55992	6.54355	7.68997	12.37545
19	1.45681	1.59865	1.75351	2.10685	2.52695	3.02560	4.31570	5.14166	6.11591	7.26334	8.61276	14.23177
20	1.48595	1.63862	1.80611	2.19112	2.65330	3.20714	4.66096	5.60441	6.72750	8.06231	9.64629	16.36654
21	1.51567	1.67958	1.86029	2.27877	2.78596	3.39956	5.03383	6.10881	7.40025	8.94917	10.80385	18.82152
22	1.54598	1.72157	1.91610	2.36992	2.92526	3.60354	5.43654	6.65860	8.14028	9.93357	12.10031	21.64475
23	1.57690	1.76461	1.97359	2.46472	3.07152	3.81975	5.87146	7.25787	8.95430	11.02627	13.55235	24.89146
24	1.60844	1.80873	2.03279	2.56330	3.22510	4.04893	6.34118	7.91108	9.84973	12.23916	15.17863	28.62518
25	1.64061	1.85394	2.09378	2.66584	3.38635	4.29187	6.84847	8.62308	10.83471	13.58546	17.00000	32.91895
26	1.67342	1.90029	2.15659	2.77247	3.55567	4.54938	7.39635	9.39916	11.91818	15.07986	19.04007	37.85680
27	1.70689	1.94780	2.22129	2.88337	3.73346	4.82235	7.98806	10.24508	13.10999	16.73865	21.32488	43.53532
28	1.74102	1.99650	2.28793	2.99870	3.92013	5.11169	8.62711	11.16714	14.42099	18.57990	23.88387	50.06561
29	1.77584	2.04641	2.35657	3.11865	4.11614	5.41839	9.31727	12.17218	15.86309	20.62369	26.74993	57.57545
30	1.81136	2.09757	2.42726	3.24340	4.32194	5.74349	10.06266	13.26768	17.44940	22.89230	29.95992	66.21177
31	1.84759	2.15001	2.50008	3.37313	4.53804	6.08810	10.86767	14.46177	19.19434	25.41045	33.55511	76.14354
32	1.88454	2.20376	2.57508	3.50806	4.76494	6.45339	11.73708	15.76333	21.11378	28.20560	37.58173	87.56507
33	1.92223	2.25885	2.65234	3.64838	5.00319	6.84059	12.67605	17.18203	23.22515	31.30821	42.09153	100.69983
34	1.96068	2.31532	2.73191	3.79432	5.25335	7.25103	13.69013	18.72841	25.54767	34.75212	47.14252	115.80480
35	1.99989	2.37321	2.81386	3.94609	5.51602	7.68609	14.78534	20.41397	28.10244	38.57485	52.79962	133.17552
36	2.03989	2.43254	2.88928	4.10393	5.79182	8.14725	15.96817	22.25123	30.91268	42.81808	59.13557	153.15185
37	2.08069	2.49335	2.98523	4.26809	6.08141	8.63609	17.24563	24.25384	34.00395	47.52807	66.23184	176.12463
38	2.12230	2.55568	3.07478	4.43881	6.38548	9.15425	18.62528	26.43668	37.40434	52.75616	74.17966	202.54332
39	2.16474	2.61957	3.16703	4.61637	6.70475	9.70351	20.11530	28.81598	41.14479	58.55934	83.08122	232.92482
40	2.20804	2.68506	3.26204	4.80102	7.03999	10.28572	21.72452	31.40942	45.25926	65.00087	93.05097	267.86355

TABLE A-2

PRESENT VALUE OF 1

(Present Value of a Single Sum)

$$P_{\overline{n}|i} = \frac{1}{(1+i)^n} = (1+i)^{-n}$$

(n) periods	2%	2½%	3%	4%	5%	6%	8%	9%	10%	11%	12%	15%
1	.98039	.97561	.97087	.96156	.95238	.94340	.92593	.91743	.90909	.90090	.89286	.86957
2	.96117	.95181	.94260	.92456	.90703	.89000	.85734	.84168	.82645	.81162	.79719	.75614
3	.94232	.92860	.91514	.88900	.86384	.83962	.79383	.77218	.75132	.73119	.71178	.65752
4	.92385	.90595	.88849	.85480	.82270	.79209	.73503	.70843	.68301	.65873	.63552	.57175
5	.90583	.88385	.86261	.82193	.78353	.74726	.68058	.64993	.62092	.59345	.56743	.49718
6	.88797	.86230	.83748	.79031	.74622	.70496	.63017	.59627	.56447	.53464	.50663	.43233
7	.87056	.84127	.81309	.75992	.71068	.66506	.58349	.54703	.51316	.48166	.45235	.37594
8	.85349	.82075	.78941	.73069	.67684	.62741	.54027	.50187	.46651	.43393	.40388	.32690
9	.83676	.80073	.76642	.70259	.64461	.59190	.50025	.46043	.42410	.39092	.36061	.28426
10	.82035	.78120	.74409	.67556	.61391	.55839	.46319	.42241	.38554	.35218	.32197	.24719
11	.80426	.76214	.72242	.64958	.58468	.52679	.42888	.38753	.35049	.31728	.28748	.21494
12	.78849	.74356	.70138	.62460	.55684	.49697	.39711	.35554	.31863	.28584	.25668	.18691
13	.77303	.72542	.68095	.60057	.53032	.46884	.36770	.32618	.28966	.25751	.22917	.16253
14	.75788	.70773	.66112	.57748	.50507	.44230	.34046	.29925	.26333	.23199	.20462	.14133
15	.74301	.69047	.64186	.55526	.48102	.41727	.31524	.27454	.23939	.20900	.18270	.12289
16	.72845	.67362	.62317	.53391	.45811	.39365	.29189	.25187	.21763	.18829	.16312	.10687
17	.71416	.65720	.60502	.51337	.43630	.37136	.27027	.23107	.19785	.16963	.14564	.09293
18	.70016	.64117	.58739	.49363	.41552	.35034	.25025	.21199	.17986	.15282	.13004	.08081
19	.68643	.62553	.57029	.47464	.39573	.33051	.23171	.19449	.16351	.13768	.11611	.07027
20	.67297	.61027	.55368	.45639	.37689	.31180	.21455	.17843	.14864	.12403	.10367	.06110
21	.65978	.59539	.53755	.43883	.35894	.29416	.19866	.16370	.13513	.11174	.09256	.05313
22	.64684	.58086	.52189	.42196	.34185	.27751	.18394	.15018	.12285	.10067	.08264	.04620
23	.63416	.56670	.50669	.40573	.32557	.26180	.17032	.13778	.11168	.09069	.07379	.04017
24	.62172	.55288	.49193	.39012	.31007	.24698	.15770	.12641	.10153	.08170	.06588	.03493
25	.60953	.53939	.47761	.37512	.29530	.23300	.14602	.11597	.09230	.07361	.05882	.03038
26	.59758	.52623	.46369	.36069	.28124	.21981	.13520	.10639	.08391	.06631	.05252	.02642
27	.58586	.51340	.45019	.34682	.26785	.20737	.12519	.09761	.07628	.05974	.04689	.02297
28	.57437	.50088	.43708	.33348	.25509	.19563	.11591	.08955	.06934	.05382	.04187	.01997
29	.56311	.48866	.42435	.32065	.24295	.18456	.10733	.08216	.06304	.04849	.03738	.01737
30	.55207	.47674	.41199	.30832	.23138	.17411	.09938	.07537	.05731	.04368	.03338	.01510
31	.54125	.46511	.39999	.29646	.22036	.16425	.09202	.06915	.05210	.03935	.02980	.01313
32	.53063	.45377	.38834	.28506	.20987	.15496	.08520	.06344	.04736	.03545	.02661	.01142
33	.52023	.44270	.37703	.27409	.19987	.14619	.07889	.05820	.04306	.03194	.02376	.00993
34	.51003	.43191	.36604	.26355	.19035	.13791	.07305	.05340	.03914	.02878	.02121	.00864
35	.50003	.42137	.35538	.25342	.18129	.13011	.06763	.04899	.03558	.02592	.01894	.00751
36	.49022	.41109	.34503	.24367	.17266	.12274	.06262	.04494	.03235	.02335	.01691	.00653
37	.48061	.40107	.33498	.23430	.16444	.11579	.05799	.04123	.02941	.02104	.01510	.00568
38	.47119	.39128	.32523	.22529	.15661	.10924	.05369	.03783	.02674	.01896	.01348	.00494
39	.46195	.38174	.31575	.21662	.14915	.10306	.04971	.03470	.02430	.01708	.01204	.00429
40	.45289	.37243	.30656	.20829	.14205	.09722	.04603	.03184	.02210	.01538	.01075	.00373

TABLE A-3

FUTURE AMOUNT OF AN ORDINARY ANNUITY OF 1

$$A_{\overline{n}|i} = \frac{(1 + i)^n - 1}{I}$$

(n) periods	2%	2½%	3%	4%	5%	6%	8%	9%	10%	11%	12%	15%
1	1.00000	1.00000	1.00000	1.00000	1.00000	1.00000	1.00000	1.00000	1.00000	1.00000	1.00000	1.00000
2	2.02000	2.02500	2.03000	2.04000	2.05000	2.06000	2.08000	2.09000	2.10000	2.11000	2.12000	2.15000
3	3.06040	3.07563	3.09090	3.12160	3.15250	3.18360	3.24640	3.27810	3.31000	3.34210	3.37440	3.47250
4	4.12161	4.15252	4.18363	4.24646	4.31013	4.37462	4.50611	4.57313	4.64100	4.70973	4.77933	4.99338
5	5.20404	5.25633	5.30914	5.41632	5.52563	5.63709	5.86660	5.98471	6.10510	6.22780	6.35285	6.74238
6	6.30812	6.38774	6.46841	6.63298	6.80191	6.97532	7.33592	7.52334	7.71561	7.91286	8.11519	8.75374
7	7.43428	7.54743	7.66246	7.89829	8.14201	8.39384	8.92280	9.20044	9.48717	9.78327	10.08901	11.06680
8	8.58297	8.73612	8.89234	9.21423	9.54911	9.89747	10.63663	11.02847	11.43589	11.85943	12.29969	13.72682
9	9.75463	9.95452	10.15911	10.58280	11.02656	11.49132	12.48756	13.02104	13.57948	14.16397	14.77566	16.78584
10	10.94972	11.20338	11.46338	12.00611	12.57789	13.18079	14.48656	15.19293	15.93743	16.72201	17.54874	20.30372
11	12.16872	12.48347	12.80780	13.48635	14.20679	14.97164	16.64549	17.56029	18.53117	19.56143	20.65458	24.34928
12	13.41209	13.79555	14.19203	15.02581	15.91713	16.86994	18.97713	20.14072	21.38428	22.71319	24.13313	29.00167
13	14.68033	15.14044	15.61779	16.62684	17.71298	18.88214	21.49530	22.95339	24.52271	26.21164	28.02911	34.35192
14	15.97394	16.51895	17.08632	18.29191	19.59863	21.01507	24.21492	26.01919	27.97498	30.09492	32.39260	40.50471
15	17.29342	17.93193	18.59891	20.02359	21.57856	23.27597	27.15211	29.36092	31.77248	34.40536	37.27972	47.58041
16	18.63929	19.38022	20.15688	21.82453	23.65749	25.67253	30.32428	33.00340	35.94973	39.18995	42.75328	55.71747
17	20.01207	20.86473	21.76159	23.69751	25.84037	28.21288	33.75023	36.97371	40.54470	44.50084	48.88367	65.07509
18	21.41231	22.38635	23.41444	25.64541	28.13238	30.90565	37.45024	41.30134	45.59917	50.39593	55.74972	75.83636
19	22.84056	23.94601	25.11687	27.67123	30.53900	33.75999	41.44626	46.01846	51.15909	56.93949	63.43968	88.21181
20	24.29737	25.54466	26.87037	29.77808	33.06595	36.78559	45.76196	51.16012	57.27500	64.20283	72.05244	102.44358
21	25.78332	27.18327	28.67649	31.96920	35.71925	39.99273	50.42292	56.76453	64.00250	72.26514	81.69874	118.81012
22	27.29898	28.86286	30.53678	34.24797	38.50521	43.39229	55.45676	62.87334	71.40275	81.21431	92.50258	137.63164
23	28.84496	30.58443	32.45288	36.61789	41.43048	46.99583	60.89330	69.53194	79.54302	91.14788	104.60289	159.27638
24	30.42186	32.34904	34.42647	39.08260	44.50200	50.81558	66.76476	76.78981	88.49733	102.17415	118.15524	184.16784
25	32.03030	34.15776	36.45926	41.64591	47.72710	54.86451	73.10594	84.70090	98.34706	114.41331	133.33387	212.79302
26	33.67091	36.01171	38.55304	44.31174	51.11345	59.15638	79.95442	93.32398	109.18177	127.99877	150.33393	245.71197
27	35.34432	37.91200	40.70963	47.08421	54.66913	63.70577	87.35077	102.72314	121.09994	143.07864	169.37401	283.56877
28	37.05121	39.85990	42.93092	49.96758	58.40258	68.52811	95.33883	112.96822	134.20994	159.81729	190.69889	327.10408
29	38.79223	41.85630	45.21885	52.96629	62.32271	73.63980	103.96594	124.13536	148.63093	178.39719	214.58275	377.16969
30	40.56808	43.90270	47.57542	56.08494	66.43885	79.05819	113.28321	136.30754	164.49402	199.02088	241.33268	434.74515
31	42.37944	46.00027	50.00268	59.32834	70.76079	84.80168	123.34587	149.57522	181.94343	221.91317	271.29261	500.95692
32	44.22703	48.15028	52.50276	62.70147	75.29883	90.88978	134.21354	164.03699	201.13777	247.32362	304.84772	577.10046
33	46.11157	50.35403	55.07784	66.20953	80.06377	97.34316	145.95062	179.80032	222.25154	275.52922	342.42945	644.66553
34	48.03380	52.61289	57.73018	69.85791	85.06696	104.18376	158.62667	196.98234	245.47670	306.83744	384.52098	765.36535
35	49.99448	54.92821	60.46208	73.65222	90.32031	111.43478	172.31680	215.71076	271.02437	341.58955	431.66350	881.17016
36	51.99437	57.30141	63.27594	77.59831	95.83632	119.12087	187.10215	236.12472	299.12681	380.16441	484.46312	1014.34568
37	54.03425	59.73395	66.17422	81.70225	101.62814	127.26812	203.07032	258.37595	330.03949	422.98249	543.59869	1167.49753
38	56.11494	62.22730	69.15945	85.97034	107.70955	135.90421	220.31595	282.62978	364.04343	470.51056	609.83053	1343.62216
39	58.23724	64.78298	72.23423	90.40915	114.09502	145.05846	238.94122	309.06646	401.44778	523.26673	684.01020	1546.16549
40	60.40198	67.40255	75.40126	95.02552	120.79977	154.76197	259.05652	337.88245	442.59256	581.82607	767.09142	1779.09031

TABLE A-4

PRESENT VALUE OF AN ORDINARY ANNUITY OF 1

$$P_{\overline{n}|i} = \frac{1 - \frac{1}{(1 + i)^n}}{i} = \frac{1 - P_{\overline{n}|i}}{i}$$

(n) periods	2%	2½%	3%	4%	5%	6%	8%	9%	10%	11%	12%	15%
1	.98039	.97561	.97087	.96154	.95238	.94340	.92593	.91743	.90909	.90090	.89286	.86957
2	1.94156	1.92742	1.91347	1.88609	1.85941	1.83339	1.78326	1.75911	1.73554	1.71252	1.69005	1.62571
3	2.88388	2.85602	2.82861	2.77509	2.72325	2.67301	2.57710	2.53130	2.48685	2.44371	2.40183	2.28323
4	3.80773	3.76197	3.71710	3.62990	3.54595	3.46511	3.31213	3.23972	3.16986	3.10245	3.03735	2.85498
5	4.71346	4.64583	4.57971	4.45182	4.32948	4.21236	3.99271	3.88965	3.79079	3.69590	3.60478	3.35216
6	5.60143	5.50813	5.41719	5.24214	5.07569	4.91732	4.62288	4.48592	4.35526	4.23054	4.11141	3.78448
7	6.47199	6.34939	6.23028	6.00205	5.78637	5.58238	5.20637	5.03295	4.86842	4.71220	4.56376	4.16042
8	7.32548	7.17014	7.01969	6.73274	6.46321	6.20979	5.74664	5.53482	5.33493	5.14612	4.96764	4.48732
9	8.16224	7.97087	7.78611	7.43533	7.10782	6.80169	6.24689	5.99525	5.75902	5.53705	5.32825	4.77158
10	8.98259	8.75206	8.53020	8.11090	7.72173	7.36009	6.71008	6.41766	6.14457	5.88923	5.65022	5.01877
11	9.78685	9.51421	9.25262	8.76048	8.30641	7.88687	7.13896	6.80519	6.49506	6.20652	5.93770	5.23371
12	10.57534	10.25776	9.95400	9.38507	8.86325	8.38384	7.53608	7.16073	6.81369	6.49236	6.19437	5.42062
13	11.34837	10.98319	10.63496	9.98565	9.39357	8.85268	7.90378	7.48690	7.10336	6.74987	6.42355	5.58315
14	12.10625	11.69091	11.29607	10.56312	9.89864	9.29498	8.24424	7.78615	7.36669	6.98187	6.62817	5.72448
15	12.84926	12.38138	11.93794	11.11839	10.37966	9.71225	8.55948	8.06069	7.60608	7.19087	6.81086	5.84737
16	13.57771	13.05500	12.56110	11.65230	10.83777	10.10590	8.85137	8.31256	7.82371	7.37916	6.97399	5.95424
17	14.29187	13.71220	13.16612	12.16567	11.27407	10.47726	9.12164	8.54363	8.02155	7.54879	7.11963	6.04716
18	14.99203	14.35336	13.75351	12.65930	11.68959	10.82760	9.37189	8.75563	8.20141	7.70162	7.24967	6.12797
19	15.67846	14.97889	14.32380	13.13394	12.08532	11.15812	9.60360	8.95012	8.36492	7.83929	7.36578	6.19823
20	16.35143	15.58916	14.87747	13.59033	12.46221	11.46992	9.81815	9.12855	8.51356	7.96333	7.46944	6.25933
21	17.01121	16.18455	15.41502	14.02916	12.82115	11.76408	10.01680	9.29224	8.64869	8.07507	7.56200	6.31246
22	17.65805	16.76541	15.93692	14.45112	13.16800	12.04158	10.20074	9.44243	8.77154	8.17574	7.64465	6.35866
23	18.29220	17.33211	16.44361	14.85684	13.48857	12.30338	10.37106	9.58021	8.88322	8.26643	7.71843	6.39884
24	18.91393	17.88499	16.93554	15.24696	13.79864	12.55036	10.52876	9.70661	8.98474	8.34814	7.78432	6.43377
25	19.52346	18.42438	17.41315	15.62208	14.09394	12.78336	10.67478	9.82258	9.07704	8.42174	7.84314	6.46415
26	20.12104	18.95061	17.87684	15.98277	14.37519	13.00317	10.80998	9.92897	9.16095	8.48806	7.89566	6.49056
27	20.70690	19.46401	18.32703	16.32959	14.64303	13.21053	10.93516	10.02658	9.23722	8.45780	7.94255	6.51353
28	21.28127	19.96489	18.76411	16.66306	14.89813	13.40616	11.05108	10.11613	9.30657	8.60162	7.98442	6.53351
29	21.84438	20.45355	19.18845	16.98371	15.14107	13.59072	11.15841	10.19828	9.36961	8.65011	8.02181	6.55088
30	22.39646	20.93029	19.60044	17.29203	15.37245	13.76483	11.25778	10.27365	9.42691	8.69379	8.05518	6.56598
31	22.93770	21.39541	20.00043	17.58849	15.59281	13.92909	11.34980	10.34280	9.47901	8.73315	8.08499	6.57911
32	23.46833	21.84918	20.38877	17.87355	15.80268	14.08404	11.43500	10.40624	9.52638	8.76860	8.11159	6.59053
33	23.98856	22.29188	20.76579	18.14765	16.00255	14.23023	11.51389	10.46444	9.56943	8.80054	8.13535	6.60046
34	24.49859	22.72379	21.13184	18.41120	16.19290	14.36814	11.58693	10.51784	9.60858	8.82932	8.15656	6.60910
35	24.99862	23.14516	21.48722	18.66461	16.37419	14.49825	11.65457	10.56682	9.64416	8.85524	8.17550	6.61661
36	25.48884	23.55625	21.83225	18.90828	16.54685	14.62099	11.71719	10.61176	9.67651	8.87859	8.19241	6.62314
37	25.96945	23.95732	22.16724	19.14258	16.71129	14.73678	11.77518	10.65299	9.70592	8.89963	8.20751	6.62882
38	26.44064	24.34860	22.49246	19.36786	16.86789	14.84602	11.82887	10.69082	9.73265	8.91859	8.22099	6.63375
39	26.90259	24.73034	22.80822	19.58448	17.01704	14.94907	11.87858	10.72552	9.75697	8.93567	8.23303	6.63805
40	27.35548	25.10278	23.11477	19.79277	17.15909	15.04630	11.92461	10.75736	9.77905	8.95105	8.24378	6.64178

TABLE A-5

PRESENT VALUE OF AN ANNUITY DUE OF 1

$$Pd_{\overline{n}|i} = 1 + \frac{1 - \frac{1}{(1+i)^{n-1}}}{i} = (1+i)\left(\frac{1 - P_{\overline{n}|i}}{i}\right) = (1+i) P_{\overline{n}|i}$$

(n) periods	2%	2½%	3%	4%	5%	6%	8%	9%	10%	11%	12%	15%
1	1.00000	1.00000	1.00000	1.00000	1.00000	1.00000	1.00000	1.00000	1.00000	1.00000	1.00000	1.00000
2	1.98039	1.97561	1.97087	1.96154	1.95238	1.94340	1.92593	1.91743	1.90909	1.90090	1.89286	1.86957
3	2.94156	2.92742	2.91347	2.88609	2.85941	2.83339	2.78326	2.75911	2.73554	2.71252	2.69005	2.62571
4	3.88388	3.85602	3.82861	3.77509	3.72325	3.67301	3.57710	3.53130	3.48685	3.44371	3.40183	3.28323
5	4.80773	4.76197	4.71710	4.62990	4.54595	4.46511	4.31213	4.23972	4.16986	4.10245	4.03735	3.85498
6	5.71346	5.64583	5.57971	5.45182	5.32948	5.21236	4.99271	4.88965	4.79079	4.69590	4.60478	4.35216
7	6.60143	6.50813	6.41719	6.24214	6.07569	5.91732	5.62288	5.48592	5.35526	5.23054	5.11141	4.78448
8	7.47199	7.34939	7.23028	7.00205	6.78637	6.58238	6.20637	6.03295	5.86842	5.71220	5.56376	5.16042
9	8.32548	8.17014	8.01969	7.73274	7.46321	7.20979	6.74664	6.53482	6.33493	6.14612	5.96764	5.48732
10	9.16224	8.97087	8.78611	8.43533	8.10782	7.80169	7.24689	6.99525	6.75902	6.53705	6.32825	5.77158
11	9.98259	9.75206	9.53020	9.11090	8.72173	8.36009	7.71008	7.41766	7.14457	6.88923	6.65022	6.01877
12	10.78685	10.51421	10.25262	9.76048	9.30641	8.88687	8.13896	7.80519	7.49506	7.20652	6.93770	6.23371
13	11.57534	11.25776	10.95400	10.38507	9.86325	9.38384	8.53608	8.16073	7.81369	7.49236	7.19437	6.42062
14	12.34837	11.98319	11.63496	10.98565	10.39357	9.85268	8.90378	8.48690	8.10336	7.74987	7.42355	6.58315
15	13.10625	12.69091	12.29607	11.56312	10.89864	10.29498	9.24424	8.78615	9.36669	7.98187	7.62817	6.72448
16	13.84926	13.38138	12.93794	12.11839	11.37966	10.71225	9.55948	9.06069	8.60608	8.19087	7.81086	6.84737
17	14.57771	14.05500	13.56110	12.65230	11.83777	11.10590	9.85137	9.31256	8.82371	8.37916	7.97399	6.95424
18	15.29187	14.71220	14.16612	13.16567	12.27407	11.47726	10.12164	9.54363	9.02155	8.54879	8.11963	7.04716
19	15.99203	15.35336	14.75351	13.65930	12.68959	11.82760	10.37189	9.75563	9.20141	8.70162	8.24967	7.12797
20	16.67846	15.97889	15.32380	14.13394	13.08532	12.15812	10.60360	9.95012	9.36492	8.83929	8.36578	7.19823
21	17.35143	16.58916	15.87747	14.59033	13.46221	12.46992	10.81815	10.12855	9.51356	8.96333	8.46944	7.25933
22	18.01121	17.18455	16.41502	15.02916	13.82115	12.76408	11.01680	10.29224	9.64869	9.07507	8.56200	7.31246
23	18.65805	17.76541	16.93692	15.45112	14.16300	13.04158	11.20074	10.44243	9.77154	9.17574	8.64465	7.35866
24	19.29220	18.33211	17.44361	15.85684	14.48857	13.30338	11.37106	10.58021	9.88322	9.26643	8.71843	7.39884
25	19.91393	18.88499	17.93554	16.24696	14.79864	13.55036	11.52876	10.70661	9.98474	9.34814	8.78432	7.43377
26	20.52346	19.42438	18.41315	16.62208	15.09394	13.78336	11.67478	10.82258	10.07704	9.42174	8.84314	7.46415
27	21.12104	19.95061	18.87684	16.98277	15.37519	14.00317	11.80998	10.92897	10.16095	9.48806	8.89566	7.49056
28	21.70690	20.46401	19.32703	17.32959	15.64303	14.21053	11.93518	11.02658	10.23722	9.54780	8.94255	7.51353
29	22.28127	20.96489	19.76411	17.66306	15.89813	14.40616	12.05108	11.11613	10.30657	9.60162	8.98442	7.53351
30	22.84438	21.45355	20.18845	17.98371	16.14107	14.59072	12.15841	11.19828	10.36961	9.65011	9.02181	7.55088
31	23.39646	21.93029	20.60044	18.29203	16.37245	14.76483	12.25778	11.27365	10.42691	9.69379	9.05518	7.56598
32	23.93770	22.39541	21.00043	18.58849	16.59281	14.92909	12.34980	11.34280	10.47901	9.73315	9.08499	7.57911
33	24.46833	22.84918	21.38877	18.87355	16.80268	15.08404	12.43500	11.40624	10.52638	9.76860	9.11159	7.59053
34	24.98856	23.29188	21.76579	19.14765	17.00255	15.23023	12.51389	11.46444	10.56943	9.80054	9.13535	7.60046
35	25.49859	23.72379	22.13184	19.41120	17.19290	15.36814	12.58693	11.51784	10.60858	9.82932	9.15656	7.60910
36	25.99862	24.14516	22.48722	19.66461	17.37419	15.49825	12.65457	11.56682	10.64416	9.85524	9.17550	7.61661
37	26.48884	24.55625	22.83225	19.90828	17.54685	15.62099	12.71719	11.61176	10.67651	9.87859	9.19241	7.62314
38	26.96945	24.95732	23.16724	20.14258	17.71129	15.73678	12.77518	11.65299	10.70592	9.89963	9.20751	7.62882
39	27.44064	25.34860	23.49246	20.36786	17.86789	15.84602	12.82887	11.69082	10.73265	9.91859	9.22099	7.63375
40	27.90259	25.73034	23.80822	20.58448	18.01704	15.94907	12.87858	11.72552	10.75697	9.93567	9.23303	7.63805

CONCEPT REVIEW

1. Presented below are a number of values taken from compound interest tables that involve the same number of periods and the same rate of interest. Indicate what each of these four values represent:
   (a) 7.36009
   (b) 1.79085
   (c) 0.55839
   (d) 13.18079

2. Harmon Co. deposits $18,000 in a money market certificate that provides interest of 8% compounded quarterly if the amount is maintained for three years. How much will Harmon have at the end of three years?

3. Phil Bayliss will receive $30,000 five years from today from a trust fund established by his mother. Assuming an interest rate of 8%, compounded semiannually, what is the present value of this amount?

4. Wendy Inc. owes $60,000 to Mike's Meat Company. How much would Wendy have to pay each year if the debt is to be retired through four equal payments made at the end of each year, and the interest rate on the debt is 15%? (Round to nearest cent.)

5. The Tsangs are planning for a retirement home. They estimate they will need $150,000 four years from now to purchase this home. Assuming an interest rate of 10%, what amount must be deposited at the end of each of the four years to fund the home price?

6. Assume the same situation as in Question 5, except that the four equal amounts are deposited at the beginning of the period rather than at the end. In this case, what amount must be deposited at the beginning of each period?

7. In a book named *Treasure*, the reader has to figure out where a 1 kg, 24 karat gold horse has been buried. If the horse is found, a prize of $25,000 per year for 20 years is provided. The actual cost to the publisher to purchase an annuity to pay the prize is $210,000. What interest rate (to the nearest percent) was used to determine the amount of the annuity? (Assume end-of-year payments.)

8. Stress Enterprises leases property to Boz Inc. Because Boz Inc. is experiencing financial difficulty, Stress agrees to receive five rents of $9,000 at the end of each year, with the rents deferred three years. What is the present value of the five rents, discounted at 12%?

9. Kitt Inc. invests $20,000 initially, which accumulates to $38,000 at the end of five years. What is the annual interest rate earned on the investment? (**Hint:** Interpolation will be needed.)

10. Recently Sam Kylyk was interested in purchasing a new Honda Acura automobile. The salesperson indicated that the price of the car was either $26,535 cash or $7,000 at the end of each of five years. Compute the effective interest rate to the nearest percent that Kylyk would have to pay if he chose to make the five annual payments.

EXERCISES

(Interest rates are per annum unless otherwise indicated.)

EA-1 **(Present Value Problem)** A hockey player was reported to have received an $11 million contract. The terms were a signing bonus of $500,000 in 1995 plus $500,000 in 2005 through the year 2008. In addition, he was to receive a base salary of $300,000 in 1995 that was to increase $100,000 a year to the year 1999; in 2000 he was to receive $1 million a year that would increase $100,000 per year to the year 2004. Assuming that the appropriate interest rate was 9% and that each payment occurred on December 31 of the respective year, compute the present value of this contract as of December 31, 1995.

EA-2 **(Future Amount and Present Value Problems)** Presented below are three unrelated situations:

1. Fishbone Company recently signed a 10-year lease for a new office building. Under the lease agreement, a security deposit of $10,000 was made that would be returned at the expiration of the lease with interest compounded at 10% per year. What amount will the company receive when the lease expires?

2. Stevenson Corporation, having recently issued a $10 million, 15-year bond, is committed to make annual sinking fund deposits of $300,000. The deposits are made on the last day of each year and yield a return of 10%. Will the fund at the end of 15 years be sufficient to retire the bonds? If not, what will the excess or deficiency be?

3. Under the terms of her salary agreement, President Joanie McKaig has an option of receiving either an immediate bonus of $35,000 or a deferred bonus of $65,000, payable in 10 years. Ignoring tax considerations and assuming a relevant interest rate of 8%, which form of settlement should President McKaig accept?

(Computations for a Retirement Fund) Greg Parent, a super salesman who is contemplating retirement on his fifty-fifth birthday, plans to create a fund that will earn 8% and enable him to withdraw $8,000 per year on June 30, beginning in 2002 and continuing through 2005. Greg intends to make equal contributions to this fund on June 30 of each of the years 1998–2001. **EA-3**

Instructions

(a) How much must the balance of the fund equal on June 30, 2001 in order for Greg Parent to satisfy his objective?

(b) What is the required amount of each of Greg's contributions to the fund?

(Unknown Periods and Unknown Interest Rate)

1. Curtis Joseph wishes to become a millionaire. His money market fund has a balance of $76,277.71 and has a guaranteed interest rate of 10%. **EA-4**

Instructions

How many years must Curtis leave the balance in the fund in order to get his desired $1,000,000?

2. Oleta Firestone desires to accumulate $1 million in 15 years using her money market fund balance of $122,894.51.

Instructions

At what interest rate must her investment compound annually?

(Computation of Bond Prices) What will you pay for a $25,000 debenture bond that matures in 15 years and pays $2,500 interest at the end of each year if you want to earn a yield of (a) 8%? (b) 10%? (c) 12%? **EA-5**

(Computation of Pension Liability) Erasure Inc. is a furniture manufacturing company with 50 employees. Recently, after a long negotiation with the local union, the company decided to initiate a pension plan as part of its compensation package. The plan will start on January 1, 1998. Each employee covered by the plan is entitled to a pension payment each year after retirement. As required by accounting standards, the controller of the company needs to report the projected pension obligation (liability). On the basis of a discussion with the supervisor of the Personnel Department and an actuary from an insurance company, the controller develops the following information related to the pension plan: **EA-6**

Average length of time to retirement	15 years
Expected life duration after retirement	10 years
Total pension payment expected each year for all retired employees.	
Payment made at the end of the year.	$600,000/year
The interest rate is 8%.	

Instructions

On the basis of the information given, determine the projected pension obligation.

(Amount Needed to Retire Shares) Debugit Inc. is a computer software development company. In recent years, it has experienced significant growth in sales. As a result, the Board of Directors has decided to raise funds by issuing redeemable preferred shares to meet cash needs for expansion. On January 1, 1997 the company issued 100,000 redeemable preferred shares with the intent to redeem them on January 1, 2007. The redemption price per share is $25. **EA-7**

As the controller of the company, Kriss Krass is asked to set up a plan to accumulate the funds that will be needed to retire the redeemable preferred shares in 2007. She expects the company to have a surplus of funds of $120,000 each year for the next 10 years, and decides to put these amounts into a sinking fund. Beginning January 1, 1998 the company will deposit $120,000 into the sinking fund annually for 10 years. The sinking fund is expected to earn 10% interest compounded annually. However, the sinking fund will not be sufficient for the redemption of the preferred shares. Therefore, Kriss plans to deposit on January 1, 2002 a single amount into a savings account that is expected to earn 9% interest.

Instructions

What is the amount that must be deposited on January 1, 2002?

EA-8 **(Analysis of Alternatives)** S.O. Simple Ltd., a manufacturer of low-sodium, low-cholesterol T.V. dinners, would like to increase its market share in Atlantic Canada. In order to do so, S.O. Simple has decided to locate a new factory in the Halifax area. S.O. Simple will either buy or lease a building, depending upon which is more advantageous. The site location committee has narrowed down the options to the following three buildings:

Building A: Purchase for a cash price of $600,000, useful life 25 years.

Building B: Lease for 25 years, making annual payments of $68,000 at the beginning of each year.

Building C: Purchase for $650,000 cash. This building is larger than needed; however, the excess space can be sub-let for 25 years at a net annual rental of $7,000. Rental payments will be received at the end of each year. S.O. Simple has no aversion to being a landlord.

Instructions

In which building would you recommend that S.O. Simple locate, assuming a 12% interest rate?

EA-9 **(Present Value of a Bond)** Your client, Gerspacher Inc., has acquired Helpless Manufacturing Company in a business combination that is to be accounted for as a purchase transaction (at fair market value). Along with the assets of Helpless, Gerspacher assumed an outstanding liability for a debenture bond issue that had a principal amount of $7,500,000 and interest payable semiannually at a rate of 8%. Helpless received $6,800,000 in proceeds from the issuance five years ago. The bonds are currently 20 years from maturity. Equivalent securities command a 12% current market rate of interest.

Instructions

Your client requests your advice regarding the amount to record for the acquired bond issue.

EA-10 **(Future Amount and Changing Interest Rates)** Melanie Doane intends to invest $20,000 in a trust on January 10 of every year, 1998 to 2012, inclusive. She anticipates that interest rates will change during that period of time as follows:

1/10/98–1/09/01	10%
1/10/01–1/09/08	11%
1/10/08–1/09/12	12%

How much will Melanie have in trust on January 10, 2012?

EA-11 **(Retirement of Debt)** Glen Chan borrowed $67,000 on March 1, 1998. This amount plus accrued interest at 12% compounded semiannually is to be repaid on March 1, 2008. To retire this debt, Glen plans to contribute five equal amounts to a debt retirement fund starting on March 1, 2003 and continuing for the next four years. The fund is expected to earn 10% per annum.

Instructions

How much must Glen Chan contribute each year to provide a fund sufficient to retire the debt on March 1, 2008?

EA-12 **(Interpolating the Interest Rate)** On July 17, 1998 Bruce Lendrum borrowed $42,000 from his grandfather to open a clothing store. Starting July 17, 1999 Bruce has to make 10 equal annual payments of $6,700 each to repay the loan.

Instructions

What interest rate is Bruce Lendrum paying? (Interpolation is required.)

EA-13 **(Interpolating the Interest Rate)** As the purchaser of a new house, Sandra Pederson signed a mortgage note to pay the Canadian Bank $16,000 every six months for 20 years, at the end of which time she will own the house. At the date the mortgage was signed, the purchase price was $198,000 and Sandra made a down payment of $20,000. The first mortgage payment is to be made six months after the date the mortgage was signed.

Instructions

Compute the exact rate of interest earned by the bank on the mortgage. (Interpolate if necessary.)

PROBLEMS

Answer each of these unrelated questions:

1. On January 1, 1998 Gadget Corporation sold a building that cost $210,000 and had accumulated depreciation of $100,000 on the date of sale. Gadget received as consideration a $275,000 noninterest-bearing note due on January 1, 2001. There was no established exchange price for the building and the note had no ready market. The prevailing rate of interest for a note of this type on January 1, 1998 was 9%. At what amount should the gain from the sale of the building be reported?

2. On January 1, 1998 Gadget Corporation purchased 100 of the $1,000 face value, 9%, 10-year bonds of Fox Inc. The bonds mature on January 1, 2008, and pay interest annually beginning January 1, 1999. Gadget Corporation purchased the bonds to yield 11%. How much did Gadget pay for the bonds?

3. Gadget Corporation bought a new machine and agreed to pay for it in equal annual instalments of $3,800 at the end of each of the next 10 years. Assuming an interest rate of 8% applies to this contract, how much should Gadget record as the cost of the machine?

4. Gadget Corporation purchased a tractor on December 31, 1998, paying $16,000 cash on that date and agreeing to pay $5,000 at the end of each of the next eight years. At what amount should the tractor be valued on December 31, 1998, assuming an interest rate of 12%?

5. Gadget Corporation wants to withdraw $50,000 (including principal) from an investment fund at the end of each year for nine years. What is the required initial investment at the beginning of the first year if the fund earns 11%?

When Norman Peterson died, he left his wife Vera an insurance policy contract that permitted her to choose any one of the following four options:

1. $55,000 immediate cash.

2. $3,700 every three months, payable at the end of each quarter for five years.

3. $20,000 immediate cash and $1,500 every three months for 10 years, payable at the beginning of each three-month period.

4. $4,000 every three months for three years and $1,200 each quarter for the following 25 quarters, all payments payable at the end of each quarter.

Instructions

If money is worth 2½% per quarter, compounded quarterly, which option will you recommend that Vera choose?

Pennywise Inc. has decided to surface and maintain for 10 years a vacant lot next to one of its discount retail outlets to serve as a parking lot for customers. Management is considering the following bids that involve two different qualities of surfacing for a parking area of 12,000 m².

Bid A. A surface that costs $5.25 per square metre. This surface will have to be replaced at the end of five years. The annual maintenance cost on this surface is estimated at 15 cents per square metre for each year except the last of its service. The replacement surface will be similar to the initial surface.

Bid B. A surface that costs $9.50 per square metre. This surface has a probable useful life of 10 years and will require annual maintenance in each year except the last year, at an estimated cost of 4 cents per square metre.

Instructions

Prepare computations that show which bid should be accepted by Pennywise Inc. You may assume that the cost of capital is 9%, that the annual maintenance expenditures are incurred at the end of each year, and that prices are not expected to change during the next 10 years.

Robyn Hood, a bank robber, is worried about her retirement. She decides to start a savings account. Robyn deposits annually her net share of the "loot," which consists of $70,000 per year, for three years beginning January 1, 1996. Robyn is arrested on January 4, 1998 (after making the third deposit) and spends the rest of 1998 and most of 1999 in jail. She escapes in September of 1999 and resumes her savings plan with semiannual deposits of $25,000 each, beginning January 1, 2000. Assume that the bank's interest rate is 9% compounded annually from January 1, 1996 through January 1, 1999, and 12% compounded semiannually thereafter.

Instructions

When Robyn retires on January 1, 2003 (six months after her last deposit), what will be the balance in her savings account?

PA-5 Provide a solution to each of the following situations by computing the unknowns (use the interest tables):

1. Leslie Rooke invests in a $125,000 annuity insurance policy at 9% compounded annually on February 8, 1998. The first of 20 receipts from the annuity is payable to Leslie 10 years after the annuity is purchased (February 8, 2008). What will be the amount of each of the 20 equal annual receipts?

2. Kevin Tait owes a debt of $20,000 from the purchase of his new sports car. The debt bears interest of 8% payable annually. Kevin wishes to pay the debt and interest in eight annual instalments, beginning one year hence. What equal annual instalments will pay the debt and interest?

3. On January 1, 1998 Mike Myers offers to buy Dan Carbey's used combine for $24,600, payable in 10 equal instalments that include 9% interest on the unpaid balance and a portion of the principal with the first payment to be made on January 1, 1998. How much will each payment be?

PA-6 During the past year, Leanne Cundall planted a new vineyard on 150 ha of land that she leases for $27,000 a year. She has asked you to assist in determining the value of her vineyard operation.

The vineyard will bear no grapes for the first five years (Years 1–5). In the next five years (Years 6–10), Leanne estimates that the vines will bear grapes that can be sold for $55,000 each year. For the next 20 years (Years 11–30), she expects the harvest to provide annual revenues of $100,000. During the last 10 years (Years 31–40) of the vineyard's life, she estimates that revenues will decline to $80,000 per year.

During the first five years the annual cost of pruning, fertilizing, and caring for the vineyard is estimated at $9,000; during the years of production, Years 6–40, these costs will rise to $10,000 per year. The relevant market rate of interest for the entire period is 12%. Assume that all receipts and payments are made at the end of each year.

Instructions
Tanya McIvor has offered to buy Leanne's vineyard business. On the basis of the present value of the business, what is the minimum price Leanne should accept?

PA-7 Handyman Inc. owns and operates a number of hardware stores on the Prairies. Recently the company has decided to locate another store in a rapidly growing area of Manitoba; the company is trying to decide whether to purchase or lease the building and related facilities.

Purchase. The company can purchase the site, construct the building, and purchase all store fixtures. The cost would be $1,650,000. An immediate down payment of $400,000 is required, and the remaining $1,250,000 would be paid off over five years at $300,000 per year (including interest). The property is expected to have a useful life of 12 years and then it will be sold for $400,000. As the owner of the property, the company will have the following out-of-pocket expenses each period:

Property taxes (to be paid at the end of each year)	$48,000
Insurance (to be paid at the beginning of each year)	27,000
Other (primarily maintenance, which occurs at the end of each year)	16,000
	$91,000

Lease. Jensen Corp. Ltd. has agreed to purchase the site, construct the building, and install the appropriate fixtures for Handyman Inc. if Handyman will lease the completed facility for 12 years. The annual costs for the lease will be $240,000. The lease would be a triple-net lease, which means that Handyman will have no responsibility related to the facility over the 12 years. The terms of the lease are that Handyman would be required to make 12 annual payments (the first payment to be made at the time the store opens and then each following year). In addition, a deposit of $100,000 is required when the store is opened that will be returned at the end of the twelfth year, assuming no unusual damage to the building structure or fixtures.

Currently the cost of funds for Handyman Inc. is 10%.

Instructions
Which of the two approaches should Handyman Inc. follow?

PA-8 Presented below are a series of time value of money problems for you to solve.

1. Your client, Kate Greenaway, wishes to provide for the payment of an obligation of $200,000 that is due on July 1, 2006. Kate plans to deposit $20,000 in a special fund each July 1 for eight years, starting July 1, 1999. She also wishes to make a deposit on July 1, 1998 of an amount that, with its accumulated interest, will bring the fund up to $200,000 at the maturity of the obligation. She expects the fund to earn interest at the rate of 4% compounded annually. Compute the amount to be deposited on July 1, 1998.

2. On January 1, 1998 Keeley Inc. initiated a pension plan under which each of its employees will receive a pension annuity of $1,000 per year beginning one year after retirement and continuing until death. Employee A will retire at the end of 2004 and, according to mortality tables, is expected to live long enough to receive eight pension payments. What is the present value of Keeley Inc.'s pension obligation for employee A at the beginning of 1998 if the interest rate is 10%?

3. McLachlan Company purchases bonds from Rankin Inc. in the amount of $400,000. The bonds are 10-year, 12% bonds that pay interest semiannually. After three years (and receipt of interest for three years), McLachlan needs money and, therefore, sells the bonds to Doyle Company, which demands interest at 16% compounded semiannually. What is the amount that McLachlan will receive on the sale of the bonds?

Answer the following questions related to Gervais Inc.

PA-9

1. Gervais Inc. has $114,400 to invest. The company is trying to decide between two alternative uses of the funds. One alternative provides $16,000 at the end of each year for 12 years; the other pays a single lump sum of $380,000 at the end of 12 years. Which alternative should Gervais select? Assume the interest rate is constant over the entire investment.

2. Gervais Inc. has just purchased a new computer. The fair market value of the equipment is $724,150. The purchase agreement specified an immediate down payment of $100,000 and semiannual payments of $76,952 that begin at the end of six months for five years. What interest rate, to the nearest percent, was used in discounting this purchase transaction?

3. Gervais Inc. loaned $300,000 to Whistler Corporation. Gervais accepted a note due in seven years at 8% compounded semiannually. After two years (and receipt of interest for two years), Gervais needed money and therefore sold the note to Royal Canadian Bank, which required interest on the note of 10% compounded semiannually. What amount did Gervais receive from the sale of the note?

4. Gervais Inc. wishes to accumulate $650,000 by December 31, 2008 to retire outstanding bonds. The company deposits $150,000 on December 31, 1998, which will earn interest at 10% per year compounded quarterly, to help in the debt retirement. The company wants to know what additional equal amounts should be deposited at the end of each quarter for 10 years to ensure that $650,000 is available at the end of 2008. (The quarterly deposits will also earn interest at a rate of 10%, compounded quarterly.) Round to even dollars.

Laird Wightman is a financial executive with Marsh Company. Although Laird has not had any formal training in finance or accounting, he has a "good sense" for numbers and has helped the company grow from a very small ($500,000 sales) to a large operation ($45 million sales). With the business growing steadily, however, the company needs to make a number of difficult financial decisions that Laird feels are a little "over his head." He has therefore decided to hire a new employee with facility in "numbers" to help him. As a basis for determining whom to employ, he asked each prospective employee to prepare answers to questions relating to the following situations he has encountered recently. Here are the questions that you are asked to answer:

PA-10

1. In 1997 Marsh Company negotiated and closed a long-term lease contract for newly constructed truck terminals and freight storage facilities. The buildings were constructed on land owned by the company. On January 1, 1998 Marsh Company took possession of the leased property. The 20-year lease is effective for the period January 1, 1998 through December 31, 2017. Rental payments of $800,000 are payable to the lessor (owner of facilities) on January 1 of each of the first 10 years of the lease term. Payments of $240,000 are due on January 1 for each of the last 10 years of the lease term. Marsh has an option to purchase all the leased facilities for $1.00 on December 31, 2017. At the time the lease was negotiated, the fair market value of the truck terminals and freight storage facilities was approximately $7,286,896. If the company had borrowed the money to purchase the facilities, it would have had to pay 10% interest. Should the company have purchased rather than leased the facilities?

2. Last year the company exchanged some land for a noninterest-bearing note. The note was to be paid at the rate of $10,000 per year for nine years, beginning one year from the date of the exchange. The interest rate for the note was 11%. At the time the land was originally purchased, it cost $90,000. What is the fair value of the note?

3. The company has always followed the policy to take any cash discounts offered on goods purchased. Recently the company purchased a large amount of raw materials at a price of $800,000 with terms 1/10, n/30 on which it took the discount. If Marsh's cost of funds was 10%, should the policy of always taking cash discounts be continued?

INDEX

WE WANT TO HEAR FROM YOU

By sharing your opinions about Intermediate Accounting 5/E, you will help us ensure that you are getting the most value for your textbook dollars. After you have used the book for a while, please fill out this form. Either fold, tape, and mail, or fax us toll free @ 1(800)565-6802!

Course name: _____ School name: _____

Your name: _____

I am using: ❑ Volume 1 ❑ Volume 2

1) Did you purchase this book (check all that apply):
   ❑ From your campus bookstore

   ❑ From a bookstore off-campus

   ❑ New ❑ Used ❑ For yourself

   ❑ For yourself and at least one other student

2) Was this text available at the bookstore when you needed it?
   ❑ Yes ❑ No

3) Was the study guide available at the bookstore when you needed it?
   ❑ Yes ❑ No ❑ Don't know

   If yes, did you purchase it?

   ❑ Yes ❑ No ❑ I intend to purchase it

4) Did you find it a useful studying aid?
   ❑ Yes ❑ No

   Comments: _____
   _____
   _____

5) How far along are you in this course (put an X where you are now)?
   ❑————————❑————————❑
   Beginning   Midway   Completed

6) How much have you used this text (put an X where you are now)?
   ❑————————❑————————❑
   Skimmed   Read half   Read entire book

7) Have you read the introductory material (i.e., the preface)?
   ❑   ❑   ❑
   Yes   No   Parts of it

8) Even if you have only skimmed this text, please rate the following features:

Features:	Very valuable/effective	Somewhat valuable/effective	Not valuable/effective
Value as a reference			
Readability			
Design & illustrations			
Study & review material			
Problems & cases			
Relevant examples			
Overall perception			

9) What do you like most about this book? _____
_____
_____
_____
_____

10) How do you think we can improve future editions?
_____
_____
_____
_____

11) Is your book ❑ New ❑ Used

Please explain your decision to buy new or used _____

_____

_____

_____

_____

12) At the end of the semester, what do you intend to do with this text?

❑ Keep it   ❑ Sell it   ❑ Unsure

13) May we quote you? ❑ Yes ❑ No

If you would like to receive information on other Wiley business books, please fill in the following information:

Name: _____

Mailing address: _____

(Street) _____ (Apt. #) _____

(City) _____ (Prov.) _____

(Postal Code) _____

Thank you for your time and feedback!

 WILEY
Publishers Since 1807

You can contact us via e-mail at: cwells@wiley.com

-------------------------------------- (fold here) --------------------------------------

MAIL ➜ POSTE
Canada Post Corporation / Société canadienne des postes

Postage paid   **Port payé**
if mailed in Canada   si posté au Canada

Business   **Réponse**
Reply   **d'affaires**

0108529899   **01**

0108529899-M9W1L1-BR01

```
COLLEGE DIVISION
JOHN WILEY & SONS CANADA LTD
22 WORCESTER RD
PO BOX 56213 STN BRM B
TORONTO ON   M7Y 9C1
```

fumed and fretted, and did not know what was the matter,
as a youth might do at one-and-twenty. And so having
done no good at St. Ewold's, he rode back much earlier
than was usual with him, instigated by some inward
unacknowledged hope that he might see Mrs. Bold before
she left.

Eleanor had not passed a pleasant morning. She was
irritated with every one, and not least with herself. She
felt that she had been hardly used, but she felt also that
she had not played her own cards well. She should have
held herself so far above suspicion as to have received her
sister's innuendoes and the archdeacon's lecture with
indifference. She had not done this, but had shown herself
angry and sore, and was now ashamed of her own petu-
lance, and yet unable to discontinue it.

The greater part of the morning she had spent alone;
but after a while her father joined her. He had fully made
up his mind that, come what come might, nothing should
separate him from his younger daughter. It was a hard
task for him to reconcile himself to the idea of seeing her
at the head of Mr. Slope's table; but he got through it.
Mr. Slope, as he argued to himself, was a respectable man
and a clergyman; and he, as Eleanor's father, had no
right even to endeavour to prevent her from marrying
such a one. He longed to tell her how he had determined
to prefer her to all the world, how he was prepared to
admit that she was not wrong, how thoroughly he differed
from Dr. Grantly; but he could not bring himself to
mention Mr. Slope's name. There was yet a chance that
they were all wrong in their surmise! and, being thus in
doubt, he could not bring himself to speak openly to her
on the subject.

He was sitting with her in the drawing-room, with his
arm round her waist, saying every now and then some
little soft words of affection, and working hard with his
imaginary fiddle-bow, when Mr. Arabin entered the room.
He immediately got up, and the two made some trite
remarks to each other, neither thinking of what he was
saying, while Eleanor kept her seat on the sofa mute and
moody. Mr. Arabin was included in the list of those
against whom her anger was excited. He, too, had dared
to talk about her acquaintance with Mr. Slope; he, too,

had dared to blame her for not making an enemy of his enemy. She had not intended to see him before her departure, and was now but little inclined to be gracious.

There was a feeling through the whole house that something was wrong. Mr. Arabin, when he saw Eleanor, could not succeed in looking or in speaking as though he knew nothing of all this. He could not be cheerful and positive and contradictory with her, as was his wont. He had not been two minutes in the room before he felt that he had done wrong to return; and the moment he heard her voice, he thoroughly wished himself back at St. Ewold's. Why, indeed, should he have wished to have aught further to say to the future wife of Mr. Slope ?

' I am sorry to hear that you are to leave us so soon,' said he, striving in vain to use his ordinary voice. In answer to this she muttered something about the necessity of her being in Barchester, and betook herself most industriously to her crochet work.

Then there was a little more trite conversation between Mr. Arabin and Mr. Harding ; trite, and hard, and vapid, and senseless. Neither of them had anything to say to the other, and yet neither at such a moment liked to remain silent. At last Mr. Harding, taking advantage of a pause, escaped out of the room, and Eleanor and Mr. Arabin were left together.

' Your going will be a great break-up to our party,' said he.

She again muttered something which was all but inaudible ; but kept her eyes fixed upon her work.

' We have had a very pleasant month here,' said he ; ' at least I have ; and I am sorry it should be so soon over.'

' I have already been from home longer than I intended,' said she ; ' and it is time that I should return.'

' Well, pleasant hours and pleasant days must come to an end. It is a pity that so few of them are pleasant ; or perhaps, rather '——

' It is a pity, certainly, that men and women do so much to destroy the pleasantness of their days,' said she, interrupting him. ' It is a pity that there should be so little charity abroad.'

' Charity should begin at home,' said he ; and he was proceeding to explain that he as a clergyman could not be

what she would call charitable at the expense of those
principles which he considered it his duty to teach, when
he remembered that it would be worse than vain to argue
on such a matter with the future wife of Mr. Slope. ' But
you are just leaving us,' he continued, ' and I will not
weary your last hour with another lecture. As it is, I fear
I have given you too many.'

' You should practise as well as preach, Mr. Arabin ? '

' Undoubtedly I should. So should we all. All of us
who presume to teach are bound to do our utmost towards
fulfilling our own lessons. I thoroughly allow my deficiency
in doing so : but I do not quite know now to what you
allude. Have you any special reason for telling me now
that I should practise as well as preach ? '

Eleanor made no answer. She longed to let him know
the cause of her anger, to upbraid him for speaking of her
disrespectfully, and then at last to forgive him, and so part
friends. She felt that she would be unhappy to leave him
in her present frame of mind ; but yet she could hardly
bring herself to speak to him of Mr. Slope. And how could
she allude to the innuendo thrown out by the archdeacon,
and thrown out, as she believed, at the instigation of Mr.
Arabin ? She wanted to make him know that he was
wrong, to make him aware that he had ill-treated her, in
order that the sweetness of her forgiveness might be
enhanced. She felt that she liked him too well to be
contented to part with him in displeasure ; and yet she
could not get over her deep displeasure without some
explanation, some acknowledgment on his part, some
assurance that he would never again so sin against her.

' Why do you tell me that I should practise what I
preach ? ' continued he.

' All men should do so.'

' Certainly. That is as it were understood and acknowledged. But you do not say so to all men, or to all
clergymen. The advice, good as it is, is not given except
in allusion to some special deficiency. If you will tell me
my special deficiency, I will endeavour to profit by the
advice.'

She paused for a while, and then looking full in his face,
she said, ' You are not bold enough, Mr. Arabin, to speak
out to me openly and plainly, and yet you expect me, a

woman, to speak openly to you. Why did you speak
calumny of me to Dr. Grantly behind my back ? '

' Calumny ! ' said he, and his whole face became suffused
with blood ; ' what calumny ? If I have spoken calumny
of you, I will beg your pardon, and his to whom I spoke it,
and God's pardon also. But what calumny have I spoken
of you to Dr. Grantly ? '

She also blushed deeply. She could not bring herself
to ask him whether he had not spoken of her as another
man's wife. ' You know that best yourself,' said she ;
' but I ask you as a man of honour, if you have not spoken
of me as you would not have spoken of your own sister ; or
rather I will not ask you,' she continued, finding that he did
not immediately answer her. ' I will not put you to the
necessity of answering such a question. Dr. Grantly has
told me what you said.'

' Dr. Grantly certainly asked me for my advice, and I
gave it. He asked me '——

' I know he did, Mr. Arabin. He asked you whether he
would be doing right to receive me at Plumstead, if I
continued my acquaintance with a gentleman who happens
to be personally disagreeable to yourself and to him ? '

' You are mistaken, Mrs. Bold. I have no personal
knowledge of Mr. Slope ; I never met him in my life.'

' You are not the less individually hostile to him. It is
not for me to question the propriety of your enmity ; but
I had a right to expect that my name should not have been
mixed up in your hostilities. This has been done, and
been done by you in a manner the most injurious and the
most distressing to me as a woman. I must confess, Mr.
Arabin, that from you I expected a different sort of usage.'

As she spoke she with difficulty restrained her tears ;
but she did restrain them. Had she given way and sobbed
aloud, as in such cases a woman should do, he would have
melted at once, implored her pardon, perhaps knelt at her
feet and declared his love. Everything would have been
explained, and Eleanor would have gone back to Barchester with a contented mind. How easily would she
have forgiven and forgotten the archdeacon's suspicions
had she but heard the whole truth from Mr. Arabin. But
then where would have been my novel ? She did not cry,
and Mr. Arabin did not melt.

' You do me an injustice,' said he. ' My advice was asked by Dr. Grantly, and I was obliged to give it.'

' Dr. Grantly has been most officious, most impertinent. I have as complete a right to form my acquaintance as he has to form his. What would you have said, had I consulted you as to the propriety of my banishing Dr. Grantly from my house because he knows Lord Tattenham Corner ? I am sure Lord Tattenham is quite as objectionable an acquaintance for a clergyman as Mr. Slope is for a clergyman's daughter.'

' I do not know Lord Tattenham Corner.'

' No ; but Dr. Grantly does. It is nothing to me if he knows all the young lords on every racecourse in England. I shall not interfere with him ; nor shall he with me.'

' I am sorry to differ with you, Mrs. Bold ; but as you have spoken to me on this matter, and especially as you blame me for what little I said on the subject, I must tell you that I do differ from you. Dr. Grantly's position as a man in the world gives him a right to choose his own acquaintances, subject to certain influences. If he chooses them badly, those influences will be used. If he consorts with persons unsuitable to him, his bishop will interfere. What the bishop is to Dr. Grantly, Dr. Grantly is to you.'

' I deny it. I utterly deny it,' said Eleanor, jumping from her seat, and literally flashing before Mr. Arabin, as she stood on the drawing-room floor. He had never seen her so excited, he had never seen her look half so beautiful.

' I utterly deny it,' said she. ' Dr. Grantly has no sort of jurisdiction over me whatsoever. Do you and he forget that I am not altogether alone in the world ? Do you forget that I have a father ? Dr. Grantly, I believe, always has forgotten it.'

' From you, Mr. Arabin,' she continued, ' I would have listened to advice because I should have expected it to have been given as one friend may advise another ; not as a schoolmaster gives an order to a pupil. I might have differed from you ; on this matter I should have done so ; but had you spoken to me in your usual manner and with your usual freedom I should not have been angry. But now——was it manly of you, Mr. Arabin, to speak of me in this way——, so disrespectful—so—— ? I cannot bring myself to repeat what you said. You must understand what I feel. Was it just of you to speak of me in such a way, and to advise my sister's husband to turn me out of my sister's house, because I chose to know a man of whose doctrine you disapprove ? '

' I have no alternative left to me, Mrs. Bold,' said he, standing with his back to the fire-place, looking down intently at the carpet pattern, and speaking with a slow measured voice, ' but to tell you plainly what did take place between me and Dr. Grantly.'

' Well,' said she, finding that he paused for a moment.

' I am afraid that what I may say may pain you.'

' It cannot well do so more than what you have already done,' said she.

' Dr. Grantly asked me whether I thought it would be prudent for him to receive you in his house as the wife of Mr. Slope, and I told him that I thought it would be imprudent. Believing it to be utterly impossible that Mr. Slope and —— '

' Thank you, Mr. Arabin, that is sufficient. I do not want to know your reasons,' said she, speaking with a terribly calm voice. ' I have shown to this gentleman the common-place civility of a neighbour ; and because I have done so, because I have not indulged against him in all the rancour and hatred which you and Dr. Grantly consider due to all clergymen who do not agree with yourselves, you conclude that I am to marry him ;—or rather you do not conclude so—no rational man could really come to such an outrageous conclusion without better ground ; —you have not thought so—but, as I am in a position in which such an accusation must be peculiarly painful, it is made in order that I may be terrified into hostility against this enemy of yours.'

As she finished speaking, she walked to the drawing-room window and stepped out into the garden. Mr. Arabin was left in the room, still occupied in counting the pattern on the carpet. He had, however, distinctly heard and accurately marked every word that she had spoken. Was it not clear from what she had said, that the archdeacon had been wrong in imputing to her any attachment to Mr. Slope ? Was it not clear that Eleanor was still free to make another choice ? It may seem strange that he should for a moment have had a doubt ; and yet he did doubt. She had not absolutely denied the charge ; she had not expressly said that it was untrue. Mr. Arabin understood little of the nature of a woman's feelings, or he would have known how improbable it was that she should make any clearer declaration than she had done. Few men do understand the nature of a woman's heart, till years have robbed such understanding of its value. And it is well that it should be so, or men would triumph too easily.

Mr. Arabin stood counting the carpet, unhappy, wretchedly unhappy, at the hard words that had been spoken to him ; and yet happy, exquisitely happy, as he thought that after all the woman whom he so regarded was not to become the wife of the man whom he so much disliked. As he stood there he began to be aware that he was himself in love. Forty years had passed over his head, and as yet woman's beauty had never given him an uneasy hour. His present hour was very uneasy.

Not that he remained there for half or a quarter of that time. In spite of what Eleanor had said, Mr. Arabin was, in truth, a manly man. Having ascertained that he loved this woman, and having now reason to believe that she was free to receive his love, at least if she pleased to do so, he followed her into the garden to make such wooing as he could.

He was not long in finding her. She was walking to and fro beneath the avenue of elms that stood in the archdeacon's grounds, skirting the churchyard. What had passed between her and Mr. Arabin, had not, alas, tended to lessen the acerbity of her spirit. She was very angry ; more angry with him than with any one. How could he have so misunderstood her ? She had been so intimate with him, had allowed him such latitude in what he had chosen to say to her, had complied with his ideas, cherished his views, fostered his precepts, cared for his comforts, made much of him in every way in which a pretty woman can make much of an unmarried man without committing herself or her feelings ! She had been doing this, and while she had been doing it he had regarded her as the affianced wife of another man.

As she passed along the avenue, every now and then an unbidden tear would force itself on her cheek, and as she raised her hand to brush it away she stamped with her little foot upon the sward with very spite to think that she had been so treated.

Mr. Arabin was very near to her when she first saw him, and she turned short round and retraced her steps down the avenue, trying to rid her cheeks of all trace of the tell-tale tears. It was a needless endeavour, for Mr. Arabin was in a state of mind that hardly allowed him to observe such trifles. He followed her down the walk, and over-took her just as she reached the end of it.

He had not considered how he would address her; he had not thought what he would say. He had only felt that it was wretchedness to him to quarrel with her, and that it would be happiness to be allowed to love her. And yet he could not lower himself by asking her pardon. He had done her no wrong. He had not calumniated her, not injured her, as she had accused him of doing. He could not confess sins of which he had not been guilty. He could only let the past be past, and ask her as to her and his hopes for the future.

'I hope we are not to part as enemies?' said he.

'There shall be no enmity on my part,' said Eleanor; 'I endeavour to avoid all enmities. It would be a hollow pretence were I to say that there can be true friendship between us after what has just passed. People cannot make their friends of those whom they despise.'

'And am I despised?'

'*I* must have been so before you could have spoken of me as you did. And I was deceived, cruelly deceived. I believed that you thought well of me; I believed that you esteemed me.'

'Thought well of you and esteemed you!' said he. 'In justifying myself before you, I must use stronger words than those.' He paused for a moment, and Eleanor's heart beat with painful violence within her bosom as she waited for him to go on. 'I have esteemed, do esteem you, as I never yet esteemed any woman. Think well of you! I never thought to think so well, so much of any human creature. Speak calumny of you! Insult you! Wilfully injure you! I wish it were my privilege to shield you from calumny, insult, and injury. Calumny! ah, me. 'Twere almost better that it were so. Better than to worship with a sinful worship; sinful and vain also.' And then he

walked along beside her, with his hands clasped behind his
back, looking down on the grass beneath his feet, and
utterly at a loss how to express his meaning. And Eleanor
walked beside him determined at least to give him no
assistance.

' Ah me ! ' he uttered at last, speaking rather to himself
than to her. ' Ah me! these Plumstead walks were
pleasant enough, if one could have but heart's ease ; but
without that the dull dead stones of Oxford were far
preferable ; and St. Ewold's too ; Mrs. Bold, I am beginning to think that I mistook myself when I came hither.
A Romish priest now would have escaped all this. Oh,
Father of heaven ! how good for us would it be, if thou
couldest vouchsafe to us a certain rule.'

' And have we not a certain rule, Mr. Arabin ? '

' Yes—yes, surely ; ' Lead us not into temptation but
deliver us from evil.' But what is temptation ? what is
evil ? Is this evil,—is this temptation ? '

Poor Mr. Arabin ! It would not come out of him, that
deep true love of his. He could not bring himself to utter
it in plain language that would require and demand an
answer. He knew not how to say to the woman by his
side, ' Since the fact is that you do not love that other
man, that you are not to be his wife, can you love me, will
you be my wife ? ' These were the words which were in
his heart, but with all his sighs he could not draw them to
his lips. He would have given anything, everything for
power to ask this simple question ; but glib as was his
tongue in pulpits and on platforms, now he could not find
a word wherewith to express the plain wish of his heart.

And yet Eleanor understood him as thoroughly as
though he had declared his passion with all the elegant
fluency of a practised Lothario. With a woman's instinct
she followed every bend of his mind, as he spoke of the
pleasantness of Plumstead and the stones of Oxford, as he
alluded to the safety of the Romish priest and the hidden
perils of temptation. She knew that it all meant love.
She knew that this man at her side, this accomplished
scholar, this practised orator, this great polemical com-
batant, was striving and striving in vain to tell her that
his heart was no longer his own.

She knew this, and felt a sort of joy in knowing it ; and

yet she would not come to his aid. He had offended her
deeply, had treated her unworthily, the more unworthily
seeing that he had learnt to love her, and Eleanor could
not bring herself to abandon her revenge. She did not ask
herself whether or no she would ultimately accept his love.
She did not even acknowledge to herself that she now
perceived it with pleasure. At the present moment it did
not touch her heart; it merely appeased her pride and
flattered her vanity. Mr. Arabin had dared to associate
her name with that of Mr. Slope, and now her spirit was
soothed by finding that he would fain associate it with his
own. And so she walked on beside him inhaling incense,
but giving out no sweetness in return.

'Answer me this,' said Mr. Arabin, stopping suddenly
in his walk, and stepping forward so that he faced his
companion. 'Answer me this one question. You do not
love Mr. Slope? you do not intend to be his wife?'

Mr. Arabin certainly did not go the right way to win
such a woman as Eleanor Bold. Just as her wrath was
evaporating, as it was disappearing before the true
warmth of his untold love, he re-kindled it by a most useless repetition of his original sin. Had he known what he
was about he should never have mentioned Mr. Slope's
name before Eleanor Bold, till he had made her all his own.
Then, and not till then, he might have talked of Mr. Slope
with as much triumph as he chose.

'I shall answer no such question,' said she; 'and what
is more, I must tell you that nothing can justify your
asking it. Good morning!'

And so saying she stepped proudly across the lawn, and
passing through the drawing-room window joined her
father and sister at lunch in the dining-room. Half an
hour afterwards she was in the carriage, and so she left
Plumstead without again seeing Mr. Arabin.

His walk was long and sad among the sombre trees that
overshadowed the churchyard. He left the archdeacon's
grounds that he might escape attention, and sauntered
among the green hillocks under which lay at rest so many
of the once loving swains and forgotten beauties of
Plumstead. To his ears Eleanor's last words sounded like
a knell never to be reversed. He could not comprehend
that she might be angry with him, indignant with him,

remorseless with him, and yet love him. He could not make up his mind whether or no Mr. Slope was in truth a favoured rival. If not, why should she not have answered his question?

Poor Mr. Arabin—untaught, illiterate, boorish, ignorant man! That at forty years of age you should know so little of the workings of a woman's heart!

CHAPTER XXXI

THE BISHOP'S LIBRARY

AND thus the pleasant party at Plumstead was broken up. It had been a very pleasant party as long as they had all remained in good humour with one another. Mrs. Grantly had felt her house to be gayer and brighter than it had been for many a long day, and the archdeacon had been aware that the month had passed pleasantly without attributing the pleasure to any other special merits than those of his own hospitality. Within three or four days of Eleanor's departure Mr. Harding had also returned, and Mr. Arabin had gone to Oxford to spend one week there previous to his settling at the vicarage of St. Ewold's. He had gone laden with many messages to Dr. Gwynne touching the iniquity of the doings in Barchester palace, and the peril in which it was believed the hospital still stood in spite of the assurances contained in Mr. Slope's inauspicious letter.

During Eleanor's drive into Barchester she had not much opportunity of reflecting on Mr. Arabin. She had been constrained to divert her mind both from his sins and his love by the necessity of conversing with her sister, and maintaining the appearance of parting with her on good terms. When the carriage reached her own door, and while she was in the act of giving her last kiss to her sister and nieces, Mary Bold ran out and exclaimed,

'Oh! Eleanor,—have you heard?—oh! Mrs. Grantly, have you heard what has happened? The poor dean!'

'Good heavens!' said Mrs. Grantly; 'what—what has happened?'

'This morning at nine he had a fit of apoplexy, and he

has not spoken since. I very much fear that by this time
he is no more.'

Mrs. Grantly had been very intimate with the dean,
and was therefore much shocked. Eleanor had not known
him so well; nevertheless she was sufficiently acquainted
with his person and manners to feel startled and grieved
also at the tidings she now received. ' I will go at once
to the deanery,' said Mrs. Grantly; ' the archdeacon,
I am sure, will be there. If there is any news to send you
I will let Thomas call before he leaves town.' And so the
carriage drove off, leaving Eleanor and her baby with
Mary Bold.

Mrs. Grantly had been quite right. The archdeacon
was at the deanery. He had come into Barchester that
morning by himself, not caring to intrude himself upon
Eleanor, and he also immediately on his arrival had heard
of the dean's fit. There was, as we have before said, a
library or reading room connecting the cathedral with the
dean's house. This was generally called the bishop's
library, because a certain bishop of Barchester was supposed to have added it to the cathedral. It was built
immediately over a portion of the cloisters, and a flight
of stairs descended from it into the room in which the
cathedral clergymen put their surplices on and off. As
it also opened directly into the dean's house, it was the
passage through which that dignitary usually went to
his public devotions. Who had or had not the right of
entry into it, it might be difficult to say; but the people
of Barchester believed that it belonged to the dean, and
the clergymen of Barchester believed that it belonged to
the chapter.

On the morning in question most of the resident clergymen who constituted the chapter, and some few others,
were here assembled, and among them as usual the archdeacon towered with high authority. He had heard of the
dean's fit before he was over the bridge which led into
the town, and had at once come to the well known clerical
trysting place. He had been there by eleven o'clock,
and had remained ever since. From time to time the
medical men who had been called in came through from
the deanery into the library, uttered little bulletins, and
then returned. There was it appears very little hope of

the old man's rallying, indeed no hope of any thing like a final recovery. The only question was whether he must die at once speechless, unconscious, stricken to death by his first heavy fit; or whether by due aid of medical skill he might not be so far brought back to this world as to become conscious of his state, and enabled to address one prayer to his Maker before he was called to meet Him face to face at the judgment seat.

Sir Omicron Pie had been sent for from London. That great man had shown himself a wonderful adept at keeping life still moving within an old man's heart in the case of good old Bishop Grantly, and it might be reasonably expected that he would be equally successful with a dean. In the mean time Dr. Fillgrave and Mr. Rerechild were doing their best; and poor Miss Trefoil sat at the head of her father's bed, longing, as in such cases daughters do long, to be allowed to do something to show her love; if it were only to chafe his feet with her hands, or wait in menial offices on those autocratic doctors; anything so that now in the time of need she might be of use.

The archdeacon alone of the attendant clergy had been admitted for a moment into the sick man's chamber. He had crept in with creaking shoes, had said with smothered voice a word of consolation to the sorrowing daughter, had looked on the distorted face of his old friend with solemn but yet eager scrutinising eye, as though he said in his heart ' and so some day it will probably be with me ; ' and then having whispered an unmeaning word or two to the doctors, had creaked his way back again into the library.

' He'll never speak again, I fear,' said the archdeacon as he noiselessly closed the door, as though the unconscious dying man, from whom all sense had fled, would have heard in his distant chamber the spring of the lock which was now so carefully handled.

' Indeed ! indeed ! is he so bad ? ' said the meagre little prebendary, turning over in his own mind all the probable candidates for the deanery, and wondering whether the archdeacon would think it worth his while to accept it. ' The fit must have been very violent.'

' When a man over seventy has a stroke of apoplexy, it seldom comes very lightly,' said the burly chancellor.

'He was an excellent, sweet-tempered man,' said one of the vicars choral. 'Heaven knows how we shall repair his loss.'

'He was indeed,' said a minor canon; 'and a great blessing to all those privileged to take a share of the services of our cathedral. I suppose the government will appoint, Mr. Archdeacon. I trust we may have no stranger.'

'We will not talk about his successor,' said the archdeacon, 'while there is yet hope.'

'Oh no, of course not,' said the minor canon. 'It would be exceedingly indecorous? but——'

'I know of no man,' said the meagre little prebendary, 'who has better interest with the present government than Mr. Slope.'

'Mr. Slope,' said two or three at once almost sotto voce. 'Mr. Slope dean of Barchester!'

'Pooh!' exclaimed the burly chancellor.

'The bishop would do anything for him,' said the little prebendary.

'And so would Mrs. Proudie,' said the vicar choral.

'Pooh!' said the chancellor.

The archdeacon had almost turned pale at the idea. What if Mr. Slope should become dean of Barchester? To be sure there was no adequate ground, indeed no ground at all, for presuming that such a desecration could even be contemplated. But nevertheless it was on the cards. Dr. Proudie had interest with the government, and the man carried as it were Dr. Proudie in his pocket. How should they all conduct themselves if Mr. Slope were to become dean of Barchester? The bare idea for a moment struck even Dr. Grantly dumb.

'It would certainly not be very pleasant for us to have Mr. Slope at the deanery,' said the little prebendary, chuckling inwardly at the evident consternation which his surmise had created.

'About as pleasant and as probable as having you in the palace,' said the chancellor.

'I should think such an appointment highly improbable,' said the minor canon, 'and, moreover, extremely injudicious. Should not you, Mr. Archdeacon?'

'I should presume such a thing to be quite out of the question,' said the archdeacon; 'but at the present moment I am thinking rather of our poor friend who is lying so near us than of Mr. Slope.'

'Of course, of course,' said the vicar choral with a very solemn air; 'of course you are. So are we all. Poor Dr. Trefoil; the best of men, but——'

'It's the most comfortable dean's residence in England,' said a second prebendary. 'Fifteen acres in the grounds. It is better than many of the bishops' palaces.'

'And full two thousand a year,' said the meagre doctor.

'It is cut down to 1200*l*.' said the chancellor.

'No,' said the second prebendary. 'It is to be fifteen. A special case was made.'

'No such thing,' said the chancellor.

'You'll find I'm right,' said the prebendary.

'I'm sure I read it in the report,' said the minor canon.

'Nonsense,' said the chancellor. 'They couldn't do it. There were to be no exceptions but London and Durham.'

'And Canterbury and York,' said the vicar choral, modestly.

'What do you say, Grantly?' said the meagre little doctor.

'Say about what?' said the archdeacon, who had been looking as though he were thinking about his friend the dean, but who had in reality been thinking about Mr. Slope.

'What is the next dean to have, twelve or fifteen?'

'Twelve,' said the archdeacon authoritatively, thereby putting an end at once to all doubt and dispute among his subordinates as far as that subject was concerned.

'Well, I certainly thought it was fifteen,' said the minor canon.

'Pooh!' said the burly chancellor. At this moment the door opened, and in came Dr. Fillgrave.

'How is he?' 'Is he conscious?' 'Can he speak?' 'I hope not dead?' 'No worse news, doctor, I trust?' 'I hope, I trust, something better, doctor?' said half a dozen voices all at once, each in a tone of extremest anxiety. It was pleasant to see how popular the good old dean was among his clergy.

'No change, gentlemen; not the slightest change—but a telegraphic message has arrived—Sir Omicron Pie will be here by the 9.15 P.M. train. If any man can do anything Sir Omicron Pie will do it. But all that skill can do has been done.'

' We are sure of that Dr. Fillgrave,' said the archdeacon ; ' we are quite sure of that. But yet you know——'

' Oh ! quite right,' said the doctor, ' quite right—I should have done just the same—I advised it at once. I said to Rerechild at once that with such a life and such a man, Sir Omicron should be summoned—of course I knew the expense was nothing—so distinguished, you know, and so popular. Nevertheless, all that human skill can do has been done.'

Just at this period Mrs. Grantly's carriage drove into the close, and the archdeacon went down to confirm the news which she had heard before.

By the 9.15 P.M. train Sir Omicron Pie did arrive. And in the course of the night a sort of consciousness returned to the poor old dean. Whether this was due to Sir Omicron Pie is a question on which it may be well not to offer an opinion. Dr. Fillgrave was very clear in his own mind, but Sir Omicron himself is thought to have differed from that learned doctor. At any rate Sir Omicron expressed an opinion that the dean had yet some days to live.

For the eight or ten next days, accordingly, the poor dean remained in the same state, half conscious and half comatose, and the attendant clergy began to think that no new appointment would be necessary for some few months to come.

CHAPTER XXXII

A NEW CANDIDATE FOR ECCLESIASTICAL HONOURS

The dean's illness occasioned much mental turmoil in other places besides the deanery and adjoining library ; and the idea which occurred to the meagre little prebendary about Mr. Slope did not occur to him alone.

The bishop was sitting listlessly in his study when the news reached him of the dean's illness. It was brought to him by Mr. Slope, who of course was not the last person in Barchester to hear it. It was also not slow in finding its way to Mrs. Proudie's ears. It may be presumed that there was not just then much friendly intercourse between

these two rival claimants for his lordship's obedience.
Indeed, though living in the same house, they had not
met since the stormy interview between them in the
bishop's study on the preceding day.

On that occasion Mrs. Proudie had been defeated. That
the prestige of continual victory should have been torn
from her standards was a subject of great sorrow to that
militant lady; but though defeated, she was not overcome. She felt that she might yet recover her lost ground,
that she might yet hurl Mr. Slope down to the dust from
which she had picked him, and force her sinning lord to
sue for pardon in sackcloth and ashes.

On that memorable day, memorable for his mutiny and
rebellion against her high behests, he had carried his way
with a high hand, and had really begun to think it possible
that the days of his slavery were counted. He had begun
to hope that he was now about to enter into a free land,
a land delicious with milk which he himself might quaff,
and honey which would not tantalise him by being only
honey to the eye. When Mrs. Proudie banged the door,
as she left his room, he felt himself every inch a bishop.
To be sure his spirit had been a little cowed by his chaplain's subsequent lecture; but on the whole he was highly
pleased with himself, and flattered himself that the worst
was over. 'Ce n'est que le premier pas qui coûte,' he
reflected; and now that the first step had been so mag-
nanimously taken, all the rest would follow easily.

He met his wife as a matter of course at dinner, where
little or nothing was said that could ruffle the bishop's
happiness. His daughters and the servants were present
and protected him.

He made one or two trifling remarks on the subject of
his projected visit to the archbishop, in order to show to
all concerned that he intended to have his own way; and
the very servants perceiving the change transferred a little
of their reverence from their mistress to their master. All
which the master perceived; and so also did the mistress.
But Mrs. Proudie bided her time.

After dinner he returned to his study where Mr. Slope
soon found him, and there they had tea together and
planned many things. For some few minutes the bishop
was really happy; but as the clock on the chimney piece

warned him that the stilly hours of night were drawing on, as he looked at his chamber candlestick and knew that he must use it, his heart sank within him again. He was as a ghost, all whose power of wandering free through these upper regions ceases at cock-crow; or rather he was the opposite of the ghost, for till cock-crow he must again be a serf. And would that be all? Could he trust himself to come down to breakfast a free man in the morning.

He was nearly an hour later than usual, when he betook himself to his rest. Rest! what rest? However, he took a couple of glasses of sherry, and mounted the stairs. Far be it from us to follow him thither. There are some things which no novelist, no historian, should attempt; some few scenes in life's drama which even no poet should dare to paint. Let that which passed between Dr. Proudie and his wife on this night be understood to be among them.

He came down the following morning a sad and thoughtful man. He was attenuated in appearance; one might almost say emaciated. I doubt whether his now grizzled locks had not palpably become more grey than on the preceding evening. At any rate he had aged materially. Years do not make a man old gradually and at an even pace. Look through the world and see if this is not so always, except in those rare cases in which the human being lives and dies without joys and without sorrows, like a vegetable. A man shall be possessed of florid youthful blooming health till, it matters not what age. Thirty— forty—fifty, then comes some nipping frost, some period of agony, that robs the fibres of the body of their succulence, and the hale and hearty man is counted among the old.

He came down and breakfasted alone; Mrs. Proudie being indisposed took her coffee in her bed-room, and her daughters waited upon her there. He ate his breakfast alone, and then, hardly knowing what he did, he betook himself to his usual seat in his study. He tried to solace himself with his coming visit to the archbishop. That effort of his own free will at any rate remained to him as an enduring triumph. But somehow, now that he had achieved it, he did not seem to care so much about it. It was his ambition that had prompted him to take his place

at the archi-episcopal table, and his ambition was now
quite dead within him.

He was thus seated when Mr. Slope made his appearance,
with breathless impatience.

' My lord, the dean is dead.'

' Good heavens ! ' exclaimed the bishop, startled out of
his apathy by an announcement so sad and so sudden.

' He is either dead or now dying. He has had an
apoplectic fit, and I am told that there is not the slightest
hope ; indeed, I do not doubt that by this time he is no
more.'

Bells were rung, and servants were immediately sent to
inquire. In the course of the morning, the bishop, leaning
on his chaplain's arm, himself called at the deanery door.
Mrs. Proudie sent to Miss Trefoil all manner of offers of
assistance. The Miss Proudies sent also, and there was
immense sympathy between the palace and the deanery.
The answer to all inquiries was unvaried. The dean was
just the same ; and Sir Omicron Pie was expected down
by the 9.15 P.M. train.

And then Mr. Slope began to meditate, as others also
had done, as to who might possibly be the new dean ; and
it occurred to him, as it had also occurred to others, that
it might be possible that he should be the new dean himself. And then the question as to the twelve hundred, or
fifteen hundred, or two thousand, ran in his mind, as it
had run through those of the other clergymen in the
cathedral library.

Whether it might be two thousand, or fifteen or twelve
hundred, it would in any case undoubtedly be a great
thing for him, if he could get it. The gratification to his
ambition would be greater even than that of his covetous-
ness. How glorious to out-top the archdeacon in his own
cathedral city ; to sit above prebendaries and canons,
and have the cathedral pulpit and all the cathedral services altogether at his own disposal !

But it might be easier to wish for this than to obtain
it. Mr. Slope, however, was not without some means of
forwarding his views, and he at any rate did not let the
grass grow under his feet. In the first place he thought—
and not vainly—that he could count upon what assistance
the bishop could give him. He immediately changed his

views with regard to his patron; he made up his mind that if he became dean, he would hand his lordship back again to his wife's vassalage; and he thought it possible that his lordship might not be sorry to rid himself of one of his mentors. Mr. Slope had also taken some steps towards making his name known to other men in power. There was a certain chief-commissioner of national schools who at the present moment was presumed to stand especially high in the good graces of the government big wigs, and with him Mr. Slope had contrived to establish a sort of epistolary intimacy. He thought that he might safely apply to Sir Nicholas Fitzwhiggin; and he felt sure that if Sir Nicholas chose to exert himself, the promise of such a piece of preferment would be had for the asking for.

Then he also had the press at his bidding, or flattered himself that he had so. The daily Jupiter had taken his part in a very thorough manner in those polemical contests of his with Mr. Arabin; he had on more than one occasion absolutely had an interview with a gentleman on the staff of that paper, who, if not the editor, was as good as the editor; and had long been in the habit of writing telling letters on all manner of ecclesiastical abuses, which he signed with his initials, and sent to his editorial friend with private notes signed in his own name. Indeed, he and Mr. Towers—such was the name of the powerful gentleman of the press with whom he was connected— were generally very amiable with each other. Mr. Slope's little productions were always printed and occasionally commented upon; and thus, in a small sort of way, he had become a literary celebrity. This public life had great charms for him, though it certainly also had its drawbacks. On one occasion, when speaking in the presence of reporters, he had failed to uphold and praise and swear by that special line of conduct which had been upheld and praised and sworn by in the Jupiter, and then he had been much surprised and at the moment not a little irritated to find himself lacerated most unmercifully by his old ally. He was quizzed and bespattered and made a fool of, just as though, or rather worse than if, he had been a constant enemy instead of a constant friend. He had hitherto not learnt that a man who aspires to be

on the staff of the Jupiter must surrender all individuality.
But ultimately this little castigation had broken no bones
between him and his friend Mr. Towers. Mr. Slope was
one of those who understood the world too well to show
himself angry with such a potentate as the Jupiter. He
had kissed the rod that scourged him, and now thought
that he might fairly look for his reward. He determined
that he would at once let Mr. Towers know that he was
a candidate for the place which was about to become
vacant. More than one piece of preferment had lately
been given away much in accordance with advice tendered
to the government in the columns of the Jupiter.

But it was incumbent on Mr. Slope first to secure the
bishop. He specially felt that it behoved him to do this
before the visit to the archbishop was made. It was really
quite providential that the dean should have fallen ill
just at the very nick of time. If Dr. Proudie could be
instigated to take the matter up warmly, he might manage
a good deal while staying at the archbishop's palace.
Feeling this very strongly Mr. Slope determined to sound
the bishop that very afternoon. He was to start on the
following morning to London, and therefore not a moment
could be lost with safety.

He went into the bishop's study about five o'clock, and
found him still sitting alone. It might have been supposed
that he had hardly moved since the little excitement
occasioned by his walk to the dean's door. He still wore
on his face that dull dead look of half unconscious suffering.
He was doing nothing, reading nothing, thinking of
nothing, but simply gazing on vacancy when Mr. Slope
for the second time that day entered his room.

' Well, Slope,' said he, somewhat impatiently ; for, to
tell the truth, he was not anxious just at present to have
much conversation with Mr. Slope.

' Your lordship will be sorry to hear that as yet the poor
dean has shown no sign of amendment.'

' Oh—ah—hasn't he ? Poor man ! I'm sure I'm very
sorry. I suppose Sir Omicron has not arrived yet ? '

' No ; not till the 9.15 P.M. train.'

' I wonder they didn't have a special. They say Dr.
Trefoil is very rich.'

' Very rich, I believe,' said Mr. Slope. ' But the truth

is, all the doctors in London can do no good; no other good than to show that every possible care has been taken. Poor Dr. Trefoil is not long for this world, my lord.'

' I suppose not—I suppose not.'

' Oh no; indeed, his best friends could not wish that he should outlive such a shock, for his intellects cannot possibly survive it.'

' Poor man! poor man!' said the bishop.

' It will naturally be a matter of much moment to your lordship who is to succeed him,' said Mr. Slope. ' It would be a great thing if you could secure the appointment for some person of your own way of thinking on important points. The party hostile to us are very strong here in Barchester—much too strong.'

' Yes, yes. If poor Dr. Trefoil is to go, it will be a great thing to get a good man in his place.'

' It will be everything to your lordship to get a man on whose co-operation you can reckon. Only think what trouble we might have if Dr. Grantly, or Dr. Hyandry, or any of that way of thinking, were to get it.'

' It is not very probable that Lord —— will give it to any of that school; why should he?'

' No. Not probable; certainly not; but it's possible. Great interest will probably be made. If I might venture to advise your lordship, I would suggest that you should discuss the matter with his grace next week. I have no doubt that your wishes, if made known and backed by his grace, would be paramount with Lord ——.'

' Well, I don't know that; Lord —— has always been very kind to me, very kind. But I am unwilling to interfere in such matters unless asked. And indeed if asked, I don't know whom, at this moment, I should recommend.'

Mr. Slope, even Mr. Slope, felt at the present rather abashed. He hardly knew how to frame his little request in language sufficiently modest. He had recognised and acknowledged to himself the necessity of shocking the bishop in the first instance by the temerity of his application, and his difficulty was how best to remedy that by his adroitness and eloquence. ' I doubted myself,' said he, ' whether your lordship would have any one immediately in your eye, and it is on this account that I venture to submit to you an idea that I have been turning over in my own mind. If poor Dr. Trefoil must go, I really do not see why, with your lordship's assistance, I should not hold the preferment myself.'

' You ! ' exclaimed the bishop, in a manner that Mr. Slope could hardly have considered complimentary.

The ice was now broken, and Mr. Slope became fluent enough. ' I have been thinking of looking for it. If your lordship will press the matter on the archbishop, I do not doubt but I shall succeed. You see I shall be the first to move, which is a great matter. Then I can count upon assistance from the public press : my name is known, I may say, somewhat favourably known to that portion of the press which is now most influential with the government, and I have friends also in the government. But, nevertheless, it is to you, my lord, that I look for assistance. It is from your hands that I would most willingly receive the benefit. And, which should ever be the chief consideration in such matters, you must know better than any other person whatsoever what qualifications I possess.'

The bishop sat for a while dumbfounded. Mr. Slope dean of Barchester ! The idea of such a transformation of character would never have occurred to his own unaided intellect. At first he went on thinking why, for what reasons, on what account, Mr. Slope should be dean of Barchester. But by degrees the direction of his thoughts changed, and he began to think why, for what reasons, on what account, Mr. Slope should not be dean of Barchester. As far as he himself, the bishop, was concerned, he could well spare the services of his chaplain. That little idea of using Mr. Slope as a counterpoise to his wife had well nigh evaporated. He had all but acknowledged the futility of the scheme. If indeed he could have slept in his chaplain's bed-room instead of his wife's there might have been something in it. But ————. And thus as Mr. Slope was speaking, the bishop began to recognise the idea that that gentleman might become dean of Barchester without impropriety ; not moved, indeed, by Mr. Slope's eloquence, for he did not follow the tenor of his speech ; but led thereto by his own cogitations.

' I need not say,' continued Mr. Slope, ' that it would be my chief desire to act in all matters connected with the

cathedral as far as possible in accordance with your views.
I know your lordship so well (and I hope you know me
well enough to have the same feelings), that I am satisfied
that my being in that position would add materially to
your own comfort, and enable you to extend the sphere
of your useful influence. As I said before, it is most
desirable that there should be but one opinion among
the dignitaries of the same diocese. I doubt much whether
I would accept such an appointment in any diocese in
which I should be constrained to differ much from the
bishop. In this case there would be a delightful uniformity
of opinion.'

Mr. Slope perfectly well perceived that the bishop did
not follow a word that he said, but nevertheless he went
on talking. He knew it was necessary that Dr. Proudie
should recover from his surprise, and he knew also that
he must give him the opportunity of appearing to have
been persuaded by argument. So he went on, and produced a multitude of fitting reasons all tending to show
that no one on earth could make so good a dean of Barchester as himself, that the government and the public
would assuredly coincide in desiring that he, Mr. Slope,
should be dean of Barchester; but that for high considerations of ecclesiastical polity it would be especially
desirable that this piece of preferment should be so
bestowed through the instrumentality of the bishop of
the diocese.

' But I really don't know what I could do in the matter,'
said the bishop.

' If you would mention it to the archbishop; if you
could tell his grace that you consider such an appointment
very desirable, that you have it much at heart with a
view to putting an end to schism in the diocese; if you
did this with your usual energy, you would probably find
no difficulty in inducing his grace to promise that he would
mention it to Lord ——. Of course you would let the archbishop know that I am not looking for the preferment
solely through his intervention; that you do not exactly
require him to ask it as a favour; that you expect that
I shall get it through other sources, as is indeed the case;
but that you are very anxious that his grace should express
his approval of such an arrangement to Lord ——'

It ended in the bishop promising to do as he was bid.
Not that he so promised without a stipulation. 'About
that hospital,' he said, in the middle of the conference.
'I was never so troubled in my life;' which was about
the truth. 'You haven't spoken to Mr. Harding since
I saw you?'

Mr. Slope assured his patron that he had not.

'Ah well, then—I think upon the whole it will be
better to let Quiverful have it. It has been half promised
to him, and he has a large family and is very poor. I think
on the whole it will be better to make out the nomination
for Mr. Quiverful.'

'But, my lord,' said Mr. Slope, still thinking that he
was bound to make a fight for his own view on this matter,
and remembering that it still behoved him to maintain
his lately acquired supremacy over Mrs. Proudie, lest he
should fail in his views regarding the deanery,—'but my
lord, I am really much afraid——'

'Remember, Mr. Slope,' said the bishop, 'I can hold
out no sort of hope to you in this matter of succeeding
poor Dr. Trefoil. I will certainly speak to the archbishop,
as you wish it, but I cannot think——'

'Well, my lord,' said Mr. Slope, fully understanding
the bishop, and in his turn interrupting him, 'perhaps
your lordship is right about Mr. Quiverful. I have no
doubt I can easily arrange matters with Mr. Harding, and
I will make out the nomination for your signature as you
direct.'

'Yes, Slope, I think that will be best; and you may
be sure that any little that I can do to forward your views
shall be done.'

And so they parted.

Mr. Slope had now much business on his hands. He
had to make his daily visit to the signora. This common
prudence should have now induced him to omit, but he
was infatuated; and could not bring himself to be commonly prudent. He determined therefore that he would
drink tea at the Stanhopes'; and he determined also,
or thought that he determined, that having done so he
would go thither no more. He had also to arrange his
matters with Mrs. Bold. He was of opinion that Eleanor
would grace the deanery as perfectly as she would the

chaplain's cottage; and he thought, moreover, that Eleanor's fortune would excellently repair any dilapidations and curtailments in the dean's stipend which might have been made by that ruthless ecclesiastical commission.

Touching Mrs. Bold his hopes now soared high. Mr. Slope was one of that numerous multitude of swains who think that all is fair in love, and he had accordingly not refrained from using the services of Mrs. Bold's own maid. From her he had learnt much of what had taken place at Plumstead; not exactly with truth, for 'the own maid' had not been able to divine the exact truth, but with some sort of similitude to it. He had been told that the archdeacon and Mrs. Grantly and Mr. Harding and Mr. Arabin had all quarrelled with 'missus' for having received a letter from Mr. Slope; that 'missus' had positively refused to give the letter up; that she had received from the archdeacon the option of giving up either Mr. Slope and his letter, or else the society of Plumstead rectory; and that 'missus' had declared with much indignation, that 'she didn't care a straw for the society of Plumstead rectory,' and that she wouldn't give up Mr. Slope for any of them.

Considering the source from whence this came, it was not quite so untrue as might have been expected. It showed pretty plainly what had been the nature of the conversation in the servants' hall; and coupled as it was with the certainty of Eleanor's sudden return, it appeared to Mr. Slope to be so far worthy of credit as to justify him in thinking that the fair widow would in all human probability accept his offer.

All this work was therefore to be done. It was desirable he thought that he should make his offer before it was known that Mr. Quiverful was finally appointed to the hospital. In his letter to Eleanor he had plainly declared that Mr. Harding was to have the appointment. It would be very difficult to explain this away; and were he to write another letter to Eleanor, telling the truth and throwing the blame on the bishop, it would naturally injure him in her estimation. He determined therefore to let that matter disclose itself as it would, and to lose no time in throwing himself at her feet.

Then he had to solicit the assistance of Sir Nicholas

Fitzwhiggin and Mr. Towers, and he went directly from
the bishop's presence to compose his letters to those
gentlemen. As Mr. Slope was esteemed an adept at letter
writing, they shall be given in full.

'(Private.)   'Palace, Barchester, Sept. 185—.

'My dear Sir Nicholas,—I hope that the intercourse
which has been between us will preclude you from regarding my present application as an intrusion. You cannot
I imagine have yet heard that poor dear old Dr. Trefoil
has been seized with apoplexy. It is a subject of profound
grief to every one in Barchester, for he has always been
an excellent man—excellent as a man and as a clergyman.
He is, however, full of years, and his life could not under
any circumstances have been much longer spared. You
may probably have known him.

'There is, it appears, no probable chance of his recovery.
Sir Omicron Pie is, I believe, at present with him. At
any rate the medical men here have declared that one
or two days more must limit the tether of his mortal
coil. I sincerely trust that his soul may wing its flight
to that haven where it may for ever be at rest and
for ever be happy.

'The bishop has been speaking to me about the preferment, and he is anxious that it should be conferred on
me. I confess that I can hardly venture, at my age, to
look for such advancement; but I am so far encouraged
by his lordship, that I believe I shall be induced to do so.
His lordship goes to —— to-morrow, and is intent on
mentioning the subject to the archbishop.

'I know well how deservedly great is your weight with
the present government. In any matter touching church
preferment you would of course be listened to. Now that
the matter has been put into my head, I am of course
anxious to be successful. If you can assist me by your
good word, you will confer on me one additional favour.

'I had better add, that Lord —— cannot as yet know of
this piece of preferment having fallen in, or rather of its
certainty of falling (for poor dear Dr. Trefoil is past hope).
Should Lord —— first hear it from you, that might probably
be thought to give you a fair claim to express your opinion.

'Of course our grand object is, that we should all be

of one opinion in church matters. This is most desirable
at Barchester; it is this that makes our good bishop so
anxious about it. You may probably think it expedient
to point this out to Lord —— if it shall be in your power
to oblige me by mentioning the subject to his lordship.
          'Believe me, my dear Sir Nicholas,
                    'Your most faithful servant,
                              'OBADIAH SLOPE.'

His letter to Mr. Towers was written in quite a different
strain. Mr. Slope conceived that he completely understood
the difference in character and position of the two men
whom he addressed. He knew that for such a man as
Sir Nicholas Fitzwhiggin a little flummery was necessary,
and that it might be of the easy everyday description.
Accordingly his letter to Sir Nicholas was written *currente
calamo*, with very little trouble. But to such a man as
Mr. Towers it was not so easy to write a letter that should
be effective and yet not offensive, that should carry its
point without undue interference. It was not difficult
to flatter Dr. Proudie or Sir Nicholas Fitzwhiggin, but
very difficult to flatter Mr. Towers without letting the
flattery declare itself. This, however, had to be done.
Moreover, this letter must, in appearance at least, be
written without effort, and be fluent, unconstrained, and
demonstrative of no doubt or fear on the part of the
writer. Therefore the epistle to Mr. Towers was studied,
and recopied, and elaborated at the cost of so many
minutes, that Mr. Slope had hardly time to dress himself
and reach Dr. Stanhope's that evening.
    When despatched it ran as follows :—

'(Private.)   'Barchester. Sept. 185—.'

(He purposely omitted any allusion to the 'palace,'
thinking that Mr. Towers might not like it. A great man,
he remembered, had been once much condemned for
dating a letter from Windsor Castle.)
    'My dear Sir,—We were all a good deal shocked here
this morning by hearing that poor old Dean Trefoil had
been stricken with apoplexy. The fit took him about
9 A.M. I am writing now to save the post, and he is still
alive, but past all hope, or possibility I believe, of living.

Sir Omicron Pie is here, or will be very shortly; but all
that even Sir Omicron can do, is to ratify the sentence of
his less distinguished brethren that nothing can be done.
Poor Dr. Trefoil's race on this side the grave is run. I do
not know whether you knew him. He was a good, quiet,
charitable man, of the old school of course, as any clergyman over seventy years of age must necessarily be.

'But I do not write merely with the object of sending
you such news as this: doubtless some one of your
Mercuries will have seen and heard and reported so much;
I write, as you usually do yourself, rather with a view to
the future than to the past.

'Rumour is already rife here as to Dr. Trefoil's successor,
and among those named as possible future deans your
humble servant is, I believe, not the least frequently
spoken of; in short I am looking for the preferment.
You may probably know that since Bishop Proudie came
to this diocese I have exerted myself here a good deal;
and I may certainly say not without some success. He
and I are nearly always of the same opinion on points of
doctrine as well as church discipline, and therefore I have
had, as his confidential chaplain, very much in my own
hands; but I confess to you that I have a higher ambition
than to remain the chaplain of any bishop.

'There are no positions in which more energy is now
needed than those of our deans. The whole of our enormous cathedral establishments have been allowed to go
to sleep,—nay, they are all but dead and ready for the
sepulchre! And yet of what prodigious moment they
might be made, if, as was intended, they were so managed
as to lead the way and show an example for all our
parochial clergy!

'The bishop here is most anxious for my success;
indeed, he goes to-morrow to press the matter on the
archbishop. I believe also I may count on the support
of at least one most effective member of the government.
But I confess that the support of the Jupiter, if I be
thought worthy of it, would be more gratifying to me
than any other; more gratifying if by it I should be
successful; and more gratifying also, if, although so
supported, I should be unsuccessful.

'The time has, in fact, come in which no government

can venture to fill up the high places of the Church in defiance of the public press. The age of honourable bishops and noble deans has gone by ; and any clergyman however humbly born can now hope for success, if his industry, talent, and character be sufficient to call forth the manifest opinion of the public in his favour.

'At the present moment we all feel that any counsel given in such matters by the Jupiter has the greatest weight—is, indeed, generally followed ; and we feel also—I am speaking of clergymen of my own age and standing—that it should be so. There can be no patron less interested than the Jupiter, and none that more thoroughly understands the wants of the people.

'I am sure you will not suspect me of asking from you any support which the paper with which you are connected cannot conscientiously give me. My object in writing is to let you know that I am a candidate for the appointment. It is for you to judge whether or no you can assist my views. I should not, of course, have written to you on such a matter had I not believed (and I have had good reason so to believe) that the Jupiter approves of my views on ecclesiastical polity.

'The bishop expresses a fear that I may be considered too young for such a station, my age being thirty-six. I cannot think that at the present day any hesitation need be felt on such a point. The public has lost its love for antiquated servants. If a man will ever be fit to do good work he will be fit at thirty-six years of age.

'Believe me very faithfully yours,
'OBADIAH SLOPE.

'T. TOWERS, ESQ
'———Court,
'Middle Temple.'

Having thus exerted himself, Mr. Slope posted his letters, and passed the remainder of the evening at the feet of his mistress.

Mr. Slope will be accused of deceit in his mode of canvassing. It will be said that he lied in the application he made to each of his three patrons. I believe it must be owned that he did so. He could not hesitate on account of his youth, and yet be quite assured that he

was not too young. He could not count chiefly on the
bishop's support, and chiefly also on that of the newspaper.
He did not think that the bishop was going to —— to press
the matter on the archbishop. It must be owned that in
his canvassing Mr. Slope was as false as he well could be.

Let it, however, be asked of those who are conversant
with such matters, whether he was more false than men
usually are on such occasions. We English gentlemen
hate the name of a lie; but how often do we find public
men who believe each other's words ?

CHAPTER XXXIII

MRS. PROUDIE VICTRIX

THE next week passed over at Barchester with much
apparent tranquillity. The hearts, however, of some of
the inhabitants were not so tranquil as the streets of the
city. The poor old dean still continued to live, just as
Sir Omicron Pie had prophesied that he would do, much
to the amazement, and some thought disgust, of Dr.
Fillgrave. The bishop still remained away. He had
stayed a day or two in town, and had also remained
longer at the archbishop's than he had intended. Mr.
Slope had as yet received no line in answer to either of
his letters; but he had learnt the cause of this. Sir
Nicholas was stalking a deer, or attending the Queen, in
the Highlands; and even the indefatigable Mr. Towers
had stolen an autumn holiday, and had made one of the
yearly tribe who now ascend Mont Blanc. Mr. Slope
learnt that he was not expected back till the last day of
September.

Mrs. Bold was thrown much with the Stanhopes, of
whom she became fonder and fonder. If asked, she would
have said that Charlotte Stanhope was her especial friend,
and so she would have thought. But, to tell the truth,
she liked Bertie nearly as well; she had no more idea of
regarding him as a lover than she would have had of
looking at a big tame dog in such a light. Bertie had
become very intimate with her, and made little speeches
to her, and said little things of a sort very different from

the speeches and sayings of other men. But then this was almost always done before his sisters; and he, with his long silken beard, his light blue eyes and strange dress, was so unlike other men. She admitted him to a kind of familiarity which she had never known with any one else, and of which she by no means understood the danger. She blushed once at finding that she had called him Bertie, and on the same day only barely remembered her position in time to check herself from playing upon him some personal practical joke to which she was instigated by Charlotte.

In all this Eleanor was perfectly innocent, and Bertie Stanhope could hardly be called guilty. But every familiarity into which Eleanor was entrapped was deliberately planned by his sister. She knew well how to play her game, and played it without mercy; she knew, none so well, what was her brother's character, and she would have handed over to him the young widow, and the young widow's money, and the money of the widow's child, without remorse. With her pretended friendship and warm cordiality, she strove to connect Eleanor so closely with her brother as to make it impossible that she should go back even if she wished it. But Charlotte Stanhope knew really nothing of Eleanor's character; did not even understand that there were such characters. She did not comprehend that a young and pretty woman could be playful and familiar with a man such as Bertie Stanhope, and yet have no idea in her head, no feeling in her heart that she would have been ashamed to own to all the world. Charlotte Stanhope did not in the least conceive that her new friend was a woman whom nothing could entrap into an inconsiderate marriage, whose mind would have revolted from the slightest impropriety had she been aware that any impropriety existed.

Miss Stanhope, however, had tact enough to make herself and her father's house very agreeable to Mrs. Bold. There was with them all an absence of stiffness and formality which was peculiarly agreeable to Eleanor after the great dose of clerical arrogance which she had lately been constrained to take. She played chess with them, walked with them, and drank tea with them; studied or pretended to study astronomy; assisted them in writing stories in rhyme, in turning prose tragedy into comic verse, or comic stories into would-be tragic poetry. She had no idea before that she had any such talents. She had not conceived the possibility of her doing such things as she now did. She found with the Stanhopes new amusements and employments, new pursuits, which in themselves could not be wrong, and which were exceedingly alluring.

Is it not a pity that people who are bright and clever should so often be exceedingly improper ? and that those who are never improper should so often be dull and heavy ? Now Charlotte Stanhope was always bright, and never heavy : but her propriety was doubtful.

But during all this time Eleanor by no means forgot Mr. Arabin, nor did she forget Mr. Slope. She had parted from Mr. Arabin in her anger. She was still angry at what she regarded as his impertinent interference ; but nevertheless she looked forward to meeting him again, and also looked forward to forgiving him. The words that Mr. Arabin had uttered still sounded in her ears. She knew that if not intended for a declaration of love, they did signify that he loved her ; and she felt also that if he ever did make such a declaration, it might be that she should not receive it unkindly. She was still angry with him, very angry with him ; so angry that she would bite her lip and stamp her foot as she thought of what he had said and done. But nevertheless she yearned to let him know that he was forgiven ; all that she required was that he should own that he had sinned.

She was to meet him at Ullathorne on the last day of the present month. Miss Thorne had invited all the country round to a breakfast on the lawn. There were to be tents, and archery, and dancing for the ladies on the lawn, and for the swains and girls in the paddock. There were to be fiddlers and fifers, races for the boys, poles to be climbed, ditches full of water to be jumped over, horse-collars to be grinned through (this latter amusement was an addition of the stewards, and not arranged by Miss Thorne in the original programme), and every game to be played which, in a long course of reading, Miss Thorne could ascertain to have been played in the good days of Queen Elizabeth. Everything of more

modern growth was to be tabooed, if possible. On one
subject Miss Thorne was very unhappy. She had been
turning in her mind the matter of a bull-ring, but could
not succeed in making anything of it. She would not for
the world have done, or allowed to be done, anything that
was cruel; as to the promoting the torture of a bull for
the amusement of her young neighbours, it need hardly
be said that Miss Thorne would be the last to think of it.
And yet there was something so charming in the name.
A bull-ring, however, without a bull would only be a
memento of the decadence of the times, and she felt herself
constrained to abandon the idea. Quintains, however,
she was determined to have, and had poles and swivels
and bags of flour prepared accordingly. She would no
doubt have been anxious for something small in the way
of a tournament; but, as she said to her brother, that had
been tried, and the age had proved itself too decidedly
inferior to its fore-runners to admit of such a pastime.
Mr. Thorne did not seem to participate much in her regret,
feeling perhaps that a full suit of chain-armour would
have added but little to his own personal comfort.

This party at Ullathorne had been planned in the first
place as a sort of welcoming to Mr. Arabin on his entrance
into St. Ewold's parsonage; an intended harvest-home
gala for the labourers and their wives and children had
subsequently been amalgamated with it, and thus it had
grown to its present dimensions. All the Plumstead
party had of course been asked, and at the time of the
invitation Eleanor had intended to have gone with her
sister. Now her plans were altered, and she was going
with the Stanhopes. The Proudies were also to be there;
and as Mr. Slope had not been included in the invitation to the palace, the signora, whose impudence never
deserted her, asked permission of Miss Thorne to bring
him.

This permission Miss Thorne gave, having no other
alternative; but she did so with a trembling heart, fearing
Mr. Arabin would be offended. Immediately on his
return she apologised, almost with tears, so dire an enmity
was presumed to rage between the two gentlemen. But
Mr. Arabin comforted her by an assurance that he should
meet Mr. Slope with the greatest pleasure imaginable

and made her promise that she would introduce them
to each other.

But this triumph of Mr. Slope's was not so agreeable to
Eleanor, who since her return to Barchester had done her
best to avoid him. She would not give way to the Plumstead folk when they so ungenerously accused her of
being in love with this odious man ; but, nevertheless,
knowing that she was so accused, she was fully alive to
the expediency of keeping out of his way and dropping
him by degrees. She had seen very little of him since her
return. Her servant had been instructed to say to all
visitors that she was out. She could not bring herself
to specify Mr. Slope particularly, and in order to avoid
him she had thus debarred herself from all her friends.
She had excepted Charlotte Stanhope, and by degrees a
few others also. Once she had met him at the Stanhopes' ;
but, as a rule, Mr. Slope's visits there were made in the
morning, and hers in the evening. On that one occasion
Charlotte had managed to preserve her from any annoyance. This was very good-natured on the part of Charlotte,
as Eleanor thought, and also very sharp-witted, as Eleanor
had told her friend nothing of her reasons for wishing to
avoid that gentleman. The fact, however, was, that
Charlotte had learnt from her sister that Mr. Slope would
probably put himself forward as a suitor for the widow's
hand, and she was consequently sufficiently alive to the
expediency of guarding Bertie's future wife from any
danger in that quarter.

Nevertheless the Stanhopes were pledged to take Mr.
Slope with them to Ullathorne. An arrangement was
therefore necessarily made, which was very disagreeable
to Eleanor. Dr. Stanhope, with herself, Charlotte, and
Mr. Slope, were to go together, and Bertie was to follow
with his sister Madeline. It was clearly visible by Eleanor's
face that this assortment was very disagreeable to her ;
and Charlotte, who was much encouraged thereby in
her own little plan, made a thousand apologies.

' I see you don't like it, my dear,' said she, ' but we
could not manage otherwise. Bertie would give his eyes
to go with you, but Madeline cannot possibly go without
him. Nor could we possibly put Mr. Slope and Madeline
in the same carriage without any one else. They'd both

be ruined for ever, you know, and not admitted inside Ullathorne gates, I should imagine, after such an impropriety.'

'Of course that wouldn't do,' said Eleanor; 'but couldn't I go in the carriage with the signora and your brother?'

'Impossible!' said Charlotte. 'When she is there, there is only room for two.' The signora, in truth, did not care to do her travelling in the presence of strangers.

'Well, then,' said Eleanor, 'you are all so kind, Charlotte, and so good to me, that I am sure you won't be offended; but I think I'll not go at all.'

'Not go at all!—what nonsense!—indeed you shall.' It had been absolutely determined in family council that Bertie should propose on that very occasion.

'Or I can take a fly,' said Eleanor. 'You know I am not embarrassed by so many difficulties as you young ladies; I can go alone.'

'Nonsense! my dear. Don't think of such a thing; after all it is only for an hour or so; and, to tell the truth, I don't know what it is you dislike so. I thought you and Mr. Slope were great friends. What is it you dislike?'

'Oh! nothing particular,' said Eleanor; 'only I thought it would be a family party.'

'Of course it would be much nicer, much more snug, if Bertie could go with us. It is he that is badly treated. I can assure you he is much more afraid of Mr. Slope than you are. But you see Madeline cannot go out without him,—and she, poor creature, goes out so seldom! I am sure you don't begrudge her this, though her vagary does knock about our own party a little.'

Of course Eleanor made a thousand protestations, and uttered a thousand hopes that Madeline would enjoy herself. And of course she had to give way, and undertake to go in the carriage with Mr. Slope. In fact, she was driven either to do this, or to explain why she would not do so. Now she could not bring herself to explain to Charlotte Stanhope all that had passed at Plumstead.

But it was to her a sore necessity. She thought of a thousand little schemes for avoiding it; she would plead illness, and not go at all; she would persuade Mary Bold to go although not asked, and then make a necessity of having a carriage of her own to take her sister-in-law; anything, in fact, she could do rather than be seen by Mr. Arabin getting out of the same carriage with Mr. Slope. However, when the momentous morning came she had no scheme matured, and then Mr. Slope handed her into Dr. Stanhope's carriage, and following her steps, sat opposite to her.

The bishop returned on the eve of the Ullathorne party, and was received at home with radiant smiles by the partner of all his cares. On his arrival he crept up to his dressing-room with somewhat of a palpitating heart; he had overstayed his allotted time by three days, and was not without much fear of penalties. Nothing, however, could be more affectionately cordial than the greeting he received : the girls came out and kissed him in a manner that was quite soothing to his spirit ; and Mrs. Proudie, ' albeit, unused to the melting mood,' squeezed him in her arms, and almost in words called him her dear, darling, good, pet, little bishop. All this was a very pleasant surprise.

Mrs. Proudie had somewhat changed her tactics ; not that she had seen any cause to disapprove of her former line of conduct, but she had now brought matters to such a point that she calculated that she might safely do so. She had got the better of Mr. Slope, and she now thought well to show her husband that when allowed to get the better of everybody, when obeyed by him and permitted to rule over others, she would take care that he should have his reward. Mr. Slope had not a chance against her ; not only could she stun the poor bishop by her midnight anger, but she could assuage and soothe him, if she so willed, by daily indulgences. She could furnish his room for him, turn him out as smart a bishop as any on the bench, give him good dinners, warm fires, and an easy life ; all this she would do if he would but be quietly obedient. But if not —— ! To speak sooth, however, his sufferings on that dreadful night had been so poignant, as to leave him little spirit for further rebellion.

As soon as he had dressed himself she returned to his room. ' I hope you enjoyed yourself at —— ' said she, seating herself on one side of the fire while he remained in his arm-chair on the other, stroking the calves of his legs. It was the first time he had had a fire in his room since the summer, and it pleased him; for the good bishop loved to be warm and cozy. Yes, he said, he had enjoyed himself very much. Nothing could be more polite than the archbishop; and Mrs. Archbishop had been equally charming.

Mrs. Proudie was delighted to hear it; nothing, she declared, pleased her so much as to think

> Her bairn respectit like the lave.

She did not put it precisely in these words, but what she said came to the same thing; and then, having petted and fondled her little man sufficiently, she proceeded to business.

'The poor dean is still alive,' said she.

'So I hear, so I hear,' said the bishop. 'I'll go to the deanery directly after breakfast to-morrow.'

'We are going to this party at Ullathorne to-morrow morning, my dear; we must be there early, you know,— by twelve o'clock I suppose.'

'Oh,—ah!' said the bishop; 'then I'll certainly call the next day.'

'Was much said about it at,——?' asked Mrs. Proudie.

'About what?' said the bishop.

'Filling up the dean's place,' said Mrs. Proudie. As she spoke a spark of the wonted fire returned to her eye, and the bishop felt himself to be a little less comfortable than before.

'Filling up the dean's place; that is, if the dean dies?—very little, my dear. It was mentioned, just mentioned.'

'And what did you say about it, bishop?'

'Why, I said that I thought that if, that is, should— should the dean die, that is, I said I thought——' As he went on stammering and floundering, he saw that his wife's eye was fixed sternly on him. Why should he encounter such evil for a man whom he loved so slightly as Mr. Slope? Why should he give up his enjoyments and his ease, and such dignity as might be allowed to him, to fight a losing battle for a chaplain? The chaplain after all, if successful, would be as great a tyrant as his wife. Why fight at all? why contend? why be uneasy?

From that moment he determined to fling Mr. Slope to the winds, and take the goods the gods provided.

' I am told,' said Mrs. Proudie, speaking very slowly, ' that Mr. Slope is looking to be the new dean.'

' Yes,—certainly, I believe he is,' said the bishop.

' And what does the archbishop say about that ? ' asked Mrs. Proudie.

' Well, my dear, to tell the truth, I promised Mr. Slope to speak to the archbishop. Mr. Slope spoke to me about it. It is very arrogant of him, I must say,—but that is nothing to me.'

' Arrogant ! ' said Mrs. Proudie ; ' it is the most impudent piece of pretension I ever heard of in my life. Mr. Slope dean of Barchester, indeed ! And what did you do in the matter, bishop ? '

' Why, my dear, I did speak to the archbishop.'

' You don't mean to tell me,' said Mrs. Proudie, ' that you are going to make yourself ridiculous by lending your name to such a preposterous attempt as this ? Mr. Slope dean of Barchester, indeed ! ' And she tossed her head, and put her arms a-kimbo, with an air of confident defiance that made her husband quite sure that Mr. Slope never would be Dean of Barchester. In truth, Mrs. Proudie was all but invincible ; had she married Petruchio, it may be doubted whether that arch wife-tamer would have been able to keep her legs out of those garments which are presumed by men to be peculiarly unfitted for feminine use.

' It is preposterous, my dear.'

' Then why have you endeavoured to assist him ? '

' Why,—my dear, I haven't assisted him—much.'

' But why have you done it at all ? why have you mixed your name up in any thing so ridiculous ? What was it you did say to the archbishop ? '

' Why, I just did mention it ; I just did say that—that in the event of the poor dean's death, Mr. Slope would—would——'

' Would what ? '

' I forget how I put it,—would take it if he could get it ; something of that sort. I didn't say much more than that.'

' You shouldn't have said anything at all. And what did the archbishop say ? '

' He didn't say anything ; he just bowed and rubbed
his hands. Somebody else came up at the moment, and
as we were discussing the new parochial universal school
committee, the matter of the new dean dropped ; after
that I didn't think it wise to renew it.'

' Renew it ! I am very sorry you ever mentioned it.
What will the archbishop think of you ? '

' You may be sure, my dear, the archbishop thought
very little about it.'

' But why did you think about it, bishop ? how could
you think of making such a creature as that Dean of
Barchester ?—Dean of Barchester ! I suppose he'll be
looking for a bishopric some of these days—a man that
hardly knows who his own father was ; a man that I
found without bread to his mouth, or a coat to his back.
Dean of Barchester, indeed ! I'll dean him.'

Mrs. Proudie considered herself to be in politics a pure
Whig ; all her family belonged to the Whig party. Now
among all ranks of Englishmen and Englishwomen (Mrs.
Proudie should, I think, be ranked among the former, on
the score of her great strength of mind), no one is so hostile
to lowly born pretenders to high station as the pure Whig.

The bishop thought it necessary to exculpate himself.
' Why, my dear,' said he, ' it appeared to me that you and
Mr. Slope did not get on quite so well as you used to do.'

' Get on ! ' said Mrs. Proudie, moving her foot uneasily
on the hearth-rug, and compressing her lips in a manner that
betokened much danger to the subject of their discourse.

' I began to find that he was objectionable to you,'—
Mrs. Proudie's foot worked on the hearth-rug with great
rapidity,—' and that you would be more comfortable if
he was out of the palace,'—Mrs. Proudie smiled, as a
hyena may probably smile before he begins his laugh,—
' and therefore I thought that if he got this place, and so
ceased to be my chaplain, you might be pleased at such
an arrangement.'

And then the hyena laughed out. Pleased at such an
arrangement ! pleased at having her enemy converted
into a dean with twelve hundred a year ! Medea, when
she describes the customs of her native country (I am
quoting from Robson's edition), assures her astonished
auditor that in her land captives, when taken, are eaten.

'You pardon them?' says Medea. 'We do indeed,' says the mild Grecian. 'We eat them!' says she of Colchis, with terrific energy. Mrs. Proudie was the Medea of Barchester; she had no idea of not eating Mr. Slope. Pardon him! merely get rid of him! make a dean of him! It was not so they did with their captives in her country, among people of her sort! 'Mr. Slope had no such mercy to expect; she would pick him to the very last bone.

'Oh, yes, my dear, of course he'll cease to be your chaplain,' said she. 'After what has passed, that must be a matter of course. I couldn't for a moment think of living in the same house with such a man. Besides, he has shown himself quite unfit for such a situation; making broils and quarrels among the clergy, getting you, my dear, into scrapes, and taking upon himself as though he were as good as bishop himself. Of course he'll go. But because he leaves the palace, that is no reason why he should get into the deanery.'

'Oh, of course not!' said the bishop; 'but to save appearances you know, my dear——'

'I don't want to save appearances; I want Mr. Slope to appear just what he is—a false, designing, mean, intriguing man. I have my eye on him; he little knows what I see. He is misconducting himself in the most disgraceful way with that lame Italian woman. That family is a disgrace to Barchester, and Mr. Slope is a disgrace to Barchester! If he doesn't look well to it, he'll have his gown stripped off his back instead of having a dean's hat on his head. Dean, indeed! The man has gone mad with arrogance.'

The bishop said nothing further to excuse either himself or his chaplain, and having shown himself passive and docile was again taken into favour. They soon went to dinner, and he spent the pleasantest evening he had had in his own house for a long time. His daughter played and sang to him as he sipped his coffee and read his newspaper, and Mrs. Proudie asked good-natured little questions about the archbishop; and then he went happily to bed, and slept as quietly as though Mrs. Proudie had been Griselda herself. While shaving himself in the morning and preparing for the festivities of Ullathorne, he fully resolved to run no more tilts against a warrior so fully armed at all points as was Mrs. Proudie.

CHAPTER XXXIV

OXFORD—THE MASTER AND TUTOR OF LAZARUS

MR. ARABIN, as we have said, had but a sad walk of it under the trees of Plumstead churchyard. He did not appear to any of the family till dinner time, and then he seemed, as far as their judgment went, to be quite himself. He had, as was his wont, asked himself a great many questions, and given himself a great many answers ; and the upshot of this was that he had set himself down for an ass. He had determined that he was much too old and much too rusty to commence the manœuvres of love-making ; that he had let the time slip through his hands which should have been used for such purposes ; and that now he must lie on his bed as he had made it. Then he asked himself whether in truth he did love this woman ; and he answered himself, not without a long struggle, but at last honestly, that he certainly did love her. He then asked himself whether he did not also love her money ; and he again answered himself that he did so. But here he did not answer honestly. It was and ever had been his weakness to look for impure motives for his own conduct. No doubt, circumstanced as he was, with a small living and a fellowship, accustomed as he had been to collegiate luxuries and expensive comforts, he might have hesitated to marry a penniless woman had he felt ever so strong a predilection for the woman herself ; no doubt Eleanor's fortune put all such difficulties out of the question ; but it was equally without doubt that his love for her had crept upon him without the slightest idea on his part that he could ever benefit his own condition by sharing her wealth.

When he had stood on the hearth-rug, counting the pattern, and counting also the future chances of his own life, the remembrances of Mrs. Bold's comfortable income had not certainly damped his first assured feeling of love for her. And why should it have done so ? Need it have done so with the purest of men ? Be that as it may, Mr. Arabin decided against himself ; he decided that it had done so in his case, and that he was not the purest of men.

He also decided, which was more to his purpose, that Eleanor did not care a straw for him, and that very probably she did care a straw for his rival. Then he made up his mind not to think of her any more, and went on thinking of her till he was almost in a state to drown himself in the little brook which ran at the bottom of the archdeacon's grounds.

And ever and again his mind would revert to the Signora Neroni, and he would make comparisons between her and Eleanor Bold, not always in favour of the latter. The signora had listened to him, and flattered him, and believed in him; at least she had told him so. Mrs. Bold had also listened to him, but had never flattered him; had not always believed in him: and now had broken from him in violent rage. The signora, too, was the more lovely woman of the two, and had also the additional attraction of her affliction; for to him it was an attraction.

But he never could have loved the Signora Neroni as he felt that he now loved Eleanor! and so he flung stones into the brook, instead of flinging in himself, and sat down on its margin as sad a gentleman as you shall meet in a summer's day.

He heard the dinner-bell ring from the churchyard, and he knew that it was time to recover his self-possession. He felt that he was disgracing himself in his own eyes, that he had been idling his time and neglecting the high duties which he had taken upon himself to perform. He should have spent this afternoon among the poor at St. Ewold's, instead of wandering about at Plumstead, an ancient love-lorn swain, dejected and sighing, full of imaginary sorrows and Wertherian grief. He was thoroughly ashamed of himself, and determined to lose no time in retrieving his character, so damaged in his own eyes. Thus when he appeared at dinner he was as animated as ever, and was the author of most of the conversation which graced the archdeacon's board on that evening. Mr. Harding was ill at ease and sick at heart, and did not care to appear more comfortable than he really was; what little he did say was said to his daughter. He thought that the archdeacon and Mr. Arabin had leagued together against Eleanor's comfort; and his wish now was to break away from the pair, and undergo in his Barchester lodgings whatever Fate had in store for him. He hated the name of the hospital; his attempt to regain his lost inheritance there had brought upon him so much suffering. As far as he was concerned, Mr. Quiverful was now welcome to the place.

And the archdeacon was not very lively. The poor dean's illness was of course discussed in the first place. Dr. Grantly did not mention Mr. Slope's name in connexion with the expected event of Dr. Trefoil's death; he did not wish to say anything about Mr. Slope just at present, nor did he wish to make known his sad surmises; but the idea that his enemy might possibly become Dean of Barchester made him very gloomy. Should such an event take place, such a dire catastrophe come about, there would be an end to his life as far as his life was connected with the city of Barchester. He must give up all his old haunts, all his old habits, and live quietly as a retired rector at Plumstead. It had been a severe trial for him to have Dr. Proudie in the palace; but with Mr. Slope also in the deanery, he felt that he should be unable to draw his breath in Barchester close.

Thus it came to pass that in spite of the sorrow at his heart, Mr. Arabin was apparently the gayest of the party. Both Mr. Harding and Mrs. Grantly were in a slight degree angry with him on account of his want of gloom. To the one it appeared as though he were triumphing at Eleanor's banishment, and to the other that he was not affected as he should have been by all the sad circumstances of the day, Eleanor's obstinacy, Mr. Slope's success, and the poor dean's apoplexy. And so they were all at cross purposes.

Mr. Harding left the room almost together with the ladies, and then the archdeacon opened his heart to Mr. Arabin. He still harped upon the hospital. 'What did that fellow mean,' said he, ' by saying in his letter to Mrs. Bold, that if Mr. Harding would call on the bishop it would be all right? Of course I would not be guided by anything he might say; but still it may be well that Mr. Harding should see the bishop. It would be foolish to let the thing slip through our fingers because Mrs. Bold is determined to make a fool of herself.'

Mr. Arabin hinted that he was not quite so sure that

Mrs. Bold would make a fool of herself. He said that he was not convinced that she did regard Mr. Slope so warmly as she was supposed to do. The archdeacon questioned and cross-questioned him about this, but elicited nothing; and at last remained firm in his own conviction that he was destined, *malgré lui*, to be the brother-in-law of Mr. Slope. Mr. Arabin strongly advised that Mr. Harding should take no step regarding the hospital in connexion with, or in consequence of, Mr. Slope's letter. 'If the bishop really means to confer the appointment on Mr. Harding,' argued Mr. Arabin, 'he will take care to let him have some other intimation than a message conveyed through a letter to a lady. Were Mr. Harding to present himself at the palace he might merely be playing Mr. Slope's game;' and thus it was settled that nothing should be done till the great Dr. Gwynne's arrival, or at any rate without that potentate's sanction.

It was droll to observe how these men talked of Mr. Harding as though he were a puppet, and planned their intrigues and small ecclesiastical manœuvres in reference to Mr. Harding's future position, without dreaming of taking him into their confidence. There was a comfortable house and income in question, and it was very desirable, and certainly very just, that Mr. Harding should have them; but that, at present, was not the main point; it was expedient to beat the bishop, and if possible to smash Mr. Slope. Mr. Slope had set up, or was supposed to have set up, a rival candidate. Of all things the most desirable would have been to have had Mr. Quiverful's appointment published to the public, and then annulled by the clamour of an indignant world, loud in the defence of Mr. Harding's rights. But of such an event the chance was small; a slight fraction only of the world would be indignant, and that fraction would be one not accustomed to loud speaking. And then the preferment had in a sort of way been offered to Mr. Harding, and had in a sort of way been refused by him.

Mr. Slope's wicked, cunning hand had been peculiarly conspicuous in the way in which this had been brought to pass, and it was the success of Mr. Slope's cunning which was so painfully grating to the feelings of the archdeacon. That which of all things he most dreaded was that he should be out-generalled by Mr. Slope : and just at present it appeared probable that Mr. Slope would turn his flank, steal a march on him, cut off his provisions, carry his strong town by a *coup de main*, and at last beat him thoroughly in a regular pitched battle. The archdeacon felt that his flank had been turned when desired to wait on Mr. Slope instead of the bishop, that a march had been stolen when Mr. Harding was induced to refuse the bishop's offer, that his provisions would be cut off when Mr. Quiverful got the hospital, that Eleanor was the strong town doomed to be taken, and that Mr. Slope, as Dean of Barchester, would be regarded by all the world as the conqueror in the final conflict.

Dr. Gwynne was the *Deus ex machinâ* who was to come down upon the Barchester stage, and bring about deliverance from these terrible evils. But how can melodramatic *dénouements* be properly brought about, how can vice and Mr. Slope be punished, and virtue and the archdeacon be rewarded, while the avenging god is laid up with the gout ? In the mean time evil may be triumphant, and poor innocence, transfixed to the earth by an arrow from Dr. Proudie's quiver, may lie dead upon the ground, not to be resuscitated even by Dr. Gwynne.

Two or three days after Eleanor's departure, Mr. Arabin went to Oxford, and soon found himself closeted with the august head of his college. It was quite clear that Dr. Gwynne was not very sanguine as to the effects of his journey to Barchester, and not over anxious to interfere with the bishop. He had had the gout but was very nearly convalescent, and Mr. Arabin at once saw that had the mission been one of which the master thoroughly approved, he would before this have been at Plumstead.

As it was, Dr. Gwynne was resolved on visiting his friend, and willingly promised to return to Barchester with Mr. Arabin. He could not bring himself to believe that there was any probability that Mr. Slope would be made Dean of Barchester. Rumour, he said, had reached even his ears, not at all favourable to that gentleman's character, and he expressed himself strongly of opinion that any such appointment was quite out of the question. At this stage of the proceedings, the master's right-hand man, Tom Staple, was called in to assist at the conference.

Tom Staple was the Tutor of Lazarus, and moreover a great man at Oxford. Though universally known by a species of nomenclature so very undignified, Tom Staple was one who maintained a high dignity in the University. He was, as it were, the leader of the Oxford tutors, a body of men who consider themselves collectively as being by very little, if at all, second in importance to the heads themselves. It is not always the case that the master, or warden, or provost, or principal can hit it off exactly with his tutor. A tutor is by no means indisposed to have a will of his own. But at Lazarus they were great friends and firm allies at the time of which we are writing.

Tom Staple was a hale strong man of about forty-five; short in stature, swarthy in face, with strong sturdy black hair, and crisp black beard, of which very little was allowed to show itself in shape of whiskers. He always wore a white neckcloth, clean indeed, but not tied with that scrupulous care which now distinguishes some of our younger clergy. He was, of course, always clothed in a seemly suit of solemn black. Mr. Staple was a decent cleanly liver, not over addicted to any sensuality; but nevertheless a somewhat warmish hue was beginning to adorn his nose, the peculiar effect, as his friends averred, of a certain pipe of port introduced into the cellars of Lazarus the very same year in which the tutor entered it as a freshman. There was also, perhaps, a little redolence of port wine, as it were the slightest possible twang, in Mr. Staple's voice.

In these latter days Tom Staple was not a happy man; University reform had long been his bugbear, and now was his bane. It was not with him as with most others, an affair of politics, respecting which, when the need existed, he could, for parties' sake or on behalf of principle, maintain a certain amount of necessary zeal; it was not with him a subject for dilettante warfare, and courteous common-place opposition. To him it was life and death. The *statu quo* of the University was his only idea of life, and any reformation was as bad to him as death. He would willingly have been a martyr in the cause, had the cause admitted of martyrdom.

At the present day, unfortunately, public affairs will allow of no martyrs, and therefore it is that there is such a deficiency of zeal. Could gentlemen of 10,000*l.* a year have died on their own door-steps in defence of protection, no doubt some half-dozen glorious old baronets would have so fallen, and the school of protection would at this day have been crowded with scholars. Who can fight strenuously in any combat in which there is no danger ? Tom Staple would have willingly been impaled before a Committee of the House, could he by such self-sacrifice have infused his own spirit into the component members of the hebdomadal board.

Tom Staple was one of those who in his heart approved of the credit system which had of old been in vogue between the students and tradesmen of the University. He knew and acknowledged to himself that it was useless in these degenerate days publicly to contend with the Jupiter on such a subject. The Jupiter had undertaken to rule the University, and Tom Staple was well aware that the Jupiter was too powerful for him. But in secret, and among his safe companions, he would argue that the system of credit was an ordeal good for young men to undergo.

The bad men, said he, the weak and worthless, blunder into danger and burn their feet ; but the good men, they who have any character, they who have that within them which can reflect credit on their Alma Mater, they come through scatheless. What merit will there be to a young man to get through safely, if he be guarded and protected and restrained like a school-boy ? By so doing, the period of the ordeal is only postponed, and the manhood of the man will be deferred from the age of twenty to that of twenty-four. If you bind him with leading-strings at college, he will break loose while eating for the bar in London ; bind him there, and he will break loose afterwards, when he is a married man. The wild oats must be sown somewhere. 'Twas thus that Tom Staple would argue of young men ; not, indeed, with much consistency, but still with some practical knowledge of the subject gathered from long experience.

And now Tom Staple proffered such wisdom as he had for the assistance of Dr. Gwynne and Mr. Arabin.

' Quite out of the question,' said he, arguing that Mr. Slope could not possibly be made the new Dean of Barchester.

' So I think,' said the master. ' He has no standing, and, if all I hear be true, very little character.'

' As to character,' said Tom Staple, ' I don't think much of that. They rather like loose parsons for deans; a little fast living, or a dash of infidelity, is no bad recommendation to a cathedral close. But they couldn't make Mr. Slope; the last two deans have been Cambridge men; you'll not show me an instance of their making three men running from the same University. We don't get our share, and never shall, I suppose; but we must at least have one out of three.'

' Those sort of rules are all gone by now,' said Mr. Arabin.

' Everything has gone by, I believe,' said Tom Staple. ' The cigar has been smoked out, and we are the ashes.'

' Speak for yourself, Staple,' said the master.

' I speak for all,' said the tutor, stoutly. ' It is coming to that, that there will be no life left anywhere in the country. No one is any longer fit to rule himself, or those belonging to him. The Government is to find us all in everything, and the press is to find the Government. Nevertheless, Mr. Slope won't be Dean of Barchester.'

' And who will be warden of the hospital ? ' said Mr. Arabin.

' I hear that Mr. Quiverful is already appointed,' said Tom Staple.

' I think not,' said the master. ' And I think, moreover, that Dr. Proudie will not be so short-sighted as to run against such a rock: Mr. Slope should himself have sense enough to prevent it.'

' But perhaps Mr. Slope may have no objection to see his patron on a rock,' said the suspicious tutor.

' What could he get by that ? ' asked Mr. Arabin.

' It is impossible to see the doubles of such a man,' said Mr. Staple. ' It seems quite clear that Bishop Proudie is altogether in his hands, and it is equally clear that he has been moving heaven and earth to get this Mr. Quiverful into the hospital, although he must know that such an appointment would be most damaging to the bishop. It is impossible to understand such a man, and dreadful to think,' added Tom Staple, sighing deeply, ' that the welfare and fortunes of good men may depend on his intrigues.'

Dr. Gwynne or Mr. Staple were not in the least aware, nor even was Mr. Arabin, that this Mr. Slope, of whom they were talking, had been using his utmost efforts to put their own candidate into the hospital; and that in lieu of being permanent in the palace, his own expulsion therefrom had been already decided on by the high powers of the diocese.

'I'll tell you what,' said the tutor, ' if this Quiverful is thrust into the hospital and Dr. Trefoil does die, I should not wonder if the Government were to make Mr. Harding Dean of Barchester. They would feel bound to do something for him after all that was said when he resigned.'

Dr. Gwynne at the moment made no reply to this suggestion; but it did not the less impress itself on his mind. If Mr. Harding could not be warden of the hospital, why should he not be Dean of Barchester?

And so the conference ended without any very fixed resolution, and Dr. Gwynne and Mr. Arabin prepared for their journey to Plumstead on the morrow.

CHAPTER XXXV

MISS THORNE'S FÊTE CHAMPÊTRE

THE day of the Ullathorne party arrived, and all the world were there; or at least so much of the world as had been included in Miss Thorne's invitation. As we have said, the bishop returned home on the previous evening, and on the same evening, and by the same train, came Dr. Gwynne and Mr. Arabin from Oxford. The archdeacon with his brougham was in waiting for the Master of Lazarus, so that there was a goodly show of church dignitaries on the platform of the railway.

The Stanhope party was finally arranged in the odious manner already described, and Eleanor got into the doctor's carriage full of apprehension and presentiment of further misfortune, whereas Mr. Slope entered the vehicle elate with triumph.

He had received that morning a very civil note from Sir Nicholas Fitzwhiggin; not promising much indeed; but then Mr. Slope knew, or fancied that he knew, that it was

not etiquette for government officers to make promises.
Though Sir Nicholas promised nothing he implied a good
deal; declared his conviction that Mr. Slope would make
an excellent dean, and wished him every kind of success.
To be sure he added that, not being in the cabinet, he was
never consulted on such matters, and that even if he spoke
on the subject his voice would go for nothing. But all this
Mr. Slope took for the prudent reserve of official life. To
complete his anticipated triumphs, another letter was
brought to him just as he was about to start to Ullathorne.

Mr. Slope also enjoyed the idea of handing Mrs. Bold
out of Dr. Stanhope's carriage before the multitude at
Ullathorne gate, as much as Eleanor dreaded the same
ceremony. He had fully made up his mind to throw himself and his fortune at the widow's feet, and had almost
determined to select the present propitious morning for
doing so. The signora had of late been less than civil to
him. She had indeed admitted his visits, and listened, at
any rate without anger, to his love; but she had tortured
him and reviled him, jeered at him and ridiculed him,
while she allowed him to call her the most beautiful of
living women, to kiss her hand, and to proclaim himself
with reiterated oaths her adorer, her slave, and worshipper.

Miss Thorne was in great perturbation, yet in great
glory, on the morning of the gala day. Mr. Thorne also,
though the party was none of his giving, had much heavy
work on his hands. But perhaps the most overtasked, the
most anxious, and the most effective of all the Ullathorne
household was Mr. Plomacy, the steward. This last
personage had, in the time of Mr. Thorne's father, when
the Directory held dominion in France, gone over to Paris
with letters in his boot heel for some of the royal party;
and such had been his good luck that he had returned safe.
He had then been very young and was now very old, but
the exploit gave him a character for political enterprise
and secret discretion which still availed him as thoroughly
as it had done in its freshest gloss. Mr. Plomacy had been
steward of Ullathorne for more than fifty years, and a very
easy life he had had of it. Who could require much
absolute work from a man who had carried safely at his
heel that which if discovered would have cost him his
head? Consequently Mr. Plomacy had never worked

hard, and of latter years had never worked at all. He had a taste for timber, and therefore he marked the trees that were to be cut down; he had a taste for gardening, and would therefore allow no shrub to be planted or bed to be made without his express sanction. In these matters he was sometimes driven to run counter to his mistress, but he rarely allowed his mistress to carry the point against him.

But on occasions such as the present Mr. Plomacy came out strong. He had the honour of the family at heart; he thoroughly appreciated the duties of hospitality; and therefore, when gala doings were going on, always took the management into his own hands and reigned supreme over master and mistress.

To give Mr. Plomacy his due, old as he was, he thoroughly understood such work as he had in hand, and did it well.

The order of the day was to be as follows. The quality, as the upper classes in rural districts are designated by the lower with so much true discrimination, were to eat a breakfast, and the non-quality were to eat a dinner. Two marquees had been erected for these two banquets, that for the quality on the esoteric or garden side of a certain deep ha-ha; and that for the non-quality on the exoteric or paddock side of the same. Both were of huge dimensions; that on the outer side was, one may say, on an egregious scale; but Mr. Plomacy declared that neither would be sufficient. To remedy this, an auxiliary banquet was prepared in the dining-room, and a subsidiary board was to be spread *sub dio* for the accommodation of the lower class of yokels on the Ullathorne property.

No one who has not had a hand in the preparation of such an affair can understand the manifold difficulties which Miss Thorne encountered in her project. Had she not been made throughout of the very finest whalebone, riveted with the best Yorkshire steel, she must have sunk under them. Had not Mr. Plomacy felt how much was justly expected from a man who at one time carried the destinies of Europe in his boot, he would have given way; and his mistress, so deserted, must have perished among her poles and canvass.

In the first place there was a dreadful line to be drawn.

Who were to dispose themselves within the ha-ha, and who without ? To this the unthinking will give an off-hand answer, as they will to every ponderous question. Oh, the bishop and such like within the ha-ha; and Farmer Greenacre and such like without. True, my unthinking friend; but who shall define these such-likes ? It is in such definitions that the whole difficulty of society consists. To seat the bishop on an arm chair on the lawn and place Farmer Greenacre at the end of a long table in the paddock is easy enough; but where will you put Mrs. Lookaloft, whose husband, though a tenant on the estate, hunts in a red coat, whose daughters go to a fashionable seminary in Barchester, who calls her farm house Rosebank, and who has a pianoforte in her drawing-room ? The Misses Lookaloft, as they call themselves, won't sit contented among the bumpkins. Mrs. Lookaloft won't squeeze her fine clothes on a bench and talk familiarly about cream and ducklings to good Mrs. Greenacre. And yet Mrs. Lookaloft is no fit companion and never has been the associate of the Thornes and the Grantlys. And if Mrs. Lookaloft be admitted within the sanctum of fashionable life, if she be allowed with her three daughters to leap the ha-ha, why not the wives and daughters of other families also ? Mrs. Greenacre is at present well contented with the paddock, but she might cease to be so if she saw Mrs. Lookaloft on the lawn. And thus poor Miss Thorne had a hard time of it.

And how was she to divide her guests between the marquee and the parlour ? She had a countess coming, an Honourable John and an Honourable George, and a whole bevy of Ladies Amelia, Rosina, Margaretta, &c.; she had a leash of baronets with their baronnettes; and, as we all know, she had a bishop. If she put them on the lawn, no one would go into the parlour; if she put them into the parlour, no one would go into the tent. She thought of keeping the old people in the house, and leaving the lawn to the lovers. She might as well have seated herself at once in a hornet's nest. Mr. Plomacy knew better than this. ' Bless your soul, Ma'am,' said he, ' there won't be no old ladies; not one, barring yourself and old Mrs. Clantantram.'

Personally Miss Thorne accepted this distinction in her

favour as a compliment to her good sense; but nevertheless she had no desire to be closeted on the coming occasion with Mrs. Clantantram. She gave up all idea of any arbitrary division of her guests, and determined if possible to put the bishop on the lawn and the countess in the house, to sprinkle the baronets, and thus divide the attractions. What to do with the Lookalofts even Mr. Plomacy could not decide. They must take their chance. They had been specially told in the invitation that all the tenants had been invited; and they might probably have the good sense to stay away if they objected to mix with the rest of the tenantry.

Then Mr. Plomacy declared his apprehension that the Honourable Johns and Honourable Georges would come in a sort of amphibious costume, half morning half evening, satin neckhandkerchiefs, frock coats, primrose gloves, and polished boots; and that, being so dressed, they would decline riding at the quintain, or taking part in any of the athletic games which Miss Thorne had prepared with so much fond care. If the Lord Johns and Lord Georges didn't ride at the quintain, Miss Thorne might be sure that nobody else would.

'But,' said she in dolorous voice, all but overcome by her cares; 'it was specially signified that there were to be sports.'

'And so there will be, of course,' said Mr. Plomacy. 'They'll all be sporting with the young ladies in the laurel walks. Them's the sports they care most about now-a-days. If you gets the young men at the quintain, you'll have all the young women in the pouts.'

'Can't they look on, as their great grandmothers did before them?' said Miss Thorne.

'It seems to me that the ladies ain't contented with looking now-a-days. Whatever the men do they'll do. If you'll have side saddles on the nags, and let them go at the quintain too, it'll answer capital, no doubt.'

Miss Thorne made no reply. She felt that she had no good ground on which to defend her sex of the present generation from the sarcasm of Mr. Plomacy. She had once declared, in one of her warmer moments, 'that now-a-days the gentlemen were all women, and the ladies all men.' She could not alter the debased character of the

age. But, such being the case, why should she take on
herself to cater for the amusement of people of such
degraded tastes ? This question she asked herself more
than once, and she could only answer herself with a sigh.
There was her own brother Wilfred, on whose shoulders
rested all the ancient honours of Ullathorne house ; it
was very doubtful whether even he would consent to ' go
at the quintain,' as Mr. Plomacy not injudiciously expressed it.

And now the morning arrived. The Ullathorne household was early on the move. Cooks were cooking in the
kitchen long before daylight, and men were dragging out
tables and hammering red baize on to benches at the
earliest dawn. With what dread eagerness did Miss Thorne
look out at the weather as soon as the parting veil of night
permitted her to look at all ! In this respect at any rate
there was nothing to grieve her. The glass had been rising
for the last three days, and the morning broke with that
dull chill steady grey haze which in autumn generally
presages a clear and dry day. By seven she was dressed
and down. Miss Thorne knew nothing of the modern
luxury of *déshabilles*. She would as soon have thought of
appearing before her brother without her stockings as
without her stays ; and Miss Thorne's stays were no trifle.

And yet there was nothing for her to do when down.
She fidgeted out to the lawn, and then back into the
kitchen. She put on her high-heeled clogs, and fidgeted
out into the paddock. Then she went into the small home
park where the quintain was erected. The pole and cross
bar and the swivel, and the target and the bag of flour
were all complete. She got up on a carpenter's bench and
touched the target with her hand ; it went round with
beautiful ease ; the swivel had been oiled to perfection.
She almost wished to take old Plomacy at his word, to get
on a side saddle and have a tilt at it herself. What must
a young man be, thought she, who could prefer maundering
among laurel trees with a wishy-washy school girl to such
fun as this ? ' Well,' said she aloud to herself, ' one man
can take a horse to water, but a thousand can't make him
drink. There it is. If they haven't the spirit to enjoy it,
the fault shan't be mine ; ' and so she returned to the
house.

At a little after eight her brother came down, and they had a sort of scrap breakfast in his study. The tea, was made without the customary urn, and they dispensed with the usual rolls and toast. Eggs also were missing, for every egg in the parish had been whipped into custards, baked into pies, or boiled into lobster salad. The allowance of fresh butter was short, and Mr. Thorne was obliged to eat the leg of a fowl without having it devilled in the manner he loved.

' I have been looking at the quintain, Wilfred,' said she, ' and it appears to be quite right.'

' Oh,—ah ; yes ; ' said he. ' It seemed to be so yesterday when I saw it.' Mr. Thorne was beginning to be rather bored by his sister's love of sports, and had especially no affection for this quintain post.

' I wish you'd just try it after breakfast,' said she. ' You could have the saddle put on Mark Antony, and the pole is there all handy. You can take the flour bag off, you know, if you think Mark Antony won't be quick enough,' added Miss Thorne, seeing that her brother's countenance was not indicative of complete accordance with her little proposition.

Now Mark Antony was a valuable old hunter, excellently suited to Mr. Thorne's usual requirements, steady indeed at his fences, but extremely sure, very good in deep ground, and safe on the roads. But he had never yet been ridden at a quintain, and Mr. Thorne was not inclined to put him to the trial, either with or without the bag of flour. He hummed and hawed, and finally declared that he was afraid Mark Antony would shy.

' Then try the cob,' said the indefatigable Miss Thorne.

' He's in physic,' said Wilfred.

' There's the Beelzebub colt,' said his sister ; ' I know he's in the stable, because I saw Peter exercising him just now.'

' My dear Monica, he's so wild, that it's as much as I can do to manage him at all. He'd destroy himself and me too, if I attempted to ride him at such a rattletrap as that.'

A rattletrap ! The quintain that she had put up with so much anxious care ; the game that she had prepared for the amusement of the stalwart yeomen of the country ; the sport that had been honoured by the affection of so many

of their ancestors! It cut her to the heart to hear it so
denominated by her own brother. There were but the two
of them left together in the world; and it had ever been
one of the rules by which Miss Thorne had regulated her
conduct through life, to say nothing that could provoke
her brother. She had often had to suffer from his indifference to time-honoured British customs; but she had
always suffered in silence. It was part of her creed that
the head of the family should never be upbraided in his
own house; and Miss Thorne had lived up to her creed.
Now, however, she was greatly tried. The colour mounted
to her ancient cheek, and the fire blazed in her still bright
eye; but yet she said nothing. She resolved that at any
rate, to him nothing more should be said about the quintain
that day.

She sipped her tea in silent sorrow, and thought with
painful regret of the glorious days when her great ancestor
Ealfried had successfully held Ullathorne against a
Norman invader. There was no such spirit now left in her
family except that small useless spark which burnt in her
own bosom. And she herself, was not she at this moment
intent on entertaining a descendant of those very Normans,
a vain proud countess with a frenchified name, who would
only think that she graced Ullathorne too highly by
entering its portals? Was it likely that an honourable
John, the son of an Earl De Courcy, should ride at a
quintain in company with Saxon yeomen? And why
should she expect her brother to do that which her brother's
guests would decline to do?

Some dim faint idea of the impracticability of her own
views flitted across her brain. Perhaps it was necessary
that races doomed to live on the same soil should give way
to each other, and adopt each other's pursuits. Perhaps
it was impossible that after more than five centuries of
close intercourse, Normans should remain Normans, and
Saxons, Saxons. Perhaps after all her neighbours were
wiser than herself. Such ideas did occasionally present
themselves to Miss Thorne's mind, and make her sad
enough. But it never occurred to her that her favourite
quintain was but a modern copy of a Norman knight's
amusement, an adaptation of the noble tourney to the
tastes and habits of the Saxon yeomen. Of this she was

ignorant, and it would have been cruelty to instruct
her.

When Mr. Thorne saw the tear in her eye, he repented
himself of his contemptuous expression. By him also it
was recognised as a binding law that every whim of his
sister was to be respected. He was not perhaps so firm in
his observances to her, as she was in hers to him. But his
intentions were equally good, and whenever he found
that he had forgotten them it was matter of grief to
him.

' My dear Monica,' said he, ' I beg your pardon ; I don't
in the least mean to speak ill of the game. When I called
it a rattletrap, I merely meant that it was so for a man of
my age. You know you always forget that I an't a young
man.'

' I am quite sure you are not an old man, Wilfred,' said
she, accepting the apology in her heart, and smiling at him
with the tear still on her cheek.

' If I was five-and-twenty, or thirty,' continued he, ' I
should like nothing better than riding at the quintain
all day.'

' But you are not too old to hunt or to shoot,' said she.
' If you can jump over a ditch and hedge I am sure you
could turn the quintain round.'

' But when I ride over the hedges, my dear—and it isn't
very often I do that—but when I do ride over the hedges
there isn't any bag of flour coming after me. Think how
I'd look taking the countess out to breakfast with the back
of my head all covered with meal.'

Miss Thorne said nothing further. She didn't like the
allusion to the countess. She couldn't be satisfied with
the reflection that the sports of Ullathorne should be
interfered with by the personal attentions necessary for
a Lady De Courcy. But she saw that it was useless for her
to push the matter further. It was conceded that Mr.
Thorne was to be spared the quintain ; and Miss Thorne
determined to trust wholly to a youthful knight of hers,
an immense favourite, who, as she often declared, was a
pattern to the young men of the age, and an excellent
sample of an English yeoman.

This was Farmer Greenacre's eldest son ; who, to tell
the truth, had from his earliest years taken the exact

measure of Miss Thorne's foot. In his boyhood he had never failed to obtain from her, apples, pocket money, and forgiveness for his numerous trespasses; and now in his early manhood he got privileges and immunities which were equally valuable. He was allowed a day or two's shooting in September; he schooled the squire's horses; got slips of trees out of the orchard, and roots of flowers out of the garden; and had the fishing of the little river altogether in his own hands. He had undertaken to come mounted on a nag of his father's, and show the way at the quintain post. Whatever young Greenacre did the others would do after him. The juvenile Lookalofts might stand aloof, but the rest of the youth of Ullathorne would be sure to venture if Harry Greenacre showed the way. And so Miss Thorne made up her mind to dispense with the noble Johns and Georges, and trust, as her ancestors had done before her, to the thews and sinews of native Ulla-thorne growth.

At about nine the lower orders began to congregate in the paddock and park, under the surveillance of Mr. Plomacy and the head gardener and head groom, who were sworn in as his deputies, and were to assist him in keeping the peace and promoting the sports. Many of the younger inhabitants of the neighbourhood, thinking that they could not have too much of a good thing, had come at a very early hour, and the road between the house and the church had been thronged for some time before the gates were thrown open.

And then another difficulty of huge dimensions arose, a difficulty which Mr. Plomacy had indeed foreseen and for which he was in some sort provided. Some of those who wished to share Miss Thorne's hospitality were not so particular as they should have been as to the preliminary ceremony of an invitation. They doubtless conceived that they had been overlooked by accident; and instead of taking this in dudgeon, as their betters would have done, they good-naturedly put up with the slight, and showed that they did so by presenting themselves at the gate in their Sunday best.

Mr. Plomacy, however, well knew who were welcome and who were not. To some, even though uninvited, he allowed ingress. 'Don't be too particular, Plomacy,' his mistress had said ; ' especially with the children. If they live anywhere near, let them in.'

Acting on this hint, Mr. Plomacy did let in many an eager urchin, and a few tidily dressed girls with their swains, who in no way belonged to the property. But to the denizens of the city he was inexorable. Many a Barchester apprentice made his appearance there that day, and urged with piteous supplication that he had been working all the week in making saddles and boots for the use of Ullathorne, in compounding doses for the horses, or cutting up carcases for the kitchen. No such claim was allowed. Mr. Plomacy knew nothing about the city apprentices ; he was to admit the tenants and labourers on the estate ; Miss Thorne wasn't going to take in the whole city of Barchester ; and so on.

Nevertheless, before the day was half over, all this was found to be useless. Almost anybody who chose to come made his way into the park, and the care of the guardians was transferred to the tables on which the banquet was spread. Even here there was many an unauthorized claimant for a place, of whom it was impossible to get quit without more commotion than the place and food were worth.

CHAPTER XXXVI

ULLATHORNE SPORTS—ACT I

THE trouble in civilised life of entertaining company, as it is called too generally without much regard to strict veracity, is so great that it cannot but be matter of wonder that people are so fond of attempting it. It is difficult to ascertain what is the *quid pro quo*. If they who give such laborious parties, and who endure such toil and turmoil in the vain hope of giving them successfully, really enjoyed the parties given by others, the matter could be understood. A sense of justice would induce men and women to undergo, in behalf of others, those miseries which others had undergone in their behalf. But they all profess that going out is as great a bore as receiving ; and to look at them when they are out, one cannot but believe them.

Entertain! Who shall have sufficient self-assurance, who shall feel sufficient confidence in his own powers to dare to boast that he can entertain his company? A clown can sometimes do so, and sometimes a dancer in short petticoats and stuffed pink legs; occasionally, perhaps, a singer. But beyond these, success in this art of entertaining is not often achieved. Young men and girls linking themselves kind with kind, pairing like birds in spring because nature wills it, they, after a simple fashion, do entertain each other. Few others even try.

Ladies, when they open their houses, modestly confessing, it may be presumed, their own incapacity, mainly trust to wax candles and upholstery. Gentlemen seem to rely on their white waistcoats. To these are added, for the delight of the more sensual, champagne and such good things of the table as fashion allows to be still considered as comestible. Even in this respect the world is deteriorating. All the good soups are now tabooed; and at the houses of one's accustomed friends, small barristers, doctors, government clerks, and such like, (for we cannot all of us always live as grandees, surrounded by an elysium of livery servants), one gets a cold potato handed to one as a sort of finale to one's slice of mutton. Alas! for those happy days when one could say to one's neighbourhood, ' Jones, shall I give you some mashed turnip?— may I trouble you for a little cabbage? ' And then the pleasure of drinking wine with Mrs. Jones and Miss Smith; with all the Joneses and all the Smiths! These latter-day habits are certainly more economical.

Miss Thorne, however, boldly attempted to leave the modern beaten track, and made a positive effort to entertain her guests. Alas! she did so with but moderate success. They had all their own way of going, and would not go her way. She piped to them, but they would not dance. She offered to them good honest household cake, made of currants and flour and eggs and sweetmeat; but they would feed themselves on trashy wafers from the shop of the Barchester pastry-cook, on chalk and gum and adulterated sugar. Poor Miss Thorne! yours is not the first honest soul that has vainly striven to recall the glories of happy days gone by! If fashion suggests to a Lady De Courcy that when invited to a *déjeûner* at twelve she ought to come at three, no eloquence of thine will teach her the advantage of a nearer approach to punctuality.

She had fondly thought that when she called on her friends to come at twelve, and specially begged them to believe that she meant it, she would be able to see them comfortably seated in their tents at two. Vain woman—or rather ignorant woman—ignorant of the advances of that civilisation which the world had witnessed while she was growing old. At twelve she found herself alone, dressed in all the glory of the newest of her many suits of raiment ; with strong shoes however, and a serviceable bonnet on her head, and a warm rich shawl on her shoulders. Thus clad she peered out into the tent, went to the ha-ha, and satisfied herself that at any rate the youngsters were amusing themselves, spoke a word to Mrs. Greenacre over the ditch, and took one look at the quintain. Three or four young farmers were turning the machine round and round, and poking at the bag of flour in a manner not at all intended by the inventor of the game ; but no mounted sportsmen were there. Miss Thorne looked at her watch. It was only fifteen minutes past twelve, and it was understood that Harry Greenacre was not to begin till the half hour.

Miss Thorne returned to her drawing-room rather quicker than was her wont, fearing that the countess might come and find none to welcome her. She need not have hurried, for no one was there. At half-past twelve she peeped into the kitchen ; at a quarter to one she was joined by her brother ; and just then the first fashionable arrival took place. Mrs. Clantantram was announced.

No announcement was necessary, indeed ; for the good lady's voice was heard as she walked across the court-yard to the house scolding the unfortunate postilion who had driven her from Barchester. At the moment, Miss Thorne could not but be thankful that the other guests were more fashionable, and were thus spared the fury of Mrs. Clantantram's indignation.

' Oh Miss Thorne, look here ! ' said she, as soon as she found herself in the drawing-room ; ' do look at my roquelaure ! It's clean spoilt, and for ever. I wouldn't but wear it because I knew you wished us all to be grand to-day ; and yet I had my misgivings. Oh dear, oh dear ! It was five-and-twenty shillings a yard.'

The Barchester post horses had misbehaved in some unfortunate manner just as Mrs. Clantantram was getting out of the chaise and had nearly thrown her under the wheel.

Mrs. Clantantram belonged to other days, and therefore, though she had but little else to recommend her, Miss Thorne was to a certain extent fond of her. She sent the roquelaure away to be cleaned, and lent her one of her best shawls out of her own wardrobe.

The next comer was Mr. Arabin, who was immediately informed of Mrs. Clantantram's misfortune, and of her determination to pay neither master nor post-boy; although, as she remarked, she intended to get her lift home before she made known her mind upon that matter. Then a good deal of rustling was heard in the sort of lobby that was used for the ladies' outside cloaks ; and the door having been thrown wide open, the servant announced, not in the most confident of voices, Mrs. Lookaloft, and the Miss Lookalofts, and Mr. Augustus Lookaloft.

Poor man !—we mean the footman. He knew, none better, that Mrs. Lookaloft had no business there, that she was not wanted there, and would not be welcome. But he had not the courage to tell a stout lady with a low dress, short sleeves, and satin at eight shillings a yard, that she had come to the wrong tent ; he had not dared to hint to young ladies with white dancing shoes and long gloves, that there was a place ready for them in the paddock. And thus Mrs. Lookaloft carried her point, broke through the guards, and made her way into the citadel. That she would have to pass an uncomfortable time there, she had surmised before. But nothing now could rob her of the power of boasting that she had consorted on the lawn with the squire and Miss Thorne, with a countess, a bishop, and the country grandees, while Mrs. Greenacre and such like were walking about with the ploughboys in the park. It was a great point gained by Mrs. Lookaloft, and it might be fairly expected that from this time forward the tradesmen of Barchester would, with undoubting pens, address her husband as T. Lookaloft, Esquire.

Mrs. Lookaloft's pluck carried her through everything, and she walked triumphant into the Ullathorne drawing-room; but her children did feel a little abashed at the sort of reception they met with. It was not in Miss Thorne's heart to insult her own guests; but neither was it in her disposition to overlook such effrontery.

'Oh, Mrs. Lookaloft, is this you,' said she; 'and your daughters and son? Well, we're very glad to see you; but I'm sorry you've come in such low dresses, as we are all going out of doors. Could we lend you anything?'

'Oh dear no! thank ye, Miss Thorne,' said the mother; 'the girls and myself are quite used to low dresses, when we're out.'

'Are you, indeed?' said Miss Thorne shuddering; but the shudder was lost on Mrs. Lookaloft.

'And where's Lookaloft?' said the master of the house, coming up to welcome his tenant's wife. Let the faults of the family be what they would, he could not but remember that their rent was well paid; he was therefore not willing to give them a cold shoulder.

'Such a headache, Mr. Thorne!' said Mrs. Lookaloft. 'In fact he couldn't stir, or you may be certain on such a day he would not have absented hisself.'

'Dear me,' said Miss Thorne. 'If he is so ill, I'm sure you'd wish to be with him.'

'Not at all!' said Mrs. Lookaloft. 'Not at all, Miss Thorne. It is only bilious you know, and when he's that way he can bear nobody nigh him.'

The fact however was that Mr. Lookaloft, having either more sense or less courage than his wife, had not chosen to intrude on Miss Thorne's drawing-room; and as he could not very well have gone among the plebeians while his wife was with the patricians, he thought it most expedient to remain at Rosebank.

Mrs. Lookaloft soon found herself on a sofa, and the Miss Lookalofts on two chairs, while Mr. Augustus stood near the door; and here they remained till in due time they were seated all four together at the bottom of the dining-room table.

Then the Grantlys came; the archdeacon and Mrs. Grantly and the two girls, and Dr. Gwynne and Mr. Harding; and as ill luck would have it, they were closely followed by Dr. Stanhope's carriage. As Eleanor looked out of the carriage window, she saw her brother-in-law helping the ladies out, and threw herself back into her seat, dreading to be discovered. She had had an odious journey. Mr. Slope's civility had been more than ordinarily greasy ; and now, though he had not in fact said anything which she could notice, she had for the first time entertained a suspicion that he was intending to make love to her. Was it after all true that she had been conducting herself in a way that justified the world in thinking that she liked the man ? After all, could it be possible that the archdeacon and Mr. Arabin were right, and that she was wrong ? Charlotte Stanhope had also been watching Mr. Slope, and had come to the conclusion that it behoved her brother to lose no further time, if he meant to gain the widow. She almost regretted that it had not been contrived that Bertie should be at Ullathorne before them.

Dr. Grantly did not see his sister-in-law in company with Mr. Slope, but Mr. Arabin did. Mr. Arabin came out with Mr. Thorne to the front door to welcome Mrs. Grantly, and he remained in the courtyard till all their party had passed on. Eleanor hung back in the carriage as long as she well could, but she was nearest to the door, and when Mr. Slope, having alighted, offered her his hand, she had no alternative but to take it. Mr. Arabin standing at the open door, while Mrs. Grantly was shaking hands with some one within, saw a clergyman alight from the carriage whom he at once knew to be Mr. Slope, and then he saw this clergyman hand out Mrs. Bold. Having seen so much, Mr. Arabin, rather sick at heart, followed Mrs. Grantly into the house.

Eleanor was, however, spared any further immediate degradation, for Dr. Stanhope gave her his arm across the courtyard, and Mr. Slope was fain to throw away his attention upon Charlotte.

They had hardly passed into the house, and from the house to the lawn, when, with a loud rattle and such noise as great men and great women are entitled to make in their passage through the world, the Proudies drove up. It was soon apparent that no every day comer was at the door. One servant whispered to another that it was the bishop, and the word soon ran through all the hangers-on and strange grooms and coachmen about the place. There was quite a little cortége to see the bishop and his ' lady ' walk across the courtyard, and the good man was pleased to see that the church was held in such respect in the parish of St. Ewold's.

And now the guests came fast and thick, and the lawn began to be crowded, and the room to be full. Voices buzzed, silk rustled against silk, and muslin crumpled against muslin. Miss Thorne became more happy than she had been, and again bethought her of her sports. There were targets and bows and arrows prepared at the further end of the lawn. Here the gardens of the place encroached with a somewhat wide sweep upon the paddock, and gave ample room for the doings of the toxophilites. Miss Thorne got together such daughters of Diana as could bend a bow, and marshalled them to the targets. There were the Grantly girls and the Proudie girls and the Chadwick girls, and the two daughters of the burly chancellor, and Miss Knowle; and with them went Frederick and Augustus Chadwick, and young Knowle of Knowle park, and Frank Foster of the Elms, and Mr. Vellem Deeds the dashing attorney of the High Street, and the Rev. Mr. Green, and the Rev. Mr. Brown, and the Rev. Mr. White, all of whom, as in duty bound, attended the steps of the three Miss Proudies.

' Did you ever ride at the quintain, Mr. Foster ? ' said Miss Thorne, as she walked with her party, across the lawn.

' The quintain ? ' said young Foster, who considered himself a dab at horsemanship. ' Is it a sort of gate, Miss Thorne ? '

Miss Thorne had to explain the noble game she spoke of, and Frank Foster had to own that he never had ridden at the quintain.

' Would you like to come and see ? ' said Miss Thorne. ' There'll be plenty here without you, if you like it.'

' Well, I don't mind,' said Frank ; ' I suppose the ladies can come too.'

' Oh yes,' said Miss Thorne ; ' those who like it ; I have no doubt they'll go to see your prowess, if you'll ride, Mr. Foster.'

Mr. Foster looked down at a most unexceptionable

pair of pantaloons, which had arrived from London only
the day before. They were the very things, at least he
thought so, for a picnic or fête champêtre; but he was
not prepared to ride in them. Nor was he more encouraged
than had been Mr. Thorne, by the idea of being attacked
from behind by the bag of flour which Miss Thorne had
graphically described to him.

'Well, I don't know about riding, Miss Thorne,' said
he; 'I fear I'm not quite prepared.'

Miss Thorne sighed, but said nothing further. She
left the toxophilites to their bows and arrows, and returned
towards the house. But as she passed by the entrance to
the small park, she thought that she might at any rate
encourage the yeomen by her presence, as she could not
induce her more fashionable guests to mix with them in
their manly amusements. Accordingly she once more
betook herself to the quintain post.

Here to her great delight she found Harry Greenacre
ready mounted, with his pole in his hand, and a lot of
comrades standing round him, encouraging him to the
assault. She stood at a little distance and nodded to him
in token of her good pleasure.

'Shall I begin, ma'am?' said Harry fingering his long
staff in a rather awkward way, while his horse moved
uneasily beneath him, not accustomed to a rider armed
with such a weapon.

'Yes, yes,' said Miss Thorne, standing triumphant as
the queen of beauty, on an inverted tub which some chance
had brought thither from the farm-yard.

'Here goes then,' said Harry as he wheeled his horse
round to get the necessary momentum of a sharp gallop.
The quintain post stood right before him, and the square
board at which he was to tilt was fairly in his way. If he
hit that duly in the middle, and maintained his pace as
he did so, it was calculated that he would be carried out
of reach of the flour bag, which, suspended at the other
end of the cross-bar on the post, would swing round when
the board was struck. It was also calculated that if the
rider did not maintain his pace, he would get a blow from
the flour bag just at the back of his head, and bear about
him the signs of his awkwardness to the great amusement
of the lookers-on.

Harry Greenacre did not object to being powdered with flour in the service of his mistress, and therefore gallantly touched his steed with his spur, having laid his lance in rest to the best of his ability. But his ability in this respect was not great, and his appurtenances probably not very good; consequently, he struck his horse with his pole unintentionally on the side of the head as he started. The animal swerved and shied, and galloped off wide of the quintain. Harry well accustomed to manage a horse, but not to do so with a twelve-foot rod on his arm, lowered his right hand to the bridle and thus the end of the lance came to the ground, and got between the legs of the steed. Down came rider and steed and staff. Young Greenacre was thrown some six feet over the horse's head, and poor Miss Thorne almost fell off her tub in a swoon.

' Oh gracious, he's killed,' shrieked a woman who was near him when he fell.

' The Lord be good to him! his poor mother, his poor mother! ' said another.

' Well, drat them dangerous plays all the world over,' said an old crone.

' He has broke his neck sure enough, if ever man did,' said a fourth.

Poor Miss Thorne. She heard all this and yet did not quite swoon. She made her way through the crowd as best she could, sick herself almost to death. Oh, his mother—his poor mother! how could she ever forgive herself. The agony of that moment was terrific. She could hardly get to the place where the poor lad was lying, as three or four men in front were about the horse which had risen with some difficulty; but at last she found herself close to the young farmer.

' Has he marked himself? for heaven's sake tell me that; has he marked his knees? ' said Harry, slowly rising and rubbing his left shoulder with his right hand, and thinking only of his horse's legs. Miss Thorne soon found that he had not broken his neck, nor any of his bones, nor been injured in any essential way. But from that time forth she never instigated any one to ride at a quintain.

Eleanor left Dr. Stanhope as soon as she could do so civilly, and went in quest of her father whom she found on the lawn in company with Mr. Arabin. She was not sorry

to find them together. She was anxious to disabuse at
any rate her father's mind as to this report which had got
abroad respecting her, and would have been well pleased
to have been able to do the same with regard to Mr.
Arabin. She put her own through her father's arm,
coming up behind his back, and then tendered her hand
also to the vicar of St. Ewold's.

' And how did you come ? ' said Mr. Harding, when the
first greeting was over.

' The Stanhopes brought me,' said she ; ' their carriage
was obliged to come twice, and has now gone back for
the signora.' As she spoke she caught Mr. Arabin's eye,
and saw that he was looking pointedly at her with a
severe expression. She understood at once the accusation
contained in his glance. It said as plainly as an eye could
speak, ' Yes, you came with the Stanhopes, but you did
so in order that you might be in company with Mr. Slope.'

' Our party,' said she, still addressing her father ' consisted of the doctor and Charlotte Stanhope, myself, and
Mr. Slope.' As she mentioned the last name she felt her
father's arm quiver slightly beneath her touch. At the
same moment Mr. Arabin turned away from them, and
joining his hands behind his back strolled slowly away by
one of the paths.

' Papa,' said she, ' it was impossible to help coming in
the same carriage with Mr. Slope ; it was quite impossible.
I had promised to come with them before I dreamt of his
coming, and afterwards I could not get out of it without
explaining and giving rise to talk. You weren't at home,
you know, I couldn't possibly help it.' She said all this
so quickly that by the time her apology was spoken she
was quite out of breath.

' I don't know why you should have wished to help it,
my dear,' said her father.

' Yes, papa, you do ; you must know, you do know all
the things they said at Plumstead. I am sure you do.
You know all the archdeacon said. How unjust he was ;
and Mr. Arabin too. He's a horrid man, a horrid odious
man, but——'

' Who is an odious man, my dear ? Mr. Arabin ? '

' No ; but Mr. Slope. You know I mean Mr. Slope.
He's the most odious man I ever met in my life, and it

was most unfortunate my having to come here in the same carriage with him. But how could I help it ? '

A great weight began to move itself off Mr. Harding's mind. So, after all, the archdeacon with all his wisdom, and Mrs. Grantly with all her tact, and Mr. Arabin with all his talent, were in the wrong. His own child, his Eleanor, the daughter of whom he was so proud was not to become the wife of a Mr. Slope. He had been about to give his sanction to the marriage, so certified had he been of the fact ; and now he learnt that this imputed lover of Eleanor's was at any rate as much disliked by her as by any one of the family. Mr. Harding, however, was by no means sufficiently a man of the world to conceal the blunder he had made. He could not pretend that he had entertained no suspicion ; he could not make believe that he had never joined the archdeacon in his surmises. He was greatly surprised, and gratified beyond measure, and he could not help showing that such was the case.

' My darling girl,' said he, ' I am so delighted, so over-joyed. My own child ; you have taken such a weight off my mind.'

' But surely, papa, *you* didn't think——'

' I didn't know what to think, my dear. The archdeacon told me that——'

' The archdeacon ! ' said Eleanor, her face lighting up with passion. ' A man like the archdeacon might, one would think, be better employed than in traducing his sister-in-law, and creating bitterness between a father and his daughter ! '

' He didn't mean to do that, Eleanor.'

' What did he mean then ? Why did he interfere with me, and fill your mind with such falsehood ? '

' Never mind it now, my child ; never mind it now. We shall all know you better now.'

' Oh, papa, that you should have thought it ! that you should have suspected me ! '

' I don't know what you mean by suspicion, Eleanor. There would be nothing disgraceful, you know ; nothing wrong in such a marriage. Nothing that could have justified my interfering as your father.' And Mr. Harding would have proceeded in his own defence to make out that Mr. Slope after all was a very good sort of man, and a very fitting second husband for a young widow, had he not been interrupted by Eleanor's greater energy.

'It would be disgraceful,' said she; 'it would be wrong; it would be abominable. Could I do such a horrid thing, I should expect no one to speak to me. Ugh——' and she shuddered as she thought of the matrimonial torch which her friends had been so ready to light on her behalf. 'I don't wonder at Dr. Grantly; I don't wonder at Susan; but, oh, papa, I do wonder at you. How could you, how could you believe it?' Poor Eleanor, as she thought of her father's defalcation, could resist her tears no longer, and was forced to cover her face with her handkerchief.

The place was not very opportune for her grief. They were walking through the shrubberies, and there were many people near them. Poor Mr. Harding stammered out his excuse as best he could, and Eleanor with an effort controlled her tears, and returned her handkerchief to her pocket. She did not find it difficult to forgive her father, nor could she altogether refuse to join him in the returning gaiety of spirit to which her present avowal gave rise. It was such a load off his heart to think that he should not be called on to welcome Mr. Slope as his son-in-law. It was such a relief to him to find that his daughter's feelings and his own were now, as they ever had been, in unison. He had been so unhappy for the last six weeks about this wretched Mr. Slope! He was so indifferent as to the loss of the hospital, so thankful for the recovery of his daughter, that, strong as was the ground for Eleanor's anger, she could not find it in her heart to be long angry with him.

'Dear papa,' she said, hanging closely to his arm, 'never suspect me again: promise me that you never will. Whatever I do, you may be sure I shall tell you first; you may be sure I shall consult you.'

And Mr. Harding did promise, and owned his sin, and promised again. And so, while he promised amendment and she uttered forgiveness, they returned together to the drawing-room windows.

And what had Eleanor meant when she declared that *whatever she did*, she would tell her father first? What was she thinking of doing?

So ended the first act of the melodrama which Eleanor was called on to perform this day at Ullathorne.

CHAPTER XXXVII

THE SIGNORA NERONI, THE COUNTESS DE COURCY, AND MRS. PROUDIE MEET EACH OTHER AT ULLATHORNE

AND now there were new arrivals. Just as Eleanor
reached the drawing-room the signora was being wheeled
into it. She had been brought out of the carriage into
the dining-room and there placed on a sofa, and was
now in the act of entering the other room, by the joint
aid of her brother and sister, Mr. Arabin, and two servants in livery. She was all in her glory, and looked so
pathetically happy, so full of affliction and grace, was so
beautiful, so pitiable, and so charming, that it was
almost impossible not to be glad she was there.

Miss Thorne was unaffectedly glad to welcome her.
In fact, the signora was a sort of lion; and though there
was no drop of the Leohunter blood in Miss Thorne's
veins, she nevertheless did like to see attractive people
at her house. The signora was attractive, and on her
first settlement in the dining-room she had whispered
two or three soft feminine words into Miss Thorne's ear,
which, at the moment, had quite touched that lady's
heart.

'Oh, Miss Thorne; where is Miss Thorne?' she said,
as soon as her attendants had placed her in her position
just before one of the windows, from whence she could
see all that was going on upon the lawn; 'How am I to
thank you for permitting a creature like me to be here?
But if you knew the pleasure you give me, I am sure you
would excuse the trouble I bring with me.' And as she
spoke she squeezed the spinster's little hand between
her own.

'We are delighted to see you here,' said Miss Thorne;
'you give us no trouble at all, and we think it a great
favour conferred by you to come and see us; don't we,
Wilfred?'

'A very great favour indeed,' said Mr. Thorne, with
a gallant bow, but of a somewhat less cordial welcome
than that conceded by his sister. Mr. Thorne had heard
perhaps more of the antecedents of his guest than his

sister had done, and had not as yet undergone the power of the signora's charms.

But while the mother of the last of the Neros was thus in her full splendour, with crowds of people gazing at her and the *élite* of the company standing round her couch, her glory was paled by the arrival of the Countess De Courcy. Miss Thorne had now been waiting three hours for the countess, and could not therefore but show very evident gratification when the arrival at last took place. She and her brother of course went off to welcome the titled grandees, and with them, alas, went many of the signora's admirers.

'Oh, Mr. Thorne,' said the countess, while in the act of being disrobed of her fur cloaks, and re-robed in her gauze shawls, 'what dreadful roads you have; perfectly frightful.'

It happened that Mr. Thorne was way-warden for the district, and not liking the attack, began to excuse his roads.

'Oh yes, indeed they are,' said the countess, not minding him in the least, 'perfectly dreadful; are they not, Margaretta? Why, my dear Miss Thorne, we left Courcy Castle just at eleven; it was only just past eleven, was it not, John? and——'

'Just past one, I think you mean,' said the Honourable John, turning from the group and eyeing the signora through his glass. The signora gave him back his own, as the saying is, and more with it; so that the young nobleman was forced to avert his glance, and drop his glass.

'I say, Thorne,' whispered he, 'who the deuce is that on the sofa?'

'Dr. Stanhope's daughter,' whispered back Mr. Thorne. 'Signora Neroni, she calls herself.'

'Whew-ew-ew!' whistled the Honourable John. 'The devil she is! I have heard no end of stories about that filly. You must positively introduce me, Thorne; you positively must.'

Mr. Thorne, who was respectability itself, did not quite like having a guest about whom the Honourable John De Courcy had heard no end of stories; but he couldn't help himself. He merely resolved that before he went to bed he would let his sister know somewhat

of the history of the lady she was so willing to welcome.
The innocence of Miss Thorne, at her time of life was
perfectly charming; but even innocence may be dangerous.

'John may say what he likes,' continued the countess,
urging her excuses to Miss Thorne; 'I am sure we were
past the castle gate before twelve, weren't we, Margaretta?'

'Upon my word I don't know,' said the Lady Margaretta,
'for I was half asleep. But I do know that I was called
sometime in the middle of the night, and was dressing
myself before daylight.'

Wise people, when they are in the wrong, always put
themselves right by finding fault with the people against
whom they have sinned. Lady De Courcy was a wise
woman; and therefore, having treated Miss Thorne very
badly by staying away till three o'clock, she assumed the
offensive and attacked Mr. Thorne's roads. Her daughter,
not less wise, attacked Miss Thorne's early hours. The
art of doing this is among the most precious of those
usually cultivated by persons who know how to live.
There is no withstanding it. Who can go systematically
to work, and having done battle with the primary accusation and settled that, then bring forward a counter-charge
and support that also? Life is not long enough for such
labours. A man in the right relies easily on his rectitude,
and therefore goes about unarmed. His very strength
is his weakness. A man in the wrong knows that he must
look to his weapons; his very weakness is his strength.
The one is never prepared for combat, the other is always
ready. Therefore it is that in this world the man that
is in the wrong almost invariably conquers the man that
is in the right, and invariably despises him.

A man must be an idiot or else an angel, who after the
age of forty shall attempt to be just to his neighbours.
Many like the Lady Margaretta have learnt their lesson
at a much earlier age. But this of course depends on the
school in which they have been taught.

Poor Miss Thorne was altogether overcome. She knew
very well that she had been ill treated, and yet she found
herself making apologies to Lady De Courcy. To do her
ladyship justice, she received them very graciously, and
allowed herself with her train of daughters to be led
towards the lawn.

There were two windows in the drawing-room wide open for the countess to pass through; but she saw that there was a woman on a sofa, at the third window, and that that woman had, as it were, a following attached to her. Her ladyship therefore determined to investigate the woman. The De Courcys were hereditarily short sighted, and had been so for thirty centuries at least. So Lady De Courcy, who when she entered the family had adopted the family habits, did as her son had done before her, and taking her glass to investigate the Signora Neroni, pressed in among the gentlemen who surrounded the couch, and bowed slightly to those whom she chose to honour by her acquaintance.

In order to get to the window she had to pass close to the front of the couch, and as she did so she stared hard at the occupant. The occupant in return stared hard at the countess. The countess who since her countess-ship commenced had been accustomed to see all eyes, not royal, ducal or marquesal, fall before her own, paused as she went on, raised her eyebrows, and stared even harder than before. But she had now to do with one who cared little for countesses. It was, one may say, impossible for mortal man or woman to abash Madeline Neroni. She opened her large bright lustrous eyes wider and wider, till she seemed to be all eyes. She gazed up into the lady's face, not as though she did it with an effort, but as if she delighted in doing it. She used no glass to assist her effrontery, and needed none. The faintest possible smile of derision played round her mouth, and her nostrils were slightly dilated, as if in sure anticipation of her triumph. And it was sure. The Countess De Courcy, in spite of her thirty centuries and De Courcy castle, and the fact that Lord De Courcy was grand master of the ponies to the Prince of Wales, had not a chance with her. At first the little circlet of gold wavered in the countess's hand, then the hand shook, then the circlet fell, the countess's head tossed itself into the air, and the countess's feet shambled out to the lawn. She did not however go so fast but what she heard the signora's voice, asking—

'Who on earth is that woman, Mr. Slope?'

'That is Lady De Courcy.'

'Oh, ah. I might have supposed so. Ha, ha, ha. Well, that's as good as a play.'

It was as good as a play to any there who had eyes to observe it, and wit to comment on what they observed.

But the Lady De Courcy soon found a congenial spirit on the lawn. There she encountered Mrs. Proudie, and as Mrs. Proudie was not only the wife of a bishop, but was also the cousin of an earl, Lady De Courcy considered her to be the fittest companion she was likely to meet in that assemblage. They were accordingly delighted to see each other. Mrs. Proudie by no means despised a countess, and as this countess lived in the county and within a sort of extensive visiting distance of Barchester, she was glad to have this opportunity of ingratiating herself.

'My dear Lady De Courcy, I am so delighted,' said she, looking as little grim as it was in her nature to do. 'I hardly expected to see you here. It is such a distance, and then you know, such a crowd.'

'And such roads, Mrs. Proudie! I really wonder how the people ever get about. But I don't suppose they ever do.'

'Well, I really don't know; but I suppose not. The Thornes don't, I know,' said Mrs. Proudie. 'Very nice person, Miss Thorne, isn't she?'

'Oh, delightful, and so queer; I've known her these twenty years. A great pet of mine is dear Miss Thorne. She is so very strange, you know. She always makes me think of the Esquimaux and the Indians. Isn't her dress quite delightful?'

'Delightful,' said Mrs. Proudie; 'I wonder now whether she paints. Did you ever see such colour?'

'Oh, of course,' said Lady De Courcy; 'that is, I have no doubt she does. But, Mrs. Proudie, who is that woman on the sofa by the window? just step this way and you'll see her, there——' and the countess led her to a spot where she could plainly see the signora's well-remembered face and figure.

She did not however do so without being equally well seen by the signora. 'Look, look,' said that lady to Mr. Slope, who was still standing near to her; 'see the high spiritualities and temporalities of the land in league together, and all against poor me. I'll wager my bracelet,

Mr. Slope, against your next sermon, that they've taken up their position there on purpose to pull me to pieces. Well, I can't rush to the combat, but I know how to protect myself if the enemy come near me.'

But the enemy knew better. They could gain nothing by contact with the Signora Neroni, and they could abuse her as they pleased at a distance from her on the lawn.

'She's that horrid Italian woman, Lady De Courcy; you must have heard of her.'

'What Italian woman?' said her ladyship, quite alive to the coming story; 'I don't think I've heard of any Italian woman coming into the country. She doesn't look Italian either.'

'Oh, you must have heard of her,' said Mrs. Proudie. 'No, she's not absolutely Italian. She is Dr. Stanhope's daughter—Dr. Stanhope the prebendary; and she calls herself the Signora Neroni.'

'Oh-h-h-h!' exclaimed the countess.

'I was sure you had heard of her,' continued Mrs. Proudie. 'I don't know anything about her husband. They do say that some man named Neroni is still alive. I believe she did marry such a man abroad, but I do not at all know who or what he was.'

'Ah-h-h-h!' said the countess, shaking her head with much intelligence, as every additional 'h' fell from her lips. 'I know all about it now. I have heard George mention her. George knows all about her. George heard about her in Rome.'

'She's an abominable woman, at any rate,' said Mrs. Proudie.

'Insufferable,' said the countess.

'She made her way into the palace once, before I knew anything about her; and I cannot tell you how dreadfully indecent her conduct was.'

'Was it?' said the delighted countess.

'Insufferable,' said the prelatess.

'But why does she lie on a sofa?' asked Lady De Courcy.

'She has only one leg,' replied Mrs. Proudie.

'Only one leg!' said Lady De Courcy, who felt to a certain degree dissatisfied that the signora was thus incapacitated. 'Was she born so?'

' Oh, no,' said Mrs. Proudie,—and her ladyship felt somewhat recomforted by the assurance,—' she had two. But that Signor Neroni beat her, I believe, till she was obliged to have one amputated. At any rate, she entirely lost the use of it.'

' Unfortunate creature ! ' said the countess, who herself knew something of matrimonial trials.

' Yes,' said Mrs. Proudie ; ' one would pity her, in spite of her past bad conduct, if she now knew how to behave herself. But she does not. She is the most insolent creature I ever put my eyes on.'

' Indeed she is,' said Lady De Courcy.

' And her conduct with men is so abominable, that she is not fit to be admitted into any lady's drawing-room.'

' Dear me ! ' said the countess, becoming again excited, happy, and merciless.

' You saw that man standing near her,—the clergyman with the red hair ? '

' Yes, yes.'

' She has absolutely ruined that man. The bishop, or I should rather take the blame on myself, for it was I,—I brought him down from London to Barchester. He is a tolerable preacher, an active young man, and I therefore introduced him to the bishop. That woman, Lady De Courcy, has got hold of him, and has so disgraced him, that I am forced to require that he shall leave the palace ; and I doubt very much whether he won't lose his gown ! '

' Why what an idiot the man must be ! ' said the countess.

' You don't know the intriguing villainy of that woman,' said Mrs. Proudie, remembering her torn flounces.

' But you say she has only got one leg ! '

' She is as full of mischief as tho' she had ten. Look at her eyes, Lady De Courcy. Did you ever see such eyes in a decent woman's head ? '

' Indeed I never did, Mrs. Proudie.'

' And her effrontery, and her voice ; I quite pity her poor father, who is really a good sort of man.'

' Dr. Stanhope, isn't he ? '

' Yes, Dr. Stanhope. He is one of our prebendaries,— a good quiet sort of man himself. But I am surprised that he should let his daughter conduct herself as she does.'

' I suppose he can't help it,' said the countess.

' But a clergyman, you know, Lady De Courcy! He should at any rate prevent her from exhibiting in public, if he cannot induce her to behave at home. But he is to be pitied. I believe he has a desperate life of it with the lot of them. That apish-looking man there, with the long beard and the loose trousers,—he is the woman's brother. He is nearly as bad as she is. They are both of them infidels.'

' Infidels!' said Lady De Courcy, ' and their father a prebendary!'

' Yes, and likely to be the new dean too,' said Mrs. Proudie.

' Oh, yes, poor dear Dr. Trefoil!' said the countess, who had once in her life spoken to that gentleman; ' I was so distressed to hear it, Mrs. Proudie. And so Dr. Stanhope is to be the new dean! He comes of an excellent family, and I wish him success in spite of his daughter. Perhaps, Mrs. Proudie, when he is dean they'll be better able to see the error of their ways.'

To this Mrs. Proudie said nothing. Her dislike of the Signora Neroni was too deep to admit of her even hoping that that lady should see the error of her ways. Mrs. Proudie looked on the signora as one of the lost,—one of those beyond the reach of Christian charity, and was therefore able to enjoy the luxury of hating her, without the drawback of wishing her eventually well out of her sins.

Any further conversation between these congenial souls was prevented by the advent of Mr. Thorne, who came to lead the countess to the tent. Indeed, he had been desired to do so some ten minutes since; but he had been delayed in the drawing-room by the signora. She had contrived to detain him, to get him near to her sofa, and at last to make him seat himself on a chair close to her beautiful arm. The fish took the bait, was hooked, and caught, and landed. Within that ten minutes he had heard the whole of the signora's history in such strains as she chose to use in telling it. He learnt from the lady's own lips the whole of that mysterious tale to which the Honourable George had merely alluded. He discovered that the beautiful creature lying before him had been more sinned against than sinning. She had owned to

him that she had been weak, confiding and indifferent
to the world's opinion, and that she had therefore been
ill-used, deceived and evil spoken of. She had spoken to
him of her mutilated limb, her youth destroyed in its
fullest bloom, her beauty robbed of its every charm, her
life blighted, her hopes withered; and as she did so, a
tear dropped from her eye to her cheek. She had told
him of these things, and asked for his sympathy.

What could a good-natured genial Anglo-Saxon Squire
Thorne do but promise to sympathise with her? Mr.
Thorne did promise to sympathise; promised also to come
and see the last of the Neros, to hear more of those fearful
Roman days, of those light and innocent but dangerous
hours which flitted by so fast on the shores of Como, and
to make himself the confidant of the signora's sorrows.

We need hardly say that he dropped all idea of warning
his sister against the dangerous lady. He had been
mistaken; never so much mistaken in his life. He had
always regarded that Honourable George as a coarse
brutal-minded young man; now he was more convinced
than ever that he was so. It was by such men as the
Honourable George that the reputations of such women
as Madeline Neroni were imperilled and damaged. He
would go and see the lady in her own house; he was fully
sure in his own mind of the soundness of his own judgment;
if he found her, as he believed he should do, an injured
well-disposed warm-hearted woman, he would get his
sister Monica to invite her out to Ullathorne.

'No,' said she, as at her instance he got up to leave her,
and declared that he himself would attend upon her wants;
'no, no, my friend; I positively put a veto upon your
doing so. What, in your own house, with an assemblage
round you such as there is here! Do you wish to make
every woman hate me and every man stare at me? I lay
a positive order on you not to come near me again to-day.
Come and see me at home. It is only at home that I can
talk; it is only at home that I really can live and enjoy
myself. My days of going out, days such as these, are
rare indeed. Come and see me at home, Mr. Thorne, and
then I will not bid you to leave me.'

It is, we believe, common with young men of five and
twenty to look on their seniors—on men of, say, double

their own age—as so many stocks and stones,—stocks and stones, that is, in regard to feminine beauty. There never was a greater mistake. Women, indeed, generally know better; but on this subject men of one age are thoroughly ignorant of what is the very nature of mankind of other ages. No experience of what goes on in the world, no reading of history, no observation of life, has any effect in teaching the truth. Men of fifty don't dance mazurkas, being generally too fat and wheezy; nor do they sit for the hour together on river banks at their mistresses' feet, being somewhat afraid of rheumatism. But for real true love, love at first sight, love to devotion, love that robs a man of his sleep, love that ' will gaze an eagle blind,' love that ' will hear the lowest sound when the suspicious tread of theft is stopped,' love that is ' like a Hercules, still climbing trees in the Hesperides,'—we believe the best age is from forty-five to seventy; up to that, men are generally given to mere flirting.

At the present moment Mr. Thorne, *ætat*. fifty, was over head and ears in love at first sight with the Signora Madeline Vesey Neroni, *nata* Stanhope.

Nevertheless he was sufficiently master of himself to offer his arm with all propriety to Lady De Courcy, and the countess graciously permitted herself to be led to the tent. Such had been Miss Thorne's orders, as she had succeeded in inducing the bishop to lead old Lady Knowle to the top of the dining-room. One of the baronets was sent off in quest of Mrs. Proudie, and found that lady on the lawn not in the best of humours. Mr. Thorne and the countess had left her too abruptly; she had in vain looked about for an attendant chaplain, or even a stray curate; they were all drawing long bows with the young ladies at the bottom of the lawn, or finding places for their graceful co-toxophilites in some snug corner of the tent. In such position Mrs. Proudie had been wont in earlier days to fall back upon Mr. Slope; but now she could never fall back upon him again. She gave her head one shake as she thought of her lone position, and that shake was as good as a week deducted from Mr. Slope's longer sojourn in Barchester. Sir Harkaway Gorse, however, relieved her present misery, though his doing so by no means mitigated the sinning chaplain's doom.

And now the eating and drinking began in earnest. Dr. Grantly, to his great horror, found himself leagued to Mrs. Clantantram. Mrs. Clantantram had a great regard ·for the archdeacon, which was not cordially returned ; and when she; coming up to him, whispered in his ear, ' Come, archdeacon, I'm sure you won't begrudge an old friend the favour of your arm,' and then proceeded to tell him the whole history of her roquelaure, he resolved that he would shake her off before he was fifteen minutes older. But latterly the archdeacon had not been successful in his resolutions ; and on the present occasion Mrs. Clantantram stuck to him till the banquet was over.

Dr. Gwynne got a baronet's wife, and Mrs. Grantly fell to the lot of a baronet. Charlotte Stanhope attached herself to Mr. Harding in order to make room for Bertie, who succeeded in sitting down in the dining-room next to Mrs. Bold. To speak sooth, now that he had love in earnest to make, his heart almost failed him.

Eleanor had been right glad to avail herself of his arm, seeing that Mr. Slope was hovering nigh her. In striving to avoid that terrible Charybdis of a Slope she was in great danger of falling into an unseen Scylla on the other hand, that Scylla being Bertie Stanhope. Nothing could be more gracious than she was to Bertie. She almost jumped at his proffered arm. Charlotte perceived this from a distance, and triumphed in her heart ; Bertie felt it, and was encouraged ; Mr. Slope saw it, and glowered with jealousy. Eleanor and Bertie sat down to table in the dining-room ; and as she took her seat at his right hand, she found that Mr. Slope was already in possession of the chair at her own.

As these things were going on in the dining-room, Mr. Arabin was hanging enraptured and alone over the signora's sofa ; and Eleanor from her seat could look through the open door and see that he was doing so.

CHAPTER XXXVIII

THE BISHOP SITS DOWN TO BREAKFAST, AND THE DEAN DIES

THE bishop of Barchester said grace over the well-spread board in the Ullathorne dining-room; and while he did so the last breath was flying from the dean of Barchester as he lay in his sick room in the deanery. When the bishop of Barchester raised his first glass of champagne to his lips, the deanship of Barchester was a good thing in the gift of the prime minister. Before the bishop of Barchester had left the table, the minister of the day was made aware of the fact at his country seat in Hampshire, and had already turned over in his mind the names of five very respectable aspirants for the preferment. It is at present only necessary to say that Mr. Slope's name was not among the five.

' 'Twas merry in the hall when the beards wagged all;' and the clerical beards wagged merrily in the hall of Ullathorne that day. It was not till after the last cork had been drawn, the last speech made, the last nut cracked, that tidings reached and were whispered about that the poor dean was no more. It was well for the happiness of the clerical beards that this little delay took place, as otherwise decency would have forbidden them to wag at all.

But there was one sad man among them that day. Mr. Arabin's beard did not wag as it should have done. He had come there hoping the best, striving to think the best, about Eleanor; turning over in his mind all the words he remembered to have fallen from her about Mr. Slope, and trying to gather from them a conviction unfavourable to his rival. He had not exactly resolved to come that day to some decisive proof as to the widow's intention; but he had meant, if possible, to re-cultivate his friendship with Eleanor; and in his present frame of mind any such re-cultivation must have ended in a declaration of love.

He had passed the previous night alone at his new parsonage, and it was the first night that he had so passed. It had been dull and sombre enough. Mrs. Grantly had

been right in saying that a priestess would be wanting
at St. Ewold's. He had sat there alone with his glass
before him, and then with his teapot, thinking about
Eleanor Bold. As is usual in such meditations, he did
little but blame her; blame her for liking Mr. Slope, and
blame her for not liking him; blame her for her cordiality
to himself, and blame her for her want of cordiality; blame
her for being stubborn, headstrong, and passionate; and
yet the more he thought of her the higher she rose in his
affection. If only it should turn out, if only it could be
made to turn out, that she had defended Mr. Slope, not
from love, but on principle, all would be right. Such
principle in itself would be admirable, loveable, womanly;
he felt that he could be pleased to allow Mr. Slope just
so much favour as that. But if—— And then Mr. Arabin
poked his fire most unnecessarily, spoke crossly to his
new parlour-maid who came in for the tea-things, and
threw himself back in his chair determined to go to sleep.
Why had she been so stiffnecked when asked a plain
question? She could not but have known in what light
he regarded her. Why had she not answered a plain
question, and so put an end to his misery? Then, instead
of going to sleep in his arm-chair, Mr. Arabin walked
about the room as though he had been possessed.

On the following morning, when he attended Miss
Thorne's behests, he was still in a somewhat confused
state. His first duty had been to converse with Mrs.
Clantantram, and that lady had found it impossible to
elicit the slightest sympathy from him on the subject of
her roquelaure. Miss Thorne had asked him whether
Mrs. Bold was coming with the Grantlys; and the two
names of Bold and Grantly together had nearly made
him jump from his seat.

He was in this state of confused uncertainty, hope,
and doubt, when he saw Mr. Slope, with his most polished
smile, handing Eleanor out of her carriage. He thought
of nothing more. He never considered whether the carriage
belonged to her or to Mr. Slope, or to any one else to whom
they might both be mutually obliged without any concert
between themselves. This sight in his present state of
mind was quite enough to upset him and his resolves.
It was clear as noonday. Had he seen her handed into

a carriage by Mr. Slope at a church door with a white veil over her head, the truth could not be more manifest. He went into the house, and, as we have seen, soon found himself walking with Mr. Harding. Shortly afterwards Eleanor came up; and then he had to leave his companion, and either go about alone or find another. While in this state he was encountered by the archdeacon.

'I wonder,' said Dr. Grantly, 'if it be true that Mr. Slope and Mrs. Bold came here together. Susan says she is almost sure she saw their faces in the same carriage as she got out of her own.'

Mr. Arabin had nothing for it but to bear his testimony to the correctness of Mrs. Grantly's eyesight.

'It is perfectly shameful,' said the archdeacon; 'or I should rather say, shameless. She was asked here as my guest; and if she be determined to disgrace herself, she should have feeling enough not to do so before my immediate friends. I wonder how that man got himself invited. I wonder whether she had the face to bring him.'

To this Mr. Arabin could answer nothing, nor did he wish to answer anything. Though he abused Eleanor to himself, he did not choose to abuse her to any one else, nor was he well pleased to hear any one else speak ill of her. Dr. Grantly, however, was very angry, and did not spare his sister-in-law. Mr. Arabin therefore left him as soon as he could, and wandered back into the house.

He had not been there long, when the signora was brought in. For some time he kept himself out of temptation, and merely hovered round her at a distance; but as soon as Mr. Thorne had left her, he yielded himself up to the basilisk, and allowed himself to be made prey of.

It is impossible to say how the knowledge had been acquired, but the signora had a sort of instinctive knowledge that Mr. Arabin was an admirer of Mrs. Bold. Men hunt foxes by the aid of dogs, and are aware that they do so by the strong organ of smell with which the dog is endowed. They do not, however, in the least comprehend how such a sense can work with such acuteness. The organ by which women instinctively, as it were, know and feel how other women are regarded by men, and how also men are regarded by other women, is equally strong, and equally incomprehensible. A glance, a word, a

motion, suffices : by some such acute exercise of her
feminine senses the signora was aware that Mr. Arabin
loved Eleanor Bold ; and therefore, by a further exercise
of her peculiar feminine propensities, it was quite natural
for her to entrap Mr. Arabin into her net.

The work was half done before she came to Ullathorne,
and when could she have a better opportunity of completing it ? She had had almost enough of Mr. Slope,
though she could not quite resist the fun of driving a very
sanctimonious clergyman to madness by a desperate and
ruinous passion. Mr. Thorne had fallen too easily to give
much pleasure in the chase. His position as a man of
wealth might make his alliance of value, but as a lover he
was very second-rate. We may say that she regarded
him somewhat as a sportsman does a pheasant. The
bird is so easily shot, that he would not be worth the
shooting were it not for the very respectable appearance
that he makes in a larder. The signora would not waste
much time in shooting Mr. Thorne, but still he was worth
bagging for family uses.

But Mr. Arabin was game of another sort. The signora
was herself possessed of quite sufficient intelligence to
know that Mr. Arabin was a man more than usually
intellectual. She knew also, that as a clergyman he was
of a much higher stamp than Mr. Slope, and that as a
gentleman he was better educated than Mr. Thorne. She
would never have attempted to drive Mr. Arabin into
ridiculous misery as she did Mr. Slope, nor would she
think it possible to dispose of him in ten minutes as she
had done with Mr. Thorne.

Such were her reflections about Mr. Arabin. As to
Mr. Arabin, it cannot be said that he reflected at all about
the signora. He knew that she was beautiful, and he felt
that she was able to charm him. He required charming
in his present misery, and therefore he went and stood
at the head of her couch. She knew all about it. Such
were her peculiar gifts. It was her nature to see that
he required charming, and it was her province to charm
him. As the Eastern idler swallows his dose of opium, as
the London reprobate swallows his dose of gin, so with
similar desires and for similar reasons did Mr. Arabin
prepare to swallow the charms of the Signora Neroni.

'Why an't you shooting with bows and arrows, Mr. Arabin?' said she, when they were nearly alone together in the drawing-room; 'or talking with young ladies in shady bowers, or turning your talents to account in some way? What was a bachelor like you asked here for? Don't you mean to earn your cold chicken and champagne? Were I you, I should be ashamed to be so idle.'

Mr. Arabin murmured some sort of answer. Though he wished to be charmed, he was hardly yet in a mood to be playful in return.

'Why, what ails you, Mr. Arabin?' said she, 'here you are in your own parish; Miss Thorne tells me that her party is given expressly in your honour; and yet you are the only dull man at it. Your friend Mr. Slope was with me a few minutes since, full of life and spirits; why don't you rival him?'

It was not difficult for so acute an observer as Madeline Neroni to see that she had hit the nail on the head and driven the bolt home. Mr. Arabin winced visibly before her attack, and she knew at once that he was jealous of Mr. Slope.

'But I look on you and Mr. Slope as the very antipodes of men,' said she. 'There is nothing in which you are not each the reverse of the other, except in belonging to the same profession; and even in that you are so unlike as perfectly to maintain the rule. He is gregarious, you are given to solitude. He is active, you are passive. He works, you think. He likes women, you despise them. He is fond of position and power, and so are you, but for directly different reasons. He loves to be praised, you very foolishly abhor it. He will gain his rewards, which will be an insipid useful wife, a comfortable income, and a reputation for sanctimony. You will also gain yours.'

'Well, and what will they be?' said Mr. Arabin, who knew that he was being flattered, and yet suffered himself to put up with it. 'What will be my rewards?'

'The heart of some woman whom you will be too austere to own that you love, and the respect of some few friends which you will be too proud to own that you value.'

'Rich rewards,' said he; 'but of little worth if they are to be so treated.'

'Oh, you are not to look for such success as awaits
Mr. Slope. He is born to be a successful man. He suggests
to himself an object, and then starts for it with eager
intention. Nothing will deter him from his pursuit. He
will have no scruples, no fears, no hesitation. His desire
is to be a bishop with a rising family, the wife will come
first, and in due time the apron. You will see all this,
and then——'

'Well, and what then ? '

'Then you will begin to wish that you had done the
same.'

Mr. Arabin looked placidly out at the lawn, and resting
his shoulder on the head of the sofa, rubbed his chin with
his hand. It was a trick he had when he was thinking
deeply ; and what the signora said made him think. Was
it not all true ? Would he not hereafter look back, if
not at Mr. Slope, at some others, perhaps not equally
gifted with himself, who had risen in the world while
he had lagged behind, and then wish that he had done
the same ?

'Is not such the doom of all speculative men of talent ? '
said she. 'Do they not all sit rapt as you now are, cutting
imaginary silken cords with their fine edges, while those
not so highly tempered sever the every-day Gordian
knots of the world's struggle, and win wealth and renown ?
Steel too highly polished, edges too sharp, do not do for
this world's work, Mr. Arabin.'

Who was this woman that thus read the secrets of his
heart, and re-uttered to him the unwelcome bodings of
his own soul ? He looked full into her face when she had
done speaking, and said, 'Am I one of those foolish blades,
too sharp and too fine to do a useful day's work ? '

'Why do you let the Slopes of the world out-distance
you ? ' said she. 'Is not the blood in your veins as warm
as his ? does not your pulse beat as fast ? Has not God
made you a man, and intended you to do a man's work
here, ay, and to take a man's wages also ? '

Mr. Arabin sat ruminating and rubbing his face, and
wondering why these things were said to him ; but he
replied nothing. The signora went on—

'The greatest mistake any man ever made is to suppose
that the good things of the world are not worth the

winning. And it is a mistake so opposed to the religion
which you preach! 'Why does God permit his bishops
one after another to have their five thousands and ten
thousands a year if such wealth be bad and not worth
having? Why are beautiful things given to us, and
luxuries and pleasant enjoyments, if they be not intended
to be used? They must be meant for some one, and what
is good for a layman cannot surely be bad for a clerk.
You try to despise these good things, but you only try;
you don't succeed.'

'Don't I?' said Mr. Arabin, still musing, and not
knowing what he said.

'I ask you the question; do you succeed?'

Mr. Arabin looked at her piteously. It seemed to him
as though he were being interrogated by some inner spirit
of his own, to whom he could not refuse an answer, and
to whom he did not dare to give a false reply.

'Come, Mr. Arabin, confess; do you succeed? Is
money so contemptible? Is worldly power so worthless?
Is feminine beauty a trifle to be so slightly regarded by
a wise man?'

'Feminine beauty!' said he, gazing into her face, as
though all the feminine beauty in the world were
concentrated there. 'Why do you say I do not regard it?'

'If you look at me like that, Mr. Arabin, I shall alter
my opinion—or should do so, were I not of course aware
that I have no beauty of my own worth regarding.'

The gentleman blushed crimson, but the lady did not
blush at all. A slightly increased colour animated her
face, just so much so as to give her an air of special interest.
She expected a compliment from her admirer, but she
was rather grateful than otherwise by finding that he did
not pay it to her. Messrs. Slope and Thorne, Messrs.
Brown, Jones and Robinson, they all paid her compliments.
She was rather in hopes that she would ultimately succeed
in inducing Mr. Arabin to abuse her.

'But your gaze,' said she, 'is one of wonder, and not
of admiration. You wonder at my audacity in asking
you such questions about yourself.'

'Well, I do rather,' said he.

'Nevertheless I expect an answer, Mr. Arabin. Why

were women made beautiful if men are not to regard them ? '

' But men do regard them,' he replied.

' And why not you ? '

' You are begging the question, Madame Neroni.'

' I am sure I shall beg nothing, Mr. Arabin, which you will not grant, and I do beg for an answer. Do you not as a rule think women below your notice as companions ? Let us see. There is the widow Bold looking round at you from her chair this minute. What would you say to her as a companion for life ? '

Mr. Arabin, rising from his position, leaned over the sofa and looked through the drawing-room door to the place where Eleanor was seated between Bertie Stanhope and Mr. Slope. She at once caught his glance, and averted her own. She was not pleasantly placed in her present position. Mr. Slope was doing his best to attract her attention ; and she was striving to prevent his doing so by talking to Mr. Stanhope, while her mind was intently fixed on Mr. Arabin and Madame Neroni. Bertie Stanhope endeavoured to take advantage of her favours, but he was thinking more of the manner in which he would by-and-by throw himself at her feet, than of amusing her at the present moment.

' There,' said the signora. ' She was stretching her beautiful neck to look at you, and now you have disturbed her. Well I declare, I believe I am wrong about you ; I believe that you do think Mrs. Bold a charming woman. Your looks seem to say so ; and by her looks I should say that she is jealous of me. Come, Mr. Arabin, confide in me, and if it is so, I'll do all in my power to make up the match.'

It is needless to say that the signora was not very sincere in her offer. She was never sincere on such subjects. She never expected others to be so, nor did she expect others to think her so. Such matters were her playthings, her billiard table, her hounds and hunters, her waltzes and polkas, her picnics and summer-day excursions. She had little else to amuse her, and therefore played at love-making in all its forms. She was now playing at it with Mr. Arabin, and did not at all expect the earnestness and truth of his answer.

'All in your power would be nothing,' said he; 'for Mrs. Bold is, I imagine, already engaged to another.'

'Then you own the impeachment yourself.'

'You cross-question me rather unfairly,' he replied, 'and I do not know why I answer you at all. Mrs. Bold is a very beautiful woman, and as intelligent as beautiful. It is impossible to know her without admiring her.'

'So you think the widow a very beautiful woman?'

'Indeed I do.'

'And one that would grace the parsonage of St. Ewold's.'

'One that would well grace any man's house.'

'And you really have the effrontery to tell me this,' said she; 'to tell me, who, as you very well know, set up to be a beauty myself, and who am at this very moment taking such an interest in your affairs, you really have the effrontery to tell me that Mrs. Bold is the most beautiful woman you know.'

'I did not say so,' said Mr. Arabin; 'you are more beautiful——'

'Ah, come now, that is something like. I thought you could not be so unfeeling.'

'You are more beautiful, perhaps more clever.'

'Thank you, thank you, Mr. Arabin. I knew that you and I should be friends.'

'But——'

'Not a word further. I will not hear a word further. If you talk till midnight, you cannot improve what you have said.'

'But Madame Neroni, Mrs. Bold——'

'I will not hear a word about Mrs. Bold. Dread thoughts of strychnine did pass across my brain, but she is welcome to the second place.'

'Her place——'

'I won't hear anything about her or her place. I am satisfied, and that is enough. But, Mr. Arabin, I am dying with hunger; beautiful and clever as I am, you know I cannot go to my food, and yet you do not bring it to me.'

This at any rate was so true as to make it necessary that Mr. Arabin should act upon it, and he accordingly went into the dining-room and supplied the signora's wants.

'And yourself?' said she.

'Oh,' said he, 'I am not hungry; I never eat at this hour.'

'Come, come, Mr. Arabin, don't let love interfere with your appetite. It never does with mine. Give me half a glass more champagne, and then go to the table. Mrs. Bold will do me an injury if you stay talking to me any longer.'

Mr. Arabin did as he was bid. He took her plate and glass from her, and going into the dining-room, helped himself to a sandwich from the crowded table and began munching it in a corner.

As he was doing so, Miss Thorne, who had hardly sat down for a moment, came into the room, and seeing him standing, was greatly distressed.

'Oh, my dear Mr. Arabin,' said she, 'have you never sat down yet? I am so distressed. You of all men too.'

Mr. Arabin assured her that he had only just come into the room.

'That is the very reason why you should lose no more time. Come, I'll make room for you. Thank'ee, my dear,' she said, seeing that Mrs. Bold was making an attempt to move from her chair, 'but I would not for worlds see you stir, for all the ladies would think it necessary to follow. But, perhaps, if Mr. Stanhope has done—just for a minute, Mr. Stanhope—till I can get another chair.'

And so Bertie had to rise to make way for his rival. This he did, as he did everything, with an air of good-humoured pleasantry which made it impossible for Mr. Arabin to refuse the proffered seat.

'His bishopric let another take,' said Bertie; the quotation being certainly not very appropriate, either for the occasion or the person spoken to. 'I have eaten and am satisfied; Mr. Arabin, pray take my chair. I wish for your sake that it really was a bishop's seat.'

Mr. Arabin did sit down, and as he did so, Mrs. Bold got up as though to follow her neighbour.

'Pray, pray don't move,' said Miss Thorne, almost forcing Eleanor back into her chair. 'Mr. Stanhope is not going to leave us. He will stand behind you like a true knight as he is. And now I think of it, Mr. Arabin, let me introduce you to Mr. Slope. Mr. Slope, Mr. Arabin.' And the two gentlemen bowed stiffly to each other across the lady whom they both intended to marry, while the other gentleman who also intended to marry her stood behind, watching them.

The two had never met each other before, and the present was certainly not a good opportunity for much cordial conversation, even if cordial conversation between them had been possible. As it was, the whole four who formed the party seemed as though their tongues were tied. Mr. Slope, who was wide awake to what he hoped was his coming opportunity, was not much concerned in the interest of the moment. His wish was to see Eleanor move, that he might pursue her. Bertie was not exactly in the same frame of mind; the evil day was near enough; there was no reason why he should precipitate it. He had made up his mind to marry Eleanor Bold if he could, and was resolved to-day to take the first preliminary step towards doing so. But there was time enough before him. He was not going to make an offer of marriage over the table-cloth. Having thus good-naturedly made way for Mr. Arabin, he was willing also to let him talk to the future Mrs. Stanhope as long as they remained in their present position.

Mr. Arabin having bowed to Mr. Slope, began eating his food without saying a word further. He was full of thought, and though he ate he did so unconsciously.

But poor Eleanor was the most to be pitied. The only friend on whom she thought she could rely, was Bertie Stanhope, and he, it seemed, was determined to desert her. Mr. Arabin did not attempt to address her. She said a few words in reply to some remarks from Mr. Slope, and then feeling the situation too much for her, started from her chair in spite of Miss Thorne, and hurried from the room. Mr. Slope followed her, and young Stanhope lost the occasion.

Madeline Neroni, when she was left alone, could not help pondering much on the singular interview she had had with this singular man. Not a word that she had spoken to him had been intended by her to be received as true, and yet he had answered her in the very spirit of truth. He had done so, and she had been aware that he had so done. She had wormed from him his secret; and he, debarred as it would seem from man's usual privilege of lying, had innocently laid bare his whole soul to her. He loved Eleanor Bold, but Eleanor was not in his eye so beautiful as herself. He would fain have Eleanor for his wife, but yet he had acknowledged that she was the less gifted of the two. The man had literally been unable to falsify his thoughts when questioned, and had been compelled to be true *malgrè lui*, even when truth must have been so disagreeable to him.

This teacher of men, this Oxford pundit, this double-distilled quintessence of university perfection, this writer of religious treatises, this speaker of ecclesiastical speeches, had been like a little child in her hands; she had turned him inside out, and read his very heart as she might have done that of a young girl. She could not but despise him for his facile openness, and yet she liked him for it too. It was a novelty to her, a new trait in a man's character. She felt also that she could never so completely make a fool of him as she did of the Slopes and Thornes. She felt that she never could induce Mr. Arabin to make protestations to her that were not true, or to listen to nonsense that was mere nonsense.

It was quite clear that Mr. Arabin was heartily in love with Mrs. Bold, and the signora, with very unwonted good nature, began to turn it over in her mind whether she could not do him a good turn. Of course Bertie was to have the first chance. It was an understood family arrangement that her brother was, if possible, to marry the widow Bold. Madeline knew too well his necessities and what was due to her sister to interfere with so excellent a plan, as long as it might be feasible. But she had strong suspicion that it was not feasible. She did not think it likely that Mrs. Bold would accept a man in her brother's position, and she had frequently said so to Charlotte. She was inclined to believe that Mr. Slope had more chance of success; and with her it would be a labour of love to rob Mr. Slope of his wife.

And so the signora resolved, should Bertie fail, to do a good-natured act for once in her life, and give up Mr. Arabin to the woman whom he loved.

CHAPTER XXXIX

THE LOOKALOFTS AND THE GREENACRES

On the whole, Miss Thorne's provision for the amusement and feeding of the outer classes in the exoteric
paddock was not unsuccessful.

Two little drawbacks to the general happiness did take
place, but they were of a temporary nature, and apparent
rather than real. The first was the downfall of young
Harry Greenacre, and the other the uprise of Mrs. Lookaloft and her family.

As to the quintain, it became more popular among the
boys on foot, than it would ever have been among the
men on horseback, even had young Greenacre been more
successful. It was twirled round and round till it was
nearly twirled out of the ground; and the bag of flour
was used with great gusto in powdering the backs and
heads of all who could be coaxed within its vicinity.

Of course it was reported all through the assemblage
that Harry was dead, and there was a pathetic scene
between him and his mother when it was found that he
had escaped scatheless from the fall. A good deal of beer
was drunk on the occasion, and the quintain was 'dratted'
and 'bothered,' and very generally anathematised by all
the mothers who had young sons likely to be placed in
similar jeopardy. But the affair of Mrs. Lookaloft was
of a more serious nature.

'I do tell 'ee plainly,—face to face,—she be there in
madam's drawing-room; herself and Gussy, and them
two walloping gals, dressed up to their very eyeses.' This
was said by a very positive, very indignant, and very fat
farmer's wife, who was sitting on the end of a bench
leaning on the handle of a huge cotton umbrella.

'But you didn't zee her, Dame Guffern?' said Mrs.
Greenacre, whom this information, joined to the recent
peril undergone by her son, almost overpowered. Mr.
Greenacre held just as much land as Mr. Lookaloft, paid
his rent quite as punctually, and his opinion in the vestry-
room was reckoned to be every whit as good. Mrs. Lookaloft's rise in the world had been wormwood to Mrs.

Greenacre. She had no taste herself for the sort of finery which had converted Barleystubb farm into Rosebank, and which had occasionally graced Mr. Lookaloft's letters with the dignity of esquirehood. She had no wish to convert her own homestead into Violet Villa, or to see her goodman go about with a new-fangled handle to his name. But it was a mortal injury to her that Mrs. Lookaloft should be successful in her hunt after such honours. She had abused and ridiculed Mrs. Lookaloft to the extent of her little power. She had pushed against her going out of church, and had excused herself with all the easiness of equality. 'Ah, dame, I axes pardon; but you be grown so mortal stout these times.' She had inquired with apparent cordiality of Mr. Lookaloft, after 'the woman that owned him,' and had, as she thought, been on the whole able to hold her own pretty well against her aspiring neighbour. Now, however, she found herself distinctly put into a separate and inferior class. Mrs. Lookaloft was asked into the Ullathorne drawing-room merely because she called her house Rosebank, and had talked over her husband into buying pianos and silk dresses instead of putting his money by to stock farms for his sons.

Mrs. Greenacre, much as she reverenced Miss Thorne, and highly as she respected her husband's landlord, could not but look on this as an act of injustice done to her and hers. Hitherto the Lookalofts had never been recognised as being of a different class from the Greenacres. Their pretensions were all self-pretensions, their finery was all paid for by themselves and not granted to them by others. The local sovereigns of the vicinity, the district fountains of honour, had hitherto conferred on them the stamp of no rank. Hitherto their crinoline petticoats, late hours, and mincing gait had been a fair subject of Mrs. Greenacre's raillery, and this raillery had been a safety valve for her envy. Now, however, and from henceforward, the case would be very different. Now the Lookalofts would boast that their aspirations had been sanctioned by the gentry of the country; now they would declare with some show of truth that their claims to peculiar consideration had been recognised. They had sat as equal guests in the presence of bishops and baronets; they had been curtseyed to by Miss Thorne on her own drawing-room

carpet; they were about to sit down to table in company
with a live countess! Bab Lookaloft, as she had always
been called by the young Greenacres in the days of their
juvenile equality, might possibly sit next to the Honourable George, and that wretched Gussy might be permitted
to hand a custard to the Lady Margaretta De Courcy.

The fruition of those honours, or such of them as fell
to the lot of the envied family, was not such as should have
caused much envy. The attention paid to the Lookalofts
by the De Courcys was very limited, and the amount of
entertainment which they received from the bishop's
society was hardly in itself a recompense for the dull
monotony of their day. But of what they endured Mrs.
Greenacre took no account; she thought only of what
she considered they must enjoy, and of the dreadfully
exalted tone of living which would be manifested by the
Rosebank family, as the consequence of their present
distinction.

'But did 'ee zee 'em there, dame, did 'ee zee 'em there
with your own eyes?' asked poor Mrs. Greenacre; still
hoping that there might be some ground for doubt.

'And how could I do that, unless so be I was there
myself?' asked Mrs. Guffern. 'I didn't zet eyes on none
of them this blessed morning, but I zee'd them as did.
You know our John; well, he will be for keeping company
with Betsey Rusk, madam's own maid, you know. And
Betsey isn't none of your common kitchen wenches. So
Betsey, she came out to our John, you know, and she's
always vastly polite to me, is Betsey Rusk, I must say.
So before she took so much as one turn with John, she
told me every ha'porth that was going on up in the house.'

'Did she now?' said Mrs. Greenacre.

'Indeed she did,' said Mrs. Guffern.

'And she told you them people was up there in the
drawing-room?'

'She told me she zee'd them come in,—that they was
dressed finer by half nor any of the family, with all their
neckses and buzoms stark naked as a born babby.'

'The minxes!' exclaimed Mrs. Greenacre, who felt
herself more put about by this than any other mark of
aristocratic distinction which her enemies had assumed.

'Yes, indeed,' continued Mrs. Guffern, 'as naked as

you please, while all the quality was dressed just as you and I be, Mrs. Greenacre.'

'Drat their impudence,' said Mrs. Greenacre, from whose well-covered bosom all milk of human kindness was receding, as far as the family of the Lookalofts were concerned.

'So says I,' said Mrs. Guffern ; ' and so says my goodman, Thomas Guffern, when he hear'd it. " Molly," says he to me, " if ever you takes to going about o' mornings with yourself all naked in them ways, I begs you won't come back no more to the old house." So says I, " Thomas, no more I wull." " But," says he, " drat it, how the deuce does she manage with her rheumatiz, and she not a rag on her : "' and Mrs. Guffern laughed loudly as she thought of Mrs. Lookaloft's probable sufferings from rheumatic attacks.

'But to liken herself that way to folk that ha' blood in their veins,' said Mrs. Greenacre.

'Well, but that warn't all neither that Betsey told. There they all swelled into madam's drawing-room, like so many turkey cocks, as much as to say, " and who dare say no to us ? " and Gregory was thinking of telling of 'em to come down here, only his heart failed him 'cause of the grand way they was dressed. So in they went ; but madam looked at them as glum as death.'

'Well now,' said Mrs. Greenacre, greatly relieved, ' so they wasn't axed different from us at all then ? '

'Betsey says that Gregory says that madam wasn't a bit too well pleased to see them where they was, and that, to his believing, they was expected to come here just like the rest of us.'

There was great consolation in this. Not that Mrs. Greenacre was altogether satisfied. She felt that justice to herself demanded that Mrs. Lookaloft should not only not be encouraged, but that she should also be absolutely punished. What had been done at that scriptural banquet, of which Mrs. Greenacre so often read the account to her family ? Why had not Miss Thorne boldly gone to the intruder and said, ' Friend, thou hast come up hither to high places not fitted to thee. Go down lower, and thou wilt find thy mates.' Let the Lookalofts be treated at the present moment with ever so cold a shoulder, they would still be enabled to boast hereafter of their position, their aspirations, and their honour.

'Well, with all her grandeur, I do wonder that she be so mean,' continued Mrs. Greenacre, unable to dismiss the subject. 'Did you hear, goodman?' she went on, about to repeat the whole story to her husband who then came up. 'There's dame Lookaloft and Bab and Gussy and the lot of 'em all sitting as grand as fivepence in madam's drawing-room, and they not axed no more nor you nor me. Did you ever hear tell the like o' that?'

'Well, and what for shouldn't they?' said Farmer Greenacre.

'Likening theyselves to the quality, as though they was estated folk, or the like o' that!' said Mrs. Guffern.

'Well, if they likes it and madam likes it, they's welcome for me,' said the farmer. 'Now I likes this place better, cause I be more at home like, and don't have to pay for them fine clothes for the missus. Every one to his taste, Mrs. Guffern, and if neighbour Lookaloft thinks that he has the best of it, he's welcome.'

Mrs. Greenacre sat down by her husband's side to begin the heavy work of the banquet, and she did so in some measure with restored tranquillity, but nevertheless she shook her head at her gossip to show that in this instance she did not quite approve of her husband's doctrine.

'And I'll tell 'ee what, dames,' continued he; 'if so be that we cannot enjoy the dinner that madam gives us because Mother Lookaloft is sitting up there on a grand sofa, I think we ought all to go home. If we greet at that, what'll we do when true sorrow comes across us? How would you be now, dame, if the boy there had broke his neck when he got the tumble?'

Mrs. Greenacre was humbled and said nothing further on the matter. But let prudent men, such as Mr. Greenacre, preach as they will, the family of the Lookalofts certainly does occasion a good deal of heart-burning in the world at large.

It was pleasant to see Mr. Plomacy, as leaning on his stout stick he went about among the rural guests, acting as a sort of head constable as well as master of the revels. 'Now, young 'un, if you can't manage to get along without that screeching, you'd better go to the other side of the twelve-acre field, and take your dinner with you. Come, girls, what do you stand there for, twirling of your thumbs? come out, and let the lads see you; you've no need to be so ashamed of your faces. Hollo! there, who are you? how did you make your way in here?'

This last disagreeable question was put to a young man of about twenty-four, who did not, in Mr. Plomacy's eye, bear sufficient vestiges of a rural education and residence.

'If you please, your worship, Master Barrell the coachman let me in at the church wicket, 'cause I do be working mostly al'ays for the family.'

'Then Master Barrell the coachman may let you out again,' said Mr. Plomacy, not even conciliated by the magisterial dignity which had been conceded to him. 'What's your name? and what trade are you, and who do you work for?'

'I'm Stubbs, your worship, Bob Stubbs; and—and—and——'

'And what's your trade, Stubbs?'

'Plaisterer, please your worship.'

'I'll plaister you, and Barrell too; you'll just walk out of this 'ere field as quick as you walked in. We don't want no plaisterers; when we do, we'll send for 'em. Come, my buck, walk.'

Stubbs the plasterer was much downcast at this dreadful edict. He was a sprightly fellow, and had contrived since his egress into the Ullathorne elysium to attract to himself a forest nymph, to whom he was whispering a plasterer's usual soft nothings, when he was encountered by the great Mr. Plomacy. It was dreadful to be thus dissevered from his dryad, and sent howling back to a Barchester pandemonium just as the nectar and ambrosia were about to descend on the fields of asphodel. He began to try what prayers would do, but city prayers were vain against the great rural potentate. Not only did Mr. Plomacy order his exit, but raising his stick to show the way which led to the gate that had been left in the custody of that false Cerberus Barrell, proceeded himself to see the edict of banishment carried out.

The goddess Mercy, however, the sweetest goddess that ever sat upon a cloud, and the dearest to poor frail erring man, appeared on the field in the person of Mr. Greenacre. Never was interceding goddess more welcome.

'Come, man,' said Mr. Greenacre, 'never stick at trifles such a day as this. I know the lad well. Let him bide at my axing. Madam won't miss what he can eat and drink, I know.'

Now Mr. Plomacy and Mr. Greenacre were sworn friends. Mr. Plomacy had at his own disposal as comfortable a room as there was in Ullathorne House; but he was a bachelor, and alone there; and, moreover, smoking in the house was not allowed even to Mr. Plomacy. His moments of truest happiness were spent in a huge arm-chair in the warmest corner of Mrs. Greenacre's beautifully clean front kitchen. 'Twas there that the inner man dissolved itself, and poured itself out in streams of pleasant chat; 'twas there that he was respected and yet at his ease; 'twas there, and perhaps there only, that he could unburden himself from the ceremonies of life without offending the dignity of those above him, or incurring the familiarity of those below. 'Twas there that his long pipe was always to be found on the accustomed chimney board, not only permitted but encouraged.

Such being the state of the case, it was not to be supposed that Mr. Plomacy could refuse such a favour to Mr. Greenacre; but nevertheless he did not grant it without some further show of austere authority.

'Eat and drink, Mr. Greenacre! No. It's not what he eats and drinks; but the example such a chap shows, coming in where he's not invited—a chap of his age too. He too that never did a day's work about Ullathorne since he was born. Plaisterer! I'll plaister him!'

'He worked long enough for me, then, Mr. Plomacy. And a good hand he is at setting tiles as any in Barchester,' said the other, not sticking quite to veracity, as indeed mercy never should. 'Come, come, let him alone to-day, and quarrel with him to-morrow. You wouldn't shame him before his lass there?'

'It goes against the grain with me, then,' said Mr. Plomacy 'And take care, you Stubbs, and behave yourself. If I hear a row I shall know where it comes from. I'm up to you Barchester journeymen; I know what stuff you're made of.'

And so Stubbs went off happy, pulling at the forelock of his shock head of hair in honour of the steward's clemency, and giving another double pull at it in honour of the farmer's kindness. And as he went he swore within his grateful heart, that if ever Farmer Greenacre wanted a day's work done for nothing, he was the lad to do it for him. Which promise it was not probable that he would ever be called on to perform.

But Mr. Plomacy was not quite happy in his mind, for he thought of the unjust steward, and began to reflect whether he had not made for himself friends of the mammon of unrighteousness. This, however, did not interfere with the manner in which he performed his duties at the bottom of the long board ; nor did Mr. Greenacre perform his the worse at the top on account of the good wishes of Stubbs the plasterer. Moreover, the guests did not think it anything amiss when Mr. Plomacy, rising to say grace, prayed that God would make them all truly thankful for the good things which Madam Thorne in her great liberality had set before them !

All this time the quality in the tent on the lawn were getting on swimmingly ; that is, if champagne without restriction can enable quality folk to swim. Sir Harkaway Gorse proposed the health of Miss Thorne, and likened her to a blood race-horse, always in condition, and not to be tired down by any amount of work. Mr. Thorne returned thanks, saying he hoped his sister would always be found able to run when called upon, and then gave the health and prosperity of the De Courcy family. His sister was very much honoured by seeing so many of them at her poor board. They were all aware that important avocations made the absence of the earl necessary. As his duty to his prince had called him from his family hearth, he, Mr. Thorne, could not venture to regret that he did not see him at Ullathorne ; but nevertheless he would venture to say—that was to express a wish—an opinion he meant to say—— And so Mr. Thorne became somewhat gravelled, as country gentlemen in similar circumstances usually do ; but he ultimately sat down, declaring that he had much satisfaction in drinking the noble earl's health, together with that of the countess, and all the family of De Courcy castle.

And then the Honourable George returned thanks. We will not follow him through the different periods of his somewhat irregular eloquence. Those immediately in his neighbourhood found it at first rather difficult to get him on his legs, but much greater difficulty was soon experienced in inducing him to resume his seat. One of two arrangements should certainly be made in these days : either let all speech-making on festive occasions be utterly tabooed and made as it were impossible ; or else let those who are to exercise the privilege be first subjected to a competing examination before the civil service examining commissioners. As it is now, the Honourable Georges do but little honour to our exertions in favour of British education.

In the dining-room the bishop went through the honours of the day with much more neatness and propriety. He also drank Miss Thorne's health, and did it in a manner becoming the bench which he adorned. The party there, was perhaps a little more dull, a shade less lively than that in the tent. But what was lost in mirth, was fully made up in decorum.

And so the banquets passed off at the various tables with great eclat and universal delight.

CHAPTER XL

ULLATHORNE SPORTS—ACT II

' THAT which has made them drunk, has made me bold.' 'Twas thus that Mr. Slope encouraged himself, as he left the dining-room in pursuit of Eleanor. He had not indeed seen in that room any person really intoxicated ; but there had been a good deal of wine drunk, and Mr. Slope had not hesitated to take his share, in order to screw himself up to the undertaking which he had in hand. He is not the first man who has thought it expedient to call in the assistance of Bacchus on such an occasion.

Eleanor was out through the window, and on the grass before she perceived that she was followed. Just at that moment the guests were nearly all occupied at the tables. Here and there were to be seen a constant couple or two,

who preferred their own sweet discourse to the jingle of
glasses, or the charms of rhetoric which fell from the
mouths of the Honourable George and the bishop of
Barchester; but the grounds were as nearly vacant as
Mr. Slope could wish them to be.

Eleanor saw that she was pursued, and as a deer, when
escape is no longer possible, will turn to bay and attack
the hounds, so did she turn upon Mr. Slope.

' Pray don't let me take you from the room,' said she,
speaking with all the stiffness which she knew how to use.
' I have come out to look for a friend. I must beg of you,
Mr. Slope, to go back.'

But Mr. Slope would not be thus entreated. He had
observed all day that Mrs. Bold was not cordial to him,
and this had to a certain extent oppressed him. But he
did not deduce from this any assurance that his aspirations
were in vain. He saw that she was angry with him. Might
she not be so because he had so long tampered with her
feelings,—might it not arise from his having, as he knew
was the case, caused her name to be bruited about in
conjunction with his own, without having given her the
opportunity of confessing to the world that henceforth
their names were to be one and the same? Poor lady!
He had within him a certain Christian conscience-stricken
feeling of remorse on this head. It might be that he had
wronged her by his tardiness. He had, however, at the
present moment imbibed too much of Mr. Thorne's
champagne to have any inward misgivings. He was right
in repeating the boast of Lady Macbeth: he was not drunk;
but he was bold enough for anything. It was a pity that
in such a state he could not have encountered Mrs. Proudie.

' You must permit me to attend you,' said he; ' I could
not think of allowing you to go alone.'

' Indeed you must, Mr. Slope,' said Eleanor still very
stiffly; ' for it is my special wish to be alone.'

The time for letting the great secret escape him had
already come. Mr. Slope saw that it must be now or never,
and he was determined that it should be now. This was
not his first attempt at winning a fair lady. He had been
on his knees, looked unutterable things with his eyes, and
whispered honeyed words before this. Indeed he was
somewhat an adept at these things, and had only to adapt

to the perhaps different taste of Mrs. Bold the well-remembered rhapsodies which had once so much gratified Olivia Proudie.

'Do not ask me to leave you, Mrs. Bold,' said he with an impassioned look, impassioned and sanctified as well, with that sort of look which is not uncommon with gentlemen of Mr. Slope's school, and which may perhaps be called the tender-pious. 'Do not ask me to leave you, till I have spoken a few words with which my heart is full; which I have come hither purposely to say.'

Eleanor saw how it was now. She knew directly what it was she was about to go through, and very miserable the knowledge made her. Of course she could refuse Mr. Slope, and there would be an end of that, one might say. But there would not be an end of it as far as Eleanor was concerned. The very fact of Mr. Slope's making an offer to her would be a triumph to the archdeacon, and in a great measure a vindication of Mr. Arabin's conduct. The widow could not bring herself to endure with patience the idea that she had been in the wrong. She had defended Mr. Slope, she had declared herself quite justified in admitting him among her acquaintance, had ridiculed the idea of his considering himself as more than an acquaintance, and had resented the archdeacon's caution in her behalf: now it was about to be proved to her in a manner sufficiently disagreeable that the archdeacon had been right, and she herself had been entirely wrong.

'I don't know what you can have to say to me, Mr. Slope, that you could not have said when we were sitting at table just now;' and she closed her lips, and steadied her eyeballs, and looked at him in a manner that ought to have frozen him.

But gentlemen are not easily frozen when they are full of champagne, and it would not at any time have been easy to freeze Mr. Slope.

'There are things, Mrs. Bold, which a man cannot well say before a crowd; which perhaps he cannot well say at any time; which indeed he may most fervently desire to get spoken, and which he may yet find it almost impossible to utter. It is such things as these, that I now wish to say to you;' and then the tender-pious look was repeated, with a little more emphasis even than before.

Eleanor had not found it practicable to stand stock still before the dining-room window, and there receive his offer in full view of Miss Thorne's guests. She had therefore in self-defence walked on, and thus Mr. Slope had gained his object of walking with her. He now offered her his arm.

'Thank you, Mr. Slope, I am much obliged to you; but for the very short time that I shall remain with you I shall prefer walking alone.'

'And must it be so short?' said he; 'must it be—'

'Yes,' said Eleanor, interrupting him; 'as short as possible, if you please, sir.'

'I had hoped, Mrs. Bold—I had hoped—'

'Pray hope nothing, Mr. Slope, as far as I am concerned; pray do not; I do not know, and need not know what hope you mean. Our acquaintance is very slight, and will probably remain so. Pray, pray let that be enough; there is at any rate no necessity for us to quarrel.'

Mrs. Bold was certainly treating Mr. Slope rather cavalierly, and he felt it so. She was rejecting him before he had offered himself, and informed him at the same time that he was taking a great deal too much on himself to be so familiar. She did not even make an attempt

> From such a sharp and waspish word as 'no'
> To pluck the sting.

He was still determined to be very tender and very pious, seeing that in spite of all Mrs. Bold had said to him, he not yet abandoned hope; but he was inclined also to be somewhat angry. The widow was bearing herself, as he thought, with too high a hand, was speaking of herself in much too imperious a tone. She had clearly no idea that an honour was being conferred on her. Mr. Slope would be tender as long as he could, but he began to think, if that failed, it would not be amiss if he also mounted himself for a while on his high horse. Mr. Slope could undoubtedly be very tender, but he could be very savage also, and he knew his own abilities.

'That is cruel,' said he, 'and unchristian too. The worst of us are all still bidden to hope. What have I done that you should pass on me so severe a sentence?' and then he paused a moment, during which the widow walked steadily on with measured step, saying nothing further.

'Beautiful woman,' at last he burst forth; 'beautiful woman, you cannot pretend to be ignorant that I adore you. Yes, Eleanor, yes, I love you. I love you with the truest affection which man can bear to woman. Next to my hopes of heaven are my hopes of possessing you.' (Mr. Slope's memory here played him false, or he would not have omitted the deanery.) 'How sweet to walk to heaven with you by my side, with you for my guide, mutual guides. Say, Eleanor, dearest Eleanor, shall we walk that sweet path together?'

Eleanor had no intention of ever walking together with Mr. Slope on any other path than that special one of Miss Thorne's which they now occupied; but as she had been unable to prevent the expression of Mr. Slope's wishes and aspirations, she resolved to hear him out to the end, before she answered him.

'Ah! Eleanor,' he continued, and it seemed to be his idea that as he had once found courage to pronounce her Christian name, he could not utter it often enough. 'Ah! Eleanor, will it not be sweet, with the Lord's assistance, to travel hand in hand through this mortal valley which his mercies will make pleasant to us, till hereafter we shall dwell together at the foot of his throne?' And then a more tenderly pious glance than ever beamed from the lover's eyes. 'Ah! Eleanor—'

'My name, Mr. Slope, is Mrs. Bold,' said Eleanor, who, though determined to hear out the tale of his love, was too much disgusted by his blasphemy to be able to bear much more of it.

'Sweetest angel, be not so cold,' said he, and as he said it the champagne broke forth, and he contrived to pass his arm round her waist. He did this with considerable cleverness, for up to this point Eleanor had contrived with tolerable success to keep her distance from him. They had got into a walk nearly enveloped by shrubs, and Mr. Slope therefore no doubt considered that as they were now alone it was fitting that he should give her some outward demonstration of that affection of which he talked so much. It may perhaps be presumed that the same stamp of measures had been found to succeed with Olivia Proudie. Be this as it may, it was not successful with Eleanor Bold.

She sprang from him as she would have jumped from an adder, but she did not spring far; not, indeed, beyond arm's length; and then, quick as thought, she raised her little hand and dealt him a box on the ear with such right good will, that it sounded among the trees like a miniature thunder-clap.

And now it is to be feared that every well-bred reader of these pages will lay down the book with disgust, feeling that, after all, the heroine is unworthy of sympathy. She is a hoyden, one will say. At any rate she is not a lady, another will exclaim. I have suspected her all through, a third will declare; she has no idea of the dignity of a matron; or of the peculiar propriety which her position demands. At one moment she is romping with young Stanhope; then she is making eyes at Mr. Arabin; anon she comes to fisty-cuffs with a third lover; and all before she is yet a widow of two years' standing.

She cannot altogether be defended; and yet it may be averred that she is not a hoyden, not given to romping, nor prone to boxing. It were to be wished devoutly that she had not struck Mr. Slope in the face. In doing so she derogated from her dignity and committed herself. Had she been educated in Belgravia, had she been brought up by any sterner mentor than that fond father, had she lived longer under the rule of a husband, she might, perhaps, have saved herself from this great fault. As it was, the provocation was too much for her, the temptation to instant resentment of the insult too strong. She was too keen in the feeling of independence, a feeling dangerous for a young woman, but one in which her position peculiarly tempted her to indulge. And then Mr. Slope's face, tinted with a deeper dye than usual by the wine he had drunk, simpering and puckering itself with pseudo piety and tender grimaces, seemed specially to call for such punishment. She had, too, a true instinct as to the man; he was capable of rebuke in this way and in no other. To him the blow from her little hand was as much an insult as a blow from a man would have been to another. It went direct to his pride. He conceived himself lowered in his dignity, and personally outraged. He could almost have struck at her again in his rage. Even the pain was a great annoyance to him, and the feeling that his clerical character had been wholly disregarded, sorely vexed him.

There are such men; men who can endure no taint on their personal self-respect, even from a woman;—men whose bodies are to themselves such sacred temples, that a joke against them is desecration, and a rough touch downright sacrilege. Mr. Slope was such a man; and, therefore, the slap on the face that he got from Eleanor was, as far as he was concerned, the fittest rebuke which could have been administered to him.

But, nevertheless, she should not have raised her hand against the man. Ladies' hands, so soft, so sweet, so delicious to the touch, so grateful to the eye, so gracious in their gentle doings, were not made to belabour men's faces. The moment the deed was done Eleanor felt that she had sinned against all propriety, and would have given little worlds to recall the blow. In her first agony of sorrow she all but begged the man's pardon. Her next impulse, however, and the one which she obeyed, was to run away.

'I never, never will speak another word to you,' she said, gasping with emotion and the loss of breath which her exertion and violent feelings occasioned her, and so saying she put foot to the ground and ran quickly back along the path to the house.

But how shall I sing the divine wrath of Mr. Slope, or how invoke the tragic muse to describe the rage which swelled the celestial bosom of the bishop's chaplain? Such an undertaking by no means befits the low-heeled buskin of modern fiction. The painter put a veil over Agamemnon's face when called on to depict the father's grief at the early doom of his devoted daughter. The god, when he resolved to punish the rebellious winds, abstained from mouthing empty threats. We will not attempt to tell with what mighty surgings of the inner heart Mr. Slope swore to revenge himself on the woman who had disgraced him, nor will we vainly strive to depict his deep agony of soul.

There he is, however, alone in the garden walk, and we must contrive to bring him out of it. He was not willing to come forth quite at once. His cheek was stinging with the weight of Eleanor's fingers, and he fancied that every one who looked at him would be able to see on his face the traces of what he had endured. He stood awhile, becoming redder and redder with rage. He stood motionless, undecided, glaring with his eyes, thinking of the pains and penalties of Hades, and meditating how he might best devote his enemy to the infernal gods with all the passion of his accustomed eloquence. He longed in his heart to be preaching at her. 'Twas thus that he was ordinarily avenged of sinning mortal men and women. Could he at once have ascended his Sunday rostrum and fulminated at her such denunciations as his spirit delighted in, his bosom would have been greatly eased.

But how preach to Mr. Thorne's laurels, or how preach indeed at all in such a vanity fair as this now going on at Ullathorne? And then he began to feel a righteous disgust at the wickedness of the doings around him. He had been justly chastised for lending, by his presence, a sanction to such worldly lures. The gaiety of society, the mirth of banquets, the laughter of the young, and the eating and drinking of the elders were, for awhile, without excuse in his sight. What had he now brought down upon himself by sojourning thus in the tents of the heathen? He had consorted with idolaters round the altars of Baal; and therefore a sore punishment had come upon him. He then thought of the Signora Neroni, and his soul within him was full of sorrow. He had an inkling—a true inkling— that he was a wicked, sinful man; but it led him in no right direction; he could admit no charity in his heart. He felt debasement coming on him, and he longed to shake it off, to rise up in his stirrup, to mount to high places and great power, that he might get up into a mighty pulpit and preach to the world a loud sermon against Mrs. Bold.

There he stood fixed to the gravel for about ten minutes. Fortune favoured him so far that no prying eyes came to look upon him in his misery. Then a shudder passed over his whole frame; he collected himself, and slowly wound his way round to the lawn, advancing along the path and not returning in the direction which Eleanor had taken. When he reached the tent he found the bishop standing there in conversation with the master of Lazarus. His lordship had come out to air himself after the exertion of his speech.

'This is very pleasant—very pleasant, my lord, is it

not ?' said Mr. Slope with his most gracious smile, and pointing to the tent; 'very pleasant. It is delightful to see so many persons enjoying themselves so thoroughly.'

Mr. Slope thought he might force the bishop to introduce him to Dr. Gwynne. A very great example had declared and practised the wisdom of being everything to everybody, and Mr. Slope was desirous of following it. His maxim was never to lose a chance. The bishop, however, at the present moment was not very anxious to increase Mr. Slope's circle of acquaintance among his clerical brethren. He had his own reasons for dropping any marked allusion to his domestic chaplain, and he therefore made his shoulder rather cold for the occasion.

'Very, very,' said he without turning round, or even deigning to look at Mr. Slope. 'And therefore, Dr. Gwynne, I really think that you will find that the hebdomadal board will exercise as wide and as general an authority as at the present moment. I, for one, Dr. Gwynne——'

'Dr. Gwynne,' said Mr. Slope, raising his hat, and resolving not to be outwitted by such an insignificant little goose as the bishop of Barchester.

The master of Lazarus also raised his hat and bowed very politely to Mr. Slope. There is not a more courteous gentleman in the queen's dominions than the master of Lazarus.

'My lord,' said Mr. Slope; 'pray do me the honour of introducing me to Dr. Gwynne. The opportunity is too much in my favour to be lost.'

The bishop had no help for it. 'My chaplain, Dr. Gwynne,' said he; 'my present chaplain, Mr. Slope.' He certainly made the introduction as unsatisfactory to the chaplain as possible, and by the use of the word present, seemed to indicate that Mr. Slope might probably not long enjoy the honour which he now held. But Mr. Slope cared nothing for this. He understood the innuendo, and disregarded it. It might probably come to pass that he would be in a situation to resign his chaplaincy before the bishop was in a situation to dismiss him from it. What need the future dean of Barchester care for the bishop, or for the bishop's wife ? Had not Mr. Slope, just as he was entering Dr. Stanhope's carriage, received an all important note from Tom Towers of the Jupiter ? had he not that note this moment in his pocket ?

So disregarding the bishop, he began to open out a conversation with the master of Lazarus.

But suddenly an interruption came, not altogether unwelcome to Mr. Slope. One of the bishop's servants came up to his master's shoulder with a long, grave face, and whispered into the bishop's ear.

' What is it, John ? ' said the bishop.

' The dean, my lord ; he is dead.'

Mr. Slope had no further desire to converse with the master of Lazarus, and was very soon on his road back to Barchester.

Eleanor, as we have said, having declared her intention of never holding further communication with Mr. Slope, ran hurriedly back towards the house. The thought, however, of what she had done grieved her greatly, and she could not abstain from bursting into tears. 'Twas thus she played the second act in that day's melodrame.

CHAPTER XLI

MRS. BOLD CONFIDES HER SORROW TO HER FRIEND MISS STANHOPE

WHEN Mrs. Bold came to the end of the walk and faced the lawn, she began to bethink herself what she should do. Was she to wait there till Mr. Slope caught her, or was she to go in among the crowd with tears in her eyes and passion in her face ? She might in truth have stood there long enough without any reasonable fear of further immediate persecution from Mr. Slope ; but we are all inclined to magnify the bugbears which frighten us. In her present state of dread she did not know of what atrocity he might venture to be guilty. Had any one told her a week ago that he would have put his arm round her waist at this party of Miss Thorne's, she would have been utterly incredulous. Had she been informed that he would be seen on the following Sunday walking down the High-street in a scarlet coat and top-boots, she would not have thought such a phenomenon more improbable.

But this improbable iniquity he had committed; and now there was nothing she could not believe of him. In the first place it was quite manifest that he was tipsy; in the next place, it was to be taken as proved that all his religion was sheer hypocrisy; and finally the man was utterly shameless. She therefore stood watching for the sound of his footfall, not without some fear that he might creep out at her suddenly from among the bushes.

As she thus stood, she saw Charlotte Stanhope at a little distance from her walking quickly across the grass. Eleanor's handkerchief was in her hand, and putting it to her face so as to conceal her tears, she ran across the lawn and joined her friend.

' Oh, Charlotte,' she said, almost too much out of breath to speak very plainly; ' I am so glad I have found you.'

' Glad you have found me!' said Charlotte, laughing: ' that's a good joke. Why Bertie and I have been looking for you everywhere. He swears that you have gone off with Mr. Slope, and is now on the point of hanging himself.'

' Oh, Charlotte, don't,' said Mrs. Bold.

' Why, my child, what on earth is the matter with you!' said Miss Stanhope, perceiving that Eleanor's hand trembled on her own arm, and finding also that her companion was still half choked by tears. ' Goodness heaven! something has distressed you. What is it? What can I do for you?'

Eleanor answered her only by a sort of spasmodic gurgle in her throat. She was a good deal upset, as people say, and could not at the moment collect herself.

' Come here, this way, Mrs. Bold; come this way, and we shall not be seen. What has happened to vex you so? What can I do for you? Can Bertie do anything?'

' Oh, no, no, no, no,' said Eleanor. ' There is nothing to be done. Only that horrid man——'

' What horrid man?' asked Charlotte.

There are some moments in life in which both men and women feel themselves imperatively called on to make a confidence; in which not to do so requires a disagreeable resolution and also a disagreeable suspicion. There are people of both sexes who never make confidences; who are never tempted by momentary circumstances to disclose their secrets; but such are generally dull, close, unimpassioned spirits, ' gloomy gnomes, who live in cold dark mines.' There was nothing of the gnome about Eleanor ; and she therefore resolved to tell Charlotte Stanhope the whole story about Mr. Slope.

' That horrid man ; that Mr. Slope,' said she : ' did you not see that he followed me out of the dining-room ? '

' Of course I did, and was sorry enough ; but I could not help it. I knew you would be annoyed. But you and Bertie managed it badly between you.'

' It was not his fault nor mine either. You know how I disliked the idea of coming in the carriage with that man.'

' I am sure I am very sorry if that has led to it.'

' I don't know what has led to it,' said Eleanor, almost crying again. ' But it has not been my fault.'

' But what has he done, my dear ? '

' He's an abominable, horrid, hypocritical man, and it would serve him right to tell the bishop all about it.'

' Believe me, if you want to do him an injury, you had far better tell Mrs. Proudie. But what did he do, Mrs. Bold ? '

' Ugh ! ' exclaimed Eleanor.

' Well, I must confess he's not very nice,' said Charlotte Stanhope.

' Nice ! ' said Eleanor. ' He is the most fulsome, fawning, abominable man I ever saw. What business had he to come to me ?—I that never gave him the slightest tittle of encouragement—I that always hated him, though I did take his part when others ran him down.'

' That's just where it is, my dear. He has heard that, and therefore fancied that of course you were in love with him.'

This was wormwood to Eleanor. It was in fact the very thing which all her friends had been saying for the last month past ; and which experience now proved to be true. Eleanor resolved within herself that she would never again take any man's part. The world with all its villainy, and all its ill-nature, might wag as it liked ; she would not again attempt to set crooked things straight.

' But what did he do, my dear ? ' said Charlotte, who was really rather interested in the subject.

' He—he—he—'

'Well—come, it can't have been anything so very horrid, for the man was not tipsy.'

'Oh, I am sure he was,' said Eleanor. 'I am sure he must have been tipsy.'

'Well, I declare I didn't observe it. But what was it, my love ?'

'Why, I believe I can hardly tell you. He talked such horrid stuff that you never heard the like ; about religion, and heaven, and love.—Oh, dear,—he is such a nasty man.'

'I can easily imagine the sort of stuff he would talk. Well,—and then— ? '

'And then—he took hold of me.'

'Took hold of you ? '

'Yes,—he somehow got close to me, and took hold of me—'

'By the waist ? '

'Yes,' said Eleanor shuddering.

'And then—'

'Then I jumped away from him, and gave him a slap on the face ; and ran away along the path, till I saw you.'

'Ha, ha, ha ! ' Charlotte Stanhope laughed heartily at the finale to the tragedy. It was delightful to her to think that Mr. Slope had had his ears boxed. She did not quite appreciate the feeling which made her friend so unhappy at the result of the interview. To her thinking, the matter had ended happily enough as regarded the widow, who indeed was entitled to some sort of triumph among her friends. Whereas to Mr. Slope would be due all those jibes and jeers which would naturally follow such an affair. His friends would ask him whether his ears tingled whenever he saw a widow ; and he would be cautioned that beautiful things were made to be looked at, and not to be touched.

Such were Charlotte Stanhope's views on such matters ; but she did not at the present moment clearly explain them to Mrs. Bold. Her object was to endear herself to her friend ; and therefore, having had her laugh, she was ready enough to offer sympathy. Could Bertie do anything ? Should Bertie speak to the man, and warn him that in future he must behave with more decorum ? Bertie, indeed, she declared, would be more angry than any one else when he heard to what insult Mrs. Bold had been subjected.

'But you won't tell him?' said Mrs. Bold with a look of horror.

'Not if you don't like it,' said Charlotte; 'but considering everything, I would strongly advise it. If you had a brother, you know, it would be unnecessary. But it is very right that Mr. Slope should know that you have somebody by you that will, and can protect you.'

'But my father is here.'

'Yes, but it is so disagreeable for clergymen to have to quarrel with each other; and circumstanced as your father is just at this moment, it would be very inexpedient that there should be anything unpleasant between him and Mr. Slope. Surely you and Bertie are intimate enough for you to permit him to take your part.'

Charlotte Stanhope was very anxious that her brother should at once on that very day settle matters with his future wife. Things had now come to that point between him and his father, and between him and his creditors, that he must either do so, or leave Barchester; either do that, or go back to his unwashed associates, dirty lodgings, and poor living at Carrara. Unless he could provide himself with an income, he must go to Carrara, or to ——. His father the prebendary had not said this in so many words, but had he done so, he could not have signified it more plainly.

Such being the state of the case, it was very necessary that no more time should be lost. Charlotte had seen her brother's apathy, when he neglected to follow Mrs. Bold out of the room, with anger which she could hardly suppress. It was grievous to think that Mr. Slope should have so distanced him. Charlotte felt that she had played her part with sufficient skill. She had brought them together and induced such a degree of intimacy, that her brother was really relieved from all trouble and labour in the matter. And moreover, it was quite plain that Mrs. Bold was very fond of Bertie. And now it was plain enough also that he had nothing to fear from his rival Mr. Slope.

There was certainly an awkwardness in subjecting Mrs. Bold to a second offer on the same day. It would have been well perhaps to have put the matter off for a week, could a week have been spared. But circumstances are frequently too peremptory to be arranged as we would wish to arrange them ; and such was the case now. This being so, could not this affair of Mr. Slope's be turned to advantage ? Could it not be made the excuse for bringing Bertie and Mrs. Bold into still closer connection ; into such close connection that they could not fail to throw themselves into each other's arms ? Such was the game which Miss Stanhope now at a moment's notice resolved to play.

And very well she played it. In the first place, it was arranged that Mr. Slope should not return in the Stanhopes' carriage to Barchester. It so happened that Mr. Slope was already gone, but of that of course they knew nothing. The signora should be induced to go first, with only the servants and her sister, and Bertie should take Mr. Slope's place in the second journey. Bertie was to be told in confidence of the whole affair, and when the carriage was gone off with its first load, Eleanor was to be left under Bertie's special protection, so as to insure her from any further aggression from Mr. Slope. While the carriage was getting ready, Bertie was to seek out that gentleman and make him understand that he must provide himself with another conveyance back to Barchester. Their immediate object should be to walk about together in search of Bertie. Bertie, in short, was to be the Pegasus on whose wings they were to ride out of their present dilemma.

There was a warmth of friendship and cordial kindliness in all this, that was very soothing to the widow ; but yet, though she gave way to it, she was hardly reconciled to doing so. It never occurred to her, that now that she had killed one dragon, another was about to spring up in her path ; she had no remote idea that she would have to encounter another suitor in her proposed protector, but she hardly liked the thought of putting herself so much into the hands of young Stanhope. She felt that if she wanted protection, she should go to her father. She felt that she should ask him to provide a carriage for her back to Barchester. Mrs. Clantantram she knew would give her a seat. She knew that she should not throw herself entirely upon friends whose friendship dated as it were but from yesterday. But yet she could not say 'no,' to one who was so sisterly in her kindness, so eager in her good nature, so comfortably sympathetic as Charlotte Stanhope. And thus she gave way to all the propositions made to her.

They first went into the dining-room, looking for their champion, and from thence to the drawing-room. Here they found Mr. Arabin, still hanging over the signora's sofa ; or, rather, they found him sitting near her head, as a physician might have sat, had the lady been his patient. There was no other person in the room. The guests were some in the tent, some few still in the dining-room, some at the bows and arrows; but most of them walking with Miss Thorne through the park, and looking at the games that were going on.

All that had passed, and was passing between Mr. Arabin and the lady, it is unnecessary to give in detail. She was doing with him as she did with all others. It was her mission to make fools of men, and she was pursuing her mission with Mr. Arabin. She had almost got him to own his love for Mrs. Bold, and had subsequently almost induced him to acknowledge a passion for herself. He, poor man, was hardly aware what he was doing or saying, hardly conscious whether he was in heaven or hell. So little had he known of female attractions of that peculiar class which the signora owned, that he became affected with a kind of temporary delirium, when first subjected to its power. He lost his head rather than his heart, and toppled about mentally, reeling in his ideas as a drunken man does on his legs. She had whispered to him words that really meant nothing, but which coming from such beautiful lips, and accompanied by such lustrous glances, seemed to have a mysterious significance, which he felt though he could not understand.

In being thus be-sirened, Mr. Arabin behaved himself very differently from Mr. Slope. The signora had said truly, that the two men were the contrasts of each other ; that the one was all for action, the other all for thought. Mr. Slope, when this lady laid upon his senses the over-powering breath of her charms, immediately attempted to obtain some fruition, to achieve some mighty triumph. He began by catching at her hand, and progressed by kissing it. He made vows of love, and asked for vows in return. He promised everlasting devotion, knelt before her, and swore that had she been on Mount Ida, Juno would have had no cause to hate the offspring of Venus. But Mr. Arabin uttered no oaths, kept his hand mostly in his trowsers pocket, and had no more thought of kissing Madam Neroni, than of kissing the Countess De Courcy.

As soon as Mr. Arabin saw Mrs. Bold enter the room, he blushed and rose from his chair; then he sat down again, and then again got up. The signora saw the blush at once, and smiled at the poor victim, but Eleanor was too much confused to see anything.

'Oh, Madeline,' said Charlotte, 'I want to speak to you particularly; we must arrange about the carriage, you know,' and she stooped down to whisper to her sister. Mr. Arabin immediately withdrew to a little distance, and as Charlotte had in fact much to explain before she could make the new carriage arrangement intelligible, he had nothing to do but to talk to Mrs. Bold.

'We have had a very pleasant party,' said he, using the tone he would have used had he declared that the sun was shining very brightly, or the rain falling very fast.

'Very,' said Eleanor, who never in her life had passed a more unpleasant day.

'I hope Mr. Harding has enjoyed himself.'

'Oh, yes, very much,' said Eleanor, who had not seen her father since she parted from him soon after her arrival.

'He returns to Barchester to-night, I suppose.'

'Yes, I believe so; that is, I think he is staying at Plumstead.'

'Oh, staying at Plumstead,' said Mr. Arabin.

'He came from there this morning. I believe he is going back; he didn't exactly say, however.'

'I hope Mrs. Grantly is quite well.'

'She seemed to be quite well. She is here; that is, unless she has gone away.'

'Oh, yes, to be sure. I was talking to her. Looking very well indeed.' Then there was a considerable pause; for Charlotte could not at once make Madeline understand why she was to be sent home in a hurry without her brother.

'Are you returning to Plumstead, Mrs. Bold?' Mr. Arabin merely asked this by way of making conversation, but he immediately perceived that he was approaching dangerous ground.

'No,' said Mrs. Bold, very quietly; 'I am going home to Barchester.'

'Oh, ah, yes. I had forgotten that you had returned.' And then Mr. Arabin, finding it impossible to say anything further, stood silent till Charlotte had completed her plans, and Mrs. Bold stood equally silent, intently occupied as it appeared in the arrangement of her rings.

And yet these two people were thoroughly in love with each other; and though one was a middle-aged clergyman, and the other a lady at any rate past the wishy-washy bread-and-butter period of life, they were as unable to tell their own minds to each other as any Damon and Phillis, whose united ages would not make up that to which Mr. Arabin had already attained.

Madeline Neroni consented to her sister's proposal, and then the two ladies again went off in quest of Bertie Stanhope.

CHAPTER XLII

ULLATHORNE SPORTS—ACT III

AND now Miss Thorne's guests were beginning to take their departure, and the amusement of those who remained was becoming slack. It was getting dark, and ladies in morning costumes were thinking that if they were to appear by candle-light they ought to readjust themselves. Some young gentlemen had been heard to talk so loud that prudent mammas determined to retire judiciously, and the more discreet of the male sex, whose libations had been moderate, felt that there was not much more left for them to do.

Morning parties, as a rule, are failures. People never know how to get away from them gracefully. A picnic on an island or a mountain or in a wood may perhaps be permitted. There is no master of the mountain bound by courtesy to bid you stay while in his heart he is longing for your departure. But in a private house or in private grounds a morning party is a bore. One is called on to eat and drink at unnatural hours. One is obliged to give up

the day which is useful, and is then left without resource
for the evening which is useless. One gets home fagged
and *désœuvré*, and yet at an hour too early for bed. There
is no comfortable resource left. Cards in these genteel days
are among the things tabooed, and a rubber of whist is
impracticable. -

All this began now to be felt. Some young people had
come with some amount of hope that they might get up a
dance in the evening, and were unwilling to leave till all
such hope was at an end. Others, fearful of staying longer
than was expected, had ordered their carriages early, and
were doing their best to go, solicitous for their servants
and horses. The countess and her noble brood were among
the first to leave, and as regarded the Hon. George, it was
certainly time that he did so. Her ladyship was in a great
fret and fume. Those horrid roads would, she was sure,
be the death of her if unhappily she were caught in them
by the dark night. The lamps she was assured were good,
but no lamp could withstand the jolting of the roads of
East Barsetshire. The De Courcy property lay in the
western division of the county.

Mrs. Proudie could not stay when the countess was
gone. So the bishop was searched for by the Revs. Messrs.
Grey and Green, and found in one corner of the tent
enjoying himself thoroughly in a disquisition on the
hebdomadal board. He obeyed, however, the behests of
his lady without finishing the sentence in which he was
promising to Dr. Gwynne that his authority at Oxford
should remain unimpaired; and the episcopal horses
turned their noses towards the palatial stables. Then the
Grantlys went. Before they did so, Mr. Harding managed
to whisper a word into his daughter's ear. Of course, he
said he would undeceive the Grantlys as to that foolish
rumour about Mr. Slope.

'No, no, no,' said Eleanor; 'pray do not—pray wait
till I see you. You will be home in a day or two, and then
I will explain to you everything.'

'I shall be home to-morrow,' said he.

'I am so glad,' said Eleanor. 'You will come and dine
with me, and then we shall be so comfortable.'

Mr. Harding promised. He did not exactly know what
there was to be explained, or why Dr. Grantly's mind

should not be disabused of the mistake into which he had
fallen ; but nevertheless he promised. He owed some
reparation to his daughter, and he thought that he might
best make it by obedience.

And thus the people were thinning off by degrees, as
Charlotte and Eleanor walked about in quest of Bertie.
Their search might have been long, had they not happened
to hear his voice. He was comfortably ensconced in the
ha-ha, with his back to the sloping side, smoking a cigar,
and eagerly engaged in conversation with some youngster
from the further side of the county, whom he had never
met before, who was also smoking under Bertie's pupilage,
and listening with open ears to an account given by his
companion of some of the pastimes of Eastern clime.

'Bertie, I am seeking you everywhere,' said Charlotte.
'Come up here at once.'

Bertie looked up out of the ha-ha, and saw the two ladies
before him. As there was nothing for him but to obey, he
got up and threw away his cigar. From the first moment
of his acquaintance with her he had liked Eleanor Bold.
Had he been left to his own devices, had she been penniless,
and had it then been quite out of the question that he
should marry her, he would most probably have fallen
violently in love with her. But now he could not help
regarding her somewhat as he did the marble workshops
at Carrara, as he had done his easel and palette, as he had
done the lawyer's chambers in London ; in fact, as he had
invariably regarded everything by which it had been
proposed to him to obtain the means of living. Eleanor
Bold appeared before him, no longer as a beautiful woman,
but as a new profession called matrimony. It was a
profession indeed requiring but little labour, and one in
which an income was insured to him. But nevertheless he
had been as it were goaded on to it ; his sister had talked
to him of Eleanor, just as she had talked of busts and
portraits. Bertie did not dislike money, but he hated the
very thought of earning it. He was now called away from
his pleasant cigar to earn it, by offering himself as a
husband to Mrs. Bold. The work indeed was made easy
enough ; for in lieu of his having to seek the widow, the
widow had apparently come to seek him.

He made some sudden absurd excuse to his auditor, and

then throwing away his cigar, climbed up the wall of the ha-ha and joined the ladies on the lawn.

'Come and give Mrs. Bold an arm,' said Charlotte, 'while I set you on a piece of duty which, as a preux chevalier, you must immediately perform. Your personal danger will, I fear, be insignificant, as your antagonist is a clergyman.'

Bertie immediately gave his arm to Eleanor, walking between her and his sister. He had lived too long abroad to fall into the Englishman's habit of offering each an arm to two ladies at the same time ; a habit, by the bye, which foreigners regard as an approach to bigamy, or a sort of incipient Mormonism.

The little history of Mr. Slope's misconduct was then told to Bertie by his sister, Eleanor's ears tingling the while. And well they might tingle. If it were necessary to speak of the outrage at all, why should it be spoken of to such a person as Mr. Stanhope, and why in her own hearing ? She knew she was wrong, and was unhappy and dispirited, and yet she could think of no way to extricate herself, no way to set herself right. Charlotte spared her as much as she possibly could, spoke of the whole thing as though Mr. Slope had taken a glass of wine too much, said that of course there would be nothing more about it, but that steps must be taken to exclude Mr. Slope from the carriage.

'Mrs. Bold need be under no alarm about that,' said Bertie, 'for Mr. Slope has gone this hour past. He told me that business made it necessary that he should start at once for Barchester.'

'He is not so tipsy, at any rate, but what he knows his fault,' said Charlotte. 'Well, my dear, that is one difficulty over. Now I'll leave you with your true knight, and get Madeline off as quickly as I can. The carriage is here, I suppose, Bertie ?'

'It has been here for the last hour.'

'That's well. Good bye, my dear. Of course you'll come in to tea. I shall trust to you to bring her, Bertie ; even by force if necessary.' And so saying, Charlotte ran off across the lawn, leaving her brother alone with the widow.

As Miss Stanhope went off, Eleanor bethought herself

that, as Mr. Slope had taken his departure, there no longer
existed any necessity for separating Mr. Stanhope from
his sister Madeline, who so much needed his aid. It had
been arranged that he should remain so as to preoccupy
Mr. Slope's place in the carriage, and act as a social policeman to effect the exclusion of that disagreeable gentleman.
But Mr. Slope had effected his own exclusion, and there
was no possible reason now why Bertie should not go with
his sister. At least Eleanor saw none, and she said as
much.

'Oh, let Charlotte have her own way,' said he. 'She
has arranged it, and there will be no end of confusion, if
we make another change. Charlotte always arranges
everything in our house; and rules us like a despot.'

'But the signora?' said Eleanor.

'Oh, the signora can do very well without me. Indeed,
she will have to do without me,' he added, thinking rather
of his studies in Carrara, than of his Barchester hymeneals.

'Why, you are not going to leave us?' asked Eleanor.

It has been said that Bertie Stanhope was a man without
principle. He certainly was so. He had no power of using
active mental exertion to keep himself from doing evil.
Evil had no ugliness in his eyes; virtue no beauty. He
was void of any of those feelings which actuate men to do
good. But he was perhaps equally void of those which
actuate men to do evil. He got into debt with utter
recklessness, thinking nothing as to whether the tradesmen
would ever be paid or not. But he did not invent active
schemes of deceit for the sake of extracting the goods of
others. If a man gave him credit, that was the man's
look-out; Bertie Stanhope troubled himself nothing
further. In borrowing money he did the same; he gave
people references to 'his governor;' told them that the
'old chap' had a good income; and agreed to pay sixty
per cent. for the accommodation. All this he did without
a scruple of conscience; but then he never contrived
active villainy.

In this affair of his marriage, it had been represented to
him as a matter of duty that he ought to put himself in
possession of Mrs. Bold's hand and fortune; and at first he
had so regarded it. About her he had thought but little.
It was the customary thing for men situated as he was to

marry for money, and there was no reason why he should not do what others around him did. And so he consented. But now he began to see the matter in another light. He was setting himself down to catch this woman, as a cat sits to catch a mouse. He was to catch her, and swallow her up, her and her child, and her houses and land, in order that he might live on her instead of on his father. There was a cold, calculating, cautious cunning about this quite at variance with Bertie's character. The prudence of the measure was quite as antagonistic to his feelings as the iniquity.

And then, should he be successful, what would be the reward ? Having satisfied his creditors with half of the widow's fortune, he would be allowed to sit down quietly at Barchester, keeping economical house with the re-mainder. His duty would be to rock the cradle of the late Mr. Bold's child, and his highest excitement a demure party at Plumstead rectory, should it ultimately turn out that the archdeacon would be sufficiently reconciled to receive him.

There was very little in the programme to allure such a man as Bertie Stanhope. Would not the Carrara work-shop, or whatever worldly career fortune might have in store for him, would not almost anything be better than this ? The lady herself was undoubtedly all that was desirable ; but the most desirable lady becomes nauseous when she has to be taken as a pill. He was pledged to his sister, however, and let him quarrel with whom he would, it behoved him not to quarrel with her. If she were lost to him all would be lost that he could ever hope to derive henceforward from the paternal roof-tree. His mother was apparently indifferent to his weal or woe, to his wants or his warfare. His father's brow got blacker and blacker from day to day, as the old man looked at his hopeless son. And as for Madeline—poor Madeline, whom of all of them he liked the best,—she had enough to do to shift for herself. No ; come what might, he must cling to his sister and obey her behests, let them be ever so stern ; or at the very least seem to obey them. Could not some happy deceit bring him through in this matter, so that he might save appearances with his sister, and yet not betray the widow to her ruin ? What if he made a confederate of

Eleanor ?   'Twas in this spirit that Bertie Stanhope set
about his wooing.

' But you are not going to leave Barchester ? ' asked
Eleanor.

' I do not know,' he replied ; ' I hardly know yet what
I am going to do.   But it is at any rate certain that I must
do something.'

' You mean about your profession ? ' said she.

' Yes, about my profession, if you can call it one.'

' And is it not one ? ' said Eleanor.   ' Were I a man, I
know none I should prefer to it, except painting.   And
I believe the one is as much in your power as the other.'

' Yes, just about equally so,' said Bertie, with a little
touch of inward satire directed at himself.   He knew in his
heart that he would never make a penny by either.

' I have often wondered, Mr. Stanhope, why you do not
exert yourself more,' said Eleanor, who felt a friendly
fondness for the man with whom she was walking.   ' But I
know it is very impertinent in me to say so.'

' Impertinent ! ' said he.   ' Not so, but much too kind.
It is much too kind in you to take any interest in so idle
a scamp.'

' But you are not a scamp, though you are perhaps idle ;
and I do take an interest in you ; a very great interest,'
she added, in a voice which almost made him resolve to
change his mind.   ' And when I call you idle, I know you
are only so for the present moment.   Why can't you settle
steadily to work here in Barchester ? '

' And make busts of the bishop, dean and chapter ? or
perhaps, if I achieve a great success, obtain a commission
to put up an elaborate tombstone over a prebendary's
widow, a dead lady with a Grecian nose, a bandeau, and
an intricate lace veil ; lying of course on a marble sofa,
from among the legs of which Death will be creeping out
and poking at his victim with a small toasting-fork.'

Eleanor laughed ; but yet she thought that if the
surviving prebendary paid the bill, the object of the artist
as a professional man would, in a great measure, be
obtained.

' I don't know about the dean and chapter and the
prebendary's widow,' said Eleanor.   ' Of course you must
take them as they come.   But the fact of your having a

great cathedral in which such ornaments are required, could not but be in your favour.'

' No real artist could descend to the ornamentation of a cathedral,' said Bertie, who had his ideas of the high ecstatic ambition of art, as indeed all artists have, who are not in receipt of a good income. ' Buildings should be fitted to grace the sculpture, not the sculpture to grace the building.'

' Yes, when the work of art is good enough to merit it. Do you, Mr. Stanhope, do something sufficiently excellent, and we ladies of Barchester will erect for it a fitting receptacle. Come, what shall the subject be ? '

' I'll put you in your pony chair, Mrs. Bold, as Dannecker put Ariadne on her lion. Only you must promise to sit for me.'

' My ponies are too tame, I fear, and my broad-rimmed straw hat will not look so well in marble as the lace veil of the prebendary's wife.'

' If you will not consent to that, Mrs. Bold, I will consent to try no other subject in Barchester.'

' You are determined, then, to push your fortune in other lands ? '

' I am determined,' said Bertie, slowly and significantly, as he tried to bring up his mind to a great resolve ; ' I am determined in this matter to be guided wholly by you.'

' Wholly by me ! ' said Eleanor, astonished at, and not quite liking, his altered manner.

' Wholly by you,' said Bertie, dropping his companion's arm, and standing before her on the path. In their walk they had come exactly to the spot in which Eleanor had been provoked into slapping Mr. Slope's face. Could it be possible that this place was peculiarly unpropitious to her comfort ? could it be possible that she should here have to encounter yet another amorous swain ?

' If you will be guided by me, Mr. Stanhope, you will set yourself down to steady and persevering work, and you will be ruled by your father as to the place in which it will be most advisable for you to do so.'

' Nothing could be more prudent, if only it were practicable. But now, if you will let me, I will tell you how it is that I will be guided by you, and why. Will you let me tell you ? '

' I really do not know what you can have to tell.'

' No,—you cannot know. It is impossible that you
should. But we have been very good friends, Mrs. Bold,
have we not ? '

' Yes, I think we have,' said she, observing in his
demeanour an earnestness very unusual with him.

' You were kind enough to say just now that you took
an interest in me, and I was perhaps vain enough to
believe you.'

' There is no vanity in that ; I do so as your sister's
brother,—and as my own friend also.'

' Well, I don't deserve that you should feel so kindly
towards me,' said Bertie ; ' but upon my word I am very
grateful for it,' and he paused awhile, hardly knowing how
to introduce the subject that he had in hand.

And it was no wonder that he found it difficult. He had
to make known to his companion the scheme that had
been prepared to rob her of her wealth ; he had to tell her
that he intended to marry her without loving her, or else
that he loved her without intending to marry her ; and he
had also to bespeak from her not only his own pardon, but
also that of his sister, and induce Mrs. Bold to protest in
her future communion with Charlotte that an offer had
been duly made to her and duly rejected.

Bertie Stanhope was not prone to be very diffident of
his own conversational powers, but it did seem to him that
he was about to tax them almost too far. He hardly knew
where to begin, and he hardly knew where he should end.

By this time Eleanor wàs again walking on slowly by
his side, not taking his arm as she had heretofore done, but
listening very intently for whatever Bertie might have to
say to her.

' I wish to be guided by you,' said he ; ' and, indeed, in
this matter, there is no one else who can set me right.'

' Oh, that must be nonsense,' said she.

' Well, listen to me now, Mrs. Bold ; and if you can help
it, pray don't be angry with me.'

' Angry ! ' said she.

' Oh, indeed you will have cause to be so. You know
how very much attached to you my sister Charlotte is.'

Eleanor acknowledged that she did.

' Indeed she is ; I never knew her to love any one so

warmly on so short an acquaintance. You know also how well she loves me ? '

Eleanor now made no answer, but she felt the blood tingle in her cheek as she gathered from what he said the probable result of this double-barrelled love on the part of Miss Stanhope.

' I am her only brother, Mrs. Bold, and it is not to be wondered at that she should love me. But you do not yet know Charlotte,—you do not know how entirely the well-being of our family hangs on her. Without her to manage for us, I do not know how we should get on from day to day. You cannot yet have observed all this.'

Eleanor had indeed observed a good deal of this ; she did not however now say so, but allowed him to proceed with his story.

' You cannot therefore be surprised that Charlotte should be most anxious to do the best for us all.'

Eleanor said that she was not at all surprised.

' And she has had a very difficult game to play, Mrs. Bold—a very difficult game. Poor Madeline's unfortunate marriage and terrible accident, my mother's ill health, my father's absence from England, and last, and worst perhaps, my own roving, idle spirit have almost been too much for her. You cannot wonder if among all her cares one of the foremost is to see me settled in the world.'

Eleanor on this occasion expressed no acquiescence. She certainly supposed that a formal offer was to be made, and could not but think that so singular an exordium was never before made by a gentleman in a similar position. Mr. Slope had annoyed her by the excess of his ardour. It was quite clear that no such danger was to be feared from Mr. Stanhope. Prudential motives alone actuated him. Not only was he about to make love because his sister told him, but he also took the precaution of explaining all this before he began. 'Twas thus, we may presume, that the matter presented itself to Mrs. Bold.

When he had got so far, Bertie began poking the gravel with a little cane which he carried. He still kept moving on, but very slowly, and his companion moved slowly by his side, not inclined to assist him in the task the performance of which appeared to be difficult to him.

' Knowing how fond she is of yourself, Mrs. Bold, cannot

you imagine what scheme should have occurred to her?'

'I can imagine no better scheme, Mr. Stanhope, than the one I proposed to you just now.'

'No,' said he, somewhat lack-a-daisically; 'I suppose that would be the best; but Charlotte thinks another plan might be joined with it.—She wants me to marry you.'

A thousand remembrances flashed across Eleanor's mind all in a moment,—how Charlotte had talked about and praised her brother, how she had continually contrived to throw the two of them together, how she had encouraged all manner of little intimacies, how she had with singular cordiality persisted in treating Eleanor as one of the family. All this had been done to secure her comfortable income for the benefit of one of the family!

Such a feeling as this is very bitter when it first impresses itself on a young mind. To the old such plots and plans, such matured schemes for obtaining the goods of this world without the trouble of earning them, such long-headed attempts to convert ' tuum ' into ' meum,' are the ways of life to which they are accustomed. 'Tis thus that many live, and it therefore behoves all those who are well to do in the world to be on their guard against those who are not. With them it is the success that disgusts, not the attempt. But Eleanor had not yet learnt to look on her money as a source of danger; she had not begun to regard herself as fair game to be hunted down by hungry gentlemen. She had enjoyed the society of the Stanhopes, she had greatly liked the cordiality of Charlotte, and had been happy in her new friends. Now she saw the cause of all this kindness, and her mind was opened to a new phase of human life.

' Miss Stanhope,' said she, haughtily, ' has been contriving for me a great deal of honour, but she might have saved herself the trouble. I am not sufficiently ambitious.'

' Pray don't be angry with her, Mrs. Bold,' said he, ' or with me either.'

' Certainly not with you, Mr. Stanhope,' said she, with considerable sarcasm in her tone. ' Certainly not with you.'

' No,—nor with her,' said he, imploringly.

' And why, may I ask you, Mr. Stanhope, have you told me this singular story? For I may presume I may judge by your manner of telling it, that—that—that you and your sister are not exactly of one mind on the subject.'

' No, we are not.'

' And if so,' said Mrs. Bold, who was now really angry with the unnecessary insult which she thought had been offered to her, ' and if so, why has it been worth your while to tell me all this ? '

' I did once think, Mrs. Bold,—that you—that you——'

The widow now again became entirely impassive, and would not lend the slightest assistance to her companion.

' I did once think that you perhaps might,—might have been taught to regard me as more than a friend.'

' Never ! ' said Mrs. Bold, ' never. If I have ever allowed myself to do anything to encourage such an idea, I have been very much to blame,—very much to blame indeed.'

' You never have,' said Bertie, who really had a good-natured anxiety to make what he said as little unpleasant as possible. ' You never have, and I have seen for some time that I had no chance ; but my sister's hopes ran higher. I have not mistaken you, Mrs. Bold, though perhaps she has.'

' Then why have you said all this to me ? '

' Because I must not anger her.'

' And will not this anger her ? Upon my word, Mr. Stanhope, I do not understand the policy of your family. Oh, how I wish I was at home ! ' And as she expressed the wish, she could restrain herself no longer, but burst out into a flood of tears.

Poor Bertie was greatly moved. ' You shall have the carriage to yourself going home,' said he ; ' at least you and my father. As for me I can walk, or for the matter of that it does not much signify what I do.' He perfectly understood that part of Eleanor's grief arose from the apparent necessity of going back to Barchester in the carriage with her second suitor.

This somewhat mollified her. ' Oh, Mr. Stanhope,' said she, ' why should you have made me so miserable ? What will you have gained by telling me all this ? '

He had not even yet explained to her the most difficult part of his proposition ; he had not told her that she was to be a party to the little deception which he intended to play off upon his sister. This suggestion had still to be

made, and as it was absolutely necessary, he proceeded to
make it.

We need not follow him through the whole of his statement. At last, and not without considerable difficulty, he
made Eleanor understand why he had let her into his
confidence, seeing that he no longer intended her the
honour of a formal offer. At last he made her comprehend
the part which she was destined to play in this little family
comedy.

But when she did understand it, she was only more
angry with him than ever : more angry, not only with him,
but with Charlotte also. Her fair name was to be bandied
about between them in different senses, and each sense
false. She was to be played off by the sister against the
father ; and then by the brother against the sister. Her
dear friend Charlotte, with all her agreeable sympathy and
affection, was striving to sacrifice her for the Stanhope
family welfare ; and Bertie, who, as he now proclaimed
himself, was over head and ears in debt, completed the
compliment of owning that he did not care to have his
debts paid at so great a sacrifice of himself. Then she
was asked to conspire together with this unwilling suitor,
for the sake of making the family believe that he had in
obedience to their commands done his best to throw himself thus away !

She lifted up her face when he had finished, and looking
at him with much dignity, even through her tears, she
said—

'I regret to say it, Mr. Stanhope ; but after what has
passed, I believe that all intercourse between your family
and myself had better cease.'

'Well, perhaps it had,' said Bertie naïvely ; 'perhaps
that will be better, at any rate for a time ; and then
Charlotte will think you are offended at what I have done.'

'And now I will go back to the house, if you please,' said
Eleanor. 'I can find my way by myself, Mr. Stanhope :
after what has passed,' she added, 'I would rather go
alone.'

'But I must find the carriage for you, Mrs. Bold, and
I must tell my father that you will return with him alone,
and I must make some excuse to him for not going with
you ; and I must bid the servant put you down at your

own house, for I suppose you will not now choose to see them again in the close.'

There was a truth about this, and a perspicuity in making arrangements for lessening her immediate embarrassment, which had some effect in softening Eleanor's anger. So she suffered herself to walk by his side over the now deserted lawn, till they came to the drawing-room window. There was something about Bertie Stanhope which gave him, in the estimation of every one, a different standing from that which any other man would occupy under similar circumstances. Angry as Eleanor was, and great as was her cause for anger, she was not half as angry with him as she would have been with any one else. He was apparently so simple, so good-natured, so unaffected and easy to talk to, that she had already half-forgiven him before he was at the drawing-room window. When they arrived there, Dr. Stanhope was sitting nearly alone with Mr. and Miss Thorne ; one or two other unfortunates were there, who from one cause or another were still delayed in getting away ; but they were every moment getting fewer in number.

As soon as he had handed Eleanor over to his father, Bertie started off to the front gate, in search of the carriage, and there waited leaning patiently against the front wall, and comfortably smoking a cigar, till it came up. When he returned to the room Dr. Stanhope and Eleanor were alone with their hosts.

' At last, Miss Thorne,' said he cheerily, ' I have come to relieve you. Mrs. Bold and my father are the last roses of the very delightful summer you have given us, and desirable as Mrs. Bold's society always is, now at least you must be glad to see the last flowers plucked from the tree.'

Miss Thorne declared that she was delighted to have Mrs. Bold and Dr. Stanhope still with her ; and Mr. Thorne would have said the same, had he not been checked by a yawn, which he could not suppress.

' Father, will you give your arm to Mrs. Bold ? ' said Bertie : and so the last adieux were made, and the prebendary led out Mrs. Bold, followed by his son.

' I shall be home soon after you,' said he, as the two got into the carriage.

' Are you not coming in the carriage ? ' said the father,

' No, no ; I have some one to see on the road, and shall walk. John, mind you drive to Mrs. Bold's house first.'

Eleanor looking out of the window, saw him with his hat in his hand, bowing to her with his usual gay smile, as though nothing had happened to mar the tranquillity of the day. It was many a long year before she saw him again. Dr. Stanhope hardly spoke to her on her way home ; and she was safely deposited by John at her own hall-door, before the carriage drove into the close.

And thus our heroine played the last act of that day's melodrame.

CHAPTER XLIII

MR. AND MRS. QUIVERFUL ARE MADE HAPPY.
MR. SLOPE IS ENCOURAGED BY THE PRESS

BEFORE she started for Ullathorne, Mrs. Proudie, careful soul, caused two letters to be written, one by herself and one by her lord, to the inhabitants of Pudding-dale vicarage, which made happy the hearth of those within it.

As soon as the departure of the horses left the bishop's stable-groom free for other services, that humble denizen of the diocese started on the bishop's own pony with the two despatches. We have had so many letters lately that we will spare ourselves these. That from the bishop was simply a request that Mr. Quiverful would wait upon his lordship the next morning at 11 A.M. ; and that from the lady was as simply a request that Mrs. Quiverful would do the same by her, though it was couched in somewhat longer and more grandiloquent phraseology.

It had become a point of conscience with Mrs. Proudie to urge the settlement of this great hospital question. She was resolved that Mr. Quiverful should have it. She was resolved that there should be no more doubt or delay, no more refusals and resignations, no more secret negotiations carried on by Mr. Slope on his own account in opposition to her behests.

' Bishop,' she said, immediately after breakfast, on the morning of that eventful day, ' have you signed the appointment yet ? '

' No, my dear, not yet ; it is not exactly signed as yet.'

' Then do it,' said the lady.

The bishop did it ; and a very pleasant day indeed he spent at Ullathorne. And when he got home he had a glass of hot negus in his wife's sitting-room, and read the last number of the ' Little Dorrit ' of the day with great inward satisfaction. Oh, husbands, oh, my marital friends, what great comfort is there to be derived from a wife well obeyed !

Much perturbation and flutter, high expectation and renewed hopes, were occasioned at Puddingdale, by the receipt of these episcopal despatches. Mrs. Quiverful, whose careful ear caught the sound of the pony's feet as he trotted up to the vicarage kitchen door, brought them in hurriedly to her husband. She was at the moment concocting the Irish stew destined to satisfy the noonday wants of fourteen young birds, let alone the parent couple. She had taken the letters from the man's hands between the folds of her capacious apron, so as to save them from the contamination of the stew, and in this guise she brought them to her husband's desk.

They at once divided the spoil, each taking that addressed to the other. ' Quiverful,' said she with impressive voice, ' you are to be at the palace at eleven to-morrow.'

' And so are you, my dear,' said he, almost gasping with the importance of the tidings : and then they exchanged letters.

' She'd never have sent for me again,' said the lady, ' if it wasn't all right.'

' Oh ! my dear, don't be too certain,' said the gentleman. ' Only think if it should be wrong.'

' She'd never have sent for me, Q., if it wasn't all right,' again argued the lady. ' She's stiff and hard and proud as pie-crust, but I think she's right at bottom.' Such was Mrs. Quiverful's verdict about Mrs. Proudie, to which in after times she always adhered. People when they get their income doubled usually think that those through whose instrumentality this little ceremony is performed are right at bottom.

' Oh Letty ! ' said Mr. Quiverful, rising from his well-worn seat.

'Oh Q.!' said Mrs. Quiverful: and then the two, unmindful of the kitchen apron, the greasy fingers, and the adherent Irish stew, threw themselves warmly into each other's arms.

'For heaven's sake don't let any one cajole you out of it again,' said the wife.

'Let me alone for that,' said the husband, with a look of almost fierce determination, pressing his fist as he spoke rigidly on his desk, as though he had Mr. Slope's head below his knuckles, and meant to keep it there.

'I wonder how soon it will be,' said she.

'I wonder whether it will be at all,' said he, still doubtful.

'Well, I won't say too much,' said the lady. 'The cup has slipped twice before, and it may fall altogether this time; but I'll not believe it. He'll give you the appointment to-morrow. You'll find he will.'

'Heaven send he may,' said Mr. Quiverful, solemnly. And who that considers the weight of the burden on this man's back, will say that the prayer was an improper one? There were fourteen of them—fourteen of them living—as Mrs. Quiverful had so powerfully urged in the presence of the bishop's wife. As long as promotion cometh from any human source, whether north or south, east or west, will not such a claim as this hold good, in spite of all our examination tests, *detur digniori's* and optimist tendencies? It is fervently to be hoped that it may. Till we can become divine we must be content to be human, lest in our hurry for a change we sink to something lower.

And then the pair sitting down lovingly together, talked over all their difficulties, as they so often did, and all their hopes, as they so seldom were enabled to do.

'You had better call on that man, Q., as you come away from the palace,' said Mrs. Quiverful, pointing to an angry call for money from the Barchester draper, which the postman had left at the vicarage that morning. Cormorant that he was, unjust, hungry cormorant! When rumour first got abroad that the Quiverfuls were to go to the hospital. this fellow with fawning eagerness had pressed his goods upon the wants of the poor clergyman. He had done so, feeling that he should be paid from the hospital funds, and flattering himself that a man with fourteen children, and money wherewithal to clothe them, could not but be an excellent customer. As soon as the second rumour reached him, he applied for his money angrily.

And 'the fourteen '—or such of them as were old enough to hope and discuss their hopes, talked over their golden future. The tall-grown girls whispered to each other of possible Barchester parties, of possible allowances for dress, of a possible piano—the one they had in the vicarage was so weather-beaten with the storms of years and children as to be no longer worthy of the name—of the pretty garden, and the pretty house. 'Twas of such things it most behoved them to whisper.

And the younger fry, they did not content themselves with whispers, but shouted to each other of their new play-ground beneath our dear ex-warden's well-loved elms, of their future own gardens, of marbles to be procured in the wished-for city, and of the rumour which had reached them of a Barchester school.

'Twas in vain that their cautious mother tried to instil into their breasts the very feeling she had striven to banish from that of their father; 'twas in vain that she repeated to the girls that ' there's many a slip 'twixt the cup and the lip; ' 'twas in vain she attempted to make the children believe that they were to live at Puddingdale all their lives. Hopes mounted high and would not have themselves quelled. The neighbouring farmers heard the news, and came in to congratulate them. 'Twas Mrs. Quiverful herself who had kindled the fire, and in the first outbreak of her renewed expectations she did it so thoroughly, that it was quite past her power to put it out again.

Poor matron! good honest matron! doing thy duty in the state to which thou hast been called, heartily if not contentedly; let the fire burn on;—on this occasion the flames will not scorch; they shall warm thee and thine. 'Tis ordained that that husband of thine, that Q. of thy bosom, shall reign supreme for years to come over the bedesmen of Hiram's hospital.

And the last in all Barchester to mar their hopes, had he heard and seen all that passed at Puddingdale that day, would have been Mr. Harding. What wants had he to set in opposition to those of such a regiment of young ravens ? There are fourteen of them living! with him at any rate, let us say, that that argument would have been sufficient for the appointment of Mr. Quiverful.

In the morning, Q. and his wife kept their appointments with that punctuality which bespeaks an expectant mind. The friendly farmer's gig was borrowed, and in that they went, discussing many things by the way. They had instructed the household to expect them back by one, and injunctions were given to the eldest pledge to have ready by that accustomed hour the remainder of the huge stew which the provident mother had prepared on the previous day. The hands of the kitchen clock came round to two, three, four, before the farmer's gig-wheels were again heard at the vicarage gate. With what palpitating hearts were the returning wanderers greeted !

'I suppose, children, you all thought we were never coming back any more ? ' said the mother, as she slowly let down her solid foot till it rested on the step of the gig. 'Well, such a day as we've had ! ' and then leaning heavily on a big boy's shoulder, she stepped once more on terra firma.

There was no need for more than the tone of her voice to tell them that all was right. The Irish stew might burn itself to cinders now.

Then there was such kissing and hugging, such crying and laughing. Mr. Quiverful could not sit still at all, but kept walking from room to room, then out into the garden, then down the avenue into the road, and then back again to his wife. She, however, lost no time so idly.

'We must go to work at once, girls ; and that in earnest. Mrs. Proudie expects us to be in the hospital house on the 15th of October.'

Had Mrs. Proudie expressed a wish that they should all be there on the next morning, the girls would have had nothing so say against it.

'And when will the pay begin ? ' asked the eldest boy.

'To-day, my dear,' said the gratified mother.

'Oh,—that is jolly,' said the boy.

'Mrs. Proudie insisted on our going down to the house,' continued the mother ; ' and when there I thought I might

save a journey by measuring some of the rooms and
windows; so I got a knot of tape from Bobbins. Bobbins
is as civil as you please, now.'

'I wouldn't thank him,' said Letty the younger.

'Oh, it's the way of the world, my dear. They all do
just the same. You might just as well be angry with the
turkey cock for gobbling at you. It's the bird's nature.'
And as she enunciated to her bairns the upshot of her
practical experience, she pulled from her pocket the
portions of tape which showed the length and breadth
of the various rooms at the hospital house.

And so we will leave her happy in her toils.

The Quiverfuls had hardly left the palace, and Mrs.
Proudie was still holding forth on the matter to her
husband, when another visitor was announced in the
person of Dr. Gwynne. The master of Lazarus had asked
for the bishop, and not for Mrs. Proudie, and therefore,
when he was shown into the study, he was surprised rather
than rejoiced to find the lady there.

But we must go back a little, and it shall be but a little,
for a difficulty begins to make itself manifest in the necessity
of disposing of all our friends in the small remainder of
this one volume. Oh, that Mr. Longman would allow me
a fourth! It should transcend the other three as the
seventh heaven transcends all the lower stages of celestial
bliss.

Going home in the carriage that evening from Ullathorne, Dr. Gwynne had not without difficulty brought
round his friend the archdeacon to a line of tactics much
less bellicose than that which his own taste would have
preferred. 'It will be unseemly in us to show ourselves in a
bad humour: and moreover we have no power in this matter,
and it will therefore be bad policy to act as though we had.'
'Twas thus the master of Lazarus argued. 'If,' he continued, 'the bishop be determined to appoint another to the
hospital, threats will not prevent him, and threats should
not be lightly used by an archdeacon to his bishop. If he
will place a stranger in the hospital, we can only leave him
to the indignation of others. It is probable that such
a step may not eventually injure your father-in-law. I will
see the bishop, if you will allow me,—alone.' At this the
archdeacon winced visibly; 'yes, alone; for so I shall

be calmer : and then I shall at any rate learn what he does mean to do in the matter.'

The archdeacon puffed and blew, put up the carriage window and then put it down again, argued the matter up to his own gate, and at last gave way. Everybody was against him, his own wife, Mr. Harding, and Dr. Gwynne. . 'Pray keep him out of hot water, Dr. Gwynne,' Mrs. Grantly had said to her guest. 'My dearest madam, I'll do my best,' the courteous master had replied. 'Twas thus he did it; and earned for himself the gratitude of Mrs. Grantly.

And now we may return to the bishop's study.

Dr. Gwynne had certainly not foreseen the difficulty which here presented itself. He,—together with all the clerical world of England,—had heard it rumoured about that Mrs. Proudie did not confine herself to her wardrobes, still-rooms, and laundries; but yet it had never occurred to him that if he called on a bishop at one o'clock in the day, he could by any possibility find him closeted with his wife; or that if he did so, the wife would remain longer than necessary to make her curtsey. It appeared, however, as though in the present case Mrs. Proudie had no idea of retreating.

The bishop had been very much pleased with Dr. Gwynne on the preceding day, and of course thought that Dr. Gwynne had been as much pleased with him. He attributed the visit solely to compliment, and thought it an extremely gracious and proper thing for the master of Lazarus to drive over from Plumstead specially to call at the palace so soon after his arrival in the country. The fact that they were not on the same side either in politics or doctrines made the compliment the greater. The bishop, therefore, was all smiles. And Mrs. Proudie, who liked people with good handles to their names, was also very well disposed to welcome the master of Lazarus.

'We had a charming party at Ullathorne, Master, had we not ?' said she. 'I hope Mrs. Grantly got home without fatigue.'

Dr. Gwynne said that they had all been a little tired, but were none the worse this morning.

'An excellent person, Miss Thorne,' suggested the bishop.

'And an exemplary Christian, I am told,' said Mrs. Proudie.

Dr. Gwynne declared that he was very glad to hear it.

'I have not seen her Sabbath-day schools yet,' continued the lady, 'but I shall make a point of doing so before long.'

Dr. Gwynne merely bowed at this intimation. He had heard something of Mrs. Proudie and her Sunday schools, both from Dr. Grantly and Mr. Harding.

'By the bye, Master,' continued the lady, 'I wonder whether Mrs. Grantly would like me to drive over and inspect her Sabbath-day school. I hear that it is most excellently kept.'

Dr. Gwynne really could not say. He had no doubt Mrs. Grantly would be most happy to see Mrs. Proudie any day Mrs. Proudie would do her the honour of calling: that was, of course, if Mrs. Grantly should happen to be at home.

A slight cloud darkened the lady's brow. She saw that her offer was not taken in good part. This generation of unregenerated vipers was still perverse, stiffnecked, and hardened in their iniquity. 'The archdeacon, I know,' said she, 'sets his face against these institutions.'

At this Dr. Gwynne laughed slightly. It was but a smile. Had he given his cap for it he could not have helped it.

Mrs. Proudie frowned again. ' "Suffer little children, and forbid them not," ' said she. ' Are we not to remember that, Dr. Gwynne ? "Take heed that ye despise not one of these little ones." Are we not to remember that, Dr. Gwynne ? ' And at each of these questions she raised at him her menacing forefinger.

'Certainly, madam, certainly,' said the master, 'and so does the archdeacon, I am sure, on week days as well as on Sundays.'

'On week days you can't take heed not to despise them,' said Mrs. Proudie, 'because then they are out in the fields. On week days they belong to their parents, but on Sundays they ought to belong to the clergyman.' And the finger was again raised.

The master began to understand and to share the intense disgust which the archdeacon always expressed when Mrs. Proudie's name was mentioned. What was he to do with such a woman as this ? To take his hat and go would have been his natural resource; but then he did not wish to be foiled in his object.

'My lord,' said he, 'I wanted to ask you a question on business, if you could spare me one moment's leisure. I know I must apologise for so disturbing you; but in truth I will not detain you five minutes.'

'Certainly, Master, certainly,' said the bishop; 'my time is quite yours,—pray make no apology, pray make no apology.'

'You have a great deal to do just at the present moment, bishop. Do not forget how extremely busy you are at present,' said Mrs. Proudie, whose spirit was now up; for she was angry with her visitor.

'I will not delay his lordship much above a minute,' said the master of Lazarus, rising from his chair, and expecting that Mrs. Proudie would now go, or else that the bishop would lead the way into another room.

But neither event seemed likely to occur, and Dr. Gwynne stood for a moment silent in the middle of the room.

'Perhaps it's about Hiram's hospital?' suggested Mrs. Proudie.

Dr. Gwynne, lost in astonishment, and not knowing what else on earth to do, confessed that his business with the bishop was connected with Hiram's hospital.

'His lordship has finally conferred the appointment on Mr. Quiverful this morning,' said the lady

Dr. Gwynne made a simple reference to the bishop, and finding that the lady's statement was formally confirmed, he took his leave. 'That comes of the reform bill,' he said to himself as he walked down the bishop's avenue. 'Well, at any rate the Greek play bishops were not so bad as that.'

It has been said that Mr. Slope, as he started for Ulla-thorne, received a despatch from his friend, Mr. Towers, which had the effect of putting him in that high good-humour which subsequent events somewhat untowardly damped. It ran as follows. Its shortness will be its sufficient apology.

'My dear Sir,—I wish you every success. I don't know that I can help you, but if I can, I will.

'Yours ever,
'T. T.
'30/9/185—'

There was more in this than in all Sir Nicholas Fitz-whiggin's flummery; more than in all the bishop's promises, even had they been ever so sincere; more than in any archbishop's good word, even had it been possible to obtain it. Tom Towers would do for him what he could.

Mr. Slope had from his youth upwards been a firm believer in the public press. He had dabbled in it himself ever since he had taken his degree, and regarded it as the great arranger and distributor of all future British terrestrial affairs whatever. He had not yet arrived at the age, an age which sooner or later comes to most of us, which dissipates the golden dreams of youth. He delighted in the idea of wresting power from the hands of his country's magnates, and placing it in a custody which was at any rate nearer to his own reach. Sixty thousand broad sheets dispersing themselves daily among his reading fellow-citizens, formed in his eyes a better depôt for supremacy than a throne at Windsor, a cabinet in Downing Street, or even an assembly at Westminster. And on this subject we must not quarrel with Mr. Slope, for the feeling is too general to be met with disrespect.

Tom Towers was as good, if not better than his promise. On the following morning the Jupiter, spouting forth public opinion with sixty thousand loud clarions, did proclaim to the world that Mr. Slope was the fitting man for the vacant post. It was pleasant for Mr. Slope to read the following lines in the Barchester news-room, which he did within thirty minutes after the morning train from London had reached the city.

' It is just now five years since we called the attention of our readers to the quiet city of Barchester. From that day to this, we have in no way meddled with the affairs of that happy ecclesiastical community. Since then, an old bishop has died there, and a young bishop has been installed; but we believe we did not do more than give some customary record of the interesting event. Nor are we now about to meddle very deeply in the affairs of the diocese. If any of the chapter feel a qualm of conscience on reading thus far, let it be quieted. Above all, let the mind of the new bishop be at rest. We are now not armed for war, but approach the reverend towers of the old cathedral with an olive-branch in our hands.

' It will be remembered that at the time alluded to, now five years past, we had occasion to remark on the state of a charity in Barchester called Hiram's Hospital. We thought that it was maladministered, and that the very estimable and reverend gentleman who held the office of warden was somewhat too highly paid for duties which were somewhat too easily performed. This gentleman— and we say it in all sincerity and with no touch of sarcasm —had never looked on the matter in this light before. We do not wish to take praise to ourselves whether praise be due to us or not. But the consequence of our remark was, that the warden did look into the matter, and finding on so doing that he himself could come to no other opinion than that expressed by us, he very creditably threw up the appointment. The then bishop as creditably declined to fill the vacancy till the affair was put on a better footing. Parliament then took it up ; and we have now the satisfaction of informing our readers that Hiram's hospital will be immediately re-opened under new auspices. Heretofore, provision was made for the maintenance of twelve old men. This will now be extended to the fair sex, and twelve elderly women, if any such can be found in Barchester, will be added to the establishment. There will be a matron ; there will, it is hoped, be schools attached for the poorest of the children of the poor, and there will be a steward. The warden, for there will still be a warden, will receive an income more in keeping with the extent of the charity than that heretofore paid. The stipend we believe will be 450*l.* We may add that the excellent house which the former warden inhabited will still be attached to the situation.

' Barchester hospital cannot perhaps boast a world-wide reputation ; but as we adverted to its state of decadence, we think it right also to advert to its renaissance. May it go on and prosper. Whether the salutary reform which has been introduced within its walls has been carried as far as could have been desired, may be doubtful. The important question of the school appears to be somewhat left to the discretion of the new warden. This might have been made the most important part of the establishment, and the new warden, whom we trust we shall not offend by the freedom of our remarks, might have been selected with some view to his fitness as schoolmaster. But we will not now look a gift horse in the mouth. May the hospital go on and prosper! The situation of warden has of course been offered to the gentleman who so honourably vacated it five years since; but we are given to understand that he has declined it. Whether the ladies who have been introduced, be in his estimation too much for his powers of control, whether it be that the diminished income does not offer to him sufficient temptation to resume his old place, or that he has in the meantime assumed other clerical duties, we do not know. We are, however, informed that he has refused the offer, and that the situation has been accepted by Mr. Quiverful, the vicar of Puddingdale.

'So much we think is due to Hiram redivivus. But while we are on the subject of Barchester, we will venture with all respectful humility to express our opinion on another matter, connected with the ecclesiastical polity of that ancient city. Dr. Trefoil, the dean, died yesterday. A short record of his death, giving his age, and the various pieces of preferment which he has at different times held, will be found in another column of this paper. The only fault we knew in him was his age, and as that is a crime of which we all hope to be guilty, we will not bear heavily on it. May he rest in peace! But though the great age of an expiring dean cannot be made matter of reproach, we are not inclined to look on such a fault as at all pardon-able in a dean just brought to the birth. We do hope that the days of sexagenarian appointments are past. If we want deans, we must want them for some purpose. That purpose will necessarily be better fulfilled by a man of forty than by a man of sixty. If we are to pay deans at all, we are to pay them for some sort of work. That work, be it what it may, will be best performed by a workman in the prime of life. Dr. Trefoil, we see, was eighty when he died. As we have as yet completed no plan for pensioning superannuated clergymen, we do not wish to get rid of any existing deans of that age. But we prefer having as few such as possible. If a man of seventy be now appointed, we beg to point out to Lord —— that he will be past all use in a year or two, if indeed he be not so at the present moment. His lordship will allow us to remind him that all men are not evergreens like himself.

'We hear that Mr. Slope's name has been mentioned for this preferment. Mr. Slope is at present chaplain to the bishop. A better man could hardly be selected. He is a man of talent, young, active, and conversant with the affairs of the cathedral; he is moreover, we conscientiously believe, a truly pious clergyman. We know that his services in the city of Barchester have been highly appreciated. He is an eloquent preacher and a ripe scholar. Such a selection as this would go far to raise the confidence of the public in the present administration of church patronage, and would teach men to believe that from henceforth the establishment of our church will not afford easy couches to worn-out clerical voluptuaries.'

Standing at a reading-desk in the Barchester newsroom, Mr. Slope digested this article with considerable satisfaction. What was therein said as to the hospital was now comparatively matter of indifference to him. He was certainly glad that he had not succeeded in restoring to the place the father of that virago who had so audaciously outraged all decency in his person; and was so far satisfied. But Mrs. Proudie's nominee was appointed, and he was so far dissatisfied. His mind, however, was now soaring above Mrs. Bold or Mrs. Proudie. He was sufficiently conversant with the tactics of the Jupiter to know that the pith of the article would lie in the last paragraph. The place of honour was given to him, and it was indeed as honourable as even he could have wished. He was very grateful to his friend Mr. Towers, and with full heart looked forward to the day when he might entertain him in princely style at his own full-spread board in the deanery dining-room.

It had been well for Mr. Slope that Dr. Trefoil had died in the autumn. Those caterers for our morning repast, the staff of the Jupiter, had been sorely put to it for the last month to find a sufficiency of proper pabulum. Just then there was no talk of a new American president. No wonderful tragedies had occurred on railway trains in Georgia, or elsewhere. There was a dearth of broken banks, and a dead dean with the necessity for a live one was a godsend. Had Dr. Trefoil died in June, Mr. Towers would probably not have known so much about the piety of Mr. Slope.

And here we will leave Mr. Slope for a while in his triumph; explaining, however, that his feelings were not altogether of a triumphant nature. His rejection by the widow, or rather the method of his rejection, galled him terribly. For days to come he positively felt the sting upon his cheek, whenever he thought of what had been done to him. He could not refrain from calling her by harsh names, speaking to himself as he walked through the streets of Barchester. When he said his prayers, he could not bring himself to forgive her. When he strove to do so, his mind recoiled from the attempt, and in lieu of forgiving ran off in a double spirit of vindictiveness, dwelling on the extent of the injury he had received. And so his prayers dropped senseless from his lips.

And then the signora; what would he not have given to be able to hate her also? As it was, he worshipped the very sofa on which she was ever lying. And thus it was not all rose colour with Mr. Slope, although his hopes ran high.

CHAPTER XLIV

MRS. BOLD AT HOME

POOR Mrs. Bold, when she got home from Ullathorne on the evening of Miss Thorne's party, was very unhappy, and moreover, very tired. Nothing fatigues the body so much as weariness of spirit, and Eleanor's spirit was indeed weary.

Dr. Stanhope had civilly but not very cordially asked her in to tea, and her manner of refusal convinced the worthy doctor that he need not repeat the invitation. He had not exactly made himself a party to the intrigue which was to convert the late Mr. Bold's patrimony into an income for his hopeful son, but he had been well aware what was going on. And he was well aware also, when he perceived that Bertie declined accompanying them home in the carriage, that the affair had gone off.

Eleanor was very much afraid that Charlotte would have darted out upon her, as the prebendary got out at his own door, but Bertie had thoughtfully saved her from this, by causing the carriage to go round by her own house. This also Dr. Stanhope understood, and allowed to pass by without remark.

When she got home, she found Mary Bold in the drawing-room with the child in her lap. She rushed forward, and, throwing herself on her knees, kissed the little fellow till she almost frightened him.

'Oh, Mary, I am so glad you did not go. It was an odious party.'

Now the question of Mary's going had been one greatly mooted between them. Mrs. Bold, when invited, had been the guest of the Grantlys, and Miss Thorne, who had chiefly known Eleanor at the hospital or at Plumstead rectory, had forgotten all about Mary Bold. Her sister-in-law had implored her to go under her wing, and had offered to write to Miss Thorne, or to call on her. But Miss Bold had declined. In fact, Mr. Bold had not been very popular with such people as the Thornes, and his sister would not go among them unless she were specially asked to do so.

'Well then,' said Mary, cheerfully, 'I have the less to regret.'

'You have nothing to regret; but oh! Mary, I have—so much—so much;'—and then she began kissing her boy, whom her caresses had aroused from his slumbers. When she raised her head, Mary saw that the tears were running down her cheeks.

'Good heavens, Eleanor, what is the matter? what has happened to you?—Eleanor—dearest Eleanor—what is the matter?' and Mary got up with the boy still in her arms.

'Give him to me—give him to me,' said the young mother. 'Give him to me, Mary,' and she almost tore the child out of her sister's arms. The poor little fellow murmured somewhat at the disturbance, but nevertheless nestled himself close into his mother's bosom.

'Here, Mary, take the cloak from me. My own, own darling, darling, darling jewel. You are not false to me. Everybody else is false; everybody else is cruel. Mamma will care for nobody, nobody, nobody, but her own, own, own little man;' and she again kissed and pressed the baby, and cried till the tears ran down over the child's face.

'Who has been cruel to you, Eleanor?' said Mary. 'I hope I have not.'

Now, in this matter, Eleanor had great cause for mental uneasiness. She could not certainly accuse her loving sister-in-law of cruelty; but she had to do that which was more galling; she had to accuse herself of imprudence against which her sister-in-law had warned her. Miss Bold had never encouraged Eleanor's acquaintance with Mr. Slope, and she had positively discouraged the friendship of the Stanhopes as far as her usual gentle mode of speaking had permitted. Eleanor had only laughed at her, however, when she said that she disapproved of married women who lived apart from their husbands, and suggested that Charlotte Stanhope never went to church. Now, however, Eleanor must either hold her tongue, which was quite impossible, or confess herself to have been utterly wrong, which was nearly equally so. So she staved off the evil day by more tears, and consoled herself by inducing little Johnny to rouse himself sufficiently to return her caresses.

'He is a darling—as true as gold. What would mamma do without him? Mamma would lie down and die if she had not her own Johnny Bold to give her comfort.' This and much more she said of the same kind, and for a time made no other answer to Mary's inquiries.

This kind of consolation from the world's deceit is very common.

Mothers obtain it from their children, and men from their dogs. Some men even do so from their walking-sticks, which is just as rational. How is it that we can take joy to ourselves in that we are not deceived by those who have not attained the art to deceive us? In a true man, if such can be found, or a true woman, much consolation may indeed be taken.

In the caresses of her child, however, Eleanor did receive consolation; and may ill befall the man who would begrudge it to her. The evil day, however, was only postponed. She had to tell her disagreeable tale to Mary, and she had also to tell it to her father. Must it not, indeed, be told to the whole circle of her acquaintance

before she could be made to stand all right with them ?
At the present moment there was no one to whom she
could turn for comfort. She hated Mr. Slope; that was
a matter of course, in that feeling she revelled. She hated
and despised the Stanhopes; but that feeling distressed
her greatly. She had, as it were, separated herself from her
old friends to throw herself into the arms of this family;
and then how had they intended to use her ? She could
hardly reconcile herself to her own father, who had
believed ill of her. Mary Bold had turned Mentor. That
she could have forgiven had the Mentor turned out to be
in the wrong; but Mentors in the right are not to be
pardoned. She could not but hate the archdeacon; and
now she hated him worse than ever, for she must in some
sort humble herself before him. She hated her sister, for
she was part and parcel of the archdeacon. And she would
have hated Mr. Arabin if she could. He had pretended to
regard her, and yet before her face he had hung over that
Italian woman as though there had been no beauty in the
world but hers—no other woman worth a moment's
attention. And Mr. Arabin would have to learn all this
about Mr. Slope ! She told herself that she hated him,
and she knew that she was lying to herself as she did so.
She had no consolation but her baby, and of that she made
the most. Mary, though she could not surmise what it
was that had so violently affected her sister-in-law, saw
at once that her grief was too great to be kept under
control, and waited patiently till the child should be in
his cradle.

' You'll have some tea, Eleanor,' she said.

' Oh, I don't care,' said she; though in fact she must
have been very hungry, for she had eaten nothing at
Ullathorne.

Mary quietly made the tea, and buttered the bread, laid
aside the cloak, and made things look comfortable.

' He's fast asleep,' said she, ' you're very tired; let me
take him up to bed.'

But Eleanor would not let her sister touch him. She
looked wistfully at her baby's eyes, saw that they were
lost in the deepest slumber, and then made a sort of couch
for him on the sofa. She was determined that nothing
should prevail upon her to let him out of her sight that night.

' Come, Nelly,' said Mary, ' don't be cross with me.
I at least have done nothing to offend you.'

' I an't cross,' said Eleanor.

' Are you angry then ? Surely you can't be angry with
me.'

' No, I an't angry ; at least not with you.'

' If you are not, drink the tea I have made for you.
I am sure you must want it.'

Eleanor did drink it, and allowed herself to be persuaded.
She ate and drank, and as the inner woman was recruited
she felt a little more charitable towards the world at large.
At last she found words to begin her story, and before she
went to bed, she had made a clean breast of it and told
everything—everything, that is, as to the lovers she had
rejected : of Mr. Arabin she said not a word.

' I know I was wrong,' said she, speaking of the blow
she had given to Mr. Slope ; ' but I didn't know what he
might do, and I had to protect myself.'

' He richly deserved it,' said Mary.

' Deserved it ! ' said Eleanor, whose mind as regarded
Mr. Slope was almost bloodthirsty. ' Had I stabbed him
with a dagger, he would have deserved it. But what will
they say about it at Plumstead ? '

' I don't think I should tell them,' said Mary. Eleanor
began to think that she would not.

There could have been no kinder comforter than Mary
Bold. There was not the slightest dash of triumph about
her when she heard of the Stanhope scheme, nor did she
allude to her former opinion when Eleanor called her late
friend Charlotte a base, designing woman. She re-echoed
all the abuse that was heaped on Mr. Slope's head, and
never hinted that she had said as much before. ' I told
you so, I told you so ! ' is the croak of a true Job's comforter. But Mary, when she found her friend lying in her
sorrow and scraping herself with potsherds, forbore to
argue and to exult. Eleanor acknowledged the merit of
the forbearance, and at length allowed herself to be
tranquilised.

On the next day she did not go out of the house.
Barchester she thought would be crowded with Stanhopes
and Slopes ; perhaps also with Arabins and Grantlys.
Indeed there was hardly any one among her friends

whom she could have met, without some cause of uneasiness.

In the course of the afternoon she heard that the dean
was dead ; and she also heard that Mr. Quiverful had been
finally appointed to the hospital.

In the evening her father came to her, and then the
story, or as much of it as she could bring herself to tell him,
had to be repeated.   He was not in truth much surprised
at Mr. Slope's effrontery ; but he was obliged to act as
though he had been, to save his daughter's feelings.   He
was, however, anything but skilful in his deceit, and she
saw through it.

' I see,' said she, ' that you think it only in the common
course of things that Mr. Slope should have treated me in
this way.'   She had said nothing to him about the embrace,
nor yet of the way in which it had been met.

' I do not think it at all strange,' said he, ' that any one
should admire my Eleanor.'

' It is strange to me,' said she, ' that any man should
have so much audacity, without ever having received the
slightest encouragement.'

To this Mr. Harding answered nothing.   With the
archdeacon it would have been the text for a rejoinder,
which would not have disgraced Bildad the Shuhite.

' But you'll tell the archdeacon ? ' asked Mr. Harding.

' Tell him what ? ' said she sharply.

' Or Susan ? ' continued Mr. Harding.   ' You'll tell
Susan ; you'll let them know that they wronged you in
supposing that this man's addresses would be agreeable
to you.'

' They may find that out their own way,' said she ;
' I shall not ever willingly mention Mr. Slope's name to
either of them.'

' But I may.'

' I have no right to hinder you from doing anything that
may be necessary to your own comfort, but pray do not do
it for my sake.   Dr. Grantly never thought well of me,
and never will.   I don't know now that I am even anxious
that he should do so.'

And then they went to the affair of the hospital.   ' But
is it true, papa ? '

' What, my dear ? ' said he.   ' About the dean ?   Yes,

I fear quite true. Indeed I know there is no doubt about it.'

'Poor Miss Trefoil. I am so sorry for her. But I did not mean that,' said Eleanor. 'But about the hospital, papa ? '

'Yes, my dear. I believe it is true that Mr. Quiverful is to have it.'

'Oh, what a shame ! '

'No, my dear, not at all, not at all a shame : I am sure I hope it will suit him.'

'But, papa, you know it is a shame. After all your hopes, all your expectations to get back to your old house, to see it given away in this way to a perfect stranger ! '

'My dear, the bishop had a right to give it to whom he pleased.'

'I deny that, papa. He had no such right. It is not as though you were a candidate for a new piece of preferment. If the bishop has a grain of justice—'

'The bishop offered it to me on his terms, and as I did not like the terms, I refused it. After that, I cannot complain.'

'Terms ! he had no right to make terms.'

'I don't know about that ; but it seems he had the power. But to tell you the truth, Nelly, I am as well satisfied as it is. When the affair became the subject of angry discussion, I thoroughly wished to be rid of it altogether.'

'But you did want to go back to the old house, papa. You told me so yourself.'

'Yes, my dear, I did. For a short time I did wish it. And I was foolish in doing so. I am getting old now ; and my chief worldly wish is for peace and rest. Had I gone back to the hospital, I should have had endless contentions with the bishop, contentions with his chaplain, and contentions with the archdeacon. I am not up to this now, I am not able to meet such troubles ; and therefore I am not ill-pleased to find myself left to the little church of St. Cuthbert's. I shall never starve,' added he, laughing, 'as long as you are here.'

'But will you come and live with me, papa ? ' she said earnestly, taking him by both his hands. 'If you will do that, if you will promise that, I will own that you are right.'

'I will dine with you to-day at any rate.'

'No, but live here altogether. Give up that close, odious little room in High Street.'

'My dear, it's a very nice little room; and you are really quite uncivil.'

'Oh, papa, don't joke. It's not a nice place for you. You say you are growing old, though I am sure you are not.'

'Am not I, my dear?'

'No, papa, not old—not to say old. But you are quite old enough to feel the want of a decent room to sit in. You know how lonely Mary and I are here. You know nobody ever sleeps in the big front bed-room. It is really unkind of you to remain up there alone, when you are so much wanted here.'

'Thank you, Nelly—thank you. But, my dear—'

'If you had been living here, papa, with us, as I really think you ought to have done, considering how lonely we are, there would have been none of all this dreadful affair about Mr. Slope.'

Mr. Harding, however, did not allow himself to be talked over into giving up his own and only little *pied à terre* in the High Street. He promised to come and dine with his daughter, and stay with her, and visit her, and do everything but absolutely live with her. It did not suit the peculiar feelings of the man to tell his daughter that though she had rejected Mr. Slope, and been ready to reject Mr. Stanhope, some other more favoured suitor would probably soon appear; and that on the appearance of such a suitor the big front bed-room might perhaps be more frequently in requisition than at present. But doubtless such an idea crossed his mind, and added its weight to the other reasons which made him decide on still keeping the close, odious little room in High Street.

The evening passed over quietly and in comfort. Eleanor was always happier with her father than with any one else. He had not, perhaps, any natural taste for baby-worship, but he was always ready to sacrifice himself, and therefore made an excellent third in a trio with his daughter and Mary Bold in singing the praises of the wonderful child.

They were standing together over their music in the evening, the baby having again been put to bed upon the sofa, when the servant brought in a very small note in a beautiful pink envelope. It quite filled the room with perfume as it lay upon the small salver. Mary Bold and Mrs. Bold were both at the piano, and Mr. Harding was sitting close to them, with the violoncello between his legs; so that the elegancy of the epistle was visible to them all.

'Please, ma'am, Dr. Stanhope's coachman says he is to wait for an answer,' said the servant.

Eleanor got very red in the face as she took the note in her hand. She had never seen the writing before. Charlotte's epistles, to which she was well accustomed, were of a very different style and kind. She generally wrote on large note-paper; she twisted up her letters into the shape and sometimes into the size of cocked hats; she addressed them in a sprawling manly hand, and not unusually added a blot or a smudge, as though such were her own peculiar sign-manual. The address of this note was written in a beautiful female hand, and the gummed wafer bore on it an impress of a gilt coronet. Though Eleanor had never seen such a one before, she guessed that it came from the signora. Such epistles were very numerously sent out from any house in which the signora might happen to be dwelling, but they were rarely addressed to ladies. When the coachman was told by the lady's maid to take the letter to Mrs. Bold, he openly expressed his opinion that there was some mistake about it. Whereupon the lady's maid boxed the coachman's ears. Had Mr. Slope seen in how meek a spirit the coachman took the rebuke, he might have learnt a useful lesson, both in philosophy and religion.

The note was as follows. It may be taken as a faithful promise that no further letter whatever shall be transcribed at length in these pages.

'My dear Mrs. Bold,—May I ask you, as a great favour, to call on me to-morrow? You can say what hour will best suit you; but quite early, if you can. I need hardly say that if I could call upon you I should not take this liberty with you.

'I partly know what occurred the other day, and I promise you that you shall meet with no annoyance if you will come to me. My brother leaves us for London to-day; from thence he goes to Italy.

'It will probably occur to you that I should not thus intrude on you, unless I had that to say to you which may be of considerable moment. Pray therefore excuse me, even if you do not grant my request, and believe me,

'Very sincerely yours,

'M. VESEY NERONI.

'Thursday Evening.'

The three of them sat in consultation on this epistle for some ten or fifteen minutes, and then decided that Eleanor should write a line saying that she would see the signora the next morning, at twelve o'clock.

CHAPTER XLV

THE STANHOPES AT HOME

WE must now return to the Stanhopes, and see how they behaved themselves on their return from Ullathorne.

Charlotte, who came back in the first homeward journey with her sister, waited in palpitating expectation till the carriage drove up to the door a second time. She did not run down or stand at the window, or show in any outward manner that she looked for anything wonderful to occur; but, when she heard the carriage-wheels, she stood up with erect ears, listening for Eleanor's footfall on the pavement or the cheery sound of Bertie's voice welcoming her in. Had she heard either, she would have felt that all was right; but neither sound was there for her to hear. She heard only her father's slow step, as he ponderously let himself down from the carriage, and slowly walked along the hall, till he got into his own private room on the ground floor. 'Send Miss Stanhope to me,' he said to the servant.

'There's something wrong now,' said Madeline, who was lying on her sofa in the back drawing-room.

'It's all up with Bertie,' replied Charlotte. 'I know, I know,' she said to the servant, as he brought up the message. 'Tell my father I will be with him immediately.'

'Bertie's wooing has gone astray,' said Madeline; 'I knew it would.'

'It has been his own fault then. She was ready enough, I am quite sure,' said Charlotte, with that sort of ill-nature which is not uncommon when one woman speaks of another.

'What will you say to him now?' By 'him,' the signora meant their father.

'That will be as I find him. He was ready to pay two hundred pounds for Bertie, to stave off the worst of his creditors, if this marriage had gone on. Bertie must now have the money instead, and go and take his chance.'

'Where is he now?'

'Heaven knows! smoking in the bottom of Mr. Thorne's ha-ha, or philandering with some of those Miss Chadwicks. Nothing will ever make an impression on him. But he'll be furious if I don't go down.'

'No; nothing ever will. But don't be long, Charlotte, for I want my tea.'

And so Charlotte went down to her father. There was a very black cloud on the old man's brow; blacker than his daughter could ever yet remember to have seen there. He was sitting in his own arm-chair, not comfortably over the fire, but in the middle of the room, waiting till she should come and listen to him.

'What has become of your brother?' he said, as soon as the door was shut.

'I should rather ask you,' said Charlotte. 'I left you both at Ullathorne, when I came away. What have you done with Mrs. Bold?'

'Mrs. Bold! nonsense. The woman has gone home as she ought to do. And heartily glad I am that she should not be sacrificed to so heartless a reprobate.'

'Oh, papa!'

'A heartless reprobate! Tell me now where he is, and what he is going to do. I have allowed myself to be fooled between you. Marriage, indeed! Who on earth that has money, or credit, or respect in the world to lose, would marry him?'

'It is no use your scolding me, papa. I have done the best I could for him and you.'

'And Madeline is nearly as bad,' said the prebendary, who was in truth very, very angry.

'Oh, I suppose we are all bad,' replied Charlotte.

The old man emitted a huge leonine sigh. If they were all bad, who had made them so? If they were unprincipled, selfish, and disreputable, who was to be blamed for the education which had had so injurious an effect?

'I know you'll ruin me among you,' said he.

'Why, papa, what nonsense that is. You are living within your income this minute, and if there are any new debts, I don't know of them. I am sure there ought to be none, for we are dull enough here.'

'Are those bills of Madeline's paid?'

'No, they are not. Who was to pay them?'

'Her husband may pay them.'

'Her husband! would you wish me to tell her you say so? Do you wish to turn her out of your house?'

'I wish she would know how to behave herself.'

'Why, what on earth has she done now? Poor Madeline! To-day is only the second time she has gone out since we came to this vile town.'

He then sat silent for a time, thinking in what shape he would declare his resolve. 'Well, papa,' said Charlotte, 'shall I stay here, or may I go up-stairs and give mamma her tea?'

'You are in your brother's confidence. Tell me what he is going to do?'

'Nothing, that I am aware of.'

'Nothing—nothing! nothing but eat and drink, and spend every shilling of my money he can lay his hands upon. I have made up my mind, Charlotte. He shall eat and drink no more in this house.'

'Very well. Then I suppose he must go back to Italy.'

'He may go where he pleases.'

'That's easily said, papa; but what does it mean? You can't let him——'

'It means this,' said the doctor, speaking more loudly than was his wont, and with wrath flashing from his eyes; 'that as sure as God rules in heaven, I will not maintain him any longer in idleness.'

'Oh, ruling in heaven!' said Charlotte. 'It is no use talking about that. You must rule him here on earth; and the question is, how you can do it. You can't turn him out of the house penniless, to beg about the street.'

'He may beg where he likes.'

'He must go back to Carrara. That is the cheapest place he can live at, and nobody there will give him credit for above two or three hundred pauls. But you must let him have the means of going.'

'As sure as——'

'Oh, papa, don't swear. You know you must do it. You were ready to pay two hundred pounds for him if this marriage came off. Half that will start him to Carrara.'

'What? give him a hundred pounds!'

'You know we are all in the dark, papa,' said she, thinking it expedient to change the conversation. 'For anything we know, he may be at this moment engaged to Mrs. Bold.'

'Fiddlestick,' said the father, who had seen the way in which Mrs. Bold had got into the carriage, while his son stood apart without even offering her his hand.

'Well, then, he must go to Carrara,' said Charlotte.

Just at this moment the lock of the front door was heard, and Charlotte's quick ears detected her brother's cat-like step in the hall. She said nothing, feeling that for the present Bertie had better keep out of her father's way. But Dr. Stanhope also heard the sound of the lock.

'Who's that?' he demanded. Charlotte made no reply, and he asked again, 'Who is that that has just come in? Open the door. Who is it?'

'I suppose it is Bertie.'

'Bid him come here,' said the father. But Bertie, who was close to the door and heard the call, required no further bidding, but walked in with a perfectly unconcerned and cheerful air. It was this peculiar *insouciance* which angered Dr. Stanhope, even more than his son's extravagance.

'Well, sir?' said the doctor.

'And how did you get home, sir, with your fair companion?' said Bertie. 'I suppose she is not up-stairs, Charlotte?'

'Bertie,' said Charlotte, 'papa is in no humour for joking. He is very angry with you.'

'Angry!' said Bertie, raising his eyebrows, as though he had never yet given his parent cause for a single moment's uneasiness.

'Sit down, if you please, sir,' said Dr. Stanhope very sternly, but not now very loudly. 'And I'll trouble you to sit down too, Charlotte. Your mother can wait for her tea a few minutes.'

Charlotte sat down on the chair nearest to the door, in somewhat of a perverse sort of manner; as much as though she would say—Well, here I am; you shan't say I don't do what I am bid; but I'll be whipped if I give way to you. And she was determined not to give way. She too was angry with Bertie; but she was not the less ready on that account to defend him from his father. Bertie also sat down. He drew his chair close to the library-table, upon which he put his elbow, and then resting his face comfortably on one hand, he began drawing little pictures on a sheet of paper with the other. Before the scene was over he had completed admirable figures of Miss Thorne, Mrs. Proudie, and Lady De Courcy, and begun a family piece to comprise the whole set of the Lookalofts.

'Would it suit you, sir,' said the father, 'to give me some idea as to what your present intentions are?—what way of living you propose to yourself?'

'I'll do anything you can suggest, sir,' replied Bertie.

'No, I shall suggest nothing further. My time for suggesting has gone by. I have only one order to give, and that is, that you leave my house.'

'To-night?' said Bertie; and the simple tone of the question left the doctor without any adequately dignified method of reply.

'Papa does not quite mean to-night,' said Charlotte, 'at least I suppose not.'

'To-morrow, perhaps,' suggested Bertie.

'Yes, sir, to-morrow,' said the doctor. 'You shall leave this to-morrow.'

'Very well, sir. Will the 4.30 P.M. train be soon enough?' and Bertie, as he asked, put the finishing touch to Miss Thorne's high-heeled boots.

'You may go how and when and where you please, so

that you leave my house to-morrow. You have disgraced me, sir; you have disgraced yourself, and me, and your sisters.'

'I am glad at least, sir, that I have not disgraced my mother,' said Bertie.

Charlotte could hardly keep her countenance; but the doctor's brow grew still blacker than ever. Bertie was executing his *chef d'œuvre* in the delineation of Mrs. Proudie's nose and mouth.

'You are a heartless reprobate, sir; a heartless, thankless, good-for-nothing reprobate. I have done with you. You are my son—that I cannot help; but you shall have no more part or parcel in me as my child, nor I in you as your father.'

'Oh, papa, papa! you must not, shall not say so,' said Charlotte.

'I will say so, and do say so,' said the father, rising from his chair. 'And now leave the room, sir.'

'Stop, stop,' said Charlotte; 'why don't you speak, Bertie? why don't you look up and speak? It is your manner that makes papa so angry.'

'He is perfectly indifferent to all decency, to all propriety,' said the doctor; and then he shouted out, 'Leave the room, sir! Do you hear what I say?'

'Papa, papa, I will not let you part so. I know you will be sorry for it.' And then she added, getting up and whispering into his ear, 'Is he only to blame? Think of that. We have made our own bed, and, such as it is, we must lie on it. It is no use for us to quarrel among ourselves,' and as she finished her whisper Bertie finished off the countess's bustle, which was so well done that it absolutely seemed to be swaying to and fro on the paper with its usual lateral motion.

'My father is angry at the present time,' said Bertie, looking up for a moment from his sketches, 'because I am not going to marry Mrs. Bold. What can I say on the matter? It is true that I am not going to marry her. In the first place——'

'That is not true, sir,' said Dr. Stanhope; 'but I will not argue with you.'

'You were angry just this moment because I would not speak,' said Bertie, going on with a young Lookaloft.

'Give over drawing,' said Charlotte, going up to him and taking the paper from under his hand. The caricatures, however, she preserved, and showed them afterwards to the friends of the Thornes, the Proudies, and De Courcys. Bertie, deprived of his occupation, threw himself back in his chair and waited further orders.

'I think it will certainly be for the best that Bertie should leave this at once, perhaps to-morrow,' said Charlotte; 'but pray, papa, let us arrange some scheme together.'

'If he will leave this to-morrow, I will give him 10*l*., and he shall be paid 5*l*. a month by the banker at Carrara as long as he stays permanently in that place.'

'Well, sir! it won't be long,' said Bertie; 'for I shall be starved to death in about three months.'

'He must have marble to work with,' said Charlotte.

'I have plenty there in the studio to last me three months,' said Bertie. 'It will be no use attempting anything large in so limited a time; unless I do my own tombstone.'

Terms, however, were ultimately come to, somewhat more liberal than those proposed, and the doctor was induced to shake hands with his son, and bid him good night. Dr. Stanhope would not go up to tea, but had it brought to him in his study by his daughter.

But Bertie went up-stairs and spent a pleasant evening. He finished the Lookalofts, greatly to the delight of his sisters, though the manner of portraying their *décolleté* dresses was not the most refined. Finding how matters were going, he by degrees allowed it to escape from him that he had not pressed his suit upon the widow in a very urgent way.

'I suppose, in point of fact, you never proposed at all?' said Charlotte.

'Oh, she understood that she might have me if she wished,' said he.

'And she didn't wish,' said the signora.

'You have thrown me over in the most shameful manner,' said Charlotte. 'I suppose you told her all about my little plan?'

'Well, it came out somehow; at least the most of it.'

'There's an end of that alliance,' said Charlotte; 'but

it doesn't matter much. I suppose we shall all be back at Como soon.'

'I am sure I hope so,' said the signora; 'I'm sick of the sight of black coats. If that Mr. Slope comes here any more, he'll be the death of me.'

'You've been the ruin of him, I think,' said Charlotte.

'And as for a second black-coated lover of mine, I am going to make a present of him to another lady with most singular disinterestedness.'

The next day, true to his promise, Bertie packed up and went off by the 4.30 P.M. train, with 20*l.* in his pocket, bound for the marble quarries of Carrara. And so he disappears from our scene.

At twelve o'clock on the day following that on which Bertie went, Mrs. Bold, true also to her word, knocked at Dr. Stanhope's door with a timid hand and palpitating heart. She was at once shown up to the back drawing-room, the folding doors of which were closed, so that in visiting the signora Eleanor was not necessarily thrown into any communion with those in the front room. As she went up the stairs, she saw none of the family, and was so far saved much of the annoyance which she had dreaded.

'This is very kind of you, Mrs. Bold; very kind, after what has happened,' said the lady on the sofa with her sweetest smile.

'You wrote in such a strain that I could not but come to you.'

'I did, I did; I wanted to force you to see me.'

'Well, signora; I am here.'

'How cold you are to me. But I suppose I must put up with that. I know you think you have reason to be displeased with us all. Poor Bertie! if you knew all, you would not be angry with him.'

'I am not angry with your brother—not in the least. But I hope you did not send for me here to talk about him.'

'If you are angry with Charlotte, that is worse; for you have no warmer friend in all Barchester. But I did *not* send for you to talk about this,—pray bring your chair nearer, Mrs. Bold, so that I may look at you. It is so unnatural to see you keeping so far off from me.'

Eleanor did as she was bid, and brought her chair close to the sofa.

'And now, Mrs. Bold, I am going to tell you something which you may perhaps think indelicate ; but yet I know that I am right in doing so.'

Hereupon Mrs. Bold said nothing, but felt inclined to shake in her chair. The signora, she knew, was not very particular, and that which to her appeared to be indelicate might to Mrs. Bold appear to be extremely indecent.

'I believe you know Mr. Arabin ? '

Mrs. Bold would have given the world not to blush, but her blood was not at her own command. She did blush up to her forehead, and the signora, who had made her sit in a special light in order that she might watch her, saw that she did so.

'Yes,—I am acquainted with him. That is, slightly. He is an intimate friend of Dr. Grantly, and Dr. Grantly is my brother-in-law.'

'Well; if you know Mr. Arabin, I am sure you must like him. I know and like him much. Everybody that knows him must like him.'

Mrs. Bold felt it quite impossible to say anything in reply to this. Her blood was rushing about her body she knew not how or why. She felt as though she were swinging in her chair ; and she knew that she was not only red in the face, but also almost suffocated with heat. However, she sat still and said nothing.

'How stiff you are with me, Mrs. Bold,' said the signora ; 'and I the while am doing for you all that one woman can do to serve another.'

A kind of thought came over the widow's mind that perhaps the signora's friendship was real, and that at any rate it could not hurt her ; and another kind of thought, a glimmering of a thought, came to her also,—that Mr. Arabin was too precious to be lost. She despised the signora ; but might she not stoop to conquer ? It should be but the smallest fraction of a stoop !

'I don't want to be stiff,' she said, 'but your questions are so very singular.'

'Well, then, I will ask you one more singular still,' said Madeline Neroni, raising herself on her elbow and turning her own face full upon her companion's. 'Do you love him, love him with all your heart and soul, with all the love your bosom can feel ? For I can tell you that he loves you, adores you, worships you, thinks of you and nothing else, is now thinking of you as he attempts to write his sermon for next Sunday's preaching. What would I not give to be loved in such a way by such a man, that is, if I were an object fit for any man to love!'

Mrs. Bold got up from her seat and stood speechless before the woman who was now addressing her in this impassioned way. When the signora thus alluded to herself, the widow's heart was softened, and she put her own hand, as though caressingly, on that of her companion which was resting on the table. The signora grasped it and went on speaking.

'What I tell you is God's own truth; and it is for you to use it as may be best for your own happiness. But you must not betray me. He knows nothing of this. He knows nothing of my knowing his inmost heart. He is simple as a child in these matters. He told me his secret in a thousand ways because he could not dissemble; but he does not dream that he has told it. You know it now, and I advise you to use it.'

Eleanor returned the pressure of the other's hand with an infinitesimal *soupçon* of a squeeze.

'And remember,' continued the signora, 'he is not like other men. You must not expect him to come to you with vows and oaths and pretty presents, to kneel at your feet, and kiss your shoe-strings. If you want that, there are plenty to do it; but he won't be one of them.' Eleanor's bosom nearly burst with a sigh; but Madeline, not heeding her, went on. 'With him, yea will stand for yea, and nay for nay. Though his heart should break for it, the woman who shall reject him once, will have rejected him once and for all. Remember that. And now, Mrs. Bold, I will not keep you, for you are fluttered. I partly guess what use you will make of what I have said to you. If ever you are a happy wife in that man's house, we shall be far away; but I shall expect you to write me one line to say that you have forgiven the sins of the family.'

Eleanor half whispered that she would, and then, without uttering another word, crept out of the room, and down the stairs, opened the front door for herself without hearing or seeing any one, and found herself in the close.

It would be difficult to analyse Eleanor's feelings as she

walked home. She was nearly stupefied by the things that had been said to her. She felt sore that her heart should have been so searched and riddled by a comparative stranger, by a woman whom she had never liked and never could like. She was mortified that the man whom she owned to herself that she loved should have concealed his love from her and shown it to another. There was much to vex her proud spirit. But there was, nevertheless, an under-stratum of joy in all this which buoyed her up wondrously. She tried if she could disbelieve what Madame Neroni had said to her; but she found that she could not. It was true; it must be true. She could not, would not, did not doubt it.

On one point she fully resolved to follow the advice given her. If it should ever please Mr. Arabin to put such a question to her as that suggested, her 'yea' should be 'yea'. Would not all her miseries be at an end, if she could talk of them to him openly, with her head resting on his shoulder ?

CHAPTER XLVI

MR. SLOPE'S PARTING INTERVIEW WITH THE SIGNORA

ON the following day the signora was in her pride. She was dressed in her brightest of morning dresses, and had quite a *levée* round her couch. It was a beautifully bright October afternoon; all the gentlemen of the neighbourhood were in Barchester, and those who had the entry of Dr. Stanhope's house were in the signora's back drawing-room. Charlotte and Mrs. Stanhope were in the front room, and such of the lady's squires as could not for the moment get near the centre of attraction had to waste their fragrance on the mother and sister.

The first who came and the last to leave was Mr. Arabin. This was the second visit he had paid to Madame Neroni since he had met her at Ullathorne. He came he knew not why, to talk about he knew not what. But, in truth, the feelings which now troubled him were new to him, and he could not analyse them. It may seem strange that he should thus come dangling about Madame Neroni because he was in love with Mrs. Bold; but it was never-

theless the fact; and though he could not understand
why he did so, Madame Neroni understood it well enough.
She had been gentle and kind to him, and had encouraged his staying. Therefore he stayed on. She pressed
his hand when he first greeted her; she made him remain
near her; and whispered to him little nothings. And
then her eye, brilliant and bright, now mirthful, now
melancholy, and invincible in either way! What man
with warm feelings, blood unchilled, and a heart not
guarded by a triple steel of experience could have with-
stood those eyes! The lady, it is true, intended to do him
no mortal injury; she merely chose to inhale a slight
breath of incense before she handed the casket over to
another. Whether Mrs. Bold would willingly have spared
even so much is another question.

And then came Mr. Slope. All the world now knew
that Mr. Slope was a candidate for the deanery, and that
he was generally considered to be the favourite. Mr. Slope,
therefore, walked rather largely upon the earth. He gave
to himself a portly air, such as might become a dean, spoke
but little to other clergymen, and shunned the bishop as
much as possible. How the meagre little prebendary,
and the burly chancellor, and all the minor canons and
vicars choral, ay, and all the choristers too, cowered and
shook and walked about with long faces when they read
or heard of that article in the Jupiter. Now were coming
the days when nothing would avail to keep the impure
spirit from the cathedral pulpit. That pulpit would
indeed be his own. Precentors, vicars, and choristers
might hang up their harps on the willows. Ichabod!
Ichabod! the glory of their house was departing from
them.

Mr. Slope, great as he was with embryo grandeur, still
came to see the signora. Indeed, he could not keep himself
away. He dreamed of that soft hand which he had kissed
so often, and of that imperial brow which his lips had
once pressed, and he then dreamed also of further favours.

And Mr. Thorne was there also. It was the first visit
he had ever paid to the signora, and he made it not without
due preparation. Mr. Thorne was a gentleman usually
precise in his dress, and prone to make the most of himself
in an unpretending way. The grey hairs in his whiskers

were eliminated perhaps once a month; those on his head were softened by a mixture which we will not call a dye; it was only a wash. His tailor lived in St. James's Street, and his bootmaker at the corner of that street and Piccadilly. He was particular in the article of gloves, and the getting up of his shirts was a matter not lightly thought of in the Ullathorne laundry. On the occasion of the present visit he had rather overdone his usual efforts, and caused some little uneasiness to his sister, who had not hitherto received very cordially the proposition for a lengthened visit from the signora at Ullathorne.

There were others also there—young men about the city who had not much to do, and who were induced by the lady's charms to neglect that little; but all gave way to Mr. Thorne, who was somewhat of a grand signior, as a country gentleman always is in a provincial city.

'Oh, Mr. Thorne, this is so kind of you!' said the signora. 'You promised to come; but I really did not expect it. I thought you country gentlemen never kept your pledges.'

'Oh, yes, sometimes,' said Mr. Thorne, looking rather sheepish, and making his salutations a little too much in the style of the last century.

'You deceive none but your consti—stit—stit; what do you call the people that carry you about in chairs and pelt you with eggs and apples when they make you a member of Parliament?'

'One another also, sometimes, signora,' said Mr. Slope, with a deanish sort of smirk on his face. 'Country gentlemen do deceive one another sometimes, don't they, Mr. Thorne?'

Mr. Thorne gave him a look which undeaned him completely for the moment; but he soon remembered his high hopes, and recovering himself quickly, sustained his probable coming dignity by a laugh at Mr. Thorne's expense.

'I never deceive a lady, at any rate,' said Mr. Thorne; 'especially when the gratification of my own wishes is so strong an inducement to keep me true, as it now is.'

Mr. Thorne went on thus awhile with antediluvian grimaces and compliments which he had picked up from

Sir Charles Grandison, and the signora at every grimace and at every bow smiled a little smile and bowed a little bow. Mr. Thorne, however, was kept standing at the foot of the couch, for the new dean sat in the seat of honour near the table. Mr. Arabin the while was standing with his back to the fire, his coat tails under his arms, gazing at her with all his eyes—not quite in vain, for every now and again a glance came up at him, bright as a meteor out of heaven.

'Oh, Mr. Thorne, you promised to let me introduce my little girl to you. Can you spare a moment?—will you see her now?'

Mr. Thorne assured her that he could, and would see the young lady with the greatest pleasure in life. 'Mr. Slope, might I trouble you to ring the bell?' said she; and when Mr. Slope got up she looked at Mr. Thorne and pointed to the chair. Mr. Thorne, however, was much too slow to understand her, and Mr. Slope would have recovered his seat had not the signora, who never chose to be unsuccessful, somewhat summarily ordered him out of it.

'Oh, Mr. Slope, I must ask you to let Mr. Thorne sit here just for a moment or two. I am sure you will pardon me. We can take a liberty with you this week. Next week, you know, when you move into the dean's house, we shall all be afraid of you.'

Mr. Slope, with an air of much indifference, rose from his seat, and, walking into the next room, became greatly interested in Mrs. Stanhope's worsted work.

And then the child was brought in. She was a little girl, about eight years of age, like her mother, only that her enormous eyes were black, and her hair quite jet. Her complexion, too, was very dark, and bespoke her foreign blood. She was dressed in the most outlandish and extravagant way in which clothes could be put on a child's back. She had great bracelets on her naked little arms, a crimson fillet braided with gold round her head, and scarlet shoes with high heels. Her dress was all flounces, and stuck out from her as though the object were to make it lie off horizontally from her little hips. It did not nearly cover her knees; but this was atoned for by a loose pair of drawers, which seemed made through-

out of lace; then she had on pink silk stockings. It was
thus that the last of the Neros was habitually dressed
at the hour when visitors were wont to call.

'Julia, my love,' said the mother,—Julia was ever a
favourite name with the ladies of that family. 'Julia,
my love, come here. I was telling you about the beautiful
party poor mamma went to. This is Mr. Thorne; will
you give him a kiss, dearest?'

Julia put up her face to be kissed, as she did to all her
mother's visitors; and then Mr. Thorne found that he
had got her, and, which was much more terrific to him,
all her finery, into his arms. The lace and starch crumpled
against his waistcoat and trowsers, the greasy black curls
hung upon his cheek, and one of the bracelet clasps
scratched his ear. He did not at all know how to hold
so magnificent a lady, nor holding her what to do with
her. However, he had on other occasions been compelled
to fondle little nieces and nephews, and now set about the
task in the mode he always had used.

'Diddle, diddle, diddle, diddle,' said he, putting the
child on one knee, and working away with it as though
he were turning a knife-grinder's wheel with his foot.

'Mamma, mamma,' said Julia, crossly, 'I don't want
to be diddle diddled. Let me go, you naughty old man,
you.'

Poor Mr. Thorne put the child down quietly on the
ground, and drew back his chair; Mr. Slope, who had
returned to the pole star that attracted him, laughed
aloud; Mr. Arabin winced and shut his eyes; and the
signora pretended not to hear her daughter.

'Go to Aunt Charlotte, lovey,' said the mamma, 'and
ask her if it is not time for you to go out.'

But little Miss Julia, though she had not exactly liked
the nature of Mr. Thorne's attention, was accustomed to
be played with by gentlemen, and did not relish the idea
of being sent so soon to her aunt.

'Julia, go when I tell you, my dear.' But Julia still
went pouting about the room. 'Charlotte, do come and
take her,' said the signora. 'She must go out; and the
days get so short now.' And thus ended the much-talked
of interview between Mr. Thorne and the last of the Neros.

Mr. Thorne recovered from the child's crossness sooner

than from Mr. Slope's laughter. He could put up with being called an old man by an infant, but he did not like to be laughed at by the bishop's chaplain, even though that chaplain was about to become a dean. He said nothing, but he showed plainly enough that he was angry.

The signora was ready enough to avenge him. 'Mr. Slope,' said she, 'I hear that you are triumphing on all sides.'

'How so?' said he, smiling. He did not dislike being talked to about the deanery, though, of course, he strongly denied the imputation.

'You carry the day both in love and war.' Mr. Slope hereupon did not look quite so satisfied as he had done.

'Mr. Arabin,' continued the signora, 'don't you think Mr. Slope is a very lucky man?'

'Not more so than he deserves, I am sure,' said Mr. Arabin.

'Only think, Mr. Thorne, he is to be our new dean; of course we all know that.'

'Indeed, signora,' said Mr. Slope, 'we all know nothing about it. I can assure you I myself——'

'He *is* to be the new dean—there is no manner of doubt of it, Mr. Thorne.'

'Hum!' said Mr. Thorne.

'Passing over the heads of old men like my father and Archdeacon Grantly——'

'Oh—oh!' said Mr. Slope.

'The archdeacon would not accept it,' said Mr. Arabin; whereupon Mr. Slope smiled abominably, and said, as plainly as a look could speak, that the grapes were sour.

'Going over all our heads,' continued the signora; 'for, of course, I consider myself one of the chapter.'

'If I am ever dean,' said Mr. Slope—'that is, were I ever to become so, I should glory in such a canoness.'

'Oh, Mr. Slope, stop; I haven't half done. There is another canoness for you to glory in. Mr. Slope is not only to have the deanery, but a wife to put in it.'

Mr. Slope again looked disconcerted.

'A wife with a large fortune too. It never rains but it pours, does it, Mr. Thorne?'

'No, never,' said Mr. Thorne, who did not quite relish talking about Mr. Slope and his affairs.

' When will it be, Mr. Slope ? '

' When will what be ? ' said he.

' Oh ! we know when the affair of the dean will be : a week will settle that. The new hat, I have no doubt, has been already ordered. But when will the marriage come off ? '

' Do you mean mine or Mr. Arabin's ? ' said he, striving to be facetious.

' Well, just then I meant yours, though, perhaps, after all, Mr. Arabin's may be first. But we know nothing of him. He is too close for any of us. Now all is open and above board with you ; which, by the bye, Mr. Arabin, I beg to tell you I like much the best. He who runs can read that Mr. Slope is a favoured lover. Come, Mr. Slope, when is the widow to be made Mrs. Dean ? '

To Mr. Arabin this badinage was peculiarly painful ; and yet he could not tear himself away and leave it. He believed, still believed with that sort of belief which the fear of a thing engenders, that Mrs. Bold would probably become the wife of Mr. Slope. Of Mr. Slope's little adventure in the garden he knew nothing. For aught he knew, Mr. Slope might have had an adventure of quite a different character. He might have thrown himself at the widow's feet, been accepted, and then returned to town a jolly, thriving wooer. The signora's jokes were bitter enough to Mr. Slope, but they were quite as bitter to Mr. Arabin. He still stood leaning against the fire-place, fumbling with his hands in his trowsers pockets.

' Come, come, Mr. Slope, don't be so bashful,' continued the signora. ' We all know that you proposed to the lady the other day at Ullathorne. Tell us with what words she accepted you. Was it with a simple " yes," or with two " no no's," which make an affirmative ? or did silence give consent ? or did she speak out with that spirit which so well becomes a widow, and say openly, " By my troth, sir, you shall make me Mrs. Slope as soon as it is your pleasure to do so ? " '

Mr. Slope had seldom in his life felt himself less at his ease. There sat Mr. Thorne, laughing silently. There stood his old antagonist, Mr. Arabin, gazing at him with all his eyes. There round the door between the two rooms were clustered a little group of people, including Miss

Stanhope and the Rev. Messrs. Gray and Green, all listening to his discomfiture. He knew that it depended solely on his own wit whether or no he could throw the joke back upon the lady. He knew that it stood him to do so if he possibly could ; but he had not a word. ' 'Tis conscience that makes cowards of us all.' He felt on his cheek the sharp points of Eleanor's fingers, and did not know who might have seen the blow, who might have told the tale to this pestilent woman who took such delight in jeering him. He stood there, therefore, red as a carbuncle and mute as a fish ; grinning just sufficiently to show his teeth ; an object of pity.

But the signora had no pity ; she knew nothing of mercy. Her present object was to put Mr. Slope down, and she was determined to do it thoroughly, now that she had him in her power.

' What, Mr. Slope, no answer ? Why it can't possibly be that the woman has been fool enough to refuse you ? She can't surely be looking out after a bishop. But I see how it is, Mr. Slope. Widows are proverbially cautious. You should have let her alone till the new hat was on your head ; till you could show her the key of the deanery.'

' Signora,' said he at last, trying to speak in a tone of dignified reproach, ' you really permit yourself to talk on solemn subjects in a very improper way.'

' Solemn subjects—what solemn subject ? Surely a dean's hat is not such a solemn subject.'

' I have no aspirations such as those you impute to me. Perhaps you will drop the subject.'

' Oh certainly, Mr. Slope ; but one word first. Go to her again with the prime minister's letter in your pocket. I'll wager my shawl to your shovel she does not refuse you then.'

' I must say, signora, that I think you are speaking of the lady in a very unjustifiable manner.'

' And one other piece of advice, Mr. Slope ; I'll only offer you one other ; ' and then she commenced singing—

> ' It's gude to be merry and wise, Mr. Slope ;
> It's gude to be honest and true ;
> It's gude to be off with the old love—Mr. Slope,
> Before you are on with the new.—

' Ha, ha, ha ! '

And the signora, throwing herself back on her sofa, laughed merrily. She little recked how those who heard her would, in their own imaginations, fill up the little history of Mr. Slope's first love. She little cared that some among them might attribute to her the honour of his earlier admiration. She was tired of Mr. Slope and wanted to get rid of him; she had ground for anger with him, and she chose to be revenged.

How Mr. Slope got out of that room he never himself knew.. He did succeed ultimately, and probably with some assistance, in getting his hat and escaping into the air. At last his love for the signora was cured. Whenever he again thought of her in his dreams, it was not as of an angel with azure wings. He connected her rather with fire and brimstone, and though he could still believe her to be a spirit, he banished her entirely out of heaven, and found a place for her among the infernal gods. When he weighed in the balance, as he not seldom did, the two women to whom he had attached himself in Barchester, the pre-eminent place in his soul's hatred was usually allotted to the signora.

CHAPTER XLVII

THE DEAN ELECT

DURING the entire next week Barchester was ignorant who was to be its new dean on Sunday morning. Mr. Slope was decidedly the favourite; but he did not show himself in the cathedral, and then he sank a point or two in the betting. On Monday, he got a scolding from the bishop in the hearing of the servants, and down he went till nobody would have him at any price; but on Tuesday he received a letter, in an official cover, marked private, by which he fully recovered his place in the public favour. On Wednesday, he was said to be ill, and that did not look well; but on Thursday morning he went down to the railway station, with a very jaunty air; and when it was ascertained that he had taken a first-class ticket for London, there was no longer any room for doubt on the matter.

While matters were in this state of ferment at Barchester, there was not much mental comfort at Plumstead. Our friend the archdeacon had many grounds for inward grief. He was much displeased at the result of Dr. Gwynne's diplomatic mission to the palace, and did not even scruple to say to his wife that had he gone himself, he would have managed the affair much better. His wife did not agree with him, but that did not mend the matter.

Mr. Quiverful's appointment to the hospital was, however, a *fait accompli*, and Mr. Harding's acquiescence in that appointment was not less so. Nothing would induce Mr. Harding to make a public appeal against the bishop; and the Master of Lazarus quite approved of his not doing so.

'I don't know what has come to the Master,' said the archdeacon over and over again. 'He used to be ready enough to stand up for his order.'

'My dear archdeacon,' Mrs. Grantly would say in reply, 'what is the use of always fighting? I really think the Master is right.' The Master, however, had taken steps of his own, of which neither the archdeacon nor his wife knew anything.

Then Mr. Slope's successes were henbane to Dr. Grantly; and Mrs. Bold's improprieties were as bad. What would be all the world to Archdeacon Grantly if Mr. Slope should become Dean of Barchester and marry his wife's sister! He talked of it, and talked of it till he was nearly ill. Mrs. Grantly almost wished that the marriage were done and over, so that she might hear no more about it.

And there was yet another ground of misery which cut him to the quick, nearly as closely as either of the others. That paragon of a clergyman, whom he had bestowed upon St. Ewold's, that college friend of whom he had boasted so loudly, that ecclesiastical knight before whose lance Mr. Slope was to fall and bite the dust, that worthy bulwark of the church as it should be, that honoured representative of Oxford's best spirit, was—so at least his wife had told him half a dozen times—misconducting himself!

Nothing had been seen of Mr. Arabin at Plumstead for the last week, but a good deal had, unfortunately, been heard of him. As soon as Mrs. Grantly had found herself

alone with the archdeacon, on the evening of the Ullathorne
party, she had expressed herself very forcibly as to Mr.
Arabin's conduct on that occasion. He had, she declared,
looked and acted and talked very unlike a decent parish
clergyman. At first the archdeacon had laughed at this,
and assured her that she need not trouble herself; that
Mr. Arabin would be found to be quite safe. But by
degrees he began to find that his wife's eyes had been
sharper than his own. Other people coupled the signora's
name with that of Mr. Arabin. The meagre little prebendary who lived in the close, told him to a nicety how
often Mr. Arabin had visited at Dr. Stanhope's, and how
long he had remained on the occasion of each visit. He
had asked after Mr. Arabin at the cathedral library, and
an officious little vicar choral had offered to go and see
whether he could be found at Dr. Stanhope's. Rumour,
when she has contrived to sound the first note on her
trumpet, soon makes a loud peal audible enough. It was
too clear that Mr. Arabin had succumbed to the Italian
woman, and that the archdeacon's credit would suffer
fearfully if something were not done to rescue the brand
from the burning. Besides, to give the archdeacon his
due, he was really attached to Mr. Arabin, and grieved
greatly at his backsliding.

They were sitting, talking over their sorrows, in the
drawing-room before dinner on the day after Mr. Slope's
departure for London; and on this occasion Mrs. Grantly
spoke out her mind freely. She had opinions of her own
about parish clergymen, and now thought it right to give
vent to them.

'If you would have been led by me, archdeacon, you
would never have put a bachelor into St. Ewold's.'

'But, my dear, you don't mean to say that all bachelor
clergymen misbehave themselves.'

'I don't know that clergymen are so much better than
other men,' said Mrs. Grantly. 'It's all very well with
a curate whom you have under your own eye, and whom
you can get rid of if he persists in improprieties.'

'But Mr. Arabin was a fellow, and couldn't have had
a wife.'

'Then I would have found some one who could.'

'But, my dear, are fellows never to get livings?'

'Yes, to be sure they are, when they get engaged.
I never would put a young man into a living unless he
were married, or engaged to be married. Now here is
Mr. Arabin. The whole responsibility lies upon you.'

'There is not at this moment a clergyman in all Oxford
more respected for morals and conduct than Arabin.'

'Oh, Oxford!' said the lady, with a sneer. 'What
men choose to do at Oxford, nobody ever hears of. A man
may do very well at Oxford who would bring disgrace on
a parish; and, to tell you the truth, it seems to me that
Mr. Arabin is just such a man.'

The archdeacon groaned deeply, but he had no further
answer to make.

'You really must speak to him, archdeacon. Only think
what the Thornes will say if they hear that their parish
clergyman spends his whole time philandering with this
woman.'

The archdeacon groaned again. He was a courageous
man, and knew well enough how to rebuke the younger
clergymen of the diocese, when necessary. But there was
that about Mr. Arabin which made the doctor feel that
it would be very difficult to rebuke him with good effect.

'You can advise him to find a wife for himself, and
he will understand well enough what that means,' said
Mrs. Grantly.

The archdeacon had nothing for it but groaning. There
was Mr. Slope; he was going to be made dean; he was
going to take a wife; he was about to achieve respectability and wealth; an excellent family mansion, and
a family carriage; he would soon be among the comfortable *élite* of the ecclesiastical world of Barchester;
whereas his own *protégé*, the true scion of the true church,
by whom he had sworn, would be still but a poor vicar,
and that with a very indifferent character for moral
conduct! It might be all very well recommending Mr.
Arabin to marry, but how would Mr. Arabin when married
support a wife!

Things were ordering themselves thus in Plumstead
drawing-room when Dr. and Mrs. Grantly were disturbed
in their sweet discourse by the quick rattle of a carriage
and pair of horses on the gravel sweep. The sound was
not that of visitors, whose private carriages are generally

brought up to country-house doors with demure propriety, but betokened rather the advent of some person or persons who were in a hurry to reach the house, and had no intention of immediately leaving it. Guests invited to stay a week, and who were conscious of arriving after the first dinner bell, would probably approach in such a manner. So might arrive an attorney with the news of a granduncle's death, or a son from college with all the fresh honours of a double first. No one would have had himself driven up to the door of a country house in such a manner who had the slightest doubt of his own right to force an entry.

'Who is it?' said Mrs. Grantly, looking at her husband.

'Who on earth can it be?' said the archdeacon to his wife. He then quietly got up and stood with the drawing-room door open in his hand. 'Why, it's your father!'

It was indeed Mr. Harding, and Mr. Harding alone. He had come by himself in a post-chaise with a couple of horses from Barchester, arriving almost after dark, and evidently full of news. His visits had usually been made in the quietest manner; he had rarely presumed to come without notice, and had always been driven up in a modest old green fly, with one horse, that hardly made itself heard as it crawled up to the hall door.

'Good gracious, Warden, is it you?' said the archdeacon, forgetting in his surprise the events of the last few years. 'But come in; nothing the matter, I hope.'

'We are very glad you are come, papa,' said his daughter. 'I'll go and get your room ready at once.'

'I an't warden, archdeacon,' said Mr. Harding. 'Mr. Quiverful is warden.'

'Oh, I know, I know,' said the archdeacon, petulantly. 'I forgot all about it at the moment. Is anything the matter?'

'Don't go this moment, Susan,' said Mr. Harding; 'I have something to tell you.'

'The dinner bell will ring in five minutes,' said she.

'Will it?' said Mr. Harding. 'Then, perhaps, I had better wait.' He was big with news which he had come to tell, but which he knew could not be told without much discussion. He had hurried away to Plumstead as fast as two horses could bring him; and now, finding himself there, he was willing to accept the reprieve which dinner would give him.

'If you have anything of moment to tell us,' said the archdeacon, 'pray let us hear it at once. Has Eleanor gone off ?'

'No, she has not,' said Mr. Harding, with a look of great displeasure.

'Has Slope been made dean ?'

'No, he has not; but—'

'But what ?' said the archdeacon, who was becoming very impatient.

'They have—'

'They have what ?' said the archdeacon.

'They have offered it to me,' said Mr. Harding, with a modesty which almost prevented his speaking.

'Good heavens!' said the archdeacon, and sank back exhausted in an easy-chair.

'My dear, dear father,' said Mrs. Grantly, and threw her arms round her father's neck.

'So I thought I had better come out and consult with you at once,' said Mr. Harding.

'Consult!' shouted the archdeacon. 'But, my dear Harding, I congratulate you with my whole heart—with my whole heart; I do indeed. I never heard anything in my life that gave me so much pleasure;' and he got hold of both his father-in-law's hands, and shook them as though he were going to shake them off, and walked round and round the room, twirling a copy of the Jupiter over his head, to show his extreme exultation.

'But—' began Mr. Harding.

'But me no buts,' said the archdeacon. 'I never was so happy in my life. It was just the proper thing to do. Upon my honour, I'll never say another word against Lord —— the longest day I have to live.'

'That's Dr. Gwynne's doing, you may be sure,' said Mrs. Grantly, who greatly liked the Master of Lazarus, he being an orderly married man with a large family.

'I suppose it is,' said the archdeacon.

'Oh, papa, I am so truly delighted!' said Mrs. Grantly, getting up and kissing her father.

'But, my dear,' said Mr. Harding.—It was all in vain that he strove to speak; nobody would listen to him.

'Well, Mr. Dean,' said the archdeacon, triumphing; 'the deanery gardens will be some consolation for the hospital elms. Well, poor Quiverful! I won't begrudge him his good fortune any longer.'

'No, indeed,' said Mrs. Grantly. 'Poor woman, she has fourteen children. I am sure I am very glad they have got it.'

'So am I,' said Mr. Harding.

'I would give twenty pounds,' said the archdeacon, 'to see how Mr. Slope will look when he hears it.' The idea of Mr. Slope's discomfiture formed no small part of the archdeacon's pleasure.

At last Mr. Harding was allowed to go up-stairs and wash his hands, having, in fact, said very little of all that he had come out to Plumstead on purpose to say. Nor could anything more be said till the servants were gone after dinner. The joy of Dr. Grantly was so uncontrollable that he could not refrain from calling his father-in-law Mr. Dean before the men; and therefore it was soon matter of discussion in the lower regions how Mr. Harding, instead of his daughter's future husband, was to be the new dean, and various were the opinions on the matter. The cook and butler, who were advanced in years, thought that it was just as it should be; but the footman and lady's maid, who were younger, thought it was a great shame that Mr. Slope should lose his chance.

'He's a mean chap all the same,' said the footman; 'and it an't along of him that I says so. But I always did admire the missus's sister; and she'd well become the situation.'

While these were the ideas down-stairs, a very great difference of opinion existed above. As soon as the cloth was drawn and the wine on the table, Mr. Harding made for himself an opportunity of speaking. It was, however, with much inward troubling that he said :—

'It's very kind of Lord —— very kind, and I feel it deeply, most deeply. I am, I must confess, gratified by the offer—'

'I should think so,' said the archdeacon.

'But, all the same, I am afraid that I can't accept it.'

The decanter almost fell from the archdeacon's hand upon the table; and the start he made was so great as

to make his wife jump up from her chair. Not accept
the deanship! If it really ended in this, there would be no
longer any doubt that his father-in-law was demented.
The question now was whether a clergyman with low
rank, and preferment amounting to less than 200*l.* a year,
should accept high rank, 1200*l.* a year, and one of the
most desirable positions which his profession had to
afford!

'What!' said the archdeacon, gasping for breath, and
staring at his guest as though the violence of his emotion
had almost thrown him into a fit.

'What!'

'I do not find myself fit for new duties,' urged Mr.
Harding.

'New duties! what duties?' said the archdeacon,
with unintended sarcasm.

'Oh, papa,' said Mrs. Grantly, 'nothing can be easier
than what a dean has to do. Surely you are more active
than Dr. Trefoil.'

'He won't have half as much to do as he has at present,'
said Dr. Grantly.

'Did you see what the Jupiter said the other day about
young men?'

'Yes; and I saw that the Jupiter said all that it could
to induce the appointment of Mr. Slope. Perhaps you
would wish to see Mr. Slope made dean.'

Mr. Harding made no reply to this rebuke, though he
felt it strongly. He had not come over to Plumstead to
have further contention with his son-in-law about Mr.
Slope, so he allowed it to pass by.

'I know I cannot make you understand my feeling,'
he said, 'for we have been cast in different moulds. I may
wish that I had your spirit and energy and power of
combating; but I have not. Every day that is added to
my life increases my wish for peace and rest.'

'And where on earth can a man have peace and rest
if not in a deanery?' said the archdeacon.

'People will say that I am too old for it.'

'Good heavens! people! what people? What need
you care for any people?'

'But I think myself I am too old for any new place.'

'Dear papa,' said Mrs. Grantly, 'men ten years older

than you are appointed to new situations day after day.'

'My dear,' said he, 'it is impossible that I should make you understand my feelings, nor do I pretend to any great virtue in the matter. The truth is, I want the force of character which might enable me to stand against the spirit of the times. The call on all sides now is for young men, and I have not the nerve to put myself in opposition to the demand. Were the Jupiter, when it hears of my appointment, to write article after article, setting forth my incompetency, I am sure it would cost me my reason. I ought to be able to bear with such things, you will say. Well, my dear, I own that I ought. But I feel my weakness, and I know that I can't. And, to tell you the truth, I know no more than a child what the dean has to do.'

'Pshaw!' exclaimed the archdeacon.

'Don't be angry with me, archdeacon: don't let us quarrel about it, Susan. If you knew how keenly I feel the necessity of having to disoblige you in this matter, you would not be angry with me.'

This was a dreadful blow to Dr. Grantly. Nothing could possibly have suited him better than having Mr. Harding in the deanery. Though he had never looked down on Mr. Harding on account of his recent poverty, he did fully recognise the satisfaction of having those belonging to him in comfortable positions. It would be much more suitable that Mr. Harding should be dean of Barchester than vicar of St. Cuthbert's and precentor to boot. And then the great discomfiture of that arch enemy of all that was respectable in Barchester, of that new low-church clerical *parvenu* that had fallen amongst them, that alone would be worth more, almost, than the situation itself. It was frightful to think that such unhoped-for good fortune should be marred by the absurd crotchets and unwholesome hallucinations by which Mr. Harding allowed himself to be led astray. To have the cup so near his lips and then to lose the drinking of it, was more than Dr. Grantly could endure.

And yet it appeared as though he would have to endure it. In vain he threatened and in vain he coaxed. Mr. Harding did not indeed speak with perfect decision of refusing the proffered glory, but he would not speak with

anything like decision of accepting it. When pressed
again and again, he would again and again allege that he
was wholly unfitted to new duties. It was in vain that
the archdeacon tried to insinuate, though he could not
plainly declare, that there were no new duties to perform.
It was in vain he hinted that in all cases of difficulty he,
the archdeacon, was willing and able to guide a weak-
minded dean. Mr. Harding seemed to have a foolish
idea, not only that there were new duties to do, but that
no one should accept the place who was not himself
prepared to do them.

The conference ended in an understanding that Mr.
Harding should at once acknowledge the letter he had
received from the minister's private secretary, and should
beg that he might be allowed two days to make up his
mind ; and that during those two days the matter should
be considered.

On the following morning the archdeacon was to drive
Mr. Harding back to Barchester.

CHAPTER XLVIII

MISS THORNE SHOWS HER TALENT AT MATCH-MAKING

On Mr. Harding's return to Barchester from Plumstead,
which was effected by him in due course in company with
the archdeacon, more tidings of a surprising nature met
him. He was, during the journey, subjected to such a
weight of unanswerable argument, all of which went to
prove that it was his bounden duty not to interfere with
the paternal government that was so anxious to make
him a dean, that when he arrived at the chemist's door
in High Street, he hardly knew which way to turn himself
in the matter. But, perplexed as he was, he was doomed
to further perplexity. He found a note there from his
daughter begging him most urgently to come to her immediately. But we must again go back a little in our story.

Miss Thorne had not been slow to hear the rumours
respecting Mr. Arabin, which had so much disturbed the
happiness of Mrs. Grantly. And she, also, was unhappy
to think that her parish clergyman should be accused of

worshipping a strange goddess. She, also, was of opinion, that rectors and vicars should all be married, and with that good-natured energy which was characteristic of her, she put her wits to work to find a fitting match for Mr. Arabin. Mrs. Grantly, in this difficulty, could think of no better remedy than a lecture from the archdeacon. Miss Thorne thought that a young lady, marriageable, and with a dowry, might be of more efficacy. In looking through the catalogue of her unmarried friends, who might possibly be in want of a husband, and might also be fit for such promotion as a country parsonage affords, she could think of no one more eligible than Mrs. Bold; and, consequently, losing no time, she went into Barchester on the day of Mr. Slope's discomfiture, the same day that her brother had had his interesting interview with the last of the Neros, and invited Mrs. Bold to bring her nurse and baby to Ullathorne and make them a protracted visit.

Miss Thorne suggested a month or two, intending to use her influence afterwards in prolonging it so as to last out the winter, in order that Mr. Arabin might have an opportunity of becoming fairly intimate with his intended bride. 'We'll have Mr. Arabin too,' said Miss Thorne to herself; 'and before the spring they'll know each other; and in twelve or eighteen months' time, if all goes well, Mrs. Bold will be domiciled at St. Ewold's;' and then the kind-hearted lady gave herself some not undeserved praise for her match-making genius.

Eleanor was taken a little by surprise, but the matter ended in her promising to go to Ullathorne for at any rate a week or two; and on the day previous to that on which her father drove out to Plumstead, she had had herself driven out to Ullathorne.

Miss Thorne would not perplex her with her embryo lord on that same evening, thinking that she would allow her a few hours to make herself at home; but on the following morning Mr. Arabin arrived. 'And now,' said Miss Thorne to herself, 'I must contrive to throw them in each other's way.' That same day, after dinner, Eleanor, with an assumed air of dignity which she could not maintain, with tears that she could not suppress, with a flutter which she could not conquer, and a joy

which she could not hide, told Miss Thorne that she was
engaged to marry Mr. Arabin, and that it behoved her
to get back home to Barchester as quick as she could.

To say simply that Miss Thorne was rejoiced at the
success of the scheme, would give a very faint idea of her
feelings on the occasion. My readers may probably have
dreamt before now that they have had before them some
terribly long walk to accomplish, some journey of twenty
or thirty miles, an amount of labour frightful to anticipate,
and that immediately on starting they have ingeniously
found some accommodating short cut which has brought
them without fatigue to their work's end in five minutes.
Miss Thorne's waking feelings were somewhat of the same
nature. My readers may perhaps have had to do with
children, and may on some occasion have promised to
their young charges some great gratification intended to
come off, perhaps at the end of the winter, or at the
beginning of summer. The impatient juveniles, however,
will not wait, and clamorously demand their treat before
they go to bed. Miss Thorne had a sort of feeling that
her children were equally unreasonable. She was like
an inexperienced gunner, who has ill calculated the length
of the train that he has laid. The gunpowder exploded
much too soon, and poor Miss Thorne felt that she was
blown up by the strength of her own petard.

Miss Thorne had had lovers of her own, but they had
been gentlemen of old-fashioned and deliberate habits.
Miss Thorne's heart also had not always been hard, though
she was still a virgin spinster; but it had never yielded
in this way at the first assault. She had intended to
bring together a middle-aged studious clergyman, and
a discreet matron who might possibly be induced to
marry again; and in doing so she had thrown fire among
tinder. Well, it was all as it should be, but she did feel
perhaps a little put out by the precipitancy of her own
success; and perhaps a little vexed at the readiness of
Mrs. Bold to be wooed.

She said, however, nothing about it to any one, and
ascribed it all to the altered manners of the new age.
Their mothers and grandmothers were perhaps a little
more deliberate; but it was admitted on all sides that
things were conducted very differently now than in

former times. For aught Miss Thorne knew of the matter, a couple of hours might be quite sufficient under the new régime to complete that for which she in her ignorance had allotted twelve months.

But we must not pass over the wooing so cavalierly. It has been told, with perhaps tedious accuracy, how Eleanor disposed of two of her lovers at Ullathorne; and it must also be told with equal accuracy, and if possible with less tedium, how she encountered Mr. Arabin.

It cannot be denied that when Eleanor accepted Miss Thorne's invitation, she remembered that Ullathorne was in the parish of St. Ewold's. Since her interview with the signora she had done little else than think about Mr. Arabin, and the appeal that had been made to her. She could not bring herself to believe or try to bring herself to believe, that what she had been told was untrue. Think of it how she would, she could not but accept it as a fact that Mr. Arabin was fond of her; and then when she went further, and asked herself the question, she could not but accept it as a fact also that she was fond of him. If it were destined for her to be the partner of his hopes and sorrows, to whom could she look for friendship so properly as to Miss Thorne? This invitation was like an ordained step towards the fulfilment of her destiny, and when she also heard that Mr. Arabin was expected to be at Ullathorne on the following day, it seemed as though all the world were conspiring in her favour. Well, did she not deserve it? In that affair of Mr. Slope, had not all the world conspired against her?

She could not, however, make herself easy and at home. When in the evening after dinner Miss Thorne expatiated on the excellence of Mr. Arabin's qualities, and hinted that any little rumour which might be ill-naturedly spread abroad concerning him really meant nothing, Mrs. Bold found herself unable to answer. When Miss Thorne went a little further and declared that she did not know a prettier vicarage-house in the county than St. Ewold's, Mrs. Bold remembering the projected bow-window and the projected priestess still held her tongue; though her ears tingled with the conviction that all the world knew that she was in love with Mr Arabin.

Well; what would that matter if they could only meet and tell each other what each now longed to tell?

And they did meet. Mr. Arabin came early in the day, and found the two ladies together at work in the drawing-room. Miss Thorne, who had she known all the truth would have vanished into air at once, had no conception that her immediate absence would be a blessing, and remained chatting with them till luncheon-time. Mr. Arabin could talk about nothing but the Signora Neroni's beauty, would discuss no people but the Stanhopes. This was very distressing to Eleanor, and not very satisfactory to Miss Thorne. But yet there was evidence of innocence in his open avowal of admiration.

And then they had lunch, and then Mr. Arabin went out on parish duty, and Eleanor and Miss Thorne were left to take a walk together.

'Do you think the Signora Neroni is so lovely as people say?' Eleanor asked as they were coming home.

'She is very beautiful certainly, very beautiful,' Miss Thorne answered; 'but I do not know that any one considers her lovely. She is a woman all men would like to look at; but few I imagine would be glad to take her to their hearths, even were she unmarried and not afflicted as she is.'

There was some little comfort in this. Eleanor made the most of it till she got back to the house. She was then left alone in the drawing-room, and just as it was getting dark Mr. Arabin came in.

It was a beautiful afternoon in the beginning of October, and Eleanor was sitting in the window to get the advantage of the last daylight for her novel. There was a fire in the comfortable room, but the weather was not cold enough to make it attractive; and as she could see the sun set from where she sat, she was not very attentive to her book.

Mr. Arabin when he entered stood awhile with his back to the fire in his usual way, merely uttering a few commonplace remarks about the beauty of the weather, while he plucked up courage for more interesting converse. It cannot probably be said that he had resolved then and there to make an offer to Eleanor. Men we believe seldom make such resolves. Mr. Slope and Mr. Stanhope had done so, it is true; but gentlemen generally propose without any absolutely defined determination as to their doing so. Such was now the case with Mr. Arabin.

'It is a lovely sunset,' said Eleanor, answering him on the dreadfully trite subject which he had chosen.

Mr. Arabin could not see the sunset from the hearth-rug, so he had to go close to her.

'Very lovely,' said he, standing modestly so far away from her as to avoid touching the flounces of her dress. Then it appeared that he had nothing further to say; so after gazing for a moment in silence at the brightness of the setting sun, he returned to the fire.

Eleanor found that it was quite impossible for herself to commence a conversation. In the first place she could find nothing to say; words, which were generally plenty enough with her, would not come to her relief. And, moreover, do what she would, she could hardly prevent herself from crying.

'Do you like Ullathorne?' said Mr. Arabin, speaking from the safely distant position which he had assumed on the hearth-rug.

'Yes, indeed, very much!'

'I don't mean Mr. and Miss Thorne. I know you like them; but the style of the house. There is something about old-fashioned mansions, built as this is, and old-fashioned gardens, that to me is especially delightful.'

'I like everything old-fashioned,' said Eleanor; 'old-fashioned things are so much the honestest.'

'I don't know about that,' said Mr. Arabin, gently laughing. 'That is an opinion on which very much may be said on either side. It is strange how widely the world is divided on a subject which so nearly concerns us all, and which is so close beneath our eyes. Some think that we are quickly progressing towards perfection, while others imagine that virtue is disappearing from the earth.'

'And you, Mr. Arabin, what do you think?' said Eleanor. She felt somewhat surprised at the tone which his conversation was taking, and yet she was relieved at his saying something which enabled herself to speak without showing her own emotion.

'What do I think, Mrs. Bold?' and then he rumbled his money with his hands in his trowsers pockets, and looked and spoke very little like a thriving lover. ' It is the bane of my life that on important subjects I acquire no fixed opinion. I think, and think, and go on thinking ; and yet my thoughts are running ever in different directions. I hardly know whether or no we do lean more confidently than our fathers did on those high hopes to which we profess to aspire.'

' I think the world grows more worldly every day,' said Eleanor.

' That is because you see more of it than when you were younger. But we should hardly judge by what we see,—we see so very very little.' There was then a pause for a while, during which Mr. Arabin continued to turn over his shillings and half-crowns. ' If we believe in Scripture, we can hardly think that mankind in general will now be allowed to retrograde.'

Eleanor, whose mind was certainly engaged otherwise than on the general state of mankind, made no answer to this. She felt thoroughly dissatisfied with herself. She could not force her thoughts away from the topic on which the signora had spoken to her in so strange a way, and yet she knew that she could not converse with Mr. Arabin in an unrestrained natural tone till she did so. She was most anxious not to show to him any special emotion, and yet she felt that if he looked at her he would at once see that she was not at ease.

But he did not look at her. Instead of doing so, he left the fire-place and began walking up and down the room. Eleanor took up her book resolutely ; but she could not read, for there was a tear in her eye, and do what she would it fell on her cheek. When Mr. Arabin's back was turned to her she wiped it away ; but another was soon coursing down her face in its place. They would come ; not a deluge of tears that would have betrayed her at once, but one by one, single monitors. Mr. Arabin did not observe her closely, and they passed unseen.

Mr. Arabin, thus pacing up and down the room, took four or five turns before he spoke another word, and Eleanor sat equally silent with her face bent over her book. She was afraid that her tears would get the better of her, and was preparing for an escape from the room, when Mr Arabin in his walk stood opposite to her. He did not come close up, but stood exactly on the spot to which his course brought him, and then, with his hands under his coat tails, thus made his confession.

'Mrs. Bold,' said he, 'I owe you retribution for a great offence of which I have been guilty towards you.' Eleanor's heart beat so that she could not trust herself to say that he had never been guilty of any offence. So Mr. Arabin thus went on.

'I have thought much of it since, and I am now aware that I was wholly unwarranted in putting to you a question which I once asked you. It was indelicate on my part, and perhaps unmanly. No intimacy which may exist between myself and your connection, Dr. Grantly, could justify it. Nor could the acquaintance which existed between ourselves.' This word acquaintance struck cold on Eleanor's heart. Was this to be her doom after all? 'I therefore think it right to beg your pardon in a humble spirit, and I now do so.'

What was Eleanor to say to him? She could not say much, because she was crying, and yet she must say something. She was most anxious to say that something graciously, kindly, and yet not in such a manner as to betray herself. She had never felt herself so much at a loss for words.

'Indeed I took no offence, Mr. Arabin.'

'Oh, but you did! And had you not done so, you would not have been yourself. You were as right to be offended, as I was wrong so to offend you. I have not forgiven myself, but I hope to hear that you forgive me.'

She was now past speaking calmly, though she still continued to hide her tears, and Mr. Arabin, after pausing a moment in vain for her reply, was walking off towards the door. She felt that she could not allow him to go unanswered without grievously sinning against all charity; so, rising from her seat, she gently touched his arm and said: 'Oh, Mr. Arabin, do not go till I speak to you! I do forgive you. You know that I forgive you.'

He took the hand that had so gently touched his arm, and then gazed into her face as if he would peruse there, as though written in a book, the whole future destiny of his life; and as he did so, there was a sober sad seriousness in his own countenance, which Eleanor found herself unable to sustain. She could only look down upon the carpet, let her tears trickle as they would, and leave her hand within his.

It was but for a minute that they stood so, but the duration of that minute was sufficient to make it ever memorable to them both. Eleanor was sure now that she was loved. No words, be their eloquence what it might, could be more impressive than that eager, melancholy gaze.

Why did he look so into her eyes? Why did he not speak to her? Could it be that he looked for her to make the first sign?

And he, though he knew but little of women, even he knew that he was loved. He had only to ask and it would be all his own, that inexpressible loveliness, those ever speaking but yet now mute eyes, that feminine brightness and eager loving spirit which had so attracted him since first he had encountered it at St. Ewold's. It might, must all be his own now. On no other supposition was it possible that she should allow her hand to remain thus clasped within his own. He had only to ask. Ah! but that was the difficulty. Did a minute suffice for all this? Nay, perhaps it might be more than a minute.

'Mrs. Bold—' at last he said, and then stopped himself.

If he could not speak, how was she to do so? He had called her by her name, the same name that any merest stranger would have used! She withdrew her hand from his, and moved as though to return to her seat. 'Eleanor!' he then said, in his softest tone, as though the courage of a lover were as yet but half assumed, as though he were still afraid of giving offence by the freedom which he took. She looked slowly, gently, almost piteously up into his face. There was at any rate no anger there to deter him.

'Eleanor!' he again exclaimed; and in a moment he had her clasped to his bosom. How this was done, whether the doing was with him or her, whether she had flown thither conquered by the tenderness of his voice, or he with a violence not likely to give offence had drawn her to his breast, neither of them knew; nor can I declare. There was now that sympathy between them which

hardly admitted of individual motion. They were one
and the same,—one flesh,—one spirit,—one life.

'Eleanor, my own Eleanor, my own, my wife!' She
ventured to look up at him through her tears, and he,
bowing his face down over hers, pressed his lips upon her
brow; his virgin lips, which since a beard first grew upon
his chin, had never yet tasted the luxury of a woman's
cheek.

She had been told that her yea must be yea, or her
nay, nay; but she was called on for neither the one nor
the other. She told Miss Thorne that she was engaged
to Mr. Arabin, but no such words had passed between
them, no promises had been asked or given.

'Oh, let me go,' said she; 'let me go now. I am too
happy to remain,—let me go, that I may be alone.' He
did not try to hinder her; he did not repeat the kiss;
he did not press another on her lips. He might have done
so had he been so minded. She was now all his own. He
took his arm from round her waist, his arm that was
trembling with a new delight, and let her go. She fled
like a roe to her own chamber, and then, having turned
the bolt, she enjoyed the full luxury of her love. She
idolised, almost worshipped this man who had so meekly
begged her pardon. And he was now her own. Oh, how
she wept and cried and laughed, as the hopes and fears
and miseries of the last few weeks passed in remembrance
through her mind.

Mr. Slope! That any one should have dared to think
that she who had been chosen by him could possibly
have mated herself with Mr. Slope! That they should
have dared to tell him, also, and subject her bright happiness to such needless risk! And then she smiled with joy
as she thought of all the comforts that she could give
him; not that he cared for comforts, but that it would
be so delicious for her to give.

She got up and rang for her maid that she might tell
her little boy of his new father; and in her own way she
did tell him. She desired her maid to leave her, in order
that she might be alone with her child; and then, while
he lay sprawling on the bed, she poured forth the praises,
all unmeaning to him, of the man she had selected to
guard his infancy.

She could not be happy, however, till she had made Mr. Arabin take the child to himself, and thus, as it were, adopt him as his own. The moment the idea struck her she took the baby up in her arms, and, opening her door, ran quickly down to the drawing-room. She at once found, by his step still pacing on the floor, that he was there; and a glance within the room told her that he was alone. She hesitated a moment, and then hurried in with her precious charge.

Mr. Arabin met her in the middle of the room. 'There,' said she, breathless with her haste; 'there, take him— take him and love him.'

Mr. Arabin took the little fellow from her, and kissing him again and again, prayed God to bless him. 'He shall be all as my own—all as my own,' said he. Eleanor, as she stooped to take back her child, kissed the hand that held him, and then rushed back with her treasure to her chamber.

It was thus that Mr. Harding's younger daughter was won for the second time. At dinner neither she nor Mr. Arabin were very bright, but their silence occasioned no remark. In the drawing-room, as we have before said, she told Miss Thorne what had occurred. The next morning she returned to Barchester, and Mr. Arabin went over with his budget of news to the archdeacon. As Doctor Grantly was not there, he could only satisfy himself by telling Mrs. Grantly how that he intended himself the honour of becoming her brother-in-law. In the ecstasy of her joy at hearing such tidings, Mrs. Grantly vouchsafed him a warmer welcome than any he had yet received from Eleanor.

'Good heavens!' she exclaimed—it was the general exclamation of the rectory. 'Poor Eleanor! Dear Eleanor! What a monstrous injustice has been done her! —Well, it shall all be made up now.' And then she thought of the signora. 'What lies people tell,' she said to herself.

But people in this matter had told no lies at all.

CHAPTER XLIX

THE BELZEBUB COLT

WHEN Miss Thorne left the dining-room, Eleanor had formed no intention of revealing to her what had occurred ; but when she was seated beside her hostess on the sofa the secret dropped from her almost unawares. Eleanor was but a bad hypocrite, and she found herself quite unable to continue talking about Mr. Arabin as though he were a stranger, while her heart was full of him. When Miss Thorne, pursuing her own scheme with discreet zeal, asked the young widow whether, in her opinion, it would not be a good thing for Mr. Arabin to get married, she had nothing for it but to confess the truth. ' I suppose it would,' said Eleanor, rather sheepishly. Whereupon Miss Thorne amplified on the idea. ' Oh, Miss Thorne,' said Eleanor, ' he is going to be married : I am engaged to him.'

Now Miss Thorne knew very well that there had been no such engagement when she had been walking with Mrs. Bold in the morning. She had also heard enough to be tolerably sure that there had been no preliminaries to such an engagement. She was, therefore, as we have before described, taken a little by surprise. But, nevertheless, she embraced her guest, and cordially congratulated her.

Eleanor had no opportunity of speaking another word to Mr. Arabin that evening, except such words as all the world might hear ; and these, as may be supposed, were few enough. Miss Thorne did her best to leave them in privacy ; but Mr. Thorne, who knew nothing of what had occurred, and another guest, a friend of his, entirely interfered with her good intentions. So poor Eleanor had to go to bed without one sign of affection. Her state, nevertheless, was not to be pitied.

The next morning she was up early. It was probable, she thought, that by going down a little before the usual hour of breakfast, she might find Mr. Arabin alone in the dining-room. Might it not be that he also would calculate that an interview would thus be possible ? Thus thinking, Eleanor was dressed a full hour before the time fixed in the Ullathorne household for morning prayers. She did not at once go down. She was afraid to seem to be too anxious to meet her lover; though, heaven knows, her anxiety was intense enough. She therefore sat herself down at her window, and repeatedly looking at her watch, nursed her child till she thought she might venture forth.

When she found herself at the dining-room door, she stood a moment, hesitating to turn the handle; but when she heard Mr. Thorne's voice inside she hesitated no longer. Her object was defeated, and she might now go in as soon as she liked without the slightest imputation on her delicacy. Mr. Thorne and Mr. Arabin were standing on the hearth-rug, discussing the merits of the Belzebub colt; or rather, Mr. Thorne was discussing, and Mr. Arabin was listening. That interesting animal had rubbed the stump of his tail against the wall of his stable, and occasioned much uneasiness to the Ullathorne master of the horse. Had Eleanor but waited another minute, Mr. Thorne would have been in the stables.

Mr. Thorne, when he saw his lady guest, repressed his anxiety. The Belzebub colt must do without him. And so the three stood, saying little or nothing to each other, till at last the master of the house, finding that he could no longer bear his present state of suspense respecting his favourite young steed, made an elaborate apology to Mrs. Bold, and escaped. As he shut the door behind him, Eleanor almost wished that he had remained. It was not that she was afraid of Mr. Arabin, but she hardly yet knew how to address him.

He, however, soon relieved her from her embarrassment. He came up to her, and taking both her hands in his, he said: ' So, Eleanor, you and I are to be man and wife. Is it so ? '

She looked up into his face, and her lips formed themselves into a single syllable. She uttered no sound, but he could read the affirmative plainly in her face.

' It is a great trust,' said he ; ' a very great trust.'

' It is—it is,' said Eleanor, not exactly taking what he had said in the sense that he had meant. ' It is a very, very great trust, and I will do my utmost to deserve it.'

' And I also will do my utmost to deserve it,' said Mr.

Arabin, very solemnly. And then, winding his arm round her waist, he stood there gazing at the fire, and she with her head leaning on his shoulder, stood by him, well satisfied with her position. They neither of them spoke, or found any want of speaking. All that was needful for them to say had been said. The yea, yea, had been spoken by Eleanor in her own way—and that way had been perfectly satisfactory to Mr. Arabin.

And now it remained to them each to enjoy the assurance of the other's love. And how great that luxury is! How far it surpasses any other pleasure which God has allowed to his creatures! And to a woman's heart how doubly delightful!

When the ivy has found its tower, when the delicate creeper has found its strong wall, we know how the parasite plants grow and prosper. They were not created to stretch forth their branches alone, and endure without protection the summer's sun and the winter's storm. Alone they but spread themselves on the ground, and cower unseen in the dingy shade. But when they have found their firm supporters, how wonderful is their beauty; how all pervading and victorious! What is the turret without its ivy, or the high garden-wall without the jasmine which gives it its beauty and fragrance? The hedge without the honeysuckle is but a hedge.

There is a feeling still half existing, but now half conquered by the force of human nature, that a woman should be ashamed of her love till the husband's right to her compels her to acknowledge it. We would fain preach a different doctrine. A woman should glory in her love; but on that account let her take the more care that it be such as to justify her glory.

Eleanor did glory in hers, and she felt, and had cause to feel, that it deserved to be held as glorious. She could have stood there for hours with his arm round her, had fate and Mr. Thorne permitted it. Each moment she crept nearer to his bosom, and felt more and more certain that there was her home. What now to her was the archdeacon's arrogance, her sister's coldness, or her dear father's weakness? What need she care for the duplicity of such friends as Charlotte Stanhope? She had found the strong shield that should guard her from all wrongs, the trusty pilot that should henceforward guide her through the shoals and rocks. She would give up the heavy burden of her independence, and once more assume the position of a woman, and the duties of a trusting and loving wife.

And he, too, stood there fully satisfied with his place. They were both looking intently on the fire, as though they could read there their future fate, till at last Eleanor turned her face towards his. ' How sad you are,' she said, smiling; and indeed his face was, if not sad, at least serious. ' How sad you are, love ! '

' Sad,' said he, looking down at her; ' no, certainly not sad.' Her sweet loving eyes were turned towards him, and she smiled softly as he answered her. The temptation was too strong even for the demure propriety of Mr. Arabin, and, bending over her, he pressed his lips to hers.

Immediately after this, Mr. Thorne appeared, and they were both delighted to hear that the tail of the Belzebub colt was not materially injured.

It had been Mr. Harding's intention to hurry over to Ullathorne as soon as possible after his return to Barchester, in order to secure the support of his daughter in his meditated revolt against the archdeacon as touching the deanery; but he was spared the additional journey by hearing that Mrs. Bold had returned unexpectedly home. As soon as he had read her note he started off, and found her waiting for him in her own house.

How much each of them had to tell the other, and how certain each was that the story which he or she had to tell would astonish the other !

' My dear, I am so anxious to see you,' said Mr. Harding, kissing his daughter.

' Oh, papa, I have so much to tell you ! ' said the daughter, returning the embrace.

' My dear, they have offered me the deanery ! ' said Mr. Harding, anticipating by the suddenness of the revelation the tidings which Eleanor had to give him.

' Oh, papa,' said she, forgetting her own love and happiness in her joy at the surprising news; ' oh, papa, can it be possible ? Dear papa, how thoroughly, thoroughly happy that makes me ! '

'But, my dear, I think it best to refuse it.'

'Oh, papa!'

'I am sure you will agree with me, Eleanor, when I explain it to you. You know, my dear, how old I am. If I live, I——'

'But, papa, I must tell you about myself.'

'Well, my dear.'

'I do so wonder how you'll take it.'

'Take what?'

'If you don't rejoice at it, if it doesn't make you happy, if you don't encourage me, I shall break my heart.'

'If that be the case, Nelly, I certainly will encourage you.'

'But I fear you won't. I do so fear you won't. And yet you can't but think I am the most fortunate woman living on God's earth.'

'Are you, dearest? Then I certainly will rejoice with you. Come, Nelly, come to me, and tell me what it is.'

'I am going——'

He led her to the sofa, and seating himself beside her, took both her hands in his. 'You are going to be married, Nelly. Is not that it?'

'Yes,' she said, faintly. 'That is if you will approve;' and then she blushed as she remembered the promise which she had so lately volunteered to him, and which she had so utterly forgotten in making her engagement with Mr. Arabin.

Mr. Harding thought for a moment who the man could be whom he was to be called upon to welcome as his son-in-law. A week since he would have had no doubt whom to name. In that case he would have been prepared to give his sanction, although he would have done so with a heavy heart. Now he knew that at any rate it would not be Mr. Slope, though he was perfectly at a loss to guess who could possibly have filled the place. For a moment he thought that the man might be Bertie Stanhope, and his very soul sank within him.

'Well, Nelly?'

'Oh, papa, promise to me that, for my sake, you will love him.'

'Come, Nelly, come; tell me who it is.'

'But will you love him, papa?'

'Dearest, I must love any one that you love.' Then she turned her face to his, and whispered into his ear the name of Mr. Arabin.

No man that she could have named could have more surprised or more delighted him. Had he looked round the world for a son-in-law to his taste, he could have selected no one whom he would have preferred to Mr. Arabin. He was a clergyman; he held a living in the neighbourhood; he was of a set to which all Mr. Harding's own partialities most closely adhered; he was the great friend of Dr. Grantly; and he was, moreover, a man of whom Mr. Harding knew nothing but what he approved. Nevertheless, his surprise was so great as to prevent the immediate expression of his joy. He had never thought of Mr. Arabin in connection with his daughter; he had never imagined that they had any feeling in common. He had feared that his daughter had been made hostile to clergymen of Mr. Arabin's stamp by her intolerance of the archdeacon's pretensions. Had he been put to wish, he might have wished for Mr. Arabin for a son-in-law; but had he been put to guess, the name would never have occurred to him.

'Mr. Arabin!' he exclaimed; 'impossible!'

'Oh, papa, for heaven's sake don't say anything against him! If you love me, don't say anything against him. Oh, papa, it's done, and mustn't be undone—oh, papa!'

Fickle Eleanor! where was the promise that she would make no choice for herself without her father's approval? She had chosen, and now demanded his acquiescence. 'Oh, papa, isn't he good? isn't he noble? isn't he religious, highminded, everything that a good man possibly can be?' and she clung to her father, beseeching him for his consent.

'My Nelly, my child, my own daughter! He is; he is noble and good and highminded; he is all that a woman can love and a man admire. He shall be my son, my own son. He shall be as close to my heart as you are. My Nelly, my child, my happy, happy child!'

We need not pursue the interview any further. By degrees they returned to the subject of the new promotion. Eleanor tried to prove to him, as the Grantlys had done, that his age could be no bar to his being a very excellent dean; but those arguments had now even less weight on him than before. He said little or nothing, but sat meditative. Every now and then he would kiss his daughter, and say ' yes,' or ' no,' or ' very true,' or ' well, my dear, I can't quite agree with you there,' but he could not be got to enter sharply into the question of ' to be, or not to be ' dean of Barchester. Of her and her happiness, of Mr. Arabin and his virtues, he would talk as much as Eleanor desired; and, to tell the truth, that was not a little; but about the deanery he would now say nothing further. He had got a new idea into his head—Why should not Mr. Arabin be the new dean?

CHAPTER L

THE ARCHDEACON IS SATISFIED WITH THE STATE OF AFFAIRS

THE archdeacon, in his journey into Barchester, had been assured by Mr. Harding that all their prognostications about Mr. Slope and Eleanor were groundless. Mr. Harding, however, had found it very difficult to shake his son-in-law's faith in his own acuteness. The matter had, to Dr. Grantly, been so plainly corroborated by such patent evidence, borne out by such endless circumstances, that he at first refused to take as true the positive statement which Mr. Harding made to him of Eleanor's own disavowal of the impeachment. But at last he yielded in a qualified way. He brought himself to admit that he would at the present regard his past convictions as a mistake; but in doing this he so guarded himself, that if, at any future time, Eleanor should come forth to the world as Mrs. Slope, he might still be able to say: ' There, I told you so. Remember what you said and what I said; and remember also for coming years, that I was right in this matter,—as in all others.'

He carried, however, his concession so far as to bring himself to undertake to call at Eleanor's house, and he did call accordingly, while the father and daughter were yet in the middle of their conference. Mr. Harding had had so much to hear and to say that he had forgotten to advertise Eleanor of the honour that awaited her, and she heard her brother-in-law's voice in the hall, while she was quite unprepared to see him.

'There's the archdeacon,' she said, springing up.

'Yes, my dear. He told me to tell you that he would come and see you; but, to tell the truth, I had forgotten all about it.'

Eleanor fled away, regardless of all her father's entreaties. She could not now, in the first hours of her joy, bring herself to bear all the archdeacon's retractions, apologies, and congratulations. He would have so much to say, and would be so tedious in saying it; consequently, the archdeacon, when he was shown into the drawing-room, found no one there but Mr. Harding.

'You must excuse Eleanor,' said Mr. Harding.

'Is anything the matter?' asked the doctor, who at once anticipated that the whole truth about Mr. Slope had at last come out.

'Well, something is the matter. I wonder now whether you will be much surprised?'

The archdeacon saw by his father-in-law's manner that after all he had nothing to tell him about Mr. Slope. 'No,' said he, 'certainly not—nothing will ever surprise me again.' Very many men now-a-days, besides the archdeacon, adopt or affect to adopt the *nil admirari* doctrine; but nevertheless, to judge from their appearance, they are just as subject to sudden emotions as their grandfathers and grandmothers were before them.

'What do you think Mr. Arabin has done?'

'Mr. Arabin! It's nothing about that daughter of Stanhope's, I hope?'

'No, not that woman,' said Mr. Harding, enjoying his joke in his sleeve.

'Not that woman! Is he going to do anything about any woman? Why can't you speak out if you have anything to say? There is nothing I hate so much as these sort of mysteries.'

'There shall be no mystery with you, archdeacon; though of course, it must go no further at present.'

'Well.'

'Except Susan. You must promise me you'll tell no one else.'

'Nonsense!' exclaimed the archdeacon, who was

becoming angry in his suspense. ' You can't have any secret about Mr. Arabin.'

' Only this—that he and Eleanor are engaged.'

It was quite clear to see, by the archdeacon's face, that he did not believe a word of it. ' Mr. Arabin! It's impossible! '

' Eleanor, at any rate, has just now told me so.'

' It's impossible,' repeated the archdeacon.

' Well, I can't say I think it impossible. It certainly took me by surprise; but that does not make it impossible.'

' She must be mistaken.'

Mr. Harding assured him that there was no mistake; that he would find, on returning home, that Mr. Arabin had been at Plumstead with the express object of making the same declaration, that even Miss Thorne knew all about it; and that, in fact, the thing was as clearly settled as any such arrangement between a lady and a gentleman could well be.

' Good heavens! ' said the archdeacon, walking up and down Eleanor's drawing-room. ' Good heavens! Good heavens! '

Now, these exclamations certainly betokened faith. Mr. Harding properly gathered from it that, at last, Dr. Grantly did believe the fact. The first utterance clearly evinced a certain amount of distaste at the information he had received; the second, simply indicated surprise; in the tone of the third, Mr. Harding fancied that he could catch a certain gleam of satisfaction.

The archdeacon had truly expressed the workings of his mind. He could not but be disgusted to find how utterly astray he had been in all his anticipations. Had he only been lucky enough to have suggested this marriage himself when he first brought Mr. Arabin into the country, his character for judgment and wisdom would have received an addition which would have classed him at any rate next to Solomon. And why had he not done so? Might he not have foreseen that Mr. Arabin would want a wife in his parsonage? He had foreseen that Eleanor would want a husband; but should he not also have perceived that Mr. Arabin was a man much more likely to attract her than Mr. Slope? The archdeacon found that he had been at fault, and of course could not immediately get over his discomfiture.

Then his surprise was intense. How sly this pair of young turtle doves had been with him. How egregiously they had hoaxed him. He had preached to Eleanor against her fancied attachment to Mr. Slope, at the very time that she was in love with his own protégé, Mr. Arabin; and had absolutely taken that same Mr. Arabin into his confidence with reference to his dread of Mr. Slope's alliance. It was very natural that the archdeacon should feel surprise.

But there was also great ground for satisfaction. Looking at the match by itself, it was the very thing to help the doctor out of his difficulties. In the first place, the assurance that he should never have Mr. Slope for his brother-in-law, was in itself a great comfort. Then Mr. Arabin was, of all men, the one with whom it would best suit him to be so intimately connected. But the crowning comfort was the blow which this marriage would give to Mr. Slope. He had now certainly lost his wife; rumour was beginning to whisper that he might possibly lose his position in the palace; and if Mr. Harding would only be true, the great danger of all would be surmounted. In such case it might be expected that Mr. Slope would own himself vanquished, and take himself altogether away from Barchester. And so the archdeacon would again be able to breathe pure air.

'Well, well,' said he. 'Good heavens! good heavens!' and the tone of the fifth exclamation made Mr. Harding fully aware that content was reigning in the archdeacon's bosom.

And then slowly, gradually, and craftily Mr. Harding propounded his own new scheme. Why should not Mr. Arabin be the new dean?

Slowly, gradually, and thoughtfully Dr. Grantly fell into his father-in-law's views. Much as he liked Mr. Arabin, sincere as was his admiration for that gentleman's ecclesiastical abilities, he would not have sanctioned a measure which would rob his father-in-law of his fairly-earned promotion, were it at all practicable to induce his father-in-law to accept the promotion which he had earned. But the archdeacon had, on a former occasion, received

proof of the obstinacy with which Mr. Harding could
adhere to his own views in opposition to the advice of all
his friends. He knew tolerably well that nothing would
induce the meek, mild man before him to take the high
place offered to him, if he thought it wrong to do so.
Knowing this, he also said to himself more than once:
' Why should not Mr. Arabin be Dean of Barchester ? '
It was at last arranged between them that they would
together start to London by the earliest train on the following morning, making a little *détour* to Oxford on their
journey. Dr. Gwynne's counsels, they imagined, might
perhaps be of assistance to them.

These matters settled, the archdeacon hurried off, that
he might return to Plumstead and prepare for his journey.
The day was extremely fine, and he came into the city
in an open gig. As he was driving up the High Street he
encountered Mr. Slope at a crossing. Had he not pulled
up rather sharply, he would have run over him. The two
had never spoken to each other since they had met on
a memorable occasion in the bishop's study. They did
not speak now ; but they looked each other full in the
face, and Mr. Slope's countenance was as impudent, as
triumphant, as defiant as ever. Had Dr. Grantly not
known to the contrary, he would have imagined that his
enemy had won the deanship, the wife, and all the rich
honours, for which he had been striving. As it was, he
had lost everything that he had in the world, and had just
received his *congé* from the bishop.

In leaving the town the archdeacon drove by the well-
remembered entrance of Hiram's hospital. There, at the
gate, was a large, untidy, farmer's wagon, laden with
untidy-looking furniture ; and there, inspecting the arrival,
was good Mrs. Quiverful—not dressed in her Sunday
best—not very clean in her apparel—not graceful as to
her bonnet and shawl ; or, indeed, with many feminine
charms as to her whole appearance. She was busy at
domestic work in her new house, and had just ventured
out, expecting to see no one on the arrival of the family
chattels. The archdeacon was down upon her before she
knew where she was.

Her acquaintance with Dr. Grantly or his family was
very slight indeed. The archdeacon, as a matter of course,

knew every clergyman in the archdeaconry, it may almost
be said in the diocese, and had some acquaintance, more
or less intimate, with their wives and families. With
Mr. Quiverful he had been concerned on various matters
of business; but of Mrs. Q. he had seen very little. Now,
however, he was in too gracious a mood to pass her by
unnoticed. The Quiverfuls, one and all, had looked for
the bitterest hostility from Dr. Grantly; they knew his
anxiety that Mr. Harding should return to his old home
at the hospital, and they did not know that a new home
had been offered to him at the deanery. Mrs. Quiverful
was therefore not a little surprised and not a little rejoiced
also, at the tone in which she was addressed.

'How do you do, Mrs. Quiverful?—how do you do?'
said he, stretching his left hand out of the gig, as he spoke
to her. 'I am very glad to see you employed in so pleasant
and useful a manner; very glad indeed.'

Mrs. Quiverful thanked him, and shook hands with
him, and looked into his face suspiciously. She was not
sure whether the congratulations and kindness were or
were not ironical.

'Pray tell Mr. Quiverful from me,' he continued, 'that
I am rejoiced at his appointment. It's a comfortable
place, Mrs. Quiverful, and a comfortable house, and
I am very glad to see you in it. Good-bye—good-bye.'
And he drove on, leaving the lady well pleased and
astonished at his good-nature. On the whole things were
going well with the archdeacon, and he could afford to
be charitable to Mrs. Quiverful. He looked forth from
his gig smilingly on all the world, and forgave every one
in Barchester their sins, excepting only Mrs. Proudie and
Mr. Slope. Had he seen the bishop, he would have felt
inclined to pat even him kindly on the head.

He determined to go home by St. Ewold's. This would
take him some three miles out of his way; but he felt
that he could not leave Plumstead comfortably without
saying one word of good fellowship to Mr. Arabin. When
he reached the parsonage the vicar was still out; but,
from what he had heard, he did not doubt but that he
would meet him on the road between their two houses.
He was right in this, for about halfway home, at a narrow
turn, he came upon Mr. Arabin, who was on horseback.

'Well, well, well, well;' said the archdeacon, loudly, joyously, and with supreme good humour; 'well, well, well, well; so, after all, we have no further cause to fear Mr. Slope.'

'I hear from Mrs. Grantly that they have offered the deanery to Mr. Harding,' said the other.

'Mr. Slope has lost more than the deanery, I find, and then the archdeacon laughed jocosely. 'Come, come, Arabin, you have kept your secret well enough. I know all about it now.'

'I have had no secret, archdeacon,' said the other with a quiet smile. 'None at all—not for a day. It was only yesterday that I knew my own good fortune, and to-day I went over to Plumstead to ask your approval. From what Mrs. Grantly has said to me, I am led to hope that I shall have it.'

'With all my heart, with all my heart,' said the arch-deacon cordially, holding his friend fast by the hand. 'It's just as I would have it. She is an excellent young woman; she will not come to you empty-handed; and I think she will make you a good wife. If she does her duty by you as her sister does by me, you'll be a happy man; that's all I can say.' And as he finished speaking, a tear might have been observed in each of the doctor's eyes.

Mr. Arabin warmly returned the archdeacon's grasp, but he said little. His heart was too full for speaking, and he could not express the gratitude which he felt. Dr. Grantly understood him as well as though he had spoken for an hour.

'And mind, Arabin,' said he, 'no one but myself shall tie the knot. We'll get Eleanor out to Plumstead, and it shall come off there. I'll make Susan stir herself, and we'll do it in style. I must be off to London to-morrow on special business. Harding goes with me. But I'll be back before your bride has got her wedding dress ready.' And so they parted.

On his journey home the archdeacon occupied his mind with preparations for the marriage festivities. He made a great resolve that he would atone to Eleanor for all the injury he had done her by the munificence of his future treatment. He would show her what was the difference in his eyes between a Slope and an Arabin. On one other thing also he decided with a firm mind: if the affair of the dean should not be settled in Mr. Arabin's favour, nothing should prevent him putting a new front and bow-window to the dining-room at St. Ewold's parsonage.

'So we're sold after all, Sue,' said he to his wife, accosting her with a kiss as soon as he entered his house. He did not call his wife Sue above twice or thrice in a year, and these occasions were great high days.

'Eleanor has had more sense than we gave her credit for,' said Mrs. Grantly.

And there was great content in Plumstead rectory that evening; and Mrs. Grantly promised her husband that she would now open her heart, and take Mr. Arabin into it. Hitherto she had declined to do so.

CHAPTER LI

MR. SLOPE BIDS FAREWELL TO THE PALACE AND ITS INHABITANTS

WE must now take leave of Mr. Slope, and of the bishop also, and of Mrs. Proudie. These leave-takings in novels are as disagreeable as they are in real life; not so sad, indeed, for they want the reality of sadness; but quite as perplexing, and generally less satisfactory. What novelist, what Fielding, what Scott, what George Sand, or Sue, or Dumas, can impart an interest to the last chapter of his fictitious history? Promises of two children and superhuman happiness are of no avail, nor assurance of extreme respectability carried to an age far exceeding that usually allotted to mortals. The sorrows of our heroes and heroines, they are your delight, oh public! their sorrows, or their sins, or their absurdities; not their virtues, good sense, and consequent rewards. When we begin to tint our final pages with *couleur de rose*, as in accordance with fixed rule we must do, we altogether extinguish our own powers of pleasing. When we become dull we offend your intellect; and we must become dull or we should offend your taste. A late writer, wishing to sustain his interest to the last page, hung his hero at

the end of the third volume. The consequence was,
that no one would read his novel. And who can apportion
out and dovetail his incidents, dialogues, characters, and
descriptive morsels, so as to fit them all exactly into 439
pages, without either compressing them unnaturally, or
extending them artificially at the end of his labour ?
Do I not myself know that I am at this moment in want
of a dozen pages, and that I am sick with cudgelling my
brains to find them ? And then when everything is done,
the kindest-hearted critic of them all invariably twits us
with the incompetency and lameness of our conclusion.
We have either become idle and neglected it, or tedious
and over-laboured it. It is insipid or unnatural, over-
strained or imbecile. It means nothing, or attempts too
much. The last scene of all, as all last scenes we fear
must be,

> Is second childishness, and mere oblivion,
> Sans teeth, sans eyes, sans taste, sans everything.

I can only say that if some critic, who thoroughly knows
his work, and has laboured on it till experience has made
him perfect, will write the last fifty pages of a novel in
the way they should be written, I, for one, will in future
do my best to copy the example. Guided by my own
lights only, I confess that I despair of success.

For the last week or ten days, Mr. Slope had seen nothing
of Mrs. Proudie, and very little of the bishop. He still
lived in the palace, and still went through his usual
routine work ; but the confidential doings of the diocese
had passed into other hands. He had seen this clearly,
and marked it well ; but it had not much disturbed him.
He had indulged in other hopes till the bishop's affairs
had become dull to him, and he was moreover aware that,
as regarded the diocese, Mrs. Proudie had checkmated
him. It has been explained, in the beginning of these
pages, how three or four were contending together as to
who, in fact, should be bishop of Barchester. Each of
these had now admitted to himself (or boasted to herself)
that Mrs. Proudie was victorious in the struggle. They
had gone through a competitive examination of considerable severity, and she had come forth the winner,
facile princeps. Mr. Slope had, for a moment, run her

hard, but it was only for a moment. It had become, as
it were, acknowledged that Hiram's hospital should be the
testing point between them, and now Mr. Quiverful was
already in the hospital, the proof of Mrs. Proudie's skill
and courage.

All this did not break down Mr. Slope's spirit, because
he had other hopes. But, alas, at last there came to him
a note from his friend Sir Nicholas, informing him that
the deanship was disposed of. Let us give Mr. Slope his
due. He did not lie prostrate under this blow, or give
himself up to vain lamentations; he did not henceforward
despair of life, and call upon gods above and gods below
to carry him off. He sat himself down in his chair, counted
out what monies he had in hand for present purposes,
and what others were coming in to him, bethought himself
as to the best sphere for his future exertions, and at once
wrote off a letter to a rich sugar-refiner's wife in Baker
Street, who, as he well knew, was much given to the
entertainment and encouragement of serious young
evangelical clergymen. He was again, he said, ' upon
the world, having found the air of a cathedral town, and
the very nature of cathedral services, uncongenial to his
spirit;' and then he sat awhile, making firm resolves
as to his manner of parting from the bishop, and also as
to his future conduct.

> At last he rose, and twitched his mantle blue (black),
> To-morrow to fresh woods and pastures new.

Having received a formal command to wait upon the
bishop, he rose and proceeded to obey it. He rang the
bell and desired the servant to inform his master that
if it suited his lordship, he, Mr. Slope, was ready to wait
upon him. The servant, who well understood that Mr.
Slope was no longer in the ascendant, brought back a
message, saying that ' his lordship desired that Mr. Slope
would attend him immediately in his study.' Mr. Slope
waited about ten minutes more to prove his independence,
and then he went into the bishop's room. There, as he
had expected, he found Mrs. Proudie, together with her
husband.

' Hum, ha,—Mr. Slope, pray take a chair,' said the
gentleman bishop.

' Pray be seated, Mr. Slope,' said the lady bishop.

' Thank ye, thank ye,' said Mr. Slope, and walking round to the fire, he threw himself into one of the arm-chairs that graced the hearth-rug.

' Mr. Slope,' said the bishop, ' it has become necessary that I should speak to you definitively on a matter that has for some time been pressing itself on my attention.'

' May I ask whether the subject is in any way connected with myself ? ' said Mr. Slope.

' It is so,—certainly,—yes, it certainly is connected with yourself, Mr. Slope.'

' Then, my lord, if I may be allowed to express a wish, I would prefer that no discussion on the subject should take place between us in the presence of a third person.'

' Don't alarm yourself, Mr. Slope,' said Mrs. Proudie, ' no discussion is at all necessary. The bishop merely intends to express his own wishes.'

' I merely intend, Mr. Slope, to express my own wishes,— no discussion will be at all necessary,' said the bishop, reiterating his wife's words.

' That is more, my lord, than we any of us can be sure of,' said Mr. Slope ; ' I cannot, however, force Mrs. Proudie to leave the room ; nor can I refuse to remain here if it be your lordship's wish that I should do so.'

' It is his lordship's wish, certainly,' said Mrs. Proudie.

' Mr. Slope,' began the bishop, in a solemn, serious voice, ' it grieves me to have to find fault. It grieves me much to have to find fault with a clergyman ; but especially so with a clergyman in your position.'

' Why, what have I done amiss, my lord ? ' demanded Mr. Slope, boldly.

' What have you done amiss, Mr. Slope ? ' said Mrs. Proudie, standing erect before the culprit, and raising that terrible forefinger. ' Do you dare to ask the bishop what you have done amiss ? does not your conscience——'

' Mrs. Proudie, pray let it be understood, once for all, that I will have no words with you.'

' Ah, sir, but you will have words,' said she ; ' you must have words. Why have you had so many words with that Signora Neroni ? Why have you disgraced yourself, you a clergyman too, by constantly consorting with such

a woman as that,—with a married woman—with one altogether unfit for a clergyman's society ? '

' At any rate, I was introduced to her in your drawing-
room,' retorted Mr. Slope.

' And shamefully you behaved there,' said Mrs. Proudie,
' most shamefully. I was wrong to allow you to remain
in the house a day after what I then saw. I should have
insisted on your instant dismissal.'

' I have yet to learn, Mrs. Proudie, that you have the
power to insist either on my going from hence or on my
staying here.'

' What ! ' said the lady ; ' I am not to have the privilege
of saying who shall and who shall not frequent my own
drawing-room ! I am not to save my servants and
dependents from having their morals corrupted by improper conduct ! I am not to save my own daughters
from impurity ! I will let you see, Mr. Slope, whether
I have the power or whether I have not. You will have
the goodness to understand that you no longer fill any
situation about the bishop ; and as your room will be
immediately wanted in the palace for another chaplain,
I must ask you to provide yourself with apartments as
soon as may be convenient to you.'

' My lord,' said Mr. Slope, appealing to the bishop,
and so turning his back completely on the lady, ' will
you permit me to ask that I may have from your own lips
any decision that you may have come to on this matter ? '

' Certainly, Mr. Slope, certainly,' said the bishop ; ' that
is but reasonable. Well, my decision is that you had
better look for some other preferment. For the situation
which you have lately held I do not think that you are
well suited.'

' And what, my lord, has been my fault ? '

' That Signora Neroni is one fault,' said Mrs. Proudie ;
' and a very abominable fault she is ; very abominable
and very disgraceful. Fie, Mr. Slope, fie ! You an
evangelical clergyman indeed ! '

' My lord, I desire to know for what fault I am turned
out of your lordship's house.'

' You hear what Mrs. Proudie says,' said the bishop.

' When I publish the history of this transaction, my lord,
as I decidedly shall do in my own vindication, I presume

you will not wish me to state that you have discarded me at your wife's bidding—because she has objected to my being acquainted with another lady, the daughter of one of the prebendaries of the chapter ? '

' You may publish what you please, sir,' said Mrs. Proudie. ' But you will not be insane enough to publish any of your doings in Barchester. Do you think I have not heard of your kneelings at that creature's feet—that is if she has any feet—and of your constant slobbering over her hand ? I advise you to beware, Mr. Slope, of what you do and say. Clergymen have been unfrocked for less than what you have been guilty of.'

' My lord, if this goes on I shall be obliged to indict this woman—Mrs. Proudie I mean—for defamation of character.'

' I think, Mr. Slope, you had better now retire,' said the bishop. ' I will enclose to you a cheque for any balance that may be due to you ; and, under the present circumstances, it will of course be better for all parties that you should leave the palace at the earliest possible moment. I will allow you for your journey back to London, and for your maintenance in Barchester for a week from this date.'

' If, however, you wish to remain in this neighbourhood,' said Mrs. Proudie, ' and will solemnly pledge yourself never again to see that woman, and will promise also to be more circumspect in your conduct, the bishop will mention your name to Mr. Quiverful, who now wants a curate at Puddingdale. The house is, I imagine, quite sufficient for your requirements : and there will moreover be a stipend of fifty pounds a year.'

' May God forgive you, madam, for the manner in which you have treated me,' said Mr. Slope, looking at her with a very heavenly look ; ' and remember this, madam, that you yourself may still have a fall ; ' and he looked at her with a very worldly look. ' As to the bishop, I pity him ! ' And so saying, Mr. Slope left the room. Thus ended the intimacy of the Bishop of Barchester with his first confidential chaplain.

Mrs. Proudie was right in this ; namely, that Mr. Slope was not insane enough to publish to the world any of his doings in Barchester. He did not trouble his friend Mr.

Towers with any written statement of the iniquity of
Mrs. Proudie, or the imbecility of her husband. He was
aware that it would be wise in him to drop for the future
all allusions to his doings in the cathedral city. Soon
after the interview just recorded, he left Barchester,
shaking the dust off his feet as he entered the railway
carriage ; and he gave no longing lingering look after the
cathedral towers, as the train hurried him quickly out
of their sight.

It is well known that the family of the Slopes never
starve : they always fall on their feet like cats, and let
them fall where they will, they live on the fat of the land.
Our Mr. Slope did so. On his return to town he found
that the sugar-refiner had died, and that his widow was
inconsolable : or, in other words, in want of consolation.
Mr. Slope consoled her, and soon found himself settled
with much comfort in the house in Baker Street. He
possessed himself, also, before long, of a church in the
vicinity of the New Road, and became known to fame as
one of the most eloquent preachers and pious clergymen
in that part of the metropolis. There let us leave him.

Of the bishop and his wife very little further need be
said. From that time forth nothing material occurred
to interrupt the even course of their domestic harmony.
Very speedily, a further vacancy on the bench of bishops
gave to Dr. Proudie the seat in the House of Lords, which
he at first so anxiously longed for. But by this time he
had become a wiser man. He did certainly take his seat,
and occasionally registered a vote in favour of Government views on ecclesiastical matters. But he had
thoroughly learnt that his proper sphere of action lay in
close contiguity with Mrs. Proudie's wardrobe. He never
again aspired to disobey, or seemed even to wish for
autocratic diocesan authority. If ever he thought of
freedom, he did so, as men think of the millennium, as
of a good time which may be coming, but which nobody
expects to come in their day. Mrs. Proudie might be
said still to bloom, and was, at any rate, strong ; and
the bishop had no reason to apprehend that he would
be speedily visited with the sorrows of a widower's life.

He is still Bishop of Barchester. He has so graced
that throne, that the Government has been averse to

translate him, even to higher dignities. There may he
remain, under safe pupilage, till the new-fangled manners
of the age have discovered him to be superannuated, and
bestowed on him a pension. As for Mrs. Proudie, our
prayers for her are that she may live for ever.

<h2 style="text-align:center">CHAPTER LII</h2>

THE NEW DEAN TAKES POSSESSION OF THE DEANERY, AND THE NEW WARDEN OF THE HOSPITAL

MR. HARDING and the archdeacon together made their
way to Oxford, and there, by dint of cunning argument,
they induced the Master of Lazarus also to ask himself this
momentous question : ' Why should not Mr. Arabin be
Dean of Barchester ? ' He of course, for a while tried his
hand at persuading Mr. Harding that he was foolish, over-
scrupulous, self-willed, and weak-minded ; but he tried
in vain. If Mr. Harding would not give way to Dr.
Grantly, it was not likely he would give way to Dr.
Gwynne ; more especially now that so admirable a scheme
as that of inducting Mr. Arabin into the deanery had been
set on foot. When the master found that his eloquence was
vain, and heard also that Mr. Arabin was about to become
Mr. Harding's son-in-law, he confessed that he also would,
under such circumstances, be glad to see his old friend and
protégé, the fellow of his college, placed in the comfortable
position that was going a-begging.

' It might be the means, you know, Master, of keeping
Mr. Slope out,' said the archdeacon with grave caution.

' He has no more chance of it,' said the master, ' than
our college chaplain. I know more about it than that.'

Mrs. Grantly had been right in her surmise. It was the
Master of Lazarus who had been instrumental in representing in high places the claims which Mr. Harding had
upon the Government, and he now consented to use his
best endeavours towards getting the offer transferred to
Mr. Arabin. The three of them went on to London
together, and there they remained a week, to the great
disgust of Mrs. Grantly, and most probably also of Mrs.
Gwynne. The minister was out of town in one direction,

and his private secretary in another. The clerks who remained could do nothing in such a matter as this, and all was difficulty and confusion. The two doctors seemed to have plenty to do; they bustled here and they bustled there, and complained at their club in the evenings that they had been driven off their legs; but Mr. Harding had no occupation. Once or twice he suggested that he might perhaps return to Barchester. His request, however, was peremptorily refused, and he had nothing for it but to while away his time in Westminster Abbey.

At length an answer from the great man came. The Master of Lazarus had made his proposition through the Bishop of Belgravia. Now this bishop, though but newly gifted with his diocesan honours, was a man of much weight in the clerico-political world. He was, if not as pious, at any rate as wise as St. Paul, and had been with so much effect all things to all men, that though he was great among the dons of Oxford, he had been selected for the most favourite seat on the bench by a Whig Prime Minister. To him Dr. Gwynne had made known his wishes and his arguments, and the bishop had made them known to the Marquis of Kensington Gore. The marquis, who was Lord High Steward of the Pantry Board, and who by most men was supposed to hold the highest office out of the cabinet, trafficked much in affairs of this kind. He not only suggested the arrangement to the minister over a cup of coffee, standing on a drawing-room rug in Windsor Castle, but he also favourably mentioned Mr. Arabin's name in the ear of a distinguished person.

And so the matter was arranged. The answer of the great man came, and Mr. Arabin was made Dean of Barchester. The three clergymen who had come up to town on this important mission dined together with great glee on the day on which the news reached them. In a silent, decent, clerical manner, they toasted Mr. Arabin with full bumpers of claret. The satisfaction of all of them was supreme. The Master of Lazarus had been successful in his attempt, and success is dear to us all. The archdeacon had trampled upon Mr. Slope, and had lifted to high honours the young clergyman whom he had induced to quit the retirement and comfort of the university. So at least the archdeacon thought; though, to speak

sooth, not he, but circumstances, had trampled on Mr.
Slope. But the satisfaction of Mr. Harding was, of all,
perhaps, the most complete. He laid aside his usual
melancholy manner, and brought forth little quiet jokes
from the inmost mirth of his heart; he poked his fun at
the archdeacon about Mr. Slope's marriage, and quizzed
him for his improper love for Mrs. Proudie. On the following day they all returned to Barchester.

It was arranged that Mr. Arabin should know nothing
of what had been done till he received the minister's letter
from the hands of his embryo father-in-law. In order that
no time might be lost, a message had been sent to him by
the preceding night's post, begging him to be at the
deanery at the hour that the train from London arrived.
There was nothing in this which surprised Mr. Arabin.
It had somehow got about through all Barchester that
Mr. Harding was the new dean, and all Barchester was
prepared to welcome him with pealing bells and full
hearts. Mr. Slope had certainly had a party; there had
certainly been those in Barchester who were prepared to
congratulate him on his promotion with assumed sincerity,
but even his own party was not broken-hearted by his
failure. The inhabitants of the city, even the high-souled
ecstatic young ladies of thirty-five, had begun to comprehend that their welfare, and the welfare of the place, was
connected in some mystèrious manner with daily chants
and bi-weekly anthems. The expenditure of the palace had
not added much to the popularity of the bishop's side of
the question; and, on the whole, there was a strong
reaction. When it became known to all the world that
Mr. Harding was to be the new dean, all the world rejoiced
heartily.

Mr. Arabin, we have said, was not surprised at the
summons which called him to the deanery. He had not
as yet seen Mr. Harding since Eleanor had accepted him,
nor had he seen him since he had learnt his future father-
in-law's preferment. There was nothing more natural,
more necessary, than that they should meet each other at
the earliest possible moment. Mr. Arabin was waiting
in the deanery parlour when Mr. Harding and Dr. Grantly
were driven up from the station.

There was some excitement in the bosoms of them all,

as they met and shook hands; by far too much to enable
either of them to begin his story and tell it in a proper
equable style of narrative. Mr. Harding was some
minutes quite dumbfounded, and Mr. Arabin could only
talk in short, spasmodic sentences about his love and good
fortune. He slipped in, as best he could, some sort of
congratulation about the deanship, and then went on with
his hopes and fears,—hopes that he might be received as
a son, and fears that he hardly deserved such good fortune.
Then he went back to the dean; it was the most thoroughly
satisfactory appointment, he said, of which he had ever
heard.

'But! but! but——' said Mr. Harding; and then
failing to get any further, he looked imploringly at the
archdeacon.

'The truth is, Arabin,' said the doctor, 'that, after all,
you are not destined to be son-in-law to a dean. Nor am
I either: more's the pity.'

Mr. Arabin looked at him for explanation. 'Is not Mr.
Harding to be the new dean?'

'It appears not,' said the archdeacon. Mr. Arabin's
face fell a little, and he looked from one to the other. It
was plainly to be seen from them both that there was no
cause of unhappiness in the matter, at least not of unhappiness to them; but there was as yet no elucidation
of the mystery.

'Think how old I am,' said Mr. Harding, imploringly.

'Fiddlestick!' said the archdeacon.

'That's all very well, but it won't make a young man
of me,' said Mr. Harding.

'And who is to be dean?' asked Mr. Arabin.

'Yes, that's the question,' said the archdeacon. 'Come,
Mr. Precentor, since you obstinately refuse to be anything
else, let us know who is to be the man. He has got the
nomination in his pocket.'

With eyes brim full of tears, Mr. Harding pulled out the
letter and handed it to his future son-in-law. He tried to
make a little speech, but failed altogether. Having given
up the document, he turned round to the wall, feigning to
blow his nose, and then sat himself down on the old dean's
dingy horse-hair sofa. And here we find it necessary to
bring our account of the interview to an end.

Nor can we pretend to describe the rapture with which Mr. Harding was received by his daughter. She wept with grief and wept with joy; with grief that her father should, in his old age, still be without that rank and worldly position which, according to her ideas, he had so well earned; and with joy in that he, her darling father, should have bestowed on that other dear one the good things of which he himself would not open his hand to take possession. And here Mr. Harding again showed his weakness. In the *mêlée* of this exposal of their loves and reciprocal affection, he found himself unable to resist the entreaties of all parties that the lodgings in the High Street should be given up. Eleanor would not live in the deanery, she said, unless her father lived there also. Mr. Arabin would not be dean, unless Mr. Harding would be co-dean with him. The archdeacon declared that his father-in-law should not have his own way in everything, and Mrs. Grantly carried him off to Plumstead, that he might remain there till Mr. and Mrs. Arabin were in a state to receive him in their own mansion.

Pressed by such arguments as these, what could a weak old man do but yield?

But there was yet another task which it behoved Mr. Harding to do before he could allow himself to be at rest. Little has been said in these pages of the state of those remaining old men who had lived under his sway at the hospital. But not on this account must it be presumed that he had forgotten them, or that in their state of anarchy and in their want of due government he had omitted to visit them. He visited them constantly, and had latterly given them to understand that they would soon be required to subscribe their adherence to a new master. There were now but five of them, one of them having been but quite lately carried to his rest,—but five of the full number, which had hitherto been twelve, and which was now to be raised to twenty-four, including women. Of these old Bunce, who for many years had been the favourite of the late warden, was one; and Abel Handy, who had been the humble means of driving that warden from his home, was another.

Mr. Harding now resolved that he himself would introduce the new warden to the hospital. He felt that many circumstances might conspire to make the men receive Mr. Quiverful with aversion and disrespect; he felt also that Mr. Quiverful might himself feel some qualms of conscience if he entered the hospital with an idea that he did so in hostility to his predecessor. Mr. Harding therefore determined to walk in, arm in arm with Mr. Quiverful, and to ask from these men their respectful obedience to their new master.

On returning to Barchester, he found that Mr. Quiverful had not yet slept in the hospital house, or entered on his new duties. He accordingly made known to that gentleman his wishes, and his proposition was not rejected.

It was a bright clear morning, though in November, that Mr. Harding and Mr. Quiverful, arm in arm, walked through the hospital gate. It was one trait in our old friend's character that he did nothing with parade. He omitted, even in the more important doings of his life, that sort of parade by which most of us deem it necessary to grace our important doings. We have housewarmings, christenings, and gala days; we keep, if not our own birthdays, those of our children; we are apt to fuss ourselves if called upon to change our residences, and have, almost all of us, our little state occasions. Mr. Harding had no state occasions. When he left his old house, he went forth from it with the same quiet composure as though he were merely taking his daily walk; and now that he re-entered it with another warden under his wing, he did so with the same quiet step and calm demeanour. He was a little less upright than he had been five years, nay, it was now nearly six years ago; he walked perhaps a little slower; his footfall was perhaps a thought less firm; otherwise one might have said that he was merely returning with a friend under his arm.

This friendliness was everything to Mr. Quiverful. To him, even in his poverty, the thought that he was supplanting a brother clergyman so kind and courteous as Mr. Harding, had been very bitter. Under his circumstances it had been impossible for him to refuse the proffered boon; he could not reject the bread that was offered to his children, or refuse to ease the heavy burden that had so long oppressed that poor wife of his; nevertheless, it had been very grievous to him to think that in going to the hospital he might encounter the ill will of his brethren in the diocese. All this Mr. Harding had fully comprehended. It was for such feelings as these, for the nice comprehension of such motives, that his heart and intellect were peculiarly fitted. In most matters of worldly import the archdeacon set down his father-in-law as little better than a fool. And perhaps he was right. But in some other matters, equally important if they be rightly judged, Mr. Harding, had he been so minded, might with as much propriety have set down his son-in-law for a fool. Few men, however, are constituted as was Mr. Harding. He had that nice appreciation of the feelings of others which belongs of right exclusively to women.

Arm in arm they walked into the inner quadrangle of the building, and there the five old men met them. Mr. Harding shook hands with them all, and then Mr. Quiverful did the same. With Bunce Mr. Harding shook hands twice, and Mr. Quiverful was about to repeat the same ceremony, but the old man gave him no encouragement.

' I am very glad to know that at last you have a new warden,' said Mr. Harding in a very cheery voice.

' We be very old for any change,' said one of them ; ' but we do suppose it be all for the best.'

' Certainly—certainly it is for the best,' said Mr. Harding. ' You will again have a clergyman of your own church under the same roof with you, and a very excellent clergyman you will have. It is a great satisfaction to me to know that so good a man is coming to take care of you, and that it is no stranger, but a friend of my own, who will allow me from time to time to come in and see you.'

' We be very thankful to your reverence,' said another of them.

' I need not tell you, my good friends,' said Mr. Quiverful, ' how extremely grateful I am to Mr. Harding for his kindness to me,—I must say his uncalled for, unexpected kindness.'

' He be always very kind,' said a third.

' What I can do to fill the void which he left here, I will do. For your sake and my own I will do so, and especially for his sake. But to you who have known him, I can never be the same well-loved friend and father that he has been.'

' No, sir, no,' said old Bunce, who hitherto had held his

peace; ' no one can be that. Not if the new bishop sent a hangel to us out of heaven. We doesn't doubt you'll do your best, sir, but you'll not be like the old master; not to us old ones.'

' Fie, Bunce, fie ! how dare you talk in that way ? ' said Mr. Harding ; but as he scolded the old man he still held him by his arm, and pressed it with warm affection.

There was no getting up any enthusiasm in the matter. How could five old men tottering away to their final resting-place be enthusiastic on the reception of a stranger? What could Mr. Quiverful be to them, or they to Mr. Quiverful ? Had Mr. Harding indeed come back to them, some last flicker of joyous light might have shone forth on their aged cheeks ; but it was in vain to bid them rejoice because Mr. Quiverful was about to move his fourteen children from Puddingdale into the hospital house. In reality they did no doubt receive advantage, spiritual as well as corporal ; but this they could neither anticipate nor acknowledge.

It was a dull affair enough, this introduction of Mr. Quiverful ; but still it had its effect. The good which Mr. Harding intended did not fall to the ground. All the Barchester world, including the five old bedesmen, treated Mr. Quiverful with the more respect, because Mr. Harding had thus walked in arm in arm with him, on his first entrance to his duties.

And here in their new abode we will leave Mr. and Mrs. Quiverful and their fourteen children. May they enjoy the good things which Providence has at length given to them !

CHAPTER LIII

CONCLUSION

THE end of a novel, like the end of a children's dinner-party, must be made up of sweetmeats and sugar-plums. There is now nothing else to be told but the gala doings of Mr. Arabin's marriage, nothing more to be described than the wedding dresses, no further dialogue to be recorded than that which took place between the archdeacon who married them, and Mr. Arabin and Eleanor who were married. ' Wilt thou have this woman to thy wedded wife,' and ' Wilt thou have this man to thy wedded husband, to

live together according to God's ordinance ? ' Mr. Arabin
and Eleanor each answered, ' I will.' We have no doubt
that they will keep their promises ; the more especially
as the Signora Neroni had left Barchester before the
ceremony was performed.

Mrs. Bold had been somewhat more than two years
a widow before she was married to her second husband,
and little Johnnie was then able with due assistance to
walk on his own legs into the drawing-room to receive the
salutations of the assembled guests. Mr. Harding gave
away the bride, the archdeacon performed the service,
and the two Miss Grantlys, who were joined in their
labours by other young ladies of the neighbourhood,
performed the duties of bridesmaids with equal diligence
and grace. Mrs. Grantly superintended the breakfast
and bouquets, and Mary Bold distributed the cards and
cake. The archdeacon's three sons had also come home
for the occasion. The eldest was great with learning, being
regarded by all who knew him as a certain future double
first. The second, however, bore the palm on this occasion,
being resplendent in a new uniform. The third was just
entering the university, and was probably the proudest
of the three.

But the most remarkable feature in the whole occasion
was the excessive liberality of the archdeacon. He literally
made presents to everybody. As Mr. Arabin had already
moved out of the parsonage of St. Ewold's, that scheme
of elongating the dining-room was of course abandoned ;
but he would have refurnished the whole deanery had he
been allowed. He sent down a magnificent piano by
Erard, gave Mr. Arabin a cob which any dean in the land
might have been proud to bestride, and made a special
present to Eleanor of a new pony chair that had gained
a prize in the Exhibition. Nor did he even stay his hand
here ; he bought a set of cameos for his wife, and a sapphire
bracelet for Miss Bold ; showered pearls and workboxes
on his daughters, and to each of his sons he presented
a cheque for 20l. On Mr. Harding he bestowed a magnificent violoncello with all the new-fashioned arrangements
and expensive additions, which, on account of these
novelties, that gentleman could never use with satisfaction
to his audience or pleasure to himself.

Those who knew the archdeacon well, perfectly understood the cause of his extravagance. 'Twas thus that he sang his song of triumph over Mr. Slope. This was his pæan, his hymn of thanksgiving, his loud oration. He had girded himself with his sword, and gone forth to the war; now he was returning from the field laden with the spoils of the foe. The cob and the cameos, the violoncello and the pianoforte, were all as it were trophies reft from the tent of his now conquered enemy.

The Arabins after their marriage went abroad for a couple of months, according to the custom in such matters now duly established, and then commenced their deanery life under good auspices. And nothing can be more pleasant than the present arrangement of ecclesiastical affairs in Barchester. The titular bishop never interfered, and Mrs. Proudie not often. Her sphere is more extended, more noble, and more suited to her ambition than that of a cathedral city. As long as she can do what she pleases with the diocese, she is willing to leave the dean and chapter to themselves. Mr. Slope tried his hand at subverting the old-established customs of the close, and from his failure she has learnt experience. The burly chancellor and the meagre little prebendary are not teased by any application respecting Sabbath-day schools, the dean is left to his own dominions, and the intercourse between Mrs. Proudie and Mrs. Arabin is confined to a yearly dinner given by each to the other. At these dinners Dr. Grantly will not take a part; but he never fails to ask for and receive a full account of all that Mrs. Proudie either does or says.

His ecclesiastical authority has been greatly shorn since the palmy days in which he reigned supreme as mayor of the palace to his father, but nevertheless such authority as is now left to him he can enjoy without interference. He can walk down the High Street of Barchester without feeling that those who see him are comparing his claims with those of Mr. Slope. The intercourse between Plumstead and the deanery is of the most constant and familiar description. Since Eleanor has been married to a clergyman, and especially to a dignitary of the church, Mrs. Grantly has found many more points of sympathy with her sister; and on a coming occasion, which is much looked forward to by all parties, she intends to spend a month or two at the deanery. She never thought of spending a month in Barchester when little Johnny Bold was born!

The two sisters do not quite agree on matters of church doctrine, though their differences are of the most amicable description. Mr. Arabin's church is two degrees higher than that of Mrs. Grantly. This may seem strange to those who will remember that Eleanor was once accused of partiality to Mr. Slope; but it is no less the fact. She likes her husband's silken vest, she likes his adherence to the rubric, she specially likes the eloquent philosophy of his sermons, and she likes the red letters in her own prayer-book. It must not be presumed that she has a taste for candles, or that she is at all astray about the real presence; but she has an inkling that way. She sent a handsome subscription towards certain very heavy ecclesiastical legal expenses which have lately been incurred in Bath, her name of course not appearing; she assumes a smile of gentle ridicule when the Archbishop of Canterbury is named, and she has put up a memorial window in the cathedral.

Mrs. Grantly, who belongs to the high and dry church, the high church as it was some fifty years since, before tracts were written and young clergymen took upon themselves the highly meritorious duty of cleaning churches, rather laughs at her sister. She shrugs her shoulders, and tells Miss Thorne that she supposes Eleanor will have an oratory in the deanery before she has done. But she is not on that account a whit displeased. A few high church vagaries do not, she thinks, sit amiss on the shoulders of a young dean's wife. It shows at any rate that her heart is in the subject; and it shows moreover that she is removed, wide as the poles asunder, from that cesspool of abomination in which it was once suspected that she would wallow and grovel. Anathema maranatha! Let anything else be held as blessed, so that that be well cursed. Welcome kneelings and bowings, welcome matins and complines, welcome bell, book, and candle, so that Mr. Slope's dirty surplices and ceremonial Sabbaths be held in due execration!

If it be essentially and absolutely necessary to choose between the two, we are inclined to agree with Mrs.

Grantly that the bell, book, and candle are the lesser evil of the two. Let it however be understood that no such necessity is admitted in these pages.

Dr. Arabin (we suppose he must have become a doctor when he became a dean) is more moderate and less outspoken on doctrinal points than his wife, as indeed in his station it behoves him to be. He is a studious, thoughtful, hard-working man. He lives constantly at the deanery, and preaches nearly every Sunday. His time is spent in sifting and editing old ecclesiastical literature, and in producing the same articles new. At Oxford he is generally regarded as the most promising clerical ornament of the age. He and his wife live together in perfect mutual confidence. There is but one secret in her bosom which he has not shared. He has never yet learned how Mr. Slope had his ears boxed.

The Stanhopes soon found that Mr. Slope's power need no longer operate to keep them from the delight of their Italian villa. Before Eleanor's marriage they had all migrated back to the shores of Como. They had not been resettled long before the signora received from Mrs. Arabin a very pretty though very short epistle, in which she was informed of the fate of the writer. This letter was answered by another, bright, charming, and witty, as the signora's letters always were; and so ended the friendship between Eleanor and the Stanhopes.

One word of Mr. Harding, and we have done.

He is still Precentor of Barchester, and still pastor of the little church of St. Cuthbert's. In spite of what he has so often said himself, he is not even yet an old man. He does such duties as fall to his lot well and conscientiously, and is thankful that he has never been tempted to assume others for which he might be less fitted.

The Author now leaves him in the hands of his readers; not as a hero, not as a man to be admired and talked of, not as a man who should be toasted at public dinners and spoken of with conventional absurdity as a perfect divine, but as a good man without guile, believing humbly in the religion which he has striven to teach, and guided by the precepts which he has striven to learn.

THE END

BOOK 3

An Eye for an Eye

CHAPTER I

SCROOPE MANOR

SOME YEARS ago it matters not how many, the old Earl of Scroope lived at Scroope Manor in Dorsetshire. The house was an Elizabethan structure of some pretensions, but of no fame. It was not known to sight-seers, as are so many of the residences of our nobility and country gentlemen. No days in the week were appointed for visiting its glories, nor was the housekeeper supposed to have a good thing in perquisites from showing it. It was a large brick building facing on to the village street—facing the village, if the hall-door of a house be the main characteristic of its face; but with a front on to its own grounds from which opened the windows of the chief apartments. The village of Scroope consisted of a straggling street a mile in length, with the church and parsonage at one end, and the Manor-house almost at the other. But the church stood within the park; and on that side of the street, for more than half its length, the high, gloomy wall of the Earl's domain stretched along in face of the publicans, bakers, grocers, two butchers, and retired private residents whose almost contiguous houses made Scroope itself seem to be more than a village to strangers. Close to the Manor and again near to the church, some favoured few had been allowed to build houses and to cultivate small gardens taken, as it were, in notches out of the Manor grounds; but these tenements must have been built at a time in which landowners were very much less jealous than they are now of such encroachments from their humbler neighbours.

The park itself was large, and the appendages to it such as were fit for an Earl's establishment—but there was little about it that was attractive. The land lay flat, and the timber, which was very plentiful, had not been made to group itself in picturesque forms. There was the Manor wood, containing some five hundred acres, lying beyond the church and far back from the road, intersected with so-called drives, which were unfit for any wheels but those of timber waggons—and round the whole park there was a broad belt of trees. Here and there about the large enclosed spaces there stood solitary oaks, in which the old Earl took pride; but at Scroope Manor there was none of that finished landscape beauty of which the owners of 'places' in England are so justly proud.

The house was large, and the rooms were grand and spacious. There was an enormous hall into one corner of which the front door opened. There was a vast library filled with old books which no one ever touched,—huge volumes of antiquated and now all but useless theology, and folio editions of the least known classics,—such as men now never read. Not a book had been added to it since the commencement of the century, and it may almost be said that no book had been drawn from its shelves for real use during the same period. There was a suite of rooms—salon with two withdrawing rooms which now were never opened. The big dining-room was used occasionally, as, in accordance with the traditions of the family, dinner was served there whenever there were guests at the Manor. Guests, indeed, at Scroope Manor were not very frequent—but Lady Scroope did occasionally have a friend or two to stay with her; and at long intervals the country clergymen and neighbouring squires were asked, with their wives, to dinner. When the Earl and his Countess were alone they used a small breakfast parlour, and between this and the big dining-room there was the little chamber in which the Countess usually lived. The Earl's own room was at the back, or if the reader pleases, front of the house, near the door leading into the street, and was, of all rooms in the house, the gloomiest.

The atmosphere of the whole place was gloomy. There were none of those charms of modern creation which now make the mansions of the wealthy among us bright and joyous. There was not a billiard table in the house. There was no conservatory nearer than the large old-fashioned greenhouse, which stood away by the kitchen garden and which seemed to belong exclusively to the gardener. The papers on the walls were dark and sombre. The mirrors were small and lustreless. The carpets were old and dingy. The windows did not open on to the terrace. The furniture was hardly ancient, but yet antiquated and uncomfortable. Throughout the house, and indeed throughout the estate, there was sufficient evidence of wealth; and there certainly was no evidence of parsimony; but at Scroope Manor money seemed never to have produced luxury. The household was very large. There was a butler, and a housekeeper, and various footmen, and a cook with large wages, and maidens in tribes to wait upon each other, and a colony of gardeners, and a coachman, and a head-groom, and under-grooms. All these lived well under the old Earl, and knew the value of their privileges. There was much to get, and almost nothing to do. A servant might live for ever at Scroope Manor,—if only sufficiently submissive to Mrs. Bunce the house-keeper. There was certainly no parsimony at the Manor, but the luxurious living of the household was confined to the servants' department.

To a stranger, and perhaps also to the inmates, the idea of gloom about the place was greatly increased by the absence of any garden or lawn near the house. Immediately in front of the mansion, and between it and the park, there ran two broad gravel terraces, one above another; and below these the deer would come and browse. To the left of the house, at nearly a quarter of a mile from it, there was a very large garden indeed—flower-gardens, and kitchen-gardens, and orchards; all ugly, and old-fashioned, but producing excellent crops in their kind. But they were away, and were not seen. Cut flowers were occasionally brought into the house— but the place was never filled with flowers as country houses are filled with them now-a-days. No doubt had Lady Scroope wished for more she might have had more.

Scroope itself, though a large village, stood a good deal out
of the world. Within the last year or two a railway has been
opened, with a Scroope Road Station, not above three miles
from the place; but in the old lord's time it was eleven miles
from its nearest station, at Dorchester, with which it had communication once a day by an omnibus. Unless a man had
business with Scroope nothing would take him there; and
very few people had business with Scroope. Now and then a
commercial traveller would visit the place with but faint
hopes as to trade. A post-office inspector once in twelve
months would call upon plethoric old Mrs. Applejohn, who
kept the small shop for stationery, and was known as the post-
mistress. The two sons of the vicar, Mr. Greenmarsh, would
pass backwards and forwards between their father's vicarage
and Malbro' school.* And occasionally the men and women of
Scroope would make a journey to their county town. But the
Earl was told that old Mrs. Brock of the Scroope Arms could
not keep the omnibus on the road unless he would subscribe
to aid it. Of course he subscribed. If he had been told by his
steward to subscribe to keep the cap on Mrs. Brock's head, he
would have done so. Twelve pounds a year his Lordship paid
towards the omnibus, and Scroope was not absolutely dissevered from the world.

The Earl himself was never seen out of his own domain,
except when he attended church. This he did twice every
Sunday in the year, the coachman driving him there in the
morning and the head-groom in the afternoon. Throughout
the household it was known to be the Earl's request to his
servants that they would attend divine service at least once
every Sunday. None were taken into service but they who
were or called themselves members of the Church Establishment. It is hardly probable that many dissenters threw away
the chance of such promotion on any frivolous pretext of
religion. Beyond this request, which, coming from the mouth
of Mrs. Bunce, became very imperative, the Earl hardly ever
interfered with his domestics. His own valet had attended
him for the last thirty years; but, beyond his valet and the

butler, he hardly knew the face of one of them. There was a
gamekeeper at Scroope Manor, with two under-gamekeepers;
and yet, for some years, no one, except the gamekeepers, had
ever shot over the lands. Some partridges and a few pheasants
were, however, sent into the house when Mrs. Bunce, moved
to wrath, would speak her mind on that subject.

The Earl of Scroope himself was a tall, thin man, something over seventy at the time of which I will now begin to
speak. His shoulders were much bent, but otherwise he
appeared to be younger than his age. His hair was nearly
white, but his eyes were still bright, and the handsome well-
cut features of his fine face were not reduced to shapeless-
ness by any of the ravages of time, as is so often the case with
men who are infirm as well as old. Were it not for the long
and heavy eyebrows, which gave something of severity to his
face, and for that painful stoop in his shoulders, he might
still have been accounted a handsome man. In youth he had
been a very handsome man, and had shone forth in the world,
popular, beloved and respected, with all the good things the
world could give. The first blow upon him was the death of
his wife. That hurt him sorely, but it did not quite crush him.
Then his only daughter died also, just as she became a bride.
High as the Lady Blanche Neville had stood herself, she had
married almost above her rank, and her father's heart had
been full of joy and pride. But she had perished childless,—
in child-birth, and again he was hurt almost to death. There
was still left to him a son—a youth indeed thoughtless, lavish,
and prone to evil pleasures. But thought would come with
the years; for almost any lavishness there were means sufficient; and evil pleasures might cease to entice. The young
Lord Neville was all that was left to the Earl, and for his heir
he paid debts and forgave injuries. The young man would
marry and all might be well. Then he found a bride for his
boy—with no wealth, but owning the best blood in the kingdom, beautiful, good, one who might be to him as another
daughter. His boy's answer was that he was already married!
He had chosen his wife from out of the streets,* and offered to

the Earl of Scroope as a child to replace the daughter who
had gone, a wretched painted prostitute from France. After
that Lord Scroope never again held up his head.

The father would not see his heir,—and never saw him
again. As to what money might be needed, the lawyers in
London were told to manage that. The Earl himself would
give nothing and refuse nothing. When there were debts—
debts for the second time, debts for the third time, the lawyers were instructed to do what in their own eyes seemed
good to them. They might pay as long as they deemed it right
to pay, but they might not name Lord Neville to his father.

While things were thus the Earl married again—the penniless daughter of a noble house—a woman not young, for
she was forty when he married her, but more than twenty
years his junior. It sufficed for him that she was noble, and
as he believed good. Good to him she was—with a duty that
was almost excessive. Religious she was, and self-denying;
giving much and demanding little; keeping herself in the
background, but possessing wonderful energy in the service
of others. Whether she could in truth be called good the
reader may say when he has finished this story.

Then, when the Earl had been married some three years
to his second wife, the heir died. He died, and as far as
Scroope Manor was concerned there was an end of him and
of the creature he had called his wife. An annuity was purchased for her. That she should be entitled to call herself
Lady Neville while she lived, was the sad necessity of the
condition. It was understood by all who came near the Earl
that no one was to mention her within his hearing. He was
thankful that no heir had come from that most horrid union.
The woman was never mentioned to him again, nor need she
trouble us further in the telling of our chronicle.

But when Lord Neville died, it was necessary that the old
man should think of his new heir. Alas; in that family,
though there was much that was good and noble, there had
ever been intestine feuds—causes of quarrel in which each
party would be sure that he was right. They were a people

who thought much of the church, who were good to the poor, who strove to be noble—but they could not forgive injuries. They could not forgive even when there were no injuries. The present Earl had quarrelled with his brother in early life—and had therefore quarrelled with all that had belonged to the brother. The brother was now gone, leaving two sons behind him—two young Nevilles, Fred and Jack, of whom Fred, the eldest, was now the heir. It was at last settled that Fred should be sent for to Scroope Manor. Fred came, being at that time a lieutenant in a cavalry regiment—a fine handsome youth of five and twenty, with the Neville eyes and Neville finely cut features. Kindly letters passed between the widowed mother and the present Lady Scroope; and it was decided at last, at his own request, that he should remain one year longer in the army, and then be installed as the eldest son at Scroope Manor. Again the lawyer was told to do what was proper in regard to money.

A few words more must be said of Lady Scroope, and then the preface to our story will be over. She too was an Earl's daughter, and had been much loved by our Earl's first wife. Lady Scroope had been the elder by ten years; but yet they had been dear friends, and Lady Mary Wycombe had passed many months of her early life amidst the gloom of the great rooms at Scroope Manor. She had thus known the Earl well before she consented to marry him. She had never possessed beauty—and hardly grace. She was strong featured, tall, with pride clearly written in her face. A reader of faces would have declared at once that she was proud of the blood which ran in her veins. She was very proud of her blood, and did in truth believe that noble birth was a greater gift than any wealth. She was thoroughly able to look down upon a parvenu millionaire—to look down upon such a one and not to pretend to despise him. When the Earl's letter came to her asking her to share his gloom, she was as poor as Charity —dependent on a poor brother who hated the burden of such claim. But she would have wedded no commoner, let his wealth and age have been as they might. She knew Lord

Scroope's age, and she knew the gloom of Scroope Manor; and she became his wife. To her of course was told the story of the heir's marriage, and she knew that she could expect no light, no joy in the old house from the scions of the rising family. But now all this was changed, and it might be that she could take the new heir to her heart.

CHAPTER II

FRED NEVILLE

WHEN FRED NEVILLE first came to the Manor, the old Earl trembled when called upon to receive him. Of the lad he had heard almost nothing—of his appearance literally nothing. It might be that his heir would be meanly visaged, a youth of whom he would have cause to be ashamed, one from whose countenance no sign of high blood would shine out; or, almost worse, he also might have that look, half of vanity, and half of vice, of which the father had gradually become aware in his own son, and which in him had degraded the Neville beauty. But Fred, to look at, was a gallant fellow— such a youth as women love to see about a house—well-made, active, quick, self-asserting, fair-haired, blue-eyed, short-lipped, with small whiskers, thinking but little of his own personal advantages, but thinking much of his own way. As far as the appearance of the young man went the Earl could not but be satisfied. And to him, at any rate in this, the beginning of their connexion, Fred Neville was modest and submissive.

'You are welcome to Scroope,' said the old man, receiving him with stately urbanity in the middle of the hall.

'I am so much obliged to you, uncle,' he said.

'You are come to me as a son, my boy—as a son. It will be your own fault if you are not a son to us in everything.'

Then in lieu of further words there shone a tear in each of the young man's eyes, much more eloquent to the Earl than could have been any words. He put his arm over his nephew's shoulders, and in this guise walked with him into the room in which Lady Scroope was awaiting them.

'Mary,' he said to his wife, 'here is our heir. Let him be a son to us.'

Then Lady Scroope took the young man in her arms and kissed him. Thus auspiciously was commenced this new connexion.

The arrival was in September, and the gamekeeper, with the under gamekeeper, had for the last month been told to be on his mettle. Young Mr. Neville was no doubt a sportsman. And the old groom had been warned that hunters might be wanted in the stables next winter. Mrs. Bunce was made to understand that liberties would probably be taken with the house, such as had not yet been perpetrated in her time —for the late heir had never made the Manor his home from the time of his leaving school. It was felt by all that great changes were to be effected—and it was felt also that the young man on whose behalf all this was to be permitted, could not but be elated by his position. Of such elation, however, there were not many signs. To his uncle, Fred Neville was, as has been said, modest and submissive; to his aunt he was gentle but not submissive. The rest of the household he treated civilly, but with none of that awe which was perhaps expected from him. As for shooting, he had come direct from his friend Carnaby's moor. Carnaby had forest as well as moor, and Fred thought but little of partridges—little of such old-fashioned partridge-shooting as was prepared for him at Scroope—after grouse and deer. As for hunting in Dorsetshire, if his uncle wished it—why in that case he would think of it. According to his ideas, Dorsetshire was not the best county in England for hunting. Last year his regiment had been at Bristol and he had ridden with the Duke's hounds.* This winter he was to be stationed in Ireland, and he had an idea that Irish hunting was good. If he found that his uncle made a point of it, he would bring his horses to Scroope for a month at Christmas. Thus he spoke to the head groom— and thus he spoke also to his aunt, who felt some surprise when he talked of Scotland* and his horses. She had thought that only men of large fortunes shot deer and kept studs— and perhaps conceived that the officers of the 20th Hussars* were generally engaged in looking after the affairs of their regiment, and in preparation for meeting the enemy.

Fred now remained a month at Scroope, and during that time there was but little personal intercourse between him and his uncle in spite of the affectionate greeting with which their acquaintance had been commenced. The old man's habits of life were so confirmed that he could not bring himself to alter them. Throughout the entire morning he would sit in his own room alone. He would then be visited by his steward, his groom, and his butler—and would think that he gave his orders, submitting, however, in almost everything to them. His wife would sometimes sit with him for half an hour, holding his hand, in moments of tenderness unseen and unsuspected by all the world around them. Sometimes the clergyman of the parish would come to him, so that he might know the wants of the people. He would have the newspaper in his hands for a while, and would daily read the Bible for an hour. Then he would slowly write some letter, almost measuring every point which his pen made—thinking that thus he was performing his duty as a man of business. Few men perhaps did less—but what he did do was good; and of self-indulgence there was surely none. Between such a one and the young man who had now come to his house there could be but little real connexion.

Between Fred Neville and Lady Scroope there arose a much closer intimacy. A woman can get nearer to a young man than can any old man—can learn more of his ways, and better understand his wishes. From the very first there arose between them a matter of difference, as to which there was no quarrel, but very much of argument. In that argument Lady Scroope was unable to prevail. She was very anxious that the heir should at once abandon his profession and sell out of the army. Of what use could it be to him now to run after his regiment to Ireland, seeing that undoubtedly the great duties of his life all centred at Scroope? There were many discussions on the subject, but Fred would not give way in regard to the next year. He would have this year, he said, to himself—and after that he would come and settle himself at Scroope. Yes; no doubt he would marry as soon as he could find a fitting wife. Of course it would be right that he should marry. He fully understood the responsibilities of his position—so he said, in answer to his aunt's eager, scrutinising, beseeching questions. But as he had joined his regiment, he thought it would be good for him to remain with it one year longer. He particularly desired to see something of Ireland, and if he did not do so now, he would never have the opportunity. Lady Scroope, understanding well that he was pleading for a year of grace from the dullness of the Manor, explained to him that his uncle would by no means expect that he should remain always at Scroope. If he would marry, the old London house should be prepared for him and his bride. He might travel—not, however, going very far afield. He might get into Parliament; as to which, if such were his ambition, his uncle would give him every aid. He might have his friends at Scroope Manor—Carnaby and all the rest of them. Every allurement was offered to him. But he had commenced by claiming a year of grace, and to that claim he adhered.

Could his uncle have brought himself to make the request in person, at first, he might probably have succeeded; and had he succeeded, there would have been no story for us as to the fortunes of Scroope Manor. But the Earl was too proud and perhaps too diffident to make the attempt. From his wife he heard all that took place; and though he was grieved, he expressed no anger. He could not feel himself justified in expressing anger because his nephew chose to remain for yet a year attached to his profession.

'Who knows what may happen to him?' said the Countess.

'Ah, indeed! But we are all in the hands of the Almighty.' And the Earl bowed his head. Lady Scroope, fully recognizing the truth of her husband's pious ejaculation, neverthless thought that human care might advantageously be added to the divine interposition for which, as she well knew, her lord prayed fervently as soon as the words were out of his mouth.

'But it would be so great a thing if he could be settled. Sophia Mellerby has promised to come here for a couple of months in the winter. He could not possibly do better than that.'

'The Mellerbys are very good people,' said the Earl. 'Her grandmother, the duchess, is one of the very best women in England. Her mother, Lady Sophia, is an excellent creature —religious, and with the soundest principles. Mr. Mellerby, as a commoner, stands as high as any man in England.'

'They have held the same property since the wars of the roses. And then I suppose the money should count for something,' added the lady.

Lord Scroope would not admit the importance of the money, but was quite willing to acknowledge that were his heir to make Sophia Mellerby the future Lady Scroope he would be content. But he could not interfere. He did not think it wise to speak to young men on such a subject. He thought that by doing so a young man might be rather diverted from than attracted to the object in view. Nor would he press his wishes upon his nephew as to next year. 'Were I to ask it,' he said, 'and were he to refuse me, I should be hurt. I am bound therefore to ask nothing that is unreasonable.'

Lady Scroope did not quite agree with her husband in this. She thought that as every thing was to be done for the young man; as money almost without stint was to be placed at his command; as hunting, parliament, and a house in London were offered to him—as the treatment due to a dear and only son was shown to him, he ought to give something in return; but she herself, could say no more than she had said, and she knew already that in those few matters in which her husband had a decided will, he was not to be turned from it.

It was arranged, therefore, that Fred Neville should join his regiment at Limerick in October, and that he should come home to Scroope for a fortnight or three weeks at Christmas. Sophia Mellerby was to be Lady Scroope's guest at that time, and at last it was decided that Mrs. Neville, who had never been seen by the Earl, should be asked to come and bring with her her younger son, John Neville, who had been successful in obtaining a commission in the Engineers. Other guests should be invited, and an attempt should be made to remove the mantle of gloom from Scroope Manor— with the sole object of ingratiating the heir.

Early in October Fred went to Limerick, and from thence with a detached troop of his regiment he was sent to the cavalry barracks at Ennis, the assize town of the neighbour-ing county Clare. This was at first held to be a misfortune by him, as Limerick is in all respects a better town than Ennis, and in county Limerick the hunting is far from being bad, whereas Clare is hardly a country for a Nimrod. But a young man, with money at command, need not regard distances; and the Limerick balls and the Limerick coverts were found to be equally within reach. From Ennis also he could attend some of the Galway meets—and then with no other superior than a captain hardly older than himself to interfere with his movements, he could indulge in that wild district the spirit of adventure which was strong within him. When young men are anxious to indulge the spirit of adventure, they generally do so by falling in love with young women of whom their fathers and mothers would not approve. In these days a spirit of adventure hardly goes further than this, unless it take a young man to a German gambling table.*

When Fred left Scroope it was understood that he was to correspond with his aunt. The Earl would have been utterly lost had he attempted to write a letter to his nephew without having something special to communicate to him. But Lady Scroope was more facile with her pen, and it was rightly thought that the heir would hardly bring himself to look upon Scroope as his home, unless some link were maintained between himself and the place. Lady Scroope therefore wrote once a week—telling everything that there was to be told of the horses, the game, and even of the tenants. She studied her letters, endeavouring to make them light and agreeable —such as a young man of large prospects would like to receive from his own mother. He was 'Dearest Fred,' and in one of those earliest written she expressed a hope that should any trouble ever fall upon him he would come to her as to his dearest friend. Fred was not a bad correspondent, and answered about every other letter. His replies were short, but that was a matter of course. He was 'as jolly as a sandboy,' 'right as a trivet'; had had 'one or two very good things,' and thought that upon the whole he liked Ennis better than Limerick. 'Johnstone is such a deuced good fellow!' Johnstone was the captain of the 20th Hussars who happened to be stationed with him at Limerick. Lady Scroope did not quite like the epithet, but she knew that she had to learn to hear things to which she had hitherto not been accustomed.

This was all very well—but Lady Scroope, having a friend in Co. Clare, thought that she might receive tidings of the adopted one which would be useful, and with this object she opened a correspondence with Lady Mary Quin. Lady Mary Quin was a daughter of the Earl of Kilfenora, and was well acquainted with all County Clare. She was almost sure to hear of the doings of any officers stationed at Ennis, and would do so certainly in regard to an officer that was specially introduced to her. Fred Neville was invited to stay at Castle Quin as long as he pleased, and actually did pass one night under its roof. But, unfortunately for him, that spirit of adventure which he was determined to indulge led him into the neighbourhood of Castle Quin when it was far from his intention to interfere with the Earl or with Lady Mary, and thus led to the following letter which Lady Scroope received about the middle of December—just a week before Fred's return to the Manor.

QUIN CASTLE, ENNISTIMON,
14 December, 18—.

'MY DEAR LADY SCROOPE,

'Since I wrote to you before Mr. Neville has been here once, and we all liked him very much. My father was quite taken with him. He is always fond of the young officers, and is not the less inclined to be so of one who is so dear and near to you. I wish he would have stayed longer, and hope that he shall come again. We have not much to offer in the way of amusement, but in January and February there is good snipe shooting.

'I find that Mr. Neville is very fond of shooting—so much so that before we knew anything of him except his name we had heard that he had been on our coast after seals and sea birds. We have very high cliffs near here—some people say the highest in the world, and there is one called the Hag's Head from which men get down and shoot sea-gulls. He has been different times in our village of Liscannor, and I think he has a boat there or at Lahinch. I believe he has already killed ever so many seals.

'I tell you all this for a reason. I hope that it may come to nothing, but I think that you ought to know. There is a widow lady living not very far from Liscannor, but nearer up to the cliffs. Her cottage is on papa's property, but I think she holds it from somebody else. I don't like to say anything to papa about it. Her name is Mrs. O'Hara, and she has a daughter.'

When Lady Scroope had read so far, she almost let the paper drop from her hand. Of course she knew what it all meant. An Irish Miss O'Hara! And Fred Neville was spending his time in pursuit of this girl! Lady Scroope had known what it would be when the young man was allowed to return to his regiment in spite of the manifold duties which should have bound him to Scroope Manor.

'I have seen this young lady,' continued Lady Mary, 'and she is certainly very pretty. But nobody knows anything about them; and I cannot even learn whether they belong to the real O'Haras. I should think not, as they are Roman Catholics. At any rate Miss O'Hara can hardly be a fitting companion for Lord Scroope's heir. I believe they are ladies, but I don't think that any one knows them here, except the priest of Kilmacrenny. We never could make out quite why they came here—only that Father Marty knows something about them. He is the priest of Kilmacrenny. She is a very pretty girl, and I never heard a word against her—but I don't know whether that does not make it worse, because a young man is so likely to get entangled.

'I daresay nothing shall come of it, and I'm sure I hope that nothing may. But I thought it best to tell you. *Pray* do not let him know that you have heard from me. Young men are so very particular about things, and I don't know what he might say of me if he knew that I had written home to you about his private affairs. All the same if I can be of any service to you, pray let me know. Excuse haste. And believe me to be,

Yours most sincerely,
MARY QUIN.'

A Roman Catholic—one whom no one knew but the priest —a girl who perhaps never had a father! All this was terrible to Lady Scroope. Roman Catholics—and especially Irish Roman Catholics—were people whom, as she thought, every one should fear in this world, and for whom everything was to be feared in the next. How would it be with the Earl if this heir also were to tell him some day that he was married? Would not his grey hairs be brought to the grave with a double load of sorrow? However, for the present she thought it better to say not a word to the Earl.

CHAPTER III

SOPHIE MELLERBY

LADY SCROOPE thought a great deal about her friend's communication, but at last made up her mind that she could do nothing till Fred should have returned. Indeed she hardly knew what she could do when he did come back. The more she considered it the greater seemed to her to be the difficulty of doing anything. How is a woman, how is even a mother, to caution a young man against the danger of becoming acquainted with a pretty girl? She could not mention Miss O'Hara's name without mentioning that of Lady Mary Quin in connexion with it. And when asked, as of course she would be asked, as to her own information what could she say? She had been told that he had made himself acquainted with a widow lady who had a pretty daughter, and that was all! When young men will run into such difficulties, it is, alas, so very difficult to interfere with them!

And yet the matter was of such importance as to justify almost any interference. A Roman Catholic Irish girl of whom nothing was known but that her mother was said to be a widow, was, in Lady Scroope's eyes, as formidable a danger as could come in the way of her husband's heir. Fred Neville was, she thought, with all his good qualities, exactly the man to fall in love with a wild Irish girl.* If Fred were to write home some day and say that he was about to marry such a bride—or, worse again, that he married her, the tidings would nearly kill the Earl. After all that had been endured, such a termination to the hopes of the family would be too cruel! And Lady Scroope could not but feel the injustice of it. Every thing was being done for this heir, for whom nothing need have been done. He was treated as a son, but

714

he was not a son. He was treated with exceptional favour as a son. Everything was at his disposal. He might marry and begin life at once with every want amply supplied, if he would only marry such a woman as was fit to be a future Countess of Scroope. Very little was required from him. He was not expected to marry an heiress. An heiress indeed was prepared for him, and would be there, ready for him at Christmas—an heiress, beautiful, well-born, fit in every respect—religious too. But he was not to be asked to marry Sophie Mellerby. He might choose for himself. There were other well-born young women about the world—duchesses' granddaughters in abundance! But it was imperative that he should marry at least a lady, and at least a Protestant.

Lady Scroope felt very strongly that he should never have been allowed to rejoin his regiment, when a home at Scroope was offered to him. He was a free agent of course, and equally of course the title and the property must ultimately be his. But something of a bargain might have been made with him when all the privileges of a son were offered to him. When he was told that he might have all Scroope to himself—for it amounted nearly to that; that he might hunt there and shoot there and entertain his friends; that the family house in London should be given up to him if he would marry properly; that an income almost without limit should be provided for him, surely it would not have been too much to demand that as a matter of course he should leave the army! But this had not been done; and now there was an Irish Roman Catholic widow with a daughter, with sea-shooting and a boat and high cliffs right in the young man's way! Lady Scroope could not analyse it, but felt all the danger as though it were by instinct. Partridge and pheasant shooting on a gentleman's own grounds, and an occasional day's hunting with the hounds in his own county, were, in Lady Scroope's estimation, becoming amusements for an English gentleman. They did not interfere with the exercise of his duties. She had by no means brought herself to like the yearly raids into Scotland made latterly by sportsmen. But if Scotch

moors and forests were dangerous, what were Irish cliffs!
Deer-stalking was bad in her imagination. She was almost
sure that when men went up to Scotch forests they did not go
to church on Sundays. But the idea of seal-shooting was much
more horrible. And then there was that priest who was the
only friend of the widow who had the daughter!

On the morning of the day in which Fred was to reach the
Manor, Lady Scroope did speak to her husband. 'Don't you
think, my dear, that something might be done to prevent
Fred's returning to that horrid country?'

'What can we do?'

'I suppose he would wish to oblige you. You are being very
good to him.'

'It is for the old to give, Mary, and for the young to accept.
I do all for him because he is all to me; but what am I to
him, that he should sacrifice any pleasure for me? He can
break my heart. Were I even to quarrel with him, the worst
I could do would be to send him to the money-lenders for a
year or two.'

'But why should he care about his regiment now?'

'Because his regiment means liberty '

'And you won't ask him to give it up?'

'I think not. If I were to ask him I should expect him to
yield; and then I should be disappointed were he to refuse. I
do not wish him to think me a tyrant.'

This was the end of the conversation, for Lady Scroope did
not as yet dare to speak to the Earl about the widow and her
daughter. She must now try her skill and eloquence with the
young man himself.

The young man arrived and was received with kindest
greetings. Two horses had preceded him, so that he might
find himself mounted as soon as he chose after his arrival,
and two others were coming. This was all very well, but his
aunt was a little hurt when he declared his purpose of going
down to the stables just as she told him that Sophia Mellerby
was in the house. He arrived on the 23rd at 4 p.m., and it
had been declared that he was to hunt on the morrow. It was

already dark, and surely he might have been content on the first evening of his arrival to abstain from the stables! Not a word had been said to Sophie Mellerby of Lady Scroope's future hopes. Lady Scroope and Lady Sophia would each have thought that it was wicked to do so. But the two women had been fussy, and Miss Mellerby must have been less discerning than are young ladies generally, had she not understood what was expected of her. Girls are undoubtedly better prepared to fall in love with men whom they had never seen, than are men with girls. It is a girl's great business in life to love and to be loved. Of some young men it may almost be said that it is their great business to avoid such a castastrophe. Such ought not to have been the case with Fred Neville now —but in such light he regarded it. He had already said to himself that Sophie Mellerby was to be pitched at his head. He knew no reason—none as yet—why he should not like Miss Mellerby well enough. But he was a little on his guard against her, and preferred seeing his horses first. Sophie, when according to custom, and indeed in this instance in accordance with special arrangement, she went into Lady Scroope's sitting-room for tea, was rather disappointed at not finding Mr. Neville there. She knew that he had visited his uncle immediately on his arrival, and having just come in from the park she had gone to her room to make some little preparation for the meeting. If it was written in Fate's book· that she was to be the next Lady Scroope, the meeting was important. Perhaps that writing in Fate's book might depend on the very adjustment which she was now making of her hair.

'He has gone to look at his horses,' said Lady Scroope, unable not to shew her disappointment by the tone of her voice.

'That is so natural,' said Sophie, who was more cunning. 'Young men almost idolize their horses. I should like to go and see Dandy whenever he arrives anywhere, only I don't dare!' Dandy was Miss Mellerby's own horse, and was accustomed to make journeys up and down between Mellerby and London.

'I don't think horses and guns and dogs should be too much thought of,' said Lady Scroope gravely. 'There is a tendency I think at present to give them an undue importance. When our amusements become more serious to us than our business, we must be going astray.'

'I suppose we always are going astray,' said Miss Mellerby.

Lady Scroope sighed and shook her head; but in shaking it she showed that she completely agreed with the opinion expressed by her guest.

As there were only two horses to be inspected, and as Fred Neville absolutely refused the groom's invitation to look at the old carriage horses belonging to the family, he was back in his aunt's room before Miss Mellerby had gone upstairs to dress for dinner. The introduction was made, and Fred did his best to make himself agreeable. He was such a man that no girl could, at the first sight of him, think herself injured by being asked to love him. She was a good girl, and would have consented to marry no man without feeling sure of his affections; but Fred Neville was bold and frank as well as handsome, and had plenty to say for himself. It might be that he was vicious, or ill-tempered, or selfish, and it would be necessary that she should know much of him before she would give herself into his keeping; but as far as the first sight went, and the first hearing, Sophie Mellerby's impressions were all in Fred's favour. It is no doubt a fact that with the very best of girls a man is placed in a very good light by being heir to a peerage and a large property.

'Do you hunt, Miss Mellerby?' he asked. She shook her head and looked grave, and then laughed. Among her people hunting was not thought to be a desirable accomplishment for young ladies. 'Almost all girls do hunt now,' said Fred.

'Do you think it is a nice amusement for young ladies?' asked the aunt in a severe tone.

'I don't see why not—that is if they know how to ride.'

'I know how to ride,' said Sophie Mellerby.

'Riding is all very well,' said Lady Scroope. 'I quite approve of it for girls. When I was young, everybody did not ride as they do now. Nevertheless it is very well, and is thought to be healthy. But as for hunting, Sophie, I'm sure your mamma would be very much distressed if you were to think of such a thing.'

'But dear Lady Scroope, I haven't thought of it, and I am not going to think of it—and if I thought of it ever so much, I shouldn't do it. Poor mamma would be frightened into fits —only that nobody at Mellerby could possibly be made to believe it, unless they saw me doing it.'

'Then there can be no reason why you should't make the attempt,' said Fred. Upon which Lady Scroope pretended to look grave, and told him that he was very wicked. But let an old lady be ever so strict towards her own sex, she likes a little wickedness in a young man—if only he does not carry it to the extent of marrying the wrong sort of young woman.

Sophia Mellerby was a tall, graceful, well-formed girl, showing her high blood in every line of her face. On her mother's side she had come from the Ancrums, whose family, as everybody knows, is one of the oldest in England; and, as the Earl had said, the Mellerbys had been Mellerbys from the time of King John, and had been living on the same spot for at least four centuries. They were and always had been Mellerbys of Mellerby—the very name of the parish being the same as that of the family. If Sophia Mellerby did not show breeding, what girl could show it? She was fair, with a somewhat thin oval face, with dark eyes, and an almost perfect Grecian nose. Her mouth was small, and her chin delicately formed. And yet it can hardly be said that she was beautiful. Or, if beautiful, she was so in women's eyes rather than in those of men. She lacked colour and perhaps animation in her countenance. She had more character, indeed, than was told by her face, which is generally so true an index of the mind. Her education had been as good as England could afford, and her intellect had been sufficient to enable her to make use of it. But her chief charm in the eyes of many consisted in the fact, doubted by none, that she was every inch a lady. She was an only daughter, too—with an only brother; and as the Ancrums were all rich, she would have a very pretty fortune of her own. Fred Neville, who had literally been nobody before his cousin had died, might certainly do much worse than marry her.

And after a day or two they did seem to get on very well together. He had reached Scroope on the 21st, and on the 23rd Mrs. Neville arrived with her youngest son Jack Neville.* This was rather a trial to the Earl, as he had never yet seen his brother's widow. He had heard when his brother married that she was fast, fond of riding, and loud. She had been the daughter of a Colonel Smith, with whom his brother, at that time a Captain Neville, had formed acquaintance—and had been a beauty very well known as such at Dublin and other garrison towns. No real harm had ever been known of her, but the old Earl had always felt that his brother had made an unfortunate marriage. As at that time they had not been on speaking terms, it had not signified much—but there had been a prejudice at Scroope against the Captain's wife, which by no means died out when the late Julia Smith became the Captain's widow with two sons. Old reminiscences remain very firm with old people—and Lord Scroope was still much afraid of the fast, loud beauty. His principles told him that he should not sever the mother from the son, and that as it suited him to take the son for his own purposes, he should also, to some extent, accept the mother also. But he dreaded the affair. He dreaded Mrs. Neville; and he dreaded Jack, who had been so named after his gallant grandfather, Colonel Smith. When Mrs. Neville arrived, she was found to be so subdued and tame that she could hardly open her mouth before the old Earl. Her loudness, if she ever had been loud, was certainly all gone—and her fastness, if ever she had been fast, had been worn out of her. She was an old woman, with the relics of great beauty, idolizing her two sons for whom all her life had been a sacrifice, in weak health, and prepared, if necessary, to sit in silent awe at the feet of the Earl who had been so good to her boy.

'I don't know how to thank you for what you have done,' she said, in a low voice.

'No thanks are required,' said the Earl. 'He is the same to us as if he were our own.' Then she raised the old man's hand and kissed it—and the old man owned to himself that he had made a mistake.

As to Jack Neville——. But Jack Neville shall have another chapter opened on his behalf.

CHAPTER IV

JACK NEVILLE

JOHN IS a very respectable name—perhaps there is no name more respectable in the English language. Sir John, as the head of a family, is certainly as respectable as any name can be. For an old family coachman it beats all names. Mr. John Smith would be sure to have a larger balance at his banker's than Charles Smith or Orlando Smith—or perhaps than any other Smith whatever. The Rev. Frederic Walker might be a wet parson,* but the Rev. John Walker would assuredly be a good clergyman at all points, though perhaps a little dull in his sermons. Yet almost all Johns have been Jacks, and Jack, in point of respectibility, is the very reverse of John. How it is, or when it is, that the Jacks become re-Johned, and go back to the original and excellent name given to them by their godfathers and godmothers, nobody ever knows. Jack Neville, probably through some foolish fondness on his mother's part, had never been re-Johned—and consequently the Earl, when he made up his mind to receive his sister-in-law, was at first unwilling to invite his younger nephew. 'But he is in the Engineers,' said Lady Scroope. The argument had its weight, and Jack Neville was invited. But even that argument failed to obliterate the idea which had taken hold of the Earl's mind. There had never yet been a Jack among the Scroopes.

When Jack came he was found to be very unlike the Nevilles in appearance. In the first place he was dark, and in the next place he was ugly. He was a tall, well-made fellow, taller than his brother, and probably stronger; and he had very different eyes—very dark brown eyes, deeply set in his head, with large dark eyebrows. He wore his black hair very short, and

722

had no beard whatever. His features were hard, and on one cheek he had a cicatrice, the remains of some misfortune that had happened to him in his boyhood. But in spite of his ugliness— for he was ugly, there was much about him in his gait and manner that claimed attention. Lord Scroope, the moment that he saw him, felt that he ought not to be called Jack. Indeed the Earl was almost afraid of him, and so after a time was the Countess.

'Jack ought to have been the eldest,' Fred had said to his aunt.

'Why should he have been the eldest?'

'Because he is so much the cleverest. I could never have got into the Engineers.'*

'That seems to be a reason why he should be the youngest,' said Lady Scroope.

Two or three other people arrived, and the house became much less dull than was its wont. Jack Neville occasionally rode his brother's horses, and the Earl was forced to acknowledge another mistake. The mother was very silent, but she was a lady. The young Engineer was not only a gentleman— but for his age a very well educated gentleman, and Lord Scroope was almost proud of his relatives. For the first week the affair between Fred Neville and Miss Mellerby really seemed to make progress. She was not a girl given to flirting —not prone to outward demonstrations of partiality for a young man; but she never withdrew herself from her intended husband, and Fred seemed quite willing to be attentive. Not a word was said to hurry the young people, and Lady Scroope's hopes were high. Of course no allusion had been made to those horrid Irish people, but it did not seem to Lady Scroope that the heir had left his heart behind him in Co. Clare.

Fred had told his aunt in one of his letters that he would stay three weeks at Scroope, but she had not supposed that he would limit himself exactly to that period. No absolute limit had been fixed for the visit of Mrs. Neville and her younger son, but it was taken for granted that they would not remain should Fred depart. As to Sophie Mellerby, her visit was elastic. She was there for a purpose, and might remain all the winter if the purpose could be so served. For the first fortnight Lady Scroope thought that the affair was progressing well. Fred hunted three days a week, and was occasionally away from home—going to dine with a regiment at Dorchester, and once making a dash up to London; but his manner to Miss Mellerby was very nice, and there could be no doubt but that Sophie liked him. When, on a sudden, the heir said a word to his aunt which was almost equal to firing a pistol at her head. 'I think Master Jack is making it all square with Sophie Mellerby.'

If there was anything that Lady Scroope hated almost as much as improper marriages it was slang. She professed that she did not understand it; and in carrying out her profession always stopped the conversation to have any word explained to her which she thought had been used in an improper sense. The idea of a young man making it 'all square' with a young woman was repulsive, but the idea of this young man making it 'all square' with this young woman was so much more repulsive, and the misery to her was so intensely heightened by the unconcern displayed by the heir in so speaking of the girl with whom he ought to have been making it 'all square' himself, that she could hardly allow herself to be arrested by that stumbling block. 'Impossible!' she exclaimed—that is if you mean—if you mean—if you mean anything at all.'

'I do mean a good deal.'

'Then I don't believe a word of it. It's quite out of the question. It's impossible. I'm quite sure your brother understands his position as a gentleman too thoroughly to dream of such a thing.'

This was Greek to Fred Neville. Why his brother should not fall in love with a pretty girl, and why a pretty girl should not return the feeling, without any disgrace to his brother, Fred could not understand. His brother was a

Neville, and was moreover an uncommonly clever fellow.
'Why shouldn't he dream of it?'

'In the first place—. Well! I did think, Fred, that you
yourself seemed to be—seemed to be taken with Miss
Mellerby.'

'Who? I? Oh, dear no. She's a very nice girl and all that,
and I like her amazingly. If she were Jack's wife, I never saw
a girl I should so much like for a sister.'

'It's quite out of the question. I wonder that you can speak
in such a way. What right can your brother have to think of
such a girl as Miss Mellerby? He has no position—no means.'

'He is my brother,' said Fred, with a little touch of anger—
already discounting his future earldom on his brother's behalf.

'Yes—he is your brother; but you don't suppose that Mr.
Mellerby would give his daughter to an officer in the
Engineers who has, as far as I know, no private means what-
ever.'

'He will have—when my mother dies. Of course I can't
speak of doing anything for anybody at present. I may die
before my uncle. Nothing is more likely. But then, if I do,
Jack would be my uncle's heir.'

'I don't believe there's anything in it at all,' said Lady
Scroope in great dudgeon.

'I dare say not. If there is, they haven't told me. It's not
likely they would. But I thought I saw something coming up,
and as it seemed to be the most natural thing in the world,
I mentioned it. As for me—Miss Mellerby doesn't care a
straw for me. You may be sure of that.'

'She would—if you'd ask her.'

'But I never shall ask her. What's the use of beating about
the bush, aunt? I never shall ask her; and if I did, she
wouldn't have me. If you want to make Sophie Mellerby your
niece, Jack's your game.'

Lady Scroope was ineffably disgusted. To be told that 'Jack
was her game' was in itself a terrible annoyance to her. But
to be so told in reference to such a subject was painful in the

extreme. Of course she could not make this young man marry as she wished. She had acknowledged to herself from the first that there could be no cause of anger against him should he not fall into the silken net which was spread for him. Lady Scroope was not an unreasonable woman, and understood well the power which young people have over old people. She knew that she couldn't quarrel with Fred Neville, even if she would. He was the heir, and in a very few years would be the owner of everything. In order to keep him straight, to save him from debts, to protect him from money-lenders, and to secure the family standing and property till he should have made things stable by having a wife and heir of his own, all manner of indulgence must be shown him. She quite understood that such a horse must be ridden with a very light hand. She must put up with slang from him, though she would resent it from any other human being. He must be allowed to smoke in his bed-room, to be late at dinner, to shirk morning prayers—making her only too happy if he would not shirk Sunday church also. Of course he must choose a bride for himself—only not a Roman Catholic wild Irish bride of whom nobody knew anything!

As to that other matter concerning Jack and Sophie Mellerby, she could not bring herself to believe it. She had certainly seen that they were good friends—as would have been quite fit had Fred been engaged to her; but she had not conceived the possibility of any mistake on such a subject. Surely Sophie herself knew better what she was about! How would she—she, Lady Scroope—answer it to Lady Sophia, if Sophie should go back to Mellerby from her house, engaged to a younger brother who had nothing but a commission in the Engineers? Sophie had been sent to Scroope on purpose to be fallen in love with by the heir; and how would it be with Lady Scroope if, in lieu of this, she should not only have been fallen in love with by the heir's younger brother, but have responded favourably to so base an affection?

That same afternoon Fred told his uncle that he was going

back to Ireland on the day but one following, thus curtailing his promised three weeks by two days.

'I am sorry that you are so much hurried, Fred,' said the old man.

'So am I, my lord—but Johnstone has to go to London on business, and I promised when I got leave that I wouldn't throw him over. You see—when one has a profession one must attend to it—more or less.'

'But you hardly need the profession.'

'Thank you, uncle—it is very kind of you to say so. And as you wish me to leave it, I will when the year is over. I have told the fellows that I shall stay till next October, and I shouldn't like to change now.' The Earl hadn't another word to say.

But on the day before Fred's departure there came a short note from Lady Mary Quin which made poor Lady Scroope more unhappy than ever. Tidings had reached her in a mysterious way that the O'Haras were eagerly expecting the return of Mr. Neville. Lady Mary thought that if Mr. Neville's quarters could be moved from Ennis, it would be very expedient for many reasons. She knew that enquiries had been made for him and that he was engaged to dine on a certain day with Father Marty the priest. Father Marty would no doubt go any lengths to serve his friends the O'Haras. Then Lady Mary was very anxious that not a word should be said to Mr. Neville which might lead him to suppose that reports respecting him were being sent from Quin Castle to Scroope.

The Countess in her agony thought it best to tell the whole story to the Earl. 'But what can I do?' said the old man. 'Young men will form these acquaintances.' His fears were evidently as yet less dark than those of his wife.

'It would be very bad if we were to hear that he was married to a girl of whom we only know that she is a Roman Catholic and friendless.'

The Earl's brow became very black. 'I don't think that he would treat me in that way.'

'Not meaning it, perhaps—but if he should become entangled and make a promise!'

Then the Earl did speak to his nephew. 'Fred,' he said, 'I
have been thinking a great deal about you. I have little else
to think of now. I should take it as a mark of affection from
you if you would give up the army—at once.'

'And not join my regiment again at all?'

'It is absurd that you should do so in your present position.
You should be here, and learn the circumstances of the property before it becomes your own. There can hardly be more
than a year or two left for the lesson.'

The Earl's manner was very impressive. He looked into
his nephew's face as he spoke, and stood with his hand upon
the young man's shoulder. But Fred Neville was a Neville all
over—and the Nevilles had always chosen to have their own
way. He had not the power of intellect nor the finished man-
liness which his brother possessed; but he could be as obstinate as any Neville—as obstinate as his father had been, or
his uncle. And in this matter he had arguments which his
uncle could hardly answer on the spur of the moment. No
doubt he could sell out in proper course,* but at the present
moment he was as much bound by military law to return as
would be any common soldier at the expiration of his fur-
lough. He must go back. That at any rate was certain. And if
his uncle did not much mind it, he would prefer to remain
with his regiment till October.

Lord Scroope could not condescend to repeat his request,
or even again to allude to it. His whole manner altered as he
took his hand away from his nephew's shoulder. But still he
was determined that there should be no quarrel. As yet there
was no ground for quarrelling—and by any quarrel the injury to him would be much greater than any that could befall
the heir. He stood for a moment and then he spoke again in
a tone very different from that he had used before. 'I hope,'
he said—and then he paused again; 'I hope you know how
very much depends on your marrying in a manner suitable
to your position.'

'Quite so—I think.'

'It is the one hope left to me to see you properly settled in life.'

'Marriage is a very serious thing, uncle. Suppose I were not to marry at all! Sometimes I think my brother is much more like marrying than I am.'

'You are bound to marry,' said the Earl solemnly. 'And you are specially bound by every duty to God and man to make no marriage that will be disgraceful to the position which you are called upon to fill.'

'At any rate I will not do that,' said Fred Neville proudly. From this the Earl took some comfort, and then the interview was over.

On the day appointed by himself Fred left the Manor, and his mother and brother went on the following day. But after he was gone, on that same afternoon, Jack Neville asked Sophie Mellerby to be his wife. She refused him—with all the courtesy she knew how to use, but also with all the certainty. And as soon as he had left the house she told Lady Scroope what had happened.

CHAPTER V

ARDKILL COTTAGE

THE CLIFFS of Moher in Co. Clare, on the western coast of Ireland, are not as well known to tourists as they should be. It may be doubted whether Lady Mary Quin was right when she called them the highest cliffs in the world, but they are undoubtedly very respectable cliffs, and run up some six hundred feet from the sea as nearly perpendicular as cliffs should be. They are beautifully coloured, streaked with yellow veins, and with great masses of dark red rock; and beneath them lies the broad and blue Atlantic. Lady Mary's exaggeration as to the comparative height is here acknowledged, but had she said that below them rolls the brightest bluest clearest water in the world she would not have been far wrong. To the south of these cliffs there runs inland a broad bay—Liscannor bay, on the sides of which are two little villages, Liscannor and Lahinch. At the latter, Fred Neville, since he had been quartered at Ennis, had kept a boat for the sake of shooting seals and exploring the coast—and generally carrying out his spirit of adventure. Not far from Liscannor was Castle Quin, the seat of the Earl of Kilfenora;* and some way up from Liscannor towards the cliffs, about two miles from the village, there is a cottage called Ardkill. Here lived Mrs. and Miss O'Hara.

It was the nearest house to the rocks, from which it was distant less than half a mile. The cottage, so called, was a low rambling long house, but one storey high—very unlike an English cottage. It stood in two narrow lengths, the one running at right angles to the other; and contained a large kitchen, two sitting rooms—of which one was never used—and four or five bed-rooms of which only three were furnished. The servant girl occupied one, and the two ladies the

others. It was a blank place enough—and most unlike that
sort of cottage which English ladies are supposed to inhabit,
when they take to cottage life. There was no garden to it,
beyond a small patch in which a few potatoes were planted.
It was so near to the ocean, so exposed to winds from the
Atlantic, that no shrubs would live there. Everything round
it, even the herbage, was impregnated with salt, and told
tales of the neighbouring waves. When the wind was from
the west the air would be so laden with spray that one could
not walk there without being wet. And yet the place was very
healthy, and noted for the fineness of its air. Rising from the
cottage, which itself stood high, was a steep hill running up
to the top of the cliff, covered with that peculiar moss which
the salt spray of the ocean produces. On this side the land
was altogether open, but a few sheep were always grazing
there when the wind was not so high as to drive them to
some shelter. Behind the cottage there was an enclosed paddock which belonged to it, and in which Mrs. O'Hara kept
her cow. Roaming free around the house, and sometimes in
it, were a dozen hens and a noisy old cock which, with the
cow, made up the total of the widow's live stock. About a
half a mile from the cottage on the way to Liscannor there
were half a dozen mud cabins which contained Mrs. O'Hara's
nearest neighbours—and an old burying ground. Half a mile
further on again was the priest's house, and then on to Liscannor there were a few other straggling cabins here and
there along the road.

Up to the cottage indeed there could hardly be said to be
more than a track, and beyond the cottage no more than a
sheep path. The road coming out from Liscannor was a real
road as far as the burying ground, but from thence onward it
had degenerated. A car, or carriage if needed, might be
brought up to the cottage door, for the ground was hard and
the way was open. But no wheels ever travelled there now.
The priest, when he would come, came on horseback, and
there was a shed in which he could tie up his nag. He himself from time to time would send up a truss of hay for his

nag's use, and would think himself cruelly used because the cow would find her way in and eat it. No other horse ever called at the widow's door. What slender stores were needed for her use, were all brought on the girls' backs from Liscannor. To the north of the cottage, along the cliff, there was no road for miles, nor was there house or habitation. Castle Quin, in which the noble but somewhat impoverished Quin family lived nearly throughout the year, was distant, inland, about three miles from the cottage. Lady Mary had said in her letter to her friend that Mrs. O'Hara was a lady—and as Mrs. O'Hara had no other neighbour, ranking with herself in that respect, so near her, and none other but the Protestant clergyman's wife within six miles of her, charity, one would have thought, might have induced some of the Quin family to notice her. But the Quins were Protestant, and Mrs. O'Hara was not only a Roman Catholic, but a Roman Catholic who had been brought into the parish by the priest. No evil certainly was known of her, but then nothing was known of her; and the Quins were a very cautious people where religion was called in question. In the days of the famine*Father Marty and the Earl and the Protestant vicar had worked together in the good cause—but those days were now gone by, and the strange intimacy had soon died away. The Earl when he met the priest would bow to him, and the two clergymen would bow to each other—but beyond such dumb salutation there was no intercourse between them. It had been held therefore to be impossible to take any notice of the priest's friends.

And what notice could have been taken of two ladies who came from nobody knew where, to live in that wild-out-of-the-way place, nobody knew why? They called themselves mother and daughter, and they called themselves O'Haras— but there was no evidence of the truth even of these assertions. They were left therefore in their solitude, and never saw the face of a friend across their door step except that of Father Marty.

In truth Mrs. O'Hara's life had been of a nature almost to

necessitate such solitude. With her story we have nothing to do here. For our purpose there is no need that her tale should be told. Suffice it to say that she had been deserted by her husband, and did not now know whether she was or was not a widow. This was in truth the only mystery attached to her. She herself was an Englishwoman, though a Catholic; but she had been left early an orphan, and had been brought up in a provincial town of France by her grandmother. There she had married a certain Captain O'Hara, she having some small means of her own sufficient to make her valuable in the eyes of an adventurer. At that time she was no more than eighteen, and had given her hand to the Captain in opposition to the wishes of her only guardian. What had been her life from that time to the period at which, under Father Marty's auspices, she became the inhabitant of Ardkill Cottage, no one knew but herself. She was then utterly dissevered from all friends and relatives, and appeared on the western coast of County Clare with her daughter, a perfect stranger to every one. Father Marty was an old man, now nearly seventy, and had been educated in France. There he had known Mrs. O'Hara's grandmother, and hence had arisen the friendship which had induced him to bring the lady into his parish. She came there with a daughter, then hardly more than a child. Between two and three years had passed since her coming, and the child was now a grown-up girl, nearly nineteen years old. Of her means little or nothing was known accurately, even to the priest. She had told him that she had saved enough out of the wreck on which to live with her girl after some very humble fashion, and she paid her way. There must have come some sudden crash, or she would hardly have taken her child from an expensive Parisian school to vegetate in such solitude as that she had chosen. And it was a solitude from which there seemed to be no chance of future escape. They had brought with them a piano and a few books, mostly French—and with these it seemed to have been intended that the two ladies should make their future lives endurable. Other resources except such as the scenery of the cliffs afforded them, they had none.

The author would wish to impress upon his readers, if it may be possible, some idea of the outward appearance and personal character of each of these two ladies, as his story can hardly be told successfully unless he do so. The elder, who was at this time still under forty years of age, would have been a very handsome woman had not troubles, suffering, and the contests of a rugged life, in which she had both endured and dared much, given to her face a look of hard combative resolution which was not feminine. She was rather below than above the average height—or at any rate looked to be so, as she was strongly made, with broad shoulders, and a waist that was perhaps not now as slender as when she first met Captain O'Hara. But her hair was still black—as dark at least as hair can be which is not in truth black at all but only darkly brown. Whatever might be its colour there was no tinge of grey upon it. It was glossy, silken, and long as when she was a girl. I do not think that she took pride in it. How could she take pride in personal beauty, when she was never seen by any man younger than Father Marty or the old peasant who brought turf to her door in creels on a donkey's back? But she wore it always without any cap, tied in a simple knot behind her head. Whether chignons had been invented then* the author does not remember—but they certainly had not become common on the coast of County Clare, and the peasants about Liscannor thought Mrs. O'Hara's head of hair the finest they had ever seen. Had the ladies Quin of the Castle possessed such hair as that, they would not have been the ladies Quin to this day. Her eyes were lustrous, dark, and very large—beautiful eyes certainly; but they were eyes that you might fear. They had been softer perhaps in youth, before the spirit of the tiger had been roused in the woman's bosom by neglect and ill-usage. Her face was now bronzed by years and weather. Of her complexion she took no more care than did the neighbouring fishermen of theirs, and the winds and the salt water, and perhaps the working of her own mind, had told upon it, to make it rough and dark.

But yet there was a colour in her cheeks, as we often see in those of wandering gypsies, which would make a man stop to regard her who had eyes appreciative of beauty. Her nose was well formed—a heaven-made nose, and not a lump of flesh stuck on to the middle of her face as women's noses sometimes are—but it was somewhat short and broad at the nostrils, a nose that could imply much anger, and perhaps tenderness also. Her face below her nose was very short. Her mouth was large, but laden with expression. Her lips were full and her teeth perfect as pearls. Her chin was short and perhaps now converging to that size which we call a double chin, and marked by as broad a dimple as ever Venus made with her finger on the face of a woman.

She had ever been strong and active, and years in that re-treat had told upon her not at all. She would still walk to Liscannor, and thence round, when the tide was low, beneath the cliffs, and up by a path which the boys had made from the foot through the rocks to the summit, though the distance was over ten miles, and the ascent was very steep. She would remain for hours on the rocks, looking down upon the sea, when the weather was almost at its roughest. When the winds were still, and the sun was setting across the ocean, and the tame waves were only just audible as they rippled on the stones below, she would sit there with her child, holding the girl's hand or just touching her arm, and would be content so to stay almost without a word; but when the winds blew, and the heavy spray came up in blinding volumes, and the white-headed sea-monsters were roaring in their fury against the rocks, she would be there alone with her hat in her hand, and her hair drenched. She would watch the gulls wheeling and floating beneath her, and would listen to their screams and try to read their voices. She would envy the birds as they seemed to be worked into madness by the winds which still were not strong enough to drive them from their purposes. To linger there among the rocks seemed to be the only delight left to her in life—except that intensive delight which a mother has in loving her child. She herself read but little, and never put a hand upon the piano. But she had a faculty of sitting and thinking, of brooding over her own past years and dreaming of her daughter's future life, which never deserted her. With her the days were doubtless very sad, but it cannot truly be said that they were dull or tedious.

And there was a sparkle of humour about her too, which would sometimes shine the brightest when there was no one by her to appreciate it. Her daughter would smile at her mother's sallies—but she did so simply in kindness. Kate did not share her mother's sense of humour—did not share it as yet. With the young the love of fun is gratified generally by grotesque movement. It is not till years are running on that the grotesqueness of words and ideas is appreciated. But Mrs. O'Hara would expend her art on the household drudge, or on old Barney Corcoran who came with the turf—though by neither of them was she very clearly understood. Now and again she would have a war of words with the priest, and that, I think, she liked. She was intensely combative, if ground for a combat arose; and would fight on any subject with any human being—except her daughter. And yet with the priest she never quarrelled; and though she was rarely beaten in her contests with him, she submitted to him in much. In matters touching her religion she submitted to him altogether.

Kate O'Hara was in face very like her mother—strangely like, for in much she was very different. But she had her mother's eyes—though hers were much softer in their lustre, as became her youth—and she had her mother's nose, but without that look of scorn which would come upon her mother's face when the nostrils were inflated. And in that peculiar shortness of the lower face she was the very echo of her mother. But the mouth was smaller, the lips less full, and the dimple less exaggerated. It was a fairer face to look upon —fairer, perhaps, than her mother's had ever been; but it was less expressive, and in it there was infinitely less capability for anger, and perhaps less capability for the agonising extremes of tenderness. But Kate was taller than her mother, and seemed by her mother's side to be slender. Nevertheless she was strong and healthy; and though she did not willingly join in those longer walks, or expose herself to the weather as did her mother, there was nothing feeble about her, nor was she averse to action. Life at Ardkill Cottage was dull, and therefore she also was dull. Had she been surrounded by friends, such as she had known in her halcyon school days at Paris, she would have been the gayest of the gay.

Her hair was dark as her mother's—even darker. Seen by the side of Miss O'Hara's, the mother's hair was certainly not black, but one could hardly think that hair could be blacker than the daughter's. But hers fell in curling clusters round her neck—such clusters as now one never sees. She would shake them in sport, and the room would seem to be full of her locks. But she used to say herself to her mother that there was already to be found a grey hair among them now and again, and she would at times show one, declaring that she would be an old woman before her mother was middle-aged.

Her life at Ardkill Cottage was certainly very dull. Memory did but little for her, and she hardly knew how to hope. She would read, till she had nearly learned all their books by heart, and would play such tunes as she knew by the hour together, till the poor instrument, subject to the sea air and away from any tuner's skill, was discordant with its limp strings. But still, with all this, her mind would become vacant and weary. 'Mother,' she would say, 'is it always to be like this?'

'Not always, Kate,' the mother once answered.

'And when will it be changed?'

'In a few days—in a few hours, Kate.'

'What do you mean, mother?'

'That eternity is coming, with all its glory and happiness. If it were not so, it would, indeed, be very bad.'

It may be doubted whether any human mind has been able to content itself with hopes of eternity, till distress in some shape has embittered life. The preachers preach very well—well enough to leave many convictions on the minds of men; but not well enough to leave that conviction. And godly men live well—but we never see them living as though such were their conviction. And were it so, who would strive and moil in this world? When the heart has been broken, and the spirit ground to the dust by misery, then—such is God's mercy—eternity suffices to make life bearable. When Mrs. O'Hara spoke to her daughter of eternity, there was but cold comfort in the word. The girl wanted something here—pleasures, companions, work, perhaps a lover. This had happened before Lieutenant Neville of the 20th Hussars had been seen in those parts.

And the mother herself, in speaking as she had spoken, had, perhaps unintentionally, indulged in a sarcasm on life which the daughter certainly had not been intended to understand. 'Yes—it will always be like this for you, for you, unfortunate one that you are. There is no other further lookout in this life. You are one of the wretched to whom the world offers nothing; and therefore—as, being human, you must hope—build your hopes on eternity.' Had the words been read clearly, that would have been their true meaning. What could she do for her child? Bread and meat, with a roof over her head, and raiment which sufficed for life such as theirs, she could supply. The life would have been well enough had it been their fate, and within their power, to earn the bread and meat, the shelter and the raiment. But to have it, and without work—to have that, and nothing more, in absolute idleness, was such misery that there was no resource left but eternity!

And yet the mother when she looked at her daughter almost persuaded herself that it need not be so. The girl was very lovely—so lovely that, were she but seen, men would quarrel for her as to who should have her in his keeping. Such beauty, such life, such capability for giving and receiving enjoyment could not have been intended to wither on a lone cliff over the Atlantic! There must be fault somewhere. But yet to live had been the first necessity; and life in cities, among the haunts of men, had been impossible with such means as this woman possessed. When she had called her daughter to her, and had sought peace under the roof which her friend the priest had found for her, peace and a roof to shelter her had been the extent of her desires. To be at rest, and independent, with her child within her arms, had been all that the woman asked of the gods. For herself it sufficed. For herself she was able to acknowledge that the rest which she had at least obtained was infinitely preferable to the unrest of her past life. But she soon learned—as she had not expected to learn before she made the experiment—that that which was to her peace, was to her daughter life within a tomb. 'Mother, is it always to be like this?'

Had her child not carried the weight of good blood, had some small grocer or country farmer been her father, she might have come down to the neighbouring town of Ennistimon, and found a fitting mate there. Would it not have been better so? From that weight of good blood—or gift, if it please us to call it—what advantage would ever come to her girl? It cannot really be that all those who swarm in the world below the bar of gentlehood are less blessed, or intended to be less blessed, than the few who float in the higher air. As to real blessedness, does it not come from fitness to the outer life and a sense of duty that shall produce such fitness? Does anyone believe that the Countess has a greater share of happiness than the grocer's wife, or is less subject to the miseries which flesh inherits? But such matters cannot be changed by the will. This woman could not bid her daughter go and meet the butcher's son on equal terms, or seek her friends among the milliners of the neighbouring town. The burden had been imposed and must be borne, even though it isolated them from all the world.

'Mother, is it always to be like this?' Of course the mother knew what was needed. It was needed that the girl should go out into the world and pair, that she should find some shoulder on which she might lean, some arm that would be strong to surround her, the heart of some man and the work of some man to which she might devote herself. The girl, when she asked her question, did not know this—but the mother knew it. The mother looked at her child and said that of all living creatures her child was surely the loveliest. Was it not fit that she should go forth and be loved—that she should at any rate go forth and take her chance with others? But how should such going forth be managed? And then— were there not dangers, terrible dangers—dangers specially terrible to one so friendless as her child? Had not she herself been wrecked among the rocks, trusting herself to one who had been utterly unworthy—loving one who had been utterly unlovely? Men so often are as ravenous wolves, merciless, rapacious, without hearts, full of greed, full of lust, looking on female beauty as prey, regarding the love of woman and her very life as a toy! Were she higher in the world there might be safety. Were she lower there might be safety. But how could she send her girl forth into the world without sending her certainly among the wolves? And yet the piteous question was always sounding in her ears. 'Mother, is it always to be like this?'

Then Lieutenant Neville had appeared upon the scene, dressed in a sailor's jacket and trousers, with a sailor's cap upon his head, with a loose handkerchief round his neck and his hair blowing to the wind. In the eyes of Kate O'Hara he was an Apollo. In the eyes of any girl he must have seemed to be as good-looking a fellow as ever tied a sailor's knot. He had made acquaintance with Father Marty at Liscannor, and the priest had dined with him at Ennis. There had been a return visit, and the priest, perhaps innocently, had taken him up on the cliffs. There he had met the two ladies, and our hero had been introduced to Kate O'Hara.

CHAPTER VI

I'LL GO BAIL SHE LIKES IT

IT MIGHT be that the young man was a ravenous wolf, but his manners were not wolfish. Had Mrs. O'Hara been a princess, supreme in her own rights, young Neville could not have treated her or her daughter with more respect. At first Kate had wondered at him, but had said but little. She had listened to him, as he talked to her mother and the priest about the cliffs and the birds and the seals he had shot, and she had felt that it was this, something like this, that was needed to make life, so sweet that as yet there need be no longing, no thought, for eternity. It was not that all at once she loved him, but she felt that he was a thing to love. His very appearance on the cliff, and the power of thinking of him when he was gone, for a while banished all tedium from her life. 'Why should you shoot the poor gulls?' That was the first question she asked him; and she asked it hardly in tenderness to the birds, but because with the unconscious cunning of her sex she understood that tenderness in a woman is a charm in the eyes of a man.

'Only because it is so difficult to get at them,' said Fred. 'I believe there is no other reason—except that one must shoot something.'

'But why must you?' asked Mrs. O'Hara.

'To justify one's guns. A man takes to shooting as a matter of course. It's a kind of institution. There ain't any tigers, and so we shoot birds. And in this part of the world there ain't any pheasants, and so we shoot sea-gulls.'

'Excellently argued,' said the priest.

'Or rather one don't, for it's impossible to get at them. But I'll tell you what, Father Marty'—Neville had already

741

assumed the fashion of calling the priest by his familiar priestly name, as strangers do much more readily than they who belong to the country—'I'll tell you what, Father Marty —I've shot one of the finest seals I ever saw, and if Morony can get him at low water, I'll send the skin up to Mrs. O'Hara.'

'And send the oil to me,' said the priest. 'There's some use in shooting a seal. But you can do nothing with those birds— unless you get enough of their feathers to make a bed.'

This was in October, and before the end of November Fred Neville was, after a fashion, intimate at the cottage. He had never broken bread at Mrs. O'Hara's table; nor, to tell the truth, had any outspoken, clearly intelligible word of love been uttered by him to the girl. But he had been seen with them often enough, and the story had become sufficiently current at Liscannor to make Lady Mary Quin think that she was justified in sending her bad news to her friend Lady Scroope. This she did not do till Fred had been induced, with some difficulty, to pass a night at Castle Quin. Lady Mary had not scrupled to ask a question about Miss O'Hara, and had thought the answer very unsatisfactory. 'I don't know what makes them live there, I'm sure. I should have thought you would have known that,' replied Neville, in answer to her question.

'They are perfect mysteries to us,' said Lady Mary.

'I think that Miss O'Hara is the prettiest girl I ever saw in my life,' said Fred boldly, 'and I should say the handsomest woman, if it were not that there may be a question between her and her mother.'

'You are enthusiastic,' said Lady Mary Quin, and after that the letter to Scroope was written.

In the meantime the seal-skin was cured—not perhaps in the very best fashion, and was sent up to Miss O'Hara with Mr. Neville's compliments. The skin of a seal that has been shot by the man and not purchased is a present that any lady may receive from any gentleman. The most prudent mamma

that ever watched over the dovecote with Argus eyes, permitting no touch of gallantry to come near it, could hardly
insist that a seal-skin in the rough should be sent back to the
donor. Mrs. O'Hara was by no means that most prudent
mamma, and made, not only the seal-skin, but the donor also
welcome. Must it not be that by some chance advent such as
this that the change must be effected in her girl's life, should
any change ever be made? And her girl was good. Why
should she fear for her? The man had been brought there
by her only friend, the priest, and why should she fear him?
And yet she did fear; and though her face was never clouded
when her girl spoke of the newcomer, though she always
mentioned Lieutenant Neville's name as though she herself
liked the man, though she even was gracious to him when he
showed himself near the cottage—still there was a deep dread
upon her when her eyes rested upon him, when her thoughts
flew to him. Men are wolves to women, and utterly merciless
when feeding high their lust. 'Twas thus her own thoughts
shaped themselves, though she never uttered a syllable to
her daughter in disparagement of the man. This was the girl's
chance. Was she to rob her of it? And yet, of all her duties,
was not the duty of protecting her girl the highest and the
dearest that she owned? If the man meant well by her girl,
she would wash his feet with her hair, kiss the hem of his
garments, and love the spot on which she had first seen him
stand like a young sea-god. But if evil—if he meant evil to
her girl, if he should do evil to her Kate—then she knew that
there was so much of the tiger within her bosom as would
serve to rend him limb from limb. With such thoughts as
these she had hardly ever left them together. Nor had such
leaving together seemed to be desired by them. As for Kate
she certainly would have shunned it. She thought of Fred
Neville during all her waking moments, and dreamed of him
at night. His coming had certainly been to her as the coming
of a god. Though he did not appear on the cliffs above once
or twice a week, and had done so but for a few weeks, his
presence had altered the whole tenour of her life. She never

asked her mother now whether it was to be always like this. There was a freshness about her life which her mother understood at once. She was full of play, reading less than was her wont, but still with no sense of tedium. Of the man in his absence she spoke but seldom, and when his name was on her lips she would jest with it—as though the coming of a young embryo lord to shoot gulls on their coast was quite a joke. The seal-skin which he had given her was very dear to her, and she was at no pains to hide her liking; but of the man as a lover she had never seemed to think.

Nor did she think of him as a lover. It is not by such thinking that love grows. Nor did she ever tell herself that while he was there, coming on one day and telling them that his boat would be again there on another, life was blessed to her, and that, therefore, when he should have left them, her life would be accursed to her. She knew nothing of all this. But yet she thought of him, and dreamed of him, and her young head was full of little plans with every one of which he was connected.

And it may almost be said that Fred Neville was as innocent in the matter as was the girl. It is true, indeed, that men are merciless as wolves to women—that they become so, taught by circumstances and trained by years; but the young man who begins by meaning to be a wolf must be bad indeed. Fred Neville had no such meaning. On his behalf it must be acknowledged that he had no meaning whatever when he came again and again to Ardkill. Had he examined himself in the matter he would have declared that he liked the mother quite as well as the daughter. When Lady Mary Quin had thrown at him her very blunt arrow he had defended himself on that plea. Accident, and the spirit of adventure, had thrust these ladies in his path, and no doubt he liked them the better because they did not live as other people lived. Their solitude, the close vicinity of the ocean, the feeling that in meeting them none of the ordinary conventional usages of society were needed, the wildness and the strangeness of the scene, all had charms which he admitted to himself. And he knew that the girl was very lovely. Of course he said so to himself and to others. To take delight in beauty is assumed to be the nature of a young man, and this young man was not one to wish to differ from others in that respect. But when he went back to spend his Christmas at Scroope, he had never told even himself that he intended to be her lover.

'Good-bye, Mrs. O'Hara,' he said, a day or two before he left Ennis.

'So you're going?'

'Oh yes, I'm off. The orders from home are imperative. One has to cut one's lump of Christmas beef and also one's lump of Christmas pudding. It is our family religion, you know.'

'What a happiness to have a family to visit!'

'It's all very well, I suppose. I don't grumble. Only it's a bore going away, somehow.'

'You are coming back to Ennis?' asked Kate.

'Coming back—I should think so. Barney Morony wouldn't be quite so quiet if I was not coming back. I'm to dine with Father Marty at Liscannor on the 15th of January, to meet another priest from Milltown Malbay—the best fellow in the world he says.'

'That's Father Creech—not half such a good fellow, Mr. Neville, as Father Marty himself.'

'He couldn't be better. However, I shall be here then, and if I have any luck you shall have another skin of the same size by that time.' Then he shook hands with them both, and there was a feeling that the time would be blank till he should be again there in his sailor's jacket.

When the second week in January had come Mrs. O'Hara heard that the gallant young officer of the 20th was back in Ennis, and she well remembered that he had told her of his intention to dine with the priest. On the Sunday she saw Father Marty after mass, and managed to have a few words with him on the road while Kate returned to the cottage alone. 'So your friend Mr. Neville has come back to Ennis,' she said.

'I didn't know that he had come. He promised to dine with me on Thursday—only I think nothing of promises from these young fellows.'

'He told me he was to be with you.'

'More power to him. He'll be welcome. I'm getting to be a very ould man, Misthress O'Hara; but I'm not so ould but I like to have the young ones near me.'

'It is pleasant to see a bright face like his.'

'That's thrue for you, Misthress O'Hara. I like to see 'em bright and ganial. I don't know that I ever shot so much as a sparrow, meself, but I love to hear them talk of their shootings, and huntings, and the like of that. I've taken a fancy to that boy, and he might do pretty much as he plazes wid me.'

'And I too have taken a fancy to him, Father Marty.'

'Shure and how could you help it?'

'But he mustn't do as he pleases with me.' Father Marty looked up into her face as though he did not understand her. 'If I were alone, as you are, I could afford, like you, to indulge in the pleasure of a bright face. Only in that case he would not care to let me see it.'

'Bedad thin, Misthress O'Hara, I don't know a fairer face to look on in all Corcomroe than your own—that is when you're not in your tantrums, Misthress O'Hara.' The priest was a privileged person, and could say what he liked to his friend; and she understood that a priest might say without fault what would be very faulty if it came from any one else.

'I'm in earnest now, Father Marty. What shall we do if our darling Kate thinks of this young man more than is good for her?' Father Marty raised his hat and began to scratch his head. 'If you like to look at the fair face of a handsome lad——'

'I do thin, Misthress O'Hara.'

'Must not she like it also?'

'I'll go bail she likes it,' said the priest.

'And what will come next?'

'I'll tell you what it is, Misthress O'Hara. 'Would you want to keep her from even seeing a man at all?'

'God forbid.'

'It's not the way to make them happy, nor yet safe. If it's to be that way wid her, she'd better be a nun all out; and I'd be far from proposing that to your Kate.'

'She is hardly fit for so holy a life.'

'And why should she? I niver like seeing too many of 'em going that way, and them that are prittiest are the last I'd send there. But if not a nun, it stands to reason she must take chance with the rest of 'em. She's been too much shut up already. Let her keep her heart till he asks her for it; but if he does ask her, why shouldn't she be his wife? How many of them young officers take Irish wives home with 'em every year. Only for them, our beauties wouldn't have a chance.'

CHAPTER VII

FATHER MARTY'S HOSPITALITY

SUCH WAS the philosophy, or, perhaps, it may be better said such was the humanity of Father Marty! But in encouraging Mrs. O'Hara to receive this dangerous visitor he had by no means spoken without consideration. In one respect we must abandon Father Marty to the judgment and censure of fathers and mothers. The whole matter looked at from Lady Scroope's point of view was no doubt very injurious to the priest's character. He regarded a stranger among them, such as was Fred Neville, as fair spoil, as a Philistine to seize whom and capture him for life on behalf of any Irish girl would be a great triumph—a spoiling of the Egyptian to the accomplishment of which he would not hesitate to lend his priestly assistance, the end to be accomplished, of course, being marriage. For Lord Scroope and his family and his blood and his religious fanaticism he could entertain no compassion whatever. Father Marty was no great politician, and desired no rebellion against England.* Even in the days of O'Connell and repeal*he had been but luke-warm. But justice for Ireland in the guise of wealthy English husbands for pretty Irish girls he desired with all his heart. He was true to his own faith, to the backbone, but he entertained no prejudice against a good looking Protestant youth when a fortunate marriage was in question. So little had been given to the Irish in these days, that they were bound to take what they could get. Lord Scroope and the Countess, had they known the priest's views on this matter, would have regarded him as an unscrupulous intriguing ruffian, prepared to destroy the happiness of a noble family by a wicked scheme. But his views of life, as judged from the other side, admitted of some excuse. As for a girl breaking her heart, he did not, perhaps, much believe in such a catastrophe. Of a sore heart a girl must run the chance—as also must a man. That young men do go about promising marriage and not keeping their promise, he knew well. None could know that better than he did, for he was the repository of half the love secrets in his parish. But all that was part of the evil coming from the fall of Adam, and must be endured till—till the Pope should have his own again, and be able to set all things right. In the meantime young women must do the best they could to keep their lovers—and should one lover break away, then must the deserted one use her experience towards getting a second. But how was a girl to have a lover at all, if she were never allowed to see a man? He had been bred a priest from his youth upwards, and knew nothing of love; but nevertheless it was a pain to him to see a young girl, good-looking, healthy, fit to be the mother of children, pine away, unsought for, uncoupled—as it would be a pain to see a fruit grow ripe upon the tree, and then fall and perish for want of plucking. His philosophy was perhaps at fault, and it may be that his humanity was unrefined. But he was human to the core—and, at any rate, unselfish. That there might be another danger was a fact that he looked full in the face. But what victory can be won without danger? And he thought that he knew this girl, who three times a year* would open her whole heart to him in confession. He was sure that she was not only innocent, but good. And of the man, too, he was prone to believe good—though who on such a question ever trusts a man's goodness? There might be danger and there must be discretion; but surely it would not be wise, because evil was possible, that such a one as Kate O'Hara should be kept from all that intercourse without which a woman is only half a woman! He had considered it all, though the reader may perhaps think that as a minister of the gospel he had come to a strange conclusion. He himself, in his own defence, would have said that having served many years in the ministry he had learned to know the nature of men and women.

Mrs. O'Hara said not a word to Kate of the doctrines which the priest had preached, but she found herself encouraged to mention their new friend's name to the girl. During Fred's absence hardly a word had been spoken concerning him in the cottage. Mrs. O'Hara had feared the subject, and Kate had thought of him much too often to allow his name to be on her tongue. But now as they sat after dinner over their peat fire the mother began the subject. 'Mr. Neville is to dine with Father Marty on Thursday.'

'Is he, mother?'

'Barney Morony was telling me that he was back at Ennis. Barney had to go in and see him about the boat.'

'He won't go boating such weather as this, mother?'

'It seems that he means it. The winds are not so high now as they were in October, and the men understand well when the sea will be high.'

'It is frightful to think of anybody being in one of those little boats now.' Kate ever since she had lived in these parts had seen the canoes from Liscannor and Lahinch about in the bay, summer and winter, and had never found anything dreadful in it before.

'I suppose he'll come up here again,' said the mother; but to this Kate made no answer. 'He is to sleep at Father Marty's I fancy, and he can hardly do that without paying us a visit.'

'The days are short and he'll want all his time for the boating,' said Kate with a little pout.

'He'll find half-an-hour, I don't doubt. Shall you be glad to see him, Kate?'

'I don't know, mother. One is glad almost to see anyone up here. It's as good as a treat when old Corcoran comes up with the turf.'

'But Mr. Neville is not like old Corcoran, Kate.'

'Not in the least, mother. I do like Mr. Neville better than Corcoran, because you see with Corcoran the excitement is very soon over. And Corcoran hasn't very much to say for himself.'

'And Mr. Neville has?'

'He says a great deal more to you than he does to me, mother.'

'I like him very much. I should like him very much indeed if there were no danger in his coming.'

'What danger?'

'That he should steal your heart away, my own, my darling, my child.' Then Kate, instead of answering, got up and threw herself at her mother's knees, and buried her face in her mother's lap, and Mrs. O'Hara knew that that act of larceny had already been perpetrated.

And how should it have been otherwise? But of such stealing it is always better that no mention should be made till the theft has been sanctified by free gift. Till the loss has been spoken of and acknowledged, it may in most cases be recovered. Had Neville never returned from Scroope, and his name never been mentioned by the mother to her daughter, it may be that Kate O'Hara would not have known that she had loved him. For a while she would have been sad. For a month or two, as she lay wakeful in her bed she would have thought of her dreams. But she would have thought of them as only dreams. She would have been sure that she could have loved him had any fair ending been possible for such love; but she would have assured herself that she had been on her guard, and that she was safe in spite of her dreams. But now the flame in her heart had been confessed and in some degree sanctioned, and she would foster it rather than quench it. Even should such a love be capable of no good fortune, would it not be better to have a few weeks of happy dreaming than a whole life that should be passionless? What could she do with her own heart there, living in solitude, with none but the sea gulls to look at her? Was it not infinitely better that she should give it away to such a young god as this than let it feed upon itself miserably? Yes, she would give it away—but might it not be that the young god would not take the gift?

On the third day after his arrival at Ennis, Neville was at Liscannor with the priest. He little dreamed that the fact of his dining and sleeping at Father Marty's house, would be known to the ladies at Castle Quin, and communicated from them to his aunt at Scroope Manor. Not that he would have been deterred from accepting the priest's hospitality or frightened into accepting that of the noble owner of the castle, had he known precisely all that would be written about it. He would not have altered his conduct in a matter in which he considered himself entitled to regulate it, in obedience to any remonstrances from Scroope Manor. Objections to the society of a Roman Catholic priest because of his religion he would have regarded as old-fashioned fanaticism. As for Earls and their daughters he would no doubt have enough of them in his future life, and this special Earl and his daughters had not fascinated him. He had chosen to come to Ireland with his regiment for this year instead of at once assuming the magnificence of his position in England, in order that he might indulge the spirit of adventure before he assumed the duties of life. And it seemed to him that in dining and sleeping at an Irish priest's house on the shores of the Atlantic, with the prospect of seal shooting and seeing a very pretty girl on the following morning, he was indulging that spirit properly. But Lady Mary Quin thought that he was misbehaving himself and taking to very bad courses. When she heard that he was to sleep at the priest's house, she was quite sure that he would visit Mrs. O'Hara on the next day.

The dinner at the priest's was very jovial. There was a bottle of sherry and there was a bottle of port, procured, chiefly for the sake of appearance, from a grocer's shop at Ennistimon—but the whiskey had come from Cork and had been in the priest's keeping for the last dozen years. He good-humouredly acknowledged that the wine was nothing, but expressed an opinion that Mr. Neville might find it difficult to beat the 'sperrits.' 'It's thrue for you, Father Marty,' said the rival priest from Milltown Malbay, 'and it's you that should know good sperrits from bad if ony man in Ireland does.'

' 'Deed thin,' replied the priest of Liscannor, 'barring the famine years, I've mixed two tumblers of punch for meself every day these forty years, and if it was all together it'd be about enough to give Mr. Neville a day's sale-shooting in his canoe.' Immediately after dinner Neville was invited to light his cigar, and everything was easy, comfortable, and to a certain degree adventurous. There were the two priests, and a young Mr. Finucane from Ennistimon—who however was not quite so much to Fred's taste as the elder men. Mr. Finucane wore various rings, and talked rather largely about his father's demesne. 'But the whole thing was new, and by no means dull. As Neville had not left Ennis till late in the day—after what he called a hard day's work in the warrior line—they did not sit down till past eight o'clock; nor did anyone talk of moving till past midnight. Fred certainly made for himself more than two glasses of punch, and he would have sworn that the priest had done so also. Father Marty, however, was said by those who knew him best to be very rigid in this matter, and to have the faculty of making his drink go a long way. Young Mr. Finucane took three or four —perhaps five or six—and then volunteered to join Fred Neville in a day's shooting under the rocks. But Fred had not been four years in a cavalry regiment without knowing how to protect himself in such a difficulty as this. 'The canoe will only hold myself and the man.' said Fred, with perfect simplicity. Mr. Finucane drew himself up haughtily and did not utter another word for the next five minutes. Nevertheless he took a most affectionate leave of the young officer when half an hour after midnight he was told by Father Marty that it was time for him to go home. Father Creech also took his leave, and then Fred and the priest of Liscannor were left sitting together over the embers of the turf fire. 'You'll be going up to see our friends at Ardkill tomorrow,' said the priest.

'Likely enough, Father Marty.'

'Of course you will. Sorrow a doubt of that.'* Then the priest paused.

'And why shouldn't I?' asked Neville.

'I'm not saying that you shouldn't, Mr. Neville. It wouldn't be civil nor yet nathural after knowing them as you have done. If you didn't go they'd be thinking there was a rason for your staying away, and that'd be worse than all. But, Mr. Neville——'

'Out with it, Father Marty.' Fred knew what was coming fairly well, and he also had thought a good deal upon the matter.

'Them two ladies, Mr. Neville, live up there all alone, with sorrow a human being in the world to protect them— barring myself.'

'Why should they want protection?'

'Just because they're lone women, and because one of them is very young and very beautiful.'

'They are both beautiful,' said Neville.

' 'Deed and they are—both of 'em. The mother can look afther herself, and after a fashion, too, she can look afther her daughter. 'I shouldn't like to be the man to come in her way when he'd once decaived her child. You're a young man, Mr. Neville.'

'That's my misfortune.'

'And one who stands very high in the world. They tell me you're to be a great lord some day.'

'Either that or a little one,' said Neville, laughing.

'Anyways you'll be a rich man with a handle to your name. To me, living here in this out of the way parish, a lord doesn't matter that.' And Father Marty gave a fillip with his fingers. 'The only lord that matters me is me bishop. But with them women yonder, the title and the money and all the grandeur goes a long way. It has been so since the world began. In riding a race against you they carry weight from the very awe which the name of an English Earl brings with it.'

'Why should they ride a race against me?'

'Why indeed—unless you ride a race against them! You wouldn't wish to injure that young thing as isn't yet out of her teens?'

'God forbid that I should injure her.'

'I don't think that you're the man to do it with your eyes open, Mr. Neville. If you can't spake her fair in the way of making her your wife, don't spake her fair at all. That's the long and the short of it, Mr. Neville. You see what they are. They're ladies, if there is a lady living in the Queen's dominions. That young thing is as beautiful as Habe,* as innocent as a sleeping child, as soft as wax to take impression. What armour has she got against such a one as you?'

'She shall not need armour.'

'If you're a gentleman, Mr. Neville—as I know you are—you will not give her occasion to find out her own wakeness. Well, if it isn't past one I'm a sinner. It's Friday morning and I mus'n't ate a morsel myself, poor papist that I am! but I'll get you a bit of cold mate and a drop of grog in a moment if you'll take it.' Neville, however, refused the hospitable offer.

'Father Marty,' he said, speaking with a zeal which perhaps owed something of its warmth to the punch, 'you shall find that I am a gentleman.'

'I'm shure of it, my boy.'

'If I can do no good to your friend, at any rate I will do no harm to her.'

'That is spoken like a Christian, Mr. Neville—which I take to be a higher name even than gentleman.'

'There's my hand upon it,' said Fred, enthusiastically. After that he went to bed.

On the following morning the priest was very jolly at breakfast, and in speaking of the ladies at Ardkill made no allusion whatever to the conversation of the previous evening. 'Ah no,' he said, when Neville proposed that they should walk up together to the cottage before he went down to his boat. 'What's the good of an ould man like me going bothering? And, signs on, I'm going into Ennistimon to see Pat O'Leary about the milk he's sending to our Union.* The thief of the world—it's wathering it he is before he sends it. Nothing kills me, Mr. Neville, but when I hear of all them English vices being brought over to this poor suffering innocent counthry.'

Neville had decided on the advice of Barney Morony, that he would on this morning go down southward along the coast to Drumdeirg rock, in the direction away from the Hag's Head and from Mrs. O'Hara's cottage; and he therefore postponed his expedition till after his visit. When Father Marty started to Ennistimon to look after that sinner O'Leary, Fred Neville, all alone, turned the other way to Ardkill.

CHAPTER VIII

I DIDN'T WANT YOU TO GO*

MRS. O'HARA had known that he would come, and Kate had known it; and, though it would be unfair to say that they were waiting for him, it is no more than true to say that they were ready for him. 'We are so glad to see you again,' said Mrs. O'Hara.'

'Not more glad than I am to find myself here once more.'

'So you dined and slept at Father Marty's last night. What will the grand people say at the Castle?'

'As I sha'n't hear what they say, it won't matter much! Life is not long enough, Mrs. O'Hara, for putting up with disagreeable people.'

'Was it pleasant last night?'

'Very pleasant. I don't think Father Creech is half as good as Father Marty, you know.'

'Oh no,' exclaimed Kate.

'But he's a jolly sort of fellow, too. And there was a Mr. Finucane there—a very grand fellow.'

'We know no one about here but the priests,' said Mrs. O'Hara, laughing. 'Anybody might think that the cottage was a little convent.'

'Then I oughtn't to come.'

'Well, no, I suppose not. Only foreigners are admitted to see convents sometimes. You're going after the poor seals again?'

'Barney says the tide is too high for the seals now. We're going to Drumdeirg.'

'What—to those little rocks?' asked Kate.

'Yes—to the rocks. I wish you'd both come with me.'

'I wouldn't go in one of these canoes all out there for the world,' said Kate.

'What can be the use of it?' asked Mrs. O'Hara.

'I've got to get the feathers for Father Marty's bed, you know. I haven't shot as many yet as would make a pillow for a cradle.'

'The poor innocent gulls!'

'The poor innocent chickens and ducks, if you come to that, Miss O'Hara.'

'But they're of use.'

'And so will Father Marty's feather bed be of use. Good-bye, Mrs. O'Hara. Good-bye, Miss O'Hara. I shall be down again next week, and we'll have that other seal.'

There was nothing in this. So far, at any rate, he had not broken his word to the priest. He had not spoken a word to Kate O'Hara, that might not and would not have been said had the priest been present. But how lovely she was; and what a thrill ran through his arm as he held her hand in his for a moment. Where should he find a girl like that in England with such colour, such eyes, such hair, such innocence —and then with so sweet a voice?

As he hurried down the hill to the beach at Coolroone, where Morony was to meet him with the boat, he could not keep himself from comparisons between Kate O'Hara and Sophie Mellerby. No doubt his comparisons were made very incorrectly—and unfairly; but they were all in favour of the girl who lived out of the world in solitude on the cliffs of Moher. And why should he not be free to seek a wife where he pleased? In such an affair as that—an affair of love in which the heart and the heart alone should be consulted, what right could any man have to dictate to him? Certain ideas occurred to him which his friends in England would have called wild, democratic, revolutionary and damnable, but which, owing perhaps to the Irish air and the Irish whiskey and the spirit of adventure fostered by the vicinity of rocks and ocean, appeared to him at the moment to be not only charming but reasonable also. No doubt he was born to high state and great rank, but nothing that his rank and state could give him was so sweet as his liberty. To be free to choose for himself in all things, was the highest privilege of man. What pleasure could he have in a love which should be selected for him by such a woman as his aunt? Then he gave the reins to some confused notion of an Irish bride, a wife who should be half a wife and half not*—whom he would love and cherish tenderly but of whose existence no English friend should be aware. How could he more charmingly indulge his spirit of adventure than by some such arrangement as this?

He knew that he had given a pledge to his uncle to contract no marriage that would be derogatory to his position. He knew also that he had given a pledge to the priest that he would do no harm to Kate O'Hara. He felt that he was bound to keep each pledge. As for that sweet, darling girl, would he not sooner lose his life than harm her? But he was aware that an adventurous life was always a life of difficulties, and that for such as live adventurous lives the duty of overcoming difficulties was of all duties the chief. Then he got into his canoe, and, having succeeded in killing two gulls on the Drumdeirg rocks, thought that for that day he had carried out his purpose as a man of adventure very well.

During February and March he was often on the coast, and hardly one visit did he make which was not followed by a letter from Castle Quin to Scroope Manor. No direct accusation of any special fault was made against him in consequence. No charge was brought of an improper hankering after any special female, because Lady Scroope found herself bound in conscience not to commit her correspondent; but very heavy injunctions were laid upon him as to his general conduct, and he was eagerly entreated to remember his great duty and to come home and settle himself in England. In the meantime the ties which bound him to the coast of Clare were becoming stronger and stronger every day. He had ceased now to care much about seeing Father Marty, and would come, when the tide was low, direct from Lahinch to the strand beneath the cliffs, from whence there was a path through the rocks up to Ardkill. And there he would remain for hours—having his gun with him, but caring little for his gun. He told himself that he loved the rocks and the wildness of the scenery, and the noise of the ocean, and the whirring of the birds above and below him. It was certainly true that he loved Kate O'Hara.

'Neville, you must answer me a question,' said the mother to him one morning when they were out together, looking down upon the Atlantic when the wind had lulled after a gale.

'Ask it then,' said he.

'What is the meaning of all this? What is Kate to believe?'

'Of course she believes that I love her better than all the world besides—that she is more to me than all the world can give or take. I have told her at least, so often, that if she does not believe it she is little better than a Jew.'

'You must not joke with me now. If you knew what it was to have one child and only that you would not joke with me.'

'I am quite in earnest. I am not joking.'

'And what is to be the end of it?'

'The end of it! How can I say? My uncle is an old man— very old, very infirm, very good, very prejudiced, and broken-hearted because his own son, who died, married against his will.'

'You would not liken my Kate to such as that woman was?'

'Your Kate! She is my Kate as much as yours. Such a thought as that would be an injury to me as deep as to you. You know that to me my Kate, our Kate, is all excellence—as pure and good as she is bright and beautiful. As God is above us she shall be my wife—but I cannot take her to Scroope Manor as my wife while my uncle lives.'

'Why should anyone be ashamed of her at Scroope Manor?'

'Because they are fools. But I cannot cure them of their folly. My uncle thinks that I should marry one of my own class.'

'Class—what class? He is a gentleman, I presume, and she is a lady.'

'That is very true—so true that I myself shall act upon the

truth. But I will not make his last years wretched. He is a Protestant, and you are Catholics.'

'What is that? Are not ever so many of your lords Catholics? Were they not all Catholics before Protestants were ever though of?'

'Mrs. O'Hara, I have told you that to me she is as high and good and noble as though she were a Princess. And I have told you that she shall be my wife. If that does not content you, I cannot help it. It contents her. I owe much to her.'

'Indeed you do—everything.'

'But I owe much to him also. I do not think that you can gain anything by quarrelling with me.'

She paused for a while before she answered him, looking into his face the while with something of the ferocity of a tigress. So intent was her gaze that his eyes quailed beneath it. 'By the living God,' she said, 'if you injure my child I will have the very blood from your heart.'

Nevertheless she allowed him to return alone to the house, where she knew that he would find her girl. 'Kate,' he said, going into the parlour in which she was sitting idle at the window—'dear Kate.'

'Well, sir?'

'I'm off.'

'You are always—off, as you call it.'

'Well—yes. But I'm not on and off, as the saying is.'

'Why should you go away now?'

'Do you suppose a soldier has got nothing to do? You never calculate, I think, that Ennis is about three-and-twenty miles from here. Come, Kate, be nice with me before I go.'

'How can I be nice when you are going? I always think when I see you go that you will never come back to me again. I don't know why you should come back to such a place as this?'

'Because, as it happens, the place holds what I love best in all the world.' Then he lifted her from her chair, and put his arm around her waist. 'Do you not know that I love you better than all that the world holds?'

'How can I know it?

'Because I swear it to you.'

'I think that you like me—a little. Oh Fred, if you were to go and never come back I should die. Do you remember Mariana?*My life is dreary. He cometh not. She said, "I am aweary, aweary; I would that I were dead!" Do you remember that? What has mother been saying to you?'

'She was bidding me to do you no harm. It was not necessary. I would sooner pluck out my eye than hurt you. My uncle is an old man—a very old man. She cannot understand that it is better that we should wait than that I should have to think hereafter that I had killed him by my unkindness.'

'But he wants you to love some other girl.'

'He cannot make me do that. All the world cannot change my heart, Kate. If you cannot trust me for that, then you do not love me as I love you.'

'Oh, Fred, you know I love you. I do trust you. Of course I can wait, if I only know that you will come back to me. I only want to see you.' He was now leaning over her, and her cheek was pressed close to his. Though she was talking of Mariana, and pretending to fear future misery, all this was Elysium to her—the very joy of Paradise. She could sit and think of him now from morning to night, and never find the day an hour too long. She could remember the words in which he made his oaths to her, and cherish the sweet feeling of his arm round her body. To have her cheek close to his was godlike. And then when he would kiss her, though she would rebuke him, it was as though all heaven were in the embrace.

'And now good-bye. One kiss darling.'

'No.'

'Not a kiss when I am going?'

'I don't want you to go. Oh, Fred! Well—there. Good-bye, my own, own, own beloved one. You'll be here on Monday?'

'Yes—on Monday.'

'And be in the boat four hours, and here four minutes.

Don't I know you?' But he went without answering this last accusation.

'What shall we do, Kate, if he deceives us?' said the mother that evening.

'Die. But I'm sure he will not deceive us.'

Neville, as he made his way down to Liscannor, where his gig was waiting for him, did ask himself some serious questions about his adventure. What must be the end of it? And had he not been imprudent? It may be declared on his behalf that no idea of treachery to the girl ever crossed his mind. He loved her too thoroughly for that. He did love her—not perhaps as she loved him. He had many things in the world to occupy his mind, and she had but one. He was almost a god to her. She to him was simply the sweetest girl that he had ever as yet seen, and one who had that peculiar merit that she was all his own. No other man had ever pressed her hand, or drank her sweet breath. Was not such a love a thousand times sweeter than that of some girl who had been hurried from drawing-room to drawing-room, and perhaps from one vow of constancy to another for half-a-dozen years? The adventure was very sweet. But how was it to end? His uncle might live these ten years, and he had not the heart —nor yet the courage—to present her to his uncle as his bride.

When he reached Ennis that evening there was a despatch marked 'Immediate,' from his aunt Lady Scroope. 'Your uncle is very ill—dangerously ill, we fear. His great desire is to see you once again. Pray come without losing an hour.'

Early on the following morning he started for Dublin, but before he went to bed that night he not only wrote to Kate O'Hara, but enclosed the note from his aunt. He could understand that though the tidings of his uncle's danger was a shock to him there would be something in the tidings which would cause joy to the two inmates of Ardkill Cottage. When he sent that letter with his own, he was of course determined that he would marry Kate O'Hara as soon as he was a free man.

CHAPTER IX

FRED NEVILLE RETURNS TO SCROOPE.

THE SUDDENNESS of the demand made for the heir's presence at Scroope was perhaps not owing to the Earl's illness alone. The Earl, indeed, was ill—so ill that he thought himself that his end was very near; but his illness had been brought about chiefly by the misery to which he had been subjected by the last despatch from Castle Quin to the Countess. 'I am most unwilling,' she said, 'to make mischief or to give unnecessary pain to you or to Lord Scroope; but I think it my duty to let you know that the general opinion about here is that Mr. Neville shall make Miss O'Hara his wife—*if he has not done so already*. The most dangerous feature in the whole matter is that it is all managed by the priest of this parish, a most unscrupulous person, who would do anything —he is so daring. We have known him many, many years, and we know to what lengths he would go. The laws have been so altered in favour of the Roman Catholics, and against the Protestants, that a priest can do almost just what he likes.* I do not think that he would scruple for an instant to marry them if he thought it likely that his prey would escape from him. My own opinion is that there has been no marriage as yet, though I know that others think that there has been.' The expression of this opinion from 'others' which had reached Lady Mary's ears consisted of an assurance from her own Protestant lady's-maid that that wicked guzzling old Father Marty would marry the young couple as soon as look at them, and very likely had done so already. 'I cannot say,' continued Lady Mary, 'that I actually know anything against the character of Miss O'Hara. Of the mother we have very strange stories here. They live in a little cottage with one

764

maid-servant, almost upon the cliffs, and nobody knows anything about them except the priest. If he should be seduced*
into a marriage, nothing could be more unfortunate.' Lady
Mary probably intended to insinuate that were young Neville
prudently to get out of the adventure, simply leaving the girl
behind him blasted, ruined, and destroyed, the matter no
doubt would be bad, but in that case the great misfortune
would have been avoided. She could not quite say this in
plain words; but she felt, no doubt, that Lady Scroope would
understand her. Then Lady Mary went on to assure her
friend that though she and her father and sisters very greatly
regretted that Mr. Neville had not again given them the pleasure of seeing him at Castle Quin, no feeling of injury on that
score had induced her to write so strongly as she had done.
She had been prompted to do so, simply by her desire to prevent *a most ruinous alliance.*

Lady Scroope acknowledged entirely the truth of these last
words. Such an alliance would be most ruinous! But what
could she do? Were she to write to Fred and tell him all that
she heard—throwing to the winds Lady Mary's stupid injunctions respecting secrecy, as she would not have scrupled
to do could she have thus obtained her object—might it not
be quite possible that she would precipitate the calamity
which she desired so eagerly to avoid? Neither had she nor
had her husband any power over the young man, except such
as arose from his own good feeling. The Earl could not disinherit him—could not put a single acre beyond his reach.
Let him marry whom he might he must be Earl Scroope of
Scroope, and the woman so married must be the Countess of
Scroope. There was already a Lady Neville about the world
whose existence was a torture to them; and if this young man
chose also to marry a creature utterly beneath him and to
degrade the family, no effort on their part could prevent him.
But if, as seemed probable, he were yet free, and if he could
be got to come again among them, it might be that he still
had left some feelings on which they might work. No doubt
there was the Neville obstinacy about him; but he had

seemed to both of them to acknowledge the sanctity of his family, and to appreciate to some degree the duty which he owed to it.

The emergency was so great that she feared to act alone. She told everything to her husband, shewing him Lady Mary's letter, and the effect upon him was so great that it made him ill. 'It will be better for me,' he said, 'to turn my face to the wall and die before I know it.' He took to his bed, and they of his household did think that he would die. He hardly spoke except to his wife, and when alone with her did not cease to moan over the destruction which had come upon the house. 'If it could have only been the other brother,' said Lady Scroope.

'There can be no change,' said the Earl. 'He must do as it lists him*with the fortune and the name and honours of the family.'

Then on one morning there was a worse bulletin than heretofore given by the doctor, and Lady Scroope at once sent off the letter which was to recall the nephew to his uncle's bedside. The letter, as we have seen, was successful, and Fred, who caused himself to be carried over from Dorchester to Scroope as fast as post-horses could be made to gallop, almost expected to be told on his arrival that his uncle had departed to his rest. In the hall he encountered Mrs. Bunce the housekeeper. 'We think my lord is a little better,' said Mrs. Bunce almost in a whisper. 'My lord took a little broth in the middle of the day, and we believe he has slept since.' Then he passed on and found his aunt in the small sitting-room. His uncle had rallied a little, she told him. She was very affectionate in her manner, and thanked him warmly for his alacrity in coming. When he was told that his uncle would postpone his visit till the next morning he almost began to think that he had been fussy in travelling so quickly.

That evening he dined alone with his aunt, and the conversation during dinner and as they sat for a few minutes after dinner had reference solely to his uncle's health. But, though they were alone on this evening, he was surprised to

find that Sophie Mellerby was again at Scroope. Lady Sophia
and Mr. Mellerby were up in London, but Sophie was not to
join them till May. As it happened, however, she was dining
at the parsonage this evening. She must have been in the
house when Neville arrived, but he had not seen her. 'Is she
going to live here?' he asked, almost irreverently, when he
was first told she was in the house. 'I wish she were,' said Lady
Scroope. 'I am childless, and she is as dear to me as a
daughter.' Then Fred apologized, and expressed himself as
quite willing that Sophie Mellerby should live and die at
Scroope.

The evening was dreadfully dull. It had seemed to him
that the house was darker, and gloomier, and more comfortless than ever. He had hurried over to see a dying man, and
now there was nothing for him to do but to kick his heels.
But before he went to bed his ennui was dissipated by a full
explanation of all his aunt's terrors. She crept down to him
at about nine, and having commenced her story by saying
that she had a matter of most vital importance on which to
speak to him, she told him in fact all that she had heard from
Lady Mary.

'She is a mischief-making gossiping old maid,' said Neville
angrily.

"Will you tell me that there is no truth in what she
writes?' asked Lady Scroope. But this was a question which
Fred Neville was not prepared to answer, and he sat silent.
'Fred, tell me the truth. Are you married?'

'No—I am not married.'

'I know that you will not condescend to an untruth.'

'If so, my word must be sufficient.'

But it was not sufficient. She longed to extract from him
some repeated and prolonged assurance which might bring
satisfaction to her own mind. 'I am glad, at any rate, to hear
that there is no truth in that suspicion.' To this he would not
condescend to reply but sat glowering at her as though in
wrath that any question should be asked him about his private concerns. 'You must feel, Fred, for your uncle in such a

matter. You must know how important this is to him. You have heard what he has already suffered; and you must know too that he has endeavoured to be very good to you.'

'I do know that he has—been very good to me.'

'Perhaps you are angry with me for interfering.' He would not deny that he was angry. 'I should not do so were it not that your uncle is ill and suffering.'

'You have asked me a question and I have answered it. I do not know what more you want of me.'

'Will you say that there is no truth in all this that Lady Mary says?'

'Lady Mary is an impertinent old maid.'

'If you were in your uncle's place, and if you had an heir as to whose character in the world you were anxious, you would not think anyone impertinent, who endeavoured for the sake of friendship, to save your name and family from a disreputable connexion.'

'I have made no disreputable connexion. I will not allow the word disreputable to be used in regard to any of my friends.'

'You do know people of the name of O'Hara?'

'Of course I do.'

'And there is a—young lady?'

'I may know a dozen young ladies as to whom I shall not choose to consult Lady Mary Quin.'

'You understand what I mean, Fred. Of course I do not wish to ask you anything about your general acquaintances. No doubt you meet many girls whom you admire, and I should be very foolish were I to make inquiries of you or of anybody else concerning them. I am the last person to be so injudicious. If you will tell me that there is not and never shall be any question of marriage between you and Miss O'Hara, I will not say another word.'

'I will not pledge myself to anything for the future.'

'You told your uncle you would never make a marriage that should be disgraceful to the position which you will be called upon to fill.'

'Nor will I.'

'But would not this marriage be disgraceful, even were the young lady ever so estimable? How are the old families of the country to be kept up, and the old blood maintained if young men, such as your are, will not remember something of all that is due to the name which they bear.'

'I do not know that I have forgotten anything.'

Then she paused before she could summon courage to ask him another question. 'You have made no promise of marriage to Miss O'Hara?' He sat dumb, but still looking at her with that angry frown. 'Surely your uncle has a right to expect that you will answer that question.'

'I am quite sure that for his sake it will be much better that no such questions shall be asked me.'

In point of fact he had answered the question. When he would not deny that such promise had been made, there could no longer be any doubt of the truth of what Lady Mary had written. Of course the whole truth had now been elicited. He was not married but he was engaged—engaged to a girl of whom he knew nothing, a Roman Catholic, Irish, fatherless, almost nameless—to one who had never been seen in good society, one of whom no description could be given, of whom no record could be made in the peerage that would not be altogether disgraceful, a girl of whom he was ashamed to speak before those to whom he owed duty and submission!

That there might be a way to escape the evil even yet Lady Scroope acknowledged to herself fully. Many men promise marriage but do not keep the promise they have made. This lady, who herself was really good—unselfish, affectionate, religious, actuated by a sense of duty in all that she did, whose life had been almost austerely moral, entertained an idea that young men, such as Fred Neville, very commonly made such promises with very little thought of keeping them. She did not expect young men to be governed by principles such as those to which young ladies are bound to submit themselves. She almost supposed that heaven had a different code of laws for men and women in her condition of life, and

that salvation was offered on very different terms to the two
sexes. The breach of any such promise as the heir of Scroope
could have made to such a girl as this Miss O'Hara would be
a perjury at which Jove might certainly be expected to laugh.
But in her catalogue there were sins for which no young
men could hope to be forgiven; and the sin of such a marriage as this would certainly be beyond pardon.

Of the injury which was to be done to Miss O'Hara, it
may be said with certainty that she thought not at all. In her
eyes it would be no injury, but simple justice—no more than
a proper punishment for intrigue and wicked ambition.
Without having seen the enemy to the family of Scroope, or
even having heard a word to her disparagement, she could
feel sure that the girl was bad—that these O'Haras were
vulgar and false impostors, persons against whom she could
put out all her strength without any prick of conscience.
Women in such mattters are always hard against women, and
especially hard against those whom they believe to belong to
a class below their own. Certainly no feeling of mercy would
induce her to hold her hand in this task of saving her husband's nephew from an ill-assorted marriage. Mercy to Miss
O'Hara! Lady Scroope had the name of being a very charitable woman. She gave away money. She visited the poor. She
had laboured hard to make the cottages on the estate clean
and comfortable. She denied herself many things that she
might give to others. But she would have no more mercy on
such a one as Miss O'Hara, than a farmer's labourer would
have on a rat!

There was nothing more now to be said to the heir—
nothing more for the present that could serve the purpose
which she had in hand. 'Your uncle is very ill,' she murmured.

'I was so sorry to hear it.'

'We hope now that he may recover. For the last two days
the doctor has told us that we may hope.'

'I am so glad to find that it is so.'

'I am sure you are. You will see him to-morrow after breakfast. He is most anxious to see you. I think sometimes you hardly reflect how much you are to him.'

'I don't know why you should say so.'

'You had better not speak to him to-morrow about this affair—of the Irish young lady.'

'Certainly not—unless he speaks to me about it.'

'He is hardly strong enough yet. But no doubt he will do so before you leave us. I hope it may be long before you do that.'

'It can't be very long, Aunt Mary.' To this she said nothing, but bade him good-night and he was left alone. It was now past ten, and he supposed that Miss Mellerby had come in and gone to her room. Why she should avoid him in this way he could not understand. But as for Miss Mellerby herself, she was so little to him that he cared not at all whether he did or did not see her. All his brightest thoughts were away in County Clare, on the cliffs overlooking the Atlantic. They might say what they liked to him, but he would never be untrue to the girl whom he had left there. His aunt had spoken of the 'affair of—the Irish young lady;' and he had quite understood the sneer with which she had mentioned Kate's nationality. Why should not an Irish girl be as good as any English girl? Of one thing he was quite sure—that there was much more of real life to be found on the cliffs of Moher than in the gloomy chambers of Scroope Manor.

He got up from his seat feeling absolutely at a loss how to employ himself. Of course he could go to bed, but how terribly dull must life be in a place in which he was obliged to go to bed at ten o'clock because there was nothing to do. And since he had been there his only occupation had been that of listening to his aunt's sermons. He began to think that a man might pay too dearly even for being the heir to Scroope. After sitting awhile in the dark gloom created by a pair of candles, he got up and wandered into the large unused dining-room of the mansion. It was a chamber over forty feet long, with dark flock paper and dark curtains, with dark painted wainscoating below the paper and huge dark mahogany furniture. On the walls hung the portraits of the

Scroopes for many generations past, some in armour, some in their robes of state, ladies with stiff bodices and high head-dresses, not beauties by Lely or warriors and statesmen by Kneller,* but wooden, stiff, ungainly, hideous figures, by artists whose works had, unfortunately, been more enduring than their names. He was pacing up and down the room with a candle in his hand, trying to realize to himself what life at Scroope might be with a wife of his aunt's choosing, and his aunt to keep the house for them, when a door was opened at the end of the room, away from that by which he had entered, and with a soft noiseless step Miss Mellerby entered. She did not see him at first, as the light of her own candle was in her eyes, and she was startled when he spoke to her. His first idea was one of surprise that she should be wandering about the house alone at night. 'Oh, Mr. Neville,' she said, 'you quite took me by surprise. How do you do? I did not expect to meet you here.'

'Nor I you!'

'Since Lord Scroope has been so ill, Lady Scroope has been sleeping in the little room next to his, downstairs, and I have just come from her.'

'What do you think of my uncle's state?'

'He is better; but he is very weak.'

'You see him?'

'Oh yes, daily. He is so anxious to see you, Mr. Neville, and so much obliged to you for coming. I was sure that you would come.'

'Of course I came.'

'He wanted to see you this afternoon; but the doctor had expressly ordered that he should be kept quiet. Good-night. I am so very glad that you are here. I am sure that you will be good to him.'

Why should she be glad, and why should she be sure that he would be good to his uncle? Could it be that she also had been told the story of Kate O'Hara? Then, as no other occupation was possible to him, he took himself to bed.

CHAPTER X

FRED NEVILLE'S SCHEME.

ON THE next morning after breakfast Neville was taken into his uncle's chamber, but there was an understanding that there was to be no conversation on disagreeable subjects on this occasion. His aunt remained in the room while he was there, and the conversation was almost confined to the expression of thanks on the part of the Earl to his nephew for coming, and of hopes on the part of the nephew that his uncle might soon be well. One matter was mooted as to which no doubt much would be said before Neville could get away. 'I thought it better to make arrangements to stay a fortnight,' said Fred—as though a fortnight were a very long time indeed.

'A fortnight!' said the Earl.

'We won't talk of his going yet,' replied Lady Scroope.

'Supposing I had died, he could not have gone back in a fortnight,' said the Earl in a low moaning voice.

'My dear uncle, I hope that I may live to see you in your own place here at Scroope for many years to come.' The Earl shook his head, but nothing more was then said on that subject. Fred, however, had carried out his purpose. He had been determined to let them understand that he would not hold himself bound to remain long at Scroope Manor.

Then he wrote a letter to his own Kate. It was the first time he had addressed her in this fashion, and though he was somewhat of a gallant gay Lothario,* the writing of the letter was an excitement to him. If so, what must the receipt of it have been to Kate O'Hara! He had promised her that he would write to her, and from the moment that he was gone she was anxious to send in to the post-office at Ennistimon for

773

the treasure which the mail car might bring to her. When she did get it, it was indeed a treasure. To a girl who really loves, the first love letter is a thing as holy as the recollection of the first kiss. 'May I see it, Kate?' said Mrs. O'Hara, as her daughter sat poring over the scrap of paper by the window.

'Yes, mamma—if you please.' Then she paused a moment. 'But I think that I had rather you did not. Perhaps he did not mean me to shew it.' The mother did not urge her request, but contented herself with coming up behind her child and kissing her. The reader, however, shall have the privilege which was denied to Mrs. O'Hara.

'DEAREST KATE,

'I got here all alive yesterday at four. I came on as fast as ever I could travel, and hardly got a mouthful to eat after I left Limerick. I never saw such beastliness as they have at the stations. My uncle is much better—so much so that I shan't remain here very long. I can't tell you any particular news—except this, that that old cat down at Castle Quin— the one with the crisp-curled wig—must have the nose of a dog and the ears of a cat and the eyes of a bird, and she sends word to Scroope of everything that she smells and hears and sees. It makes not the slightest difference to me—nor to you I should think. Only I hate such interference. The truth is old maids have nothing else to do. If I were you I wouldn't be an old maid.

'I can't quite say how long it will be before I am back at Ardkill, but not a day longer than I can help. Address to Scroope, Dorsetshire—that will be enough—to F. Neville, Esq. Give my love to your mother—As for yourself, dear Kate, if you care for my love, you may weigh mine for your own dear self with your own weights and measures. Indeed you have all my heart.

                                        Your own F.N.'

'There is a young lady here whom it is intended that I shall marry. She is the pink of propriety and really very pretty—but you need not be a bit jealous. The joke is that my brother is furiously in love with her, and I fancy she would be just as much in love with him only that she's told not to—A thousand kisses.'

It was not much of a love letter, but there were a few words in which sufficed althogether for Kate's happiness. She was told that she had all his heart—and she believed it. She was told that she need not be jealous of the proper young lady, and she believed that too. He sent her a thousand kisses; and she, thinking that he might have kissed the paper, pressed it to her lips. At any rate his hand had rested on it. She would have been quite willing to show to her mother all these expressions of her lover's love; but she felt that it would not be fair to him to expose his allusions to the 'beastliness' at the stations. He might say what he liked to her; but she understood that she was not at liberty to show to others words which had been addressed to her in the freedom of perfect intimacy.

'Does he say anything of the old man?' asked Mrs. O'Hara.

'He says that his uncle is better.'

'Threatened folks live long. Does Neville tell you when he will be back?'

'Not exactly; but he says that he will not stay long. He does not like Scroope at all. I knew that. He always says that —that—.'

'Says what, dear?'

'When we are married he will go away somewhere—to Italy or Greece or somewhere. Scroope he says is so gloomy.'

'And where shall I go?'

'Oh mother—you shall be with us, always.'

'No dear, you must not dream of that. When you have him you will not want me.'

'Dear mother. I shall want you always.'

'He will not want me. We have no right to expect too much from him, Kate. That he shall make you his wife we have a right to expect. If he were false to you——'

'He is not false. Why should you think him false?'

'I do not think it; but if he were——! Never mind. If he be true to you, I will not burden him. If I can see you happy, Kate, I will bear all the rest.' That which she would have to bear would be utter solitude for life. She could look forward and see how black and tedious would be her days; but all that would be nothing to her if her child were lifted up on high.

It was now the beginning of April, which for sportsmen in England is of all seasons the most desperate. Hunting is over. There is literally nothing to shoot. And fishing—even if there were fishing in England worth a man's time—has not begun. A gentleman of enterprise driven very hard in this respect used to declare that there was no remedy for April but to go and fly hawks in Holland.* Fred Neville could not fly hawks at Scroope, and found that there was nothing for him to do. Miss Mellerby suggested—books. 'I like books better than anything,' said Fred. 'I always have a lot of novels down at our quarters. But a fellow can't be reading all day, and there isn't a novel in the house except Walter Scott's and a lot of old rubbish. Bye-the-by have you read "All isn't Gold that Glitters?"'* Miss Mellerby had not read the tale named. 'That's what I call a good novel.'

Day passed after day and it seemed as though he was expected to remain at Scroope without any definite purpose, and, worse still, without any fixed limit to his visit. At his aunt's instigation he rode about the property and asked questions as to the tenants. It was all to be his own, and in the course of nature must be his own very soon. There could not but be an interest for him in every cottage and every field. But yet there was present to him all the time a schoolboy feeling that he was doing a task; and the occupation was not pleasant to him because it was a task. The steward was with him as a kind of pedagogue, and continued to instruct him during the whole ride. This man only paid so much a year, and the rent ought to be so much more; but there were circumstances. And 'My Lord' had been peculiarly good. This farm was supposed to be the best on the estate, and that other

the worse. Oh yes, there were plenty of foxes. 'My Lord' had
always insisted that the foxes should be preserved. Some of
the hunting gentry no doubt had made complaints, but it
was a great shame. Foxes had been seen, two or three at a
time, the very day after the coverts had been drawn blank.
As for game, a head of game could be got up very soon, as
there was plenty of corn and the woods were large; but 'My
Lord' had never cared for game. The farmers all shot the
rabbits on their own land. Rents were paid to the day. There
was never any mistake about that. Of course the land would
require to be re-valued,* but 'My Lord' wouldn't hear of such
a thing being done in his time. The Manor wood wanted
thinning very badly. The wood had been a good deal neglected. 'My Lord' had never liked to hear the axe going. That
was Grumby Green and the boundary of the estate in that
direction. The next farm was college property,* and was
rented five shillings an acre dearer than 'My Lord's' land. If
Mr. Neville wished it the steward would show him the limit
of the estate on the other side tomorrow. No doubt there was
a plan of the estate. It was in 'My Lord's' own room, and
would show every farm with its acreage and bounds. Fred
thought that he would study this plan on the next day instead of riding about with the steward.

He could not escape from the feeling that he was being
taught his lesson like a school-boy, and he did not like it. He
longed for the freedom of his boat on the Irish coast, and
longed for the devotedness of Kate O'Hara. He was sure that
he loved her so thoroughly that life without her was not to
be regarded as possible. But certain vague ideas very injurious
to the Kate he so dearly loved crossed his brain. Under the
constant teaching of his aunt he did recognize it as a fact that
he owed a high duty to his family. For many days after that
first night at Scroope not a word was said to him about Kate
O'Hara. He saw his uncle daily—probably twice a day; but
the Earl never alluded to his Irish love. Lady Scroope spoke
constantly of the greatness of the position which the heir was
called upon to fill and of all that was due to the honour of the

family. Fred, as he heard her, would shake his head impatiently, but would acknowledge the truth of what she said. He was induced even to repeat the promise which he had made to his uncle, and to assure his aunt that he would do nothing to mar or lessen the dignity of the name of Neville. He did become, within his own mind, indoctrinated with the idea that he would injure the position of the earldom which was to be his were he to marry Kate O'Hara. Arguments which appeared to him to be absurd when treated with ridicule by Father Marty, and which in regard to his own conduct he had determined to treat as old women's tales, seemed to him at Scroope to be true and binding. The atmosphere of the place, the companionship of Miss Mellerby, the reverence with which he himself was treated by the domestics, the signs of high nobility which surrounded him on all sides, had their effect upon him. Noblesse oblige. He felt that it was so. Then there crossed his brain visions of a future life which were injurious to the girl he loved.

Let his brother Jack come and live at Scroope and marry Sophie Mellerby. As long as he lived Jack could not be the Earl, but in regard to money he would willingly make such arrangements as would enable his brother to maintain the dignity and state of the house. They would divide the income. And then he would so arrange his matters with Kate O'Hara that his brother's son should be heir to the Earldom. He had some glimmering of an idea that as Kate was a Roman Catholic a marriage ceremony might be contrived of which this would become the necessary result. There should be no deceit. Kate should know it all, and everything should be done to make her happy. He would live abroad, and would not call himself by his title. They would be Mr. and Mrs. Neville. As to the property that must of course hereafter go with the title, but in giving up so much to his brother, he could, of course, arrange as to the provision necessary for any children of his own. No doubt his Kate would like to be the Countess Scroope—would prefer that a future son of her own should be the future Earl. But as he was ready to abandon so much, surely she would be ready to abandon something. He must explain to her—and to her mother—that under no other circumstances could he marry her. He must tell her of pledges made to his uncle before he knew her, of the duty which he owed to his family, and of his own great dislike to the kind of life which would await him as acting head of the family. No doubt there would be scenes—and his heart quailed as he remembered certain glances which had flashed upon him from the eyes of Mrs. O'Hara. But was he not offering to give up everything for his love? His Kate should be his wife after some Roman Catholic fashion in some Roman Catholic country. Of course there would be difficulties—the least of which would not be those glances from the angry mother; but it would be his business to overcome difficulties. There were always difficulties in the way of any man who chose to leave the common grooves of life and to make a separate way for himself. There were always difficulties in the way of adventures. Dear Kate! He would never desert his Kate. But his Kate must do as much as this for him. Did he not intend that, whatever good things the world might have in store for him, his Kate should share them all?

His ideas were very hazy, and he knew himself that he was ignorant of the laws respecting marriage. It occurred to him, therefore, that he had better consult his brother, and confide everything to him. That Jack was wiser than he, he was always willing to allow; and although he did in some sort look down upon Jack as a plodding fellow, who shot no seals and cared nothing for adventure, still he felt it to be almost a pity that Jack should not be the future Earl. So he told his aunt that he proposed to ask his brother to come to Scroope for a day or two before he returned to Ireland. Had his aunt, or would his uncle have, any objection? Lady Scroope did not dare to object. She by no means wished that her younger nephew should again be brought within the influence of Miss Mellerby's charms; but it would not suit her purpose to give offence to the heir by refusing so reasonable request. He would have been off to join his brother at Woolwich* immediately. So the invitation was sent, and Jack Neville promised that he would come.

Fred knew nothing of the offer that had been made to Miss Mellerby, though he had been sharp enough to discern his brother's feelings. 'My brother is coming here tomorrow,' he said one morning to Miss Mellerby when they were alone together.

'So Lady Scroope has told me. I don't wonder that you should wish to see him.'

'I hope everybody will be glad to see him. Jack is just about the very best fellow in the world—and he's one of the cleverest too.'

'It is nice to hear one brother speak in that way of another.'

'I swear by Jack. He ought to have been the elder brother —that's the truth. Don't you like him?'

'Who—I. Oh, yes, indeed. What I saw of him I liked very much.'

'Isn't it a pity that he shouldn't have been the elder?'

'I can't say that, Mr. Neville.'

'No. It wouldn't be just civil to me. But I can say it. When we were here last winter I thought that my brother was—'

'Was what, Mr. Neville?'

'Was getting to be very fond of you. Perhaps I ought not to say so.'

'I don't think that much good is ever done by saying that kind of thing,' said Miss Mellerby gravely.

'It cannot at any rate do any harm in this case. I wish with all my heart that he was fond of you and you of him.'

'That is all nonsense. Indeed it is.'

'I am not saying it without an object. I don't see why you and I should not understand one another. If I tell you a secret will you keep it?'

'Do not tell me any secret that I must keep from Lady Scroope.'

'But that is just what you must do.'

'But then suppose I don't do it,' said Miss Mellerby

But Fred was determined to tell his secret. 'The truth is that both my uncle and my aunt want me to fall in love with you.'

'How very kind of them,' said she with a little forced laugh.

'I don't for a moment think that, had I tried it on ever so, I could have succeeded. I am not at all the sort of man to be conceited in that way. Wishing to do the best they could for me, they picked you out. It isn't that I don't think well of you as they do, but——'

'Really, Mr. Neville, this is the oddest conversation.'

'Quite true. It is odd. But the fact is you are here, and there is nobody else I can talk to. And I want you to know the exact truth. I'm engaged to—somebody else.'

'I ought to break my heart—oughtn't I?'

'I don't in the least mind your laughing at me. I should have minded it very much if I had asked you to marry me, and you had refused me.'

'You haven't given me the chance, you see.'

'I didn't mean. What was the good?'

'Certainly not, Mr. Neville, if you are engaged to someone else. I shouldn't like to be Number Two.'

'I'm in a peck of troubles—that's the truth. I would change places with my brother tomorrow if I could. I daresay you don't believe that, but I would. I will not vex my uncle if I can help it, but I certainly shall not throw over the girl who loves me. If it wasn't for the title, I'd give up Scroope to my brother tomorrow, and go and live in some place where I could get lots of shooting, and where I should never have to put on a white choker.'*

'You'll think better of all that.'

'Well!—I've just told you everything because I like to be on the square. I wish you knew Kate O'Hara. I'm sure you would not wonder that a fellow should love her. I had rather you didn't tell my aunt what I have told you; but if you choose to do so, I can't help it.'

CHAPTER XI

THE WISDOM OF JACK NEVILLE

NEVILLE HAD been forced to get his leave of absence renewed on the score of his uncle's health, and had promised to prolong his absence till the end of April. When doing so he had declared his intention of returning to Ennis in the beginning of May; but no agreement to that had as yet been expressed by his uncle or aunt. Towards the end of the month his brother came to Scroope, and up to that time not a word further had been said to him respecting Kate O'Hara.

He had received an answer from Kate to his letter, prepared in a fashion very different from that of his own. He had seated himself at a table and in compliance with the pledge given by him, had scrawled off his epistle as fast as he could write it. She had taken a whole morning to think of hers, and had recopied it after composing it, and had then read it with the utmost care, confessing to herself, almost with tears, that it was altogether unworthy of him to whom it was to be sent. It was the first love letter she had ever written—probably the first letter she had ever written to a man, except those short notes which she would occasionally scrawl to Father Marty in compliance with her mother's directions. The letter to Fred was as follows—

ARDKILL COTTAGE
10th April, 18—.

MY DEAREST FRED,

'I received your dear letter three or four days ago, and it made me so happy. We were sorry that you should have such an uncomfortable journey; but all that would be over and soon forgotten when you found yourself in your comfortable home and among your own friends. I am very glad to hear that your uncle is better. The thought of finding him so ill must have made your journey very sad. As he is so much better, I suppose you will come back soon to your poor little Kate.

'There is no news at all to send you from Liscannor. Father Marty was up here yesterday and says that your boat is all safe at Lahinch. He says that Barney Morony is an idle fellow, but as he has nothing to do he can't help being idle. You should come back and not let him be idle any more. I think the sea gulls know that you are away, because they are wheeling and screaming about louder and bolder than ever.

'Mother sends her best love. She is very well. We have had nothing to eat since you went because it has been Lent. So, if you had been here, you would not have been able to get a bit of luncheon. I dare say you have been a great deal better off at Scroope. Father Marty says that you Protestants will have to keep your Lent hereafter—eighty days at a time instead of forty; and that we Catholics will be allowed to eat just what we like, while you Protestants will have to look on at us. If so, I think I'll manage to give you a little bit.

'Do come back to your own Kate as soon as you can. I need not tell you that I love you better than all the world because you know it already. I am not a bit jealous of the proper young lady, and I hope that she will fall in love with your brother. Then some day we shall be sisters—shan't we? I should like to have a proper young lady for my sister so much. Only, perhaps she would despise me. Do come back soon. Everything is so dull while you are away! You would come back to your own Kate if you knew how great a joy it is to her when she sees you coming along the cliff.

'Dearest, dearest love, I am always your own, own

KATE O'HARA.'

Neville thought of showing Kate's letter to Miss Mellerby, but when he read it a second time he made up his mind that he would keep it to himself. The letter was all very well, and as regarded the expressions towards himself, just what it should be. But he felt that it was not such a letter as Miss Mellerby would have written herself, and he was a little ashamed of all that was said about the priest. Neither was he proud of the pretty, finished, French hand-writing, over every letter of which his love had taken so much pains. In truth, Kate O'Hara was better educated than himself, and perhaps knew as much as Sophie Mellerby. She could have written her letter quite as well in French as in English, and she did understand something of the formation of her sentences. Fred Neville had been at an excellent school, but it may be doubted whether he could have explained his own written language. Nevertheless he was a little ashamed of his Kate, and thought that Miss Mellerby might perceive her ignorance if he shewed her letter.

He had sent for his brother in order that he might explain his scheme and get his brother's advice—but he found it very difficult to explain his scheme to Jack Neville. Jack, indeed, from the very first would not allow that the scheme was in any way practicable. 'I don't quite understand, Fred, what you mean. You don't intend to deceive her by a false marriage?'

'Most assuredly not. I do not intend to deceive her at all.'

'You must make her your wife, or not make her your wife.'

'Undoubtedly she will be my wife. I am quite determined about that. She has my word—and over and above that, she is dearer to me than anything else.'

'If you marry her, her eldest son must of course be the heir to the title.'

'I am not at all so sure of that. All manner of queer things may be arranged by marriage with Roman Catholics.'

'Put that out of your head,' said Jack Neville. 'In the first place you would certainly find yourself in a mess, and in the next place the attempt itself would be dishonest. I daresay men have crept out of marriages because they have been illegal; but a man who arranges a marriage with the intention of creeping out of it is a scoundrel.'

'You needn't bully about it, Jack. You know very well that I don't mean to creep out of anything.'

'I am sure you don't. But as you ask me I must tell you what I think. You are in a sort of dilemma between this girl and Uncle Scroope.'

'I'm not in any dilemma at all.'

'You seem to think you have made some promise to him which will be broken if you marry her—and I suppose you certainly have made her a promise.'

'Which I certainly mean to keep,' said Fred.

'All right. Then you must break your promise to Uncle Scroope.'

'It was a sort of half and half promise. I could not bear to see him making himself unhappy about it.'

'Just so. I suppose Miss O'Hara can wait.'

Fred Neville scratched his head. 'Oh yes—she can wait. There's nothing to bind me to a day or a month. But my uncle may live for the next ten years now.'

'My advice to you is to let Miss O'Hara understand clearly that you will make no other engagement, but that you cannot marry her as long as your uncle lives. Of course I say this on the supposition that the affair cannot be broken off.'

'Certainly not,' said Fred with a decision that was magnanimous.

'I cannot think the engagement a fortunate one for you in your position. Like should marry like. I'm quite sure of that. You would wish your wife to be easily intimate with the sort of people among whom she would naturally be thrown as Lady Scroope—among the wives and daughters of other Earls and such like.'

'No; I shouldn't.'

'I don't see how she would be comfortable in any other way.'

'I should never live among other Earls, as you call them. I hate that kind of thing. I hate London. I should never live here.'

'What would you do?'

'I should have a yacht and live chiefly in that. I should go about a good deal, and get into all manner of queer places. I don't say but what I might spend a winter now and then in Leicestershire or Northamptonshire, for I am fond of hunting. But I should have no regular home. According to my scheme you should have this place—and sufficient of the income to maintain it of course.'

'That wouldn't do Fred,' said Jack, shaking his head— 'though I know how generous you are.'

'Why wouldn't it do?'

'You are the heir, and you must take the duties with the privileges. You can have your yacht if you like a yacht—but you'll soon get tired of that kind of life. I take it that a yacht is a bad place for a nursery, and inconvenient for one's old boots. When a man has a home fixed for him by circumstances—as you will have—he gravitates towards it, let his own supposed predilections be what they may. Circumstances are stronger than predilections.'

'You're a philosopher.'

'I was always more sober than you, Fred.'

'I wish you had been the elder—on the condition of the younger brother having a tidy slice out of the property to make himself comfortable.'

'But I am not the elder, and you must take the position with all encumbrances. I see nothing for it but to ask Miss O'Hara to wait. If my uncle lives long the probability is that one or the other of you will change your minds and that the affair will never come off.'

When the younger and wiser brother gave this advice he did not think it all likely that Miss O'Hara would change her mind. Penniless young ladies don't often change their minds when they are engaged to the heirs of Earls. It was not at all probable that she should repent the bargain that she had made. But Jack Neville did think it very probable that his brother might do so—and, indeed, felt sure that he would do so if years were allowed to intervene. His residence in County Clare would not be perpetual, and with him in his circumstances it might well be that the young lady, being out of sight should be out of mind. Jack could not exactly declare his opinion on this head. His brother at present was full of his promise, full of his love, full of his honour. Nor would Jack have absolutely counselled him to break his word to the young lady. But he thought it probable that in the event of delay poor Miss O'Hara might go to the wall—and he also thought that for the general interests of the Scroope family it would be better that she should do so.

'And what are you going to do yourself?' asked Fred.

'In respect of what?'

'In respect of Miss Mellerby?'

'In respect of Miss Mellerby I am not going to do anything,' said Jack as he walked away.

In all that the younger brother said to the elder as to poor Kate he was no doubt wise and prudent; but in what he said about himself he did not tell the truth. But then the question asked was one which a man is hardly bound to answer, even to a brother. Jack Neville was much less likely to talk about his love affairs than Fred, but not on that account less likely to think about them. Shophie Mellerby had refused him once, but young ladies have been known to marry gentlemen after refusing them more than once. He at any rate was determined to persevere, having in himself and in his affairs that silent faith of which the possessor is so often unconscious, but which so generally leads to success. He found Miss Mellerby to be very courteous to him if not gracious; and he had the advantage of not being afraid of her. It did not strike him that because she was the granddaughter of a duke, and because he was a younger son, that therefore he ought not to dare to look at her. He understood very well that she was brought there that Fred might marry her—but Fred was intent on marrying someone else, and Sophie Mellerby was not a girl to throw her heart away upon a man who did not want it. He had come to Scroope for only three days, but, in spite of some watchfulness on the part of the Countess, he found his opportunity for speaking before he left the house. 'Miss Mellerby,' he said, 'I don't know whether I ought to thank Fortune or to upbraid her for having again brought me face to face with you.'

'I hope the evil is not so oppressive as to make you very loud in your upbraidings.'

'They shall not at any rate be heard. I don't know whether there was any spice of malice about my brother when he asked me to come here, and told me in the same letter that you were at Scroope.'

'He must have meant it for malice, I should think,' said the young lady, endeavouring, but not quite successfully, to imitate the manner of the man who loved her.

'Of course I came.'

'Not on my behalf, I hope, Mr. Neville.'

'Altogether on your behalf. Fred's need to see me was not very great, and, as my uncle had not asked me, and as my aunt, I fancy, does not altogether approve of me, I certainly should not have come—were it not that I might find it difficult to get any other opportunity of seeing you.'

'That is hardly fair to Lady Scroope, Mr. Neville.'

'Quite fair, I think. I did not come clandestinely. I am not ashamed of what I am doing—or of what I am going to do. I may be ashamed of this—that I should feel my chance of success to be so small. When I was here before I asked you to—allow me to love you. I now ask you again.'

'Allow you!' she said.

'Yes—allow me. I should be too bold were I to ask you to return my love at once. I only ask you to know that because I was repulsed once, I have not given up the pursuit.'

'Mr. Neville, I am sure that my father and mother would not permit it.'

'May I ask your father, Miss Mellerby?'

'Certainly not—with my permission.'

'Nevertheless you will not forget that I am suitor for your love?'

'I will make no promise of anything, Mr. Neville.' Then,

fearing that she had encouraged him, she spoke again. 'I think you ought to take my answer as final.'

'Miss Mellerby, I shall take no answer as final that is not favourable. Should I indeed hear that you were to be married to another man, that would be final; but that I shall not hear from your own lips. You will say goodbye to me,' and he offered her his hand.

She gave him her hand—and he raised it to his lips and kissed it, as men were wont to do in the olden days.

CHAPTER XII

FRED NEVILLE MAKES A PROMISE

FRED NEVILLE felt that he had not received from his brother the assistance or sympathy which he had required. He had intended to make a very generous offer—not indeed quite understanding how this offer could be carried out, but still of a nature that should, he thought, have bound his brother to his service. But Jack had simply answered him by sermons —by sermons and an assurance of the impracticability of his scheme. Nevertheless he was by no means sure that his scheme was impracticable. He was at least sure of this—that no human power could force him to adopt a mode of life that was distasteful to him. No one could make him marry Sophie Mellerby, or any other Sophie, and maintain a grand and gloomy house in Dorsetshire, spending his income, not in a manner congenial to him, but in keeping a large retinue of servants and taking what he called the 'heavy line' of an English nobleman. The property must be his own—or at any rate the life use of it. He swore to himself over and over again that nothing should induce him to impoverish the family or to leave the general affairs of the house of Scroope worse than he found them. Much less than half of that which he understood to be the income coming from the estates would suffice for him. But let his uncle or aunt—or his strait-laced methodical brother, say what they would to him, nothing should induce him to make himself a slave to an earldom.

But yet his mind was much confused and his contentment by no means complete. He knew that there must be a disagreeable scene between himself and his uncle before he returned to Ireland, and he knew also that his uncle could, if he so minded, stop his present very liberal allowance

altogether. There had been a bargain, no doubt, that he
should remain with his regiment for a year, and of that year
six months were still unexpired. His uncle could not quarrel
with him for going back to Ireland; but what answer should
he make when his uncle asked him whether he were engaged
to marry Miss O'Hara—as of course he would ask; and what
reply should he make when his uncle would demand of him
whether he thought such a marriage fit for a man in his position. He knew that it was not fit. He believed in the title, in
the sanctity of the name, in the mysterious grandeur of the
family. He did not think that an Earl of Scroope ought to
marry a girl of whom nothing whatever was known. The
pride of the position stuck to him—but it irked him to feel
that the sacrifices necessary to support that pride should fall
on his own shoulders.

One thing was impossible to him. He would not desert his
Kate. But he wished to have his Kate, as a thing apart. If he
could have given six months of each year to his Kate, living
that yacht-life of which he had spoken, visiting those strange
sunny places which his imagination had pictured to him, un-
shackled by conventionalities, beyond the sound of church
bells, unimpeded by any considerations of family—and then
have migrated for the other six months to his earldom and his
estates, to his hunting and perhaps to Parliament, leaving his
Kate behind him, that would have been perfect. And why
not? In the days which must come so soon, he would be his
own master. Who could impede his motions or gainsay his
will? Then he remembered his Kate's mother, and the
glances which would come from the mother's eyes. There
might be difficulty even though Scroope were all his own.

He was not a villain—simply a self-indulgent spoiled young
man who had realized to himself no idea of duty in life. He
never once told himself that Kate should be his mistress. In
all the pictures which he drew for himself of a future life
everything was to be done for her happiness and for her
gratification. His yacht should be made a floating bower for
her delight. During those six months of the year which, and

which only, the provoking circumstances of his position would enable him to devote to joy and love, her will should be his law. He did not think himself to be fickle. He would never want another Kate. He would leave her with sorrow. He would return to her with ecstasy. Everybody around him should treat her with the respect due to an empress. But it would be very expedient that she should be called Mrs. Neville instead of Lady Scroope. Could things not be so arranged for him—so arranged that he might make a promise to his uncle, and yet be true to his Kate without breaking his promise? That was his scheme. Jack said that his scheme was impracticable. But the difficulties in his way were not, he thought, so much those which Jack had propounded as the angry eyes of Kate O'Hara's mother.

At last the day was fixed for his departure. The Earl was already so much better as to be able to leave his bedroom. Twice or thrice a day Fred saw his uncle, and there was much said about the affairs of the estate. The heir had taken some trouble, had visited some of the tenants, and had striven to seem interested in the affairs of the property. The Earl could talk for ever about the estate, every field, every fence, almost every tree on which was familiar to him. That his tenants should be easy in their circumstances, a protestant, church-going, rent-paying, people, son following father, and daughters marrying as their mothers had married, unchanging, never sinking an inch in the social scale, or rising—this was the wish nearest to his heart. Fred was well disposed to talk about the tenants as long as Kate O'Hara was not mentioned. When the Earl would mournfully speak of his own coming death, as an event which could not now be far distant, Fred with fullest sincerity would promise that his wishes should be observed. No rents should be raised. The axe should be but sparingly used. It seemed to him strange that a man going into eternity should care about this tree or that—but as far as he was concerned the trees should stand while Nature supported them. No servant should be dismissed. The carriage horses should be allowed to die on the place. The old charities should be maintained. The parson of the parish should always be a welcome guest at the Manor. No promise was difficult for him to make so long as that one question were left untouched.

But when he spoke of the day of his departure as fixed— as being 'the day after tomorrow'—then he knew that the question must be touched. 'I am sorry—very sorry, that you must go,' said the Earl.

'You see a man can't leave the service at a moment's notice.'

'I think that we could have got over that, Fred.'

'Perhaps as regards the service we might, but the regiment would think ill of me. You see, so many things depend on a man's staying or going. The youngsters mayn't have their money ready.* I said I should remain till October.'

'I don't at all wish to act the tyrant to you.'

'I know that, uncle.'

Then there was a pause. 'I haven't spoken to you yet, Fred, on a matter which has caused me a great deal of uneasiness. When you first came I was not strong enough to allude to it, and I left it to your aunt.' Neville, knew well what was coming now, and was aware that he was moved in a manner that hardly became his manhood. 'Your aunt tells me that you have got into some trouble with a young lady in the west of Ireland.'

'No trouble, uncle, I hope.'

'Who is she?'

Then there was another pause, but he gave a direct answer to the question. 'She is a Miss O'Hara.'

'A Roman Catholic?'

'Yes.'

'A girl of whose family you know nothing?'

'I know that she lives with her mother.'

'In absolute obscurity—and poverty?'

'They are not rich,' said Fred.

'Do not suppose that I regard poverty as a fault. It is not necessary that you should marry a girl with any fortune.'

'I suppose not, Uncle Scroope.'

'But I understand that this young lady is quite beneath yourself in life. She lives with her mother-in a little cottage, without servants——'

'There is a servant.'

'You know what I mean, Fred. She does not live as ladies live. She is uneducated.'

'You are wrong there, my lord. She has been at an excellent school in France.'

'In France! Who was her father, and what?'

'I do not know what her father was—a Captain O'Hara, I believe.'

'And you would marry such a girl as that—a Roman Catholic; picked up on the Irish coast—one of whom nobody knows even her parentage or perhaps her real name? It would kill me, Fred.'

'I have not said that I mean to marry her.'

'But what do you mean? Would you ruin her—seduce her by false promises and then leave her? Do you tell me that in cold blood you look forward to such a deed as that?'

'Certainly not.'

'I hope not, my boy; I hope not that. Do not tell me that a heartless scoundrel is to take my name when I am gone.'

'I am not a heartless scoundrel,' said Fred Neville, jumping up from his seat.

'Then what is it that you mean? You have thought, have you not, of the duties of the high position to which you are called? You do not suppose that wealth is to be given to you, and a great name, and all the appanages and power of nobility, in order that you may eat more, and drink more, and lie softer than others. It is because some think so, and act upon such base thoughts, that the only hereditary peerage left in the world is in danger of encountering the ill will of the people. Are you willing to be known only as one of those who have disgraced their order?'

'I do not mean to disgrace it.'

'But you will disgrace it if you marry such a girl as that. If

she were fit to be your wife, would not the family of Lord
Kilfenora have known her?'

'I don't think much of their not knowing her, uncle.'

'Who does know her? Who can say that she is even what
she pretends to be? Did you not promise me that you would
make no such marriage?'

He was not strong to defend his Kate. Such defence would
have been in opposition to his own ideas, in antagonism
with the scheme which he had made for himself. He understood, almost as well as did his uncle, that Kate O'Hara ought
not to be made Countess of Scroope. He too thought that
were she to be presented to the world as the Countess of
Scroope, she would disgrace the title. And yet he would not
be a villain! And yet he would not give her up! He could
only fall back upon his scheme. Miss O'Hara is as good as
gold,' he said; 'but I acknowledge that she is not fit to be
mistress of this house.'

'Fred,' said the Earl, almost in a passion of affectionate
solicitude, 'do not go back to Ireland. We will arrange about
the regiment. No harm shall be done to anyone. My health
will be your excuse, and the lawyers shall arrange it all.'

'I must go back,' said Neville. Then the Earl fell back in
his chair and covered his face with his hands. 'I must go
back; but I will give you my honour as a gentleman to do
nothing that shall distress you.'

'You will not marry her?'

'No.'

'And, oh, Fred, as you value your own soul, do not injure
a poor girl so desolate as that. Tell her and tell her mother
the honest truth. If there be tears, will not that be better
than sorrow, and disgrace, and ruin?' Among evils there
must always be a choice; and the Earl thought that a broken
promise was the lightest of those evils to a choice among
which his nephew had subjected himself.

And so the interview was over, and there had been no
quarrel. Fred Neville had given the Earl a positive promise
that he would not marry Kate O'Hara—to whom he had

sworn a thousand times that she should be his wife, Such a promise, however—so he told himself—is never intended to prevail beyond the lifetime of the person to whom it is made. He had bound himself not to marry Kate O'Hara while his uncle lived, and that was all.

Or might it not be better to take his uncle's advice altogether and tell the truth—not to Kate, for that he could not do—but to Mrs. O'Hara or to Father Marty? As he thought of this he acknowledged to himself that the task of telling such a truth to Mrs. O'Hara would be almost beyond his strength. Could he not throw himself upon the priest's charity, and leave it all to him? Then he thought of his own Kate, and some feeling akin to genuine love told him that he could not part with the girl in such fashion as that. He would break his heart were he to lose his Kate. When he looked at it in that light it seemed to him that Kate was more to him than all the family of the Scroopes with all their glory. Dear, sweet, soft, innocent, beautiful Kate! His Kate who, as he knew well, worshipped the very ground on which he trod! It was not possible that he should separate himself from Kate O'Hara.

On his return to Ireland he turned that scheme of his over and over again in his head. Surely something might be done if the priest would stand his friend! What, if he were to tell the whole truth to the priest, and ask for such assistance as a priest might give him? But the one assurance to which he came during his journey was this—that when a man goes in for adventures, he requires a good deal of skill and some courage too to carry him through them.

AN EYE FOR AN EYE

VOLUME II

CHAPTER I

FROM BAD TO WORSE

AS HE was returning to Ennis, Neville was so far removed from immediate distress as to be able to look forward without fear to his meeting with the two ladies at Ardkill. He could as yet take his Kate in his arms without any hard load upon his heart, such as would be there if he knew that it was incumbent upon him at once to explain his difficulties. His uncle was still living, but was old and still ill. He would naturally make the most of the old man's age and infirmities. There was every reason why they should wait, and no reason why such waiting should bring reproaches upon his head. On the night of his arrival at his quarters he despatched a note to his Kate. 'Dearest love. Here I am again in the land of freedom and potatoes. I need not trouble you with writing about home news, as I shall see you the day after tomorrow. All tomorrow and Wednesday morning I must stick close to my guns here. After one on Wednesday I shall be free. I will drive over to Lahinch, and come round in the boat. I must come back here the same night, but I suppose it will be the next morning before I get to bed. I sha'n't mind that if I get something for my pains. My love to your mother. Your own, F.N.'

In accordance with this plan he did drive over to Lahinch. He might have saved time by directing that his boat should come across the bay to meet him at Liscannor, but he felt that he would prefer not to meet Father Marty at present. It might be that before long he would be driven to tell the priest a good deal, and to ask for the priest's assistance; but at present he was not anxious to see Father Marty. Barney Morony was waiting for him at the stable where he put up

799

his horse, and went down with him to the beach. The ladies, according to Barney, were quite well and more winsome than ever. But—and this information was not given without much delay and great beating about the bush—there was a rumour about Liscannor that Captain O'Hara had 'turned up.' Fred was so startled at this that he could not refrain from showing his anxiety by the questions which he asked. Barney did not seem to think that the Captain had been at Ardkill or any-where in the neighbourhood. At any rate he, Barney, had not seen him. He had just heard the rumour. 'Shure, Lieutenant, I wouldn't be telling yer honour a lie; and they do be saying that the Captain one time was as fine a man as a woman ever sot eyes on—and why not, seeing what kind the young lady is, God bless her!' If it were true that Kate's father had 'turned up' such an advent might very naturally alter Neville's plans. It would so change the position of things, as to relieve him in some degree from the force of his past promises.

Nevertheless when he saw Kate coming along the cliffs to meet him, the one thing more certain to him than all other things was that he would never abandon her. She had been watching for him almost from the hour at which he had said that he would leave Ennis, and, creeping up among the rocks, had seen his boat as it came round the point from Liscannor. She had first thought that she would climb down the path to meet him; but the tide was high and there was now no strip of strand below the cliffs; and Barney Morony would have been there to see and she resolved that it would be nicer to wait for him on the summit. 'Oh Fred, you have come back,' she said, throwing herself on his breast.

'Yes; I am back. Did you think I was going to desert you?'

'No; no. I knew you would not desert me. 'Oh, my darling!'

'Dear Kate—dearest Kate.'

'You have thought of me sometimes?'

'I have thought of you always—every hour.' And so he swore to her that she was was as much to him as he could possibly be to her. She hung on his arm as she went down to the cottage, and believed herself to be the happiest and most fortunate girl in Ireland. As yet no touch of the sorrows of love had fallen upon her.

He could not all at once ask her as to that rumour which Morony had mentioned to him. But he thought of it as he walked with his arm round her waist. Some question must be asked, but it might, perhaps, be better that he should ask it of the mother. Mrs. O'Hara was at the cottage and seemed almost as glad to see him as Kate had been. 'It is very pleasant to have you back again,' she said. 'Kate has been counting first the hours and then the minutes.'

'And so have you, mother.'

'Of course we want to hear all the news,' said Mrs. O'Hara. Then Neville, with the girl who was to be his wife, sitting close beside him on the sofa—almost within his embrace— told them how things were going at Scroope. His uncle was very weak—evidently failing; but still so much better as to justify the heir in coming away. He might perhaps live for another twelve months, but the doctors thought it hardly possible that he should last longer than that. Then the nephew went on to say that his uncle was the best and most generous man in the world—and the finest gentleman and the truest Christian. He told also of the tenants who were not to be harassed, and the servants who were not to be dismissed, and the horses that were to be allowed to die in their beds, and the trees that were not to be cut down.

'I wish I knew him,' said Kate. 'I wish I could have seen him once.'

'That can never be,' said Fred, sadly.

'No—of course not.'

Then Mrs. O'Hara asked a question. 'Has he ever heard of us?'

'Yes—he has heard of you.'

'From you?'

'No—not first from me. There are many reasons why I would not have mentioned your names could I have helped it. He has wished me to marry another girl—and especially a Protestant girl. That was impossible.'

'That must be impossible now, Fred,' said Kate, looking up into his face.

'Quite so, dearest; but why should I have vexed him, seeing that he is so good to me, and that he must be gone so soon?'

'Who had told him of us?' asked Mrs. O'Hara.

'That woman down there at Castle Quin.'

'Lady Mary?'

'Foul-tongued old maid that she is,' exclaimed Fred. 'She writes to my aunt by every post, I believe.'

'What evil can she say of us?'

'She does say evil. Never mind what. Such a woman always says evil of those of her sex who are good-looking.'

'There, mother—that's for you,' said Kate, laughing. 'I don't care what she says.'

'If she tells your aunt that we live in a small cottage, without servants, without society, with just the bare necessaries of life, she tells the truth of us.'

'That's just what she does say—and she goes on harping about religion. Never mind her. You can understand that my uncle should be old-fashioned. He is very old, and we must wait.'

'Waiting is so weary,' said Mrs. O'Hara.

'It is not weary for me at all,' said Kate.

Then he left them, without having said a word about the Captain. He found the Captain to be a subject very uncomfortable to mention, and thought as he was sitting there that it might perhaps be better to make his first enquiries of this priest. No one said a word to him about the Captain beyond what he had heard from his boatman.* For, as it happened, he did not see the priest till May was nearly past, and during all that time things were going from bad to worse. As regards any services which he rendered to the army at this period of his career, the excuses which he had made to his uncle were certainly not valid. Some pretence at positively necessary routine

duties it must be supposed that he made; but he spent more
of his time either on the sea, or among the cliffs with Kate,
or on the road going backwards and forwards, than he did
at his quarters. It was known that he was to leave the regiment and become a great man at home in October, and his
brother officers were kind to him. And it was known also, of
course, that there was a young lady down on the sea coast
beyond Ennistimon, and doubtless there were jokes on the
subject. But there was no one with him at Ennis having such
weight of fears or authority as might have served to help to
rescue him. During this time Lady Mary Quin still made her
reports, and his aunt's letters were full of cautions and entreaties. 'I am told,' said the Countess, in one of her now
detested epistles, 'that the young woman has a reprobate
father who has escaped from the galleys.* Oh, Fred, do not
break our hearts.' He had almost forgotten the Captain when
he received this further rumour which had circulated to him
round by Castle Quin and Scroope Manor.

It was all going from bad to worse. He was allowed by the
mother to be at the cottage as much as he pleased, and the
girl was allowed to wander with him when she would among
the cliffs. It was so, although Father Marty himself had more
than once cautioned Mrs. O'Hara that she was imprudent.
'What can I do?' she said. 'Have not you yourself taught
me to believe that he is true?'

'Just spake a word to Miss Kate herself.'

'What can I say to her now? She regards him as her
husband before God.'

'But he is not her husband in any way that would prevent
his taking another wife an' he plases. And, believe me,
Misthress O'Hara, them sort of young men like a girl a dale
better when there's a little "Stand off" about her.'

'It is too late to bid her to be indifferent to him now,
Father Marty.'

'I am not saying that Miss Kate is to lose her lover. I hope
I'll have the binding of 'em together myself, and I'll go bail

I'll do it fast enough. In the meanwhile let her keep herself to herself a little more.'

The advice was very good, but Mrs. O'Hara knew not how to make use of it. She could tell the young man that she would have his heart's blood if he deceived them, and she could look at him as though she meant to be as good as her word. She had courage enough for any great emergency. But now that the lover had been made free of the cottage she knew not how to debar him. She could not break her Kate's heart by expressing doubts to her. And were he to be told to stay away, would he not be lost to them forever? Of course he could desert them if he would, and then they must die.

It was going from bad to worse certainly; and not the less so because he was more than ever infatuated about the girl. When he had calculated whether it might be possible to desert her he had been at Scroope. He was in County Clare now, and he did not hesitate to tell himself that it was impossible. Whatever might happen, and to whomever he might be false —he would be true to her. He would at any rate be so true to her that he would not leave her. If he never made her his legal wife, his legal wife at all points, he would always treat her as his legal wife. When his uncle the Earl should die, when the time came in which he would be absolutely free as to his own motions, he would discover the way in which this might best be done. If it were true that his Kate's father was a convict escaped from the galleys, that surely would be an additional reason why she should not be made Countess of Scroope. Even Mrs. O'Hara herself must understand that. With Kate, with his own Kate, he thought that there would be no difficulty.

From bad to worse! Alas, alas; there came a day in which the pricelessness of the girl he loved sank to nothing, vanished away, and was as a thing utterly lost, even in his eyes. The poor unfortunate one—to whom beauty had been given, and grace, and softness—and beyond all these and finer than these, innocence as unsullied as the whiteness of the plumage on the breast of a dove; but to whom, alas, had not been given

a protector strong enough to protect her softness, or guardian
wise enough to guard her innocence! To her he was godlike,
noble, excellent, all but holy. He was the man whom Fortune, more than kind, had sent to her to be the joy of her
existence, the fountain of her life, the strong staff for her
weakness. Not to believe in him would be the foulest treason!
To lose him would be to die! To deny him would be to deny
her God! She gave him all—and her pricelessness in his eyes
was gone for ever.

He was sitting with her one day towards the end of May on
the edge of the cliff, looking down upon the ocean and listening to the waves, when it occurred to him that he might as
well ask her about her father. It was absurd he thought to
stand upon any ceremony with her. He was very good to her,
and intended to be always good to her, but it was essentially
necessary to him to know the truth. He was not aware, perhaps, that he was becoming rougher with her than had been
his wont. She certainly was not aware of it, though there was
a touch of awe sometimes about her as she answered him.
She was aware that she now shewed to him an absolute
obedience in all things which had not been customary with
her; but then it was so sweet to obey him; so happy a thing
to have such a master! If he rebuked her, he did it with his
arm round her waist, so that she could look into his face and
smile as she promised that she would be good and follow his
behests in all things. He had been telling her now of some
fault in her dress, and she had been explaining that such
faults would come when money was so scarce. Then he had
offered her gifts. A gift she would of course take. She had
already taken gifts which were the treasures of her heart. But
he must not pay things for her till—till—. Then she again
looked up into his face and smiled. 'You are not angry with
me?' she said.

'Kate—I want to ask you a particular question.'

'What question?'

'You must not suppose, let the answer be what it may, that
it can make any difference between you and me.'

'Oh—I hope not,' she replied trembling.

'It shall make none,' he answered with all a master's assurance and authority. 'Therefore you need not be afraid to answer me. Tidings have reached me on a matter as to which I ought to be informed.'

'What matter? Oh Fred, you do so frighten me. I'll tell you anything I know.'

'I have been told that—that your father—is alive.' He looked down upon her and could see that her face was red up to her very hair. 'Your mother once told me that she had never been certain of his death.'

'I used to think he was dead.'

'But now you think he is alive?'

'I think he is—but I do not know. I never saw my father so as to remember him; though I do remember that we used to be very unhappy when we were in Spain.'

'And what have you heard lately? Tell me the truth, you know.'

'Of course I shall tell you the truth, Fred. I think mother got a letter, but she did not shew it me. She said just a word, but nothing more. Father Marty will certainly know if she knows.'

'And you know nothing?'

'Nothing.'

'I think I must ask Farther Marty.'

'But will it matter to you?' Kate asked.

'At any rate it shall not matter to you,' he said, kissing her. And then again she was happy; though there had now crept across her heart the shadow of some sad foreboding, a foretaste of sorrow that was not altogether bitter as sorrow is, but which taught her to cling closely to him when he was there and would fill her eyes with tears when she thought of him in his absence.

On this day he had not found Mrs. O'Hara at the cottage. She had gone down to Liscannor, Kate told him. He had sent his boat back to the strand near that village, round the point and into the bay, as it could not well lie under the rocks at high tide, and he now asked Kate to accompany him as he walked down. They would probably meet her mother on the road. Kate, as she tied on her hat, was only too happy to be his companion. 'I think,' he said, 'that I shall try and see Father Marty as I go back. If your mother has really heard anything about your father, she ought to have told me.'

'Don't be angry with mother, Fred.'

'I won't be angry with you, my darling,' said the master with masterful tenderness.

Although he had intimated his intention of calling on the priest that very afternoon, it may be doubted whether he was altogether gratified when he met the very man with Mrs. O'Hara close to the old burying ground. 'Ah, Mr. Neville,' said the priest, 'and how's it all wid you this many a day?'

'The top of the morning to you thin, Father Marty,' said Fred, trying to assume an Irish brogue. Nothing could be more friendly than the greeting. The old priest took off his hat to Kate, and made a low bow, as though he should say— to the future Countess of Scroope I owe a very especial respect. Mrs. O'Hara held her future son-in-law's hand for a moment, as though she might preserve him for her daughter by some show of affection on her own part. 'And now, Misthress O'Hara,' said the priest, 'as I've got a companion to go back wid me, I'm thinking I'll not go up the hill any further.' Then they parted, and Kate looked as though she were being robbed of her due because her lover could not give her one farewell kiss in the priest's presence.

CHAPTER II

IS SHE TO BE YOUR WIFE?

'IT'S QUITE a stranger you are, these days,' said the priest as soon as they had turned their backs upon the ladies.

'Well; yes. We haven't managed to meet since I came back —have we?'

'I've been pretty constant at home, too. But you like them cliffs up there, better than the village no doubt.'

'Metal more attractive, Father Marty,' said Fred laughing —'not meaning however any slight upon Liscannor or the Cork whisky.'

'The Cork whisky is always to the fore, Mr. Neville. And how did you lave matters with your noble uncle?'

Neville at the present moment was anxious rather to speak of Kate's ignoble father rather than of his own noble uncle. He had declared his intention of making inquiry of Father Marty, and he thought that he should do so with something of a high hand. He still had that scheme in his head, and he might perhaps be better prepared to discuss it with the priest if he could first make this friend of the O'Hara family understand how much he, Neville, was personally injured by this 'turning up' of a disreputable father. But, should he allow the priest at once to run away to Scroope and his noble uncle, the result of such conversation would simply be renewed promises on his part in reference to his future conduct to Kate O'Hara.

'Lord Scroope wasn't very well when I left him. By the bye, Father Marty, I've been particularly anxious to see you.'

' 'Deed thin I was aisy found, Mr. Neville.'

'What is this I hear about—Captain O'Hara?'

'What is it that you have heard, Mr. Neville?' Fred looked

into the priest's face and found that he, at least, did not
blush. It may be that all power of blushing had departed
from Father Marty.

'In the first place I hear that there is such a man.'

'Ony way there was once.'

'You think he's dead then?'

'I don't say that. It's a matter of—faith, thin, it's a matter
of nigh twenty years since I saw the Captain. And when I
did see him I didn't like him. I can tell you that, Mr. Neville.'

'I suppose not.'

'That lass up there was not born when I saw him. He was
à handsome man too, and might have been a gentleman av'
he would.'

'But he wasn't.'

'It's a hard thing to say what is a gentleman, Mr. Neville.
I don't know a much harder thing. Them folk at Castle
Quin now, wouldn't scruple to say that I'm no gentleman,
just because I'm a Popish priest. I say that Captain O'Hara
was no gentleman because he ill-treated a woman.' Father
Marty as he said this stopped a moment on the road, turning
round and looking Neville full in the face. Fred bore the look
fairly well. Perhaps at the moment he did not understand its
application. It may be that he still had a clear conscience in
that matter, and thought that he was resolved to treat Kate
O'Hara after a fashion that would in no way detract from his
own character as a gentleman. 'As it was,' continued the
priest, 'he was a low blag-guard.'

'He hadn't any money, I suppose?'

' 'Deed and I don't think he was iver throubled much in
respect of money. But money doesn't matter, Mr. Neville.'

'Not in the least,' said Fred.

'Thim ladies up there are as poor as Job, but anybody that
should say that they weren't ladies would just be shewing
that he didn't know the difference. The Captain was well
born, Mr. Neville, av' that makes ony odds.'

'Birth does go for something, Father Marty.'

'Thin let the Captain have the advantage. Them O'Haras

of Kildare weren't proud of him I'm thinking, but he was a
chip of that block; and some one belonging to him had seen
the errors of the family ways, in respect of making him a
Papist. 'Deed and I must say, Mr. Neville, when they send us
any offsets* from a Prothestant family it isn't the best that
they give us.'

'I suppose not, Father Marty.'

'We can make something of a bit of wood that won't take
ony shape at all, at all along wid them. But there wasn't
much to boast of along of the Captain.'

'But is he alive, Father Marty—or is he dead? I think I've
a right to be told.'

'I am glad to hear you ask it as a right, Mr. Neville. You
have a right if that young lady up there is to be your wife.'
Fred made no answer here, though the priest paused for a
moment, hoping that he would do so. But the question could
be asked again, and Father Marty went on to tell all that he
knew, and all that he had heard of Captain O'Hara. He was
alive. Mrs. O'Hara had received a letter purporting to be
from her husband, giving an address in London, and asking
for money. He, Father Marty, had seen the letter; and he
thought that there might perhaps be a doubt whether it was
written by the man of whom they were speaking. Mrs. O'Hara
had declared that if it were so written the handwriting was
much altered. But then in twelve years the writing of a man
who drank hard will change. It was twelve years since she
had last received a letter from him.

'And what do you believe?'

'I think he lives, and that he wrote it, Mr. Neville. I'll
tell you God's truth about it as I believe it, because as I
said before I think you are entitled to know the truth.'

'And what was done?'

'I sent off to London—to a friend I have.'

'And what did your friend say?'

'He says there is a man calling himself Captain O'Hara.'

'And is that all?'

'She got a second letter. She got it the very last day you

was down here. Pat Cleary took it up to her when you was
out wid Miss Kate.'

'He wants money, I suppose.'

'Just that, Mr. Neville.'

'It makes a difference—doesn't it?'

'How does it make a difference?'

'Well; it does. I wonder you don't see it. You must see it.'
From that moment Father Marty said in his heart that Kate
O'Hara had lost her husband. Not that he admitted for a
moment that Captain O'Hara's return, if he had returned,
would justify the lover in deserting the girl; but that he perceived that Neville had already allowed himself to entertain
the plea. The whole affair had in the priest's estimation been
full of peril; but then the prize to be won was very great!
From the first he had liked the young man, and had not
doubted—did not now doubt—but that once married he
would do justice to his wife. Even though Kate should fail
and should come out of the contest with a scorched heart—
and that he had thought more than probable—still the prize
was very high and the girl he thought was one who could survive such a blow. Latterly in that respect he had changed his
opinion. Kate had shewn herself to be capable of so deep a
passion that he was now sure that she would be more than
scorched should the fire be one to injure and not to cherish
her. But the man's promises had been so firm, so often reiterated, were so clearly written, that the priest had almost
dared to hope that the thing was assured. Now, alas, he perceived that the embryo English lord was already looking for
a means of escape, and already thought that he had found it
in this unfortunate return of the father. The whole extent of
the sorrow even the priest did not know. But he was determined to fight the battle to the very last. The man should
make the girl his wife, or he, Father Marty, parish priest of
Liscannor, would know the reason why. He was a man who
was wont to desire to know the reason why, as to matters
which he had taken in hand. But when he heard the words
which Neville spoke and marked the tone in which they

were uttered he felt that the young man was preparing for himself a way of escape.

'I don't see that it should make any difference,' he said shortly.

'If the man be disreputable—'

'The daughter is not therefore disreputable. Her position is not changed.'

'I have to think of my friends.'

'You should have thought of that before you declared yourself to her, Mr. Neville,' How true this was now, the young man knew better than the priest, but that, as yet, was his own secret. 'You do not mean to tell me that because the father is not all that he should be, she is therefore to be thrown over. That cannot be your idea of honour. Have you not promised that you would make her your wife?' The priest stopped for an answer, but the young man made him none. 'Of course you have promised her.'

'I suppose she has told you so.'

'To whom should she tell her story? To whom should she go for advice? But it was you who told me so, yourself.'

'Never.'

'Did you not swear to me that you would not injure her? And why should there have been any talk with you and me about her, but that I saw what was coming? When a young man like you chooses to spend his hours day after day and week after week with such a one as she is, with a beautiful young girl, a sweet innocent young lady, so sweet as to make even an ould priest like me feel that the very atmosphere she breathes is perfumed and hallowed, must it not mean one of two things—that he desires to make her his wife or else—or else something so vile that I will not name it in connection with Kate O'Hara? Then as her mother's friend, and as hers —as their only friend near them, I spoke out plainly to you, and you swore to me that you intended no harm to her.'

'I would not harm her for the world.'

'When you said that, you told me as plainly as you could spake that she should be your wife. With her own mouth

she never told me. Her mother has told me. Daily Mrs.
O'Hara has spoken to me of her hopes and fears. By the Lord
above whom I worship and by His Son in whom I rest all
my hopes, I would not stand in your shoes if you intend to
tell that woman that after all that has passed you mean to
desert her child.'

'Who has talked of deserting?' asked Neville angrily.

'Say that you will be true to her, that you will make her
your wife before God and man, and I will humbly ask your
pardon.'

'All that I say is that this Captain O'Hara's coming is a
nuisance.'

'If that be all, there is an end of it. It is a nuisance. Not
that I suppose he ever will come. If he persists she must
send him a little money. There shall be no difficulty about
that. She will never ask you to supply the means of keeping
her husband.'

'It isn't the money. I think you hardly understand my
position, Father Marty.' It seemed to Neville that if it was
ever his intention to open out his scheme to the priest, now
was his time for doing so. They had come to the cross roads
at which one way led down to the village and to Father
Marty's house, and the other to the spot on the beach where
the boat would be waiting. 'I can't very well go on to Liscannor,' said Neville.

'Give me your word before we part that you will keep
your promise to Miss O'Hara,' said the priest.

'If you will step on a few yards with me I will tell you
just how I am situated.' Then the priest assented, and they
both went on towards the beach, walking very slowly. 'If I
alone were concerned, I would give up everything for Miss
O'Hara. I am willing to give up everything as regards myself.
I love her so dearly that she is more to me than all the
honours and wealth that are to come to me when my uncle
dies.'

'What is to hinder but that you should have the girl you
love and your uncle's honours and wealth into the bargain?'

'That is just it.'

'By the life of me I don't see any difficulty. You're your own masther. The ould Earl can't disinherit you if he would.'

'But I am bound down.'

'How bound? Who can bind you?'

'I am bound not to make Miss O'Hara Countess of Scroope.'

'What binds you? You are bound by a hundred promises to make her your wife.'

'I have taken an oath that no Roman Catholic shall become Countess Scroope as my wife.'

'Then, Mr. Neville, let me tell you that you must break your oath.'

'Would you have me perjure myself?'

'Faith I would. Perjure yourself one way you certainly must, av' you've taken such an oath as that, for you've sworn many oaths that you would make this Catholic lady your wife. Not make a Roman Catholic Countess of Scroope! 'It's the impudence of some of you Prothestants that kills me entirely. As though we couldn't count Countesses against you and beat you by chalks! I ain't the man to call hard names, Mr. Neville; but if one of us is upstarts, it's aisy seeing which. Your uncle's an ould man, and I'm told nigh to his latter end. I'm not saying but what you should respect even his wakeness. But you'll not look me in the face and tell me that afther what's come and gone that young lady is to be cast on one side like a plucked rose, because an ould man has spoken a foolish word, or because a young man has made a wicked promise.'

They were now standing again, and Fred raised his hat and rubbed his forehead as he endeavoured to arrange the words in which he could best propose his scheme to the priest. He had not yet escaped from the idea that because Father Marty was a Roman Catholic priest, living in a village in the extreme west of Ireland, listening night and day to the roll of the Atlantic and drinking whisky punch, therefore he would be found to be romantic, semi-barbarous, and perhaps more than semi-lawless in his views of life. Irish priests have been made by chroniclers of Irish story to do marvellous things;* and Fred Neville thought that this priest, if only the matter could be properly introduced, might be persuaded to do for him something romantic, something marvellous, perhaps something almost lawless. In truth it might have been difficult to find a man more practical or more honest than Mr. Marty. And then the difficulty of introducing the subject was very great. Neville stood with his face a little averted, rubbing his forehead as he raised his sailor's hat. 'If you could only read my heart,' he said, 'you'd know that I am as true as steel.'

'I'd be loathe to doubt it, Mr. Neville.'

'I'd give up everything to call Kate my own.'

'But you need give up nothing, and yet have her all your own.'

'You say that because you don't completely understand. It may as well be taken for granted at once that she can never be Countess of Scroope.'

'Taken for granted!' said the old man as the fire flashed out of his eyes.

'Just listen to me for one moment. I will marry her to-morrow, or at any time you may fix, if a marriage can be so arranged that she shall never be more than Mrs. Neville.'

'And what would you be?'

'Mr. Neville.'

'And what would her son be?'

'Oh—just the same—when he grew up perhaps there wouldn't be a son.'

'God forbid that there should. on those terms. You intend that your children and her children shall be—bastards. That's about it, Mr. Neville.' The romance seemed to vanish when the matter was submitted to him in this very prosaic manner. 'As to what you might choose to call yourself, that would be nothing to me and not very much I should say, to her. I believe a man needn't be a lord unless he likes to be a lord

—and needn't call his wife a countess. But, Mr. Neville, when you have married Miss O'Hara, and when your uncle shall have died, there can be no other Countess of Scroope, and her child must be the heir to your uncle's title.'

'All that I could give her except that, she should have.'

'But she must have that. She must be your wife before God and man, and her children must be the children of honour and not of disgrace.' Ah—if the priest had known it all!

'I would live abroad with her, and her mother should live with us.'

'You mean that you would take Kate as your misthress! And you make this as a proposal to me! Upon my word, Mr. Neville, I don't think that I quite understand what it is that you're maning to say to me. Is she to be your wife?'

'Yes,' said Neville, urged by the perturbation of his spirit to give a stronger assurance than he had intended.

'Then must her son if she have one be the future Earl of Scroope. He may be Protesthant—or what you will?'

'You don't understand me, Father Marty.'

'Faith, and that's thrue. But we are at the baich, Mr. Neville, and I've two miles along the coast to Liscannor.'

'Shall I make Barney take you round in the canoe?'

'I believe I may as well walk it. Good-bye, Mr. Neville. I'm glad at any rate to hear you say so distinctly that you are resolved at all hazards to make that dear girl your wife.' This he said, almost in a whisper, standing close to the boat, with his hand on Neville's shoulder. He paused a moment as though to give special strength to his words, and Neville did not dare or was not able to protest against the assertion. Father Marty himself was certainly not romantic in his manner of managing such an affair as this in which they were now both concerned.

Neville went back to Ennis much depressed, turning the matter over in his mind almost hopelessly. This was what had come from his adventures! No doubt he might marry the girl—postponing his marriage till after his uncle's death.

For aught he knew as yet that might still be possible. But were he to do so, he would disgrace his family, and disgrace himself by breaking the solemn promise he had made. And in such case he would be encumbered, and possibly be put beyond the pale of that sort of life which should be his as Earl of Scroope, by having Captain O'Hara as his father-in-law. He was aware now that he would be held by all his natural friends to have ruined himself by such a marriage.

On the other hand he could, no doubt, throw the girl over. They could not make him marry her though they could probably make him pay very dearly for not doing so. If he could only harden his heart sufficiently he could escape in that way. But he was not hard, and he did feel that so escaping, he would have a load on his breast which would make his life unendurable. Already he was beginning to hate the coast of Ireland, and to think that the gloom of Scroope Manor was preferable to it.

CHAPTER III

FRED NEVILLE RECEIVES A VISITOR AT ENNIS.

FOR SOMETHING over three weeks after his walk with the priest Neville saw neither of the two ladies of Ardkill. Letters were frequent between the cottage and the barracks at Ennis, but—so said Fred himself, military duties detained him with the troop. He explained that he had been absent a great deal, and that now Captain Johnson* was taking his share of ease. He was all alone at the barracks, and could not get away. There was some truth in this, created perhaps by the fact that as he didn't stir, Johnson could do so. Johnson was backwards and forwards, fishing at Castle Connel, and Neville was very exact in explaining that for the present he was obliged to give up all the delights of the coast. But the days were days of trial to him.

A short history of the life of Captain O'Hara was absolutely sent to him by the Countess of Scroope. The family lawyer, at the instance of the Earl—as she said, though probably her own interference had been more energetic than that of the Earl—had caused enquiries to be made. Captain O'Hara, the husband of the lady who was now living on the coast of County Clare, and who was undoubtedly the father of the Miss O'Hara whom Fred knew, had passed at least ten of the latter years of his life at the galleys in the south of France. He had been engaged in an extensive swindling transaction at Bordeaux, and had thence been transferred to Toulon, had there been maintained by France—and was now in London. The Countess in sending this interesting story to her nephew at Ennis, with ample documentary evidence, said that she was sure that he would not degrade his family utterly by thinking of allying himself with people who were so thoroughly disreputable; but that, after all that was passed, his uncle expected from him a renewed assurance on the matter. He answered this in anger. He did not understand why the history of Captain O'Hara should have been raked up. Captain O'Hara was nothing to him. He supposed it had come from Castle Quin, and anything from Castle Quin he disbelieved. He had given a promise once and he didn't understand why he should be asked for any further assurance. He thought it very hard that his life should be made a burden to him by foul-mouthed rumours from Castle Quin. That was the tenor of his letter to his aunt; but even that letter sufficed to make it almost certain that he could never marry the girl. He acknowledged that he had bound himself not to do so. And then, in spite of all that he said about the mendacity of Castle Quin, he did believe the little history. And it was quite out of the question that he should marry the daughter of a returned galley-slave. He did not think that any jury in England would hold him to be bound by such a promise. Of course he would do whatever he could for his dear Kate; but, even after all that had passed, he could not pollute himself by marriage with the child of so vile a father. Poor Kate! Her sufferings would have been occasioned not by him, but by her father.

In the meantime Kate's letters to him became more and more frequent, more and more sad—filled ever with still increasing warmth of entreaty. At last they came by every post, though he knew how difficult it must be for her to find daily messengers into Ennistimon. Would he not come and see her? He must come and see her. She was ill and would die unless he came to her. He did not always answer these letters, but he did write to her perhaps twice a week. He would come very soon—as soon as Johnson had come back from his fishing. She was not to fret herself. Of course he could not always be at Ardkill. He too had things to trouble him. Then he told her that he had received letters from home which caused him very much trouble; and there was a something of sharpness in his words, which brought from her a string of lamentations in which, however, the tears and wailings did not as yet take the form of reproaches. Then there came a short note from Mrs. O'Hara herself. 'I must beg that you will come to Ardkill at once. It is absolutely necessary for Kate's safety that you should do so.'

When he received this he thought that he would go on the morrow. When the morrow came he determined to postpone the journey for yet another day! The calls of duty are so much less imperious than those of pleasure! On that further day he still meant to go, as he sat about noon unbraced, only partly dressed in his room at the barracks. His friend Johnson was back in Ennis, and there was also a Cornet with the troop. He had no excuse whatever on the score of military duty for remaining at home on that day. But he sat idling his time, thinking of things. All the charm of the adventure was gone. He was sick of the canoe and of Barney Morony. He did not care a straw for the seals or wild gulls. The moaning of the ocean beneath the cliff was no longer pleasurable to him—and as to the moaning at their summit, to tell the truth, he was afraid of it. The long drive thither and back was tedious to him. He thought now more of the respectability of his family than of the beauty of Kate O'Hara.

But still he meant to go—certainly would go on this very day. He had desired that his gig should be ready, and had sent word to say that he might start at any moment. But still he sat in his dressing-gown at noon, unbraced, with a novel in his hand which he could not read, and a pipe by his side which he could not smoke. Close to him on the table lay that record of the life of Captain O'Hara, which his aunt had sent him, every word of which he had now examined for the third or fourth time. Of course he could not marry the girl. Mrs. O'Hara had deceived him. She could not but have known that her husband was a convict—and had kept the knowledge back from him in order that she might allure him to the marriage. Anything that money could do, he would do. Or, if they would consent, he would take the girl away with him to some sunny distant clime, in which adventures might still be sweet, and would then devote to her—some portion of his time. He had not yet ruined himself, but he would indeed ruin himself were he, the heir to the earldom of Scroope, to marry the daughter of a man who had been at the French galleys! He had just made up his mind that he would be firm in this resolution—when the door opened and Mrs. O'Hara entered his room. 'Mrs. O'Hara.'

She closed the door carefully behind her before she spoke, excluding the military servant who had wished to bar her entrance. 'Yes, sir; as you would not come to us I have been forced to come to you. I know it all. When will you make my child your wife?'

Yes. In the abjectness of her misery the poor girl had told her mother the story of her disgrace; or, rather, in her weakness had suffered her secret to fall from her lips. That terrible retribution was to come upon her which, when sin has been mutual, falls with so crushing a weight upon her who of the two sinners has ever been by far the less sinful. She, when she knew her doom, simply found herself bound by still stronger ties of love to him who had so cruelly injured her. She was his before; but now she was more than ever his. To have him near her, to give her orders that she might obey them, was the consolation that she coveted—the only consolation that could have availed anything to her. To lean against him, and to whisper to him, with face averted, with half-formed syllables, some fervent words that might convey to him a truth which might be almost a joy to her if he would make it so—was the one thing that could restore hope to her bosom. Let him come and be near to her, so that she might hide her face upon his breast. But he came not. He did not come, though, as best she knew how, she had thrown all her heart into her letters. Then her spirit sank within her, and she sickened, and as her mother knelt over her, she allowed her secret to fall from her.

Fred Neville's sitting-room at Ennis was not a chamber prepared for the reception of ladies. It was very rough, as are usually barrack rooms in outlying quarters in small towns in the west of Ireland—and it was also very untidy. The more prudent and orderly of mankind might hardly have understood why a young man, with prospects and present wealth such as belonged to Neville, should choose to spend a twelve-month in such a room, contrary to the wishes of all his friends, when London was open to him, and the continent, and scores of the best appointed houses in England, and all the glories of ownership at Scroope. There were guns about, and whips, hardly half a dozen books, and a few papers. There were a couple of swords lying on a table that looked like a dresser. The room was not above half covered with its carpet, and though there were three large easy chairs, even they were torn and soiled. But all this had been compatible with adventures—and while the adventures were simply romantic and not a bit troublesome, the barracks at Ennis had been to him by far preferable to the gloomy grandeur of Scroope.

And now Mrs. O'Hara was there, telling him that she knew of all! Not for a moment did he remain ignorant of the meaning of her communication. And now the arguments to be used against him in reference to the marriage would be stronger than ever. A silly, painful smile came across his handsome face as he attempted to welcome her, and moved a chair for her accommodation. 'I am so sorry that you have had the trouble of coming over,' he said.

'That is nothing. When will you make my child your wife?' How was he to answer this? In the midst of his difficulties he had brought himself to one determination. He had resolved that under no pressure would be marry the daughter of O'Hara, the galley-slave. As far as that he had seen his way. Should he now at once speak of the galley-slave, and, with expressions of regret, decline the alliance on that reason? Having dishonoured this woman's daughter should he shelter himself behind the dishonour of her husband? That he meant to do so ultimately is true; but at the present moment such a task would have required a harder heart than his. She rose from her chair and stood close over him as she repeated her demand, 'When will you make my child your wife?'

'You do not want me to answer you at this moment?'

'Yes—at this moment. Why not answer me at once? She has told me all. Mr. Neville, you must think not only of her, but of your child also.'

'I hope not that,' he said.

'I tell you that it is so. Now answer me. 'When shall my Kate become your wife?'

He still knew that any such consummation as that was quite out of the question. The mother herself as she was now present to him, seemed to be a woman very different from the quiet, handsome, high-spirited, but low-voiced widow whom he had known, or thought that he had known, at Ardkill. Of her as she had there appeared to him he had not been ashamed to think as one who might at some future time be personally related to himself. He had recognized her as a lady whose outward trappings, poor though they might be, were suited to the seclusion in which she lived. But now, although it was only to Ennis that she had come from her nest among the rocks, she seemed to be unfitted for even so much intercourse with the world as that. And in the demand which she reiterated over him she hardly spoke as a lady would speak. Would not all they who were connected with him at home have a right to complain if he were to bring such a woman with him to England as the mother of his wife. 'I can't answer such a question as that on the spur of the moment,' he said.

'You will not dare to tell me that you mean to desert her?'

'Certainly not. I was coming over to Ardkill this very day. The trap is ordered. I hope Kate is well?'

'She is not well. How should she be well?'

'Why not? I didn't know. If there is anything that she wants that I can get for her, you have only to speak.'

In the utter contempt which Mrs. O'Hara now felt for the man she probably forgot that his immediate situation was one in which it was nearly impossible that any man should conduct himself with dignity. Having brought himself to his present pass by misconduct, he could discover no line of good conduct now open to him. Moralists might tell him that let the girl's parentage be what it might, he ought to marry her; but he was stopped from that, not only by his oath, but by a conviction that his highest duty required him to preserve his family from degradation. And yet to a mother, with such a demand on her lips as that now made by Mrs. O'Hara—whose demand was backed by such circumstances—how was it possible that he should tell the truth and plead the honour of his family? His condition was so cruel that it was no longer possible to him to be dignified or even true. The mother again made her demand. 'There is one thing that you must do for her before other things can be thought of. When shall she become your wife?'

It was for a moment on his tongue to tell her that it could not be so while his uncle lived—but to this he at once felt that there were two objections, directly opposed to each other, but each so strong as to make any such reply very dangerous. It would imply a promise, which he certainly did not intend to keep, of marrying the girl when his uncle should be dead; and, although promising so much more than he intended to perform, would raise the ungovernable wrath of the woman before him. That he should now hesitate—now, in her Kate's present condition—as to redeeming those vows of marriage which he had made to her in her innocence, would raise a fury in the mother's bosom which he feared to encounter. He got up and walked about the room, while she stood with her eyes fixed upon him, ever and anon reiterating her demand. 'No day must now be lost. When will you make my child your wife?'

At last he made a proposition to which she assented. The tidings which she had brought him had come upon him very suddenly. He was inexpressibly pained. Of course Kate, his dearest Kate, was everything to him. Let him have that afternoon to think about it. On the morrow he would assuredly visit Ardkill. The mother, full of fears, resolving that should he attempt to play her girl false and escape from her she would follow him to the end of the world, but feeling that at the present moment she could not constrain him, accepted his repeated promise as to the following day; and at last left him to himself.

CHAPTER IV

NEVILLE'S SUCCESS

NEVILLE SAT in his room alone, without moving, for a couple of hours after Mrs. O'Hara had left him. In what way should he escape from the misery and ruin what seemed to surround him? An idea did cross his mind that it would be better for him to fly and write the truth from the comparatively safe distance of his London club. But there would be a meanness in such conduct which would make it impossible that he should ever again hold up his head. The girl had trusted to him and by trusting to him had brought herself to this miserable pass. He could not desert her. It would be better that he should go and endure all the vials of their wrath than that. To her he would still be tenderly loving, if she would accept his love without the name which he could not give her. His whole life he would sacrifice to her. Every luxury which money could purchase he would lavish on her. He must go and make his offer. The vials of wrath which would doubtless be poured out upon his head would not come from her. In his heart of hearts he feared both the priest and the mother. But there are moments in which a man feels himself obliged to encounter all that he most fears—and the man who does not do so in such moments is a coward.

He quite made up his mind to start early on the following morning; but the intermediate hours were very sad and heavy, and his whole outlook into life was troublesome to him. How infinitely better would it have been for him had he allowed himself to be taught a twelve month since that his duty required him to give up the army at once! But he had made his bed, and now he must lie upon it. There was no escape from this journey to Ardkill. Even though he should be stunned by their wrath he must endure it.

He breakfasted early the next day, and got into his gig before nine. He must face the enemy, and the earlier that he did it the better. His difficulty now lay in arranging the proposition that he would make and the words that he should speak. Every difficulty would be smoothed and every danger dispelled if he would only say that he would marry the girl as quickly as the legal forms would allow. Father Marty, he knew, would see to all that, and the marriage might be done effectually. He had quite come to understand that Father Marty was practical rather than romantic. But there would be cowardice in this as mean as that other cowardice. He believed himself to be bound by his duty to his family.* Were he now to renew his promise of marriage, such renewal would be caused by fear and not by duty, and would be mean. They should tear him piecemeal rather than get from him such a promise. Then he thought of the Captain, and perceived that he must make all possible use of the Captain's character. Would anybody conceive that he, the heir of the Scroope family, was bound to marry the daughter of a convict returned from the galleys? And was it not true that such promise as he had made had been obtained under false pretences? Why had he not been told of the Captain's position when he first made himself intimate with the mother and daughter?

Instead of going as was his custom to Lahinch, and then rowing across the bay and round the point, he drove his gig to the village of Liscannor. He was sick of Barney Morony and the canoe, and never desired to see either of them again. He was sick indeed, of everything Irish, and thought that the whole island was a mistake. He drove, however, boldly through Liscannor and up to Father Marty's yard, and, not finding the priest at home, there left his horse and gig. He had determined that he would first go to the priest and boldly declare that nothing should induce him to marry the daughter of a convict. But Father Marty was not at home. The old woman who kept his house believed that he had gone into Ennistimon. He was away with his horse, and would not be back till dinner time. Then Neville, having seen his own nag taken from the gig, started on his walk up to Ardkill.

How ugly the country was to his eyes as he now saw it. Here and there stood a mud cabin, and the small, half-cultivated fields, or rather patches of land, in which the thin oat crops were beginning to be green were surrounded by low loose ramshackle walls, which were little more than heaps of stone, so carelessly had they been built and so negligently preserved. A few cocks and ·hens with here and there a miserable, starved pig seemed to be the stock of the country. Not a tree, not a shrub, not a flower was there to be seen. The road was narrow, rough, and unused. The burial ground which he passed was the liveliest sign of humanity about the place. Then the country became still wilder, and there was no road. The oats also ceased, and the walls. But he could hear the melancholy moan of the waves, which he had once thought to be musical and had often sworn that he loved. Now the place with all its attributes was hideous to him, distasteful, and abominable. At last the cottage was in view, and his heart sank very low. Poor Kate! He loved her dearly through it all. He endeavoured to take comfort by assuring himself that his heart was true to her. Not for worlds would he injure her—that is, not for worlds, had any worlds been exclusively his own. On account of the Scroope world—which was a world general rather than particular—no doubt he must injure her most horribly. But still she was his dear Kate, his own Kate, his Kate whom he would never desert.

When he came up to the cottage the little gate was open, and he knew that somebody was there besides the usual inmates. His heart at once told him that it was the priest. His fate had brought him face to face with his two enemies at once! His breath almost left him, but he knew that he could not run away. However bitter might be the vials of wrath he must encounter them. So he knocked at the outer door and, after his custom walked into the passage. Then he knocked again at the door of the one sitting-room—the door which hitherto he had always passed with the conviction that he should bring delight—and for a moment there was no answer. He heard no voice and he knocked again. The door was opened for him, and as he entered he met Father Marty. But he at once saw that there was another man in the room, seated in an armchair near the window. Kate, his Kate, was not there, but Mrs. O'Hara was standing at the head of the sofa, far away from the window and close to the door. 'It is Mr. Neville,' said the priest. 'It is as well that he should come in.'

'Mr. Neville,' said the man rising from his chair, 'I am informed that you are a suitor for the hand of my daughter. Your prospects in life are sufficient, sir, and I give my consent.'

The man was a thing horrible to look at, tall, thin, cadaverous, ill-clothed, with his wretched and all but ragged overcoat buttoned close up to his chin, with long straggling thin grizzled hair, red-nosed, with a drunkard's eyes, and thin lips drawn down at the corners of the mouth. This was Captain O'Hara; and if any man ever looked like a convict returned from work in chains, such was the appearance of this man. This was the father of Fred's Kate—the man whom it was expected that he, Frederic Neville, the future Earl of Scroope, should take as his father-in-law! 'This is Captain O'Hara,' said the priest. But even Father Marty, bold as he was, could not assume the voice with which he had rebuked Neville as he walked with him, now nearly a month ago, down to the beach.

Neville did feel that the abomination of the man's appearance strengthened his position. He stood looking from one to another, while Mrs. O'Hara remained silent in the corner. 'Perhaps,' said he, 'I had better not be here. I am intruding.'

'It is right that you should know it all,' said the priest. 'As regards the young lady it cannot now alter your position. This gentleman must be—arranged for.'

'Oh, certainly,' said the Captain. 'I must be——arranged for, and that so soon as possible.' The man spoke with a slightly foreign accent and in a tone, as Fred thought, which

savoured altogether of the galleys. 'You have done me the
honour, I am informed, to make my daughter all your own.
These estimable people assure me that you hasten to make
her your wife on the instant. I consent. The O'Haras, who
are of the very oldest blood in Europe, have always connected
themselves highly. Your uncle is a most excellent nobleman
whose hand I shall be proud to grasp.' As he thus spoke he
stalked across the room to Fred, intending at once to commence the work of grasping the Neville family.

'Get back,' said Fred, retreating to the door.

'Is it that you fail to believe that I am your bride's father?'

'I know not whose father you may be. Get back.'

'He is what he says he is,' said the priest. 'You should bear
with him for a while.'

'Where is Kate?' demanded Fred. It seemed as though, for
the moment, he were full of courage. He looked round at
Mrs. O'Hara, but nobody answered him. She was still standing with her eyes fixed upon the man, almost as though she
thought that she could dart out upon him and destroy him.
'Where is Kate?' he asked again. 'Is she well?'

'Well enough to hide herself from her old father,' said the
Captain, brushing a tear from his eye with the back of his
hand.

'You shall see her presently, Mr. Neville,' said the priest.

Then Neville whispered a word into the priest's ear. 'What
is it that the man wants?'

'You need not regard that,' said Father Marty.

'Mr. Marty,' said the Captain, 'you concern yourself too
closely in my affairs. I prefer to open my thoughts and desires
to my son-in-law. He has taken measures which give him a
right to interfere in the family. Ha, ha, ha.'

'If you talk like that I'll stab you to the heart,' said Mrs.
O'Hara, jumping forward. Then Fred Neville perceived that
the woman had a dagger in her hand which she had hitherto
concealed from him as she stood up against the wall behind
the head of the sofa. He learnt afterwards that the priest,
having heard in Liscannor of the man's arrival, had hurried

up to the cottage, reaching it almost at the same moment with the Captain. Kate had luckily at the moment been in her room and had not seen her father. She was still in her bed* and was ill—but during the scene that occurred afterwards she roused herself. But Mrs. O'Hara, even in the priest's presence, had at once seized the weapon from the drawer— showing that she was prepared even for murder, had murder been found necessary by her for her relief. The man had immediately asked as to the condition of his daughter, and the mother had learned that her child's secret was known to all Liscannor. The priest now laid his hand upon her and stopped her, but he did it in all gentleness. 'You'll have a fierce pig of a mother-in-law, Mr. Neville,' said the Captain, 'but your wife's father—you'll find him always gentle and open to reason. You were asking what I wanted.'

'Had I not better give him money?' suggested Neville.

'No,' said the priest shaking his head.

'Certainly,' said Captain O'Hara.

'If you will leave this place at once,' said Neville, 'and come to me to-morrow morning at the Ennis barracks, I will give you money.'

'Give him none,' said Mrs. O'Hara.

'My beloved is unreasonable. You would not be rid of me even were he to be so hard. I should not die. Have I not proved to you that I am one whom it is hard to destroy by privation. The family has been under a cloud. A day of sunshine has come with this gallant young nobleman. Let me partake the warmth. I will visit you, Mr. Neville, certainly— but what shall be the figure?'

'That will be as I shall find you then.'

'I will trust you. I will come. The journey hence to Ennis is long for one old as I am, and would be lightened by so small a trifle as—shall I say a banknote of the meanest value.' Upon this Neville handed him two banknotes for £1 each, and Captain O'Hara walked forth out of his wife's house.

'He will never leave you now,' said the priest.

'He cannot hurt me. I will arrange with some man of business to pay him a stipend as long as he never troubles our friend here. Though all the world should know it, will it not be better so?'

Great and terrible is the power of money. When this easy way out of their immediate difficulties had been made by the rich man, even Mrs. O'Hara with all her spirit was subdued for the moment, and the reproaches of the priest were silenced for that hour. The young man had seemed to behave well, had stood up as the friend of the suffering women, and had been at any rate ready with his money. 'And now,' he said, 'where is Kate?' Then Mrs. O'Hara took him by the hand and led him into the bedroom in which the poor girl had buried herself from her father's embrace. 'Is he gone?' she asked before even she would throw herself into her lover's arms.

'Neville has paid him money,' said the mother.

'Yes, he has gone,' said Fred; 'and I think—I think that he will trouble you no more.'

'Oh, Fred, oh, my darling, oh, my own one. At last, at last you have come to me. Why have you stayed away? You will not stay away again? Oh, Fred, you do love me? Say that you love me.'

'Better than all the world,' he said pressing her to his bosom.

He remained with her for a couple of hours, during which hardly a word was said to him about his marriage. So great had been the effect upon them all of the sudden presence of the Captain, and so excellent had been the service rendered them by the trust which the Captain had placed in the young man's wealth, that for this day both priest and mother were incapacitated from making their claim with the vigour and intensity of purpose which they would have shown had Captain O'Hara not presented himself at the cottage. The priest left them soon—but not till it had been arranged that Neville should go back to Ennis to prepare for his reception of the Captain, and return to the cottage on the day after that interview was over. He assumed on a sudden the practical views of a man of business. He would take care to have an Ennis attorney with him when speaking to the Captain, and would be quite prepared to go to the extent of two hundred a year for the Captain's life, if the Captain could be safely purchased for that money. 'A quarter of it would do,' said Mrs. O'Hara. The priest thought £2 a week would be ample. 'I'll be as good as my word,' said Fred. Kate sat looking into his face thinking that he was still a god.

'And you will certainly be here by noon on Sunday?' said Kate, clinging to him when he rose to go.

'Most certainly.'

'Dear, dear Fred.' And so he walked down the hill to the priest's house almost triumphantly. He thought himself fortunate in not finding the priest who had ridden off from Ardkill to some distant part of the parish—and then drove himself back to Ennis.

CHAPTER V

FRED NEVILLE IS AGAIN CALLED HOME TO SCROOPE

NEVILLE WAS intent upon business, and had not been back in Ennis from the cottage half an hour before he obtained an introduction to an attorney. He procured it through the sergeant-major of the troop. The sergeant-major was intimate with the innkeeper, and the innkeeper was able to say that Mr. Thaddeus Crowe was an honest, intelligent, and peculiarly successful lawyer. Before he sat down to dinner Fred Neville was closeted at the barracks with Mr. Crowe.

He began by explaining to Mr. Crowe who he was. This he did in order that the attorney might know that he had the means of carrying out his purpose. Mr. Crowe bowed, and assured his client that on that score he had no doubts whatever. Nevertheless Mr. Crowe's first resolve, when he heard of the earldom and of the golden prospects, was to be very careful not to pay any money out of his own pocket on behalf of the young officer, till he made himself quite sure that it would be returned to him with interest. As the interview progressed, however, Mr. Crowe began to see his way, and to understand that the golden prospects were not pleaded because the owner of them was himself short of cash. Mr. Crowe soon understood the whole story. He had heard of Captain O'Hara, and believed the man to be as thorough a blackguard as ever lived. When Neville told the attorney of the two ladies, and of the anxiety which he felt to screen them from the terrible annoyance of the Captain's visits, Mr. Crowe smiled, but made no remark. 'It will be enough for you to know that I am earnest about it,' said the future Earl, resenting even the smile. Mr. Crowe bowed, and asked his client to finish the story.

'The man is to be with me tomorrow, here, at twelve, and I wish you to be present. Mr. Crowe, my intention is to give him two hundred pounds a year as long as he lives.'

'Two hundred a year!' said the Ennis attorney, to whom such an annuity seemed to be exorbitant as the purchase-money for a returned convict.

'Yes—I have already mentioned that sum to his wife, though not to him.'

'I should reconsider it, Mr. Neville.'

'Thank you—but I have made up my mind. The payments will be made, of course, only on condition that he troubles neither of the ladies either personally or by letter. It might be provided that it shall be paid to him weekly in France, but will not be paid should he leave that country. You will think of all this, and will make suggestions tomorrow. I shall be glad to have the whole thing left in your hands, so that I need simply remit the cheques to you. Perhaps I shall have the pleasure of seeing you tomorrow at twelve.' Mr. Crowe promised to turn the matter over in his mind and to be present at the hour named. Neville carried himself very well through the interview, assuming with perfect ease the manners of the great and rich man who had only to give his orders with a certainty that they would be obeyed. Mr. Crowe, when he went out from the young man's presence, had no longer any doubt on his mind as to his client's pecuniary capability.

On the following day at twelve o'clock, Captain O'Hara, punctual to the minute, was at the barracks; and there also sitting in Neville's room, was the attorney. But Neville himself was not there, and the Captain immediately felt that he had been grossly imposed upon and swindled. 'And who may I have the honour of addressing, when I speak to you, sir?' demanded the Captain.

'I am a lawyer.'

'And Mr. Neville—my own son-in-law—has played me that trick!'

Mr. Crowe explained that no trick had been played, but

did so in language which was no doubt less courteous than would have been used had Mr. Neville been present. As, however, the cause of our hero's absence is more important to us than the Captain's prospects that must be first explained.

As soon as the attorney left him Neville had sat down to dinner with his two brother officers, but was not by any means an agreeable companion. When they attempted to joke with him as to the young lady on the cliffs, he showed very plainly that he did not like it; and when Cornet Simpkinson after dinner raised his glass to drink a health to Miss O'Hara, Neville told him that he was an impertinent ass. It was then somewhat past nine, and it did not seem probable that the evening would go off pleasantly. Cornet Simpkinson lit his cigar, and tried to wink at the Captain. Neville stretched out his legs and pretended to go to sleep. At this moment it was a matter of intense regret to him that he had ever seen the West of Ireland.

At a little before ten Captain Johnson retired, and the Cornet attempted an apology. He had not meant to say anything that Neville would not like. 'It doesn't signify, my dear boy; only as a rule, never mention women's names,' said Neville, speaking as though he were fully fitted by his experience to lay down the law on a matter so delicate. 'Perhaps one hadn't better,' said the Cornet—and then that little difficulty was over. Cornet Simpkinson however thought of it afterwards, and felt that that evening and that hour had been more important than any other evening or any other hour in his life.

At half-past ten, when Neville was beginning to think that he would take himself to bed, and was still cursing the evil star which had brought him to County Clare, there arose a clatter at the outside gate of the small barrack-yard. A man had posted all the way down from Limerick and desired to see Mr. Neville at once. The man had indeed come direct from Scroope—by rail from Dublin to Limerick, and thence without delay on to Ennis. The Earl of Scroope was dead, and

Frederic Neville was Earl of Scroope. The man brought a letter from Miss Mellerby, telling him the sad news and conjuring him in his aunt's name to come at once to the Manor. Of course he must start at once for the Manor. Of course he must attend as first mourner at his uncle's grave before he could assume his uncle's name and fortune.

In that the first hour of his greatness the shock to him was not so great but that he at once thought of the O'Haras. He would leave Ennis the following morning at six, so as to catch the day mail train out of Limerick for Dublin. That was a necessity; but though so very short a span of time was left to him, he must still make arrangements about the O'Haras. He had hardly heard the news half an hour before he himself was knocking at the door of Mr. Crowe the attorney. He was admitted, and Mr. Crowe descended to him in a pair of slippers and a very old dressing-gown. Mr. Crowe, as he held his tallow candle up to his client's face, looked as if he didn't like it. 'I know I must apologize,' said Neville, 'but I have this moment received news of my uncle's death.'

'The Earl?'

'Yes.'

'And I have now the honour of—speaking to the Earl of Scroope.'

'Never mind that. I must start for England almost immediately. I haven't above an hour or two. You must see that man, O'Hara, without me.'

'Certainly, my lord.'

'You shouldn't speak to me in that way yet,' said Neville angrily. 'You will be good enough to understand that the terms are fixed two hundred a year as long as he remains in France and never molests anyone either by his presence or by letter. Thank you. I shall be so much obliged to you! I shall be back here after the funeral, and will arrange about payments. Good-night.'

So it happened that Captain O'Hara had no opportunity on that occasion of seeing his proposed son-in-law. Mr. Crowe, fully crediting the power confided to him, did as he was

bidden. He was very harsh to the poor Captain; but in such
a condition a man can hardly expect that people should not
be harsh to him. The Captain endeavoured to hold up his
head, and to swagger, and to assume an air of pinchbeck
respectability. But the attorney would not permit it. He
required that the man should own himself to be penniless, a
scoundrel, only anxious to be bought; and the Captain at last
admitted the facts. The figure was the one thing important to
him—the figure and the nature of the assurance. Mr. Crowe
had made his calculations, and put the matter very plainly.
A certain number of francs—a hundred francs—would be
paid to him weekly at any town in France he might select—
which however would be forfeited by any letter written either
to Mrs. O'Hara, to Miss O'Hara, or to the Earl.

'The Earl!' ejaculated the Captain.

Mr. Crowe had been unable to refrain his tongue from the
delicious title, but now corrected himself. 'Nor Mr. Neville,
I mean. No one will be bound to give you a farthing, and any
letter asking for anything more will forfeit the allowance
altogether.' The Captain vainly endeavoured to make better
terms, and of course accepted those proposed to him. He
would live in Paris—dear Paris. He took five pounds for his
journey, and named an agent for the transmission of his
money.

And so Fred Neville was the Earl of Scroope. He had still
one other task to perform before he could make his journey
home. He had to send tidings in some shape to Ardkill of
what had happened. As he returned to the barracks from Mr.
Crowe's residence he thought wholly of this. That other
matter was now arranged. As one item of the cost of his adventure in County Clare he must pay two hundred a year
to that reprobate, the Captain, as long as the reprobate chose
to live—and must also pay Mr. Crowe's bill for his assistance.
This was a small matter to him as his wealth was now great,
and he was not a man by nature much prone to think of
money. Nevertheless it was a bad beginning of his life.
Though he had declared himself to be quite indifferent

on that head, he did feel that the arrangement was not
altogether reputable—that it was one which he could not explain to his own man of business without annoyance, and
which might perhaps give him future trouble. Now he must
prepare his message for the ladies at Ardkill—especially to
the lady whom on his last visit to the cottage he had found
armed with a dagger for the reception of her husband. And
as he returned back to the barracks it occurred to him that
a messenger might be better than a letter. 'Simpkinson,' he
said, going at once into the young man's bedroom, 'have you
heard what has happened to me?' Simpkinson had heard all
about it, and expressed himself as 'deucedly sorry' for the old
man's death, but seemed to think that there might be consolation for that sorrow. 'I must go to Scroope immediately
said Neville. 'I have explained it all to Johnson, and shall
start almost at once. I shall first lie down and get an hour's
sleep. I want you to do something for me.' Simpkinson was
devoted. Simpkinson would do anything. 'I cut up a little
rough just now when you mentioned Miss O'Hara's name.'
Simpkinson declared that he did not mind it in the least, and
would never pronounce the name again as long as he lived.
'But I want you to go and see her tomorrow,' said Neville.
Then Simpkinson sat bolt upright in bed.

Of course the youthful warrior undertook the commission.
What youthful warrior would not go any distance to see a
beautiful young lady on a cliff, and what youthful warrior
would not undertake any journey to oblige a brother officer
who was an Earl? Full instructions were at once given to him.
He had better ask to see Mrs. O'Hara—in describing whom
Neville made no allusion to the dagger. He was told how to
knock at the door, and send in word by the servant to say
that he had called on behalf of Mr. Neville. He was to drive
as far as Liscannor, and then get some boy to accompany him
on foot as a guide. He would not perhaps mind walking two
or three miles. Simpkinson declared that were it ten he
would not mind it. He was then to tell Mrs. O'Hara—just the
truth. He was to say that a messenger had come from Scroope

announcing the death of the Earl, and that Neville had been obliged to start at once for England.

'But you will be back?' said Simpkinson.

Neville paused a moment. 'Yes, I shall be back, but don't say anything of that to either of the ladies.'

'Must I say I don't know? They'll be sure to ask, I should say.'

'Of course they'll ask. Just tell them that the whole thing has been arranged so quickly that nothing has been settled, but that they shall hear from me at once. You can say that you suppose I shall be back, but that I promised that I would write. Indeed that will be the exact truth, as I don't at all know what I may do. Be as civil to them as possible.'

'That's of course.'

'They are ladies, you know.'

'I supposed that.'

'Am I most desirous to do all in my power to oblige them. You can say that I have arranged that other matter satisfactorily.'

'That other matter?'

'They'll understand. The mother will at least, and you'd better say that to her. You'll go early.'

'I'll start at seven if you like.'

'Eight or nine will do. Thank you, Simpkinson. I'm so much obliged to you. I hope I shall see you over in England some day when things are a little settled.' With this Simpkinson was delighted—as he was also with the commission entrusted to him.

And so Fred Neville was the Earl of Scroope. Not that he owned even to himself that the title and all belonging to it were as yet in his own possession. Till the body of the old man should be placed in the family vault he would still be simply Fred Neville, a lieutenant in Her Majesty's 20th Hussars. As he travelled home to Scroope, to the old gloomy mansion which was now in truth not only his home, but his own house, to do just as he pleased with it, he had much to fill his mind. He was himself astonished to find with how great a weight his new dignities sat upon his shoulders, now that they were his own. But a few months since he had thought and even spoken of shifting them from himself to another so that he might lightly enjoy a portion of the wealth which would belong to him without burdening himself with the duties of his position. He would take his yacht, and the girl he loved, and live abroad, with no present record of the coronet which would have descended to him, and with no assumption of the title. But already that feeling had died away within him. A few words spoken to him by the priest and a few serious thoughts within his own bosom had sufficed to explain to him that he must be the Earl of Scroope. The family honours had come to him, and he must support them —either well or ill as his strength and principles might govern him. And he did understand that it was much to be a peer, an hereditary legislator, one who by the chance of his birth had a right to look for deferential respect even from his elders. It was much to be the lord of wide acres, the ruler of a large domain, the landlord of many tenants who would at any rate regard themselves as dependent on his goodness. It was much to be so placed that no consideration of money need be a bar to any wish—that the considerations which should bar his pleasures need be only those of dignity, character and propriety. His uncle had told him more than once how much a peer of England owed to his country and to his order—how such a one is bound by no ordinary bonds to a life of high resolves, and good endeavours. "Sans reproche" was the motto of his house, and was emblazoned on the wall of the hall that was now his own. If it might be possible to him he would live up to it and neither degrade his order nor betray his country.

But as he thought of all this, he thought also of Kate O'Hara. With what difficulties had he surrounded the commencement of this life which he purposed to lead! How was he to escape from the mess of trouble which he had prepared for himself by his adventures in Ireland. An idea floated across his mind that very many men who stand in their

natural manhood high in the world's esteem, have in their
early youth formed ties such as that which now bound him
to Kate O'Hara—that they have been silly as he had been,
and had then escaped from the effects of their folly without
grievous damage. But yet he did not see his mode of escape.
If money could do it for him he would make almost any
sacrifice. If wealth and luxury could make his Kate happy,
she should be happy as a Princess. But he did not believe
either of her or of her mother that any money would be
accepted as a sufficient atonement. And he hated himself for
suggesting to himself that it might be possible. The girl was
good, and had trusted him altogether. The mother was self-
denying, devoted, and high-spirited. He knew that money
would not suffice.

He need not return to Ireland unless he pleased. He could
send over some agent to arrange his affairs, and allow the two
women to break their hearts in their solitude upon the
cliffs. Were he to do so he did not believe that they would
follow him. They would write doubtless, but personally he
might, probably, be quit of them in this fashion. But in this
there would be a cowardice and a meanness which would
make it impossible that he should ever again respect himself.

And thus he again entered Scroope, the lord and owner of
all that he saw around him—with by no means a happy
heart or a light bosom.

CHAPTER VI

THE EARL OF SCROOPE IS IN TROUBLE

NOT A word was said to the young lord on his return home respecting the O'Haras till he himself had broached the subject. He found his brother Jack Neville at Scroope on his arrival, and Sophie Mellerby was still staying with his aunt. A day had been fixed for the funeral, but no one had ventured to make any other arrangement till the heir and owner should be there. He was received with solemn respect by the old servants who, as he observed, abstained from calling him by any name. They knew that it did not become them to transfer the former lord's title to the heir till all that remained of the former lord should be hidden from the world in the family vault; but they could not bring themselves to address a real Earl as Mr. Neville. His aunt was broken down by sorrow, but nevertheless, she treated him with a courtly deference. To her he was now the reigning sovereign among the Nevilles, and all Scroope and everything there was at his disposal. When he held her by the hand and spoke of her future life she only shook her head. 'I am an old woman, though not in years old as was my lord. But my life is done, and it matters not where I go.'

'Dear aunt, do not speak of going. Where can you be so well as here?' But she only shook her head again and wept afresh. Of course it would not be fitting that she should remain in the house of the young Earl who was only her nephew by marriage. Scroope Manor would now become a house of joy, would be filled with the young and light of heart; there would be feasting there and dancing; horses neighing before the doors, throngs of carriages, new furniture, bright draperies, and perhaps, alas, loud revellings. It would

843

not be fit that such a one as she should be at Scroope now that her lord had left her.

The funeral was an affair not of pomp but of great moment in those parts. Two or three Nevilles from other counties came to the house, as did also sundry relatives bearing other names. Mr. Mellerby was there, and one or two of the late Earl's oldest friends; but the great gathering was made up of the Scroope tenants, not one of whom failed to see his late landlord laid in his grave. 'My Lord,' said an old man to Fred, one who was himself a peer and was the young lord's cousin though they two had never met before, 'My Lord,' said the old man, as soon as they had returned from the grave, 'you are called upon to succeed as good a man as ever it has been my lot to know. I loved him as a brother. I hope you will not lightly turn away from his example.' Fred made some promise which at the moment he certainly intended to perform.

On the next morning the will was read. There was nothing in it, nor could there have been anything in it, which might materially affect the interests of the heir. The late lord's widow was empowered to take away from Scroope anything that she desired. In regard to money she was provided for so amply that money did not matter to her. A whole year's income from the estates was left to the heir in advance, so that he might not be driven to any momentary difficulty in assuming the responsibilities of his station. A comparatively small sum was left to Jack Neville, and a special gem to Sophie Mellerby. There were bequests to all the servants, a thousand pounds to the vicar of the parish—which perhaps was the only legacy which astonished the legatee—and his affectionate love to every tenant on the estate. All the world acknowledged that it was as good a will as the Earl could have made. Then the last of the strangers left the house, and the Earl of Scroope was left to begin his reign and do his duty as best he might.

Jack had promised to remain with him for a few days, and Sophie Mellerby, who had altogether given up her London season, was to stay with the widow till something should be settled as to a future residence. 'If my aunt will only say that she will keep the house for a couple of years, she shall have it,' said Fred to the young lady—perhaps wishing to postpone for so long a time the embarrassment of the large domain; but to this Lady Scroope would not consent. If allowed she would remain till the end of July. By that time she would find herself a home.

'For the life of me, I don't know how to begin my life,' said the new peer to his brother as they were walking about the park together.

'Do not think about beginning it at all. You won't be angry, and will know what I mean, when I say that you should avoid thinking too much of your own position.'

'How am I to help thinking of it? It is so entirely changed from what it was.'

'No Fred—not entirely; nor as I hope, is it changed at all in those matters which are of most importance to you. A man's self, and his ideas of the manner in which he should rule himself, should be more to him than any outward accidents. Had that cousin of ours never died——'

'I almost wish he never had.'

'It would then have been your ambition to live as an honourable gentleman. To be that now should be more to you than to be an Earl and a man of fortune.'

'It's very easy to preach, Jack. You were always good at that. But here I am, and what am I to do? How am I to begin? Everybody says that I am to change nothing. The tenants will pay their rents, and Burnaby will look after things outside, and Mrs. Bunce will look after the things inside, and I may sit down and read a novel. When the gloom of my uncle's death has passed away, I suppose I shall buy a few more horses and perhaps begin to make a row about the pheasants. I don't know what else there is to do.'

'You'll find that there are duties.'

'I suppose I shall. Something is expected of me. I am to keep up the honour of the family; but it really seems to me that the best way of doing so would be to sit in my uncle's arm chair and go to sleep as he did.'

'As a first step in doing something you should get a wife for yourself. If once you had a settled home, things would arrange themselves round you very easily.'

'Ah, yes—a wife. You know, Jack, I told you about that girl in County Clare.'

'You must let nothing of that kind stand in your way.'

'Those are your ideas of high moral grandeur! Just now my own personal conduct was to be all in all to me, and the rank nothing. Now I am to desert a girl I love because I am an English peer.'

'What has passed between you and the young lady, of course I do not know.'

'I may as well tell you the whole truth,' said Fred. And he told it honestly—almost honestly. It is very hard for a man to tell a story truly against himself, but he intended to tell the whole truth. 'Now what must I do? Would you have me marry her?' Jack Neville paused for a long time. 'At any rate you can say yes, or no.'

'It is very hard to say yes, or no.'

'I can marry no one else. I can see my way so far. You had better tell Sophie Mellerby everything, and then a son of yours shall be the future Earl.'

'We are both of us young as yet, Fred, and need not think of that. If you do mean to marry Miss O'Hara you should lose not a day—not a day.'

'But what if I don't. You are always very ready with advice, but you have given me none as yet.'

'How can I advise you? I should have heard the very words in which you made your promise before I could dare to say whether it should be kept or broken. As a rule a man should keep his word.'

'Let the consequences be what they may?'

'A man should keep his word certainly. And I know no promise so solemn as that made to a woman when followed by conduct such as yours has been.'

'And what will people say then as to my conduct to the family? How will they look on me when I bring home the daughter of that scoundrel?'

'You should have thought of that before.'

'But I was not told. Do you not see that I was deceived there. Mrs. O'Hara clearly said that the man was dead. And she told me nothing of the galleys.'

'How could she tell you that?'

'But if she has deceived me, how can I be expected to keep my promise? I love the girl dearly. If I could change places with you, I would do so this very minute, and take her away with me, and she should certainly be my wife. If it were only myself, I would give up all to her. I would, by heaven. But I cannot sacrifice the family. As to solemn promises, did I not swear to my uncle that I would not disgrace the family by such a marriage? Almost the last word that I spoke to him was that. Am I to be untrue to him? There are times in which it seems impossible that a man should do right.'

'There are times in which a man may be too blind to see the right,' said Jack—sparing his brother in that he did not remind him that those dilemmas always come from original wrongdoing.

'I think I am resolved not to marry her,' said Fred.

'If I were in your place I think I should marry her,' said Jack—'but I will not speak with certainty even of myself.'

'I shall not. But I will be true to her all the same. You may be sure that I shall not marry at all.' Then he recurred to his old scheme. 'If I can find any mode of marrying her in some foreign country, so that her son and mine shall not be the legitimate heir to the title and estates, I would go there at once with her, though it were to the further end of the world. You can understand now what I mean when I say that I do not know how to begin.' Jack acknowledged that in that matter he did understand his brother. It is always hard for a man to commence any new duty when he knows that he has a millstone round his neck which will probably make that duty impracticable at last

He went on with his life at Scroope for a week after the funeral without resolving upon anything, or taking any steps towards solving the O'Hara difficulty. He did ride about among the tenants, and gave some trifling orders as to the house and stables. His brother was still with him, and Miss Mellerby remained at the Manor. But he knew that the thunder-cloud must break over his head before long, and at last the storm was commenced. The first drops fell upon him in the soft form of a letter from Kate O'Hara.

'DEAREST FRED,

I am not quite sure that I ought to address you like that; but I always shall unless you tell me not. We have been expecting a letter from you every day since you went. Your friend from Ennis came here and brought us the news of your uncle's death. We were very sorry; at least I was certainly. I liked to think of you a great deal better as my own Fred, than as a great lord. But you will still be my own Fred always; will you not?

Mother said at once that it was a matter of course that you should go to England; but your friend, whose name we never heard, said that you had sent him especially to promise that you would write quite immediately, and that you would come back very soon. I do not know what he will think of me, because I asked him whether he was quite, quite sure that you would come back. If he thinks that I love you better than my own soul, he only thinks the truth.

Pray—pray write at once. Mother is getting vexed because there is no letter. I am never vexed with my own darling love, but I do so long for a letter. If you knew how I felt, I do think you would write almost every day—if it were only just one short word. If you would say, "Dear Love," that would be enough. And pray come. Oh do, do, pray come! Cannot you think how I must long to see you! The gentleman who came here said that you would come, and I know you will. But pray come soon. Think now, how you are all the world to me. You are more than all the world to me.

'I am not ill as I was when you were here: But I never go outside the door now. I never shall go outside the door again till you come. I don't care now for going out upon the rocks. I don't care even for the birds as you are not here to watch them with me. I sit with the skin of the seal you gave me behind my head and I pretend to sleep. But though I am quite still for hours I am not asleep, but thinking always of you.

We have neither seen or heard anything more of my father, and Father Marty says that you have managed about that very generously. You are always generous and good. I was so wretched all that day, that I thought I should have died. You will not think ill of your Kate, will you, because her father is bad?

Pray write when you get this, and above all things let us know when you will come to us.

Always, always, and always,

Your own

KATE.'

Two days after this, while the letter was still unanswered, there came another from Mrs. O'Hara which was, if possible, more grievous to him than that from her daughter.

'My Lord,' the letter began. When he read this he turned from it with a sickening feeling of disgust. Of course the woman knew that he was now Earl of Scroope; but it would have been so desirable that there should have been no intercourse between her and him except under the name by which she had hitherto known him. And then in the appellation as she used it there seemed to be a determination to reproach him which must, he knew, lead to great misery.

'My Lord,

The messenger you sent to us brought us good news, and told us that you were gone home to your own affairs. That I suppose was right, but why have you not written to us before this? Why have you not told my poor girl that you will come to her, and atone to her for the injury you have done in the only manner now possible? I cannot and do not believe that you intend to evade the solemn promises that you have made her, and allow her to remain here a ruined outcast, and the mother of your child. I have thought you to be both a gentleman and a christian, and I still think so. Most assuredly you would be neither were you disposed to leave her desolate, while you are in prosperity.

I call upon you, my lord, in the most solemn manner, with all the energy and anxiety of a mother—of one who will be of all women the most broken-hearted if you wrong her—to write at once and let me know when you will be here to keep your promise. For the sake of your own offspring I implore you not to delay.

We feel under deep obligations to you for what you did in respect of that unhappy man. We never for a moment doubted your generosity.

Yours, My Lord,
With warmest affection, if you will admit it,
C. O'HARA.

'P.S. I ask you to come at once and keep your word. Were you to think of breaking it, I would follow you through the world.'*

The young Earl, when he received this, was not at a loss for a moment to attribute the body of Mrs. O'Hara's letter to Father Marty's power of composition, and the postscript to the unaided effort of the lady herself. Take it as he might —as coming from Mrs. O'Hara or from the priest—he found the letter to be a great burden to him. He had not as yet answered the one received from Kate, as to the genuineness of which he had entertained no doubt. How should he answer such letters? Some answer must of course be sent, and must be the forerunner of his future conduct. But how should he write his letter when he had not as yet resolved what his conduct should be?

He did attempt to write a letter, not to either of the ladies, but to the priest, explaining that in the ordinary sense of the word he could not and would not marry Miss O'Hara, but that in any way short of that legitimate and usual mode of marriage, he would bind himself to her, and that when so bound he would be true to her for life. He would make any settlement that he, Father Marty, might think right either upon the mother or upon the daughter. But Countess of Scroope the daughter of that Captain O'Hara should not become through his means. Then he endeavoured to explain the obligation laid upon him by his uncle, and the excuse which he thought he could plead in not having been informed of Captain O'Hara's existence. But the letter when written seemed to him to be poor and mean, cringing and at the same time false. He told himself that it would not suffice. It was manifest to him that he must go back to County Clare, even though he should encounter Mrs. O'Hara, dagger in hand. What was any personal danger to himself in such an affair as this? And if he did not fear a woman's dagger, was he to fear a woman's tongue—or the tongue of a priest? So he tore the letter, and resolved that he would write and name a day on which he would appear at Ardkill. At any rate such a letter as that might be easily written, and might be made soft with words of love.

'DEAREST KATE,

I will be with you on the 15th or on the 16th at latest. You should remember that a man has a good deal to do and think of when he gets pitchforked into such a new phase of life as mine. Do not, however, think that I quarrel with you, my darling. That I will never do. My love to your mother.

Ever your own,
FRED.

I hate signing the other name.'

This letter was not only written but sent.

CHAPTER VII

SANS REPROCHE.

THREE or four days after writing his letter to Kate O'Hara, the Earl told his aunt that he must return to Ireland, and he named the day on which he would leave Scroope. 'I did not think that you would go back there,' she said. He could see by the look of her face and by the anxious glance of her eye that she had in her heart the fear of Kate O'Hara—as he had also.

'I must return. I came away at a moment's notice.'

'But you have written about leaving the regiment.'

'Yes—I have done that. In the peculiar circumstances I don't suppose they will want me to serve again. Indeed I've had a letter, just a private note, from one of the fellows at the Horse Guards explaining all that.'

'I don't see why you should go at all—indeed I do not.'

'What am I to do about my things? I owe some money. I've got three or four horses there. My very clothes are all about just as I left them when I came away.'

'Anybody can manage all that. Give the horses away.'

'I had rather not give away my horses,' he said laughing. 'The fact is I must go.' She could urge nothing more to him on that occasion. She did not then mention the existence of Kate O'Hara. But he knew well that she was thinking of the girl, and he knew also that the activity of Lady Mary Quin had not slackened. But his aunt, he thought, was more afraid of him now that he was the Earl than she had been when he was only the heir; and it might be that this feeling would save him from the mention of Kate O'Hara's name.

To some extent the dowager was afraid of her nephew. She knew at least that the young man was all-powerful and

might act altogether as he listed. In whatever she might say she
could not now be supported by the authority of the Lord of
Scroope. He himself was lord of Scroope; and were he to tell
her simply to hold her tongue and mind her own business
she could only submit. But she was not the woman to allow
any sense of fear, or any solicitude as to the respect due to
herself, to stand in the way of the performance of a duty. It
may be declared on her behalf that had it been in her
nephew's power to order her head off in punishment for her
interference, she would still have spoken had she conceived
it to be right to speak.

But within her own bosom there had been dreadful con-
flicts as to that duty. Lady Mary Quin had by no means
slackened her activity. Lady Mary Quin had learned the exact
condition of Kate O'Hara, and had sent the news to her
friend with greedy rapidity. And in sending it Lady Mary
Quin entertained no slightest doubt as to the duty of the
present Earl of Scroope. According to her thinking it could
not be the duty of an Earl of Scroope in any circumstances
to marry a Kate O'Hara. There are women, who in regard
to such troubles as now existed at Ardkill cottage, always
think that the woman should be punished as the sinner and
that the man should be assisted to escape. The hardness of
heart of such women—who in all other views of life are perhaps tender and soft-natured—is one of the marvels of our
social system. It is as though a certain line were drawn to include all women—a line, but, alas, little more than a line—
by overstepping which, or rather by being known to have
overstepped it, a woman ceases to be a woman in the estimation of her own sex. That the existence of this feeling has
strong effect in saving women from passing the line, none of
us can doubt. That its general tendency may be good rather
than evil, is possible. But the hardness necessary to preserve
the rule, a hardness which must be exclusively feminine but
which is seldom wanting, is a marvellous feature in the
female character. Lady Mary Quin probably thought but little
on the subject. The women in the cottage on the cliff, who

were befriended by Father Marty, were to her dangerous scheming Roman Catholic adventurers. The proper triumph of Protestant virtue required that they should fail in their adventures. She had always known that there would be something disreputable heard of them sooner or later. When the wretched Captain came into the neighbourhood—and she soon heard of his coming—she was gratified by feeling that her convictions had been correct. When the sad tidings as to poor Kate reached her ears, she had 'known that it would be so.' That such a girl should be made Countess of Scroope in reward for her wickedness would be to her an event horrible, almost contrary to Divine Providence—a testimony that the Evil One was being allowed peculiar power at the moment, and would no doubt have been used in her own circles to show the ruin that had been brought upon the country by Catholic emancipation. She did not for a moment doubt that the present Earl should be encouraged to break any promises of marriage to the making of which he might have been allured.

But it was not so with Lady Scroope. She, indeed, came to the same conclusion as her friend, but she did so with much difficulty and after many inward struggles. She understood and valued the customs of the magic line. In her heart of hearts she approved of a different code of morals for men and women. That which merited instant, and as regarded this world, perpetual condemnation in a woman might in a man be very easily forgiven. A sigh, a shake of the head, and some small innocent stratagem that might lead to a happy marriage and settlement in life with increased income, would have been her treatment of such sin for the heirs of the great and wealthy. She knew that the world could not afford to ostracise the men—though happily it might condemn the women. Nevertheless, when she came to the single separated instance, though her heart melted with no ruth for the woman—in such cases the woman must be seen before the ruth is felt—though pity for Kate O'Hara did not influence her, she did acknowledge the sanctity of a gentleman's word. If, as Lady

Mary told her, and as she could so well believe, the present
Earl of Scroope had given to this girl a promise that he would
marry her, if he had bound himself by his pledged word, as
a nobleman and a gentleman, how could she bid him become
a perjured knave? Sans reproche!* Was he thus to begin to
live and to deserve the motto of his house by the conduct of
his life?

But then the evil that would be done was so great! She
did not for a moment doubt all that Lady Mary told her about
the girl. The worst of it had indeed been admitted. She was
a Roman Catholic, ill-born, ill-connected, damaged utterly
by a parent so low that nothing lower could possibly be raked
out of the world's gutters. And now the girl herself was—a
castaway. Such a marriage as that of which Lady Mary spoke
would not only injure the house of Scroope for the present
generation, but would tend to its final downfall. Would it
not be known throughout all England that the next Earl of
Scroope would be the grandson of a convict? Might there not
be questions as to the legitimacy of the assumed heir? She
herself knew of noble families which had been scattered,
confounded, and almost ruined by such imprudence. Hitherto the family of Scroope had been continued from generation
to generation without stain—almost without stain. It had
felt it to be a fortunate thing that the late heir had died because of the pollution of his wretched marriage. And now
must evil as bad befall it, worse evil perhaps, through the
folly of this young man? Must that proud motto be taken
down from its place in the hall from very shame? But the
evil had not been done yet, and it might be that her words
could save the house from ruin and disgrace.

She was a woman of whom it may be said that whatever
difficulty she might have in deciding a question she could
recognise the necessity of a decision and could abide by it
when she had made it. It was with great difficulty that she
could bring herself to think that an Earl of Scroope should
be false to a promise by which he had seduced a woman, but
she did succeed in bringing herself to such thought. Her very

heart bled within her as she acknowledged the necessity. A lie to her was abominable. A lie, to be told by herself, would have been hideous to her. A lie to be told by him, was worse. As virtue, what she called virtue, was the one thing indispensable to men. And yet she must tell him to lie, and having resolved so to tell him, must use all her intellect to defend the lie—and insist upon it.

He was determined to return to Ireland, and there was nothing that she could do to prevent his return. She could not bid him shun a danger simply because it was a danger. He was his own master, and were she to do so he would only laugh at her. Of authority with him she had none. If she spoke, he must listen. Her position would secure so much to her from courtesy—and were she to speak of the duty which he owed to his name and to the family he could hardly laugh. She therefore sent to him a message. Would he kindly go to her in her own room? Of course he attended to her wishes and went. 'You mean to leave us tomorrow, Fred,' she said. We all know the peculiar solemnity of a widow's dress—the look of self-sacrifice on the part of the woman which the dress creates; and have perhaps recognised the fact that if the woman be deterred by no necessities of economy in her toilet—as in such material circumstances the splendour is more perfect if splendour be the object—so also is the self-sacrifice more abject. And with this widow an appearance of melancholy solemnity, almost of woe, was natural to her. She was one whose life had ever been serious, solemn, and sad. Wealth and the outward pomp of circumstances had conferred upon her a certain dignity; and with that doubtless there had reached her some feeling of satisfaction. Religion too had given her comfort, and a routine of small duties had saved her from the wretchedness of ennui. But life with her had had no laughter, and had seldom smiled. Now in the first days of her widowhood she regarded her course as run, and looked upon herself as one who, in speaking almost, spoke from the tomb. All this had its effect upon the young lord. She did inspire him with a certain awe; and though her weeds gave her no authority, they did give her weight.

'Yes; I shall start tomorrow,' he replied.

'And you still mean to go to Ireland?'

'Yes—I must go to Ireland. I shan't stay there, you know.'

Then she paused a moment before she proceeded. 'Shall you see—that young woman when you are there?'

'I suppose I shall see her.'

'Pray do not think that I desire to interfere with your private affairs. I know well that I have no right to assume over you any of that affectionate authority which a mother might have—though in truth I love you as a son.'

'I would treat you just as I would my own mother.'

'No, Fred; that cannot be so. A mother would throw her arms round you and cling to you if she saw you going into danger. A mother would follow you, hoping that she might save you.'

'But there is no danger.'

'Ah, Fred, I fear there is.'

'What danger?'

'You are now the head of one of the oldest and the noblest families in this which in my heart I believe to be the least sinful among the sinful nations of the wicked world.'

'I don't quite know how that may be—I mean about the world. Of course I understand about the family.'

'But you love your country?'

'Oh yes. I don't think there's any place like England—to live in.'

'And England is what it is because there are still some left among us who are born to high rank and who know how to live up to the standard that is required of them. If ever there was such a man, your uncle was such a one.'

'I'm sure he was—just what he ought to have been.'

'Honourable, true, affectionate, self-denying, affable to all men, but ever conscious of his rank, giving much because much had been given to him, asserting his nobility for the benefit of those around him, proud of his order for the sake

of his country, bearing his sorrows with the dignity of silence,
a nobleman all over, living on to the end sans reproche! He
was a man whom you may dare to imitate, though to follow
him may be difficult.' She spoke not loudly, but clearly, looking him full in the face as she stood motionless before him.

'He was all that,' said Fred, almost overpowered by the
sincere solemnity of his aunt's manner.

'Will you try to walk in his footsteps?'

'Two men can never be like one another in that way. I
shall never be what he was. But I'll endeavour to get along
as well as I can.'

'You will remember your order?'

'Yes, I will. I do remember it. Mind you, aunt, I am not
glad that I belong to it. I think I do understand about it all,
and will do my best. But Jack would have made a better
Earl than I shall do. That's the truth.'

'The Lord God has placed you—and you must pray to
Him that He will enable you to do your duty in that state of
life to which it has pleased Him to call you. You are here
and must bear his decree; and whether it be a privilege to
enjoy, you must enjoy it, or a burden to bear, you must endure it.'

'It is so of course.'

'Knowing that, you must know also how incumbent it is
upon you not to defile the stock from which you are sprung.'

'I suppose it has been defiled,' said Fred, who had been
looking into the history of the family. 'The ninth Earl seems
to have married nobody knows whom. And his son was my
uncle's grandfather.'

This was a blow to Lady Scroope, but she bore it with
dignity and courage. 'You would hardly wish it to be said that
you had copied the only one of your ancestors who did amiss.
The world was rougher then than it is now, and he of whom
you speak was a soldier.'

'I'm a soldier too,' said the Earl.

'Oh, Fred, is it thus you answer me! He was a soldier in

rough times, when there were wars. I think he married when
he was with the army under Marlborough.'

'I have not seen anything of that kind, certainly.'

'Your country is at peace, and your place is here, among
your tenantry, at Scroope. You will promise me, Fred, that
you will not marry this girl in Ireland?'

'If I do, the fault will be all with that old maid at Castle
Quin.'

'Do not say that, Fred. It is impossible. Let her conduct
have been what it may, it cannot make that right in you
which would have been wrong, or that wrong which would
have been right.'

'She's a nasty meddlesome cat.'

'I will not talk about her. What good would it do? You
cannot at any rate be surprised at my extreme anxiety. You
did promise your uncle most solemnly that you would never
marry this young lady.'

'If I did, that ought to be enough.' He was now waxing
angry and his face was becoming red. He would bear a good
deal from his uncle's widow, but he felt his own power and
was not prepared to bear much more.

'Of course I cannot bind you. I know well how impotent
I am—how powerless to exercise control. But I think, Fred,
that for your uncle's sake you will not refuse to repeat your
promise to me if you intend to keep it. Why is it that I am
so anxious? It is for your sake, and for the sake of a name
which should be dearer to you than it is even to me.'

'I have no intention of marrying at all.'

'Do not say that.'

'I do say it. I do not want to keep either you or Jack in
the dark as to my future life. This young lady—of whom, by
the by, neither you nor Lady Mary Quin know anything,
shall not become Countess of Scroope. To that I have made
up my mind.'

'Thank God.'

'But as long as she lives I will make no woman Countess of
Scroope. Let Jack marry this girl that he is in love with. They

shall live here and have the house to themselves if they like it. He will look after the property and shall have whatever income old Mellerby thinks proper. I will keep the promise I made to my uncle—but the keeping of it will make it impossible for me to live here. I would prefer now that you should say no more on the subject.' Then he left her, quitting the room with some stateliness in his step, as though conscious that at such a moment as this it behoved him to assume his rank.

The dowager sat alone all that morning thinking of the thing she had done. She did now believe that he was positively resolved not to marry Kate O'Hara, and she belived also that she herself had fixed him in that resolution. In doing so had she or had she not committed a deadly sin? She knew almost with accuracy what had occurred on the coast of Clare. A young girl, innocent herself up to that moment, had been enticed to her ruin by words of love which had been hallowed in her ears by vows of marriage. Those vows which had possessed so deadly an efficacy, were now to be simply broken! The cruelty to her would be damnable, devilish— surely worthy of hell if any sin of man can be so called! And she, who could not divest herself of a certain pride taken in the austere morality of her own life, she who was now a widow anxious to devote her life solely to God, had persuaded the man to this sin, in order that her successor as Countess of Scroope might not be, in her opinion, unfitting for nobility! The young lord had promised her that he would be guilty of this sin, so damnable, so devilish, telling her as he did so, that as a consequence of his promise he must continue to live a life of wickedness! In the agony of her spirit she threw herself upon her knees and implored the Lord to pardon her and to guide her. But even while kneeling before the throne of heaven she could not drive the pride of birth out of her heart. That the young Earl might be saved from the damning sin and also from the polluting marriage—that was the prayer she prayed.

CHAPTER VIII

LOOSE ABOUT THE WORLD

THE COUNTESS was seen no more on that day—was no more seen at least by either of the two brothers. Miss Mellerby was with her now and again, but on each occasion only for a few minutes, and reported that Lady Scroope was ill and could not appear at dinner. She would, however, see her nephew before he started on the following morning.

Fred himself was much affected by the interview with his aunt. No doubt he had made a former promise to his uncle, similar to that which had now been extracted from him. No doubt he had himself resolved, after what he had thought to be mature consideration that he would not marry the girl, justifying to himself this decision by the deceit which he thought had been practised upon him in regard to Captain O'Hara. Nevertheless, he felt that by what had now occurred he was bound more strongly against the marriage than he had ever been bound before. His promise to his uncle might have been regarded as being obligatory only as long as his uncle lived. His own decision he would have been at liberty to change when he pleased to do so. But, though his aunt was almost nothing to him—was not in very truth his aunt, but only the widow of his uncle, there had been a solemnity about the engagement as he had now made it with her, which he felt to be definitely binding. He must go to Ardkill prepared to tell them absolutely the truth. He would make any arrangements they pleased as to their future joint lives, so long as it was an arrangement by which Kate should not become Countess of Scroope. He did not attempt to conceal from himself the dreadful nature of the task before him. He knew what would be the indignation of the priest. He could picture to himself the ferocity of the mother, defending her young as a lioness would her whelp. He could imagine that that dagger might again be brought from its hiding place. And, worse than all, he would see the girl prostrate in her woe, and appealing to his love and to his oaths, when the truth as to her future life should be revealed to her. But yet he did not think of shunning the task before him. He could not endure to live a coward in his own esteem.

He was unlike himself and very melancholy. 'It has been so good of you to remain here' he said to Sophie Mellerby. They had now become intimate and almost attached to each other as friends. If she had allowed a spark of hope to become bright within her heart in regard to the young Earl that had long since been quenched. She had acknowledged to herself that had it been possible in other respects they would not have suited each other—and now they were friends.

'I love your aunt dearly and have been very glad to be with her.'

'I wish you would learn to love somebody else dearly.'

'Perhaps I shall, some day—somebody else; though I don't at all know who it may be.'

'You know whom I mean.'

'I suppose I do.'

'And why not love him? Isn't he a good fellow?'

'One can't love all the good fellows, Lord Scroope.'

'You'll never find a better one than he is.'

'Did he commission you to speak for him?'

'You know he didn't. You know that he would be the last man in the world to do so?'

'I was surprised.'

'But I had a reason for speaking.'

'No doubt.'

'I don't suppose it will have any effect with you—but it is something you ought to know. If any man of my age can be supposed to have made up his mind on such a matter, you may believe that I have made up my mind that I will—never marry.'

'What nonsense, Lord Scroope.'

'Well—yes; perhaps it is. But I am so convinced of it my-self that I shall ask my brother to come and live here—per-manently—as master of the place. As he would have to leave his regiment it would of course be necessary that his position here should be settled—and it shall be settled.'

'I most sincerely hope that you will always live here your-self.'

'It won't suit me. Circumstances have made it impossible. If he will not do so, nor my aunt, the house must be shut up. I am most anxious that this should not be done. I shall im-plore him to remain here, and to be here exactly as I should have been—had things with me not have been so very un-fortunate. He will at any rate have a house to offer you if——'

'Lord Scroope!'

'I know what you are going to say, Sophie.'

'I don't know that I am as yet disposed to marry for the sake of a house to shelter me.'

'Of course you would say that; but still I think that I have been right to tell you. I am sure you will believe my assurance that Jack knows nothing of all this.'

That same evening he said nearly the same thing to his brother, though in doing so he made no special allusion to Sophie Mellerby. 'I know that there is a great deal that a fellow should do, living in such a house as this, but I am not the man to do it. It's a very good kind of life, if you happen to be up to it. I am not but you are.'

'My dear Fred, you can't change the accidents of birth.'

'In a great measure I can; or at least we can do so between us. You can't be Lord Scroope, but you can be master of Scroope Manor.'

'No I can't—and, which is more, I won't. 'Don't think I am uncivil.'

'You are uncivil, Jack.'

'At any rate I am not ungrateful. I only want you to under-stand thoroughly that such an arrangement is out of the question. In no condition of life would I care to be the locum tenens for another man. You are now five or six and twenty. At thirty you may be a married man with an absolute need for your own house.'

'I would execute any deed.'

'So that I might be enabled to keep the owner of the property out of the only place that is fit for him! It is a power which I should not use, and do not wish to possess. Believe me, Fred, that a man is bound to submit himself to the circumstances by which he is surrounded, when it is clear that they are beneficial to the world at large. There must be an Earl of Scroope, and you at present are the man.'

They were sitting together out upon the terrace after dinner, and for a time there was silence. His brother's arguments were too strong for the young lord, and it was out of his power to deal with one so dogmatic. But he did not forget the last words that had been spoken. It may be that 'I shall not be the man very long,' he said at last.

'Any of us may die today or tomorrow,' said Jack.

'I have a kind of presentiment—not that I shall die, but that I shall never see Scroope again. It seems as though I were certainly leaving for ever a place that has always been distasteful to me.'

'I never believe anything of presentiments.'

'No; of course not. You're not that sort of fellow at all. But I am. I can't think of myself as living here with a dozen old fogies about the place all doing nothing, touching their hats, my-lording me at every turn, looking respectable, but as idle as pickpockets.'

'You'll have to do it.'

'Perhaps I shall, but I don't think it.' Then there was again silence for a time. 'The less said about it the better, but I know that I've got a very difficult job before me in Ireland.'

'I don't envy you, Fred—not that.'

'It is no use talking about it. It has got to be done, and the sooner done the better. What I shall do when it is done, I have not the most remote idea. Where I shall be living this day month I cannot guess. I can only say one thing certainly, and that is that I shall not come back here. There never was a fellow so loose about the world as I am.'

It was terrible that a young man who had it in his power to do so much good or so much evil should have had nothing to bind him to the better course! There was the motto of his house, and the promises which he had made to his uncle persuading him to that which was respectable and as he thought dull; and opposed to those influences there was an unconquerable feeling on his own part that he was altogether unfitted for the kind of life that was expected of him. Joined to this there was the fact of that unfortunate connection in Ireland from which he knew that it would be base to fly, and which, as it seemed to him, made any attempt at respectability impossible to him.

Early on the following morning, as he was preparing to start, his aunt again sent for him. She came out to him in the sitting-room adjoining her bedroom and there embraced him. Her eyes were red with weeping, and her face wan with care. 'Fred,' she said; 'dear Fred.'

'Goodbye, aunt. The last word I have to say is that I implore you not to leave Scroope as long as you are comfortable here.'

'You will come back?'

'I cannot say anything certain about that.'

She still had hold of him with both hands and was looking into his face with loving, frightened, wistful eyes. 'I know,' she said, 'that you will be thinking of what passed between us yesterday.'

'Certainly I shall remember it.'

'I have been praying for you, Fred; and now I tell you to look to your Father which is in Heaven for guidance, and not to take it from any poor frail sinful human being. Ask Him to keep your feet steady in the path, and your heart pure, and your thoughts free from wickedness. Oh, Fred, keep your mind and body clear before Him, and if you will kneel to Him for protection, He will show you a way through all difficulties.' It was thus that she intended to tell him that his promise to her, made on the previous day, was to count for nought, and that he was to marry the girl if by no other way he could release himself from vice. But she could not bring herself to declare to him in plain terms that he had better marry Kate O'Hara, and bring his new Countess to Scroope in order that she might be fitly received by her predecessor. It might be that the Lord would still show him a way out of the two evils.

But his brother was more clear of purpose with him, as they walked together out to the yard in which the young Earl was to get into his carriage. 'Upon the whole, Fred, if I were you I should marry that girl.' This he said quite abruptly. The young lord shook his head. 'It may be that I do not know all the circumstances. If they be as I have heard them from you, I should marry her. Goodbye. Let me hear from you, when you have settled as to going anywhere.'

'I shall be sure to write,' said Fred as he took the reins and seated him in the phaeton.

His brother's advice he understood plainly, and that of his aunt he thought that he understood. But he shook his head again as he told himself that he could not now be guided by either of them.

CHAPTER IX

AT LISCANNOR

THE YOUNG lord slept one night at Ennis, and on the third morning after his departure from Scroope, started in his gig for Liscannor and the cliffs of Moher. He took a servant with him and a change of clothes. And as he went his heart was very heavy. He could not live a coward in his own esteem. Were it not so how willingly would he have saved himself from the misery of this journey, and have sent to his Kate to bid her come to him in England! He feared the priest, and he feared his Kate's mother—not her dagger, but her eyes and scorching words. He altogether doubted his own powers to perform satisfactorily the task before him. He knew men who could do it. His brother Jack would do it, were it possible that his brother Jack should be in such a position. But for himself, he was conscious of a softness of heart, a feminine tenderness, which—to do him justice—he did not mistake for sincerity, that rendered him unfit for the task before him. The farther he journeyed from Scroope and the nearer that he found himself to the cliffs the stronger did the feeling grow within him, till it had become almost tragical in its dominion over him. But still he went on. It was incumbent on him to pay one more visit to the cliffs and he journeyed on.

At Limerick he did not even visit the barracks to see his late companions of the regiment. At Ennis he slept in his old room, and of course the two officers who were quartered there came to him. But they both declared when they left him that the Earl of Scroope and Fred Neville were very different persons, attributing the difference solely to the rank and wealth of the new peer. Poor Simpkinson had expected long whispered confidential conversations respecting the ladies of Ardkill; but the Earl had barely thanked him for his journey; and the whispered confidence, which would have been so delightful, was at once impossible. 'By Heaven, there's nothing like rank to spoil a fellow. He was a good fellow once.' So spoke Captain Johnson, as the two officers retreated together from the Earl's room.

And the Earl also saw Mr. Crowe the attorney. Mr. Crowe recognized at its full weight the importance of a man whom he might now call 'My Lord' as often as he pleased, and as to whose pecuniary position he had made some gratifying inquiries. A very few words sufficed. Captain O'Hara had taken his departure, and the money would be paid regularly. Mr. Crowe also noticed the stern silence of the man, but thought that it was becoming in an Earl with so truly noble a property. Of the Castle Quin people who could hardly do more than pay their way like country gentlefolk, and who were mere Irish, Mr. Crowe did not think much.

Every hour that brought the lord nearer to Liscannor added a weight to his bosom. As he drove his gig along the bleak road to Ennistimon his heart was very heavy indeed. At Maurice's mills,* the only resting-place on the road, it had been his custom to give his horse a mouthful of water; but he would not do so now though the poor beast would fain have stopped there. He drove the animal on ruthlessly, himself driven by a feeling of unrest which would not allow him to pause. He hated the country now, and almost told himself that he hated all whom it contained. How miserable was his lot, that he should have bound himself in the opening of his splendour, in the first days of a career that might have been so splendid, to misfortune that was squalid and mean as this. To him, to one placed by circumstances as he was placed, it was squalid and mean. By a few soft words spoken to a poor girl whom he had chanced to find among the rocks he had so bound himself with vile manacles, had so crippled, hampered and fettered himself, that he was forced to renounce all the glories of his station. Wealth almost unlimited was at his command—and rank, and youth, and such personal gifts of appearance and disposition as best serve to win general love. He had talked to his brother of his unfitness for his earldom; but he could have blazoned it forth at Scroope and up in London, with the best of young lords, and have loved well to do so. But this adventure, as he had been wont to call it, had fallen upon him, and had broken him as it were in pieces. Thousands a year he would have paid to be rid of his adventure; but thousands a year, he knew well, were of no avail. He might have sent over some English Mr. Crowe with offers almost royal; but he had been able so to discern the persons concerned as to know that royal offers, of which the royalty would be simply money royalty, could be of no avail. How would that woman have looked at any messenger who had come to her with offers of money—and proposed to take her child into some luxurious but disgraceful seclusion? And in what language would Father Marty have expressed himself on such a proposed arrangement? And so the Earl of Scroope drove on with his heart falling ever lower and lower within his bosom.

It had of course been necessary that he should form some plan. He proposed to get rooms for one night at the little inn at Ennistimon, to leave his gig there, and then to take one of the country cars on to Liscannor. It would, he thought, be best to see the priest first. Let him look at his task which way he would, he found that every part of it was bad. An interview with Father Marty would be very bad, for he must declare his intentions in such a way that no doubt respecting them must be left on the priest's mind. He would speak only to three persons—but to all those three he must now tell the certain truth. There were causes at work which made it impossible that Kate O'Hara should become Countess of Scroope. They might tear him to pieces, but from that decision he would not budge. Subject to that decision they might do with him and with all that belonged to him almost as they pleased. He would explain this first to the priest if it should chance that he found the priest at home.

He left his gig and servant at Ennistimon and proceeded as he had intended along the road to Liscannor on an outside car. In the mid-distance about two miles out of the town he met Father Marty riding on the road. He had almost hoped— nay, he had hoped—that the priest might not be at home. But here was the lion in his path. 'Ah, my Lord,' said the priest in his sweetest tone of good humour—and his tones when he was so disposed were very sweet—'Ah, my Lord, this is a sight for sore eyes. They tould me you were to be here today or tomorrow, and I took it for granted therefore it'd be the day afther. But you're as good as the best of your word.' The Earl of Scroope got off the car, and holding the priest's hand, answered the kindly salutation. But he did so with a constrained air an with a solemnity which the priest also attributed to his newly-begotten rank. Fred Neville—as he had been a week or two since—was almost grovelling in the dust before the priest's eyes; but the priest for the moment thought that he was wrapping himself up in the sables and ermine of his nobility. However, he had come back—which was more perhaps than Father Marty had expected—and the best must be made of him with reference to poor Kate's future happiness. 'You're going on to Ardkill, I suppose, my Lord,' he said.

'Yes—certainly; but I intended to take the Liscannor road on purpose to see you. I shall leave the car at Liscannor and walk up. You could not return, I suppose?'

'Well—yes—I might.'

'If you could, Father Marty——'

'Oh, certainly.' The priest now saw that there was some- thing more in the man's manner than lordly pride. As the Earl got again up on his car, the priest turned his horse, and the two travelled back through the village without further conversation. The priest's horse was given up to the boy in the yard, and he then led the way into the house. 'We are not much altered in our ways, are we, my Lord?' he said as he moved a bottle of whisky that stood on the sideboard. 'Shall I offer you lunch?'

'No, thank you, Father Marty—nothing, thank you.' Then he made a gasp and began. The bad hour had arrived, and it must be endured. 'I have come back, as you see, Father Marty. That was a matter of course.'

'Well, yes, my Lord. As things have gone it was a matter of course.'

'I am here. I came as soon as it was possible that I should come. Of course it was necessary that I should remain at home for some days after what has occurred at Scroope.'

'No doubt—no doubt. But you will not be angry with me for saying that after what has occurred here, your presence has been most anxiously expected. However here you are, and all may yet be well. As God's minister I ought perhaps to up-braid. But I am not given to much upbraiding, and I love that dear and innocent young face too well to desire anything now but that the owner of it should receive at your hands that which is due to her before God and man.'

He perceived that the priest knew it all. But how could he wonder at this when that which ought to have been her secret and his had become known even to Lady Mary Quin? And he understood well what the priest meant when he spoke of that which was due to Kate O'Hara before God and man; and he could perceive, or thought that he perceived, that the priest did not doubt of the coming marriage, now that he, the victim, was again back in the west of Ireland. And was he not the victim of a scheme? Had he not been allured on to make promises to the girl which he would not have made had the truth been told him as to her father? He would not even in his thoughts accuse Kate—his Kate—of being a parti-cipator in these schemes. But Mrs. O'Hara and the priest had certainly intrigued against him. He must remember that. In the terrible task which he was now compelled to begin he must build his defence chiefly upon that. Yes; he must begin his work, now upon the instant. With all his golden prospects—with all 'his golden honours already in his possession—he could wish himself dead rather than begin it. But he could not die and have done it. 'Father Marty,' he said, 'I cannot make Miss O'Hara Countess of Scroope.'

'Not make her Countess of Scroope! What will you make her then?'

'As to that, I am here to discuss it with you.'

'What is it you main, sir? Afther you have had your will of her, and polluted her sweet innocence, you will not make her your wife! You cannot look me in the face, Mr. Neville, and tell me that.'

There the priest was right. The young Earl could not look him in the face as he stammered out his explanation and proposal. The burly, strong old man stood perfectly still and silent as he, with hesitating and ill-arranged words, tried to gloze over and make endurable his past conduct and intentions as to the future. He still held some confused idea as to a form of marriage which should for all his life bind him to the woman, but which should give her no claim to the title, and her child no claim either to the title or the property. 'You should have told me of this Captain O'Hara,' he said, as with many half-formed sentences he completed his suggestions.

'And it's on me you are throwing the blame?'

'You should have told me, Father Marty.'

'By the great God above me, I did not believe that a man could be such a villain! As I look for glory I did not think it possible! I should have told you! Neither did I nor did Mistress O'Hara know or believe that the man was alive. And what has the man to do with it? Is she vile because he has been guilty? Is she other than you knew her to be when you first took her to your bosom, because of his sin?

'It does make a difference, Mr. Marty.'

'Afther what you have done it can make no difference. When you swore to her that she should be your wife, and conquered her by so swearing, was there any clause in your contract that you were not to be bound if you found aught displaising to you in her parentage?'

'I ought to have known it all.'

'You knew all that she knew—all that I knew. You knew all that her mother knew. No, Lord Scroope. It cannot be that you should be so unutterably a villain. You are your own masther. Unsay what you have said to me, and her ears shall never be wounded or her heart broken by a hint of it.'

'I cannot make her Countess of Scroope. You are a priest, and can use what words you please to me—but I cannot make her Countess of Scroope.'

'Faith—and there will be more than words used, my young lord. As to your plot of a counterfeit marriage——'

'I said nothing of a counterfeit marriage.'

'What was it you said, then? I say you did. You proposed to me—to me a priest of God's altar—a false counterfeit marriage, so that those two poor women, who you are afraid to face, might be cajoled and chaited and ruined.'

'I am going to face them instantly.'

'Then must your heart be made of very stone. Shall I tell you the consequences?' Then the priest paused awhile, and the young man bursting into tears, hid his face against the wall. 'I will tell you the consequences, Lord Scroope. They will die. The shame and sorrow which you have brought on them, will bring them to their graves—and so there will be an end of their troubles upon earth. But while I live there shall be no rest for the sole of your foot. I am ould, and may soon be below the sod, but I will lave it as a legacy behind me that your iniquity shall be proclaimed and made known in high places. While I live I will follow you, and when I am gone there shall be another to take the work. My curse shall rest on you—the curse of a man of God, and you shall be accursed. Now, if it suits you, you can go up to them at Ardkill and tell them your story. She is waiting to receive her lover. You can go to her, and stab her to the heart at once. Go, sir! Unless you can change all this and alter your heart even as you hear my words, you are unfit to find shelter beneath my roof.'

Having so spoken, waiting to see the effect of his indignation, the priest went out, and got upon his horse, and went away upon his journey.* The young lord knew that he had been insulted, was aware that words had been said to him so severe that one man, in his rank of life, rarely utters them to another; and he had stood the while with his face turned to the wall speechless and sobbing! The priest had gone, telling him to leave the house because his presence disgraced it; and he had made no answer. Yet he was the Earl of Scroope—the thirteenth Earl of Scroope—a man in his own country full of honours. Why had he come there to be called a villain? and why was the world so hard upon him that on hearing himself so called he could only weep like a girl? Had he done worse than other men? Was he not willing to make any retribution for his fault—except by doing that which he had been taught to think would be a greater fault? As he left the house he tried to harden his heart against Kate O'Hara. The priest had lied to him about her father. They must have known that the man was alive. They had caught him among them, and the priest's anger was a part of the net with which they had intended to surround him. The stake for which they had played had been very great. To be Countess of Scroope was indeed a chance worth some risk. Then, as he breasted the hill up towards the burial ground, he tried to strengthen his courage by realizing the magnitude of his own position. He bade himself remember that he was among people who were his inferiors in rank, education, wealth, manners, religion and nationality. He had committed an error. Of course he had been in fault. Did he wish to escape the consequences of his own misdoing? Was not his presence there so soon after the assumption of his family honours sufficient evidence of his generous admission of the claims to which he was subject? Had he not offered to sacrifice himself as no other man would have done? But they were still playing for the high stakes. They were determined that the girl should be Countess of Scroope. He was determined that she should not be Countess of Scroope. He was still willing to sacrifice himself, but his family honours he would not pollute.

And then as he made his way past the burial ground and on towards the cliff there crept over him a feeling as to the girl very different from that reverential love which he had bestowed upon her when she was still pure. He remembered the poorness of her raiment, the meekness of her language, the small range of her ideas. The sweet soft coaxing loving smile, which had once been so dear to him, was infantine and ignoble. She was a plaything for an idle hour, not a woman to be taken out into the world with the high name of Countess of Scroope.

All this was the antagonism in his own heart against the indignant words which the priest had spoken to him. For a moment he was so overcome that he had burst into tears. But not on that account would he be beaten away from his decision. The priest had called him a villain and had threatened and cursed him! As to the villainy he had already made up his mind which way his duty lay. For the threats it did not become him to count them as anything. The curses were the result of the man's barbarous religion. He remembered that he was the Earl of Scroope, and so remembering summoned up his courage as he walked on to the cottage.

CHAPTER X

AT ARDKILL

SHARP EYES had watched for the young lord's approach. As he came near to the cottage the door was opened and Kate O'Hara rushed out to meet him. Though his mind was turned against her—was turned against her as hard and fast as all his false reasonings had been able to make it—he could not but accord to her the reception of a lover. She was in his arms and he could not but press her close to his bosom. Her face was held up to his, and of course he covered it with kisses. She murmured to him sweet warm words of passionate love, and he could not but answer with endearing names. 'I am your own—am I not?' she said as she still clung to him. 'All my own,' he whispered as he tightened his arm round her waist.

Then he asked after Mrs. O'Hara. 'Yes; mother is there. She will be almost as glad to see you as I am. Nobody can be quite so glad. Oh Fred—my darling Fred—am I still to call you Fred?'

'What else, my pet?'

'I was thinking whether I would call you—my Lord.'

'For heaven's sake do not.'

'No. You shall be Fred—my Fred; Fred to me, though all the world besides may call you grand names.' Then again she held up her face to him and pressed the hand that was round her waist closer to her girdle. To have him once more with her—this was to taste all the joys of heaven while she was still on earth.

They entered the sitting-room together and met Mrs. O'Hara close to the door. 'My Lord,' she said, 'you are very welcome back to us. Indeed we need you much. I will not upbraid you as you come to make atonement for your fault. If you will let me I will love you as a son.' As she spoke she held his right hand in both of hers, and then she lifted up her face and kissed his cheek.

He could not stay her words, nor could he refuse the kiss. And yet to him the kiss was as the kiss of Judas, and the words were false words, plotted words, pre-arranged, so that after hearing them there should be no escape for him. But he would escape. He resolved again, even then, that he would escape; but he could not answer her words at the moment. Though Mrs. O'Hara held him by the hand, Kate still hung to his other arm. He could not thrust her away from him. She still clung to him when he released his right hand, and almost lay upon his breast when he seated himself on the sofa. She looked into his eyes for tenderness, and he could not refrain himself from bestowing upon her the happiness. 'Oh, mother,' she said, 'he is so brown—but he is handsomer than ever.' But though he smiled on her, giving back into her eyes her own soft look of love, yet he must tell his tale.

He was still minded that she should have all but the one thing—all if she would take it. She could not be Countess of Scroope; but in any other respect he would pay what penalty might be required for his transgression. But in what words should he explain this to those two women? Mrs. O'Hara had called him by his title and had claimed him as her son. No doubt she had all the right to do so which promises made by himself could give her . . . He had sworn that he would marry the girl, and in point of time had only limited his promise by the old Earl's life. The old Earl was dead, and he stood pledged to the immediate performance of his vow—doubly pledged if he were at all solicitous for the honour of his future bride. But in spite of all promises she should never be Countess of Scroope!

Some tinkling false-tongued phrase as to lover's oaths*had once passed across his memory and had then sufficed to give him a grain of comfort. There was no comfort to be found in it now. He began to tell himself, in spite of his manhood,

that it might have been better for him and for them that he
should have· broken this matter to them by a well-chosen
messenger. But it was too late for that now. He had faced
the priest and had escaped from him with the degradation of
a few tears. Now he was in the presence of the lioness and
her young. The lioness had claimed him as denizen of the
forest; and, would he yield to her, she no doubt would be
very tender to him. But, as he was resolved not to yield, he
began to find that he had been wrong to enter her den. As
he looked at her, knowing that she was at this moment softened by false hopes, he could nevertheless see in her eye
the wrath of the wild animal. How was he to begin to make
his purpose known to them.

'And now you must tell us everything,' said Kate, still en-
circled by his arm.

'What must I tell you?'

'You will give up the regiment at once?'

'I have done so already.'

'But you must not give up Ardkill—must he, mother?'

'He may give it up when he takes you from it, Kate.'

'But he will take you too, mother?'

The lioness at any rate wanted nothing for herself. 'No,
love. I shall remain here among my rocks, and shall be happy
if I hear that you are happy.'

'But you won't part us altogether—will you, Fred?'

'No, love.'

'I knew he wouldn't. And mother may come to your grand
house and creep into some pretty little corner there, where
I can go and visit her, and tell her that she shall always be
my own, own darling mother.'

He felt that he must put a stop to this in some way, though
the doing of it would be very dreadful. Indeed in the doing
of it the whole of his task would consist. But still he shirked it
and used his wit in contriving an answer which might still
deceive without being false in words. 'I think,' said he, 'that
I shall never live at any grand house, as you call it.'

'Not live at Scroope?' asked Mrs. O'Hara.

'I think not. It will hardly suit me.'

'I shall not regret it,' said Kate. 'I care nothing for a grand house. I should only be afraid of it. I know it is dark and sombre, for you have said so. Oh, Fred, any place will be Paradise to me, if I am there with you.'

He felt that every moment of existence so continued was a renewed lie. She was lying in his arms, in her mother's presence, almost as his acknowledged wife. And she was speaking of her future home as being certainly his also. But what could he do? How could he begin to tell the truth? His home should be her home, if she would come to him—not as his wife. That idea of some half-valid morganatic marriage* had again been dissipated by the rough reproaches of the priest, and could only be used as a prelude to his viler proposal. And, though he loved the girl after his fashion, he desired to wound her by no such vile proposal. He did not wish to live a life of sin, if such life might be avoided.* If he made his proposal, it would be but for her sake; or rather that he might show her that he did not wish to cast her aside.* It was by asserting to himself that for her sake he would relinquish his own rank, were that possible, that he attempted to relieve his own conscience. But in the meantime, she was in his arms talking about their joint future home! 'Where do you think of living?' asked Mrs. O'Hara in a tone which shewed plainly the anxiety with which she asked the question.

'Probably abroad,' he said.

'But mother may go with us?' The girl felt that the tension of his arm was relaxed, and she knew that all was not well with him. And if there was ought amiss with him, how much more must it be amiss with her? 'What is it, Fred?' she said. 'There is some secret. Will you not tell it to me?' Then she whispered into his ear words intended for him alone, though her mother heard them. 'If there be a secret you should tell it me now. Think how it is with me. Your words are life and death to me now.' He still held her with loosened arms, but did not answer her. He sat, looking out into the middle of the room with fixed eyes, and he felt that drops of perspiration were on his brow. And he knew that the other woman was glaring at him with the eyes of an injured lioness, though he did not dare to turn his own to her face. 'Fred, tell me; tell me.' And Kate rose up, with her knees upon the sofa, bending over him, gazing into his countenance and imploring him.

'There must be disappointment,' he said; and he did not know the sound of his own voice.

'What disappointment? Speak to me. What disappointment?'

'Disappointment!' shrieked the mother. 'How disappointment? There shall be no disappointment.' Rising from her chair, she hurried across the room, and took her girl from his arms. 'Lord Scroope, tell us what you mean. I say there shall be no disappointment. Sit away from him, Kate, till he has told us what it is.' Then they heard the sound of a horse's foot passing close to the window, and they all knew that it was the priest. 'There is Father Marty,' said Mrs. O'Hara. 'He shall make you tell it.'

'I have already told him.' Lord Scroope as he said this rose and moved towards the door; but he himself was almost unconscious of the movement. Some idea probably crossed his mind that he would meet the priest, but Mrs. O'Hara thought that he intended to escape from them.

She rushed between him and the door and held him with both her hands. 'No; no; you do not leave us in that way, though you were twice an Earl.'

'I am not thinking of leaving you.'

'Mother, you shall not hurt him; you shall not insult him,' said the girl. 'He does not mean to harm me. He is my own, and no one shall touch him.'

'Certainly I will not harm you. Here is Father Marty. Mrs. O'Hara you had better be tranquil. You should remember that you have heard nothing yet of what I would say to you.'

'Whose fault is that? Why do you not speak? Father Marty, what does he mean when he tells my girl that there must be disappointment for her? Does he dare to tell me that he hesitates to make her his wife?'

The priest took the mother by the hand and placed her on the chair in which she usually sat. Then, almost without a word, he led Kate from the room to her own chamber, and bade her wait a minute till he should come back to her. Then he returned to the sitting-room and at once addressed himself to Lord Scroope. 'Have you dared,' he said, 'to tell them what you hardly dared to tell to me?'

'He has dared to tell us nothing,' said Mrs. O'Hara.

'I do not wonder at it. I do not think that any man could say to her that which he told me that he would do.'

'Mrs. O'Hara,' said the young lord, with some return of courage now that the girl had left them, 'that which I told Mr. Marty this morning, I will now tell to you. For your daughter I will do anything that you and she and he may wish —but one thing. I cannot make her Countess of Scroope.'

'You must make her your wife,' said the woman shouting at him.

'I will do so to-morrow if a way can be found by which she shall not become Countess of Scroope.'

'That is, he will marry her without making her his wife,' said the priest. 'He will jump over a broomstick with her and will ask me to help him—so that your feelings and hers may be spared for a week or so. Mrs. O'Hara, he is a villain—a vile, heartless, cowardly reprobate, so low in the scale of humanity that I degrade myself by spaking to him. He calls himself an English peer! Peer to what? Certainly to no one worthy to be called a man!' So speaking, the priest addressed himself to Mrs. O'Hara, but as he spoke his eyes were fixed full on the face of the young lord.

'I will have his heart out of his body,' exclaimed Mrs. O'Hara.

'Heart—he has no heart. You may touch his pocket—or his pride, what he calls his pride, a damnable devilish in-human vanity; or his name—that bugbear of a title by which he trusts to cover his baseness; or his skin, for he is a coward.

Do you see his cheek now? But as for his heart—you cannot get at that.'

'I will get at his life,' said the woman.

'Mr. Marty, you allow yourself a liberty of speech which even your priesthood will not warrant.'

'Lay a hand upon me if you can. There is not blood enough about you to do it. Were it not that the poor child has been wake and too trusting, I would bid her spit on you rather than take you for a husband.' Then he paused, but only for a moment. 'Sir, you must marry her, and there must be an end of it. In no other way can you be allowed to live.'

'Would you murder me?'

'I would crush you like an insect beneath my nail. Murder you! Have you thought what murder is—that there are more ways of murder than one? Have you thought of the life of that young girl who now bears in her womb the fruit of your body? Would you murder her—because she loved you, and trusted you, and gave you all simply because you asked her; and then think of your own life? As the God of Heaven is above me, and sees me now, and the Saviour in whose blood I trust, I would lay down my life this instant, if I could save her from your heartlessness.' So saying he too turned away his face and wept like a child.

After this the priest was gentler in his manner to the young man, and it almost seemed as though the Earl was driven from his decision. He ceased, at any rate, to assert that Kate should never be Countess of Scroope, and allowed both the mother and Father Marty to fall into a state of doubt as to what his last resolve might be. It was decided that he should go down to Ennistimon and sleep upon it. On the morrow he would come up again, and in the meantime he would see Father Marty at the inn. There were many prayers addressed to him both by the mother and the priest, and such arguments used that he had been almost shaken. 'But you will come to-morrow?' said the mother, looking at the priest as she spoke.

'I will certainly come to-morrow.'

'No doubt he will come to-morrow,' said Father Marty—who intended to imply that if Lord Scroope escaped out of Ennistimon without his knowledge, he would be very much surprised.

'Shall I not say a word to Kate?' the Earl asked as he was going.

'Not till you are prepared to tell her that she shall be your wife,' said the priest.

But this was a matter as to which Kate herself had a word to say. When they were in the passage she came out from her room, and again rushed into her lover's arms. 'Oh, Fred, I will go with you anywhere if you will take me.'

'He is to come up to-morrow, Kate,' said her mother.

'He will be here early to-morrow, and everything shall be settled then,' said the priest, trying to assume a happy and contented tone.

'Dearest Kate, I will be here by noon,' said Lord Scroope, returning the girl's caresses.

'And you will not desert me?'

'No, darling, no.' And then he went leaving the priest behind him at the cottage.

Father Marty was to be with him at the inn by eight, and then the whole matter must be again discussed. He felt that he had been very weak, that he had made no use—almost no use at all—of the damning fact of the Captain's existence. He had allowed the priest to talk him down in every argument, and had been actually awed by the girl's mother, and yet he was determined that he would not yield. He felt more strongly than ever, now that he had again seen Kate O'Hara, that it would not be right that such a one as she should be made Countess of Scroope. Not only would she disgrace the place, but she would be unhappy in it, and would shame him. After all the promises that he had made he could not, and he would not, take her to Scroope as his wife. How could she hold up her head before such women as Sophie Mellerby and others like her? It would be known by all his friends that he had been taken in and swindled by low people in the County Clare, and he would be regarded by all around him as one who had absolutely ruined himself. He had positively resolved that she should not be Countess of Scroope, and to that resolution he would adhere. The foul-mouthed priest had called him a coward, but he would be no coward. The mother had said that she would have his life. If there were danger in that respect he must encounter it. As he returned to Ennistimon he again determined that Kate O'Hara should never become Countess of Scroope.

For three hours Father Marty remained with him that night, but did not shake him. He had now become accustomed to the priest's wrath and could endure it. And he thought also that he could now endure the mother. The tears of the girl and her reproaches he still did fear.

'I will do anything that you can dictate short of that,' he said again to Father Marty.

'Anything but the one thing that you have sworn to do?'

'Anything but the one thing that I have sworn not to do.' For he had told the priest of the promises he had made both to his uncle and to his uncle's widow.

'Then,' said the priest, as he crammed his hat on his head, and shook the dust off his feet, 'if I were you I would not go to Ardkill to-morrow if I valued my life.' Nevertheless Father Marty slept at Ennistimon that night, and was prepared to bar the way if any attempt at escape were made.

CHAPTER XI

ON THE CLIFFS

NO ATTEMPT at escape was made. The Earl breakfasted by himself at about nine, and then lighting a cigar, roamed about for a while round the Inn, thinking of the work that was now before him. He saw nothing of Father Marty though he knew that the priest was still in Ennistimon. And he felt that he was watched. They might haved saved themselves that trouble, for he certainly had no intention of breaking his word to them. So he told himself, thinking as he did so, that people such as these could not understand that an Earl of Scroope would not be untrue to his word. And yet since he had been back in County Clare he had almost regretted that he had not broken his faith to them and remained in England. At half-past ten he started on a car, having promised to be at the cottage at noon, and he told his servant that he should certainly leave Ennistimon that day at three. The horse and gig were to be ready for him exactly at that hour.

On this occasion he did not go through Liscannor, but took the other road to the burial ground. There he left his car and slowly walked along the cliffs till he came to the path leading down from them to the cottage. In doing this he went somewhat out of his way, but he had time on his hands and he did not desire to be at the cottage before the hour he had named. It was a hot midsummer day, and there seemed to be hardly a ripple on the waves. The tide was full in, and he sat for a while looking down upon the blue waters. What an ass had he made himself, coming thither in quest of adventures! He began to see now the meaning of such idleness of purpose as that to which he had looked for pleasure and excitement. Even the ocean itself and the very rocks had lost their charm for him. It was all one blaze of blue light, the sky above and the water below, in which there was neither beauty nor variety. How poor had been the life he had chosen! He had spent hour after hour in a comfortless dirty boat, in company with a wretched ignorant creature, in order that he might shoot a few birds and possibly a seal. All the world had been open to him, and yet how miserable had been his ambition! And now he could see no way out of the ruin he had brought upon himself.

When the time had come he rose from his seat and took the path down to the cottage. At the corner of the little patch of garden ground attached to it he met Mrs. O'Hara. Her hat was on her head, and a light shawl was on her shoulders as though she had prepared herself for walking. He immediately asked after Kate. She told him that Kate was within and should see him presently. Would it not be better that they two should go up on the cliffs together, and then say what might be necessary for the mutual understanding of their purposes? 'There should be no talking of all this before Kate,' said Mrs. O'Hara.

'That is true.'

'You can imagine what she must feel if she is told to doubt. Lord Scroope, will you not say at once that there shall be no doubt? You must not ruin my child in return for her love!'

'If there must be ruin I would sooner bear it myself,' said he. And then they walked on without further speech till they had reached a point somewhat to the right, and higher than that on which he had sat before. It had ever been a favourite spot with her, and he had often sat there between the mother and daughter. It was almost the summit of the cliff, but there was yet a higher pitch which screened it from the north, so that the force of the wind was broken. The fall from it was almost precipitous to the ocean, so that the face of the rocks immediately below was not in view; but there was a curve here in the line of the shore, and a little bay in the coast, which exposed to view the whole side of the opposite cliff, so that the varying colours of the rocks might be seen. The two ladies had made a seat upon the turf, by moving the loose stones and levelling the earth around, so that they could sit securely on the very edge. Many many hours had Mrs. O'Hara passed upon the spot, both summer and winter, watching the sunset in the west, and listening to the screams of the birds. 'There are no gulls now,' she said as she seated herself—as though for a moment she had forgotten the great subject which filled her mind.

'No—they never show themselves in weather like this.* They only come when the wind blows. I wonder where they go when the sun shines.'

'They are just the opposite to men and women who only come around you in fine weather. How hot it is!' and she threw her shawl back from her shoulders.

'Yes, indeed. I walked up from the burial ground and I found that it was very hot. Have you seen Father Marty this morning?'

'No. Have you?' she asked the question turning upon him very shortly.

'Not to-day. He was with me till late last night.'

'Well.' He did not answer her. He had nothing to say to her. In fact everything had been said yesterday. If she had questions to ask he would answer them. 'What did you settle last night? When he went from me an hour after you were gone, he said that it was impossible that you should mean to destroy her.'

'God forbid that I should destroy her.'

'He said that—that you were afraid of her father.'

'I am.'

'And of me.'

'No—not of you, Mrs. O'Hara.'

'Listen to me. He said that such a one as you cannot endure the presence of an uneducated and ill-mannered mother-in-law. Do not interrupt me, Lord Scroope. If you will marry her, my girl shall never see my face again; and I will cling to that man and will not leave him for a moment, so that he shall never put his foot near your door. Our name shall never be spoken in your hearing. She shall never even write to me if you think it better that we shall be so separated.'

'It is not that,' he said.

'What is it, then?'

'Oh, Mrs. O'Hara, you do not understand. You—you I could love dearly.'

'I would have you keep all your love for her.'

'I do love her. She is good enough for me. She is too good; and so are you. It is for the family, and not for myself.'

'How will she harm the family?'

'I swore to my uncle that I would not make her Countess of Scroope.'

'And have you not sworn to her again and again that she should be your wife? Do you think that she would have done for you what she has done, had you not so sworn? Lord Scroope, I cannot think that you really mean it.' She put both her hands softly upon his arm and looked up to him imploring his mercy.

He got up from his seat and roamed along the cliff, and she followed him, still imploring. Her tones were soft, and her words were the words of a suppliant. Would he not relent and save her child from wretchedness, from ruin and from death. 'I will keep her with me till I die,' he said.

'But not as your wife?'

'She shall have all attention from me—everything that a woman's heart can desire. 'You two shall never be separated.'

'But not as your wife?'

'I will live where she and you may please. She shall want nothing that my wife would possess.'

'But not as your wife?'

'Not as Countess of Scroope.'

You would have her as your mistress then?' As she asked this question the tone of her voice was altogether altered, and the threatening lion-look had returned to her eyes. They were now near the seat, confronted to each other; and the fury of her bosom, which for a while had been dominated

by the tenderness of the love for her daughter, was again
raging within her. Was it possible that he should be able to
treat them thus—that he should break his word and go from
them scathless, happy, joyous, with all the delights of the
world before him, leaving them crushed into dust beneath his feet. She had been called upon from her youth upwards to bear injustice—but of all injustice surely this
would be the worst. 'As your mistress,' she repeated—'and I
her mother, am to stand by and see it, and know that my girl
is dishonoured! Would your mother have borne that for
your sister? How would it be if your sister were as that girl
is now?

'I have no sister.'

'And therefore you are thus hard-hearted. She shall never
be your harlot—never. I would myself sooner take from her
the life I gave her. You have destroyed her, but she shall
never be a thing so low as that.'

'I will marry her—in a foreign land.'

'And why not here? She is as good as you. Why should she
not bear the name you are so proud of dinning into our ears?
Why should she not be a Countess? Has she ever disgraced
herself? If she is disgraced in your eyes you must be a Devil.'

'It's not that,' he said hoarsely.

'What is it? What has she done that she should be thus
punished? Tell me, man, that she shall be your lawful wife.'
As she said this she caught him roughly by the collar of his
coat and shook him with her arm.

'It cannot be so,' said the Earl of Scroope.

'It cannot be so! But I say it shall—or—or—! What are
you, that she should be in your hands like this? Say that she
shall be your wife, or you shall never live to speak to another
woman.' The peril of his position on the top of the cliff
had not occurred to him—nor did it occur to him now. He
had been there so often that the place gave him no sense of
danger. Nor had that peril—as it was thought afterwards by
those who most closely made inquiry on the matter—ever
occurred to her. She had not brought him there that she

might frighten him with that danger, or that she might avenge herself by the power which it gave her. But now the idea flashed across her maddened mind. 'Miscreant,' she said. And she bore him back to the very edge of the preci-pice.

'You'll have me over the cliff,' he exclaimed hardly even yet putting out his strength against her.

'And so I will, by the help of God. Now think of her! Now think of her! And as she spoke she pressed him backwards towards his fall. He had power enough to bend his knee, and to crouch beneath her grasp on to the loose crumbling soil of the margin of the rocks. He still held her by her cuff and it seemed for a moment as though she must go with him. But, on a sudden, she spurned him with her foot on the breast, the rag of cloth parted in his hand, and the poor wretch tumbled forth alone into eternity.

That was the end of Frederic Neville, Earl of Scroope, and the end, too, of all that poor girl's hopes in this world. When you stretch yourself on the edge of those cliffs and look down over the abyss on the sea below it seems as though the rocks were so absolutely perpendicular, that a stone dropped with an extended hand would fall amidst the waves. But in such measurement the eye deceives itself, for the rocks in truth slant down; and the young man, as he fell, struck them again and again; and at last it was a broken mangled corpse that reached the blue waters below.

Her Kate was at last avenged. The woman stood there in her solitude for some minutes thinking of the thing she had done. The man had injured her—sorely—and she had pun-ished him. He had richly deserved the death which he had received from her hands. In these minutes, as regarded him, there was no remorse. But how should she tell the news to her child? The blow which had thrust him over would, too probably, destroy other life than his. Would it not be better that her girl should so die? What could prolonged life give her that would be worth her having? As for herself—in these first moments of her awe she took no thought of her own danger. It did not occur to her that she might tell how the man had ventured too near the edge and had fallen by mischance. As regarded herself she was proud of the thing she had accomplished; but how should she tell her child that it was done?

She slowly took the path, not to the cottage, but down towards the burial ground and Liscannor, passing the car which was waiting in vain for the young lord. On she walked with rapid step, indifferent to the heat, still proud of what she had done—raging with a maddened pride. How little had they two asked of the world! And then this man had come to them and robbed them of all that little, had spoiled them ruthlessly, cheating them with lies, and then excusing himself by the grandeur of his blood! During that walk it was that she first repeated to herself the words that were ever afterwards on her tongue; An Eye for an Eye. Was not that justice? And, had she not taken the eye herself, would any Court in the world have given it to her? Yes—an eye for an eye! Death in return for ruin! One destruction for another! The punishment had been just. An eye for an eye! Let the Courts of the world now say what they pleased, they could not return to his earldom the man who had plundered and spoiled her child. He had sworn that he would not make her Kate Countess of Scroope! Nor should he make any other woman a Countess!

Rapidly she went down by the burying ground, and into the priest's house. Father Marty was there, and she stalked at once into his presence. 'Ha—Mrs. O'Hara! And where is Lord Scroope?'

'There,' she said, pointing out towards the ocean. 'Under the rocks!'

'He has fallen!'

'I thrust him down with my hands and with my feet.' As she said this, she used her hand and her foot as though she were now using her strength to push the man over the edge. 'Yes, I thrust him down, and he fell splashing into the waves.

I heard it as his body struck the water. He will shoot **no** more of the seagulls now.'

'You do not mean that you have murdered him?'

'You may call it murder if you please, Father Marty! An eye for an eye, Father Marty! It is justice, and I have done it. An Eye for an Eye!'

CHAPTER XII

CONCLUSION

THE STORY of the poor mad woman who still proclaims in
her seclusion the justice of the deed which she did, has now
been told. It may perhaps be well to collect the scattered
ends of the threads of the tale for the benefit of readers who
desire to know the whole of a history.

Mrs. O'Hara never returned to the cottage on the cliffs
after the perpetration of the deed. On the unhappy priest de-
volved the duty of doing whatever must be done. The police
at the neighbouring barracks were told that the young lord
had perished by a fall from the cliffs, and by them search was
made for the body. No real attempt was set on foot to screen
the woman who had done the deed by any concealment of the
facts. She herself was not alive to the necessity of making any
such attempt. 'An eye for an eye!' she said to the head-
constable when the man interrogated her. It soon became
known to all Liscannor, to Ennistimon, to the ladies at
Castle Quin, and to all the barony of Corcomroe that Mrs.
O'Hara had thrust the Earl of Stroope over the cliffs of
Moher, and that she was now detained at the house of Father
Marty in the custody of a policeman. Before the day was
over it was declared also that she was mad—and that her
daughter was dying.

The deed which the woman had done and the death of
the young lord were both terrible to Father Marty; but there
was a duty thrown upon him more awful to his mind even
than these. Kate O'Hara, when her mother appeared at the
priest's house, had been alone at the cottage. By degrees
Father Marty learned from the wretched woman something
of the circumstances of that morning's work. Kate had not

seen her lover that day, but had been left in the cottage while her mother went out to meet the man, and if possible to persuade him to do her child justice. The priest understood that she would be waiting for them or more probably searching for them on the cliffs. He got upon his horse and rode up the hill with a heavy heart. What should he tell her; and how should he tell it?

Before he reached the cottage she came running down the hillside to him. 'Father Marty, where is mother? Where is Mr. Neville? You know. I see that you know. Where are they?' He got off his horse and put his arm round her body and seated her beside himself on the rising bank by the wayside. 'Why don't you speak?' she said.

'I cannot speak,' he murmured. 'I cannot tell you.'

'Is he—dead?' He only buried his face in his hands. 'She has killed him! Mother—mother!' Then, with one loud long wailing shriek, she fell upon the ground.

Not for a month after that did she know anything of what happened around her. But yet it seemed that during that time her mind had not been altogether vacant, for when she awoke to self-consciousness, she knew at least that her lover was dead. She had been taken into Ennistimon and there, under the priest's care, had been tended with infinite solicitude; but almost with a hope on his part that nature might give way and that she might die. Overwhelmed as she was with sorrows past and to come would it not be better for her that she should go hence and be no more seen? But as Death cannot be barred from the door when he knocks at it, so neither can he be made to come as a guest when summoned. She still lived, though life had so little to offer to her.

But Mrs. O'Hara never saw her child again. With passionate entreaties she begged of the police that her girl might be brought to her, that she might be allowed if it were only to see her face or to touch her hand. Her entreaties to the priest, who was constant in his attendance upon her in the prison to which she was removed from his house, were piteous—almost heartbreaking. But the poor girl, though she was meek,

silent, and almost apathetic in her tranquillity, could not even
bear the mention of her mother's name. Her mother had destroyed the father of the child that was to be born to her,
her lover, her hero, her god; and in her remembrance of
the man who had betrayed her, she learned to execrate the
mother who had sacrificed everything—her very reason—in
avenging the wrongs of her child!

Mrs. O'Hara was taken away from the priest's house to the
County Gaol, but was then in a condition of acknowledged
insanity. That she had committed the murder no one who
heard the story doubted, but of her guilt there was no evidence whatever beyond the random confession of a maniac.
No detailed confession was ever made by her. 'An eye for an
eye,' she would say when interrogated—Is not that justice?
A tooth for a tooth!' Though she was for a while detained in
prison it was impossible to prosecute her—even with a view
to an acquittal on the ground of insanity; and while the
question was under discussion among the lawyers, provision
for her care and maintenance came from another source.

As also it did for the poor girl. For a while everything was
done for her under the care of Father Marty—but there was
another Earl of Scroope in the world, and as soon as the
story was known to him and the circumstances had been made
clear, he came forward to offer on behalf of the family whatever assistance might now avail them anything. As months
rolled on the time of Kate O'Hara's further probation came,
but Fate spared her the burden and despair of a living infant. It was at last thought better that she should go to her
father and live in France with him, reprobate though the
man was. The priest offered to find a home for her in his
own house at Liscannor; but as he said himself, he was an
old man, and one who when he went would leave no home
behind him. And then it was felt that the close vicinity of
the spot on which her lover had perished would produce a
continued melancholy that might crush her spirits utterly.
Captain O'Hara therefore was desired to come and fetch his
child—and he did so, with many protestations of virtue for

the future. If actual pecuniary comfort can conduce to virtue in such a man, a chance was given him. The Earl of Scroope was only too liberal in the settlement he made. But the settlement was on the daughter and not the father; and it is possible therefore that some gentle restraint may have served to keep him out of the deep abyss of wickedness.

The effects of the tragedy on the coast of Clare spread beyond Ireland, and drove another woman to the verge of insanity. When the Countess of Scroope heard the story, she shut herself up at Scroope and would see no one but her own servants. When the succeeding Earl came to the house which was now his own, she refused to admit him into her presence, and declined even a renewed visit from Miss Mellerby who at that time had returned to her father's roof. At last the clergyman of Scroope prevailed, and to him she unburdened her soul—acknowledging, with an energy that went perhaps beyond the truth, the sin of her own conduct in producing the catastrophe which had occurred. 'I knew that he had wronged her, and yet I bade him not to make her his wife.' That was the gist of her confession and she declared that the young man's blood would be on her hands till she died. A small cottage was prepared for her on the estate, and there she lived in absolute seclusion till death relieved her from her sorrows.

And she lived not only in seclusion, but in solitude almost to her death. It was not till four years after the occurrences which have been here related that John fourteenth Earl of Scroope brought a bride home to Scroope Manor. The reader need hardly be told that that bride was Sophie Mellerby. When the young Countess came to live at the Manor the old Countess admitted her visits and at last found some consolation in her friend's company. But it lasted not long, and then she was taken away and buried beside her lord in the chancel of the parish church.

When it was at last decided that the law should not interfere at all as to the personal custody of the poor maniac who had sacrificed everything to avenge her daughter, the Earl of

Scroope selected for her comfort the asylum in which she still continues to justify from morning to night, and, alas, often all the night long, the terrible deed of which she is ever thinking. 'An eye for an eye,' she says to the woman who watches her.

'Oh, yes, ma'am; certainly.'

'An eye for an eye, and a tooth for a tooth!* Is it not so? An eye for an eye!'

THE END

EXPLANATORY NOTES

xxxvii *in the west of England*: in the manuscript, Trollope first wrote, then crossed out, 'Ireland'.

xxxviii *who was its head*: the manuscript and first edition continue: 'Others there, who were cognisant of the conditions of the various patients, only knew that from quarter to quarter the charges for this poor lady's custody were defrayed by the Earl of Scroope.' This was removed in later editions presumably because the fact that there are three Earls of Scroope in the subsequent narrative might confuse the reader.

4 *Marlbro' school*: i.e. Marlborough College, in Wiltshire. The school was started in its modern form in 1843. (Trollope's spelling, incidentally, was normal in the nineteenth century.) Marlborough was originally set up for the sons of clergy, and in Trollope's day a large number of scholarships were reserved for them. The fact that Mr Greenmarsh's sons are evidently dayboys who walk to the school suggests that in describing the Scroope family and their estate, Trollope had the Seymours in mind (that noble family's old mansion formed the central building of the new school). See also note to p. 81.

5 *from out of the streets*: Trollope initially wrote, and crossed out, 'London streets' deciding almost immediately to make the abandoned woman French.

10 *the Duke's hounds*: the eighth Duke of Beaufort (1824–99) whose seat was Stoke Park, near Bristol. The Duke (who also served in the Hussars in his youth) presided over one of the country's most famous hunts and was, in Trollope's day, the greatest authority on the sport in England.

when he talked of Scotland: Trollope originally wrote 'the moors' and crossed it out. What he meant was 'grouse moors' but evidently thought that 'Scotland', where Britain's best

"No." She sighed. "But since I'm practically an only child, what do I know? And you know *Asian* mothers—"

"I already apologized for that crack." Ben sat down. "I'm a good guy. Don't be a brat."

"I'm not a brat. Well, maybe a little bit of a brat." She waved her hand in the air. "As long as you're here, maybe you can make yourself useful." She showed him a problem. "I have to find the area underneath the curve as it expands at the rate of the function of time."

"Just integrate."

"I'm not allowed to integrate. I have to do it with simple geometry at any given point."

"Oh."

"Yeah. *Oh.*"

Ben smiled. She had fight in her and that was good. He picked up the pencil and started dividing the figure into workable polygons. It took sixteen divisions. "This should do it."

She looked at the work. "Maybe you should enter the contest instead of me."

"Maybe you should just tell your mom you don't want to do it."

"Maybe you should just leave me alone." She was muttering under her breath but loud enough so he could hear it. "Can't a girl get a little solitude?"

"Lilly, I know my sister and Griff are wrapped up in

one another and she's probably being a little inconsiderate. But she isn't going anywhere and neither is your friendship."

Lilly shrugged. "I don't care, Ben. And what's wrong with being alone, Mr. Asocial extraordinaire? Or should I call you Mr. Popular now?"

"That's a very interesting point. Because now that I'm with the in-crowd, I'm still a fish with a bicycle. It's weird sitting with Ro now that she's back with JD."

"So just get back with Ro," she blurted out. "You obviously still love her. She obviously still loves you. You should try a little forgiveness."

"This is none of your business, but I'm gonna tell you anyway." Ben waited until he got her attention. She finally put her pencil down. "Ro and I are magnets. If the proper poles are aligned, it's instant attraction. But if you align them the wrong way, the poles repel and no amount of forcing them together will change the physics." He erased his sectioning of the math problem and pointed to the smudged paper. "Let me see you solve this without integration."

Her dark eyes shifted from Ben's to the paper in front of her. She stared at the figure in front of her, at first copying his erased lines and arcs, but then she slowly started improving on the solution, her brainpower clicking in as she chewed on the eraser of the pencil, her hair once again hiding her face. Gently, he tucked an errant tress behind her ear. It was an intimate gesture for a guy to do to a fourteen—well, almost fifteen-year-old girl. She looked up and blushed.

He pointed to the paper. "Go on."

She straightened up and cleared her throat. She was a beautiful girl and would be an even more beautiful woman. She glowed, especially when she did something that engaged her. Looking at her was like seeing a memory of his lost innocence.

When Ben was thirteen, he vaguely remembered "liking" Lisa Holloway. And she "liked him back." And that's what it was for the better part of a year: shy smiles and awkward conversations. And he had some kind of recollection of planning a movie date with her. But then Ellen went missing and around the same time Lisa's parents got divorced. The date never materialized, and shortly afterward, Lisa became enamored of the dark side of everything. She went through a slew of older boyfriends, became truant, and was almost kicked out of high school. But then some unseen force reeled her back in during their senior year, although she still dressed in silly costumes. Ben wondered how it would have been if they had gotten together. Would she have cheated on him like Ro did?

Possibly . . . probably. Once bitten, twice shy.

Ben looked over Lilly's shoulder. She had produced an elegant solution. "Very good. Way better than mine."

"You started me off in the right direction."

"Then I'll take the credit." He stood up. "I'm going back to Albuquerque. You have my e-mail. If you need any more help, don't be afraid to use it."

"Thanks." This time her smile was real. "I'm not mad at you, Ben. I could never be mad at you."

"How about Haley?"

"I love Haley. She's my sister and best friend all rolled into one. It's my problem, not anything she and Griff are doing . . . other than being in love. I'll deal." She shrugged. "Honestly, I don't mind the solitude. I do need to study for state finals. I have a fighting chance of winning, but I'll get wiped out in regionals. I can't compete against all those Texas private schools. My mom will be disappointed but she'll get over it. She's working on other things besides math competitions to get me into the Ivies."

"You know you're a lock for the Ivies. You're half Indian and I found out from Ro that it means that you have underrepresented minority status. Plus, you come from a state that's underrepresented in the Ivies. And you are a master silversmith, judging from my recent Christmas gift. And as an aside, you happen to be brilliant."

Her face was filled with electricity. She closed her

workbook, got up, stuffed her pages into her backpack, and slung it over her shoulder. "Maybe I'll go say hi to Haley."

"Maybe you should."

She smiled and left, skipping down the hallway.

Chapter 4

As the time approached, he was getting nervous. Not nervous excitement, but actually nervous, and that gave him pause. He had a wife. He had a child. He had a life beyond this and he certainly wasn't getting any younger. Maybe . . . just maybe it was time to quit.

Each time he had done something, he'd sworn it was the last time. If he kept going, he'd eventually get caught. Something would trip him up and he knew the police had his DNA. If he kept his nose clean, he'd be fine, and that wasn't a hard thing to do because when he wasn't abducting, raping, and murdering girls, he was living a fairly conventional life. When he didn't travel, he worked regular hours. Kara wasn't a church-goer, but she was civic-minded. She was involved with the school, volunteered at the library, and ran its book club. She did Pilates with her friends. She spent too much on ridiculous things: designer clothes and handbags, tennis lessons, and absurdly expensive shoes for their son. Not to mention the cost of private school tuition. It seemed that the school was raising its fees every six months. And if he even mentioned putting Ivan in public school, she'd chew his head off. No wonder he was tense.

No wonder he took out his frustration on others.

He hated to admit it but he was more like his dad than he thought. And Kara was more like his mother than he wanted to believe. Not that his parents had been abusive, but his mother was demanding.

Dad had been an engineer. He provided for the family and never raised his voice in anger. As far as he knew, Dad had never been unfaithful because Dad never had a friend. Nor did he seem to care about having friends. He also never cared about material possessions. He drove an old Buick and dressed every day in short-sleeved white shirts, black slacks, and a clip-on tie. Dad had lived life as a loner, sequestering himself behind a locked door whenever his wife started to nag. But even when he was physically around, it was as if he wasn't there. He read a lot—biographies and nonfic-

tion. If they talked at all, it was always about a book. So maybe Dad did teach him something—the importance of being well read and well educated.

School had been his solace. It wasn't the best school, but he was the best. It afforded him the luxury of going to a top university on someone else's dime. But at least his education hadn't gone to waste. He used it, he plied it, he availed himself of all the perks it gave him.

And there were perks. Free travel, free rentals, and lots of open roads. He had always loved to drive. It calmed him down, it gave him perspective, and in the end, it gave him the greatest thing of all—not freedom, although that was important.

What the open road gave him was access to prey.

June answered the door. Her hair was pulled back in a tight ponytail, yanking on her temples, giving her a temporary facelift. Not that she needed it. Her skin was smooth, with high cheekbones and dark eyes that always looked suspicious and a bit angry. "Yes?"

She wasn't even bothering with the bare minimum of civility. It wasn't her fault. Math heads were different. Ben said, "Hi, June, I was wondering if George was around."

"Why do you want to see George?"

"I've got a couple of questions for him." He zipped up his parka.

June realized it was cold outside. "Come in."

"Thank you."

June closed the door. "You want some tea, Ben? You look cold."

"No, I'm fine, thank you."

"Suit yourself." She disappeared and the house went silent. Ben suspected that Lilly was in her room and didn't feel like talking. Okay by him. He didn't feel like facing another emotional female. June could be very cool, but it wasn't because she was mean. She was a controlled person and probably somewhat controlling. She didn't come across as a tiger mom, but from Lilly, he knew that she had expectations. And that wasn't a bad thing. Without pressure, a tire went flat.

He thought about Haley, slipping into adolescence, replete with boyfriend and social status. Lilly was becoming more and more withdrawn, and he was helpless to stop it. But she would blossom eventually. Lilly had always had an inner strength.

George came out. "Hey, Ben."

"Feel like having some pie?" Ben asked.

June made a face. "Pie? What pie? You already ate."

"There's always room for pie," George said.

"You had two pieces of cake, George. If you eat any more desserts, you'll go into a diabetic coma."

"My insulin is fine, thank you very much, and don't look at me like that. You made the cake."

"That doesn't mean you have to eat it all." June hit his belly. "You're getting fat."

Instead of being angry, George just laughed. "You need me to pick up anything while I'm out, June?"

"I can't believe you're really going out for pie."

"Yes, I am really going out for pie."

"Then pick me up a piece of anything sugarless." Again she patted his stomach. "Some of us have self-control. Others just succumb." She shook her head and disappeared from view.

George was still smiling. "I take it you want to drive?"

"Absolutely."

They were three blocks away from George's house when he spoke. "What is it?"

Ben pulled over to the curb and liberated the ten images he'd found through Google from his backpack. "Do you know any of these people?"

George shuffled the faces. "Who are they?"

"They might be associated with the labs."

He continued to study the images. "Vicksburg, just what did you hack into?"

"I didn't hack into anything." George gave him a sour look. Ben said, "Honest. You can check the hard drive of my computer."

"Hard drives come and hard drives go. How'd you get these names?"

"That's a complicated question."

The old man rubbed his eyes and returned half the stack. "I don't know these." He had handed Ben back images of four scientists and Jason Fillmore, the security analyst. "They may be associated with the labs, but I've never had any dealings with them."

"And the others?"

"I've worked with Percy Sellers, Robert Yin, Kim Dok Park, and Stu Greenberg. I've known Yin and Greenberg for years. They're plasma physicists. Yin is from Fermi, Stu is from Lawrence Livermore."

Ben sat up. "What do you know about Stu Greenberg?"

"He's around sixty. A senior scientist and a brilliant, brilliant guy. June and I had dinner with his wife and him about a year ago when we were in the Bay Area. They're lovely people." He laughed. "I guarantee he isn't who you're looking for."

"You never know what's inside a person's head."

"Stu's head is stuffed with remarkable and ingenious ideas. There's no room for anything else. He also has osteoarthritis and has had several surgeries. I believe he walks with a cane."

Rule *him* out. Ben said, "What about the others?"

"Dr. Park is a biochemist, Sellers's specialty is medical radiology." He pointed to Kevin Barnes. "This guy. He's not a scientist, he's a lawyer."

"I know that." Ben's heart took off and he forced himself to speak slowly. "What kind of a lawyer is he?"

"Immigration. I've dealt with him a few times because he needed character references from some of the scientists in the labs for visa extensions or permanent residence." George handed him back the remaining stack. "How'd you get these names, Ben?"

"I can't tell you."

"I know you did something illegal. It's going to come back to bite you on the butt. Get rid of your hard drive."

"I didn't do anything illegal, but I can switch drives if you think I should."

"Do it. Now tell me what's going on. Why are you narrowing down your searches to the faces you showed me?"

Ben was prepared for the question and for his answer. "I got these names by looking at scientists who go to a lot of conventions."

"All scientists travel a lot. We present our research.

We're always exchanging information with one another. There are hundreds of scientists. How did you narrow it down to these men? And why the lawyer? And stop bullshitting me. It's pissing me off."

Ben cleared his throat. "These particular men have traveled more than once to Los Alamos and over extended periods of time. They've also traveled between the other labs."

"How'd you find that out? I know you don't have the skills to hack into a national laboratory. So you did it in some other way. Are you hacking into the airlines?"

That would have been a good idea, Ben thought. He said, "I can't tell you, George."

"Ben, you have to stop what you're doing right now! I know you didn't get this information from a Google search."

"That is true. But that doesn't mean the feds are coming after me."

George sized him up. "Why the lawyer?"

"He's been to Los Alamos at least six times in the last four years."

"How do you know that?"

"I can't tell you."

"But you didn't do anything illegal." A pause. "Did you pay someone to do something illegal?"

"No, I did not."

George shook his head. "Let's go get some pie."

Ben restarted the motor and put the car into gear. "Tell me about the immigration lawyer, Kevin Barnes. There's not much on him in the search engines. He doesn't have a Facebook or LinkedIn page. He's kind of a cipher."

"Not all of us waste our time being social on the Internet."

"You'd think he'd want some kind of professional page just for business."

"Maybe he has enough clients without going digital."

"Is he a government employee?"

"He works for the labs, but I don't know if he's on the government payroll or he's someone Uncle Sam has outsourced."

"If he works for the government, it would make sense that he wouldn't advertise anything." George didn't comment. "Do you know him?"

"I mind my own business, Ben. I focus on my own work and that's why the lab keeps old guys like me around."

"What are you? Like fifty?"

"None of your damn business." George thought a moment. "Barnes must be doing a good job. He's been around for a while."

"How old is he?"

"In his forties."

"Any personal impressions of the guy?"

George was silent, but he was thinking about the question. "He's weird."

Ben opened and closed his mouth. "He's *weird*?"

"Scientists are not the most social people in the world. We like what we do and what we do requires solitude. I'm always thinking in numbers. So is June. But you don't expect odd behavior from a lawyer. Most of the other lawyers I've met are slick."

"I see you've never met my dad or grandpa." George laughed and then Ben said, "What kind of weird are we talking about?"

"Let me backtrack. If Barnes was a mathematician, I wouldn't have used the adjective 'weird.' It's just you think of a lawyer as being aggressive or forward. From the very few dealings I've had with him, he didn't seem like a lawyerly type. He certainly didn't dress like a lawyer, but that could be because he works around scientists so much he's adopted the dress."

Ben was silent.

George said, "Like I said, he must be competent, otherwise he wouldn't have lasted this long."

"You're defending him."

"I can see you're jumping to conclusions and it's my fault. I stoked the fires. Do me a favor and I won't rat you out to Shanks."

Ben was stunned. If he hadn't been driving, he would have gotten out of the car and slammed the door. "You're thinking of ratting me out?"

"It's my only weapon to get you to stop doing stupid things."

"I *trusted* you."

"Actually, Ben, it had nothing to do with trust. You came to me for *information,* and assumed I wouldn't say anything. And I haven't. But that will change if you keep hacking into systems."

"I haven't hacked into anything." Ben was furious, but George seemed oblivious to his anger. He was in his own world.

Finally, he said, "Let me poke around . . . see what I can dig up." He turned to Ben. "Stop doing what you're doing."

"I'm not doing anything illegal." Ben pulled into a parking space at the Pie House.

"Well, you didn't get these names by picking them out of a hat." George patted his stomach. "All this talking to you isn't good for my waistline. June is right. I'm getting pudgy. Let's go see if we can find something sugarless."

He pulled on the door handle and Ben followed him to the shop. There were quite a few sugarless fruit pies. George chose cherry and Ben went for the sugarless apple.

George said, "You're as skinny as a stork. Why are you buying a sugarless pie?"

Ben said nothing. He didn't know why. Perhaps it was because "sugarless" was an apt description for the better portion of the last three years.

Chapter 5

Whoa. Finally! I know where I've seen Kevin Barnes." Ro stopped typing on her computer, looked up, and waited for Ben to continue. "The night of the equinox . . . while I waited for you to finish up at the Jackson . . ." He hit the image. "He bumped into my shoulder in the parking lot."

Ro got up from Ben's bed. "Are you sure?"

"Positive. I even asked you about him. You were going to look him up the next day." No response. "Do you remember this at all?"

"I do remember your asking." A deep sigh. "I'm sorry, Ben, I forgot to do it."

"'S'right."

"No, it's not all right. I could have gotten his room

key when he turned it in and we could have tested it for DNA."

"Dorothy, if he's the one, I guarantee you he didn't turn in his room key." Ben continued to stare at the picture. "The guy was heavier . . . older." He closed his eyes, trying to revive a memory. "He was smelly . . . no, not smelly. Sweaty . . . the kind of musty odor you get when you're nervous or you've done physical labor."

Ro was already going down the list of hotel guests on that date. "There's no Kevin Barnes."

"Can I see the list of patrons?"

"Of course." She handed it to him.

Quickly, Ben's eyes scanned down the names. "Nike B. Ravens is an anagram of Kevin Barnes."

"Nike's a girl's name."

"Did you say anything to him when you checked him in?"

"I didn't check him in, Vicks, but I would have noticed the name."

"Well, maybe your coworkers aren't as astute. And if I were looking for a sexual psychopath, I wouldn't be looking for a girl. It's a good dodge."

"Then why use an anagram of the name when he's used his real name before?"

"Because if you're using aliases, it's good not to stray too far from your real name. Otherwise you forget who you are. As for using his true name, the guy is keeping it real once in a while. Probably to confuse the police if they were looking." Immediately he fished out the names that were registered at the Jackson around the time of Ellen's abduction. "Holy shit! Here it is! Karen Bevins." He regarded Ro. "He's using girls' names. I've got to tell George Tafoya—"

"Ben, you've got to tell Shanks."

"And say what, Ro? That you've been hacking the Jackson Lodge registration database?"

"I haven't hacked into anything."

"Not technically, but all this information was illegally obtained. You'll get into trouble. It'll ruin your life. We can't tell Shanks unless we can come across it in some other way."

"You bumped into him on the night of the equinox, right?"

"How would I know his name? He didn't introduce himself." Ben was frantic. "Let me think . . . I should talk to George Tafoya . . . wait. I can't call him."

"Why not?"

"Because his phones are bugged."

"He told you that his phones are bugged?"

"Yes, and probably his house and his car. Maybe even his cell phone."

"Is Lilly's phone bugged?"

"I haven't the slightest idea. But that's a very good plan." He called up Haley. "Hi, is Lilly with you? Do you know where she is? No, never mind, it's not important." He looked at Ro. "Lilly is at the library. Maybe I'll go down there."

"Can you at least wait until JD arrives here so you don't abandon me since I'm helping you out? Unless you want me to leave."

"No, no, no. You're right. Let's see what else I can find out about this dude or Karen Bevins or Nike B. Ravens." Ben paused. "You try to figure out how we can get this name to Shanks without having you arrested."

She said, "How about . . . I noticed him . . . that he was coming in very late on the equinox . . . and it got me thinking. So I looked him up—"

"No, you can't look him up." He thought a moment. "You would have to know who he is . . . his name. And like you said, you didn't check him in. Furthermore, he was registered under a different name."

She blew out air. "Fiction writing was never my forte. I'm a terrible liar."

"I know that firsthand."

She threw a pillow at him. That was her usual behavior when she became frustrated with him. When the doorbell rang, Ben checked his watch and Ro checked hers. She said, "JD isn't due for another hour."

"Be back in a moment." Ben opened the front door. Lisa Holloway was wearing her usual black dress with an irregular hemline and combat boots. She had dyed a purple streak in her hair. Her nails were painted black. Her eyes were ringed with dark eyeliner and her lips were bright blue.

"Hey." He stepped outside rather than invite her in. "What's up?"

"Not much."

"You okay?"

"Yeah, I'm fine." Her eyes furrowed. "Do I look not okay?"

"No, you look . . . like you always do. What's up?"

"I was just wondering if you'd like . . . to get a cup of coffee or something."

"Ro's here. We're working on some stuff together. Then I'm going down to Albuquerque. I have work tomorrow and classes at UNM."

"Okay." She dragged her toe across the porch. "Some other time."

"Sure."

"You wanna go to prom together?" she blurted out.

When Ben didn't answer right away, she crossed her arms over her chest. "Don't feel obligated. Josh Martin has already asked me but . . . I'd rather go with you."

"I'm taking Ro."

Her face was confused. "So who's JD taking?"

"He's taking Ro too."

"You're *both* taking her?"

"Yeah, that was the deal when she started dating JD again, that we'd both take her to prom."

She nodded. "Two dates . . ." She nodded again. "Sweet." She shrugged and started to head to her car. "See you."

Ben held up his hand. "Wait." She turned and looked at him. Ben beckoned her with a crooked finger and she stepped back up onto the porch. He said, "Sure, let's go to prom together. But I'm not going to any after party or any hotel or—"

"You don't have to fuck me, okay?" Her eyes were hard and sad at the same time. "I know you're not interested, okay? Especially after . . ." She averted her glance. "You know."

"Yeah, that was kind of unfortunate."

She faced him. "I'll pay for the limo, your tux rental, and the corsage. Just show up, okay?"

"Don't waste money on a limo. I'll drive. And I'll pay for my own tux rental and I'll pay for the corsage.

I was gonna do that anyway, so it's fine. What kind of corsage do you want? Pin-on or wrist?"

"I don't know. I haven't bought my dress." Her voice softened. "Any color you like?"

"Color? You mean you're not wearing black?"

"I'm not going Goth, okay." She rolled her eyes. "I don't want my kids looking at my prom picture and saying, 'God, Mom, what were you thinking?' I've already said that enough times to myself."

"You and me both." He smiled at her and she smiled back. "There's nothing wrong with a signature look."

"If you don't care, I will probably wear black . . . but not Goth black. There you have it. Are you really going down to Albuquerque, Vicks, or are you trying to get rid of me?"

"No, I'm really going back to Albuquerque. High school is over for me and I've got a major topology test—" He heard muffled footsteps and turned around.

Ro had come outside. "If this was going to take a while, the least you could have done was let me know."

"I'm going." Lisa waved. "Bye."

"Bye." Ben turned to Ro. "Sorry." He walked back into the house and to his room.

She followed. "What was that all about?"

"She asked me to prom."

"Lisa did?"

"Yep."

"What'd you say?"

"I said okay."

Ro glared at him. "Aren't you taking me?"

"JD's taking you."

"I thought both of you were taking me."

"That's what I told her at first . . . that I was taking you and JD was taking you as well. And then I realized how stupid that sounded, so I said I'd take her."

"Thank you very much." She was angry.

"Ro, c'mon. Do you really need two dates? JD's your boyfriend."

"That wasn't my choice."

"Well, it wasn't my choice either."

"Well then, who the hell's choice was it if it wasn't yours?"

"No, no, no." He turned to her. "Don't lay that on me. *You* made the choice."

"I told you I was drunk. I didn't even want to do it."

"But you did it anyway."

"What do you *want* from me, Ben? I said I was sorry about a million times. Obviously, everything I did for you . . ." She took up a pile of paper and threw it at him. "All this shit . . . all my sleepless nights illegally poking into computers, wiggling my ass for disgusting businessmen, working myself to the bone just wasn't enough to atone for my sin! I don't know who's stupider. You or me."

She picked up her purse. Ben caught her by the arm. "Why are we fighting about this? It's ancient history."

"You're an asshole, that's why we're fighting."

"I'm an asshole? *I'm* an asshole?"

"Yes, you're an asshole. You promised to take me to prom and now you're taking Lisa." She turned on him. "She *fucked* him too, you know."

"I know, Ro, I was there." But Lisa wasn't his girlfriend at the time. He didn't point that out. Ro was already too worked up. He let go of her arm. "What are you getting so upset about anyway? In a couple of months, you'll be gone for good and I'll just be a small footnote in your life."

There were tears in her eyes. "Well, then *excuse me* for thinking that maybe as my first love and my first lover, you saw me as something more than a footnote."

"No, no, no. You got it wrong. I said that *I'd* be the footnote in *your* life."

"But what you really mean is *I'm* the footnote in *your* life."

"No, I meant what I said. That *I'm* the footnote in *your* life." He covered his face with his hands. "Can we stop fighting, please?"

"Why are you taking Lisa Holloway to prom? Everyone will just snicker behind your back."

"As long as it's behind my back, what do I care?"

She hit him. "She's a slut."

"She's not a slut. She's just . . . friendly."

"I can't believe you're going with her."

"I'm going with her because she asked me. And because I felt I owed her one from a long time ago. And because you have a real boyfriend and a legitimate date without me. And to tell you the truth, I'm tired of being second in line behind that idiot. I don't enjoy being his straight man and I don't enjoy sitting with you guys and I'm really not going to enjoy sharing you with him at prom. I'd rather go with Lisa, as . . . *friendly* as she is . . . because I'd rather have a whole date with someone I like than half a date with someone I love. I don't want to hang out with your crowd, I don't want to stand in the shadows while you dance with him, and I don't want to be someone I'm not! What I want to do is find the monster that killed my sister so he doesn't do it again. And if it's Kevin Barnes, I'm going to find him and rip him to shreds. And if it *is* him, you've helped me out like nobody else. I love you dearly. You know that. Can we please just stop fighting!"

She looked at him. "I love you too."

Ben smiled. "You know we broke up at the perfect time: before our love could turn into contempt. How good is that?" She didn't answer. He tried out a weak smile. "I'd still love to dance with you."

She remained silent.

"Please, let's get along. It's like two months before you leave River Remez for good." He looked at her and then looked down. "Ro, if it isn't Kevin Barnes, I need your help. You know all the codes and the abbreviations and everything. And if it is Kevin Barnes, you're my eyes and ears at the Jackson. I know that's being selfish, but I can't do this without you, Dorothy."

He had expected her to take his head off. Instead she said, "Even if I hated you—which I do sometimes—I would continue to help you, Vicks. I realize we're dealing with a greater issue than stupid teenage love."

"I knew there was a reason I loved you so much."

"Don't sweet-talk me. I am so . . . pissed at you." She hit his chest. "You threw me over."

"Do you really want me to call Lisa up and tell her I changed my mind?"

"Yes."

"Well . . . I'm not going to do it." She hit him again. "I'd still love to dance with you." No response. "Please?"

She folded her arms across her chest. "I want a prom picture with both you and JD, one on either arm."

"Fine."

"*Two* pictures with both of you. Then I want one alone with you and one alone with JD."

"Whatever you want."

"And I want two corsages, Vicks, one from you and one from JD."

"Done."

"And the one you get me better be bigger and more expensive than Lisa's."

"You are ruthless."

"Yes or no."

"Yes."

"Go with Lisa." Ro waved him away. "I give you my permission."

"Thank you very much, Your Grace."

She looked at the mess in his room. "I can't concentrate anymore." She thought a moment. "I don't have all the registers from the Lodge in Albuquerque—just for some selected days. Let me hunt around a little more."

"No way, no way!" Ben shook his head. "George knows that I obtained the names illegally, but he doesn't know how. We've gotten out of this alive. If you get caught, it'll ruin your life. Please promise me you'll stop."

"Why should I? You don't promise me anything. And even when you do, you renege."

Ben took her in his arms. "It's bad enough that you're still working at the Jackson. You really shouldn't press your luck. You should quit."

"Vicks, if he's onto us—and just maybe he is—he knows what I'm doing there, so . . . maybe it's better that I'm there." She pulled away but kept her arms around his waist. "You know what that crime show says: keep your friends close but your enemies closer."

"Actually, I think Sun Tzu said it in *The Art of War.*" Ro was silent. He said, "I looked it up."

This time she broke away. "I'm hungry. To make up for your sins with Lisa, you may take me out for dinner. You can clean all this up later."

"I should clean it up now. I have to get back to Albuquerque. I've got a big test tomorrow and . . ." Her look made him wilt. "I thought you were going out to the movies with JD."

"We'll catch a later show. And if he gets pissed, I don't care." She was glaring at him, daring Ben to contravene her orders.

Pick your battles, Vicks.

He said, "Where would you like to go eat?"

She picked up her purse, flipped her hair, and tossed him a look over her shoulder. "Kiki's is just fine. Although if you should opt for something better, I wouldn't say no."

Chapter 6

*W*eapons weren't his thing. If it couldn't be done with the hands and the brain, it was a cop-out. *Still, there was something thrilling about holding a killing machine in one's hands. Something so powerful, so strong, yet so compact. Weapons were the ultimate combination of art and mechanics.*

He knew he was taking chances. It wasn't that he wanted to be caught—that would be disastrous—but it seemed that over the years he'd needed more and more to keep up the thrill. It was like sex. The act was fine, but sometimes the foreplay was even finer. And as he got older, it seemed he needed more and more foreplay, hence the weapon. It produced a thrill, holding something potentially lethal. It gave him power.

And that's what it was all about really.
Power.

"Stop squirming." Laura Vicksburg put down her phone and adjusted the camera attachment. "If you stop moving, I can finish quicker."

"I'm not moving on purpose. The tux doesn't fit." Ben was annoyed. "Why are you even doing this? There's a photographer at the prom. I promise I'll order extra photos."

"He or she will not have a mother's love. And stop glaring at me. It wrinkles your forehead."

His father, hiding behind a newspaper, was laughing. Haley put up her hand. "Wait." She straightened his clip-on bow tie. "I can't wait for my prom."

"Want to go instead of me?"

She ignored him. "We have morp in two weeks, but it's not the real thing. It's, like, homemade decorations and weak punch. And we're not allowed to wear strapless or minidresses or gowns. That doesn't leave too much in the fashion department."

"You've hit on something," Ben told her. "Prom is really all about chick fashion."

"You just realized this?" Haley patted his cheek. "You really do look handsome, Ben. You clean up very nicely." She backed away and his mother took another picture.

"Can I go now?"

"Where are your six friends, Grumpy?" Laura waved her hand. "Yes, you can go now!"

"If I had my choice, I'd rather take you or Haley or even Lilly . . ." He looked at his sister. "Where *is* Lilly? I never see her anymore."

"We're going shopping together this weekend for dresses." She looked peevish. "She's going with Ezra to morp. She has a life without me."

"I'm just used to seeing her, that's all. No need to get snippy."

She stuck her tongue out. Laura's eyes had turned wet. "Promise me you'll *try* to have a good time. I know this isn't your thing, Ben, but you won't regret it. It's what . . . you should be doing at your age."

Ben nodded, knowing exactly what she meant.

This first time should have been Ellen's moment. He was a piss-poor substitute, but he was all that Mom had.

Lisa decided to do a modern twist on her usual garb. The dress was black lace but had an underlay of gold. Supersexy and contemporary and very short, like a baby-doll nightgown. Her long legs were encased in seamed stockings held up by a garter belt that peeked from under the micromini hemline. Her shoes were ultrahigh heels and they glittered like the stars.

Ben complimented her. She complimented him. Her mom took pictures while criticizing Lisa's dress (too short), her makeup (too much), and her hair ("you should have done an updo"). Had she been Ben's mother, he would have taken drugs too. On the ride over, Lisa was sulky and silent.

"You look great," he told her.

"Thanks." She was fiddling with her hair, which had been tied in an elaborate braid. "My mom's a bitch." Her eyes were hot. "God, I can't wait to get out of there 'cause it's either I leave or I'll commit homicide."

"If she meant to embarrass you in front of me, it didn't work. You look superhot." He parked the car and helped her out. "Take it from me as a guy: you couldn't do any better."

"Should I have done an updo?"

"You should let your hair loose. Guys love long hair."

She began to undo the braid, her carefully designed coif falling over her shoulders in waves.

"Perfect," Ben said. "Should we go in or would you like more time?"

"I suppose we have to take the plunge."

Ben took her hand and together they walked inside. The gym wasn't exactly transformed—it still smelled of sweat and dirty socks—but it did look festive. There was bunting and banners, there was colored lighting, and there was a disco ball. Onionfeather—the band—was dressed in retro suits with skinny ties: white jackets and black cuffed pants that showed their socks. There was a full-sized buffet table with desserts and punch and coffee. The dance floor was half filled with couples gyrating to terrible music. The guys were in rented tuxes and the girls glittered like tinsel. Ro was holding court near the coffee urn. JD had his arm around her waist. Ben sighed. The girl was an absolute knockout, wearing something long and slinky, with silver and gold threaded through it and a big slit that revealed a good deal of leg. The entire dress showed off that incredible body.

"Balenciaga," Lisa said.

"Pardon?"

"Ro's gown. It's designer. You can't even get the label here. She must have bought it in New York or something. There's one thing I can guarantee you: it must have cost a fortune."

"Waste of money."

"Not on her." She turned to him. "You know she told us like the first week she came here that she was approached at sixteen to model for the Katy's Intimates junior catalog. That's lingerie, in case you didn't know."

"Oh, I know all about Katy's Intimates."

"I bet you do. But her mother didn't want her to do it and then they moved to River Remez. She's still bitter."

Ben laughed. "I . . . did not know that."

Lisa smoothed out her dress. "Some of us just have to be happy with the H&M catalog." She raised her eyebrows and began pointing around the room. "That dress, that dress, and that dress. They're from Forever 21. That one's H&M. Those two are Ross Dress for Less—"

"Lisa, you look hot. Let's get our picture taken."

They waited in line for the photographer, and when they were done, Ro took Ben's arm, glaring at Lisa while smiling at the same time. It was a feat. "My turn."

"Ro—"

"Go ahead," Lisa said. "You two look nice together."

"Thank you," Ben said.

Ro's whisper was more of a growl. "I hate it when she's nice. It means she's planning on fucking you."

"Will you please stop?"

"She looks like a blow-up doll."

"You're nasty."

She said, "Where's my corsage?"

"In the trunk of my car."

"Go get it."

"I agreed to buy you a corsage that was bigger and better than Lisa's. Which I did. But I didn't agree to give it to you so you can embarrass her, which you've already done by looking so hot and classy. So you win, Ro. Can we all try to get through this civilly?"

"As long as you agree that I've won."

When it was their turn in front of the camera, Ro turned on the fake wattage. When it was over, Ben said, "It's no contest, okay." He kissed her cheek and broke away, trying to find Lisa. But before he could get to her, JD cornered him near the popcorn machine.

"Man, you don't even have to take anything off," he said. "Just slam her against the wall and shove it in."

"You have the soul of a poet."

"Get it while you can, dude. Girls get hot when you look fly."

"More penguin than fly." Ben checked his watch. "How much longer?"

"Around three hours."

"What the fuck do you do here for three hours?" When JD pulled out a plastic bag filled with dried vegetable material, Ben laughed. "Put it away, dude. You need that scholarship."

"They wouldn't have the balls. I'm the finest thing that ever happened to this dump." He looked around. "I lit up before I got here. Makes the food taste a hell of a lot better. The rest is for the after party. Believe me, Vicks, I've got a lot of tricks up my sleeve." He smiled. "Are you gonna be there?"

"Not a chance."

"She's practically flashing you." He furrowed his brow. "Tell me righteous, dude. Are you gay?"

"Seriously? You're really asking me that?"

"Then why turn down pussy? Even if it's not number one pussy, it's still pussy. And she's good, dude. She's certainly had enough experience."

Ro was walking toward them. Ben smiled. "Have fun at the after party, but wear a condom. Oh right. I forgot. You carry those in your car just in case you want to fuck other guys' girlfriends."

"Vicks—"

"I'm just sayin' . . ." He walked away and went looking for Lisa. She was happily chatting away with Shannon Stork. But she was perceptive. She took one look at his face and excused herself. "You okay?"

"Just bored."

"Do you wanna dance?"

The music was off-key and earsplittingly loud. "Sure, let's dance."

"We can sit it out, Vicks." She smiled. "Or we can sit out the entire prom."

"No, no . . ." Ben sighed. "I'm just being a jerk. Sure, let's dance."

"Vicks, we can go. All I wanted to do was show up with you. This isn't my idea of fun either."

"But they haven't crowned the king and queen yet."

"Be still, my beating heart."

Ben laughed. "Do you really want to leave?"

"I wouldn't mind some air. It's kind of stuffy in here."

"Sounds like a good idea." Ben paused. "No tokes or snorts or pills, please. I'd like to graduate."

"I'm clean and sober."

"Perfect." When they got outside, Lisa took his hand and started pulling him away from the gym. "Uh, what's going on?"

"Just come."

They crossed the quad, walking to the front of the school toward the administration building. "Where are we going exactly?"

"It's a surprise."

"I don't like surprises."

"Well, you'll like this one." She took out a key and opened a door to the administration building. It was deserted and dark, but since there were windows to the parking lot, some lamppost illumination and starlight streamed through.

"Uh, how'd you get a key to the school?"

"I used to have a lot of friends with iffy ethics. Is it my fault that the stupid school never bothers to change their locks? C'mon!" She led him to the stairwell, and in near blackness, they climbed to the second floor.

Ben had a sneaking suspicion where they were going. And when she turned right and left and zigzagged across the hallway, he knew. She stopped right in front of the math supply closet, took out another key, and opened the door.

"Lisa, c'mon."

"You c'mon."

"No, this isn't right."

"What are you afraid of?" She pushed him into the closet and closed the door. "I know you're not gay."

"This isn't right. It isn't respectful."

"I know. It's very sleazy." She started fooling around with his tux's zipper. "Listen to me, Vicks. I'm not doing it for you. I'm doing it for *me*. It's important to me to give you a different memory—other than the *unfortunate* one, okay?"

"Lisa, you don't have to do this."

"But I want to do this." She dropped to her knees, and in a matter of seconds, Ben's "No, Lisas" became "Oh, Lisas." It didn't take long. Five minutes later they were in the dark hallway, alone, silent, and awkward. Instead of feeling relaxed, Ben was tense.

Lisa, on the other hand, was very matter-of-fact. "I need a bathroom. Wait here, okay?"

"I'm not going anywhere." He was on the floor, sitting against the hallway lockers. When she came out of the bathroom, she called his name.

"Over here."

She looked around and sat by his side. Her breath had turned minty. She massaged his neck. "You okay?"

"I'm fine." He was suddenly annoyed. "I'm not a virgin, by the way."

"I know."

He turned to face her. "You girls yak with one another?"

"All the time."

He was quiet. Then he said, "What'd she say about me?"

"That you were big." She patted his knee. "She wasn't lying."

Ben's face went hot. "What else did she say?"

"Who listened? Ro was rubbing my nose in it because she knew I liked you. Well, the joke's on her now." Her eyes held his. "And don't look so scared. I don't expect anything from you, Vicks. All I wanted was bragging rights about nailing you."

"Shouldn't I be bragging about nailing you?"

"Nah." She waved him off. "I'm easy. But you're not." She leaned her head against his shoulder. "I used to feel bad about it—being so . . . slutty. But then I found out that Shannon was not only doing JD when she was going with Weekly, she was also doing Salinez because she found out that Chelsea was doing Weekly. And then, of course, Ro did JD while she was going with you." She shrugged. "I mean, if everyone is a skank, why be embarrassed?"

"Your logic is impeccable." Ben regarded her face. He lifted her chin and kissed her minty mouth. They started making out. The order of events was backward, but it felt nice, so what the hell.

Lisa purred. "She also said you were a good kisser."

"Just good?"

"Well, maybe she said great." Her hands drifted to his crotch. "You want to do it? I mean *really* do it?"

"No, no. This is fine."

"Your words don't match other parts of you."

"That is true enough." Ben pulled her hand away and kissed it very gallantly. "No, Lisa, although you are gorgeous and I am still horny, I will be a gentleman and pass. So remember this moment. There are nice guys in this world."

"You're a dying breed."

"That is probably true but I'm not dead yet."

"Some other time, then, but don't wait too long." She sat up. "In a month I'm gone. My dad can't wait for me to come and my mom can't wait for me to go."

"Where's your dad? Houston?"

"Dallas. But I'll be dorming at school. You should think about UT, Vicks. It's not that far from New Mexico and Austin's a great city."

"Yeah, it *is* a great city."

"Why are you hanging around here? You should be at MIT or Harvard."

Ben just laughed.

"What's so funny?"

"Nothing at all." He took her hand and pulled her up. "Wanna go back to the gym before we both get expelled?"

"Nah, let's just get out of here for good. I'm hungry."

"Sure. Where do you want to go?"

"Kiki's. I want to run into Ro and let her know we were up to something."

"You girls are very catty."

"Vicks, that's what prom is all about. Looking hot so the boys leer at you and the girls give you dirty looks. In that regard, I consider my senior prom a big, big success." She kissed his nose. "And it's all because of you."

"I am happy to have fulfilled your revenge fantasy."

"It wasn't a fantasy, dude. I really did blow you."

Now, how do you respond to that? Ben laughed again. Hand in hand, they walked out of the school and toward the parking lot, which was filled to capacity. It took him a while to remember where he parked. When he found his wheels—the car had been blocked by a limo—he pulled out his keys. But as he got closer, Ben stopped dead and yanked Lisa back. Blood rushed to his brain. His heart was going haywire. "My tires are flat."

Lisa dropped his hand. "Wow."

Ben walked around the car. "All four of them."

"Someone pranked you—let the air out."

He knelt down and looked at the squashed rubber. "This isn't a prank. They're cut."

"What?" There was fear in Lisa's voice. "You mean like someone slashed them?"

"Yep. All four of them." It kicked something into his brain. He felt his head go light. "Oh my *God!*"

He took off toward the gym, did a U-turn, grabbed Lisa's hand, and dragged her with him.

"What's wrong, Ben?"

He didn't answer. Couldn't get the words out. When they arrived back inside, Ben scanned the room, but he couldn't find Ro anywhere. He did see JD talking to Weekly and Salinez and ran up to them. "Where's Ro?"

"Hey, Vicks." He was smirking. "How'd it go?"

Apparently, his dread wasn't apparent in the dim light. Ben grabbed JD's shoulders tightly and enunciated very clearly. "Where? Is? *Ro?*"

"In the bathroom or something. What the hell is wrong with you?"

Ben raced to the girls' bathroom and flung open the door. There were a few gasps and a few screams, but he saw her in a corner, talking to Shannon while putting on lipstick. Before he could get a word out, she was glaring at him. "Where've *you* been?"

Ben hugged her tightly. Lisa followed him inside. He was about to offer an explanation, but horror seized his insides. He began to shake as he took out his cell and called home. Thank God for speed dial. He was sure that he couldn't have come up with his own phone number right then. Haley answered and relief washed over him.

"Where are you?" he shouted into his cell.

"Uh, you called me," she answered.

"Are Mom and Dad home?" Someone asked him to leave the girls' bathroom. Ben took the conversation outside. To Haley, he said, "Mom and Dad are home, right?"

"Yeah."

"Lock the doors and don't open them, no matter what." He heard a voice in the background. "Who's there with you? Griff?"

"For your information, it happens to be Lilly. We're looking at dresses in the fashion mags for morp."

"Lilly's there? Even better. She's sleeping over, right?"

"Yeah, of course." A pause. "Ben, what's going on?"

"I'll call you later." He hung up.

Ro emerged from the bathroom. "What is wrong with you?"

Lisa said, "Someone slashed all the tires on his car."

Ro gasped and brought her hand to her mouth. The color drained from her face. "Slashed? Like with a knife?"

"Yeah, like with a knife."

Lisa said, "Ben, you need to call the police."

Ro said, "Ben, call Shanks."

Call Shanks.

His thoughts exactly.

Chapter 7

There seemed to be as many people around the car as there were inside the gym. A gaggle of girls had gathered in a circle, worried looks on their faces, rubbing each other's arms to keep warm and yakking away with one another. The guys chose to say nothing. Instead they walked around the car, examining the situation, nodding as if they were having profound thoughts. Ben distanced himself and made phone calls. Within a half hour, he had a genuine powwow: Mom and Dad, Haley and Lilly, two squad cars from the River Remez Police, the girls' and boys' VPs, and the school's illustrious, fuming principal, Mr. Beltran.

"Whoever did this is not going to get away with it!" He too was orbiting the car, eyeing the damage. "Not on my watch." He looked at Ben. "You have no idea who did this?"

Of course he had an idea. But he wasn't going to share it. "It was probably random, sir." *Liar, liar, pants on fire.* "I'm never in school anymore. Who'd even care about me enough to piss me off?"

"Well, we'll see about that."

As soon as Ben saw Sam's car pull up, he knew he was in for it. Shanks stormed through the yellow crime-scene ribbon and surveyed the compromised car. After a thorough look at four flat pieces of rubber, he said, "What do you know about this?"

Ben threw up his hands.

"Don't give me that bullshit."

"Talk about blaming the victim."

Within moments, Shanks was surrounded by Ben's parents and the principal. Mr. Beltran said, "Do you have any ideas about this, Detective?"

Sam eyed Ben. "We haven't had a recent rash of slashed tires, if that's what you're asking."

"I'm talking about punks and vandalism. What about those idiots who spray-painted the Palace of the Governors?"

Ben turned so his hot face wouldn't be noticed. Sam said, "That was Santa Fe. I'll check with them. Maybe they've had some similar property crimes."

"You do that," Beltran said. "One of the things that makes this community great is the people. If we let them down, what do we have?"

"A bunch of let-down people," Sam answered.

Beltran bristled. "Just find out who did this. It would be a sad state of affairs if the school district had to resort to policing their own property. Let's not waste any more taxpayer dollars, okay?"

Shanks kept his expression flat. "I'll give it my full attention, Mr. Beltran. Last thing I want to do is deal with angry parents."

After the principal left, Sam pulled Ben away from the crowd, and none too gently. "Okay, Vicksburg, spit it out!"

His parents followed. Dad wagged a finger in Sam's face. "Why are you coming down on him, Sam?"

"Because he knows something about this."

"I don't know anything!" Ben insisted. "Why are you yelling at me?"

"I'm not yelling, I'm asking. And I'm asking because you've been up to something. You know how I know that? Because you're always up to something."

"Why are you connecting this juvenile act to what I do?"

"First of all, it's not juvenile. Juveniles spray-paint. Juveniles key cars. Juveniles even steal cars. But juveniles generally do not slash the tires of random people. And if they do, they don't slash all four tires. To do that, it takes muscle. It takes time. It takes deliberation. Are you honestly telling me that this was random?"

"I'm honestly telling you I don't know who did it. I parked my car and went into my prom. When I came out with my date, my tires were cut."

Sam softened his tone. "The uniformed guys handle things like this. I'm a detective. You called me down and you must have had a reason for it."

"Actually, Ro called you."

"I thought you didn't see her anymore."

Mom said, "She's been at the house for the last few weekends. They're doing something that has to do with my daughter's incident."

His own mother was ratting him out. Ben looked around. The crowds had thinned a bit. Haley and Lilly were talking to Ro.

Sam said, "Should I be talking to Ro? Was she your prom date?"

"No. I went with Lisa Holloway." Ben pointed her out. "She was with me the entire time. Maybe she saw something that I didn't."

Shanks eyed him suspiciously. "You stay here while I get a statement from her."

As soon as Shanks left, William Vicksburg turned

to his son. "What the hell is going on? And be honest because this is scaring the crap out of your mother and me."

Mom burst into tears. "What have you gotten yourself into?" She was openly sobbing. "I haven't suffered enough?" She stepped away and tried to get control of her emotions.

"Ben, does this have something to do with Ellen's murder?" Dad didn't wait for an answer. "You and I are going to have a serious talk."

"Dad, I will tell you everything I know." Ben lowered his voice. "But do you honestly think that this is the work of a sexual psychopath? Slashing tires? C'mon!"

"Do you *know* who did it, Ben? And I don't mean who slashed the tires."

Ben knew he meant Ellen's murder. He was beginning to feel very uncomfortable sitting on the information, no matter how it was obtained. He was going to have to tell Shanks everything. And that was going to happen tonight. "No, I don't know who did it, Dad. If I did, he'd be dead. But I have some ideas."

His mother butted in. "What are you talking about? Ellen?"

"Nothing," Dad said.

"Now you're keeping information from me too?"

Dad weighed his options. "He has ideas about Ellen."

"About who did it?"

Shanks was still talking to Lisa. Ben said, "I don't know who did it. That's the truth. I have lists of names . . . of who it might be."

"And you haven't told the police?"

Ben regarded his parents—his father and then his mother. "I got the names illegally."

His father licked his lips. "What did you hack into?"

"I didn't hack into anything. And if you ask how I got the names, I won't tell you. I'd rather go to jail—"

"Ben, stop being so damn melodramatic. That's Haley's department."

"It has to be Ro," Mom said.

"No, it's not Ro," Ben lied. "She has nothing to do with anything. She was just there for moral support. I didn't hack into a computer system. But what I did wasn't legal."

Laura shook her head. She wasn't buying it. "Where does Ro work, Ben?"

"Ro works?" Dad said.

"She does. She got a job when they broke up. And now they're seeing each other again. They lock the door to his room. They're in there for hours. And I know it's not about sex."

Ben's face went hot. "Mom!"

"What do you do with her, Benjamin?"

"Nothing."

"Six hours every Sunday, you two sit around and do nothing?" Mom was furious. "Where does she work?"

"She's a waitress."

"*Where?*"

"Ask her."

"I'm asking *you!*"

"She works as a cocktail waitress at the Jackson Lodge."

Mom turned pale. "You hacked into the database at the Lodge and found *his* name in the registry. And you haven't told us? You haven't told *Shanks?*"

"I don't know his name, Mom! If I knew his name, I'd tell the world!"

"Who are you even looking for? Why do you think he stayed at the Jackson?"

"It's a long story, Mom."

"Then it looks like we're staying up all night."

Ro had materialized. Ben's mother stared at her. "Lovely dress, Dorothy."

"Thank you." Ro's eyes were on the ground. Then they looked up at Ben's dad. "I'm eighteen now. And I'm hiring you as my lawyer."

"Done," Dad said. "What's going on?"

She kept her voice very low. "I overheard you, Mrs.

Vicksburg, and you're right. We do have information from the database. We don't know exactly who we're after, but we have ideas." She turned to her ad hoc lawyer. "I didn't hack into anything, Mr. Vicksburg, because I was allowed to use the computer system when I worked the desk. But I went beyond my duties as a desk clerk. I've been printing out data: names of guests starting from roughly six months before Ellen's murder and going forward. Ben and I have been going through the names one by one by one."

Ben's father was stunned, half in disbelief and half in admiration. He said, "What makes you think that the son of a bitch stayed at the Jackson?"

"Los Alamos puts its scientists up there because the Jackson gives them discounts. If there's a scientific meeting that involves more than a couple of people, the lab uses that hotel. There are smaller hotels in the city of Los Alamos, but the Jackson's the biggest that has a deal with the lab. And since I couldn't take a job everywhere, I picked the Jackson."

"You think he's a *scientist*?" Ben's mom asked.

"Ben thinks it's someone with an affiliation with Los Alamos." Ro turned to Ben. "You haven't said anything to your parents?"

Laura was throwing her son dagger eyes. "What . . . is . . . going . . . on?"

Ben took a deep breath and let it out. "Over the years I've been looking at things that were similar to Ellen's case."

"I know that, Benjamin. What have you found out?"

"Similar cases that have taken place near other national labs—geographically. I have told Shanks. He knows my theories. But I have no idea if I'm right or wrong."

Dad said, "How did you find out that this hotel deals with Los Alamos National Lab, Ro?"

"It was very high tech, Mr. Vicksburg. I made phone calls."

Ben said, "It's my fault. She did it for me."

Ro's face remained impassive. "No, Ben, I did it for Ellen."

Laura's eyes overflowed. "Oh dear."

Ben said, "Dorothy, I'm so sorry I got you involved in this mess."

"I'm not sorry at all. But I don't know where to go from here." She smiled at Ben's parents. "I'm open to ideas."

"Well, it's clear you can't tell anyone without compromising yourself. Furthermore, even if you did tell Shanks, he couldn't use the information because you obtained everything in an illegal manner. Ellen's case is still open. We could suggest that Shanks go back and get a subpoena for all hotel registries at the time of the incident. If you figured out some names, he should be able to do the same thing."

"Why didn't he go to the hotels when it first happened?" Laura asked.

"He did, Mom. He investigated every single hotel in the area and looked at the names of people staying in town around the dates of the abduction. But he didn't know he was looking for someone associated with the labs. Also, it could be that the perpetrator's name wasn't on any local guest list."

"Or not in a form he recognized," Ro said. When Ben glared at her, she said, "The jig is up, Vicks. Just come clean."

"*What?*" Ben's dad asked.

"It's possible he could be using aliases."

"Like women's names," Ro added.

"You know this for a fact?"

"No. That's why we're looking at the data from way before and way after the incident. Shanks can't get access to that data without reasonable cause."

"I want to see your files."

"Bad idea, Dad. You work for the government. No one would benefit from you being disbarred."

"Cut the sarcastic shit."

"William, please."

Dad said, "Stop trying to stonewall me, Ben, I don't like it."

Shanks was done interviewing Lisa and was walking toward them. Ben said, "We'll continue this conversation at home."

"What conversation?" Shanks asked.

"Sorry, Sam," William said. "Privileged information."

"What the hell is going on?" When no one answered him, Shanks took Ben's arm. "You're coming to the police station. We're going to have a nice talk, Vicksburg."

Ro said, "He won't admit to anything there because everything is recorded. But he may tell you stuff off the record if he knows what's good for him." She smiled widely. "How about if we go to Ben's house? I'll make a nice pot of coffee and Mr. Vicksburg—the senior Mr. Vicksburg—can tell us what to say and what not to say so no one ends up in prison."

"Just go home, Dorothy," Ben told her.

"Uh, let me think about that, Vicks." She was still smiling. "No."

William turned to Laura. "Go home with the girls and I'll meet you there." To Shanks: "The kids and I will come with you."

"Dad, I have to wait for the tow truck."

Shanks said, "I'm impounding your car."

"Sam, I have finals. I have to get to Albuquerque."

"Take a bus." He shook his head. "Ro's right. The kids aren't going to talk at the police station. Mind if we use your house? That way I can also see what they've been up to."

Dad put his hand on Sam's shoulder. His eyes grew watery. "Just like old times."

Ben said, "You don't have to get involved, Dad. I'll tell him everything."

"Maybe *I* need your father, hotshot." Ro punched his shoulder. "God, I hate you right now."

"Someone slashed my tires and you hate me?"

"You ruined homecoming by cutting out on my special day, you ruined the winter dance by not going with me, you ruined the spring fling with your slugfest, and now you've ruined prom. Grad night is my last hurrah in this godforsaken place. It would be nice to have one event here that you didn't spoil."

"I don't believe you," Ben said. "Let me remind you that I saved you from a very bad Christmas Eve and I took you out to a very nice and expensive dinner for your eighteenth birthday. I also gave you exactly what you wanted as far as birthday presents are concerned. And while we're talking about people spoiling things, guess who spoiled Valentine's Day?"

She yanked him aside and whispered furiously, "That was awful. You know how remorseful I feel. Everything I've done has been for you because I feel so ashamed. You call yourself a nice guy. *Stop* it already."

Her eyes were pure wrath. "I won't mention it again," he told her. "Just go home, Dorothy. I'm trying to save your ass."

"My ass doesn't need to be saved by you. And I'd like to remind you that you weren't making any headway in your 'research' until I helped you out."

"All true, but what does that have to do with anything? I don't want you involved!"

"Too late for that because I'm already involved!" She hit him again. Abruptly, she burst into tears. "Now JD is taking Lisa to the after party and he's probably going to bang her."

"No, he won't." He took her in his arms and kissed the top of her updo. "I promise you he won't."

"Why?" Her eyes were ablaze. "Did you already bang her?" She pushed him away. "Where the hell were you two for so long?"

"I didn't bang anyone. All I'm saying is that JD is loyal to you—"

Shanks broke in. "Sorry to interrupt your little lovers' spat, but there's work to do. Shall we go?"

Ro dried her eyes on the back of her hand. Then she slipped her arm under Ben's. "Let's."

Chapter 8

Stewing and feeling violated, Ben said nothing as his father sifted through his carefully constructed files, reading what had been meant for his eyes only. He squirmed and sighed, showing his resentment, but his father was uninterested. Ro held his hand and glanced at him in understanding. At long last, they had reached a truce.

Shanks, in the meantime, had gone back to the police station to get his own files and they were waiting for him to return. He hadn't looked at any of the purloined material because as of yet, no one could figure out how to legitimize the files. Shanks knew that if he nabbed someone, he'd have to justify his investigation under oath. The saving grace was the life that all this activity had injected into Ellen's stalled case.

William Vicksburg shook his head. "The police can't use any of this stuff. It was obtained illegally. Who are you two looking at?"

Ro pulled out Kevin Barnes. "Him."

William began to read the data. "He's not a scientist, he's a lawyer."

Ben said, "An immigration lawyer who works for the government getting visas for its foreign scientists. He was at the hotel on the vernal equinox, Dad. I bumped into him. He smelled dirty—wet and musty—like he had just done some gardening. And this was at midnight."

The man paled. "Oh Jesus! We've got to tell Shanks." He wagged a finger. "Son, you are not going to start searching the mountains again."

"No one in the area was reported missing, Dad. I don't think he did anything, although I don't know that for sure."

"So why was he here?"

"Reliving something maybe."

"If this is the guy, I'll kill him myself."

"You'll have to stand in line," Ben said.

Ro said, "No one is killing anyone." She turned to Ben. "How'd you find out he was an immigration lawyer? I couldn't find anything on him except that he's a lawyer."

"George Tafoya told me. He knows him from the lab. He thinks he's weird."

"George Tafoya thinks he's weird?" William said. *"How?"*

"Nothing he can put his finger on."

"Get me George's phone number."

"You can't call him up," Ben said. "His phone lines might be bugged."

"Bugged?" his dad said. "He told you his phone is bugged?"

"He thinks his entire house is bugged. Whenever we talk, we go out and drive in my car. I told him everything I know about Barnes. He told me to back off and let him poke around."

Dad said, "Exactly how many people have you enlisted for help?"

"Just Ro and George. And of course, Shanks."

"What else haven't you told me?"

"We think that Kevin Barnes is using aliases," Ro said. "Specifically girls' names so he's less likely to be noticed."

"How did he check into the Jackson using girls' names?"

"We don't question things like that, Mr. Vicksburg. It would be bad for business. We just smile and do the job."

The doorbell rang. Ben got up. "Must be Sam."

"I'll get it," William said. "Don't tell Shanks any of this. I've got to think of a way to make this all legal. And certainly do not tell your mother any of it. I'll tell her in my own time."

Ben looked at Ro, who said, "The jig is up, Vicksburg. You've been officially outed."

"I'm happy to let the experts do their thing."

"I wonder if that's true." She stood. "Shall we join the others?"

"I suppose we have to."

Ben's parents were having a powwow with Sam. Haley and Lilly were on the couch in their pj's, looking very scared. Shanks noticed it. "Might be better if the girls weren't here."

"I want to know what's going on," Haley said.

"Fair enough," Shanks said. "After all your family and you have been through, you deserve to know. But first let me find out what's going on, okay, Haley?"

Lilly tugged on Haley's sleeve. "They'll tell us when they know. Let's continue on with our search for the perfect morp dress."

Laura was still fuming at her son. Ben asked her, "You okay?"

"I have a terrible headache."

"I'll get you an Advil."

"What I have can't be remedied with pills."

"Mom, I'm really sorry. But at least we're getting somewhere."

There were tears in her eyes. "Ben, our family has suffered horribly. In a single stroke, our lives were in shambles. A wound can't heal if you keep picking at the scab."

"I know. I'm sorry for all the misery I've caused you."

"You didn't cause me misery. *He* did. I just want some of the pieces put back together, even if the clay pot is badly damaged. Is that too much to ask?"

Ben's dad said, "Laura, why don't you lie down? I'll catch you up in the morning."

"What do they need you for, William?"

"One of us should be here. And Ro hired me as her lawyer. I have to stay."

"So now you're involved?"

"Do I have a choice?"

"No, I suppose not." She walked out of the living room.

Shanks was already sitting at the dining room table, booting up his laptop. Ro said, "I'll make some coffee."

"I'll make it." Ben got up and started a pot. Ro was

smoothing out her prom dress. It was then that Ben realized he was still wearing his rented tux. "I'm going to change. You want some sweats, Ro?"

"That would be nice."

They went into his room and he tossed her sweatpants and a sweatshirt. "You've contacted your parents?"

"It was all I could do to keep my father from charging down here."

"He's welcome to join the gang."

"Not on your life, Vicks. I also told them I'm sleeping over."

"Why? I'll take you home."

"I'm not going out in the dark and neither should you. We don't know where he is. Can I take a shower in your bathroom? My makeup is itching my skin."

"Of course. You can sleep here. I'll use Ellen's room."

"That's okay with your mom?"

"Sometimes I sleep there. Sometimes my mom sleeps there. You know . . ."

"Yes, unfortunately, I do know."

When they came back into the living room, Ro had changed into sloppy clothes, her wet hair in a towel. Without the dress and the makeup, she looked about fifteen, especially with the sprinkling of freckles across her nose.

Shanks was staring at his laptop screen. He opened up a briefcase. "Over my many, many years as a cop, I've learned to only ask questions if I want to hear the answers. Right now, I'm interested in getting information without landing either one of you in jail."

"Same goal here," William said. "I'm here as Ro's lawyer."

"That's fine." Sam took out a piece of paper. "Here is a list of scientists that I have been looking into since Ben told me his theory about the killer being involved in the labs." He handed a sheet of paper to Ro and the same one to Ben. "Anyone strike your fancy?"

Ben scanned the names. Some were the people whom Ro and he had been looking into. "How'd you get these names, Sam?"

He gave Ben a long, hard look. "What do you think I do with my time, Vicksburg? Throw paper airplanes across the squad room?"

"Don't take offense. You know me by now."

"Yes, I do." He tousled the kid's hair, an act that was more appropriate three years ago. In Sam's eyes, Ben was still a kid. "These names were chosen because the men on this list have been to three out of the four labs for business. We've investigated all of them, and by our thinking, none of them seems like a suitable candidate." He paused. "But some of them do travel a lot. If you're brilliant and happen to be a sexual psychopath, it's a good deal for you. Talk to me about these names."

Ben took a pencil and checked the names he recognized. To Ro, he said, "How are you doing?"

She made a face. "I remember looking up Peter Chesney and Neville Armand . . . Paul Arons . . . Michael Swit. I know we eliminated them, Vicks, but I don't remember why."

"Neither do I, but if these guys were at all of the labs—"

"Three out of four," Sam corrected.

"At the times of the murders—"

"I didn't say anything about that," Sam said. "What I told you was that they've been to at least three of the four labs."

"Katie Doogan?" William asked.

"Katie Doogan and two others—Julia Rehnquist, who was buried near Lawrence Livermore, and Jamey Moore, who was found not too far from Oak Ridge National Lab."

The elder Vicksburg turned to his son. "You knew

about other murders?" When Ben didn't say anything, he said, "I suppose you've been doing this because I haven't done anything. My bad."

"No, that's not it." Ben put his hand on his father's shoulder. "I started doing it so you didn't have to."

"Can we stick to the case here?" Shanks said. "So you've seen some of these names."

"Some . . ." Ro was still looking at the names. "Why don't you like them as the bad guy?"

"Age, rank, and serial number. They don't fit the profile. Their time is accounted for. They didn't rack up a lot of miles on their rentals. They didn't stay in strange places and they don't have a lot of unexplained absences. Milton Ortiz and Derek Whitecliffe agree. What do you think?"

Ben said, "If you don't like them, that's good enough for me."

"A rare compliment." Sam took the list away. "So . . . for the time being, we'll put them on the bottom." He turned to the kids. "Don't either of you tell me more than I'm asking for."

"Just phrase your questions in a yes-or-no format," William said.

"Do you two have lists of more names?"

"Yes."

"Obviously, I'd like to look at your research, Ben, but if you've gotten the names in a suspicious manner, I can't. Should I look at your names?"

"No."

"That's what I thought. Did you hack into anything, Ben?"

He looked at his father, who said, "No, he did not."

Sam said, "When Ben told me his lab theories, I called up hotels in the area that deal with Los Alamos. Then I got a court order that allowed me to look at the guest lists from those hotels for certain dates. Now I know the Jackson deals with Los Alamos." He looked at Ro. "And I know that you work at the Jackson. Am I right about that?"

"You are correct," she said.

Ben was stunned. "Why didn't you tell me you got lists from the Jackson?" he asked Shanks.

"Because you're not a cop, Vicks, and you're not privy to the same information that I am. And while I could get a court order for some dates, I couldn't exactly justify looking through three years' worth of registry. But unlike you, I can get court orders for hotels in addition to the Jackson. So I have some advantages. The way I figure it, you have some advantages and I have some advantages." Sam smiled. "I'm going to show you

KILLING SEASON · 735

a lot of lists of names. I shouldn't be showing them to you. But we're not going to tell anyone, right?"

"Our lips are sealed," Ro said.

"Will, does this make you uncomfortable?"

"Not at all."

"Great." Sam opened a briefcase and pulled out sheaves of paper. "It's a long list. I want you to point out anyone who you think I might want to investigate further."

It was a long roster of names, presented in alphabetical order. Kevin Barnes hadn't made the cut. Ben cleared his throat and handed it back to him. "Do you have the original rosters? The ones directly off the hotel computers?"

"This is the original list. I just alphabetized it."

"It isn't complete."

"Yes it is."

"No it isn't, Sam. It's only men."

His eyes widened. "You're *shittin'* me."

"Do you have the lists from before you winnowed them down to men?"

"They're not organized."

Ro said, "We know who we're looking for."

Sam rubbed his forehead. "Hold on. Let me bring up the files. I'll link them all together . . . it's forty-five pages."

"That's okay."

"They're alphabetized. That should help you out." He showed the kids his screen. "Knock yourself out."

Ben and Ro sorted through the names. She spotted one first. "Venika Berns . . ."

"Who?"

"This one." Ro pointed it out. "And Senna Berkiv. And here's Karen Bevins again."

"Eva Birnskin," Ben said.

Ro scrolled down and down and down. "Oh, here's one. Anne V. Kerbis."

"What are you looking at?" Sam stared at the names. "They're all anagrams." He looked at their faces. "Who?"

Ben said, "The name is not on your list, so do you really want me to say something out loud?"

"I should be able to figure it out." Shanks was talking more to himself than to anyone else. "It's an odd combination of letters . . . *V-I-K* . . . is it Vik . . . wait, don't answer."

Ben said, "I could write an algorithm that would spit out all the possible combinations of names."

"How long would it take you?"

"There might be something I could download off the Internet. Give me about a half hour."

"Go. I'll keep working at this."

Ro yawned. Ben said, "Do you want to go to bed?"

"Not on your life." She smiled at Mr. Vicksburg. "Do you mind if I stay over? I don't feel like traveling the open roads."

"Of course, honey." William stood up. "I'm going to check on my wife."

"Sure, sure," Shanks said.

Ro said, "I think I'll lie down on the couch for a moment and dream about a real prom . . . where there's a disco ball and a king and a queen and they dance together while everyone applauds."

Shanks was muttering to himself. "Vik . . . Kiv . . . Ben . . . is it Ben?"

Ro said, "It's not Ben."

"Don't tell me."

"Stop asking me."

"I'm talking to myself. Ben . . . Benk . . ."

Ben said, "I'll go try to figure out an algorithm."

Shanks went on, muttering to himself until a half hour had passed. Ben returned with a printout in his hand.

Shanks said, "Kiv . . . Kev . . . Kevin? Is it Kevin?"

"It's very warm in here." Ro made a point of fanning herself. "You must be very warm as well. As a matter of fact, Detective, I think you're sizzling."

"I'm sizzling," Ben said.

Shanks said, "Okay, it's Kevin. Kevin what?"

Ben handed Shanks the printout. He spotted the name right away. It was the combination that made the most sense. "Kevin Barnes." When neither of the kids said anything, Shanks grinned. "Okay. Now we're cooking with gas. He's not the football player."

"Unlikely."

"There's an art dealer, a shop owner, a lawyer—"

Ben cleared his throat. Shanks looked up and then back at the screen. "Why would I be interested in a lawyer?" More taps on the keyboard. "I can't even find out what kind of lawyer he is."

"Just off the top of my head, it might be immigration," Ro told him. "He might get foreign visas for visiting scientists, but that's just a guess."

Shanks was stunned. "How'd you find that out?"

"Just a guess."

"Kevin Barnes works for the national labs?" No one spoke. Shanks closed his laptop and stowed it in his briefcase. "I'm going down to the station house to make some phone calls."

"Who are you going to call?"

"There are just a handful of people you know who could give you that information, Vicks. Specifically people who work for the lab."

"If you're thinking about George Tafoya, don't call him. His lines are bugged."

"What?"

"Honest to goodness. When we talk, we talk in my car."

Shanks just shook his head. "What is he doing for you? Specifically?"

"He said he'd poke around quietly. He told me to stop doing anything I'm doing. And now I've told you everything I know. Can I come back to the station house with you?"

"Absolutely not." He stood up. "This guy . . . who-ever he is . . . you think you know something about him. But after tonight, I suspect he knows even more about you." His eyes turned to Ro. "And you." Back to Ben. "I know you can shoot. You might want to go down to the range."

"I was thinking about doing that tomorrow . . . if I get a car."

"What about you?" Shanks was addressing Ro. "Will you be joining him?"

"I don't know how to shoot," Ro told him. "I don't believe in guns."

Shanks licked his lips. "Young lady, maybe it's time to change your religion."

Chapter 9

*I*t was an *idiotic thing to do, so unlike him. He was, above all, methodical and calculating and conservative in thought as well as action. He planned meticulously. Something that impulsive was way beyond his understanding of himself.*

Why did he do it? He obsessed about his actions as he drove through the darkness, through fog and shadows, until the wee hours of the morning were upon him. Why had he done something so moronic when he knew the kid was onto something? As soon as the girl took the job . . . something was up. He could tell.

Maybe he did it to scare the little shit, let him know that his actions were not without consequences. He knew the kid wouldn't give up—after going in and out of the police station for years—but sometimes you had to show someone who was boss.

He drove on and on, through miles and miles of darkness: north through New Mexico, passing near Farmington and the Four Corners until he slid over the border into Colorado. As soon as he got to Denver, he'd camp out for the night. He had driven by mountains and flatlands and areas that were remote and perfect for his passion except they were far away. The next day he'd pass the Great Salt Lake and drive on until he reached Idaho.

It was two days of driving, but none of that bothered him much. He loved to drive as much as he loved to hunt. Not that he expected to find anyone on this lonesome highway and at this time of night. He didn't even want to find anyone because then the temptation would be just too much.

Once every nine months: his season, his quota, his passion, his obsession. Any more than that, he'd be making a spectacle of himself.

Ben aimed and peeled off six shots in rapid succession. He pushed the button and the paper felon came forward, pierced like a sieve: two between the eyes, two elsewhere in the face, and two in the top half of his head.

JD studied his handiwork. "You've been practicing?"

"Here and there."

"Remind me not to piss you off."

"Too late for that." They both laughed. Ro was not amused with ther camaraderie. Nor was she happy to be at a shooting range. She fiddled with her earmuffs. She examined her nails. She alternated between being bored and being sulky, talking in monosyllabic grunts.

JD put his paper felon on the line and pushed the button. Mr. Criminal was about thirty yards away. He loaded his pistol and took aim, sighting down to the target. His nose was just about healed, but there was a slight tilt as well as a chink in the bridge. He'd been playing contact sports since he was five, but it took a girl to screw up his perfect Roman slope. JD claimed he liked the result, that the asymmetry made him look tougher.

Ro said, "When is this going to be over?"

JD put the pistol down. "What's your problem?"

"The *problem* is I'm bored. Let's just leave."

"It's not as easy as it looks," Ben said. "We're doing this for your protection."

JD said, "You could act a little grateful. I spent a fortune on a tux, a corsage, a limo, a room, and a great bottle of champagne, and you crapped out on me last night."

"I'd much rather have been with you than where I was." She glared at him. "And may I add for the record that you looked very happy to be with Lisa."

"I didn't screw her." JD looked at Ben. "Can't say the same for him."

"I didn't screw her either," Ben said. "Don't get me involved in your spat." He turned to Ro. "You didn't have to come here."

"You insisted I come."

That was true. "I thought you might want to learn something."

"I hate guns!"

"Your loss," JD said.

Ro knew she was acting bratty, but it was a cover-up. Secretly, she was fascinated that the two guys in her life were doing something she absolutely abhorred, and doing it for her.

JD sighted down to his target and emptied the chamber. When he was done, he'd hit two in the face, two in the body, and missed two altogether. "He'd still be dead. That's all that matters."

Ben said, "Give it a go, girl, even if it's just this once."

"A gun in my hand is a weapon for someone else. I could never shoot it. I'd freeze."

"Which is exactly why you should learn to shoot a gun," JD said. "So you won't freeze."

Ro didn't say anything. Instead she gave both of them the full force of her steely eyes. It was weird. When she first started at Remez High, all she wanted was to rule the student body, be adored, and as an afterthought, she hoped that JD and Vicks would get along because she really did like them both. Now that they were friends again, it irritated her. Sometimes it seemed that they enjoyed each other's company more than hers.

"Fine," she said. "I'll try it."

JD put another paper felon on the line. He started at ten yards. He gave her his gun and stood behind her. He showed her how to hold the weapon, how to brace it with both hands to avoid kickback as much as possible. He said, "See that little thing sticking out? That's the sight. Line it up with where you want to shoot."

"This thing is heavy."

"Only because you've been holding up your arms so long." His body was close to hers. "Okay, aim for the chest. That's a much bigger target than the head."

"I can hit the head."

"Give it a whirl, then."

She took a shot. The kickback brought her hands

up and she didn't even hit the target. She was pissed. "What the hell happened?"

"Physics," Ben told her. "Bullet goes forward, your hands go back. You've got to brace your entire body so that your hands remain steady. Try it again."

She emptied the chamber. All her shots were wide. "This sucks. I suck." She handed JD the empty gun. "Put some more bullets inside. I want to try again."

JD smiled. "Sure thing, sugar."

"You should try my gun," Ben told her. "It has a little less kickback. Might be easier."

"I can handle this one, thank you very much," Ro barked. "I just need practice."

"We created a monster," JD said.

"Nonsense," Ro said. "I still loathe guns. But I have my pride. I will quit as soon as I get a bullet on the target paper."

After another try, she managed to hit the paper but not on the target area. JD held out his hand for the gun.

Ro balked. "Give me another round of bullets. Just let me get one on the body."

"Ammo ain't cheap."

"Just give it to me."

Another round, and she hit the body—twice.

By the time they left, she had peeled off a clean head shot and felt good about it.

Ben thought, *Good for her, good for JD, and good for me.*

Good for all of us good guys.

A week later Ben was cleaning up three years of an obsession; it was liberating, to be sure, but just like a drug addict, he had twinges of longing. Just one more file; just one more fix. The shredder was going full force. When he was done, the family would have a hell of a compost pile.

"You know, you never answered my question," Ro said to him. She was wearing jeans and a T-shirt and heels. She looked good, as always.

"What question?" As usual, he was listening with half an ear, rereading the file on Kevin Barnes, trying to figure out his next move. "I sure hope we have this right." He looked at her. "Do you think we have it right?"

"Probably, but now it's Shanks's problem." She ripped the file out of his hand and placed it in the shredder. "Stop second-guessing yourself and answer my question."

"What question?"

"On prom night, you disappeared." She was couching her anger in a saccharine-sweet smile. "You were gone for quite a while."

"That's not a question."

"Okay. How about this? Where were you?"

"I was dealing with slashed tires, Ro. I wasn't looking at my watch."

"I'm just saying that it took a long time to examine four flat pieces of rubber."

"What do you want me to say?"

She walked over to him until they were nose to nose. Her eyes were smoldering. "You don't have to say anything because I already know." She pushed him hard. "You dumped me as a date after you promised to take me to the prom. And then you go ahead and screw that skank?"

"I told you I didn't screw her."

"To paraphrase someone we *both* know: You may not have screwed her, but you did something! Because her description of you was way too accurate to be chance!" She pushed him again. "Okay, bud." She wagged a finger in his face. "Now we're *even*!"

"Not quite."

"You're right. We're not even. *You* didn't take on a menial, thankless job and suffer through sleepless nights just to help *me* out. As of right now, you owe me one, Mr. Big."

Ben liked the moniker. It made him smile and that

made her angrier. She threw something at him and it whizzed past his head. It crashed into the wall and fell with a thud.

"Okay, okay," Ben said. "We're even."

"No . . . we . . . are . . . not!" This time she threw his calculator.

Ben caught it with one hand. "Okay, now that's expensive. Can you stop destroying my room?"

"This is the deal. I want both you and JD to take me to grad night! And if you stand me up again, I will kill you."

"What about Lisa?"

"The poor dear will just have to go stag." She kissed him hard on the mouth. "Understood?"

He was breathless from her kiss. Whenever he felt out of control, he obsessed about one thing. "Can we finish up with this? It's making me anxious. Plus, the solstice is only a few days away."

She broke away and plopped down on the papers that were covering his bed. "Ben, it's over. Shanks is monitoring the situation. You should be writing your speech for graduation, not playing detective when we have a real detective. And stop trying to wriggle out of grad night. You're going."

He changed the subject. "What kind of speech should I be writing?"

She was incredulous. "Aren't you valedictorian?"

"Salutatorian."

"Salut . . ." She frowned. "How'd that happen? You're the smartest person in the school."

"JD's done way more for the school than I have. I'm fine with it."

She was quiet. "That doesn't seem fair."

"Ro, I don't give a rat's ass. I am so over high school. I don't even know why I'm going to graduation. It's meaningless. And so is grad night. Just go with JD. I'll stay home. I'm tired of tailing after you two lovebirds."

"We're not lovebirds. We're dates of convenience, and as soon as we graduate, it's so, so over. How can I ever be serious with someone who cheated on me?" She realized what she said and put her hand to her mouth. "Strike that."

Ben laughed.

She walked over to him and played with his curls. "I hate to admit this, but you're right. It's stupid for me to have two dates for grad night. Or any date at all, for that matter. Let's all go together as a group: you, me, JD, Lisa, Shannon, Chelsea, Mark, and Weekly. It's fun that way."

"Great." Ben winced. "It'll be one big happy orgy because, apparently, there has been lots of swapping that, in my perpetual haze, I've not been aware of."

She slapped his shoulder. "Stop it." Then her eyes misted up. She blinked back tears. "I'll miss you, Vicks, even with all your quirks and craziness. I've never met anyone like you."

"I'll miss you too, Dorothy." He meant it with every fiber of his being. "But right now, I'm still here and I'm still obnoxious. I've got three years of a fixation here. Help me clean it up."

She said, "You're still speaking at graduation, right?"

"Yeah, I think I welcome everyone."

"What are you going to say?"

"It's like a couple of sentences. I'll wing it."

"You can't wing it, Vicks. You'll have to say the same thing at rehearsal and at graduation."

"We have a rehearsal?"

"Yes, we have a rehearsal." She mocked his voice.

He put down a stack of papers. "When?"

"In three days, Mr. Space Cadet, the day before graduation."

"That's June twenty-first. It's the *day* of the solstice. I can't be there. I'll be watching Haley and Lilly."

"You have to make it or the school won't graduate you."

"Then I won't graduate—"

"Vicks, stop it!" She put her hands on his shoulders.

Her voice was soft. "Griff and Ezra will watch the girls. We'll keep them locked up in the house until we come back. They'll be fine."

"No way—"

"Shanks is on it. Albuquerque is on it. You're *done* with this." She stared at him. "I'll be really upset if you don't come to graduation." She paused. "And if you're with the girls . . . who'll be watching me?"

He hadn't thought about that. "Have JD drive you to rehearsal. Tell him to take a gun."

She pushed him away. "Anytime you don't want to deal with me, you palm me off on JD." She picked up her purse. "I'm leaving."

"Wait, wait, wait." Of course, what she said was true. He said, "Okay. I'll come to rehearsal. I'll work it out with the girls."

"Your parents will be home, right?"

"Maybe, but I kinda didn't want them dealing with this."

"So let the girls go to my house. My mom should be home. And we'll emphasize to the boys that they have to be with them at home with the door locked the entire time."

"Let them stay at my house. It's closer to the school."

"I'm down with that."

"Does Griff know how to shoot?"

"The guy is not going to come knocking at your door, Ben. That's just stupid."

"Why am I not reassured?"

"I know you're worried, but it'll only be a couple of hours." She put her purse down and kissed him like she did way back when. "Please come to rehearsal. I really want us to go through graduation together."

Ben was quiet.

"I know we can't go backward," Ro said. "After graduation, we'll all be scattered across the four corners of the globe. And I'm looking forward to the future. Within a few months at college, I'll be pledged with the top sorority and I'll be dating the best-looking guy on campus. But . . ." She blew out air. "You can only have one first love . . . and you'll always be my first love."

He kissed her back and there was instant electricity. Dear Lord, protect him from being seventeen. "And you'll always be my first love."

"So, my first love . . . you'll come to rehearsal with me?"

It was against his better judgment. "I'll go for a couple of hours, okay. That's the best I can do."

"Fair enough." A sad smile. "When I'm gone, think of me from time to time."

"Ro, it's the *not* thinking about you that'll be difficult." He suddenly felt very blue. "How the hell do I move on when you've set the bar so high?"

"I hate it when you say things like that." She was choked up. "It makes me think about what I'm losing."

"You'll always have me here." He pointed to her chest. "And I'll always have you here." He pointed to his own heart.

She wiped her wet eyes. "Now it's my turn to say let's get back to work." She threw another pile into the shredder. It made a god-awful sound that had Ben cringing.

But his mind was still on the conversation.

She was his first love, no doubt about that.

And she cheated on him, no doubt about that either.

There was first love.

And then there was true love.

Chapter 10

*B*ack in New Mexico, he broke into a sweat and it wasn't because of the warm weather. He shouldn't have come back. After his stunt with the tires they were onto him, and he'd have better luck elsewhere.

But compulsion was compulsion and he knew that nothing was going to satisfy him except a hit in this territory. So why did he take a chance on doing something that he'd ultimately find hollow?

It didn't have to be a certain person. Any female that fit the categories would do. But it would be extra-special sweet to do it right under their proverbial noses, prove that lightning could strike twice, and just maybe it would give him the same thrill that she gave him three years ago.

She had fought like a tiger, scratching and clawing

and screaming, but she didn't have a chance. Eventually he had subdued her by sheer force. It was because of her spirit that he decided to start using chemicals to get from point A to point B to point C . . . well, they were dead by point C—limp and lifeless, unable to respond in any way.

Some guys got off on the fight. He got off on the helplessness. He was ashamed to admit it, even to himself, but he sometimes liked it better when they were dead than when they were alive. He could take his time, whisper things to the girls that he really wanted to say, let them know that he did care about them. That it wasn't personal . . . just . . . it was who he was.

He had passed the Four Corners on the rez, passed Shiprock, and was going into Farmington. He'd be in Albuquerque by evening, ready to set up shop. He knew better than to check in at the Jackson Santa Fe—pretty little Dorothy wasn't there by chance—so he'd hit the Jackson down south, where he still had business at Sandia NL. That way the government would be paying for his room and meals and he could go in and out of Santa Fe without being noticed.

That was if all went as planned. And when things didn't go as planned, well, that was okay too.

Creativity spawned excitement. And that's all he wanted in his dull, dull life. A little fun now and then.

———

Ro was chipper while Ben was pissed off and anxiety-ridden. She zipped across the threshold with Griffen following her like the tail to her comet. She had on a bright pink polo shirt that screamed summer. All it did was remind Ben of the significance of the day.

"I don't like this plan." Ben closed the door. "I should be here."

"Stop worrying." She sighed heavily. "We've been over this a thousand times."

Ben looked around. "Where's Ezra?"

"Sick," Griffen said.

"So there's just the three of you?" He shook his head. "Uh-uh, I'm staying home."

"Vicks, Griff is here, the girls are together, and Shanks said he'll make at least three drive-bys."

"I'm not going unless they wait at the police station."

"And I told you I'm not waiting at a police station," Haley said.

She seemed as pissed off as he was. It was the time of the year when she and Ben became orphans. Their mother was barely functioning, managing just to work and sleep. Their dad, on the other hand, was all work. Both of them were as absent as they were absent-minded. Ben and Haley were left to fend for themselves, and since

Ben drove, Haley was dependent on him. He became bossy. She became defiant. Nothing worked for either of them.

Haley said, "I've got a ton of work to do for my final papers. And Mom said something about leaving early from work."

Ben said, "She has a doctor's appointment."

"Oh . . ." Haley's complexion darkened. "I thought maybe she actually wanted to spend some time with me."

"She does, Haley." Ben exhaled "She just can't function right now." Silence. "You haven't said anything to her about today, right?"

"God, don't you trust me at all?"

"I'm sorry if it comes across like that."

Haley was somewhat mollified. "Honestly, it's stupid that she doesn't know."

"I wanted here her, Haley. Dad overruled me."

"You haven't told your mom about what's going on?" Ro was genuinely surprised.

"The official anniversary of my sister's death is in spitting distance. She's been in a dark place for days. My dad told me that he doesn't want to unnecessarily worry her."

Ro made a face. "But she knows about the slashed tires. She knows that Shanks was grilling us about

Barnes. You need to tell her what's going on. She won't wilt, you know."

"You've never been with her at this time of year." Ben looked at his sister. "Should I tell her?"

"Call Dad and ask him again."

He phoned his father. The conversation was very short. "Don't tell Mom, but he'll be here in an hour or so to oversee, okay?"

"Oh please," Haley shot back. "Call him back and tell him we're fine."

"None of this would be necessary if you guys would wait at the police station."

"And what would Mom think about that?" Haley looked at him with hard eyes. "Ben, we're *fine*. I mean, like how long are you going to be gone? Like two hours? I mean, like, c'mon!"

"Here, here," Ro said.

To Lilly, Ben said, "You okay with this?"

"I can study anywhere." She gave a weak smile. "If you have to go to rehearsal to go to graduation, then go to rehearsal. We'll be fine."

"Can we go already?" Ro was tugging on Ben's T-shirt.

"I'm halfway done with college. Why do I need to graduate high school?" To Ro, he said, "Go on without me."

"I don't believe this!" She was angry.

Lilly stepped in. "Ben, the graduation ceremony isn't for you. It's for your parents. You owe it to them."

Ben knew she was right and that stank.

He wasn't meant to be the oldest child, to be the first one to go to prom, the first one to wear a cap and gown or go to college or get married or have kids or experience any of those milestones. He was born second in line. He should have *been* second in line. Totally wrong but what could he do?

Ben turned to Griff. "You don't answer the door for anyone, right? Even if he says he's Shanks. Even if it *is* Shanks . . . well, if it is Shanks, you call me first. No one goes through that door unless I say so!"

"Dude, I hear you."

"Don't dude me right now," Ben said. "It doesn't inspire confidence."

Griff turned serious. "It's a little embarrassing that you don't trust me."

Ben took his arm and spoke in a low voice. "Griff, he killed four people."

"I'm on it, Ben. Besides, the guy would have to be a moron to come to the house."

Sometimes you've just got to let go. Ben said, "Did you preprogram your cell phones with the numbers?"

"We all did: yours, Shanks's, your dad's, my dad's, and nine-one-one."

"And you'll keep the lines free at all times, right?"

"I got the memo." Griff was staring with his big blue eyes. "I can *handle* it."

Ben finally saw what he wanted: genuine concern in Griff's eyes. The past year the boy had not only grown taller, he had filled out. He had broader shoulders and muscle in his arms. If he kept going this way, he'd make varsity football. In an arm wrestling match, Ben wouldn't be surprised if Griff could take him down. But in a life-and-death struggle, Ben had an advantage over any of them. He had the passion because he knew what he was fighting for. "I'm counting on you. Don't let me down."

"I got it, Vicks."

Ro was pushing Ben out the door. "See you guys. Lock up!" She dragged him to her car. "Will you relax?"

"That is *out* of the question." They got into her Explorer and he pulled out a gun from a boot holster. It was only a little mouse gun, but it was better than nothing. Ro's eyes went wide. He shrugged. "Just in case."

"You're nuts."

He stowed the gun in her glove compartment. "Look, I know I'm being ridiculous, but it's the way I'm wired, okay?" He took out his phone.

"Vicks, c'mon!"

"I just want to make sure that Haley's keeping the line open."

When she answered, she said, "I'm still here."

"Keep the line open."

"I can't if I'm talking to you." She hung up.

He didn't feel right about leaving them, but as long as they toed the line—stayed inside the house with the doors locked—he supposed that they would last a few hours.

That's what Ben told himself over and over and over.

Fifteen minutes into the hour, Haley put down her laptop. "How much longer is that damn truck going to beep?"

Lilly looked up from her workbook. She furrowed her brow as she listened to the incessant *wheep, wheep, wheep* in a high-pitched range. "I hadn't noticed it until you said something."

"How could you not notice it?"

"I was concentrating."

"Well, bully for you."

Lilly forced her lips shut to prevent herself from saying something she'd later regret. It wasn't that Haley was grumpy, it was that she was selectively grumpy. With Griff, she was all smiles. Lilly was a third wheel, again. She got up and went to the window. "It's street repair. The truck is hauling away broken asphalt."

"So why is it beeping?"

"It does that every time it backs up."

"Well, it's driving me crazy! I hate studying to begin with and I've got four finals and a paper." Haley regarded Lilly. "Did you do the English paper yet?" She didn't wait for an answer. "Of course you did. And I bet you already studied for finals?"

Lilly sighed. "How can I help you, Haley?"

"By not being so condescending. You and my brother are really a pair." She stood up. "I'm going to the library."

Griffen said, "You know you can't do that."

"Why? Because Ben said I can't?" She made a face. "Who made him lord and protector?"

"Haley—"

"I understand where he's coming from." Her eyes got moist. "She was my sister too, you know. He acts like he's the only one who's suffered. Just because I'm not hunting around for some phantom killer doesn't mean I don't care or I'm inferior."

Lilly said, "Haley, he's not trying to be superior, he's just worried about your personal safety."

"He's bossy."

Griffen said, "You know we're not going anywhere. Put cotton in your ears or something."

"Let's look at this logically," Haley said. "The library is like ten blocks away. If we all go together and we all stay together, it's probably even a better place to be because it's public."

"Why didn't you say anything to him about the library when he was here?" Griffen asked. "I promised him I'd look after you two."

"So look after us in the library. We'll all stay in the same place at the same table." Haley looked at Lilly. "You just said you can do work anywhere."

"It's not a problem for me," Lilly said. "But if he comes back and finds us gone, he'll freak. Why don't you call him up and tell him your plans."

"How about if we go to the library *first* and then I'll call him up and tell him the change of plans? Because if I call him now, he'll come rushing home and I don't want to deal with him because he'll be pissed. He's always pissed. It's hard being with someone so pissed off."

Tell me about it, Lilly thought.

"With my mom being a zombie and my dad never around, things suck, okay? I know that Ben's being protective, but you know he truly likes bossing me around."

"That's not fair," Lilly said.

764 • FAYE KELLERMAN

"Earth to Lilly. Ben is not God."

Lilly felt her face go hot. Griffen broke in. "Haley, let's just stick with the plan, and when he comes back, we'll all go to the library, okay? Let's just take a break and—"

"I have way too much work to take a break, okay?"

"Jesus! Sorry!" Griffen threw up his hands. The truck continued to beep every time it backed up into the roadway.

"I'm sick of Ben saying jump and we say how high. I'm going with or without you."

Lilly said, "Haley, you know that if you go, then we all have to go."

"So come with me. You know . . . like, strength in numbers."

Griffen said, "You're not worried even though this guy has killed other girls?"

"If it's the guy Ben thinks it is—and there's no proof of that yet—he killed in three other cities. It's been three years. He's not coming back here. It would be stupid."

Lilly said, "What about Ben's slashed tires?"

"It was probably a prank."

"Haley, no one slashes four tires for a prank."

She shrugged. "I don't see why I have to rearrange my life just because Ben says so."

"Because it makes sense? Why are you picking now of all times to be rebellious?"

"I'm not being rebellious." Haley zeroed in on Lilly. "Ben is not my father and I'm not his child. Stop insulting me."

"Could everyone just chill?" Griffen said. "You're just fighting because you're tense. That's normal—"

"Stop psychoanalyzing me, Griff. It just makes me even angrier." Haley was red-faced with moist eyes. She scooped up her books. "This guy has destroyed my family. I'm not letting him destroy me. I'll see you all later."

Griffen picked up his laptop. "We'll all go together."

"Fine, we'll go together," Lilly said. "You should call Ben and let him know."

"Later."

"Haley, stop acting stupid."

"Excuse me?" Haley glared at her. "I certainly know whose side *you're* on."

"I'm not taking sides. This isn't an election."

"I am so gone."

"Wait, wait." Griffen took her arm. "Just wait, okay?"

"Fine."

Haley tapped her foot until Griffen and Lilly had gathered up their belongings. Within minutes, they were out the door and on the street. The first day of summer had turned out to be spectacular. The sun was strong, the sky was a rich teal blue, and the air smelled of lavender and roses. The trio walked down the hillside, the mountains in the distance boasting an array of colors from deep greens to earthy rusts. Birds had roosted in the treetops and bees flitted from sage plant to sage plant.

With the warmth on her face, Haley felt better. The trip to the library was an easy walk, and fifteen minutes later the group reached the building without incident. They found an empty table, sat down, and Haley settled in, taking out her laptop and her books. Griffen sat next to her and Lilly sat across the table from them.

Lilly whispered, "Before you forget, you should text Ben and tell him where we are."

"You do it."

Such a baby, Lilly thought. "Fine, I'll do it." She texted him, then put her phone ringer on vibrate and slipped it in her purse. Finals would be over in ten days along with her first year of high school.

How time flies.

Chapter 11

The lineup was in alphabetical order, which would have been great if Ben had actually been at the back. Instead, because he was salutatorian—a title akin to the country's vice president and equally meaningful—he had to march in the front of the line, but behind JD. The order of importance was not lost on JD's ego and he ribbed Ben mercilessly.

At the beginning of lineup, the boys' VP made the announcement to turn off all cell phones, that anyone caught disobeying the edict would miss graduation—clearly an incentive for Ben to keep his phone on the loudest ring possible. Instead he played the semigood citizen and put his phone on vibrate and in his pants pocket, where he could check it at regular intervals.

The rehearsal was clearly not going to be an hour.

After thirty minutes, the faculty was still arranging the students. The sun was hot and everyone was sweating and fanning themselves with their hands. In the chaos, Ben sneaked a glance at his phone messages.

The text message from Lilly set his heart racing.

SHIT!

He pulled out his phone. JD said, "What are you doing, Vicks? Put that away."

Ben heard his voice but not the words. He read Lilly's message. "FUCK!"

Heads turned in his direction.

"What's wrong?" JD said.

The boys' VP said, "Vicks, what are you doing? Put that phone away."

"I've gotta go, sir."

"What's wrong?"

"I . . . have to pick up my sister at the library."

"Can't someone else do it?"

"No! No one else can do it. I am the only one who can do it and I have to go *now!*"

"Is she sick?"

"No, she's just very stupid."

"This is very poor timing on your part," the veep told him. "You know if you miss rehearsal, you can't attend graduation."

"With all due respect, sir, *screw* graduation."

He jogged away, trying to call Haley and trying to find Ro at the same time. "Answer the phone, you stupid idiot!" Her cell rang twice and then went to voice mail. At that point, Ben's head got fuzzy. He didn't know if it was heat or fear, but his knees buckled. He managed to catch himself before he hit the ground. Ro came over to him. "Ben, what's wrong?"

"I need your car keys!"

"What?"

"Haley went to the library. I can't reach her. Give me your fucking keys!"

"You're in no state to drive—"

Ben grabbed her purse and rooted through her belongings. She was pulling it back by a strap. "Vicks, you have to calm down."

"Don't tell me that!" He yanked her purse away from her, catching her off balance. She stumbled back and fell to the ground on her butt. He pulled out the keys and tossed her back her purse. "I knew I should have stayed back."

He took off, but she ran after him.

"Vicks, wait! Wait! . . ." A pause. "WAIT."

When he got to Ro's car, the temptation was strong to just hop in and speed away. But she looked so pathetic, panting and wheezing. He threw open the passenger door and dove into the driver's seat. He took off before she could fully close the door. "The kids went to the library."

"What? Why?"

"'Cause they're idiots. Call up your brother."

She already had her phone out. "It's going to voice mail."

"I can't believe how fucking stupid they are. Call up Lilly."

Ro went through the contact list until she found the number.

"Voice mail." Ben saw Ro wipe her eyes. She said, "He couldn't have kidnapped all three. Goddamn them! How could they do this! How could they be so damn stupid!"

Ben glanced at her. It was rare for Ro to swear. She was red-faced, sweating and crying at the same time. She was texting with shaking hands. By leaving with him, Ben knew she'd miss the graduation ceremony. She was as upset as he was and that made him get a grip. She said, "Should I call Shanks?"

"Hold off. I'll be there in five minutes."

"I'll try my brother again." Silence. "I'm going to kill him! I am sincerely going to kill him!"

Every second was interminable. Finally, he pulled into the library lot, found a space, and jumped out of the driver's seat. Ro was on his heels.

Since the library wasn't the proper place to start screaming out names, Ben's eyes were in frantic search mode. The public reading room wasn't all that big, and within a few moments, he saw Haley, sitting at a table, typing on her laptop.

He didn't know whether to kill her or hug her.

Walking over, he scream-whispered, "What the fuck!" He glared at Griffen. "Is this what you call *handling* it?"

"She stormed out of the house. I had about two seconds to decide and I thought it was better if we all went together rather than split up."

Ro hissed at him, "Why wasn't your phone on?"

"It was. I had it on vibrate—"

"You didn't answer it."

"I probably didn't feel it." Griff sighed. "Honestly, Ben, what should I have done? Tied her up?"

"That would have been a great idea!"

They were promptly shushed by the librarian, who told them to take it outside.

Ben sat next to his sister. She was blushing, sweating, and had yet to speak. He lowered his voice. "Why did you *do* this to me, Haley? I know I can be a tyrant, but you gotta read the metamessage. I only wanted you to be safe. Now we're both gonna miss graduation because I panicked and left rehearsal!"

Her lower lip trembled and her eyes teared up. "I'm . . . sorry. I just wanted to get out of the house."

"You wanted to assert your independence because I'm bossy . . . which is fine any other day except today. You know you totally screwed me!"

She was trying to hold back sobs. "The truck was beeping and I couldn't concentrate and that house has so many bad memories sometimes!" She wiped her tears on her sleeve. "I'm sorry."

He sincerely wanted to strangle her. Instead he threw his arms around her and hugged her tightly. "It doesn't matter. Just as long as you're okay. That's all I care about."

"I'm so sorry!"

"Forget it." To Ro, Ben said, "Go back to rehearsal and tell them I was stealing your car. Everyone saw me acting like a maniac. You'll be fine."

Her eyes were wet as well. "It's fine. I don't even care anymore. I'll drive everyone back. I'm just glad for a happy ending."

"Sorry, Griff," Ben told him. "You did the right thing."

"No, I should have insisted—"

"Let's just get out of here. I feel like I'm gonna puke and I'd rather do it outside." Ben got up and looked around. "Where's Lilly?" The question was met with silence. Haley's eyes went to Lilly's purse and open laptop. A stack of books and papers sat next to the computer.

Haley couldn't speak. Griffen stammered out, "I was studying . . . I . . ."

Instantly came the sinking feeling in the pit of Ben's gut, just like when they got the phone call from his father three years ago.

"Do you know where Ellen is?"

Ro stammered out, "I'll check out the bathroom."

"Yeah . . . phew! That's it!" Haley hit her head. "She said she was going to the bathroom, that I should watch her purse."

Ben's heart was racing. "How long has she been gone?"

"A few minutes—"

He caught up with Ro. Through the door, he heard her call Lilly's name.

"Is she there?"

Silence.

"Ro, is she—"

"I hear you!" Ro threw open the door. "She's not here!"

"Oh God!" Panic set in once again. Ben ran back to Haley and grabbed her shoulders. "She's not in the bathroom. How long has it been since she left?"

When Haley couldn't speak, Griffen said, "Maybe five minutes. I guess I shoulda gone with her."

Ya think? Ben said, "Just five minutes?"

"Maybe a little longer. I wasn't paying attention—"

"Lilly!" He shouted her name out loud. Everyone turned around. "We have a lost girl. *Lilly!*"

Everyone around them started yelling out her name, but after a minute it was crystal clear that she wasn't in the building. The fact that her purse and computer *were* in the building meant only one thing in Ben's mind.

Ro's voice was trembling. "He couldn't have dragged her out the front door."

She was right. Unless there was an alternate escape route, Lilly had to be somewhere in the building. Ben backtracked to the bathroom, and to his horror found an unlocked emergency exit. When he opened it, there wasn't a single chime or beep to let anyone know that the barrier had been breached. The exit led right to the library's parking lot, where the light hit his eyes like a nuclear blast. After a moment to adjust, he scanned the asphalt, but no one was there. He didn't recall exactly how many cars had been parked when he came in, but he distinctly remembered a white compact that was no longer there. There was an empty spot with a few drops of fluid where that white compact *might* have been. The liquid should have dried up very quickly in the direct sun. Ben figured that at most the car had been gone for less than ten minutes.

Ro suddenly materialized, the other two kids on her heels. They appeared shell-shocked. "Gimme your keys," Ben barked to her.

"Where are we going?"

"I don't know where I'm going, but I'm looking for a white compact, a Toyota or a Honda."

"There must be a million white Toyota or Honda compacts."

He didn't bother to answer, needing to marshal all his energy for the hunt. His mind was reeling like a movie in reverse. "It was four-door . . . not a Honda. It was a Hyundai . . . probably an Elantra." Brain snapping to the present, his eyes scoured the lot until he found what he was looking for. He pointed to a video camera.

"Ro, call up Shanks and meet him here at the library. You tell him what's going on—"

"I'm coming with you, dude."

Too frantic to argue, Ben said, "Okay, come with me. Griffen, *you* wait here for Shanks and show him that video camera. Tell him to put out an APB for a white Hyundai four-door compact that's probably an Elantra. Tell him to call me if he finds the car or if he sees anything else on the tape. Even if he doesn't see anything, tell him to look for that car." He grabbed Ro's hand. "Let's go."

"Anything else?" Griffen shouted to his back.

"Yeah. Tell him the motherfucker's got Lilly!"

Chapter 12

He was like a chicken without a head, all impulses but without a working brain behind it. Ben knew that the fiend would end up burying her in the dead of night, near the River Remez in the mountains. The trouble was Ben didn't have a clue as to where he'd do his monstrous activities. In all of the cases, the kill spot had been different from the burial spot.

Where, where, where?

Ro was talking to Shanks in a calm, cool voice that belied her panic. Finally, she hung up the cell. "He's on his way to the library. He put out an APB for a white Elantra."

"God, I hope I'm right."

"Where are you going?"

"North. Toward Los Alamos. It's the only thing I

can think of right now. He's familiar with the areas around the lab. Any ideas? I'm open."

Suddenly Ro hit her forehead. "God, I'm an idiot!" She turned to him. "When we take the reservations at the hotel, we take the license plate of the rental car." With shaking hands she started punching in numbers. A few moments later she said, "Hi, Tom, this is Gretchen Majors . . . I'm fine . . . yes, it *is* a beautiful day."

Ben looked at her and whispered, "What *the fuck*?"

She shushed him. "Good to hear. Uh, I need your help. Can you look up the license plate of a guest for me? I got a call that he's stranded and he doesn't—"

"Get to the point!"

"Shut up!" she whispered. "Kevin Barnes, but he could be under the name Karen Bevins or Eva . . . I don't know why but I do know he uses aliases."

Another interminable pause. *"Hurry up!"*

She ignored him. "I really don't know why he uses false names, but I need to get the license . . . I got a call from someone at the airport . . . I don't know why they didn't call the hotel. I gave him my card and maybe that's why . . . Yeah, I had my cell on it."

"Goddammit, Ro! He's got Lilly—"

"Shut up!" She turned to her phone. "No, not you. I'm talking to my dog. Yes, I know giving out your cell is against policy. I'm sorry. But if you could look up that plate, please?"

She was really winging it. *C'mon! Hurry up!*

"Yeah, he might be staying elsewhere but he usually stays at the Jackson Santa Fe or the Jackson Albuquerque. Could you check with Albuquerque? Thank you so much. I'll wait." She turned to Ben. "I'm doing something illegal. He's doing something illegal. Don't say a freakin' word."

"What's taking him so fucking long?"

"Vicks!"

"It's LILLY."

"I'm just as nervous as you are, so shut up! Hi, Tom, I'm still here . . . Uh, yeah, that's probably the person I'm looking for."

"What's the alias?" he shouted.

She plugged up her free ear with her finger so she couldn't hear Ben. "Thank you, Tom. That's a white Hyundai Elantra, right? Good. Would you happen to know what rental company he used? Avis? Great. And would you happen to have the license plate?" She began scribbling something down. "That really helps. Thanks, Tom, I owe you one." She ended the call.

"You got the *license plate*?"

"I did."

"I love you. Call it in to Shanks."

"I will, but right now, I've got a better idea." She made another phone call. "Hi, this is Gretchen Majors from the Jackson . . . Yes, I'm calling because I need a location on a car that was stranded . . . a white Hyundai Elantra." She gave the person on the other end the license plate. "The customer called me from the spot, but in his panic he forgot to tell me where he is. I don't know why he called me. I must have given him my phone number . . . I'd do it myself, but I'm busy with something else, so if you could just give me the location . . . thank you, I'll wait."

Ben was drowning in tension. He couldn't breathe as the seconds droned on, his heart like a steam drill. His eyes were blurry, which was especially bad because he had just entered the highway at top speed, racing to nowhere. Finally, he heard her voice.

"Route 501 toward Los Alamos . . . No, I don't understand why the car is still moving. He said he was stranded."

Ben's instincts had put him in the right area but now that he knew he was close, he had an even bigger sense of urgency, putting pedal to the metal. Both he and Ro were jolted backward and Ro gasped. But she continued to sound professional over the phone. "I really don't understand it either. I'll get to the bottom of it and call you back. Thank you very much." She hung up. She was clutching the door, her complexion something in between white and gray. "You heard what he told me?"

"I did."

"So you know where he's going?"

"I know what route he's taking. Call Shanks."

"I'm a step ahead of you."

Ben's brain was on overdrive. The fact that *his* car was still en route somewhere was a good omen. "After you speak to Shanks, call back the guy at the desk and check up on the car's location."

"Vicks, I've used up my goodwill. I won't get any more out of him. But Shanks can call back and get a bead on him."

She was thinking way more clearly than he was. She clicked off her phone. "Shanks's number goes to voice mail. Nine-one-one?"

"Text him first."

She did. Thirty seconds later her cell rang. Without saying hello, she said, "I got his license plate and a rough idea where he is." She gave him the information. "The car is on the move. Avis has a locator on the vehicle. They can give you the exact point-by-point location. Last time I checked, the car was moving down—"

She stopped talking. Ben could hear shouting over the line, even though the phone wasn't on speaker. Ro was stuttering. "But . . . but . . . but . . . No, I don't

know where we are, sir. Ben's driving." More scream-
ing. "I'll tell him, sir. Yes . . . yes . . . yes . . . thank you.
Bye." She hung up. "He wants you to go back to River
Remez pronto and let the police handle it."

"Fuck that." He exited the highway heading toward 501.

"Do you know where we're going?"

"I know exactly where we're going. I hope that's exactly where *he's* going." Suddenly he was seized with
dread. He banged his fist against his head. "Oh shit!"

"*What?*"

"The road to the Los Alamos highway is guarded by
national security. There's a checkpoint we have to pass.
I'm sure the motherfucker got through easily because
he has a security badge."

"So we can't get through?"

"No, we *can* get through. It's not a problem . . . un-
less the guards have been notified and they've closed
off the road. Then we're screwed. Not to mention that
I'm so nervous I'm probably going to be questioned.
The guard's gonna ask for ID. Do you have a New
York driver's license?"

"I have a local driver's license."

"Under Gretchen Majors. Right. But do you have a
New York driver's license?"

"Yeah, I've got that too."

"Use that one." They were approaching the stop, the roadway narrowed by concrete barricades and continuing on the other side of the checkpoint. Ben brought the car down to a crawl. "Okay. This is the story. We're going to the Caldera to hike. We're in casual clothes, so it's plausible. Just play along, okay?"

"What's the Caldera?"

"Stop asking questions and just go along with it."

"I'd like to know what it is so if they ask me questions, I can answer them without looking stupid."

"I don't have time for a fucking history lesson."

"God, you don't have to shout."

"I'm fucking nervous."

"Well, join the fucking club," Ro shot back. "Jesus, you're terrible under pressure." Then she burst into tears.

Ben swung the car over to the curb, but didn't turn off the engine. "The Caldera is the cone of a dormant volcano. It's now wide-open space where people hike. I'm sorry I'm shouting, but any minute, those guys are gonna get a call from Shanks about the Elantra. And then they're going to block off the road. And we'll be too late. Let's hold it together for another minute, and then once we get past the security guards, you can swear at me all you want."

"You're right." She dried her eyes. "Sorry."

"I'm sorry too. Let's just . . ." He was still pant-ing. "No problem." He pulled away from the curb and up to the checkpoint. Rolling down the window, Ben was greeted with a blast of hot wind in his face. He put on his best stupid-teenage-boy grin, the kind of dumb look that a dude has when he's with a good-looking girl. It probably came out halfway between a leer and a sneer. "Hello, sir."

The man was wearing a brown uniform; he had a military crew cut and suspicious brown eyes. "Where are you headed?"

"To the Caldera for a hike."

"Little late in the day."

It was four P.M. "We've got at least three hours of good daylight. I just want to show my friend around New Mexico. She's from New York."

The officer peered in the window. Ro smiled and waved. Ben tried to control his tension, hoping that he'd have just a minute before the guard's walkie-talkie buzzed. He smiled again. "Beautiful day." It came out as suck-up and he immediately regretted talking. He had never been good at chitchat.

"It's hot."

"Not as hot as it will be in a month. Besides, the Caldera is usually a few degrees cooler."

"True." The officer asked for ID and Ben showed

him his license. Then he checked their laps to make sure their seat belts were fastened. "Try to get back before dark."

"I will. I know the roads are dark after sunset."

"So you go there often?"

God, just close your fucking mouth, Vicksburg. "I used to board around the area in the winter. Now I go in the summertime and hike. It helps me think."

The officer continued to stare at Ben and Ro. Then he waved them on. "Go ahead."

"Thank you." Ben slowly pulled onto the road. As soon as the checkpoint was out of eyesight, he punched the accelerator.

The road was two lanes and sinuous, cutting through the mountains. The temperature was at least ten degrees hotter because the elevation had dropped and the afternoon sun was strong, seeping through the front windshield as they went northwest toward Los Alamos. After a few minutes, the lab buildings came into view. They were low-slung and set back from the road, white buildings with white signs that had LANL and identifying sector numbers in blue lettering. There was no indication of what went on inside, but since the buildings were only closed off by a chain link fence, the structures were probably not the homes of bunker busters. There were dozens of little buildings in the area, all through the Sangres, bleeding into the western Jemez Mountains. Ben had traveled these roads hundreds of times to get to the San Ildefonso and the Santa Clara pueblos, but never in his life had he traveled with such purpose and urgency.

He slowed the car as both of them hunted for a white Hyundai Elantra, his head whirling as they searched. Once the Elantra stopped moving, it meant that the monster had taken Lilly inside one of those buildings. And then they only had minutes before it was too late. "Ro, call Shanks and tell him that we're on top of the guy. Tell him that if he stops the car and takes her out, it's all over. We need a *location!*"

"Got it." She phoned Shanks while peering out the window. He heard Shanks's voice over the line, but then Ro disconnected her cell and punched his shoulder hard. *"Stop!"* She rolled down the window and pointed. "What about *that* car?"

A white Elantra sat behind the gate of a high chain link fence. There was barbed wire on top, so climbing it was a last-resort option. The building wasn't marked with a lab sector sign. It was two stories and might have been used for storage. But seeing as this was Los Alamos, who knew what was inside.

Ro's cell rang again and it was probably Shanks. In the distance, Ben heard sirens.

"Get out of the car!" he ordered.

"What?"

"Just do it! And stay way back from the gate!"

She jumped out of the passenger seat. He slammed the car into reverse, then backed down the road. He shoved the gear back into drive with one foot on the brake and the other on the accelerator. He pressed down and the engine roared, then he steeled himself for the inevitable, gluing his head and neck and back against the seat and the neck rest. As he lifted his left foot from the brake, he depressed the accelerator to the floor and the car shot forward like a ball from a cannon.

It smashed through the chain link fence with that spine-tingling sound of metal against metal—warping, scraping, and gouging. Ben had crashed into the Elantra and sent it hurling into a tree. When that happened, the windshield of the Explorer cracked and the airbags deployed. He braked hard, and the beast came to a halt.

He was in one piece and that was all that mattered. He somehow managed to open the glove compartment and grab the gun, worming himself out of the hunk of metal that had once been Ro's Explorer. By the time he was free, Ro had caught up with him. The two of them raced toward the building.

Coming from the inside was the sickening sound of desperate screaming. The door was secured, so Ben took aim, shot the lock, and rammed the door with his shoulder. The barrier didn't collapse but enough of it broke away from the hinges that he could crawl through the splinters. Inside, it was dim, some light coming in from a few windows. The afternoon sun was sinking fast.

"Lilly!"

Another shriek.

"LILLY!" Ben's voice was raw. "Get the fuck away from her!"

Then he realized that the only thing more sickening than the screaming was the sudden silence. Ro yanked on his T-shirt. "It was coming from this way."

They wound and wound their way in the encroaching twilight. The horror scene was tucked into a corner. Ben's knees weakened and his gorge rose.

Lilly's throat had been cut, blood oozing out of the wound. Her hands were around her neck, trying to stanch the flow. She was in shock, her black eyes trembling in their orbs. Her entire body was seized with the shakes. Ro ripped off her T-shirt and knelt down, wrapping the cloth around Lilly's neck while Ben called 911, stuttering out an approximation of where they were and what had just happened. He heard his own voice speak, but he was disembodied, trapped in a nightmare, in a horrific, disorienting daze, until he heard Ro's voice. "She's alive." Ro was gently pressing her shirt against her neck. "It's deep but it isn't spurting. She's gonna make it if I have to rip open a vein and give her a transfusion on the spot! Just hang in there, Lilly. You're gonna be fine. Help is coming, baby, help is coming!"

A distant wail turned louder. They could both hear sirens. Ben dropped to his knees and held Lilly's clammy, bloody hand. He felt fingers wrap around his. To Ro, he said, "What can I do?"

"Barnes!" She looked up. "Go *get* him!"

Ben froze, looking back and forth between Ro and Lilly.

"I've got this, Ben. Help is seconds away. Go get him! Go! *Go!*"

As if to propel him forward, Lilly let go of his hand. His legs found their strength. Gun in hand, he stood up and took off to parts unknown.

Chapter 13

His body was slowly returning from the shock, his brain kicking into logic mode.

Ben took in his surroundings.

The first floor of the building was around twenty-five hundred to three thousand square feet, roughly a five-hundred-foot square. The second story was a cat-walk that went around the entire perimeter. Every square inch appeared to be taken up by something, mostly boxes that were piled, stacked, and pushed against the wall.

Boxes meant hiding spaces—good for him as protection, bad for him because they could hide a monster known as Kevin Barnes.

The building had a front entrance and a set of back double doors that were still locked from the inside with a double iron bar across the jamb. As far as he could tell, those were the only two ways in or out. But Ben didn't know the building and Barnes probably did. It was also possible that he had escaped through the front when Ben and Ro were busy with Lilly. He could be long gone, but he could also be within reach.

Take nothing for granted.

Into the bowels of the warehouse. Ben knew he couldn't get a good sense of the layout from the first floor. There were too many boxes breaking up his sight line. He had to go up. A metal staircase was in the corner of the back wall, near the locked and barred double doors. He tiptoed upward, pausing to make sure that each step was silent. When he reached the second story, he immediately hid behind a wall of cardboard. He crouched down, scanning the lower level. He couldn't see everything because of all the obstacles, but he could see enough to orient himself in relation to the building. Most importantly, he could see the back doors. He suspected that Barnes was doing exactly what he was doing. Barnes's goal was to get out. Ben's goal was to stop him.

The sirens kept getting louder and louder until the wailing finally stopped. The lull was followed by a surge of humanity bursting through the front door. First the police, then three EMTs with doctor's bags and equipment. Ben could hear Ro shouting to them and the cops shouting back. The police began to fan out inside the warehouse, taking up positions on the lower floor and upper area with two of them keeping watch over the double doors in the back. If Barnes was still inside, there was no way that he could make it through those babies. The only way he could leave was through the front entrance.

The police were calling out Ben's name, wanting him visible and out of their way so they could continue with the manhunt without shooting him. The smart thing to do would be to say something and wait for them to retrieve him. Get the hell back to safety. Let the pros be the pros. Live to see another day.

But that train had long left the station. Ben had become a heat-seeking missile, homed in on a target and with a predetermined trajectory. Barnes was out there and Ben *had* to be the one to bring him down. He owed it to Ellen—to Katie and Julia and Jamey, and now more than ever, to Lilly. He had to go one-on-one, knowing full well there was a good chance that it would end badly for him.

Ignoring their pleas to come down to safety. After a minute or two, they stopped calling his name, focusing on the monster. They started calling out to Kevin Barnes.

Kevin, you're surrounded.

Kevin, give yourself up.

Kevin, don't make this more difficult than it needs to be.

Kevin, it's over.

It was over for him, but not for Ben.

Feeling the weight of the gun in his hand.

He was not a vegetarian. He ate meat and fish and animal protein and never thought much of it. But he also wasn't a hunter. He wasn't even much for fishing. Sport killing didn't hold much interest for him. If he could get flesh from a grocery store, that was fine.

But this was different. It wasn't bloodlust. That waste of space simply didn't deserve to live. Even if a jury would decide otherwise, Ben had decided long ago that taking Barnes's life would be a righteous killing. He had no trouble imagining what Barnes would look like with a bullet exploding his brain. The thought didn't bother him. Rather, it excited him, feeding him with adrenaline. His vision became clearer and more focused. The hardest thing for him to do was not to react too quickly.

Patience . . . patience.

More people were storming the warehouse. Within twenty minutes, police were everywhere, including Sam Shanks—Ben could hear him yelling out his name.

There was concern in Shanks's voice but also anger. He was pleading and chastising at the same time. But Ben remained rooted.

Either catch me or watch me shoot him dead.

They'd arrest him for murder.

Whatever.

He didn't know anything about SWAT procedure, but he figured that the cops would divide the area into sectors. That meant a lot of inch-by-inch searching, clearing each space until they found predator and prey.

When the cops stopped shouting Kevin's name, the space became quieter, but not silent. Ben could hear the static of radios and muffled voices, but sound became dampened, like a mute had been applied to an instrument. There was a good chance he could be shot by accident. All it took was one wrong step.

Silence wasn't just golden, it was a necessity.

Standing up from a squat, taking soundless steps, trying to gauge the situation, knowing that Barnes was doing the same thing. There was conversation among the cops. When it grew louder, he moved. When the talking got softer, Ben stopped.

Both of the doors were heavily guarded.

He threw himself into the mind of the beast. Suppose he was trapped, surrounded. Would he try for an escape or hang tight? Probably he'd stuff himself into a box and wait, thinking that the police probably wouldn't open every single carton in the warehouse.

Barnes had to be hiding. And if that was the case, Ben had no choice but to flush him out before the police did. To do that, Barnes would need a glimmer of hope for an escape.

Which meant drawing the police away from the doors.

Thinking of a plan, Ben stayed put. Let the police do a little of the work for him. They had started opening boxes, going from the front to the back. Cops had arrived by the dozens, the action concentrated near the front doors. The back doors were harder to open, harder to escape from. And they were guarded by two cops with high-powered rifles. But there was still way less going on in the back than in the front. And since the cops were working from front to back, it meant they were pushing Barnes to the rear of the building. If Barnes had any brains in his head, he had to know that his only hope was through the back.

Silently, Ben turned on his heel as he inched toward the rear of the warehouse. There was a cop at the foot of the metal staircase he had climbed, and several cops on the second story in front of the staircase.

Again, Shanks called out his name.

The posse kept searching.

If something was gonna happen, it had to happen quickly. He loaded his gun and stuck it in his back pocket. He squatted down.

Looking around for just the right implement to make the right amount of noise, he spotted a piece of a two-by-four about twenty feet away.

That would work.

Creeping toward the fragment of wood, moving with stealth and silence until it was within grabbing distance. He stretched out his fingers, seized it, then gripped it in his hand. Still hidden behind the boxes, he stood up, listening to the police clear one area after another. Inching toward the railing of the catwalk, he stationed himself close to the edge, but still blocked from the view of the cops.

Ben hurled the two-by-four across the room until it crashed on the opposite side from where he stood. The noise was a magnet, everyone running to the spot. The backdoor guards temporarily stepped forward and away from their positions.

And that's when the mouse darted out, seconds away from making it to the locked door.

Now or never.

Ben flung himself over the railing—a cat in a tree

leaping on its prey. Maybe they'd shoot him in the process, but he was so amped he didn't care.

Flying, flying, flying. His body airborne for what seemed like hours.

His mind at peace with his decision.

Chapter 14

Falling on him with a thud, both of them now on the ground. Immediately Ben tried to land punches but Barnes fought back like a wounded animal, scratching, clawing, biting, punching, kicking. The dance of life and death. A few moments into the fight, Ben felt a sharp stab in his ribs, but it did nothing to slow him down. He clawed at Barnes's throat, getting his hand around the monster's neck. But Barnes bit back, hitting him in the face. He got free and rolled over.

Ben saw the gleam of a knife, but kept going, falling on Barnes, pinning him down. Barnes managed to slip away and tried to get to his feet, screaming for help from the police. But the monster had nowhere to go; he was backed up against the wall. Ben grabbed his waist and took him down, the knife clanking to the floor. Ben quickly kicked it away.

The police were closing in.

Ben had to act and act now. He managed enough leverage to wrap his arms around Barnes's neck. He pulled out his gun, and with that, three years of pain, agony, and fury came spilling out.

"You ruined my life!" He whacked Barnes over the head with the butt. "You ruined my fucking *life!*" Another whack. "You ruined my sister, you ruined my family, you ruined me!" A final whack until Barnes went limp in his arms.

Ben still had Barnes in a headlock. He jammed the gun into Barnes's mouth, bracing himself for exploding brains.

But then time suddenly stopped.

He looked around.

There were weapons drawn toward his face, and people yelling, *screaming* at him to put the gun down.

Not just yet, my friends.

Ben used Barnes's body as a shield. With his back to the wall, the police couldn't come from behind. And with the gun down Barnes's throat, Ben knew they wouldn't move on him until they thought they had no choice.

He realized he was enjoying himself. Exhilarated, in fact. Barnes started stirring, then struggling when he found that the gun was down his throat.

"Make a move and I'll turn your head to pulp." Ben was whispering. "You liked when they were all helpless. How do you like the feeling now?"

He pushed the gun down Barnes's throat until he gagged. "Do it now, Barnes. Beg for mercy like they did. Tell me about your wife and kids and all the other shit. Just maybe I'll change my mind."

Gurgles were coming from Barnes's throat. Ben's voice was a hush. His hands were steady, his mind was clear.

"Nah, I don't give a solitary fuck about your kids and your wife. And I certainly don't give a solitary fuck about your worthless life! I'm just thinking how to do it.

"See, this is what I'm thinking. I've got this little gun with little bullets that'll kill you if I put enough of them inside your brain. But if I only do one or two, they'll rattle around your skull, turning all your gray matter to scrambled eggs, but your lower brain'll still be working. So you'll exist but you won't live. What'll it be, Kev? Death or vegetable?"

A wall of uniforms was slowly advancing. Ben noticed and yelled out, "Get back or I *will* shoot him."

When no one stopped, he fired the gun at Barnes's feet and screamed, "Back! Now!"

That did the trick.

Shanks's voice cut through the silence, his body emerging from the crowd. He said, "Son of a bitch, Vicks, you did it. You got him. You made a promise to your sister and you kept it. Everyone else failed, but you did it, kiddo. Now just drop the gun and everything will be okay. We'll take it from here. It's over, Ben."

Silence.

Shanks moved a step closer. "You're about to become a hero—"

"A *hero?* Are you out of your mind?" Ben hoisted Barnes to his feet so that he continued to act as a shield. "This piece of shit is still breathing, Sam. So it ain't over."

Shanks tried another approach. "Ben, you want justice, right? Justice for Ellen and the others. How do you think she'd feel about a justice that sent you to jail? Ben, you can't do this to your parents. You can't do it to your mom and dad and your sister. They need you."

"Nah, they don't," Ben said. "Their lives are ruined anyway. This is exactly what they want. They want him dead just like I do."

"Ben, that's ridiculous—"

"Don't fucking tell me I'm ridiculous."

"Sorry . . ." Sam took a deep breath and let it out. "You're right, Ben. That was a rotten thing to say. I'm nervous, dude. I'm really, really nervous. I'm nervous for me, I'm nervous for you. Sorry."

The warehouse went quiet . . . Barnes was now awake; with the revolver in his mouth, his breathing was labored. Ben knew the SWAT team would charge him in a matter of minutes, so he had a real decision to make.

He heard Ro's voice this time. "Ben, don't do it. I'm begging you."

Ben saw tears on her cheeks. Ro sure cried a lot.

She said, "I love you, Ben. Please, for me, don't do it."

He didn't move.

She kept pleading. "Ben, don't do it. I love you. I need you—"

"No you don't," Ben interrupted. The gun was still down Barnes's throat. "If I went away to prison tomorrow, I'm sure you'd be sad. And you'd write me letters. And maybe you'd even visit me. But then you'd move on. And that would be fine with me. Even if I can't move on, you should, Dorothy. The world doesn't stop just because I checked out a long time ago."

Again the room went quiet. Ro blinked several

times. Her voice was one step above a whisper. "Ben, Lilly's still alive. *She* needs you."

With the mention of the young teen's name, Ben's brain returned to earth. "Oh shit!" He shoved the body onto the floor and charged forward. "Oh my God. Lilly!"

Immediately he was pounced upon, bodies of men shoving him onto his stomach, whipping his hands behind his back, holding down his legs as he struggled, screaming for them to let him go. Someone took his gun away. He heard Sam telling him to shut up and stop moving. Over and over and over.

Eventually, Ben got the message and went limp. Pressure eased off his back and he was hoisted to his feet, cuffed and surrounded. A gorilla was on either side of him, but Ben was looking into Sam's eyes. "You gotta let me go to her." Tears down his cheeks. "She needs me. I need to *see* her."

"What you need to do is calm down. You're not in your right mind at this moment."

"I'm okay, I swear. Please take the cuffs off." He was begging. "I need to see her." No response. "Sam, she's *dying!*"

Sam sighed, but said nothing.

"I'm not going anywhere. Just let me go to her."

"I'll take you to her, but the cuffs stay on—" Shanks

stared at him and his eyes went dark. "Oh shit." He lifted up the kid's shirt. "You've been stabbed. You need medical attention."

"Tell them to let me go and I'll get attention."

"Let him go," Sam said.

As soon as he was freed, Ben bolted to Lilly, hands still manacled behind his back. A huddle of EMTs was working on her. He bent down, his eyes fixed on hers. Her body was shaking even though she had a blanket over her. There was a pool of blood by her side and blood-soaked gauze around her neck. Tubes were down her nose. Monitors and needles were on and in her arms. An oxygen mask was over her nose. Her complexion was gray.

"You're okay, Lilly, you're okay." Saying it just as much to himself as to her. "Just hang in there, baby. I'm not leaving, okay. You're gonna be okay."

Wide dark eyes focused in on his face. He knew she had heard him. Her jeans and underwear had been ripped off and her panties were soaked with blood. Ben felt like his head was about to explode.

I should have fucking shot him.

Shanks was at his side. "You're a fucking idiot, Vicks, you know that? A stupid, fucking moron!"

"Please just take off the cuffs."

"I have to take the cuffs off because you need medical attention. If you bolt, I will haul your ass into jail now and that will be that."

"I'm not going anywhere."

Shanks took off the cuffs and whispered in the boy's ear. "The stab wound. You got it immediately, the second he jumped on you. You were in fear of your life. You understand what I'm saying, Ben?"

"Yes, I got it." One of the EMTs had lifted his shirt. Sam was still holding his shirt. Ben said, "Just let me go to her."

Shanks finally let Ben go. He said, "I'll be right back."

A gaggle of people was talking all at once, mostly medical conversations. Someone told Ben to get the hell away from Lilly, but then someone countermanded the order and said to leave him alone, that he was calming down the girl and her blood pressure was going up. Her body was still shaking, but when Ben took her hand, her fingers weakly tightened around his.

He whispered to her, "Just hold on. Lilly, you're gonna be fine. You're gonna be okay. I'm here for you. I'm not going anywhere."

His T-shirt sported a big wet blob, and blood was dripping onto the floor. He knew he should be hurting, but he was so jacked up he felt numb. The EMTs were talking to some kind of doctor over the radio.

Words were being bandied back and forth: "blood loss," "shock," "possible severed vocal cords." Lilly's violent shakes had subsided but she was still trembling. Ben could feel his brain working even if he wasn't at his best. His phone was still in his back pocket. He reached for it and began to look up doctors. The nearest specialist was someone in Dallas.

He pulled his hand from Lilly's. "I'm not going anywhere, honey. Just making a phone call." He stood up from his kneeling position and immediately felt woozy, the room spinning around him. He knelt back down—about a foot away from Lilly so she couldn't hear—deciding he could call from a sitting position. Anything was better than passing out. His breathing was shallow and his ribs began to hurt. The adrenaline was wearing off and pain was replacing the high. He was shaking as he punched in the numbers.

"C'mon . . . answer you motherfu—yes, ma'am, my name is Benjamin Vicksburg. I need to talk to Dr. Jacob Winslow. It's a dire emergency! My friend's neck was slashed . . . no, it isn't a joke. I'd let you talk to the EMTs but they're pretty busy saving her life . . . yes, I will hold, thank you."

The wait seemed interminable. A male voice came on the line. "Who is this?"

"My name is Benjamin Vicksburg. My friend was just viciously attacked and her throat was cut. The EMTs working on her said something about her vocal cords being cut. We need a specialist and you're the nearest one to where we are."

"Where are you?"

"Los Alamos, New Mexico."

"Is this a joke?"

"No, sir, I guarantee you that this is not a joke. I guarantee you this will be in the papers tomorrow morning. She's not even fifteen years old. You've got to help. Can you get a chopper from Dallas and meet us here in New Mexico?"

A pause.

"Hello?"

"I'm still here. If she's with EMTs, put one of them on the line."

"Sir—"

"Put an EMT on the goddamn line or I'm going to hang up."

Ben crawled back to one of the EMTs and put his phone on speaker and up against the medic's ear. He said, "You gotta talk to him. He's a throat doctor that specializes in vocal-cord surgery. Please tell him what's going on!"

The woman looked at him, paused, but then complied. The conversation was brief. The doctor asked questions, the EMT answered. Words were exchanged: Lilly's condition, her neck, her vocal cords, her blood pressure, her core temperature, other technical things. Finally, the doctor asked to speak "to the kid." The EMT pulled back from the phone and Ben turned off the speakerphone.

Dr. Winslow said, "They're trying to stabilize her enough to take her to the medical center in Albuquerque. I have a few colleagues there. I'll make some calls. It'll take me at least three hours to get there."

"Thank you, thank you—"

"What is your relationship to her?" he asked.

"Friend."

"You're not a relative?"

"No."

"Where are her parents?"

Oh shit!

What the hell was he going to tell George and June?

"I'll get her parents down there."

"I can't do anything without her parents' permission. What's her name?"

"Lilly Tafoya."

"Her parents?"

"George and June Tafoya."

"And your name again?"

"Benjamin Vicksburg. As in the Civil War battle."

"And give me a couple of phone numbers where I can reach you or people who are involved in this."

Ben gave him his cell number, but he couldn't think of any other number aside from Haley's. He looked up and Sam was nearby. He shoved the phone in his hand. "This is a throat doctor for Lilly. Please tell him I'm legit."

Sam took the phone. "This is Detective Sam Shanks of the River Remez PD. Who am I talking to?"

Ben went back to Lilly, who was now on a gurney. He took her hand. "I'm coming with you, baby."

Sam went up to Ben and gave him back the phone. "How'd you find that guy?"

"The wonders of the Internet. I'm going with her to Albuquerque."

"To the medical center?"

Ben nodded.

"We need to talk, but first you need to get yourself treated."

"Whatever."

"Not whatever. Now."

They were loading Lilly into the ambulance. "I gotta

go with her, Sam. I'll meet you in Albuquerque." Ben climbed inside.

No one bothered to object.

The hatch closed. The sirens blared and the ambulance took off. Ben closed his eyes and prayed.

Chapter 15

They were separated as soon as they hit the emergency corridor in the medical center—Lilly to the OR and Ben into an ER examining room. Slowly, he took off his clothes and put on a robe.

Suddenly he was a patient.

A nurse swabbed his chest. He hadn't really felt the stab beyond the initial jolt, but he sure as hell felt the cleansing. He was dressed with a temporary bandage to stop the bleeding, although by that point, it had trickled down to a slow leak. With an IV in his arm, he waited on an examining table—alone and utterly depleted.

He reached into the back pocket of his pants and made the hardest call of his life. How the hell did Shanks or any of them do this? The line clicked in. He heard himself talk although he didn't even recognize his own voice.

"George Tafoya, please. It's an emergency."

"Name?"

"Benjamin Vicksburg."

Several minutes later: "Ben, what's going on?"

His throat momentarily seized up. Then he said, "Something's happened to Lilly—"

"Oh my God! Is she *okay*?"

"She's . . . in surgery at the Albuquerque medical center. You and June have to come down—"

"What the fuck happened?" When the kid didn't answer immediately, George said, "Ben, what the fuck happened? Tell me!"

A long pause. "She was attacked, George—"

"How?" Then a gasp. "Is it the guy you asked me about? Kevin Barnes?"

"Yes."

"Is she okay?"

"She's in surgery—"

"Answer the fucking question, Ben!" His voice became clogged. "Is my baby okay?"

"I rode with her in the ambulance. When they took her into surgery, she was alive and conscious. You've got to get down here. The surgeon is going to need your permission to operate on her beyond emergency measures."

"Oh my God! How the fuck did this happen?" Ben heard panting over the line. "Fuck this. June and I will be down as soon as I can figure out—"

"I'm sorry, George." But the line was already dead.

Detective Milton Ortiz came into the room. Ben hadn't seen him since Katie Doogan's body had been found. The detective's eyes went to Ben's bandaged chest and then to his face.

"Sam asked you to keep an eye on me?"

"He asked me to check in on you—make sure you got treated."

"I got treated."

"Are you all right?"

"I think it's going to be a very long time before I'm all right." He swiped at his wet face. "Have you heard anything about Lilly?"

Ortiz shook his head. "Sam's on his way."

"I've got to call my parents. Let them know I'm okay."

"They've been contacted."

"I can talk if you want to ask me questions."

"I'll leave that up to Sam."

"He's mad at me."

"You scared the shit out of him." Ortiz looked at him. "We all know it was self-defense."

With a gun down his throat?

Ortiz went on. "He stabbed you, and you were jacked up, not in your right mind. It was self-defense and that's all there is to it. I don't want to hear anything else. Got it?"

Ben got it. "What'd they do with Barnes?"

"I'm sure he's locked up somewhere, demanding to speak to his lawyer."

"He *is* a lawyer."

"Then I'm sure he knows the ropes."

"I fucked up, Detecive. He got her right under my nose. It's totally my fault."

Ortiz's eyes narrowed. "Son, you listen to me and listen good. You need to put the blame where it belongs. On Kevin Barnes. He did it. He is solely responsible. Not you."

"But—"

"There are no buts, Vicksburg."

Ben didn't answer. Nothing was going to help until he was sure that Lilly would be all right—at least medically. She'd never, ever truly be all right again, and that was on him.

Some guy in a white coat came into the room. His name tag said DR. NORMAN MILLSTEIN. He looked about sixty: steel-wool thinning gray hair and a mustache. He washed his hands, introducing himself, and then he started to peel away the gauze. "You've got quite a fan club out there asking about you. There must be over a dozen kids clogging up the waiting room, wondering if you're okay."

"You mean if Lilly's okay . . . the girl who came in with me. Do you know what's happening with her?"

"She's still in surgery."

"Is she okay?"

"I don't know."

"Do you know who's doing the surgery?"

"There is a team."

"Is she stabilized?"

"I don't know." He took off the bandages. "You need stitches, young man."

"Whatever."

"Not whatever. You may not realize it, but you've got some pretty nasty-looking wounds."

"I know. I hurt."

Ortiz took out his phone. "I'd like to take pictures before you close him up. It may help him down the line . . . with the case."

"Go ahead."

As the detective zeroed in on the wounds, Ben looked down. He had been stabbed and sliced in several places—nasty-looking gashes.

Ortiz finished up his photo taking. To Millstein he asked, "Do you know if the River Remez police have arrived?"

"Not sure."

He turned to Ben. "I'll go see if I can find Shanks. I know he wants to talk to you."

"Thanks," Ben said, although he didn't know why. After Ortiz left, he said, "Could you find out about the girl?"

The doctor was opening drawers and taking stuff out, preparing to sew him up. He said, "I'll do what I can, but truthfully, you'll know when I know."

"You can't peek in?"

"No, it doesn't work that way." He was holding a hypodermic needle. "This will hurt. Hold still if you can." He started injecting around the wounds. When he saw the boy wincing in pain, he said, "Just a few more."

"It's fine." Ben was angry at Ro, at Haley, at Griff, at the world, but most of all, he was furious at himself. He rarely wasted time on emotions. They just got in the way of everything. But anger was something that came naturally. The adrenaline was definitely wearing off and he was sinking into a deep funk. He also did depression pretty well. The shrink he had seen after Ellen died said that depression was just anger turned inward. It sounded a little convenient at the time. Now he understood.

I should never have left them alone.

His belly and sides started tingling. Five minutes later Millstein started to stitch him up.

"Feel anything?"

"Nope."

It was weird because he could sense the needle going in, but it didn't hurt. As the doctor worked, Ben's wrath began to subside. What was the use of screaming at anyone? They probably felt worse than he did. He had done something—fought back and brought down the monster. Ro had battled for Lilly's life. But Haley . . . poor Haley. Lilly was her best friend. There were no words right now that would comfort her. And Griff? He surely had enough guilt to last a lifetime.

More invisible damage done by that waste of space.

Ben knew that when he saw the kids, he'd have to be a source of compassion and understanding even if he didn't feel that way inside. Because he wasn't about to let that bastard have any more power over him. The idea of seeing George and June was nauseating, but he had to face them as well. If they decided to hate him, what could he do? Join the club. He hated himself.

"You're a good patient," Millstein told him.

"Thanks." Ben was thinking, *I should have killed him.*

Then he thought of his parents, of Haley, and of Lilly, of course. He'd have to be there for them. He would dedicate his life to her recovery. He couldn't do that if he was in jail.

Shanks walked into the room, looking old and weary. Dr. Millstein looked up. "We're a little busy in here."

"He's a detective," Ben said. "He needs to talk to me."

"Not while I'm doing this. You can't move, and if you talk, you move."

"I won't say anything," Shanks said.

Millstein didn't answer, but continued sewing.

"How's it looking?" Ben asked Shanks.

"Nasty."

"Stop talking," Millstein said.

"I meant how's it looking for Lilly."

"I don't know, Ben."

Millstein stopped and regarded Shanks. "Please?" He pointed to the door.

"Let him stay," Ben told the doc. "He makes me feel better . . . someone who looks as shitty and worn out as I do."

Shanks managed a very weak smile. "Stop talking. Let him finish up."

"Thank you," Millstein said.

Finally, the doctor stood up. "I'll be back in a moment."

When he left, Ben looked down at his stomach, a patchwork quilt done by an Amish person on crack. Shanks saw him staring. "You'll have stories to tell."

"It would have been a better story to see his head explode." Ben looked up. "Can you find out how Lilly's doing?"

"She's in surgery, Ben. That's all anyone knows."

"Are her parents out there?"

"They arrived about five minutes ago."

"Have you talked to them?"

"I introduced myself. I told them we had the bad guy behind bars. I don't think they heard me."

"Do they hate me?"

"Don't be ridiculous."

"That's the second time you've told me that today."

"Ben, I want to tell you something." Shanks bit his lip. "You know you saved her life. If you had waited for us . . . for the cops to break down that door, she would have been long gone."

"I'm sure George and June don't see it that way."

"George and June are completely focused on Lilly. I guarantee you they're not giving you any thought. But when they do, they'll be very grateful."

"If she's okay, maybe." Silence. "I don't even know

what okay means anymore. How can she recover from this?"

"The human spirit is very resilient if you give it a chance."

"Yeah . . . right." Ben rubbed his forehead and felt a pull on his stitches. As soon as the anesthetic wore off, it was going to hurt whenever he moved. "If she doesn't make it, I'll kill myself."

"She made it down to the hospital," Shanks said. "That's step one."

"I just want to wake up six months from now and be normal. Or as normal as I was before all this happened. I'm so frickin' tired of living a nightmare!"

The doctor walked in along with Ben's parents. Laura's eyes immediately started watering. Ben said, "Mom, please don't."

"Oh my God!" She turned her head and stifled a sob. Even his dad had watery eyes.

He asked, "Are you all right?"

"I'm talking and walking, Dad. So I guess the answer is yes. How's Haley? She really needs you two more than I do."

Laura had managed to calm herself down. She kissed her son's cheek and Ben took her hand. He said, "I'm fine. Go tell Haley that I love her and I'm glad she's okay. Tell her that."

William wiped his eyes. "I love you, son."

"I love you too, Dad."

After washing his hands and gloving up, Millstein said, "I'm going to need a little elbow room. He should be out in about a half hour."

"You're not keeping him overnight?" William asked.

"It's not necessary. But someone will need to bring him in tomorrow to re-dress the wounds."

"If I need to sleep somewhere, I'll stay at Grandma and Grandpa's."

Laura said, "There is no way you're going to go there looking like this. It'll kill them."

"Mom, they're going to find out."

"Ben, you're coming home."

"That's stupid."

William said, "Laura, you can't hide this from them. It'll probably be in the papers. It's news, honey. We'll have to prep them."

Laura started crying again. Millstein said, "Maybe it's better if you two wait outside."

Shanks stood up. "Let's give him some room."

Laura handed Ben a bag of clothing. "Sam said he'll need your clothes."

"Yeah, right. Thanks."

"Let's go," his dad said.

The three of them left. Millstein started cleaning

the wounds. Ben felt a faint sting and told him so. "I'll give you some pain medication." He unwrapped some gauze. "I'm going to mummify you now. It's the only way that the bandages are going to stay on." As the doc worked, the quiet was haunting. Millstein stood up. "I need some more gauze."

As soon as he left, Ro peeked her head through the door. Her eyes were wet, swollen, and red-rimmed. "Hi."

"How's Lilly?"

"No word."

Ben couldn't think of anything else to say. He beckoned her in with a crook of the finger and she came over. She looked him up and down, covered with gauze, his face and arms splotched with blood. Her own shirt was bloody red, evidence of her heroism. Her hair was matted, her face was drained of color. If there was such a thing as a zombie, she was it.

Ben licked his lips. "You did good."

Water fell from her eyes and rushed down her cheeks. Her voice was a whisper. "It's all my fault." A pause. "You must hate me."

Ben smiled. "I will admit . . . that I've been thinking a lot. And . . . I will admit . . . that I went down that road. That if it hadn't been for that stupid rehearsal, this wouldn't have happened. And if you hadn't insisted that I go, this wouldn't have happened. But then . . . honestly, probably something else would have happened. Because he wasn't going to stop. So . . ." It was getting hard to breathe. "We could do the blame game. Or . . . we can put the blame where it belongs . . . on a psychopathic serial killer . . . and save ourselves a lot of misery. So let's hate the monster and not each other."

She wiped her tears. "That's kind of you to say."

"Ro, we're all sick about Lilly. That's what we're all thinking about. But it's still better than thinking about a burial. And that's because of you."

Millstein came back in and regarded Ro, who immediately burst into tears. The doctor waited a few moments until she had regained some control. Then he said, "He'll be out in a little bit. It would be better if you waited outside."

She kissed his cheek. "Are you okay?"

"Sure."

Millstein cleared his throat and she left. He finished up about a half hour later, giving Ben an armful of medication along with several prescriptions. Ben put on his new and blood-free clothes—jeans and a T-shirt—but his sneakers were still blood-spattered. Pain was seeping in where before it had just felt numb.

Numbness wears off quickly.

Pain lasts a long, long time.

Chapter 16

Dozens of pairs of eyes were upon him. Ben figured that there must have been around forty people, although who they were barely registered. But they included people from the pueblo—some of them outside doing a healing chant. His mother relieved him of the bag of medication along with a bag of bloodstained clothes. "Sit down, Ben."

"I'm okay."

She was pulling vials out of the bag. "Sit down!"

"I'm fine." But he wasn't. He hurt, but he didn't want any pain medication. Nothing to dull him. His eyes scanned the faces around him and his eyes eventually landed on Haley. She saw him and looked away. To his mom he said, "One moment."

Limping over to his baby sister—each step agonizing—Ben put his arm around her, taking her to a private corner. "Don't talk, okay?" His breathing was labored. "It's hard for me to talk, so you've got to listen. It's no one's fault except his." She kept shaking her head no, her eyes pouring out tears. "Haley, blaming ourselves is a waste of time. We've got to keep it all together, okay? Whatever happens, we can't let him fuck us up any more. If he does that, he really wins. And everything that happened today will be for nothing. So let's just . . . hold it together until we get some news about Lilly, okay?"

Haley bit her lip and wiped her eyes. "Okay."

Her voice was a mouse squeak. Ben kissed her head, and when she started to hug him, he gasped in pain. "Oh my God. Sorry."

"I'm fine. Just . . ." He pointed to his cheek. "You can kiss me here."

She did and they both walked back to the group. Ben looked around for an empty seat and the whole waiting room stood up. But then he saw George and June and Lilly's two half brothers in a corner by themselves. June was facing the wall, rocking back and forth. Lilly's half brothers were talking to George. His eyes were downcast, but when he looked up, he noticed Ben. He made the first move. They met in the middle of the room. George's broad face was drawn and colorless. His dark eyes were piercing as they regarded Ben's face.

"No one is telling us a fucking thing . . . just that she was attacked and she's now in surgery. What the hell is going on?" When Ben tried to talk, the words jammed in his throat. George said, "Are you going to man up or stonewall like everyone else? I know it's bad." Tears ran down his cheeks. "Just tell me *something*!"

Ben pointed to his throat. "He cut her."

George's voice grew faint. "Her cut her throat? Dear God! How bad?"

Ben tried to think of something positive. "Like I said . . . she never lost consciousness. She was staring at me on the ride over. And she knew it was me." Ben's voice cracked. "She held my hand. They got her here, George. That's the main thing."

"Did she say anything to you?"

Ben ran his tongue along the inside of his cheek. "No."

"Could she talk?"

"I . . . don't know." He looked down. "There's a neck specialist flying in from Dallas. You'll need to sign some stuff so he can operate."

"I know. They told me that."

"He's a vocal-cord specialist. She was hurt in that area, so they called him down."

He stared at Ben. "What else did the monster do?" When the boy didn't answer, he said, "Was she—"

"Yes." Ben looked away and George swore under his breath. "How'd he even get to her? I thought she was studying at your house. I was going to pick her up from there."

"They walked over to the library. I think he was stalking them—"

"He got her in the *library*?"

Ben nodded.

"The *public* library?"

"There was an emergency exit near the women's bathroom. Most of the time they don't bother to lock it. I think he waited until one of them went to the bathroom."

"He was waiting until Lilly went to the bathroom?"

"I think if it had been Haley, he would have taken her instead." Ben looked down. "I should have killed him when I had the chance."

"Yeah, you damn well should have killed him. Why the hell didn't you?" When Ben was silent, George said, "I don't know what I'm saying. I'm not in my right mind now." His eyes went to Ben's red-stained arms. He lifted the hem of Ben's shirt and looked at his bandaged body. "What the hell happened to you?"

"I'm fine."

"Did you fight him off?"

"I don't remember what I did, except I stuck a gun in his mouth. Other than that, it's all one big nightmarish blur."

"How'd you find out where he took her?"

"Ro managed to track him using her hotel connections. We got there ahead of the police. We called in the police."

"And you're sure it's Kevin Barnes?"

"Yeah . . . it's him."

"I'll kill him. I'll fucking put a gun to his head and shoot his brains out." He paused. "I should have taken you more seriously—confronted the bastard." He shook his head. "This is my fault."

"No, it's not your fault. It's not my fault either. It's Kevin Barnes who did it."

The big man blew out air. "You're right. I should be thanking you . . . you and whatsherface."

Ben smiled. "Ro Majors. She kept her . . ." *Alive.* "She kept Lilly going until the paramedics came."

"Thank her for me, will you? I can't talk to anyone right now."

Ben glanced at his watch. It was eight in the evening—

those had been both the fastest and the slowest four hours that had ever passed in his life. They both saw a nurse approach June. George moved in to intercept her and Ben tagged along.

She said, "These are consent forms for Dr. Winslow."

"That's the throat doctor. Is he here at the hospital?"

"Yes."

"Can I talk to him?" George asked.

"He's getting ready for surgery, Dr. Tafoya. He needs your permission before he can do anything."

"What's going on with my little girl?"

"I don't know, sir."

"C'mon!" There was desperation in his voice. "You must know something."

"I'm sorry, sir, but I honestly don't know anything."

George sighed, grabbed the clipboard, signed it, and shoved it into the nurse's chest. Then he walked back to June.

Ben shrugged at the nurse. "He's not himself."

"He's well behaved compared to others. I've been screamed at, cursed at, spit at, name-called, grabbed, shaken, and occasionally a few people have tried to land a punch in my face. Stress brings out all sorts of hidden demons. How are you feeling?"

"I'm still here, so I guess that's good news." Ben smiled, she smiled, and then he turned and went back to the crowd.

His presence brought the soft conversation to a halt. The faces began to take on names—his parents and grandparents; Ro and Haley, of course; but also Griffen, JD, Weekly, Mark Salinez, Lisa, Shannon, Chelsea; Mr. Beltran, the principal; Tom Gomez. Lilly's grandmother and grandfather. Ben's cousin Henry was there, looking completely sober. If there was ever a time to get hammered, Ben felt it was now. Shanks was sitting next to Ben's father. He offered the kid his chair, but Ben shook his head. Within a few minutes, conversation picked up again—something along the lines of whether or not the school should hold graduation. JD, Weekly, Griffen, and Salinez got up and left. Ben wondered where they were going but was too tired to ask.

He went over to the far wall, away from everyone, and sat down on the floor, legs straight out in front of him so as not to pull his stitches. Ro brought him a chair and walked away. He managed to stand long enough to sit in it, stitches burning and pulling and his whole body enveloped in pain. He threw back his head, looking up at an acoustical-tiled light green ceiling.

For just a little while he needed to be alone.

Everyone respected that.

You don't bother the injured wolf.

Half an hour later Ben went over to Shanks. "Where is he? Barnes."

"Locked up. Have a seat, Vicks."

Ben sat down. Shanks's jaw muscles were working overtime. He looked like he was chewing on imaginary gum.

"Is he talking?"

"Barnes? Of course not."

"No bail, right?"

"He's a suspect in four murders. Not a chance."

"What's gonna be his story?" A pause. "He's not gonna plead guilty."

"I have no idea what his story will be," Shanks said. "They've just finished processing him, Ben. Then he has to talk to a lawyer. Then he has to be officially arraigned. These things take a while."

"If I were him, I'd say that he heard screaming, went in, and was trying to help Lilly, and that we scared him away. And he stabbed me because I scared him."

Shanks whispered, "And this is your rebuttal story. You found him . . . on top of Lilly and he started cutting at you with his knife. That's why you have those gashes. You ran after him, jumped him, and he stabbed you. And you do have a stab wound. It was at that point when you took out your gun. In fear for your life. Got it?"

"Sounds good except I beat him up."

"He was wielding the knife. You were in fear for your life. It's the total truth, son . . . maybe not in that exact order, but the truth. Case closed. Stop talking about it, all right?"

Ben nodded. "You can legally take his DNA now."

"Yes we can."

"You must really feel sorry for me." Shanks looked at the kid, who said, "The old Shanks would have said, 'Thank you for reminding me. Otherwise, I would have forgotten about that.'"

Shanks smiled. "We put a rush on it, but it'll still take about twenty-four hours. The judge already agreed to hold him without bail until the tests come back. As soon as we get the matches with the other murders, he's a goner. It's over." Shanks ran his hand through his messy hair. "I'm going to need a statement from you when you're feeling better."

"I can do it now. It's torture just to sit here and wait. Go get a pad and paper."

"I'll be right back." As soon as Shanks left, Ro came over. Ben's dad got up. "Take a seat, honey."

"Thank you." She sat down and put a hand on Ben's knee.

"Looks like I fucked up grad night, Dorothy." He shrugged. "Sorry about that."

She let out a sad laugh. "God . . . was I ever *that* superficial?"

"All the time." When she slapped his leg, Ben said, "Okay. I know you're all right. You're hitting me."

Ro smiled with wet eyes. "She's gonna make it, right?"

"Of course." JD, Weekly, Salinez, and Griffen had returned. There were cotton balls taped to the insides of their arms. "They gave blood?"

"Yeah," Ro said. "My turn." She stood up.

"I'll go with you," Ben told her.

"You stay put."

"I'm okay."

"Ben, there are like thirty people in this room who are all willing to donate. Just sit down and concentrate on making more of your own erythrocytes, okay?"

She got up and JD immediately took her place. He was wearing the same shirt and jeans that he had on for graduation rehearsal. "You okay?"

"I'm fine. Why does everyone keep asking me that?"

JD lifted Ben's shirt, looked at the bandages, and let

it fall back down. He wiped his hand across his mouth. "How bad was it? I mean, how bad was she?"

"She'll recover . . . I hope."

JD turned away. He said, "We should be graduating tomorrow. It was my day, Vicksburg. I fucking knew you'd figure out a way to upstage me."

Ben laughed and it hurt. "I'm the man, dude."

JD laughed too. "Yep, just for today, you *are* the man. Do you hurt?"

"Kills."

"You need anything?"

"Nah."

"How about something to eat? You want a Doogie burger or something?"

"If I put anything in my stomach, I'll puke."

JD nodded. "Did the doc give you meds?"

"Yeah."

"Pain meds?"

"Yeah, my mom's got the bag."

"What'd they give you for pain?"

"I dunno. Probably Vicodin . . . maybe OxyContin. I really don't know."

JD raised his eyebrows. He whispered, "Wanna get high together?"

Ben didn't know if he was serious, but the comment

made him smile. "I'll tell you what, JD. Whatever I don't use, it's yours. My graduation gift to you."

"Cool."

Shanks had come back with a yellow legal pad and a pen. JD stood up. "If you need something . . ."

"I'll let you know."

Shanks walked Ben into a secluded spot with a couple of empty chairs. "Walk me through the day."

Ben did so, with the modifications suggested to him by Ortiz and Shanks. The entire recitation took longer than he thought it would and wore him out.

Shanks said, "You did good."

"You're satisfied?"

"I am. You were clearly acting in self-defense and you were in fear for your life. I—and everyone around me—will recommend that no charges be brought against you."

"You're sure about that? Barnes is going to tell a different story."

"His DNA is going to put him at the scene of four murders. There were forty cops there to witness what happened and to back you up. A little girl is fighting for her life." Shanks closed his notebook. "There are things in life you'll worry about. This won't be one of them."

Chapter 17

L imbo is defined as the place between heaven and hell, but it's way more hell than heaven. The waiting was interminable, but the group kept saying if it was taking this long it must be good news.

At midnight—around eight hours after the attack—two surgeons dressed in green scrubs, still wearing caps and shoe covers, came out of a locked door and looked around the waiting room. George bounced up and so did June. The surgeons spoke to the Tafoyas, who kept nodding—no wailing. Ben took that as a good sign.

George looked around, eyes falling on Ben. He motioned the kid over, then put a protective arm around him. One of the surgeons was tall and graying, and had piercing blue eyes. "Are you the kid who called me? Vicksburg?"

"That was me. You're Dr. Winslow?"

"I am. That was quick thinking on your feet."

Ben had a thousand questions, but knew better than to ask any. Not with Lilly's parents around. George said, "She made it through the surgery. She's in guarded condition."

Relief did not even begin to describe Ben's emotions. "Guarded is good, right?"

"It's a very good outcome considering what she went through," Winslow said. "She's in recovery. We'll transfer her to the ICU and then you can see her. That's going to take a couple of hours."

Ben couldn't help himself. "What about her . . . you know." He touched his neck.

"Her vocal cords?" Winslow said. "There was damage, but not as bad as it could have been. Vocal cords aren't really cords like a string. They are more like an accordion. I can't say anything definite, but I'm optimistic. She'll likely need another operation—maybe two—and vocal rehabilitation."

"But she'll talk again?"

"I'm optimistic."

"Enough questions," George said. "Go home, Ben. Take care of yourself."

June was staring at Ben with dry eyes. "George is right. Go home. And thank you, Ben."

"Honestly, I'm gonna stick around. Do you guys need coffee or anything?"

"No. If you're not going home, then go back to your crowd. Give us a moment to digest all this shit." George kissed the top of the boy's head. "You know how grateful I am to you and whatsherface, right?"

"Right."

"Okay. Go away."

"What should I tell everyone? They're gonna ask."

"Just tell them that she made it through surgery. Everyone should leave and give us some peace and quiet. It's hard looking at everyone with them pretending not to see me. Tell them all to pack it in, including the tribe. I don't need their fucking incantations. I mean, if they want to do it in Santa Clara, that's fine. I will appreciate the community support later on, but right now, I'm too sick to deal with anyone, including you. So go away."

"I'm leaving."

He was greeted by expectant faces.

Ben gave a thumbs-up, which was answered by spontaneous smiles and sighs of relief. "She made it through surgery and is in guarded condition. That's all I know." He rubbed his eyes. "George wants everyone to leave. Our presence is making him nervous."

Slowly, people started to gather up their belongings.

Henry came up and he and Ben fist-bumped. Ben's grandparents came over, his grandma saying, "Are you coming to the house, Benny?"

"Eventually. I'm gonna stick around here for now."

Ro said, "You just said everyone should leave."

"I'm not included in everyone." To his grandma: "I'll be here for a while. I'll call you to pick me up when I'm ready, okay?"

"When will that be?"

"Tomorrow morning, probably."

"Benny, you need to rest."

"I know, I know. Go. I'll call you later." He turned to Ro. "George says thank you for what you did with Lilly."

"He did? I didn't think he even knew my name."

"He didn't. He called you 'whatsherface.'"

"Okay, that figures."

The crowd had thinned to Sam Shanks and the families—Ro's as well as Ben's. Ben looked at Griff. "No long faces, okay, dude? We're all just doing the best we can. And it's gonna be okay."

"I'm staying with you," Haley said.

Ben knew this was something she had to do. "Okay, Hales. Stay with me. A little company might not be bad."

"I'm staying with her," Griff said.

"And I'm staying with you," Ro said to Griff.

"And we're staying with you," Ro's dad told them.

Ben's dad said, "Mom and I are not leaving without Haley and you, Ben. What if you start to bleed and you need help?"

"Dad, I'm in a hospital."

His mom said, "If you stay, we're staying. End of discussion."

"Whatever. Do what you want."

The group was silent for a few minutes, but eventually people started to talk—slowly at first, then the pace picked up. Shanks got coffee and doughnuts. He took some over to the Tafoyas, who joined the crowd until they were all chatting away about things both big and trivial. From graduation to Ellen's childhood. From Ro's college choices to Gretchen's illness. And of course, they all told stories about Lilly. It was nonsense talk, but it was serious conversation. There were a lot of wet eyes interspersed with the occasional smile and even a chuckle or two.

Just passing time.

As soon as Lilly was moved to the ICU, the powwow started to break up. June and George immediately left to be with their daughter. George's sons left for Las Cruces. Griff and his parents called it a day. Shanks needed to get back to River Remez to begin his paper-work. And Ben's parents insisted that Haley go home and get some sleep.

It was down to Ro and Ben. Since Lilly was still alive, it was a safe bet that graduation would go on and that was okay because life goes on. At the ceremony, there would probably be the requisite moment of si-lence, and even though it was nonsense, it made people feel better, so why not?

It was five in the morning when Ro called a taxi to take her back to River Remez. Ben walked out and waited with her by the curb. Sunrise was coming—a new day filled with a new hope. And after three years of the chase, perhaps it was in the cards to finally see a little light.

"Sorry about your car."

"It's collateral damage," Ro said. "You're not going to come to graduation, are you."

"Nope. Looks like my parents will have to wait for Haley."

"What about your speech?"

"You can talk in my place. People would much rather look at you than at me."

"They want to see you."

"They want to see a freak."

"More like a hero."

"You're way more of a hero than I am."

"So from one hero to another . . ." She wiped away tears. "Come to graduation. If you won't do that, at least come to grad night. Allow yourself one teeny bit of high school. It won't change anything. But just maybe it'll make you feel a little better to be, like . . . normal."

"'Normal' is not on my vocab list. Besides, I can barely move, let alone party."

"We'll rent a wheelchair."

Ben kissed her softly on the lips. "Have fun, honey. Really. You deserve it."

Her cheeks were wet. "It's so ironic. I've always been such an attention hog. Now that everyone's gonna be focused on me, I don't know if I'll be able to handle it."

"You have to handle it," Ben told her. "Someone has to be the socially adroit one." They both saw the cab coming down the street. "You'd better have fun, Dorothy. That's an order. I'll want to hear every detail about graduation and grad night, okay?"

"Okay."

"I mean it. Who got stoned, who got arrested, who got drunk and puked on himself, and most important, who banged whom."

"Well . . . that just about sums up high school." She dried her eyes. They kissed again and then she slipped into the cab, disappearing from sight.

Slowly and painfully, he made his way inside to the waiting room.

Everything he had done—all that research and running around and all the promises and hours and toil and sweat and even getting knifed—he had told himself that he was doing it for Ellen. But truthfully, he'd been doing it for himself. If he ever wanted to look in the mirror without flinching, he couldn't let that bastard win. And now that Barnes was caught, and Ben had won, he was floundering, more than a little lost. Superfluous to everyone except maybe Lilly. And Ben needed her way, way more than she had ever needed him.

He had fallen asleep in a chair and woke up with a start around two hours later. It was a little before eight in the morning and he stank. Feeling like shit, he went into the men's room and washed his face and arms and scrubbed his hair with liquid hand soap. The water was pinkish as it flowed down the drain. He stuck his head under the hand dryer and shook out his hair like a wet dog. Then he bought coffee and muffins for the Tafoyas.

Since he wasn't allowed into the ICU, he left the goodies at the nurses' station. The nurse on duty said she'd tell George that he dropped by and that he was still here. Ben was convinced that George would never get the message, but an hour later he showed up. "Go home."

"I've got an appointment. They're gonna change my bandages. What's going on?"

"She's still heavily sedated. But . . ." A deep exhale. "She's improving. Her blood pressure is coming up." He paused. "We're trying to keep it real—no false hopes—but I'm . . . I'm optimistic." George shook his head. "You're not going to leave until you see her."

"I'm a mule, George. You should know that by now."

"Okay, Ben, this is the deal. If I let you see her, will you leave?"

"After they change my bandages, yes."

"And you'll go home to River Remez."

"Actually, I'm going to stay with my grandparents. It's closer and I've been living there anyway. They're just waiting for me to call so they can pick me up."

"Great. Stay there. Recuperate. Take care of yourself and let us take care of Lilly. That's the deal."

"I promise I'll leave and rest up for a while. But I know myself. I'm gonna come back. I think my grandparents got me a tablet for a graduation present. I'll bring it with me. It'll keep me busy for hours."

"You don't need to be here, Ben. You need to take care of yourself." Ben didn't answer and George dry-washed his face. "I'm talking to a wall."

"Yes, you are."

"There can't be more than two people in the ICU. June won't leave. That's a given. I suppose I could use a few minutes to take a piss and just organize my scrambled brain. I want to check in with work and get that out of the way. I'll see if June will allow you to visit."

"Is she mad at me?"

"No." George was taken aback. "Why on earth would she be mad at you?"

"I left them alone in the house, George. I shouldn't have gone to graduation rehearsal—"

George cut him off. "No one's mad. You're family. Don't be stupid. Wait here while I ask June if it's okay."

As soon as he left, Ben closed his eyes, but the images were too awful and too bloody. Instead he stared at nothing. George returned around a half hour later. "June says okay, but just for a few minutes." A pause. "Ben, she's doing better but she looks bad. You've got to steel yourself, for June's sake. Keep it up-tempo."

"Got it."

George had taken ten steps before Ben managed to stand up. He turned around and saw Ben struggling. "Sorry." He came back. "Lean on me."

"I'm okay. I just move *slowly.*"

Together they crept over to the ICU. Ben was in a lot of pain but it felt right. He wasn't supposed to be okay while Lilly was not okay. The nurse had him gown up and cover his feet and head. The ICU room was glassed in. Ben could see a body on the bed with tubes running in and out all over the place. Machines were beeping and chiming. The beat of his heart only added to the rhythm. He went inside.

June was sitting next to Lilly, her delicate fingers wrapped around her daughter's limp hand. She had looked up when Ben came in, but then her eyes went back at Lilly's face. She was a small woman to begin with, but the psychic pain had somehow made her diminutive. There was an empty chair—George's seat—and Ben took it.

Lilly had tubes in her nose and mouth and an oxygen mask over her face. Her neck was completely wrapped in white bandages and gauze. Her left hand was on a board attached to the bed railing and there were needles in her arm and wrist and a couple of IVs dripping clear liquid. Her complexion was gray, as if all the life force had been sucked out of her.

Keep it positive, Vicksburg. But keep it real.

He had wanted to tell her that everything would be all right, that she would be fine and things would go back to the way they were. He had wanted to tell her how beautiful she looked, healthy and rosy and full of spit and fire. He had wanted to tell her all of that. But it wasn't true, and deep inside Lilly would know it wasn't true. She always had a great bullshit detector.

"Can I talk to her?" he whispered to June.

She turned, her eyes reaching deep within his soul. "A few minutes."

He ran a finger across Lilly's ashen cheek. "Hi, hon. It's Ben."

For just a moment she opened her eyes, but then the lids fluttered and closed. Her heart rate quickened. Then it slowed until the intervals between each beat lengthened. The monitor read a sluggish forty-five beats per minute, but she was sedated.

Keep it positive, keep it real.

Again he touched her cheek. "We got him, honey." Her heart rate sped up a bit. More than hearing him, he knew she understood. "We got him and he's behind bars. He's never, ever gonna get out and he's never, ever, ever gonna hurt anyone else again. It's over and done with. He's toast. Your job is to just get well."

Ben paused to keep the emotion out of his voice.

"You just get well and heal up so that I can give you and Haley a hard time like I always do. We're all here for you, Lilly—anything you need and anything you want. I'm here as long as you want. I'm not going anywhere. Right now, I've got nothing but time. So when you wake up and you're better, if you want to hang out and annoy me, I'm here, okay?"

No response. But her blood pressure was stable, her breathing was stable, and so was her heart rate. So that was as good a response as anything.

"I know your dad wants to come back and be with you here in this room. And since there can only be two people with you, I gotta leave the ICU. But I'll be close. I'm gonna stay with my grandparents so I can come back and forth easily. So . . . so . . . I guess I'll talk to you in a little bit. Because your dad wants to be here and we can't have more than two people in the room . . . I think I already said that.

"Take care, hon. Get well . . . get well real soon. I'll be waiting." Ben looked at June. "Thanks."

She leaned over and kissed his cheek. Then she continued her vigil.

George was just outside the ICU. He helped Ben walk back to the waiting room, offering him coffee and a croissant once the kid was seated.

"Thanks. I actually *am* a little hungry." Ben nibbled the croissant.

"Call your grandparents."

"I'll go to the house as soon as I get my bandages changed."

"When's that?"

Ben looked at his watch and took out the vial of antibiotics. He swallowed a pill dry. "At ten. In an hour." He took a sip of the coffee. It felt warm and soothing. "I'll leave when that's done. Thank you for letting me see her." Another sip of coffee. "You know, she opened her eyes for a second."

"She *did*?"

"Just for a second. But she did react to my voice. Her heart rate went up. She heard me, George. And I really, really think she understood what I was saying."

"You kept it positive?"

"I kept it positive."

George dry-washed his face again. "I've got something in my car that I've been carrying around for months."

"What?"

"Just wait here."

"Sure. Where else would I go?"

George was back about five minutes later, carrying a manila envelope. "This is Lilly's graduation present to you. And today is officially your graduation, whether you're there or not." He handed Ben the package.

"What is it?"

"Just open it."

The flap had been taped shut. Ben ripped it off and

pulled out a stack of paper. The first thing he saw was a letter from the California Institute of Technology congratulating him on his acceptance. He hadn't applied to Caltech. He hadn't applied anywhere except St. John's and UNM. Looking at George, he said, "Excuse me?"

"It was Lilly's idea. She wanted to make it happen. So a few of us got together and did what needed to be done."

"A few of you being . . ."

"Lilly, me, your parents, of course, Tom Gomez, your teachers who felt you were selling yourself short. Even your principal was in on it."

"You *forged* an application to a major university."

"We didn't forge anything." George was irritated. "You got the grades, you got the scores, you got the National Merit Scholarship. Your teachers in high school and at UNM wrote the recommendations. They certainly weren't forged. I have no idea what your boss at Circuitchip wrote, but I assume it was okay 'cause you got in."

A pause.

"Lilly wrote your essays. Did a damn good job. They sounded just like you . . . actually, smarter than you. And she didn't mention Ellen, even though everyone said she should. She figured you wouldn't have liked that."

"I wouldn't have liked it."

"The only thing that was forged was your signature—courtesy of your dad. Big effing deal."

Ben regarded the letter. "This is ridiculous. I'm not going anywhere . . . especially not now. She needs me."

"Lilly has two parents, Ben. She doesn't need a third." George weighed his words. "You know you're a little like me, kid. And maybe that's why Lilly always had a thing for you." He paused. "Benjamin, it's time for you to stop being a grown-up and start acting your age."

"I'm not going anywhere," Ben repeated. "I can't leave her alone."

"You're not leaving her alone, you're going away to college. Thousands of kids just like you do it every year. Stop being a baby."

Ben was furious. "Me? A baby?"

"Ben, you're fine as long as you're facing death in the eye. It's life that gives you problems."

Ben was too angry to talk, then a few moments passed and a cooler head prevailed. Ben said, "George, I can't leave her now. It'll break her heart." Silence. "She *loves* me."

"I know she does. I've seen enough of her doodling: 'Ben,' 'Benny,' 'Benjamin' written across the insides of her notebooks . . . all the hearts with your and her initials in them. The true question is, do you love her?"

"Of course I love her."

"I mean, do you really *love* her?"

"George, she's not even fifteen yet."

"Well, she won't be fifteen forever." When the kid didn't answer, George said, "Ben, if you love her, you'll go to Caltech. She *wants* you to go."

Dumbfounded, Ben stammered out, "That was then. This is now."

George stared at the kid with wet eyes. "If you want to do something for her—something very, very important for her—*blaze* the fucking trail. She chose Caltech for you because *she* wants to go to Caltech. She wants to go to L.A. She always wanted to learn how to surf."

George looked upward.

"After what happened, I should never let her go. Never, ever, ever. All I want to do is hold her hand and tell her I love her. And June . . . pssh . . . she's superprotective to begin with. If it's up to us, we'd keep her under lock and key forever. What good will that do? We'll cripple her.

"But if she has a guardian angel out there, someone who can take care of her if she needs it down the road, maybe . . . just maybe . . . June will relent and let my beautiful daughter spread her beautiful wings. That monster took a lot from her, but he didn't take her brain. He didn't take her soul. If you want to help her, get yourself educated and help my daughter to do the same."

Ben was still looking at the letter. "I can't believe my dad forged my signature."

"Stop making a federal case out of it."

"This is going to cost a fortune."

"Your parents would mortgage the house if they had to. Fortunately, they don't have to. There should be another letter inside." George grabbed the envelope from Ben. "Here we go. Work-study. Eighty percent reduction in tuition, room, and board. You'll need to go by the third week in August, Ben. There's orientation and entrance exams to determine your level in math and physics. We've already sent in your acceptance letter. It's a done deal. If you pull out now, you'll expose us all to being charged with fraud."

"I'll just say I changed my mind."

"If you do that, it's like spitting in Lilly's face." George was snorting. "You think about it." He stood up. "You think about what the people who love you did for you. And when you're done thinking about it, you get on that fucking plane and make us all proud."

With that, he left.

Ben had never wanted to go away for college. New situations were torture. He was out of his element at parties and social gatherings. He wasn't a talker or a good team player. He was a loner who lived in his head. He liked numbers more than words and was happiest when he was by himself with a pencil and piece of paper, working on abstract concepts that had nothing to do with real life.

Then he thought for a moment.

He suspected he had just described a lot of the student body at Caltech.

A class full of Vicksburgs. Now, that was a scary thought.

It was Lilly's graduation present to him. Under the current circumstances, he had no choice but to accept.

Lilly, Lilly, Lilly.

Why couldn't she be like most girls her age? Why didn't she just hang up posters of rock stars, chase boys, shop for makeup, and call it a day? Why did she have to be so much like him?

Chapter 18

B en kept a diary, so he would remember.

DAY ONE

Ninety-six hours after being viciously attacked, Lilly celebrated her fifteenth birthday by being moved from the ICU to a room in the special-care ward. Her vitals were stable, but she still had a fever and she still needed oxygen and a glucose drip. She hadn't eaten because she couldn't swallow, let alone talk. Disoriented, confused, and loopy from the medicine, she needed time to even realize she was in a hospital. She became agitated. She had to be sedated a number of times. She moved in and out of consciousness, her eyes scanning her environment, soaking in whatever she could.

There were so many tests; in and out and in and out. That in itself would tire out a normal person, let alone someone as compromised as Lilly. June yelled each time they took her away. She yelled when they brought her back. Ben had to keep on reminding himself that despite everything, Lilly was making progress. She had some moments of lucidity. And she recognized people. When he talked to her, he was positive that she knew who he was.

DAY TWO

The nurses liked to keep the number of visitors in her room to two. June was a fixture. George, Haley, and Ben took shifts. Lilly began to have longer periods of consciousness and became aware of her surroundings. At one point, when Ben was visiting her, she was coherent enough to understand that she had neck surgery and couldn't talk. She lifted her hand and pantomimed writing in the air.

Ben hunted in his backpack and took out a notebook of lined paper and a pencil.

She wrote: *???????*

June became paralyzed, but recovered quickly. She told Lilly that she had been in an accident. That her throat had been injured, so she needed to rest her voice and try to recover.

Her eyes narrowed, and Ben knew that look. She didn't fully believe her mother, but she didn't argue. She lay silently until she fell asleep. She seemed a bit more peaceful when she slept. That is, until they woke her up to change her dressing.

Dr. Winslow was there. He talked to June. He talked to George. He told them that Lilly was making remarkable progress. Then he patted Ben's shoulder and told him that he had done a good job.

After fucking it up in the first place.

DAY THREE

When he arrived at nine, Lilly was up and watching TV. Her fever was down and she no longer needed an oxygen mask. The IV was dripping and she was being fed through tubes, but without the mask, she looked healthier than before, even if her complexion was still wan. George finished up his coffee, stood, and said, "I'm going to go in to work and try to clear my desk for a few hours. You'll stay with June until I get back?"

"Of course."

George kissed his daughter's forehead and Ben took

his chair beside the bed. He leaned over the bed so Lilly could see him and she gave him a slight wave. Then her eyes went upward to the TV. She didn't initiate any contact for a while. Then she picked up a tablet Ben had brought for her, wrote something, and handed it to Ben. *What kind of accident?*

Her voice wasn't working but her mind sure was. Ben showed the tablet to June, who was momentarily stymied. Ben said, "Do you remember the ambulance?"

She snapped her fingers and pointed to the tablet still in June's hands. Her mom gave it back to her.

No.

"Okay. You were in an ambulance and I was with you when they took you to the hospital."

I remember you.

"Right. I was with you the entire ride."

She wrote and showed Ben the tablet: *What happened?*

June blanched when he showed her Lilly's words. She said, "It was a car accident, Lilly. A very bad accident. We'll tell you everything once you're completely better. All that matters is that you get better."

Lilly lifted her eyes back to the TV. When her mother spoke to her, she refused to engage her. At some level, she knew that June wasn't telling the truth.

DAY FOUR

Lilly's eyes were moving back and forth when Ben came into the room. She sensed his presence before he spoke, already writing in her tablet.

What happened?

Her mother was furious with Lilly's insistence on knowing. She said, "Ben got in a car accident. You're very lucky to be alive."

He'd take the blame. Not a problem. But Lilly didn't buy it.

She wrote: *Why isn't Ben hurt?*

"I *was* hurt." Ben leaned over and lifted his T-shirt. He had healed sufficiently to have equal amounts of pain and itch, but was still bandaged up. Lilly slowly lifted her free hand and touched the gauze. "I was hurt, but not nearly as bad as you were. Lilly, it was all my fault. When you get better, when you truly, truly get better, I hope you'll forgive me."

She didn't answer, but he could almost smell things percolating in her brain. She looked away and stared at the wall until she closed her eyes and fell asleep. While she napped he went down to the cafeteria to get lunch for June. When he came back, Lilly was up again.

"Hey." Ben spoke so she knew he was in the room.

"Just went to get your mom and me some lunch. Do you mind us eating here?"

She wrote: *Tell me about the accident.*

June was smoldering. She couldn't figure out why Lilly wouldn't let it go. It was what made her a fine math mind. Ben took a bite of an apple. "I was driving Ro's Explorer and plowed into a chain link fence." All of that was true. "The windshield shattered and pieces flew all over the place." True too. "Your throat got cut." That was true, although it had nothing to do with the car. "You almost died. If Ro hadn't been there, you *would* have died. She saved you. Do you forgive me?"

Her eyes were boring into his. *I forgive you. But I don't believe you.*

Ben didn't say anything and neither did June. She took the tablet away. "You need to rest."

Lilly didn't argue, but they knew she was angry. When Ben talked, she wouldn't respond with any kind of gesture or written word. Eventually, she fell back asleep and so did June. Neither one woke when George came in. Ben got up and left.

DAY FIVE

Haley wanted to hang out with her best friend without her brother horning in. Ben relinquished his vigil, spending the day with Ro at his grandparents' house, filling out an excessive amount of college forms. After a lot of deliberation, Ro had decided on the University of Pennsylvania.

It was the first time he'd been alone with her since *that* day. He owed her for saving Lilly's life, for allowing him to catch a monster, and he owed her big-time because she had dealt with everyone—all the phone calls and questions, the media—TV, radio, and newspaper interviews. She allowed Ben to remain in the background. She allowed him to heal.

She said, "Do you think if I wrote up what happened at Los Alamos Brown would reconsider?"

"Ro, after what happened at Los Alamos, you could get in anywhere. You caught a serial killer."

"*We* caught a serial killer."

"You can take all the credit. I certainly don't give a shit."

"The way I figure it is that if the school didn't want me for who I am before this happened, then screw it!"

"Brown didn't reject you. You're on the waiting list. If you want to go, let them know what happened. At the very least, send them one of the million articles and let them see what you're made of."

She sat back and blew out air. "How's Lilly?"

"Getting better." Ben regarded her. "Did you know about this collusion behind my back?"

"Of course. Lilly told me. I thought it was a great idea, although in the back of my mind I thought you'd never go. Now, of course, you have to go."

Of course, she was right.

Suck it up, Ben.

He was filling out forms for a roommate. It creeped him out—someone sleeping where he'd also be sleeping. He'd never gone to sleep-away camp for precisely that reason.

"You could have told me."

"Right." Ro looked at him. "You know, maybe you'll actually like it."

"Maybe." And that was as much of a concession as he was going to give her. "Will you text me from time to time?"

"I'll text you every day . . . until I get a boyfriend. Then it might be every other day."

"Ha ha." *Suck it up, Ben.* "I'll miss you."

"I'll be back for holidays. Griff decided to spend another year here, so my fam is staying on."

"How's he doing?"

"Feeling guilty like the rest of us. But by staying here, he and Haley figure they can be there for Lilly."

"I should be here for her."

"She needs her peers, not someone overprotecting her like her parents. Do her a favor and learn the ropes at Caltech so when she gets there, she'll have a tour guide."

"That's what George said."

"He's right. Go try to salvage whatever teen years you have left, Vicks. That's what I'm doing."

"You're more resilient than I am."

"Bullshit. What's your ideal roommate?"

"Besides you?"

"Good answer." Ro got up and peeked over his shoulder. His roommate requests were nonexistent. "Should I fill it out for you?"

"Sure. That way I'll have absolutely nothing to do with this fiasco and a lot of people to blame."

"Or thank."

Ben looked at her. "Thank you. For everything."

"You're welcome." She grabbed the application out of his hands and began to fill it out. "You want a mixed floor?"

"No. If it were up to me, I wouldn't even want a mixed dorm."

"C'mon, Vicks, have some fun. Besides, I'm sure the girls are just like the boys there."

"No mixed floor." He looked over her shoulder and tried to see what she was writing, but she covered the sheet.

"I want it to be a surprise."

"No thanks. I've had enough of those."

"Yeah, but not good ones. This'll be a good one. I know what's good for you. Now sit down or pace or go away."

Ben smiled. "Seriously, I will miss you."

"I know. I'll miss you too." Ro looked at him with dewy eyes. "It's probably better this way. I can't deal with any more intensity. I want to go back to my former superficial life."

"Don't you know you can't go home again?"

"Yeah, but I can go to college. And I don't even have to reinvent myself. I'm a legitimate hero. I now deserve all the adulation that comes with it. I am invincible." When Ben laughed, she pouted. "I'm serious."

"I know. That's what's so funny, but also charming. It must be wonderful to know who you are."

"You'll get attention too, you know. While I know you'll never relish it like I do, don't brush people off. Try . . . talking about it even if it's just a sentence or two. It'll make the people you're talking to feel important and it's a lot cheaper than psychotherapy."

He was about to protest, but what would be the point? "I'll try."

"As my dad always says: 'Good enough for government work.' And it's good enough for me."

DAY SIX

When Ben arrived at the hospital in the afternoon, Haley had been with Lilly all morning. This time she'd brought Griffen. The three of them were watching TV. Haley and Griff left when Ben came in and Lilly seemed to be in a good mood. She was down to one IV drip and just a nasal tube. Haley said she had actually managed to swallow some juice. She coughed, of course, but she kept at least half of it down.

The graph was on the upswing.

Lilly's largesse did not extend to Ben. When she saw him, she scribbled on her tablet. *What really happened, Ben?*

Of course June was there. Ben showed her the message and again she took the tablet away. "You were up all morning with your friends. You need to rest."

This time Lilly wasn't about to relent. She kept snapping her fingers until her mother gave in and gave her the tablet. *I want to talk to Ben alone.*

"No," June said. "You need something, you talk to me."

You're not telling me the truth.

"I'm telling you what you need to know." June looked at Ben. "You should leave now."

He got up but Lilly slammed her free hand onto the

bed railing. Then she grabbed her mother's arm. June gave her the tablet. She wrote: *Stop treating me like a child.*

"Should I go?" Ben asked June.

"Yes."

Lilly threw the tablet at her mother's chest, where it landed with a thud. For the first time ever, Ben saw June cry, although it was silent. Big fat tears ran down her cheeks. Ben touched June's arm and she looked away.

"Can I have a word with you, please?" When they were out of Lilly's earshot, he whispered, "I can handle this. I'm not gonna overload her with details."

"What are you going to tell her?"

"That she was attacked. She knows it wasn't a car accident. Give me a chance, okay?"

June wiped her eyes. "Just a few minutes—and nothing, *nothing,* about the rape."

"Fair enough."

She left the room, but lingered outside and that was certainly her right. Ben went back to Lilly and handed her the tablet.

I feel bad.

"Do you want me to call the nurse for more pain medication?"

Not that kind of bad. I feel bad for throwing the tab-let at her. I know she's worried.

"Are you worried?"

Should I be worried?

"You're going to need more surgery, Lilly. And voice therapy." When she didn't answer, Ben said, "I'm so sorry."

She still didn't answer. Then she wrote: *What happened?*

Ben exhaled. "The truth? You were attacked. But we got the guy who did it. He's behind bars and he's never going to see freedom again. So you're safe. Absolutely safe."

Lilly's hand went to her neck. *He cut my throat?*

"Yes."

She didn't write anything for a few minutes—a very long time to sit in tension. Finally, Lilly scribbled, *I don't remember.* Tears fell onto her cheeks. Ben pulled out a Kleenex and gave it to her. *I don't remember anything!*

Barnes had no doubt knocked her out in order to get her into the car. It wasn't surprising that she had no recollection of the kidnapping. "That's a good thing, Lilly. It's a self-protective thing."

Who was he? Ellen's killer?

"Yes."

You caught him?

"The police did, yes."

How did you get hurt?

"He stabbed me with the same knife that he used to attack you. We're blood brothers . . . blood siblings." A small smile played on her lips. "You're not going to have to testify, if that's what you're worried about. We got his DNA matched to my sister and three other murdered girls. There might even be more. So like I said, you're safe. He's never getting out."

So you fought him off?

"I fought with him, yes, but by that time the police were all around, so he knew he was doomed. My only regret is that I didn't shoot him when I had a chance."

You had a gun?

"I did."

Again she didn't immediately respond. Then she wrote: *I'm glad you didn't shoot him. Why ruin your life?*

"That's what everyone kept telling me. Lilly, you should know that Ro saved you. She kept you going until the ambulance got there."

You were with Ro?

"Yes."

She paused a long time. *This happened the day before graduation, right? The graduation rehearsal.*

Ben's eyes moistened. "So you do remember that day."

Only that we went to the library. Another protracted silence. *Nothing after that.* A pause. *Except your face. I remember your face.*

"We were in the ambulance together speeding off to the medical center. I was talking to you and you were looking at me the whole time." He stood up. "Now that's enough questions. Don't ask me anything else 'cause I won't answer you. I'm gonna go get your mom, okay?" She held his arm. "What is it, hon?"

She waited a few moments, then she wrote: *Am I still a virgin?*

Fury swept through his body. His vision went blurry for a few moments. "Unless you know something that I don't, of course you are," he snapped. "Stop asking silly questions."

She held his chin and brought his face in front of hers, staring with big, black eyes. Determined eyes, but he certainly wasn't going to be the one to tell her.

The sad truth was he didn't need to tell her, because deep in her heart, she already knew. She could read his eyes and that made him feel low. But Lilly was always one to throw a curve ball.

She managed a smile for his benefit. She picked up the tablet and wrote one word.

Dang.

DAY SEVEN

With her fever gone and her vitals stabilized, Lilly was allowed to go home. June and George had fixed up her room with enough medical equipment to staff a small hospital—IVs, oxygen tanks, monitors, and a fridge filled with juices and sports water. Even though June took a leave of absence from her job, she and George hired a full-time nurse for Lilly.

Outside the house were banners and balloons welcoming Lilly back home. Inside the living room, there were more flowers than were blooming outside in the garden. As she was wheeled out of the hospital, Lilly smiled and waved, and then George made an announcement.

No one was permitted to visit her until after the weekend.

The no one extended to Ben. That was okay with him. The Sabbath was a day of rest.

Chapter 19

The summer passed in a heartbeat.

A nationwide scan of missing girls uncovered possible links to three more victims whose bodies had yet to be discovered. In exchange for the whereabouts of the bodies and of course with the permission of all of the families involved, the D.A. took the death penalty off the table. Barnes was allowed to plead out the seven murders and the attempted murder for seven life sentences without the possibility of parole. Ben figured it was good that he hadn't whacked him. It gave three other families a chance to bury their dead.

Before he could blink, he was at the Sunport in Albuquerque, standing in the security line with Ro and JD and other kids from his class, waiting to catch planes, to take the next step. Families were fussing over their children and Ben's mom and dad were no exception. Ro's mom had actually wanted to come and help move Ro into her dorm, but Ro insisted that after all that had happened, it would look funny to have her mommy there.

It was never an expectation that JD's parents would help him move into his dorm. It wasn't an expectation for Ben's parents as well, although his grandfather really wanted to come. Ben figured he was more curious about Caltech than he was concerned about Ben, but that was Grandpa Ed. Parents' weekend would come very soon and Grandpa and Grandma were invited. His buddy Grant was going to meet Ben at the airport and show him around L.A. Ben knew he'd be in good hands.

Ben was healed but still a little raw around the edges. He couldn't bike or run or lift weights, but he did take lots of long, long walks alone, thinking and planning and just trying to figure it all out. He couldn't move as fluidly as he wanted, but with a little time and patience, he knew he'd be fine.

Three weeks before, his classmates had thrown him a surprise eighteenth birthday party. He hated surprises, but this was a nice one and he had a good time—it was his last chance to say good-bye to everyone who was leaving.

As they got closer to security, Ben gave his parents a semi–bear hug good-bye. His mom had dry eyes but his dad did not. Then it was Ben's turn to take out his laptop and remove his shoes.

"Bye." Another series of hugs all around. "I'll call you went I get to L.A."

Ben, JD, and Ro passed through security, then checked for their respective flights. Ro was going to Philadelphia via Midway, JD was going to Durham via Baltimore, and Ben was going straight to L.A.

The Sunport was pink and green with little booths selling turquoise jewelry and knickknacks that were supposed to remind people that they were in the Southwest. JD was going to a bigger town, although Durham was still small compared to many other cities. The adjustment wouldn't be too hard, especially since he'd be breathing football, parties, and girls—there would be no time to be lonely. Ro had lived in or near a big city almost her entire life. She was going back to her roots.

Ben was alone—a small-town boy going to the big city for the first time. Ro and JD had regular backpacks, while Ben had a wheelie bag. He felt like a six-year-old, but better to feel infantile than to rip something open.

The boys sat with Ro between them. While Ben began fussing with his laptop, JD and Ro carried on a semiprivate conversation revolving around JD's football games and Ro's choice of a sorority. Ben thought about navigating life without a quest.

Within a half hour, there was a boarding announcement for the flight to Baltimore, and that's when JD got up. He hugged Ben first.

"Take care, Vicks. And when your start-up offers its IPO, let me in on it."

"You'll be the first one I call."

"And when we make it into the finals, give me a call and I'll wrangle you a ticket."

"I'll be there, James David, making sure you don't do anything felonious in the after-game celebration. Take care."

Ben took his wheelie and went over to his gate, giving JD and Ro some privacy to say their good-byes.

Five minutes later Ro sat down next to him. "I have a little time."

"You want to sit by your gate? You're leaving first."

"This is fine. I'll hear the boarding announcements."

"What boarding group are you?"

"C."

"I'm C too."

"I'll probably get seated next to a sleazy guy or a wailing baby. God forbid there should be a cute guy on board."

"You never know."

"I guess I'll see you around Thanksgiving." She fiddled with her chipped nails. "You'll be home, right?"

"Of course. If it had been up to me, I would have never left home."

He laughed and so did she. It was strained for both of them.

She said, "It's really time for both of us. Although I have my doubts how much four years of parties, drinking, and sex can help me become productive."

"I see what your priorities are."

"And what are your priorities, Vicks?"

"Getting up in the morning."

She hit him. The first garbled boarding announcement for Midway came across the loudspeaker. She stood up and so did he.

"I'll walk you over."

"It's just across the aisle."

"I want to be with you."

"That's different." She put her backpack on and took his arm. She said, "So you'll come visit me in Philadelphia?"

Ben couldn't help it. His eyes moistened.

Ro said, "Okay, okay, you don't have to visit me."

He hugged her tightly. "Of course I'll visit you."

She leaned her head on his chest. "I will never, ever find another boy like you, Benjamin Vicksburg. You are an original. I love you."

"I love you too."

She broke away. "Let's talk when we get settled."

"Good idea. And tell me what you think of Grant when you go for a weekend in Boston. He's already planning a million things."

"You know, you don't have to set me up. I think I can do okay on my own."

"I'm not setting you up. It's his idea, Ro. He's dying to meet you. That boy knows a good thing when he sees it."

They heard the boarding announcement for the B group. Ro said, "I'd better stand in line."

They walked hand in hand up to the gate until her group was called. Ben said, "Knock 'em dead, Dorothy. Philadelphia will never know what hit it."

"Philadelphia is just the start, baby. Because once you're in the majors, there is no going back." She broke away and handed her ticket to the airline attendant. "Bye, Vicks. Go out and own the world." She pranced down the Jetway: tall, proud, and full of herself. Ben wouldn't have wanted it any other way.

Back in front of the gate for the Southwest flight to LAX, Ben was alone until his group was called. The flight was full, but he managed to snag an aisle seat next to a mother and a four-year-old kid who was already bouncing in his seat. Ben didn't care. He liked the energy.

Before he stuffed his wheelie underneath his seat, he retrieved a college guidebook, well-worn and dog-eared, that took him back to an earlier time. Ellen and he were sitting at the breakfast bar at their house, just the two of them. It was before school and their mom was busy getting Haley dressed. He was wolfing down sugar cereal, listening to Spotify on his phone—a recent gift for his birthday. Ellen was drinking juice and munching on toast. She wore a red T-shirt and jeans, and her hair was in her eyes as she studied the book.

"I've found it, Benny." He hadn't heard her initially because of his earbuds. She hit his arm and he took them out.

"Huh?"

"I said I found where I want to go to college."

"Where?"

"Bryn Mawr."

"Bryn Mawr?" With his usual tact at fourteen, he said, "What's so good about Bryn Mawr?"

"Well, it's near Philadelphia."

"What's so good about Philadelphia?"

"It's near Bryn Mawr."

He had laughed. That much he remembered. "That's crack-ass." He checked his watch. He was meeting his buds before school started. They often did that. Also, he liked to bike when the roads were clear. He picked up his backpack and Ellen handed him the book.

"You keep this. I don't need it anymore."

He tucked the book into the pocket of his backpack. "Are you really going away to college?"

"Of course I'm going away to college," she answered.

Something came over him. Even at fourteen, he knew he'd miss her when she left. "Then I guess I'll have to visit you in Philadelphia."

She gave him a thousand-watt smile. "I'd like that, Benny."

That was the last time he ever saw his sister in the flesh. At least it had been a good memory. And perhaps because it was, he was able to keep his promise. Holding her book, he paged through until he found Bryn Mawr. She had checked it off with a smiley face, writing: *This is it!*

Her writing made him smile.

And then it made him cry.

Instead of her, he was the one going off to school—for all the people who believed in him, all the people who worked so hard—family, teachers, mentors, and friends. But most of all, it was for Ellen. Always and forever.

The four-year-old was looking at him. Embarassed, Ben wiped his face. His phone beeped: a text from Lilly. R U there?

He texted back, Just sitting on the plane, waiting to take off.

There was a pause.

I envy you.

So you come join me, hon. Least you could do since it was your idea.

Another long pause.

I don't know, Ben . . . I've got a long road ahead.

And what could he say to that?

She texted, I'm scared, Ben. I'm scared of EVERY-THING.

He replied, So come join me at Caltech and I promise I'll hold your hand.

What if therapy doesn't work? What if I can't talk ever again beyond a squeak? I can't even scream for help.

So come join me and I promise I'll be your voice. Your brainpower is still off the charts. You have no excuses, young lady.

Another pause.

I may have the brains, Ben, but I no longer have the heart.

Again, his eyes went wet.

So take my heart. You own it anyway.

He could picture her face, and see her eyes moisten with tears. They had spent a lot of time together once she was out of the hospital. At first, the conversations had centered around her: what she needed and how she felt, questions asked and answered, until there was nothing left to tell her. The endless writing seemed to exhaust her. So to fill in the silences, Ben began to talk about himself. And as he talked, she began to answer with an occasional mouthing of words. And the funny thing about lipreading is you concentrate very hard because some words look alike if you're not paying close enough attention. It means looking intensely at someone's face. And when you really look at the face, you notice a lot more.

And the more he looked at Lilly and read her mouthed but unspoken communication, the more he truly understood Lilly Tafoya. It was like meeting her for the first time. And talking about himself . . . it was like he was meeting himself for the first time as well.

He confided in her, things that he hadn't admitted in a long, long time. And as he did, she ceased to be just his little sister's best friend. Lilly Tafoya became *his* friend.

Girlfriend?

Not yet.

But like George said, she wouldn't be fifteen forever.

Ben saw his future. Lilly would come to school with him. If she couldn't talk, he'd shadow her in class if she wanted. And if she didn't want it, he'd still be around in case she changed her mind. And they'd get educated together. They'd get advanced degrees. Eventually, they'd go back to New Mexico, where, like her parents, they would probably wind up with jobs at one of the many labs. They'd get married—two ceremonies: one in a church and the other at the pueblo. They'd go to local sports games, take long walks in the mountains, play Scrabble and video games. They'd be on school boards and community boards and make the system better. They'd throw birthday parties and block parties and holiday parties. They'd make a family together, a life together. They'd grow old together.

For most guys his age, this was surely a vision of hell. To him, it was exactly what he'd wanted for the last three-plus years: a chance to live a normal life.

She still hadn't texted him back, so he texted her again.

I've got to turn off the phone. They're making announcements and the flight attendant is giving me the stink eye.

He was about to press the off button when his phone chimed. He looked down at the text.

I love you, Ben.

A huge smile planted itself across his face.

"Sir, you have to turn off your phone."

He looked up. The flight attendant, a woman in her fifties with short blond hair and muddy blue eyes, wore a very stern expression.

"She just told me she loves me." He showed her the text.

The woman sighed and rolled her hand in the air as if to say, *Hurry up.* He texted Lilly back but didn't push the send button. To the flight attendant, he asked, "'I love you too' or 'I love you, Lilly'?"

"'I love you, Lilly,'" she whispered.

"Yeah, I thought so." He pushed the send button. Once he saw that the message had gone through, he turned off the phone and stowed it away.

Then, for the first time in what seemed like a very long time, he sat back to enjoy the ride.

About the Author

FAYE KELLERMAN lives with her husband, *New York Times* bestselling author Jonathan Kellerman, in Los Angeles, California, and Santa Fe, New Mexico.

Praise for Faye Kellerman's Decker/Lazarus Novels

"Hands down, the most refreshing mystery couple around."

—*People*

RITUAL BATH	THE FORGOTTEN
SACRED AND PROFANE	STONE KISS
MILK AND HONEY	STREET DREAMS
DAY OF ATONEMENT	THE BURNT HOUSE
FALSE PROPHET	THE MERCEDES COFFIN
GRIEVOUS SIN	BLINDMAN'S BLUFF
SANCTUARY	HANGMAN
JUSTICE	GUN GAMES
PRAYERS FOR THE DEAD	THE BEAST
SERPENT'S TOOTH	MURDER 101
JUPITER'S BONES	THEORY OF DEATH
STALKER	BONE BOX

ALSO BY FAYE KELLERMAN

THE QUALITY OF MERCY	THE GARDEN OF EDEN
PRISM	MOON MUSIC
CAPITAL CRIMES	KILLING SEASON
DOUBLE HOMICIDE	

DISCOVER GREAT AUTHORS, EXCLUSIVE OFFERS, AND MORE AT HC.COM

AVAILABLE WHEREVER BOOKS ARE SOLD

HARPER LUXE

THE NEW LUXURY IN READING

We hope you enjoyed reading
our new, comfortable print size and found it
an experience you would like to repeat.

Well — you're in luck!

HarperLuxe offers the finest in fiction and
nonfiction books in this same larger print size and
paperback format. Light and easy to read, HarperLuxe
paperbacks are for book lovers who want to see
what they are reading without the strain.

For a full listing of titles and
new releases to come, please visit our website:

www.HarperLuxe.com

SEEING IS BELIEVING!